www.wadsworth.com

wadsworth.com is the World Wide Web site for Wadsworth Publishing Company and is your direct source to dozens of on-line resources.

At *wadsworth.com* you can find out about supplements, demonstration software, and student resources. You can also send e-mail to many of our authors and preview new publications and exciting new technologies.

wadsworth.com
Changing the way the world learns®

CRIMINAL LAW

Fourth Edition

George E. Dix
A.W. Walker Centennial Chair in Law,
University of Texas

M. Michael Sharlot
Dean and John Jeffers Research Chair in Law,
University of Texas

West/Wadsworth

I(T)P An International Thomson Publishing Company

Belmont, CA • Albany, NY • Boston • Cincinnati • Johannesburg • London • Madrid • Melbourne
Mexico City • New York • Pacific Grove, CA • Scottsdale, AZ • Singapore • Tokyo • Toronto

Criminal Justice Editor: Sabra Horne
Development Editor: Dan Alpert
Assistant Editor: Claire Masson
Editorial Assistant: Cherie Hackelberg
Marketing Manager: Mike Dew
Project Editor: Tanya Nigh
Print Buyer: Karen Hunt
Permissions Editor: Yanna Walters
Production: Tobi Giannone, Michael Bass & Associates
Designer: Harry Voigt
Copy Editor: Helen Walden
Cover Design: Harry Voigt
Compositor: JR Bidwell / Tactical Graphics
Printer: RR Donnelley & Sons

Printed in the United States of America
1 2 3 4 5 6 7 8 9 10

For more information, contact Wadsworth Publishing Company, 10 Davis Drive, Belmont, CA 94002,
or electronically at http://www.wadsworth.com

International Thomson Publishing Europe
Berkshire House
168-173 High Holborn
London, WC1V 7AA, United Kingdom

International Thomson Editores
Seneca, 53
Colonia Polanco
11560 México D.F. México

Nelson ITP, Australia
102 Dodds Street
South Melbourne
Victoria 3205 Australia

International Thomson Publishing Asia
60 Albert Street
#15-01 Albert Complex
Singapore 189969

Nelson Canada
1120 Birchmount Road
Scarborough, Ontario
Canada M1K 5G4

International Thomson Publishing Japan
Hirakawa-cho Kyowa Building, 3F
2-2-1 Hirakawa-cho, Chiyoda-ku
Tokyo 102 Japan

International Thomson Publishing Southern Africa
Building 18, Constantia Square
138 Sixteenth Road, P.O. Box 2459
Halfway House, 1685 South Africa

 This book is printed on acid-free recycled paper.

Library of Congress Cataloging-in-Publication Data
Dix, George E.
    Criminal law / George E. Dix, M. Michael Sharlot.—4th ed.
        p.   cm.
    ISBN 0-534-54684-6 (acid-free paper)
    1. Criminal law—United States—Cases.   I. Sharlot, M. Michael.
II. Title.
KF9218.D53 1998
345.73—dc21   98–16978

PREFACE TO THE FOURTH EDITION

Substantive criminal law, the subject of this book, deserves careful attention for several reasons. It is, of course, important because it affects the manner in which the government intrudes into the lives of numerous persons in an exceptionally significant way—by convicting them of criminal offenses. In addition, however, substantive criminal law is a uniquely effective vehicle for examining the great questions about the relationship of the individual to the state. The goals of the criminal law and the continuing debate as to how they may best be achieved and what costs should be paid in the effort to accomplish them should be a part of the intellectual life of every thinking citizen. A course in substantive criminal law is an excellent opportunity to explore these matters.

This book was prepared on the assumption that the study of criminal law should not be limited to consideration of the "general rules" concerning what conduct is criminal under what circumstances. Students considering criminal law issues should also address what the criminal law *should* provide, in light of the social and private interests involved and the ability of the law to influence behavior. Fortunately, our nation is sufficiently diverse that most options worth consideration are actual law in one or more (although perhaps a minority of) states, or at least have been considered in reported opinions. The materials here present many such options as well as discussions of current general rules. This book exposes readers to what the criminal law "is" as well as to what it best "should be."

Part I of the book consists of a single chapter, introducing students to law in general, the legal proceedings in which substantive criminal law matters arise, and some general background that is helpful in using the rest of the material. The Chapter 1 discussion of the origin and current status of the Model Penal Code is of special importance, given the use of the Code's positions in nearly all the areas covered later in the materials.

Part II turns to general principles of the criminal law. After a short introduction in Chapter 2, this part considers the criminal law's formulations of the actions required for criminal liability (Chapter 3), the culpable mental state demanded (Chapter 4), the results sometimes required and causation issues presented when this is the case (Chapter 5), and finally, in Chapter 6, the law defining liability for a crime on the part of those who are not the primary actors.

Part III addresses specific crimes. Chapter 7 presents the homicide offenses. Other offenses against physical integrity are presented next: assault, kidnapping, and related matters in Chapter 8 and sexually assaultive crimes in Chapter 9. Crimes against property are considered in Chapter 10 and offenses against the habitation—burglary and arson—are examined in Chapter 11. Finally, Chapter 12 addresses the inchoate or preparatory crimes: attempt, solicitation, and conspiracy.

Defenses to criminal liability are presented in Part IV. Chapter 13 introduces readers to the differences among the various defensive doctrines and relates these to the law governing claims of ignorance and mistake regarding both fact and law. Self-defense and related matters—defense of others and property—are the subject of Chapter 14. Defensive implications of showings that accuseds are "abnormal" in some way are considered in Chapter 15, which deals with infancy, intoxication, insanity, and similar conditions. Finally, necessity, duress, entrapment, and law enforcement are considered collectively in Chapter 16.

Some students may be interested in pursuing study of criminal law beyond the coverage of this book. An excellent source of further information and discussion on substantive criminal law questions and issues is the "hornbook," *Criminal Law*, by Professor Wayne R. LaFave and the late Austin W. Scott, Jr. The second edition was published in 1986. Professor George P. Fletcher's provocative book, *Rethinking Criminal Law*, published in 1978, is quite useful as well. The commentaries contained in the tentative drafts of the American Law Institute's Model Penal Code are older but not outdated. No finer overall view of the problems of the criminal law exists than the late Professor Herbert Packer's short 1968 volume, *The Limits of the Criminal Sanction*.

We would like to extend our gratitude to the following reviewers: James Hague, Virginia Commonwealth University; Leroy Maxwell, Missouri Western State College; Steven Murray, Community College of Rhode Island; Gayle Tronvig-Carper, Western Illinois University; and John Watkins, University of Alabama.

G.E.D.

M.M.S.

Austin, Texas
February 25, 1998

Summary of Contents

Part 3 Substantive Elements of Crimes 147

Part 4 Defenses 383

TABLE OF CONTENTS

PART 1

INTRODUCTION TO CRIMINAL LAW

Chapter 1

SUBSTANTIVE CRIMINAL LAW ISSUES AND THEIR PROCEDURAL CONTEXT

CHAPTER CONTENTS

A. Sources of Law.

B. Relationship of Constitutional Law and Substantive Criminal Law.

C. The Model Penal Code and Legislative Revision.

D. Selecting Cases for Inclusion.

E. Procedural Context of Criminal Litigation.

    1. The Roles of Judge and Jury.

    2. Matters in Issue and "Burdens."

    3. Pleading Sufficiency.

    4. Admissibility of Evidence.

    5. Evidential Sufficiency.

    6. Jury Instructions.

    7. Argument of Counsel.

    8. Appellate Review.

    9. Collateral Attack.

    10. State Defendant's Access to Federal Courts.

Some students using this book are probably about to experience their first contact with legal materials and, specifically, the published opinions of courts. Nonlawyers may have some difficulty understanding these opinions. Therefore, this chapter offers some preliminary explanations concerning the sources of law in general and criminal law in particular, and the procedural context from which published court opinions develop.

A. SOURCES OF LAW

Our secular law system draws upon three different sources of law, and consequently three different "kinds" of law. Substantive criminal law draws from all three sources and therefore embodies all three kinds of law.

The first source of law consists of constitutions, of both United States and individual states. These constitutions, of course, by their nature are supreme over the other kinds of law, and in the event of a conflict, constitutional rules must dominate over others. Similarly, the federal Constitution is dominant over state law as well as over nonconstitutional federal law. If a rule of federal constitutional law conflicts with a rule of state law—whether that state rule is of constitutional dimensions or not—the federal constitutional rule must be followed.

The second source of law consists of judges and courts, which provide the "common law." Common law is the law developed by courts through the process of resolving particular cases. As more and more cases are decided, patterns appear from which "rules" can be ascertained. These rules constitute the common law. In some strict usages, common law means court-made rules in effect as of a specific time, such as the date of the adoption of the federal Constitution. For most purposes, however, common law is best regarded as judge-made law.

The third source consists of legislatures. Law from this source is, of course, embodied in statutes. For the modern substantive criminal law, this type of law is often most important, because all American jurisdictions have extensive statutes dealing with crimes and criminal law. Not infrequently, however, these statutes are intended to merely restate the definition of crimes or defenses developed in judge-made law, and consequently the full meaning of the statutes can only be discerned by study of the cases in light of which the statutes were passed.

This tripartite division often breaks down in practice, and the three types of law become interrelated. Although crimes are almost always defined by statute, for example, these statutes quite frequently contain ambiguities that must be resolved through litigation. In many states, moreover, legislation covering substantive criminal law contains gaps, especially regarding defenses to crimes. These gaps are often filled by judicial decisions, which sometimes create or recognize defenses not provided for in the jurisdiction's statutes.

B. RELATIONSHIP OF CONSTITUTIONAL LAW AND SUBSTANTIVE CRIMINAL LAW

Constitutional law affects substantive criminal law in several ways. Sometimes it is reasonably clear that a certain interpretation of a statute defining a crime would make the statute unconstitutional. In such cases, courts will frequently assume that the legislature did not intend to enact an unconstitutional statute and will reject the interpretation of the statute that would render it invalid. Sometimes, of course, unconstitutionality cannot be avoided by a judicial interpretation of a statute relating to substantive criminal law and a statute must be held unconstitutional. Because constitutional considerations render such statutes invalid and thus of no effect, constitutional law can be said to sometimes have a very direct effect upon substantive criminal law.

In other situations, the courts will stop short of holding a statute entirely unconstitutional but will hold that particular defendants cannot constitutionally be convicted under the statute because to do so would violate their constitutional rights. Thus some applications of facially valid statutes may be constitutionally prohibited.

Constitutional requirements affect substantive law in many of the areas covered by this book. Chapter 3, for example, begins with consideration of a federal constitutional requirement that crimes be defined as including some "act." Chapter 4 makes clear that courts often assume that federal constitutional considerations limit the extent to which the states may impose so-called "strict liability," liability for crimes that do not require a culpable mental state. The precise nature and extent of any such requirement is, however, far from clear.

Similarly, Chapter 15 presents the United States Supreme Court's consideration in *Montana v. Egelhoff* of a possible federal constitutional requirement that defendants be permitted to rely defensively upon evidence of voluntary intoxication. In *Egelhoff,* the Court as a whole refused to hold that a state defendant's federal constitutional rights were violated when he was not permitted to have the jury in his intentional homicide prosecution consider his voluntary intoxication in determining whether the prosecution had proved he killed with the culpable mental state required by that crime. In that discussion, the federal constitutional question in *Egelhoff* is related to a number of less dramatic and less obvious issues, including the authority of the United States Supreme Court to consider the propriety of the Montana courts' interpretation of Montana statutes. Although these other issues are highly technical and clearly beyond the concern of this book, they cannot be completely ignored because they are essential to understanding the split among the Justices of the Supreme Court in *Egelhoff.*

Supreme Court case law is useful for purposes other than identifying the specific binding federal constitutional requirements. It may be a source in which to find analyses, principles, and values that can be applied to tasks beyond the formulation of specific constitutional rules.

As a general matter, constitutional rules in general and federal constitutional rules in particular impose only a broad outer limit beyond which state legislatures and courts cannot go in creating and defining crimes and imposing criminal liability. Those broad outer limits reflect only the most important aspects of the most important values related to such constitutional requirements as "due process of law" and the unacceptability of "cruel and unusual punishment." However, Supreme Court decisions and opinions may offer guidance as to important values that *should* be taken into account by state legislatures and courts in exercising the considerable flexibility they have to operate within the outer limits defined by federal constitutional case law.

Chapter 3, for example, develops the federal constitutional requirement that a crime include a requirement of physical conduct (or a sufficient omission) by the accused. This appears to be based in part upon the Supreme Court's conclusion that a crime consisting of only a status—and no specific act—creates an unacceptably high risk that people will be convicted for criminal thoughts or propensities that would not, if the people were left unprosecuted, ever materialize into actually harmful behavior.

State judges and legislators might find convincing the Supreme Court's basic position: that very important values held by most in our society are endangered by criminal prosecution of persons not for what they have actually done or caused, but because we believe they have a propensity to do or cause harm. If so, concern that state criminal law not unjustifiably infringe upon these values might cause them to draft or interpret statutes so as to require conduct by defendants that adequately demonstrates the defendants' dangerous propensities are real.

Such a requirement, for example, might be useful in addressing the question raised in Section C of Chapter 3. How should courts interpret laws prohibiting "control" of a vehicle while intoxicated? Because these crimes require the act of controlling the vehicle, they are not status crimes and thus do not violate the apparent specific requirements of the federal constitutional case law prohibiting status offenses. However, a state court might find the basic concerns of the Supreme Court case law convincing and therefore opt to interpret "control" to require some conduct strongly suggesting that the person would actually drive the car if not interrupted by authorities. Such an interpretation would minimize the risk that the crime would result in conviction and punishment for acts of "control" that would not in fact have led to the dangerous conduct of driving while intoxicated.

United States Supreme Court case law, then, is important not simply for the specific rules and requirements of federal constitutional law it imposes. It may also help identify values and positions that suggest the *most appropriate*—although not constitutionally required—way for courts and legislatures to go about defining crimes and defenses.

C. THE MODEL PENAL CODE AND LEGISLATIVE REVISION

Throughout this book, provisions of the Model Penal Code are included. This complication has played a major role in recent development of criminal law, and an appreciation of its nature and significance is necessary to understand the significance of its provisions.

The Model Penal Code was drafted by a committee of the American Law Institute, an organization composed of leading scholars that formulates proposed legislation dealing with a variety of subjects. A number of preliminary, or "tentative," drafts were prepared and the positions taken in these drafts were supported by extensive commentary. These were then discussed by the membership of the Institute and, in some cases with modification, approved. In 1962, a final product was published as the Proposed Official Draft. This was approved in its entirety by the Institute.

Despite its title, then, the Model Penal Code is not in any sense "law." It is, rather, a proposed formulation of statutes relating to criminal law that is available to legislatures, which may—or may not—use and perhaps adopt some or all of it. In actual fact, it has served as the basis for existing statutory provisions in many states.

Since 1962, a number of American jurisdictions have undertaken extensive revision of their statutory provisions relating to substantive criminal law. One discussion noted that between 1962 and 1983, 34 legislative substantive criminal law revisions of varying degrees of thoroughness occurred. Wechsler, Foreword to Model Penal Code and Commentaries Part I xi (Official Draft and Rev. Comments 1985). These revisions have often relied heavily upon the Model Penal Code. Even where the positions taken in the Model Penal Code have not been adopted, they have often served as the basis for discussion in the revision process. As a result of these comprehensive revision efforts, many jurisdictions now have quite detailed statutory provisions covering not only the definitions of particular offenses but also general principles concerning criminal liability and defenses to criminal charges.

An "official" draft of the Model Penal Code, with explanatory notes, was published in 1985. This followed the preparation of a multivolume set of revised and expanded commentaries that were published in 1980 and 1985, together with the text of the Code. As a result, it is now possible to make reference to this "official draft" of the Code, although that official version contains few differences in substance from the "proposed official draft" published in 1962 and used so extensively in legislative work from the early 1960s through the present.

Despite this legislative activity in the substantive criminal law area, no comprehensive revision of federal substantive criminal law has occurred. Preliminary efforts, however, have been made. In 1966, Congress created the National Commission on Reform of Federal Criminal Laws. The commission was chaired by Edmund G. Brown, former San Francisco District Attorney and eight-year governor of California. A "study draft" of a possible revision of federal statutes, with comments, was published in 1970. National Commission on Reform of Federal Criminal Laws, Study Draft of a New Federal Criminal Code (1970). The same year, the commission published a compilation of consultants' reports and staff memoranda. National Commission on Reform of Federal Criminal Laws, Working Papers of the National Commission on Reform of Federal Criminal Laws (1970). One year later a final report, consisting of a proposed new federal criminal code and comments, was published. National Commission on Reform of Federal Criminal Laws, Final Report of the Commission on Reform of Federal Criminal Laws (1971).

Legislation seeking the sort of reforms and revisions proposed by the commission was introduced into Congress and gave rise to considerable discussion. In large part because of the controversy generated by some provisions, no congressional action was taken. In 1984, however, Congress passed the Comprehensive Crime Control Act of 1984, which included some of the features of earlier efforts at comprehensive reform. Provisions of this legislation affecting the insanity defense in federal prosecutions are considered in Chapter 15. Despite the efforts and discussions, however, federal statutes have not undergone the sort of revision that has occurred in many states.

The provisions of the Model Penal Code are included in this book for several reasons. First, in some areas the Institute embodied in the Code merely what it perceived as existing law. Provisions reflecting this approach are therefore valuable as skillful restatements of what is—or was as of 1962—the "majority approach" of the law in various areas. Second, as was previously pointed out, the Code has been quite influential in the numerous statutory revisions that have taken place since 1962.

Consequently, the Model Penal Code often is consistent with modern statutory law and therefore can usefully be studied as a typical statement of present substantive criminal law. Third, even if the Code's provisions differ from traditional and modern law, they often reflect the well-considered views of a respected institution advised by excellent scholars and practitioners concerning what the law ought to be. They are useful, then, in undertaking the sort of critical examination of substantive criminal law that is a necessary part of any study of the area.

D. SELECTING CASES FOR INCLUSION

This book is designed for teaching by means of the "case method." While techniques used by teachers differ significantly, many instructors using the case method organize class discussion around the principal cases in the teaching materials. Discussion often involves identifying the issue or issues in the case, understanding the resolution of them by the court that authored the opinion, and perhaps consideration of other ways in which the issues might have been resolved. Principal cases are not selected for inclusion here because they necessarily state the only, best, or even majority view of the law or because they apply the law correctly or well to the facts. Rather, they are selected because they will serve effectively as the basis for discussion. This may be because the court's discussion is unusually informative, because the facts present a unique or otherwise interesting opportunity to discuss how the law should be applied to them, or even because the case arguably was wrongly decided so that discussion would be useful.

If the members of the court were divided on how to decide the case, the opinions of the dissenting judges (who would have resolved the case differently than the majority of the members of the court voted to do) are sometimes included. It is important to understand the arguments both ways on the issues presented, and consideration of such dissenting opinions is often helpful in this regard.

Sometimes an opinion is included in the materials even though the case was appealed further and the opinion printed is therefore not the final disposition of the case. Chapter 15's material on intoxication, for example, includes the opinion in *Weaver v. State* of the Indiana Court of Appeals, an "intermediate" appellate court. (The distinction between intermediate and other appellate courts is explained on page 24.) As the note following *Weaver* indicates, the case was appealed further to the Indiana Supreme Court, where the decision printed in the materials was reversed. The intermediate appellate court's opinion and that of the judge who dissented in that court were included, however, because those opinions contain the most effective discussion of the issues.

In preparing for class, students would generally be well advised to read the materials—and especially the principal cases—keeping in mind the reasons for their inclusion in the book.

E. PROCEDURAL CONTEXT OF CRIMINAL LITIGATION

This book relies heavily upon cases as vehicles for presenting the substantive criminal law. Obviously, the study of criminal law through the case method requires that students have an understanding of the ways in which substantive criminal law issues arise in criminal litigation and how these issues become embodied in written judicial opinions of the sort used in these materials.

The material in this casebook consists largely of appellate judicial decisions in criminal litigation. Trial judges generally do not write elaborate opinions explaining their rulings, and few jurisdictions publish any trial judges' opinions that are written. Some jurisdictions do, however, and those trial judge opinions are often quite interesting even though—as the views of "only" trial judges—they are of relatively little value as precedent. Chapter 15's material on the defense of insanity includes an opinion of a federal district judge—in *United States v. Pollard*—to whom the case was submitted for decision after the defendant waived his right to trial by jury. Judge Levin's thoughtful opinion is an unusual and valuable example of how a conscientious "trier of fact"— the body at the trial level that decides the factual question of guilt or innocence—dealt with a particularly hard question regarding the defendant's ability, given his mental illness, to avoid committing the charged crimes.

Most opinions in this book, as well as most opinions available to lawyers, are those of appellate courts. Perhaps unfortunately, the appellate courts seldom address directly many of the substantive criminal law issues with which the casebook is concerned. Because of the division of functions between trial and appellate courts, the latter commonly deal with the procedural regularity of the trial, and are seldom called upon to determine whether, on particular facts, a criminal accused is or is not guilty of a particular crime. Because substantive criminal law issues arise in this complex procedural context, some preliminary understanding of the procedural context may be useful in reading, evaluating, and using the decisions reprinted in this casebook.

Substantive criminal law issues may arise in trial litigation in a number of ways. Usually the issues will find their way to an appellate court only if the defendant is convicted and appeals from that conviction. In other situations, however, the issue may get to the appellate tribunal in other ways.

1. *The Roles of Judge and Jury*

Understanding criminal procedure demands an appreciation for the very different roles of judge and jury in the trial of a criminal case. In all major criminal prosecutions, the defendant has a federal (and perhaps state as well) constitutional right to trial by jury. The jury, however, has a somewhat limited role in the trial.

Basically, the role of the jury is to determine the facts and apply the law to the facts. The judge's role, on the other hand, is to determine the law. The judge's conclusions regarding the law are reflected in the instructions given the jury, which tell the jury the law governing the crime charged and any defenses relied upon by the defendant.

In theory, the jury is bound in most jurisdictions to accept the law as given by the trial judge. Thus the jury's duty is to resolve factual disputes, such as whether the prosecution's eyewitnesses or the defendant's alibi witnesses told the truth in their trial testimony. It is also the jury's duty to apply the law as given by the judge to the facts of the case. If the crime charged requires proof of the *mens rea* of recklessness, for example, the judge will tell the jury how the law defines recklessness. Whether the prosecution's evidence shows recklessness, however, is an application matter for the jury to undertake.

If a defendant wants to argue for a particular definition of a legal term—such as recklessness—this argument will usually be directed to the judge, pursuant to a request for jury instructions including this definition. (Jury instructions are considered in more detail later in this chapter.) If a defendant wants to argue a factual or application matter, such as that the prosecution's eyewitnesses are not telling the truth, this will usually be directed to the jury.

The jury's obligation to accept the law as given by the judge means that the lawyers cannot argue that the jury should convict or acquit despite the law, that is, by applying law different from that given it by the judge. In actual fact, a jury has the power to ignore the law in favor of the accused. If a jury acquits a defendant because it believes the law should not—although it does—cover what the prosecution proved the defendant did, the prosecution has no recourse and the defendant goes free. However, courts generally regard this as a necessary although regrettable incidental effect of a defendant's right to trial by jury. A defendant is not permitted to exploit that side effect of jury trial by explicitly arguing to the jury that it should acquit the defendant despite—or because it disagrees with—the law.

The trial judge also decides procedural matters. Thus whether the pleadings are sufficient, whether particular evidence is admissible, or whether particular arguments by the lawyers are proper are all generally determined by the judge. As is developed later in this chapter, these questions, although they are in a sense only *procedural*, may put before the judge the need to address and resolve matters of *substantive* criminal law.

2. Matters in Issue and "Burdens"

What matters are in issue in any criminal trial is determined by interaction among the applicable substantive criminal law, the pleadings of the parties, and the evidence introduced by the parties.

It is universally agreed in the United States that in a criminal trial, the prosecution bears the extraordinarily high burden of proof beyond a reasonable doubt. Not until 1970, in *In re Winship*, 397 U.S. 358, 90 S.Ct. 1068, 25 L.Ed.2d 368 (1970), however, did the United States Supreme Court have occasion to announce that this was a federal constitutional requirement. In the course of his opinion for the Court in *Winship*, Justice Brennan explained the importance of this basic procedural requirement:

The reasonable-doubt standard plays a vital role in the American scheme of criminal procedure. It is a prime instrument for reducing the risk of convictions resting on factual error. The standard provides concrete substance for the presumption of innocence * * * .

The requirement of proof beyond a reasonable doubt has this vital role in our criminal procedure for several cogent reasons. The accused during a criminal prosecution has at stake interest of immense importance, both because of the possibility that he may lose his liberty upon conviction and because of the certainty that he would be stigmatized by the conviction. Accordingly, a society that values the good name and freedom of every individual should not condemn a man for commission of a crime when there is reasonable doubt about his guilt. * * *

Moreover, use of the reasonable doubt standard is indispensable to command the respect and confidence of the community in application of the criminal law. It is critical that the moral force of the criminal law not be diluted by a standard of proof that leaves people in doubt whether innocent men are being condemned. It is also important in our free society that every individual going about his ordinary affairs have confidence that his government cannot adjudge him guilty of a criminal offense without convincing a proper factfinder of his guilt with utmost certainty.

Lest there remain any doubt about the constitutional stature of the reasonable-doubt standard, we explicitly hold that the Due Process Clause protects the accused against conviction except upon proof beyond a reasonable doubt of every fact necessary to constitute the crime with which he is charged.

However, as a great deal of later litigation has demonstrated, it is not always clear what this means.

It is necessary as a preliminary matter to distinguish several different trial burdens that might be placed upon the prosecution. One is the burden of persuasion. This, of course, is the duty to convince the trier of fact—jury or (if the defendant has waived jury trial) the judge—of the matter at issue. A second is the burden of proceeding or coming forward with—or production of—evidence. This is, in effect, the duty to produce a certain amount of evidence on a matter in order to make that matter an issue in the case. A third is the burden of pleading. This is the duty to address a matter in the pleadings.

Pleading matters will be discussed in the next section and the burdens of persuasion and coming forward with evidence will also be developed. At this point, however, these matters can be distinguished by considering the following District of Columbia abortion statute at issue in *United States v. Vuitch*, 402 U.S. 62, 91 S.Ct. 1294, 28 L.Ed.2d 601 (1971):

Whoever, by means of any instrument, medicine, drug or other means whatever, procures or produces, or attempts to procure or produce an abortion or miscarriage on any woman, unless the same were done as necessary for the preservation of the mother's life or health and under the direction of a competent licensed practitioner of medicine, shall be imprisoned in the penitentiary not less than one year or not more than ten years * * *

D.C.Code Ann. § 22-201. This statute criminalized conduct that is now constitutionally protected under the Supreme Court's more recent case law restricting on federal constitutional grounds the extent to which abortions may be prohibited. However, the statute and its application in *Vuitch* are useful illustrations of certain substantive and procedural law issues.

The terms of the statute make clear that under the substantive criminal law, the necessity of an abortion to preserve the woman's life or health might be an issue in a prosecution under the statute. If it is an issue, this will require that evidence on the matter be introduced by someone and will require that the trier of fact address the matter. What must be done to make what can be called "medical necessity" an issue in a particular prosecution?

Medical necessity might be regarded as in issue in all prosecutions under the statute. The prosecution might be required to plead in each case that no medical necessity existed. This would, in effect, make the lack of medical necessity an element of the offense, which the prosecution must allege and prove in each case. Or, it might be regarded as in issue only if the defense raised it by an appropriate pleading. The defense, for example, might be required to file some sort of responsive pleading alleging that the abortion alleged in the prosecution's charging instrument was medically necessary within the meaning of the statute. Or, the matter might be regarded in issue only if the defense, during trial, produced some evidence indicating that the particular abortion at issue was medically necessary.

Once it is determined that medical necessity is an issue in the case, it is then necessary to determine who has the burden of persuasion on that matter. It could, of course, be regarded—once raised—as part of the prosecution's case and thus the prosecution might be required to prove the lack of medical necessity by its usual burden, beyond a reasonable doubt. Or, it could be regarded as a matter that the defense must establish. If, therefore, the prosecution proves that an abortion was produced or procured by the defendant, this could be regarded as justifying conviction unless the defendant establishes that this abortion was medically necessary within the meaning of the statute. If the latter course is chosen, the defense's burden might be the usual civil burden of a preponderance of the evidence, it might be the prosecution's criminal burden of proof beyond a reasonable doubt, or it might be some intermediate standard, such as proof by clear and convincing evidence.

3. Pleading Sufficiency

The basic pleading in a criminal case is the formal charge against the defendant; this is usually an indictment returned by a grand jury or an information filed by the prosecutor. Local law dictates how the prosecution will be titled (or, as lawyers often say, how it will be "styled"), but the initiating entity is always the public prosecuting official representing the government. Thus a federal "lawsuit" constituting a federal court prosecution of Mary Smith will be styled, *"United States v. Mary Smith."* Some states style prosecution, *"State* (perhaps *"of Texas")* v. *Mary Smith"* or, instead of *"State"* use *"People"* or *"Commonwealth."* Cases reprinted in this book reflect this varied practice.

There is substantial variation among jurisdictions as to how detailed and specific a criminal pleading must be. In many jurisdictions, however, it is necessary for the indictment or information to allege sufficient facts so that those facts, if proved, will establish the defendant's guilt. Rule 7(c)(1) of the Federal Rules of Criminal Procedure, for example, provides: "The indictment or information shall be a plain, concise, and definite written statement of the essential facts constituting the offense charged." Often the requirement is met by simply using the language of the statute creating the crime with specific references for such details as the name of the victim. However, the general rule is that if, at trial, the prosecution has to prove a fact to secure the defendant's conviction, that fact must—in a general way, at least—be pleaded in the indictment or information.

If an indictment or information does not allege sufficient facts, it must—upon motion of the defense—be dismissed as failing to charge an offense.

If the defense moves before trial to dismiss a charging instrument on these grounds, the motion to dismiss may raise issues of substantive criminal law. Whether particular facts need to be alleged obviously turns upon the substantive criminal law defining the crime that is charged. In deciding whether to dismiss an indictment, then, a trial judge must often identify the elements of the crime charged and determine whether the indictment alleges facts constituting all such elements. Dismissal before trial because of insufficiency of the charge does not preclude the prosecution from seeking a new indictment or filing new information. This is because the defendant is not regarded as having been placed in jeopardy so as to have the Double Jeopardy Clause of the Constitution apply and bar a new prosecution.

If a defense motion to dismiss is overruled, no appeal may ordinarily be taken unless and until the defendant is ultimately convicted. On an appeal from a conviction, the trial court's improper failure to dismiss the indictment may constitute reversible error. However, if the motion to dismiss is granted and the indictment is dismissed, the prosecution is sometimes authorized to appeal from the order dismissing the charge.

Generally, no specific pleading is required of a criminal defendant. At the arraignment, the defendant is asked for a plea. If the defendant refuses to plead, a plea of not guilty is entered for him. There are some exceptions. A few jurisdictions demand that the defense disclose before trial the general nature of any defenses it will raise at trial. And in most jurisdictions, a defendant who intends to raise the defense of insanity (see Chapter 15) must provide the prosecution with pretrial notice of this.

Some of the facts of *United States v. Vuitch* can be used to illustrate how substantive criminal law issues can arise in the context of criminal pleadings. Vuitch was charged with a violation of the District of Columbia abortion statute by means of an indictment along the following lines:

UNITED STATES DISTRICT COURT
FOR THE DISTRICT OF COLUMBIA

Criminal No. 1043-68

Violation: D.C. Code 201 (Abortion)

The United States of America
v.
Milan Vuitch

The Grand Jury Charges:

On or about February 1, 1968, within the District of Columbia, Milan Vuitch, by means of instruments, medicines, drugs and substances, a more particular description of which is unknown to the Grand Jury, did procure and produce an abortion and miscarriage of Inez M. Fradin, she being then and there pregnant.

Mary Smith
_____
Attorney of the United States
in and for the District of Columbia

A TRUE BILL: ___*Larry Jones*_____Foreman

Although the major issues in *Vuitch* did not involve pleading or proof, the defense could reasonably have moved to dismiss the indictment on the ground that the government failed to allege that the abortion and miscarriage were not "done as necessary for the preservation of the mother's life or health and under the direction of a competent licensed practitioner of medicine." This, of course, would have raised the question of whether the inapplicability of the statutory exception is an element of the offense that the prosecution must allege.

It is widely agreed that defenses created by case law or statutes other than those defining the charged crime need not be negated in criminal pleadings. Thus the existence of an insanity defense does not require that in each indictment the prosecution allege that the defendant was not insane. However, where there is an exception to liability created by the same statute defining the crime, there is less agreement. In *Vuitch,* the Supreme Court indicated that the government should have alleged that the defendant's actions were not done as necessary to preserve the woman's life or health and under the direction of a medical practitioner. Where an exception is created by the same statutory provisions as define the elements of the crime, the Court explained, it is generally necessary that the prosecution both plead in the indictment and then prove at trial that the defendant is not within the exception.

Another issue might have been raised in *Vuitch* by a defense attack upon the indictment. The statute itself contains no *mens rea* or culpable mental state element. Despite this, however, judicial construction of the statute may nevertheless impose a requirement of *mens rea;* this is considered in Chapter 4. If intent must be proved in order to convict a defendant under the statute, it is arguable that this intent must be pleaded in the indictment. The defense, then, might have moved to dismiss the indictment on the ground that the crime charged requires criminal intent, and since this is not alleged in the indictment, the indictment fails to allege all elements of the crime. In order to rule on this motion, the trial court would have to address and resolve the substantive criminal law question as to what criminal intent, if any, is required by the District's abortion statute.

In *Vuitch*, the actual issue before the Supreme Court was whether the abortion statute was unconstitutionally vague. A defense motion to dismiss the indictment claimed that the statute was unconstitutionally vague and therefore unenforceable and consequently that no prosecution could be brought under it. The trial judge dismissed the indictment on this ground and the government appealed. As *Vuitch* itself indicates, pretrial attacks upon the validity of the statute defining the crime may require both the trial court and appellate tribunals to address, before trial, the substantive criminal law issues raised in these materials.

4. Admissibility of Evidence

During trial, objections may be made to the admissibility of evidence offered by either side. Resolving objections to evidence may require addressing issues of substantive criminal law. If a conviction is appealed, the defendant may offer errors in the admissibility of evidence as grounds for reversing the conviction.

Suppose, for example, that a defendant charged with murder seeks to establish the defense of insanity. In support of this defense, he offers the testimony of a psychiatrist. If permitted to testify, the psychiatrist will say that at the time the defendant killed the victim, the defendant was mentally ill and, because of that illness, he was unable to control his behavior. Suppose further that the prosecution objects to this evidence. As a general matter, evidence is admissible only if it is relevant to some issue in the case. The evidence here is relevant only to the defendant's ability to exercise conscious control over his behavior at the time of the crime. Whether his ability to control his behavior is a possible issue in the case depends in part upon the substantive law defining the crime charged and the defenses to that crime.

In this example, the trial judge must, in ruling on the objection to the testimony of the psychiatrist, determine the criterion for insanity in the jurisdiction. If insanity is defined so as to permit a defendant to base a defense on the contention that he was unable to control his conduct, the offered evidence is relevant to insanity and probably admissible. If, on the other hand, insanity is defined so that a defense is established only if the defendant proves that he was unable to "understand" that his conduct was contrary to the law, the offered testimony may not be relevant. It may not, in other words, tend to show insanity as the law defines it. It is important to note that in ruling on the evidence objection, the trial judge must make a substantive criminal law determination—what is "insanity" for purposes of the insanity defense.

If the trial judge excludes the evidence, the defendant is convicted, and an appeal is taken, the defendant may seek reversal of the conviction on the ground that the psychiatrist's testimony was erroneously excluded at trial. To determine whether the trial court's action was in error, the appellate court must resolve the substantive criminal law issue of the content of the insanity defense.

5. Evidential Sufficiency

In a trial, of course, the ultimate question is the sufficiency of the evidence to prove the defendant guilty. If trial is by jury, this is—generally speaking—a matter for the jury to determine.

Even in a jury trial, however, the sufficiency of the evidence may be subjected to a preliminary test before the jury has an opportunity to evaluate it. The defense may move for a directed verdict of acquittal. If this motion is granted, the court's action has the effect of taking the case from the jury and acquitting the defendant without the need for jury consideration. Principles of double jeopardy and defendants' right to trial by jury mean that the acquittal is final; the prosecution cannot appeal and cannot try the defendant again for the offense. Because the prosecution has no recourse from a directed verdict and since guilt-or-innocence is generally to be determined by a jury, it is clear that trial judges should be quite reluctant to grant defense motions for directed verdicts.

A defendant's right to jury trial means that a defendant has a complete right to have a jury decide guilt or innocence. This right exists no matter how conclusive the prosecution's evidence. Therefore, the trial judge cannot grant the prosecution's motion for a directed verdict of guilty.

In determining evidential sufficiency, as just discussed, federal constitutional requirements demand that the prosecution establish the defendant's guilt by "proof beyond a reasonable doubt." Generally, this means that each element of the charged offense must be identified and proven beyond a reasonable doubt.

As a criminal trial develops, however, issues may arise concerning matters other than proof of the elements of the charged offense. Allocating the burden of proof concerning these matters is a complex task. Basically, there are two major positions that are taken concerning the burden of proof on issues other than the elements of the charged offense.

One position is that the defendant bears the burden of proof. In the murder situation discussed in the previous section, for example, it is clear that the prosecution must prove that the defendant caused the victim's death and the defendant did so with the state of mind required for murder. These matters are all elements of the crime of murder. However, the defendant's claim of insanity may be viewed as imposing upon the defense the burden of proving that the defendant was insane within the meaning given that term by the criminal law. Of course, the jury should not reach the question of whether the defendant has met this burden unless it first finds the state has proven, beyond a reasonable doubt, all elements of the offense charged. If it finds the state has met its burden, however, it might appropriately convict the defendant unless it finds the defense has proven the "elements" of a "defense" of insanity.

The major alternative approach distinguishes between assignment of the burden of "production," on the one hand, and the burden of "persuasion," on the other. The defendant may, under this approach, have the burden of raising an issue by producing a certain amount of evidence bearing upon that issue. However, when the defendant does this and the issue is thus "raised," the prosecution then has the burden of persuasion.

Under this approach, no issue of insanity would be regarded as present unless the defendant produced a certain—usually rather small—amount of evidence suggesting that he was insane. Producing this evidence would have the effect of raising the issue. Once it is raised, the burden of persuasion is on the prosecution. Thus, once the issue of insanity is raised by defense evidence, the prosecution must negate it by proof beyond a reasonable doubt. It must, in other words, prove beyond a reasonable doubt that the defendant was sane at the time of the offense. This burden does not arise, however, until and unless the defendant meets the burden of production on that issue.

Under this second approach, the following issues are presented: Did the state prove the elements of murder beyond a reasonable doubt? If so, did the defendant produce sufficient evidence to raise the issue of insanity? If so, did the prosecution produce sufficient evidence on the issue of insanity, that is, did it produce evidence showing beyond a reasonable doubt that the defendant was not insane?

Terminology differs among jurisdictions. However, a common pattern is to characterize matters on which the defense has the burden of persuasion as "affirmative defenses." Other matters are characterized as simply "defenses." These tend to be matters on which the prosecution has the burden of persuasion if the defendant raises the matter by sufficient evidence. Terminology for defensive matters is discussed further in Chapter 13.

Burdens of producing and persuasion are closely tied to the question of whether the trial judge was obligated to instruct the jury on matters other than the elements of the charged offense. This is considered in the next section.

It is somewhat unclear what limits if any the federal constitutional requirement of due process—as construed in *In re Winship*, discussed previously—places upon the allocation of burdens of production and persuasion. The Supreme Court reaffirmed that "[p]lacing upon the defendant the burden of going forward with evidence on an affirmative defense is normally permissible." *Simopoulos v. Virginia*, 462 U.S. 506, 510, 103 S.Ct. 2532, 2535, 76 L.Ed.2d 755, 760 (1983). Moreover, the Court has held that a state may place upon a defendant the burden of persuasion on at least some matters, such as the defense of insanity. In *Leland v. Oregon,* 343 U.S. 790, 72 S.Ct. 1002, 96 L.Ed. 1302 (1952), the Court held that a state could constitutionally require a defendant to prove insanity and to do so by proof beyond a reasonable doubt. These issues are considered in more detail later, specifically in the Editors' Introduction to Chapter 13 and the Editors' Introduction to "B. Intoxication" in Chapter 15.

It is clearly constitutionally impermissible to relieve the prosecution of its burden of proof by means of certain "presumptions" that indirectly have this effect. If, for example, the prosecution has the burden of proving beyond a reasonable doubt that the defendant acted "intentionally" in committing a crime, due process is violated if the jury is told that "[t]he law presumes that a person intends the ordinary consequences of his voluntary acts." *Sandstrom v. Montana,* 442 U.S. 510, 99 S.Ct. 2450, 61 L.Ed.2d 39 (1979).

6. Jury Instructions

In a criminal case tried to a jury, it is, as a general rule, necessary to adequately instruct the jury on all issues raised by the charge against the defendant and the evidence introduced at trial. This involves two significantly different although interrelated questions: When must the jury be instructed on an issue? What is necessary for instructions on an issue to be sufficient?

On the first question, it is clear that the jury must always be informed with regard to the elements of the crime charged and must be told that the prosecution must prove each element beyond a reasonable doubt. Upon proper request, the jury must be similarly instructed concerning any other offense of which the defendant might be convicted. Generally speaking, of course, a defendant can be convicted only of that offense (or those offenses) charged in the indictment. A defendant charged with burglary, for example, cannot at trial be convicted of robbery, even if the prosecution's evidence undeniably shows the defendant guilty of robbery rather than burglary.

Like many aspects of criminal procedure, this submission of the charged offense to the trial jury is to some extent a matter of federal constitutional right. In *Sullivan v. Louisiana,* 508 U.S. 275, 277, 113 S.Ct. 2078, 2081, 124 L.Ed.2d 182 (1993), the Supreme Court made clear that the Fifth Amendment requirement of proof beyond a reasonable doubt and the Sixth Amendment right to jury trial are "interrelated." These provisions together, the Court added in *United States v. Gaudin,* 515 U.S. 506, 510, 115 S.Ct. 2310, 2313, 132 L.Ed.2d 444, 449–450 (1995), demand that a criminal conviction rest upon a jury determination that the defendant is guilty of every element of the crime charged, beyond a reasonable doubt.

In *Gaudin,* the defendant was charged with making false statements on federal loan documents. One element of this offense requires the prosecution to prove that the false statement by the defendant was "material." The trial judge instructed the jury that the government was required to prove that the alleged false statements were material but he added:

> [t]he issue of materiality . . . is not submitted to you for your decision but rather
> is a matter for the decision of the court. You are instructed that the statements
> charged in the indictment are material statements.

The trial judge's refusal to allow the jury to determine the materiality of the statement, the Supreme Court held, violated Gaudin's constitutional "right to have a jury determine, beyond a reasonable doubt, his guilt of every element of the crime with which he is charged."

Defendants' federal constitutional right to have a conviction rest on a fair jury determination that the prosecution has proved each element of the crime beyond a reasonable doubt may have other implications. These are considered later in this book. Chapter 13, for example, raises the possibility that a defendant relying on a defensive theory of mistake of fact may have a right under *Sullivan* and *Gaudin* to have the defensive theory explained to the jury by the trial judge.

As a general rule, the trial judge may permit the jury to convict the defendant of only those crimes actually charged in the indictment. There is an important exception, however. A defendant may be convicted of offenses other than those charged in the indictment if those offenses are "lesser included offenses" of an offense charged. An offense is a lesser included offense of a charged offense if it is established by some of the same but less than all of the evidence necessary to prove the charged, "greater," offense. The "lesser" offense, in other words, must require for its proof no evidence not also required for proof of the "greater."

Suppose, for example, a defendant is charged with the felony of burglary. In the jurisdiction, burglary is defined as an entry into another's dwelling with the intent therein to commit a felony, where the entry is made without the other person's effective consent. The jurisdiction also prohibits as a misdemeanor what is labeled "criminal trespass." This is defined as entry onto the property of another without effective consent. It is quite likely that criminal trespass is a lesser included offense of burglary. Burglary requires proof of everything that is required for criminal trespass, plus something further: that at the time of the entry, the accused had the intent to commit a felony. Or, to put the matter another way, criminal trespass is established by proof of some but not all of the facts necessary to show burglary, and no other facts.

Again speaking generally, a defendant charged with and tried for burglary will be entitled to have the jury instructed on criminal trespass if it is clear that criminal trespass is a lesser included offense of burglary and there is some basis in the proof at trial for the jury to conclude that the defendant is guilty only of criminal trespass. If, for example, there is some evidence that the defendant did enter the premises without consent but at the time lacked the intent to commit a felony, then the jury should be instructed on criminal trespass as well as the charged offense of burglary.

If the jury is "charged on" criminal trespass, the instructions should tell the jury the elements of both it and burglary. They should further tell the jury to first consider whether the prosecution has proved beyond a reasonable doubt the defendant's guilt of the charged offense of burglary. However, the instructions should make clear that if the jury concludes the prosecution has not met its burden on the charged offense, the jury should then consider whether the prosecution has proved beyond a reasonable doubt all elements of criminal trespass. If the jury concludes that the prosecution has done so, the instructions should state, the defendant should be convicted of criminal trespass but not burglary.

Whether criminal juries are instructed on defensive matters presents more difficult questions. If a defendant seeks an instruction on what might be called a "true" defense—one that assumes all elements of the charged crime have been showed but relies upon *additional* facts as entitling the accused to acquittal—there is general agreement that the jury should be told about the offense if, but only if, the evidence "raises" it.

Suppose in the burglary prosecution just discussed, for example, the defense introduces evidence—consisting of testimony by the defendant's brother—that the defendant was crazy and that this may have affected his ability to refrain from entering the victim's dwelling. In the jurisdiction, there is a "defense" of insanity and insanity is defined as mental abnormality that renders a person unable to control his actions. As a general matter, it should be clear that insanity is not a matter that challenges the sufficiency of the prosecution's evidence concerning the elements of the crime. The accused's ability to control his conduct is not something the prosecution must prove in each case and, generally speaking, juries are not told in burglary prosecutions that the prosecution must prove beyond a reasonable doubt that the defendant was able to, but chose not to, avoid entering the victim's dwelling. If insanity exists, it consists of additional evidence (that is, evidence not tending to prove or disprove any element of the crime) that is given the effect of requiring acquittal despite the sufficiency of the evidence to prove, beyond a reasonable doubt, each element of the crime.

If the jury is "instructed on" insanity, it will be told that insanity is a defense and that insanity consists of a condition in which the defendant is, because of mental illness, unable to control his action. The instructions should tell the jury that it should consider insanity only if it first finds that the prosecution has proven each element of the charged offense—burglary—beyond a reasonable doubt. If the jury finds the evidence sufficient on these matters, it should then but only then consider insanity. If it finds the defendant insane, the instruction should make clear, the jury is to acquit the defendant despite its earlier conclusion that the prosecution's evidence sufficiently established each element of the offense.

Generally speaking, a jury needs to be instructed on defensive issues such as insanity only if they are "raised by the evidence." Also the instructions should make clear to the jury who has the burden of proof or persuasion on the defensive issue and what that burden is. Normally, a defensive issue is raised only if some evidence has been introduced from which the jury might find that the "defense" has been established. In the burglary example just discussed, whether the defense of insanity has been so "raised" is arguable. The defense introduced no expert testimony. Whether "lay" testimony that the defendant was sufficiently crazy to be insane in the legal sense is sufficient to raise the issue of insanity and thus to require a jury instruction is a matter of legitimate debate.

As a general matter, a defensive matter is raised if some evidence has been introduced that, if believed, would mean that a defense exists. For example, if the defendant takes the witness stand and testifies to a version of the facts that, if accepted, mean that the defendant had a defense for the conduct constituting the crime, the matter should go to the jury. See, for example, *Brown v. State,* 698 P.2d 671, 674 (Alaska App.1985) (the jury should be instructed on self-defense even if the only evidence supporting that theory was the defendant's own testimony). That the evidence supporting the defense version of the facts is weak and unlikely to be believed by the jury is not a legitimate basis for refusing to submit the issue to the jury. Defendants' right to jury trial means that they have the right to have the jury, under proper instruction, evaluate the credibility or "believability" of testimony supporting their version of the events on which the prosecution is based.

The matter can become quite complex. In *United States v. Bailey,* 444 U.S. 394, 100 S.Ct. 624, 62 L.Ed.2d 575 (1980), reprinted in part in Chapter 16, the members of the Supreme Court were arguably divided not on the issue of the substantive criminal law—under what circumstances is duress or necessity a defense to charge of prison escape—but rather on whether the defense testimony raised a jury issue on that defense in the particular cases before the Court.

If an instruction is required because the issue has been raised, what the jury is told concerning the burden of persuasion depends, as was discussed, upon local law relating to the particular defensive matter at issue. The defendant may have the burden of persuasion on insanity and this burden may be one of a "preponderance of the evidence," by proof "beyond a reasonable doubt," or some intermediate one, as by "clear and convincing" evidence. Or, once the defendant has raised the issue of insanity by evidence sufficient to require a jury instruction, the prosecution may have the burden of proving, probably by proof beyond a reasonable doubt, that the accused was sane at the time of the events constituting the crime. In any case, the jury instructions must make clear to the jury what the burden of proof on the defensive issue is and upon which party that burden rests.

When a defendant relies not upon a true defense but rather upon a defensive theory that challenges the sufficiency of the prosecution's evidence regarding the elements of the crime, there is considerable variation as to whether and when the jury must be instructed on that specific theory.

Suppose, for example, a defendant is charged with burglary, which was previously defined. At trial the defense introduces evidence of alibi, that is, that at the time of the offense the defendant was elsewhere and therefore could not have been the burglar. The defense evidence challenges the sufficiency of the prosecution's evidence to establish one element of the offense—that the defendant committed the act of entering another's dwelling. If the defendant was elsewhere it necessarily follows that he did not commit the act of entry, and thus could not have committed burglary as that crime is defined.

Is the defendant entitled to have the jury instructed specifically on the "issue" of alibi? Jurisdictions differ. Some courts emphasize the risk that juries may misallocate the burden of proof and require that the defendant "prove" his claim of alibi; these courts tend to require that juries be instructed that such alibi evidence relates to a matter on which the prosecution has the burden of proof, so that if this evidence raises a reasonable doubt as to whether the accused was the perpetrator, the accused should be acquitted.

Other courts, in contrast, reason that instructions placing the burden of proof on the prosecution generally are sufficient and no specific instruction on such a defensive theory that the prosecution has not met its burden is necessary. Some regard such instructions as raising a risk that a jury may misinterpret the instructions as suggesting that the burden of proof should be placed on the accused or that the judge regards the defendant's alibi evidence as particularly worthy of belief. Because instructions on a defensive theory simply challenging the prosecution's proof are unnecessary and potentially misleading, they are not given.

Generally, then, jury instructions must adequately inform the jury as to the law relating to all matters that must be addressed. Obviously, the sufficiency of jury instructions in this regard presents numerous substantive criminal law issues. Whether particular jury instructions are erroneous in content presents some of the most difficult questions in criminal law and procedure.

Many American jurisdictions have developed so-called " pattern" instructions for criminal as well as civil cases. Thus a trial judge's task, with the help of both the prosecutor and defense counsel, is to identify on what matters the jury must be instructed and then to choose and give the portions of the pattern instructions relating to those matters. As a result, however, the instructions are obviously drafted in a general fashion and are not "individualized" for particular cases.

Jury instructions in criminal cases have come under substantial attack, especially by social scientists. A major consideration in drafting instructions, these critics claim, is the need to avoid reversal on appeal for legal inaccuracies in the instructions. As a result, the instructions tend to use "safe" language found in statutes or in old judicial opinions. Although such language may survive scrutiny by appellate courts, the critics suggest, it is often ineffective in helping jurors to understand the law that they are called upon to apply. Severance, Greene and Loftus, Towards Criminal Jury Instructions That Jurors Can Understand, 75 J.Crim.L. & Crim. 198, 201 (1984), noted that a 1950 book of approved jury instructions contained the following comment:

> The one thing an instruction must do above all else is correctly state the law. This is true regardless of who is capable of understanding it.

Severance and Loftus, Improving the Ability of Jurors to Comprehend and Apply Criminal Jury Instructions, 17 L. & Soc.Rev. 153 (1982), studied a series of criminal trials in which deliberating juries had specifically asked the trial judge for additional information or guidance. They concluded that these requests showed that despite the trial judge's instructions, juries experienced confusion concerning the elements of the crime that needed to be proved and, in particular, were uncertain concerning the intent that was necessary for guilt.

Kramer and Koenig, Do Jurors Understand Criminal Jury Instructions?, 23 U. Mich. J.L.Ref. 401 (1990), reported on questionnaires given to actual jurors after cases were concluded that asked about some matters on which the jurors were instructed and some on which they were not. They concluded that instructions sometimes at least had little impact on jurors' comprehension. Most discouraging, sometimes instructions seemed to *decrease* comprehension; jurors who had listened to instructions about a matter responded less accurately to questions about that matter than jurors who had not been instructed on it.

The problem is probably more than one of drafting. Tanford, The Law and Psychology of Jury Instructions, 69 Neb.L.Rev. 71, 82–83 (1990), suggested that the widespread practice of formulating jury instructions in abstract form may impede jurors' comprehension. Yet there is a risk that if judges relate instructions to facts—by referring to the actual evidence, using examples from everyday experience, and using specific names rather than abstract generic terms such as "parties"—those judges would be improperly interfering with juries by making prohibited comments on the evidence. He also offered that in some situations "it is the law itself that is incomprehensible." "If the law itself is incoherent," he added, "no amount of redrafting of pattern instructions is going to result in jurors understanding it."

7. Argument of Counsel

Substantive criminal law issues may also arise in disputes concerning jury arguments made by either or both defense counsel or prosecutors. Generally speaking, lawyers' arguments are limited to the facts in evidence and the law applicable to cases of this sort. Lawyers may not—to put the matter negatively—argue on the basis of information not in evidence or propositions of law contrary to the jurisdiction's law.

In the burglary case previously hypothesized, for example, the prosecutor could not properly argue to the jury that they should convict the defendant of burglary even if they find that because of insanity he could not control his conduct. Because the jurisdiction's insanity law, it is posited, provides that an inability, due to mental abnormality, to control conduct is a defense, the prosecutor may not urge the jury to apply a different rule of law. Defense counsel is similarly limited. If under the jurisdiction's definition of legal insanity loss of control does not amount to insanity, defense counsel cannot urge that the jury acquit the defendant on the ground that the evidence shows he was unable to control his conduct at the time of the incident.

If objection is made to a lawyer's argument on the basis that it goes beyond or is inconsistent with the applicable law or with the evidence that has been introduced, the trial judge must, in ruling on the objection, often make a substantive criminal law determination. Thus substantive criminal law issues can arise in the procedural context of objections to argument of counsel.

8. *Appellate Review*

Although procedures exist for the prosecution, under some circumstances, to obtain appellate review of trial court decisions, most appeals in criminal cases are appeals taken by convicted defendants from their convictions.

Many American jurisdictions have so-called "two tier" appellate court structures. In such structures, convicted defendants have a virtually absolute right to appeal to the first, or "intermediate," appellate court. When that appellate court has acted, the highest appellate court—often, in the state context, the state "supreme court"—has the authority but not the obligation to review the decision of the intermediate appellate court. This often means that the party losing before the intermediate appellate court—whether that party is the convicted defendant or the prosecution—may seek review by the higher court. Whether or not to undertake review, however, is discretionary with that tribunal; neither party has a "right" to review by the highest court. Schemes of this sort are often subject to exceptions in cases of maximum severity, that is, those in which the death penalty has been imposed. Defendants sentenced to death are often absolutely entitled to review of their conviction and sentence by the jurisdiction's highest appellate court.

The general public often has the perception that appellate tribunals "release" convicted defendants with some frequency and for mere "technicalities." This perception is, however, unlikely to be true. One study, Davies, Affirmed: A Study of Criminal Appeals and Decision-Making Norms in a California Court of Appeals, 1982 Am.Bar Ass.Research J. 543 (1982), carefully studied criminal appeals in one state intermediate appellate court. In only 14 percent of criminal cases did the appellate court give an appealing defendant some relief. In contrast, 31 percent of appellants in civil litigation were, to some extent, successful before the appellate court. Even those defendants who secured relief on appeal often obtained only some modification of their situation, such as a reduction in sentence or a reversal of some but not all convictions from which they appealed. In only 4.8 percent of the cases did the appellate court reverse all convictions and therefore require that the appealing defendant either be released or retried. In terms of convictions obtained, Davies estimated that about 2.6 convictions in every thousand (or 0.26 percent) were reversed on appeal.

Convicted defendants can appeal on a variety of grounds, but most defendant appeals fall into one of two categories. In both categories, the role of the appellate court is limited, which helps explain the low reversal rate.

First, defendants may argue that there was insufficient evidence to convict. Davies' study reported that about 24 percent of appeals raised issues of this sort, but that relief was seldom granted on this ground. Appellate courts, generally speaking, have no authority to address directly whether the evidence presented at trial proves guilt beyond a reasonable doubt. They may, however, depending upon local law, subject the evidence to scrutiny of two sorts. This is of special importance, because of the double jeopardy implications of an appellate ruling on evidential sufficiency.

If an appellate court finds that the evidence is insufficient to support a conviction, this is—for double jeopardy purposes—the equivalent of acquittal. It means that the appellate court cannot remand the case for a new trial but must instead see that the defendant is acquitted. *Burks v. United States,* 437 U.S. 1, 98 S.Ct. 2141, 57 L.Ed.2d 1 (1978). Under double jeopardy doctrine, an acquittal bars a defendant from being prosecuted again for the offense of which he was acquitted.

The standard for appellate review of evidential sufficiency is designed to require appellate courts to accord great deference to the trier of fact, whether a jury or, when the defendant has waived a jury trial, the judge. As a result, the issue for the appellate court on an appeal from a conviction is usually only whether there is some evidence in the record on each matter that the prosecution was obligated to establish from which a reasonable trial judge or jury *could* conclude that guilt was shown beyond a reasonable doubt. If such evidence exists, a conviction should be affirmed against an insufficient evidence attack, even if the appellate judges would—had they been the trial judge or the jurors—have acquitted.

Some jurisdictions, however, authorize appellate courts to engage in a more rigorous scrutiny of the evidence than is permissible under the "insufficient evidence" standard. Under this approach, an appellate court can grant relief if the court determines that the verdict of guilty is against "the weight of the evidence." Moreover, the double jeopardy clause of the federal constitution permits a state to enable its appellate courts to direct a new trial rather than an acquittal upon determinations that the record of case contains sufficient evidence to support the conviction but also that the verdict of guilty was contrary to the weight of the evidence presented at trial. *Tibbs v. Florida,* 457 U.S. 31, 102 S.Ct. 2211, 72 L.Ed.2d 652 (1982). Application of the second criterion obviously gives the appellate tribunal greater authority to consider the evidence. The Supreme Court explained in *Tibbs:*

> [A] conviction rests upon insufficient evidence when, even after viewing the evidence in the light most favorable to the prosecution, no rational factfinder could have found the defendant guilty beyond a reasonable doubt. A reversal based on the weight of the evidence, on the other hand, draws the appellate court into questions of credibility. The "weight of the evidence" refers to "a determination [by] the trier of fact that a greater amount of credible evidence supports one side of an issue or cause than the other."

Defendants can also attack convictions on grounds in a second category. This category consists of procedural errors related to the trial. Davies found that various issues of this sort were raised in appeals to the court he studied with the following frequency: evidence improperly admitted under the rules of evidence (raised in 39.7 percent of cases); evidence improperly admitted because of invalid searches (27.8 percent of cases); improper jury instructions (25.9 percent of cases); improper argument or comments by prosecutor (22.6 percent of cases); evidence offered by the defense improperly excluded (15.6 percent of cases). A conviction may be reversed for trial error of this sort, of course, even if the evidence to support the conviction is sufficient.

Whether there was procedural error during trial or not is often a matter presenting the appellate court with only a limited question. When a defendant claims that a trial judge erred by admitting certain evidence, for example, whether the judge's ruling admitting that evidence was error is often relegated to the discretion of the trial judge. On appeal, then, the appellate court judges do not ask whether they would have ruled differently had they been the trial judge and conclude that the trial judge erred if they would have ruled differently. Rather, the appellate court asks only whether the trial judge's ruling was so clearly contrary to what the appellate judges would have done as to constitute "abuse of discretion" and thus error.

The appellate courts' role in reviewing errors in this second category is affected by widespread acceptance in criminal litigation of what is often called the "harmless error" rule. Under this doctrine, an error in a criminal trial does not justify reversal of the conviction if it is "harmless." Sometimes the rule is put otherwise—trial error constitutes reversible error requiring that a conviction be invalidated only if it is "prejudicial." Whether an error was "prejudicial" or "harmless" within the meaning of this rule generally turns upon whether the appellate court determines that there is a sufficiently high risk that it affected the outcome of the trial, that is, that it "caused" or contributed to the conviction. No significant interests are served, the reasoning goes, by reversal of a conviction for an error if the record makes sufficiently certain that the error did not affect the outcome of the trial.

Whether an error is harmless or not often involves a complex inquiry that depends in large part upon the nature of the error found. A conclusion that the record shows that the defendant is clearly guilty, of course, does not automatically mean that the conviction should be upheld despite the occurrence of error in the trial. In many cases, however, the sufficiency of the evidence supporting the defendant's guilt is a relevant consideration. The stronger the evidence showing guilt, the more likely it is that a procedural error in the trial did not affect the outcome. Overwhelming evidence of guilt, in other words, often indicates that had the trial been conducted without the error, the defendant would nevertheless have been convicted.

In any event, appellate court opinions constitute a major source of the substantive criminal law area, as is true in other areas of law. In evaluating the significance of appellate holdings and discussions, however, it is necessary to consider carefully the manner in which the substantive criminal law issue arose in the trial court. It is also necessary to consider what is often the limited role of the appellate tribunal in reviewing a conviction from which a defendant appeals. Seldom does an appellate court have occasion to address whether on particular evidence a defendant is or is not guilty of a particular offense.

9. Collateral Attack

A defendant who has unsuccessfully appealed his or her conviction as high in the court system as is possible or who failed to take advantage of the right to appeal after conviction may also, in some situations, challenge the conviction in what are called proceedings for "collateral" attack. The procedural device for doing this is often the writ of habeas corpus. A convicted (and imprisoned) defendant files an application for the writ claiming that his or her incarceration is impermissible because the conviction on which it rests is flawed. Such a proceeding is called a collateral attack because in theory it is not a continuing part of the litigating constituting the original prosecution (as was any appeal). Rather, it is a new lawsuit that in some sense occurs collateral to the lawsuit constituting the original prosecution.

A defendant convicted in state court may often mount collateral attack in first state courts and, if that fails, seek similar relief from the federal courts. A defendant convicted in federal court can only seek habeas corpus relief from the federal courts.

The ability to collaterally attack a conviction infringes even more than appeal upon the prosecution's legitimate interest in having convictions be final. Consequently, the grounds on which collateral attack can be made are quite limited. A defendant as a general rule cannot collaterally attack a conviction on a ground that would require reversal if raised on direct appeal. Rather, the defendant must show a particularly serious defect in the prosecution, such as an error of constitutional dimensions or what the courts often call a "jurisdictional" error or one that renders a conviction entirely "void."

A defendant convicted in state court who seeks habeas corpus relief from the federal courts is further limited to contentions that the state court proceedings were tainted by a federal constitutional error. Federal courts have no authority to hold a state conviction invalid because the federal judges are convinced the state courts made an error in defining or applying state law.

One example of an opinion in a habeas corpus proceeding appears in Chapter 13, which reprints the opinion of a federal district judge in *Wilson v. Tard*. Wilson was convicted of manslaughter in the New Jersey state courts and unsuccessfully appealed his conviction as far in the state court system as he could. In the state proceedings, he argued in part that the trial judge's instructions on mistake of fact were wrong as a matter of New Jersey state criminal law. He then applied to the federal district court for habeas corpus relief.

Note that the case—*Wilson v. Tard*—is styled differently from that of most other cases in these materials. Wilson is the incarcerated state defendant, who was suing Tard, who in turn was the warden of the state facility in which Wilson was incarcerated. Because this is not a part of the original litigation (which was styled *State v. Wilson),* it has a new title that reflects the different procedural context.

Because Wilson was a state defendant seeking relief from a federal court, he could not rely on the claim of New Jersey law error that he had asserted on his appeal in state court. Rather, he had to argue that because of the way in which the trial judge instructed the jury in his state trial, his conviction was obtained in violation of his federal constitutional right to due process of law and its requirement that a conviction rest upon proof of all elements of the crime beyond a reasonable doubt. He relied upon the same events as in the state proceeding, but because he was seeking federal habeas corpus relief he had to establish that those events denied him a federal constitutional right.

10. State Defendant's Access
to Federal Courts

Most of the opinions reprinted in this book arise out of state criminal prosecutions. Some, however, are opinions of federal courts. How does a state defendant get into federal court regarding a matter that began as and is essentially a state court proceeding? There are two ways.

First, a defendant who has appealed his or her conviction to the highest state court that under state law can consider the case may, if denied relief by the state courts, seek review of the state's courts' denial of relief from the United States Supreme Court. This review is sought by applying to the Supreme Court for what is called a writ of certiorari. Whether to accept the case is discretionary with the Supreme Court, and the defendant has no right to such review.

The United States Supreme Court has authority on writ of certiorari only to review state courts' holdings on federal law. It has no authority to review state courts' interpretations of law. Usually, certiorari is sought on the ground that the state courts misinterpreted or misapplied federal constitutional law.

The second way in which a state defendant can get into federal court was described in Section 9 of this chapter—the defendant may apply to the federal courts for habeas corpus relief from a state conviction. A defendant who does this applies not to the United States Supreme Court but rather to the lowest level of federal court, the United States District Court. The action of the district court can often be appealed by the losing party to the intermediate federal courts, the United States Courts of Appeal. A party who loses before the court of appeal, like the defendant who loses a state court appeal, may seek review from the United States Supreme Court by application for the writ of certiorari. Again, whether to accept the case is discretionary with the Supreme Court.

The first case in this book illustrates a state defendant getting into federal court. In Section A of Chapter 3, the book reprints the opinions in *Robinson v. California*. Robinson was convicted in the California courts in a prosecution styled *People v. Robinson*. When the state appellate courts found no error in his trial, he sought certiorari from the United States Supreme Court. He asserted that the California courts erred in failing to recognize that his conviction violated his right under the Eighth Amendment of the United States Constitution to be free of cruel and unusual punishment; thus he raised a federal constitutional issue. The Supreme Court agreed to consider his case and, doing so, found that the highest California court to consider the case erred in holding that federal Eighth Amendment law did not bar the conviction.

PART 2

GENERAL PRINCIPLES

Chapter 2

GENERAL PRINCIPLES OF CRIMINAL LIABILITY: INTRODUCTION

Courts often say that a crime consists of both *mens rea* and *actus reus* or, to abandon "law Latin," that a crime consists of a mental state and a physical act. To some extent, however, this may suggest an oversimplified analysis, depending upon how each term, especially *actus reus,* is defined.

Actus reus might be defined as simply the physical activity that a person must perform in order to incur liability for a crime. Then, however, the often-repeated statement that *mens rea* and *actus reus* make up a crime ignores the fact that many crimes require proof of other types of matters, such as certain results that must occur (the victim's death in homicide offenses, for example) and attendant circumstances that must exist (such as "nighttime" in burglary).

It is also possible to define *actus reus* as including all nonmental elements: the physical activity, any results that must occur, and any circumstances that must exist. Cohen, Actus Reus, in 1 Encyclopedia of Crime & Justice 15 (1983) ("the *actus reus* designates all the elements of the criminal offense except the *mens rea"*). This is the sense in which the term will be used in this book. Thus the "act" required for criminal liability by a particular crime—the physical movement or omission by the defendant—must be distinguished from the *actus reus* of that crime. The act is part of, but often not the complete, *actus reus* of the offense.

The Model Penal Code follows a somewhat similar approach, although it does not use the traditional law Latin terms *actus reus* and *mens rea.* "Act" (or "action") is defined in section 1.13 as "a bodily movement whether voluntary or involuntary." "Conduct," on the other hand, is defined as "an action or omission and its accompanying state of mind." "Elements of an offense" are defined as possibly including—depending upon the particular offense being considered—conduct, attendant circumstances, and results of conduct.

It is perhaps best, insofar as can be done, to avoid reference to such terms and instead to adopt as functional an approach as possible. This book proposes a scheme of analysis designed to facilitate careful analysis of issues that might arise in applying a crime to a particular set of facts. Given the widespread trend towards adoption of comprehensive criminal codes often based upon the American Law Institute's Model Penal Code, this almost always involves consideration and application of statutory provisions creating and defining the offense and providing for defenses to liability. Sometimes, however, the contents of modern statutory provisions and definitions can only be meaningfully established by considering the common law definitions of their predecessors. Even more frequently, reference to early common law and more recent judicial development of defenses and general principles is necessary, due to the tendency of American legislation to focus on the definition of particular offenses rather than on traditional general matters.

The analysis proposed here is a three-step process. The first step is to ascertain the elements of the offense, that is, those matters that the prosecution must usually plead in the charging instrument and that it must always prove at trial.

For the sake of convenience and clarity, it is valuable to consider elements of offenses in terms of four categories. A particular crime may not contain an element in each category, although to some extent constitutional considerations may require proof of some element in each of the first two categories.

Act. It is most useful to think of the act required for liability in terms of what physical activities must be shown on the part of the accused. The statute creating and defining the crime may specifically describe (and limit) the type of physical activity that can constitute the crime, as, for example, by requiring that the defendant have been "driving." Or, as in the case with most homicide offenses, the definition of the crime may make no effort to describe the required physical activity. In this case, any action or failure to act that meets general requirements will suffice.

State of Mind. For a number of reasons, the criminal law is deeply concerned with the accused's conscious state of mind at the time of the act constituting the offense. Nearly all offenses require that the trier of fact be convinced beyond a reasonable doubt that the accused was, at that time, aware of something. However, the state of mind—the culpable mental state—required differs drastically among offenses.

Results. A number of offenses require that a particular result be shown to have occurred. When this is the case, the prosecution must also show that there was a causal relationship between the defendant's act and state of mind, on the one hand, and the occurrence of the result, on the other.

Attendant Circumstances. Some offenses require a showing that particular circumstances existed at the time of the offense. These differ from results (those elements in the third category just described) in that the prosecution need not show a causal relationship between the accused's actions and state of mind, on the one hand, and the attendant circumstances, on the other.

Circumstances may serve an important policy purpose in defining or limiting the conduct made criminal. Or, they may be of relatively minor importance. Federal crimes, for example, often require the showing of certain circumstances for the sole purpose of justifying federal jurisdiction over the offense.

Frequently, circumstances are included in the definition of a crime to distinguish the offense from less serious crimes and to provide the basis for a more severe penalty. Many jurisdictions have several burglary offenses, for example, which define as a more serious category of burglary (with a more serious penalty) those prohibited entries occurring at a time when the circumstance of "nighttime" existed.

The second step of the analysis requires consideration of any so-called defenses that are really means of disproving one of the elements of the offense. Most often this amounts to disproving the state of mind required for the crime. Proof of a defendant's mistake as to the facts existing at the time of his or her actions, for example, may serve to raise in the jurors' minds a reasonable doubt as to whether the defendant entertained the requisite state of mind.

The final step in the analysis is to address defenses in the true sense. These are matters that, if established, prevent or reduce liability despite proof of all elements of the offense. One who kills to preserve her own life, for example, will have entertained an awareness that her actions would cause the death of the victim; this suffices (under most statutes) for murder. Yet if, in addition, the elements of self-defense are established, she is relieved of liability.

The remainder of this book is organized with reference to this analysis. Part 2 considers general principles or rules relating to criminal liability. Chapter 3 deals with problems in identifying the act required for liability. Chapter 4 addresses state of mind requirements. When a crime includes an element consisting of a result, this necessarily raises potential problems of causation, since the defendant's act must have caused any result required. Causation questions are addressed in Chapter 5.

Although as a general rule a defendant can be convicted of only those crimes personally committed by the defendant, in some situations a defendant is criminally responsible for crimes actually committed by someone else. The law defining such responsibility for offenses committed by others is the law of complicity, which is considered in Chapter 6.

In Part 3 of the book, attention is turned—with the basic principles covered in Part 2 in mind—to the requirements of specific crimes. Homicide crimes are of particular importance, because of both their impact upon victims and the penalties imposed upon conviction; these are considered in Chapter 7. Other crimes against the person are next addressed in Chapter 8. Crimes of sexual aggressiveness are covered separately in Chapter 9.

Property crimes have traditionally been a matter of particular complexity, and these are presented in Chapter 10. Traditional criminal law gave particular protection to interests in the security of the dwelling, and the two crimes that implemented this—burglary and arson—are covered in Chapter 11.

As a general rule, a person who engages in conduct preparatory to committing at least a serious criminal offense may well incur criminal liability for that preparatory conduct itself. Such liability is for the "inchoate" or "preparatory" offenses, considered in Chapter 12.

Finally, the book turns in Part 4 to defenses in a broad sense. Mistake regarding either fact or law is covered in Chapter 13. Self-defense and related matters are addressed in Chapter 14. Defenses relating to a person's capacity for criminal responsibility are covered in Chapter 15, and other defenses—necessity, entrapment, and law enforcement—are dealt with in Chapter 16.

No pretense can be made that substantive criminal law may be analyzed "scientifically." It may be helpful, however, to visualize the basic framework of analysis previously described above through the following formula:

$$\left[\left(\text{Act} + \text{State of Mind}\right) \xrightarrow{\text{(Causation)}} \text{Results}\right] + \begin{array}{l}\text{Attendant}\\\text{Circumstances}\end{array} = \text{Liability}$$

This formula reflects the need to show for liability the required physical conduct, the necessary state of mind, any required result (and causation between the conduct and intent and that result), and any demanded attendant circumstances.

Chapter 3

GENERAL PRINCIPLES OF CRIMINAL LIABILITY: THE ACT

CHAPTER CONTENTS

Editors' Introduction: The General Requirement of an "Act"

As explained in Chapter 2, this book uses the term actus reus to refer to all the non-mental elements of a crime: the physical activity that the accused must be shown to have performed, the consequences of that activity that must be proved, and the circumstances attendant upon the accused's activity that the prosecution must establish. This encourages a differentiation of each category of element and forces a more thorough examination of the proof necessary for liability for particular crimes.

This chapter deals with the first aspect of *actus reus* so defined—the physical activity that the accused must be shown to have performed. Conceptually, the general rule that a defendant must not only have had a criminal *mens rea* but also must have engaged in prohibited activity serves as a major limitation upon the government's power to intervene in the lives and situations of its citizens. One court explained:

> [Making such things as the planning of a crime the commission of the crime itself] would run counter to a fundamental concept that underlies our criminal justice system. Until an individual actually commits an offense, he is innocent. Thinking about perpetrating a crime is not unlawful. The evil lies in the commission of the illegal act. Prior to the time one actually crosses the line and acts, there is always the possibility that conscience, civic responsibility or plain good judgment will prevail.

United States v. Washington Water Power Co., 793 F.2d 1079,1 1082 (9th Cir.1986). Whether in actual practice the requirement of an act imposes a meaningful limitation upon criminal liability is more problematic.

Some offenses are defined so as to specify with great particularity what action is required. This is explored in some of the chapters later in this book that concern the definition of particular offenses. What action constitutes "entry" for purposes of burglary, for example, is addressed in some detail by the definition of that offense.

Other offenses make no effort whatsoever to define the necessary physical activity by the accused. The homicide offenses, for example, define the various crimes in terms of the result caused (the death of the victim), the accused's mental state (as, for example, "malice aforethought"), and certain circumstances (as, for example, "adequate provocation"). In regard to such offenses, then, whether an accused has performed an act upon which criminal liability can be based depends not upon the law defining the charged offense but rather on some general principles concerning criminal activity.

Even when a crime does require a quite specifically described type of action—such as "entry" for burglary—it is still, and therefore in addition, necessary that the defendant's physical activity constitute an acceptable act for criminal liability within the meaning of these general principles. The general principles governing such matters are the main subject of this chapter.

Usually, of course, crimes are defined in ways that as applied require proof of affirmative action on the part of an accused, and usually the prosecution relies upon its proof as showing that the accused affirmatively acted in such a manner as to constitute the charged offense. Sections A, B, and C present several general concerns reflecting the requirement of an affirmative act. Section A addresses the federal constitutional prohibition against status crimes, which arguably imposes a requirement that crimes be defined in terms of specified action on the part of accused persons. Section B presents the requirement that action be voluntary and the resulting doctrine that unconsciousness renders a person incapable of incurring criminal liability. Section C considers the task of construing the act required by particular crimes, using the offense of operating a vehicle while intoxicated.

Those portions of section 2.01 of the Model Penal Code reprinted following this introduction offer a proposed statutory restatement of what are generally agreed upon as the rules or requirements in this area. Portions of this section dealing with omissions are reprinted in Section D of this chapter.

MODEL PENAL CODE*

Official Draft, 1985

Section 2.01. Requirement of Voluntary Act; * * *
Possession as an Act

(1) A person is not guilty of an offense unless his liability is based on conduct which includes a voluntary act or the omission to perform an act of which he is physically capable.

(2) The following are not voluntary acts within the meaning of this Section:

(a) a reflex or convulsion;

(b) a bodily movement during unconsciousness or sleep;

(c) conduct during hypnosis or resulting from hypnotic suggestion;

(d) a bodily movement that otherwise is not a product of the effort or determination of the actor, either conscious or habitual.

* * *

(4) Possession is an act, within the meaning of this Section, if the possessor knowingly procured or received the thing possessed or was aware of his control thereof for a sufficient period to have been able to terminate his possession.

*©1985 by the American Law Institute, as adopted
at the 1962 Annual Meeting of The American Law
Institute. Reprinted with permission.

A. THE FEDERAL CONSTITUTIONAL PROHIBITION AGAINST "STATUS" CRIMES

The principal case in this section, *Robinson v. California,* has been widely construed as barring the imposition of criminal liability for a status. Consider whether this is a correct interpretation of the case. Was the conviction of Robinson violative of his federal constitutional rights because he was convicted on the basis of his status rather than because of specific demonstrated activity on his part? If so, why was this the case? Why is conviction on the basis of a demonstrated status cruel and unusual punishment within the meaning of the Eighth Amendment?

A major question posed by the principal case is whether it suggests a broader federal constitutional limit upon the power of the states to define criminal conduct. Does it hold or suggest that the Eighth Amendment bars holding persons like Robinson liable for crimes based upon their status, condition, or acts if those are involuntary in some sense?

Robinson v. California

Supreme Court of the United States, 1962
370 U.S. 660, 82 S.Ct. 1417, 8 L.Ed.2d 758 (1962).

MR. JUSTICE STEWART delivered the opinion of the Court.

A California statute makes it a criminal offense for a person to "be addicted to the use of narcotics." This appeal draws into question the constitutionality of that provision of the state law as construed by the California courts in the present case.

The appellant was convicted after a jury trial in the Municipal Court of Los Angeles. * * * [The prosecution's evidence came from two Los Angeles police officers who testified that at the time of defendant's arrest they had examined his arms which were discolored and had scar tissue. The officers opined that these conditions were due to the use of hypodermic needles. Both testified that Robinson had admitted to narcotics use in the past, although at arrest he neither appeared to be under the influence of narcotics, nor to be suffering from withdrawal. Defendant denied he had ever used narcotics or admitted such use. He claimed that the condition of his arms was the result of an allergy. His testimony in this regard was corroborated by two witnesses.]

The trial judge instructed the jury that the statute made it a misdemeanor for a person "either to use narcotics, or to be addicted to the use of narcotics * * *. That portion of the statute referring to the 'use' of narcotics is based upon the 'act' of using. That portion of the statute referring to 'addicted to the use' of narcotics is based upon a condition or status. They are not identical. * * * To be addicted to the use of narcotics is said to be a status or condition and not an act. It is a continuing offense and differs from most other offenses in the fact that [it] is chronic rather than acute; that it continues after it is complete and subjects the offender to arrest at any time before he reforms. The existence of such a chronic condition may be ascertained from a single examination, if the characteristic reactions of that condition be found present."

The judge further instructed the jury that the appellant could be convicted under a general verdict if the jury agreed *either* that he was of the "status" *or* had committed the "act" denounced by the statute. "All that the People must show is either that the defendant did use a narcotic in Los Angeles County, or that while in the City of Los Angeles he was addicted to the use of narcotics * * *."

Under these instructions the jury returned a verdict finding the appellant "guilty of the offense charged."

The broad power of a State to regulate the narcotic drug traffic within its borders is not here in issue. * * *

Such regulation, it can be assumed, could take a variety of valid forms. A State might impose criminal sanctions, for example, against the unauthorized manufacture, prescription, sale, purchase, or possession of narcotics within its borders. In the interest of discouraging the violation of such laws, or in the interest of the general health or welfare of its inhabitants, a State might establish a program of compulsory treatment for those addicted to narcotics. Such a program of treatment might require periods of involuntary confinement. And penal sanctions might be imposed for failure to comply with established compulsory treatment procedures. Or a State might choose to attack the evils of narcotics traffic on broader fronts also—through public health education, for example, or by efforts to ameliorate the economic and social conditions under which those evils might be thought to flourish. In short, the range of valid choice which a State might make in this area is undoubtedly a wide one, and the wisdom of any particular choice within the allowable spectrum is not for us to decide. Upon that premise we turn to the California law in issue here.

It would be possible to construe the statute under which the appellant was convicted as one which is operative only upon proof of the actual use of narcotics within the State's jurisdiction. But the California courts have not so construed this law. Although there was evidence in the present case that the appellant had used narcotics in Los Angeles, the jury were instructed that they could convict him even if they disbelieved that evidence. The appellant could be convicted, they were told, if they found simply that the appellant's "status" or "chronic condition" was that of being "addicted to the use of narcotics." And it is impossible to know from the jury's verdict that the defendant was not convicted upon precisely such a finding.

* * *

This statute, therefore, is not one which punishes a person for the use of narcotics, for their purchase, sale or possession, or for antisocial or disorderly behavior resulting from their administration. It is not a law which even purports to provide or require medical treatment. Rather, we deal with a statute which makes the "status" of narcotic addiction a criminal offense, for which the offender may be prosecuted "at any time before he reforms." California has said that a person can be continuously guilty of this offense, whether or not he has ever used or possessed any narcotics within the State, and whether or not he has been guilty of any antisocial behavior there.

It is unlikely that any State at this moment in history would attempt to make it a criminal offense for a person to be mentally ill, or a leper, or to be afflicted with a venereal disease. A State might determine that the general health and welfare require that the victims of these and other human afflictions be dealt with by compulsory treatment, involving quarantine, confinement, or sequestration. But, in the light of contemporary human knowledge, a law which made a criminal offense of such a disease would doubtless be universally thought to be an infliction of cruel and unusual punishment in violation of the Eighth and Fourteenth Amendments. * * *

We cannot but consider the statute before us as of the same category. In this Court counsel for the State recognized that narcotic addiction is an illness.[8] Indeed, it is apparently an illness which may be contracted innocently or involuntarily.[9] We hold that a state law which imprisons a person thus afflicted as a criminal, even though he has never touched any narcotic drug within the State or been guilty of any irregular behavior there, inflicts a cruel and unusual punishment in violation of the Fourteenth Amendment. To be sure, imprisonment for ninety days is not, in the abstract, a punishment which is either cruel or unusual. But the question cannot be considered in the abstract. Even one day in prison would be a cruel and unusual punishment for the "crime" of having a common cold.

We are not unmindful that the vicious evils of the narcotics traffic have occasioned the grave concern of government. There are, as we have said, countless fronts on which those evils may be legitimately attacked. We deal in this case only with an individual provision of a particularized local law as it has so far been interpreted by the California courts.

Reversed.

MR. JUSTICE DOUGLAS, concurring.

While I join the Court's opinion, I wish to make more explicit the reasons why I think it is "cruel and unusual"

punishment in the sense of the Eighth Amendment to treat as a criminal a person who is a drug addict. * * * [T]he principle that would deny power to exact capital punishment for a petty crime would also deny power to punish a person by fine or imprisonment for being sick. * * *

MR. JUSTICE HARLAN, concurring.

I am not prepared to hold that on the present state of medical knowledge it is completely irrational and hence unconstitutional for a State to conclude that narcotics addiction is something other than an illness nor that it amounts to cruel and unusual punishment for the State to subject narcotics addicts to its criminal law. * * * Since addiction alone cannot reasonably be thought to amount to more than a compelling propensity to use narcotics, the effect of [the] instruction was to authorize criminal punishment for a bare desire to commit a criminal act.

If the California statute reaches this type of conduct, it is an arbitrary imposition which exceeds the power that a State may exercise in enacting its criminal law. Accordingly, I agree that the application of the California statute was unconstitutional in this case and join the judgment of reversal.

MR. JUSTICE CLARK, dissenting.

* * *

[T]he majority admits that "a State might establish a program of compulsory treatment for those addicted to narcotics" which "might require periods of involuntary confinement." I submit that California has done exactly that. The majority's error is in instructing the California Legislature that hospitalization is the *only* treatment for narcotics addiction—that anything less is a punishment denying due process. California has found otherwise after a study which I suggest was more extensive than that conducted by the Court. Even in California's program for hospital commitment of nonvolitional narcotic addicts * * * it is recognized that some addicts will not respond to or do not need hospital treatment. * * * The [proper due process] test is the overall purpose and effect of a State's act, and I submit that California's program relative to narcotic addicts—including both the "criminal" and the "civil" provisions—is inherently one of treatment and lies well within the power of a State.

MR. JUSTICE WHITE, dissenting.

If appellant's conviction rested upon sheer status, condition or illness or if he was convicted for being an addict who had lost his power of self-control, I would have other thoughts about this case. But this record presents neither

---

[8] In its brief the appellee stated: "Of course it is generally conceded that a narcotic addict, particularly one addicted to the use of heroin, is in a state of mental and physical illness. So is an alcoholic." Thirty-seven years ago this Court recognized that persons addicted to narcotics "are diseased and proper subjects for [medical] treatment." *Linder v. United States,* 268 U.S. 5, 18, 45 S.Ct. 446, 449, 69 L.Ed. 819.

[9] Not only may addiction innocently result from the use of medically prescribed narcotics, but a person may even be a narcotics addict from the moment of his birth. * * *

situation. * * * [T]here was no evidence at all that appellant had lost the power to control his acts. * * * He was an incipient addict, a redeemable user, and the State chose to send him to jail for 90 days rather than to attempt to confine him by civil proceedings under another statute which requires a finding that the addict has lost the power of self-control. In my opinion, on this record, it was within the power of the State of California to confine him by criminal proceedings for the use of narcotics or for regular use amounting to habitual use.

Notes and Questions

The Supreme Court returned to the requirements of the Eighth Amendment in *Powell v. Texas,* 392 U.S. 514, 88 S.Ct. 2145, 20 L.Ed.2d 1254 (1968). Powell had been convicted under the following Texas statute:

> Whoever shall get drunk or be found in a state of intoxication in any public place, or at any private house except his own, shall be fined not exceeding one hundred dollars.

The charge and proof was that Powell had been found in a state of public intoxication in a public place. The defense was that Powell was a chronic alcoholic and unable therefore to avoid the situation on which his conviction was based. Evidence in support of these contentions was presented. The members of the Court split on the meaning of the Eighth Amendment as applied in *Robinson* as well as on the sufficiency of Powell's showing to bring himself within the *Robinson* holding. In a plurality opinion announcing the judgment of the Court[a] affirming Powell's conviction, Justice Marshall explained:

The entire thrust of *Robinson's* interpretation of the Cruel and Unusual Punishment Clause is that criminal penalties may be inflicted only if the accused has committed some act, has engaged in some behavior, which society has an interest in preventing, or perhaps in historical common law terms, has committed some *actus reus*.

This opinion was joined by Chief Justice Warren and Justices Black and Harlan. Justice Black, in a concurring opinion, amplified the reasons he favored this interpretation of *Robinson:*

> [I believe] our attempt in *Robinson* to limit our holding to pure status crimes, involving no conduct whatever, was a sound one. * * * [Some] problems raised by status crimes are in no way involved when the State attempts to punish for conduct, and these * * * problems were, in my view, the controlling aspects of our decision.
>
> Punishment for a status is particularly obnoxious, and in many instances can reasonably be called cruel and unusual, because it involves punishment for a mere propensity, a desire to commit an offense; the mental element is not simply one part of the crime but may constitute all of it. This is a situation universally sought to be avoided in our criminal law; the fundamental requirement that some action be proved is solidly established even for offenses most heavily based on propensity, such as attempt, conspiracy, and recidivist crimes. * * *
>
> The reasons for this refusal to permit conviction without proof of an act are difficult to spell out, but they are nonetheless perceived and universally expressed in our criminal law. Evidence of propensity can be considered relatively unreliable and more difficult for a defendant to rebut; the requirement of a specific act thus provides some protection against false charges. Perhaps more fundamental is the difficulty of distinguishing, in the absence of any conduct, between desires of the day-dream variety and fixed intentions that may pose a real threat to society; extending the criminal law to cover both types of desires would be unthinkable, since "[t]here can hardly be anyone who has never thought evil. When a desire is inhibited it may find expression in fantasy; but it would be absurd to condemn this natural

---

[a]The opinion is the textual explanation for the court's action. For an opinion to be an opinion "of the court," when the court is composed of multiple judges, the opinion must receive the votes of a majority of the judges. The judgment, in contrast, is the procedural disposition. In *Robinson,* the judgment was the single directive, "Reversed," at the end of Justice Stewart's opinion. This judgment indicated that the decision of the California court under review was reversed by the Supreme Court. Since five other justices joined Justice Stewart's opinion in *Robinson,* that opinion was one of the Supreme Court as an institution. Pursuant to the practice of this Court, Justice Stewart's opinion was introduced by a phrase explicitly stating the opinion was "of the Court."

When the vote of the judges on a multijudge court is such that no opinion receives the votes of a majority of the judges, there is nevertheless generally a majority for one particular disposition of the case, that is, to affirm, reverse, remand for further consideration, or some other specific action. That judgment must be articulated, and practice is for this to be done in an opinion supporting the judgment that receives more votes for this disposition of the case than were received by any other opinion supporting that action. Such an opinion is often referred to as a plurality opinion. The Supreme Court's practice is to label an opinion of this sort one "announcing the judgment of the Court."

Some judges will agree with the disposition of the case

psychological mechanism as illegal." [R. Perkins, Criminal Law 762 (1957)]

In contrast, crimes that require the State to prove that the defendant actually committed some proscribed act involve none of these special problems.

Under this approach, why was not Powell's conviction nevertheless subject to attack under *Robinson*? Did the theory under which Powell was charged and convicted require proof of an "act" or behavior such as to distinguish it from a constitutionally prohibited status offense? Is being found in a public place an act on Powell's part? Justice Marshall offered:

> The State of Texas * * * has not sought to punish a mere status, as California did in *Robinson* * * *. Rather, it has imposed upon [Powell] a criminal sanction for public behavior * * *. This seems a far cry from convicting one for being an addict [or for] being a chronic alcoholic * * *.

Four members of the Court, in an opinion by Justice Fortas, urged that *Robinson* stands upon

> a principle which is the foundation of individual liberty and the cornerstone of the relations between a civilized state and its citizens: Criminal penalties may not be inflicted upon a person for being in a condition he is powerless to change.

They further found that Powell had sufficiently proved that he was powerless to avoid the condition upon which his conviction rested and thus his conviction could not stand. Thus the four justices dissented and argued that Powell's conviction should be held invalid.

The 4-to-4 tie among the justices was broken by Justice White, who agreed with those justices joining Justice

Marshall's decision that Powell's conviction should be upheld. Justice White's reasons were quite different from those given by Justice Marshall, and he expressed his views in an opinion stating clearly that he concurred in the result announced in Justice Marshall's opinion but not in that opinion itself. Justice White reasoned that the Eighth Amendment barred the conviction of a chronic alcoholic even for conduct that, as a result of his alcoholism, he was powerless to avoid. However, Justice White further concluded that Powell had not demonstrated that he was unable to avoid being found in public while intoxicated. Therefore, in his view, Powell had not shown the Eighth Amendment prohibition applied to him and his conviction was therefore not barred by the Eighth Amendment.

In light of Justice White's analysis, it is arguable that a majority of five justices in *Powell* read *Robinson* as prohibiting the criminalization of at least some conduct because that conduct is the product of an impairment and thus involuntary in some sense. Justice White apparently agreed with the dissenters on this point but imposed a more stringent standard for what a defendant would have to show to demonstrate that the conduct for which he was prosecuted was the result of his underlying illness. Nevertheless, *Powell* is widely regarded as establishing the reading of *Robinson* embodied in Justice Marshall's opinion and explained further by Justice Black. Under this reading, the involuntariness of conduct is simply irrelevant to whether *Robinson* and the Eighth Amendment prohibit criminal prosecution for that conduct. It is simply necessary under *Robinson* for the crime to require some conduct rather than define the offense in terms of a "status."

So read, *Robinson* makes the traditional criminal law requirement of conduct into a federal constitutional demand. It does not, however, provide any basis for defendants to argue that they cannot be convicted because their prohibited conduct was in some sense involuntary.

---

announced in such a plurality opinion but not with the explanation given in the opinion. In *Robinson,* for example, Justice Harlan voted to reverse the decision of the California court but did not join Justice Stewart's explanatory opinion. Justice Harlan's opinion announced his concurrence in the judgment but made clear he did not join the Court's opinion. Justice Douglas, on the other hand, voted both for the reversal announced in Justice Stewart's opinion and to join in that opinion. He wished to articulate further matters reflecting only his own view, so he wrote an opinion simply "concurring." This meant concurring in both the judgment

announced in the opinion of the Court and in the opinion itself. Justice Black's opinion in *Powell* was of the same sort.

Only an opinion of the court is ordinarily entitled to full binding effect as legal precedent. Several justices of the Supreme Court have indicated that discussion in a plurality opinion, although not binding precedent, reflects "the considered opinion" of several members of the Court and thus "should obviously be the point of reference for further discussion of the issue." *Texas v. Brown,* 460 U.S. 730, 737, 103 S.Ct. 1535, 1541, 75 L.Ed.2d 502 (1983) (opinion of Rehnquist, J., announcing the judgment of Court).

B. THE REQUIREMENT OF CONSCIOUSNESS AND THE "DEFENSE" OF "AUTOMATISM"

Editors' Introduction: The Act Requirement, Voluntariness, and Consciousness

The terms of section 2.01(l) of the Model Penal Code, reprinted after the Editors' Introduction, require that the act upon which criminal liability is based be a "voluntary" one. This simply restates a widely accepted proposition that is, nevertheless, subject to misinterpretation and is often misunderstood. This requirement may easily be confused with the requirement of *mens rea* or criminal "intent," considered in detail in Chapter 4. It may also be confused with the defense of insanity, which in some jurisdictions permits an accused to escape conviction upon proof that a mental impairment rendered the accused incapable of resisting a striving or impulse to commit the crime; this defense is addressed in Chapter 15.

In regard to the limited implications of the requirement under discussion here—that the act be voluntary—consider the view of Professor Perkins:

> It is sometimes said that no crime has been committed unless the harmful result was brought about by a "voluntary act." Analysis of such a statement will disclose, however, that as so used the phrase "voluntary act" means no more than the word "act." An act must be a willed movement or the omission of a possible and legally-required performance. This is essential to the *actus reus* rather than to the *mens rea*. "A spasm is not an act."
>   * * * A positive act (willed movement) always has a voluntary element and hence the phrase "voluntary act" is merely tautological as so applied. * * * Hence the assertion that there is no crime without a "voluntary act" is redundant * * *.

R. Perkins, Criminal Law 749 (1969).

The need for the act to be voluntary has served as the conceptual basis for what is sometimes called the "defense" of "automatism." In *Evans v. State,* 322 Md. 24, 585 A.2d 204 (1991), the Maryland Court of Appeals indicated that a defendant's expert testimony that he suffered from an amnesiac episode at the time he shot another "may approach what has been described * * * as automatism." It continued:

> The Supreme Court of Wyoming explained automatism in these words:
>
>> Automatism is the state of a person who, though capable of action, is not conscious of what he is doing. While in an automatistic state, an individual performs complex actions without an exercise of will. Because these actions are performed in a state of unconsciousness, they are involuntary. Automatistic behavior may be followed by complete or partial inability to recall the actions performed while unconscious. Thus, a person who acts automatically does so without intent, exercise of free will, or knowledge of the act.

Fulcher v. State, 633 P.2d 142, 145 (Wyo.1981). The same Court pointed out that "[a]utomatism may be caused by an abnormal condition of the mind capable of being designated a mental illness or deficiency" or it "may also be manifest in a person with a perfectly healthy mind."

In W. LaFave & A. Scott, Substantive Criminal Law, § 4.9 (1986), the authors distinguish automatism from insanity:

> A defense related to but different from the defense of insanity is that of unconsciousness, often referred to as automatism: one who engages in what would otherwise be criminal conduct is not guilty of a crime if he does so in state of unconsciousness or semi-consciousness.

In *People v. Martin,* 87 Cal.App.2d 581, 197 P.2d 379, 383 (1948), the court said: "[t]he defense of insanity is one thing, and the defense of unconsciousness is another." * * * Other courts hold that the loss of cognitive ability resulting from a condition such as epilepsy is available as a defense in a criminal case as an "insanity" or lack of criminal responsibility defense. The latter approach is sometimes favored because the defendant is required to interpose a plea of "insanity," thus giving reasonable notice to the State of the contention being made; and, because treatment, where appropriate, can be required after a finding that the defendant committed the offense but is not criminally responsible.

State v. Mercer

Supreme Court of North Carolina, 1969.
275 N.C. 108, 165 S.E.2d 328.

Separate indictments charged defendant with the first degree murder on September 14, 1967, of (1) Myrtle R. Mercer, defendant's wife, (2) Ida Mae Dunn, and (3) Jeffrey Lane Dunn, Ida's five-year-old son.

There was evidence tending to show the facts narrated below.

Defendant, a member of the United States Army for 19 1/2 years, was stationed at Fort Benning, Georgia, at the time of the trial.

Defendant and Myrtle Mercer were married in Fayetteville, N.C., in April, 1965. Thereafter, he was stationed at duty posts in and out of the United States. Myrtle Mercer, Ida Mae Dunn, and Jeffrey Lane Dunn, Ida's five-year-old boy, lived together in Wilson, N.C. Defendant visited Myrtle in Wilson from time to time when on leaves. He was thirty-nine; Myrtle was twenty-three.

Marital difficulties developed. Defendant had heard that Myrtle was having affairs with other men. He thought Myrtle's relationship with Ida involved more than normal affection. As time passed, defendant's strong affection for Myrtle was not reciprocated.

On July 6, 1967, defendant received a letter from Myrtle, referred to in the evidence as a "Dear John" letter, in which she told him she was tired of being tied down and wanted to come and go as she pleased. In a letter mailed August 10th from Kentucky (where he was then stationed), defendant wrote Myrtle: "Please don't make me do something that will send both of us to our graves." Also: "I could never see you with another man, and I would die and go to hell before I would see you with some other man, and take myself with you."

In September, 1967, defendant obtained a ten-day leave "to come home and see if he could get straightened out with his wife. * * * " Defendant told his first sergeant that "if he did not get straightened out he would not be back."

On September 13, 1967, defendant visited the house in Wilson where Myrtle, Ida, and Jeffrey lived. He talked with Myrtle. However, she would not discuss their marital problems and did not want him to stay at that house.

Defendant stayed at the home of his cousin, Mrs. Mable Owens, in Tarboro. He left there on the morning of September 14, 1967, and arrived at Myrtle's around noon. She would not talk with him. (Note: Defendant testified Myrtle at that time gave him some clothes, a camera and a paper bag containing a pistol he had given to her for her protection.) At the conclusion of this visit, he returned to the home of Mrs. Owens. Sometime during the day defendant bought a pint of vodka and had two drinks from it.

About 8:30 P.M., Mrs. Owens, at the request of defendant, drove defendant to Myrtle's house in Wilson. The two children of Mrs. Owens accompanied them. Defendant knocked. There was no response. The house was unlighted and apparently no one was there. They left and visited defendant's brother (in Wilson) for some twenty-five or thirty-five minutes. While there, defendant telephoned Myrtle's house. The line was busy. They went back to Myrtle's house. Defendant asked Mrs. Owens if she and her children would go into the house with him. She replied that they would wait in the car.

Defendant went to the front door and knocked several times. There was no answer. Defendant shot at the door twice, pushed it open with his foot and went inside. At that time, a light came on in the front bedroom. Someone said, "Ervin, don't do that." Defendant fired three or four shots killing Myrtle instantly and fatally wounding Ida and Jeffrey. He then left the house. A neighbor called the police.

Defendant was arrested at the home of his brother in Wilson, a few hours after the fatal shots were fired. He accompanied the officers to a lot behind Myrtle's house where the gun which inflicted the fatal injuries was hidden.

Testimony of defendant, in addition to that referred to above, is set out in the opinion. It tended to show he was completely unconscious of what transpired when Myrtle, Ida and Jeffrey were shot.

In each case, the jury returned a verdict of guilty of murder in the second degree. * * *

BOBBITT, JUDGE.

* * *

The court's final instructions were as follows: "(T)he Court instructs you that the evidence in regard and surrounding the alleged loss of memory by the defendant will be considered by you *on the question of premeditation and deliberation in the charge of murder in the first degree.* * * * if you find from the evidence, not by the greater weight, nor by the preponderance, but if the defendant has satisfied you — merely satisfied you—that he lost consciousness, sufficient consciousness, to the extent that he did not have sufficient time to *premeditate or deliberate,* that is, if he did not have sufficient time to form in his mind the intent to kill, under the definition of premeditation and *deliberation,* then it would be your duty to return a verdict of not guilty of murder in the first degree, because the Court has instructed you if the State has failed to satisfy you of the element of *premeditation or deliberation,* or if there arises in your minds a reasonable doubt in regard to those two elements or either one of those two elements, it would be your duty to

return a verdict of not guilty. And further in regard, when you come to consider those elements of *premeditation and deliberation,* if the defendant has satisfied you, not beyond a reasonable doubt, not by the greater weight of the evidence, but has merely satisfied you that he lost consciousness to such an extent that he was unable to *premeditate,* and was unable to *deliberate,* according to the definition of those terms that the law has given you, then he could not be guilty of murder in the first degree, and it would be your duty to return a verdict of not guilty as to murder in the first degree, under those circumstances. Now, *the Court feels that those are the only two elements in the case in which this evidence in regard to his loss of consciousness applies,* and the Court has ruled that there is no element of legal insanity in the evidence." (Our italics.)

Defendant's assignment of error, based on his exception to the foregoing portion of the charge, must be sustained. Defendant testified he was completely unconscious of what transpired when Myrtle, Ida and Jeffrey were shot. The court instructed the jury that this evidence was for consideration only in respect of the elements of premeditation and deliberation in first degree murder. This restriction of the legal significance of the evidence as to defendant's unconsciousness was erroneous.

* * *

"If a person is in fact unconscious at the time he commits an act which would otherwise be criminal, he is not responsible therefor. The absence of consciousness not only precludes the existence of any specific mental state, but also excludes the possibility of a voluntary act without which there can be no criminal liability." 1 Wharton's Criminal Law and Procedure (Anderson), § 50, p. 116.

"Unconsciousness is a complete, not a partial, defense to a criminal charge." 21 Am.Jur.2d, Criminal Law § 29, p. 115.

"Unconsciousness. A person cannot be held criminally responsible for acts committed while he is unconscious. Some statutes broadly exempt from responsibility persons who commit offenses without being conscious thereof. Such statutes, when construed in connection with other statutes relating to criminal capacity of the insane and voluntarily intoxicated, do not include within their protection either insane or voluntarily intoxicated persons, and are restricted in their contemplation to persons of sound mind suffering from some other agency rendering them unconscious of their acts * * *. 22 C.J.S. Criminal Law § 55, p. 194.

Defendant contends he had no knowledge of and did not consciously commit the act charged in the indictments. He does not contend he was insane. Unconsciousness and insanity are separate grounds of exemption from criminal responsibility.

* * * Unconsciousness is never an *affirmative* defense. * * *

There was no evidence defendant was a somnambulist or an epileptic. Nor was there evidence he was under the influence of intoxicants or narcotics. Under cross-examination, defendant testified his only previous "blackout" experience, which was of brief duration, occurred when he received and read the "Dear John" letter.

Upon the present record, defendant was entitled to an instruction to the effect the jury should return verdicts of not guilty if in fact defendant was completely unconscious of what transpired when Myrtle, Ida and Jeffrey were shot.

* * *

It should be understood that unconsciousness, although always a factor of legal significance, is not a complete defense under all circumstances. Without undertaking to mark the limits of the legal principles applicable to varied factual situations that will arise from time to time, but solely by way of illustration, attention is called to the following: In California, "unconsciousness produced by voluntary intoxication does not render a defendant incapable of committing a crime." *People v. Cox,* 67 Cal.App.2d 166, 153 P.2d 362, and cases cited. In Colorado, a person who precipitates a fracas and as a result is hit on the head and rendered semi-conscious or unconscious cannot maintain that he is not criminally responsible for any degree of homicide above involuntary manslaughter, or that he is not criminally responsible at all. *Watkins v. People,* 158 Colo. 485, 408 P.2d 425. In Oklahoma, a motorist is guilty of manslaughter if he drives an automobile with knowledge that he is subject to frequent blackouts, when his continued operation of the automobile is in reckless disregard to the safety of others and constitutes culpable or criminal negligence. *Carter v. State*[, 376 P.2d 351 (Okl.Cr.1962)]; *Smith v. Commonwealth*[, 268 S.W.2d 937 (Ky.1954)]. As to somnambulism, see *Fain v. Commonwealth*[, 78 Ky. 183 (1879)], and *Lewis v. State,* 196 Ga. 755, 27 S.E.2d 659.

Notes and Questions

1. In a subsequent decision, the *Mercer* court further discussed the relationship of the voluntary act requirement to potential causes for unconsciousness:

   The defenses of insanity and unconsciousness are not the same in nature, for unconsciousness at the time of the alleged criminal act need not be the result of a disease or defect of the mind. As a consequence, the two defenses are not the same in effect, for a defendant found not guilty by reason of unconsciousness, as distinct from insanity, is not subject to commitment to a hospital for the mentally ill.

   * * *

   Sources of unconsciousness, recognized as a defense by courts and textwriters, include somnambulism, somnolenture, hypnotism, cerebral concussion, delirium from fever or drugs, diabetic shock; epileptic black-outs; and drunkenness. * * *

   State v. Caddell, 287 N.C. 266, 285, 215 S.E.2d 348, 360 (1975).

   Should some—or perhaps all— of these conditions be regarded as mental illnesses potentially raising insanity but not the absence of a voluntary act? A defendant who successfully asserts insanity also triggers a procedure by which that defendant is evaluated and retained in hospital custody until no longer dangerous; see Chapter 15.

   In *McClain v. State,* 678 N.E.2d 104 (Ind.1997), the Indiana Supreme Court adopted the view that automatism could be—but is not necessarily— caused by a mental illness or defect, and therefore automatism is not simply part of the insanity defense. Under *McClain,* a defendant is apparently free to show, if he can, that he was unconscious for a reason other than a mental illness or defect and if successful he is entitled to acquittal without having to submit to evaluation and hospitalization. On the other hand, the prosecution is apparently free to counter with evidence that *if* the defendant was unconscious, it was for reasons that establish insanity and any acquittal thus required should be on insanity grounds.

   In *McClain,* the defendant—charged with assaulting police officers—offered expert testimony that he suffered from sleep deprivation that triggered his attack upon the officers. This was not a mental illness or defect raising insanity, he claimed, because it was externally caused and unlikely to reoccur; the prosecution made no contention that the cause of his unconsciousness was a mental illness or defect. However, consider the evidence in *People v. Cegers,* 7 Cal.App.4th 988, 9 Cal.Rprt.2d 297 (1992), in which Cegers was shown to have assaulted his victim with a knife when she nudged him awake. The defense offered the testimony of Dr. Merrill M. Mitler, a psychologist and expert on sleep disorders, who had administered an oximeter test to Cegers. The oximeter measures the level of oxygen saturation in the blood.

Dr. Mitler was prepared to testify that Cegers suffered from apnea, and that on the day of the assault he also suffered from "confusional arousal syndrome." The oximeter showed that at times during Cegers's sleep his oxygen level diminished, caused by some defect in breathing patterns. This condition, called "sleep apnea," causes confusion and abnormal behavior upon being awakened, such as sleepwalking. The condition is exacerbated by excess alcohol consumption. Sleep apnea is a well-recognized condition * * *.

　* * * Dr. Mitler's testimony * * * would [also] have explored the syndrome called "confusional arousal syndrome." The syndrome is associated with people who have sleep apnea and are awakened during a period of depressed mental functioning. They are able to perform motor functions, such as walking, while still mentally asleep. In severe cases such persons can be violent, causing injury or death to others, in which event their condition has been termed "homicidal somnambulism." The condition is properly termed physiological rather than psychological, because it results from an anomaly of the brain.

　Dr. Mitler was prepared to testify that Cegers suffered from confusional arousal syndrome on the night of the assault. * * *

If Dr. Mitler's testimony is credited, and Cegers is exonerated from criminal liability, perhaps that exoneration should be on the basis of insanity, which triggers a procedure for determining whether he should be civilly detained because of the danger he poses.

2. The principle embraced by the cases distinguishing insanity and automatism is apparently that if unconsciousness is caused by something covered by a different and more specific criminal law doctrine, it does not raise the simple voluntariness of the defendant's conduct but should be considered under that other doctrine. The *Mercer* court later followed this principle, and the suggestion in *Mercer* itself, by holding that unconsciousness due to voluntary ingestion of alcohol or drugs does not raise the defense recognized in *Mercer*. *State v. Fisher,* 336 N.C. 684, 445 N.E.2d 866 (1994). As is developed in Chapter 15, most jurisdictions have separate doctrines addressing intoxication and rigorously limiting the defensive effect of showing that the defendant was intoxicated at the time of criminal conduct.

3. In *Caddell,* discussed in note 1, the court noted that *Mercer* was the only case it found holding that a jury question regarding unconsciousness was raised by "the defendant's uncorroborated and unexplained testimony that, at the moment of his otherwise criminal act, he 'blacked-out,' and so does not remember what, if anything, he did * * *." *Caddell* did not reach whether this holding of *Mercer* was correct. Other courts, however, have shared the underlying concern, and at least one has indicated that testimony such as Mercer apparently gave is not sufficient to raise the matter:

> Mere inability to remember an event, in and of itself, cannot establish automatism, since the relevant inquiry involves the accused's knowledge and control at the time of the conduct, not at the time of trial.

Sellers v. State, 809 P.2d 676, 686–87 (Okla.Crim. App.1991).

4. *Caddell* also reconsidered *Mercer*'s comments concerning the burden of persuasion on the matter at issue and concluded that, for burden of proof purposes, automatism or unconsciousness could not be distinguished from insanity. Therefore, it overruled *Mercer*'s comments and held that automatism is an affirmative defense on which the defendant has the burden of proof.

5. If the evidence shows that a defendant was unconscious at the time of the conduct directly constituting the crime, criminal liability can sometimes nevertheless be imposed for earlier conduct. This is the case, as *Mercer* itself suggested, where a driver of a car becomes unconscious and in that state strikes and kills another. Although the doctrine applied in *Mercer* may preclude prosecution on the basis of the actual act of steering the car into the victim, it does not prevent prosecution on the basis of the defendant's earlier act of driving with a tendency to become unconscious. If the prosecution can show the defendant did this with the required culpable mental state, liability can exist on this ground. In *State v. Freeman,* No. 02C01-9406-CR-00113 (Tenn.Crim.App.1995) (not reported), for example, the defendant was the driver of a car that proceeded through a red light and struck a crowd of elementary school children. Two children died and two others were seriously injured. Freeman testified that she had experienced seizures about once a month, but never while driving, and that she must have had a seizure on this

occasion. She testified that she had consulted a physician, who advised her to see a specialist, which she did not do because she could not afford it. Nevertheless, her convictions for criminally negligent homicide and aggravated assault (recklessly causing serious bodily injury) were affirmed. The court explained:

The general rule appears to be that an accused who causes the death of another as a result of becoming unconscious because of an epileptic seizure is criminally responsible in undertaking to drive knowing that he or she may become unconscious. The critical factor is knowledge that one is subject to epileptic seizures.

C. SPECIAL PROBLEM: DRIVING WHILE INTOXICATED

Editors' Introduction: Crimes Prohibiting the Creation of Risks

What act, activity, or conduct by the defendant must be proven by the prosecution in a criminal case obviously must be considered on a case-by-case basis in light of the definition of the particular crimes with which the defendant has been charged or of which he or she can be convicted and the evidence on which the prosecution's case rests. It is possible, however, to make some useful generalizations.

First, it is often necessary to interpret the requirements of the crime charged, and more specifically of the crime's requirement of particular conduct, in light of both general principles relating to the act requirement and the social purpose of the crime at issue. What definition of the conduct required best serves to implement the purpose of the legislature in creating the crime, while also respecting the general principle— underlying the requirement of conduct—that citizens should not be held criminally responsible until they have acted, as well as thought, in a dangerous manner?

Second, it is also often necessary to recognize that crimes are often drafted so as to permit apprehension and conviction of persons who do not actually cause the real underlying harm with which the legislature was concerned but rather only *create a risk* that such harm will occur. The decision reprinted in this section involves a statute criminalizing conduct by intoxicated persons with automobiles. Almost certainly, the main—and perhaps only—concern of the legislature was harm to persons and property caused by intoxicated drivers of vehicles. Yet these crimes are often drafted and construed so as to cover persons who actually cause no such harm but rather create too high a risk that such harm will occur.

In a sense, this involves criminal liability for a "propensity" to cause harm. It therefore creates a risk of convicting persons who, if left uninterrupted, would in actual fact, not cause the harm at which the law is aimed. The real task of legislatures and courts in drafting and construing these crimes is to determine how best to identify those persons who have created a high enough risk that if left alone, they would cause harm to the persons or property by actually driving while intoxicated.

Crimes of the sort under consideration here tend to define the act required for liability in one or more of three alternative terms: (1) "driving" a vehicle; (2) "operating" a vehicle"; and (3) "controlling" (or "actually" or "physically" controlling) a vehicle. Obviously these alternatives cover progressively more conduct further removed from the basic harm actually at the core of legislative concern—the causing of injury or harm. Also, however, the risk of including people who if left alone would not cause harm to others is greater if the crime prohibits "control" than if it encompasses only "driving." The task is to balance the need to create liability for creation of a sufficient risk against the need to avoid convicting those not actually dangerous.

State v. Starfield

Supreme Court of Minnesota, 1992
481 N.W.2d 834.

SIMONETT, Justice.

* * *

On February 24, 1989, at around 1:47 A.M., Ramsey County deputy sheriffs responded to a report of a car in the ditch in Gem Lake. The car was stuck in a snow-filled ditch. The headlights were on, but the motor was not running. Deputy Lopez approached the driver's side of the car and testified he found defendant Sandra Starfield sitting in the driver's seat. Through a closed window, Lopez asked Starfield if she was okay. Starfield replied that she was not hurt. Lopez then testified he opened the car door and asked for Starfield's driver's license. Starfield could not find it in her purse. From the odor of alcohol and bloodshot eyes, Lopez believed that Starfield was intoxicated. Lopez noticed the keys were not in the ignition, so he asked for them. Starfield replied that the keys were "in the car," but Lopez could not find them.

Minutes later more deputies arrived. A pick-up truck came by and the driver offered to pull Starfield's car out of the ditch, but the offer was not accepted. After being given an implied consent advisory, Starfield refused to submit to a blood alcohol test. While in the squad car, when asked if she was operating the car, she replied, "Nope," but did not elaborate. At the Ramsey County Jail, a set of car keys was found in Starfield's coat pocket. While being booked, Starfield contended she was not driving the car; but she never mentioned that she was waiting in the car for her son.

Eventually, Starfield's car was removed from the ditch by a tow truck. One of the deputies testified that the car was stuck in the snow, and that Starfield could not have driven the car out of the snow.

The next day, Starfield was questioned (after a *Miranda* warning) and, for the first time, said that her son was driving the car when it went into the ditch. She said her son had gone for help and had left her in the car. An officer also testified that Starfield told him she had tried to drive the car out of the ditch.

At trial, Starfield testified that her son had driven the car into the ditch, had then gone for help, and that the deputies arrived while the son was gone. Starfield's son, Scott, corroborated his mother's story. He said the car had a tire blow-out, causing the car to go into the ditch, and that he had then walked to a Perkins restaurant to call a friend for help. On cross-examination, the prosecution inquired of Scott why he had left his intoxicated mother in the car to walk to Perkins one-half mile away rather than seek help at a house near the car; why he had shut off the motor and heater in sub-zero temperatures before going to Perkins; and why he would walk through a snow-filled field to get to Perkins rather than walk along the road.

Defendant was charged under Minn.Stat. § 169.121, subd. 1(a) (Supp.1989), making it a crime to "drive, operate, or be in physical control of any motor vehicle * * * when the person is under the influence of alcohol." At the close of the State's case, the trial judge granted defendant Starfield's motion to acquit on the charge of "driving" under the influence of alcohol, reasoning that the evidence was insufficient to support such a conviction. Consequently, the case went to the jury solely on the question whether Starfield was in "physical control" of a motor vehicle while under the influence of alcohol.

Defense counsel requested the following instruction on physical control:

The purpose behind Minn.Stat. § 169.121, subd. 1 is to deter drunken individuals from getting into their vehicles except as passengers. The State must prove beyond a reasonable doubt that the Defendant was at or near her vehicle for the purpose of operating it or controlling it. Further, the State must prove beyond a reasonable doubt that the Defendant's car was capable of being operated.

The trial court denied the requested instruction and instead gave [the standard] instruction * * *:

A person is in physical control of a motor vehicle when he or she is present in a vehicle and is in a position to either direct the movement of the vehicle or keep the vehicle from moving. It is not necessary for the engine to be running in order for a person to be in physical control of a motor vehicle.

While deliberating, the jury returned with the following written question: "Does the car have to be *able* to be moved for a person to have physical control of the vehicle?" (Emphasis in the original.) The trial judge responded by repeating his earlier instruction. The jury returned a verdict of guilty.

On appeal, the court of appeals vacated the conviction and remanded for a new trial. For there to be "physical control," the court concluded, the prosecution must show the defendant drove the car to the location or into the predicament in which it was found, or that the driver had the ability to continue on an inebriated journey at any moment. Because the trial court had dismissed the "driving" charge, the court of appeals assumed Starfield to be a passenger in her own car, and as a passenger, she was entitled to an instruction on operability. The appeals panel declined to suggest an appropriate instruction, but noted that in fashioning an instruction the trial court should take into account evidence that Starfield was merely a passenger in a disabled vehicle. We granted the State's petition for further review.

Arguably, the evidence was sufficient to have submitted to the jury the charge of "driving" under the influence; however, this is not what happened. The only charge here is having "physical control" of a motor vehicle. The issue then becomes whether the physical control contemplated by the statute includes a motor vehicle so stuck in a snow-filled ditch that it cannot move. In the following discussion, we will use the terms "inoperable" or "disabled" to refer either to a mechanical breakdown of the car or to the car being in some predicament where it cannot move, such as being out of gas or stuck in the snow or mud.

The term "physical control" is more comprehensive than either "drive" or "operate." In *State v. Juncewski,* 308 N.W.2d 316, 319 (Minn.1981), the last time we spoke on the subject, we said that the term "physical control" should be given "the broadest possible effect" and that the intent was to deter inebriated persons from getting into vehicles except as passengers. *Juncewski* did not involve, however, a disabled vehicle. Since then the court of appeals has been faced with a variety of fact situations involving disabled vehicles.

The court of appeals has found physical control where the vehicle had a flat tire, *State v. Woodward,* 408 N.W.2d 927 (Minn.App.1987); a dead battery, *Abeln v. Commissioner of Public Safety,* 413 N.W.2d 546 (Minn.App.1987); and where the car was stuck in a snow-filled ditch, *State v. Duemke,* 352 N.W.2d 427 (Minn.App.1984). The State stressed the disabilities in these three cases were all temporary disabilities. A flat tire can be changed; a dead battery can be jump-started; and a car can be towed from a snow-filled ditch.

The court of appeals in this appeal, however, relied on two of its prior decisions where "physical control" was not found. In *State v. Pazderski,* 352 N.W.2d 85 (Minn.App. 1984), the defendant was found asleep in the front seat of his car parked in his driveway. Defendant claimed he had driven home but not gone inside the house because he wished to avoid a domestic dispute. Because he was at his destination and not going anywhere, the appeals panel reversed his conviction. In *Roberts v. Commissioner of Public Safety,* 371 N.W.2d 605 (Minn.App.1985), review denied, Oct. 11, 1985, the defendant, after passing out from drinking, had been placed by friends in the front seat of his car parked in a dance hall parking lot; the keys were left on the dashboard but the friends pulled the coil wire to the ignition so defendant could not drive off. The appeals panel affirmed the trial court's ruling that defendant was not in physical control of the vehicle. While the appeals panel noted that the car was mechanically inoperable, at least temporarily, the decision also suggests that the defendant had a passenger status because he had been placed in the car without his knowledge.

Both *Pazderski* and *Roberts* have been somewhat limited by subsequent court of appeals' decisions. *Pazderski* has been limited to cases where the defendant is in his or her driveway. When the vehicle is located elsewhere, the appeals court has found physical control because the intoxicated individual might proceed on his journey and attempt to get home. See *Martin v. Commissioner of Public Safety,* 358 N.W.2d 734, 737 (Minn.App.1984) (car located in front of a house, not his own, and defendant could at any time begin to drive); *Palme v. Commissioner of Public Safety,* 366 N.W.2d 343, 345 (Minn.App.1985) (defendant found asleep in pick-up truck next to a bar claimed his friend had put him there; keys on the seat next to the defendant, so defendant could at any time start the pick-up and attempt to go home), review denied, June 24, 1985. And as we have seen, both *Abeln* (dead battery) and *Woodward* (flat tire) suggest that mechanical inoperability as noted in *Roberts* (disconnected coil wire) may not be enough to exclude physical control. See also *State v. Thurmer,* 348 N.W.2d 776, 779 (Minn.App.1984) (defendant admitted driving car found stuck in snow-filled ditch; court found physical control because keys were in the ignition and defendant admitted he drove the car there).

Insofar as "physical control" refers to something other than "driving" or "operating," the foregoing cases suggest that physical control is meant to cover situations where an inebriated person is found in a parked vehicle under circumstances where the car, without too much difficulty, might again be started and become a source of danger to the operator, to others, or to property. In *Juncewski,* we indicated that the purpose of the physical control offense is to act as a preventive measure to deter the drunk driver from again driving. The danger addressed by the physical control offense is the concern that the intoxicated person "could have at any time started the automobile and driven away." Or as stated in *State v. Webb,* 78 Ariz. 8, 274 P.2d 338, 339 (1954), the purpose of the offense is to "enable the drunken driver to be apprehended before he strikes."

Alcoholic behavior can be unpredictable. A person may get or be put into a car to "sleep it off," but then decide to drive away. It is, of course, no crime for an intoxicated person to be in a motor vehicle as a passenger. A passenger, by definition, is someone who is merely along for the ride. When, however, only one person is found in or about a stopped car, the question arises whether that person is a passenger or a person in physical control of the motor vehicle. Mere presence in or about the vehicle is not enough for physical control; it is the overall situation that is determinative.

In most cases, the jury is asked to decide if the defendant was driving, operating, or was in physical control of a motor vehicle while under the influence of alcohol. This three-pronged charge is submitted even when the defendant is found in a stationary vehicle with no direct testimony—no eye witness, no admission by the defendant—that the defendant drove the vehicle to where it was found at rest. In such a case, there still may be circumstantial evidence from which the jury could find that defendant had driven the car to its resting place; and, because this driving is included within "physical control," the inebriated defendant may, with consistency, be found guilty of driving, operating or being in control of the motor vehicle. But this is not all. Moreover, when it appears that the defendant drove the car to where it came to rest, this is also evidence that the defendant, when found in the parked car, was in physical control of the car while it was parked.

In the case now before us, * * * the jury could find beyond a reasonable doubt from the circumstantial evidence—Starfield behind the wheel, in her own car, keys in her pocket, towing assistance likely available—that Starfield was in physical control of the car when it was in the ditch.

This brings us, then, to the question of operability.

There was evidence from which the jury could have found that the snow-stuck car was incapable of immediate self-powered mobility. While stuck in the ditch, the car was not a danger to anyone, and, arguably, whatever physical control Starfield had over the car was ineffectual and, therefore, noncriminal. Consequently, Starfield argues she cannot be convicted of a crime for sitting in a car incapable of going anywhere and a hazard to nobody. And while the State also charged Starfield with driving under the influence of alcohol, she points out it was unable to prove that charge, and this should end the matter.

The fact remains, however, that a car incapable of immediate self-propelled mobility may still be a potential traffic hazard, and it is this potential for harm, as we have seen, that the "physical control" offense is meant to encompass. The person in physical control may, while still inebriated, correct the disability and meander down the road.[1] Here, for example, Starfield might have enlisted the aid of a passerby to extricate her car from the ditch (indeed, such a driver came along after the deputies arrived) and, even if one of the tires was flat (we have only the son's word for this), the car could have been driven on the highway with the flat tire or the flat tire could have been changed. In other words, temporary inoperability does not necessarily preclude criminal liability. See also *State v. Smelter,* [36 Wash.App. 439, 674 P.2d 690 (1984)] (car out of gas, but a gas station nearby).

Other courts have held, and we agree, that the state does not need to prove operability of the motor vehicle. Operability does not appear in our statute as an element of physical control. One court at least has indicated that inoperability may, in certain circumstances, be treated as an affirmative defense to a prosecution for a physical control offense. *Jones v. State,* 510 So.2d 1147, 1149 (Fla. Dist.Ct. App.1987). We do not, however, think that treating inoperability as an affirmative defense is appropriate either.

Drunk-driving cases, especially those where the officer comes upon a stationary car with an inebriated person inside, seem to provoke a remarkable variety of explanations to test the factfinder's credibility-determining powers. Inoperability or, more precisely, the nature and duration of any inoperability, is simply a factor or circumstance to be evaluated with all the surrounding facts and circumstances

---

[1]Of course, a stationary, disabled vehicle, even if it cannot readily be rendered capable of movement, may be a hazard in its stationary, disabled condition. For example, a disabled car may protrude somewhat onto the roadway; or the car may be imbedded in a snow-filled ditch in such a way that running the motor creates a danger of asphyxiating the person inside.

by the jury in determining whether the situation gives rise to physical control.[2]

In a case where the State is claiming "physical control" of a disabled motor vehicle, we think the standard * * * instruction on physical control [as given here] might appropriately be supplemented by an instruction along the following lines:

> In considering whether or not the defendant was in physical control of the motor vehicle while under the influence of alcohol, you may consider defendant's location in or by the vehicle, the location of the ignition keys, whether the defendant had been a passenger in the vehicle before it came to rest, who owned the vehicle, the extent to which the vehicle was inoperable, and whether the vehicle if inoperable might have been rendered operable so as to be a danger to persons or property. You may consider these as well as any other facts or circumstances bearing on whether or not the defendant was then in physical control of a motor vehicle which was or reasonably could become a danger to persons or property while the defendant was under the influence of alcohol.

Ordinarily, instructions drawing attention to particular kinds of evidence should be avoided in criminal cases. In this instance, however, directing the jury's attention in nonargumentative fashion to a number of relevant factors bearing on physical control could be helpful by providing focus to the arguments of counsel and the deliberations of the jurors. An instruction along the foregoing lines should be given if requested in cases where inoperability is involved.

In this case, the defendant requested an instruction which would have been error to give. Operability of the motor vehicle is not an element of the crime of being in physical control of a motor vehicle while under the influence of alcohol, and the State did not—contrary to the requested instruction—have a duty to prove operability beyond a reasonable doubt. Neither must the State prove that the defendant was in the vehicle for the purpose of operating the motor vehicle, as defendant's instruction also requested. An intent to operate is not an element of the

criminal offense; if it were, defendants found in a drunken stupor behind the wheel could argue they lacked any intent to move the vehicle. A drunken intent is highly problematic and too easily manipulated after the fact. Indeed, an attempt to make lack of intent an affirmative defense was defeated in the 1989 legislature.

Consequently, the trial court did not err in denying defendant's requested instruction. Nor can we say it was reversible error for the trial court not to have given a supplementary instruction on relevant facts to consider for physical control in the absence of counsel's request for the instruction. Under the standard * * * instruction that was given, the parties were free to argue, and did argue, the conflicting inferences to be drawn from the fact that defendant's car was stuck in the snow-filled ditch.

We reverse and reinstate the conviction.

Reversed.

TOMLJANOVICH, Justice (concurring in part and dissenting in part).

I concur in the majority's result but respectfully dissent as to one section of its opinion. Contrary to the majority's assertion, inoperability is never relevant to the issue of whether a defendant was in control of a motor vehicle. Operability is relevant to only one question: whether the thing at issue is, in fact, a motor vehicle.

The statute makes it a crime to "be in physical control of any motor vehicle * * * when the person is under the influence of alcohol." I would not read the word "operable" into the statute to permit the jury to require physical control of an operable motor vehicle.

Operability has nothing to do with control, and allowing the defense to raise it needlessly complicates what should be a straightforward determination. If defendants can claim, and juries can consider, inoperability, police officers will be forced to test drive every car they stop and parties will be forced to bring in automotive experts to testify. In the end, any trial involving this issue is what will be inoperable.

* * *

I respectfully dissent from the court's conclusion that inoperability is potentially relevant.

Notes and Questions

1. Some statutes require "actual physical control," which would seem to require more than simple physical control. Nevertheless, some courts have construed these crimes more broadly than the *Starfield* court defined the Minnesota statute. In

---

[2]Considering a motor vehicle's potential for operability will not, as the dissent suggests, require police officers to test-drive every car they stop, or, more to the point, every stopped car they come upon; nor is there any particular need for automotive experts. Cases in which potential operability may be a factor are quite rare, and even in these rare cases it is the overall situation that is important.

Adams v. State, 697 P.2d 622 (Wyo.1985), for example, the court upheld a conviction for being in "actual physical control" of a vehicle while intoxicated upon proof that the defendant was found unconscious in his vehicle parked twenty feet off the highway with the engine off, the lights off, and the key in the ignition but off. "As long as a person is physically or bodily able to assert dominion in the sense of movement by starting the car and driving away, then he has substantially as much control over the vehicle as he would if he were actually driving it," the court explained, and thus is in actual physical control. A Utah court has gone even further and indicated that a person need only have "an *apparent* ability to start and move the vehicle in order to be in actual physical control." *State v. Barnhart,* 850 P.2d 473, 478 (Utah App.1993) (emphasis supplied).

2. The Maryland Court of Appeals characterized the approach of *Adams,* discussed in note 1 as "overly broad and excessively rigid." It suggested:

> [W]e must give the word "actual" some significance. Further, when interpreting a statute, we assume that the words of the statute have their ordinary and natural meaning, absent some indication to the contrary. We have no such contrary indications here, so we examine the ordinary meaning of "actual physical control." Webster's Third New International Dictionary 1706 (1986) defines "physical" as "relating to the body ... often opposed to *mental."* (Emphasis in original). Webster's also defines "control" as "to exercise restraining or directing influence over." Most importantly, "actual" is defined as "present," "current," "existing in fact or reality," and "in existence or taking place at the time." Webster's also contrasts "actual" with "potential and possible" as well as with "hypothetical." By using the word "actual," the legislature implied a current or imminent restraining or directing influence over a vehicle. Accordingly, a person is in "actual physical control" if the person is presently exercising or is imminently likely to exercise "restraining or directing influence" over a motor vehicle while in an intoxicated condition.
>
> We believe that, by using the term "actual physical control," the legislature intended to differentiate between those inebriated people who represent no threat to the public because they are only using their vehicles as shelters

until they are sober enough to drive and those people who represent an imminent threat to the public by reason of their control of a vehicle. When the occupant is totally passive, has not in any way attempted to actively control the vehicle, and there is no reason to believe that the inebriated person is imminently going to control the vehicle in his or her condition, we do not believe that the legislature intended for criminal sanctions to apply.

As a practical matter, we recognize that any definition of "actual physical control," no matter how carefully considered, cannot aspire to cover every one of the many factual variations that one may envision. What constitutes "actual physical control" will inevitably depend on the facts of the individual case. The inquiry must always take into account a number of factors, however, including the following:

1) whether or not the vehicle's engine is running, or the ignition on;

2) where and in what position the person is found in the vehicle;

3) whether the person is awake or asleep;

4) where the vehicle's ignition key is located;

5) whether the vehicle's headlights are on;

6) whether the vehicle is located in the roadway or is legally parked.

No one factor alone will necessarily be dispositive of whether the defendant was in "actual physical control" of the vehicle. Rather, each must be considered with an eye towards whether there is in fact present or imminent exercise of control over the vehicle or, instead, whether the vehicle is merely being used as a stationary shelter. Courts must in each case examine what the evidence showed the defendant was doing or had done, and whether these actions posed an imminent threat to the public.

Perhaps the strongest factor informing this inquiry is whether there is evidence that the defendant started or attempted to start the vehicle's engine. The policy of allowing an intoxicated individual to "sleep it off" in safety, rather than attempt to drive home, arguably need not encompass the privilege of starting the engine, whether for the sake of running the radio, air conditioning, or heater. Indeed, once an individual has started the vehicle, he or she has come as close as possible to actually driving without doing so and will generally be in "actual physical control" of the vehicle. Other factors may militate against a court's determination on this point, however. For example, a person asleep on the back seat, under a blanket, might not be found in "actual physical control," even if the engine is running. The location of the vehicle can be a determinative factor in the inquiry because a person whose vehicle is parked illegally or stopped in the roadway is obligated by law to move the vehicle, and because of this obligation could more readily be deemed in "actual physical control" than a person lawfully parked on the shoulder or on his or her own property. In sum, the primary focus of the inquiry is whether the person is merely using the vehicle as a stationary shelter or whether it is reasonable to assume that the person will, while under the influence, jeopardize the public by exercising some measure of the vehicle.

Atkinson v. State, 331 Md. 199, 215–17, 627 A.2d 1019, 1027–28 (1993).

3. Many crimes that cover conduct criminalized because of the propensity created by that conduct for leading to further harm define the crime in part by requiring a culpable mental state that when present suggests the offender poses a high risk of ulti-mately causing the target harm. Larceny (and modern theft), for example, is often said to be intended to protect only persons' interest in not being *permanently* deprived of their property. As is developed in Chapter 4, this interest is reflected in the crime by the required culpable mental state rather than the conduct. A person need not actually cause permanent loss to the owner to complete larceny, but that person must act with the intent that the owner be permanently deprived.

As *Starfield* suggests, statutes dealing with intoxicated vehicle drivers have tended not to take this approach. There is widespread agreement that actual physical control does not require proof of intent to drive, although several courts have expressed reservations that this may render the offense at least sometimes counterproductive to the goal of providing safe highways. *State v. Kitchens,* 498 N.W.2d 649, 653 (S.D. 1993). Apparently legislatures and courts are concerned that any such requirement of intent to drive could too often be successfully challenged by defendants on the reasoning that their intoxication shows they lacked this intent.

Could this concern be met by regarding an exculpatory intent not to drive as a defensive matter? Courts have not been receptive. In *State ex rel. McDougall v. Superior Court,* 173 Ariz. 582, 845 P.2d 508 (App.1992), review dismissed, for example, the trial court had held that although proof of intent to drive is not necessary to establish exercise of control under the Arizona statute, conviction was precluded where the undisputed facts established that the defendant had not driven, did not intend to drive, and had turned on the engine of the vehicle to keep warm. Holding this error, the appellate tribunal reasoned that the defendant's intent is simply irrelevant.

D. LIABILITY BASED ON FAILURE TO ACT

It is clear that normally a crime must include the element of an act. Can the absence of an act—that is, an omission—ever constitute the equivalent of an act for purposes of holding a person criminally liable? There are two situations in which the answer is yes.

The first category is easily understood and consists of situations in which a statute both imposes a duty and creates a crime consisting of violating that duty. There are many statutes that impose duties on us to act and employ the criminal sanction if we fail to do so. For example, all owners of cars are under a duty in many states to have them inspected, most adults have a duty to file a federal income tax return, and young men of a certain age have a duty to register for a possible draft. Such statutes announce a clearly defined course of required conduct. Criminal liability for failing to undertake that conduct presents few if any problems in terms of the act requirement for criminal liability.

Far more problematic are those situations in which the charged crime creates no explicit command to act but the prosecution proceeds on the theory that the defendant's liability nevertheless rests on a failure to act. Usually, these are prosecutions for crimes that require some harmful and prohibited result to have occurred, and the prosecution's theory is that the result in the case can be attributed to the accused in the sense that it would not have occurred had the accused taken action to prevent it. Most common are prosecutions for homicide offenses, based on the accused's failure to take action that would or might have prevented the death of the victim.

In cases of the second sort, the courts (and legislatures) have been reluctant to impose extensive criminal liability. This is apparently in large part because of fear that criminal liability for failure to act might be too broadly applied and also because of an inability to formulate limited liability of this sort.

As is illustrated by the case reprinted in this section (*Commonwealth v. Pestinikas*), courts and legislatures have generally limited liability in such situations to cases in which the accused had a *legal* duty to act. In *Jones v. United States,* 113 U.S.App.D.C. 352, 308 F.2d 307 (1962), for example, the defendant was convicted of involuntary manslaughter for the death of a 10-month-old infant who had been left in her care by the child's mother. The death was attributed to severe malnutrition and lack of adequate medical care. Yet the court held that the jury could not convict without first finding beyond a reasonable doubt that the defendant was under a legal duty to supply food and medical care to the victim

The case that follows, *Commonwealth v. Pestinikas,* was widely regarded at the time it was decided as the first case to result in liability for *murder* by omission. As is developed in Chapter 7, murder requires a culpable mental state in addition to proof that the defendant's conduct—or omission—caused the death of the victim. These defendants were charged with first degree intentional murder and, alleging that the murder was committed "by means of torture," the prosecution sought the death penalty. At trial, the defendants were convicted of the lesser included offense of third degree murder, which under Pennsylvania law consists of all murders not made first or second degree murder. Because murder requires "malice aforethought," that culpable mental state had to be proved. Most likely, the jury found that the defendants acted with at least malicious disregard of a high risk that the victim would die as a result of their inaction. On appeal, in any case, the defendants apparently did not challenge the sufficiency of the evidence to show their culpable mental states. Rather, they argued that the evidence failed to establish an omission sufficient for criminal liability. In considering the case, however, keep in mind that establishing that an omission will suffice for liability does not establish the separate requirement that the culpable mental state be proved.

Commonwealth v. Pestinikas

Superior Court of Pennsylvania, 1992
421 Pa.Super. 371, 617 A.2d 1339.

Before WIEAND, McEWEN, OLSZEWSKI, DEL SOLE, BECK, TAMILIA, POPOVICH, JOHNSON and HUDOCK, JJ.

WIEAND, Judge:

The principal issue in this appeal is whether a person can be prosecuted criminally for murder when his or her failure to perform a contract to provide food and medical care for another has caused the death of such other person. The trial court answered this question in the affirmative and instructed the jury accordingly. The jury thereafter found Walter and Helen Pestinikas guilty of murder of the third degree in connection with the starvation and dehydration death of ninety-two (92) year old Joseph Kly. On direct appeal from the judgment of sentence,[3] the defendants contend that the trial court misapplied the law and gave the jury incorrect instructions. They argue, therefore, that they are entitled to an arrest of judgment because of the insufficiency of the evidence against them or at least a new trial because of the trial court's erroneous instructions to the jury.

* * *

Joseph Kly met Walter and Helen Pestinikas in the latter part of 1981 when Kly consulted them about pre-arranging his funeral. In March, 1982, Kly, who had been living with a stepson, was hospitalized and diagnosed as suffering from Zenker's diverticulum, a weakness in the walls of the esophagus, which caused him to have trouble swallowing food. In the hospital, Kly was given food which he was able to swallow and, as a result, regained some of the weight which he had lost. When he was about to be discharged, he expressed a desire not to return to his stepson's home and sent word to appellants that he wanted to speak with them. As a consequence, arrangements were made for appellants to care for Kly in their home on Main Street in Scranton, Lackawanna County.

Kly was discharged from the hospital on April 12, 1982. When appellants came for him on that day they were instructed by medical personnel regarding the care which was required for Kly and were given a prescription to have filled for him. Arrangements were also made for a visiting nurse to come to appellants' home to administer vitamin B-12 supplements to Kly. Appellants agreed orally to follow the medical instructions and to supply Kly with food, shelter, care and the medicine which he required.

According to the evidence, the prescription was never filled, and the visiting nurse was told by appellants that Kly did not want the vitamin supplement shots and that her services, therefore, were not required. Instead of giving Kly a room in their home, appellants removed him to a rural part of Lackawanna County, where they placed him in the enclosed porch of a building, which they owned, known as the Stage Coach Inn. This porch was approximately nine feet by thirty feet, with no insulation, no refrigeration, no bathroom, no sink and no telephone. The walls contained cracks which exposed the room to outside weather conditions. Kly's predicament was compounded by appellants' affirmative efforts to conceal his whereabouts. Thus, they gave misleading information in response to inquiries, telling members of Kly's family that they did not know where he had gone and others that he was living in their home.

After Kly was discharged from the hospital, appellants took Kly to the bank and had their names added to his savings account. Later, Kly's money was transferred into an account in the names of Kly or Helen Pestinikas, pursuant to which moneys could be withdrawn without Kly's signature. Bank records reveal that from May, 1982, to July, 1983, appellants withdrew amounts roughly consistent with the three hundred ($300) dollars per month which Kly had agreed to pay for his care. Beginning in August, 1983 and continuing until Kly's death in November, 1984, however, appellants withdrew much larger sums so that when Kly died, a balance of only fifty-five ($55) dollars remained. In the interim, appellants had withdrawn in excess of thirty thousand ($30,000) dollars.

On the afternoon of November 15, 1984, when police and an ambulance crew arrived in response to a call by appellants, Kly's dead body appeared emaciated, with his ribs and sternum greatly pronounced. Mrs. Pestinikas told police that she and her husband had taken care of Kly for three hundred ($300) dollars per month and that she had given him cookies and orange juice at 11:30 A.M. on the morning of his death. A subsequent autopsy, however, revealed that Kly had been dead at that time and may have been dead for as many as thirty-nine (39) hours before his body was found. The cause of death was determined to be starvation and dehydration. Expert testimony opined that Kly would have experienced pain and suffering over a long period of time before he died.

---

[3]Each appellant was sentenced to serve a term of imprisonment for not less than five (5) years nor more than ten (10) years. * * *

At trial, the Commonwealth contended that after contracting orally to provide food, shelter, care and necessary medicine for Kly, appellants engaged in a course of conduct calculated to deprive Kly of those things necessary to maintain life and thereby cause his death. The trial court instructed the jury that appellants could not be found guilty of a malicious killing for failing to provide food, shelter and necessary medicines to Kly unless a duty to do so had been imposed upon them by contract. The court instructed the jury, inter alia, as follows:

> In order for you to convict the defendants * * *, you must first find beyond a reasonable doubt that the defendants had a legal duty of care to Joseph Kly.
>
> There are but two situations in which Pennsylvania law imposes criminal liability for the failure to perform an act. One of these is where the express language of the law defining the offense provides for criminal [liability] based upon such a failure. The other is where the law otherwise imposes a duty to act.
>
> Unless you find beyond a reasonable doubt that an oral contract imposed a duty to act upon Walter and Helen Pestinikas, you must acquit the defendants.

Appellants contend that this was error.

The applicable law appears at 18 Pa.C.S. § 301(a) and (b) as follows:

> (a) General rule.—A person is not guilty of an offense unless his liability is based on conduct which includes a voluntary act or the omission to perform an act of which he is physically capable.
>
> (b) Omission as basis of liability.—Liability for the commission of an offense may not be based on an omission unaccompanied by action unless:
>
> (1) the omission is expressly made sufficient by the law defining the offense; or
>
> (2) a duty to perform the omitted act is otherwise imposed by law.

With respect to subsection (b), Toll, in his invaluable work on the Pennsylvania Crimes Code, has commented

> . . . [Subsection (b)] states the conventional position with respect to omissions unaccompanied by action as a basis of liability. Unless the omission is expressly made sufficient by the law defining the offense, a duty to perform the omitted act must have been otherwise imposed by law for the omission to have the same standing as a voluntary act for purposes of liability. *It should, of course, suffice, as the courts now hold, that the duty arises under some branch of the civil law. If it does, this minimal requirement is satisfied, though whether the omission constitutes an offense depends as well on many other factors.*

Toll, Pennsylvania Crimes Code Annotated, § 301, at p. 60, quoting Comment, Model Penal Code § 2.01 (emphasis added).

In *State v. Brown,* 129 Ariz. 347, 631 P.2d 129 (1981), the Court of Appeals for Arizona affirmed a manslaughter conviction of the operator of a boarding home in connection with the starvation death of a ninety-eight year old resident. The Arizona Court interpreted a statutory provision which is similar to Section 301 of the Pennsylvania Crimes Code in the following manner:

> As stated in A.R.S. Sec. 13-201 and demonstrated by the case law, the failure to perform a duty imposed by law may create criminal liability. In the case of negligent homicide or manslaughter, the duty must be found outside the definition of the crime itself, perhaps in another statute, or in the common law, or in a contract. The most commonly cited statement of the rule is found in *People v. Beardsley,* 150 Mich. 206, 113 N.W. 1128 (1907):
>
> > "The law recognizes that under some circumstances the omission of a duty owed by one individual to another, where such omission results in the death of the one to whom the duty is owing, will make the other chargeable with manslaughter.... This rule of law is always based upon the proposition that the duty neglected must be a legal duty, and not a mere moral obligation. It must be a duty imposed by law or by contract, and the omission to perform the duty must be the immediate and direct cause of death. (citations omitted)"

In *Jones v. United States,* 308 F.2d 307 (C.A.D.C.1962), the court stated:

> "There are at least four situations in which the failure to act may constitute breach of a legal duty. One can be held criminally liable: first, where a statute imposes a duty to care for another; second, where one stands in a certain status relationship to another; third, where one has assumed a contractual duty to care for another; and fourth, where one has voluntarily assumed the care of another and so secluded the helpless person as to prevent others from rendering aid."
>
> * * *

Consistently with this legal thinking we hold that when, in 18 Pa.C.S. § 301(b)(2), the statute provides that an omission to do an act can be the basis for criminal liability if a duty to perform the omitted act has been imposed by law, the legislature intended to distinguish between a legal duty to act and merely a moral duty to act. A duty to act imposed by contract is legally enforceable and, therefore, creates a legal duty. It follows that a failure to perform a duty imposed by contract may be the basis for a charge of criminal homicide if such failure causes the death of another person and all other elements of the offense are present. Because there was evidence in the instant case that Kly's death had been caused by appellants' failure to provide the food and medical care which they had agreed by oral contract to provide for him, their omission to act was sufficient to support a conviction for criminal homicide, and the trial court was correct when it instructed the jury accordingly.

Our holding is not that every breach of contract can become the basis for a finding of homicide resulting from an omission to act. A criminal act involves both a physical and mental aspect. An omission to act can satisfy the physical aspect of criminal conduct only if there is a duty to act imposed by law. A failure to provide food and medicine, in this case, could not have been made the basis for prosecuting a stranger who learned of Kly's condition and failed to act. Even where there is a duty imposed by contract, moreover, the omission to act will not support a prosecution for homicide in the absence of the necessary *mens rea*. For murder, there must be malice. Without a malicious intent, an omission to perform duties having their foundation in contract cannot support a conviction for murder. In the instant case, therefore, the jury was required to find that appellants, by virtue of contract, had undertaken responsibility for providing necessary care for Kly to the exclusion of the members of Kly's family. This would impose upon them a legal duty to act to preserve Kly's life. If they maliciously set upon a course of withholding food and medicine and thereby caused Kly's death, appellants could be found guilty of murder.

Appellants' reliance upon *Commonwealth v. Konz,* 498 Pa. 639, 450 A.2d 638 (1982), is misplaced. In that case, the Court did not consider criminal responsibility for an omission to perform a duty imposed by contract, but considered only the nature of the duties arising from the marital relationship. The Court held that where a husband was aware of his condition, i.e., diabetes, and competently made a voluntary decision to forego further treatment, i.e., insulin, his wife was not criminally liable for failing to summon medical help. Because *Konz* was carefully limited by the Court to its own facts, it provides little, if any, guidance in the instant case.

With respect to the alleged insufficiency of the evidence, it may also be observed that appellants' culpable conduct, according to the evidence, was not limited merely to an omission to act. It consisted, rather, of an affirmative course of conduct calculated to deprive Kly of the food and medical care which was otherwise available to him and which was essential to continued life. It included efforts to place Kly beyond the ability of others to provide such needs. Such a course of conduct, the jury could find, as it did, had been pursued by appellants willfully and maliciously, who thereby caused Kly's death.

Appellants argue that, in any event, the Commonwealth failed to prove an enforceable contract requiring them to provide Kly with food and medical attention. It is their position that their contract with Kly required them to provide only a place for Kly to live and a funeral upon his death. This obligation, they contend, was fulfilled. * * * [I]t seems readily apparent from the * * * record * * * that the evidence was sufficient to create an issue of fact for the jury to resolve. The issue was submitted to the jury on careful instructions by the learned trial judge and does not present a basis entitling appellants to post-trial relief.

* * *

Having found no valid reason for disturbing the jury's verdicts, we conclude that the judgments of sentence must be, as they are,

AFFIRMED.

[The concurring opinion of Judge Tamila and the dissenting opinion of Judge McEwen are omitted.]

DEL SOLE, Judge, dissenting.

* * * I believe that the Majority * * * error[s] by equating "legal duty" with a "duty imposed by law." Resolution of the instant case is controlled by the definition of the phrase "a duty imposed by law." I believe that this phrase, as it appears in 18 Pa.C.S.A. § 301(b)(2), encompasses only those duties which are imposed by statute or regulation and specifically does not include a contractual obligation.

* * *

Generally to be convicted of a crime the performance of a voluntary act is necessary, but an omission may be a basis for criminal liability in certain situations. * * *

Duties which are "imposed by law" do not encompass those which arise out of a contract or agreement. A person who enters a contract does so freely. The duties contained in a contract are those which the person who is entering the contract agrees to undertake voluntarily in exchange for some other consideration. The duties themselves are not "imposed by law" they are assumed by the terms of the agreement. Although breach of the agreement may result in some legal recourse, the law will fashion a remedy only if the injured party seeks one. The Pestinikases' omissions which resulted in a breach of their agreement to care for Mr. Kly do not constitute an omission which could be the basis of liability under § 301(b)(2).

* * *

I am concerned that the position argued by the Commonwealth in this case would subject those parties who breach a contract to criminal responsibility even though no specific crime involving their actions has been defined by the legislature. These concerns require us to remain mindful that a penal statute such as that found in the instant case should be strictly construed in favor of the defendant. The strict construction rule regarding penal statutes is based on the rationale that it would be unjust to convict a person without clear notice that the contemplated conduct is unlawful, as well as providing that individual with notice of the potential penalties. This rationale provides sound reasoning for the conclusion that the term "duties imposed by law" does not encompass those duties contained in a contract. * * *

Because the statute we are asked to examine * * * refers solely to "duties imposed by law," and because a contractual duty alone is not one "imposed by law," I * * * dissent * * *.

McEWEN, J., joins.

Notes and Questions

1. The most commonly recognized duty that will provide a basis for liability for omissions is that of parents to minor children. A duty to act may also arise when the defendant is responsible for a condition that required assistance that the defendant failed to provide. Thus, in *Herman v. State,* 472 So.2d 770 (Fla.App. 1985), the defendant's conviction for manslaughter was affirmed where the victim, a cocaine addict, died from the hemorrhaging of her nose and mouth due to a cocaine overdose administered by the defendant, who failed to call medical assistance when the victim began convulsing.

2. Whatever the source of the duty, it is crucial that the victim be unable to take remedial action herself. This is apparently the basis on which *Pestinikas* distinguished *Commonwealth v. Konz,* 498 Pa. 639, 450 A.2d 638 (1982).

3. Would the following statute be appropriate? It would change the traditional and general rule that criminal liability can exist for an omission only if the defendant had a preexisting *legal* obligation to act.

   Liability for Omission. A person shall be criminally responsible for a result if he fails to take action to prevent that result, but for his failure to take action the result would not have occurred, and the failure to take action constitutes a substantial deviation from common decency. In determining whether a failure to act constitutes a substantial deviation from common decency the following factors shall be taken into account:

   1. the seriousness of the result,

   2. the likelihood that the result would occur without action,

   3. any burden or risk which taking action would have required the person to assume, and

   4. any responsibility of the person for creating the need for action.

Statutes quite similar to the proposal are found in European Codes. Feldbrugge, "Good and Bad Samaritans," 14 Am.J. Comp.L. 630 (1966).

MODEL PENAL CODE*

Official Draft, 1985

Section 2.01. * * * Omission as Basis of Liability
* * *

(3) Liability for the commission of an offense may not be based on an omission unaccompanied by action unless:

(a) the omission is expressly made sufficient by the law defining the offense; or

(b) a duty to perform the omitted act is otherwise imposed by law.

Chapter 4

GENERAL PRINCIPLES OF CRIMINAL LIABILITY: THE STATE OF MIND

CHAPTER CONTENTS

Editors' Introduction: Criminal Law's Emphasis on Mental States

Criminal law differs from other forms of criminal liability perhaps most importantly in its emphasis upon the subjective state of mind of the person whose legal liability is at issue. Cowman, Towards an Experimental Definition of Criminal Mind, in F. Clarke and M. Nahm eds., Philosophical Essays in Honor of Edgar Arthur Singer, Jr. 163 (1942) explained:

> In the 17th year of the reign of Edward IV, Brian pronounced his celebrated dictum that a man is responsible only for his words and deeds and not for his thoughts, because "the devil himself knoweth not the mind of man." What the learned judge apparently took to be an axiomatic rule of evidence has become a part of the substantive law of contracts in the form of the doctrine of objective intent. Contract law is now taken to be concerned only with intent as outwardly manifested by the conduct of the parties.
>
> Similarly, the law of torts is almost exclusively occupied with the external behavior of the parties. * * * Anglo-American civil law, therefore, has from the earliest times indicated that, with certain few exceptions, objective intent is the only kind of intent with which it is prepared to deal.
>
> The theory of the criminal law is different. Here it is still felt necessary to investigate a man's secret thought, or absence of thought, whenever intention, or malice, or even negligence is an element of the crime in question.

The historical development of the criminal law's emphasis upon an alleged offender's state of mind (the *mens rea* requirement) was traced by Sayre, Mens Rea, 45 Harv.L.Rev. 974, 981–83, 988–89, 993–94 (1932):

> [S]tudy of the early law seems to show that up to the twelfth century the conception of *mens rea* in anything like its present sense was nonexistent. In certain cases at least criminal liability might attach irrespective of the actor's state of mind. But because the old records fail to set forth a *mens rea* as a general requisite of criminality one must not reach the conclusion that even in very early times the mental element was entirely disregarded. The very nature of the majority of the early offenses rendered them impossible of commission without a criminal intent. Waylaying and robbery are impossible without it; so is rape; and the same is roughly true of housebreaking. * * *
>
> Furthermore, the intent of the defendant seems to have been a material factor, even from the very earliest times, in determining the extent of punishment.
>
> By the end of the twelfth century two influences were making themselves strongly felt. One was the Roman law[;] * * * the Roman law conceptions of *dolus* and *culpa* required careful consideration of the mental element in crime.
>
> A second influence, even more powerful, was the canon law, whose insistence upon moral guilt emphasized still further the mental element in crime. * * * Henceforth, the criminal law of England, developing in the general direction of moral blameworthiness, begins to insist upon a *mens rea* as an essential element of criminality.
>
> We can trace the changed attitude in the new generalizations concerning the necessity of an evil intent which are found scattered through the Year Books in the

remarks of judges and counsel * * *. We sense it in the growing insistence upon more and more sharply defined mental requisites as essentials of the common-law felonies. We find it fermenting in the form of new defenses which show the absence of an evil mind and therefore of criminal liability-defenses such as infancy or insanity or compulsion.

By the second half of the seventeenth century, it was universally accepted law that an evil intent was as necessary for felony as the act itself. * * *

At the outset when the *mens rea* necessary for criminality was based on general moral blameworthiness, the conception was an exceedingly vague one. As a result of the slow judicial process of discriminating one case from another and "talking of diversities," much sharper and more precise lines gradually came to be drawn as to the exact mental requisites for various crimes. Since each felony involved different social and public interests, the mental requisites for one almost inevitably came to differ from those of another.[a]

As Sayre suggested, the criminal law's emphasis on subjective mental state is based upon two basic assumptions. The first is that criminal liability should only be imposed upon those who have demonstrated both their dangerousness and their moral blameworthiness. The second assumption is that moral blameworthiness is demonstrated only if a person acts with awareness of the relevant facts.

Since Sayre's writing, the mental requisites for crimes have in many jurisdictions become even more carefully defined. As was developed in Chapter 1, the Model Penal Code has offered an elaborate framework for defining mental state requirements more specifically and carefully than was the case under traditional law. Even in those jurisdictions that have not adopted a comprehensive statutory framework based on the Model Penal Code, the Code's basic approach is often influential with the courts. As a result of this increased emphasis upon mental states, the criminal law has become even more subjective in nature in the years since the development of the Model Penal Code.

Modern criminal law's more detailed attention to the subjective mental state of those charged with crime is due in part to a desire to go beyond simply assuring moral blameworthiness in a general sense. The definitions of many modern crimes reflect an effort on the part of legislatures to define crimes to assure *proportionate* blameworthiness, that is, moral reprehensibility proportionate to the seriousness of the crime as reflected in the penalty applicable upon conviction.

The criminal law's so-called subjective approach to criminal liability assumes, of course, that state of mind and therefore "mind" itself are ascertainable. This underlying assumption has been called into question on both practical and theoretical grounds.

The practical ground is based upon difficulty of proof. If there is such a thing as state of mind, it is nevertheless so subjective and difficult of proof that it is unrealistic to believe that an individual's state of mind at a past time can generally be reliably

---

[a]Reprinted from 45 Harvard Law Review 974 (1932).

determined. Thus, it is argued, the criminal law should not attempt to make criminal liability turn on state of mind.

The theoretical ground is more basic. This view holds that "mind" is a mere abstraction and therefore it is artificial to treat states of mind as if they actually existed. Rather than waste time attempting to infer an offender's state of mind from his or her behavior, this view holds that the law would better serve its purposes if it regarded the so-called mind as the criminal behavior itself rather than using the behavior as evidence from which to infer "mind." See T. Cowan, Towards an Experimental Definition of Criminal Mind, in F. Clarke and M. Nahm, eds., Philosophical Essays in Honor of Edgar Arthur Singer, Jr. (1942; Cowan, A Critique of the Moralistic Conception of Criminal Law, 97 U.Pa.L.Rev. 502, 510 (1949). In fact, Cowan represented, the law does this by procedural devices such as the presumption that a person "intends" the natural consequences of his or her act. Inserting the concept of "state of mind," he concluded, merely serves to confuse analysis.

Despite these misgivings, however, criminal law continues to be in large part a matter of defining what subjective culpable mental states are required by particular crimes and then determining whether persons accused of those crimes acted with those required mental states.

There is a widespread assumption that constitutional law imposes some limits on the extent to which criminal liability can be imposed without a subjective mental state requirement. Just as constitutional considerations demand that crimes be defined in terms of conduct rather than status—as discussed in Chapter 3—these fundamental requirements almost certainly demand that some crimes require proof of *mens rea.* *When* proof of awareness is constitutionally required, and *what* awareness must be shown as a constitutional necessity, however, remain quite unclear.

The existence of minimal constitutional demands is confirmed by the United States Supreme Court's decision in *Lambert v. California,* 355 U.S. 225, 78 S.Ct. 240, 2 L.Ed.2d 228 (1967). Lambert was prosecuted under section 52.39 of the Los Angeles Municipal Code, which made it unlawful for "any convicted person" to be or remain in Los Angeles for more than five days without registering with the Chief of Police. "Convicted person" was defined by section 52.38(a) as, "Any person * * * convicted of an offense punishable as a felony * * *." Each day that a person covered by the ordinance failed to register was made a separate offense.

At trial, Lambert was proved to have lived in Los Angeles for seven years after being convicted of forgery, a felony, but without registering. She offered testimony that she was unaware of the requirement that she register, but this was refused. Upon conviction under the ordinance, she was fined $250 and placed on probation for three years. The Supreme Court, by a 5-to-4 vote and in an opinion by Justice Douglas, held that "the registration provisions of the Code as sought to be applied here violate the Due Process requirements of the Fourteenth Amendment." Justice Douglas explained:

> The question is whether a registration act of this character violates due process where it is applied to a person who has no actual knowledge of his duty to register, and where no showing is made of the probability of such knowledge.
> We do not go with Blackstone in saying that "a vicious will" is necessary to

constitute a crime, for conduct alone without regard to the intent of the doer is often sufficient. There is wide latitude in the lawmakers to declare an offense and to exclude elements of knowledge and diligence from its definition. But we deal here with conduct that is wholly passive—mere failure to register. It is unlike the commission of acts, or the failure to act under circumstances that should alert the doer to the consequences of his deed. The rule that "ignorance of the law will not excuse" is deep in our law, as is the principle that of all the powers of local government, the police power is "one of the least limitable." On the other hand, due process places some limits on its exercise. Engrained in our concept of due process is the requirement of notice. Notice is sometimes essential so that the citizen has the chance to defend charges. * * * [This] principle is * * * appropriate where a person, wholly passive and unaware of any wrongdoing, is brought to the bar of justice for condemnation in a criminal case.

Registration laws are common and their range is wide. Many such laws are akin to licensing statutes in that they pertain to the regulation of business activities. But the present ordinance is entirely different. Violation of its provisions is unaccompanied by any activity whatever, mere presence in the city being the test. Moreover, circumstances which might move one to inquire as to the necessity of registration are completely lacking. * * * We believe that actual knowledge of the duty to register or proof of the probability of such knowledge and subsequent failure to comply are necessary before a conviction under the ordinance can stand. As Holmes wrote in The Common Law, "A law which punished conduct which would not be blameworthy in the average member of the community would be too severe for that community to bear." Its severity lies in the absence of an opportunity either to avoid the consequences of the law or to defend any prosecution brought under it. Where a person did not know of the duty to register and where there was no proof of the probability of such knowledge, he may not be convicted consistently with due process. Were it otherwise, the evil would be as great as it is when the law is written in print too fine to read or in a language foreign to the community.

Did *Lambert* turn on the fact that the crime at issue was defined in terms of inaction, that is, *not* registering? The Court seems to rely at least in part upon the proposition that when a crime consists of failing to act rather than acting, particular care needs to be taken to assure that potential offenders have adequate opportunity to avoid committing the crime. Or did *Lambert* turn on a conclusion that the duty to register was so unusual that *Lambert* and others like her were quite unlikely to be aware of the need to register to avoid their conduct—remaining in Los Angeles—from being a criminal offense? Perhaps *Lambert* stands for the proposition that when a crime consists of conduct or inaction that is quite unlikely to be criminal, particular care needs to be taken to assure that potential offenders have adequate opportunity to avoid what they know will be criminal conduct.

What would have been sufficient in *Lambert* to avoid the due process defect? Obviously no due process violation would have occurred if the ordinance had defined the offense as requiring for conviction that a person "be or remain in Los Angeles for a period of more than five days, aware of his or her duty to register, but without registering." Suppose, however, that the crime requires only proof that the accused was or remained in Los Angeles for the designated period "under circumstances in which a reasonable person would be aware of his or her duty to register, but without register-ing?" In the first situation, the crime would require actual subjective awareness of the critical fact—the duty to register. In the second, the crime would require what is later defined in this chapter as negligence, that is, circumstances in which a reasonable person exercising reasonable care would have been aware of that critical fact.

Suppose the crime had imposed no such requirement but had provided that one prosecuted under the ordinance was to be acquitted if that person proved, by a pre-ponderance of the evidence, that he did not know of the duty to register? In this situa-tion, the matter would be addressed without putting any additional burden on the prosecution but instead by giving an accused an opportunity to raise a *defense*.

Keep *Lambert* in mind while addressing the material in the remainder of this chap-ter. Consider the extent to which the federal constitutional demands created by the decision, or the underlying values stressed by Justice Douglas, should affect the way in which modern criminal statutes are drafted, construed, and applied.

Lambert seemed to say that due process requires that criminal defendants have a fair opportunity to avoid committing a crime and thus incurring criminal liability. This fair opportunity to avoid liability, in turn, demands in at least some situations that crimes require awareness of the facts making up the crime. Only a person who is aware of the facts is placed on notice that the person's conduct will constitute a crime and thus is given a fair notice of the need to avoid criminal liability.

Mens rea may be required by other constitutional considerations than the due process demand applied in *Lambert*. The Eighth Amendment prohibition against cruel and unusual punishment imposes at least a minimal demand that criminal punishment not be grossly disproportionate to the conduct on which it is based. Thus the death penalty for rape of an adult woman is so disproportionate as to constitute cruel and unusual punishment. *Coker v. Georgia*, 433 U.S. 584, 97 S.Ct. 2861, 53 L.Ed.2d 982 (1977). If a crime may be committed without awareness of those facts that make the conduct blameworthy, serious criminal liability—or perhaps any criminal liability at all—may be so disproportionate as to similarly violate the Eighth Amendment.

Despite the uncertainty as to precisely what constitutional considerations demand of crimes in this area, courts' interpretation of statutory offenses are often influenced by what the courts perceive are actual or potential constitutional demands. Decisions to construe crimes as requiring *mens rea* are with some frequency supported in part by explanations that this construction avoids the difficult constitutional question that would be presented if the crime at issue was interpreted otherwise.

Some courts, however, conclude that despite *Lambert*, constitutional considerations are minimally applicable here. In *State v. Maldonado*, 137 N.J. 536, 556, 645 A.2d 1165, 1174 (1992), for example, the New Jersey Supreme Court reasoned that "the State has the power to define a crime without proof of *mens rea* so long as the defini-tion does not offend fundamental notions of justice. Thus, constitutional-due-process limitations on strict-liability criminal statutes apply [only] when the underlying conduct is so passive, so unworthy of blame, that the persons violating the proscription would have no notice that they were breaking the law."

This chapter begins by exploring the basic approach of the Model Penal Code. It then develops what can usefully be regarded as the general rule of criminal liability—that general criminal intent is required. Next, it explores the additional culpable mental states required by some crimes and then the reduced standards applied by some crimes, the so-called strict liability offenses.

Defensive theories that consist of challenges to proof of *mens rea* are considered later in Part 4 of the book. Mistake, for example, is considered in Chapter 13 and both intoxication and diminished capacity are addressed in Chapter 15.

A. STATE OF MIND ANALYSIS AND TYPES OF MENTAL STATES

Editors' Introduction: Defining the Terms Used in Describing the Mental Elements of Crimes

Despite long-standing agreement that the actor's state of mind is of major, if not critical, importance in determining whether criminal liability exists for an act, and, where appropriate, the gradation of liability, the precise state-of-mind requirements demanded for conviction of particular crimes remains amazingly unclear. Even less certainty exists concerning some general terms often used in judicial and textual discussions of criminal intent, particularly the phrases "general intent" and "specific intent."

These terms are widely used in formulating what are often regarded as generally accepted rules. For example, the defenses of voluntary intoxication and diminished capacity are sometimes defined as available only where the crime at issue requires proof of a specific intent; this is considered further in Chapter 15. A mistake of fact is often required to be reasonable as well as honestly entertained unless it shows the lack of a specific intent required by the crime charged; this is considered further in Chapter 13.

In view of this widespread use of the terms general and specific intent, it is surprising that there is not more widespread agreement on their meaning. The United States Supreme Court observed:

> At common law, crimes generally were classified as requiring either "general intent" or "specific intent." This venerable distinction, however, has been the source of a good deal of confusion. As one treatise explained:
>
> > "Sometimes 'general intent' is used in the same way as 'criminal intent' to mean the general notion of *mens rea,* while 'specific intent' is taken to mean the mental state required for a particular crime. Or, 'general intent' may be used to encompass all forms of the mental state requirement, while 'specific intent' is limited to the one mental state of intent. Another possibility is that 'general intent' will be used to characterize an intent to do something on an undetermined occasion, and 'specific intent' to denote an intent to do that

thing at a particular time and place." W. LaFave & A. Scott, Handbook on Criminal Law § 28, pp. 201–02 (1972) (footnotes omitted).

This ambiguity has led to a movement away from the traditional dichotomy of intent [between specific and general intent] and towards an alternative analysis of *mens rea*. This new approach, exemplified in the American Law Institute's Model Penal Code, is based on two principles. First, the ambiguous and elastic term "intent" is replaced with a hierarchy of culpable states of mind. The different levels in this hierarchy are commonly identified, in descending order of culpability, as purpose, knowledge, recklessness, and negligence. * * *

[Second,] there is another ambiguity inherent in the traditional distinction between specific intent and general intent. Generally, even time-honored common-law crimes consist of several elements, and complex statutorily defined crimes exhibit this characteristic to an even greater degree. Is the same state of mind required of the actor for each element of the crime, or may some elements require one state of mind and some another. * * * [T]he American Law Institute stated: "[C]lear analysis requires that the question of the kind of culpability required to establish the commission of an offense be faced separately with respect to each material element of the crime. MPC Comments 123.

United States v. Bailey, 444 U.S. 394, 403–06, 100 S.Ct. 624, 631–32, 62 L.Ed.2d 575, 586–88 (1980).

The analysis of mental states embodied in the Model Penal Code has been widely followed in legislative criminal code revision, and constitutes one of the major contributions of the Code to the development of American substantive criminal law. Because of its prominence in contemporary substantive criminal law, the Model Penal Code's approach is a major focus of this chapter.

This analysis suggests and perhaps requires that the states of mind required for criminal liability be considered with regard to two dimensions. First, it is necessary to identify what the state of mind must concern. This might usefully be characterized as the "object dimension." Second, it is necessary to identify what state of mind concerning what object is required. This might usefully be characterized as the "level dimension." As the Supreme Court's *Bailey* discussion indicates, a single crime may require mental states that differ in level depending upon which object they concern.

The federal statute at issue in *United States v. Feola*, 420 U.S. 671, 95 S.Ct. 1255, 43 L.Ed.2d 541 (1975), provides an example:

> Whoever forcibly assaults * * * any person designated [a federal officer] while engaged in * * * the performance of his official duties, shall be fined not more than $5,000 or imprisoned not more than three years, or both.

18 U.S.C.A. § 111. The nonmental elements of this crime can be identified as follows:

1. forcibly assault[ing];

2. a person designated a federal officer;

3. who is, at the time, engaged in the performance of his or her official duties.

A mental state might be required concerning each of these matters or, in the terminology just used, concerning each of these objects. However, if a decision is made to require a mental state with regard to each of these objects, those mental states might differ with regard to—again in the terminology used above—their level. For example, it might well be appropriate to require that a defendant act with at least knowledge concerning element 1, that is, that the defendant at least be aware that he or she is (depending upon the applicable definition of assault) injuring another person, putting that person in apprehension of injury, or touching that person in an offensive way without his or her consent. However, with regard to elements 2 and 3, it may be equally appropriate that recklessness or perhaps even negligence be sufficient, that is, that the defendant need only have been aware (or should have been aware) of a substantial and unjustifiable risk that the victim was a federal officer and that the federal officer was, at the time, engaged in the performance of his or her official duties. Indeed, no state of mind at all might be required as to either or both of these elements.

In any case, all such mental states would concern objects that are themselves elements of the offense. Congress might, however, have concluded that liability for this offense should require proof that the actor had a state of mind concerning matters other than the act of assault and the attendant circumstances of the victim's federal identity and activity. For example, it is not necessary under § 111 for the government to prove that a defendant's conduct impeded the victim's performance of his official duties. However, Congress might have determined that such assaults should constitute a federal offense only if they were made with the intent to impede the federal officer's performance of his or her official duties. Such a conclusion could have been embodied in a somewhat different version of § 111:

> Whoever forcibly assaults * * * any person designated [a federal officer] while engaged in * * * the performance of his official duties, with the purpose of impeding the officer's performance of those duties, shall be fined not more than $5,000 or imprisoned not more than three years, or both.

Now, by the precise terms of the offense, one element of the crime is a mental state concerning an object—impediment of the victim's performance of his official duties—that need not itself be proved to establish guilt. The quality of that mental state is "purpose," that is, the defendant must—using the distinctions of the Model Penal Code—have had the conscious objective of impeding the officer's performance of his or her duties.

This distinction, then, is between states of mind that concern or have as their objects matters—acts, circumstances, or results—that are themselves nonmental elements of the crime, and other states of mind that concern matters not elements of the offense.

Is this distinction useful? It may assist in understanding what at least some courts mean when they use the term, general intent. Although, as the preceding *Bailey* discussion suggested, use of this terminology has been inconsistent, many courts appear to use the phrase "general intent" to refer to the mental state or states required by the crime that have as their object or objects the defendant's acts or, perhaps, other matters that are elements of the offense. In *State v. McVey*, 376 N.W.2d 585, 586 (Iowa 1985), for example, the court regarded theft by exercising control over stolen goods as only a general intent crime because it does not require proof of any intent beyond the voluntary act of exercising the prohibited control over property the accused knows to have been stolen. In *Dean v. State*, 668 P.2d 639, 642 (Wyo.1983), the court treated arson—defined as willfully and maliciously burning a house—as not a specific intent crime, but it commented that a revised statute defining the crime as maliciously starting a fire with intent to damage an occupied structure would create specific intent offense. The revised crime discussed in *Dean* would be a specific intent crime because it requires a state of mind regarding an object—damage to an occupied structure—that is not an element of the offense, since the prosecution need not prove that damage to an occupied structure in fact occurred.

Is there any utility in continuing to use the terms specific and general intent? Given the inconsistencies in the meaning given the terms, it is arguable that they contribute little but further confusion to an already uncertain area. Of course, to the extent that courts and legislatures use them, they cannot be ignored.

The distinction drawn by the definition previously suggested, however, may have some analytical value. It is useful in careful analysis to distinguish and address separately two points with regard to particular crimes. First, what mental states ought to be required with regard to those matters that are themselves part of the *actus reus* of the crime (that is, what general intent in the terminology previously discussed ought to be required)? Second, what mental states ought to be required with regard to other matters (that is, what specific intent ought to be required)? Because different considerations may apply to the issues posed by these inquiries, analysis that separates them will encourage independent resolution of the issues.

Given the rationales for stressing the actor's state of mind in deciding whether criminal liability ought to exist, it is arguable that as a general rule some level of mental state ought to be required with regard to each part of the *actus reus* of the offense. This is the position taken in Section 2.02 of the Model Penal Code, which is reprinted in this section.

However, other mental states—or specific intents—may not, as a general rule, be suggested by basic principles of criminal liability. Perhaps they should be imposed only where a specifically identifiable function would be served. Also, proving a specific intent may pose special difficulties for the prosecution and may trigger the operation of so-called defenses such as intoxication. Therefore, given these considerations, perhaps courts willing to find requirements of general intent even in the absence of statutory language requiring this should be more reluctant to find specific intents required by crimes where the legislative language does not impose such requirements.

Specific intent, then, may usefully be regarded as meaning mental states that have as their objects matters that are not elements of the crime. Cf. W. LaFave and A. Scott, Criminal Law 389–90 (2nd ed. 1986) (in case law discussing intoxication, specific intent sometimes means intent in addition to the intent to do the physical act that the crime requires); R. Perkins and R. Boyce, Criminal Law 832 (3rd ed. 1982).

The federal statute just considered provides an opportunity for an illustrative example. Those states of mind, if any, required by § 111 that concern the three nonmental elements of the offense—forcible assault, that the victim be a federal officer, and that the victim be engaged in the performance of official duties—would constitute the general intent required by the offense. As actually embodied in the federal code, § 111 would not require any specific intent. However, the further culpable mental state demanded by the previously given hypothetical version of the statute would require such a specific intent, because it would require a mental state concerning a matter—impediment of the victim's performance of his official duties—that is not itself an element of the offense.

As so defined, the characterization of mental states does not depend on their level within the hierarchy of mental states. The fact that the specific intent required by the hypothetical version of § 111 demands purpose does not, in itself, make that a specific intent.

It is important to stress that there is not general agreement on this use of the terminology. In *Bailey,* for example, the Supreme Court observed that, "In a general sense, 'purpose' corresponds loosely with the common-law concept of specific intent, while 'knowledge' corresponds loosely with the concept of general intent." Under the previously used definition of the terms, of course, this is simply not the case. The Minnesota Supreme Court asserted in *State v. Orsello,* 554 N.W.2d 70 (Minn.1996), that "General intent requires only that the defendant engaged intentionally in specific, prohibited conduct. In contrast, specific intent requires that the defendant acted with the intention to produce a specific *result* * * *." *Orsello* characterized the stalking offense there before the court as a specific intent crime because it required that the defendant intend to cause the victim to feel oppressed, prosecuted, or intimidated. Because the crime required that in fact this result occur—that the victim in fact be caused to feel oppressed, prosecuted, or intimidated—under the definitions previously used this offense would *not* involve a specific intent.

Often, however, the approach just set out explains what courts mean by other language used in an effort to define general and specific intents. The approach is consistent, for example, with the explanation in *Ford v. State,* 330 Md. 682, 625 A.2d 984, 993 (1993) that general intent is the intent to do the *actus reus* of the crime, while a specific intent is an intention to accomplish something more.

This and the next several sections of this chapter assume that this distinction between general and specific intents, as so defined, has analytical value and use this distinction as a basis for the subdivision of the chapter. This section reprints those portions of the Model Penal Code that define and distinguish among various states of mind according to what was previously characterized as their level. Section B deals with general intent as previously defined—the state of mind required concerning those matters that are part of the *actus reus* of the crime. In contrast, Section C concerns what under these definitions would be specific intents. Section D, on the other hand, addresses those situations in which a decision is or may be made that even general intent in this sense is not required.

MODEL PENAL CODE*

Official Draft, 1985

Section 2.02. General Requirements of Culpability

* * *

(2) *Kinds of Culpability Defined.*

(a) *Purposely.*

A person acts purposely with respect to a material element of an offense when:

(i) if the element involves the nature of his conduct or a result thereof, it is his conscious object to engage in conduct of that nature or to cause such a result; and

(ii) if the element involves the attendant circumstances, he is aware of the existence of such circumstances or he believes or hopes that they exist.

(b) *Knowingly.*

A person acts knowingly with respect to a material element of an offense when:

(i) if the element involves the nature of his conduct or the attendant circumstances, he is aware that his conduct is of that nature or that such circumstances exist; and

(ii) if the element involves a result of his conduct, he is aware that it is practically certain that his conduct will cause such a result.

(c) *Recklessly.*

A person acts recklessly with respect to a material element of an offense when he consciously disregards a substantial and unjustifiable risk that the material element exists or will result from his conduct. The risk must be of such a nature and degree that, considering the nature and purpose of the actor's conduct and the circumstances known to him, its disregard involves a gross deviation from the standard of conduct that a law-abiding person would observe in the actor's situation.

(d) *Negligently.*

A person acts negligently with respect to a material element of an offense when he should be aware of a substantial and unjustifiable risk that the material element exists or will result from his conduct. The risk must be of such a nature and degree that the actor's failure to perceive it, considering the nature and purpose of his conduct and the circumstances known to him, involves a gross deviation from the standard of care that a reasonable person would observe in the actor's situation.

Note

The "kinds" (or dimensions or levels) of culpable mental states distinguished and defined in the Model Penal Code are designed for use in a statutory scheme containing crimes defined by use of the terms used in § 2.02(2). Nevertheless, they are sometimes used by courts in describing or defining the mental states required by crimes that are not part of such a statutory scheme and thus do not explicitly use the terms of Model Penal Code analysis.

The United States Supreme Court, for example, has used the Model Penal Code's distinctions in formulating the culpable mental states required by several federal crimes. In *United States v. United States Gypsum Co.*, 438 U.S. 422, 444, 98 S.Ct. 2864, 2877, 57 L.Ed.2d 854, 874 (1978), the Court commented that the Model Penal Code "is one source of guidance" upon which Court has relied to "illuminate" questions regarding the practical aspects of the mental element of federal crimes. See also, *Posters 'N' Things, Ltd.,* 511 U.S. 513, 524–24, 114 S.Ct. 1747, 1753–54, 128 L.Ed.2d 539, 550–51 (1994) (using Model Penal Code terminology to frame mental state required by Mail Order Drug Paraphernalia Control Act).

However, when terms such as knowledge or recklessness are used in statutes that are not part of a statutory scheme with precise definitions of those terms, the terms may not be defined or used by the courts in the same way they are defined in the Model Penal Code.

Federal law, for example, has not been revised so as to include any such definition of these terms, although they are sometimes used in federal statutes and judicial decisions. The Supreme Court has imposed requirements of "knowledge" for some federal crimes, but the Court's working definition of knowledge may be less demanding than that of the Model Penal Code. Under the Code's definition, knowledge regarding a result of conduct requires that the defendant be "practically certain" that his conduct will cause the result. In *United States Gypsum Co.,* however, the Court described the mental state required by its version of knowledge as "knowledge that [anticompetitive] effects would *most likely* follow, and "knowledge of [one's actions] probable consequences." (Emphasis supplied.) In *Posters 'N' Things, Ltd.,* the Court described the effect of its requirement that the defendant act with knowledge regarding the use of the items at issue as requiring that "the Government must establish that the defendant knew that the items at issue are *likely* to be used with illegal drugs * * *." (Emphasis supplied.) Quite possibly the Court is imposing what is functionally a requirement of recklessness in the Model Penal Code sense, but is calling it knowledge.

B. THE STANDARD STATE OF MIND REQUIREMENT FOR CRIMINAL LIABILITY: "GENERAL INTENT"

Under the approach suggested in the Editors' Introduction to Section A of this chapter, analysis most usefully begins with consideration of what state of mind is required concerning each element of the crime charged. Thus it is necessary to consider whether a defendant must have entertained purpose, knowledge, recklessness, or perhaps negligence with regard to the act constituting the crime, any result required, and any circumstances that the crime requires be proved. This is the subject of the present section.

   Those portions of the Model Penal Code defining and distinguishing the different levels of state of mind were reprinted in Section A, at page 70. This section begins with the provisions of the Code governing the application of those definitions to particular criminal offenses. The principal case presents the task of implementing a somewhat similar statutory structure with regard to a particular crime. As the Texas statute being applied in that case suggests, the approach of the Model Penal Code has been widely used as a model for actual legislation, but it has sometimes been modified.

MODEL PENAL CODE*

Official Draft, 1985

Section 2.02. General Requirements of Culpability

(1) Minimum *Requirements of Culpability.* * * * [A] person is not guilty of an offense unless he acted purposely, knowingly, recklessly or negligently, as the law may require, with respect to each material element of the offense.

(3) *Culpability Required Unless Otherwise Provided.* When the culpability sufficient to establish a material element of an offense is not prescribed by law, such element is established if a person acts purposely, knowingly or recklessly with respect thereto.

(4) *Prescribed Culpability Requirement Applies to All Material Elements.* When the law defining an offense prescribes the kind of culpability that is sufficient for the commission of an offense, without distinguishing among the material elements thereof, such provision shall apply to all the material elements of the offense, unless a contrary purpose plainly appears.

(5) *Substitutes for Negligence, Recklessness and Knowledge.* When the law provides that negligence suffices to establish an element of an offense, such element also

is established if a person acts purposely, knowingly or recklessly. When reck-lessness suffices to establish an element, such element also is established if a person acts purposely or knowingly. When acting knowingly suffices to estab-lish an element, such element also is established if a person acts purposely.

(6) *Requirement of Purpose Satisfied if Purpose Is Conditional.* When a particular purpose is an element of an offense, the element is established although such purpose is conditional, unless the condition negatives the harm or evil sought to be prevented by the law defining the offense.

(7) *Requirement of Knowledge Satisfied by Knowledge of High Probability.* When knowledge of the existence of a particular fact is an element of an offense, such knowledge is established if a person is aware of a high probability of its existence, unless he actually believes that it does not exist.

(8) *Requirement of Wilfulness Satisfied by Acting Knowingly.* A requirement that an offense be committed wilfully is satisfied if a person acts knowingly with respect to the material elements of the offense, unless a purpose to impose further requirements appears.

(9) *Culpability as to Illegality of Conduct.* Neither knowledge nor recklessness or negligence as to whether conduct constitutes an offense or as to the exis-tence, meaning or application of the law determining the elements of an offense is an element of such offense, unless the definition of the offense or the Code so provides.

(10) *Culpability as Determinant of Grade of Offense.* When the grade or degree of an offense depends on whether the offense is committed purposely, knowingly, recklessly or negligently, its grade or degree shall be the lowest for which the determinative kind of culpability is established with respect to any material element of the offense.

Notes and Questions

1. Section 2.02(4) provides that if a crime provides generally for a culpable mental state without specifying to which elements that culpable mental state applies, the mental state is to apply to all "*material* elements" of the crime. What is added by the qualification "material"? In the definitional section, the Code specifies that "material element of an offense" means "an element that does not relate exclusively to the statute of limitations, jurisdiction, venue, or to any other matter similarly unconnected with (i) the harm or evil, incident to conduct, sought to be prevented by the law defining the offense, or (ii) the existence of a justification or excuse for such, conduct." Model Penal Code § 1.13 (10) (Official Draft 1985).

   This means that if an element of a crime is included only for one of these essentially procedural reasons, no awareness of it is required. Essentially, material elements are those that are used in an effort to define the crime as covering all dangerous and blameworthy behavior but not conduct lacking these characteristics.

2. The position of the Model Penal Code—that in the absence of a specific indication to the contrary with respect to any material element of an offense a culpability of at least "recklessness" would be required—was defended by the drafters of the Model Penal Code as representing "what usually is regarded as the common law position." Model Penal Code, Comments to § 2.02, 244 (Official Draft 1985). It also, according to the comments, "represents the most convenient norm for drafting purposes. When purpose or knowledge is required, it is conventional to be explicit. And since negligence is an exceptional basis of liability, it should be excluded as a basis unless explicitly prescribed."

3. Not all jurisdictions that following the general approach of the Model Penal Code have followed these two basic "default" rules of the Code—that generally at least recklessness is required as to all significant elements of a crime. Alaska, for example, provides that generally the conduct constituting the crime must be shown to have been committed "knowingly," but the accused need only be shown to have been reckless regarding circumstances and results. Alaska Stat. § 11.81.610(b). Indiana first adopted the Model Penal Code approach but in 1977 changed its statute so that as a general rule recklessness is required, but only "with respect to every element of the prohibited conduct." Ind. Code 35-41-2-2, § 2(d). This is considered in *Tyson v. State,* reprinted in Chapter 9.

Alvarado v. State

Court of Criminal Appeals of Texas, 1986
704 S.W.2d 36.

CLINTON, JUDGE.

[Appellant Amelia Alvarado was charged with injury to a child in violation of § 22.04 of the Texas Penal Code:

(a) A person commits an offense if he intentionally, knowingly, recklessly or with criminal negligence engages in conduct that causes serious bodily injury to a child who is 14 years of age or younger.

[Only if the prosecution alleged and proved that the defendant caused the injury intentionally or knowingly, however, was the offense a felony.] The indictment alleged that appellant "intentionally and knowingly * * * caused serious bodily injury [to the child] by * * * placing him in a tub of hot water." At trial, appellant testified in her own behalf. She acknowledged that she had been angry with the victim for resisting his bath and refusing to disrobe and that she placed him, fully clothed, into the water without first test-

ing it. She denied, however, that she knew the water was hot enough to cause burning as serious bodily injury is defined.

The Texas Penal Code also provides:
§ 6.02 Requirements of Culpability

(a) Except as provided in Subsection (b) of this section, a person does not commit an offense unless he intentionally, knowingly, recklessly, or with criminal negligence engages in conduct as the definition of the offense requires.

(b) If the definition of an offense does not prescribe a culpable mental state, a culpable mental state is nevertheless required unless the definition plainly dispenses with any mental element.

(c) If the definition of an offense does not prescribe a culpable mental state, but one is nevertheless required under Subsection (b) of this section, intent, knowledge, or recklessness suffices to establish criminal responsibility.

* * *

Another provision of the Code, Section 6.03, defines the various mental states in terms somewhat similar to those used in the Model Penal Code; see page 70. "Intentionally," however, is used instead of "purposely." Moreover, both recklessness and negligence are defined only with respect to "circumstances surrounding [the actor's] conduct or the results of his conduct." Tex. Penal Code §§ 6.03(c), 6.03(d). No definition is provided for recklessness or negligence concerning the nature of the actor's conduct.

On original submission, a panel of the court affirmed the judgment of conviction. Appellant was granted leave to file a motion for rehearing.

[At trial] appellant argued the focus of the pertinent culpable mental states in the statute, is on the "result of conduct," here, "serious bodily injury." She accordingly requested that the trial court limit the definitions of the culpable mental states to that which relates in each to the "result" of the offense as follows:

"A person acts intentionally, or with intent, *with respect to a result of* his conduct when it is his conscious objective or desire to cause the result."

"A person acts knowingly, or with knowledge, *with respect to a result of* his conduct when he is aware that his conduct is reasonably certain to cause the result."

The trial judge denied these charges because they "lack everything that is in the definition in the Code," and instead charged the jury [:

"A person acts intentionally, or with intent, with respect to the nature of her conduct or to a result of her conduct *when it is her conscious objective or desire to engage in the conduct* or cause the result."

"A person acts knowingly, or with knowledge, with respect to the nature of her conduct or to circumstances surrounding her conduct *when she is aware of her conduct* or that the circumstances exist. A person acts knowingly, or with knowledge, with respect to a result of her conduct when she is aware that her conduct is reasonably certain to cause the result."]

In his final argument to the jury, defense counsel stressed the fact that in order to find his client guilty * * * the jury must find it was her conscious objective or desire to cause serious bodily injury to the child or that she was aware that putting the child in the water was reasonably certain to cause serious bodily injury to the child. In response, the district attorney pointed out to the jury that

what defense counsel had said was a misstatement of the court's charge; he urged the jury to read the charge and observed that a finding that appellant had engaged in the conduct of putting the child in "hot water" knowingly or intentionally was sufficient for a conviction.

On appeal, the * * * panel asserted that the language of § 22.04, supra, (which includes the phrase "engages in conduct,") "clearly focuses on the conduct *and* the result of that conduct" [emphasis original]. However, without addressing the contention that the court's charge allowed conviction if appellant had requisite culpability as to *either* the result or the conduct alone, the panel overruled appellant's ground of error.

[A]ll the culpable mental states do not apply to all possible "elements of conduct." Section 22.04 provides an offense is committed if a person intentionally, knowingly, *recklessly or with criminal negligence* causes injury to a child, but, as was acknowledged in *Lugo-Lugo* [v. *State,* 650 S.W.2d 72, 77 (Tex.Crim.App.1983),] "[a] person cannot be reckless or negligent with respect to the 'nature of conduct.'" See §§ 6.03(c) and (d).[5] The only "element of conduct" which can be the object of all four of the culpable mental states is, "result of conduct." See §§ 6.03(a), (b), (c) and (d). Indeed, experience teaches that when all four culpable mental states have been prescribed by the Legislature in defining an offense, it is a strong indication that the offense is a "specific result" type of crime.

* * * [I]t is usually a simple matter to look at a penal proscription and determine whether the Legislature intended to punish "specified conduct" as opposed to a "specified result." For example, before 1983 amendments, V.T.C.A. Penal Code, § 21.02(a) prohibited a person from "having sexual intercourse with a female" when certain "circumstances surrounding" the intercourse were extant. By specifying the "nature of the conduct" prohibited (having sexual intercourse) the Legislature indicated rape is a "nature of conduct" crime and the required culpability must go to that element of conduct.

By contrast, the injury to a child statute, like the homicide and other assaultive proscriptions, does not specify the "nature of conduct." Clearly then, the "nature of conduct" in these offenses is inconsequential (so long as it includes a voluntary act) to commission of the crimes. What matters is that the conduct (whatever it may be) is done with the required culpability to effect the *result* the Legislature has specified.

---

[5] Thus, under the rationale of the panel—that the pertinent culpable mental state goes to the "nature of conduct"—neither "recklessly" or "with criminal negligence" could be utilized.

On original submission the panel stated that even if the trial court erred in refusing appellant's request, no harm was apparent because appellant made "what amounted to a confession on the witness stand." The panel then cited other evidence, presumably from which the jury could have inferred scienter on the part of appellant.

Our reading of the record, however, discloses the appellant steadfastly denied through the trial that she knew the water was hot enough to cause burning as serious bodily injury is defined, even though she admitted she was angry at the child for resisting his bath and refusing to disrobe, and placed him, fully clothed, into the water, without first testing it. In other words, the issue of appellant's mental culpability was contested.

But the court's charge permitted the jury to convict appellant if they found she knowingly or intentionally placed the child in "a tub of hot water," without requiring a finding that she intended or knew serious bodily injury would result.

No matter how incredible appellant's defense may have appeared to the panel, the accused was entitled to have the jury properly instructed on all matters affecting that defense. And in view of her specially requested instructions, the trial court's failure to limit its charge on the applicable culpable mental states to those appropriate to this case, constituted reversible error.

Accordingly, this cause is reversed and remanded to the trial court.

ONION, P.J., and W.C. DAVIS and McCORMICK, J.J., dissent.

Notes and Questions

1. Under the statute, either recklessness or negligence is a sufficient level of culpability. Because the state in this case pleaded that the defendant acted either knowingly or intentionally, it was precluded from relying on either of these levels of culpability.

2. On retrial, should the defendant be convicted? Has the state proven beyond a reasonable doubt that she acted with the state of mind required by the crime charged as construed by the appellate court? If negligence were sufficient, would the state have met its burden of proof? If recklessness were sufficient?

3. The analysis would have been easier if section 6.02 of the Texas Penal Code had used the language of section 2.02(4) of the Model Penal Code. Section 2.02(4) makes clear that as a general rule a required culpable mental state applies to *all* material elements of the crime. Thus the culpable mental state required for injury to a child would have applied to the element of "conduct" and to that requiring the conduct to have caused serious bodily injury. It would also have applied to that element consisting of proof that the person to whom the serious injury was done be a "child."

4. Under the specific terms of the statute involved in *Alvarado,* negligence is a sufficient level of culpability. The position of the Model Penal Code—and to some extent of section 6.02(c) of the Texas Penal Code—is that negligence is and ought to be "an exceptional basis of liability." Model Penal Code Comments to § 2.02, 127 (Tent. Draft No. 4, 1955). Why should negligence be an exceptional basis of liability, presumably to be used only where specific and important reasons for reducing the required level of culpability exist? Consider the following:

   Since negligence involves no *mens rea,* the question is raised as to the advisability of punishing negligent conduct with criminal sanctions. Professor Edwin Keedy responded to this question as follows: "If the defendant, being mistaken as to the material facts, is to be punished because his mistake is one an average man would not make, punishment will sometimes be inflicted *when the criminal mind does not exist.* Such a result is contrary to fundamental principles, and is plainly unjust, for a man should not be held criminal because of lack of intelligence." This argument is persuasive, especially when considered in conjunction with the traditional concepts and goals of criminal punishment.

   The concept of criminal punishment is based on one, or a combination, of four theories: deterrence, retribution, rehabilitation and incapacitation.

   The deterrence theory of criminal law is based on the hypotheses that the prospective offender knows that he will be punished for any criminal activity, and, therefore, will adjust his behavior to avoid committing a criminal act. This theory rests on the idea of "rational utility," i.e., prospective offenders will weigh the evil of the sanction against the gain of the contemplated crime. However, punishment of a negligent offender in no way implements this theory, since the negligent harmdoer is, by definition, unaware of the risk he imposes on society. It is questionable whether holding an individual criminally liable for acts the risks of which he has failed to perceive will deter him from failing to perceive in the future.

   The * * * retributive theory of criminal law presupposes a "moral guilt," which justifies society in seeking its revenge against the offender. This "moral guilt" is ascribed to those forms of conduct which society deems threatening to its very existence, such as murder and larceny. However, the negligent harm-doer has not actually committed this type of morally reprehensible act, but has merely made an error in judgment. This type of error is an everyday occurrence, although it may deviate from a normal standard of care. Nevertheless, such conduct does not approach the moral turpitude against which the criminal law should seek revenge. It is difficult to comprehend how retribution requires such mistakes to be criminally punished.

It is also doubtful whether the negligent offender can be rehabilitated in any way by criminal punishment. Rehabilitation presupposes a "warped sense of values" which can be corrected. Since inadvertence, and not a deficient sense of values, has caused the "crime," there appears to be nothing to rehabilitate.

The underlying goal of the incapacitation theory is to protect society by isolating an individual so as to prevent him from perpetrating a similar crime in the future. However, this approach is only justifiable if less stringent methods will not further the same goal of protecting society. For example, an insane individual would not be criminally incarcerated, if the less stringent means of medical treatment would afford the same societal protection. Likewise, with a criminally negligent individual, the appropriate remedy is not incarceration, but "to exclude him from the activity in which he is a danger."

[T]here appears to be no reasonable justification for punishing negligence as a criminal act under any of these four theories. It does not further the purposes of deterrence, retribution, rehabilitation or incapacitation; hence, there is no rational basis for the imposition of criminal liability on negligent conduct.

This view, favoring exclusion of negligence from the criminal law, is not without support. The chief exponent of this position is Professor Jerome Hall, who maintains that there are persuasive historical, ethical and scientific reasons to support the exclusionary argument.

Hall's historical ground rests upon a continuing trend toward restricting criminal negligence in many Anglo-American legal systems. * * *

Professor Hall's ethical argument is based on the premise that, throughout the long history of ethics, the essence of fault has been voluntary harm-doing. He maintains that this requirement of voluntary action becomes even more persuasive in the penal law, because no one should be criminally punished unless he has clearly acted immorally, by voluntarily harming someone. Negligence, of course, cannot be classified as voluntary harm-doing. Therefore, no fault is involved and accordingly no punishment is justified.

In addition, Hall suggests scientific arguments for the exclusion of negligence from penal liability. One contention is that the incorporation of negligence into the penal law imposes an impossible function on judges, namely, to determine whether a person, about whom very little is known, had the competence and sensitivity to appreciate certain dangers in a particular situation when the facts plainly indicate that he did not exhibit that competence. Also, Hall maintains that "the inclusion of negligence bars the discovery of a scientific theory of penal law, i.e., a system of propositions interrelating variables that have a realistic foundation in fact and values."

Comment, Is Criminal Negligence A Defensible Basis for Penal Liability?, 16 Buffalo L.Rev. 749, 750–52 (1967).5*

5. Insofar as Alvarado could be convicted if she acted with knowledge—awareness of a reasonable certainty that her conduct of putting the baby in the water would cause serious bodily injury—many courts would also make clear to the jury that Alvarado could not avoid the necessary knowledge by refusing to consider the situation.

The Model Penal Code's section 2.02(7) is widely regarded as having given rise to what are variously called "conscious-indifference," "willful blindness," or "ostrich" instructions to juries. These instructions tell the juries that knowledge cannot be avoided by willful or conscious indifference (or "blindness") or by putting one's head in the sand as an ostrich might do.

United States v. Rodriguez, 983 F.2d 455 (2d Cir. 1993), illustrates use of such a jury charge. Rodriguez was arrested at JFK airport in New York in possession of a suitcase that had 1,939 grams of cocaine concealed in its sides. She told police, and testified at trial, that she had purchased the suitcase at a flea market in Venezuela, was unaware of the drugs in it, and had not noticed that its sides were unusually thick. The trial judge instructed the jury:

Now, with regard to the element of knowledge, one may not willfully and intentionally remain ignorant of a fact, material and important to her conduct, to escape the consequences of the criminal law. If you find beyond a reasonable doubt that the defendant was aware that there was a high probability that she possessed a drug that is a controlled substance, but that she deliberately and consciously avoided confirming this fact so she could deny knowledge if apprehended, then you may treat this deliberate avoidance as the equivalent of knowledge, unless you find the defendant actually believed that she was not possessing a drug that is a controlled substance.

These instructions have been characterized as creating risks that juries will convict on the basis of negligence—in *Rodriguez*, on the basis of a conclusion that the defendant *should have* known drugs were in the suitcase—or will regard the burden of proof as shifting to the defendants to prove their innocence. *United States v. de Francisco-Lopez*, 939 F.2d 1405, 1410–11 (10th Cir. 1991). Consequently, at least some federal courts have stressed that it is to be given only if the government has shown some deliberate acts by the defendant to avoid actual knowledge of the fact at issue.

In *Rodriguez*, the instruction was held proper. Rodriguez was quite likely to have noticed the thick and bulging sides of the suitcase and its added weight. The manner in which the cocaine was concealed precluded the possibility that it had been quickly placed in the suitcase without her knowledge after she acquired it. Her claim that she accidentally came by a four-pound quantity of cocaine through purchase of an empty suitcase at a flea market was "inherent[ly] implausibl[e]." In *de Francisco-Lopez*, however, the defendant was apprehended driving an automobile in which a large amount of cocaine was found concealed in secret compartments; he denied knowledge of the drug and contended he had been hired to drive the car from Los Angeles to New York by a stranger he knew only as Juan. A deliberate ignorance instruction was error, the court held, because the circumstances, although "suspicious," were too equivocal to show with sufficient strength that the defendant acted to deliberately avoid knowledge of the presence of drugs in the car.

Chadwell v. State

Court of Appeals of Arkansas, 1992
37 Ark.App. 9, 822 S.W.2d 402.

CRACRAFT, Chief Judge.

Christopher Chadwell was charged with * * * class C felony theft of property, and was convicted * * * at a non-jury trial. He appeals * * *.

The evidence reflects that on April 14, 1990, Gerard Joubert, the operator of Joubert's Tavern, observed a car stop on the parking lot of the tavern. Appellant got out of the car and went into the tavern for a moment. Appellant then returned to the parking lot, where Joubert saw him removing property from a vehicle which he knew belonged to Ed Morgan. When Joubert came out of the tavern, appellant fled to the car in which he had arrived and attempted to enter it through a window. Joubert apprehended him and held him until police arrived.

Ed Morgan testified that a jacket had been taken from his vehicle and that, at the time of the taking, his wallet had been in one of its pockets. He also testified that the wallet contained his driver's license and a credit card. The jacket was found partially hidden on the backseat of the vehicle appellant had attempted to enter. Morgan's wallet was found later that evening lying on the parking lot near the area where Morgan's car had been parked. In Morgan's opinion, the value of the jacket and wallet did not exceed $140.00.

At the close of the evidence, appellant moved that the felony theft charge be reduced to a misdemeanor because there was no proof that he knowingly took the wallet and credit card, and the evidence established that the value of the coat and wallet would only sustain a conviction of misdemeanor theft. The trial court agreed that the value of the stolen articles did not equal the amount required to constitute a class C felony * * *, but held that the theft of the credit card alone constituted a class C felony * * *.

Arkansas Code Annotated § 5-36-103(a)(1) (Supp.1991) provides that one commits theft of property if he knowingly takes or exercises unauthorized control over the property of another person with the purpose of depriving the owner thereof. Subsequent provisions of § 5-36-103 classify the degree of the crime of theft based largely on the value of the property stolen. Where the value of the property does not exceed $200.00, the crime is ordinarily classified as a misdemeanor. However, subsection (b)(2)(D) provides that theft of property is a class C felony if the property is a credit card. Credit cards are singled out in the statute for special treatment regardless of value since such items almost invariably end up in illicit channels where they are used to commit additional offenses.

Appellant * * * contends that the evidence is insufficient to support his conviction for felony theft of property. He argues, as he did in the trial court, that since there was no proof that he knew that the jacket contained the wallet or that the wallet contained a credit card, he could not be held to have knowingly taken control of the credit card. We do not agree.

* * *

In this context, Ark. Code Ann. § 5-36-103(a)(1) requires only that one knowingly take unauthorized control over the property of another; it does not require that he know either the value or the true character of the property taken. Here, the court could easily find from the evidence that appellant knowingly took control of the jacket, whatever its pockets may have contained, with the intent of depriving the owner. Knowledge on his part of the contents of the pockets was not necessary for conviction. The unauthorized taking of the jacket, which contained the wallet and the credit card, was one act, and the party committing it is liable for all of the property thus taken by him.

* * *

Affirmed.

Notes and Questions

1. Arkansas, like many jurisdictions, has a statute similar to section 2.02(4) of the Model Penal Code, reprinted on page 72, directing that a provision in a crime for a culpable mental state is to apply to all the material elements of the crime unless a contrary legislative purpose plainly appears. Ark.Code Ann. § 5-2-203. Arguably the nature of the property—that it is a credit card—is an element of felony theft and the requirement that the defendant act knowingly should apply to that element as well as others. However, perhaps that fact is not an element of the offense, because it does not distinguish theft from noncriminal conduct but only determines the grade of a theft offense.

2. *Chadwell* illustrates the reluctance of courts to require a culpable mental state regarding a fact (whether or not it is an element of the crime) that

serves rather than to determine the grade or severity of the crime committed to distinguish conduct constituting the crime from noncriminal conduct. This approach is applied to drug offenses in which the amount of the drug determines the severity of the crime. Most courts do not require a culpable mental state regarding the amount of the drug, so the prosecution need not show the defendant was aware of the amount or that it was within the range necessary for the crime.

The major exception is *People v. Ryan,* 82 N.Y.2d 497, 626 N.E.2d 51, 605 N.Y.S.2d 235 (1993), a prosecution under a New York statute providing that "A person is guilty of criminal possession of a controlled substance in the second degree when he knowingly and unlawfully possesses * * * six hundred twenty-five milligrams of a hallucinogen." New York has a statute similar to section 2.02(4) of the Model Penal Code. *Ryan* held that under the two statutes a defendant must know that the hallucinogen he possessed was six hundred twenty-five milligrams or more in weight. Asserting that this interpretation was consistent with the general purpose of a culpable mental state, the court explained:

> The Legislature has decided that persons who illegally possess larger quantities of controlled substances should be punished more severely; their conduct is more repugnant and presents a greater threat to society. Because drug possession is not a strict liability crime, however, an individual is not deserving of enhanced punishment unless he or she is aware that the amount possessed is greater. A purpose of the knowledge requirement, then, is to avoid overpenalizing someone who unwittingly possesses a larger amount of a controlled substance than anticipated.

Ryan's specific prosecution was based on a shipment of hallucinogenic mushrooms. The prosecution's testimony was that the total weight of the mushrooms was 932.8 grams and that a 140-gram sample was found to contain 796 milligrams of psilocybin, a hallucinogen. On these facts, the appellate court reasoned, the prosecution's evidence did not permit the jury to find that Ryan knew that the requisite amount of psilocybin was involved. There was no evidence that Ryan had ordered the requisite quantity of the drug. Evidence that Ryan had ordered an amount of mushroom that would ordinarily contain 625 milligrams of the drug might be

sufficient, the court noted, but prosecution had produced no evidence as to how psilocybin comes to be
in mushrooms (whether by injection or natural
processes) or as to the amount of psilocybin that
would typically appear in the amount of mushrooms

that Ryan ordered. In other cases, the court noted,
defendants' knowledge of the weights could be
deduced from the potency of the drugs, the prices
paid for them, or the negotiations by which the
drugs were obtained.

Editors' Note: Transferred Intent

Mens rea analysis as applied to some situations is facilitated by what has become
known as the doctrine of transferred intent. It traditionally is applied when a defendant, intending to kill A, shoots at A but misses and hits B, killing B. Under transferred intent, the defendant's liability for actually killing B is analyzed as if the
defendant intended to kill B. The accused's intent to kill his intended victim is "transferred" from that victim to his actual victim.

The doctrine is justified on the ground that the accidental difference between the
victim intended and the one actually harmed does not affect any of the considerations
properly determining criminal liability. As the California Supreme Court commented
in *People v. Scott,* 14 Cal.4th 544, 927 P.2d 288, 59 Cal.Rptr.2d 178 (1996):

> [U]nder such circumstances, the accused is deemed as culpable, and society is
> harmed as much, as if the defendant had accomplished what he had initially
> intended, and justice is achieved by punishing the defendant for a crime of the
> same seriousness as the one he tried to commit against his intended victim.
> Under the classic formulation of the common law doctrine of transferred intent,
> the defendant's guilt is thus "exactly what it would have been had the blow fallen
> upon the intended victim instead of the bystander."

The doctrine does not require a literal miss by the defendant. Thus in *Poe v.
State,* 341 Md. 523, 671 A.2d 501 (1996), the defendant pointed a gun toward his
estranged wife, shouted, "Take this, bitch," and pulled the trigger. The shot hit and
passed through his wife, causing a nonfatal wound, and then struck a six-year-old
girl in the head, killing her. Application of transferred intent was not precluded simply
because the defendant not only accidentally inflicted a fatal injury on an unintended
victim but also hit his intended victim.

Although transferred intent is most often invoked in homicide cases, it is not limited to such prosecutions. It can apply to prosecutions for assault, and could be used as
well in a prosecution for harm to property where the defendant sought to do harm to
one item but accidentally did similar harm to another item.

In *Scott,* the California Supreme Court held that the doctrine of transferred intent
does not assume a single "intent" that can be used only once. Thus on facts somewhat
like those in *Poe,* the court held that use of transferred intent to prosecute for murder
of the accidentally struck victim was not precluded by charges for assault against the
intended victim. The court explained:

> Courts and commentators have long recognized that the notion of creating a
> whole crime by "transferring" a defendant's intent from the object of his assault to

the victim of his criminal act is * * * a "bare-faced" legal fiction. The legal fiction of transferring a defendant's intent helps illustrate why, as a theoretical matter, a defendant can be convicted of murder when she did not intend to kill the person actually killed. The transferred intent doctrine does not, however, denote an actual "transfer" of "intent" from the intended victim to the unintended victim. Rather, as applied here, it connotes a policy—that a defendant who shoots at an intended victim with intent to kill but misses and hits a bystander instead should be subject to the same criminal liability that would have been imposed had he hit his intended mark. It is the policy underlying the doctrine, rather than its literal meaning, that compels the conclusion that * * * transferred intent * * * was properly [used] in this case.

The doctrine only applies where the harm actually caused is the same (or at least quite similar) to that intended. Thus in *In the Interest of J.G.,* 655 So.2d 1284 (Fla.App.1995), the proof showed J.G. struck at the victim with a closed fist but instead struck and shattered the rear window of the victim's car. The trial judge concluded that J.G. did not intend to hit or harm the window but that the intent to hit the victim could be transferred to the window, and therefore J.G. was guilty of criminal mischief. "The doctrine of transferred intent could only operate to transfer J.G.'s intent to commit an offensive touching (i.e., a battery)," the appellate court held in reversing, and thus transferred intent could *not* provide the intent to damage property of another needed for criminal mischief.

The Model Penal Code embodies the traditional approach, but in its section on causation. Under section 2.03, an actual but unintended result (the death of the person accidentally hit by the shot) gives rise to liability if "it differs from that [result] designed or contemplated * * * only in the respect that a different person or different property is injured or affected * * *." In *Poe,* just discussed, what actually happened— the death of the girl—differed from what Poe intended—the death of his wife—only in that a different person was injured. Thus he would be treated as if he had intended the death of the girl. The Code does not, of course, use the term transferred intent.

C. STATE OF MIND BEYOND "GENERAL INTENT"

Editors' Introduction: "Specific Intents" and Other Unusually Stringent Culpable Mental State Requirements

Once it is determined what if any state of mind is required by a crime concerning those matters that are themselves elements of the offense, it is useful to address whether an additional mental state must be proved for guilt to be established. In the terms proposed for convenient usage in the Editor's Introduction to Section A of this chapter, these mental states would be identified as specific intents. Again, however, it is important to note that this use of the term does not coincide with the manner in which some courts define general and specific intents.

At this point, it may be useful to reconsider the formula presented in Chapter 2 as an aid in visualizing the framework of analysis described in that chapter. As presented at that point, the formula oversimplifies the state-of-mind issues that may arise in determining the requirements imposed by a particular offense. A more refined and complete formula would be:

$$\left[\left(\text{Act} + \text{Mental State}\right) \xrightarrow{\text{Causation}} \left(\text{Result} + \text{Mental State}\right)\right] +$$

$$\left(\begin{array}{c}\text{Attendant} \\ \text{Circumstances}\end{array} + \begin{array}{c}\text{Mental} \\ \text{State}\end{array}\right) + \begin{array}{c}\text{Specific} \\ \text{Intent}\end{array} = \text{Liability}$$

Many of the traditional specific intents, such as the intent to steal required by larceny, are covered in later chapters of this book. The principal cases in this section deal with the possibility that in some exceptional situations crimes may require awareness of the illegality of the conduct constituting the crime.

Federal constitutional considerations may sometimes require such awareness. Reconsider the discussion of *Lambert v. California* at pages 62–64. The awareness that *Lambert* held impermissibly missing was really awareness of a matter of law—the ordinance's duty to register. Also, consider the discussion in the principal case of another important Supreme Court decision requiring awareness of law, *Liparota v. United States.*

Ratzlaf v. United States

Supreme Court of the United States, 1994
510 U.S. 135, 114 S.Ct. 655, 126 L.Ed.2d 615.

Justice GINSBURG delivered the opinion of the Court.

Federal law requires banks and other financial institutions to file reports with the Secretary of the Treasury whenever they are involved in a cash transaction that exceeds $10,000. It is illegal to "structure" transactions—i.e., to break up a single transaction above the reporting threshold into two or more separate transactions—for the purpose of evading a financial institution's reporting requirement. "A person willfully violating" this antistructuring provision is subject to criminal penalties. This case presents a question on which Courts of Appeals have divided: Does a defen-

dant's purpose to circumvent a bank's reporting obligation suffice to sustain a conviction for "willfully violating" the antistructuring provision? * * *

I

On the evening of October 20, 1988, defendant-petitioner Waldemar Ratzlaf ran up a debt of $160,000 playing blackjack at the High Sierra Casino in Reno, Nevada. The casino gave him one week to pay. On the due date, *Ratzlaf* returned to the casino with cash of $100,000 in hand. A casino official informed Ratzlaf that all transactions involving more than $10,000 in cash had to be reported to state and federal authorities. The official added that the casino could accept a cashier's check for the full amount due without triggering any reporting requirement. The casino helpfully placed a limousine at Ratzlaf's disposal, and assigned an employee to accompany him to banks in the vicinity. Informed that banks, too, are required to report cash transactions in excess of $10,000, Ratzlaf purchased cashier's checks, each for less than $10,000 and each from a different bank. He delivered these checks to the High Sierra Casino.

Based on this endeavor, Ratzlaf was charged with "structuring transactions" to evade the banks' obligation to report cash transactions exceeding $10,000 * * *. The trial judge instructed the jury that the Government had to prove defendant's knowledge of the banks' reporting obligation and his attempt to evade that obligation, but did not have to prove defendant knew the structuring was unlawful. Ratzlaf was convicted, fined, and sentenced to prison.

Ratzlaf maintained on appeal that he could not be convicted of "willfully violating" the antistructuring law solely on the basis of his knowledge that a financial institution must report currency transactions in excess of $10,000 and his intention to avoid such reporting. To gain a conviction for "willful" conduct, he asserted, the Government must prove he was aware of the illegality of the "structuring" in which he engaged. The Ninth Circuit upheld the trial court's construction of the legislation and affirmed Ratzlaf's conviction. We granted certiorari * * *.

II

A

Congress enacted the Currency and Foreign Transactions Reporting Act (Bank Secrecy Act) in 1970, in response to increasing use of banks and other institutions as financial intermediaries by persons engaged in criminal activity. The Act imposes a variety of reporting requirements on individuals and institutions regarding foreign and domestic financial transactions. The reporting requirement relevant here, § 5313(a), applies to domestic financial transactions. Section 5313(a) reads:

"When a domestic financial institution is involved in a transaction for the payment, receipt, or transfer of United States coins or currency (or other monetary instruments the Secretary of the Treasury prescribes), in an amount, denomination, or amount and denomination, or under circumstances the Secretary prescribes by

regulation, the institution and any other participant in the transaction the Secretary may prescribe shall file a report on the transaction at the time and in the way the Secretary prescribes. . . ."[3]

To deter circumvention of this reporting requirement, Congress enacted an antistructuring provision, as part of the Money Laundering Control Act of 1986. Section 5324, which Ratzlaf is charged with "willfully violating," reads:

"No person shall for the purpose of evading the reporting requirements of section 5313(a) with respect to such transaction —

     . . .

"(3) structure or assist in structuring, or attempt to structure or assist in structuring, any transaction with one or more domestic financial institutions."[6]

The criminal enforcement provision at issue, 31 U.S.C. § 5322(a), sets out penalties for "[a] person willfully violating," inter alia, the antistructuring provision. Section 5322(a) reads:

"A person willfully violating this subchapter [31 U.S.C. § 5311 et seq.] or a regulation prescribed under this subchapter (except section 5315 of this title or a regulation prescribed under section 5315) shall be fined not more than $250,000, or imprisoned for not more than five years, or both."

B

Section 5324 forbids structuring transactions with a "purpose of evading the reporting requirements of section 5313(a)." Ratzlaf admits that he structured cash transactions, and that he did so with knowledge of, and a purpose to avoid, the banks' duty to report currency transactions in excess of $10,000. The statutory formulation (§ 5322)

---

[3] By regulation, the Secretary ordered reporting of "transaction[s] in currency of more than $10,000." Although the Secretary could have imposed a report-filing requirement on "any...participant in the transaction," the Secretary chose to require reporting by the financial institution but not by the customer.

[6] Regarding enforcement of § 5324, the Secretary considered, but did not promulgate, a regulation requiring banks to inform currency transaction customers of the section's proscription. * * *

under which Ratzlaf was prosecuted, however, calls for proof of "willful[ness]" on the actor's part. The trial judge in Ratzlaf's case, with the Ninth Circuit's approbation, treated § 5322(a)'s "willfulness" requirement essentially as surplusage—as words of no consequence. Judges should hesitate so to treat statutory terms in any setting, and resistance should be heightened when the words describe an element of a criminal offense.

"Willful," this Court has recognized, is a "word of many meanings," and "its construction [is] often . . . influenced by its context." Accordingly, we view §§ 5322(a) and 5324(3) mindful of the complex of provisions in which they are embedded. In this light, we count it significant that § 5322(a)'s omnibus "willfulness" requirement, when applied to other provisions in the same subchapter, consistently has been read by the Courts of Appeals to require both "knowledge of the reporting requirement" and a "specific intent to commit the crime," i.e., "a purpose to disobey the law."

* * *

A term appearing in several places in a statutory text is generally read the same way each time it appears. We have even stronger cause to construe a single formulation, here § 5322(a), the same way each time it is called into play.

The United States urges, however, that § 5324 violators, by their very conduct, exhibit a purpose to do wrong, which suffices to show "willfulness":

"On occasion, criminal statutes—including some requiring proof of 'willfulness'—have been understood to require proof of an intentional violation of a known legal duty, i.e., specific knowledge by the defendant that his conduct is unlawful. But where that construction has been adopted, it has been invoked only to ensure that the defendant acted with a wrongful purpose. See *Liparota v. United States,* 471 U.S. 419, 426, 105 S.Ct. 2084, 2088, 85 L.Ed.2d 434 (1985). . . .

. . .

"The anti-structuring statute, 31 U.S.C. § 5324, satisfies the 'bad purpose' component of willfulness by explicitly defining the wrongful purpose necessary to violate the law: it requires proof that the defendant acted with the purpose to evade the reporting requirement of Section 5313(a)."

Brief for United States 23–25.

"'[S]tructuring is not the kind of activity that an ordinary person would engage in innocently,'" the United States asserts. It is therefore "reasonable," the Government concludes, "to hold a structurer responsible for evading the reporting requirements without the need to prove specific knowledge that such evasion is unlawful."

Undoubtedly there are bad men who attempt to elude official reporting requirements in order to hide from Government inspectors such criminal activity as laundering drug money or tax evasion. But currency structuring is not inevitably nefarious. Consider, for example, the small business operator who knows that reports filed under 31 U.S.C. § 5313(a) are available to the Internal Revenue Service. To reduce the risk of an IRS audit, she brings $9,500 in cash to the bank twice each week, in lieu of transporting over $10,000 once each week. That person, if the United States is right, has committed a criminal offense, because she structured cash transactions "for the specific purpose of depriving the Government of the information that Section 5313(a) is designed to obtain." Nor is a person who structures a currency transaction invariably motivated by a desire to keep the Government in the dark. But under the Government's construction an individual would commit a felony against the United States by making cash deposits in small doses, fearful that the bank's reports would increase the likelihood of burglary, or in an endeavor to keep a former spouse unaware of his wealth.

Courts have noted "many occasions" on which persons, without violating any law, may structure transactions "in order to avoid the impact of some regulation or tax." * * * [C]ountless taxpayers each year give a gift of $10,000 on December 31 and an identical gift the next day, thereby legitimately avoiding the taxable gifts reporting required by 26 U.S.C. § 2503(b).

In light of these examples, we are unpersuaded by the argument that structuring is so obviously "evil" or inherently "bad" that the "willfulness" requirement is satisfied irrespective of the defendant's knowledge of the illegality of structuring. Had Congress wished to dispense with the requirement, it could have furnished the appropriate instruction.

C

* * *

We do not dishonor the venerable principle that ignorance of the law generally is no defense to a criminal charge. In particular contexts, however, Congress may decree otherwise. That, we hold, is what Congress has done with respect to 31 U.S.C. § 5322(a) and the provisions it controls. To convict Ratzlaf of the crime with which he was charged, violation of 31 U.S.C. §§ 5322(a) and 5324(3), the jury had to find he knew the structuring in which he engaged was unlawful.[19] Because the jury was not properly instructed in this regard, we reverse the judgment of the Ninth Circuit and remand this case for further proceedings consistent with this opinion.

It is so ordered.

Justice BLACKMUN, with whom THE CHIEF JUSTICE, Justice O'CONNOR, and Justice THOMAS join, dissenting.

* * *

"The general rule that ignorance of the law or a mistake of law is no defense to criminal prosecution is deeply rooted in the American legal system." *Cheek v. United States,* 498 U.S. 192, 199, 111 S.Ct. 604, 609, 112 L.Ed.2d 617 (1991). The Court has applied this common-law rule "in numerous cases construing criminal statutes."

Thus, the term "willfully" in criminal law generally "refers to consciousness of the act but not to consciousness that the act is unlawful." *Cheek,* 498 U.S., at 209, 111 S.Ct., at 614 (Scalia, J., concurring in judgment); American Law Institute, Model Penal Code § 2.02(8) (1985) ("A requirement that an offense be committed willfully is satisfied if a person acts knowingly with respect to the material elements of the offense, unless a purpose to impose further requirements appears").

* * *

Unlike other provisions of the subchapter, the antistructuring provision identifies the purpose that is required for a § 5324 violation: "evading the reporting requirements." The offense of structuring, therefore, requires (1) knowledge of a financial institution's reporting requirements, and (2) the structuring of a transaction for the purpose of evading those requirements. These elements define a violation that is "willful" as that term is commonly interpreted. The majority's additional requirement that an actor have actual knowledge that structuring is prohibited strays from the statutory text, as well as from our precedents interpreting criminal statutes generally and "willfulness" in particular.

* * *

The majority * * * contends that § 5322(a)'s willfulness element, when applied to the subchapter's other provisions, has been read by the courts of appeals to require knowledge of and a purpose to disobey the law. In fact, the cases to which the majority refers stand for the more subtle proposition that a willful violation requires knowledge of the pertinent reporting requirements and a purpose to avoid compliance with them. Consistent with and in light of that construction, Congress' 1986 enactment prohibited structuring "for the purpose of evading the reporting requirements." The level of knowledge imposed by the term "willfully" as it applies to all the underlying offenses in the subchapter on reporting requirements is "knowledge of the reporting requirements."

The Court * * * concludes that its interpretation of "willfully" is warranted because structuring is not inherently "nefarious." It is true that the Court, on occasion, has imposed a knowledge-of-illegality requirement upon criminal statutes to ensure that the defendant acted with a wrongful purpose. See, e.g., *Liparota v. United States,* 471 U.S. 419, 426, 105 S.Ct. 2084, 2088, 85 L.Ed.2d 434 (1985). I cannot agree, however, that the imposition of such a requirement is necessary here. First, the conduct at issue—splitting up transactions involving tens of thousands of dollars in cash for the specific purpose of circumventing a bank's reporting duty—is hardly the sort of innocuous activity involved in cases such as *Liparota,* in which the defendant had been convicted of fraud for purchasing food stamps for less than their face value. Further, an individual convicted of structuring is, by definition, aware that cash transactions are regulated, and he cannot seriously argue that he lacked notice of the law's intrusion into the particular sphere of activity. Cf. *Lambert v. California,* 355 U.S. 225, 229, 78 S.Ct. 240, 243, 2 L.Ed.2d 228 (1957). By requiring knowledge of a bank's reporting requirements as well as a "purpose of evading" those requirements, the antistructuring provision targets those who knowingly act to deprive the Government of information to which it is entitled. In my view, that is not so plainly innocent a purpose as to justify reading into the statute the additional element of knowledge of illegality. In any event, Congress has determined that purposefully structuring transactions is not innocent conduct.

In interpreting federal criminal tax statutes, this Court has defined the term "willfully" as requiring the "voluntary, intentional violation of a known legal duty." *Cheek v. United States,* 498 U.S., at 200, 111 S.Ct., at 610. Our rule in the

---

[19] The dissent asserts that our holding "largely nullifies the effect" of § 5324 by "mak[ing] prosecution for structuring difficult or impossible in most cases." Even under the dissent's reading of the statute, proof that the defendant knew of the bank's duty to report is required for conviction; we fail to see why proof that the defendant knew of his duty to refrain from structuring is so qualitatively different that it renders prosecution "impossible." A jury may, of course, find the requisite knowledge on defendant's part by drawing reasonable inferences from the evidence of defendant's conduct, and the Government has not found it "impossible" to persuade a jury to make such inferences in prosecutions for willful violations of §§ 5313, 5314, or 5316.

tax area, however, is an "exception to the traditional rule," applied "largely due to the complexity of the tax laws." The rule is inapplicable here, where, far from being complex, the provisions involved are perhaps among the simplest in the United States Code.

[I]t cannot be ignored that the majority's interpretation of § 5324 as a practical matter largely nullifies the effect of that provision. In codifying the currency transaction reporting requirements in 1970, "Congress recognized the importance of reports of large and unusual currency transactions in ferreting out criminal activity." Congress enacted the antistructuring law to close what it perceived as a major loophole in the federal reporting scheme due to easy circumvention. Because requiring proof of actual knowledge of illegality will make prosecution for structuring difficult or impossible in most cases, the Court's decision reopens the loophole that Congress tried to close.

* * *

The petitioner in this case was informed by casino officials that a transaction involving more than $10,000 in cash must be reported, was informed by the various banks he visited that banks are required to report cash transactions in excess of $10,000, and then purchased $76,000 in cashier's checks, each for less than $10,000 and each from a different bank. Petitioner Ratzlaf, obviously not a person of limited intelligence, was anything but uncomprehending as he traveled from bank to bank converting his bag of cash to cashier's checks in $9,500 bundles. I am convinced that his actions constituted a "willful" violation of the antistructuring provision embodied in 31 U.S.C. § 5324. As a result of

today's decision, Waldemar Ratzlaf—to use an old phrase—will be "laughing all the way to the bank."

The majority's interpretation of the antistructuring provision is at odds with the statutory text, the intent of Congress, and the fundamental principle that knowledge of illegality is not required for a criminal act. Now Congress must try again to fill a hole it rightly felt it had filled before. I dissent.

Notes and Questions

1. Did *Ratzlaf* mean that a defendant must have knowledge of his legal duties as the term knowledge is defined by the Model Penal Code? In a pre-*Ratzlaf* decision, *United States v. Aversa*, 984 F.2d 493 (1st Cir. 1993) (en banc), vacated and remanded, 510 U.S. 1069, 114 S.Ct. 873, 127 L.Ed.2d 70 (1994), the First Circuit held that the statute requires either knowledge of one's legal duty or a reckless disregard for the law. In *United States v. London*, 66 F.3d 1227, 1239–42 (1st Cir.1995), cert. denied, ___ U.S. ___, 116 S.Ct. 1542, 134 L.Ed.2d 646 (1996), the court held that *Ratzlaf* did not intend to change this and that a reckless disregard of legal duties was sufficient.

2. Later in the same year that *Ratzlaf* was decided, Congress apparently negated it by changing the federal statutes. A new federal crime consisting of violating the structuring provisions was created, which leaves out the term "willfully" and instead provides for criminal punishment of "[w]hoever violates this section * * *." 31 U.S.C. § 5324(c)(1).

D. STATE OF MIND LESS THAN "GENERAL INTENT": THE "STRICT LIABILITY" OFFENSES

Despite general acceptance of the proposition that criminal liability is fairly imposed only if the accused has been proven to have acted with awareness of those factual matters constituting the crime, the law has with some frequency recognized that exceptions must be made. Consequently, some offenses require less than awareness of the facts making up the crime. These offenses are often described as imposing "strict liability." The case reprinted in this section, *Staples v. United States*, reflects the United States Supreme Court's treatment of the prosecution's argument that the National Firearms Act imposes criminal liability that is strict in nature.

As the opinions in the case reflect, courts seldom define the issue as whether a particular crime imposes wholly strict liability. Rather, there is usually widespread agreement that the requirement of general intent applies in part, and therefore that an accused must be shown to have been aware of at least some of those facts that make up the offense. The prosecution's contention is generally that no awareness is required regarding one or more—but less than all—of those factual elements making up the crime. In *Staples*, for example, the charged crime can be summarized as requiring proof of three factual elements:

1. The defendant possessed an object.
2. The object possessed was a "firearm," which under the part of the statutory definition at issue meant that the object was a weapon capable of automatic firing.
3. The firearm was "not properly registered" under the Act.

In reading the case, consider which of these elements the defendant must have had awareness, of either under the parties' implicit agreement or under prior case law of the Supreme Court. At issue in *Staples* was whether the crime created by the National Firearms Act creates liability that is *partially* strict in nature.

Constitutional considerations discussed in the Editors' Introduction to this chapter suggest that in some circumstances criminal liability that is wholly or partially strict may offend constitutional requirements.

Staples v. United States

Supreme Court of the United States, 1994
511 U.S. 600, 114 S.Ct. 1793, 128 L.Ed.2d 608.

Justice THOMAS delivered the opinion of the Court.

The National Firearms Act makes it unlawful for any person to possess a machinegun that is not properly registered with the Federal Government. Petitioner contends that, to convict him under the Act, the Government should have been required to prove beyond a reasonable doubt that he knew the weapon he possessed had the characteristics that brought it within the statutory definition of a machinegun. * * *

I

The National Firearms Act (Act), 26 U.S.C. §§ 5801–5872, imposes strict registration requirements on statutorily defined "firearms." The Act includes within the term "firearm" a machinegun, and further defines a machinegun as "any weapon which shoots . . . or can be readily restored to shoot, automatically more than one shot, without manual reloading, by a single function of the trigger." Thus, any fully automatic weapon is a "firearm" within the meaning of the Act.[1] Under the Act, all firearms must be registered in the National Firearms Registration and Transfer Record maintained by the Secretary of the Treasury. Section 5861(d) makes it a crime, punishable by up to 10 years in prison, for any person to possess a firearm that is not properly registered.

Upon executing a search warrant at petitioner's home, local police and agents of the Bureau of Alcohol, Tobacco and Firearms (BATF) recovered, among other things, an AR-15 assault rifle. The AR-15 is the civilian version of the military's M-16 rifle, and is, unless modified, a semiautomatic weapon. The M-16, in contrast, is a selective fire rifle that allows the operator, by rotating a selector switch, to choose semiautomatic or automatic fire. Many M-16 parts are interchangeable with those in the AR-15 and can be used to convert the AR-15 into an automatic weapon. No doubt to inhibit such conversions, the AR-15 is manufactured with a metal stop on its receiver that will prevent an M-16 selector switch, if installed, from rotating to the fully automatic position. The metal stop on petitioner's rifle, however, had been filed away, and the rifle had been assembled with an M-16 selector switch and several other M-16 internal parts, including a hammer, disconnector, and trigger. Suspecting that the AR-15 had been modified to be capable of fully

---

[1] As used here, the terms "automatic" and "fully automatic" refer to a weapon that fires repeatedly with a single pull of the trigger. That is, once its trigger is depressed, the weapon will automatically continue to fire until its trigger is released or the ammunition is exhausted. Such weapons are "machineguns" within the meaning of the Act. We use the term "semi-automatic" to designate a weapon that fires only one shot with each pull of the trigger, and which requires no manual manipulation by the operator to place another round in the chamber after each round is fired.

automatic fire, BATF agents seized the weapon. Petitioner subsequently was indicted for unlawful possession of an unregistered machinegun in violation of § 5861(d).

At trial, BATF agents testified that when the AR-15 was tested, it fired more than one shot with a single pull of the trigger. It was undisputed that the weapon was not registered as required by § 5861(d). Petitioner testified that the rifle had never fired automatically when it was in his possession. He insisted that the AR-15 had operated only semi-automatically, and even then imperfectly, often requiring manual ejection of the spent casing and chambering of the next round. According to petitioner, his alleged ignorance of any automatic firing capability should have shielded him from criminal liability for his failure to register the weapon. He requested the District Court to instruct the jury that, to establish a violation of § 5861(d), the Government must prove beyond a reasonable doubt that the defendant "knew that the gun would fire fully automatically."

The District Court rejected petitioner's proposed instruction and instead charged the jury as follows:

> "The Government need not prove the defendant knows he's dealing with a weapon possessing every last characteristic [which subjects it] to the regulation. It would be enough to prove he knows that he is dealing with a dangerous device of a type as would alert one to the likelihood of regulation."

Petitioner was convicted and sentenced to five years' probation and a $5,000 fine.

The Court of Appeals affirmed. * * * We granted certiorari to resolve a conflict in the Courts of Appeals concerning the *mens rea* required under § 5861(d).

II

A

Whether or not § 5861(d) requires proof that a defendant knew of the characteristics of his weapon that made it a "firearm" under the Act is a question of statutory construction. As we observed in *Liparota v. United States,* 471 U.S. 419, 105 S.Ct. 2084, 85 L.Ed.2d 434 (1985), "[t]he definition of the elements of a criminal offense is entrusted to the legislature, particularly in the case of federal crimes, which are solely creatures of statute." Thus, we have long recognized that determining the mental state required for commission of a federal crime requires "construction of the statute and . . . inference of the intent of Congress." *United States v. Balint,* 258 U.S. 250, 253, 42 S.Ct. 301, 302, 66 L.Ed. 604 (1922).

The language of the statute, the starting place in our inquiry, provides little explicit guidance in this case. Section 5861(d) is silent concerning the *mens rea* required for a violation. It states simply that "[i]t shall be unlawful for any person . . . to receive or possess a firearm which is not registered to him in the National Firearms Registration and Transfer Record." Nevertheless, silence on this point by itself does not necessarily suggest that Congress intended to dispense with a conventional *mens rea* element, which would require that the defendant know the facts that make his conduct illegal. See *Balint,* supra, at 251, 42 S.Ct., at 302 (stating that traditionally, "scienter" was a necessary element in every crime). On the contrary, we must construe the statute in light of the background rules of the common law, in which the requirement of some *mens rea* for a crime is firmly embedded. As we have observed, "[t]he existence of a *mens rea* is the rule of, rather than the exception to, the principles of Anglo-American criminal jurisprudence." [*United States v. United States Gypsum Co.,* 438 U.S. 422, 436, 98 S.Ct. 2864, 2873, 57 L.Ed.2d 854 (1978)]. See also *Morissette v. United States,* 342 U.S. 246, 250, 72 S.Ct. 240, 243, 96 L.Ed. 288 (1952) ("The contention that an injury can amount to a crime only when inflicted by intention is no provincial or transient notion. It is as universal and persistent in mature systems of law as belief in freedom of the human will and a consequent ability and duty of the normal individual to choose between good and evil.").

There can be no doubt that this established concept has influenced our interpretation of criminal statutes. Indeed, we have noted that the common law rule requiring *mens rea* has been "followed in regard to statutory crimes even where the statutory definition did not in terms include it." Relying on the strength of the traditional rule, we have stated that offenses that require no *mens rea* generally are disfavored, and have suggested that some indication of congressional intent, express or implied, is required to dispense with *mens rea* as an element of a crime.

According to the Government, however, the nature and purpose of the National Firearms Act suggest that the presumption favoring *mens rea* does not apply to this case. The Government argues that Congress intended the Act to regulate and restrict the circulation of dangerous weapons. Consequently, in the Government's view, this case fits in a line of precedent concerning what we have termed "public welfare" or "regulatory" offenses, in which we have understood Congress to impose a form of strict criminal liability through statutes that do not require the defendant to know the facts that make his conduct illegal. In construing such statutes, we have inferred from silence that Congress did not intend to require proof of *mens rea* to establish an offense.

For example, in *Balint,* supra, we concluded that the Narcotic Act of 1914, which was intended in part to minimize the spread of addictive drugs by criminalizing undocumented sales of certain narcotics, required proof only that the defendant knew that he was selling drugs, not that he knew the specific items he had sold were "narcotics" within the ambit of the statute. Cf. *United States v. Dotterweich,* 320 U.S. 277, 281, 64 S.Ct. 134, 136, 88 L.Ed. 48 (1943) (stating in dicta that a statute criminalizing the shipment of adulterated or misbranded drugs did not require knowledge that the items were misbranded or adulterated). As we explained in *Dotterweich, Balint* dealt with "a now familiar type of legislation whereby penalties serve as effective means of regulation. Such legislation dispenses with the conventional requirement for criminal conduct—awareness of some wrongdoing."

Such public welfare offenses have been created by Congress, and recognized by this Court, in "limited circumstances." Typically, our cases recognizing such offenses involve statutes that regulate potentially harmful or injurious items. Cf. *United States v. International Minerals & Chemical Corp.,* 402 U.S. 558, 564–565, 91 S.Ct. 1697, 1701–1702, 29 L.Ed.2d 178 (1971) (characterizing *Balint* and similar cases as involving statutes regulating "dangerous or deleterious devices or products or obnoxious waste materials"). In such situations, we have reasoned that as long as a defendant knows that he is dealing with a dangerous device of a character that places him "in responsible relation to a public danger," he should be alerted to the probability of strict regulation, and we have assumed that in such cases Congress intended to place the burden on the defendant to "ascertain at his peril whether [his conduct] comes within the inhibition of the statute." Thus, we essentially have relied on the nature of the statute and the particular character of the items regulated to determine whether congressional silence concerning the mental element of the offense should be interpreted as dispensing with conventional *mens rea* requirements.[3]

B

The Government argues that § 5861(d) defines precisely the sort of regulatory offense described in *Balint.* In this view, all guns, whether or not they are statutory "firearms," are dangerous devices that put gun owners on notice that they must determine at their hazard whether their weapons come within the scope of the Act. On this understanding, the District Court's instruction in this case was correct, because a conviction can rest simply on proof that a defendant knew he possessed a "firearm" in the ordinary sense of the term.

The Government seeks support for its position from our decision in *United States v. Freed,* 401 U.S. 601, 91 S.Ct. 1112, 28 L.Ed.2d 356 (1971), which involved a prosecution for possession of unregistered grenades under § 5861(d).[4] The defendant knew that the items in his possession were grenades, and we concluded that § 5861(d) did not require the Government to prove the defendant also knew that the grenades were unregistered. To be sure, in deciding that *mens rea* was not required with respect to that element of the offense, we suggested that the Act "is a regulatory measure in the interest of the public safety, which may well be premised on the theory that one would hardly be surprised to learn that possession of hand grenades is not an innocent act." Grenades, we explained, "are highly dangerous offensive weapons, no less dangerous than the narcotics involved in *United States v. Balint.*" But that reasoning provides little support for dispensing with *mens rea* in this case.

As the Government concedes, *Freed* did not address the issue presented here. In *Freed,* we decided only that § 5861(d) does not require proof of knowledge that a firearm is unregistered. The question presented by a defendant who possesses a weapon that is a "firearm" for purposes of the Act, but who knows only that he has a "firearm" in the general sense of the term, was not raised or considered. And our determination that a defendant need not

---

[3]By interpreting such public welfare offenses to require at least that the defendant know that he is dealing with some dangerous or deleterious substance, we have avoided construing criminal statutes to impose a rigorous form of strict liability. See, e.g., *United States v. International Minerals & Chemical Corp.,* 402 U.S. 558, 563–564, 91 S.Ct. 1697, 1700–1701, 29 L.Ed.2d 178 (1971) (suggesting that if a person shipping acid mistakenly thought that he was shipping distilled water, he would not violate a statute criminalizing undocumented shipping of acids). True strict liability might suggest that the defendant need not know even that he was dealing with a dangerous item. Nevertheless, we have referred to public welfare offenses as "dispensing with" or "eliminating" a *mens rea* requirement or "mental element," and have described them as strict liability crimes. While

use of the term "strict liability" is really a misnomer, we have interpreted statutes defining public welfare offenses to eliminate the requirement of *mens rea*; that is, the requirement of a "guilty mind" with respect to an element of a crime. Under such statutes we have not required that the defendant know the facts that make his conduct fit the definition of the offense. Generally speaking, such knowledge is necessary to establish *mens rea,* as is reflected in the maxim *ignorantia facti excusat.* Cf. *Regina v. Tolson,* 23 Q.B. 168, 187 (1889) (Stephen, J.) ("[I]t may, I think, be maintained that in every case knowledge of fact [when not appearing in the statute] is to some extent an element of criminality as much as competent age and sanity").

[4] A grenade is a "firearm" under the Act.

know that his weapon is unregistered suggests no conclusion concerning whether § 5861(d) requires the defendant to know of the features that make his weapon a statutory "firearm"; different elements of the same offense can require different mental states. Moreover, our analysis in *Freed* likening the Act to the public welfare statute in *Balint* rested entirely on the assumption that the defendant knew that he was dealing with hand grenades—that is, that he knew he possessed a particularly dangerous type of weapon (one within the statutory definition of a "firearm"), possession of which was not entirely "innocent" in and of itself. The predicate for that analysis is eliminated when, as in this case, the very question to be decided is whether the defendant must know of the particular characteristics that make his weapon a statutory firearm.

Notwithstanding these distinctions, the Government urges that *Freed*'s logic applies because guns, no less than grenades, are highly dangerous devices that should alert their owners to the probability of regulation. But the gap between *Freed* and this case is too wide to bridge. In glossing over the distinction between grenades and guns, the Government ignores the particular care we have taken to avoid construing a statute to dispense with *mens rea* where doing so would "criminalize a broad range of apparently innocent conduct." In *Liparota,* we considered a statute that made unlawful the unauthorized acquisition or possession of food stamps. We determined that the statute required proof that the defendant knew his possession of food stamps was unauthorized, largely because dispensing with such a *mens rea* requirement would have resulted in reading the statute to outlaw a number of apparently innocent acts. Our conclusion that the statute should not be treated as defining a public welfare offense rested on the common sense distinction that a "food stamp can hardly be compared to a hand grenade."

Neither, in our view, can all guns be compared to hand grenades. Although the contrast is certainly not as stark as that presented in *Liparota,* the fact remains that there is a long tradition of widespread lawful gun ownership by private individuals in this country. Such a tradition did not apply to the possession of hand grenades in *Freed* or to the selling of dangerous drugs that we considered in *Balint.* In fact, in *Freed* we construed § 5861(d) under the assumption that "one would hardly be surprised to learn that possession of hand grenades is not an innocent act." Here, the Government essentially suggests that we should interpret the section under the altogether different assumption that "one would hardly be surprised to learn that owning a gun is not an innocent act." That proposition is simply not supported by common experience. Guns in general are not "deleterious devices or products or obnoxious waste materials," that put their owners on notice that they stand "in responsible relation to a public danger."

* * *

On a slightly different tack, the Government suggests that guns are subject to an array of regulations at the federal, state, and local levels that put gun owners on notice that they must determine the characteristics of their weapons and comply with all legal requirements. But regulation in itself is not sufficient to place gun ownership in the category of the sale of narcotics in *Balint.* The food stamps at issue in *Liparota* were subject to comprehensive regulations, yet we did not understand the statute there to dispense with a *mens rea* requirement. Moreover, despite the overlay of legal restrictions on gun ownership, we question whether regulations on guns are sufficiently intrusive that they impinge upon the common experience that owning a gun is usually licit and blameless conduct. Roughly 50 per cent of American homes contain at least one firearm of some sort, and in the vast majority of States, buying a shotgun or rifle is a simple transaction that would not alert a person to regulation any more than would buying a car.

If we were to accept as a general rule the Government's suggestion that dangerous and regulated items place their owners under an obligation to inquire at their peril into compliance with regulations, we would undoubtedly reach some untoward results. Automobiles, for example, might also be termed "dangerous" devices and are highly regulated at both the state and federal levels. Congress might see fit to criminalize the violation of certain regulations concerning automobiles, and thus might make it a crime to operate a vehicle without a properly functioning emission control system. But we probably would hesitate to conclude on the basis of silence that Congress intended a prison term to apply to a car owner whose vehicle's emissions levels, wholly unbeknownst to him, began to exceed legal limits between regular inspection dates.

Here, there can be little doubt that, as in *Liparota,* the Government's construction of the statute potentially would impose criminal sanctions on a class of persons whose mental state—ignorance of the characteristics of weapons in their possession—makes their actions entirely innocent.[10] The Government does not dispute the contention that virtually any semiautomatic weapon may be converted, either by internal modification or, in some cases, simply by wear and tear, into a machinegun within the meaning of the Act. Such a gun may give no externally visible indication that it

---

[10] We, of course, express no view concerning the inferences a jury may have drawn regarding petitioner's knowledge from the evidence in this case.

is fully automatic. But in the Government's view, any person who has purchased what he believes to be a semiautomatic rifle or handgun, or who simply has inherited a gun from a relative and left it untouched in an attic or basement, can be subject to imprisonment, despite absolute ignorance of the gun's firing capabilities, if the gun turns out to be an automatic.

We concur in the Fifth Circuit's conclusion on this point: "It is unthinkable to us that Congress intended to subject such law-abiding, well-intentioned citizens to a possible ten-year term of imprisonment if . . . what they genuinely and reasonably believed was a conventional semiautomatic [weapon] turns out to have worn down into or been secretly modified to be a fully automatic weapon." As we noted in *Morissette,* the "purpose and obvious effect of doing away with the requirement of a guilty intent is to ease the prosecution's path to conviction."[11] We are reluctant to impute that purpose to Congress where, as here, it would mean easing the path to convicting persons whose conduct would not even alert them to the probability of strict regulation in the form of a statute such as § 5861(d).

C

The potentially harsh penalty attached to violation of § 5861(d)—up to 10 years' imprisonment—confirms our reading of the Act. Historically, the penalty imposed under a statute has been a significant consideration in determining whether the statute should be construed as dispensing with *mens rea.* Certainly, the cases that first defined the concept of the public welfare offense almost uniformly involved statutes that provided for only light penalties such as fines or short jail sentences, not imprisonment in the state penitentiary.

---

[11] The Government contends that Congress intended precisely such an aid to obtaining convictions, because requiring proof of knowledge would place too heavy a burden on the Government and obstruct the proper functioning of § 5861(d). But knowledge can be inferred from circumstantial evidence, including any external indications signaling the nature of the weapon. And firing a fully automatic weapon would make the regulated characteristics of the weapon immediately apparent to its owner. In short, we are confident that when the defendant knows of the characteristics of his weapon that bring it within the scope of the Act, the Government will not face great difficulty in proving that knowledge. Of course, if Congress thinks it necessary to reduce the Government's burden at trial to ensure proper enforcement of the Act, it remains free to amend § 5861(d) by explicitly eliminating a *mens rea* requirement.

As commentators have pointed out, the small penalties attached to such offenses logically complemented the absence of a *mens rea* requirement: in a system that generally requires a "vicious will" to establish a crime, imposing severe punishments for offenses that require no *mens rea* would seem incongruous. Indeed, some courts justified the absence of *mens rea* in part on the basis that the offenses did not bear the same punishments as "infamous crimes," and questioned whether imprisonment was compatible with the reduced culpability required for such regulatory offenses. Similarly, commentators collecting the early cases have argued that offenses punishable by imprisonment cannot be understood to be public welfare offenses, but must require *mens rea.*

* * * [W]here, as here, dispensing with *mens rea* would require the defendant to have knowledge only of traditionally lawful conduct, a severe penalty is a further factor tending to suggest that Congress did not intend to eliminate a *mens rea* requirement. In such a case, the usual presumption that a defendant must know the facts that make his conduct illegal should apply.

III

In short, * * * to obtain a conviction, the Government should have been required to prove that petitioner knew of the features of his AR-15 that brought it within the scope of the Act.

* * *

For the foregoing reasons, the judgment of the Court of Appeals is reversed and the case remanded for further proceedings consistent with this opinion.

So ordered.

[The opinion of Justice Ginsburg, with whom Justice O'Connor joined, concurring in the judgment, is omitted.]

Justice STEVENS, with whom Justice BLACKMUN joins, dissenting.

* * *

The question presented is whether the National Firearms Act imposed on the Government the burden of proving beyond a reasonable doubt not only that the defendant knew he possessed a dangerous device sufficient to alert him to regulation, but also that he knew it had all the characteristics of a "firearm" as defined in the statute. Three unambiguous guideposts direct us to the correct answer to that question: the text and structure of the Act, our cases construing both this Act and similar regulatory legislation, and the Act's history and interpretation.

I

* * * Although the lack of an express knowledge requirement in § 5861(d) is not dispositive, its absence suggests that Congress did not intend to require proof that the defendant knew all of the facts that made his conduct illegal. * * * [T]o interpret statutory offenses such as § 5861(d), we look to "the nature of the statute and the particular character of the items regulated" to determine the level of knowledge required for conviction. An examination of § 5861(d) in light of our precedent dictates that the crime of possession of an unregistered machinegun is in a category of offenses described as "public welfare" crimes.[9] Our decisions interpreting such offenses clearly require affirmance of petitioner's conviction.

II

"Public welfare" offenses share certain characteristics: (1) they regulate "dangerous or deleterious devices or products or obnoxious waste materials,"; (2) they "heighten the duties of those in control of particular industries, trades, properties or activities that affect public health, safety or welfare,"; and (3) they "depend on no mental element but consist only of forbidden acts or omissions[.]" Examples of such offenses include Congress' exertion of its power to keep dangerous narcotics, hazardous substances, and impure and adulterated foods and drugs out of the channels of commerce.

Public welfare statutes render criminal "a type of conduct that a reasonable person should know is subject to stringent public regulation and may seriously threaten the community's health or safety." *Liparota v. United States,* 471 U.S. 419, 433, 105 S.Ct. 2084, 2092, 85 L.Ed.2d 434 (1985). Thus, under such statutes, "a defendant can be convicted even though he was unaware of the circumstances of his conduct that made it illegal." * * *

The National Firearms Act unquestionably is a public welfare statute. Congress fashioned a legislative scheme to regulate the commerce and possession of certain types of dangerous devices, including specific kinds of weapons, to protect the health and welfare of the citizenry. To enforce this scheme, Congress created criminal penalties for certain acts and omissions. The text of some of these offenses—including the one at issue here—contains no knowledge requirement.

* * *

Cases arise, of course, in which a defendant would not know that a device was dangerous unless he knew that it was a "firearm" as defined in the Act. * * *

The enforcement of public welfare offenses always entails some possibility of injustice. Congress nevertheless has repeatedly decided that an overriding public interest in health or safety may outweigh that risk when a person is dealing with products that are sufficiently dangerous or deleterious to make it reasonable to presume that he either knows, or should know, whether those products conform to special regulatory requirements. The dangerous character of the product is reasonably presumed to provide sufficient notice of the probability of regulation to justify strict enforcement against those who are merely guilty of negligent rather than willful misconduct.* * *[20]

* * *

Accordingly, I would affirm the judgment of the Court of Appeals.

Notes and Questions

1. When a crime explicitly requires a culpable mental state but is not clear regarding whether the awareness required applies to one or more factual elements of the crime, the issue is in a sense one of whether strict liability will be imposed regarding that element. *United States v. X-Citement Video, Inc.,* 513 U.S. 64, 115 S.Ct. 464, 130 L.Ed.2d 372 (1994), illustrates these problems. The defendant was convicted under the following provision of The Protection Against Sexual Exploitation Act of 1977:

   (a) Any person who—
      (1) knowingly transports or ships in interstate or foreign commerce by any means including by computer or mails, any visual depiction, if—
         (A) the producing of such visual depiction involves the use of a minor engaging in sexually explicit conduct; and

---

[9] These statutes are sometimes referred to as "strict liability" offenses. As the Court notes, because the defendant must know that he is engaged in the type of dangerous conduct that is likely to be regulated, the use of the term "strict liability" to describe these offenses is inaccurate. I therefore use the term "public welfare offense" to describe this type of statute.

[20] The Court also supports its conclusion on the basis of the purported disparity between the penalty provided by this statute and those of other regulatory offenses. Although a modest penalty may indicate that a crime is a public welfare offense, such a penalty is not, as the Court recognizes, a requisite characteristic of public welfare offenses. For example, the crime involved in *Balint* involved punishment of up to five years' imprisonment. Moreover, congressional authorization of a range of penalties in some cases—petitioner, for instance, is on probation—demonstrates a recognition that relatively innocent conduct should be punished less severely.

(B) such visual depiction is of such conduct;
(2) knowingly receives, or distributes, any visual depiction that has been mailed, or has been shipped or transported in interstate or foreign commerce, or which contains materials which have been mailed or so shipped or transported, by any means including by computer, or knowingly reproduces any visual depiction for distribution in interstate or foreign commerce or through the mails, if—
(A) the producing of such visual depiction involves the use of a minor engaging in sexually explicit conduct; and
(B) such visual depiction is of such conduct;

. . .

shall be [guilty of a crime].

On appeal, the Ninth Circuit Court of Appeals held, first, that the statute did not require that a defendant be aware that the person depicted was a minor and, second and consequently, that the statute was facially invalid as violating First Amendment free speech requirements. The Supreme Court held the Ninth Circuit erred in its first conclusion. Chief Justice Rehnquist began for the majority:

The critical determination which we must make is whether the term "knowingly" in subsections (1) and (2) modifies the phrase "the use of a minor" in subsections (1)(A) and (2)(A). The most natural grammatical reading, adopted by the Ninth Circuit, suggests that the term "knowingly" modifies only the surrounding verbs: transports, ships, receives, distributes, or reproduces. Under this construction, the word "knowingly" would not modify the elements of the minority of the performers, or the sexually explicit nature of the material, because they are set forth in independent clauses separated by interruptive punctuation. But we do not think this is the end of the matter, both because of anomalies which result from this construction, and because of the respective presumptions that some form of scienter is to be implied in a criminal statute even if not expressed, and that a statute is to be construed where fairly possible so as to avoid substantial constitutional questions.

* * *

Some applications of respondents' position would produce results that were not merely odd, but positively absurd. If we were to conclude that

"knowingly" only modifies the relevant verbs in § 2252, we would sweep within the ambit of the statute actors who had no idea that they were even dealing with sexually explicit material. For instance, a retail druggist who returns an uninspected roll of developed film to a customer "knowingly distributes" a visual depiction and would be criminally liable if it were later discovered that the visual depiction contained images of children engaged in sexually explicit conduct. Or, a new resident of an apartment might receive mail for the prior resident and store the mail unopened. If the prior tenant had requested delivery of materials covered by § 2252, his residential successor could be prosecuted for "knowing receipt" of such materials. Similarly, a Federal Express courier who delivers a box in which the shipper has declared the contents to be "film" "knowingly transports" such film. We do not assume that Congress, in passing laws, intended such results.

The Court's analysis continued:

Our reluctance to simply follow the most grammatical reading of the statute is heightened by our cases interpreting criminal statutes to include broadly applicable scienter requirements, even where the statute by its terms does not contain them. * * *

[Our case law] instructs that the presumption in favor of a scienter requirement should apply to each of the statutory elements which criminalize otherwise innocent conduct. *Staples* held that the features of a gun as technically described by the firearm registration act was such an element. Its holding rested upon "the nature of the particular device or substance Congress has subjected to regulation and the expectations that individuals may legitimately have in dealing with the regulated items." Age of minority in § 2252 indisputably possesses the same status as an elemental fact because non-obscene, sexually explicit materials involving persons over the age of 17 are protected by the First Amendment. In the light of these decisions, one would reasonably expect to be free from regulation when trafficking in sexually explicit, though not obscene, materials involving adults. Therefore, the age of the performers is the crucial element separating legal innocence from wrongful conduct.

In addition, the majority noted, a statute such as section 2252 lacking a scienter requirement as to the age of the performers would raise serious constitutional doubts. Courts should, it continued, read a statute so as to eliminate constitutional doubts if such a reading is not plainly contrary to the intent of Congress. Consequently, the Court held, the term "knowingly" extends to both the sexually explicit nature of the material and to the age of the performers.

2. Perhaps the classic examples of completely strict liability criminal offenses are at least relatively minor traffic offenses. Speeding, for example, requires no culpable mental state, so a speeding defendant's guilt is not affected by evidence that his speedometer was broken and he therefore did not know that he was traveling at a prohibited speed. *People v. Caddy,* 189 Colo. 353, 540 P.2d 1089 (1975). Strict liability has also been found under an ordinance prohibiting driving with improper lights, *Smith v. City of Tuscaloosa,* 666 So.2d 101 (Ala.Crim.App.1995), cert. denied, and an ordinance requiring motorcycle headlights to be illuminated at all times the motorcycle is being operated, *City of Toledo v. Wacenski,* 95 OhioApp.3d 282, 642 N.E.2d 407 (1994). Because conviction of these crimes carries little or no stigma of moral blameworthiness and the penalties are low, the reasons for requiring a culpable mental state arguably do not apply. Moreover, perhaps requiring proof of a culpable mental state might encourage enough persons cited for violations to contest their guilt that prosecution of traffic laws violations would become difficult or impossible, at least with the kind of regularity necessary to make prosecution an effective deterrent.

3. Is "strict liability" appropriate or defensible in regard to those "regulatory offenses" as to which it has traditionally been imposed? Consider the following comments from Mueller, *Mens Rea* and the Law Without It, 58 W.Va.L.Rev. 34, 37–38, 50, 59–60 (1955):

> The reasons for * * * [imposing strict liability in regard to such offenses] have been variously stated: If *"mens rea"* were required, (1) the enforcement of the statute would be impeded; or (2) the courts would be overburdened; or (3) justice would be hampered; or (4) fraudulent defenses could be fabricated, etc. Prima facie such claims can be just as easily made as refuted. The often stated reason here listed under (1), for instance, seems to be nothing more than a "because", and proves no more.

(2) supra, is a little more specific. It is certainly true that there is hardly any aspect of human activity which has escaped control by the law. When we eat, the (pure food and drug) law eats with us; when we walk, the (traffic) law walks with us; and even the health and soundness of our sleep is regulated by law. To litigate every one of the regulated problems of daily life would surely hamper the administration of justice. But what good will it do to punish indiscriminately, regardless of guilt or innocence, merely to save the time it would take to determine the validity of a defense? And what of the deterrent effect of such a frustrating law? Would it not ease the burden on the court and reduce the length of the court calendar much more if, for instance, in January we would prosecute only blond culprits, in February only bald ones, in March brunettes, etc.? That would at least deter some of the culprits some of the time, whereas absolute criminal liability is totally without deterrent effect. * * *

Ad (3) it might be answered that absolute criminal liability surely is not the vehicle to unhamper criminal justice. If anything, it does away with justice altogether by distributing penalties indiscriminately. *Ad* (4) it will suffice to ask: what crime is there which is not subject to the interposition of fraudulent defenses? Surely the temptation for tricking one's way out of a jam is much greater in crimes threatening serious consequences than it is in petty offenses.

* * *

[It has been feared that the enforcement of the regulatory schemes would bog down if strict liability were not imposed.]

Now then, how can a law deter anybody which inflicts punishment for the mere doing of the outward act? Is it not manifest that a law which punishes without caring about the factual and moral blamelessness of a defendant thereby frustrates him and the community at large? Why should the citizen bother to use care if the courts do not bother whether or not he used care, inflicting punishment in any event? Punishment which befalls the innocent and the guilty alike, like hay fever, hail or hurricane, can have no good effect at all, except perhaps for insurance companies, for whom it creates a new insurable interest.

[It has also been argued that unless strict liability were imposed, "many unscrupulous persons would not hesitate to fabricate such facts as would be needful to accomplish" the assertion of a defense of mistake of fact.]

* * *

The ease of manufacturing surreptitious or fraudulent defenses is, as any lawyer knows, not confined to such cases. * * * Since the temptation to fabricate defenses is even greater in prosecutions in which the stakes are higher, for instance in murder prosecutions, why then not dispense with "*mens rea*" altogether and make every act, e.g., the killing of a human being, conclusive evidence of a criminal intent to do the act, e.g., killing a human being conclusive evidence of a criminal intent, thus murder?

* * * All other arguments in favor of absolute criminal liability failing, it has sometimes been reasoned that the raising of issues in defense of regulatory violations would require dealing with collateral and irrelevant issues. Hence, too much time, in proportion to the slightness of the offense, would have to be devoted to the matter if the defendant were permitted to present an elaborate defense or, indeed, any defense. It has been said that courts would never be able to clear their calendars if in this vast mass of petty offenses a judge, or a jury, were to try all defensive facts. Speediness of "justice" is said to be the compelling reason for absolute criminal liability.

If this were truly the only, or major, reason for resort to absolute criminal liability, then it would be sheer folly to dispense with the "*mens rea*" and nevertheless to consider all defensive arguments for the purpose of possibly mitigating the punishment * * *. Of course, this only goes to show

that the "speediness of justice" argument is absurd. The choice does not lie between speedy justice and slow justice, but between speedy injustice and justice of whatever celerity we can achieve by whatever court reform may be necessary. Justice ought to be speedy, but absolute criminal liability is not apt to achieve it.

* * *

[It has also been argued in support of strict liability that "as the penalty is slight, no great injustice is perpetrated by enforcing this type of statute regardless of knowledge".]

Are we compelled to prefer small injustice over justice? I do not think that the writer regarded this point as a major reason for the imposition of absolute criminal liability. But even as collateral support it fails miserably. Such reasoning may be appropriate in a country where absolutism and dictatorial utility sacrifice life, liberty and property to the Moloch state, but not here.

4. Despite judicial hostility toward strict liability for other than public welfare offenses, one area in which the absence of *mens rea* has long been accepted is that of statutory rape. At least with respect to statutory rape involving a victim below the age of consent, the reasonableness of the adult defendant's mistaken belief that the willing partner was of age has long been deemed irrelevant to criminal liability. Thus, it may be said that this is a strict liability crime insofar as no state of mind need be shown by the prosecution with respect to the element of the victim's age, nor may the defendant offer evidence on that point. This issue is explored in *People v. Olsen* (reprinted in Chapter 9) and the notes that follow it.

Chapter 5

GENERAL PRINCIPLES OF CRIMINAL LIABILITY: CAUSATION

CHAPTER CONTENTS

Editors' Introduction: Causation as a Requirement for Criminal Liability

Many crimes require proof of an element that is properly regarded as a "result." All such crimes raise potential problems of "causation." The arson requirement of a burning, for example, can be regarded as a result, and an arson prosecution can therefore involve a question of whether the defendant caused what the proof clearly shows was a burning of property sufficient to constitute arson.

All of the homicide offenses require proof that the defendant caused the death of the victim, and almost all litigated causation matters arise in homicide cases. Causation rules and principles, although developed almost exclusively in homicide situations, will nevertheless be applied in nonhomicide cases when and if causation issues arise.

Precisely what causation requires when it is demanded is sometimes difficult to determine, although the law's requirements are often less than might be supposed. The case law contains numerous, various, and sometimes conflicting analyses, often provided with elaborate, seemingly technical terminology: legal cause, proximate cause, intervening factors, superseding causes, intervening causes that are coincidences, and the like. Perhaps this reflects uncertainty as to the real importance of causation and thus ambivalence as to how rigorously to define it.

In any case, causation problems can be addressed only if they are identified. This requires consideration of when causation is required by a crime and—when it is required—what must be shown to have caused what particular result.

Determining What (If Any) Causation Is Required: Injury or Death Occurring While Driving When Intoxicated

Whether a crime requires a result is sometimes a difficult question to answer. A crime may even leave some question as to what conduct by the defendant must be shown to have caused the result. Considerable judicial attention has been paid to the second issue in cases under statutes creating crimes consisting of causing death or injury to another in connection with intoxicated operation of a vehicle. Prosecutors have sometimes argued that the only causation required is a showing that the victim's death or injury was caused by the operation of a vehicle, the operator of which was at the time intoxicated.

The issue was presented in *State v. Benoit,* 650 A.2d 1230 (R.I.1994), in which the victim was a passenger in a car driven by one Cynthia Murray. The vehicle driven by Murray suddenly veered from its lane, crossed the highway median, and struck a vehicle driven by defendant Benoit. As a consequence of the collision the victim died. Benoit, found to be intoxicated, was prosecuted for offenses defined by statute as committed if "[death or serious bodily injury] of any person other than the operator is caused by the operation of any motor vehicle, the operator of which is under the influence of any intoxicating liquor * * *." If the only causation required was that urged by the prosecutors as just set out, Benoit could of course be convicted; if Benoit had not been operating his vehicle where and when he was doing so, his car and that driven by Murray would not have collided and the victim would not have died as and when she did.

The Rhode Island court noted that no court has adopted the prosecutors' interpretation of these kinds of statutes. It then held that the Rhode Island crime requires proof that the manner in which the defendant operated the vehicle while intoxicated caused the injury to or death of the victim. Because the prosecution in *Benoit* could offer no evidence that the manner in which Benoit operated his car contributed to the accident and thus the victim's death, the prosecution was unsuccessful.

Prosecutors' argument that such crimes should require only the minimal causation just described is not, however, without judicial support. Justice Lederberg dissented in *Benoit,* arguing that the history of the crime at issue showed that the legislature intended to impose the maximum disincentive to driving while intoxicated. This legislative intent, he continued, would best be implemented by adopting the prosecutors' view that the death or injury need only be shown to have been caused by the fact that the defendant was operating the vehicle rather than by the manner in which the defendant was operating it. This would create the legislatively-intended "compelling deterrent to an individual who is about to engage in the criminal behavior of driving while under the influence of an intoxicating liquor."

In contrast to *Benoit,* the Michigan Supreme Court in *People v. Lardie,* 452 Mich. 231, 551 N.W.2d 656 (1996), gave that state's similar statute a much narrower construction. First, the court held that the statute did not impose the sort of strict liability for which the prosecution there argued. The legislature sought to deter motorists from deciding to drive after they have become intoxicated. However, the court found insufficient indication that the legislature intended to wholly abandon the general rule that criminal liability is only imposed for the intentional commission of a wrongful act. Therefore, the majority concluded, the prosecution must show that "the defendant purposefully drove while intoxicated."

The *Lardie* court then rejected the reading that *Benoit* had given to the Rhode Island statute. Instead, it held that under the Michigan statute the prosecution must prove that the victim's death was caused by the defendant's wrongful act *in deciding to drive while intoxicated.* "Therefore," it explained, "the [prosecution] must establish that the particular defendant's decision to drive while intoxicated produced a change in that driver's operation of the vehicle that caused the death of the victim." The legislature must not have intended the statute to apply where there was no causation between the manner in which the intoxication caused the driver to operate the vehicle and the victim's death:

> [T]his interpretation would not directly further the Legislature's purpose of reducing fatalities because there is no reason to penalize an intoxicated driver with a fifteen-year felony when there is an accident resulting in a fatality if that driver, even if not intoxicated, would still have been the cause in fact of the victim's death. There would be no reason because it would not prevent that fatality from occurring again.

As *Benoit* and *Lardie* make clear, there are at least three ways these crimes can be construed with regard to results and causation. The prosecution can be required to prove that the victim's death or injury was caused by (a) the fact that the defendant was operating his vehicle; (b) the manner in which the defendant was operating his vehicle (regardless of whether the manner of operation was affected by the defendant's intoxication); or (c) the manner in which the defendant was operating his vehicle, which in turn must be shown to have been caused by the defendant's intoxication. *Benoit* adopted position (b), while *Lardie* opted for position (c).

The Importance and Possible Constitutional Necessity of Causation

How important is causation, and why should crimes require proof of it? The issue must be put in perspective before it can be addressed.

Often, a conclusion that a defendant did not actually cause a required result does not result in exonerating the defendant from all criminal liability but only in reducing the seriousness of the offense. One who tries to kill another but does not cause the death of the victim will usually be guilty of attempted murder. The defendant in *Benoit* was probably provably guilty of driving while intoxicated. Whether causation exists or not will often not determine whether there is any criminal liability but rather will affect the seriousness of the crime for which a defendant is liable.

If a person acts in an effort to kill someone else, why should the severity of the crime committed be affected by whether the defendant was successful or not? To some extent, the requirement that the defendant has actually caused the necessary result provides assurance that each defendant actually poses maximum danger to the protected interest. One who attempts but fails to kill another has not demonstrated his ability to take the life of another. Perhaps he has not demonstrated his inclination to retain the intent to kill even when faced with the final step necessary to accomplish that intention. One who is shown to have intentionally *caused* the death of another, on the other hand, has demonstrated both of these and therefore that he poses maximum danger to the protected interest in preserving the lives of others.

Further, causation may be important to determining the blameworthiness of a situation and thus to determining the moral culpability of an accused. Causation may therefore be suggested by the basic policy demand of proportionality between the defendant's behavior and the seriousness of the criminal liability imposed for that behavior. It may also be constitutionally required if constitutional rules demand such proportionality.

In *Lardie,* the defendant argued that the constitutional requirement of due process imposes a demand that a crime require blameworthiness somewhat proportional to the severity of the penalty imposed. Unless the crime at issue there required proof of causation between the culpable act (the decision to drive while intoxicated) and the consequence (death of the victim), he argued, the crime would not assure sufficient blameworthiness to survive due process challenge.

The Michigan court assumed in *Lardie* that its criminal law derived from the common law a "basic premise" that the culpable mental state required for a crime should have a causal connection to the defendant's conduct and that this be causally connected to any result involved in the crime. It further assumed that serious criminal liability based on an occurrence, such as the death of another, without a showing of causation between the defendant's *mens rea* and his conduct, on the one hand, and that occurrence, on the other, might violate due process. It concluded, however, that the causation it found required by the statute, described earlier in this introduction, was sufficient to satisfy any such basic premise of law and constitutional requirement.

The *Lardie* court's inclination to find the comparatively stringent causation requirement it found may have been stimulated by the court's perception that without such a causation requirement the crime at issue was constitutionally vulnerable. In any case, its inclination to construe the statute as it did was certainly influenced by its perception of sound criminal law policy: When the occurrence of a necessary event is a major factor in regarding a crime as a serious one—as is the occurrence of death or serious injury in crimes such as those applied in *Benoit* and *Lardie*—the existence of a causal relationship between the conduct required of a defendant and that occurrence is critical to assuring that the crime covers only those who are demonstratedly and proportionately blameworthy.

Causation, like a culpable mental state, is an important aspect of the criminal law's effort to assure adequate and appropriate moral blameworthiness before criminal liability is attached.

Causation Defined Generally

When causation must be proved, as it clearly must be in homicide offenses, what does that causation require?

In *State v. Guess*, 244 Conn.App. 790, 797–98, 692 A.2d 849, 855–56 (1997), the court explained general causation rules as follows:

> In order for legal causation to exist in a criminal prosecution, the state must prove beyond a reasonable doubt that the defendant was both the cause in fact, or actual cause, as well as the proximate cause of the victim's injuries. See W. LaFave & A. Scott, Criminal Law (1972) § 35, pp. 246–51. "In order that conduct be the actual cause of a particular result it is almost always sufficient that the result would not have happened in the absence of the conduct; or, putting it another way, that 'but for' the antecedent conduct the result would not have occurred." Id., p. 249. On the other hand, proximate cause requires that "the forbidden result which actually occurs must be enough similar to, and occur in a manner enough similar to, the result or manner which the defendant intended (in the case of crimes of intention), or the result or manner which his reckless or negligent conduct created a risk of happening (in the case of crimes of recklessness and negligence) that the defendant may fairly be held responsible for the actual result even though it does differ or happens in a different way from the intended or haz-arded result…." Id., p. 248. *State v. Leroy*, 232 Conn. 1, 17 n. 6, 653 A.2d 161 (1995).

As this suggested, causation requirements are of two types: legal or factual causation and proximate causation.

Legal or Factual Causation

Legal or factual causation, as *Guess* indicated, requires a showing that "but for" the defendant's conduct, the result would not have occurred or, as it is sometimes put, that the defendant's conduct was a "but for" antecedent of the result, without which the result would not have occurred.

The traditional factual causation issue was raised in *Commonwealth v. Soto*, 693 A.2d 226 (Pa.Super.1997), in which the evidence showed that Soto and his cousin Torres lured the victim, Pacheco, to a desolate quarry to resolve a drug dealing dispute. Torres first shot Pacheco five times in the body. Having run out of ammunition, the two ran to an acquaintance's home a mile away and procured more bullets. Upon their return to the quarry, Soto took the reloaded gun and shot Pacheco three times in the head. At Soto's murder trial he was convicted on evidence that included the following:

> Dr. Isadore Mihalakis, who testified as an expert witness for the Commonwealth[,] * * * stated unequivocally that the five body wounds suffered by the victim were inflicted prior to the three head wounds and that at least two of the five body wounds were lethal independent of the later-inflicted head wounds. When asked, in his expert opinion, whether the victim was alive at the time the last three bul-

lets were fired, Dr. Mihalakis testified that "he was either in profound shock [or] at or near death's door when he suffered these."

Soto argued on appeal that either he shot a dead body or a victim who was so near to death that his shots could not be a cause of death. The court first held that the jury could have found that Pacheco was alive when Soto shot him. Then, rejecting Soto's contention that the victim was so near death at the time of Soto's shots that his shots did not factually cause the victim's death, the court explained:

> In order for an act to be a * * * cause of death, it must be a substantial, although not the sole, cause of the death. * * * Moreover, "an accused may not escape criminal liability on the ground that, prior to the criminal act, his victim was not in perfect health."
>   Applied to the instant case, it is evident that, although the victim's very life-blood was seeping out of him and his pulse and breathing were strained, he was alive when appellant shot him three times in the face at close range. Appellant's argument that he is somehow less culpable because the victim was doomed to death at the time appellant shot him is specious and outlandish.

Thus a defendant factually or legally causes a victim's death if the defendant's actions simply speed up—or otherwise become a substantial cause of—death as it actually occurs.

The essence of factual causation, as *Soto* illustrates, is that the defendant's actions constituted a substantial factor in the result occurring *as and when it did.* If Soto's shots caused Pacheco to die before he would have died from Torres' shots, Soto factually caused the death. If Soto's shots did not speed up the death but when Pacheco expired his death resulted from bleeding caused by both Soto's shots and those fired by Torres, Soto factually caused the death.

Arguably the effect of Torres' shots could have been so pervasive and the impact of Soto's shots so minimal that a jury could find that Soto's shots did not amount to the necessarily *substantial* contributing cause. Clearly, however, in situations like *Soto* if the jury finds the defendant's actions a substantial cause of death that decision will be respected.

Only in unusual appellate cases is factual causation found lacking. One such case was *People v. Phippen,* 649 N.Y.S.2d 191 (N.Y.App.1996). Phippen, owner of a trucking company, directed his driver to continue to operate a truck despite repeated information that one front tire "hopped" and vibrated. The tire blew out, the truck crossed the street into the opposite traffic lane, and in a resulting collision another motorist was killed. Phippen was charged with reckless manslaughter and convicted. On appeal, the court held that the prosecution's evidence permitted the jury to find that Phippen was actually aware that using the truck with the "faulty" tire created a substantial risk of death of another and thus that he acted recklessly. An expert had testified at trial that a blowout can be caused by many things and he was unable to recover enough of the tire from the truck to have an opinion as to what caused the specific blowout on Phippen's truck. As a result, the appellate court held, the evidence was insufficient for the jury to find that Phippen's recklessness caused the accident and therefore the victim's death. The prosecution, in other words, failed to prove beyond a reasonable doubt that the victim's death would not have occurred when and as it did "but for" Phippen's recklessness.

Proximate Causation

Proximate causation requirements are more difficult to describe and apply than factual causation demands. As the previously quoted discussion from *Guess* suggested, proximate causation issues usually arise when the result intended by the defendant— the death of the homicide victim, for example—occurs but the chain of events between the defendant's conduct and that result is different from what the defendant anticipated. *Guess*'s formulation of the general proximate causation requirement, taken from a leading text, is somewhat more functional than many courts would give. Often, courts simply say that a result is proximately caused by the defendant's act if the result occurred as a consequence of a natural (or "probable" or "continuous") sequence of events, unbroken by an efficient intervening (or by a "superseding") cause.

The requirement that the result be a "natural" consequence of the defendant's actions adds little and perhaps nothing. Usually, if legal or factual causation exists, the real question is whether the defendant can establish that proximate causation is lacking because the events were interrupted or broken by an intervening cause or factor that the courts will regard as breaking the chain of proximate causation.

Generally speaking, courts have been quite reluctant to find that such intervening factors relieve defendants of responsibility for their victims' death, that is, that such factors become "superseding causes" of those deaths.

The problem is illustrated by *State v. Hall,* 129 Ariz. 589, 633 P.2d 398 (1981). Hall, an inmate at an Arizona prison, beat Robert Phillips, another inmate, with a pipe. Phillips remained unconscious for ten days. He then made medical progress until, 27 days after the attack, he suffered a pulmonary embolism in his lungs and died. Hall was prosecuted for intentional murder. Expert testimony established that the risk of embolism was increased by prolonged periods of inaction, such as remaining in bed. Despite Hall's argument that his actions did not "cause" Phillips' death, he was convicted. This was affirmed on appeal. The facts showed, the appellate court reasoned, that Hall intended to cause Phillips' death and did so. Hall may not have intended or anticipated that Phillips' death occur as it did, that is, as a result of an embolism. However, this does not mean that causation, even proximate causation, was lacking:

> The wounds inflicted need not have been fatal or even the direct cause of death. It is sufficient if the wounds caused death indirectly through a chain of natural effects and causes unchanged by human action. This is true even though the death-causing condition was anatomically disassociated from the wound inflicted. [Hall's actions] would not be a proximate cause of Phillips' death if the chain of natural effects and causes was either non-existent because of or broken by intervening events which were unforeseeable and hence were superseding events.

In dealing with cases where the intended death was achieved in an unintended manner because of an intervening event, courts usually distinguish cases where the intervening event was a coincidence from cases where the intervening event was a response to the defendant's prior actions. * * * [A]n intervening cause that was a coincidence will be a superseding cause when it was unforeseeable. On the other hand, an intervening cause that was a response will be a superseding cause only where it was abnormal and unforeseeable.

* * * Phillips' hospitalization and immobility were caused by blows to the head delivered by [Hall]. A normal response to such immobility is the development of leg vein thrombosis which could result in a pulmonary embolism. Since the intervening responses of thrombosis and pulmonary embolism were not abnormal, [Hall's] actions were a proximate cause of Phillips' death.

As *Hall* makes clear, proximate causation remains as long as the defendant's actions were *a* proximate cause of the result. Causation does not require that the defendant's actions be the only cause in any sense. It is sufficient that despite an intervening factor the defendant's actions remained one of several "contributing" causes. For an intervening cause to break the chain of proximate causation, then, it must become the *sole* cause of the result.

Causation Distinguished from Culpable Mental State Requirements

Where causation is required, as in homicide prosecutions, it is separate from the requirement of a culpable mental state. Confusion may be reduced by recognition that the culpable mental states required by most result crimes do not require proof that the defendant consciously anticipate the sequence of events by which the result occurs.

Hall, previously discussed, illustrates this. If the prosecution's theory was that Hall was guilty of murder because he acted with intent to kill Phillips, the prosecution's proof of *mens rea* required only that it show Hall desired Phillips' death to occur. The prosecution was under no obligation to prove that Hall desired any particular sequence of events between his act (striking Phillips with the pipe) and the result (Phillips' death). When the prosecution proved that Hall struck Phillips with the pipe, that Hall had at that time the desire by that act to cause Phillips' death, and that Phillips' death occurred as a factual and natural result of Hall's action in striking him with the pipe, the prosecution had made its basic case against Hall.

Hall's apparent anticipation that Phillips would die as a result of internal or external bleeding from the blow and shortly after that blow became legally significant only because of Hall's argument that the embolism was a superseding cause of Phillips' death. Only Hall's contention interjected into the case the difference between the manner in which Hall anticipated the death occurring and the manner in which it actually did occur.

Both factual and proximate causation are, of course, elements of the charged offense that the prosecution must prove beyond a reasonable doubt. In *Hall,* once Hall raised the issue of intervening and superseding cause, the prosecution clearly had the burden of convincing the jury beyond a reasonable doubt that the wounds inflicted by Hall caused Phillips' death in a manner unbroken by an intervening and superseding cause such as the embolism. The principal case reprinted next addresses more specifically when juries must be instructed on intervening causes.

State v. Munoz

Supreme Court of Connecticut, 1995
233 Conn. 106, 659 A.2d 683.

BORDEN, Associate Justice.

The dispositive issue in this appeal is whether, under the circumstances of this case, the trial court's jury instruction regarding the element of causation of the death of the victim requires a new trial. The defendant, Juan Carlos Munoz, appeals from the judgment of conviction, following a jury trial, of murder * * *.

[At 6:30 A.M., on May 30, 1990, the body of Mariano Herrera was discovered near a stone wall on the grounds of the Bishop Meadows condominium complex in Stamford, Connecticut. The body bore three major stab wounds, in the chest, back and neck, and twenty-four superficial wounds. Later evidence established that the three major wounds were the cause of death. Trial testimony for the prosecution indicated that Herrera had not died where his body was found. Herrera's keys were discovered on roadway of the complex about fifty feet from the body and the evidence indicated that the body had been dragged backwards from the location of the keys to the place it was discovered.

At 10:45 P.M. the evening of the 29th, defendant Munoz drove up to the home of his cousin, Gonzalo Garcia, in Stamford. Munoz was soaking wet and his hands were cut and bleeding. He told Garcia that he had been attacked by robbers in New York City. At Munoz' request, Garcia took him for treatment to a nearby hospital in Portchester, New York, and Munoz there gave medical authorities the same explanation for his wounds that he had given his cousin.

On June 4 Munoz returned to the hospital for followup treatment. When interviewed there by police, he gave the same explanation. He went with officers to the police station in Stamford, where he was shown a picture of Herrera and denied knowing him. Munoz then changed his story and stated that he and a friend, Carlos Perez, had met Herrera on the night of the 29th under an Interstate 95 overpass. The meeting was for Munoz to refuse Herrera's request that Munoz become a drug courier. When Herrera was told of the refusal, he produced a knife and attacked Munoz. Munoz then—without having harmed Herrera—left, and Perez stayed with Munoz.

In response to police expressions of disbelief, Munoz then produced another version in which he and Manuel Cruz went together to meet Herrera under the overpass because Cruz wanted Munoz to become a drug courier for Herrera. When Munoz declined to join the venture—according to this version—Herrera became angry and attacked Munoz with a knife. Munoz first defended himself and then grabbed the knife and stabbed Herrera once or twice in the back. Munoz became scared, dropped the knife, and left for his cousin's home. When he fled, Munoz asserted, Herrera was "fine."

Munoz was charged with and convicted of the intentional murder of Herrera. First, the appellate court concluded that the evidence was sufficient to support the conviction. The evidence permitted the jury to find that Munoz inflicted all of Herrera's wounds.]

The defendant * * * claims that the trial court improperly failed to instruct the jury regarding the element of causation of Herrera's death in accordance with the defendant's request to charge. * * * We agree.

In order to place this claim in its proper context, it is necessary to focus on the defendant's theories of defense * * *. He had two, albeit not entirely consistent, theories: (1) self-defense; and (2) alibi. A necessary component of the defendant's alibi defense was the notion that, in the presence of a third person, he had fought with Herrera under the highway overpass, left Herrera wounded but not fatally so, and that someone else, presumably the third person, inflicted the fatal wounds and later transported Herrera's body to the condominium complex. Thus, under this version of what had occurred, the defendant was somewhere else, namely, either at the hospital or at Garcia's house, when Herrera was killed.

The defendant's alibi defense was based, in part, on uncertainty in the evidence regarding the time of Herrera's

death. There was evidence, based on an analysis by [state medical examiner] Katsnelson of the contents of Herrera's stomach, from which the jury could have concluded that Herrera died at approximately 1 A.M., when the defendant was at the hospital in Portchester. * * * The other part of the defendant's alibi defense, namely, that someone other than the defendant inflicted the fatal wounds after the defendant had fled from the fight scene under the highway overpass, was based on the following evidence and arguments of the defendant to the jury.

The defendant's statement, read in a light favorable to him, indicated that when he met Herrera and the third person under the overpass at some time between 10 and 10:45 P.M., he and Herrera had fought, and that he had stabbed Herrera, but that Herrera was not fatally wounded when he fled. Although the police, several days later, unsuccessfully searched the area under the overpass for the knife and for other evidence of a bloody and fierce knife fight, their failure to find any such evidence arguably was explained by the torrential rains [the night of the 29th] that could have washed away the evidence, and by the possibility that someone else picked up the knife.

In addition, there was evidence from which the jury could have found, and the defendant argued to the jury, that Herrera's body had been transported to the condominium complex during the early morning hours, when the defendant was back at Garcia's house. Edmund H. Miller, a resident of the complex whose condominium was approximately seventy feet from where Herrera's body was discovered, testified that during the night of May 29–30, 1990, he was awake until approximately 2 A.M., that he heard no voices or noises out of the ordinary, and that his dog, which ordinarily barked when quiet is interrupted by noise, was silent.

In addition, there was no forensic evidence to support the state's theory that Herrera had been stabbed at the place on the condominium complex roadway from which his body had been dragged fifty feet to the stone wall. The presence of his keys at that location, together with the condition of his body and clothing, suggested that his body had been dragged from that location, and [assistant state medical examiner] Breakell testified that Herrera had not died at the location where his body had been found. Breakell did not testify, however, that Herrera had died at the location from which his body had been dragged, and the torrential rains on the night in question could have explained any lack of blood or other evidence at that location.

Furthermore, traces of blood on the defendant's jacket were consistent only with his blood type, and a search of the defendant's car disclosed no evidence of Herrera's blood. Although there was considerable evidence of blood in the car, all of it was consistent with only the defendant's blood type, and inconsistent with Herrera's. This evidence supported a potential inference that someone other than the defendant had transported Herrera's body from the overpass area, where the defendant said he had stabbed Herrera, to the condominium complex where Herrera's body was found.

Against this evidentiary background, the defendant filed the following request to charge on the element of causation: "The second element is that the defendant, acting with that intent to cause the death of another person, caused the death of that person. This means that the defendant's conduct was the proximate cause of the victim's death. An act or omission to act is the proximate cause of death when it substantially and materially contributes in a natural and continuous sequence, *unbroken by an intervening cause,* to the resulting death. It is the cause without which the death would not have occurred, and it is the predominating cause, the substantial factor, from which death followed as a natural, direct and immediate consequence. It is not necessary that the particular kind of harm that results from the defendant's act be intended by him. Where the death or injury caused by the defendant's conduct is a foreseeable and natural result of that conduct, the law considers the chain of legal causation unbroken and holds the defendant criminally responsible. . . .

"With regard to this element of the crime it is important for you to consider the testimony of Dr. Katsnelson that the cause of death was multiple stabbing of the head, neck and chest, as well as the testimony of [the police officers to whom the defendant made his statements] that the defendant described only one stab of the back." (Emphasis added.)

The trial court declined to instruct the jury in accordance with the defendant's request to charge. In its instructions on causation, the court [told the jury] that "[a] person is guilty of murder when, with the intent to cause the death of another person, he causes the death of such person," and then elaborated that this meant that the state was required to prove beyond a reasonable doubt that the defendant, acting with the requisite intent, "in fact caused the death of Mariano Herrera."

The court then stated: "In order to convict * * * this defendant of murder . . . you must first find that he caused the death of Mariano Herrera, and you must find proved beyond a reasonable doubt, that Mariano Herrera died as a result of this defendant's actions."

"Now, you have heard testimony about the number of wounds inflicted on the victim's body. You also heard testimony about at least one wound and possibly a second wound, which the defendant has admitted to having inflict-

ed. I have to tell you that it is not essential that the wound or wounds inflicted by the defendant, be the sole cause of the victim's death. It is sufficient if the wound or wounds . . . has or have been a substantial factor in causing his death. It's up to you to decide whether there was one or two wounds, or many wounds—or one, two, or more wounds inflicted by this defendant."

The defendant's claim requires us to determine, in light of the evidentiary basis for his alibi defense described above, whether: (1) the trial court's failure to include an instruction on intervening cause was improper; and, if so, (2) the impropriety requires a new trial. We answer both these inquiries in the affirmative.

* * *

Very recently, in *State v. Leroy,* [232 Conn. 1, 653 A.2d 161 (1995)], we reviewed "our cases that have discussed proximate causation in criminal prosecutions." The context of that review was a claim by the state that the Appellate Court had misapplied our [earlier] language * * * that, in order to satisfy the causation element of a crime, a defendant's conduct must have been *"the* substantial factor," or *"the* predominating cause" of the victim's injuries. (Emphasis added.) The Appellate Court had reversed the defendant's conviction because the trial court had instructed the jury that the defendant's conduct must have been " '*a* substantial factor' " of the victim's injuries. (Emphasis in original.)

In sustaining the state's claim in *Leroy,* we held that the proper formulation of the rule of law, and therefore of the underlying requirements of a proper jury instruction on proximate cause, was as follows: "[W]hen several factors contribute, in a chain of events, to cause a victim's injury, in order to be the proximate cause of that injury, the defendant's conduct must have been a cause that necessarily set in operation the factors that accomplish the injury. In short, *a jury instruction with respect to proximate cause must contain, at a minimum, the following elements: (1) an indication that the defendant's conduct must contribute substantially and materially, in a direct manner, to the victim's injuries; and (2) an indication that the defendant's conduct cannot have been superseded by an efficient, intervening cause that produced the injuries."* (Emphasis added.) * * *[8]

Accordingly, we conclude that the jury instruction in this case was improper because the court did not indicate that, for the defendant to be found guilty, "the defendant's conduct cannot have been superseded by an efficient, intervening cause that produced" Herrera's death. The evidence described previously * * * was susceptible of any of the following determinations by the jury: (1) the defendant's stabbing of Herrera did not in any way cause Herrera's death because that stab wound was not fatal, all of the fatal stab wounds having been inflicted by someone else after the defendant had fled; (2) although the defendant stabbed Herrera under the highway overpass, and although that stabbing may have contributed substantially and directly to Herrera's death by virtue of providing one of the ultimately fatal stab wounds, some third party's conduct in inflicting additional stab wounds, in the defendant's absence, was so significant that it amounted to an efficient, intervening cause; or (3) although the defendant stabbed Herrera under the highway overpass, the state's proof of whether that stabbing, as opposed to the stabbing of Herrera by someone else after the defendant had fled, resulted in Herrera's death was sufficiently inconclusive as to give rise to a reasonable doubt, based on the doctrine of efficient, intervening cause, about whether the defendant's conduct was the proximate cause of Herrera's death.

The first potential determination described above was sufficiently covered by the trial court's instruction as given, and would be encompassed by the requirement in *Leroy* that the instruction indicate that the defendant's conduct "must contribute substantially and materially, in a direct manner, to the victim's injuries." The second and third potential determinations, however, were not sufficiently covered by the trial court's instructions, and required an instruction indicating that in order for the defendant to be found guilty, "the defendant's conduct cannot have been superseded by an efficient, intervening cause that produced" Herrera's death. * * *

We cannot conclude, moreover, that there is no reasonable possibility that the inadequacy of the court's instruction affected the jury's verdict. As the state concedes, the state's case was not overwhelming. * * * Indeed * * * one of the potential determinations by the jury, based on the defendant's theory of defense, could have been a reasonable

---

[8] We emphasize that * * * the requirement of language in the jury instructions regarding an efficient, intervening cause is not ironclad. It arises in those cases in which the evidence could support a finding by the jury that the defendant's conduct was overcome by an efficient, intervening cause, or in which the evidence regarding proximate causation was such that, based on the doctrine of efficient, intervening cause, the jury could have a reasonable doubt about the defendant's guilt. Thus, in the general run of cases, in which the evidence is susceptible of a finding of only one cause of

the harm contemplated by the statute, a statement in the jury instruction referring to an efficient, intervening cause might well be unnecessary. In other cases, however, such as this case, where the evidence would support a finding by the jury that the defendant's conduct, although a "but for" cause of the victim's injuries, may nonetheless have been overcome by an efficient, intervening cause, or may nonetheless provide a basis for a reasonable doubt as to the effect of the defendant's conduct, an appropriate instruction on the doctrine of intervening cause is required.

doubt about who caused Herrera's death. Furthermore, the defendant's version of the events, although perhaps somewhat implausible, was not so bizarre that it fell beyond the bounds of the credible.

* * *

Because our determination of this issue requires a new trial, on the remand the trial court will be required to include an appropriate instruction to the jury on the doctrine of efficient, intervening cause. Although our case law has referred to that doctrine, those cases have not focused on the contours of that doctrine. We take this occasion, therefore, to elaborate somewhat on that doctrine as it applies to a criminal case in order to provide some guidance to the trial court.

The doctrine of intervening cause, which has deep roots in the law of proximate cause, both criminal and civil, has been referred to several times in our case law. It refers to a situation in which the defendant's conduct is a "but for" cause, or cause in fact, of the victim's injury, but nonetheless some other circumstance subsequently occurs—the source of which may be an act of the victim, the act of some other person, or some nonhuman force—that does more than supply a concurring or contributing cause of the injury, but is unforeseeable and sufficiently powerful in its effect that it serves to relieve the defendant of criminal responsibility for his conduct. Thus, the doctrine serves as a dividing line between two closely related factual situations: (1) where two or more acts or forces, one of which was set in motion by the defendant, combine to cause the victim's injuries, in which case the doctrine will not relieve the defendant of criminal responsibility; and (2) where an act or force intervenes in such a way as to relieve a defendant, whose conduct contributed in fact to the victim's injuries, from responsibility, in which case the doctrine will apply. Furthermore, in a case in which the evidence, viewed in favor of the defendant, justifies an instruction on the doctrine of intervening cause it will ordinarily be a question of fact for the jury, to be resolved pursuant to appropriate instructions by the trial court, whether the subsequent circumstance constitutes a concurring or contributing cause, in which case the defendant will not be relieved of criminal responsibility, or an efficient, intervening cause, in which case he will be so relieved.

These principles are illustrated by *State v. Alterio* [154 Conn. 23, 220 A.2d 451 (1966)]. In that case, a vehicular homicide prosecution, the defendant and another person engaged in an automobile race, as a result of which the other person's car collided at an intersection with a car driven by Harold DeSanty, Jr., in which the fatal victim, Harold DeSanty, Sr., was a passenger. The defendant had unsuccessfully requested the trial court to charge the jury that he must be acquitted if Harold DeSanty, Jr., had been negligent. On appeal, this court rejected the defendant's claim that he was entitled to that instruction. We stated: "The only bearing which the conduct of the driver of the DeSanty car could have upon the result . . . would relate to the issue of causation. This issue formed the substance of two other of Alterio's requests to charge.

"It was the state's burden to prove that a proximate cause of the death was the unlawful acts of the defendants or of either of them. Consequently, under the circumstances of this accident, *only if the conduct of the driver of the DeSanty car was shown to be the independent and efficient cause of his father's death would the state fail to meet its burden.* If, however, the requisite causal connection was established between an unlawful act of either of the defendants and the death, then both defendants, who joined in the common design to commit the unlawful act, would be responsible.

"Every person is held to be responsible for the natural consequences of his acts, and if he commits a felonious act and death follows, it does not alter its nature or diminish its criminality to prove that other causes co-operated to produce that result. It was incumbent upon the court, therefore, to point out to the jury that in order to establish the guilt of the defendants the state was required to prove the essential element of causation and the effect of participation by Alterio in the common undertaking which ended fatally." (Emphasis added; internal quotation marks omitted.)

Thus, in *Alterio,* the court indicated that, where the defendant's conduct combined with that of another to cause the victim's death, the defendant was not relieved from responsibility. The court also suggested, however, that if the conduct of the driver of the car in which the victim had been a passenger had been sufficient to overcome the causative effect of the defendant's conduct, that conduct could have been an "independent and efficient cause of [the victim's] death," in which case the state would not have met its burden on the element of proximate cause.

* * *

The judgment is reversed and the case is remanded for a new trial.

Notes and Questions

1. Homicide defendants sometimes argue that improper medical care of the victim constituted a superseding cause that broke the chain of proximate causation between their conduct and the victim's death. In *People v. Saavedra-Rodriguez,* 949 P.2d 86 (Colo.App.1997), for example, the proof showed that the defendant stabbed the victim with a knife and that the victim was conscious and talking when he arrived at a hospital. After emergency surgery was performed, however, he died. The defendant offered

evidence that one of the two emergency room physicians had filed an incident report claiming that the other physician had provided the victim with substandard care: He first failed to recognize the possibility of serious internal injury, he failed to take appropriate procedures to remove accumulated blood from the victim's chest, he withheld administration of fluids and blood, he canceled the "Trauma Red" alert that had been called to summon an anesthesiologist, he failed to promptly begin a thoracotomy, once he began a thoracotomy he failed to find the cut in the victim's heart, he failed to undertake aortic cross-clamping, when he did perform the cross-clamping he may have caused a "caval injury," and he failed to approve a resuscitative procedure involving administration of blood directly to the heart. The complaining physician added that he himself undertook cardiac massage and refused the first physician's directive to discontinue this action. Nevertheless, the trial court refused to instruct the jury on intervening causes, reasoning that only "affirmatively injurious" medical treatment could interrupt proximate causation.

The appellate court found error. It agreed with other courts that simply negligect medical care cannot constitute an intervening cause. However, it concluded, as have a considerable number of other courts, that medical care that is so deficient as to amount to "gross negligence" can interrupt proximate causation. Saavedra-Rodriguez had made a credible case that the care given to his victim was this deficient. Thus he was entitled to have the jury instructed to determine whether his victim's treatment was in fact such gross negligence and, if so, whether it was an intervening and superseding cause that broke the chain of proximate causation between Saavedra-Rodriguez's stabbing of the victim and the victim's death.

2. A more unusual contention was raised in *People v. Velez,* 159 Misc.2d 38, 602 N.Y.S.2d 758 (1993), another murder prosecution. Velez was shown to have shot the victim, Bittner, in the head during a robbery on October 17, 1991. Bittner was taken to Lincoln Hospital, where he was diagnosed as suffering from facial nerve paralysis. Pneumonia developed but was cured. Bittner continued to have difficulty speaking and walking. On December 4, he was transferred to Metropolitan Hospital for rehabilitation and on admission was found to be unable to swallow and thus require feeding by tube. In response to his slow progress, Bittner became depressed and dis-

traught, and on December 19 he pulled out his feeding tube and refused its reinsertion. He expressed a desire to return to regular food but failed to eat the food provided. He took only liquids and refused all medical tests and procedures. On December 24, he died. Medical testimony showed that Bittner had suffered brain damage from the gunshot that caused the difficulty in swallowing. Had he accepted feeding, he would have lived but would have had permanent disability. The medical examiner concluded that Bittner committed suicide by refusing food and medical treatment but that the gunshot by Velez was a contributing factor in the death.

Velez waived jury trial and the trial judge wrote an extensive opinion in response to Velez's contention that Bittner's suicidal refusal of treatment and food broke the chain of proximate causation between Velez's gunshot and Bittner's death. The judge identified and reviewed several appellate decisions from other jurisdictions upholding convictions despite evidence that the victim in a sense intervened and committed suicide. Some suggested that since the victims' suicides were themselves attributable to the injuries inflicted by the defendants, they simply could not as a matter of law interrupt proximate causation.

In *Hall,* discussed in the Editors' Introduction to this chapter, the Arizona Supreme Court suggested that "an intervening cause that was a response [to the defendant's conduct] will be a superseding cause only where it was abnormal and unforeseeable." This, of course, suggests that Bittner's suicide might have constituted a superseding cause but only if it was abnormal and unforeseeable.

The *Velez* trial judge held that despite the evidence showing Bittner's actions, the prosecution had shown Velez caused Bittner's death and was therefore guilty of murder. He explained:

> [T]his Court concludes that the People have met their burden of proving causation. The victim acted voluntarily in refusing nourishment and medical treatment. However, his inability to ingest food orally was directly caused by the gunshot wound he suffered. The gunshot wound created the difficulty swallowing and the difficulty swallowing prevented him from ingesting food orally. The gunshot wound set in motion a chain of events resulting in hospitalization, difficult swallowing, and forced feeding, the cessation

of which resulted in death. The gunshot wound forged a causative link between the initial injury and death and was a sufficiently direct and contributing event which eventually resulted in death. The suicide does not operate as an intervening act that excuses criminal liability because death was not solely attributable to this secondary agency. Death was caused by both the gunshot wound and the malnutrition. Perhaps criminal liability would be excused if the victim had recovered sufficiently to be discharged from the hospital and committed suicide at a more remote time to the initial injury. However, that is not the situation here and this Court is not called upon to answer that question. Here, the People established causation beyond a reasonable doubt.

MODEL PENAL CODE*

Official Draft, 1985

Section 2.03. Causal Relationship Between Conduct and Result, Divergence Between Result Designed or Contemplated and Actual Result or Between Probable and Actual Result

(1) Conduct is the cause of a result when:

    (a) it is an antecedent but for which the result in question would not have occurred; and

    (b) the relationship between the conduct and result satisfies any additional causal requirements imposed by the Code or by the law defining the offense.

(2) When purposely or knowingly causing a particular result is an element of an offense, the element is not established if the actual result is not within the purpose or the contemplation of the actor unless * * * the actual result involves the same kind of injury or harm as that designed or contemplated and is not too remote or accidental in its occurrence to have a [just] bearing on the actor's liability or on the gravity of his offense.

(3) When recklessly or negligently causing a particular result is an element of an offense, the element is not established if the actual result is not within the risk of which the actor is aware or, in the case of negligence, of which he should be aware unless * * * the actual result involves the same kind of injury or harm as the probable result and is not too remote or accidental in its occurrence to have a [just] bearing on the actor's liability or on the gravity of his offense.

(4) When causing a particular result is a material element of an offense for which absolute liability is imposed by law, the element is not established unless the actual result is a probable consequence of the actor's conduct.

Note

Consider how *Munoz* would be analyzed by the jury under the Model Penal Code approach, if the jury concluded that Munoz inflicted some of the knife wounds upon Herrera but that a third party later inflicted further wounds and transported Herrera's body to the condo complex. The "actual result" would be Herrera's dying as he did, from the wounds inflicted by Munoz and other wounds inflicted by the third person. The "designed or contemplated [result]" would be Herrera dying from the injuries inflicted by Munoz and probably doing so shortly after Munoz stabbed Herrera. Munoz was charged with intentional murder so the charged crime required that he purposefully cause the result. Therefore, section 2.03(2) would apply.

Under section 2.03(2), the actual result and the designed result both involved "the same kind of injury or harm": death. Consequently, liability would exist only if the jury determined that "the actual result * * * is not too remote or accidental in its occurrence to have a [just] bearing on [Munoz'] liability or on the gravity of his offense." Instead of deciding whether there was a reasonable doubt that a third person's actions constituted an "efficient, intervening cause," the jury would address whether the way in which matters developed was too remote or accidental as compared with what Munoz anticipated to have a just bearing on his criminal responsibility for Herrera's death. Would this be a better way of resolving the matter than the more traditional proximate cause instructions required by *Munoz*?

In *State v. Maldonado*, 137 N.J. 536, 645 A.2d 1165 (1994), the New Jersey Supreme Court rejected a contention that a causation criterion similar to that in section 2.03 of the Model Penal Code was so unclear or unfair as to be unconstitutional. The drafters of the Model Penal Code, *Maldonado* noted, concluded that the terms used in traditional causation analysis left juries with great flexibility but without substantial practical guidance in making a decision. They decided that the nature of the problem meant it is inevitable that juries will make these decisions on the basis of "a community's sense of justice on whether a defendant, otherwise clearly responsible under the criminal law, should be relieved of punishment because the [actual] result appear[s] too distant from his act." The New Jersey legislature could reasonably conclude that the Code's drafters were correct and that the language focusing upon whether the actual events were "too remote or accidental" was a valid way for the legislature to provide for juries to apply the community's common "conscience" under as much guidance as the nature of the problem permits. Thus use of the Code's language was held constitutionally permissible.

Chapter 6

GENERAL PRINCIPLES OF CRIMINAL LIABILITY: COMPLICITY

CHAPTER CONTENTS

Editors' Introduction: Liability for the Crimes of Others, Vicarious Liability, and Liability of Organizations

Traditionally, criminal liability has often extended to persons other than those who actually engaged in the specific conduct amounting to particular offenses. This chapter deals with the doctrines underlying such liability. Several somewhat overlapping but nevertheless distinct bodies of law are considered. Attention is first focused upon what has traditionally been the major significance of the law of parties, liability for "aiding and abetting" another's commission of a crime. Next, liability arising as a result of a precrime conspiracy is considered. Finally, liability for conduct committed after the primary offense has been committed is examined.

Several preliminary matters must, however, be addressed: so-called vicarious criminal liability, liability based on membership in or one's relationship to an organization, the background law of common law "parties," and the general ways modern law differs from traditional common law.

Vicarious Liability

In some sense, of course, one who under the law of parties or its modern equivalents is liable for a crime actually committed by someone else is held vicariously liable for that offense. However, such liability rests upon the defendant's participation, albeit indirect participation, in the offense. Liability for crimes committed by a person's coconspirators, considered in Section B, might also be regarded as vicarious in nature, but in reality it rests upon the defendant's even less direct participation in the offense by virtue of participation in the conspiracy.

In better reasoned discussions, the term vicarious liability is reserved for those situations in which liability for the crimes of others is imposed not because of such indirect participation in the crimes but rather merely because of a relationship between the defendant and the person committing the crime by her own actions. Most commonly, this involves making employers liable for crimes committed by their employees because of the employer-employee relationship rather than on the basis of the employers' participation, direct or indirect, in the offense.

Although strict liability (as discussed in Chapter 4, D) and vicarious liability often occur in the same situations, these terms refer to different aspects of the criminal liability. The Wisconsin Supreme Court explained:

> [I]t is helpful to an understanding of vicarious liability to compare it with the doctrine of strict liability. Strict liability allows for criminal liability absent the elements of *mens rea* found in the definition of most crimes. Thus under strict liability the accused has engaged in the act or omission; the requirement of mental fault, *mens rea*, is eliminated.
>
> * * *
>
> Vicarious liability, in contrast to strict liability, dispenses with the requirement of the *actus reus* and imputes the criminal act of one person to another.

State v. Beaudry, 123 Wis.2d 40, 48, 50, 365 N.W.2d 593, 597 (1985).

Sometimes statutes specifically provide for vicarious liability by defining a crime as capable of being committed by doing certain things "by an employee." However, courts may interpret a crime as involving such liability for violations committed by an employee even in the absence of such specific language.

The Wisconsin Supreme Court in *Beaudry,* for example, construed the Wisconsin liquor laws as imposing vicarious liability upon the designated agent of a corporation holding a liquor license for violations—such as remaining open after designated closing hours—committed by employees of the corporation. Several considerations persuaded the court that the purpose of the liquor laws would be promoted by vicarious liability and therefore that the legislature must have intended it. First, the criminal offenses under the liquor laws impose "strict" liability; vicarious liability is more likely with regard to such strict liability offenses. Second, the offenses at issue are misdemeanors; vicarious liability is more likely with regard to relatively minor offenses. Third, it would often be difficult for the prosecution to prove that employers participated in the commission of particular violations, although they in fact did. Finally, enforcement of the general regulatory scheme of which the offenses are a part requires frequent prosecutions. Therefore, imposing upon the prosecution the task of proving that employers actually participated in specific violations would be an especially heavy burden. The last two considerations strongly suggest that vicarious liability will be favored where the offenses are part of a broad regulatory scheme and imposing ordinary requirements of proof of participation upon the prosecution is likely to create such great difficulties as to frustrate effective enforcement of that scheme.

There may be constitutional limits upon the circumstances in which vicarious liability can be imposed. In *Commonwealth v. Koczwara,* 397 Pa. 575, 155 A.2d 825 (1959), cert. denied, 363 U.S. 848, 80 S.Ct. 1624, 4 L.Ed.2d 1731 (1960), a tavern licensee and operator was convicted of sale of beer to minors although he was not present and his bartender employee had made the sales. He received a fine and a three-month jail term. The Pennsylvania Supreme Court held that due process was violated by the imposition of a jail term based on vicarious liability and vacated that part of the penalty.

Even vicarious liability resulting in only a fine may be unconstitutional at least in some situations. In *Davis v. Peachtree City,* 251 Ga. 219, 304 S.E.2d 701 (1983), the defendant, president of a chain of convenience stores, was found guilty of sale of wine to a minor on Sunday by an employee of one store. The Georgia Supreme Court concluded that the State's interests in implementing its liquor laws could be enforced by methods—such as revoking liquor licenses in a civil proceeding—less onerous than vicarious criminal liability. As a result, due process was found violated even though only a fine was imposed as a penalty. A similar result was reached by the Minnesota Supreme Court in *State v. Guminga,* 395 N.W.2d 344 (Minn.1986).

Although this is a largely unexplored area, there may be various methods for one vicariously liable for crimes of another to avoid liability. In *United States v. Park,* 421 U.S. 658, 95 S.Ct. 1903, 44 L.Ed.2d 489 (1975), the president of a national grocery chain was held properly convicted of a violation of the National Pure Food and Drug Act consisting of receiving food shipped in interstate commerce and permitting it to be exposed to rodent infestation. However, the Supreme Court indicated, at a trial on the merits a defendant like Park could raise "defensively" a claim that he was power-less to prevent or correct the violation. A defendant making such a claim, the court continued, has the burden of coming forward with evidence supporting it. Once such evidence is produced, however, the Government then has the ultimate burden of proving beyond a reasonable doubt that the defendant had the power to prevent or correct the violation.

It is unclear whether a defendant such as the designated corporate agent held liable in *Beaudry* is entitled at trial to raise a defensive claim that she had been unable to pre-vent the prohibited sale by the corporation's employee. It is, of course, also unclear—if she is entitled to raise such a claim—what she must show (or what the prosecution must "disprove"). The few cases also leave unclear what is a sufficient showing that a vicariously liable defendant was powerless to prevent another, such as an employee, from committing a criminal act.

Organizational Criminal Liability

Under some circumstances, corporations and sometimes other organizations such as partnerships are liable for criminal offenses. Obviously an organization itself cannot commit an offense, so organizational liability of this sort must be based upon a rule that makes the organization criminally responsible for certain actions of its employees or agents. Although an organization obviously cannot be imprisoned, a fine can, of course, be levied upon it. In such cases, some of the burden imposed by the penalty may fall upon persons who did not participate in the offense. If a corporation is convicted and fined, for example, shareholders may suffer financially because of the corporation's need to pay the fine. In a sense, then, the shareholders are penalized for conduct committed by others.

In part because of concern regarding the propriety of penalizing such nonpartici-pants, courts and legislatures have struggled with the appropriate standard for deter-mining when an organization (and its members) may be punished for an offense committed by only a few employees or agents. Generally speaking, a corporation may be found guilty of certain offenses—usually minor ones—upon a showing that the offenses were committed by a corporate agent or employee acting within the scope of his authority. However, more serious offenses—and especially those requiring particu-lar intents or mental states—can give rise to corporate liability only if the offense was directed or acquiesced in by a relatively highly placed corporate officer. See Model Penal Code § 207 (Official Draft 1985).

Common Law of Parties

Criminal liability for crimes committed by others has most commonly been imposed under the traditional common law of parties and its modern equivalent. Modern statutes, such as the provision of the Model Penal Code reprinted after this introduc-tion, are easier to understand against the background of the parties to a crime at common law, superseded by such modern statutes.

At common law, participants in—or "parties" to—felonies were distinguished and categorized as follows:

Principal in the First Degree	Principal in the Second Degree	Accessory Before the Fact	Accessory After the Fact
One who, with the requisite state of mind, performed the criminal act or directly caused the criminal result, either with his own hand, with an instrument or a nonhuman agent, or by means of an innocent human agent.	One who was actually or constructively present at the scene of the crime and who, with the required state of mind, aided, counseled, commanded, or encouraged the principal in the first degree.	One neither actually nor constructively present at the scene of the crime who, with the requisite state of mind, ordered, counseled, encouraged or otherwise assisted or encouraged the principal in the first degree.	One who, with knowledge of the commission of an offense by an offender, concealed the offender or gave him some other assistance to prevent his detection, arrest, trial, or punishment.

The involvement necessary to render someone a principal in the second degree or an accessory before the fact was often referred to as "aiding and abetting."

These distinctions were not drawn at common law with regard to misdemeanors. All participants in a misdemeanor—meaning those who would fit in any of the first three categories of felony participants—were guilty of the misdemeanor but all were regarded as principals. Concealment of or assistance to a misdemeanant did not give rise to criminal liability at all.

At common law, the law of parties had a number of complex procedural implications. Venue and jurisdictional problems arose because of the rule that an accessory was punishable only at the place where the act of accessoryship was committed and not where the final offense was committed. Strict attitudes toward pleading demanded that a defendant be charged with the specific form of liability that the trial proof would show. One charged as a principal in the first degree could not be convicted if the proof at trial showed that the defendant was an accessory before the fact. Finally, the liability of an accessory was tied to that of the principal. Thus an accessory could not be tried before the principal and anything that prevented the conviction of the principal also prevented conviction of the accessory. This was even expanded to require that reversal of a principal's conviction also result in reversal of the conviction of an accessory. See *Standefer v. United States,* 447 U.S. 10, 14–19, 100 S.Ct. 1999, 2003–05, 64 L.Ed.2d 689, 695–96 (1980).

Modern Liability for Crimes Committed by Others

No American jurisdiction still retains unmodified the common law of parties, but the changes have varied widely. Modern statutes generally provide for the liability of all who at common law would have been principals in either degree or accessories before the fact. Section 2.06 of the Model Penal Code, reprinted after this introduction, would do this by making all such persons liable for crimes committed by others if the persons were accomplices of the individuals who committed those offenses. This is essentially aiding and abetting liability, covered in Section A. Most states have supplemented this with liability for certain crimes committed by coconspirators; such liability is covered in Section B.

The procedural ramifications of the traditional distinctions among the participants or parties has been minimized and often the distinctions themselves have been abolished. Title 18 of the U.S. Code Ann., for example, provides:

§ 2. Principals

   (a) Whoever commits an offense against the United States or aids, abets, counsels, commands, induces or procures its commission, is punishable as a principal.

   (b) Whoever willfully causes an act to be done which if directly performed by him or another would be an offense against the United States is punishable as a principal.

Other statutes provide in more detail for the requirements of liability. Many follow the pattern of section 2.06 of the Model Penal Code (reprinted below) and address the matter directly in terms of when one person is "liabl[e] for conduct of another." Liability for a crime of persons other than the actual perpetrator is often, even under provisions such as 18 U.S.C.A. § 2 or section 2.06 of the Model Penal Code, referred to as "accomplice" or "aiding and abetting" liability.

Liability for assistance *after* the commission of a crime—accessoryship after the fact in common law terminology—has generally been separated from liability for the offense itself and made a distinct offense. Such liability is, therefore, treated separately in this book in Section C .

MODEL PENAL CODE*

Official Draft, 1985

Section 2.06. Liability for Conduct of Another; Complicity

(1) A person is guilty of an offense if it is committed by his own conduct or by the conduct of another person for which he is legally accountable, or both.

(2) A person is legally accountable for the conduct of another person when:

   (a) acting with the kind of culpability that is sufficient for the commission of the offense, he causes an innocent or irresponsible person to engage in such conduct; or

(b) he is made accountable for the conduct of such other person by the Code or by the law defining the offense; or

(c) he is an accomplice of such other person in the commission of the offense.

(3) A person is an accomplice of another person in the commission of an offense if —

(a) with the purpose of promoting or facilitating the commission of the offense, he

(i)   solicits such other person to commit it; or

(ii) aids or agrees or attempts to aid such other person in planning or committing it; or

(iii) having a legal duty to prevent the commission of the offense, fails to make proper effort so to do; or

(b) his conduct is expressly declared by law to establish his complicity.

(4) When causing a particular result is an element of an offense, an accomplice in the conduct causing such result is an accomplice in the commission of that offense, if he acts with the kind of culpability, if any, with respect to that result that is sufficient for the commission of the offense.

(5) A person who is legally incapable of committing a particular offense himself may be guilty thereof if it is committed by the conduct of another person for which he is legally accountable, unless such liability is inconsistent with the purpose of the provision establishing his incapacity.

(6) Unless otherwise provided by the Code or by the law defining the offense, a person is not an accomplice in an offense committed by another person if —

(a) he is a victim of that offense; or

(b) the offense is so defined that his conduct is inevitably incident to its commission; or

(c) he terminates his complicity prior to the commission of the offense and

(i) wholly deprives it of effectiveness in the commission of the offense; or

(ii) gives timely warning to the law enforcement authorities or otherwise makes proper effort to prevent the commission of the offense.

(7) An accomplice may be convicted on proof of the commission of the offense and of his complicity therein, though the person claimed to have committed the offense has not been prosecuted or convicted or has been convicted of a different offense or degree of offense or has an immunity to prosecution or conviction or has been acquitted.

A. LIABILITY AS AN AIDER AND ABETTOR
Editors' Introduction: Aiding and Abetting or "Accomplice" Liability

Liability for a crime actually committed by someone else has traditionally been based primarily upon what is often described as aiding and abetting liability. As the term suggests, this type of liability borrows significantly from the substance of the common law of parties. The Model Penal Code provision reprinted earlier describes one liable under provisions of this sort as being an accomplice of the person who actually commits it.

Despite the simplification of liability of this sort provided by many modern statutes, the task of determining when a person's participation in a crime is sufficient to create liability for that crime is often a difficult one. In resolving particular cases, courts frequently use general language that is of little help in understanding why the case was decided as it was or in predicting how future cases will be decided.

Some distinctions, however, are clearly required by the demands of sound analysis and better-articulated judicial discussions. One federal court, for example, has explained:

> The seminal [federal] case [on aiding and abetting] is *United States v. Peoni,* 100 F.2d 401, 401 (2d Cir.1938), in which Judge Learned Hand states that aiding and abetting requires that the defendant "in some sort associate himself with the venture, that he participate in it as in something that he wishes to bring about, that he seek by his action to make it succeed." This suggests two general components of aiding and abetting—an act on the part of a defendant which contributes to the execution of a crime and the intent to aid in its commission."

United States v. Greer, 467 F.2d 1064 (7th Cir.1972). As the cases in this section demonstrate, however, it is not always easy to separate what act the defendant must have performed (and perhaps what impact that act must have had) from the intent that the defendant must have harbored.

Several general aspects of this liability can usefully be addressed before detailed attention is turned to the basic requirements of the required participation—the act—and a sufficient culpable mental state—the intent.

Situations in Which Participation Does Not Create Liability

As a general rule, participation in any offense renders a person liable for that offense as an accomplice. Despite the general rule, however, some situations do not permit the imposition of liability on an accomplice basis.

The law defining these situations was discussed in *United States v. Southard,* 700 F.2d 1 (1st Cir.1983), cert. denied, 464 U.S. 823, 104 S.Ct. 89, 78 L.Ed.2d 97 (1983). Southard was tried and convicted of aiding and abetting a violation of 18 U.S.C.A. § 1084(a):

> Whoever being engaged in the business of betting or wagering knowingly uses a

wire communication facility for the transmission in interstate or foreign commerce of bets or wagers or information assisting in the placing of bets or wagers on any sporting event or contest [commits an offense].

The government's theory was that one Brian was in the gambling business and that the other defendants (Banker and Ferris) assisted his actions violative of the statute. Government evidence showed that the defendants placed bets for Brian with various bookmakers and that they exchanged with Brian various information ("line information") of significance in the wagering business. The defendants urged that the evidence failed to show that they were engaged in the gambling business and therefore they must be considered to have done nothing more than place bets. Further, they argued, one who merely placed bets with another could not—on that basis alone—be an accessory to the other's violation of section 1084(a).

The court, however, held that on the specific facts of the case, a conviction for aiding and abetting a violation of § 1804(a) was permissible:

[N]ot every substantive crime is susceptible to an aiding and abetting charge. The question is whether section 1084(a) falls within one of the exceptions to the general rule that aiding and abetting goes hand-in-glove with the commission of a substantive crime.

The first exception is that the victim of a crime may not be indicted as an aider or abettor even if his conduct significantly assisted in the commission of the crime. Examples are persons who pay extortion, blackmail, or ransom monies. It is obvious that section 1084(a) does not involve victims; even a compulsive gambler cannot be described as a "victim" of the bookmakers with whom he bets.

The next exception embraces criminal statutes enacted to protect a certain group of persons thought to be in need of special protection. Accomplice liability will not be imposed upon the protected group absent an affirmative legislative policy to include them as aiders and abettors. For example, a woman who is transported willingly across state lines for the purpose of engaging in illicit sexual intercourse is not an accomplice to the male transporter's Mann Act violation. Appellant claims that he was a mere bettor, not one "engaged in the business of betting or wagering," and therefore falls within the same category as the woman transported across state lines. This, of course, is primarily a question of proof. But even if we assume that defendant was only a bettor, he is not helped any. Section 1084(a) was not passed to protect bettors from their gambling proclivities. Its stated purpose was to assist the states in enforcing their own laws against gambling.

The final exception to accomplice liability upon which appellant relies occurs when the crime is so defined that participation by another is necessary to its commission. The rationale is that the legislature, by specifying the kind of individual who is to be found guilty when participating in a transaction necessarily involving one or more other persons, must not have intended to include the participation by others in the offense as a crime. This exception applies even though the statute was not intended to protect the other participants. Thus, one having intercourse with a prostitute is not liable for aiding and abetting prostitution, and a purchaser is not an accomplice to an illegal sale. Appellant argues that here the legislature has made criminally liable only those "engaged in the business of bet-

ting or wagering" and that the other participants are not within the compass of
the statute. Therefore, appellant contends, he should only have been charged with
the substantive crime, not aiding and abetting.

The flaw in this argument is that it assumes that the other participant is only a
bettor who does nothing to assist the principal in carrying on his gambling activities. The question, as the district court recognized, is not whether a mere bettor
can be prosecuted as an aider and abettor, but whether a person not "in the business of betting or wagering" can be found guilty of assisting one who is. We think
it clear that he can.

We have been unable to find any cases that discuss directly the propriety of an
aiding and abetting prosecution in conjunction with a section 108(a) offense. * * *

The evidence, viewed in the light most favorable to the government, establishes
clearly that none of the appellants raising this issue was a "mere bettor." The jury
could reasonably have found, based on the telephone intercepts, that Banker and
Southard were "engaged in the business of betting or wagering," that they
exchanged line information with Brian and that they placed bets for him with
other bookmakers. Ferris, whose involvement in this prosecution was the most
tenuous of all the appellants, placed at least one bet for Brian for another book-
maker. Because the actions of these three appellants exceeded those of mere bettors, we have no difficulty finding they were properly indicted.

The court, however, carefully took no position on whether persons who were "mere
bettors" could be held liable as participants in a violation of section 1084(a).

The final exception recognized by *Southard* is generally applied to crimes consisting
of the sale of drugs. Sale requires both a seller and a purchaser, and a purchaser is
therefore necessary to any commission of the crime. Since these crimes impose liability
only for participating as a seller, however, the legislative intent is read as excluding the
purchaser from liability despite that purchaser's participation.

Southard's analysis may have been or become incomplete. A federal court addressed
what it characterized as the problem of applying principles of accomplice liability to
complex statutory crimes:

> As the number of complex criminal statutory crimes has proliferated over the last
> 30 years, and as the government has attempted to expand the net of criminal liabil-
> ity under them by charging accomplices in addition to principals, the case law and
> therefore the theory of federal accomplice liability has fallen into some disarray.
> Even in the days of relatively simple crimes at common law and in earlier federal
> statutes, the various theories of accomplice liability were often difficult to apply. In
> this new era of "predicate offenses" with multiple "ancillary conditions" and
> mandatory and other sentencing enhancements, the new complexity of the statutes
> is causing disparate results based on conflicting ideas of accomplice liability.

United States v. Hill 55 F.3d 1197, 1200 (6th Cir.1995). Some offenses, Hill
observed, may indicate a legislative intention that accomplice liability be unavailable.
Under the federal continuing enterprise statute, 21 U.S.C.A. § 848, certain drug
"kingpins" are treated harshly if they have five or more employees and certain other
conditions are met. Federal courts are split, Hill noted, on whether a person can be

charged as an accomplice to a kingpin violation. Arguably, accomplice liability would permit some small-time drug dealers to be treated as principals and thus frustrate the apparent intent of Congress to limit kingpin liability to those running large drug enterprises.

Hill concluded that in some situations at least the problems of imposing accomplice liability can be handled if courts carefully define the requirements of accomplice liability as they apply to particular offenses. Special care, the court suggested, must be paid to the mental state requirement.

Aider and Abettor's Inability to Commit Offense by Own Actions

Should an aider and abettor's liability be affected by proof that given the crime involved, he could not commit the offense as a principal, that is, by his own conduct as the actual perpetrator?

The general law governing such contentions was set out and applied in *People v. Fraize,* 36 Cal.App.4th 1722, 43 Cal.Reptr. 64 (1995). Fraize was convicted under Cal. Penal Code § 288a, which provides for liability of "[a]ny person who participates in an act of oral copulation while confined * * * in any local detention facility * * *." The evidence showed that Fraize was a court bailiff who approached two prisoners in the courthouse lockup and directed one to orally copulate the other and then to copulate Fraize. Noting that only jail inmates could violate the statute by their own actions, Fraize contended that he could not be prosecuted under it. Rejecting this, the court elaborated:

> The contention lacks merit for it fails to recognize that under an aiding and abetting theory—a theory the People pled against defendant and argued to the trial court—a defendant can properly be convicted of a crime even though by statutory definition the defendant would be incapable of committing the substantive offense by himself. * * * For instance, although rape is statutorily defined as "an act of sexual intercourse accomplished with a person not the spouse of the perpetrator," it is proper to prosecute, on an aiding and abetting theory, a man for the rape of his wife, or a woman for the rape of another woman. And in an even more relevant vein, it has been held that an adult can be prosecuted for aiding and abetting children to commit lewd acts on themselves. It therefore follows that the People's use of the aiding and abetting theory against defendant was proper.

Prosecution and Conviction of the Actual Perpetrator

Should the prosecution of an aider and abettor be affected by proof that the primary actor has not been prosecuted or even captured? Should it be affected by proof that the primary actor has been tried and acquitted?

At common law, an accessory's prosecution required the prior conviction of the principal. *Sandefer v. United States,* 447 U.S. 10, 15, 100 S.Ct. 1999, 2001, 64 L.Ed.2d

689, 695 (1980). A very few jurisdictions may still link the liability of an aider and abettor to the guilt of the principal, at least to some degree. In *State v. Suites,* 109 N.C.App. 37, 427 S.E.2d 318, review denied, 333 N.C. 794, 431 S.E.2d 29 (1993), for example, an aider and abettor's conviction for murder, based upon a plea of guilty, was held invalid because at a later trial the principal was acquitted.

Most jurisdictions, however, treat the liability of the various participants in a crime as independent matters. The Arizona Supreme Court explained:

> [W]hen a principal has been acquitted of a criminal act, can the accomplice, in a separate trial, be convicted of aiding and abetting that criminal act? We hold that he can.
>
> The State is never required to prove more than the allegations contained in [a charge] in order to sustain the conviction of an aider and abettor. * * * What is required at the trial of the aider and abettor is proof, complete and convincing, of the guilt of the principal. Justice demands that the principal crime be fully proved, since the guilt of the aider and abettor depends upon the commission of the principal crime. Thus, whether or not the principal is convicted or acquitted in a separate trial can have no bearing on the trial of the aider and abettor, if the evidence shows the latter guilty. Society is no less injured by the illegal acts of the aider and abettor even though the principal himself escapes conviction. In order to convict an aider and abettor, justice demands no more than [that] * * * the evidence convincingly show that a crime was committed by the principal.

State v. Spillman, 105 Ariz. 523, 525, 468 P.2d 376, 378 (1970). In *Sandefer,* the Supreme Court held that the legislative history of 18 U.S.C.A. § 2 (reprinted on page 116) reveals a Congressional intention to permit prosecution of an aider and abettor despite prior acquittal of the actual perpetrator of the crime.

Should it make any difference if the principal's acquittal occurs in the same trial as that in which the aider and abettor is convicted? Generally, as the North Carolina Supreme Court noted in *State v. Reid,* 335 N.C. 647, 656–57, 440 S.E.2d 776, 781–82 (1994), it does not. In *United States v. Robins,* 978 F.2d 875 (5th Cir.1992), for example, the trial was a joint trial of Allison for possession of marijuana with intent to distribute and Robins for aiding and abetting that crime. The jury acquitted Allison but convicted Robins, and this was held permissible. The courts generally reason that the principal's acquittal may be the result of jury leniency or compromise that gives the aider and abettor no right to escape conviction. The aider and abettor's interests are sufficiently protected by the prosecution's obligation to prove the principal's guilt and the aider and abettor's right to appellate review to assure that such proof is made.

Change of Heart

If one provides encouragement or assistance to another sufficient to create accomplice liability for any crime the other person may commit, is there any way to escape liability? If, of course, the other person is prevented from committing the offense, there is no offense for which the aiding and abettor party can be liable. However, is there any way short of this to prevent liability?

It is widely agreed that that such liability can be avoided by undoing the encouragement or assistance earlier provided. Where only verbal encouragement was provided, it may be sufficient to simply voice disapproval of the plan in a timely fashion. If more was done, however, further action may be necessary to avoid liability. If a weapon was provided, for example, reacquisition of that weapon may be necessary. See *Commonwealth v. Huber,* 15 D. & C.2d 726 (Pa.Q. Sessions 1958). The Model Penal Code (see page 116) and some statutes based on it require that the person "wholly deprive [his complicity] of effectiveness in the commission of the offense" or "[make] proper effort to prevent the commission of the offense."

There are few cases on the matter, but those courts that have considered claims of change of heart have not been sympathetic. In *State v. O'Neal,* 618 S.W.2d 31 (Mo.1981), for example, O'Neal participated with another person in a robbery. He saw that his companion was about to shoot the victims and he turned and walked away. According to his testimony at trial, he was afraid of his companion and therefore did not try to stop him. He did think, according to his testimony, that his walking away might make his companion change his mind about shooting the victims. It did not. At his trial for the killings actually committed by his companion, was he entitled to have the jury instructed on withdrawal? Applying a statute based on the Model Penal Code provision, the Missouri court held that no instruction was required. Apparently by letting events progress to the point where his companion was pointing a gun at the victims, O'Neil had forfeited any opportunity to withdraw by delaying his effort to withdraw too long. At least, by so waiting he made it necessary to do more to effectively withdraw than silently walk away.

Liability of Aider and Abettor for Additional Crimes

The two subsections that follow address in considerable detail the requirements for aiding and abetting liability for what can best be considered the first crime at issue. This is because in contrast to the strict requirements for finding some guilt on this basis, once such liability for the first crime is found many courts apply a much looser analysis for determining whether the aider and abettor is guilty of additional crimes committed by the actual perpetrator of the first offense.

Liability is quite often found for additional crimes that the aider and abettor may not have intended to encourage or assist, even if liability for the first offense requires an intent to encourage or assist in the commission of that offense. Thus many courts hold that the aider and abettor is liable for the offense he intended to facilitate and others committed by the primary actor "in furtherance of their * * * common purpose." See *State v. Bacon,* 658 A.2d 54, 60 (Vt.1995).

Some courts go further and impose liability for crimes committed by the primary actor that are the "natural or probable result" of the common purpose. In *State v. Marr,* 113 N.C.App. 774, 440 S.E.2d 275, 278 (1994), aff'd in part and rev'd in part, 342 N.C. 607, 467 S.E.2d 236 (1996), for example, the evidence was clear that Marr encouraged Smith and Jaynes to go to the property of one Acker when Acker was not there and steal equipment from a shed. Smith and Jaynes went to the property when Acker's vehicles were there, knocked on the door, shot Acker dead when he respond-ed, and entered the residence as well as the shed. Then they burned the residence. Was Marr liable for the burglary committed by entering the residence, the arson (of the residence), and the murder, all as the natural or probable results of the theft from the shed, which he did aid and abet? The intermediate court applied the "natural and probable consequences" standard, acknowledging that it was "more easily stated than applied." It found liability for all the offenses on the basis of case law, which it read as holding that "once an accessory before the fact has counseled, procured or planned a criminal event, he must answer for all crimes flowing from the accomplished event." When the North Carolina Supreme Court granted review, the prosecution admitted that it could not support the convictions for murder and arson and the higher court reversed those convictions. It affirmed conviction for the burglary, however, on the ground that Marr could have assumed that Smith and Jaynes would steal other items and would enter the residence to do so.

This rule is often applied in the homicide context in connection with the felony murder rule, but it is by no means limited to that type of situation.

Careful reevaluation of this broad liability may persuade courts to limit the responsi-bility of the aider and abetter. The Vermont Supreme Court in *Bacon,* for example, reconsidered this body of law in light of the required culpable mental state for aiding and abetting liability. Holding the aider and abettor liable for crimes that are part of the common understanding or purpose is appropriate, it concluded, because this per-mits the conviction of those who participate in an offense with "the equivalent [of] * * * the requisite mental state." However, it rejected liability for crimes that are sim-ply the "natural and probable consequence" of an offense planned, because such lia-bility "violates one of the most basic principles of criminal law by allowing the jury to convict a person for causing a bad result without determining that the person had some culpable mental state with respect to that result."

How far does liability extend under the "natural and probable consequences" rule? The difference in the results in the two decisions in *Marr,* previously discussed, make clear the truth of the intermediate court's comment that the rule is "more easily stated than applied." This is reaffirmed by *Roy v. United States,* 652 A.2d 1098 (D.C.App.1995), in which the evidence showed that Peppi Miller, working for police, arranged with Roy for Miller to purchase a handgun. Miller went to meet Roy to make the purchase:

> Roy * * * explained that Miller would have to wait for "Steve" [Ross], who was to bring the handgun.
>
> Ross arrived [and] walked towards the grounds of a nearby school. Roy told Miller that Steve had brought the handgun and that Miller should "go talk to Steve and get it from Steve."
>
> Miller followed Ross through a gate into the school yard and down some steps to a location approximately thirty yards from the entrance. Roy remained in the vicinity of a blue trash can which was near the gate. Miller caught up with Ross, and at trial he described the ensuing events as follows:

> He [Ross] said, "What's up?" I said, "What's up?" He said, "[Y]ou got the
> money?" I said, "Yes, I have the money." And then, I pulled the money out
> [of] my pocket * * *. [T]hen he put the clip into the chamber, pulled the
> round back, pointed the gun in my face and said for me to drop the money.
> * * * [H]e had told me to put the money on the ground. . . . Then I started
> to back up, and then he said, "I'm not playing with you, I told you." He
> said, "Better yet, jump the fence," so I jumped the fence. . . . Then I gave off
> the distress signal * * *.

Officers promptly responded to Miller's distress signal. Within two minutes,
they had apprehended Roy, Ross, and several other individuals who were in the
area. Roy and Ross were standing approximately five feet apart near the entrance
to the school at the time of their capture. The officers recovered $600 in cash
from Ross' front pants pocket; bills totaling $400 were bundled separately from
the other money, and a[n] * * * agent testified that these bills were in the same
denominations as those which had been provided to Miller earlier. A loaded
handgun bearing Ross' fingerprint was found near the gate.

Roy was prosecuted for the armed robbery. One government theory was that Roy
aided and abetted Ross' sale of the gun to Miller and the robbery committed by
Ross was a "natural and probable consequences" of the gun sale for which Roy was
responsible. Rejecting this theory, the appellate court explained:

> Armed robbery is a felony punishable by life imprisonment; selling a handgun, on
> the other hand, constitutes CPWOL, a misdemeanor * * *. The government's
> application of the "natural and probable consequences" doctrine would thus dra-
> matically expand Roy's exposure even where * * * he did not intend that a crime
> of violence be committed.
>
> This court has stated that "an accessory is liable for any criminal act which
> *in the ordinary course of things* was the *natural and probable* consequence of the
> crime that he advised or commanded, although such consequence may not have
> been intended by him." The italicized words place a number of obvious restric-
> tions on the * * * [rule]. The phrase "in the ordinary course of things" refers to
> what may reasonably ensue from the planned events, not to what might conceiv-
> ably happen, and in particular suggests the absence of intervening factors. "Natural"
> has many meanings, but the most apposite dictionary definition is "in accordance
> with or determined by nature." A natural consequence is thus one which is within
> the normal range of outcomes that may be expected to occur if nothing unusual
> has intervened. We need not define "probable," except to note that, even stand-
> ing alone, this adjective sets a significantly more exacting standard than the word
> "possible." Accordingly, if we accord to the words of our cases their ordinary
> everyday meaning, it is not enough for the prosecution to show that the accom-
> plice knew or should have known that the principal might conceivably commit
> the offense which the accomplice is charged with aiding and abetting. Without
> inserting additional phrases or adjectives into the calculus, we think that our
> precedents require the government to prove a good deal more than that. A "natur-
> al and probable" consequence in the "ordinary course of things" presupposes an
> outcome within a reasonably predictable range.

We turn to the facts at hand. * * * The government argues that Peppi Miller was a logical target of a robbery because, "given the illegal nature of the activity in which he was involved, [he] was unlikely to file a complaint with the police about the robbery." This reasoning, however, recognizes no apparent limiting principle. If we were to accept the government's position, then the robbery of any buyer or seller in a drug or unlicensed pistol sale would be viewed as the "natural and probable consequence" of that transaction, for a participant in any illegal project may well be reluctant to invoke the aid of the constabulary. * * *

* * * Viewed in the light most favorable to the prosecution, the evidence would perhaps support a finding that Roy should have known that it was conceivable that Ross might rob Miller. The evidence was insufficient, however, to show that a robbery would follow in the "ordinary course of events," or that it was a "natural and probable consequence" of the activities in which Roy was shown to have engaged. We must therefore reverse for evidentiary insufficiency Roy's conviction for armed robbery.

Roy was a close case, however, and some courts—such as the intermediate court in *Marr*—would undoubtedly have upheld the conviction on the ground that a jury could have reasonably concluded that the robbery was a natural and probable consequence of the crime of sale of a gun.

1. Required Participation

Courts sometimes use language that suggests an aider and abettor must do something that has a discernible impact upon the commission of the crime. Thus the Massachusetts Supreme Judicial Court commented in *Commonwealth v. Raposo,* 413 Mass. 182, 185, 595 N.E.2d 773, 776 (1992), that "what is required to be convicted as an accessory before the fact is not only knowledge of the crime and a shared intent to bring it about but also some sort of act that contributes to its happening." Whether this is actually demanded is not clear as a matter of either theory or practice. In actual fact, the issue seldom arises. In *State v. Marr,* 113 N.C.App. 774, 778, 440 S.E.2d 275, 278 (1994), aff'd in part and rev'd in part, 342 N.C. 607, 467 S.E.2d 236 (1996), the court explained:

> The requirement for conviction of an accessory before the fact is that the State must prove beyond a reasonable doubt that the action or statements of the defendant somehow caused or contributed to the actions of the principal. Generally, there is not a great deal of dispute over whether an accessory's words or acts caused or contributed to the actions of the principal. Rather, the factual issue is more likely to focus on whether the accessory "counseled, procured, or commanded the principal *at all*."

Perhaps in part because the issue is litigated relatively infrequently, those cases that do raise the question sometimes present courts with considerable difficulty.

Evans v. State

District Court of Appeal of Florida, 1994
643 So.2d 1204.

WEBSTER, Judge.

In this direct criminal appeal, appellant seeks review of convictions, based upon an aiding and abetting theory, for shooting into a building and criminal mischief. He argues that the trial court erroneously denied his motion for a judgment of acquittal as to both charges, because the evidence was legally insufficient to establish that he had aided or abetted the commission of either offense. We agree and, accordingly, reverse.

The only evidence presented at trial which tied appellant in any way to the offenses charged was a statement voluntarily given by appellant to law enforcement officers shortly after the offenses had been committed. No other evidence was offered which suggested any involvement by appellant in either offense.

Viewed in a light most favorable to the state, the evidence presented at trial consisted of the following. At about 9:15 P.M. on a Sunday evening, the victims' home and store were sprayed with bullets. (Some 57 rounds were later counted.) Miraculously, nobody was injured. Having heard the gunfire, a witness looked out and saw "a sporty" "stepside, new modeled Chevrolet pickup" which was "fancy colored," either "a teal blue or a teal green." All that the witness was able to say about the occupants of the truck was that there were at least three black people in the rear. Approximately an hour later, a truck matching the description given to law enforcement was stopped, some 14 or 15 miles from the site where the shooting had occurred. There were two black males in the rear of the truck, and three in the cab. The witness who had seen the truck earlier was brought to the site where it had been stopped, and positively identified it. The occupants of the truck were transported to a detention facility for questioning. After having been advised of his rights, appellant agreed to give a statement, a tape recording of which was played for the jury.

In his statement, appellant said that, earlier that day, Kelvin Godfrey had called him and told him that a friend of theirs had been beaten up by the owner of the store. He and Wendell Scott, who owned the truck, drove to Godfrey's house, to see the friend who had been beaten. When they arrived, the friend was not there. They settled in to watch a ball game on television. Godfrey and two other individuals, Tim Garrett and "a black guy we don't know," began discussing shooting out the windows of the store in retribution for the earlier beating of their friend. It seemed

to appellant as though the other three had discussed such a plan earlier, before he and Scott had arrived. When the ball game ended, all five got into Scott's pickup. Scott was driving, and appellant was in the passenger seat. The other three individuals were all in the rear. They drove by the store, and one or more of the individuals in the rear fired at the store. Appellant was not paying too much attention, because he was listening to the radio. After the shooting, Scott drove back to Godfrey's house, where Godfrey, Garrett and the third person got out. Scott and appellant then left. The other three people in the truck when it was stopped had had nothing to do with the incident. Appellant was familiar with firearms because he had formerly been a correctional officer. However, he had not "touched a gun" since he had left that job.

To secure a conviction on an aider and abettor theory, the state must establish (1) that the defendant helped the person who actually committed the crime by doing or saying something that caused, encouraged, incited or otherwise assisted that person to commit the crime; and (2) that the defendant intended to participate in the crime. Given the evidence presented at trial, both the trial court and the jury were obliged to accept appellant's statement as true, because it was reasonable, unrebutted and unimpeached. In fact, but for appellant's statement, there was no evidence even placing appellant at the scene of the offenses.

We are unable to distinguish the facts of this case from those in *C.P.P. v. State,* 479 So.2d 858 (Fla. 1st DCA 1985). There, the appellant had been found to have committed the offenses of burglary and grand theft, based upon an aider and abettor theory, and adjudicated a delinquent child. On appeal, he argued that the evidence had been legally insufficient to establish his guilt. The court summarized the evidence as follows:

> The evidence against appellant consists essentially of the testimony of a store manager stating that his store was burglarized, . . . and appellant's confession, admitting his presence in an automobile at the store premises while two other persons left the car, and returned two and one-half hours later, placing four or five bags in the trunk. Appellant also admitted having prior knowledge that the two others intended to burglarize the store and take goods therefrom. Finally, he admitted that another person remained in the car for the purpose of serving as a lookout.

Noting that "'mere knowledge that an offense is being committed is not the same as participation with the requisite criminal intent,'" and that "presence at the scene of the offense and flight from the scene are insufficient to establish participation", the court reversed, holding that, as a matter of law, the state had failed to establish that the appellant was guilty, on an aider and abettor theory, of either offense.

Viewed in a light most favorable to the state (but accepting as true appellant's uncontradicted and unimpeached version of what transpired), the evidence presented at trial established that appellant knew, when he got into the truck, that one or more of the persons in the rear intended to shoot out the windows of the store; that one or more of the persons in the rear of the truck did shoot at the store as the truck drove by; and that appellant was a passenger in the cab of the truck when the shooting occurred. Based upon *C.P.P. v. State,* such evidence is legally insufficient to establish appellant's guilt on an aider and abettor theory, and his convictions must be set aside. Accordingly, appellant's convictions for shooting into a building and criminal mischief are reversed, and the case is remanded with directions that appellant be discharged.

REVERSED and REMANDED, with directions.

LAWRENCE, Judge, dissenting.

I respectfully dissent, for I am of the view that the trial judge did not err in refusing to set aside the jury verdict finding Evans guilty. The controlling authority in this case is our decision in *A.B.G. v. State,* 586 So.2d 445 (Fla. 1st DCA 1991), dismissed, 605 So.2d 1261 (Fla.1992). The facts recited in that case are as follows:

The only witness at the adjudicatory hearing was a security officer at an Albertson's store in Jacksonville, Florida. He testified that on October 25, 1990, he saw four boys, including the appellant, enter the store. The group proceeded directly to the condom section. Three of the boys, including the appellant, stood elbow-to-elbow directly in front of the condoms. The other two boys began removing boxes of condoms from the display. One of the boys broke open a box of two condoms, removed them from the box, and placed them in the inside pocket of his jacket. The boy who stood immediately next to appellant put two boxes into the right front pocket of his jacket. Appellant (at least four or five times) looked down at the condoms, then to the front of the store and to the rear of the store. Appellant's actions were continuous, occurring both before and after the other boys stuffed the condoms into their pockets. Appellant and the other boys also conversed

during the theft. The fourth boy stood behind the other three and also looked to the front and back of the store. The boys walked together to the front of the store and past the cash register without paying for the merchandise. As they attempted to exit the store, they were confronted by the manager. Appellant turned away from the store manager and walked back into the lobby.

In concluding that the evidence was sufficient for the fact-finder to find that A.B.G. was an active participant in the crime, the *A.B.G.* court said:

[T]he fact finder could reasonably infer from the evidence presented that appellant's hypothesis of innocence, that he didn't know the other boys were going to take the condoms and that he was just nervously looking around, was not reasonable. The boys entered the store together and proceeded directly to the condom display. Appellant stood elbow-to-elbow with a boy who was stuffing condom packages into his front jacket pocket. He was observed talking with the other boys during the commission of the crime. The appellant demonstrated a deliberate pattern of conduct, both before and after the other boys had concealed the condoms. These factors, taken in the light most favorable to the state, are inconsistent with appellant's purported lack of knowledge and mere nervous presence at the crime scene. A fact finder could reasonably infer that, as a result of appellant's consistent actions both before and after the actual taking of the property, the only reasonable hypothesis from the evidence presented was that appellant intended to be, and was, an active participant in the theft as a lookout.

In the instant case, Evans does not argue any hypothesis of innocence, except that he "merely went along for the ride." As acknowledged by the majority, the evidence must be viewed in a light most favorable to the State. I can only conclude (as did both the jury and trial judge) that Evans' statement and argument, suggesting that he was not an active participant, should be rejected as unreasonable on its face.

The majority view relies on *Dudley v. State,* 511 So.2d 1052 (Fla. 3d DCA 1987), for the proposition that the jury had no choice but to accept the statement of the defendant (Evans) as true in its entirety, because it was reasonable, unrebutted, and unimpeached. The *Dudley* court also said:

On the other hand, where the defendant's exonerating testimony (a) is not reasonable on its face, or (b) is contradicted by other evidence in the case, or (c) is otherwise impeached, the trier of fact is privileged to reject such testimony and convict the defendant of the crime charged, providing, of course, there is otherwise sufficient evidence of guilt.

The jury was justified in rejecting portions of Evans' statement, while believing other portions, because some of it was facially unreasonable. In analyzing the statement, the jury could have concluded that the following facts were significant in determining whether to believe or disbelieve some or all of the statement. Evans was a former correctional officer, and thus no stranger to the law enforcement profession. He was familiar with firearms, having previously "qualified" with a ".38" and an "AR . . . 15"; he identified the multiple shots fired from the truck as probably having come from a .22 rifle, and not from a larger caliber weapon; he saw a .22 rifle at the house before the group entered the truck. Evans had a motive for committing the crime, in that the victim of the instant offense had allegedly hit Evans' good friend with a gun. Evans heard about the incident, and decided to look for the friend and "see what it was all, what all this was about and stuff." He went to another friend's house in pursuit of this effort, when other friends also arrived. These friends discussed, in Evans' presence at the house, a plan to "ride by the store and they say they was going to shoot in the windows." The friends had a .22 rifle "just laying on the chair" in the house at the time of the conversation. While still at the house, Evans related:

> We was—we was like watching the game and then they was talking about what happened to Max [Evans' good friend] and talking about they was wanting to shoot, shoot the windows out the, out the store because the guy worked there or owned it or whatever, and then we left.

Other evidence from witnesses reflected the following facts. Approximately fifty-seven rounds were fired at the scene of the crime. The pick-up truck was stopped by police approximately one hour following the incident, at which time all five of the persons still occupied the truck, although there were now three persons in the cab, including Evans, and only two persons in the cargo bed.

The jury was warranted in rejecting portions of Evans' statement as facially unreasonable, and could have reached that conclusion on the following basis. A reasonable person, especially a former correctional officer, with no intent to commit a crime, would not have left the house with friends in the same motor vehicle, knowing that his companions were en route to commit a crime and that its commission was imminent. There was no suggestion from Evans' statement, or any other evidence, that Evans was under any coercion or pressure to accompany those committing the crime. Following the criminal episode, Evans remained

with those committing the crime in the same truck until all were detained by the police, approximately one hour later; he, otherwise, did nothing to disassociate himself from them. A reasonable person, with no criminal intent, would have sought to sever any association with those involved in the crime, however belated such an attempt might take place. A reasonable person would have known that, under the circumstances of this case, his mere presence and election to accompany his companions on the criminal episode would have communicated a subtle message of approval and encouragement. A reasonable person, with no criminal intent, would have attempted to dissuade his companions from a serious violation of the law, especially when the potential for serious bodily injury or death was a reasonable or probable result.

* * *

Notwithstanding the majority's view that there was no participation (and thus no intent) on Evans' part, intent to commit a crime can be proven in other ways. * * * [I]ntent may be proven either by showing that the aider and abettor had the requisite intent himself, or that he knew that the principal had the intent.

Evans admitted by his own statement that he knew that the principals had the intent to commit the crime before they left the house. Thus, there is ample authority for concluding that Evans had the requisite intent.

The majority view relies on *C.P.P. v. State,* 479 So.2d 858 (Fla. 1st DCA 1985), to conclude that Evans lacked the requisite criminal intent. However, *C.P.P.* may be distinguished from *Evans.* In *C.P.P.,* the facts leave open the hypothesis that C.P.P. acted under coercion, or similar constraint, that he was thwarted in any attempt to disassociate himself from the principals, or that he did not take seriously his principals' announced plans until it was too late. However, Evans' statement reflects that he was not acting under constraint, but could have distanced himself from the principals at any time, had it not been for an intent to participate in the crime.

I would affirm the judgment of the trial court.

Note and Questions

Must the aider and abettor's conduct (or omission) have had any particular impact upon the primary offender? Language used by courts sometimes suggests so but seldom provides a clear standard for determining how much or what kind of impact. In *People v. Sims,* 136 Cal.App.3d 942, 186 Cal.Rptr. 793, 798 (1983), for example, the court simply said that an aider and abettor must be shown to have "acted in a manner which either directly or indirectly increased the probability that the crime would be completed successfully."

Where liability as an "accomplice" under section 2.06 of

the Model Penal Code is based upon affirmative action rather than an omission, what does the Code require? Note that section 2.06(3)(ii) provides that it is sufficient if the defendant "aids" or "attempts to aid" the other person. This suggests that liability can be based on actions that were intended to aid but did not.

In *State v. Gelb,* 212 N.J.Super. 582, 515 A.2d 1246 (1986), Gelb was prosecuted for a number of crimes (including manslaughter and criminal mischief) committed when a railroad switch was thrown causing a passenger train to derail. Had the switch been thrown before the train reached a particular point—Marlot Avenue—the engineer would have seen a warning light and stopped in time to avoid the accident. Gelb was part of a group of young men gathered around the switch. Although there had been some discussion of throwing the switch, it was not clear that any firm decision to do so had been made. As the train's lights came into view, one Held said, "Throw the switch." Wade began pulling on the switch. Gelb then yelled at Wade to "wait until the train passed Marlot Avenue so the engineer doesn't know the switch is pulled." Wade let go of the switch. Venton, however, reached across and pulled the handle the rest of the way down. The location of the train at this time was unclear. It also was not clear whether Wade had pulled the switch handle sufficiently to throw the switch. At his trial, Gelb requested that the jury be instructed that if he performed some act designed to aid, abet, or incite the commission of the crimes but did so after the switch had been thrown, he did not participate in the offenses so as to be liable for them under a statutory provision similar to section 2.06 of the Model Penal Code. Finding no error in the trial court's refusal to give such an instruction, the appellate court explained:

> [B]y the very terms of the statute, accomplice liability will attach if an individual merely attempts to aid in the commission of a crime; such an attempt need not actually facilitate the commission of the offense to support a finding of liability.

Thus no impact on the actual commission of the offense was required.

2. Required Culpable Mental State

A number of American courts have construed accomplice liability law as requiring "intent." The California Supreme Court, for example, reviewed that state's law and concluded:

> [T]he weight of authority and sound law require proof that an aider and abettor act with knowledge of the criminal purpose of the perpetrator and with an intent or purpose either of committing, or of encouraging or facilitating commission of, the offense.
>
> When the definition of the offense includes the intent to do some act or achieve some consequence beyond the *actus reus* of the crime, the aider and abettor must share the specific intent of the perpetrator. By "share" we mean neither that the aider and abettor must be prepared to commit the offense by his or her own act should the perpetrator fail to do so, nor that the aider and abettor must seek to share the fruits of the crime. Rather, an aider and abettor will "share" the perpetrator's specific intent when he or she knows the full extent of the perpetrator's criminal purpose and gives aid or encouragement with the intent or purpose of facilitating the perpetrator's commission of the crime. * * *

People v. Beeman, 35 Cal.3d 547, 560, 199 Cal.Rptr. 60, 68, 674 P.2d 1318, 1325–26 (1984). See also, *Hensel v. State,* 604 P.2d 222, 234 (Alaska 1979) ("liability for the crime of another will attach only upon a showing that an individual had knowledge of the criminal enterprise and specifically intended, by his conduct, to aid, abet, assist, or participate in the criminal enterprise").

The major issue is whether this requirement demands that in Model Penal Code terms the defendant have acted with purpose rather than merely knowledge. Thus the distinction between these two levels of culpable mental state, developed in Chapter 4, becomes quite significant.

The question concerning the mental state that ought to be required for accomplice liability was described in the Comments to section 2.06 of the Model Penal Code, (reprinted on page 116) as "a much debated issue." In explanation, the Comments continued:

> The issue is whether knowingly facilitating the commission of a crime ought to be sufficient for complicity, absent a true purpose to advance the criminal end. The problem, to be sure, is narrow in its focus: often, if not usually, aid rendered with guilty knowledge implies purpose since it has no other motivation. But there are many and important cases where this is the central question in determining a liability. A lessor rents with knowledge that the premises will be used to establish a bordello. A vendor sells with knowledge that the subject of the sale will be used in commission of crime. * * * An employee puts through a shipment in the course of his employment though he knows the shipment is illegal. A farm boy clears the ground for setting up a still, knowing that the venture is illicit. Such cases can be multiplied indefinitely; they have given courts much difficulty when they have been brought * * *.

Model Penal Code, Comments to Section 2.04, pp. 27–28 (Tent. Draft No. 1, 1953).

Even if the formal law purports to require an intent or purpose to encourage or facilitate commission of the offense, there is some question whether in fact this is really demanded as a practical matter of the law in application. The case that follows purports to recognize what is careless application of a strict intent standard.

United States v. Ortega

United States Court of Appeals, Seventh Circuit, 1995
44 F.3d 505.

Before POSNER, Chief Judge, and BAUER and FLAUM, Circuit Judges.
POSNER, Chief Judge.

The defendant, Agustin Ortega, was sentenced to 63 months in prison following his conviction by a jury of aiding and abetting the possession of heroin with intent to distribute it. He had also been charged with conspiracy to distribute heroin but that charge was dismissed after the jury hung on it. * * *

The charges against Ortega arose out of a deal that Jesus Villasenor and Mario Gomez (who was Ortega's nephew) made to sell heroin to a pair of individuals who, unbeknownst to them, were an FBI agent and an FBI informant. The deal was struck at a restaurant and afterward the parties repaired to Villasenor's van, which was parked outside. Ortega was sitting in the van, behind the driver's seat. Villasenor went to the rear of the van and poked around, looking for something. Then he asked (in Spanish, as was the entire conversation among the parties), "Where is it?," and Ortega pointed to an area on the floor of the van and said, "Over there." Villasenor went to the place indicated and came up with a plastic bag, which he opened. The informant tasted it, and pronounced it heroin. The bag emitted a pungent odor and Ortega remarked—depending on the translation—either, "The damn aroma comes from that thing," or, "It still fuckin' smells like that's what it is." There was also testimony that after the informant declared the substance in the bag to be heroin, Ortega commented, "the best."

The evidence was not sufficient to convict Ortega of possession of heroin beyond a reasonable doubt. Possession, including constructive possession, implies a right—not necessarily a legal right, but a right recognized by the relevant community, which may be an illegal community—to control. There is a sense in which, when Ortega was alone in the van with the heroin, he had "control" over it. He could have picked up the bag of heroin and run. But the power to make off with someone else's property is not equivalent to a right to the property. There is no evidence that the heroin was Ortega's in that sense. The heroin was Villasenor's. It is no answer that if only Ortega knew where it was, only Ortega could possess it. You can be the only person to know where something is, yet not own the thing; it may be inaccessible to you, and even if accessible may be the rightful possession of another. We doubt very much whether by the usages and customs of the heroin trade Ortega could have played finders keepers with Villasenor and expected to live to tell about it.

But if Ortega did not possess the heroin, Villasenor did; and the question then becomes whether Ortega aided and abetted Villasenor's possession. If the evidence that Ortega said "the best" is credited, the answer is clearly yes. The canonical definition of aiding and abetting a federal offense, stated by Judge Learned Hand in *United States v. Peoni*, 100 F.2d 401, 402 (2d Cir.1938), and repeated in innumerable subsequent cases, e.g., *Nye & Nissen v. United States*, 336 U.S. 613, 619, 69 S.Ct. 766, 769–70, 93 L.Ed. 919 (1949), requires not only that the defendant have aided his principal to commit a crime but also that he have wanted the principal to succeed in committing it. Obviously this rules out inadvertent assistance * * *.

If Ortega pronounced the heroin "the best," this makes him an aider and abettor. He was speaking to a customer and warranting the quality of the seller's product. He was assisting the sale in circumstances that made clear that he wanted it to succeed. But the evidence that Ortega, rather than the informant or the FBI agent, said "the best" is so weak that we hesitate to base our decision on the assumption that he did say it. If he did not, he still assisted the sale by pointing to the bag of heroin, and he did so knowingly. His remarks (quite apart from "the best") showed that he knew the bag contained heroin, as his reply brief concedes; and he must also have known—or so at least a reasonable jury could have found—that Villasenor wanted the heroin in order to make a sale.

Even so, if the evidence that Ortega said "the best" is discounted there is no evidence that he wanted the sale to succeed. He might have pointed to the bag because Villasenor asked him where it was and he knew, not

because he wanted Villasenor to succeed in selling the heroin in it. The jury, recall, could not agree on a verdict on the conspiracy charge. Presumably it failed because there was very little evidence that Ortega, who happened to be an uncle of Gomez, Villasenor's partner in the sale of the heroin, was a member of the Villasenor-Gomez conspiracy. One of the alternative possibilities is that he was someone along for the ride who rendered one-time assistance by watching over the heroin (the van's door was broken, and as a result could not be locked, and there had been a previous theft) while Villasenor and Gomez were in the restaurant negotiating with the FBI agent and the informant. If we knew that Ortega was to be paid, as corrupt policemen are paid to look the other way when a drug deal is about to come off, it would be plain enough that he wanted the deal to succeed, as that would greatly enhance the probability of his actually being paid; and all the elements of the traditional test for aiding and abetting would then be satisfied. Likewise as we have said if he joined actively in the selling by talking up the quality of the product, showing that he wanted the sale to go through.

But what if he merely rendered assistance, without being compensated or otherwise identifying with the goals of the principal? We do not think it should make a difference, provided the assistance is deliberate and material. One who, knowing the criminal nature of another's act, deliberately renders what he knows to be active aid in the carrying out of the act is, we think, an aider and abettor even if there is no evidence that he wants the act to succeed—even if he is acting in a spirit of mischief. The law rarely has regard for underlying motives. *Peoni's* formula for aiding and abetting, if read literally, implies that the defendant must to be convicted have some actual desire for his principal to succeed. But in the actual administration of the law it has always been enough that the defendant, knowing what the principal was trying to do, rendered assistance that he believed would (whether or not he cared that it would) make the principal's success more likely—in other words did what he could do or what he was asked to do to help make success more likely. No more is required to make the defendant guilty of joining the principal's venture and adopting its aims for his own within the meaning of *Peoni* and the cases that follow it.

AFFIRMED.

Notes and Questions

1. One approach to the problem of the culpable mental state required for aiding and abetting is to provide separately for, first, purposeful and, second, knowing involvement in an offense. The Proposed Federal Criminal Code defined the liability of an accomplice,

generally speaking, as requiring "intent that an offense be committed." Section 401(l)(b). However, it also proposed the following additional offense:

§ 1002. Criminal Facilitation

(1) Offense. A person is guilty of criminal facilitation if he knowingly provides substantial assistance to a person intending to commit a felony, and that person, in fact, commits the crime contemplated, or a like or related felony, employing the assistance so provided. The ready lawful availability from others of the goods or services provided by a defendant is a factor to be considered in determining whether or not his assistance was substantial * * *.

* * *

(3) Grading. Facilitation of a Class A felony is a Class C felony. Facilitation of a Class B or Class C felony is a Class A misdemeanor.

The Comment notes that this would provide a solution to the dilemma created by other approaches, which require that any facilitator either be treated as a full accomplice or be completely absolved of criminal liability. Proposed Federal Criminal Code, Comments to § 1002.

Some jurisdictions take this approach. See, for example, New York Penal Law §§ 115.00–115.08 (McKinney's 1986 Supp.) (four degrees of criminal facilitation). Under the New York provisions, criminal facilitation consists of aiding another in committing an offense, "believing it probable that he is rendering aid." New York Penal Law § 115.00(l) (McKinney's 1986 Supp.) (aiding commission of any felony is fourth degree criminal facilitation).

Would the proposed federal statute provide a more appropriate result in cases like *Ortega?* If the prosecution proved that Ortega had an affirmative desire that Villasenor successfully possess the heroin with intent to distribute it, he would be guilty of that crime. However, if he was only aware that his actions would assist Villasenor's commission of the offense and thus was indifferent as to this, liability would exist only if he provided *substantial* assistance to Villasenor. Further, in the second situation his liability would not be the same as that of Villasenor, since he would not be guilty of the crime of possession. Rather, he would be guilty of the separate offense of "criminal facilitation" and subject to a less severe penalty than Villasenor.

2. There is general agreement with the comment of the California Supreme Court set out in the introduction to this subsection that the aider and abettor must "share the specific intent of the perpetrator." This means, however, that in some unusual situations the aider and abettor may be guilty of a different crime than the actual perpetrator:

All [participants] in a crime are not necessarily guilty of the same grade of offense. A [participant] may be convicted of a higher or lower degree of the crime, depending upon the mental element proved at trial.

State v. Smith, 450 So.2d 714 (La.App.1984) In *Smith,* for example, defendant Haley Smith clearly aided his brother Rodney's robbery of a store. During the robbery, Rodney picked up a hammer lying under the store counter and shook it at the clerks. Rodney was convicted of *armed* robbery with a dangerous weapon. Haley, however, was held to have aided and abetted only Rodney's commission of simple robbery, because he did not know that Rodney would use a dangerous weapon. In the terms used by the California Supreme Court, Haley shared with Rodney the culpable mental state necessary for simple robbery but not that necessary for armed robbery.

Editors' Note: Aiding and Abetting a Drug Sale

Some courts are reluctant to uphold convictions for aiding and abetting the sale of controlled substances despite proof of sufficient involvement by the defendants that on the surface at last appears to satisfy the general requirements for liability. These cases are illustrated by *People v. Johnson,* 657 N.Y.S.2d 27 (App.1997), in which Johnson had been convicted of a sale actually made by his codefendant. The court set out the facts in summary form without disclosing where the events took place:

[I]n response to the undercover's inquiry of whether "anyone" was working, the defendant replied "Yeah. My boy right here will hook you up." He then motioned to his codefendant, who was standing approximately five feet away. The under-cover subsequently walked away with the codefendant and purchased drugs approximately fifteen feet from where the defendant remained.

Finding the evidence insufficient to support Johnson's conviction, the court first stressed that the prosecution was obligated to prove that the defendant "'intentionally aided' his codefendant in the sale of drugs, as opposed to merely providing assistance 'believing it probable' that he was rendering aid." It then held, "[The] evidence, stand-ing alone, was legally insufficient to hold that the defendant acted in concert with the requisite mental culpability for the illicit transaction."

In *Johnson* and similar cases, the courts' decisions leave somewhat unclear the basis on which these courts find the prosecution's evidence lacking. Perhaps the courts regard the proved participation in the sale too minimal; thus the defect in *Johnson* may have been the prosecution's failure to prove that Johnson "acted in concert" with his codefendant. Yet as developed in the last subsection, aiding and abetting law generally requires relatively little participation in the events.

Perhaps, alternatively, the courts regard the evidence of a *purpose* to assist or facili-tate the sale insufficient; thus the defect in *Johnson* may have been the prosecution's failure to prove that Johnson *intended* that his referral aid his codefendant in selling drugs to the undercover officer. If the prosecution failed to show that the defendant had anything to gain from the sale being successfully completed, perhaps the evidence did not support an inference that the defendant consciously wanted his referral to facilitate the sale. That these cases turn on proof of the required culpable mental state is suggested by another New York court's explanation for *upholding* a conviction in *People v. Fernandez,* 193 A.D. 406, 597 N.Y.S.2d 68 (1993): "Defendant's unprompted communication to the seller of his approval of the buyer, and his role as a lookout at the request of the seller, combined with his observed close interaction with the seller before, during and after the sale, creates a reasonable inference that defendant was acting intentionally to aid the seller in safely consummating the sale."

Other courts have had much less difficulty upholding convictions in what appear to be similar situations. This approach is illustrated by *Turner v. State,* 573 So.2d 1340 (Miss.1990). Undercover agent Lawrence Vaughan, assisted by confidential informant Anthony Cole, made a purchase of cocaine from Turner on May 18, 1989; Turner's conviction for this sale was affirmed in another appellate decision. On May 19, Vaughan and Cole returned to the same area—near the Cat's Den—to again meet Turner for another sale. Turner approached their car and told them that they were too late. The "package," he explained, "was too much stuff to hold" and he had therefore "sent the package back." Turner added that Vaughan and Cole should move on up the street and "someone would take care of [them]." Shortly thereafter, a woman named Betty Gandy approached Vaughan and Cole and sold them cocaine. Turner was con-victed of the sale by Gandy on the ground that he aided and abetted it. On appeal, Turner challenged the sufficiency of the evidence to support his conviction. Rejecting this, the court explained that the evidence was "more than legally sufficient" to show that Turner aided and abetted the sale actually made by Gandy. It then added:

[I]f we were to credit Turner's argument today, we would be opening a hole a mile
wide in our defenses against drug trafficking in this state. If on this evidence
Turner has committed no offense, it would be a simple matter for drug dealers to
send flunkies to make their deliveries and thus avoid prosecution and punishment.

It is not entirely clear that Turner specifically made the same argument as Johnson
apparently successfully asserted—that the prosecution was required but failed to prove
that he *intended* by his referral of the officer to the actual seller to facilitate the sale.
The court in *Turner* did note, however, that Turner argued that the evidence failed to
show that he received any pecuniary advantage from the sale and the court obviously
rejected this.

Perhaps cases such as *Johnson* reflect a perception on the part of some courts that
drug sale laws are exceptionally harsh. This, in turn, might suggest that those who are
only indirectly involved should not incur liability unless they participate in a more significant manner than is required generally by aiding and abetting liability. If this is the
case, however, decisions such as *Johnson* appear to implement this view by applying a
very rigorous requirement of proof that the defendant had the *purpose* of encouraging
or facilitating the sale.

B. LIABILITY UNDER THE COCONSPIRATOR RULE

Editors' Introduction: The Coconspirator Liability Rule

A number of jurisdictions provide, in addition to accessorial liability, that under certain circumstances one person is liable for an offense committed by another because
the two were both members of a criminal conspiracy.

The leading case adopting the doctrine that accomplishes this result (the *"Pinkerton
rule"*) is *Pinkerton v. United States,* 328 U.S. 640, 66 S.Ct. 1180, 90 L.Ed. 1489 (1946).
Walter and Daniel Pinkerton were convicted of criminal conspiracy to violate the
United States Internal Revenue Code and of a number of substantive violations of that
code. There was no evidence tending to show that Daniel participated in the commission of the offenses of which he was convicted. The jury had not been instructed on
his potential liability as an aider or abettor. Rather, it had been told that he could be
found guilty of crimes committed by Walter if at the time of the offenses both were
parties to a criminal conspiracy and Walter committed the offenses in furtherance of
this conspiracy. Upholding the convictions, the United States Supreme Court
explained:

We have here a continuous conspiracy. There is here no evidence of the affirmative action on the part of Daniel which is necessary to establish his withdrawal
from it. *Hyde v. United States,* 225 U.S. 347, 369, 32 S.Ct. 793, 803, 56 L.Ed.
1114, Ann.Cas.1914A, 614. As stated in that case, "having joined in an unlawful
scheme, having constituted agents for its performance, scheme and agency to be

continuous until full fruition be secured, until he does some act to disavow or defeat the purpose he is in no situation to claim the delay of the law. As the offense has not been terminated or accomplished, he is still offending. And we think consciously offending,—offending as certainly, as we have said, as at the first moment of his confederation, and consciously, through every moment of its existence." And so long as the partnership in crime continues, the partners act for each other in carrying it forward. It is settled that "an overt act of one partner may be the act of all without any new agreement specifically directed to that act." *United States v. Kissel,* 218 U.S. 601, 608, 31 S.Ct. 124, 126, 54 L.Ed. 1168. Motive or intent may be proved by the acts or declarations of some of the conspirators in furtherance of the common objective. A scheme to use the mails to defraud, which is joined in by more than one person, is a conspiracy. Yet all members are responsible, though only one did the mailing. The governing principle is the same when the substantive offense is committed by one of the conspirators in furtherance of the unlawful project. The criminal intent to do the act is established by the formation of the conspiracy. Each conspirator instigated the commission of the crime. The unlawful agreement contemplated precisely what was done. It was formed for the purpose. The act done was in execution of the enterprise. The rule which holds responsible one who counsels, procures, or commands another to commit a crime is founded on the same principle. That principle is recognized in the law of conspiracy when the overt act of one partner in crime is attributable to all. An overt act is an essential ingredient of the crime of conspiracy * * *. If that can be supplied by the act of one conspirator, we fail to see why the same or other acts in furtherance of the conspiracy are likewise not attributable to the others for the purpose of holding them responsible for the substantive offense.

A different case would arise if the substantive offense committed by one of the conspirators was not in fact done in furtherance of the conspiracy, did not fall within the scope of the unlawful project, or was merely a part of the ramifications of the plan which could not be reasonably foreseen as a necessary or natural consequence of the unlawful agreement. But as we read this record, that is not this case.

Some jurisdictions appear to have adopted the same approach but use different terminology. Illinois, for example, follows a "common design" rule, which permits the conviction of all participants of a "common criminal design or agreement" of any criminal acts committed by other members of the agreement in furtherance of the common design. See *People v. Terry,* 99 Ill.2d 508, 77 Ill.Dec. 442, 460 N.E.2d 746 (1984).

If accomplices can be convicted for foreseeable but unintended offenses committed by those whom they aid or encourage (see Section A of this chapter), does the *Pinkerton* rule really increase the liability of one who assists another in a criminal enterprise? The existence of *Pinkerton* liability obviously makes a difference in some cases. *United States v. Gallo,* 763 F.2d 1504 (6th Cir.1985), modified on reh., 774 F.2d 106 (6th Cir.1985), cert. denied, 475 U.S. 1017, 106 S.Ct. 1200, 89 L.Ed.2d 314 (1986), was a very complex prosecution for a variety of federal crimes arising out of organized gambling and drug activities in Cleveland. In addition to the appellant Fritz Graewe, the events involved, among others, Newman, Odom, and Hoven. Graewe was convicted of a number of substantive crimes, including several violations of the federal "Travel Act," 18 U.S.C.A. § 1952 (aiding racketeering through interstate travel) committed by Newman and Hoven and of possession of cocaine found in a rental car used by Odom. On appeal, his convictions were at first upheld on a *Pinkerton* theory. On rehearing, however, the appellate court was persuaded that the jury instructions had not adequately put this theory before the trial jury and therefore the *Pinkerton* rule could not be used to support those convictions. It nevertheless upheld Graewe's convictions for some substantive crimes on the grounds that the evidence showed he aided and abetted their commission. With regard to others, however, the court concluded that without the *Pinkerton* rule the evidence failed to support Graewe's guilt:

> There is no evidence that [Graewe] knew of, participated in, or otherwise aided and abetted in [the] Travel Act violations. * * * Similarly, * * * [n]o evidence directly linked [Graewe] to [the] rental car, and thus his conviction on [the possession of cocaine charge] also must fall.

There is still substantial support for the *Pinkerton* rule. In *State v. Barton,* 424 A.2d 1033 (R.I.1981), the Supreme Court of Rhode Island noted that it had adopted the same approach as the *Pinkerton* rule thirteen years before *Pinkerton* and that the rule was "sound and viable" as well as the majority approach. It continued:

> The *Pinkerton* rule has found favor with many states under a variety of theories. Under one view, vicarious liability is supported on the premise that criminal acts, apart from the object of the conspiracy, are dependent upon the encouragement and material support of the group as a whole and therefore justify treating each member of the conspiracy as an agent for the others. * * * Under another view, the *Pinkerton* rule is supported on the theory that group activity presents a greater potential threat to the public than individual action. * * * In a similar vein, others have suggested that conspiracy provides a vehicle whereby criminals will engage in more elaborate and complex schemes than they would attempt if working alone, and therefore such activity should be discouraged via the *Pinkerton* rule.

The *Pinkerton* rule has, however, been rejected by a number of courts. This is often on the technical ground that in revising statutory criminal codes, legislatures have provided in some detail for liability for crimes committed by others but have failed to provide for liability under the coconspirator rule. Thus, as the Arizona Supreme Court reasoned in *State ex rel. Woods v. Cohne,* 173 Ariz. 497, 844 P.2d 1147 (1992), the legislature must have intended that coconspirator liability for the crimes of others be abolished.

In *State v. Small,* 301 N.C. 407, 272 S.E.2d 128 (1980), the North Carolina Supreme Court reasoned more expansively that the coconspirator rule was weakly based:

> [T]he erroneous idea that a conspirator automatically becomes liable as a principal to all crimes committed as a result of or in furtherance of the illegal agreement has largely resulted from too broad a reading of case law statements which either

(1) discussed the application of the coconspirator rule as a rule of evidence [making the admissions of one conspirator admissible against the others], or (2) applied established principles of accomplice liability to evidence of conspiracy and preconcert.

The New York Court of Appeals in *People v. McGee,* 49 N.Y.2d 48, 424 N.Y.S.2d 157, 399 N.E.2d 1177 (1979), cert. denied, 446 U.S. 942, 100 S.Ct. 2167, 64 L.Ed.2d 797 (1980) added:

> [I]t is repugnant to our system of jurisprudence, where guilt is generally personal to the defendant, to impose punishment, not for the socially harmful agreement to which the defendant is a party, but for substantive offenses in which he did not participate.

A number of federal courts have indicated that imposition of liability under the *Pinkerton* analysis would violate the federal constitutional requirement of due process of law "where the relationship between the defendant and the substantive offense [for which the defendant is liable under *Pinkerton*] is slight." *United States v. Castaneda,* 9 F.3d 761, 766 (9th Cir.1993). In such situations, to find the substantive offense "foreseeable" under *Pinkerton* would be unconstitutional. Only in *Castaneda,* however, has a federal court found that due process was actually violated. Defendant Leticia Castaneda was a minor participant in an extensive heroin and cocaine distribution network; her husband Uriel was a much more active participant. Nevertheless, Leticia Castaneda was found guilty of seven violations of 18 U.S.C. § 924(c) (using or carrying a firearm in relation to a crime of drug trafficking) committed by other members of the network. Evidence showed only that Leticia answered the telephone at the home she shared with Uriel, taking messages from callers and passing those messages along to Uriel. Her role in the conspiracy was "passive," the court concluded, and she assisted Uriel "only insofar as she acted as his spouse." The seven firearms offenses committed by the others, the appellate tribunal concluded, could not be found foreseeable to Leticia without violating due process, and it therefore reversed her convictions for those offenses. Her conviction for the conspiracy itself, however, was upheld.

State v. Stein

Supreme Court of New Jersey, 1976
70 N.J. 369, 360 A.2d 347.

CONFORD, P.J.A.D., Temporarily Assigned.

This appeal emanates from * * * a judgment of the Appellate Division partly affirming and partly reversing a series of convictions of defendant arising from a number of connected occurrences. * * *

The evidence adduced on the State's case indicates that defendant, a Trenton lawyer, suggested to a certain underworld figure that the house of one Dr. Gordon in Trenton was a likely target for a successful breaking and entering or burglary, as large amounts of cash were kept there. Defendant expected to share in the gains. As a result, there was an armed robbery at that home about a year later. While attempting to evade the police, who had been alerted to the affair, the perpetrators abducted members of the family and injured two policemen. They were caught and arrested. * * *

[Defendant was charged with and convicted of conspiracy to steal currency, armed robbery, assault with an offensive weapon on Edith Gordon, assault with an offensive weapon on Shelly Gordon, kidnapping, kidnapping while armed, and assault on a police officer. He was] sentenced concurrently to terms of imprisonment aggregating 30 years to 30 years and one day.

On March 17, 1972 Testa and Stasio, impersonating police officers, gained entrance to the Trenton home of Dr. Arnold Gordon. The pair produced pistols and demanded money and jewelry from Gordon. While Testa and Stasio obtained $470 from Gordon and bound him and his wife Edith, a maid telephoned the police. When the police arrived, the robbers took Edith and her 14 year old daughter Shelly from the house at gunpoint as hostages and attempted an escape at high speed in a getaway car. A chase ensued. Ultimately, the getaway car crashed into a police car barrier, seriously injuring two police officers. The police arrested Testa and Stasio and freed Edith and Shelly. * * *

Subsequent investigation aroused the suspicions of the county prosecutor as to the possible involvement of others in the crime. Testa testified before the grand jury as follows: In September 1971 Joe Bradley introduced him to Pontani. Pontani gave Testa particulars about the layout of the Gordon home. Pontani wanted to be sure the children were not in the house at the time of the robbery. Pontani, Testa and Bradley met three times between September and October 18, 1971, the date of Bradley's death. Tassone was present on a few occasions. Testa stated that from the outset it was intended that the crime would be an armed robbery. Although burglary had been initially discussed, it was discarded as an impossibility. After Bradley's death, Pontani spoke to a lawyer who guaranteed the amount of money that would be in the house, the movements of the family and the layout of the telephone system. Pontani had indicated that the lawyer was "Jewish" and a close friend of the Gordons. Testa was present when Pontani telephoned the lawyer. The latter advised Pontani that $200,000 would be found in the house.

[The investigation led to defendant, who subsequently gave police a statement. In this statement,] Stein gave his age, 46, and stated that he was an attorney who was also engaged in real estate development. He became involved with Pontani as an attorney. Stein was introduced to Pontani by a woman, Wilson Marcello. Stein knew that Pontani was a professional secondstory man who was in financial difficulty. Stein was also in financial straits. It was suggested that if they could locate a home where there was cash, Pontani would burglarize the home. In the course of a casual "almost flippant" conversation on the subject, Stein ventured some names from the area in which he resided, including that of Dr. Gordon. Stein knew that Gordon, a

dentist, took cash home. He estimated the amount at less than $10,000 but he did not know where the money was kept. During the course of subsequent conversations over a long period of time, Stein, in response to Pontani's questions, offered such information as the number of people in the Gordon household and where and when the children went to school. Although there was no specific discussion as to Stein's share of the money to be stolen, Stein anticipated that he would participate therein. The attempted robbery occurred anywhere from 9 months to a year after the last conversation on the matter. After two months Stein assumed that no crime would occur. However, he did nothing in the interim to prevent it from happening. After the robbery and other crimes took place, Pontani advised Stein by telephone that the people who had tried to pull off the job had no right to do it, since "they had really in effect stolen information that he had given to another party [Joe Bradley] and that he had abandoned the idea long since." Pontani insisted he had nothing to do with it. Stein had assumed that any attempted larceny would be in the form of breaking and entering while the Gordons were away, not a "personal confrontation." He gave Pontani the information as to when the Gordons were on vacation. * * *

The Appellate Division reversed the convictions of the defendant on the substantive charges of assault with an offensive weapon (against Edith and Shelly Gordon), kidnapping, kidnapping while armed and assaults on a police officer. It sustained that of armed robbery. The former were deemed not within the scope of the original conspiracy * * *. We review this ruling * * *.

The question as to the criminal responsibility of a conspirator for the commission by others of substantive offenses having some causal connection with the conspiracy but not in the contemplation of the conspirator has been a matter of considerable debate and controversy. Here there is no question but that Stein did not actually contemplate any criminal consequence of his "tip" to Pontani beyond a burglary and theft of money from the Gordon home. The trial court applied the conventionally stated rule that each conspirator is responsible for "anything done by his confederates which follows incidentally in the execution of the common design as one of its probable and natural consequences, even though it was not intended as part of the original design."

We regard the rule as just stated to be sound and viable. * * * We hold it represents the law of this State.

It remains to apply the rule to the instant fact situation. Ordinarily the matter of factual application of the rule would be submitted to the jury under appropriate instructions. Here the matter was for the trial judge in the first instance as fact-finder. The Appellate Division found correct the trial ruling that the armed robbery was within the scope

Rationale

Rationale

of the conspiracy to steal currency from the Gordon home. We are in agreement. The robbery was a "natural" or "probable" consequence of the conspiracy. But the Appellate Division concluded that the assaults with an offensive weapon on the wife and daughter of Dr. Gordon were "not connected with the robbery as such" but "with the preliminary acts of taking the Gordons as hostages and the eventual kidnappings" and therefore "not fairly * * * part of the conspiratorial agreement". The assault convictions were therefore set aside.

We are not in complete agreement with this last determination. The brandishing of handguns by the robbers when they first encountered Dr. and Mrs. Gordon in the house was clearly a foreseeable event in the course of an unlawful invasion of the house for criminal purposes by armed men. * * * Thus the assault conviction as to Mrs. Gordon should not have been set aside as too remote from the conspiracy.

As to the charge of assault with an offensive weapon on Shelly Gordon (daughter of the Gordons), since the evidence indicates that offense occurred only at the time of the attempted escape from the police, its disposition depends on the determination as to the other associated charges, discussed next below.

Liability of the defendant for the kidnapping, kidnapping while armed and assaults on a police officer presents a much closer question. The Appellate Division held that these substantive acts were "offenses committed by the criminals effecting the conspiratorial specific crime after that crime had been committed, as part of a plan to flee when it became evident that they were about to be apprehended" and that defendant could not be charged therefor. On balance, we are satisfied that this is a correct result, particularly in relation to the kidnapping phases of the episode. This holding will also apply to the reversal by the Appellate Division of the conviction for assault with an offensive weapon on Shelly Gordon. However, we rest our concurrence with the Appellate Division not on the ground that the substantive offenses took place subsequent to the commission of the crime conspired or that the offenses were part of a plan to flee, but rather that it would be unreasonable for a fact-finder to find as a fact beyond a reasonable doubt that they were necessary, natural or probable consequences of the conspiracy, having in mind the unique fact-complex presented.

[The charges of kidnapping, kidnapping while armed, assault on an officer, and assault on Shelly Gordon are to be dismissed. Defendant could be validly convicted on the charges of conspiracy, armed robbery and assault on Edith Gordon, but because there was procedural error in the trial (not discussed here) he is entitled to a new trial on these charges. The case is thus remanded for a new trial on those charges.]

Notes and Questions

1. *In State v. Bridges,* 133 N.J. 447, 628 A.2d 270 (1993), the *Stein* court reaffirmed the vitality of the coconspirator rule under a revised statutory version of criminal conspiracy. It also held that juries should be told to consider whether substantive crimes committed by other conspirators were objectively foreseeable "and whether the substantive crime occurred or was committed in a manner that was too far removed or too remote from the objectives of the original conspiracy." Apparently (although this is not entirely clear) the second inquiry that *Bridges* directed juries to make is more flexible than the foreseeability standard and permits a jury to refuse to convict a defendant on the ground that the substantive crime committed by a coconspirator was not "sufficiently connected to the original conspirational plan to provide a just basis for a determination of guilt for that substantive crime."

2. The case law often assumes that if a conspirator effectively withdraws from a conspiracy before a crime is committed by a coconspirator, the withdrawal—even if it is not defense to the criminal conspiracy—precludes liability under the *Pinkerton* rule for the substantive offense committed by a coconspirator. However, it is not entirely clear what is necessary to make a withdrawal effective for this purpose.

   Collins v. State, 561 P.2d 1373 (Okl.Crim.App.), cert. denied, 434 U.S. 906, 98 S.Ct. 306, 54 L.Ed.2d 193 (1977), illustrates the matter. Collins was charged with a murder arising out of a burglary-murder episode. Some evidence tended to show that Collins' codefendant (and coconspirator) Prowess held a gun on the victims while Collins bound them. Several times Collins said, "Let's get out of here." When Prowess told him to get the car, Collins ran from the house. Prowess then shot the victims and killed them. The trial court refused to instruct the jury on any possible abandonment by Collins of the venture before the killings by Prowess. Affirming, the appellate court explained:

   > [I]n order to successfully abandon the scheme [a] party must communicate to the others involved his intention to do so. * * * [T]he defendant at no point told Jerry Prowess he was withdrawing; he left only upon Prowess' instructions to get the car.

Where the defendant's action is sufficient to indicate an intention to withdraw from the venture, it is generally assumed that this "notice" must be actually communicated to *all* other members of the conspiracy before it becomes effective. In two-person situations such as *Collins,* this is unlikely to be a problem. In more complex arrangements involving many individuals, however, such full communication to all other persons involved may present a difficult or perhaps impossible task.

According to some courts, withdrawal requires more than a communicated notice indicating an intent to withdraw. See *United States v. Quesada-Rosadal,* 685 F.2d 1281, 1284 (11th Cir.1982), which indicated that effective withdrawal requires some affirmative action to defeat or disavow the purpose of the conspiracy. It has also been suggested that a withdrawal must occur before the commission of the crime by the coconspirator "becomes so imminent that avoidance is out of the question." *Commonwealth v. Laurin,* 269 Pa.Super. 368, 372, 409 A.2d 1367, 1369 (1979).

C. LIABILITY FOR ASSISTANCE AFTER THE FACT

Editors' Introductory Note: Postcrime Assistance

As discussed in the Editors' Introduction to this chapter, the common law of parties made an accessory after the fact a party to the crime and punishable as if he had himself committed it. Modern criminal codes have abandoned this approach. One who provides postcrime assistance is not thereby rendered liable for the crime that was committed by the person assisted. However, such a person is often guilty of a separate offense.

Title 18 of the United States Code, for example, uses common law party terminology but a much different substantive approach than was followed under the law of parties. The statute creates a separate offense, although the penalty is tied to the penalty affixed to the crime committed by the person assisted.

§ 3. Accessory after the fact

Whoever, knowing that an offense against the United States has been committed, receives, comforts or assists the offender in order to hinder or prevent his apprehension, trial or punishment is an accessory after the fact.

* * * [A]n accessory after the fact shall be imprisoned not more than one-half the maximum term of imprisonment or fined not more than one-half the maximum fine prescribed for the punishment of the principal, or both; or if the principal is punishable by death, the accessory shall be imprisoned for not more than ten years.

The federal statute uses old common law terminology, at least as the name for the offense. A quite different approach was taken by the Model Penal Code, which proposed the following offense:

Section 242.3. Hindering Apprehension or Prosecution

A person commits an offense if, with purpose to hinder the apprehension, prosecution, conviction or punishment of another for crime, he:

(1) harbors or conceals the other; or

(2) provides or aids in providing a weapon, transportation, disguise or other means of avoiding apprehension or effecting escape; or

(3) conceals or destroys evidence of the crime, or tampers with a witness, informant, document or other source of information, regardless of its admissibility in evidence; or

(4) warns the other of impending discovery or apprehension, except that this paragraph does not apply to a warning given in connection with an effort to bring another into compliance with law; or

(5) volunteers false information to a law enforcement officer.

The offense is a felony of the third degree if the conduct which the actor knows has been charged or is liable to be charged against the person aided would be a felony of the first or second degree. Otherwise it is a misdemeanor.

Some cases give rise to difficulty in determining whether assistance was provided at such a time as to render the assisting person a participant in the offense or, instead, liable only under provisions such as 18 U.S.C.A. § 3. This is obviously important. If a person provides assistance *during* the offense, he is guilty of the crime and subject to the full penalty attaching to the offense. If he assists the perpetrator *after* the offense, he is subject to what is generally a much lower penalty. There is agreement that in order to create liability for the offense itself the assistance or encouragement must occur either before the crime or while it is in process. If one assists in the escape of another known to have committed an offense, on the other hand, he is properly convicted as accessory after the fact or under modern statutory equivalents. *United States v. Balano,* 618 F.2d 624, 631 (10th Cir.1979), cert. denied, 449 U.S. 840, 101 S.Ct. 118, 66 L.Ed.2d 47 (1980).

However, despite the technical completion of the offense, for purposes of this analysis offenses are sometimes regarded as having "escape phases." One who assists the perpetrator during this "escape phase" joins the offense. Thus, persons like getaway car drivers are regarded as "entangled in the consummation of the crime itself" and properly charged with complicity in it. For example, in *United States v. Willis,* 559 F.2d 443 (5th Cir.1977), according to Willis, the evidence showed only that he took the other participants to the bank and, when they ran out after robbing it, drove them away. The court assumed that the facts failed to show Willis' guilty knowledge of the others' purpose until they ran out of the bank and into the waiting car. It held, however, that Willis had been properly convicted of aiding and abetting the robbery because of his role as driver of the getaway car. For purposes of characterizing the involvement of those who join in the "escape phase" only, the court noted, the crime of robbery continues throughout the escape.

If, on the other hand, the day after the robbery the perpetrators had come to Willis' home seeking assistance and he had then assisted them in fleeing to Brazil, he almost certainly would have violated only 18 U.S.C.A. § 3. In part, confusion in this area is due to the use of "escape" in two different senses. The flight of the perpetrators to Brazil in the hypothetical may be referred to as an "escape." However, this must be distinguished from the "escape phase" of the robbery itself. Assistance provided to the perpetrators during this "escape phase" creates liability for the robbery itself.

State v. Chism

Supreme Court of Louisiana, 1983
436 So.2d 464.

DENNIS, JUSTICE.

The defendant, Brian Chism, was convicted by a judge of being an accessory after the fact, and sentenced to three years in the parish prison, with two and one-half years suspended. The defendant was placed upon supervised probation for two years. * * *

On the evening of August 26, 1981 in Shreveport, Tony Duke gave the defendant, Brian Chism, a ride in his automobile. Brian Chism was impersonating a female, and Duke was apparently unaware of Chism's disguise. After a brief visit at a friend's house the two stopped to pick up some beer at the residence of Chism's grandmother. Chism's one-legged uncle, Ira Lloyd, joined them, and the three continued on their way, drinking as Duke drove the automobile. When Duke expressed a desire to have sexual relations with Chism, Lloyd announced that he wanted to find his ex-wife Gloria for the same purpose. Shortly after midnight, the trio arrived at the St. Vincent Avenue Church of Christ and persuaded Gloria Lloyd to come outside. As Ira Lloyd stood outside the car attempting to persuade Gloria to come with them, Chism and Duke hugged and kissed on the front seat as Duke sat behind the steering wheel.

Gloria and Ira Lloyd got into an argument, and Ira stabbed Gloria with a knife several times in the stomach and once in the neck. Gloria's shouts attracted the attention of two neighbors, who unsuccessfully tried to prevent Ira from pushing Gloria into the front seat of the car alongside Chism and Duke. Ira Lloyd climbed into the front seat also, and Duke drove off. One of the bystanders testified that she could not be sure but she thought she saw Brian's foot on the accelerator as the car left.

Lloyd ordered Duke to drive to Willow Point, near Cross Lake. When they arrived Chism and Duke, under Lloyd's direction, removed Gloria from the vehicle and placed her on some high grass on the side of the roadway, near a wood line. Ira was unable to help the two because his wooden leg had come off. Afterwards, as Lloyd requested, the two drove off, leaving Gloria with him.

There was no evidence that Chism or Duke protested, resisted or attempted to avoid the actions which Lloyd ordered them to take. Although Lloyd was armed with a knife, there was no evidence that he threatened either of his companions with harm.

Duke proceeded to drop Chism off at a friend's house, where he changed to male clothing. He placed the blood-stained women's clothes in a trash bin. Afterward, Chism went with his mother to the police station at 1:15 A.M. He gave the police a complete statement, and took the officers to the place where Gloria had been left with Ira Lloyd. The police found Gloria's body in some tall grass several feet from that spot. An autopsy indicated that stab wounds had caused her death. Chism's discarded clothing disappeared before the police arrived at the trash bin.

An accessory after the fact is any person, who, after the commission of a felony, shall harbor, conceal, or aid the offender, knowing or having reasonable ground to believe that he has committed the felony, and with the intent that he may avoid or escape from arrest, trial, conviction, or punishment. La.R.S. 14:25.

* * *

[W]e conclude that a person may be punished as an accessory after the fact if he aids an offender personally, knowing or having reasonable ground to believe that he has committed the felony, and has a specific or general intent that the offender will avoid or escape from arrest, trial, conviction, or punishments.[2] See W. Lafave & A. Scott, Criminal Law § 66 at 522–23 (1972); R. Perkins, Criminal Law § 8.4 at 667 (2d ed. 1969).

An accessory after the fact may be tried and convicted [under Louisiana law], notwithstanding the fact that the principal felon may not have been arrested, or amenable to justice. However, it is still necessary to prove the guilt of the principal beyond a reasonable doubt, and an accessory after the fact cannot be convicted or punished where the princi-

---

[2] The Louisiana offense, therefore, is a compromise between the traditional common law crime of accessory after the fact, which required actual knowledge of a completed crime plus specific intent to aid the felon avoid justice, and the emerging modern trend, which recharacterizes the offense of accessory after the fact as obstruction of justice, and which dispenses with the requirement of a completed felony and knowledge of that fact by the accessory, allowing for conviction so long as the obstructive purpose is present. See A.L.I., Model Penal Code, part 2, article 242.3 and comment 3 (1980).

pal felon has been acquitted. Furthermore, it is essential to prove that a felony was committed and completed prior to the time the assistance was rendered the felon, although it is not also necessary that the felon have been already charged with the crime.

Defendant appealed from his conviction and sentence and argues that the evidence was not sufficient to support the judgment. Consequently, in reviewing the defendant's assigned error, we must determine whether, after viewing the evidence in the light most favorable to the prosecution, any rational trier of fact could have found beyond a reasonable doubt that (a) a completed felony had been committed by Ira Lloyd before Brian Chism rendered him the assistance described below; (b) Chism knew or had reasonable grounds to know of the commission of the felony by Lloyd, and (c) Chism gave aid to Lloyd personally under circumstances that indicate either that he actively desired that the felon avoid or escape arrest, trial, conviction, or punishment or that he believed that one of these consequences was substantially certain to result from his assistance.

There was clearly enough evidence to justify the finding that a felony had been completed before any assistance was rendered to Lloyd by the defendant. The record vividly demonstrates that Lloyd fatally stabbed his ex-wife before she was transported to Willow Point and left in the high grass near a wood line. Thus, Lloyd committed the felonies of attempted murder, aggravated battery, and simple kidnapping, before Chism aided him in any way. A person cannot be convicted as an accessory after the fact to a murder because of aid given after the murderer's acts but before the victim's death, but under these circumstances the aider may be found to be an accessory after the fact to the felonious assault. * * *

The evidence overwhelmingly indicates that Chism had reasonable grounds to believe that Lloyd had committed a felony before any assistance was rendered. In his confessions and his testimony Chism indicates that the victim was bleeding profusely when Lloyd pushed her into the vehicle, that she was limp and moaned as they drove to Willow Point, and that he knew Lloyd had inflicted her wounds with a knife. The Louisiana offense of accessory after the fact deviates somewhat from the original common law offense in that it does not require that the defendant actually know that a completed felony has occurred. Rather, it incorporates an objective standard by requiring only that the defendant render aid "knowing or having reasonable grounds to believe" that a felony has been committed.

The closest question presented is whether any reasonable trier of fact could have found beyond a reasonable

doubt that Chism assisted Lloyd under circumstances that indicate that either Chism actively desired that Lloyd would avoid or escape arrest, trial, conviction, or punishment, or that Chism believed that one of these consequences was substantially certain to result from his assistance. After carefully reviewing the record, we conclude that the prosecution satisfied its burden of producing the required quantity of evidence.

* * * Despite evidence supporting some contrary inferences, a trier of fact reasonably could have found that Chism acted with at least a general intent to help Lloyd avoid arrest because: (1) Chism did not protest or attempt to leave the car when his uncle, Lloyd, shoved the mortally wounded victim inside; (2) he did not attempt to persuade Duke, his would-be lover, exit out the driver's side of the car and flee from his uncle, whom he knew to be one-legged and armed only with a knife; (3) he did not take any of these actions at any point during the considerable ride to Willow Point; (4) at their destination, he docilely complied with Lloyd's directions to remove the victim from the car and leave Lloyd with her, despite the fact that Lloyd made no threats and that his wooden leg had become detached; (5) after leaving Lloyd with the dying victim, he made no immediate effort to report the victim's whereabouts or to obtain emergency medical treatment for her; (6) before going home or reporting the victim's dire condition he went to a friend's house, changed clothing and discarded his own in a trash bin from which the police were unable to recover them as evidence; (7) he went home without reporting the victim's condition or location; (8) and he went to the police station to report the crime only after arriving home and discussing the matter with his mother.

* * *

Therefore, we affirm the defendant's conviction. * * *

DIXON, CHIEF JUSTICE (dissenting).

I respectfully dissent from what appears to be a finding of guilt by association. The majority lists five instances of inaction, or failure to act, by defendant: (1) did not protest or leave the car; (2) did not attempt to persuade Duke to leave the car; (3) did neither (1) nor (2) on [the] ride to Willow Point; (5) made no immediate effort to report crime or get aid for the victim; (7) failed to report victim's condition or location after changing clothes. The three instances of defendant's action relied on by the majority for conviction were stated to be: (4) complying with Lloyd's direction to remove the victim from the car and leave the victim and Lloyd at Willow Point; (6) changing clothes and discarding bloody garments; and (8) discussing the matter with defendant's mother before going to the police station to report the crime.

None of these actions or failures to act tended to prove defendant's intent, specifically or generally, to aid defendant avoid arrest, trial, conviction or punishment.

Notes and Questions

1. Another means of addressing conduct after the commission of an offense by another has traditionally been the offense of misprision of felony. As the Supreme Court of South Carolina noted in *State v. Carson*, 274 S.C. 316, 262 S.E.2d 918 (1980), the common law offense of this name consisted of a criminal neglect either to prevent a felony from being committed or to bring an offender to justice (as by coming forward to authorities), but without the sort of previous relationship with the offender as to make the person an accessory before the fact and without providing the sort of assistance to the offender as would make the person an accessory after the fact. Modern state statutes sometimes create a misdemeanor of misprision of felony and the offense is incorporated into the following provision of Title 18 of the United States Code:

> § 4. Misprision of felony
> Whoever, having knowledge of the actual commission of a felony cognizable by a court of the United States, conceals and does not as soon as possible make known the same to some judge or other person in civil or military authority under the United States, shall be fined not more than $500 or imprisoned not more than three years, or both.

The common law offense may have been committed by mere failure to inform authorities of the commission of a felony by another, but American courts have tended to construe statutory crimes of this sort as requiring some "active" concealment of the offender. In *Carson,* for example, the defendant was shown to have witnessed a murder and to have left the scene upon arrival of police. In addition, however, when police located and questioned him, he denied being present at the murder or having any information, and when he later made a statement to police he admitted being present but provided no information regarding the perpetrator. Upholding his conviction for misprision of felony, the court described the proof as showing that he was "a witness who concealed valuable information from investigating officers."

American courts have overwhelmingly and perhaps uniformly interpreted not only misprision of felony crimes but similar offenses as requiring more than mere passive failure to come forward with information. In *People v. Donelson,* 45 Ill.App.3d 609, 359 N.E.2d 1225, 4 Ill.Dec. 273 (1977), the court reversed a conviction for a statutory offense consisting of concealing an offender where the proof showed only that the defendant was told by one Devault that Devault had committed a burglary and then took no affirmative act to come forward with that information. The court noted no evidence tending to show that Donelson had lied to anyone about the matter or even that had refused to answer questions about it. After surveying the case law, the court reported, it had not been able to find a single case in any American jurisdiction directly holding that a person commits any criminal offense by merely remaining silent as to the commission of an offense.

Should there be criminal liability for mere failure to come forward with information regarding others' guilt of at least serious crimes? Goldberg, *Misprision of Felony: An Old Concept in a New Context,* 52 A.B.A.J. 148 (1966), argued that a properly limited duty of this sort would be desirable:

> It may be * * * objected that a legal duty to report criminal acts to the authorities would be so novel in most American jurisdictions that even responsible citizens would unavoidably break the law. But all Americans are familiar with their legal duty to report serious traffic accidents to the police. It is about time we consider violent assault on persons as important as automobile crashes.

Legislation has frequently created a duty to report acts of child abuse or abuse of disabled persons, and failure to do so is often made a crime. American legislatures have been unwilling, however, to criminalize mere failure to report criminal acts.

2. Many of the offenses governing postcrime assistance have exceptions covering assistance to relatives. A New Mexico statute defining such an offense, for example, provides:

> Harboring or aiding a felon consists of any person, not standing in the relation of husband or wife, parent or grandparent, child or grandchild, brother or sister by consanguinity or

affinity, who knowingly conceals any offender or gives such offender any other aid, knowing that he has committed a felony, with the intent that he escape or avoid arrest, trial, conviction or punishment.

N.M.Stat.Ann. § 30-224. The rationale for a similar provision in a Florida statute was explained as follows:

The statute represents a legislatively determined balance between two competing societal interests. The first is society's interest in appre-
hending suspected offenders. The second is society's interest in safeguarding the family unit from unnecessary fractional pressures. [The statute] achieves a balance between these two goals by restricting its application to a select group of family members and by conferring immunity so that these individuals need never choose between love of family and obedience to the law.

State v. C.H., 421 So.2d 62, 65 (Fla.App.1982).

Part 3

Substantive Elements of Crimes

Chapter 7

HOMICIDE: GRADING THE CRIMINAL CAUSATION OF DEATH

CHAPTER CONTENTS

Editors' Introduction: The Distinctions Among the Homicide Offenses

The homicide offenses present an almost unique situation in the criminal law. All, of course, are based upon defendants' liability for the deaths of other persons. However, the existence of several (or more) different crimes all based upon the fact of causing death reflects recognition of a need to distinguish among killings according to varying degrees of culpability of the killer and perhaps according to the danger that the killer presents of future additional killings or assaultive criminal acts. In order to accomplish this need to distinguish, virtually all jurisdictions recognize several homicide offenses that differ from each other in terms of the state of mind required and to some extent by the presence of certain circumstances.

Grading offenses according to culpability and dangerousness and doing this by carefully defining state of mind requirements and attendant mitigating circumstances, of course, is not unique to homicide. However, the perceived need to create so many different offenses—constituting in effect graded degrees of criminal liability for the single crime of killing another person—has made homicide law stand out as posing an especially difficult task for the law.

Modern criminal homicide's pattern is the result of a complicated historical development, as was explained in *Comber v. United States,* 584 A.2d 26, 35–36 (D.C.Ct. App.1990):

> "What we now know as murder and manslaughter constituted just one offense under the common law of England." R. PERKINS & R. BOYCE, CRIMINAL LAW 125 (3d ed. 1982). At the turn of the sixteenth century, all homicides, with the exception of accidental homicides, homicides committed in self-defense, or homicides committed "in the enforcement of justice," "were deemed unlawful and were punished by death." The harsh effects of this regime were mitigated, however, by the extension of ecclesiastic jurisdiction. Ecclesiastic courts, which retained jurisdiction to try clerics accused of criminal offenses, did not impose capital punishment. Rather, under ecclesiastic law, a person who committed an unlawful homicide "received a one-year sentence, had his thumb branded and was required to forfeit his goods." The transfer of a case from the secular to the ecclesiastic jurisdiction, a procedural device known as "benefit of clergy," thus "resulted in leniency

of the most important sort." Moreover, "[b]y the fifteenth century, the courts began to accept proof of literacy as the test for clerical status, with the result that benefit of clergy became a 'massive fiction' that 'tempered in practice the harshness of the common law rule that virtually all felonies were capital offenses.'"

Perhaps because of concern about "the accretion of ecclesiastic jurisdiction at the expense of the secular," or perhaps because "'the number of serious offenses appeared to increase,'" England's monarchs, beginning in the late fifteenth century and into the first half of the sixteenth, enacted a series of statutes which excluded a class of the most heinous homicides from benefit of clergy. These killings were referred to in the various statutes as "willful prepense murders," "murder upon malice prepensed," and "murder of malice prepensed." 3 J. STEPHEN, A HISTORY OF THE CRIMINAL LAW OF ENGLAND 44 (1883). "Unlawful homicides that were committed without such malice were designated 'manslaughter,' and their perpetrators remained eligible for benefit of clergy." The offenses encompassed by the new statutes were designated "murder"; perpetrators of these offenses were subject to secular jurisdiction and capital punishment. This distinction between murder and manslaughter persisted "[e]ven after ecclesiastic jurisdiction was eliminated for all secular offenses." These early statutory developments thus led to the division of criminal homicides into murder, which retained its status as a capital crime, and the lesser offense of manslaughter. The courts defined murder in terms of the evolving concept of "malice aforethought" and treated manslaughter as a residual category for all other criminal homicides. MODEL PENAL CODE § 210.3 comment 1, at 44 (Official Draft and Revised Comments 1980) (footnotes omitted).

This evolution continued:

The broad and undifferentiated early definition of manslaughter created pressure for refinement. In the same way that the early common law concept of unlawful homicide had evolved into murder and manslaughter, so too did manslaughter divide into separate categories of voluntary and involuntary manslaughter, depending on the type of conduct involved. The distinction between the two varieties of manslaughter was noted by Blackstone as early as 1769. * * * [T]his distinction was based at least in part on the perception that voluntary manslaughters ordinarily involve more culpable behavior than involuntary manslaughters, and that voluntary manslaughter frequently warrants a more severe sentence than involuntary manslaughter. 2 W. LAFAVE & A. SCOTT, [SUBSTANTIVE CRIMINAL LAW] § 7.9, at 251 [(1986)] * * *, § 7.9, at 251 ("[t]oday many American jurisdictions maintain the old distinction between voluntary and involuntary manslaughter, usually awarding a less severe punishment for involuntary than for voluntary manslaughter").

Both voluntary and involuntary manslaughter may still be accurately defined as "homicide[s] without malice aforethought on the one hand and without justification or excuse on the other." The two offenses are distinguishable by virtue of the perpetrator's state of mind; specifically, the difference between the two offenses lies in the basis for concluding that the perpetrator acted without malice aforethought. * * * [I]n all voluntary manslaughters, the perpetrator acts with a state of mind which, but for the presence of legally recognized mitigating circumstances, would constitute malice aforethought, as the phrase has been defined for purposes of second-degree murder. All involuntary manslaughters, in contrast, are killings in which the perpetrator's state of mind, without any consideration of any issues of mitigation, would not constitute malice aforethought.

The need to distinguish among the homicide offenses may have been somewhat reduced by recently imposed constitutional limits on capital punishment. The creation of a separate offense of first degree murder in many American jurisdictions was motivated in large part by what was seen as the need to identify those killings for which death would be the appropriate and sometimes mandatory penalty. However, it is now clear that the Eighth Amendment prohibition against cruel and unusual punishment prohibits a mandatory penalty of death for any particular homicide crime, *Woodson v. North Carolina,* 428 U.S. 280, 96 S.Ct. 2978, 49 L.Ed.2d 944 (1976), *Roberts v. Louisiana,* 428 U.S. 325, 96 S.Ct. 3001, 49 L.Ed.2d 974 (1976), and that the death penalty may be imposed only if the sentencing authority is permitted to consider a wide variety of possibly mitigating considerations relating to the offense and the offender. Thus there is less need to use the definition of the homicide crimes to identify those killers deserving maximum harshness.

Although homicide law is to a large extent a matter of statute in most jurisdictions, many statutes retain to a greater or lesser extent the flavor and substance of common law distinctions. This chapter first presents several typical statutory schemes for grading criminal homicide. It then examines the traditional distinctions among murder, premeditated murder, voluntary manslaughter, and involuntary manslaughter. Finally, the last section of this chapter considers what are in a sense forms of strict liability for homicide: felony murder and misdemeanor manslaughter.

> Homicide offenses sometimes give rise to difficult questions of causation
> based on the links between defendants' actions and the deaths of the victims.
> Causation is a more general aspect of criminal liability, however, and therefore
> it is treated separately in Chapter 5.

A. STATUTORY FORMULATIONS

As in most areas, statutory homicide schemes vary from jurisdiction to jurisdiction. Moreover, there is a discernible difference between modern schemes and more traditional ones, which embody with varying degrees of specificity old common law concepts and terminology. This section presents one scheme of each sort.

1. The California Penal Code:
A Traditional Approach

This subsection reprints those sections of the California Penal Code that create and define homicide offenses. Amendments, primarily in 1981, added to several of these sections language designed to eliminate or minimize the "defense" of diminished capacity as that developed in the California case law. The diminished capacity case law and the responsive portions of sections 188 and 189 of the California Penal Code are discussed in Chapter 15 on pages 524–529.

CALIFORNIA PENAL CODE

§ 187. Murder defined; death of fetus

(a) Murder is the unlawful killing of a human being, or a fetus, with malice aforethought.

(b) This section shall not apply to any person who commits an act which results in the death of a fetus if any of the following apply:

(1) The act complied with the Therapeutic Abortion Act * * *.

(2) The act was committed by a holder of a physician's and surgeon's certificate * * * in a case where, to a medical certainty, the result of a childbirth would be death of the mother of the fetus or where her death from childbirth, although not medically certain, would be substantially certain or more likely than not.

(3) The act was solicited, aided, abetted, or consented to by the mother of the fetus.

§ 188. Malice, express malice, and implied malice defined

Malice Defined. Such malice may be express or implied. It is express when there is manifested a deliberate intention unlawfully to take away the life of a fellow creature. It is implied, when no considerable provocation appears, or when the circumstances attending the killing show an abandoned and malignant heart.

§ 189. Murder, degrees

All murder which is perpetrated by means of a destructive device or explosive, poison, lying in wait, torture, or by any other kind of willful, deliberate, and premeditated killing, or which is committed in the perpetration of, or attempt to perpetrate, arson, rape, carjacking, robbery, burglary, mayhem, or any act punishable under Section 288 [prohibiting "any lewd or lascivious act * * * upon or with the body, or any part or member thereof, of a child under the age of fourteen years, with the intent of arousing, appealing to, or gratifying the lust or passions or sexual desires of such person or of such child * * * "], or any murder which is perpetrated by means of discharging a firearm from a motor vehicle, intentionally at another person outside of the vehicle with the intent to inflict death, is murder of the first degree: and all other kinds of murders are of the second degree.

§ 190. Murder, punishment; discretion of jury

Every person guilty of murder in the first degree shall suffer death, confinement in state prison for life without possibility of parole, or confinement in state prison for life. * * * [Subject to certain exceptions,] every person guilty of murder in the second degree is punishable by imprisonment in the state prison for a term of 15 years to life.

§ 192. Manslaughter, voluntary, involuntary, and in driving a vehicle defined, construction of section

Manslaughter is the unlawful killing of a human being, without malice. It is of three kinds:

1. Voluntary—upon a sudden quarrel or heat of passion.

2. Involuntary—in the commission of an unlawful act, not amounting to felony; or in the commission of a lawful act which might produce death, in an unlawful manner, or without due caution and circumspection. This subdivision shall not apply to acts committed in the driving of a vehicle.

3. Vehicular—

   (1) * * * [D]riving a vehicle in the commission of an unlawful act, not amounting to felony, and with gross negligence; or driving a vehicle in the commission of a lawful act which might produce death, in an unlawful manner, and with gross negligence.

   (2) * * * [D]riving a vehicle in the commission of an unlawful act, not amounting to felony, but without gross negligence; or driving a vehicle in the commission of a lawful act which might produce death, in an unlawful manner, but without gross negligence.

* * *

This section shall not be construed as making any homicide in the driving of a vehicle punishable which is not a proximate result of the commission of an unlawful act, not amounting to felony, or of the commission of a lawful act which might produce death, in an unlawful manner.

"Gross negligence," as used in this section, shall not be construed as prohibiting or precluding a charge of murder under Section 188 upon facts exhibiting wantonness and a conscious disregard for life to support a finding of implied malice, or upon facts showing malice, consistent with the holding of the California Supreme Court in *People v. Watson*, 30 Cal.3d 290.

§ 193. Voluntary manslaughter, involuntary manslaughter and vehicular manslaughter; punishment

(a) Voluntary manslaughter is punishable by imprisonment in the state prison for three, six, or eleven years.

(b) Involuntary manslaughter is punishable by imprisonment in the state prison for two, three, or four years.

(c) Vehicular manslaughter is punishable as follows:

   (1) A violation of paragraph (1) of subdivision (c) of Section 192 is punishable either by imprisonment in the county jail for not more than one year or by imprisonment in the state prison for two, four, or six years.

   (2) A violation of paragraph (2) of subdivision (c) of Section 192 is punishable by imprisonment in the county jail for not more than one year.

2. The Model Penal Code: A Modern Statutory Approach

The homicide provisions of the Model Penal Code, reprinted in this subsection, have provided the basis for many modern statutory revisions.

MODEL PENAL CODE*

Official Draft 1985

ARTICLE 210. CRIMINAL HOMICIDE

Section 210.0. Definitions

In Articles 210–213, unless a different meaning plainly is required:

(1) "human being" means a person who has been born and is alive;

(2) "bodily injury" means physical pain, illness or any impairment of physical condition;

(3) "serious bodily injury" means bodily injury which creates a substantial risk of death or which causes serious, permanent disfigurement, or protracted loss or impairment of the function of any bodily member or organ;

(4) "deadly weapon" means any firearm, or other weapon, device, instrument, material or substance, whether animate or inanimate, which in the manner it is used or is intended to be used is known to be capable of producing death or serious bodily injury.

Section 210.1. Criminal Homicide

(1) A person is guilty of criminal homicide if he purposely, knowingly, recklessly or negligently causes the death of another human being.

(2) Criminal homicide is murder, manslaughter or negligent homicide.

Section 210.2. Murder

(1) Except as provided in Section 210.3(l)(b), criminal homicide constitutes murder when:

    (a) it is committed purposely or knowingly; or

    (b) it is committed recklessly under circumstances manifesting extreme indifference to the value of human life. Such recklessness and indifference are presumed if the actor is engaged or is an accomplice in the commission of, or an attempt to commit, or flight after committing or attempting to commit robbery, rape or deviate sexual intercourse by force or threat of force, arson, burglary, kidnapping or felonious escape.

---

(2) Murder is a felony of the first degree [but a person convicted of murder may be sentenced to death, as provided in Section 210.6].

Section 210.3. Manslaughter

(1) Criminal homicide constitutes manslaughter when:

    (a) it is committed recklessly; or

    (b) a homicide which would otherwise be murder is committed under the influence of extreme mental or emotional disturbance for which there is reasonable explanation or excuse. The reasonableness of such explanation or excuse shall be determined from the viewpoint of a person in the actor's situation under the circumstances as he believes them to be.

(2) Manslaughter is a felony of the second degree.

Section 210A. Negligent Homicide

(1) Criminal homicide constitutes negligent homicide when it is committed negligently.

(2) Negligent homicide is a felony of the third degree.

Notes and Questions

1. Traditionally, homicide occurred only when the death of a "person" was caused. A fetus was not a person; homicide was committed only if a fetus was born alive and expired as a result of injuries sustained either before or after birth. *People v. Bolar,* 109 Ill.App.3d 384, 64 Ill.Dec.919, 440 N.E.2d 639 (1982). In those jurisdictions following the traditional rule, no homicide occurs even if the defendant intentionally destroyed the fetus. This is illustrated by *Hollis v. Commonwealth,* 652 S.W.2d 61 (Ky.1983), in which the defendant, announcing he did not want a baby, forced his hand into his wife's body and destroyed the fetus.

   Whether a fetus was born alive and thus could be the victim of a homicide offense may present a difficult question. In *Bolar,* for example, the fetus was removed and regular but faint heartbeats were heard. After several minutes of resuscitation efforts, the heartbeats stopped and the fetus or child was pronounced dead. The trial court's determination that the fetus had been born alive was upheld on appeal as within the discretion of the trial court.

   In some jurisdictions, the common law rule has been judicially modified. In *Hughes v. State,* 868 P.2d 730 (Okla.Crim.App.1994), the Oklahoma court adopted what it acknowledged was the minority view that a homicide prosecution can be based upon causing the death of a viable fetus. The traditional rule, the court noted, is based upon the difficulty of determining whether the fetus was alive at the time of the defendant's action, whether the defendant's act killed it, and whether the fetus would have been born alive except for the defendant's conduct. Modern medical skills, it concluded, have sufficiently reduced the difficulty of making these decisions to justify abandoning the rule:

We think that the better rule is that infliction of prenatal injuries resulting in the death of a viable fetus, before or after it is born, is homicide. If a person were to commit violence against a pregnant woman and destroy the fetus within her, we would not want the death of the fetus to go unpunished. We believe that our criminal law should extend its protection to viable fetuses.

Those portions of section 187 of the California Penal Code that deal with killing a fetus are a legislative reaction to *Keeler v. Superior Court,* 2 Cal.3d 619, 87 Cal.Rptr. 481, 470 P.2d 617 (1970), which applied the common law rule. The California Supreme Court considered the resulting statutory provisions at length in *People v. Davis,* 7 Cal.4th 797, 872 P.2d 591, 30 Cal.Rptr.2d 50 (1994), and rejected challenges to the state's ability to so criminalize the killing of a fetus. Specifically, the plurality reasoned that Supreme Court decisions, which hold that a woman's right to privacy prohibited criminalizing her actions in aborting a fetus, did not limit the state's ability to criminalize the killing of such a fetus without the woman's consent. Further, six of the seven members of the court concluded that the legislature did not intend to require that a fetus be viable to make the killing of that fetus murder. In *Davis,* the defendant was shown to have shot Maria Flores, who was at the time between 23 and 25 months pregnant. Flores lived but the fetus was stillborn as a result of the gunshot. Expert testimony was that the fetus's statistical chances of survival outside of the womb were between 2 and 47 percent. Although the conviction was reversed for procedural error, the California Supreme Court's disposition made clear that a conviction for murdering the fetus would be permissible.

2. When does death occur for purposes of homicide analysis? Suppose the following situation: Defendant inflicts wound on victim. Victim's physician, after treating victim, decides that because victim's brain evidences no electrical activity, victim is dead despite the fact that victim's heart and lungs are functioning because of a respirator. Physician then removes victim from the respirator and, as a result, victim's heart and lungs cease functioning. When did victim die or, to put the question in different terms, did defendant "cause" death of victim or did physician? The traditional definition of death defined it in terms of cessation of heartbeat and respiration. However, courts have indicated a willingness to accept a definition of death in terms of an absence of brain activity, that is, "brain death." See *Commonwealth v. Golston,* 373 Mass. 249, 366 N.E.2d 744 (1977). Thus in the hypothetical, the victim died— as a result of the defendant's action — when the victim became brain dead, and the physician's actions did not in any sense "cause" the victim's death for purposes of homicide law analysis.

3. The common law rule was that a person could not be convicted of murder unless the victim died within a year and a day from the time the fatal blow was given or the cause of death administered. See, for example, *Louisville E. & St. L. R. Co. v. Clarke,* 152 U.S. 230, 239, 14 S.Ct. 579, 581, 38 L.Ed. 422, 424 (1894). Some American jurisdictions still follow this rule.

Courts or legislatures have abrogated the rule in many jurisdictions. See *People v. Carrillo,* 164 Ill.2d 144, 646 N.E.2d 582, 207 Ill.Dec. 16, cert. denied, 515 U.S. 1146, 115 S.Ct. 2586, 132 L.Ed.2d 834 (1995). Sometimes judicial holding to this effect rest on the rationale that by enacting a comprehensive penal code without the rule, the legislature has implicitly rejected it. Where the matter rests within judicial discretion, the courts have regarded the rationale for the rule as no longer viable. The New Mexico Court of Appeals explained in *State v. Gabehart,* 114 N.M. 183, 836 P.2d 102 (App.1992):

> The original reason for recognition of the rule was grounded upon the uncertainty of causation for the death of an individual where the death occurs more than a year and a day following the infliction of injuries upon the victim. As noted by 1 Wayne R. LaFave & Austin W. Scott, Jr., Substantive Criminal Law Section 3.12(i), at 421 (1986), "[t]he difficulty in proving that the blow caused the death after so long an interval was obviously the basis of the rule." Recent precedent, however, points out that due to modern advances in medical and criminal science and technology, the rationale behind the rule no longer exists. In fact, retention of the rule is inconsistent with demonstrable medical evidence in "lingering death" situations. Advances in medical technology now permit victims, although severely injured, to be kept alive for extended periods of time. We agree * * * that the basis for the rule has disappeared, and that it would be incongruous if developments in medical science that allow a victim's life to be prolonged were permitted to be used to bar prosecution of an assailant, where scientific evidence is presented to establish beyond a reasonable doubt that the defendant's acts proximately caused the victim's death.

Where the rule has been abolished, considerable time may elapse between the defendant's death-causing actions and the victim's death. In *Commonwealth v. Correa,* 437 Pa.Super. 1, 648 A.2d 1199 (1994), appeal denied, 548 Pa. 617, 657 A.2d 487 (1995), for example, a manslaughter conviction was obtained and upheld where the victim died nine years after being shot by the defendant.

Some legislatures have retained the rule but expanded the time limit. As a result of a 1969 amendment, for example, § 194 of the California Penal Code provides, "To make the killing either murder or manslaughter, it is requisite that the party die within three years and a day after the stroke received or the cause of death administered. * * * "

B. KILLINGS WITH "MALICE AFORETHOUGHT"
Editors' Introduction: "Malice Aforethought" and the Culpable Mental State Required for Murder

Murder—traditionally, a killing with "malice aforethought"—is the basic homicide offense. Analysis of a criminal homicide situation will ordinarily begins with an inquiry into the possibility of the killing being murder.

Unfortunately, the traditional definition of the crime leaves some uncertainty as to the state of mind required. The problem was explained by the Michigan Court of Appeals in *People v. Morrin*, 31 Mich.App. 301, 310–18, 187 N.W.2d 434, 438–43 (1971):

> A person who kills another is guilty of the crime of murder if the homicide is committed with malice aforethought. Malice aforethought is the intention to kill, actual or implied, under circumstances which do not constitute excuse or justification or mitigate the degree of the offense to manslaughter. The intent to kill may be implied where the actor actually intends to inflict great bodily harm or the natural tendency of his behavior is to cause death or great bodily harm. (The common-law felony-murder rule is an example of implied intent or implied malice aforethought.)

> Thus, as "malice aforethought" is now defined, a killing may be murder even though the actor harbored no hatred or ill will against the victim and even though he "acted on the spur of the moment." Whatever may be the philological origin of the words "malice aforethought," today "each word has a different significance in legal usage than in ordinary conversation."

> The nature of malice aforethought is the source of much of the confusion that attends the law of homicide. The cause of this confusion has been the evolution of malice aforethought from an independently significant element of murder to a "term of art" whose significance is largely historical and procedural.

> The precise roots of malice aforethought are uncertain. Common law courts spoke of "malice prepense" as early as the 13th century. The requirement that malice aforethought be established in all murder prosecutions represented the common law's recognition that a rational legal system will punish certain homicides (for example, those that are intentional) while excusing others (accidental homicides, for example).

> From the beginning malice aforethought was defined principally in functional terms. We know what it did; it both distinguished criminal from innocent homicide and murder from manslaughter. Yet what it was, the precise state of mind which it described, eluded symmetrical definition.

> The common-law courts were faced with a difficult problem: malice aforethought was a requisite element of murder, but one so elusive that in many cases it resisted direct proof. Their solution was to create a presumption of malice. As early as the 16th century proof that the accused person killed the victim gave rise to a "presumption" that the act was done with malice aforethought. Once it was established that the accused killed the victim, the burden was upon the accused to prove circumstances of justification, excuse, or mitigation.

> This rule, firmly rooted in English law, has taken hold in a great many American jurisdictions * * *.

The merits of the rule are that it relieves the prosecution from the necessity of proving the nonexistence of circumstances of excuse, justification, and mitigation—frequently an impossible burden—and instead allocates the burden of proving such circumstances to the defendant, who, arguably, has greater ability to do so than the prosecution.

There is also, however, a grave drawback to this presumptive device. This defect arises in connection with jury instructions, to instruct a jury that malice is presumed from the fact of killing is to invite confusion concerning the ultimate burden of proof in the trial. The prosecution must always prove the defendant guilty beyond a reasonable doubt; a rule of law that shifts the burden of proof with respect to "malice" tends to cloud the dimensions of the prosecution's ultimate burden.

Despite this history, malice aforethought has developed a reasonably clear meaning in modern law. The District of Columbia Court of Appeals explained:

"[M]alice aforethought" has evolved into "a term of art" embodying several distinct mental states. As the commentary to the Model Penal Code explains:

> Whatever the original meaning of [the] phrase [malice aforethought], it became over time an "arbitrary symbol" used by judges to signify any of a number of mental states deemed sufficient to support liability for murder. Successive generations added new content to "malice aforethought" until it encompassed a variety of mental attitudes bearing no predictable relation to the ordinary sense of the two words.

MODEL PENAL CODE, § 210.2 comment 1, at 14 [(Official Draft and Revised Comments 1980)]. Following the common law trend, this court has recognized that malice aforethought, in the District of Columbia, "denotes four types of murder, each accompanied by distinct mental states."

First, a killing is malicious where the perpetrator acts with the specific intent to kill. Second, a killing is malicious where the perpetrator has the specific intent to inflict serious bodily harm. Third, "an act may involve such a wanton and willful disregard of an unreasonable human risk as to constitute malice aforethought even if there is not actual intent to kill or injure." R. PERKINS & R. BOYCE, [CRIMINAL LAW] at 59 [(3d ed.1982)]. In *Byrd v. United States,* [500 A.2d 1376, 1385 (D.C.1985) adopted en banc, *Byrd v. United States,* 510 A.2d 1035 (D.C.1986)], we referred to this kind of malicious killing as "depraved heart" murder.

Historically, a fourth kind of malice existed when a killing occurred in the course of the intentional commission of a felony. Under this "felony-murder" rule, "[m]alice, an essential element of murder, is implied from the intentional commission of the underlying felony even though the actual killing might be accidental."

Comber v. State, 584 A.2d 26, 38–39 (D.C.Ct.App.1990).

Some modern statutes, such as the California statutory scheme reprinted in Section A of this chapter, define homicide offenses in terms that differ little from those used by the early common law courts in homicide discussions. Other modern statutes, including those based upon the Model Penal Code's proposals also reprinted in Section A, employ different terminology and, sometimes, different categories, but these schemes often embody requirements and distinctions similar or identical to those used in early common law homicide analysis.

Intentional killings—those accomplished with the conscious purpose of causing death—are universally murder under modern statutory schemes, at least in the absence of considerations that excuse, justify, or mitigate. Murder of this type raises few conceptual problems, although the inquiries as to whether particular murder defendants in fact intended to kill sometimes pose difficult tasks. *State v. Raguseo,* reprinted in Section D of this chapter, is an example of the factual questions often presented by these cases.

Killings accomplished with the intent to cause grievous bodily harm seldom give rise to judicial discussion. Some difficulty is posed by the question of what sort of injuries to the victim must have been intended by the defendant. *People v. Geiger,* 10 Mich.App. 339, 159 N.W.2d 383 (1968), suggested that the defendant must have intended injury of a very serious nature, naturally and commonly involving loss of life or "grievous mischief."

Killings in the course of criminal acts present special problems. These killings and the so-called "felony murder" doctrine are considered in Section F of this chapter.

Those killings potentially falling within the third type distinguished by the District of Columbia court have presented continuing difficulty. Many modern statutes provide for such killings to be murder, although the statutory language varies in content and specificity. Courts and statutes vary in referring to such murders as "depraved mind" murder, "depraved heart" murder, or "depraved indifference" murder. Section 210.2(1)(b) of the Model Penal Code, reprinted on page 155, defines murder as including a killing committed "recklessly under circumstances manifesting extreme indifference to the value of human life * * *." Section 188 of the California Penal Code, reprinted on page 153, provides for these cases by permitting malice to be implied "when the circumstances attending the killing show an abandoned and malignant heart." The case reprinted in this section applied the New York "depraved indifference" type of murder.

Does the colorful terminology sometimes used to describe and define this type of murder create practical and perhaps constitutional problems? In *Waters v. State,* 443 A.2d 500 (Del.1982), the jury was instructed in terms of § 635, Del.Code.Ann., which provided that a person is guilty of second degree murder if the person

> recklessly causes the death of another person under circumstances which manifest
> a cruel, wicked and depraved indifference to human life * * *.

Waters argued that the failure to define "cruel, wicked and depraved indifference to human life" left the jurors without sufficiently objective (and constitutional) standards for determining whether he was guilty of second degree murder. The appellate court noted that instructions of the sort at issue had been used as early as 1903 and concluded:

[T]he words "cruel, wicked and depraved indifference to human life" are words with a commonly accepted meaning, time-honored in this State's jurisprudence. Over the years, instructions [involving this language] have been given to innumerable juries in this State. Apparently, they have been able to understand and apply the concepts inherent therein to the facts before them. With this long history in mind, we find no vagueness problem, rising to constitutional levels, created by the instant charge.

People v. Roe

Court of Appeals of New York, 1989
74 N.Y.2d 20, 542 N.E.2d 610, 544 N.Y.S.2d 297.

HANCOCK, Judge.

In defendant's appeal from his conviction for depraved indifference murder (Penal Law § 125.25[2])[1] for the shooting death of a 13-year-old boy, the sole question we address is the legal sufficiency of the evidence. Defendant, a 15 1/2-year-old high school student, deliberately loaded a mix of "live" and "dummy" shells at random into the magazine of a 12-gauge shotgun. He pumped a shell into the firing chamber not knowing whether it was a "dummy" or a "live" round. He raised the gun to his shoulder and pointed it directly at the victim, Darrin Seifert, who was standing approximately 10 feet away. As he did so, he exclaimed "Let's play Polish roulette" and asked "Who is first?" When he pulled the trigger, the gun discharged sending a "live" round into Darrin's chest. Darrin died as a result of the massive injuries.

Defendant was convicted after a bench trial and the Appellate Division unanimously affirmed, holding that the evidence was legally sufficient to establish defendant's guilt. That court concluded, moreover, upon an exercise of its independent factual review power, that the verdict was not against the weight of the evidence. * * * [W]e address only the central legal issue presented: sufficiency of the proof—i.e., "whether 'after viewing the evidence in the light most favorable to the prosecution, any rational trier of fact could have found the essential elements of the crime beyond a reasonable doubt.'" * * *

* * *

Before analyzing the evidence and its legal sufficiency, a brief examination of the crime of depraved indifference murder and its elements is instructive. Depraved indifference murder, like reckless manslaughter is a *nonintentional* homicide. It differs from manslaughter, however, in that it must be shown that the actor's reckless conduct is imminently dangerous and presents a grave risk of death; in manslaughter, the conduct need only present the lesser "substantial risk" of death (see, *People v. Register,* 60 N.Y.2d 270, 276, 469 N.Y.S.2d 599, 457 N.E.2d 704). Whether the lesser risk sufficient for manslaughter is elevated into the very substantial risk present in murder depends upon the wantonness of defendant's acts—i.e., whether they were committed "[u]nder circumstances evincing a depraved indifference to human life". This is not a *mens rea* element which focuses "upon the subjective intent of the defendant, as it is with intentional murder"; rather it involves "an objective assessment of the degree of risk presented by defendant's reckless conduct".

The only culpable mental state required * * *, we have made clear, is recklessness—the same mental state required for manslaughter, second degree * * *. In a trial for murder under Penal Law § 125.25(2), proof of defendant's subjective mental state is, of course, relevant to the element of recklessness, the basic element required for both manslaughter in the second degree and depraved indifference murder. Evidence of the actor's subjective mental state, however, *is not pertinent* to a determination of the additional element required for depraved indifference murder: whether the objective circumstances bearing on the nature of a defendant's reckless conduct are such that the conduct creates a very substantial risk of death.

---

[1] Penal Law "§ 125.25 *Murder in the second degree.*
"A person is guilty of murder in the second degree when:

* * *

"2. Under circumstances evincing a depraved indifference to human life, he recklessly engages in conduct which creates a grave risk of death to another person, and thereby causes the death of another person."

Generally, the assessment of the objective circumstances evincing the actor's "depraved indifference to human life"— i.e., those which elevate the risk to the gravity required for a murder conviction—is a qualitative judgment to be made by the trier of the facts. If there is evidence which supports the jury's determination, it is this court's obligation to uphold the verdict. Examples of conduct which have been held sufficient to justify a jury's finding of depraved indifference include: driving an automobile on a city sidewalk at excessive speeds and striking a pedestrian without applying the brakes; firing several bullets into a house (see *People v. Register,* supra); continually beating an infant over a five-day period; and playing "Russian roulette" with one "live" shell in a six-cylinder gun.

With this background, we turn to the issue before us, now more fully stated: whether, viewing the evidence in the light most favorable to the People, any rational trier of the fact could have concluded that the objective circumstances surrounding defendant's reckless conduct so elevated the gravity of the risk created as to evince the depraved indifference to human life necessary to sustain the murder conviction. A brief summary of the evidence is necessary.

On the afternoon of August 14, 1984, the day of the shooting, defendant was at his home in the Village of Buchanan, Westchester County. There is uncontroverted proof that defendant, who had completed his first year in high school, had an intense interest in and detailed knowledge of weapons, including firearms of various kinds.[2] He was familiar with his father's 12-gauge shotgun and, indeed, had cleaned it approximately 50 times. The cleaning process involved oiling the firing pin and pulling the trigger, using a "dummy" shell to avoid "dry firing" the weapon.[3]

At approximately 3:00 P.M., Darrin and his friend, Dennis Bleakley, also a 13 year old, stopped by to await the arrival of Darrin's older brother who was expected shortly.

Defendant entertained the two boys by showing them his sawed-off shotgun, gravity knife, and Chuka sticks which he kept in a bag under his bed; he demonstrated how he assembled and disassembled the sawed-off shotgun.

Defendant then escorted Darrin and Dennis to his parents' room where he took out his father's 12-gauge shotgun. He asked Darrin to go back to his bedroom to get the five shotgun shells which were on the shelf. Defendant knew that three of these shells were "live" and two were "dummies". He randomly loaded four of the five shells into the magazine and pumped the shotgun, thereby placing one shell in the firing chamber. Because he loaded the magazine without any regard to the order in which the shells were inserted, he did not know if he had chambered a "live" or "dummy" round.

It was at this point, according to Dennis's testimony, that defendant raised the shotgun, pointed it directly at Darrin, and said "Let's play Polish roulette. Who is first?" He pulled the trigger discharging a "live" round which struck the 82-pound Darrin at close range. The shot created a gaping wound in Darrin's upper right chest, destroyed most of his shoulder, produced extensive damage to his lung, and eventually caused his death.

Defendant disputed this version of the incident. He testified that he had one foot on his parents' bed and was resting the butt of the gun on his inner thigh with the barrel pointing up and away from the victim. While he was demonstrating how the gun worked, he claimed, his foot slipped and the shotgun became airborne momentarily. Defendant testified that when he attempted to catch the gun, the butt kicked up under his armpit and he accidentally hit the trigger and discharged the gun.

The evidence of the objective circumstances surrounding defendant's point-blank discharge of the shotgun is, in our view, sufficient to support a finding of the very serious risk of death required for depraved indifference murder. Because the escalating factor—depraved indifference to human life—is based on an objective assessment of the circumstances surrounding the act of shooting and not the *mens rea* of the actor, the evidence stressed by the dissent concerning defendant's *mens rea*—his emotional condition in the aftermath of the killing—is beside the point. Also without relevance are the dissent's references to defendant's claimed ignorance concerning the order in which cartridges, once loaded in the magazine, would enter the firing chamber. Such lack of knowledge can make no difference when, as is concededly the case here, the shooter knowingly loaded the mix of "live" and "dummy" cartridges with no regard to the order of their insertion into the magazine.

The comparable case here is not that of a person, uneducated in use of weapons, who, while playing with a gun that he does not know is loaded, accidentally discharges it;

---

[2] In addition to proof that defendant had handled and used his sawed-off shotgun and his father's shotgun, the People introduced evidence that defendant had previously used a .22-caliber rifle, an air rifle, a .22- caliber air pistol, and a BB gun. Defendant had read magazine articles and books concerning guns, given several speeches in school about weapons, and drawn pictures of various guns. This evidence was admissible to prove recklessness—i.e., that defendant was aware of the risks involved—by showing that he was familiar with weapons in general and with this gun in particular.

[3] According to defendant, "dry firing" is releasing the firing pin when there is no cartridge in the chamber and nothing for the pin to strike against. To avoid the damage to the pin which "dry firing" can cause, "dummy" cartridges are used.

rather, the apt analogy is a macabre game of chance where the victim's fate—life or death—may be decreed by the flip of a coin or a roll of a die. It is no different where the odds are even that the shell pumped into the firing chamber of a 12-gauge shotgun is a "live" round, the gun is aimed at the victim standing close by, and the trigger is pulled (see, 2 LaFave & Scott, Substantive Criminal Law § 7.4, at 202 ["Russian roulette" with one "live" shell in a six-chamber gun is a classic example of depraved indifference murder]).

The sheer enormity of the act—putting another's life at such grave peril in this fashion—is not diminished because the sponsor of the game is a youth of 15. As in *Register,* where bullets which might kill or seriously injure someone, or hit no one at all, were fired at random into a crowded bar, the imminent risk of death was present here. That in one case the gamble is that a bullet might not hit anyone and in the other that the gun might not fire is of no moment. In each case, the fact finder could properly conclude that the conduct was so wanton as to amount to depraved indifference to human life.

It is conceivable that another trier of fact hearing this evidence could have been persuaded to arrive at a different verdict. From the dissenter's extensive discussion of the proof and the inferences he would draw therefrom, it is evidence that he would have done so. Our proper function on appeal, however, is vastly different from that of the prosecutor in determining which crimes to charge, that of the Judge or jury in hearing the evidence and making factual conclusions * * *. We do not find facts * * *. Our sole authority is to review legal questions such as the one considered here: whether the evidence was legally insufficient. As to this question, we have little difficulty in concluding that the unanimous Appellate Division correctly held that the evidence was sufficient to support the verdict.

* * * [T]he order of the Appellate Division should be affirmed.

BELLACOSA, Judge (dissenting).

I vote to reverse this conviction of a 15-year-old person for the highest degree of criminal homicidal responsibility—depraved indifference murder. The evidence adduced, the statutory scheme under which defendant was charged, and the legislative intent behind it do not support the disproportionate level of maximum blameworthiness imposed here. Moreover, this result finalizes the obliteration of the classical demarcation between murder and manslaughter in this State * * *.

While the tangible content of "depraved indifference to human life" is * * * elusive, the wantonness of the conduct

augmenting the reckless culpable mental state must also manifest a level of callousness and extreme cruelty as to be "equal in blameworthiness to intentional murder." I allude to some of the same case illustrations in this regard as the majority does, except I emphasize the particular escalating depravity facts that the majority avoids: firing a gun *three times* in a packed barroom, *having boasted in advance an intention to kill someone;* driving a car at high speed on a crowded urban street *and failing to apply the brakes after striking one person; continuously* beating a young child *over a five-day period.*

The depraved indifference category of murder reflects the Legislature's policy refinement that there is a type of reckless homicide that is so horrendous as to qualify, in a legal fiction way, for blameworthiness in the same degree as the taking of another's life intentionally, purposefully and knowingly. * * *

In this case, a 15-year-old person stands convicted of the tragic and senseless killing of the 13-year-old brother of his best friend. The shooting occurred around three o'clock in defendant's home on a summer afternoon. Thirteen-year-old Darrin Seifert and another youngster, Dennis Bleakley, went to defendant's home where they were invited to defendant's upstairs bedroom. They examined defendant's weapons collection, which included a sawed-off shotgun. After the weapons were returned to their storage places, defendant and his two companions walked down the hallway to defendant's parents' room where defendant removed a 12-gauge shotgun from a gun case. Defendant asked Darrin to retrieve some shotgun shells located on a shelf in defendant's room. Darrin and Dennis went to defendant's room and took five shells. Three were live ammunition and two were "dummies". Returning to the master bedroom, Darrin handed the shells to defendant, who proceeded to load the shotgun with four shells. Testimony established that defendant knew two of the shells he loaded into the gun were "live" and two were "dummies". There was also conflicting testimony as to whether the defendant understood that the gun worked in such a manner that the first shell inserted into the gun would be the last fired from the gun or vice versa. The two police investigators testified that, shortly after the incident, defendant indicated he thought he had chambered a "dummy" shell and appeared stunned when he learned the gun operated on a "first in-last out" order of fire. Defendant contradicted this testimony when he testified he had not paid attention to the order in which he loaded the shells into the gun. Both theories, in any event, suggest only recklessness, not depravity.

Moreover, after loading the gun and while standing 10 feet away from the other two boys, defendant exclaimed, "Let's play Polish roulette. Who's first?" Defendant raised the shotgun, pointed it at his two companions and pulled the trigger. The gun fired a live shell which hit Darrin's right chest and shoulder area, knocking him to the floor. Defendant dropped the shotgun and ran over to Darrin, screaming, "Don't die. I killed my best friend's brother." He quickly directed Dennis to go downstairs to call an ambulance, which was done. A neighbor, hearing the shot, entered the house and ran upstairs. She observed defendant straddled over Darrin's body and heard him say, "Is he alright? Is he alright? Tell me." When the police arrived shortly thereafter, they observed the defendant pounding his fists against the wall, crying, "I can't believe I shot him. I can't believe I shot my best friend. Help, please, oh my God, help." The ambulance arrived and Darrin was taken to the hospital where he was pronounced dead on arrival.

The * * * question is whether defendant's conduct "was of such gravity that it placed the crime upon the same level as the taking of life by premeditated design * * * [and whether] defendant's conduct, though reckless, was equal in blameworthiness to intentional murder."

I disagree that defendant's conduct qualifies for this lofty homicidal standard. He acted recklessly, of that there can be no doubt. * * * But the accusation and the conviction at the highest homicidal level, predicated on callous depravity and complete indifference to human life, are not supportable against this 15 year old on a sufficiency review and are starkly contradicted by the whole of the evidence adduced.

This "crime is classified as murder and the murder penalty should be imposed 'only when the degree of risk *approaches certainty;* that is, at the point where reckless homicide becomes knowing homicide.'" Here, defendant's actions cannot be said to have created an almost certain risk of death. The mathematical probabilities, the objective state of mind evidenced at and around the critical moment, the ambiguity in the evidence as to the operational order in the firing of the weapon, and all the circumstances surrounding this tragic incident all render the risk uncertain and counterindicate depravity, callousness and indifference of the level fictionally equaling premeditated, intentional murder. That central and essential element of the crime charged was not proved beyond a reasonable doubt and that has been for a very long time a classically reviewable issue in this court.

* * *

The testimony of the only other eyewitness, Dennis Bleakley, established that defendant was shaken and distraught immediately upon realizing that he had shot their companion. Defendant also immediately ran to his victim and instructed Dennis to call an ambulance; the neighbor testified that when she arrived on the scene, seconds after hearing the shot, defendant was kneeling over his friend's body and crying. Similarly, the police officer who arrived on the scene testified that defendant was extremely distraught and overcome with grief. This is not evidence beyond a reasonable doubt of that hardness of heart or that malignancy of attitude qualifying as "depraved indifference". Frankly, the evidence proves the opposite.

* * * [T]o uphold this defendant's conviction on the uppermost and most heinous level of criminal homicidal responsibility cheapens the gravity with which we treat far more serious murders, e.g., cold-blooded contract killings and the like. In the eyes of the law all the slayers are now made alike, when the perpetrators themselves know and our best instincts and intelligence tell us, too, that they are very different. Justice is disfigured by the punishment of offenders so homogeneously and, yet, so disproportionately.

Notes and Questions

1. Should a person's conviction of this type of murder require that the person have created a high risk of death to something more than just a single target victim? Some courts require this. The Alabama statutes provide that a person commits murder if,

   Under circumstances manifesting extreme indifference to human life, he recklessly engages in conduct which creates a gave risk of death to a person other than himself, and thereby causes the death of another person.

Ala. Code § 13A-6-2(a)(2). In *Northington v. State,* 413 So.2d 1169 (Ala. Crim.App.1981), writ quashed as improvidently granted, 413 So.2d 1172 (1982), the evidence showed that the defendant withheld food and medical care from her five-month-old daughter, causing the daughter's death. She was convicted of murder under the provision set out above. This statute, the appellate court reasoned, restates prior Alabama law under which first degree murder included homicides perpetrated by conduct greatly dangerous to the lives of others and evincing a depraved mind regardless of human life. The doctrine of "depraved heart murder" is intended to embrace those situations in which the perpetrator harbors a disregard for human life generally. Thus it is necessary that the perpetrator have no deliberate intent to injure or kill any particular individual. Here, the evidence indicated that the defendant's actions and omissions were specifically directed toward the daughter and no others:

   [W]hile the defendant's conduct did indeed evidence an extreme indifference to the life of her child, there was nothing to show that the conduct displayed an extreme indifference to human life generally.

Reversing the conviction, the court continued:

The function of this section is to embrace those homicides caused by such acts as driving an automobile in a grossly wanton manner, shooting a firearm into a crowd or moving train, and throwing a timber from a roof onto a crowded street.

The New York statute applied in *Roe,* however, has been construed as not requiring indifference to the lives of many persons or to human life "generally." See *People v. LeGrand,* 61 A.D.2d 815, 815, 402 N.Y.S.2d 209, 211 (1978) (liability need not be based on conduct that places many persons in danger).

In *Windham v. State*, 602 So.2d 798 (Miss.1992), the majority of a split court indicated that under the traditional view, an act directed at and endangering only one person would not suffice under such a statute because the accused's act "must have manifested a reckless indifference to human life in general." It rejected that approach, however, on the ground that the distinction between the risk of death to one specific person and the risk to more than one "is a senseless and outmoded [distinction]."

Several members of the *Windham* court expressed concern that free of a requirement that the conduct demonstrate indifference to the lives of multiple persons, the crime is too uncertain. Justice Roberts, concurring, struggled with the statutory terms:

"Evincing a depraved heart" is the puzzler. I doubt it would mean much to a cardiologist. Resort to the dictionary seems similarly unavailing. In *Gentry v. State,* 92 Miss. 141, 154, 45 So.2d 721 (1908), we read this phrase "a spirit of malignancy," but hardly advanced the ball. I take it no one will dispute that the phrase must be seen a metaphor, a euphemism, regarding the actor's cognitive, not cardiac, function. I am open to the suggestion otherwise, but I do not see that it says anything of consequence independent of "eminently dangerous to others" and "regardless of human life."

2. The difference between this type of murder and involuntary manslaughter is in part that for this type of murder the defendant must have created a higher risk of death than is required for manslaughter. What culpable mental state is required for this type of murder is a matter on which the courts have disagreed. *Roe* mentioned that New York requires only the same mental state as it requires for manslaughter. However, the District of Columbia Court of Appeals has required for this type of murder that "the perpetrator was subjectively aware that his or her conduct created an extreme risk of death or serious bodily injury." *Comber v. United States*, 584 U.S. 26, 39 (D.C.Ct.App.1980). Thus the defendant must be aware of the extreme magnitude of the risk that he or she creates.

C. PREMEDITATED KILLINGS: FIRST DEGREE MURDER

The common law crime of murder was not divided into degrees and premeditation was not an element of the single offense of murder. American statutes, however, often created different offenses of first and second degree murder; the California statute, reprinted on page 153, is reasonably typical. Under this approach, among the distinguishing features is the premeditation requirement for one type of first degree murder.

As the following case illustrates, the reported appellate decisions most often address the appellate review process, that is, when does the evidence support a conviction for first degree murder when a properly instructed jury has convicted a defendant of that offense? Consider also, however, how juries should be instructed. On a more general level, consider whether it is sound policy to separate out premeditated killings for the imposition of more severe penalties than are imposed for other murders.

State v. Bingham

Supreme Court of Washington, 1986
105 Wash.2d 820, 719 P.2d 109.

GOODLOE, Justice.

In this case, we review the sufficiency of the evidence of the premeditation element in an aggravated first degree murder conviction. * * *

On February 18, 1982, the raped and strangled body of Leslie Cook, a retarded adult, was found in a pasture in Sequim. Cook was last seen alive on February 15, 1982 with respondent Charles Dean Bingham. The Clallam County Prosecutor * * * charged Bingham with aggravated first degree (premeditated) murder, rape being the aggravating circumstance. The prosecutor also notified Bingham that the State would seek the death penalty.

The evidence presented at trial showed that on February 15, Cook and Bingham got off a bus together in Sequim about 6 P.M. There was no evidence that they knew each other before this time. They visited a grocery store and two residences. Cook was last seen at the residence of Wayne Humphrey and Enid Pratt where Bingham asked for a ride back to Port Angeles. When he was told no, Bingham said they would hitchhike. They left together heading toward the infrequently traveled Old Olympic Highway. None of the witnesses who saw the two heard any argument or observed any physical contact between them. Three days later, Cook's body was found in a field about a 1/4 mile from the Humphrey-Pratt residence.

At trial, King County Medical Examiner Reay described the results of the autopsy he performed on Cook's body. The cause of death was "asphyxiation through manual strangulation", accomplished by applying continuous pressure to the windpipe for approximately 3 to 5 minutes. Cook had a bruise on her upper lip, more likely caused by a hand being pressed over her mouth than by a violent blow. Tears were found in Cook's vaginal wall and anal ring. Spermatozoa was present. These injuries were inflicted antemortem. Also, there was a bite mark on each of Cook's breasts. Reay testified that these occurred perimortem or postmortem.

Two forensic odontologists testified that the bite mark on one breast matched Bingham's teeth. No conclusive determination could be made with respect to the other bite mark.

The prosecutor's theory, as revealed in both his opening statement and closing argument, was that Bingham wanted to have sex with Cook and that he had to kill her in order to do so. The prosecutor hypothesized that Bingham had

started the act while Cook was alive, and that he put his hand over her mouth and then strangled her in order to complete the act. The prosecutor also told the jury that the murder would be premeditated if Bingham had formed the intent to kill when he began to strangle Cook, and thought about that intent for the 3 to 5 minutes it took her to die.

The court instructed the jury on aggravated first degree murder and on the lesser included offenses of first and second degree murder and first degree manslaughter. * * *

The jury found Bingham guilty of aggravated first degree murder. The jury also found, in the penalty phase, that the State had failed to prove that there were insufficient mitigating circumstances to warrant leniency. The trial court therefore sentenced Bingham to life imprisonment without the possibility of release or parole.

* * *

We must determine whether evidence of premeditation was sufficiently demonstrated in order for the issue to go to the jury and in order to sustain a finding of premeditated killing.

The constitutional standard for reviewing the sufficiency of the evidence in a criminal case is "whether, after reviewing the evidence in the light most favorable to the prosecution, any rational trier of fact could have found the essential elements of the crime beyond a reasonable doubt." The element challenged in this case is "premeditated intent".

Bingham was charged with first degree murder pursuant to RCW 9A.32.030(1)(a), which requires for conviction "a premeditated intent to cause the death of another". The element of premeditation distinguishes first and second degree murder. Section (1)(a) of the second degree murder statute, RCW 9A.32.050, requires for conviction "intent to cause the death of another person but without premeditation".

The only statutory elaboration on the meaning of premeditation is found in RCW 9A.32.020(1), which states that premeditation "must involve more than a moment in point of time." Washington case law further defines premeditation as "the mental process of thinking beforehand, deliberation, reflection, weighing or reasoning for a period of time, however short." We recently approved an instruction which defined premeditation as "the deliberate formation of and reflection upon the intent to take a human life."

Premeditation may be shown by direct or circumstantial evidence. Circumstantial evidence can be used where the inferences drawn by the jury are reasonable and the evidence supporting the jury's verdict is substantial. In this case, the State presented no direct evidence. The issue thus becomes whether sufficient circumstantial evidence of premeditation was presented. * * *

To show premeditation, the State relied on the pathologist's testimony that manual strangulation takes 3 to 5 minutes. The State argues this time is an appreciable amount of time in which Bingham could have deliberated. Bingham argues that time alone is not enough and that other indicators of premeditation must be shown.

One case, *State v. Smith,* 12 Wash.App. 720, 531 P.2d 843 (1975), aff'd, 88 Wash.2d 127, 559 P.2d 970, cert. denied, 434 U.S. 876, 98 S.Ct. 226, 54 L.Ed.2d 155 (1977), was relied heavily upon by the parties * * *. In *Smith,* the defendant was convicted of the premeditated first degree murder of his son. The facts showed that the defendant took his son for a midnight walk by a creek near his house. The next morning he returned home alone and disoriented. The boy's body was found in the river. He had been drowned.

The *entire Smith* discussion on premeditation is as follows:

Premeditation. Although no definite motive was proven, the jury was presented with substantial evidence of the existence of premeditation. The Smiths had discussed separation, though at the time of the incident had decided not to do so. They had concluded, however, that if they separated, Kathy Smith would receive custody of the children. For premeditation to be inferable by the jury, there must have been a period of time during which the intent to kill is *deliberated.* This time may be very short provided it is an "appreciable period of time." Looking at the circumstances surrounding the child's death, it is clear that an appreciable period of time did elapse. As recognized by our State Supreme Court, choking takes an appreciable time. *State v. Harris,* 62 Wn.2d 858, 385 P.2d 18 (1963); *State v. Gaines,* 144 Wash. 446, 258 P. 508 (1927), cert. denied, 277 U.S. 81, 72 L.Ed. 793, 48 S.Ct. 468 (1928).

(Some italics ours.)

* * * *Smith* [may hold] * * * premeditation can be shown by only evidence of choking because choking takes an appreciable amount of time. The *Smith* facts could also be found to reflect a deliberated decision to kill the child by holding the child's head under water.

A review of the two cases cited in *Smith* for the proposition that choking takes an appreciable amount of time also shows that more than choking was involved in those cases. In both *State v. Harris,* 62 Wash.2d 858, 385 P.2d 18 (1963), and *State v. Gaines,* 144 Wash. 446, 258 P. 508 (1927), the facts show that the injuries were inflicted by various means over some period of time. In *Harris,* the victim

had been struck on the head several times with a blunt instrument with such force that in one place her skull had been fractured into her brain. Also, additional blows had severely damaged one ear and cheek and fractured her jaw, breaking two teeth. *After* this terrific beating, her assailant, while she was still alive, tied the vacuum cleaner cord around her neck and strangled her, which was the immediate cause of her death . . .

(Italics ours.) In *Gaines,*

the deceased was first choked into insensibility to an extent which could have produced death. A choking, to have this effect, takes some appreciable time. *After* the deceased was choked into insensibility, her assailant went to a garbage dump nearby, got a rock, returned and inflicted the wounds upon the head. It cannot be held, under the facts and circumstances of this case, that there was no evidence from which the jury had a right to find deliberation or premeditation.

(Italics ours.)

We find all of these cases, while helpful in understanding the premeditation element, are not determinative of whether manual strangulation alone is sufficient. We agree * * * that to allow a finding of premeditation only because the act takes an appreciable amount of time obliterates the distinction between first and second degree murder. Having the opportunity to deliberate is not evidence the defendant did deliberate, which is necessary for a finding of premeditation. Otherwise, any form of killing which took more than a moment could result in a finding of premeditation, without some additional evidence showing reflection. Holding a hand over someone's mouth or windpipe does not necessarily reflect a decision to kill the person, but possibly only to quiet her or him. Furthermore, here a question of the ability to deliberate or reflect while engaged in sexual activity exists.

The position of the State * * * appears to be that, if the defendant has the opportunity to deliberate and chooses not to cease his actions, then it is proper to allow the jury to infer deliberation. They offer three cases for the proposition that premeditation may properly be inferred from evidence of the lapse of time to death. *State v. Harris,* supra; *State v. Griffith,* 91 Wash.2d 572, 589 P.2d 799 (1979); *State v. Luoma,* [88 Wash.2d 28, 558 P.2d 756 (1977)]. While *Harris, Griffith,* and *Luoma* do use language regarding reliance on circumstances of the crime to show premeditation, the circumstances showed more action or thought than mere infliction of the fatal act.

In *Harris,* the assailant, after inflicting a terrific head beating, tied a vacuum cleaner cord around the victim's neck and strangled her. The interim time period between the beating and the strangulation, as well as the presence and use of a vacuum cleaner cord in effectuating the victim's death distinguish this case from the manual strangulation situation with which we are presented.

In *Griffith,* some children were hitting a basketball against the house where defendant lived with his mother. The defendant took the ball from the children. He went to his car, got a gun, and placed it on a table next to the front door. Within 5 minutes, two adults went to the house to retrieve the ball. The defendant, while talking to the adults at the front door, reached for the gun, pointed it at the adults, and shot one of them. The court said:

Although the period of time in which these events transpired was approximately 5 minutes, there was sufficient evidence from which the jury could have found that the defendant formulated an intent and deliberated upon it prior to the shooting.

The planned presence of a weapon necessary to facilitate a killing has been held to be adequate evidence to allow the issue of premeditation to go to the jury.

In *Luoma,* the defendant transported the victim to the crime scene, took her down a bank, positioned her and then crushed her head with a large rock. From the facts in *Luoma,* "[t]he jury could properly conclude that the death was not the result of an impulsive, spontaneous act." We note that the language in *Luoma* focuses on intent, not premeditation. As is clear from the statutory requirements * * *, premeditation is a separate and additional element to the intent requirement for first degree murder.

Here, *no* evidence was presented of deliberation or reflection before or during the strangulation, only the strangulation. The opportunity to deliberate is not sufficient.

As was recognized in *Austin v. United States,* 382 F.2d 129, 138–39 (D.C.Cir.1967):

The facts of a savage murder generate a powerful drive, almost a juggernaut for jurors, and indeed for judges, to crush the crime with the utmost condemnation available, to seize whatever words or terms reflect maximum denunciation, to cry out murder "in the first degree." But it is the task and conscience of a judge to transcend emotional momentum with reflective analysis. The judge is aware that many murders most brutish and bestial are committed in a consuming frenzy or heat of passion, and that these are in law only murder in the second degree. The [State's] evidence suffice[s] to establish an intentional and horrible murder—the kind that could be committed in a frenzy or heat of passion. However the core responsibility of the court requires it to reflect on the sufficiency of the [State's] case.

Exercising our responsibility, we find manual strangulation alone is insufficient evidence to support a finding of premeditation.

We affirm the Court of Appeals decision [reversing the conviction].

DOLLIVER, C.J., and UTTER, BRACHTENBACH and PEARSON, JJ., concur.

CALLOW, Justice (dissenting).

I would reinstate the aggravated first degree murder conviction of defendant. Sufficient evidence was presented on premeditation for that issue to be submitted to the jury. The decision on that issue is the function of the jury; not to be taken away.

* * *

The majority * * * ignore[s] numerous items of evidence which corroborate the presence of premeditation. I believe a review of the record compels the conclusion that there was sufficient evidence for the jury to conclude that the defendant acted with premeditation. The evidence meets the required standard since it could lead a rational trier of fact to find the essential elements of first degree murder beyond a reasonable doubt. The rule announced by the majority seems to be that premeditation must take place before the commencement of the act that results in death. Take the farmer's son who begins to fill the bin with wheat as a joke on his brother sleeping at its bottom. Then, realizing that he will inherit the whole farm if he persists, he does so and causes his brother's death. He had time to premeditate and did so in the middle of the act. He has committed aggravated first degree murder. That a murderer originally commenced an act without intending death does not grant him a carte blanche to persist when he realizes that to do so will kill his victim.

* * *

The majority argues that "[t]he *Smith* facts could also be found to reflect a deliberated decision to kill the child by holding the child's head under water." Likewise, the facts in this case could be found to reflect a deliberated decision to kill Leslie Cook by applying between 3 and 5 minutes of continuous and steady pressure to her neck. The act of strangulation inflicted by the defendant upon the deceased is considerably more than just the "[h]olding [of] a hand over someone's mouth or windpipe . . ." * * *

Here it can be inferred that the defendant thought about the consequences as he choked his victim. The period of premeditation might not have been during the initial squeeze, but the evidence of premeditation certainly was present in the continued application of force, knowing it would bring about death.

* * *

Regarding the type of circumstantial evidence that is relevant to the issue of premeditation, the court in *People v. Irby,* 129 Mich.App. 306, 323, 342 N.W.2d 303 (1983), leave to appeal denied, 418 Mich. 951 (1984), listed the following nonexclusive factors pertinent to establish premeditation: (1) A prior relationship showing motive; or (2) a murder weapon acquired and positioned as an indication of preparation; or (3) evidence which supports an inference the killer transported the victim to a secluded location for an illicit or criminal purpose; or (4) circumstances suggesting premeditation and deliberation; or (5) subsequent organized conduct which suggests the existence of a plan. * * *

The circumstances of Leslie Cook's death are replete with evidence besides the manual strangulation which raise the inference the defendant did premeditate: (1) the defendant took the deceased to a secluded location; (2) the defendant raped the deceased; (3) the time that is necessary to cause death by strangulation; (4) the defendant had plenty of opportunity to desist after the deceased lapsed into unconsciousness, but nevertheless, he chose to continue to strangle Leslie Cook to death; (5) there is no evidence of provocation; (6) the defendant is a large man and there is little sign of struggle; and (7) the defendant bit the breasts of the deceased and left the near-naked body exposed to the winter elements. The jury heard the testimony of Dr. Reay that it takes 3 to 5 minutes to effect death by manual strangulation. Continuous and steady pressure on the victim's neck is required. The amount of pressure required is sufficiently greater than the amount required to keep someone from crying out. The strangulation of Leslie Cook was cruel and brutal. The jury would be justified in concluding from the circumstances of this case that the death was not the result of an impulsive or spontaneous act flowing from an attempt to overcome resistance or to effect sexual contact and that the defendant chose to kill in order to silence his victim and conceal a rape.

* * *

Premeditation cannot automatically be inferred from elapsed time. Even so, the jury should be permitted to examine the evidence to glean what it can about intent and premeditation. I find the evidence of elapsed time, of the crime scene and other pertinent circumstances compel the conclusion the defendant had ample opportunity to premeditate. Further, the defendant caused Leslie Cook's death by strangulation. What one does is highly indicative of what one intended to do. The jury should not be precluded from considering the method of killing if its very nature provides clues to the mental process of the perpetrator.

* * *

The State presented substantial circumstantial evidence on the issue of premeditation. The trial court properly left that issue to the jury. The jury found that the defendant did premeditate. I would reinstate the first degree murder conviction of the defendant.

ANDERSEN, DURHAM and DORE, JJ., concur.

Notes and Questions

1. Generally, appellate courts defer to jury findings that premeditation was proved. This approach is illustrated by the North Carolina court's discussion of a defendant's contention that the evidence was insufficient to justify submission of premeditated murder to the jury:

   Under the "felled victim theory" of premeditation and deliberation, "when numerous wounds are inflicted, the defendant has the opportunity to premeditate from one shot to the next." Even where the gun is capable of being fired rapidly, "some amount of time, however brief, for thought and deliberation must elapse between each pull of the trigger." Here, [the witness] Harrell testified that at the time of the shooting, she heard four shots: "first a 'pow' and just a little hesitation and then three more consecutive from there." Agent Creasy, assigned to the Trace Evidence Section of the SBI Crime Laboratory, testified that one explanation for the concentration of gunshot residue on the victim's left hand is that the victim had raised his left hand to fend off an attack.

   We conclude the trial court did not err in denying defendant's motion to dismiss for lack of evidence showing premeditation and deliberation.

   State v. Watson 338 N.C. 168, 179, 449 S.E.2d 694, 701 (1994).

2. Where the evidence tends to show provocation (although insufficient to reduce the killing to manslaughter) or concern by the defendant for his safety (although insufficient to constitute a complete

defense), appellate courts are sometimes willing to reverse convictions for premeditated murder. In *State v. Corn*, 303 N.C. 293, 278 S.E.2d 221 (1981), for example, Melton and a companion entered Corn's home and found him lying on a sofa. Melton was intoxicated and said something—it may have been an accusation that Corn was homosexual—to which Corn responded, "You son-of-a-bitch, don't accuse me of that." He then jumped off the sofa, grabbed a nearby rifle, and shot Melton several times in the chest. Reversing a conviction for premeditated murder, the court explained:

> There is no evidence that defendant acted in accordance with a fixed design or that he had sufficient time to weigh the consequences of his actions. Defendant did not threaten Melton before the incident or exhibit any conduct which would indicate that he formed any intent to kill him prior to the incident in question. There was no significant history of arguments or ill will between the parties. Although defendant shot deceased several times, there is no evidence that any shots were fired after he fell or that defendant dealt any blows to the body once the shooting ended
>
> All the evidence tends to show that defendant shot Melton after a quarrel, in a state of passion, without aforethought or calm consideration. * * *

3. Does—or should—premeditation require a "calm" or perhaps "normal" mental process? In *People v. Hamm*, 120 Mich.App. 388, 328 N.W.2d 51 (1982), Hamm killed a psychiatrist, Dr. Hoyt, who had treated him during hospitalization. Hoyt had become a focal point of Hamm's delusions and Hamm was obsessed with the false belief that Hoyt was conspiring with local physicians to keep Hamm from obtaining treatment for what he believed to be arsenic poisoning. Several hours before the killing, Hamm attempted to get some shells for his gun, explaining that he wanted them "to kill Dr. Hoyt." A friend attempted to calm him down and the two discussed Hamm's problem and several options open to him, such as having his father help him, or going to the police or prosecuting attorney.

On appeal from his conviction for premeditated murder, Hamm urged that his mental illness and delusion precluded him from adequately considering "rational, viable alternatives" to killing so as to be guilty of first degree murder. The court first found no authority for construing premeditation as requir-

ing this sort of consideration. However, it continued:

> In any event, there was ample evidence to suggest that defendant considered several alternatives to killing Dr. Hoyt. Defendant had considered going to his father for help, suing Dr. Hoyt in a civil action, calling the police or prosecuting attorney, or shooting Dr. Hoyt in the legs and making him "confess" to defendant's father. Therefore, under the defendant's standard for determining deliberation, there was sufficient evidence to sustain a conviction.

Is it likely that Hamm's consideration of these alternatives was affected by his delusional beliefs? If so, perhaps Hamm did not engage in the sort of mental process that justifies treating his act of intentionally killing Hoyt as more serious than second degree murder.

4. Is premeditation, under any definition, an appropriate criterion with which to select those cases in which the maximum penalty—whatever it is—may be imposed? Consider the following.

The Significance of Deliberation and Impulse

Whether and to what extent homicidal behavior was preceded by deliberation is plainly of evidential value in determining what the actor knew and intended when he acted. The more extensive the deliberation, the more probable it is that at least the more palpable risks created by the homicidal act were clearly perceived, and at least its more immediate consequences intended. From this point of view, however, gradations in homicidal behavior from the purely impulsive to the completely deliberate bear directly upon the question whether the actor created the homicidal risk inadvertently or advertently and, if advertently, whether or not he intended to kill, and only indirectly upon his character. The difficult question is whether the impulsiveness or deliberateness of his behavior has direct and independent significance in relation to his character. Assuming that other factors indicative of his character, such as knowledge, intent and motive are the same, of what additional importance is it that his act was the product of or was preceded by more or less deliberation? It may be argued that the more carefully considered and the less impulsive the act is, the more it indicates basic perversion of the actor's conceptions of good and evil. But it is surely not self-evident that the man who acts on wrong principles is a more dangerous man than one who acts without considering what is good. There are, moreover, other objections to this view of the significance of deliberation. In the first place, it ignores that passion may influence deliberation as well as lead to action without deliberation, so that deliberate as well as impulsive action may be contrary to the actor's real notions of good and evil. In the second place, it does not embrace either deliberation about means rather than ends or acts which are preceded by but are not in accord with the results of deliberation. And yet it is extremely difficult in most cases to discover in what terms the actor deliberated or what was the relationship between deliberation and act. These objections are not avoided by stating the significance of deliberation in another way. Thus it may be said that reflection prior to action indicates that the actor lacks the sort of desires that will prevent such an act, since reflection is the opportunity to bring such desires into play, an opportunity which, by hypothesis, is not afforded by impulsive action; whereas action without reflection does not permit of that inference because if the actor had deliberated he might not have acted as he did. But in order to draw from these premises the conclusion that the man who acts deliberately is more dangerous than the man who acts impulsively, it must be asserted that the probability that the former's deliberations will result in wrong judgments is greater than the probability that the latter will not reflect before acting. This proposition also requires proof. The truth is, we think, that deliberation has no independent significance in relation to character and that the importance usually accorded it properly belongs to other factors which are its concomitants such, for example, as lapse of time, or to still other factors which it evidences, such as knowledge and intent. When the matter is viewed in that way, no difficulty is experienced in dealing with cases in which deliberation itself results in the intensification of passion, as it may when the enormity of an injury done the actor or the value of an end to be served by a homicidal act becomes apparent only after thought.

Wechsler and Michael, *A Rationale of the Law of Homicide,* 37 Colum.L. Rev. 701, 1261, 1282–84 (1937).

Editors' Note: Choosing Life or Death for a Convicted Murderer

As was pointed out in the introduction to this chapter, premeditated murders were originally distinguished from other murders for purposes of separate classification in large part to identify those killings for which the death penalty should be required or at least available. As a result of the Supreme Court's application of the Eighth Amendment in the death penalty context, a number of jurisdictions have revised their homicide classification schemes to distinguish in what is regarded as a more appropriate—and constitutionally acceptable—manner those situations in which the death penalty will be available. Some of these jurisdictions have rejected the pattern in which murder is divided into degrees and rather have created the offense of "capital murder" for which death may be imposed.

Definitions of capital murder sometimes incorporate the premeditation requirement. Under the Virginia statute, for example, capital murder is defined as "the willful, deliberate and premeditated killing" of another under certain circumstances, as for example, if the victim was a law enforcement officer killed for the purpose of interfering with the officer's official duties, the killing was "for hire," more than one person was killed as a part of the same transaction, or the killing was related to the commission of rape, abduction, or robbery. Va. Code § 18.2–31.

Other jurisdictions limit the death penalty to those situations in which the defendant has been convicted of a specified homicide offense and, in addition, "special" or "aggravating" circumstances are shown by the prosecution to exist. Illinois, for example, makes a defendant eligible for the death penalty if the conviction is for murder and any one of eight aggravating factors is shown. Ill.Stat.Ann. ch. 38, § 9-1(b). California permits imposition of the death penalty upon conviction of first degree murder (see page 153) and a finding by the jury that at least one of nineteen "special circumstances" is found to be true. Cal. Penal Code § 190.2(a). Among those special circumstances are:

(1) The murder was intentional and carried out for financial gain.

(2) The defendant was previously convicted of murder in the first or second degree. * * *

* * *

(5) The murder was committed for the purpose of avoiding or preventing a lawful arrest or to perfect an escape from lawful custody.

* * *

(7) The victim was a peace officer * * * who, while engaged in the course of the performance of his or her duties was intentionally killed, and the defendant knew or reasonably should have known that the victim was a police officer engaged in the performance of his or her duties; or the victim was a peace officer * * * and was intentionally killed in retaliation for the performance of his or her official duties.

* * *

(10) The victim was a witness to a crime who was intentionally killed for the purpose of preventing his or her testimony in any criminal proceeding, and the killing was not committed during the commission, or attempted commission of the crime to which he or she was a witness; or the victim was a witness to a crime and was intentionally killed in retaliation for his or her testimony in any criminal proceeding.

* * *

(14) The murder was especially heinous, atrocious, or cruel, manifesting exceptional depravity. As utilized in this section, the phrase especially heinous, atrocious or cruel manifesting exceptional depravity means a conscienceless, or pitiless crime which is unnecessarily torturous to the victim.

(15) The defendant intentionally killed the victim while lying in wait.

(16) The victim was intentionally killed because of his or her race, color, religion, nationality or country of origin.

(17) The murder was committed while the defendant was engaged in or was an accomplice in the commission of, or attempted commission of, or the immediate flight after committing or attempting to commit the following felonies: [robbery, kidnapping, rape, sodomy, lewd acts upon a child, oral copulation, burglary, arson, and train wrecking].

(18) The murder was intentional and involved the infliction of torture. For purpose of this section torture requires proof of the infliction of extreme physical
pain no matter how long its duration.

(19) The defendant intentionally killed the victim by the administration of
poison.

The making of the requisite finding of the truth of the allegation that a special circumstance exists does not require the imposition of the death sentence, but triggers
further proceedings to determine whether death or life imprisonment is the appropriate penalty.

D. PROVOKED KILLINGS: VOLUNTARY MANSLAUGHTER

Editors' Introduction: Voluntary Manslaughter, Reasonable Provocation, and the Objective "Reasonable Person" Standard

Homicide law has long given some significance to provoking circumstances that
are insufficient to justify relieving the defendant of all criminal responsibility for
the killing. Traditionally, this has been accomplished by providing that a killing
will be reduced from murder to voluntary manslaughter if the facts show "adequate
provocation."

Perhaps because provocation only reduces the seriousness of the offense for which
the accused may be convicted, the law has restricted those who can benefit from
the doctrine to accuseds who meet a partially objective standard. Thus the need for the
provocation to be "adequate" includes a requirement that it have been sufficient to
provoke a reasonable person.

Tradition has also included substantial concern that juries might abuse the power to
mitigate a killing on provocation grounds. As a result, much of the law in this area has
addressed the power of the trial judge to characterize provocation as inadequate "as a
matter of law" and consequently neither instruct the jury on voluntary manslaughter
nor give them that offense as a possible verdict choice.

Modern statutes often retain much of the traditional approach, even if manslaughter
is not formally subdivided between voluntary and involuntary manslaughter. However,
courts are increasingly uncomfortable with traditional law's reluctance to entrust to
juries the task of deciding whether particular provocation was adequate. This is best
illustrated by modern courts' treatment of the traditionally rigid rule that "mere words"
cannot give rise to provocation. This rule has, to some extent, been modified by some
courts.

The issue was raised in *Speake v. State,* 610 So.2d 1238 (Ala.Crim.App.1992).
Larry Wayne Speake was convicted of the murder of his wife. On appeal, he argued
that the trial court committed reversible error in refusing to charge the jury on the
criminal offense of manslaughter as a lesser included offense of murder. His confes-

sion, he argued, contained sufficient evidence of provocation to raise a jury question. The significant part of his confession stated:

> On Thursday, December 13, 1990, my wife and I went to bed about 10:00 p.m. and watched the news. After the news was over, I wanted to make love to Charlotte. Charlotte did not want to make love and she brought up the ring she had been wanting to buy. We got into a fuss about the ring. Charlotte got out of bed and put her clothes on. She put on a black sweater with a print on the front and black pants. Charlotte told me she was going to leave me alone, and said she was going to find someone else to have sex with. Then Charlotte went into the kitchen and I got out of bed and followed her. In the kitchen, Charlotte got her purse and car keys and went outside onto the back porch. I followed her. I was telling her not to go. At this point, Charlotte said some very hurting stuff to me and I lost my temper. I choked her with a belt type rope. When I realized what I had done, I panicked. I couldn't believe what I had done. It shouldn't have happened. I cried and begged Charlotte to forgive me. After this, I put Charlotte's body into the back of my pickup truck and took her clothes off.

Finding no error in the trial court's refusal to permit the jury to consider provoked manslaughter, the court explained:

> Fundamentally, the question in this case is whether the provocation was sufficient and the appellant's "fit of temper" and passion was justified in any degree. Legally, the issue is whether a wife's admission that she is going "to find someone else to have sex with" constitutes legal provocation so as to reduce the commission of an intentional killing from murder to manslaughter. We hold that, as a matter of law, the comments in this case do not constitute sufficient provocation.
>
> * * * "The law does not accord impunity to unbridled passions, nor suffer an individual to dispose of the life of his fellow being on his own judgment and belief." "The well established rule in Alabama is that mere words, no matter how insulting or abusive, cannot reduce a killing to manslaughter. *Watson v. State*, 82 Ala. 10, 2 So. 455 (1886)." "It is laid down by the most approved authors on criminal law, that 'words of reproach, how grievous soever, are not a provocation sufficient to free the party killing from the charge of murder, and neither are provoking actions and questions, without an assault.'—Roscoe's Cr.Ev., 683, marg.; Fost. 290; 1 Hawk.Pl.Cr. chap. 31, § 33; 1 Hale, 455. Mr. Russell says, 'no affront by bare words or gestures, however false and malicious, and aggravated with the most provoking circumstances, will free the party killing from the guilt of murder.'—1 Russ. 434–5." *Felix v. State*, 18 Ala. 720, 723 (1851).
>
> In Alabama, it is well settled that witnessing the act of adultery is recognized as legal provocation for the intentional homicide of either the unfaithful spouse or the paramour. However, it is also settled that mere admissions of infidelity do not constitute legal provocation.
>
> * * *
>
> We note that "[t]he modern tendency is to extend the rule of mitigation beyond the narrow situation where one spouse actually catches the other in the act of committing adultery." 2 W. LaFave and A. Scott, *Substantive Criminal Law* § 7.10(b)(5) (1986).

> "The formerly well-established rule that words alone (or words plus gestures) will never do for reducing an intentional killing to voluntary manslaughter has in many jurisdictions changed into a rule that words also will sometimes do, at least if the words are informational (conveying information of a fact which constitutes a reasonable provocation when that fact is observed) rather than merely insulting or abusive words. Thus a sudden confession of adultery by a wife, or information from a third person that a wife has been unfaithful, has sometimes been held to constitute a provocation to the husband of the same sort as if he had made an 'ocular observation' of his wife's adultery."

2 Substantive Criminal Law at § 7.10(b)(6) (footnotes omitted). Despite this "modern tendency," this Court is bound by the decisions of the Alabama Supreme Court. Furthermore, in this case, the wife's "threat" to "find someone else to have sex with" is not an admission of past adultery. Rather, it is a threat of future misconduct that does not even imply the present existence of a specific paramour with whom she intended to commit the act of adultery. Here, the threatened act of adultery was neither so imminent nor so certain that the suggestion of adultery lessened the appellant's culpability for the intentional killing. * * *

Although there is evidence that the wife also said some "very hurting stuff" to the appellant, there is no evidence of what that "stuff" was. Therefore, that "very hurting stuff" has no legal significance under the traditional rule that mere words, however offensive or insulting, will not reduce a homicide from murder to manslaughter.

Modern statutes based upon the Model Penal Code—see § 210.3(1)(a) on page 156 often replace traditional "adequate provocation" with "extreme emotional disturbance for which there is reasonable explanation or excuse." Under such statutes, courts agree that trial judges should be particularly unwilling to hold that specific situations show insufficient "extreme" disturbance of the defendant or an insufficiently "reasonable" basis for that disturbance to create an issue for the jury to decide. Under such a statute, Larry Speake would quite likely be entitled to have the jury consider whether his wife's words caused him "extreme emotional disturbance" and, if so, whether they constituted an objectively reasonable basis for that disturbance.

In determining the objective reasonableness of provocation or the "explanation or excuse" for a defendant's "extreme emotional disturbance," the defendant's showing must be judged against a reasonable person standard. A major issue is the extent to which, if any, the objective reasonable person should be regarded as having the defendant's characteristics.

The issue was presented by *State v. Thunberg,* 492 N.W.2d 534 (Minn.1992), in which the evidence indicated the defendant had been intoxicated at the time of the killing. The prosecution persuaded the trial judge to tell the jury it should evaluate the defendant's claim of provocation by asking whether the situation would have provoked a *sober* person of ordinary self-control. The court explained how the Model Penal Code's approach would affect traditional law on this matter:

The traditional approach of the courts that have considered this issue is that the adequacy of provocation is to be judged from the perspective of the reasonable sober person. 2 W. LaFave and A. Scott, Substantive Criminal Law § 7.10(b)(10) (1986). See, e.g., *Bishop v. United States*, 107 F.2d 297, 302-03 (D.C.Cir.1939) ("If a defendant is intoxicated, there is no requirement that provocation for 'heat of passion' be greater than that that would arouse a reasonable, sober man to act.").

However, as LaFave and Scott point out, there has been movement in the criminal codes away from the strictly objective reasonable person test for determining the adequacy of provision. The Model Penal Code provides for reduction from murder to manslaughter if the killing was "committed under the influence of extreme mental or emotional disturbance for which there is a reasonable explanation or excuse," with reasonableness to be "determined from the viewpoint of a person in the actor's situation under the circumstances as [the actor] believes them to be." Model Penal Code § 210.3 (Official Draft and Revised Comments 1980). The comment to this section states in relevant part:

> The critical element in the Model Code formulation is the clause requiring that reasonableness be assessed "from the viewpoint of a person in the actor's situation." The word "situation" is designedly ambiguous. On the one hand, it is clear that personal handicaps and external circumstances must be taken into account. Thus, blindness, shock from traumatic injury, and extreme grief are all easily read into the term "situation." This result is sound, for it would be morally obtuse to appraise a crime for mitigation of punishment without reference to these factors. On the other hand, it is equally plain that idiosyncratic moral values are not part of the actor's situation. * * * The Model Code endorses a formulation that affords sufficient flexibility to differentiate in particular cases between those special aspects of the actor's situation that should be deemed material for purpose of grading and those that should be ignored. There thus will be room for interpretation of the word "situation," and that is precisely the flexibility desired. There will be opportunity for argument about the reasonableness of explanation or excuse, and that too is a ground on which argument is required. In the end, the question is whether the actor's loss of self-control can be understood in terms that arouse sympathy in the ordinary citizen. Section 210.3 faces this issue squarely and leaves the ultimate judgment to the ordinary citizen in the function of a juror assigned to resolve the specific case.

Model Penal Code § 210.3 commentary (Official Draft and Revised Comments 1980). In other words, the Model Penal Code leaves it to the parties to argue the relevance of the defendant's intoxication to the issue of whether adequate provocation exists.

According to LaFave and Scott, a "substantial minority" of the modern criminal codes contain a provision "along these lines," although some of the provisions, while not following the strictly objective traditional test, "seem less subjective than the Model Penal Code provision." This middle category includes those provisions such as Montana's ("from the viewpoint of a reasonable person in the actor's situation") and Oregon's ("from the standpoint of an ordinary person in the actor's situation").

Concluding that the Minnesota statute was one within the middle category, the court held that a trial judge should not specify for the jury whether the reasonable person was intoxicated or sober. Thus the defendant and the prosecutor are free to argue to the jurors that they should or should not judge the defendant by whether a reasonable and intoxicated person would have been provoked.

With regard to the burden of proof on those matters that distinguish provoked killings from those treated more severely, the case law shows some confusion. Traditionally, as the Editors' Introduction to Section B made clear, the malice afore-thought required for murder is conceptualized as the culpable mental state required for murder in the absence of circumstances that mitigate the killing to manslaughter. Thus provocation negated malice aforethought, on which the prosecution has the burden of proof. Essentially, then, the defendant has the obligation to raise the issue by producing evidence of provocation, or the jury need not be told about it. If the issue is so raised, however, the prosecution's burden of proving malice aforethought requires it to prove that the defendant killed under circumstances *not* giving rise to adequate provocation. How explicit this must be told to the jury is a matter of judg-ment. Massachusetts, for example, has held that the better practice is to explicitly tell the jury that the prosecution has the burden of proving the absence of provocation. A conviction will not be reversed, however, if the judge does not make this explicit but does tell the jury that provocation negates malice and the prosecution must prove malice. *Commonwealth v. Todd*, 408 Mass. 724, 727, 563 N.E.2d 211, 214 (1990).

The United States Supreme Court held in *Mullaney v. Wilbur*, 421 U.S. 684, 95 S.Ct. 1881, 44 L.Ed.2d 508 (1975), that if the applicable law in such a case requires the prosecution to prove malice aforethought, the defendant's due process rights are violat-ed if the jury is told that malice is "presumed" unless the defendant proves adequate provocation. Yet the Court two years later in *Patterson v. New York*, 432 U.S. 197, 97 S.Ct. 2319, 53 L.Ed.2d 281 (1977), held that New York's more modern statutory scheme did not violate due process when it distinguished murder and manslaughter by the provocation-like concept of extreme emotional distress and imposed upon a defendant proved guilty of murder the burden of then proving extreme emotional dis-tress sufficient to reduce his liability to manslaughter.

This confusing case law is discussed in the Editors' Introduction to Chapter 13. Most likely, however, *Mullaney* does not mean that the federal constitution requires the traditional position just described, in which the defendant must raise the issue as to whether a killing should be reduced from murder to manslaughter, but when the issue is raised the prosecution must prove the absence of adequate provocation. Most likely, *Mullaney* held that due process barred placing the burden of proof regarding adequate provocation on the defendant only because the Maine statutory scheme there at issue required no real showing by the prosecution to first establish that the killing was mur-der. The jury instead was told that malice aforethought is "presumed" from proof that the defendant killed the victim. If a jury is told in realistic terms that the prosecution must prove intent to kill or one of the other culpable mental states ordinarily sufficient for malice aforethought in order to establish the accused's guilt of murder, the jury could then be told—*Mullaney* notwithstanding—that the jury should reduce the killing from murder to voluntary manslaughter only if the accused proved by a preponderance of the evidence that he killed in reaction to adequate provocation.

In any case, *Patterson* explicitly holds that under a modern statutory scheme based on the Model Penal Code model, like that applied in the principal case that follows, once the prosecution proves the defendant guilty of murder the burden of establishing extreme emotional distress—the modern equivalent of adequate provocation—can be placed on the defendant. The trend is toward this approach.

State v. Raguseo

Supreme Court of Connecticut, 1993
225 Conn. 114, 622 A.2d 519.

BORDEN, Associate Justice.

The defendant, John Raguseo, appeals from the judgment of conviction, after a jury trial, of murder * * *. The defendant claims that the trial court improperly: (1) denied his motions for a judgment of acquittal and for a new trial because the evidence did not establish that he had the intent to cause the death of the victim; (2) denied his motions for a judgment of acquittal and for a new trial because the evidence established the affirmative defense of extreme emotional disturbance; [and] (3) instructed the jury regarding the affirmative defense of extreme emotional distress * * *. We affirm the judgment of the trial court.

The jury reasonably could have found the following facts. The defendant lived in an apartment building on Clinton Avenue in Norwalk. The apartment building had its own parking lot for its tenants, and each tenant had an assigned parking space. The defendant owned a 1983 Camaro automobile that he parked in the space, and a 1979 Plymouth van that he parked at his mother's house. He took meticulous care of both vehicles and the parking space at his apartment building. He posted a no parking sign in front of the space, and he often swept the space, painted the lines on either side of the space, and clipped the shrubbery on a nearby fence. Prior to the crime, the defendant had repeatedly complained to the apartment building's superintendent about the unauthorized use of his parking space by the guests of other tenants.

At approximately 12:20 A.M., on June 21, 1990, the defendant returned home to find that someone had parked in his space. The defendant parked his vehicle directly behind the automobile in his space so that the other automobile could not be moved. The defendant then went inside the building to his apartment. He called 911 to com-

plain that someone had parked in his space but the police informed him that they could not tow the vehicle because it was parked on private property. He also telephoned a friend, Carol Bakinowski, to complain that someone had parked in his space and that he did not know what he would do if "someone comes to the door and starts abusing me." While they were speaking, Bakinowski could hear a loud banging noise in the background. The defendant told her that he was banging a knife on the kitchen table.

At approximately 2 A.M., the defendant saw from his window that the victim in this case, Philip Iacozza, had parked in his space, and had returned to his automobile and was trying to back out of the parking space. When the defendant saw the victim almost back the automobile into his vehicle, he took the knife and went down to the parking lot.

After a brief verbal exchange, the defendant repeatedly stabbed the victim in the head and torso. The defendant then returned to his apartment and called the police. When police officers arrived, he stated that "he couldn't take it any more, that he had done it, and that he was tired of people parking in his parking space." The defendant told the officers that they could find the knife with which he had stabbed the victim in the kitchen. The officers then found a blood-stained, eight inch knife in the kitchen sink.

The state charged the defendant in an information with murder * * *. The defendant at trial did not deny that he had caused Iacozza's death, but instead claimed that: (1) he did not have the intent to cause the death of Iacozza; (2) he was not guilty because of a mental disease or defect; and (3) he had acted under the influence of an extreme emotional disturbance. The jury returned a guilty verdict and the court rendered a judgment on the information. The defendant was then committed to the Whiting Forensic

Institute, but later was transferred to the Somers correctional facility.

I

The defendant first claims that the trial court improperly denied his motions for a judgment of acquittal and a new trial because the evidence did not establish that he had the intent to cause the death of the victim. We disagree.

The defendant was charged with murder * * *. "'In order to be convicted under our murder statute, the defendant must possess the specific intent to cause the death of the victim. To act intentionally, the defendant must have had the conscious objective to cause the death of the victim. Ordinarily, intent can only be proved by circumstantial evidence; it may be and usually is inferred from the defendant's conduct. Intent to cause death may be inferred from the type of weapon used, the manner in which it was used, the type of wound inflicted and the events leading to and immediately following the death. . . . Furthermore, it is a permissible, albeit not a necessary or mandatory, inference that a defendant intended the natural consequences of his voluntary conduct. . . .'"

On the basis of the evidence and the inferences reasonably drawn therefrom, the jury could have concluded beyond a reasonable doubt that the defendant had intended to kill the victim. The defendant had been angry because, upon returning home from work, he discovered a vehicle parked in his parking space. He blocked the victim's vehicle from leaving and watched the space from the window to see when the driver would return. While waiting, he repeatedly banged the murder weapon against his kitchen table. As soon as he saw the victim, he left his apartment, carrying an eight inch knife, and attacked the victim. He inflicted approximately fifteen stab wounds, most in vital areas of the body. Many of the wounds were deep and reached vital organs of the victim. In light of these facts, we conclude that there was ample evidence from which the jury could have concluded beyond a reasonable doubt that the defendant had the intent to kill the victim.

* * *

II

The defendant claims that the trial court improperly denied his motions for a judgment of acquittal and for a new trial because the evidence established the affirmative defense of extreme emotional disturbance. We disagree.

Conflicting evidence was introduced at trial regarding the defendant's mental state both before and after the attack on the victim. Bakinowski testified that she had known the defendant for several years and that he had a history of reacting poorly to unexpected events. She also testified concerning the defendant's repeated concern about people parking in his space, and his meticulous care of the van and automobile. Finally, she testified that the defendant, prior to the time of the murder, had become increasingly depressed, and that, during the telephone conversation just prior to the attack, he had sounded desperate.

The defendant's mother testified that her son had had emotional problems for many years, and had been hospitalized on several occasions, including one instance following a suicide attempt. The defendant also elicited testimony from police officers that he had been agitated and upset when they arrived at his apartment shortly after the attack. The defendant also presented his medical records and the testimony of James R. Merikangas, a neurologist and psychiatrist, who had examined the defendant for trial. Merikangas testified that it was his diagnosis that, on June 21, 1990, the defendant suffered from paranoid schizophrenia and that, as a result, the defendant's thinking was illogical and irrational.

The state presented testimony, however, disputing the defendant's evidence as to his degree of emotional disturbance. John Sullivan, a psychiatrist, testified for the state that, although the defendant had difficulty controlling his anger at times, there was nothing to indicate that the defendant had been psychotic or out of touch with reality. Several police officers testified that the defendant had not appeared to be agitated or shaking, and responded to questions calmly. Moreover, one police officer testified that the defendant did not appear to be "at the end of his rope."

Section 53a–54a(a) provides in relevant part that "it shall be an affirmative defense [to the crime of murder] that the defendant committed the proscribed act or acts under the influence of extreme emotional disturbance for which there was a reasonable explanation or excuse, the reasonableness of which is to be determined from the viewpoint of a person in the defendant's situation under the circumstances as the defendant believed them to be." Extreme emotional disturbance "is a mitigating circumstance which will reduce the crime of murder to manslaughter."

The burden is on the defendant to prove the affirmative defense of extreme emotional disturbance by a preponderance of the evidence. "In the final analysis, the ultimate determination of the presence or absence of extreme emotional disturbance [is] one of fact for the trier, aided by the expert testimony of both sides, but left to its own factual determinations."

The state concedes that there was substantial evidence that the defendant acted under an extreme emotional disturbance. The defendant, on the other hand, also concedes that there was some evidence suggesting that he did not act under an extreme emotional disturbance. In light of these concessions, we rely on the fundamental role of the jury as the finder of fact. In a case in which the evidence is conflicting, it is the quintessential jury function to reject or accept certain evidence, and to believe or disbelieve any expert testimony.

* * *

In the present case, the defendant has not demonstrated that the jury incorrectly applied the law to the facts or was governed by ignorance, prejudice, corruption or partiality. To the contrary, there were substantial facts from which the jury could have concluded that the defendant did not act under an extreme emotional disturbance. The jury heard testimony from the state's expert witness that the defendant was not psychotic and that he was not unreasonable in desiring not to have anyone else park in his space. Furthermore, there was ample testimony that the defendant, immediately following the attack on the victim, was not in a state of extreme emotional disturbance but instead remained calm, called the police, and understood the import of his actions. From these facts, and the jury's right to reject any or all of the defendant's evidence, we conclude that the trial court properly denied the defendant's motions for a judgment of acquittal and a new trial.

III

The defendant claims that the trial court improperly instructed the jury regarding the affirmative defense of extreme emotional disturbance. We are not persuaded.

The following facts are relevant to this claim. The trial court instructed the jury on extreme emotional disturbance, in relevant part, as follows: "Our statute on the affirmative defense of extreme emotional disturbance insofar as it applies to this case provides that, 'in any prosecution for murder, it shall be an affirmative defense that the defendant committed the proscribed act or acts under the influence of extreme emotional disturbance for which there was a reasonable explanation or excuse, the reasonableness of which is to be determined from the viewpoint of a person in the defendant's situation under the circumstances as the defendant believed them to be.' . . .

"I will now discuss with you the elements of the affirmative defense of extreme emotional disturbance. There are three elements to this affirmative defense.

"First; the defendant's emotional disturbance was not a mental disease or defect that rises to the level of the affirmative defense of mental disease or defect as that has been defined [for] you. That is, that he was not suffering from a mental disease or defect that caused him to lack substantial capacity as a result of that mental disease or defect either to appreciate the wrongfulness of his act or to adjust his conduct to the requirements of the law.

"Secondly; that the defendant was exposed to an extremely unusual and overwhelming stress that is more than mere annoyance or unhappiness. While this emotional stress might often be caused by a sudden triggering situation, hot blood as you say, it might as well arise by virtue of a significant mental trauma caused—causing a long period of brooding or dwelling on some presumed injustice.

"And thirdly; the defendant had an extreme emotional reaction to this state as a result of which there was a loss of self control and his reason was overborne by intense feelings, such as passion or anger or distress or grief, or excessive agitation or other similar emotions. You should give consideration as to whether the intensity of these feelings was such that the defendant's usual intellectual and emotional controls failed, and that his normal rational thinking no longer prevailed at the time of the act.

"As used in this affirmative defense, the word 'extreme' means the greatest degree of intensity away from the norm, away from the normal or usual state for the defendant.

"If you find that the defendant acted under extreme emotional disturbance as I have defined that term for you, you must also find . . . that there was a reasonable explanation . . . for any emotional disturbance suffered by the defendant at the time of the stabbing. The reasonableness of this explanation or excuse is to be determined from the viewpoint of a reasonable person in the defendant's situation under the circumstances as the defendant believed them to be."

The jury deliberated for more than four days. The jury asked for reinstruction on this affirmative defense on three separate occasions. The reinstructions were, for the most part, the same as the original instruction. After the second reinstruction, the court also stated: "And here if the evidence and the claims of the defendant, as I understand it, is that the—there was a trauma causing a long period of dwelling on presumed injustice with regard to the circumstances involving himself and involving his parking—allotted parking space."

After further deliberation, the jury sought reinstruction again on extreme emotional disturbance, requesting that the trial court focus on: (1) the three factors that make up the defense and whether all three must be met; (2) the definition of the "norm" and whose norm is relevant, society's or the defendant's; and (3) the reasonable person's perspective. The trial court repeated its prior instructions and also stated that the reasonableness of the explanation for the emotional disturbance must be "determined from the viewpoint of a reasonable person; that is, a person of ordinary intellect and faculties, who finds him—who would find himself in the defendant's situation under the circumstances as the defendant believed it to be."

* * *

The defendant * * * argues that the charge on extreme emotional disturbance was improper because the jury was instructed that the reasonableness of the explanation or excuse for the emotional disturbance was to be determined from the viewpoint of a reasonable person in the defendant's situation under the circumstances as the defendant believed them to be. The defendant contends that the jury should be instructed that the reasonableness of the explanation or excuse must be determined from his perspective rather than a reasonable person's perspective. Additionally, the defendant argues that this instruction is improper in any case in which the defendant has also raised the affirmative defense of mental disease or defect because the jury is likely to become confused about the relationship between the affirmative defenses. We disagree.

In *State v. Ortiz*, 217 Conn. 648, 652-53, 588 A.2d 127 (1991), we rejected a virtually identical challenge to such an instruction. In *Ortiz*, the defendant claimed that § 53a–54a(a) required an instruction that the jury must consider the reasonableness of the explanation or excuse as determined from the defendant's viewpoint rather than from the viewpoint of a reasonable person in the defendant's situation under the circumstances as he believed them to be. * * * [W]e concluded that the legislature intended to establish "'a standard that is objective in its overview, but subjective as to the defendant's belief'; and, with regard to the objective element contained in the statute, [we stated] that 'the reasonable man yardstick is only used to determine the reasonableness of the explanation or excuse of the action of the defendant from the viewpoint of a person in the defendant's situation under the circumstances as the defendant believed them to be.'"

We reasoned in *Ortiz* that the defendant's challenge to the instruction, as in the present case, would "eviscerate the element of objectivity that the drafters intended to preserve," and would make the inquiry entirely subjective. * * * In the present case, the defendant has not presented any significant justification for overruling *Ortiz* other than an unsupported claim that the standard is unworkable.[4] "'[A] court should not overrule its earlier decisions unless the most cogent reasons and inescapable logic require it.'"

* * *

V

[In the course of ruling on several claims of procedural error, the court observed that Dr. Merikangas, the psychiatrist who testified for the defense, had elicited from the defendant that the defendant had consumed a six pack of beer and some wine prior to returning home on the evening of the attack. Dr. Merikangas's report concluded in part that "Mr. Raguseo is a chronic paranoid schizophrenic . . . who under the stress of the circumstance felt threatened and because of a defect of mind and reason exacerbated by alcohol and diabetes was substantially incapable of conforming his conduct to the requirements of law."]

* * *

The judgment is affirmed.

In this opinion PETERS, C.J., and NORCOTT and SANTANIELLO, JJ., concurred.

BERDON, Associate Justice, dissenting.

I disagree with the majority, which upholds the trial court's jury instruction on the defense of extreme emotional disturbance pursuant to General Statutes § 53a–54a(a). The trial court stated that the reasonableness of the explanation or excuse for the emotional disturbance was to be determined from the viewpoint of a reasonable person in the defendant's situation under circumstances as the defendant believed them to be. * * * I believe that *Ortiz* was wrongfully decided on this issue. The trial court's injection of the term "reasonable" into the language of the extreme emotional disturbance defense created an overly objective test that prevented the jury from considering the defendant's mental abnormalities.

For this defense to make any sense, the jury's determination of whether there was a reasonable explanation or excuse for the extreme emotional disturbance (the objective test) must be determined from the defendant's viewpoint under circumstances as the defendant believed them to be (the subjective test), not the viewpoint of a reasonable person in the defendant's situation. The jury must be able to consider the defendant's eccentricities in order to assess the situation from the defendant's viewpoint. I have concluded that this subjective/objective test must be employed for several reasons.

The plain language of the statute directs us to determine the reasonableness of the explanation or excuse for the emotional disturbance "from the viewpoint of a person in the defendant's situation under the circumstances as the defendant believed them to be." General Statutes § 53a–54a(a). This clearly means the defendant's situation under the circumstances as the defendant perceived them to be.

* * *

---

[4] The defendant concedes that no state has adopted a totally subjective extreme emotional disturbance defense, as would be required if we were to agree with his claim.

Our extreme emotional disturbance defense, as provided in § 53a-54a(a), is based on the Model Penal Code of the American Law Institute, Tentative Draft No. 9, § 201.3. If there is any ambiguity in the language of § 53a–54a(a), the comments accompanying the Model Penal Code clarify that the jury must consider the defendant's situation in applying the defense. The important—and necessary—terms are "situation" and "circumstances." As the Model Penal Code comments explain, "[t]he word 'situation' is designedly ambiguous. On the one hand, it is clear that personal handicaps and some external circumstances must be taken into account. Thus, blindness, shock from traumatic injury, and extreme grief are all easily read into the term 'situation.' This result is sound, for it would be morally obtuse to appraise a crime for mitigation of punishment without reference to these factors. On the other hand, it is equally plain that idiosyncratic *moral* values are not part of the actor's situation." (Emphasis added.) II A.L.I., Model Penal Code and Commentaries (1980) § 210.3(1)(b), comment, p. 62. Thus, the drafters intended the word "situation" to focus the jury's attention on the defendant's unique mental and emotional attributes, while still allowing the jury to determine whether a reasonable person would agree that the explanation or excuse for the defendant's emotional disturbance was objectively reasonable.

* * *

In sum, the test for determining whether the extreme emotional disturbance defense should apply is both subjective, in that it permits the jury to consider the defendant's particular eccentricities, and objective, in that the jury is asked to determine whether the *explanation or excuse* for the defendant's disturbance was reasonable in light of his subjective situation and perception of the circumstances.

I can understand why the jury had difficulty applying the court's instructions—having been instructed on the extreme emotional disturbance defense four times—to the substantial evidence indicating extreme emotional disturbance. On the third reinstruction, the jury asked the trial court to focus on whether the definition of "norm" referred to the norm for the defendant or the norm for society. The jury was obviously struggling to consider the defendant's emotional or mental imbalance in its determination of the defendant's situation. The court's use of the reasonable person standard, however, effectively precluded any consideration of the defendant's emotional or mental imbalance.

* * *

Because the conduct of a person who has taken the life of another can rarely, if ever, be characterized as reasonable from the viewpoint of a reasonable person, the majority takes the heart out of the extreme emotional disturbance defense by upholding the "reasonable person" instruction.

By adopting the extreme emotional disturbance defense, the legislature sought to bridge the gap between insanity and cold-blooded intent to kill. The majority's interpretation eliminates this bridge and forces the jury to choose one extreme or the other.

Accordingly, I would order a new trial.

Notes and Questions

1. Traditionally, a killing is not reduced to voluntary manslaughter if an objectively sufficient "cooling period" occurred between the provocation and the killing. This matter was presented in an usual procedural posture in *People v. Wofford*, 196 Mich.App. 275, 492 N.W.2d 747 (1992), in which the facts were as follows:

> The fatal shooting of Spencer Thomas arose out of an altercation involving the decedent and defendant the previous day. While at work, defendant was informed by Toya Reed, Kevin Lee, and defendant's boss that "a guy was threatening him," apparently because defendant was romantically involved with Toya Reed, who was Kevin Lee's girl friend. Later, while looking for Lee in order to find out more about the threat, defendant encountered the decedent, who was Lee's cousin, and asked him whether he was threatening defendant because of Toya Reed and why. An argument ensued, and the decedent took out a gun. The decedent then fired a shot, missing defendant as he was leaving in his car. On the evening of the following day, May 24, 1989, the decedent was sitting on his porch when defendant and Toya Reed arrived in defendant's car. Defendant got out of his car, took a gun from the back of the vehicle, and confronted the decedent, who also had a gun. Defendant shot the decedent three times, hitting him in the back at least twice. According to the autopsy report, the decedent died of a gunshot wound to the right upper back.

Wofford was charged with second degree murder but in a trial to the court without a jury was found guilty of voluntary manslaughter. The trial judge specifically found:

> I think that he was still mad about what happened to him before and he did not take it lightly.
>
> I believe beyond any reasonable doubt that the defendant at the time of the act, was

disturbed by mental or emotional excitement which make an ordinary person likely to act rationally without due deliberation or reflection and from passion rather than judgment. Secondly, I believe that the killing was a result of provocation or passion and that occurred before reasonable time had elapsed and that this defendant had time to cool, even though 24 hours is a considerable period of time. However, the law does not say how long a reasonable time is and I think that this defendant when he went over there fired at [the] decease[d] three times, hitting him in the back at least twice. This indicates that he was not, his life was not threatened to the point where he had no other alternative but to kill the defendant.

On appeal by the defendant on unrelated procedural grounds, the appellate court commented:

In finding defendant guilty of voluntary manslaughter, the trial court concluded that the killing occurred in circumstances of passion and provocation before sufficient time had elapsed to enable defendant to control his passions. While the trial court correctly noted that, as a matter of law, no precise time has been established during which passion must subside, the "cooling off" period must be reasonable. Recently, in [People v. Pouncey, 437 Mich. 382, 471 N.W.2d 346 (1991)], the Supreme Court reversed this Court's decision and held that the trial court correctly refused the requested jury instruction on voluntary manslaughter where approximately thirty seconds was sufficient to constitute a "cooling off" period.

In this case, we believe that sufficient time had passed for defendant to control his passions and that a "cooling off" period of twenty-four hours was not reasonable. The trial court's findings reveal that defendant chose to return to the decedent's house with a gun because defendant was angry about what had happened to him the day before. Defendant was not compelled to go back to the decedent's house and could have stayed away. Although the trial court committed clear error in finding that sufficient time had not passed to enable defendant to indulge in cool reflection, this error benefited the defendant and is not appealable by the prosecutor.

However, events occurring before a cooling period may be considered if they are related to an event that takes place sufficiently close to the killing, as was made clear in *Commonwealth v. Voytko*, 349 Pa.Super. 320, 503 A.2d 20 (1986). The facts were as follows:

[A]pproximately seven weeks prior to the shooting, Voytko had found his wife, Michelle, in bed with Robert Cole at the latter's home. Six weeks later, about a week before the shooting, Voytko and Cole became involved in a fight. About the same time, Voytko and his wife had an argument, and she left the marital home to return to the home of her parents. On May 23, 1983, at or about 5:00 A.M., Cole returned Michelle to her parents' home following a date. As Cole was parking his truck, Voytko pulled in behind him, stopped and walked over to the truck. He screamed that his wife should get out of the truck. When Cole opened the door on the driver's side of the truck, Voytko shot Cole in the head with a shotgun. * * * Cole died later the same day.

Other evidence showed that four days before the shooting, police had been summoned to the parents' home and found Voytko in a wooded area behind the home. When asked what he was doing, Voytko explained that he was checking up on his wife because of marital problems. The jury was instructed on voluntary manslaughter.

What factors could be considered, however, in determining whether adequate provocation existed? Could the jury consider Boytko's discovery of the victim in bed with Voytko's wife, given the seven-week gap between that event and the killing? Should the fight be regarded as relevant? Perhaps any "cooling" that should have occurred between the discovery of the couple in bed or the fight and the events on the morning of May 23, 1983 was offset or negated by the events immediately preceding the killing. The trial judge refused a defense request to instruct the jury that in determining what constitutes adequate provocation, "reliance may be placed upon the cumulative impact of a series of related events." This was held error, under "the well-settled principle that 'preceding events' may have a 'final culmination'" which in combination may constitute adequate provocation. The jury should be left free, then, to consider that although seeing his wife on a date with Cole was not itself and in isolation sufficient, that observation could be considered together with his earlier discovery of the couple together in bed, and when evaluated together the circumstances might be found sufficient.

2. Cases frequently speak of "mutual combat" as adequate provocation to reduce a killing from murder to manslaughter. Mutual combat arises where the victim and the defendant intend to fight and are ready to do so, and the defendant acts in the "heat of blood" engendered by the situation. It is not necessary that blows have actually been struck for mutual combat to exist, but if any blows have been struck it is not material which participant struck the first blow or that the deceased may have struck no blows at all. See *People v. Villegas*, 222 Ill.App.3d 546, 558, 584 N.E.2d 248, 257, 165 Ill.Dec. 69, 78 (1991), appeal denied, 144 Ill.2d 642, 591 N.E.2d 30, 169 Ill.Dec. 150 (Ill.1992) ("Mutual combat is a fight or struggle which both parties enter willingly or where two persons, upon a sudden quarrel and in hot blood, mutually fight upon equal terms and where death results from the combat."). *United States v. Hardin*, 443 F.2d 735, 738 n. 6 (D.C. Cir.1970), however, suggested, "[M]utual combat alone is not a true alternative ground for mitigating a murder to manslaughter; it is merely one of the circumstances from which the jury could find adequate provocation."

Under what circumstances should mutual combat—however it is conceptualized—constitute adequate provocation? A New Jersey court offered in

State v. Pridgen, 245 N.J.Super. 239, 249, 584 A.2d 869, 873–74 (1991):

> Passion/provocation manslaughter is "[a] homicide which would otherwise be murder . . . [that] is committed in the heat of passion resulting from a reasonable provocation." N.J.S.A. 2C:11-4b(2). As was pointed out in *State v. Crisantos* (Arriagas), 102 N.J. 265, 508 A.2d 167 (1986):
>
> > Another common-law rule was that mutual combat under certain circumstances could constitute adequate provocation to reduce murder to manslaughter . . . However, "to reduce the offense from murder to manslaughter the contest must have been waged on equal terms and no unfair advantage taken of the deceased. * * * The offense is not manslaughter but murder where the defendant alone was armed; and took an unfair advantage of the deceased." 1 *Warren on Homicide*, § 110 at 525–526 [(1938)]. Another authority expresses the same rule in these terms: "But if a person, under color of fighting on equal terms, kills the other with a deadly weapon which he used from the beginning or concealed on his person from the beginning, the homicide constitutes murder". 2 *Wharton's Criminal Law*, § 110 at 254 [(14th ed.1979)].

E. RECKLESS AND NEGLIGENT KILLINGS: INVOLUNTARY MANSLAUGHTER AND NEGLIGENT HOMICIDE

Traditionally, some unintended killings not sufficient for murder were nevertheless made criminal. As the District of Columbia Court of Appeals has explained:

> [W]here a killing is not committed with a specific intent to kill or do serious bodily injury, or in conscious disregard of an extreme risk of death or serious bodily injury, there is no question that the killing was without malice. However, even such an unintentional or accidental killing is unlawful, and thus constitutes involuntary manslaughter, unless it is justifiable or excusable. Indeed, it is the absence of circumstances of justification or excuse which renders a non-malicious killing "unlawful." Accordingly, one key to distinguishing those unintentional killings which are unlawful, and hence manslaughter, from those to which no homicide liability attaches is determining the circumstances under which a killing will be legally excused.

Generally, at common law, where a person kills another in doing a "lawful act in a lawful manner," the homicide is excusable. As this phrase implies, two categories of unintentional killings were not excused and thus were manslaughter: killings in the course of lawful acts carried out in an unlawful, i.e., criminally negligent, fashion, and killings in the course of unlawful, i.e., criminal, acts.

* * *

The law pertaining to the first category, which may be labeled "criminal-negligence" manslaughter, has undergone considerable transformation, and the cases have steadily narrowed the range of conduct deemed sufficiently culpable to sustain a manslaughter conviction. In the thirteenth century, it appears that even a person who caused death "by misadventure," or in a completely non-negligent fashion, had no legal defense to a homicide charge. By the mid-eighteenth century, however, if a death-producing act "was done with due caution, or was accompanied only by slight negligence," the perpetrator lacked the "culpable negligence" required to render the homicide manslaughter. Cf. 4 W. BLACKSTONE, [COMMENTARIES] at *192 [(originally published 1769)] (involuntary manslaughter occurs "where a person does an act, lawful in itself, but in an unlawful manner and without due caution and circumspection").

Comber v. United States, 584 A.2d 26, 46–47 (D.C.Ct.App.1990).

The major difficulty in applying this body of law has been presented when a defendant's negligence is sufficient to give rise to criminal liability. Judicial descriptions of the sort of negligence necessary for criminal liability are often colorful but almost equally often of little guidance. A Florida court, for example, has stated:

Culpable negligence * * * means action of such a gross and flagrant character that it evidences a reckless disregard for human life or safety equivalent to an intentional violation of the rights of others.

Dominique v. State, 435 So.2d 974, 974 (Fla.App.1983). The negligence necessary for such liability must, of course, be distinguished from the state of mind sufficient to make a killing a "depraved mind" murder, as was discussed in Section B of this chapter.

Modern manslaughter statutes following the pattern of the Model Penal Code often impose liability for recklessly killing another. In *Comber,* the court described the modern law of manslaughter:

Most jurisdictions appear to permit the imposition of involuntary manslaughter liability on death-producing conduct involving something less than an "extreme" risk of death or serious bodily; a "high degree of risk of death or serious bodily injury" will suffice. 2 W. LAFAVE & A. SCOTT, [SUBSTANTIVE CRIMINAL LAW] § 7.12, at 278 (1986). See, e.g., *Commonwealth v. Catalina*, 407 Mass. 779, 783, 556 N.E.2d 973, 976 (1990) (involuntary manslaughter is homicide "unintentionally caused . . . by an act which constitutes such disregard of probable harmful consequences to another as to constitute wanton or reckless conduct" (emphasis added)). Moreover, the "modern view, evidenced by the position taken in most of the recent comprehensive criminal codes, is to require for involuntary manslaughter a consciousness of risk." 2 W. LAFAVE & A. SCOTT, supra note 6, § 7.12, at 280. Accordingly, generally it is the gravity of the risk created by the actor, rather than his or her awareness of that risk, which serves as the principal distinguishing feature between "depraved heart" murder and involuntary manslaughter. However, many of these jurisdictions have also enacted negligent homicide statutes which permit imposition of at least minor homicide liability even in cases where the perpetrator did not realize the risk created by his or her conduct.

The case that follows was decided under a quite traditional approach.

Cable v. Commonwealth

Supreme Court of Virginia, 1992
243 Va. 236, 415 S.E.2d 218.

COMPTON, Justice.

Tried by a jury in the Circuit Court of Warren County, appellant Alfred Morris Cable was convicted of involuntary manslaughter for the killing of his hunting companion. The defendant appeals * * *, with the sole appellate issue being whether the evidence was sufficient to support the jury's verdict.

The facts are undisputed, although some are susceptible of conflicting inferences. Therefore, applying settled appellate principles, we will state the facts in the light most favorable to the Commonwealth, which prevailed in the trial court.

In the early morning of November 6, 1989, the first day of turkey hunting season, defendant, age 44, and the victim, David Virgil Clowers, age 37, arrived together in a Warren County section of the George Washington National Forest, known as Shaw Gap, to hunt for turkeys.

The area was open to the public. The most popular activity conducted there was hunting, although it was "common to find backpackers, hikers, birdwatchers, [and] people that look at trees and flowers" present in the area. The homicide took place about 3:30 P.M. on a Massanutten Mountain range where the terrain was steep with dense vegetation and small trees "very close together." The weather was "partly overcast" but the visibility was "very good."

The defendant, an experienced hunter, and the victim were legally dressed in camouflage attire and their faces were blackened. The defendant was armed with a 12-gauge semi-automatic shotgun. He was carrying two types of ammunition in shells that looked "just alike" although labeled differently. Some shells were packed with double-aught buckshot, "capable of inflicting very serious, grievous wounds at a distance," and others were packed with No. 4 birdshot, used for hunting small game.

During the morning hours, and into the early after-

noon, the pair had been hunting separately without success. They saw no other persons in the woods, nor any turkeys. After they met for lunch, they decided to hunt for squirrels, which were also in season. Defendant decided to change the load in his weapon. He removed the double-aught buckshot shells and thought he inserted shells with No. 4 birdshot. The duo decided to separate again and the defendant "walked about 30 yards over the hill." The victim remained "on top of the mountain."

About 10 to 15 minutes passed and defendant heard gunshot to his right rear and behind him; he thought it was the victim shooting. "Maybe 20 minutes" later, defendant heard a squirrel "barking off to the right." Defendant started walking towards the sound of the squirrel, which defendant estimated came from 20 yards away. Defendant continued walking towards the sound and a ravine, approaching "a big old tree."

According to the defendant, "when I got to the edge of it, I just stopped because I did not want to cross it, because it was thick through there." Continuing, defendant said: "So, when I stopped, I heard something like a squirrel jumping out of the tree. I turned, put my gun up, and I seen a flash of movement and I shot . . . it was just a flash of movement," black in color.

After defendant fired, the victim "hollered, 'Alfred, damn it, you shot me, buddy.'" Defendant stated that the vegetation was so thick at the scene that even if the victim had been wearing an orange vest, he would not have seen him through the foliage. Defendant, who was not wearing eyeglasses, admitted that "for a long time" his distance vision had been impaired but he had not obtained glasses before the incident.

At the time he fired, defendant had "no idea" the victim "was in that area." The record does not reveal the distance between the defendant and the victim when he was shot. According to defendant, "He was, I guess, across the ravine like, on the other side sort of."

The victim immediately had difficulty breathing. After rendering aid to the victim, the distraught defendant went down the mountain seeking medical assistance for his friend. The defendant, along with rescue personnel, returned to the scene about two hours later to find that the victim had died. He had sustained two penetrating buckshot wounds, one entering the left rear rib cage and the other entering the waist area at the left rear. The former wound caused the death.

Subsequently, the defendant was indicted, tried, and sentenced in accordance with the jury's verdict to 12 months in jail. The trial court suspended the execution of all but four months of the jail sentence, and imposed other conditions including a prohibition against the defendant hunting with a firearm for five years. Execution of the sentence was stayed pending appeal.

Settled principles pertinent to this case should be reviewed. Where a defendant has been convicted by a jury whose verdict has been approved by the trial judge, and where the defendant assails the sufficiency of the evidence, under familiar rules it is the appellate court's duty to examine the evidence which tends to support the verdict and to permit the verdict to stand unless plainly wrong. If there is evidence to sustain the verdict, the reviewing court "should not overrule it and substitute its own judgment, even if its opinion might differ from that of the jury."

"Involuntary manslaughter is defined as the accidental killing of a person, contrary to the intention of the parties, during the prosecution of an unlawful, but not felonious, act, or during the improper performance of some lawful act. The 'improper' performance of the lawful act, to constitute involuntary manslaughter, must amount to an unlawful commission of such lawful act, not merely a negligent performance. The negligence must be criminal negligence. The accidental killing must be the proximate result of a lawful act performed in a manner 'so gross, wanton, and culpable as to show a reckless disregard of human life.'

In this context, the term "gross, wanton, and culpable" describes conduct. The word "gross" means "aggravated or increased negligence" while the word "culpable" means "deserving of blame or censure." "'Gross negligence' is culpable or criminal when accompanied by acts of commission or omission of a wanton or wilful nature, showing a reckless or indifferent disregard of the rights of others, under circumstances reasonably calculated to produce injury, or

which make it not improbable that injury will be occasioned, and the offender knows, or is charged with the knowledge of, the probable result of his acts."

[T]he defendant contends that * * * affirmance of his conviction [would] improperly establish[] a rule of strict liability in criminal cases arising from hunting accidents. Conceding that he was careless and failed to exercise due care, defendant maintains that he was not criminally negligent.

He points out that the victim "was wearing camouflage clothing, had blackened his face, and was in a ravine in dense vegetation." He points to testimony that he "had neither seen nor heard anyone else in the area in the nine or ten hours he had been on the mountain." He argues that he "had ample reason to believe that no one was or could be in the vicinity." He says, "Based upon his experience, the acuity of his hearing, and his knowledge of the terrain that lay between where he had last seen Clowers and his own position, he was certain that he could have heard Clowers moving through the woods and since he had not heard him, he reasonably believed that Clowers was still up on the mountain, high and to his right."

Defendant argues that the evidence is uncontradicted that he believed his weapon was loaded with No. 4 birdshot which, he says, is not likely to inflict serious bodily injury or death, that he thought he was shooting at a squirrel, and that he shot only once. Thus, defendant contends, his conduct, as revealed by all the evidence, "cannot be said to evince a callous and reckless disregard for human life." We do not agree.

As we examine the evidence which tends to support the jury's verdict, we conclude that the judgment of conviction is neither plainly wrong nor without evidence to support it. * * *

Some of the very factors upon which the defendant relies to exonerate himself of criminal negligence actually tend to support the conviction. The defendant knew that his companion was nearby dressed in camouflage clothing with a blackened face, so attired to conceal his presence. The defendant was fully aware that the thickness of the foliage would render a person so attired still more obscure. Being an experienced hunter, the defendant knew, or should have known, one of the basic principles of hunting safety, as stated by the Commonwealth's expert witness, "always be sure of your target and what is behind it before you fire."

Although possessing this knowledge, the defendant, with impaired vision, nonetheless fired at "a flash of movement" without identifying the target, having mistakenly inserted a lethal load into his weapon. He seeks to excuse his conduct by saying that he believed he was shooting at a squirrel. Yet, he never saw a squirrel. Given the conditions existing in this thicket of foliage in this public section of a national park, the defendant had a duty to identify his target before shooting. A person who is criminally negligent in omitting to perform a duty is guilty of involuntary manslaughter, although no malice is shown. This defendant never even attempted identification.

Indeed, the defendant did not have to shoot at all. He could have waited until his view of a target was unobstructed, especially since he knew that at least one other human was in the immediate area.

[W]e believe defendant's conduct amounted to aggravated negligence evidenced by acts of omission of a wanton nature, showing an indifferent disregard of the rights of others, under circumstances which made it not improbable that injury would occur, the defendant being charged with knowledge of the probable result of his acts.

Accordingly, the judgment of the [trial court] will be

Affirmed.

STEPHENSON, Justice, with whom CARRICO, Chief Justice, and HARRISON, Retired Justice, join, dissenting.

I respectfully dissent.

A higher degree of negligence is required to establish criminal negligence than to establish simple or gross negligence. To establish criminal negligence, the evidence must prove beyond a reasonable doubt that a defendant's conduct was so gross and wanton as to show a reckless disregard of human life.

"[A]n actual or constructive consciousness of the danger involved" is essential to prove wanton negligence. Thus, "[t]he act done must be intended or it must involve a reckless disregard for the rights of another and will probably result in an injury."

In the present case, the victim was dressed in camouflage attire, and his face was blackened. The defendant had no reason to believe that the victim was nearby. They had gone their separate ways approximately 30 minutes earlier. They had seen no other persons all day. The defendant, an experienced hunter, thought he heard a squirrel "bark," then "heard something like a squirrel jumping out of [a] tree." He fired his shotgun upon seeing "a flash of movement" in a thicket. The defendant thought that he was shooting at a squirrel. He also believed that his gun was loaded with "bird shot."

The defendant and the victim were not only good friends and hunting companions but the victim soon would have been the defendant's son-in-law. It is inconceivable

that the defendant would consciously show a reckless disregard of the victim's life.

The only other involuntary manslaughter case arising out of a hunting accident that we have decided is *Gooden v. Commonwealth*, 226 Va. 565, 311 S.E.2d 780 (1984). In *Gooden*, a majority held that the evidence was sufficient to sustain the defendant's conviction. Although I joined the dissent, I think the evidence in *Gooden* was much stronger for conviction than is the evidence in the present case.

In *Gooden,* the victim wore a red hat and red bandannas pinned to the front and back of his jacket, and he stood "on top of a knoll," in the "clear," upon a power line easement. Further, the defendant fired his gun even though "too many" hunters had been observed that afternoon along the easement. Finally, the victim's companion saw no deer in the vicinity either before or during the shooting.

Justice Cochran's dissent in *Gooden* contains the following statement which is equally appropriate in the present case:

No one can deny that this was a tragic accident. But [the defendant] was engaged in the lawful pursuit of a form of recreation sponsored by the Commonwealth. He was not required to insure the safety of all other hunters within the range of his [weapon]. The devotees of this sport are aware of a certain inherent risk of danger where high-powered weapons may lawfully be used. To convict [the defendant] of manslaughter, under the most favorable view of the evidence, is in effect to impose a rule of strict liability. We have not approved such a rule in civil litigation and we are not justified in applying it in a criminal prosecution. Although the evidence is sufficient to establish ordinary negligence, I do not agree that it is sufficient to establish criminal negligence.

Accordingly, I would hold that the evidence, as a matter of law, is insufficient to establish criminal negligence. Upon that issue, I do not think that reasonable minds could differ. Therefore, I would reverse the trial court's judgment.

Notes and Questions

1. Is it clear from the court's discussion in *Cable* whether the defendant must in fact have actually been aware of the risk of death? It is not uncommon for courts to leave this unaddressed.

2. If *Cable* had arisen in a jurisdiction that distinguished reckless and criminally negligent killings, which would have been the most appropriate charge?

F. DEATHS CAUSED IN THE PERPETRATION OF CRIMES: FELONY MURDER AND MISDEMEANOR MANSLAUGHTER

Editors' Introduction: The Felony Murder Rule and Misdemeanor Manslaughter

The basic felony murder doctrine is easily stated:

> The theory of felony murder is that a defendant does not have to have intended to kill one who dies during the course of * * * felonies, in order to be charged with murder. The intent to commit the underlying felony will be imputed to the homicide, and a defendant may thus be charged with murder on the basis of the intent to commit the underlying felony.

State v. Stewart, 663 A.2d 912, 920 (R.I.1995). A somewhat corresponding rule provides that causing death in the perpetration of an unlawful act not a felony constitutes involuntary manslaughter; this is the misdemeanor manslaughter rule. Few criminal law doctrines have given rise to more discussion and debate than these rules, although the harsh consequences of a murder conviction have caused most discussion to focus upon the felony murder rule.

The significance of the felony murder rule increases when it is combined with the doctrine making all members of a conspiracy liable for the crimes committed by other members of the conspiracy, at least where those crimes are committed in furtherance of the conspiracy and are a foreseeable result of it. This doctrine is covered in detail in Section B of Chapter 6.

Combination of the two doctrines means, of course, that in jointly committed felonies, all of the participants may be liable for the felony murder committed by one of their number. The impact of this is illustrated by *People v. Friedman*, 205 N.Y. 161, 98 N.E. 471 (1912), in which Friedman stood guard while Kuhn, his cofelon, entered a store to rob it. In a struggle, Kuhn killed the victim and Friedman was charged and convicted of felony murder. On appeal, the court held that the trial judge properly refused the following instruction requested by Friedman:

> If * * * the scope and plan of execution of [the] unlawful enterprise did not involve the use of force or violence which might result in the taking of human life, then the defendant is not responsible for the act of Kuhn in taking human life * * *.

Explaining, the court reasoned that the trial court had properly left to the jury the task of deciding whether the killing was a "natural and probable consequence" of the joint undertaking:

> If the natural and probable consequence of the common enterprise was the killing of Mr. Schuchart in case of resistance on his part, the defendant was liable for murder * * *, although he did not do the actual killing. The request assumes that, if the appellant did not fire the fatal shot, he could escape liability unless the conspiracy expressly contemplated the use of force or violence as might cause

death. This is an erroneous view of the law. An express agreement by intending robbers not to kill in carrying out a plan of robbery would not save any of the conspirators from responsibility for a homicide by one of them in committing or attempting to commit the robbery, if such killing was the natural and probable result of the robbery or attempt to rob in such a contingency as actually occurred in this case.

On the other hand, one who joins a felony *after* one of the felons has caused a death most likely does not incur liability for felony murder. In *People v. Pulido*, 15 Cal.4th 713, 936 P.2d 1235, 63 Cal.Rptr.2d 625 (1997), defendant Pulido testified that he accompanied Michael Aragon to a gas station, thinking Aragon sought matches. In fact, Aragon robbed the station and killed the clerk. Although he realized what Aragon had done, Pulido admitted, he accompanied—and assisted—Aragon in leaving the scene and escaping. After acknowledging that its earlier discussions were unclear, the California Supreme Court held that under Pulido's version of the events he would not be guilty of the felony murder committed by Aragon. The "nonkiller" must, at a minimum, have been a conspirator or aider and abettor in the felony *at the time of the killing*. Complicity in a felony murder does not extend to one who joins the felonious enterprise after the killing has been completed.

The Michigan Supreme Court has discussed the origin and traced the general history of the felony murder rule:

Lord Coke's statement of the felony-murder rule [was as follows]:

"If the act be unlawful it is murder. As if A. meaning to steale a deere in the park of B., shooteth at the deer, and by the glance of the arrow killeth a boy that is hidden in a bush: this is murder, for that the act was unlawfull, although A. had no intent to hurt the boy, nor knew not of him. But if B. the owner of the park had shot at his own deer, and without any ill intent had killed the boy by the glance of his arrow, this had been homicide by misadventure, and no felony.

"So if one shoot at any wild fowle upon a tree, and the arrow killeth any reasonable creature afar off, without any evill intent in him, this is per infortunium [misadventure]: for it was not unlawful to shoot at the wilde fowle: but if he had shot at a cock or hen, or any tame fowle of another mans, and the arrow by mischance had killed a man, this had been murder, for the act was unlawfull."

The above excerpt from Coke is most often cited as the origin of the felony-murder doctrine. Unfortunately, Coke's statement has been criticized as completely lacking in authority. * * *

At early common law, the felony-murder rule went unchallenged because at that time practically all felonies were punishable by death. It was, therefore, "of no particular moment whether the condemned was hanged for the initial felony or for the death accidentally resulting from the felony." Thus * * * no injustice was caused directly by application of the rule at that time.

Case law of Nineteenth-Century England reflects the efforts of the English courts to limit the application of the felony-murder doctrine. * * *, culminating

in *Regina v. Serne*, 16 Cox, Crim.Cas. 311 (1887). In the latter case, involving a
death resulting from arson, Judge Stephen instructed the jury as follows:

"[I]nstead of saying that any act done with intent to commit a felony and which
causes death amounts to murder, it should be reasonable to say that any act
known to be dangerous to life and likely in itself to cause death, done for the purpose of committing a felony which causes death, should be murder."

In this century, the felony-murder doctrine was comparatively rarely invoked in
England and in 1957 England abolished the felony-murder rule. * * *
    While only a few states have followed the lead of Great Britain in abolishing
felony murder, various legislative and judicial limitations on the doctrine have
effectively narrowed the scope of the rule in the United States. Perkins states that
the rule is "somewhat in disfavor at the present time" and that "courts apply it
where the law requires, but they do so grudgingly and tend to restrict its application where circumstances permit."
    Some courts, recognizing the questionable wisdom of the rule, have refused to
extend it beyond what is required. "[W]e do want to make clear how shaky are
the basic premises on which [the felony murder rule] rests. With so weak a foundation, it behooves us not to extend it further and indeed, to restrain it within the
bounds it has always known." Commonwealth ex rel. *Smith v. Myers*, 438 Pa. 218,
227, 261 A.2d 550, 555 (1970).

                                        * * *

    Many state legislatures have also been active in restricting the scope of felony
murder by imposing additional limitations.

People v. Aaron, 409 Mich. 672, 692–703, 299 N.W.2d 304, 309–14 (1980). The
misdemeanor manslaughter rule has been somewhat similarly limited and perhaps
more frequently abandoned, although with less fanfare.
    To the extent that the felony murder and misdemeanor manslaughter rules create
liability for causing death without regard to whether the defendant intended or contemplated that death result, they obviously deviate from the general approach that
criminal liability should attach only for contemplated results. What social interests
might be served by this deviation?
    Several rationales or justifications for the felony murder rule have been offered. In
State v. Goodseal, 220 Kan. 487, 493, 553 P.2d 279, 286 (1976), the Kansas Supreme
Court explained that the rationale of the felony murder rule is "to furnish an added
deterrent to the perpetration of felonies * * *." A somewhat different explanation was
given in *People v. Washington*, 62 Cal.2d 777, 781, 44 Cal.Rptr. 442, 445, 402 P.2d 130,
133 (1965): "The purpose of the felony-murder rule is to deter felons from killing negligently or accidentally by holding them strictly responsible for killings they commit."
    Another discussion of felony murder offered the following:

Felony murder reflects a societal judgment that an intentionally committed robbery that causes the death of a human being is qualitatively more serious than an

identical robbery that does not * * * [and] that a robbery that causes death is more closely akin to murder than to robbery. If this conclusion accurately reflects social attitudes, and if classification of crimes is to be influenced by such attitudes in order to avoid depreciation of the seriousness of the offense and to encourage respect for the law, then the felony murder doctrine is an appropriate classificatory device.

There is impressive empirical evidence that this classification does indeed reflect widely shared societal attitudes. Recently, the Bureau of Justice Standards of the United States Department of Justice released a national survey of public evaluations of the seriousness of 204 hypothetical legal events, ranging from the heinous to the trivial. [Bureau of Justice Statistics of the United States Department of Justice, Report to the Nation on Crime and Justice: The Data 4–5 (1983).] Respondents assigned widely differing scores to various differences in result, without reference to *mens rea*. Although the events were not described in terms making them unambiguously felony murders or express-malice murders, many were described so as to make intentional killing impossible. Some such ostensible felony murders were ranked by the respondents as more serious than other, apparently intentional killings; in particular, rape- or robbery-homicides were graded far more severely than express-malice family killings.

Jurors provide another index of the public's attitude towards felony murder. Kalven and Zeisel [The American Jury 443 n. 18 (1966)] were surprised to find that jurors faced with actual felony murder cases agreed with the doctrine. * * *

Crump and Crump, In Defense of The Felony Murder Doctrine. 9 Harv.J.L. & Public Policy 359, 363–65 (1985).

A few courts have simply abandoned the felony murder rule. In *Aaron*, for example, the Michigan Supreme Court held that the definition of murder in the Michigan statutes did not make killings in the course of felonies murder for that reason alone. A showing that the defendant killed the victim in the course of committing a felony, the court stressed, may be considered in determining whether the defendant killed with malice aforethought. However, "the jury may not find malice from the intent to commit the underlying, felony alone." The New Mexico Supreme Court, clearly concerned that broad felony murder liability might be unconstitutional, reached much the same result. *State v. Ortega*, 112 N.M. 554, 817 P.2d 1196 (1991).

Given the increasing number of statutes defining homicide offenses and the variety of approaches taken under these statutes, generalizations concerning the felony murder rule are difficult. Quite commonly, however, statutory schemes—like the California one, see page 153, which divide murder into degrees and define second degree murder and traditional malice aforethought terms, are read as creating a general rule that killings in the course of felonies are second degree murder. Some statutes, like Section 189 of the California Penal Code (see page 153), specifically provide for certain felony murders to be first degree murders.

The District of Columbia Court of Appeals has traced the development of the body of law imposing felony murder-like liability for deaths caused by the commission of less serious crimes:

* * * Centuries ago, the "unlawful act" category of involuntary manslaughter included all killings occurring in the course of a criminal act not amounting to a felony, i.e., a misdemeanor. The doctrine became known as the "misdemeanor-manslaughter rule," something of an analogue to the felony-murder rule. As time passed, however, the misdemeanor-manslaughter rule "came to be considered too harsh," and "the courts began to place limitations upon it." 2 W. LAFAVE & A. SCOTT, [SUBSTANTIVE CRIMINAL LAW], § 7.13, at 287 [(1986)]. Thus, in many jurisdictions, a homicide occurring in the course of a misdemeanor is involuntary manslaughter only if the offense is malum in se, rather than malum prohibitum.

Malum in se is defined as "[a] wrong in itself. . . . An act is said to be malum in se when it is inherently and essentially evil, that is, immoral in its nature and injurious in its consequences, without any regard to the fact of its being noticed or punished by the law of the state." BLACK'S LAW DICTIONARY 865 (5th ed. 1979). Malum prohibitum is defined as "[a] wrong prohibited . . .; an act which is not inherently immoral, but becomes so because its commission is expressly forbidden by positive law. . . ."

Where the misdemeanor manslaughter doctrine applies, involuntary manslaughter liability attaches even where the defendant does not act with the degree of recklessness ordinarily required for involuntary manslaughter predicated on criminally negligent behavior. In effect, the defendant's intentional commission of a misdemeanor supplies the culpability required to impose homicide liability.

* * * [W]e have been mindful of the danger that the traditional misdemeanor-manslaughter rule, imposing involuntary manslaughter liability whenever a killing occurs in the commission of a misdemeanor malum in se, might cast too wide a net.

Despite its long-standing roots, the misdemeanor-manslaughter rule has been criticized in recent years. This criticism has been directed primarily at the absence of a foreseeability of harm requirement in misdemeanor-manslaughter. "[A]bout two-thirds of the modern [state] codes do not contain a manslaughter crime grounded in the defendant's death-causing unlawful act." 2 W. LAFAVE & A. SCOTT, supra * * *, § 7.13, at 287. In other jurisdictions, courts have abolished or refused to apply the misdemeanor-manslaughter rule. See, e.g., [Commonwealth v.] Catalina, [407 Mass. 779, 787, 556 N.E.2d 978, 976 (1990)] (abandoning unlawful-act involuntary manslaughter except in cases where a battery causes death under "circumstances in which the defendant is, or should be, cognizant of the fact that the battery he is committing endangers human life").

The risk of an unreasonable application of involuntary manslaughter liability is especially pronounced in view of the massive increase since the early common-law era in the number and forms of misdemeanors. * * *

Comber v. United States, 584 A.2d 26, 49–50 (D.C.Ct.App. 1990) (paragraphing modified and footnote material inserted into text). The modern trend is illustrated by two recent decisions.

In *State v. Collins*, 67 Ohio St.3d 115, 616 N.E.2d 224 (1993), the defendant was convicted of manslaughter based on having caused the death of another as a result of his commission of the misdemeanor of failing to stop at a clearly marked stop sign. Under Ohio law, this misdemeanor and most other traffic offenses are classified as "minor" misdemeanors. Persons charged with such minor misdemeanors have no right to jury trial and can be punished on conviction by only a fine of up to $100. Although the manslaughter statute defined the crime as causing the death of another "as a proximate result of the offender's committing or attempting to commit a misdemeanor," the Ohio Supreme Court (by a 7–5 vote) held that the legislature did not intend that the prosecution be able to use a minor misdemeanor as a predicate offense. It noted that some traffic offenses were classified as more serious offenses than minor misdemeanors: driving under the influence of drugs or alcohol, driving faster than thirty-five m.p.h. in a school zone during recess or arrival or departure times, and drag racing. "These strict liability traffic offenses," the court noted, "may serve as valid underlying offenses to [misdemeanor-manslaughter]." With regard to minor misdemeanors, however, the court observed:

> We also find persuasive [the following] quote from *LaFave & Scott*, Criminal Law (2 Ed. 1986) 683, Section 7.13: " * * * There is no logical reason for inflicting manslaughter punishment on one who unintentionally kills another simply because he is committing a traffic violation, unless it makes sense to punish the one-in-a-thousand traffic violation, which by bad luck produces an unexpected death, far more severely than the nine hundred and ninety-nine violations which happily do not produce any such devastating result. * * * It is true that, in the case of crimes defined in terms of bad results, it is often something of an accident whether the specified result occurs or not. Where one seriously wounds another by shooting at him with intent to kill, or severely but unintentionally injures him by reckless driving, chance often takes a hand in deciding whether the victim dies or recovers, and thus whether the defendant receives a greater or lesser punishment. If the bad result which happens is actually intended, or if it is recklessly produced (especially by one conscious of the risk), it does not seem too harsh to make the severity of his punishment depend somewhat on the actual result, however accidental. Where, however, the result is both unintended and produced without any consciousness of the risk of producing it, it seems too harsh and illogical. * * * "

The New Mexico Supreme Court has been even more restrictive. In *State v. Yarborough*, 930 P.2d 131 (N.M.1996), the defendant failed to notice cars involved in a prior accident on an interstate highway and struck them with his vehicle; a four-year-old child in one car was killed. The defendant was convicted of involuntary manslaughter based on the theory that he caused the boy's death as a result of violating section 66-8-11(B) of the Motor Vehicle Code:

> B. Any person who operates a vehicle in a careless, inattentive or imprudent manner, without due regard for the width, grade, curves, corners, traffic, weather and road conditions and all other attendant circumstances is guilty of a misdemeanor.

The court reviewed the case law and concluded that most jurisdictions still applying misdemeanor manslaughter require that the predicate misdemeanor involve criminal negligence or recklessness. It continued:

Involuntary manslaughter is a fourth-degree felony in New Mexico. * * *
[C]onviction of a fourth-degree felony carries with it a presumptive sentence of
eighteen months in the New Mexico State Penitentiary, a fine of up to $5000, a
lifetime loss of the right to vote, and the loss of the right to hold an elective office
or an appointive public office. * * * In addition to these and other legal consequences of a felony conviction, there are many intangible social repercussions. We
must be sure that the penalties associated with a felony conviction are imposed
only in response to an act done with at least the minimum culpable state of mind.

* * *

[C]riminal negligence has been required in this jurisdiction for involuntary-
manslaughter convictions arising out of automobile accidents, and it is required
by most of the jurisdictions that still apply the misdemeanor-manslaughter rule.
We believe that the law in this area mandates that a felony conviction be based
upon more than ordinary negligence. * * * [W]e [therefore] hold that the State
must show at least criminal negligence to convict a criminal defendant of involuntary manslaughter. * * *

* * * Careless driving * * * requires only a showing of ordinary or civil negligence. Therefore, careless driving cannot be used as a predicate for an involun-
tary-manslaughter conviction.

Despite this trend in the case law, a conviction for misdemeanor manslaughter was
upheld by the Michigan Supreme Court in *People v. Datema*, 448 Mich. 585, 533
N.W.2d 272 (1995). The facts were as follows:

In the early morning hours of December 22, 1988, defendant and his wife,
Pamela Datema, were sitting in their living room with two friends. All four had
been smoking marijuana and both defendant and his wife had been drinking
throughout the evening.

As the evening wore on, the conversation turned to the topic of previous
romances, and the defendant and his wife began to argue about various para-
mours with whom they had slept. During the argument, Mrs. Datema started to
rise from her chair, claiming to have had sexual intercourse with other men in
front of defendant's sons. As she rose, defendant slapped her once across the face
with an open hand. Mrs. Datema slumped back into her chair, screamed that she
hoped defendant would "go to Florida and stay there," then slipped from the
chair onto the floor. Initially, defendant and the two others present in the room
thought that Mrs. Datema had passed out from drinking too much but, after five
to ten minutes, they became concerned and tried to wake her. When they were
unable to do so, they called an ambulance. Mrs. Datema never regained consciousness and died soon after.

The jury was told it could convict Datema if it found he committed an assault and
battery on Mrs. Datema, that she died, and that the cause of her death was Datema's
assault and battery. It was also told that to find that Datema committed assault and battery upon the victim, it would have to find that he intended to injure her. Given that the
predicate misdemeanor required the "specific intent" to injure the victim, the appellate
court held, the "inequities and harsh results" possible under the felony murder rule and
perhaps under some other applications of misdemeanor manslaughter were not present.

1. Basic Limitations on the Felony Murder Rule

Editors' Introduction: Judicial Approaches to Limiting Felony Murder

Applied literally, felony murder would impose a form of strict liability for those killings it covers, since a defendant could be convicted of murder without any showing of any awareness at all on the defendant's part *that death would be caused.* Any *mens rea* required for the underlying felony, of course, is almost certain to involve no actual anticipation that the death of another will be caused. Many courts have regarded felony murder as at least potentially imposing conviction and punishment disproportionately severe to the elements of the crime. Some have expressed concern that on at least some facts such liability may be so disproportionate to the defendant's blameworthiness as to be unconstitutional.

As a result, many courts have been receptive to arguments that they should limit the felony murder rule so as to provide assurance that it is not applied more broadly than is justified by its rationale. There are three primary approaches to limiting felony murder that can usefully be distinguished.

Limiting Predicate Felonies to Dangerous Crimes

One approach to so restricting the rule is to limit those felonies that can serve as "predicate" felonies for felony murder. The Delaware Supreme Court explained its actions in adopting such an approach in language that has been widely quoted by other courts:

> The only rational function of the felony murder rule is to furnish an added deterrent to the perpetration of felonies, which, by their nature or by the attendant circumstances, create a foreseeable risk of death. This function is not served by application of the rule to felonies not foreseeably dangerous. The rule should not be extended beyond the rational function. Moreover, the application of the rule to felonies not foreseeably dangerous would be unsound analytically because there is no logical basis for imputing malice from the intent to commit a felony not dangerous to human life.

Jenkins v. State, 230 A.2d 262 (Del. 1967).

Whether felonies are dangerous under such an analysis can be determined in either of two ways. A minority of courts—but including the California Supreme Court—permit a felony to suffice for felony murder only if that felony is inherently dangerous in the abstract. Only if a felony cannot be committed without causing a substantial risk or a high probability that death will result is it inherently dangerous; only if a person contemplates committing such a felony can the felony murder rule be expected to have its deterrent impact. Under this approach, practicing medicine without a license is not inherently dangerous. However, the California court has held inherently dangerous the crimes of furnishing a poisonous substance, reckless possession of a destructive device, kidnapping for ransom, and maliciously discharging a firearm at an occupied dwelling house. *People v. Hansen*, 9 Cal.4th 300, 885 P.2d 1022, 36 Cal.Rptr.2d 609 (1994).

Most courts using the dangerous felony approach, in contrast, look to the manner in which particular felonies were committed in the cases before them. As the Rhode Island Supreme Court explained:

> We believe that the better approach is for the trier of fact to consider the facts and circumstances of the particular case to determine whether such felony was inherently dangerous in the manner and the circumstances in which it was committed, rather than have a court make the determination by viewing the elements of a felony in the abstract.

State v. Stewart, 663 A.2d 912, 919 (R.I.1995). In *Ford v. State*, 262 Ga. 602, 423 S.E.2d 255 (1992), the facts were as follows:

> Ford was the boyfriend of the daughter of Louise Robinson. The victim, Redding, lived in a basement apartment at Robinson's house. On May 13, 1991, appellant went to Robinson's house, bringing with him a semi-automatic pistol. While there he attempted to unload the pistol, but in the process of being unloaded the weapon fired, sending a bullet through the floor and into Redding's apartment, where it struck and killed Redding. There is no evidence that at the time of the shooting appellant was aware of the existence of the apartment or of Redding's presence in it. * * * [B]efore the date of the killing appellant had been convicted of the felony of possession of cocaine with intent to distribute.

Under Georgia law possession of a firearm by a convicted felon is itself a felony offense. Under the circumstances in which Ford committed that felony, however, it was not dangerous and thus his accidental killing of Redding did not permit his conviction for murder.

Requirement That the Deaths Have Been Foreseeable

Some jurisdictions do not phase the felony murder rule in terms requiring a dangerous felony but instead require that the victim's death have been reasonably foreseeable to the defendant on the facts of the case. Often this requirement is treated as arising from a need for the felonious activity to be the "proximate" cause of the victim's death.

This second approach is illustrated by New York law and its application in *People v. Matos*, 83 N.Y.2d 509, 634 N.E.2d 157, 611 N.Y.S.2d 785 (1994). Matos fled—with a police officer in pursuit—over Manhattan rooftops from a nighttime robbery and burglary. The officer apparently slipped and fell to his death. Upholding a conviction for felony murder, the court explained:

The trial court stressed to the jury that * * * it must * * * find that defendant's conduct was a sufficiently direct cause of the ensuing death before it could impose criminal responsibility. The defendant's conduct qualifies as a sufficiently direct cause when the ultimate harm should have been reasonably foreseen.

* * * [T]he jury was correctly given the issue as to whether it was foreseeable that upon defendant's attempt to escape by way of the roof, he would be pursued by an officer. In those circumstances it should also be foreseeable that someone might fall while in hot pursuit across urban roofs in the middle of the night.

Requirement of Direct Causation

The requirement of "causation" between the felonious conduct and the victim's death is a flexible one. Some courts have used it to limit felony murder in much the same manner as the dangerous felony and foreseeability requirements.

The District of Columbia courts, for example, have interpreted the District's felony murder statute as not requiring foreseeability. The statute does, however, require a direct causal link between the felonious conduct and the death, and therefore if an "extraordinary intervening event" occurs in the chain of events this constitutes a "legal cause defense" to felony murder.

This third approach to limiting felony murder was unsuccessfully invoked in *Bonhart v. United States*, 691 A.2d 160 (D.C.Ct.App.1997). Bonhart was shown to have been the drug supplier to the victim, Della. When Della did not pay, Bonhart set fire to Della's apartment. Della initially escaped from the apartment but returned in an effort to rescue his dog; he was ultimately killed in the blaze. Rejecting Bonhart's legal cause defense to felony murder, the court explained:

> If [an] extraordinary event [relied upon as giving rise to a legal cause defense] is the victim's own response to the circumstances that the defendant created, the victim's reaction must be an abnormal one in order to supersede the defendant's act. Therefore, the question here is whether Della's response was abnormal if he entered his burning apartment building to save his dog's life.
>
> This question admits of only one answer, because the impulse to protect one's personal property from a fire is generally recognized to be normal and ordinary rather than abnormal and extraordinary. Experience teaches us that even if one's dwelling is burning, it is quite common for a person to reenter it to try to rescue property. This normal human instinct to rescue can be especially pronounced when an animal's life is at stake.

The case that follows considers several other possible limitations on felony murder liability. Note that the first decision was by the intermediate appellate court and the second was by the state's highest appellate tribunal in its further consideration of the same case.

State v. Leech

Court of Appeals of Washington, 1989
54 Wash.App. 597, 775 P.2d 463.

PEKELIS, Judge.

Clyde Dale Leech appeals his conviction for first degree felony murder stemming from an arson fire in which a Seattle fire fighter died. * * * He * * * contends that he was improperly convicted of felony murder. We agree and reverse.

On July 12, 1987, a fire broke out at the Crest apartment building (the "Crest") located at Pike and Boren streets in Seattle. Among the nearly 70 fire fighters who fought the blaze was Robert Earhart, a 15-year veteran who died in the course of fighting the fire. Fire investigators suspected arson, and Leech was arrested at the scene.

Many witnesses testified about the circumstances of Robert Earhart's death. Sometime during the fire, Earhart was reported missing. Another fire fighter discovered his body in a room on the third floor of the building, his breathing apparatus lying on the floor with the air tank reading at or near zero. Earhart's autopsy showed that he died of carbon monoxide poisoning.

George Franz of the Washington State Department of Labor and Industries investigated the circumstances of Earhart's death. He testified that Earhart's death could have been prevented had he followed the rules and obtained a new air tank when his air supply reached a critically low level. Earhart's breathing apparatus, which was not defective, was designed to sound an alarm when there was less than 5 minutes of oxygen left in the tank.

Franz also testified that he issued a citation to the Seattle Fire Department for violation of state regulations prohibiting fire fighters from "freelancing" (fighting a fire without supervision). Franz opined that had Earhart been properly supervised, he would have been instructed to obtain a new air tank when the alarm sounded and his death would have been prevented.

The jury found Leech guilty of first degree murder committed "in the course of and in furtherance of" first degree arson. Leech appeals.

Leech contends that he was improperly convicted of first degree felony murder because: (1) Earhart's negligence was not a "specifically foreseeable" result of the arson; (2) the arson fire was not the "proximate cause" of Earhart's death; and (3) Earhart's death was not caused "in the course of *and in furtherance of* " the crime of arson as required by RCW 9A.32.030. (Emphasis added.)

RCW 9A.32.030(1) provides that a person is guilty of first degree murder when:

(c) He commits or attempts to commit the crime of . . . arson in the first degree, . . . and; *in the course of and in furtherance of* such a crime or in immediate flight therefrom, he, or another participant, causes the death of a person other than one of the participants . . .

(Emphasis added.) Thus, to convict Leech of felony murder, the State must show that (1) Earhart's death was proximately caused by the arson; and (2) his death was caused "in the course of and in furtherance of" the arson.

Leech first contends that Earhart's negligence was not a "specifically foreseeable" result of the arson and, therefore, the application of the felony murder statute violated his due process rights. Leech's contention is without merit. RCW 9A.48.020 defines first degree arson as including fires that are knowingly and maliciously set which are "manifestly dangerous to any human life, including firemen". In addition, this court has held that "[i]n setting a hostile fire, the arsonist can anticipate that firemen will be endangered." *State v. Levage*, 23 Wash.App. 33, 35, 594 P.2d 949 (1979). Thus, both the court and the Legislature have determined that a fire fighter's death that occurs in the course of combating an arson fire is a foreseeable consequence of arson.

Leech next contends that the felony murder statute was improperly applied in this case because the arson did not proximately cause Earhart's death. He argues that Earhart's own negligence in failing to use his breathing apparatus, rather than the arson, caused Earhart's death. The facts of this case amply support a finding that Leech's arson fire proximately caused Earhart's death, however.

"[I]t is not necessary that defendant's act should have been the sole cause of the harm[;] . . . a contributory cause is sufficient." (Italics omitted.) *State v. Neher*, 52 Wash.App. 298, 301, 759 P.2d 475 (1988) (quoting R. Perkins, *Criminal Law*, ch. 6, § 9, at 608–09 (1957)), aff'd, 112 Wash.2d 347, 771 P.2d 330 (1989). Here, the arson was at least a contributory cause of Earhart's death. But for the arson fire, Earhart would not have been exposed to the poisonous fumes that ultimately killed him.

Moreover, a victim's contributory negligence does not relieve a defendant of criminal responsibility for homicide unless it is a supervening cause of death, that is, the sole cause of death. Earhart's alleged negligence in failing to use his breathing apparatus properly did not intervene in the chain of causation in such a way as to become the sole cause of his death. Earhart's failure to use his breathing apparatus would not have resulted in his death if Leech had not set the arson fire. Thus, Leech's conduct in setting the fire proximately caused Earhart's death.

Notwithstanding sufficient evidence of proximate cause, however, the State must prove that Earhart's death was caused "in the course of and[5] in furtherance of" the arson. Earhart's death certainly occurred "in the course of", i.e. during, the fire. Our analysis is therefore limited to the narrow question presented here: whether Earhart's death was "in furtherance of" the arson.

The State contends that it may prove a death is caused "in furtherance" of a felony by showing that the death is committed within the "res gestae" of the felony. In support, the State cites *State v. Dudrey*, 30 Wash.App. 447, 635 P.2d 750 (1981), review denied, 96 Wash.2d 1026 (1982). There, the court held that "a homicide is deemed committed during the perpetration of a felony, for the purpose of felony-murder, if the homicide is within the 'res gestae' of the felony, i.e., whether there was a close proximity in terms of time and distance between the felony and the homicide."

Dudrey is inapposite, however. There, the court determined that the homicide was within the "res gestae" of the felony by focusing on the fact that the defendants killed the victim when she interrupted their burglary. The *Dudrey* court did not have to define "in furtherance of" since the murder was clearly committed in furtherance of the burglary scheme.

The State cites numerous additional cases to support its argument, none of which is on point because each involves the application of a felony murder law that is distinctly different from Washington's statute. Moreover, we are unable to find any Washington case which has defined 'in furtherance of' within the meaning of RCW 9A.32.030. "'Absent a statutory definition, words of a statute must be accorded their ordinary meaning.'" In addition, punitive statutes must "'be literally and strictly construed in favor of the accused.'"

"Furtherance" means "a helping forward: ADVANCEMENT, PROMOTION." Webster's Third New Internat'l Dictionary, 924 (1976). Therefore, the plain terms of the felony murder statute require the State to prove that in acting to promote or advance his arson, Leech caused Earhart's death.

* * *

Here, there is no evidence from which any reasonable juror could conclude that in acting to advance or promote the arson, Leech caused Earhart's death. Indeed, by the time Earhart arrived, the fire was well under way and Leech had left the premises. Thus, Leech did not cause Earhart's death "in furtherance" of the arson.

Accordingly, we vacate Leech's conviction for felony murder. In reaching its verdict, the jury necessarily convicted Leech of the lesser included offense of first degree arson. Therefore, we order the trial court to enter a conviction of first degree arson and resentence Leech accordingly.

Reversed and remanded.

State v. Leech

Supreme Court of Washington, 1990
114 Wash.2d 700, 790 P.2d 160.

ANDERSEN, Justice

Facts of Case

At issue in this case is whether a fire fighter's death occurred in the furtherance of an arson, thus rendering the arsonist liable for the crime of first degree felony murder.

* * *

---

[5] We note that RCW 9A.32.030(1)(c) requires the State to prove that the killing occurred both "in the course of" *and* "in furtherance of" the felony. Other jurisdictions have enacted similar felony murder statutes but with an important difference: these statutes require only that the State prove either that the killing occurred "in the course of" *or* "in furtherance of" an enumerated felony. * * *.

* * * The Court of Appeals held that the arson was a proximate cause of Earhart's death but also held that the death did not occur in "furtherance of" the arson. * * *

Thereupon the State sought discretionary review of the Court of Appeals decision in this court and we granted review.

The main issue presented is * * * [:] Did the fire fighter's death occur in the furtherance of the arson as required by the felony murder statute?

Decision

CONCLUSION. A death that is caused by an arson fire before it is extinguished occurs in furtherance of the arson and renders the arsonist liable for felony murder.

* * *

We agree with the Court of Appeals disposition of the defendant's first two contentions. With regard to the claim that Earhart's alleged negligence was not foreseeable, * * * [i]t does not seem to us that human error in fighting a fire is an extraordinary occurrence. The implication of the defendant's argument is that an arsonist is entitled to have his fire fought in a perfect, risk-free manner by a fire department; this is not the law. Thus, the Court of Appeals properly rejected the contention that the defendant was not guilty of felony murder because Earhart's alleged negligence was not specifically foreseeable.

We also agree with the Court of Appeals conclusion that the arson fire proximately caused Earhart's death. We find it sufficient to simply note here that the fire fighter's alleged negligence in using his breathing apparatus was not the sole cause of his death. Since his failure to use the apparatus would not have killed him had the defendant not set the arson fire, the defendant's conduct in setting the fire was a proximate cause of Earhart's death.

We next turn to the Court of Appeals analysis regarding the defendant's third contention: whether Earhart's death was caused "in the course of and in furtherance of" the arson. The Court of Appeals held that Earhart's death clearly occurred "in the course of" the arson, i.e., during the fire. It concluded, however, that the death did not occur "in furtherance of" the arson, since the defendant did not cause Earhart's death in acting to promote or advance the arson * * *. It is this conclusion that is at issue.

A homicide is deemed committed during the perpetration of a felony, for the purpose of felony murder, if the homicide is within the "res gestae" of the felony, i.e., if there was a close proximity in terms of time and distance between the felony and the homicide.

The defendant argues (and the Court of Appeals apparently agreed) that the act of arson is complete once a fire is set and has a potential for harm and that any subsequent death caused by the still-burning fire is not sufficiently related in time to the arson to occur within the res gestae of that felony or in the furtherance thereof. According to this argument, the arsonist is not liable for felony murder unless he or she accidentally kills someone who is attempting to prevent the arsonist from starting the fire.

This argument is addressed by a leading treatise in discussing the time connection required by felony murder statutes that use phrases such as "in the furtherance of" and "in the commission of."

Burglary is committed when the defendant breaks and enters the building with the appropriate intent; nothing further, like the caption and asportation necessary for robbery, is required for burglary. Arson is committed when the building first catches fire; the further consumption of the building by fire adds nothing further to the arson already committed. Rape is committed upon the first penetration; further sexual activity by the defendant after this initial connection adds nothing to the crime of rape already committed.

Yet for purposes of the time connection implicit in the expression "in the commission of," the crimes of arson, burglary and rape may be considered to continue while the building burns, while the burglars search the building and while the sexual connection is maintained.

2 W. LaFave & A. Scott [Substantive Criminal Law] § 7.5, at 224–25 [(1986)].

* * *

The purpose of the felony murder rule is to deter felons from killing negligently or accidentally by holding them strictly responsible for killings they commit. In Washington, "the intent of the legislature to punish those who commit a homicide in the course of a felony under the applicable murder statute is clear."

This court has held that "statutes should be construed to effect their purpose, and strained, unlikely, or absurd consequences resulting from a literal reading are to be avoided." To apply the "in furtherance of" language only to the time in which an arson fire is being set is to achieve an absurd consequence, i.e., a situation in which an arsonist whose fire kills will almost never be liable for murder.

We hold that because the fire fighter's death in this case occurred while the arson fire was still engaged, the death was sufficiently close in time and place to the arson to be part of the res gestae of that felony. Thus, the death of Seattle fire fighter Robert Earhart occurred "in furtherance of" the arson and the defendant was properly charged and convicted of the crime of felony murder; the Court of Appeals holding to the contrary is reversed.

* * *

The Court of Appeals is reversed and the defendant's conviction of the crime of first degree felony murder is affirmed.

Notes and Questions

1. In 1990, the Washington legislature amended the felony murder statute at issue in *Leech* so that it provides that a person is guilty of first degree murder when:

   (c) He commits or attempts to commit the crime of . . . arson in the first degree, . . . and; in the course of *or* in furtherance of such a crime or in immediate flight therefrom, he, or another participant, causes the death of a person other than one of the participants . . .

2. Most courts agree with the Washington Supreme Court in *Leech* that the felony murder rule is not rendered inapplicable simply because the felony was technically completed before the fatal harm was done to the victim. The North Carolina court generalized in *State v. Rinck*, 303 N.C. 551, 564, 280 S.E.2d 912, 922 (1981), that "a killing is committed in the perpetration of a felony when there is no break in the chain of events leading from the initial felony to the act causing death."

Most of the cases involve robberies. In *Rinck*, the robbers left the victim who called police and reported the robbery. Before officers arrived, however, the robbers returned and killed the victim, apparently to prevent him from identifying them. This killing was held to have been in the perpetration of the robbery. Killings caused during "immediate flight" from a robbery are generally regarded as felony murders because of the robbery. *People v. Hickam*, 684 P.2d 228, 231 (Colo.1984).

The California courts have tended to define a robbery as continuing until the robbers reach a place of temporary safety. In *People v. Johnson*, 5 Cal.App. 4th 552, 7 Cal.Reptr.2d 23 (1992), review denied, for example, the facts were as follows:

> * * * Elaine Williams died as the result of an automobile accident. The car she was driving was struck by a car driven by appellant John Edward Johnson, Jr. Thirty minutes earlier, Johnson had robbed two men of cash and a ring and had fled in a stolen vehicle. The robberies had been immediately reported to police, who set up a county-wide roadblock in an attempt to apprehend the robber. * * *
>
> Before Williams' vehicle was hit, Johnson had lost control of the stolen car which was moving at least 58 miles per hour. After impact, Johnson left the car and entered a nearby marsh. He was arrested on the other side of it. Police later retrieved a revolver and cash from the marsh and found a ring and a warm-up suit in the car.
>
> * * *
>
> At trial, Johnson testified that after the * * * robberies, he drove south on Highway 101 to Highway 92 and saw no one follow him. He drove to Highway 280, but no one was chasing him. Driving north on Highway 280, he first saw what appeared to be a law enforcement officer in a vehicle. When the officer turned on his red and blue flashing lights, Johnson sped up. When he lost sight of the pursuing car, Johnson turned off the freeway and drove for eight or nine minutes in a residential area. During this period, he saw no police and thought he was safe. Johnson testified that he then drove through the residential area to El Camino Real in Burlingame and headed back to Highway 101. Heading north, Johnson thought he saw another police officer, so he got off the freeway at the Millbrae exit. Then, Johnson spotted the airport police, who began to pursue him. He drove on toward the airport, where another police vehicle began to follow him. Johnson testified that this vehicle did not have lights or sirens on. He passed a van and hit another car very hard. Dizzy and shaken, he fled the scene but was soon arrested.

After his conviction for first degree felony murder, Johnson challenged the sufficiency of the evidence. He argued that whether he had reached a place of temporary safety or not should be determined on a subjective basis, and since no evidence contradicted his testimony that he felt safe before the final chase, the jury could not have found that he caused Williams' death in immediate flight from the robberies. Stressing that whether a defendant has reached a place of temporary safety is primarily a jury question, the appellate court affirmed. A subjective standard would thwart application of the felony murder rule, it concluded, since the felony murder rule minimizes the prosecution's need to prove the accused's mental state. Whether immediate flight has ended, therefore, is to be determined objectively by addressing whether a robber actually reached a place of temporary safety, although his belief may be considered in making this determination. In *Johnson*, the prosecution had offered evidence that Johnson's version of the events was not accurate and that given the distance covered he did not have time for a leisurely drive through a residential area. It also emphasized that he apparently lacked time to dispose of the gun or to change into the warm-up suit he had placed in the car apparently to alter his appearance. Given this evidence, the court concluded, the jury's implicit finding that he had not reached a place of temporary safety was supported by the record.

3. There are a few indications that the approach of the intermediate court in *Leech* may have merit. Several courts have indicated that felony murder liability does not exist where the defendant felo-

niously provides drugs to the victim, who then injects them into himself, because the crime of sale has terminated before the victim's death. See *State v. Mauldin*, 215 Kan. 956, 959, 529 P.2d 124, 127 (1974). *Mauldin* was followed in *State v. Aarsvold*,

376 N.W.2d 518, 523 (Minn.App.1985), review denied (alternative ground). Perhaps, however, these decisions reflect misgivings regarding the use of drug offenses as a predicate for felony murder rather than sound application of felony murder principles.

Editors' Note: The Merger Rule as a Limitation on Felony Murder

Another limitation on felony murder applied by many courts is the so-called "merger" rule. This rule requires that the predicate felony, in order to make the killing felony murder, be one that is in some sense "independent" of the homicide. If the felony is not independent in this sense, it is said to "merge" into the homicide and thus be unavailable for purposes of making the killing felony murder.

There is widespread agreement, for example, that if the defendant killed the victim by means of an assault that constituted a felonious assault, this assault "merges" with the homicide and does not make the killing felony murder. See, for example, *People v. Ireland*, 70 Cal.2d 522, 75 Cal.Rptr. 188, 450 P.2d 580 (1969). In part, the rationale for the merger rule seems to be that without it the felony murder rule would render the general requirement of malice meaningless because felony murder would apply so frequently. In *Ireland*, the California Supreme Court explained that "the great majority of all homicides" are committed "as a result of a felonious assault[.]" If the intent to commit the assaults can substitute for malice aforethought, therefore, the general rule that malice must be established is rendered inapplicable to most cases.

However, whether particular felonies are sufficiently "parts" of the homicide—or sufficiently like assault—so as to merge with it has been a troublesome question. The California Supreme Court's decisions illustrate this. In *People v. Wilson*, 1 Cal.3d 431, 82 Cal.Rptr. 494, 462 P.2d 22 (1969), for example, the prosecution's theory was that death was caused in the commission of an entry that, in turn, was felony burglary because Wilson had entered the premises with the intent to commit felony assault upon the victim. Rejecting this, the court held that the felony murder rule does not apply to a burglary-killing case in which the entry is a felony only because of the intent to commit the assault and the assault itself, under *Ireland*, could not be used to make the killing felony murder. In *People v. Smith*, 35 Cal.3d 798, 201 Cal.Rptr. 311, 678 P.2d 886 (1984), the court considered whether felony child abuse constituted a felony independent of the resulting homicide of the child victim so as to make the homicide felony murder. Holding that it was not, the court explained:

> [Our cases bar] the application of the felony murder rule "where the purpose of the conduct was the very assault which resulted in death." In cases in which [felony child abuse] is a direct assault on a child that results in death * * *, it is plain that the purpose of the child abuse was the "very assault which resulted in death." It would be wholly illogical to allow this kind of assaultive child abuse to be bootstrapped into felony murder merely because the victim was a child.

In *People v. Hansen*, 9 Cal.4th 300, 885 P.2d 1022, 36 Cal.Rptr.2d 609 (1994), the California court noted that some other jurisdictions—particularly New York—apply the merger rule only where the predicate felony involves no criminal intent or design independent of the attack on the victim. A felony that *does* involve "a collateral and independent felonious design," then, does not merge and can support felony murder. *Hansen* rejected this approach, however, because under it "a felon who acts with a purpose other than specifically to inflict injury upon someone—for example, with the intent to sell narcotics for financial gain, or to discharge a firearm at a building solely to intimidate the occupants—is subject to greater criminal liability for an act resulting in death than a person who actually intends to injure the person of the victim."

Instead, *Hansen* held, a felony should merge only if permitting the felony to serve as the predicate for felony murder would make most homicides into murder without proof of malice and thus frustrate legislative intent to require a showing of malice in most cases. Hansen had fired a gun at an apartment in an apparent effort to persuade the occupants to return money they had taken in a drug ripoff. His shot hit and killed a young girl. Holding that the felony of shooting at an inhabited dwelling did not merge and thus could support felony murder liability, *Hansen* reasoned that most homicides do not result from actions that constitute this felony. Thus, felony murder with this crime as the predicate felony would not result in removing the requirement of malice aforethought in most homicide cases.

A few jurisdictions reject the merger rule entirely and permit even felony assaults on the victim to serve as the basis for making a death into felony murder. See *Sheridan v. State*, 253 Ga. 712, 324 S.E.2d 472 (1985) (felony murder conviction upheld on the ground that defendant killed victim during assault with a deadly weapon); *State v. Beeman*, 315 N.W.2d 770 (Iowa 1982).

2. Killings by Resisting Victims or Pursuing Police Officers

Courts have had special difficulty applying the felony murder rule in situations where the "direct" or "immediate" cause of the deceased's death was an action—almost always a gunshot—of the victim of the felony or a police officer seeking to prevent the felony or pursuing the felons. Should the felony murder rule apply in these situations? Should it make any difference whether the deceased was one of the felons, a by-stander, or someone else?

State v. Canola

Supreme Court of New Jersey, 1977
73 N.J. 206, 374 A.2d 20.

CONFORD, P.J.A.D., Temporarily Assigned.

Defendant, along with three confederates, was in the process of robbing a store when a victim of the robbery, attempting to resist the perpetration of the crime, fatally shot one of the co-felons. The sole issue for our resolution is whether, under N.J.S.A. 2A:113-1, defendant may be held liable for felony murder. * * *

The facts of this case * * * may be summarized as follows. The owner of a jewelry store and his employee, in an attempt to resist an armed robbery, engaged in a physical skirmish with one of the four robbers. A second conspirator, called upon for assistance, began shooting, and the store owner returned the gunfire. Both the owner and the felon, one Lloredo, were fatally shot in the exchange, the latter by the firearm of the owner.

Defendant and two others were indicted on two counts of murder, one count of robbery and one count of having been armed during the robbery. The murder counts were based on the deaths, respectively, of the robbery victim and the co-felon. After trial on the murder counts defendant was found guilty on both and was sentenced to concurrent terms of life imprisonment. * * *. Conventional formulations of the felony murder rule would not seem to encompass liability in this case. * * * A recent study of the early formulations of the felony murder rule by such authorities as Lord Coke, Foster and Blackstone and of later ones by Judge Stephen and Justice Holmes concluded that they were concerned solely with situations where the felon or a confederate did the actual killing. Comment, 24 Rutgers L.Rev. 591, 600–601(1970). * * *

The precise issue in the present case is whether a broader concept than the foregoing—specifically, liability of a felon for the death of a co-felon effected by one resisting the felony—is required by the language of our statute applicable to the general area of felony murder. N.J.S.A. 2A:113–1. This reads:

If any person, in committing or attempting to commit arson, burglary, kidnapping, rape, robbery, sodomy or any unlawful act against the peace of this state, of which the probable consequences may be bloodshed, kills another, *or if the death of anyone ensues from the* committing *or attempting to* commit *any such crime or act * * * then such person so killing is guilty of* murder. (emphasis added).

Before attempting, through analysis of the statutory language itself, a resolution of the contrasting views of the statute entertained below, it will be helpful to survey the progress of the pertinent law in the other American jurisdictions. * * *

It is clearly the majority view throughout the country that, at least in theory, the doctrine of felony murder does not extend to a killing, although growing out of the commission of the felony, if directly attributable to the act of one other than the defendant or those associated with him in the unlawful enterprise. * * * This rule is sometimes rationalized on the "agency" theory of felony murder.[6]

A contrary view, which would attach liability under the felony murder rule for any death proximately resulting from the unlawful activity—even the death of a co-felon—notwithstanding the killing was by one resisting the crime, does not seem to have the present allegiance of any court. * * * [In all the cases,] either an officer or other innocent person was killed. * * *

At one time the proximate cause theory was espoused by the Pennsylvania Supreme Court, *Commonwealth v. Moyer*, 357 Pa. 181, 53 A.2d 736 (Sup.Ct.1947) (murder conviction for death of gas station attendant in exchange of gunfire during robbery, without proof that a felon fired fatal shot); *Commonwealth v. Almeida*, 362 Pa. 596, 68 A.2d 595 (Sup.Ct.1949); cert. den. 339 U.S. 924, 70 S.Ct. 614, 94 L.Ed. 1346, reh. den. 339 U.S. 950, 70 S.Ct. 798, 94 L.Ed. 1364, cert. den. 340 U.S. 867, 71 S.Ct. 83, 95 L.Ed. 633 (1950). The reasoning of the *Almeida* decision, involving the killing of a policeman shot by other police attempting to apprehend robbers, was distinctly circumvented when the question later arose whether it should be applied to an effort to inculpate a defendant for the killing of his co-felon at the hands of the victim of the crime. *Commonwealth v. Redline* 391 Pa. 486 137 A.2d 472 (Sup.Ct.1958). The court there held against liability. Examining the common-law authorities relied upon by the *Almeida* majority, the *Redline* court concluded:

As already indicated, *Almeida* was, itself, an extension of the felony murder doctrine by judicial decision and is not to be extended in its application beyond facts such as those to which it was applied.

The court then held that *"in order to convict for felony-murder, the killing must have been done by the defendant or by* an *accomplice or confederate or by one acting in furtherance of the felonious undertaking."* (emphasis in original). The court refused, however, actually to overrule the *Almeida* decision,

---

[6] The classic statement of the theory is found in an early case applying it in a context pertinent to the case at bar, *Commonwealth v. Campbell*, 89 Mass. (7 Allen) 541, 544 (Sup.Jud.Ct.1863), as follows:

No person can be held guilty of homicide unless the act is either actually or constructively his, and it cannot be his act in either sense unless committed by his own hand or by someone acting in concert with him or in furtherance of a common object or purpose.

thereby creating a distinction (although the opinion indicates it was a halfhearted one) between the situation in which the victim was an innocent party and the killing therefore merely "excusable" and that in which the deceased was a felon and the killing thus "justifiable". Twelve years later the Pennsylvania court did overrule Almeida in a case involving Almeida's companion, Smith. (Commonwealth ex rel. *Smith v. Myers*, 438 Pa. 218, 261 A.2d 550 (Sup.Ct.1970)). The court noted, *inter alia*, the harsh criticism leveled against the common-law felony rule, its doubtful deterrent effect, the failure of the cases cited in *Almeida* to support the conclusions reached therein, the inappropriateness of tort proximate-cause principles to homicide prosecution, and the "will-of-the-wisp" distinction drawn by the *Almeida* court between justifiable and excusable homicides. It concluded, "beyond a shadow of a doubt * * * *Almeida* * * * constituted [an] aberration [] in the annals of Anglo-American adjudicature."

* * *

To be distinguished from the situation before us here, and from the generality of the cases discussed above, are the so-called "shield" cases. The first of these were the companion cases of *Taylor v. State*, 41 Tex. Cr.R. 564, 55 S.W. 961 (Cr.App.1900) affd 63 S.W. 330 (Cr.App.1901), and *Keaton v. State*, 41 Tex.Cr.R. 621, 57 S.W. 1125 (Cr.App.1900). In attempting to escape after robbing a train, defendants thrust the brakeman in front of them as a shield, as a result of which he was fatally shot by law officers. The court had no difficulty in finding defendants guilty of murder. * * * In *Keaton*, the court said defendant would be responsible for the "reasonable, natural and probable result of his act" of placing deceased in danger of his life. The conduct of the defendants in cases such as these is said to reflect "express malice", justifying a murder conviction.

This review of the development in this country of the felony murder rule in relation to culpability for lethal acts of non-felons shows that, despite its early limitation to deadly acts of the felons themselves or their accomplices, the rule has undergone several transformations and can no longer be stated in terms of universal application. * * * [I]t appears from the reported cases that up until 1922 all cases in the general field denied liability; the period from 1922 to 1935 was one of vacillation; and cases from 1935 * * * to 1956 tended to impose liability on the grounds of proxi-. mate causation where the defendant knew that forceful resistance could be expected. But when the Pennsylvania court in *Redline*, supra, overruled its prior holding of liability, in apparent return to the original position of the common law, a number of other jurisdictions followed suit, and the trend since has been towards nonliability.

Reverting to our immediate task here, it is to determine whether our own statute necessarily mandates the proximate cause concept of felony murder * * *.

Most modern progressive thought in criminal jurisprudence favors restriction rather than expansion of the felony murder rule. A leading text states: "The felony murder rule is somewhat in disfavor at the present time. The courts apply it when the law requires, but they do so grudgingly and tend to restrict its application where the circumstances permit." Perkins on Criminal Law (2d ed. 1969) 44. It has frequently been observed that although the rule was logical at its inception, when all felonies were punishable by death, its survival to modern times when other felonies are not thought to be as blameworthy as premeditated killings is discordant with rational and enlightened views of criminal culpability and liability. * * *.

The final report of the New Jersey Criminal Law Revision Commission was, however, unwilling totally to reject the felony murder rule, concluding instead:

> It is true that we have no way of knowing how many of the homicides resulting in felony murder convictions were committed purposefully, knowingly or recklessly and how many were negligent or accidental. But it is our belief that this rule of law does lead some to refuse to assume a homicidal risk in committing other crimes. Vol. II Commentary, New Jersey Penal Code, p. 158.

The proposed New Jersey Penal Code * * * confines the rule to deaths caused by the felon or his co-felons "in the course of and in furtherance of [the felony]." New Jersey Penal Code § 2011–3 (Final Report 1971). This is standard "agency theory" formulation and would seem intended to exclude liability for acts of persons other than felons or co-felons though generally arising out of the criminal episode.

In view of all of the foregoing, it appears to us regressive to extend the application of the felony murder rule beyond its classic common-law limitation to acts by the felon and his accomplices, to lethal acts of third persons not in furtherance of the felonies scheme. The language of the statute does not compel it, and, as indicated above, is entirely compatible with the traditional limitations of the rule. Tort concepts of foreseeability and proximate cause have shallow relevance to culpability for murder in the first degree. Gradations of criminal liability should accord with degree of moral culpability for the actor's conduct. * * *

It is our judgment that if the course of the law as understood and applied in this State for almost 200 years is to be altered so drastically, it should be by express legislative enactment.

The judgment of the [court below] is modified so as to strike the conviction and sentencing of defendant for murder of the co-felon Lloredo.

HUGHES, C.J., dissenting.

I respectfully dissent from the opinion of the majority here, and would affirm the decision of the Appellate Division, for the precise reasons stated in its majority opinion * * *:

> The proximate cause theory, simply stated, is that when a felon sets in motion a chain of events which were or should have been within his contemplation when the motion was initiated, the felon, and those acting in concert with him, should be held responsible for any death which by direct and almost inevitable consequences results from the initial criminal act. [*State v. Canola*, 135 N.J.Super. 224, 235, 343 A.2d 110, 116 (1975)].

Resistance whether by victim or police, and even unintended or accidental deaths which occur in the confused res gestae of violent felony, can hardly be deemed outside the contemplation of the initiator of such criminal violence.

Notes and Questions

1. *Canola* reflects the "agency" theory of felony murder liability: that a felon is guilty of felony murder only if the fatal shot was fired by, or the victim's death was otherwise directly caused by, either the felon or one of his co-felons for whose acts the felon is responsible, that is, the felon or one of the felon's agents. In *State v. Branson*, 487 N.W.2d 880, 882 (Minn.1992), this was described as the approach of courts in most jurisdictions.

   There have, however, been some decisions imposing felony murder liability in these cases, generally on the ground that the language or history of the jurisdiction's particular murder statutes shows that the legislature rejected the agency approach. A surviving robber, for example, was held guilty of felony murder for the death of the other robber who was shot and killed by the robbery victim. *State v. Oimen*, 184 Wis.2d 423, 516 N.W.2d 399 (1994). In *People v. Hernandez*, 82 N.Y.2d 309, 624 N.E.2d 661, 604 N.Y.S.2d 524 (1993), Hernandez attempted to rob an undercover police officer. Other officers opened fire when he resisted their efforts to arrest him and one of the officers' shots hit and killed another officer. Holding Hernandez liable for felony murder, the court stressed that the New York statute

imposed such liability for a felon who "causes" the death of a nonparticipant in the felony. Causation generally in homicide analysis, it continued, imposes no requirement that the shooter be one of the felons and nothing suggested the legislature intended an unusually strict requirement of causation in these cases.

2. Might persons like Canola be guilty of murder because of the death of their co-felons on some theory other than felony murder? The California Supreme Court held in *People v. Washington*, 62 Cal.2d 777, 44 Cal.Rptr. 442, 402 P.2d 130 (1965), that the felony murder rule could not be invoked to hold one felon liable for the death of his co-felon occasioned by resistance to the underlying robbery by the victim. It noted, however:

> Defendants who initiate gun battles may also be found guilty of murder if their victims resist and kill. Under such circumstances, "the defendant for a base, anti-social motive and with wanton disregard for human life, does an act that involves a high degree of probability that it will result in death" * * *, and it is unnecessary to imply malice by invoking the felony-murder doctrine.

This possibility was developed in *Taylor v. Superior Court*, 3 Cal.3d 578, 91 Cal.Rptr. 275, 477 P.2d 131 (1970). Taylor waited outside a liquor store while his companions, Smith and Daniels, went in to rob it. Smith pointed a gun at the proprietors, Mr. and Mrs. West. According to the Wests' testimony, Daniels "chattered insanely," saying to Mr. West, "Put the money in the bag. * * * Don't move or I'll blow your head off. * * * Don't move or we'll have an execution right here." Mrs. West testified that Smith appeared "intent," "apprehensive," and as if "waiting for something to happen;" his apparent apprehension and nervousness were manifested by the manner in which he stared at Mr. West. As Smith and Daniels were forcing the Wests to lie on the floor, the Wests obtained weapons and shot at the robbers. Smith was fatally wounded. Taylor (and Daniels) were charged with murder. At a preliminary hearing the magistrate found probable cause to believe them guilty of murder. The magistrate's action was challenged by means of an application for a writ of prohibition. The California Supreme Court denied the writ, finding that evidence supported the magistrate's finding of probable cause. Noting that Taylor, as an accomplice to the robbery, would be vicariously responsible for any killing attributable to the intentional acts of his associates committed with "conscious disregard for life, and likely to cause death," the court concluded:

> [T]he evidence * * * discloses acts of provocation on the parts of Daniels and Smith from which the trier of fact could infer malice, including Daniels' coercive conduct towards Mr. West and his repeated threats of "execution," and Smith's intent and nervous apprehension as held Mrs. West at gunpoint. The foregoing conduct was sufficiently provocative of lethal resistance to lead a man of ordinary caution and prudence to conclude that Smith "initiated" the gun battle, or that such conduct was done with conscious disregard for human life and with natural consequences dangerous to life.

Chapter 8

OTHER CRIMES AGAINST THE PERSON

CHAPTER CONTENTS

The basic purpose of civil society and the criminal law is to protect the bodily integrity of all persons from illicit aggression. Homicide, the most important of all crimes against the person and, indeed, of all crimes, is treated separately and at considerable length in Chapter 7. Rape, another crime of special gravity, along with other forms of sexual assault, is examined in some detail in Chapter 9. Robbery might be considered as a crime against the person but is commonly analyzed as an aggravated form of larceny and is therefore addressed in Chapter 10 along with other crimes against property.

This chapter covers the remaining offenses consisting of aggression against the person of the victim: assault, battery, and kidnapping.

A. ASSAULT AND BATTERY

Assault and battery were treated at common law as separate and distinct crimes. A battery was any unlawful application of force to the person of another. Modern law generally requires some injury or an offensive touching.

Assault at common law was more difficult to define. One form of assault was a failed attempt at battery. Another form consisted of putting another person in fear of a battery. Under modern codes, the crime of assault generally includes what previously were assaults and batteries. The definitions often provide that although a completed battery type of assault—causing injury or an offensive touching—can be committed recklessly, an "assault" of the other type—an attempted battery—requires that the defendant have acted purposely or with knowledge.

Increased sensitivity to the need to discourage persons from placing others at risk has often resulted in the creation of other crimes covering risk-creating conduct not within assault. The Model Penal Code provision for such an offense of reckless endangerment, reprinted at page 214, is frequently used as a model for such offenses.

In a minority of jurisdictions an assault of the attempted battery type requires that the defendant have had "present ability" to commit the battery. Thus, if the accused has pointed a gun at his victim and pulled the trigger but unknown to either the gun is unloaded, there would be no assault. This is inconsistent with the traditional position taken in attempt law as considered in Chapter 12, which provides that such factual impossibility of success does not preclude liability for attempt. This form of assault is considered further in note 2 after the first principal case.

Simple assault is normally a misdemeanor as it was at common law. There are also many different forms of aggravated assault of the battery type that are punished as felonies. The aggravation is based on various characteristics of the victim or the results or means of the accused's attack. Examples of aggravation are where the assault causes serious bodily injury or is committed with a deadly weapon or is committed against peace officers who are acting in the line of duty, or against a child or an elderly person.

Under what circumstances the consent of the victim prevents liability for assault or battery is a question that is best considered part of the definition of the crimes rather than a defensive matter, and the second case reprinted in this section addresses that question.

Mihas v. United States

District of Columbia Court of Appeals, 1992
618 A.2d 197.

BELSON, Senior Judge:

A Superior Court judge found appellant John Mihas guilty of assault * * * and sentenced him to time served (two months). Mihas contends that the evidence was insufficient to sustain a conviction * * *. We disagree, and therefore affirm.

I.

In the late afternoon of October 11, 1990, the complaining witness, Paul Rinehart, was walking down an alley in his neighborhood, Cleveland Park, headed in the direction of a Seven-Eleven store on Connecticut Avenue. In the alley, he encountered appellant, a sixty-one year old man who was "living on the street" and carrying his possessions with him. According to Rinehart, he glanced at appellant Mihas as

they passed each other and, shortly thereafter, heard something drop. When Rinehart turned in the direction of the sound, he saw Mihas bend down and pick something up. The two men were about ten to twelve feet apart at that time. Until that time Rinehart had seen no knife in Mihas' possession.

At that juncture, according to Rinehart, Mihas spoke first, saying "[w]hat are you looking at, punk? Get out of here," and repeated that statement a couple of times. Mihas then took several steps toward Rinehart, and it was during that approach that Rinehart first saw the knife. Rinehart feared that he might actually be assaulted—that Mihas might cut him. As Mihas approached, he held the knife pointed in the direction of Rinehart, holding it in his right hand at about belt-high, with the knife pointed downward at about a 45 degree angle. Mihas approached to within

four or five feet of Rinehart. In response to Mihas' belliger-
ent remarks, Rinehart responded, "What the hell do you
want?" a couple of times. Rinehart made no further gestures
toward Mihas; Rinehart then turned and left the alley;
Mihas did not follow.

Testifying in his own behalf, Mihas said that he had the
knife out before encountering Rinehart and was using it to
clean his fingernails. When he confronted Rinehart, Mihas
said, Rinehart looked at him "in a strange funny way, like
that, you know, like who are you, but not speaking. . . ."
According to his own testimony, Mihas then said, "What are
you looking at, Jocko?" and then as Rinehart passed by he
added "reckless eyeballing can get you locked up," and then
said "You're [sic] best bet, keep on going, you know, get
back there." Rinehart, according to Mihas, might have tried
to mumble something, and by then the individuals were
twenty-five feet apart. When Mihas was later stopped by
police, he was identified by Rinehart, and found to have in
his possession a paring knife with a blade two and three
quarters inches long.

The trial judge made several findings of fact, including
"that there came a time when Mr. Mihas, with the knife still
in his hand, displayed in a way in which Mr. Rinehart could
see it, did approach Mr. Rinehart who remained stationary,
and that the two gentlemen were close. That is, within five
feet of each other." Without resolving whether Mr. Mihas
said "what are you looking at, punk?" as distinguished from
"what are you looking at, Jocko?" the trial judge found it
was clear that from a close distance, with a knife held in his
hand, Mihas did say "[y]our best bet is to keep on going" or
"get out of here," words which ordered Rinehart to move
along. The court went on to find that appellant committed
the act of carrying the knife at the time of the confrontation—whether or not it had earlier been carried for the purpose of cleaning nails—and also found that the carrying of
the knife was accompanied by several steps in the direction
of Rinehart accompanied by words of commanding tone,
and that Mihas' actions constituted a menacing threat,
although not with any specific intent to injure. The trial
court also found that Mihas had the apparent present ability
to hurt Rinehart, that any person in the position of Rinehart
would have felt concern for his safety, and that Mihas had
the intent to act as he did, i.e., to tell Mr. Rinehart to be on
his way—at the point of a knife.

On the basis of the aforementioned findings of fact, the
trial judge concluded that appellant was guilty of criminal
assault of the "intent-to-frighten" type. * * *

II.

* * * To prevail * * *, Mihas must establish that the government presented "no evidence" upon which a reasonable

mind could find guilt beyond a reasonable doubt. * * *

* * * [W]e are unable to agree with Mihas' contention
that the evidence failed to establish that he committed an
act which constituted an assault, or had the necessary criminal intent to do so. This jurisdiction recognizes two types
of assault: (1) "[a]ttempted battery assault which requires
proof of an attempt to cause a physical injury, 'which may
consist of any act tending to such corporal injury, accompanied with such circumstances as denoted at the time an
intention, coupled with the present ability, of using actual
violence against the person'"; and (2) intent-to-frighten
assault which requires proof of "threatening conduct
intended either to injure or frighten the victim." In order to
establish the latter type of assault, the government must
offer "proof that the defendant intended either to cause
injury or to create apprehension in the victim by engaging
in some threatening conduct; and actual battery need not
be attempted." In addition, the requisite intent is the general "intent to perform the acts which constitute the assault."
We are satisfied that the record here clearly supports the
trial court's conclusion that Mihas had engaged in this type
of assault, and that the findings of fact provided an adequate basis for that conclusion. The actions of Mihas
included initiating the conversation between the two with
the hostile question "What are you looking at?" followed by
the appellation "Jocko" or "punk," and further followed by
Mihas' instruction to Rinehart that he should "get out of
here." These utterances were combined with Mihas'
approach from ten to twelve feet away to within four or five
feet of Rinehart, while holding a knife pointed in the direction of Rinehart belt high, and pointed downward at a 45
degree angle. On this record, we cannot overturn the trial
court's finding that any person in Rinehart's position would
have felt concern for his safety, the crucial inquiry in a case
of this sort.

* * * [W]e therefore affirm.

Affirmed.

PRYOR, Senior Judge, dissenting:
* * * [T]his case causes me to pause. It is notable in my
view because the result is driven, almost imperceptibly,
by inference built upon other inferences. Appellant was
charged with a less common form of assault: conduct
deemed an intentional effort to frighten another. In the
prosecution of most criminal offenses, we normally focus
on the state of mind of the accused. But in this instance,
the guilt of the accused, depends, in part, on the subjective
perceptions of the complaining witness. Thus on the barest
of evidence, where, it seems to me, that more attention
has been given to the complainant's perceptions than the

mens rea required of appellant, we are ultimately urged to give the prosecution the benefit of all inferences.

In an urban setting which includes a diverse range of many different types of people, it is undoubtedly true that appellant, a homeless person, and the complainant, a resident of an affluent section of the city, had a harsh encounter in an alley. However, when we look, on balance, at what happened, the government, in order to prevail, can only depend on a network of inferences. Even applying the customary litmus, the evidence is, in my opinion, insufficient. What we have is an unfortunate argument between two citizens which has been transformed into [a] criminal conviction[]. I respectfully dissent.

Notes

1. Unlike the law in some other jurisdictions, the District of Columbia law defining the second type of assault distinguished by the court does not require that the victim have actually experienced fear. See *Anthony v. United States*, 361 A.2d 202, 206 (D.C.App.1976), reaffirmed in *Robinson v. United States*, 506 A.2d 572, 575 (D.C.App.1986). In *Robinson*, the defendant Robinson was shown to have pointed a gun at a police officer. Robinson's conviction did not require, the court noted, that the officer actually have experienced apprehension or fear. If, for example, his training as a police officer made him "resistant" to threats such as that conveyed by Robinson's actions, this would not have rendered Robinson innocent of assault. The critical question, according to the court, is whether the defendant "acted in such a manner as would under the circumstances portend an immediate threat of danger to a person of reasonable sensibility." This had been explained in *Anthony*. Criminal assault, the court reasoned, is designed to discourage acts that increase the potential for injury and the tendency toward resistance, conflict, and violence. If a defendant acts in such a manner as would convey a threat of immediate danger to a reasonable person, his conduct is within the concern of the criminal law. The fact that his victim, because of exceptional fortitude (or perhaps because of stupidity), did not react to or realize the danger does not mean that the defendant's conduct and other conduct like it should not be punished and thereby discouraged.

2. Some formulations of "attempted battery" assault impose a requirement that the defendant have the "present ability to carry out the attempt." *People v. Valdez*, 175 Cal.App.3d 103, 220 Cal.Rptr. 538 (1985), illustrates the significance of this. Defendant Valdez had become embroiled with the cashier at a self-service gas station over his claim for the refund of one dollar. He displayed a pistol and while the cashier, who was inside a booth, called the police, the defendant fired three shots at the cashier. The shots were stopped by the bulletproof glass window. Valdez appealed his conviction (and four-year sentence) for assault on the grounds that there was insufficient evidence to prove he had the present ability to injure the victim.

The Court of Appeal first inquired as to whether under California law "present ability" would be satisfied by "apparent present ability." The difference is significant. Under the *objective* "present ability" requirement, a defendant who points an unloaded or nonfunctional gun at a victim is not guilty of assault because the condition of the weapon establishes that he lacked the ability to carry out his presumed intent to shoot the victim. This view would excuse some but would vindicate the principle that an act claimed to constitute an assault should bring the actor closer to the commission of the assault than would be required for a mere attempt. In contrast, if only an apparent present ability is required, this defendant does commit assault, if either he or his victim believes that the gun can be fired. If a jurisdiction defines assault as consisting only of an attempted battery but further provides that an apparent present ability to succeed is sufficient, the end result is probably very close to adopting a rule that provides that assault is committed by putting the victim in fear. See *Anthony v. United States*, discussed in note 1, holding that assault under District of Columbia law requires only the apparent ability to complete the attempt.

The court in *Valdez* concluded that California required *objective* "present ability." Nevertheless, it upheld the conviction on the grounds that this test referred solely to the defendant's actions. If the defendant has an operable firearm and has put himself within striking distance of his victim he has "present ability." The fact that his victim takes effective steps to avoid injury as by flight or here by taking refuge in a bulletproof cage, or that other external circumstances doom the actor's attack to failure, does not negate the required "present ability."

MODEL PENAL CODE*

Official Draft, 1985

§ 211.1 Assault

(1) *Simple Assault.* A person is guilty of assault if he:

  (a) attempts to cause or purposely, knowingly or recklessly causes bodily injury to another; or

  (b) negligently causes bodily injury to another with a deadly weapon; or

  (c) attempts by physical menace to put another in fear of imminent serious bodily injury.

Simple assault is a misdemeanor unless committed in a fight or scuffle entered into by mutual consent, in which case it is a petty misdemeanor.

(2) Aggravated *Assault.* A person is guilty of aggravated assault if he:

  (a) attempts to cause serious bodily injury to another, or causes such injury purposely, knowingly or recklessly under circumstances manifesting extreme indifference to the value of human life; or

  (b) attempts to cause or purposely or knowingly causes bodily injury to another with a deadly weapon.

Aggravated assault under paragraph (a) is a felony of the second degree; aggravated assault under paragraph (b) is a felony of the third degree.

§ 211.2 Recklessly Endangering Another Person

A person commits a misdemeanor if he recklessly engages in conduct which places or may place another person in danger of death or serious bodily injury. Recklessness and danger shall be presumed where a person knowingly points a firearm at or in the direction of another, whether or not the actor believed the firearm to be loaded.

State v. Shelley

Court of Appeals of Washington, 1997
85 Wash.App. 24, 929 P.2d 489.

GROSSE, Judge.

During a rough basketball game, Jason Shelley struck another player and broke his jaw in three places. He was convicted of assault in the second degree after the State successfully argued to the jury that Shelley intentionally punched the other player. On appeal, Shelley claims that he was entitled to argue that the victim consented to the possibility of injury when he decided to play pickup basketball. While we agree that consent may be a defense to assault in athletic competitions, Shelley has failed to establish a factual basis for that defense. Further, while we hold that the consent defense is not limited to conduct within the rules of the games, rather it is to the conduct and harm that are the reasonably foreseeable hazards of joint participation in an athletic contest, we conclude that Shelley's conduct was not a reasonably foreseeable hazard.

On March 31, 1993, Jason Shelley and Mario Gonzalez played "pickup" basketball on opposing teams at the University of Washington Intramural Activities Building (the IMA). Pickup games are not refereed by an official; rather, the players take responsibility for calling their own fouls. During the course of three games, Gonzalez fouled Shelley several times. Gonzalez had a reputation for playing overly aggressive defense at the IMA. Toward the end of the evening, after trying to hit the ball away from Shelley, he scratched Shelley's face, and drew blood. After getting scratched, Shelley briefly left the game and then returned.

Shelley and Gonzalez have differing versions of what occurred after Shelley returned to the game. According to Gonzalez, while he was waiting for play in the game to return to Gonzalez's side of the court, Shelley suddenly hit him. Gonzalez did not see Shelley punch him. According to Shelley's version of events, when Shelley rejoined the game, he was running down the court and he saw Gonzalez make "a move towards me as if he was maybe going to prevent me from getting the ball." The move was with his hand up "across my vision." Angry, he "just reacted" and swung. He said he hit him because he was afraid of being hurt, like the previous scratch. He testified that Gonzalez continually beat him up during the game by fouling him hard.

A week after the incident, a school police detective interviewed Shelley and prepared a statement for Shelley to sign based on the interview. Shelley reported to the police that Gonzalez had been "continually slapping and scratching him" during the game. Shelley "had been getting mad" at Gonzalez and the scratch on Shelley's face was the "final straw." As the two were running down the court side by side, "I swung my right hand around and hit him with my fist on the right side of his face." Shelley asserted that he also told the detective that Gonzalez waved a hand at him just before throwing the punch and that he told the detective that he was afraid of being injured.

Gonzalez required emergency surgery to repair his jaw. Broken in three places, it was wired shut for six weeks. His treating physician believed that a "significant" blow caused the damage.

During the course of the trial, defense counsel told the court he intended to propose a jury instruction that: "A person legally consents to conduct that causes or threatens bodily harm if the conduct and the harm are reasonably

foreseeable hazards of joint participation in a lawful, athletic contest or competitive sport." Although the trial court agreed that there were risks involved in sports, it stated that "the risk of being intentionally punched by another player is one that I don't think we ever do assume." The court noted, "In basketball . . . you consent to a certain amount of rough contact. If they were both going for a rebound and Mr. Shelley's elbow or even his fist hit Mr. Gonzalez as they were both jumping for the rebound and Mr. Gonzalez'[s] jaw was fractured in exactly the same way . . . then you would have an issue." Reasoning that "our laws are intended to uphold the public peace and regulate behavior of individuals," the court ruled "that as a matter of law, consent cannot be a defense to an assault." The court indicated that Shelley could not claim consent because his conduct "exceed[ed] what is considered within the rules of that particular sport[:]"

> [C]onsent is to contact that is contemplated within the rules of the game and that is incidental to the furtherance of the goals of that particular game.
>
> If you can show me any rule book for basketball at any level that says an intentional punch to the face in some way is a part of the game, then I would take another—second look at your argument. I don't believe any such rule book exists.

Later Shelley proposed jury instructions on the subject of consent:

> An act is not an assault, if it is done with the consent of the person alleged to be assaulted.
>
> It is a defense to a charge of second degree assault occurring in the course of an athletic contest if the conduct and the harm are reasonably foreseeable hazards of joint participation in a lawful athletic contest or competitive sport.

The trial court rejected these and Shelley excepted. The trial court did instruct the jury about self-defense.

Consent

First, we hold that consent is a defense to an assault occurring during an athletic contest. This is consistent with the law of assault as it has developed in Washington. A person is guilty of second degree assault if he or she "[i]ntentionally assaults another and thereby recklessly inflicts substantial bodily harm." One common law definition of assault recognized in Washington is "'an unlawful touching with criminal intent.'" At the common law, a touching is unlawful when the person touched did not give consent to it, and was either harmful or offensive. As our Supreme Court stated in *State v. Simmons*, [59 Wash.2d 381, 388, 368 P.2d 378 (1962)] "where there is consent, there is no assault."' The State argues that because *Simmons* was a sexual assault case, the defense consent should be limited to that realm. We decline to apply the defense so narrowly. Logically, consent must be an issue in sporting events because a person participates in a game knowing that it will involve potentially offensive contact and with this consent the "touchings" involved are not "unlawful."

Our review of the cases and commentary on the issue of consent reveals that although the defense of consent is applied in the realm of sexual assault, it has been sparingly applied by the courts in other areas. The rationale that courts offer in limiting it is that society has an interest in punishing assaults as breaches of the public peace and order, so that an individual cannot consent to a wrong that is committed against the public peace. Urging us to reject the defense of consent because an assault violates the public peace, the State argues that this principle precludes Shelley from being entitled to argue the consent defense on the facts of his case. In making this argument, the State ignores the factual contexts that dictated the results in the cases it cites in support.

When faced with the question of whether to accept a school child's consent to hazing or consent to a fight, or a gang member's consent to a beating, courts have declined to apply the defense. Obviously, these cases present "touchings" factually distinct from "touchings" occurring in athletic competitions.

If consent cannot be a defense to assault, then most athletic contests would need to be banned because many involve "invasions of one's physical integrity." Because society has chosen to foster sports competitions, players necessarily must be able to consent to physical contact and other players must be able to rely on that consent when playing the game. This is the view adopted by the drafters of the Model Penal Code:

> There are, however, situations in which consent to bodily injury should be recognized as a defense to crime.
> . . . There is . . . the obvious case of participation in an athletic contest or competitive sport, where the nature of the enterprise often involves risk of serious injury. Here, the social judgment that permits the contest to flourish necessarily involves the companion judgment that reasonably foreseeable hazards can be consented to by virtue of participation.[12]

The more difficult question is the proper standard by which to judge whether a person consented to the particular conduct at issue.

The State argues that "when the conduct in question is not within the rules of a given sport, a victim cannot be deemed to have consented to this act." The trial court apparently agreed with this approach. Although we recognize that there is authority supporting this approach, we reject a reliance on the rules of the games as too limiting. Rollin M. Perkins on Criminal Law explains:

> The test is not necessarily whether the blow exceeds the conduct allowed by the rules of the game. Certain excesses and inconveniences are to be expected beyond the formal rules of the game. It may be ordinary and expected conduct for minor assaults to occur. However, intentional excesses beyond those reasonably contemplated in the sport are not justified.[14]

Instead, we adopt the approach of the Model Penal Code which provides that:

> (2) *Consent to Bodily Injury.* When conduct is charged to constitute an offense because it causes or threatens bodily injury, consent to such conduct or to the infliction of such injury is a defense if:
>
>   . . .
>
> (b) the conduct and the injury are reasonably foreseeable hazards of joint participation in a lawful athletic contest or competitive sport or other concerted activity not forbidden by law.[15]

The State argues the law does not allow "the victim to 'consent' to a broken jaw simply by participating in an unrefereed, informal basketball game." This argument presupposes that the harm suffered dictates whether the defense is available or not. This is not the correct inquiry.

The correct inquiry is whether the conduct of defendant constituted foreseeable behavior in the play of the game. Additionally, the injury must have occurred as a by-product of the game itself. In construing a similar statutory defense, the Iowa court required a "nexus between defendant's acts and playing the game of basketball." In *State v. Floyd*, [466 N.W.2d 919, 922 (Iowa.Ct.App.1990),] a fight broke out during a basketball game and the defendant, who was on

---

[12] Model Penal Code, supra, § 2.11 cmt. 2, at 396 (footnotes omitted).

[14] Rollin M. Perkins & Ronald N. Boyce, Criminal Law, at 154 (3d ed. 1982) (citing *Regina v. Watson*, 26 CCC 2nd 150 (Prov.Ct. Ont.1975) (upholding conviction of hockey player who pursued an opponent and beat him with fists)).

[15] Model Penal Code, supra § 2.11, at 393. * * *

the sidelines, punched and severely injured several opposing team members. Because neither defendant nor his victims were voluntarily participating in the game, the defense did not apply because the statute "contemplated a person who commits acts during the course of play, and the exception seeks to protect those whose acts otherwise subject to prosecution are committed in furtherance of the object of the sport." As the court noted in *Floyd*, there is a "continuum, or sliding scale, grounded in the circumstances under which voluntary participants engage in sport . . . which governs the type of incidents in which an individual volunteers (i.e., consents) to participate[.]"

The New York courts provide another example. In a football game, while tackling the defendant, the victim hit the defendant. After the play was over and all of the players got off the defendant, the defendant punched the victim in the eye. The court in *People v. Freer* held that this act was not consented to:

Initially it may be assumed that the very first punch thrown by the complainant in the course of the tackle was consented to by defendant. The act of tackling an opponent in the course of a football game may often involve "contact" that could easily be interpreted to be a "punch". Defendant's response after the pileup to complainant's initial act of "aggression" cannot be mistaken. Clearly, defendant intended to punch complainant.

This was not a consented to act.

People v. Freer, 86 Misc.2d 280, 381 N.Y.S.2d 976, 978 (1976).

As a corollary to the consent defense, the State may argue that the defendant's conduct exceeded behavior foreseeable in the game. Although in "all sports players consent to many risks, hazards and blows," there is "a limit to the magnitude and dangerousness of a blow to which another is deemed to consent." This limit, like the foreseeability of the risks, is determined by presenting evidence to the jury about the nature of the game, the participants' expectations, the location where the game has been played, as well as the rules of the game.

Here, taking Shelley's version of the events as true, the magnitude and dangerousness of Shelley's actions were beyond the limit. There is no question that Shelley lashed out at Gonzalez with sufficient force to land a substantial blow to the jaw, and there is no question but that Shelley intended to hit Gonzalez. There is nothing in the game of basketball, or even rugby or hockey, that would permit consent as a defense to such conduct. Shelley admitted to an assault and was not precluded from arguing that the assault justified self-defense; but justification and consent are not the same inquiry.

* * *

We affirm.

B. KIDNAPPING AND FALSE IMPRISONMENT

False imprisonment at common law was the unlawful confinement of another person. As the Model Penal Code provisions contained in this section illustrate, it is still frequently defined in the same way in modern criminal codes.

At common law, kidnapping involved the forcible asportation — carrying away — of a person from his or her own country to another. The crime has evolved in many jurisdictions to prohibit as a very serious felony any malicious and unlawful abduction or confinement of another with the intent to hold for ransom or other benefit, or to facilitate the commission of some other crime. Abduction and confinement are susceptible to definition in ways that would include a great range of conduct. The breadth of many such statutes has posed problems for courts.

Perhaps the most troublesome issues concern the offense of kidnapping when it is committed as part of a course of conduct that also involves another serious offense, most often robbery or sexual assault. When may an offender be convicted of both the other serious offense and kidnapping? If the prosecution cannot secure conviction for both and if kidnapping is more serious than the other offense, when do the situations give rise to kidnapping?

These issues — in part ones of multiple punishment — may be viewed as a question of double jeopardy, as one of "merger," or as one of the definition of the crime of kidnapping. If the question is posed as one of the last sort, it requires consideration of, first, the general definition of the offense and, second, whether the offense is somehow differently defined when it is applied to facts involving another serious offense.

The general definitional question was posed by *State v. Wagner*, 191 Wis.2d 322, 528 N.W.2d 85 (1995). Defendant Wagner was convicted of kidnapping based upon proof that he accosted the victim in a laundromat, placed a gun in her side, and forced her into the rest room of the laundromat. The statute under which he was charged provided that a person is guilty of kidnapping who

> [b]y force or threat of imminent force carries another from one place to another without his consent and with intent to cause him to be secretly confined or imprisoned or to be carried out of this state or to be held to service against his will.

Wis. Stat. § 940.31(1)(a). Rejecting Wagner's contention that the evidence was insufficient, the court explained:

> Whether the forced movement of a person from one room to another in the same building satisfies the "carries another from one place to another" element of § 940.31(1)(a) is a question of first impression in Wisconsin. * * * [W]e conclude that it does.
>
> Although under the common law, kidnapping "was the forcible abduction of a person from one country to another," the focus of modern-day kidnapping statutes is generally on the harm caused by the confinement. The confinement, however, "need not exist for any particular length of time." By the same token, the critical aspect of the asportation element is "not the distance the victim is transported but the unlawful compulsion against the will to go somewhere." *State v. Williams*, 111 Ariz. 222, 526 P.2d 1244, 1246 (1974) (forced movement from one room to another within house). See also *Ellis v. State*, 211 Ga.App. 605, 440 S.E.2d 235, 239 (1994) (forced movement of victim "from her den to her bedroom was sufficient evidence" to support defendant's kidnapping conviction). Here, Wagner forced Megan M. from an area of the laundromat that was open to public view into the bathroom—an area that was hidden from the public. There, according to the evidence that the jury could believe, he intended to sexually assault her, thus satisfying the "[holding] to service against [her] will" element of the statute.

However, American courts have tended overwhelmingly to read into statutory language a requirement that the defendant's action go beyond what is required by the apparent meaning of the words used in kidnapping statutes, at least when the statutes are applied to defendants who are clearly guilty of a different serious offense committed in connection with the charged kidnapping.

State v. Anthony

Supreme Court of Tennessee, 1991
817 S.W.2d 299.

DAUGHTREY, Justice.

We have before us [a] criminal case[] in which the defendant [was] convicted of both armed robbery and aggravated kidnapping, * * * growing out of a single criminal episode. * * *

On a superficial level, the question presented is whether the facts * * * support convictions for both robbery and kidnapping. The real issue involves the propriety of a kidnapping conviction where detention of the victim is merely incidental to the commission of another felony, such as robbery or rape. * * *

At the outset, it is helpful to identify the principles implicated in the discussion that follows, and to separate the relevant from the irrelevant. [This case does] not involve double jeopardy analysis under either the state or federal constitution—there is no question that the offenses of robbery and kidnapping have separate elements and that dual convictions, even for conduct arising from the same criminal episode, would not violate double jeopardy provisions. At the same time, the conviction and punishment of a defendant for kidnapping, based on facts insufficient to sustain that conviction, would clearly violate the due process guarantees found in both constitutions. It is from this vantage point that we proceed to a review of the facts * * * and of the action taken in the trial and appellate courts.

* * *

The episode giving rise to the convictions * * * occurred shortly after 11:00 P.M. one night, when the defendant, Dennis Anthony, and another man robbed the Shoney's Restaurant on Lovell Road in Knox County. The restaurant had just closed, and three employees—Christopher Smith, Brian Seals, and Jimmy Joyce Livingood—were emptying trash into dumpsters behind the building when the defendant and his companion drove up in a red Camaro. After requesting a cigarette from Seals, the defendant asked Seals and Livingood if they knew where Magnolia Avenue was. Before they could answer, the defendant, who was carrying a revolver, got out of the car and ordered the three employees to lie on the ground near the dumpsters. Leaving his confederate to watch Smith, Seals, and Livingood, the defendant entered the restaurant through the back door. The accomplice detained the three employees until the defendant returned and they fled the scene together.

Manager Al Kesterson was in the front section of the restaurant when he heard a shout. He turned around to find the defendant pointing a gun at him. The defendant

ordered Kesterson to accompany him to the office. As they went, the defendant spotted another employee, waitress Laurie Lexvold. The defendant grabbed Lexvold, held the gun to her head, and took both Kesterson and Lexvold back through the kitchen into the office. When the defendant demanded that the safe be opened, Kesterson informed him that the safe was in the front of the restaurant by the cash register. At the defendant's orders, Lexvold remained in the office while the two men returned to the front of the restaurant, where the defendant directed Kesterson to open the safe and a separate cash box. After taking some of the contents of the safe and the money from the box, the defendant headed through the kitchen on his way out of the restaurant.

While the defendant was making his way through the building, he happened upon another employee, Floyd Lundy, Jr., as Lundy was coming out of the restroom. The defendant "stuck his gun in [Lundy's] face" and told him to "get back in the men's room and stay there." Lundy remained in the restroom until the defendant left the restaurant.

The defendant and his accomplice left as soon as the defendant came out of the building. Once they were certain that the two robbers had gone, the victims called the police. The entire episode took slightly more than five minutes.

The defendant was convicted of the armed robbery of Al Kesterson, the armed burglary of the restaurant, and the aggravated kidnappings of Kesterson, Lexvold, Lundy, Smith, Livingood, and Seals. The Court of Criminal Appeals, in a split opinion, held that none of the kidnapping convictions could stand. * * *

* * *

In seeking to overturn the intermediate court decision[] in [this case], the state relies chiefly on our analysis in State v. Black, 524 S.W.2d 913 (Tenn.1975), in which we adopted the well-known "Blockburger test" for determining when to sustain multiple convictions which are based upon the same acts or transaction. The broad question, of course, is whether or not the offenses in question constitute the "same offense" under the double jeopardy clause. As Black notes, multiple convictions do not violate double jeopardy if "[t]he statutory elements of the two offenses are different, and neither offense is included in the other." Id. at 920, citing Iannelli v. United States, 420 U.S. 770, 95 S.Ct. 1284, 43 L.Ed.2d 616 (1975), in which the United States Supreme Court held that:

In determining whether separate punishment might be imposed, *Blockburger* requires that courts examine the offenses to ascertain "whether each [statutory] provision requires proof of a fact which the other does not." As *Blockburger* and other [double jeopardy] decisions applying its principle reveal . . . the Court's application of the test focuses on the statutory elements of the offense.

Id. at 785, 95 S.Ct. at 1293, quoting *Blockburger v. United States*, 284 U.S. 299, 304, 52 S.Ct. 180, 182, 76 L.Ed. 306 (1932).

In this appeal, by contrast, the result does not turn on an examination of the statutory elements of the two offenses for which * * * Martin w[as] convicted. The essential elements of kidnapping and robbery are obviously separate and distinct, and simultaneous convictions on these two charges would not necessarily violate the rule in *Blockburger*. But since the dispositive question here does not raise double jeopardy implications, much of the analysis which the state brings to bear on the question is, simply, irrelevant. * * *

The problem recurs frequently because modern, broadly-drawn kidnapping statutes, like the Tennessee statute in these cases,[1] no longer require common law elements once necessary in kidnapping, such as secrecy and asportation. Literally construed, the offense of kidnapping defined in these statutes at times

> . . . could literally overrun several other crimes, notably robbery and rape, and in some circumstances assault, since detention and sometimes confinement, against the will of the victim, frequently accompany these crimes * * *. It is a common occurrence in robbery, for example, that the victim be confined briefly at gunpoint or bound and detained, or moved into and left in another room or place.

---

[1] At the time the * * * offenses in this appeal were committed, in 1986 and 1988, T.C.A. § 39-2-301 (aggravated kidnapping) mandated the conviction of anyone "who unlawfully seizes, confines, inveigles, entices, decoys, abducts, conceals, kidnaps or carries away another with the felonious intent to (1) cause the other to be confined secretly against his will; (2) detain the other against his will; or (3) send the other out of the state against his will. . . ." Under the superseding statute which took effect on November 1, 1989, as amended effective April 30, 1990, T.C.A. § 39-13-303, kidnapping is defined as false imprisonment "under circumstances exposing the other person to substantial risk of bodily injury. . . ." * * *

People v. Levy, 15 N.Y.2d 159, 256 N.Y.S.2d 793, 204 N.E.2d 842, 844 (1965), cert. den. 381 U.S. 938, 85 S.Ct. 1770, 14 L.Ed.2d 701. Various approaches have been adopted by other courts in an attempt to solve this problem * * *.

* * *

Because the statutory elements of kidnapping and other associated felonies rarely coincide, double jeopardy analysis has frequently been rejected in other jurisdictions as a method of resolving the inequities that may result from simultaneous convictions of kidnapping and of a separate felony, like robbery, that inherently involves some detention or asportation of the victim. The courts often rule that, despite the wording of the relevant statutes, they were not intended to apply in these situations, or that to so apply them would allow abuse of prosecutorial discretion or violate due process. See, e.g., *People v. Daniels*, [71 Cal.2nd 1119, 80 Cal.Rptr. 897, 459 P.2d 225 (1969)]; *People v. Adams*, 34 Mich.App. 546, 192 N.W.2d 19 (1971)]; *People v. Levy*, supra.

The extreme example is presented in *People v. Levy*, a case in which the defendants accosted a husband and wife as they arrived at their house, forced them at gunpoint into their car, and drove the couple a distance of 27 blocks over a 20-minute period, during which time they robbed the victims of their jewelry and a wallet. The New York Court of Appeals reversed the kidnapping convictions as a matter of law and left the first degree robbery conviction standing, finding that the restraint involved was incidental to the robbery and of the type that had long been treated as an inherent part of such other offenses as robbery, rape, and the like. In *People v. Daniels*, the California Supreme Court reversed kidnapping convictions where the victims had been forced to move about in their apartments during the commission of the offenses of robbery and rape. Citing both *Levy* and *Daniels*, the Supreme Court of Michigan in *People v. Adams* reversed a kidnapping conviction where, during a prison disturbance, the defendant and other inmates seized a prison official at knife point and, threatening to kill the official, moved him from one part of the prison to another during negotiations.

By an overwhelming margin, the majority view in other jurisdictions is that kidnapping statutes do not apply to unlawful confinements or movements incidental to the commission of other felonies. In general, three basic tests have evolved under the majority rule. The first is exemplified by *Adams*, *Levy*, and *State v. Innis*, 433 A.2d 646 (R.I.1981), cert. den. 456 U.S. 930, 102 S.Ct. 1980, 72 L.Ed.2d 447 (1982). It asks whether the confinement, movement, or detention was merely incidental to the accompanying felony or whether it was significant enough

in and of itself to warrant independent prosecution. * * *
The California test adds to this question (i.e., whether the
kidnapping was incidental) the further question of whether
the detention or movement substantially increased the risk
of harm over and above that necessarily present in the
accompanying felony. *People v. Daniels*, supra, 459 P.2d at
238 (movement within victims' business during course of
robbery held not kidnapping); see also *People v. Timmons*,
4 Cal.3d 411, 93 Cal.Rptr. 736, 482 P.2d 648 (1971) (victims driving own car for some five blocks while defendant
robbed them held not kidnapping); *People v. Thomas*, 3
Cal.App.3d 859, 83 Cal.Rptr. 879 (1970) (brief movement
of young female victims during robbery from lighted street
with pedestrians and motorists to darkened alley held separate kidnapping). * * * A more formulaic, although not
substantially different, test * * * has * * * been promulgat-
ed by the Florida Supreme Court in *Faison v. State*, as follows:

> [I]f a taking or confinement is alleged to have been done
> to facilitate the commission of another crime, to be kid-
> napping the resulting movement or confinement: (a)
> Must not be slight, inconsequential and merely inciden-
> tal to the other crime; (b) Must not be of the kind inher-
> ent in the nature of the other crime; and (c) Must have
> some significance independent of the other crime in that
> it makes the other crime substantially easier of commis-
> sion or substantially lessens the risk of detection.

426 So.2d 963, 965 (Fla.1983) * * *.

* * *

[W]hile we recognize the difficulties that Tennessee
courts may face in applying a rule that lacks the apparent
clarity of the "Blockburger test," we find ourselves in agreement with the majority view that holds double jeopardy
analysis to be inadequate in resolving the question raised by
this appeal. We conclude that the better rule is * * *
whether the confinement, movement, or detention is essentially incidental to the accompanying felony and is not,
therefore, sufficient to support a separate conviction for
kidnapping, or whether it is significant enough, in and of
itself, to warrant independent prosecution and is, therefore,
sufficient to support such a conviction. We further agree
* * * that one method of resolving this question is to ask
whether the defendant's conduct "substantially increased
[the] risk of harm over and above that necessarily present
in the crime of robbery itself."

We rest this holding not on a concern for constitutional
protection against double jeopardy, but on our understanding of the constitutional guarantee of due process. * * *

Furthermore, we believe that this approach is fully consistent with the intent of the General Assembly in enacting
the prohibition against kidnapping. As previously noted,
every robbery, by definition, involves some detention
against the will of the victim, if only long enough to take
goods or money from the person of the victim. This does
not mean that the legislature intended that every robbery
should also constitute a kidnapping, even though a literal
reading of the statute might suggest otherwise. We conclude that the courts' task is to apply the statute narrowly,
so as to make its reach fundamentally fair and to protect
the due process rights of every citizen, even those charged
with robbery, rape, or the like.

* * *

Applying the test announced today to the facts of the
* * * case[] now before us, we find * * * the facts present a
close[] case as to some of his six kidnapping convictions.
However, we conclude that the intermediate court should
be affirmed * * *. Clearly, the restaurant manager,
Kesterson, was not kidnapped. Although there was some
interference with Kesterson's liberty when he was forced at
gunpoint to open the safe, his movements in this regard
were essentially incidental to the robbery. Indeed, they were
part and parcel of that offense. Likewise, we do not find
Anthony's treatment of employees Lexvold and Lundy to be
sufficiently "significant in and of itself" to support separate
convictions for kidnapping.

That leaves us to determine the propriety of the three
verdicts returned against Anthony for kidnapping the
remaining Shoney's employees, Smith, Seals, and Livingood,
who were forcibly detained behind the restaurant while the
actual robbery was going on inside.

Superficially at least, this conduct might appear adequate to constitute a separate offense. * * * We conclude
[, however,] that the activity in question here was incidental
[to the robbery].

There is no significant difference between what happened to the employees who were inside the building and
those who were not. The only distinguishing factor is their
location at the time of the robbery. Indeed, had Smith,
Seals, and Livingood been standing just inside the back
door, rather than a few feet outside it, there would be no
question that their detention was essentially incidental to
the robbery.

We conclude that geography alone should not control
the outcome in this case. Nothing that occurred in connection with the detention of Smith, Seals, and Livingood was
sufficiently significant, in and of itself, to warrant separate
convictions for their kidnapping. These three employees
were held only briefly; they were not harmed in any way;
nor were they forced to move to a different location where
additional harm might have befallen them. They were not,

in short, subjected to any "substantially increased risk of harm over and above that necessarily present in the crime of robbery itself."

Having concluded that not every robber can or should be held criminally liable for kidnapping, we nevertheless would not want this opinion interpreted to mean that a defendant can never be convicted of both offenses, simply because they arise out of the same episode. If, for example, the three employees behind the restaurant had been taken hostage following the robbery, or if they had been moved from the scene of the robbery under circumstances giving rise to "a substantially increased likelihood of harm to the victims," * * * then the result might well be different from the one we reach here. Focusing solely on the facts in these two cases, however, we must conclude that the convictions for kidnapping cannot be sustained.

We therefore affirm the judgment of the Court of Criminal Appeals * * *.

Notes

1. Under many statutes, kidnapping (and false imprisonment, as well) can be committed by deceit or fraud as well as by force or threats. The federal kidnapping statute, for example, covers victims who have been "inveigled" or "decoyed." 18 U.S.C.A. § 1201(a). A defendant who persuaded women to enter his vehicle and remain in it by falsely promising to drive them home or to a job interview kidnapped them within the meaning of the statute. *United States v. Hoog*, 504 F.2d 45 (8th Cir.1974), cert. denied, 420 U.S. 961, 95 S.Ct. 1349, 43 L.Ed.2d 437 (1975). A defendant who persuaded a 15-year old youth to walk with him to a wooded area by falsely representing to the youth that there were squirrels in the area and the two of them would observe those squirrels was held to have "kidnapped" the youth within the meaning of a statute that did not define the offense further. The court explained:

   > [I]n the last century this and other courts have progressively recognized that one's will may be coerced as effectively by fraud as by force. Accordingly, this Court has interpreted the common law definition of kidnapping to encompass not only the unlawful taking and carrying away of a person by force but also the unlawful taking and carrying away of a person by false and fraudulent representations amounting substantially to a coercion of the will. * * * [F]raud has become synonymous with force in the common law definition of kidnapping, and the equation of fraud with force has been accepted in the legal encyclopedias and approved in numerous jurisdictions.

   State v. Murphy, 280 N.C. 1, 184 S.E.2d 845, 847 (1971).

2. Kidnapping, of course, requires that the defendant be aware that he is confining or moving a person. A few courts have held that a person who mistakenly believes he has killed his victim and then moves what he believes to be the victim's body does not commit kidnapping because the victim was in fact alive, because the crime requires the person to know that what he is moving is another person. *People v. Tolbert*, 56 Cal.Rptr.2d 604 (Cal.App.1996), ordered not officially published.

MODEL PENAL CODE*

(Official Draft, 1985)

§ 212.1 Kidnapping

A person is guilty of kidnapping if he unlawfully removes another from his place of residence or business, or a substantial distance from the vicinity where he is found, or if he unlawfully confines another for a substantial period in a place of

---

isolation, with any of the following purposes:

(a) to hold for ransom or reward, or as a shield or hostage; or

(b) to facilitate commission of any felony or flight thereafter; or

(c) to inflict bodily injury on or to terrorize the victim or another; or

(d) to interfere with the performance of any governmental or political function.

Kidnapping is a felony of the first degree unless the actor voluntarily releases the victim alive and in a safe place prior to trial, in which case it is a felony of the second degree. A removal or confinement is unlawful within the meaning of this Section if it is accomplished by force, threat or deception, or, in the case of a person who is under the age of 14 or incompetent, if it is accomplished without the consent of a parent, guardian or other person responsible for general supervision of his welfare.

§ 212.2 Felonious Restraint

A person commits a felony of the third degree if he knowingly:

(a) restrains another unlawfully in circumstances exposing him to risk of serious bodily injury; or

(b) holds another in a condition of involuntary servitude.

§ 212.3 False Imprisonment

A person commits a misdemeanor if he knowingly restrains another unlawfully so as to interfere substantially with his liberty.

Chapter 9

RAPE AND RELATED SEX OFFENSES

CHAPTER CONTENTS

Sexually motivated or sexually related misconduct presents special problems for substantive criminal law. Despite widespread changes in attitudes, frank, open, and objective discussion of such conduct is still often difficult. Similarly, courts, legislatures, judges, jurors, lawyers, and others may have difficulty in engaging in objective and accurate assessment of the seriousness of such conduct and the relative merits of various ways by which society might respond to it. This difficulty may lead to errors of both excessive leniency and excessive severity.

There is increasing acknowledgment, for example, that the criminal justice system, including the substantive criminal law, has reflected our society's attitudes toward this form of misconduct in several ways. These include an undervaluation of the significance of sexually assaultive behavior to its victims, an overestimation of the significance of the victim's prior behavior to the assault, and an insensitivity to the anguish associated with the victim's role in prosecuting such offenses. On the other hand, highly emotional reactions to sexually related criminal conduct may lead some to seek control mechanisms that ignore other systemic values such as proportionality and the special importance of accurate fact finding.

In any case, many jurisdictions have recently undertaken substantial revision of their substantive criminal law in this area. Such revision frequently includes the replacement of the traditional crime of rape by a more broadly defined offense often called sexual assault. This chapter considers issues raised by sexually related misconduct in light of these recent reform trends in the underlying substantive criminal laws.

The sexual offenses also provide an opportunity to consider, in this particular context, those elements of crimes that consist of attendant circumstances. As was emphasized in the introductory note to Chapter 2, "The General Principles of Criminal Liability," it is useful to consider those elements of crimes consisting of attendant circumstances separately from other elements consisting of the act required of the accused, the state of mind required concerning matters other than attendant circumstances, and any result that must have been caused by the accused's conduct. The traditional circumstance required by rape—that the victim not consent—has itself given rise to considerable controversy and the courts have had similar difficulty dealing with claims that rape defendants, because of mistake, were not aware that their victims had not consented.

The first section of this chapter addresses traditional or "forcible" rape or its modern statutory successor, sexual assault. The second addresses what has traditionally been called "statutory" rape: sexual behavior with a victim who lacks legal capacity to consent and whose consent (or lack of consent) is therefore of no technical legal significance.

A. FORCIBLE RAPE
Editors' Introduction: Rape Law, Reform, and Related Procedural Matters

The existence of sexual offenses obviously represents a basic decision—today almost exclusively a legislative decision—that certain types of sexually related conduct are distinguishable from other misconduct and consequently should be included within distinct criminal proscriptions. Usually, of course, this is done in order to assure or at least provide the opportunity to penalize them more severely than other but not sexually related misconduct.

Rape has traditionally been the major serious offense involving sexually related misconduct. However, recent reform efforts have persuaded many legislatures that it is necessary to reconsider what kinds of sexually related misconduct engaged in under what circumstances should be distinguished and included within the major sex crime or crimes. Such reconsideration has often led to the conclusion that it is appropriate and perhaps necessary to distinguish among the various types of activity that are included in the major sexual crimes. As a result, modern offenses such as sexual assault reflect a number of important decisions relating to the comparative seriousness with which various forms of sexually related conduct should be regarded.

In the context of sexual offenses, the decisions involve a variety of subconsiderations. What basic activity should be made criminal? Should this be limited to coitus? Should only conduct upon female victims be encompassed? However the conduct is defined in terms of the sex of the victim, what other limits should be placed upon it? Should it extend to, but no farther than, other penetrations of the victim? Or should it extend as far as physical touchings, perhaps of what are regarded as exceptionally personal or private areas of the body?

As part of this process, of course, it is necessary to consider what attendant circumstances to require in particular areas of the offense. Should all aspects of the conduct be regarded as criminal if, but only if, the victim is shown not to have consented? Should any general requirement of proof of nonconsent be dispensed with upon a showing that the victim was under what is perceived to be some disability, such as youth, mental impairment, or unconsciousness? Or perhaps even the absence of consent should not be regarded as sufficient unless the prosecution also shows that the act—whether intercourse or something "less"—was accomplished by certain defined types of force or threats.

Most of the conduct at issue—putting aside its sexual aspects—has long constituted a criminal offense of some sort, if nothing more serious than misdemeanor battery or assault. The legislative question is therefore, more accurately, how to describe the activity to be treated together as a distinguishable—and more serious—sexual offense.

Traditionally, the question was posed as how the single offense of rape is appropriately defined. More recently, legislatures have shown a tendency to define degrees of rape. And since the mid-1970s, a number of legislatures have entertained proposals to replace the traditional offense of rape with more broadly defined offenses often labeled "sexual assault," "criminal sexual conduct," or "sexual contact." The model for these latter efforts has generally been the Michigan legislation enacted in 1974 and reprinted after this introduction at page 232. The redefinition of the substantive crime or crimes of which the sexual assaulter might be convicted is only one part of what is often regarded as the reform of rape laws. Discussion of that reform, however, requires some preliminary consideration of the traditional offense of rape.

Traditional Rape Law

At early common law, rape was a felony involving unlawful and nonconsensual sexual intercourse with a female.

Rape has been fraught with enormous emotional significance for the participants in the processes of criminal justice as well as for the victims. The investigation and prosecution of rape cases, according to some commentators, has reflected the deep sexism of the law and the criminal justice system.

The New Jersey Supreme Court explained what many perceived to be the basic defect in the approach taken by traditional rape law:

* * * Under the [English] common law, rape was defined as "carnal knowledge of a woman against her will." American jurisdictions generally adopted the English view, but over time states added the requirement that the carnal knowledge have been forcible, apparently in order to prove that the act was against the victim's will. * * *

Under traditional rape law, in order to prove that a rape had occurred, the state had to show both that force had been used and that the penetration had been against the woman's will. Force was identified and determined not as an independent factor but in relation to the response of the victim, which in turn implicated the victim's own state of mind. "Thus, the perpetrator's use of force became criminal only if the victim's state of mind met the statutory requirement. The perpetrator could use all the force imaginable and no crime would be committed if the state could not prove additionally that the victim did not consent." National Institute of Law Enforcement and Criminal Justice, Forcible Rape—An Analysis of Legal Issues 5 (March 1978). Although the terms "non-consent" and "against her will" were often treated as equivalent, under the traditional definition of rape, both formulations squarely placed on the victim the burden of proof and of action. Effectively, a woman who was above the age of consent had actively and affirmatively to withdraw that consent for the intercourse to be against her will. * * *

The presence or absence of consent often turned on credibility. To demonstrate that the victim had not consented to the intercourse, and also that sufficient force had been used to accomplish the rape, the state had to prove that the victim had resisted. According to the oft-quoted Lord Hale, to be deemed a credible witness, a woman had to be of good fame, disclose the injury immediately, suffer signs of injury, and cry out for help. 1 Matthew Hale, History of the Pleas of the Crown 633 (1st ed. 1847). Courts and commentators historically distrusted the testimony of victims, "assuming that women lie about their lack of consent for various reasons: to blackmail men, to explain the discovery of a consensual affair, or because of psychological illness." Evidence of resistance was viewed as a solution to the credibility problem; it was the "outward manifestation of nonconsent, [a] device for determining whether a woman actually gave consent."

The resistance requirement had a profound effect on the kind of conduct that could be deemed criminal and on the type of evidence needed to establish the crime. Courts assumed that any woman who was forced to have intercourse against her will necessarily would resist to the extent of her ability. In many jurisdictions the requirement was that the woman have resisted to the utmost. * * * Other states followed a "reasonableness" standard, while some required only sufficient resistance to make non-consent reasonably manifest.

* * *

The judicial interpretation of the pre-reform rape law * * *, with its insistence on resistance by the victim, greatly minimized the importance of the forcible and assaultive aspect of the defendant's conduct. Rape prosecutions turned then not so much on the forcible or assaultive character of the defendant's actions as on the nature of the victim's response. * * * That the law put the rape victim on trial was clear.

The resistance requirement had another untoward influence on traditional rape law. Resistance was necessary not only to prove non-consent but also to demonstrate that the force used by the defendant had been sufficient to overcome the victim's will. The amount of force used by the defendant was assessed in relation to the resistance of the victim. In New Jersey the amount of force necessary to establish rape was characterized as "the degree of force sufficient to overcome any resistance that had been put up by the female." *State v. Terry*, 89 N.J. Super. [445, 449] (quoting jury charge by trial court). Resistance, often demonstrated by torn clothing and blood, was a sign that the defendant had used significant force to accomplish the sexual intercourse. Thus, if the defendant forced himself on a woman, it was her responsibility to fight back, because force was measured in relation to the resistance she put forward. Only if she resisted, causing him to use more force than was necessary to achieve penetration, would his conduct be criminalized. Indeed, the significance of resistance as the proxy for force is illustrated by cases in which victims were unable to resist; in such cases the force incident to penetration was deemed sufficient to establish the "force" element of the offense.

The importance of resistance as an evidentiary requirement set the law of rape apart from other common-law crimes, particularly in the eyes of those who advocated reform of rape law in the 1970s. However, the resistance requirement was not the only special rule applied in the rape context. A host of evidentiary rules and standards of proof distinguished the legal treatment of rape from the treatment of other crimes. Many jurisdictions held that a rape conviction could not be sustained if based solely on the uncorroborated testimony of the victim. Often judges added cautionary instructions to jury charges warning jurors that rape was a particularly difficult charge to prove. Courts * * * allowed greater latitude in cross-examining rape victims and in delving into their backgrounds than in ordinary cases. Rape victims were required to make a prompt complaint or have their allegations rejected or viewed with great skepticism. Some commentators suggested that there be mandatory psychological testing of rape victims.

In the Interest of M.T.S., 129 N.J. 422, 431–36, 609 A.2d 1266, 1270–73 (1992).

Reform of Substantive Rape Law

Reforms of rape law often involved its replacement with a new crime of sexual assault, sometimes divided into several offenses of varying seriousness. The problem presented by some of these reformed crimes, and addressed in the case reprinted in this subsection, was in part the result of the reformers' basic approach. The New Jersey Supreme Court in *M.T.S.* explained:

> Critics of rape law agreed that the focus of the crime should be shifted from the victim's behavior to the defendant's conduct, and particularly to its forceful and assaultive, rather than sexual, character. Reformers also shared the goals of facilitating rape prosecutions and of sparing victims much of the degradation involved in bringing and trying a charge of rape. There were, however, differences over the best way to redefine the crime. Some reformers advocated a standard that defined rape as unconsented-to sexual intercourse; others urged the elimination of any reference to consent from the definition of rape. Nonetheless, all proponents of reform shared a central premise: that the burden of showing non-consent should not fall on the victim of the crime. In dealing with the problem of consent the

reform goal was not so much to purge the entire concept of consent from the law as to eliminate the burden that had been placed on victims to prove they had not consented.

Similarly, with regard to force, rape law reform sought to give independent significance to the forceful or assaultive conduct of the defendant and to avoid a definition of force that depended on the reaction of the victim. Traditional interpretations of force were strongly criticized for failing to acknowledge that force may be understood simply as the invasion of "bodily integrity." In urging that the "resistance" requirement be abandoned, reformers sought to break the connection between force and resistance.

Thus, substantive rape law reform has been designed to remove the prior focus upon the victims' nonconsent and resistance and to substitute an emphasis upon the nature of the assailants' conduct.

As a result, modern statutes often attempt to give greater emphasis to the culpable conduct of the defendant rather than focusing on the behavior of the victim. This is illustrated by the 1980 amendment of section 261 of the California Penal Code. The crime had required proof that the victim had resisted but was overcome by force or prevented from resistance by the threat of great and immediate harm. The amendment modified the section to define rape as

> an act of sexual intercourse accomplished with a person not the spouse of the perpetrator, under any of the following circumstances; * * *
>
> (2) Where it is accomplished against a person's will by means of force or fear of immediate and unlawful bodily injury on the person or another.

The principal case in the first subsection that follows illustrates the difficulty that can arise as a result of these changes in the focus and terms of the offense.

The Marital Exemption— Rape by a Spouse

One longstanding issue in rape law was put in terms of whether or to what extent the law should recognize a "marital exemption" from the crime covering spouses of the victims or the scope of any such marital privilege as should be provided.

In traditional rape law, the requirement that the act of intercourse be "unlawful" was regarded as demanding the absence of a spousal relationship. The explanation was sometimes put in terms concluding that marriage constituted irrevocable consent by the wife to sexual intercourse with the husband. R. Perkins and R. Boyce, Criminal Law 202–03 (3rd ed. 1982). Thus rape was said to be subject to a so-called "marital exemption," under which a husband was immunized from liability for rape if the victim was his wife. In 1984, some form of marital exemption existed in over 40 states. *People v. Liberta*, 64 N.Y.2d 152, 163 n. 6, 485 N.Y.S.2d 207, 212 n. 6, 474 N.E.2d 567, 572 n. 6 (1984).

This marital exemption has been widely repealed or at least modified. Thus, under many current rape or sexual assault crimes, the prosecution need not prove that the victim was not the spouse of the perpetrator, and a defendant has no "defense" consisting of proof that the victim was the defendant's spouse.

Given the tendency of some legislatures to provide no marital exemption for some but less than all sexually assaultive crimes, there is some question as to the constitutional validity of legislative selectivity in this area. The opinions addressing such issues also discuss possible rationales for exempting spouses of the victim from liability for crimes of this sort.

Several cases arose under the Illinois statutory scheme, which previously exempted spouses from liability for some sexual offenses—particularly those involving sexually motivated touchings without penetration—but did create spousal liability for serious sexual assaults involving penetration. In *People v. M.D.*, 231 Ill.App.3d 176, 595 N.E.2d 702, 172 Ill.Dec. 341, appeal denied, 146 Ill.2d 643, 602 N.E.2d 467, 176 Ill.Dec. 813 (1992), the Illinois Court of Appeals explored at length possible justifications for marital exemptions from sexually related offenses and found them so wanting that the remaining marital exemptions were held unconstitutional and unenforceable. This did not, however, affect the enforceability of the serious sexual assault crimes against accuseds charged with such assaults upon their wives.

The Illinois court first rejected as possible justifications the suggested reduced "seriousness" of conduct perpetrated against a spouse and a purported need to promote reconciliation by removing the threat of criminal prosecution from situations where one spouse had criminally assaulted the other. It then turned to more "practical" considerations:

> The final rationales that have been asserted in support of the marital exemption are that a marital sexual assault would be difficult to prove and that a possibility of fabricated complaints from vindictive spouses exists. The former argument is based upon the problem of proving lack of consent. What this argument fails to take into account is that the problem of proving lack of consent is likely to be present in most cases in which the alleged victim and perpetrator have had a prior consensual sexual relationship regardless of whether they were married or unmarried. With regard to the other contention, we find no basis for believing that a vindictive spouse is more likely to fabricate a sexual assault charge than a vindictive unmarried former lover. Accordingly, we conclude that these two rationales do not provide any support for the marital exemption for acts of forcible sexual conduct.

Following these cases, the Illinois legislature repealed the remaining marital exemptions in this area.

Other Aspects of Rape Law Reform

Modification of the definition of rape or its replacement by some more broadly defined offense has been only a part—and perhaps a relatively minor part—of efforts to reform the criminal prosecution of sexual offenses. Another aspect of these reform efforts has been the development of limitations upon trial exploration of the victim's prior sexual conduct. Such exploration is widely regarded as exceptionally intrusive into the privacy of the victim, of little relevance to the proper issues in prosecutions, and creating a significant risk that judges' and juries' attention will be diverted from those issues. The resulting "rape shield" laws have been attacked, however, as impeding defendants' ability to fully develop before juries grounds that may exist for doubting the credibility of the testimony of the victim, which is often the major evidence indicating the defendant's guilt.

Other changes have also taken place. The rules that reflected a special distrust of complainants' testimony have been almost entirely rejected. See, for example *People v. Barnes*, 42 Cal.3d 284, 301–302, 228 Cal. Rptr. 228, 238–39, 721 P.2d 110, 120 (1986). In addition, in an effort to encourage the filing of complaints and to ease the prosecution's burden, innovative and sometimes controversial legal practices have evolved in some jurisdictions with respect to the trial of such crimes. One has been the use of expert testimony to the effect that the behavior of the complaining witness after the events in issue was consistent with a "rape trauma syndrome." Such testimony is usually offered to help establish that the intercourse was without consent. It has also been offered to explain the special difficulty—repression engendered by the trauma of the experience—that a rape victim might have in making a positive identification of her assailant.

There has also been a widespread movement to authorize children who are complaining witnesses in sexual offense cases to provide their evidence without having to confront their alleged assailants. This is often accomplished by permitting the testimony of such children to be presented in filmed or taped form. However, such laws have been under sharp attack as violative of defendants' right of confrontation under the Sixth Amendment to the United States Constitution.

How successful have these reforms been? If they have not been adequate, what else is needed? To what extent should reform efforts be focused upon the "substantive" criminal law—as, for example, the definitions of the offenses—rather than procedural matters or perhaps the attitudes of those involved in the processing of cases?

A Task Force on Women in the Courts, appointed by the Chief Judge of the State of New York, reported in 1986 on the administration of New York rape laws. Historically, the report observed, rape was "virtually unprosecutable" in the state. After examining reforms and practice following them, the Task Force found the following:

1. Until recently, New York's rape law codified the view that women's claims of rape are to be skeptically received. Through a slow process of reform, the most detrimental provisions have been repealed or struck down as unconstitutional.

2. The attitudes embodied in the former law and which resisted its reform continue to operate in the minds of some judges, jurors, defense attorneys, and prosecutors.

3. As a result, cultural stigma and myths about rape's perpetrators and victims still narrow the law's protective reach.

    a. Elements of a woman's character unrelated to her powers of observation and veracity—such as her manner of dress, perceived reaction to the crime, and lifestyle—continue to be unfairly deemed relevant to a determination of the defendant's guilt or innocence.

    b. Victims of rape who had any level of past relationship or acquaintanceship with the perpetrator are less likely to see his conviction and appropriate punishment.

4. Certain legislative and prosecutorial measures can offer a more appropriate response to the unique trauma rape victims suffer.

    a. Specialized prosecution units trained to recognize rape victims' psychological trauma and designed to minimize the need for the victim to repeat her story to many individuals and to appear in court have been successfully implemented in a number of counties.

    b. A statute creating victim–rape counsel confidentiality, similar to that applied to communications between psychiatrists and patients, would permit victims to utilize important crisis services without fear that privately related statements would be admitted in court.

Report of the New York Task Force on Women in the Court 89–90 (1986). The Task Force heard testimony that grand juries would be more likely to indict in cases of acquaintance rape if they were offered an option that would categorize such attacks as less serious offenses than attacks by strangers. As a result, the Task Force also recommended that the legislature consider adding one or more additional felony grades to the crime of rape.

After this introduction, some of the provisions of the extraordinarily elaborate and complex Michigan statute are reprinted. These rather than the Model Penal Code provisions are used because, as previously noted, the Michigan provisions have been widely relied upon for revision of rape offenses.

The two subsections that follow address the two major problems arising under, and perhaps in part created by, modern rape or sexual assault crimes. First is defining the force that must be used. Second is the significance that should be given to evidence that the accused incorrectly believed the victim consented to the conduct.

MICHIGAN PENAL CODE

Sec. 750.520a. As used in sections 520a to 520i:

    (a) "Actor" means a person accused of criminal sexual conduct.

    (b) "Intimate parts" includes the primary genital area, groin, inner thigh, buttock, or breast of a human being.

    (c) "Mentally defective" means that a person suffers from a mental disease or defect which renders that person temporarily or permanently incapable of appraising the nature of his or her conduct.

    (d) "Mentally incapacitated" means that a person is rendered temporarily incapable of appraising or controlling his or her conduct due to the influence of a narcotic, anesthetic, or other substance administered to that person without his or her consent, or due to any other act committed upon that person without his or her consent.

(e) "Physically helpless" means that a person is unconscious, asleep, or for any other reason is physically unable to communicate unwillingness to an act.

* * *

(g) "Sexual contact" includes the intentional touching of the victim's or actor's intimate parts or the intentional touching of the clothing covering the immediate area of the victim's or actor's intimate parts, if that intentional touching can reasonably be construed as being for the purpose of sexual arousal or gratification.

(h) "Sexual penetration" means sexual intercourse, cunnilingus, fellatio, anal intercourse, or any other intrusion, however slight, of any part of a person's body or of any object into the genital or anal openings of another person's body, but emission of semen is not required.

750.520b. (1) A person is guilty of criminal sexual conduct in the first degree if he or she engages in sexual penetration with another person and if any of the following circumstances exists:

(a) That other person is under 13 years of age.

(b) The other person is at least 13 but less than 16 years of age and the actor is a member of the same household as the victim, the actor is related to the victim, * * * or the actor is in a position of authority over the victim and used this authority to coerce the victim to submit.

(c) Sexual penetration occurs under circumstances involving the commission of any other felony.

(d) The actor is aided or abetted by 1 or more persons and either of the following circumstances exists:

   (i)   The actor knows or has reason to know that the victim is mentally defective, mentally incapacitated, or physically helpless.

   (ii) The actor uses force or coercion to accomplish the sexual penetration. * * *

(e) The actor is armed with a weapon or any article used or fashioned in a manner to lead the victim to reasonably believe it to be a weapon.

(f) The actor causes personal injury to the victim and force or coercion is used to accomplish sexual penetration. Force or coercion includes but is not limited to any of the following circumstances:

   (i)   When the actor overcomes the victim through the actual application of physical force or physical violence.

   (ii) When the actor coerces the victim to submit by threatening to use force or violence on the victim, and the victim believes that the actor has the present ability to execute these threats.

   (iii) When the actor coerces the victim to submit by threatening to retaliate in the future against the victim, or any other person, and the victim believes that the actor has the ability to execute this threat. As used in this subdivision, "to retaliate" includes threats of physical punishment, kidnapping, or extortion.

(iv)   When the actor engages in the medical treatment or examination of the victim in a manner or for purposes which are medically recognized as unethical or unacceptable.

(v)   When the actor, through concealment or by the element of surprise, is able to overcome the victim.

(g) The actor causes personal injury to the victim, and the actor knows or has reason to know that the victim is mentally defective, mentally incapacitated, or physically helpless.

(2) Criminal sexual conduct in the first degree is a felony punishable by imprisonment in the state prison for life or for any term of years.

750.520c. (1) A person is guilty of criminal sexual conduct in the second degree if the person engages in sexual contact with another person and if any of the following circumstances exists:

[The circumstances which are omitted are essentially the same as those for first degree sexual conduct. The crucial difference is that the actor here engages in "sexual contact" rather than "penetration."]

(2) Criminal sexual conduct in the second degree is a felony punishable by imprisonment for not more than 15 years.

750.520d. (1) A person is guilty of criminal sexual conduct in the third degree if the person engages in sexual penetration with another person and if any of the following circumstances exists:

(a) That other person is at least 13 years of age and under 16 years of age.

(b) Force or coercion is used to accomplish the sexual penetration. Force or coercion includes but is not limited to any of the circumstances listed in section 520b(l)(f)(i) to (v).

(c) The actor knows or has reason to know that the victim is mentally defective, mentally incapacitated, or physically helpless.

(2) Criminal sexual conduct in the third degree is a felony punishable by imprisonment for not more than 15 years.

750.520e. (1) A person is guilty of criminal sexual conduct in the fourth degree if he or she engages in sexual contact with another person and if either of the following circumstances exists:
[The circumstances are the same as those listed in 750.520d(b) and (c).]

(2) Criminal sexual conduct in the fourth degree is a misdemeanor punishable by imprisonment for not more than 2 years, or by a fine of not more than $500.00, or both.

750.520i. A victim need not resist the actor in prosecution under sections 520b to 520g.

Note
The provisions just given are reprinted as enacted in 1974. 1974 Mich.Pub. Acts No. 266. In 1983, a great many amendments were enacted. The thrust of these changes was to make the law even more detailed and expansive in its coverage.

1. The Force Required

Modern sexual assault crimes often reflect an effort to define the offense without reference to the victim's resistance or consent. As developed earlier, this reflects the view that avoiding reference to these matters in the definition of the offense encourages trials to focus upon the behavior of the accused and not that of the victim.

As a result, however, the criminal law may have left insufficiently addressed the conduct of an accused that must be proved to establish the defense. The case reprinted next presents this problem under a modern statute that continues to define the crime as rape.

Commonwealth v. Berkowitz

Superior Court of Pennsylvania, 1992
415 Pa.Super. 505, 609 A.2d 1338.

Before WIEAND, KELLY and CERCONE, JJ.

PER CURIAM:

Appellant appeals from judgment of sentence imposed following convictions of rape and indecent assault. We are called upon to determine the degree of physical force necessary to complete the act of rape in Pennsylvania. * * *

I. Facts and Procedural History

In the spring of 1988, appellant and the victim were both college sophomores at East Stroudsburg State University, ages twenty and nineteen years old, respectively. They had mutual friends and acquaintances. On April nineteenth of that year, the victim went to appellant's dormitory room. What transpired in that dorm room between appellant and the victim thereafter is the subject of the instant appeal.

During a one day jury trial held on September 14, 1988, the victim gave the following account during direct examination by the Commonwealth. At roughly 2:00 on the afternoon of April 19, 1988, after attending two morning classes, the victim returned to her dormitory room.

There, she drank a martini to "loosen up a little bit" before going to meet her boyfriend, with whom she had argued the night before. Roughly ten minutes later she walked to her boyfriend's dormitory lounge to meet him. He had not yet arrived.

Having nothing else to do while she waited for her boyfriend, the victim walked up to appellant's room to look for Earl Hassel, appellant's roommate. She knocked on the door several times but received no answer. She therefore wrote a note to Mr. Hassel, which read, "Hi Earl, I'm drunk. That's not why I came to see you. I haven't seen you in a while. I'll talk to you later, [victim's name]." She did so, although she had not felt any intoxicating effects from the martini, "for a laugh."

After the victim had knocked again, she tried the knob on the appellant's door. Finding it open, she walked in. She saw someone lying on the bed with a pillow over his head, whom she thought to be Earl Hassel. After lifting the pillow from his head, she realized it was appellant. She asked appellant which dresser was his roommate's. He told her, and the victim left the note.

Before the victim could leave appellant's room, however, appellant asked her to stay and "hang out for a while." She complied because she "had time to kill" and because she didn't really know appellant and wanted to give him "a fair chance." Appellant asked her to give him a back rub but she declined, explaining that she did not "trust" him. Appellant then asked her to have a seat on his bed. Instead, she found a seat on the floor, and conversed for a while about a mutual friend.[1] No physical contact between the two had, to this point, taken place.

Thereafter, however, appellant moved off the bed and down on the floor, and "kind of pushed [the victim] back with his body. It wasn't a shove, it was just kind of a leaning-type of thing." Next appellant "straddled" and started kissing the victim. The victim responded by saying, "Look, I gotta go. I'm going to meet [my boyfriend]." Then appellant lifted up her shirt and bra and began fondling her. The victim then said "no."

After roughly thirty seconds of kissing and fondling, appellant "undid his pants and he kind of moved his body up a little bit." The victim was still saying "no" but "really couldn't move because [appellant] was shifting at [her] body so he was over [her]." Appellant then tried to put his penis in her mouth. The victim did not physically resist, but rather continued to verbally protest, saying "No, I gotta go, let me go," in a "scolding" manner.

Ten or fifteen more seconds passed before the two rose to their feet. Appellant disregarded the victim's continual complaints that she "had to go," and instead walked two feet away to the door and locked it so that no one from the outside could enter.[2]

Then, in the victim's words, "[appellant] put me down on the bed. It was kind of like—he didn't throw me on the bed. It's hard to explain. It was kind of like a push but no. . . ." She did not bounce off the bed. "It wasn't slow like a romantic kind of thing, but it wasn't a fast shove either. It was kind of in the middle."

Once the victim was on the bed, appellant began "straddling" her again while he undid the knot in her sweatpants. He then removed her sweatpants and underwear from one of her legs. The victim did not physically resist in any way while on the bed because appellant was on top of her, and she "couldn't like go anywhere." She did not scream out at anytime because, "[i]t was like a dream was happening or something."

Appellant then used one of his hands to "guide" his penis into her vagina. At that point, after appellant was inside her, the victim began saying "no, no to him softly in a moaning kind of way . . . because it was just so scary." After about thirty seconds, appellant pulled out his penis and ejaculated onto the victim's stomach.

Immediately thereafter, appellant got off the victim and said, "Wow, I guess we just got carried away." To this the victim retorted, "No, we didn't get carried away, you got carried away." The victim then quickly dressed, grabbed her school books and raced downstairs to her boyfriend who was by then waiting for her in the lounge.

Once there, the victim began crying. Her boyfriend and she went up to his dorm room where, after watching the victim clean off appellant's semen from her stomach, he called the police.

Defense counsel's cross-examination elicited more details regarding the contact between appellant and the victim before the incident in question. The victim testified that roughly two weeks prior to the incident, she had attended a school seminar entitled, "Does 'no' sometimes mean[] 'yes'?" Among other things, the lecturer at this seminar had discussed the average length and circumference of human penises. After the seminar, the victim and several of her friends had discussed the subject matter of the seminar over a speaker-telephone with appellant and his roommate Earl Hassel. The victim testified that during that telephone conversation, she had asked appellant the size of his penis. According to the victim, appellant responded by suggesting that the victim "come over and find out." She declined.

When questioned further regarding her communications with appellant prior to the April 19, 1988 incident, the victim testified that on two other occasions, she had stopped by appellant's room while intoxicated. During one of those times, she had laid down on his bed. When asked whether she had asked appellant again at that time what his penis size was, the victim testified that she did not remember.

Appellant took the stand in his own defense and offered an account of the incident and the events leading up to it which differed only as to the consent involved. According to appellant, the victim had begun communication with him after the school seminar by asking him of the size of his penis and of whether he would show it to her. Appellant had suspected that the victim wanted to pursue a sexual relationship with him because she had stopped by his room twice after the phone call while intoxicated, laying down on his bed with her legs spread and again asking to see his penis. He believed that his suspicions were confirmed when she initiated the April 19, 1988 encounter by stopping by his room (again after drinking), and waking him up.

Appellant testified that, on the day in question, he did initiate the first physical contact, but added that the victim warmly responded to his advances by passionately returning his kisses. He conceded that she was continually "whisper-

---

[1] On cross-examination, the victim testified that during this conversation she had explained she was having problems with her boyfriend.

[2] The victim testified that she realized at the time that the lock was not of a type that could lock people inside the room.

ing . . . no's," but claimed that she did so while "amorously . . . passionately" moaning. In effect, he took such protests to be thinly veiled acts of encouragement. When asked why he locked the door, he explained that "that's not something you want somebody to just walk in on you [doing.]"

According to appellant, the two then laid down on the bed, the victim helped him take her clothing off, and he entered her. He agreed that the victim continued to say "no" while on the bed, but carefully qualified his agreement, explaining that the statements were "moaned passionately." According to appellant, when he saw a "blank look on her face," he immediately withdrew and asked "is anything wrong, is something the matter, is anything wrong." He ejaculated on her stomach thereafter because he could no longer "control" himself. Appellant testified that after this, the victim "saw that it was over and then she made her move. She gets right off the bed . . . she just swings her legs over and then she puts her clothes back on." Then, in wholly corroborating an aspect of the victim's account, he testified that he remarked, "Well, I guess we got carried away," to which she rebuked, "No, we didn't get carried, you got carried away."

After hearing both accounts, the jury convicted appellant of rape and indecent assault. * * * Appellant was then sentenced to serve a term of imprisonment of one to four years for rape and a concurrent term of six to twelve months for indecent assault. Post-trial bail was granted pending this timely appeal.

* * *

[We address first whether there is sufficient evidence to support a rape conviction.]

II. Sufficiency of the Evidence

Appellant's argument in this regard was well summarized by appellant's counsel in his brief.

* * *

Mr. Berkowitz prays that this Court overturns his rape conviction. He asks that this Court define the parameters between what may have been unacceptable social conduct and the criminal conduct necessary to support the charge for forcible rape.

We contend that upon review, the facts show no more than what legal scholars refer to as "reluctant submission". * * * The uncontroverted evidence fails to establish forcible compulsion.

The Commonwealth counters:

Viewing the evidence and its inferences in the light most favorable to the Commonwealth, the jury's conclusion that the Defendant's forcible conduct overcame [the victim's] will is reasonable. The assault was rapid and the victim was physically overcome. Because she was acquainted with the Defendant, [the victim] had no

reason to be fearful or suspicious of him and her resorting to verbal resistance only is understandable. More importantly, perhaps, it is only her lack of consent that is truly relevant. It is entirely reasonable to believe that the Defendant sat on her, pushed her on the bed and penetrated her before she had time to fully realize her plight and raise a hue and cry. If the law required active resistance, rather the simple absence of consent, speedy penetration would immunize the most violent attacks and the goal-oriented rapist would reap an absurd reward. Certainly a victim must communicate her objections. But, contrary to the Defendant's arguments, Pennsylvania law says she can "just say no." [The victim] said "no." She said it repeatedly, clearly and sternly. She was rapidly, forcibly raped and deserves the protection of the law.

With the Commonwealth's position, the trial court agreed. We cannot.

In viewing the evidence, we remain mindful that credibility determinations were a matter solely for the fact finder below. * * * If a jury could have reasonably determined from the evidence adduced that all of the necessary elements of the crime were established, then the evidence will be deemed sufficient to support the verdict.

In Pennsylvania, the crime of rape is defined by statute as follows:

A person commits a felony of the first degree when he engages in sexual intercourse with another person not his spouse:
(1) by forcible compulsion;
(2) by threat of forcible compulsion that would prevent resistance by a person of reasonable resolution;
(3) who is unconscious; or
(4) who is so mentally deranged or deficient that such person is incapable of consent.

18 Pa.C.S.A. § 3121. A statutory caveat to this rule may be found in section 3107 of title 18.

Resistance Not Required
The alleged victim need not resist the actor in prosecution under this chapter: Provided, however, that nothing in this section shall be construed to prohibit a defendant from introducing evidence that the alleged victim consented to the conduct in question.

The contours of Pennsylvania's rape statute, however, are not immediately apparent. As our Supreme Court explained in the landmark case, *Commonwealth v. Rhodes*, 510 Pa. 537, 510 A.2d 1217 (1986):

"[F]orcible compulsion" as used in section 3121(1) includes not only physical force or violence but also moral, psychological or intellectual force used to compel a person to engage in sexual intercourse against that person's will.

Closely related to section 3121(1) is section 3121(2) which applies to the situation where "forcible compulsion" is not actually used but is threatened. That section uses the phrase "by threat of forcible compulsion that would prevent resistance by a person of reasonable resolution." The Model Penal Code used the terminology "compels her to submit by any threat that would prevent resistance by a woman of ordinary resolution" and graded that offense as gross sexual imposition, a felony of the third degree. The Pennsylvania legislature rejected the concept that sexual intercourse compelled by "gross imposition" should be graded as a less serious offense and, therefore, enacted section 3121(2). By use of the phrase "person of reasonable resolution," the legislature introduced an objective standard regarding the use of threats of forcible compulsion to prevent resistance (as opposed to actual application of "forcible compulsion.")

The determination of whether there is sufficient evidence to demonstrate beyond a reasonable doubt that an accused engaged in sexual intercourse by forcible compulsion (which we have defined to include "not only physical force or violence, but also moral, psychological or intellectual force used to compel a person to engage in sexual intercourse against that person's will,"), or by the threat of such forcible compulsion that would prevent resistance by a person of reasonable resolution *is, of course, a determination that will be made in each case based upon the totality of the circumstances that have been presented to the fact finder.* Significant factors to be weighed in that determination would include the respective ages of the victim and the accused, the respective mental and physical conditions of the victim and the accused, the atmosphere and physical setting in which the incident was alleged to have taken place, the extent to which the accused may have been in a position of authority, domination or custodial control over the victim, and whether the victim was under duress. This list of possible factors is by no means exclusive.

(emphasis added).

Before us is not a case of mental coercion. There existed no significant disparity between the ages of appellant and the victim. They were both college sophomores at the time of the incident. Appellant was age twenty; the victim was nineteen. The record is devoid of any evidence suggesting that the phys-

ical or mental condition of one party differed from the other in any material way. Moreover, the atmosphere and physical setting in which the incident took place was in no way coercive. The victim walked freely into appellant's dorm room in the middle of the afternoon on a school day and stayed to talk of her own volition. There was no evidence to suggest that appellant was in any position of authority, domination or custodial control over the victim. Finally, no record evidence indicates that the victim was under duress. Indeed, nothing in the record manifests any intent of appellant to impose "moral, psychological or intellectual" coercion upon the victim. See and compare *Commonwealth v. Rhodes,* supra (position of authority, isolated area of the incident and explicit commands sufficient to prove mental coercion); *Commonwealth v. Ables,* [404 Pa.Super 169, 177–179, 590 A.2d 334, 338 (1991)] (position of trust and confidence coupled with emotional exploitation sufficient to establish moral coercion); *Commonwealth v. Ruppert,* 397 Pa.Super. 132, 579 A.2d 966 (1990) (father–daughter relationship coupled with showing of sexually explicit pictures sufficient to establish psychological coercion); *Commonwealth v. Frank,* 395 Pa.Super. 412, 577 A.2d 609 (1990) (therapist–patient relationship coupled with threat sufficient for psychological coercion); *Commonwealth v. Dorman,* [377 Pa.Super. 419, 547 A.2d 757 (1988)] (appellant's position of authority and trust and remote location of the incident sufficient to establish psychological coercion).

Nor is this a case of a threat of forcible compulsion. When asked by defense counsel at trial whether appellant had at any point threatened her in any manner, the victim responded, "No, he didn't." Moreover, careful review of the record fails to reveal any express or even implied threat that could be viewed as one which, by the objective standard applicable herein, "would prevent resistance by a person of reasonable resolution." Compare *Commonwealth v. Poindexter,* 372 Pa.Super. 566, 539 A.2d 1341 (1989) (father's reproaches and threats sufficient to establish coercion toward daughters); *Commonwealth v. Williams,* 294 Pa.Super. 93, 439 A.2d 765 (1982) (threat that victim would be killed if she resisted sufficient to establish forcible compulsion).

Rather, the Commonwealth contends that the instant rape conviction is supported by the evidence of actual physical force used to complete the act of intercourse. Essentially, the Commonwealth maintains that, viewed in the light most favorable to it, the record establishes that the victim did not consent to engage in the intercourse, and thus, any force used to complete the act of intercourse thereafter constituted "forcible compulsion."

In response, appellant urges that the victim's testimony itself precludes a finding of "forcible compulsion." Appellant essentially argues that the indisputable lack of physical injuries and physical resistance proves that the evidence was insufficient to establish rape.

In beginning our review of these arguments, it is clear that any reliance on the victim's absence of physical injuries or physical resistance is misplaced. Although it is true that the instant victim testified that she was not "physically hurt in any fashion," and that it was "possible that [she] took no physical action to discourage [appellant]," such facts are insignificant in a sufficiency determination. * * * Similarly, our legislature has expressly commanded that the "victim *need not resist* the actor in prosecutions under" Chapter 31. See 18 Pa.C.S.A. § 3107. (emphasis added). As the *Rhodes* Court observed, this legislative mandate was intended to make it clear that "lack of consent is not synonymous with lack of resistance." Thus, while the presence of actual injury or physical resistance might well indicate "forcible compulsion," we are compelled to conclude that the absence of either or both is not fatal to the Commonwealth's case.

What is comparatively uncertain, however, in the absence of either an injury or resistance requirement, is the precise degree of actual physical force necessary to prove "forcible compulsion." As the *Rhodes* Court has made clear, no precise definition of the term "forcible compulsion" may be found.

> The "force necessary to support convictions for rape and involuntary deviate sexual intercourse need only be such as to establish lack of consent and to induce the woman to submit without additional resistance'. . . . The degree of force required to constitute rape [or involuntary deviate sexual intercourse] is relative and depends upon the facts and particular circumstances of the case."

The *Rhodes* Court specifically refused to "delineate all of the possible circumstances that might tend to demonstrate that sexual intercourse was engaged in by forcible compulsion or by threat of forcible compulsion within the meaning of [title 18] section 3121(1) and (2)." Rather, the Court left that delineation to evolve "in the best tradition of the common law—by development of a body of case law. . . . [W]hether there is sufficient evidence to demonstrate . . . that an accused engaged in sexual intercourse by forcible compulsion . . . is, of course, a determination that will be made in each case based on the *totality of the circumstances*. . . ." Thus, the ultimate task for the fact finder remains the question of whether, under the totality of circumstances, "the victim . . . was forced to . . . engage in sexual intercourse . . . *against his or her will*." (emphasis added).

Here, the victim testified that the physical aspects of the encounter began when appellant "kind of pushed me back with his body. It wasn't a shove, it was just kind of a leaning-type thing." Compare *Commonwealth v. Rough*, [275 Pa.Super 93, 439 A.2d 765, 768 (1982)] (victim forced to

floor and struck). She did not testify that appellant "pinned" her to the floor with his hands thereafter; she testified that he "started kissing me . . . [and] lift[ing] my shirt [and] bra . . . straddling me kind of . . . shifting at my body so that he was over me." Compare *Commonwealth v. Meadows*, 381 Pa.Super. 354, 356–60, 553 A.2d 1006, 1008–09 (1989) (victim "pinned" to the ground despite physical resistance). When he attempted to have oral sex with her, appellant "knelt up straight . . . [and] tried to put his penis in my mouth . . . and after he obviously couldn't . . . he, we got up." Although appellant then locked the door, his act cannot be seen as an attempt to imprison the victim since she knew and testified that the type of lock on the door of appellant's dorm room simply prevented those on the outside from entering but could be opened from the inside without hindrance. Compare *Commonwealth v. Rhodes*, supra (victim imprisoned in car brought to isolated area). Appellant did not push, shove or throw the victim to his bed; he "put" her on the bed, not in a "romantic" way, but not with a "fast shove either." Once on the bed, appellant did not try to restrain the victim with his hands in any fashion. Compare *Commonwealth v. Irvin* [260 Pa.Super. 122, 393 A.2d 1042, 1044 (1978)] (victim choked and her screams muffled by defendant's hands). Rather, while she was "just kind of laying there," he "straddled" her, "quick[ly] undid" the knot in her sweatpants, "took off" her sweatpants and underwear, placed the "weight of his body" on top of her and "guided" his penis inside her vagina.

Even in the light most favorable to the Commonwealth, the victim's testimony as to the physical aspects of the encounter cannot serve as a basis to prove "forcible compulsion." The cold record is utterly devoid of any evidence regarding the respective sizes of either appellant or the victim. As such, we are left only to speculate as to the coercive effect of such acts as "leaning" against the victim or placing the "weight of his body" on top of her. This we may not do. Moreover, even if the record indicated some disparity in the respective weights or strength of the parties, such acts are not themselves inconsistent with consensual relations. Except for the fact that appellant was on top of the victim before and during intercourse, there is no evidence that the victim, if she had wanted to do so, could not have removed herself from appellant's bed and walked out of the room without any risk of harm or danger to herself whatsoever. These circumstances simply cannot be bootstrapped into sexual intercourse by forcible compulsion.

Similarly inconclusive is the fact that the victim testified that the act occurred in a relatively brief period of time. The short time frame might, without more, indicate that the victim desired the sexual encounter as easily as it might that she didn't, given the fact that no threats or mental coercion were alleged. At most, therefore, the physical aspects of the encounter establish that appellant's sexual advances may have been unusually rapid, persistent and virtually uninterrupted. However inappropriate, undesirable or unacceptable such conduct may be seen to be, it does not, standing alone, prove that the victim was "forced to engage in sexual intercourse against her will."

The only evidence which remains to be considered is the fact that both the victim and appellant testified that throughout the encounter, the victim repeatedly and continually said "no."[3] Unfortunately for the Commonwealth, under the existing statutes, this evidence alone cannot suffice to support a finding of "forcible compulsion."

Evidence of verbal resistance is unquestionably relevant in a determination of "forcible compulsion." At least twice previously this Court has given weight to the failure to heed the victim's oral admonitions. * * * In each such case, however, evidence of verbal resistance was only found sufficient where coupled with a sufficient threat of forcible compulsion, mental coercion, or actual physical force of a type inherently inconsistent with consensual sexual intercourse. Thus, although evidence of verbal protestations may be relevant to prove that the intercourse was against the victim's will, it is not dispositive or sufficient evidence of "forcible compulsion."

If the legislature had intended to define rape, a felony of the first degree, as non-consensual intercourse, it could have done so. It did not do this. It defined rape as sexual intercourse by "forcible compulsion." Compare 18 Pa.C.S.A. § 3126 (defining indecent assault as "indecent contact with another not [the actor's] spouse . . . *without the consent* of the other person.") (emphasis added). If the legislature means what it said, then where as here no evidence was adduced by the Commonwealth which established either that mental coercion, or a threat, or force inherently inconsistent with consensual intercourse was used to com-

plete the act of intercourse, the evidence is insufficient to support a rape conviction. Accordingly, we hold that the trial court erred in determining that the evidence adduced by the Commonwealth was sufficient to convict appellant of rape.

* * *

[With regard to the conviction for indecent assault, the court found that the trial court erred in excluding evidence offered by the defense. The Rape Shield Law generally bars evidence of the victim's past sexual conduct "unless it can be established that to exclude such evidence would lay victim to the very raison d'être of the trial itself: the pursuit of truth." The defense should have been permitted to introduce evidence that the victim and her boyfriend had engaged in a series of arguments regarding his jealousy and her alleged infidelity to their relationship. This was in large part because the prosecution had argued to the jury that the victim had no reason to falsify. Since the prosecution had contended that in part because of the victim's relationship with her boyfriend she had no reason to lie regarding whether she consented to intercourse with the defendant, the defendant had a right to argue that her relationship with her boyfriend did provide a reason to lie and to produce evidence supporting that contention. The court stressed that the defense would not be entitled to introduce evidence as to the truth or falsity of any alleged instance of the victim's infidelity; it was entitled to prove "the existence of the boyfriend's jealousy, not its validity." For this error in excluding evidence, the conviction for indecent assault was reversed.]

IV. Conclusion

For the foregoing reasons, we conclude that the evidence adduced by the Commonwealth was insufficient to convict appellant of rape, and that a new trial is warranted on the indecent assault charge. * * * Accordingly, we discharge appellant as to the rape conviction and reverse and remand for a new trial in accordance with this opinion.

Notes and Questions

1. On further appeal in *Berkowitz* to the Pennsylvania Supreme Court, the action of the intermediate superior court reversing the rape conviction was affirmed. With regard to the conviction for indecent assault, the Supreme Court held that the evidence that the victim and her boyfriend argued over her possible infidelity was so closely tied to the victim's fidelity itself that the Rape Shield law barred the defense from going into it. Thus the superior court was mistaken in holding that the trial judge erred in excluding this evidence. The conviction and sentence on

---

[3] The accounts differed in this respect only as to the tone in which the word was spoken. Appellant claimed it was whispered "passionately." The victim testified that she voiced her objections before the intercourse in a "scolding" manner. At trial, it was peculiarly for the jury to determine the credibility of the parties. On appeal, we must view the record in the light most favorable to the Commonwealth. Viewed in this way, we must consider the victim's admonitions before the intercourse to be sincere protests. Although the victim testified that during the intercourse she "moaned" the word "no," the degree of the ambiguity of her protests at that point is inconsequential for a sufficiency determination. By that time, penetration had occurred and the crime, if any, was complete. Such evidence merely went to the weight to attach to the victim's credibility. Moreover, the victim carefully explained that her "moaning" during intercourse was in no way "passionate."

the indecent assault charge were therefore reinstated. 537 Pa. 143, 641 A.2d 1161 (1994).

2. The New Jersey Supreme Court took a much different approach to a similar statute in *In the Interest of M.T.S.*, 129 N.J. 422, 609 A.2d 1266 (1992). M.T.S., a 15-year-old youth at the time of the incident at issue, was alleged to be delinquent on the basis of facts that petitioners contended established second degree sexual assault. At 11:30 P.M., M.T.S. went to the bedroom of C.G., a 15-year-old female with whose family M.T.S. was staying, and vaginally penetrated her. He testified C.G. consented to the penetration. C.G. testified that she was asleep and awoke to find that M.T.S. had penetrated her. Because this was a juvenile court delinquency proceeding, the judge made specific findings. In those findings, the judge concluded that the evidence failed to show that C.G. was asleep at the time of the penetration but did establish that she did not consent to that act. On this basis, the judge held that sexual assault had occurred. The Appellate Division reversed, reasoning that the lack of evidence of force beyond that involved in the act of sexual penetration precluded a finding of sexual assault. On further review, the New Jersey Supreme Court reasoned:

> The New Jersey Code of Criminal Justice defines "sexual assault" as the commission "of sexual penetration" "with another person" with the use of "physical force or coercion." * * *
>
> The parties offer two alternative understandings of the concept of "physical force" as it is used in the statute. The State would read "physical force" to entail any amount of sexual touching brought about involuntarily. A showing of sexual penetration coupled with a lack of consent would satisfy the elements of the statute. The Public Defender urges an interpretation of "physical force" to mean force "used to overcome lack of consent." That definition equates force with violence and leads to the conclusion that sexual assault requires the application of some amount of force in addition to the act of penetration.
>
> * * *
>
> The reform statute defines sexual assault as penetration accomplished by the use of "physical force" or "coercion," but it does not define either "physical force" or "coercion" or enumerate examples of evidence that would establish those elements. * * * The task of defining "physical force" therefore was left to the courts.

That definitional task runs the risk of undermining the basic legislative intent to reformulate rape law. * * *

Because the statute eschews any reference to the victim's will or resistance, the standard defining the role of force in sexual penetration must prevent the possibility that the establishment of the crime will turn on the alleged victim's state of mind or responsive behavior. We conclude, therefore, that any act of sexual penetration engaged in by the defendant without the affirmative and freely-given permission of the victim to the specific act of penetration constitutes the offense of sexual assault. Therefore, physical force in excess of that inherent in the act of sexual penetration is not required for such penetration to be unlawful. The definition of "physical force" is satisfied * * * if the defendant applies any amount of force against another person in the absence of what a reasonable person would believe to be affirmative and freely-given permission to the act of sexual penetration.

Under the reformed statute, permission to engage in sexual penetration must be affirmative and it must be given freely, but that permission may be inferred either from acts or statements reasonably viewed in light of the surrounding circumstances. Persons need not, of course, expressly announce their consent to engage in intercourse for there to be affirmative permission. Permission to engage in an act of sexual penetration can be and indeed often is indicated through physical actions rather than words. Permission is demonstrated when the evidence, in whatever form, is sufficient to demonstrate that a reasonable person would have believed that the alleged victim had affirmatively and freely given authorization to the act.

Applying this to the facts of the case before it, the court concluded that the record provided reasonable support for the trial court's conclusion that the victim had not expressed consent to the act of intercourse, either through her words or actions. Therefore, it reversed the judgment of the intermediate court and reinstated the disposition of juvenile delinquency for the commission of second degree sexual assault.

3. There is general agreement that submission or consent given in response to threats—explicit or implied—to do serious physical harm will be ineffective and render resulting sexual activity criminal under literally all sexual assault and similar offenses. What other influences are or should be sufficient? In *State v. Thompson*, 243 Mont. 28, 792 P.2d 1103 (1990), the defendant was principal and basketball coach of a high school. He was charged with the offense of sexual intercourse without consent, based on allegations that he forced a female student at the school—"Jane Doe"—to engage in an oral sexual act with him by threatening that she would not graduate unless she participated. Under the statute defining the charged offense, sexual conduct is "without consent" if "the victim is compelled to submit by force or by threat of imminent death, bodily injury, or kidnapping to be inflicted on anyone." The trial court dismissed the charges on the grounds that the allegations did not constitute the offense because they did not include a threat sufficient to render the act without consent. On the prosecution's appeal, the Montana Supreme Court reasoned:

> The State * * * contends that Thompson, in his position of authority as the principal, intimidated Jane Doe into the alleged acts. Furthermore, the State argues the fear and apprehension of Jane Doe show Thompson used force against her. We agree with the State that Thompson intimidated Jane Doe; however, we cannot stretch the definition of force to include intimidation, fear, or apprehension. * * * The State argues that the definition "threat of bodily injury" includes psychological impairment. Unfortunately, the statute sets forth bodily injury, not psychological impairment. A threat that eventually leads to psychological impairment is not sufficient under the statute. The statute only addresses the results of three specific kinds of threats, and psychological impairment is not one of them.
>
> * * *
>
> This case is one of considerable difficulty for us * * *. The alleged facts, if true, show disgusting acts of taking advantage of a young person by an adult who occupied a position of authority over the young person. If we could rewrite the statutes to define the alleged acts here as sexual intercourse without consent, we would willingly do so. The business of courts, however, is to interpret statutes, not to rewrite them, nor to insert words not put

> there by the legislature. With a good deal of reluctance, and with strong condemnation of the alleged acts, we affirm the District Court.

4. If consent to sexual acts is given but deception was used to generate it, under what circumstance is that consent ineffective and the sexual acts criminal? The issue was presented by *People v. Hough*, 159 Misc.2d 997, 607 N.Y.S.2d 884 (1994), in which the facts were as follows:

> [A]t approximately 3:30 A.M. complainant was sleeping in her apartment which she left unlocked because she was expecting her boyfriend, Lenny Hough, to come over. Complainant was awoken by a knock and believed that it was her boyfriend at the door. * * *
>
> Complainant instructed the male to come in * * *. After the light was turned on, complainant realized that the male was not Lenny but was his twin brother, the defendant, Lamont Hough. They talked shortly and complainant told defendant to lock the door when he left. The complainant then went back to sleep but was again awoken at approximately 5:00 A.M. when she heard a knock at the door and heard a male say "open the door." Complainant believed the male was her boyfriend because it sounded like him. Complainant got out of bed and * * * turned off the light located near the door * * *. Complainant opened the door and thought it was Lenny who entered the apartment, as it was dark and she couldn't see. The two spoke momentarily and then complainant returned to bed. The male, who smelt of alcohol, also got into bed next to the complainant. Complainant began talking to the male as if it were her boyfriend Lenny but was looking away from him while they were in the bed. The complainant asked the male why he didn't use the key she gave him and he said he either lost it or left it at his father's house.
>
> The male * * * asked her to have sex with him and she told him to make it quick because she had to work in the morning. Complainant removed her clothing and was calling him Lenny. * * * They had intercourse for several minutes during which time complainant wasn't looking at the male's face. When the act was over, the male said * * * "What are you going to tell Lenny?" Complainant got out of bed, turned the light on and saw that it was Lamont and not Lenny that she had sexual intercourse with.

Complainant threw the defendant's clothes out the door and defendant left. Shortly thereafter, complainant contacted the police.

Defendant Lamont Hough was charged with sexual misconduct under N.Y. Penal Law section 130.20(1), which defines the crime as "engag[ing] in sexual intercourse with a female without her consent." Section 130.05 provides that lack of consent results from forcible compulsion or incapacity to consent. A person is incapable of consent when he or she is less than 17 years old or mentally defective or mentally incapacitated or physically helpless. Hough moved to dismiss the charges on the grounds that the facts alleged did not amount to the charged crime. The trial judge wrote:

> The lack of consent which forms the basis of the charge against defendant * * * results from the complainant's mistaken belief resulting from defendant's alleged fraud that the body she made love with was that of her boyfriend.

* * *

This Court has been unable to discover any authority for the factual circumstances presented in this case where the charge is sexual misconduct. Even where the charge is rape in the classic situation where the woman is forced to submit to sexual intercourse, there is little authority. Truly, these facts present a novel issue.

In general, in the absence of a statute, where a woman is capable of consenting and does consent to sexual intercourse, a man is not guilty of rape even though he obtained the consent through fraud or surprise. * * * The reason is that in the traditional definition of the crime of rape, the sexual intercourse must have been achieved "by force", or "forcibly".

A few courts have indicated that consent to sexual intercourse may be vitiated, and the crime committed where defendant achieved the sexual intercourse by impersonating the woman's husband. * * *

A number of states have enacted statutes which extend the traditional definition of rape to include sexual intercourse achieved by fraud or impersonation. * * *

* * *

Additionally, the Model Penal Code makes it a crime for a male to have sexual intercourse with a female when he knows that she submits because she mistakenly supposes that he is her husband. Model Penal Code (U.L.A.) § 213.1(2).

* * *

The legislature defined lack of consent in Penal Law § 130.05 and intended to exclude cases of fraud or impersonation. Where the legislature intended to extend the definition of lack of consent, it did. For instance, lack of consent as applied to the crime of sexual abuse is extended to "any circumstances . . . in which the victim does not expressly or impliedly acquiesce in the actor's conduct."

For the charge of sexual misconduct, however, lack of consent has been defined by the legislature and does not include the particular circumstances in the present case. Consequently, assuming that defendant did deceive the complainant into having sexual intercourse with him, defendant cannot be found guilty of sexual misconduct.

* * *

Based upon the foregoing, defendant's motion is granted and the information is hereby dismissed.

The traditional assumption has been that fraud will render the victim's consent ineffective only if the fraud deceives the victim regarding the "nature of the act," that is, regarding whether the defendant's actions constitute sexual intercourse. In *People v. Minkowski*, 204 Cal.App.2d 832, 23 Cal.Reptr. 92 (1962), for example, the defendant, an actual physician, obtained the victims' consent to insertion into their bodies of medical instruments but then in fact inserted his penis into them, and his conviction was upheld.

However, the courts have been reluctant to read "nature of the act" more broadly. In *Boro v. Superior Court*, 163 Cal.App.3d 1224, 210 Cal.Reptr. 122 (1985), for example, a split court reversed a conviction on proof that the defendant represented himself to be a physician and persuaded the victim that sexual intercourse with him was necessary to her medical treatment for a fatal disease he falsely represented she had. The prosecution's theory was that the victim was unconscious of the nature of the act, because the defendant's misrepresentations caused her to believe it was in the nature of medical treatment and not a simple, ordinary act of sexual intercourse. This theory was not successful, because the victim was not subjected to fraud as to the nature of the act.

2. Mistake Regarding Consent

What if any effect should result from evidence that although the victim of sexual assault did not in fact consent, the accused incorrectly believed that the victim was consenting? This has proven to be a troublesome matter for courts.

In a sense, this should simply be an application to a specific situation of general rules concerning mistake of fact, presented in Chapter 13. Thus, a defendant who produces evidence that he was mistaken about consent is arguably entitled to have the jury consider that evidence in deciding whether the prosecution has proved beyond a reasonable doubt that the defendant was aware that the victim was not consenting, *if* the absence of consent is an element of the crime *and* the crime also requires a culpable mental state regarding that element. As the case reprinted next suggests, then, a preliminary question must be whether the charged crime requires awareness of lack of consent. Some modern formulations of sexual assault that do not explicitly mention the victim's consent, of course, make more difficult the task of deciding whether these statutes require awareness of the lack of consent.

In addition, the rape–sexual assault context presents again the question developed in Chapter 13 as to whether a mistake of fact should have to be objectively reasonable if it was actually made by the accused.

Should mistake of fact law be applied with special restrictiveness in sexual assault cases? The approach of the court in the case reprinted here is similar to that taken by the California Supreme Court in a series of cases arising out of *People v. Mayberry*, 15 Cal.3d 143, 125 Cal.Rptr. 745, 542 P.2d 1337 (1975) and reaffirmed in *People v. Williams*, 4 Cal.4th 354, 14 CAl.Rptr.2d 441, 841 P.2d 961 (1992). In *Williams*, dissenting Justice Mosk criticized this approach as tainted by several improper considerations. First, he suggested, the majority was motivated by a fear that in these cases defendants would too easily fabricate reasonable-and-honest-belief defenses through their own false testimony. Thus, he claimed, the majority was imposing what amounts to a requirement of evidence corroborating sexual assault defendants' testimony. Second, he speculated, the majority seemed to fear that juries would misconstrue or misapply a "reasonable-and-honest-belief defense" to acquit defendants contrary to the law and the evidence. Any such fears, he responded, are unjustified. Whatever was the case in the past, he claimed, statistics compiled by the United States Department of Justice establish that prosecutions for rape are as successful as other prosecutions, and thus there is no need to fear that such cases pose special risks of jury error or disobedience.

Tyson v. State

Court of Appeals of Indiana, 1993
619 N.E.2d 276.

SHIELDS, Judge.

Michael G. Tyson appeals his conviction[] of rape * * * [a class B felony].

* * *

Tyson argues the trial court committed reversible error when it refused to give his Tendered Instructions

Nos. 5 and 6, both of which deal with Tyson's belief regarding D.W.'s consent to sexual acts. The instructions in question read as follow:

Tendered Instruction No. 5:

Before you may return a conviction on any count, you must be satisfied that the State has proved beyond a reasonable doubt that the defendant knowingly forced the complainant to engage in the sexual acts charged. This means that the State must prove beyond a reasonable doubt that the complainant did not consent and, in addition, that the defendant did not reasonably believe that she had consented.

Tendered Instruction No. 6:

The defense of mistake of fact is defined by law as follows: It is a defense that the person who engaged in the prohibited conduct was reasonably mistaken about a matter of fact, if the mistake negates the culpability required for the commission of the offense. The reasonable mistake about a fact must have prevented the defendant from acting intentionally or knowingly as those terms are defined by law. In this case, it is a defense to all the charges that the defendant was reasonably mistaken about whether the complainant consented to the sexual acts in question. The State has the burden of disproving this defense beyond a reasonable doubt.

* * *

Jury instructions lie largely within the sound discretion of the trial court and are reviewed only for an abuse of that discretion. When the trial court refuses to give an instruction, we must determine whether the tendered instruction correctly states the law, whether there is evidence in the record to support the giving of the instruction, and whether the substance of the tendered instruction is covered by instructions which were given by the trial court.

Although not argued by the State on appeal, a credible argument can be made that the tendered instructions do not correctly state the law in Indiana because they incorrectly focus on Tyson's perception of D.W.'s consent.

The culpability required for the commission of an offense is defined in IC 35-41-2-2(d) (1988) which provides: "Unless the statute defining the offense provides otherwise, if a kind of culpability is required for commission of an offense, it is required with respect to every material element of the prohibited conduct." Thus, unlike the Model Penal Code, which requires culpability with respect to every material element of the offense, the Indiana Criminal Code requires culpability only with respect to the prohibited conduct. This distinction was emphasized by the amendment to the culpability statute which occurred in 1977. A prior version of IC 35-41-2-2(d) required culpability with respect to material elements of "prohibited conduct and its atten-

dant circumstances." IC 35-41-2-2(d) (1976). By deleting the phrase "and its attendant circumstances," the legislature expressed its intent to limit the culpability requirement to prohibited conduct only.

The significance of the fact that culpability is not required for attendant circumstances is illustrated by the statutory definition of the mistake of fact defense. IC 35-41-3-7 (1988) defines the defense as follows: "It is a defense that the person who engaged in the prohibited conduct was reasonably mistaken about a matter of fact, if the mistake negates the *culpability* required for commission of the offense." (emphasis added). Thus, an alleged mistake of fact with reference to an attendant circumstance for which there is no culpability required is not within the parameters of the defense.

To determine if the defense is available, therefore, the elements of a statute must be broken down into those of prohibited conduct and those of attendant circumstances. In rape, for example, the statute provides in relevant part: "A person who knowingly or intentionally has sexual intercourse with a member of the opposite sex when . . . the other person is compelled by force or imminent threat of force . . . commits rape." IC 35-42-4-1 (1992 Supp.) The prohibited conduct in the offense of rape is sexual intercourse with a member of the opposite sex by force or imminent threat of force. Compulsion of the victim, while an element of the offense, is an attendant circumstance, not prohibited conduct. * * *

Of course, although lack of consent is not an element of rape * * *per se, evidence which has a tendency to prove either consent or lack of consent is relevant to the element of compulsion * * *. Evidence that the alleged victim consented to the sexual act is evidence that negates compulsion, while evidence that the alleged victim did not consent may be evidence that the victim was compelled.

Arguably, then, in order to raise the defense of mistake of fact in a rape * * * case, there must be evidence that suggests the defendant was reasonably mistaken as to whether a sexual act occurred or whether force or threatened force was used, the prohibited conduct components of the offenses. Evidence that the sexual act or force or threat of force did not occur cannot raise a mistake of fact "defense" because that evidence denies the prohibited conduct, and there cannot have been a mistake about conduct which did not occur. For example, Tyson testified that he did not, at any time, force D.W. to engage in sexual conduct. Accordingly, he neither argues that he was reasonably mistaken as to the occurrence of sexual conduct or as to his use of force, nor does he claim that evidence of such a mistake was presented. Instead, he claims he was reasonably mistaken as to D.W.'s consent, a mistake which, arguably, is not a defense to rape * * *.

Assuming that Tendered Instructions Nos. 5 and 6 correctly state the law in Indiana, the instructions do not meet the second prong of the test, that is, there is no evidence in the record from which a reasonable juror could conclude that Tyson reasonably believed D.W. consented to the sexual conduct.

Indiana has long recognized that an honest and reasonable mistake concerning a fact excuses criminal conduct which would not be criminal if the fact had been as the defendant reasonably believed. "Honesty is a subjective test dealing with what [the defendant] actually believed. Reasonableness is an objective test inquiring what a reasonable man situated in similar circumstances would do. To require the giving of [the defendant's] instruction, we must find some evidence of both."

Thus, if the State presents a prima facie case of guilt, the defendant has the burden of going forward with an evidentiary basis for his mistaken belief of fact which could create a reasonable doubt in the jury's mind that he acted without the requisite mental state. * * *

Tyson asserts that his testimony provides ample evidence to support Tendered Instructions Nos. 5 and 6. During direct examination, Tyson testified that "I believe that we had both made it clear earlier that day what was going to happen, and that she came to my room at 2 o'clock in the morning. I'm sure we made it clear;"[21] that D.W. responded in a positive manner to his kissing in the limousine while riding to his hotel; and that while he was kissing her in the hotel room she was "dropping her jacket, you know, getting her jacket off quick." He also testified that he complied with D.W.'s request not to ejaculate in her and that he asked her to stay the night.

Assuming Tyson's assertions, that he believed he and D.W. "made it clear" earlier in the day that they were going to have sexual intercourse and that, after the sexual conduct occurred, he asked her to spend the night with him, provide some evidence that he honestly believed D.W. consented to sexual intercourse, the assertions are not evidence of the reasonableness of that belief. To determine whether there is evidence that Tyson's assumed belief was reasonable, we look to his description of the encounter:

Q.: Did you undress her?

A.: I did.

* * * * * *

Q.: What happened then, Mr. Tyson?

A.: As I'm kissing her, she's moving fast. I'm kissing her. She dropping [sic] her jacket [and taking off her clothes] * * *

Q.: Then what happened?

* * * * * *

A.: We were having oral sex a little while, and she had told me to stop, and she had told me to come up, come up. She said, "No, come up."

Q.: Meaning what?

A.: Indicating that she wanted me to insert my penis in her.

* * * * * *

Q.: And what did you do then?

A.: She had told me not to come in her. She said, "Don't come in me, don't come in me. I'm not on the pill," and I pulled back and I ejaculated on her stomach and her leg.

Tyson's description is a plain assertion of actual consent. From this testimony, a reasonable jury could infer only that D.W. actually consented to sexual intercourse. There is no recitation of equivocal[22] conduct by D.W. which reasonably could have led Tyson to believe that D.W. only appeared to consent to the charged sexual conduct; no gray area exists from which Tyson can logically argue that he misunderstood D.W.'s actions. According to Tyson, he exerted no force and D.W. offered no resistance; instead, she was an active and equal participant in the conduct. While this testimony would negate an element of the crime—that Tyson forcibly engaged in sexual conduct with D.W.—and challenges D.W.'s credibility, it does not support the giving of a mistake of fact instruction.

Tyson further argues that "many of the statements [D.W.] admitted she had made to [Tyson] during the sexual conduct itself were consistent with a reasonable belief on his part that the sex was consensual." Specifically, D.W. testified that when Tyson saw she was crying during the rape * * *, he asked if she wanted to "get on top," to which she responded in the affirmative without "then explaining to him that she agreed to go on top only because she thought it would enable her to get away;" and that she asked Tyson to, "Please put a condom on" and said, "I don't need a

---

[21] Tyson testified that earlier in the day, soon after he had met D.W., he explained to her "That I wanted to fuck her," and she responded, "Sure, just give me a call."

[22] Equivocal is defined as "having two or more significations: capable of more than one interpretation: of doubtful meaning: ambiguous." Webster's Third New International Dictionary 769 (1976).

baby." Tyson argues that "[a] properly instructed jury could have found (or entertained a reasonable doubt) that these exchanges could have led a reasonable person to believe that [D.W.] consented, even if in her own mind she may not have been consenting." However, in the context in which these statements occurred, that is, amidst D.W.'s unequivocal description of a sexual assault, they could not, as a matter of law, lead a reasonable person to believe that Tyson was reasonably mistaken as to D.W.'s consent to sexual intercourse. * * *

* * *

Tyson asks us to consider that D.W. "met Tyson later, under circumstances which suggested an interest in sex— she accepted an invitation at 1:40 A.M.., voluntarily accompanied Tyson to his hotel room, and willingly sat on his bed with him." This conduct may support a determination that a reasonable person in Tyson's position reasonably could have believed D.W. would at some point be willing to consent to sexual conduct; it also is consistent with Tyson's testimony of consensual sexual conduct. However, considering D.W.'s testimony of unequivocal compulsion at the time the sexual conduct occurred, her willingness to meet him and her alleged "interest in sex" does not support the determination that a reasonable person in Tyson's position reasonably, but mistakenly, could have believed that D.W. consented to sexual conduct at the pertinent time—immediately preceding the sexual conduct.

Tyson testified to one set of events, D.W. to another. Tyson's testimony compels the conclusion that D.W. unequivocally gave her actual consent to sexual conduct and participated in it; D.W.'s testimony compels the conclusion that Tyson forcibly performed sexual conduct upon her. Thus, neither witness's testimony provides the basis for a reasonable mistake because neither testimony contains equivocal conduct which reasonably could have been misunderstood by Tyson. * * *[26]

"In spite of our preference to leave determinations of reasonableness to the jury, which embodies the values of the community, we find no evidence here from which the jury could have determined that [Tyson's] belief was reasonable," as required by Indiana law.[27]

In contrast, the trial court's instructions to the jury were accurate. The trial court gave Final Instruction No. 19, which articulates the elements of the crime of rape, including "the State must have proved . . . [Tyson] . . . knowingly or intentionally . . . had sexual intercourse with [D.W.] when . . . [D.W.] was compelled by force or imminent threat of force" * * *. It also gave Final Instruction No. 18, which defines the terms intentionally and knowingly. These instructions properly instructed the jury regarding the culpability required for the offenses with which Tyson was charged, and properly focused the jury on the task of determining whether the State proved beyond a reasonable doubt that Tyson knowingly or intentionally used force to have sexual conduct with D.W. when D.W. was compelled by the force. The trial court did not err in refusing Tyson's Tendered Instructions Nos. 5 and 6.

* * *

Judgment affirmed.

SULLIVAN, Judge, dissenting.

* * *

Instructions Nos. 5 and 6 tendered by the defense were erroneously and prejudicially refused by the trial court. * * *

Consent or the lack thereof is a fact. D.W. either consented or she did not. If she consented, that is a fact. If she did not consent, that is a fact. Resolution of that fact question, however, does not end the inquiry. The law provides that if a person accused of rape is reasonably mistaken as to the fact of consent when the alleged victim, in fact, did not consent, such mistake negates the culpability required for the crime. * * *

Whether a defendant's mistake or belief is reasonable depends upon the attendant circumstances. In the case before us, those relevant and crucial circumstances are not restricted to the occurrences in the hotel room beginning with the point at which Tyson "undress[ed]" D.W. They include other circumstances of the day and night preceding the encounter and the activities of the early morning hours which led to the occurrences which transpired in Tyson's hotel room. * * *

---

[26] Tyson argues that a "properly instructed jury might well have concluded that the truth of what occurred in the hotel room lay *somewhere between* Washington's inculpatory account and Tyson's exculpatory one." Appellant's Brief at 46 (emphasis in original). This, however, is not a criteria for our review of a tendered instruction; rather, we review the record to see if the evidence presented could support the instruction.

[27] The dissent cites *People v. Burnham* (1986), 176 Cal.App.3d 1134, 222 Cal.Rptr. 630, rev. denied, in which the California Court of Appeals states that whenever a defendant testifies to the

complainant's unequivocal consent to sexual conduct he also triggers the "defense of a bona fide belief in the victim's consent" and a mistake of fact instruction is required. Thus, under *Burnham*, as long as a defendant expresses his subjective belief that the victim consented, a mistake of fact instruction is warranted whether or not that belief was reasonable. This view is not uniformly held in other jurisdictions. In Indiana, evidence from which a reasonable jury could find both an honest and reasonable belief on the part of the defendant is required before a mistake of fact instruction may be given. * * *

The evidence quoted and analyzed by the majority, when taken together with the surrounding circumstances, permit a reasonable belief as to the fact of consent. Stated conversely, if the jury believed that Tyson used only such "force" as would be involved in a consensual sexual act, they may well have concluded that Tyson reasonably believed that D.W. was consenting. Regardless of whether D.W.'s subjective mental state reflected actual consent, and even if as a fact she did not consent, Tyson may have reasonably believed that she was consenting. That question is peculiarly within the prerogative of the jury. They were not permitted to exercise this prerogative * * * because they were not advised of the appropriate legal principles which would constitute the essential framework within which to assess the evidence and to consider the relevant attendant circumstances. In short, by refusing to give defendant's tendered instructions, the trial court denied the jury the proper tools necessary for performance of their duty. They were effectively forced, in this regard, to make factual determinations in a vacuum.

It is improper to deny a reasonable belief instruction, as does the majority here, based upon an evaluation of the weight of the evidence or the credibility of the witnesses. * * *

While the word "consent" does not appear in I.C. 35-42-4-1, the word "compelled" is used. It is clear, therefore, that the force or threat of force must have compelling effect upon the alleged victim. The fact of coercion is therefore an indispensable element of the crime. * * *

The majority seeks to draw a significant distinction between our culpability statute and that of the Model Penal Code. Model Code § 2.02(4) does not use the word "conduct" in referring to material elements of the offense. This is not, however, particularly meaningful. Again, the prohibited conduct is force which coerces. The fact of coercion is without question a "material element" of the act of "force". Without coercion, there has been no crime of rape or deviate conduct committed. Our statute and our law is wholly consistent with the Model Penal Code.

The fact of coercion is not merely an "attendant circumstance" * * *. It is an essential element of the act itself. * * *

* * *

It cannot be emphasized too strongly that the question is not sufficiency of the evidence to convict of rape * * *. The question in regard to the instructions is, rather, whether Michael Tyson was entitled to have the jury assess that evidence in the light of applicable law.

* * *

The instructions, if given, might have resulted in the same verdict. But they might not have. The jury, in light of the instructions might have reasonably concluded that while D.W. did not consent, Tyson did have an honest and reasonable belief that she did so. The jury was entitled to make that determination, not the trial court and certainly not this court.

The erroneous rulings herein considered dictate reversal and remand for a new trial.

B. "STATUTORY" RAPE AND RELATED CRIMES INVOLVING YOUNG VICTIMS

Editors' Introduction: Sexual Offenses Against Young Victims

Statutory rape traditionally consisted of sexual intercourse by a male with a female who was beneath the age at which her consent would be given effect. Whether consent was given or not was irrelevant, since any consent given by the victim was ineffective. In modern criminal statutes, statutory rape is often superseded by some aspect of sexual assault and perhaps other crimes covering sexual behavior other than intercourse with young persons.

Traditionally, statutory rape is regarded as a strict liability offense in the sense that no culpable mental state is required regarding the victim's age. Consequently, a person accused of statutory rape has no defense of mistake of fact based on a misperception as to the victim's age; even a completely reasonable belief on the part of the accused that the victim was above the age of consent is completely irrelevant to the accused's guilt. The majority view is that modern statutory rape or its successor crimes will similarly be construed as imposing the traditional form of strict liability. See for example, *Jenkins v. State*, 110 Nev. 865, 877 P.2d 1063 (1994) (interpreting crime of statutory seduction). In *Gannert v. State*, 332 Md. 571, 584 , 632 A.2d 797, 803 (1993), however, the court acknowledged that two-fifths of the states recognize at least a limited defense of reasonable mistake as to age.

Strict liability in this context is often supported on the ground that sexual exploitation of young persons is an exceptionally harmful activity that mandates maximum efforts of discouragement. Moreover, the argument goes, requiring proof of awareness of age or even permitting accuseds' to assert mistake as to age would unacceptably reduce the effectiveness of the criminal sanction as a means of discouraging such behavior. In *Jenkins*, for example, the court commented, "Requiring proof that the perpetrator was aware of the victim's age would emasculate the salutary purpose of the statute." Whatever the cost in terms of convicting persons who did not engage in morally culpable behavior, proponents of strict liability urge, this is acceptable given the need for strict liability to implement the exceptionally important legislative purpose.

The Idaho court concluded in *State v. Stiffler*, 117 Idaho 405, 788 P.2d 220 (1990), that neither the objective of preventing the exploitation of young girls "from conscienceless men" nor that of preventing "the exploitation of persons deemed legally incapable of giving consent" justified strict liability, apparently because—the court believed   only persons acting with culpable awareness of their victims' ages pose the dangers at which the crime, so construed, is aimed. Nevertheless, it reasoned that the crime has now come to also serve the purpose of preventing teenage pregnancies. This objective, the court concluded, justifies strict liability in these cases because such pregnancies can result regardless of the male awareness of the female's age.

Several courts have construed crimes of this sort as at least permitting accused to assert a defense of an honest—and perhaps objectively reasonable—belief that the person with whom the accused engaged in sexual behavior was of an age at which the person's consent would be effective. Probably the leading decision is *People v. Hernandez*, 61 Cal.2d 529, 393 P.2d 673, 39 Cal.Reptr. 361 (1964), discussed in *People v. Olsen*, reprinted in this section.

Some states have by statute modified the traditional position and accommodated some claims of mistake as to the victims' ages. Under Alaska Stat. 11.41.445(b), for example, it is an affirmative defense that the defendant reasonably believed the victim to be of an age under which the sexual conduct would not constitute the offense. No such defense is available, however, if the victim was under 13 years of age at the time of the offense. One Alaska court has rejected the argument that constitutional requirements are violated by placing the burden of proof on a defendant to show a reasonable mistaken belief that the victim was of an age that would make the defendant's sexual conduct legally permissible. *Steve v. State*, 875 P.2d 110 (Alaska App.1994).

There is some reason to question whether courts (and legislatures) have carefully examined whether requiring proof of a culpable mental state would in fact impede the effectiveness of these statutes. A requirement that the accused have been no more than reckless regarding whether the object of his sexual behavior was old enough to give effective consent, for example, might involve far fewer difficulties than would a requirement that the accused act with knowledge of the victim's age, and yet avoid conviction of those whose behavior is not sufficiently blameworthy to warrant such criminal liability.

People v. Olsen

Supreme Court of California, 1984
36 Cal.3d 638, 205 Cal.Rptr. 492, 685 P.2d 52.

BIRD, CHIEF JUSTICE

Is a reasonable mistake as to the victim's age a defense to a charge of lewd or lascivious conduct with a child under the age of 14?[1]

* * *

[The complaining witness, Shawn M., was 13 years and 10 months old on the evening in question. Her testimony was that two young men had entered the camper trailer located in the driveway of her home. However, there were no signs of forced entry despite her testimony that she had locked the door. Employing a knife as a threat, she testified, one—James Garcia—forced her to have intercourse with the other, Edward Olsen, in his presence. Her father testified that he came to the trailer because he heard male voices within, that he saw three persons on the bed and struggled with Olsen until Garcia stabbed him in the shoulder.

Shawn acknowledged that she knew both men and had been very good friends with Olsen although at the time of the incident considered Garcia her boyfriend. She testified to having previously engaged in intercourse and with having sexual relations short of intercourse with both of these men. She admitted having told both that she was over 16 and that she looked over 16.

Garcia gave a very different version of the event. His claim, supported by the circumstantial evidence of other witnesses, was that he had frequently had consensual intercourse with Shawn and that both he and Olsen had been invited into the trailer for that purpose.]

At the conclusion of the trial, the court found Garcia and appellant guilty of violating section 288, subdivision (a). In reaching its decision, the court rejected defense counsel's argument that a good faith belief as to the age of the victim was a defense to the section 288 charge. Appellant was sentenced to the lower term of three years in state prison. This appeal followed.

Appellant's sole contention on appeal is that a good faith, reasonable mistake of age is a defense to a section 288 charge.

II.

The language of section 288 is silent as to whether a good faith, reasonable mistake as to the victim's age constitutes a defense to a charge under that statute. * * *

Twenty years ago, this court in *People v. Hernandez* (1964) 61 Cal. 2d 529, 39 Cal.Rptr. 361, 393 P.2d 673, overruled established precedents and held that an accused's good faith, reasonable belief that a victim was 18 years or more of age was a defense to a charge of statutory rape.

In *Hernandez*, the accused was charged with statutory rape of a girl who was 17 years and 9 months old, and who had voluntarily engaged in an act of sexual intercourse. The trial court refused to allow the accused to present evidence of his good faith, reasonable belief that the prosecutrix was 18 or over. On appeal, this court held it reversible error to exclude such evidence.

The *Hernandez* court acknowledged that an accused possesses criminal intent when he acts without a belief that his victim is 18 or over. However, the court determined that if one engages in sexual intercourse with a female and reasonably believes she is 18 or over, then the essential element of criminal intent is missing.

---

[1] Section 288, subdivision (a) provides in relevant part: "Any person who shall willfully and lewdly commit any lewd or lascivious act * * * upon or with the body, or any part or member thereof, of a child under the age of 14 years, with the intent of arousing, appealing to, or gratifying the lust or passions or sexual desires of such person or of such child, shall be guilty of a felony and shall be imprisoned in the state prison for a term of three, six, or eight years." * * *

Relying on sections 20[12] and 26[13] and on *People v. Vogel* (1956) 46 Cal.2d 798, 299 P.2d 850, the court noted that it had recently "given recognition to the legislative declarations" in those two sections when it held in *Vogel* that a good faith belief that a previous marriage had been terminated was a valid defense to a charge of bigamy. The court stated, "the reluctance to accord to a charge of statutory rape the defense of a lack of criminal intent has no greater justification than in the case of other statutory crimes [such as bigamy], where the Legislature has made identical provision with respect to intent." Thus, "it cannot be a greater wrong to entertain a bona fide but erroneous belief that a valid consent to an act of sexual intercourse has been obtained." The court went on to hold that a charge of statutory rape is defensible where a criminal intent is lacking unless there is a "legislative direction otherwise."

The *Hernandez* court, however, cautioned that its holding was not "indicative of a withdrawal from the sound policy that it is in the public interest to protect the sexually naive female from exploitation. No responsible person would hesitate to condemn as untenable a claimed good faith belief in the age of consent of an 'infant' female whose obviously tender years preclude the existence of reasonable grounds for that belief." The court then concluded that there was nothing to indicate that "the purposes of the law [could] be better served by foreclosing the defense of a lack of intent."

In deciding whether to apply the philosophy of *Hernandez* to the offense of lewd or lascivious conduct with a child under the age of 14, this court is guided by decisions of the Court of Appeal. The * * * post-*Hernandez* Court of Appeal decisions which have considered the issue have refused to apply *Hernandez*. *People v. Toliver* (1969) 270 Cal.App.2d 492, 494–496, 75 Cal.Rptr. 819, cert. den., 396 U.S. 895, 90 S.Ct. 193, 24 L.Ed.2d 172; *People v. Tober* (1966) 241 Cal.App.2d 66, 71–73, 50 Cal.Rptr. 228.)

In *People v. Tober,* the accused was convicted of lewd or lascivious acts on the body of a 10-year-old child. On appeal, the court rejected the premise that lewd or lascivious acts on a 10-year-old child "may be indulged in under a claimed good faith belief that the child is either an adult or has reached the age of 14 years." The Court of Appeal explained that "[t]he very refusal to distinguish between a child of tender years and an adult may be said to be characteristic of some of those who engage in the sort of conduct of which defendant has been convicted." The court refused to apply *Hernandez* to section 288 cases, relying on that court's caution that a good faith, mistaken belief as to age is untenable when the victim involved is of "tender years."

People v. Toliver, also rejected the *Hernandez* rule in the section 288 context. * * *

As *Toliver* explained, *Hernandez* "in effect considered that section 288 is for protection of infants or children as to whom persons commit lewd and lascivious acts at their peril." *Hernandez* points out that consent can be an element of statutory rape, since a male may reasonably believe that a female is older than 18 and, therefore, can consent to an act of intercourse. "On the other hand, [a] violation of section 288 does not involve consent of any sort, thereby placing the public policies underlying it and statutory rape on different footings." The court also found it significant that the Legislature provided harsher penalties for violating section 288 than for statutory rape.

* * *

Moreover, other language in *Hernandez* strongly suggests that a reasonable mistake as to age would not be a defense to a section 288 charge. As *Hernandez* noted, when [the earlier case law rejecting such a defense] was decided, an accused could be convicted of statutory rape only if the victim were under 14. *Hernandez* also found it "noteworthy that the purpose of the [earlier] rule was to afford protection to young females therein described as 'infants.'" Thus, an "infant" at the time of [these earlier cases] was any child under 14. The *Hernandez* court's use of that term, therefore, evidenced a belief that a mistake of age defense would be untenable when the offense involved a child that young.

The language in *Hernandez,* together with the reasoning in *Tober* [and] *Toliver* * * *, compel the conclusion that a reasonable mistake as to the victim's age is not a defense to a section 288 charge.

It is significant that a violation of section 288 carries a much harsher penalty than does unlawful sexual intercourse (§ 261.5), the crime involved in *Hernandez*. Section 261.5 carries a maximum punishment of one year in the county jail or three years in state prison (§ 264), while section 288 carries a maximum penalty of eight years in state prison. The different penalties for these two offenses further supports the view that there exists a strong public policy to protect children under 14.

---

[12] Section 20 provides: "In every crime or public offense there must exist a union, or joint operation of act and intent, or criminal negligence."

[13] Section 26 provides in relevant part: "All persons are capable of committing crimes except those belonging to the following classes: * * * [¶] Three—Persons who committed the act or made the omission charged under an ignorance or mistake of fact, which disproves any criminal intent."

* * *

It is true that at common law "an honest and reasonable belief in the existence of circumstances, which, if true, would make the act for which the person is indicted an innocent act, has always been held to be a good defense." However, it is evident that the public policy considerations in protecting children under the age of 14 from lewd or lascivious conduct are substantial—far more so than those associated with unlawful sexual intercourse. These strong public policies are reflected in several Penal Code statutes, and they compel a different rule as to section 288.

The legislative purpose of section 288 would not be served by recognizing a defense of reasonable mistake of age. Thus, one who commits lewd or lascivious acts with a child, even with a good faith belief that the child is 14 years of age or older, does so at his or her peril.

* * *

Accordingly, the judgment of conviction is affirmed.

GRODIN, JUSTICE, concurring and dissenting.

I agree that * * * in the eyes of the Legislature [an honest and reasonable belief that the victim was 14 years or older] is not a defense to the crime. What troubles me is the notion that a person who acted with such belief, and is not otherwise shown to be guilty of any criminal conduct, may not only be convicted but be sentenced to prison notwithstanding his eligibility for probation when it appears that his belief did not accord with reality. To me, that smacks of cruel or unusual punishment.

* * * [A] person's belief in the victim's age being over 14 may be not only honest but reasonable. No doubt the standard of what is reasonable must be set relatively high in order to accomplish the legislative objective of protecting persons under 14 years of age against certain conduct. Perhaps it is not enough that a person "looks" to be more than 14; perhaps there is a duty of reasonable inquiry besides. At some point, however, the belief becomes reasonable by any legitimate standard, so that one would say the defendant is acting in a way which is no different from the way our society would expect a reasonable, careful, and law-abiding citizen to act.

At that point, it seems to me, the imposition of criminal sanctions, particularly imprisonment, simply cannot be tolerated in a civilized society.

In this case we cannot ascertain from the record on appeal whether the trial court found some merit in defendant's claim that he honestly and reasonably believed the victim to be over 14 years of age. * * * [I]t is possible that the claim was given credence. If so, and defendant's conduct was in other respects that which we would expect of a reasonable, careful, and law-abiding citizen, I would conclude that imposition of a sentence of imprisonment on defendant is impermissible. Inasmuch as the record is inadequate to resolve either question, however, I would remand for a new probation and sentence hearing at which the court, if probation is again denied, should make express findings as to whether defendant honestly and reasonably believed the victim to be over 14 years of age and, if so, whether his conduct with her otherwise reflected that *mens rea* traditionally accepted as a prerequisite to the imposition of serious penal sanctions.

Note and Questions

If criminal sanctions are appropriate for consensual sexual conduct involving young persons, is it desirable—or constitutionally acceptable—for liability to be imposed only on male participants? In *Michael M. v. Superior Court*, 450 U.S. 464, 101 S.Ct. 1200, 67 L.Ed.2d 437 (1981), the Supreme Court considered the argument that California's statutory rape provision violated the Fourteenth Amendment's requirement of equal protection because it permitted only the conviction of males for having intercourse with females. A majority rejected the contention and upheld the statute. Justice Rehnquist's plurality opinion reasoned, first, that the statute served the legitimate state interest of preventing teenage pregnancies. Second, the legislative decision to attack that problem by creating a crime that is not "gender neutral" was acceptable because females were more likely to be deterred by the threat of pregnancy, and the threat of prosecution might reduce the female's willingness to report violations

Chapter 10

CRIMES AGAINST PROPERTY

CHAPTER CONTENTS

Editors' Introduction: Classification of the Crimes Against Property

The offenses discussed in this chapter all involve wrongful actions directed at property. The first four sections deal with crimes—larceny, embezzlement, false pretenses, and theft—in which the misappropriation threatens only the owner's enjoyment of the property. No risk to the safety of the person of another is involved. Computer-related conduct has posed special problems, and the criminal law's response is considered in the next section. The last two sections concern offenses—robbery and extortion— that involve invasions of—or threats to—other interests as well as ownership.

The cases in the first four sections of this chapter illustrate only a handful of the many judicial and statutory formulations of these offenses that, largely as a function of history, distinguish among various crimes of property acquisition. Among these crimes are theft, theft by false pretext, conversion by a bailee, theft from the person, shoplifting, swindling, embezzlement, and receiving or concealing embezzled or stolen property.

Historically, the application of the various crimes of property acquisition depended on incredible intricacies concerning the nature of the property involved, the relationship of the accused to the property, and the accused's behavior with respect to the property. For example, as will be seen from Sections A and B that follow, whether an accused obtained possession of property by trespass or not would control as to whether she committed larceny rather than embezzlement.

Modern criminal codes almost always create a single property offense intended to incorporate what traditionally were the different offenses discussed in the first three sections of this chapter. In many jurisdictions, this is labeled "theft." The Model Penal Code provisions defining theft, widely used as the basis for these codes, are presented in Section D. In some jurisdictions, more traditional terminology has been preserved. For example, the New York statute, at issue and reprinted in the principal case presented in Section A (see footnote 5 of *People v. Olivo*, page 260), defined the offense of larceny as including what were previously larceny, larceny by trick, embezzlement, and false pretenses.

In part, the many fine distinctions concerning the elements of larceny generated by the common law courts were aimed at ensuring that only persons whose conduct manifested criminality in totally unambiguous ways were to be punished. Another important reason for some of these distinctions, however, was the fact that all property offenses were capital crimes. A judge faced with an accused whose conduct varied from the paradigm of larceny might have been reluctant to find the crime had been committed if such a finding would place the defendant in jeopardy of the gallows. The fine distinctions among the crimes often permitted judges to acquit such defendants.

Society has more recently, of course, adopted less rigorous penalties for all property crimes. Judges, juries, and legislatures are consequently less reluctant to conclude that such persons have committed no criminal conduct. In addition, society has undoubtedly become more sensitive to invasions of personal interests, including interests in property. Decreasing emphasis on the traditional distinctions drawn in property crime law certainly reflects in part a resulting willingness to use the extreme tool of the criminal law to respond to and discourage less direct and harmful intrusions upon property interests than were the sole concern of the early traditional offenses.

Over the centuries, courts and legislatures have moved away from emphasis on the act constituting property crimes and toward increasing emphasis on the alleged violator's state of mind. Fletcher, The Metamorphosis of Larceny, 89 Harv.L.Rev. 469 (1976). The act and circumstances required for particular acquisition offenses remain important as to both the fact and level of liability. However, it is clear that today the accused's culpable mental state is often the central factor in making these determinations.

A. LARCENY
Editors' Introduction: Traditional Larceny Issues

Larceny was the only common law property acquisition crime, that is, the only property acquisition offense originating in English judge-made case law. Subsequently developed offenses, such as embezzlement and false pretenses, were created by Parliament rather than the English courts.

Both the terms and concepts used in defining larceny and other crimes recognized in early English law are sometimes used in modern statutes consolidating what were previously the different property offenses into a single offense often labeled "theft." Even when the terminology has been changed, however, the meaning of the modern language is often deeply colored by its early English antecedents. As a result, an understanding of the limitations of common law larceny, (covered in this section) and the coverage of the legislatively created offenses designed largely to respond to these limitations (covered in the next two sections) is useful in understanding the contents of modern statutory theft offenses.

The elements of larceny were (1) the taking (or caption); (2) by trespass; (3) and carrying away (or asportation); (4) of the tangible personal property of another; (5) with the intent to steal. The contents of each of these elements gave rise to much dispute and litigation, some of which is reflected in the next two subsections. Several issues, however, can be discussed more summarily.

Property That Could Be the Subject of Larceny

The task of defining what property could be the subject of larceny posed many questions for the common law. Modern law sometimes raises issues based on the remaining remnants of those distinctions.

Because of the need for the property to be *personal*, real property or things attached thereto ("fixtures") were excluded. Growing crops could not be the subject of larceny unless and until they had been harvested by the owner or his agents. In *People v. Dillon*, 34 Cal.3d 441, 668 P.2d 697, 194 Cal.Rptr. 390 (1983), the defendant was charged with first degree felony murder on facts showing that he and others went to an illicit marijuana field intending to steal the crop and in the course of the events one of those tending the crop was killed. Dillon argued that although the California legislature had changed the traditional rule regarding crops for purposes of larceny, it had not similarly modified robbery, so that he did not cause the death in the course of committing robbery. The court responded by rejecting this contention and holding that Dillon could commit robbery of the crops:

> Defendant's argument finds apparent support in the common law definition of property subject to larceny * * *
>   The common law rule limiting larceny to the unlawful taking of personalty derived from the undeniable fact that realty, in the sense of land subject to description by metes and bounds, cannot be "carried away." (See Perkins, Criminal Law (2d ed. 1969) p. 234.) * * * When restricted to land, the logic of the rule was unassailable. But for various reasons unrelated to the criminal law, "realty" was defined in due course to include many items that can be more or less readily detached and removed from the land. Unfortunately, the legal fiction that these objects are "immovable" has never hindered would-be thieves from moving most of them. Nevertheless, probably because larceny was a felony at common law and therefore a capital offense, judges resisted its application to those who had merely pilfered growing food or wood. Courts therefore clung to the artificial distinction between personal property and things that "savour of the realty," and held that if the thief maintained possession continuously during severance and asportation, the property never became personalty in the possession of its owner and hence no larceny could occur. Put conversely, "if a man come to steal trees, or the lead of a church or house, and sever it, and after about an hour's time, or so, come and fetch it away, this hath been held felony, because the act is not continuated but interpolated, and in that interval the property lodgeth in the right owner as a chattel." (1 Hale, *458 Pleas of the Crown (1st Am. ed. 1847) p. 510.) Thus, in a perverse and unintended application of the work ethic, thieves industrious

enough to harvest what they stole and to carry it away without pause were guilty at most of trespass, while those who tarried along the way, or enjoyed fruits gathered by the labor of others, faced the hangman's noose.

The rule has long been the subject of ridicule and limitation. * * * Today, the old rule is less justifiable and more mischievous than ever. As the Maine court observed, "In a modern mobile society in which the attachment of all manner of valuable appliances and gadgets to the realty is commonplace, we see no occasion to attribute to the Legislature any intention to so narrowly circumscribe the meaning of the words 'goods or chattels' in our larceny statute as to make the stealing of chattels severed from realty an attractive and lucrative occupation." We perceive no reason to reach a different conclusion regarding the words "goods" and "chattels" as they apply to robbery in our statute. We believe it would come as a great surprise to the potential victim of crime to learn that the more precautions he takes to guard his valuables, and the more violence that must be done to take them from him, the less severe the penalty the law will impose. Because we find no reasoned support for the continued application of the common law rule, * * * we refrain from extending it to the crime of robbery.

Because larceny was limited to *tangible* property, intangible personal property, such as checks, could not be the subject of the offense. Moreover, "base" animals such as dogs and cats were regarded as incapable of value and thus they could not be the subject of larceny. For example, *State v. Arbogast*, 133 W.Va. 672, 57 S.E.2d 715 (1950), applied the common law rule and held that an indictment for larceny of a dog did not charge a criminal offense, although the reasons given for the rule do not seem logical or sound at this time. "The usefulness of the dog now makes it one of the most valuable animals to man." Generally, however, dogs are now treated as personal property subject to larceny or modern theft. *State v. Hernandez*, 121 Ariz. 544, 592 P.2d 378 (1979), review denied.

Modern codes often define the property subject to larceny or theft very broadly and thus eliminate these traditional limitations. Because asportation is no longer required by many modern crimes, the reason for limiting larceny to exclude real property no longer applies. Under the Model Penal Code theft provisions reprinted later in this chapter at page 280, for example, a person can commit theft by exercising unlawful control over real property, even if the person cannot "take" or move it.

Application of even modern property crimes to computer-related situations has given rise to special problems. These are addressed in Section E later in this chapter.

Services

Larceny, of course, was limited to property and thus did not cover services or similar matters. Some modern crimes may be similarly restricted.

In *Commonwealth v. Rivers*, 31 Mass.App.Ct. 669, 583 N.E.2d 867 (1991), for example, a town operated a landfill site at which, for a price, it permitted commercial haulers to deposit material. Rivers was convicted of larceny upon evidence that he used the landfill without paying for doing so. Finding that Rivers had not taken "property" within the meaning of larceny, the court explained:

The Commonwealth argues that here the "property involved was the money owed to the town" for the use of the landfill. To consider the price or value of what is taken or used as "money" would be a substantial departure from the concept of common law larceny which was limited to the taking of tangible personal property.

Many jurisdictions have created separate offenses consisting of larceny or theft of services to supplement traditional property crimes. The Model Penal Code provisions include one creating the offense of theft of services (see page 283). Rivers' actions would most likely constitute theft of services under such a statute.

1. The Act Required

Traditional larceny required two acts by the defendant: a taking of the property *and* an asportation of that property. In addition, the crime required a circumstance—that these actions have been trespassory.

The taking referred to the exercise of control over the property, either directly by the accused or through an innocent third party. Asportation, in contrast, required some movement, however slight, of the property as part of the process of removing it. In practice, the distinction was seldom of importance given the ease with which both requirements were met. This remains true today under modern statutes, as a general matter.

The requirement that the taking and asportation have been trespassory meant that it must have been wrongful. This meant either without the consent of the person from whose possession the property was taken or by consent secured by deception. If the crime was committed by consent obtained by deception, it was called larceny by trick.

Modern property crimes often abandon any requirement of asportation, although they demand a wrongful taking of—or, as section 223.2(1) of the Model Penal Code provides, an unlawful exercise of control over—the property. The nature and extent of movement is, of course, relevant to whether an accused has taken the property. As the following case makes clear, whether a defendant has done enough with property to complete a modern larceny or theft remains a troublesome question.

People v. Olivo

Court of Appeals of New York, 1981
52 N.Y.2d 309, 438 N.Y.S.2d 242, 420 N.E.2d 40.

COOKE, CHIEF JUDGE.

These cases present a recurring question in this era of the self-service store which has never been resolved by this court: may a person be convicted of larceny for shoplifting if the person is caught with goods while still inside the store? For reasons outlined below, it is concluded that a larceny conviction may be sustained, in certain situations, even though the shoplifter was apprehended before leaving the store.

I

In *People v. Olivo*, defendant was observed by a security guard in the hardware area of a department store. Initially conversing with another person, defendant began to look around furtively when his acquaintance departed. The security agent continued to observe and saw defendant assume a crouching position, take a set of wrenches and secret it in his clothes. After again looking around, defendant began walking toward an exit, passing a number of cash registers en route. When defendant did not stop to pay for the merchandise, the officer accosted him a few feet from the exit. In response to the guard's inquiry, denied having the wrenches, but as he proceeded to the security office, defendant removed the wrenches and placed them under his jacket. At trial, defendant testified that he had placed the tools under his arm and was on line at a cashier when apprehended. The jury returned a verdict of guilty on the charge of petit larceny. The conviction was affirmed by Appellate Term.

II

In *People v. Gasparik*, defendant was in a department store trying on a leather jacket. Two store detectives observed him tear off the price tag and remove a "sensormatic" device designed to set off an alarm if the jacket were carried through a detection machine. There was at least one such machine at the exit of each floor. Defendant placed the tag and the device in the pocket of another jacket on the merchandise rack. He took his own jacket, which he had been carrying with him, and placed it on a table. Leaving his own jacket, defendant put on the leather jacket and walked through the store, still on the same floor, bypassing several cash registers. When he headed for the exit from that floor, in the direction of the main floor, he was apprehended by security personnel. At trial, defendant denied removing the price tag and the sensormatic device from the jacket, and testified that he was looking for a cashier without a long line when he was stopped. The court, sitting without a jury, convicted defendant of petit larceny. Appellate Term affirmed.

III

In *People v. Spatzier*, defendant entered a bookstore on Fulton Street in Hempstead carrying an attaché case. The two co-owners of the store observed the defendant in a ceiling mirror as he browsed through the store. They watched defendant remove a book from the shelf, look up and down the aisle, and place the book in his case. He then placed the case at his feet and continued to browse. One of the owners approached defendant and accused him of stealing the book. An altercation ensued and when defendant allegedly struck the owner with the attaché case, the case opened and the book fell out. At trial, defendant denied secreting the book in his case and claimed that the owner had suddenly and unjustifiably accused him of stealing. The jury found defendant guilty of petit larceny, and the conviction was affirmed by the Appellate Term.

IV

The primary issue in each case is whether the evidence, viewed in the light most favorable to the prosecution, was

sufficient to establish the elements of larceny as defined by the Penal Law. To resolve this common question, the development of the common-law crime of larceny and its evolution into modern statutory form must be briefly traced.

Larceny at common law was defined as a trespassory taking and carrying away of the property of another with intent to steal it. The early common-law courts apparently viewed larceny as defending society against breach of the peace, rather than protecting individual property rights, and therefore placed heavy emphasis upon the requirement of a *trespassory taking*. Thus, a person such as a bailee who had rightfully obtained possession of property from its owner could not be guilty of larceny. The result was that the crime of larceny was quite narrow in scope.

Gradually, the courts began to expand the reach of the offense, initially by subtle alterations in the common-law concept of possession. Thus, for instance, it became a general rule that goods entrusted to an employee were not deemed to be in his possession, but were only considered to be in his custody, so long as he remained on the employer's premises.[2] And, in the case of *Chisser* (Raym. Sir.T. 275, 83 Eng. Rep. 142), it was held that a shop owner retained legal possession of merchandise being examined by a prospective customer until the actual sale was made. In these situations, the employee and the customer would not have been guilty of larceny if they had first obtained lawful possession of the property from the owner. By holding that they had not acquired possession, but merely custody, the court was able to sustain a larceny conviction.

As the reach of larceny expanded, the intent element of the crime became of increasing importance, while the requirement of a trespassory taking became less significant. As a result, the bar against convicting a person who had initially obtained lawful possession of property faded. In *King v. Pear* (1 Leach 212, 168 Eng.Rep. 208), for instance, a defendant who had lied about his address and ultimate destination when renting a horse was found guilty of larceny for later converting the horse. Because of the fraudulent misrepresentation, the court reasoned, the defendant had never obtained legal possession. Thus, "larceny by trick" was born.

Later cases went even further, often ignoring the fact that a defendant had initially obtained possession lawfully, and instead focused upon his later intent. The crime of larceny then encompassed, not only situations where the defendant initially obtained property by a trespassory taking, but many situations where an individual, possessing

---

[2] In 1529, a statute was passed subjecting employees to the law of larceny as to all valuable property entrusted to them by their employers (21 Hen. VIII, ch. 7).

the requisite intent, exercised control over property inconsistent with the continued rights of the owner. During this evolutionary process, the purpose served by the crime of larceny obviously shifted from protecting society's peace to general protection of property rights.[4]

Modern penal statutes generally have incorporated these developments under a unified definition of larceny (see e.g., American Law Institute, Model Penal Code [Tent. Draft No. 1], § 206.1 [theft is appropriation of property of another, which includes unauthorized exercise of control]). Case law, too, now tends to focus upon the actor's intent and the exercise of dominion and control over the property. Indeed, this court has recognized, in construing the New York Penal Law,[5] that the "*ancient* common-law concepts of larceny" no longer strictly apply.

This evolution is particularly relevant to thefts occurring in modern self-service stores. In stores of that type, customers are impliedly invited to examine, try on, and carry about the merchandise on display. Thus in a sense, the owner has consented to the customer's possession of the goods for a limited purpose. That the owner has consented to that possession does not, however, preclude a conviction for larceny. If the customer exercises dominion and control wholly inconsistent with the continued rights of the owner, and the other elements of the crime are present, a larceny has occurred.[6] Such conduct on the part of a customer satisfies the "taking" element of the crime.

It is this element that forms the core of the controversy in these cases. The defendants argue, in essence, that the crime is not established, as a matter of law, unless there is evidence that the customer departed the shop without paying for the merchandise.

Although this court has not addressed the issue, case law from other jurisdictions seems unanimous in holding that a shoplifter need not leave the store to be guilty of larceny. This is because a shopper may treat merchandise in a manner inconsistent with the owner's continued rights—and in a manner not in accord with that of prospective purchaser—without actually walking out of the store. Indeed, depending upon the circumstances of each case, a variety of conduct may be sufficient to allow the trier of fact to find a taking. It would be well-nigh impossible, and unwise, to attempt to delineate all the situations which would establish a taking. But it is possible to identify some of the factors used in determining whether the evidence is sufficient to be submitted to the fact finder.

In many cases, it will be particularly relevant that defendant concealed the goods under clothing or in a container. Such conduct is not generally expected in a self-service store and may in a proper case be deemed an exercise of dominion and control inconsistent with the store's continued rights. Other furtive or unusual behavior on the part of the defendant should also be weighed. Thus, if the defendant surveys the area while secreting the merchandise or abandoned his or her own property in exchange for the concealed goods, this may evince larcenous rather than innocent behavior. Relevant too is the customer's proximity to or movement towards one of the store's exits. Certainly it is highly probative of guilt that the customer was in possession of secreted goods just a few short steps from the door or moving in that direction. Finally, possession of a known shoplifting device actually used to conceal merchandise, such as a specially designed outer garment or false bottomed carrying case, would be all but decisive.

* * * So long as it bears upon the principal issue—whether the shopper exercised control wholly inconsistent with the owner's continued rights—any attending circumstance is relevant and may be taken into account.

---

[4] One commentator has argued that the concept of possessorial immunity—i.e., that one who obtains possession of property by delivery from the owner cannot be guilty of larceny—stems from a general reluctance of the early common law to criminalize acts arising out of private relationships (Fletcher, Metamorphosis of Larceny, 89 Harv.L.Rev. 469, 472–476). Thus, although an owner deprived of property by a bailee could seek a civil remedy * * *, the harm was deemed private and not a matter for societal intervention. Over time, the public–private dichotomy waned and the criminal law increasingly was viewed as an instrument for protecting certain interests and controlling social behavior. As a concomitant development, the criminal law changed its main focus from the objective behavior of the defendant to his subjective intent.

[5] Section 155.05 of the Penal Law defines larceny: "1. A person steals property and commits larceny when, with intent to deprive another of property or to appropriate the same to himself or to a third person, he wrongfully takes, obtains, or withholds such property from an owner thereof. 2. Larceny includes a wrongful taking, obtaining or withholding of another's property, with the intent prescribed in subdivision one of this section, committed in any of the following ways: (a) By conduct heretofore defined or known as common law larceny by trespassory taking, common law larceny by trick, embezzlement, or obtaining property by false pretenses."

[6] Also, required, of course, is the intent prescribed by subdivision 1 of section 155.05 of the Penal Law, and some movement * * *. As a practical matter in shoplifting cases the same evidence which proves the taking will usually involve movement.

The movement, or asportation, requirement has traditionally been satisfied by a slight moving of the property. This accords with the purpose of the asportation element which is to show that the thief had indeed gained possession and control of the property.

V

Under these principles, there was ample evidence in each case to raise a factual question as to the defendants' guilt. In *People v. Olivo,* defendant not only concealed goods in his clothing, but he did so in a particularly suspicious manner. And, when defendant was stopped, he was moving towards the door, just three feet short of exiting the store. It cannot be said as a matter of law that these circumstances failed to establish a taking.[8]

In *People v. Gasparik,* defendant removed the price tag and sensor device from a jacket, abandoned his own garment, put the jacket on and ultimately headed for the main floor of the store. Removal of the price tag and sensor device, and careful concealment of those items, is highly unusual and suspicious conduct for a shopper. Coupled with defendant's abandonment of his own coat and his attempt to leave the floor, those factors were sufficient to make out a prima facie case of a taking.

In *People v. Spatzier,* defendant concealed a book in an attaché case. Unaware that he was being observed in an overhead mirror, defendant looked furtively up and down

the aisle before secreting the book. In these circumstances, given the manner in which defendant concealed the book and his suspicious behavior, the evidence was not insufficient as a matter of law.

VII

In sum, in view of the modern definition of the crime of larceny, and its purpose of protecting individual property rights, a taking of property in the self-service store context can be established by evidence that a customer exercised control over merchandise wholly inconsistent with the store's continued rights. Quite simply, a customer who crosses the line between the limited right he or she has to deal with merchandise and the store owner's rights may be subject to prosecution for larceny. Such a rule should foster the legitimate interests and continued operation of self-service shops, a convenience which most members of the society enjoy.

Accordingly, in each case, the order of the Appellate Term should be affirmed.

Note

As *Olivo* suggests, modern property crime law governing the kind of action covered by common law larceny has tended more and more to focus upon an accused's culpable mental state rather than on whether the accused acted sufficiently to complete the crime. Very seldom do appellate courts reverse convictions because the prosecution has failed to show the defendant exercised sufficient control over the property.

---

[8] As discussed, the same evidence which establishes dominion and control in these circumstances will often establish movement of the property. And, the requisite intent generally may be inferred from all the surrounding circumstances. It would be the rare case indeed in which the evidence establishes all the other elements of the crime but would be insufficient to give rise to an inference of intent.

---

2. The State of Mind Required: The Intent to Steal

The culpable mental state required by traditional larceny is the intent to *permanently* deprive another of that person's interest in the property at issue. This reflects traditional law's position that owners' interest in being free of temporary dispossession of their property was not important enough to deserve protection of the criminal law. The civil law could properly be relied upon to remedy risks of only temporary loss and to discourage people from temporarily depriving others of their property.

This aspect of traditional larceny law survived the revision of property crime law. Essentially the same culpable mental state required for common law larceny is today required by most jurisdictions for theft or its modern equivalent.

The major problem arises when, as in the case that follows, the evidence suggests the accused may not have intended to himself keep the property or even have wanted it to be permanently lost to the owner but rather took the property intending to do something with it that he knew created some risk of permanent loss to the owner. As note 1 after the case suggests, the analysis of the court is questionable at best. Perhaps, however, this analysis suggests that the court was not in sympathy with property crime's general approach to protecting only owners' interest in avoiding permanent loss of their property. There is a real possibility that society has become sufficiently sensitive to property rights so that the criminal law should cover takings with only an intent to temporarily deprive owners of their property.

The case that follows involves a prosecution for robbery. Because robbery in this jurisdiction incorporates larceny, the culpable mental state at issue is that required for both larceny and robbery.

State v. Gordon

Supreme Judicial Court of Maine, 1974
321 A.2d 352.

[Defendant was convicted by a jury of armed robbery and appeals from this conviction.]

One Edwin Strode, and defendant had escaped in Vermont from the custody of the authorities who had been holding them on a misdemeanor charge. In the escape defendant and Strode had acquired two hand guns and also a blue station wagon in which they had fled from Vermont through New Hampshire into Maine. Near Standish, Maine, the station wagon showed signs of engine trouble, and defendant and Strode began to look for another vehicle. They came to the yard of one Franklin Prout. In the yard was Prout's 1966 maroon Chevelle and defendant, who was operating the station wagon, drove it parallel to the Prout Chevelle. Observing that the keys were in the Chevelle, Strode left the station wagon and entered the Chevelle. At this time Prout came out of his house into the yard. Strode pointed a gun at him, and defendant and Strode then told Prout that they needed his automobile, were going to take it but they "would take care of it and see he [Prout] got it back as soon as possible." With defendant operating the station wagon and Strode the Chevelle, defendant and Strode left the yard and proceeded in the direction of Westbrook. Subsequently, the station wagon was abandoned in a sand pit, and defendant and Strode continued their flight in the Chevelle. A spectacular series of events followed—including the alleged assault (with intent to kill) upon Westbrook police officer, Stultz, a shoot-out on Main Street in Westbrook, and a high speed police chase, during which the Chevelle was driven off the road in the vicinity of the Maine Medical Center in Portland where it was abandoned, Strode and defendant having commandeered another automobile to resume their flight. Ultimately, both the defendant and Strode were apprehended, defendant having been arrested on the day following the police chase in the vicinity of the State Police Barracks in Scarborough.

* * * [D]efendant maintains that the evidence clearly established that (1) defendant and Strode had told Prout that they "would take care of * * * [the automobile] and see [that] he [Prout] got it back as soon as possible" and (2) defendant intended only a temporary use of Prout's Chevelle. Defendant argues that the evidence thus fails to warrant a conclusion beyond a reasonable doubt that defendant had the specific intent requisite for "robbery." (Hereinafter, reference to the "specific intent" necessary for "robbery" signifies the "specific intent" incorporated into "robbery" as embracing "larceny.")

Although defendant is correct that robbery is a crime requiring a particular specific intent,[1] defendant wrongly apprehends its substantive content.

A summarizing statement appearing in defendant's brief most clearly exposes his misconception of the law. Acknowledging that on all of the evidence the jury could properly

" * * * have inferred * * * that [defendant and Strode] intended to get away from the authorities by going to New York or elsewhere *where they would abandon* the car * * * (emphasis supplied)

---

[1] It is generally required that the necessary specific intent exist simultaneously with the wrongful taking of the property. *State v. McKeough*, [Me., 300 A.2d 755, 757 (1973)] makes clear that * * *:

"Maine is one of the jurisdictions which has recognized as an exception to the simultaneous intent rule the principle that if the property is taken from the owner against his will, by a trespass or fraud, a *subsequently* formed intent * * * [of the requisite content] will constitute larceny."

Defendant concludes that, nevertheless, the State had failed to prove the necessary specific intent because it is

" * * * entirely irrational to conclude * * * that the defendant himself intended at the time he and Strode took the car, *to keep the car in their possession for any length of time*." (emphasis supplied)

Here, defendant reveals that he conceives as an essential element of the specific intent requisite for "robbery" that the wrongdoer must intend: (1) an advantageous relationship between himself and the property wrongfully taken, and (2) that such relationship be permanent rather than temporary.

Defendant's view is erroneous. The law evaluates the "animus furandi" of "robbery" in terms of the detriment projected to the legally protected interests of the owner rather than the benefits intended to accrue to the wrongdoer from his invasion of the rights of the owner.

* * * [M]any of the earlier decisions reveal language disagreements, as well as conflicts as to substance, concerning whether a defendant can be guilty of "robbery" without specifically intending a gain to himself (whether permanent or temporary), so-called "lucri causa." In the more recent cases, there is overwhelming consensus that "lucri causa" is not necessary.

We now decide, in confirmatory clarification of the law of Maine, that "lucri causa" is not an essential element of the "animus furandi" of "robbery." [T]he specific intent requisite for "robbery" is defined solely in terms of the injury projected to the interests of the property owner:—specific intent "to deprive permanently the owner of his property."

The instant question thus becomes: on the hypothesis, arguendo, that defendant here actually intended to use the Prout automobile "only temporarily" (as he would need it to achieve a successful flight from the authorities), is defendant correct in his fundamental contention that this, *in itself*, negates, *as a matter of law*, specific intent of defendant to deprive permanently the owner of his property? We answer that defendant's claim is erroneous.

Concretely illustrative of the point that a wrongdoer may intend to use wrongfully taken property "only temporarily" and yet, without contradiction, intend that the owner be deprived of his property permanently is the case of a defendant who proposes to use the property only for a short time and then to destroy it. At the opposite pole, and excluding (as a matter of law) specific intent to deprive permanently the owner of his property, is the case of a defendant who intends to make a temporary use of the property and then by his own act to return the property to its owner. Between these two extremes can lie various situations in which the legal characterization of the wrongdoer's intention, as assessed by the criterion of whether it is a specific

intent to deprive permanently the owner of his property, will be more or less clear and raise legal problems of varying difficulty.

In these intermediate situations a general guiding principle may be developed through recognition that a "taking" of property is by definition "temporary" only if the possession, or control, effected by the taking is relinquished. Hence, measured by the correct criterion of the impact upon the interests of the owner, the wrongdoer's "animus furandi" is fully explored for its true legal significance only if the investigation of the wrongdoer's state of mind extends beyond his anticipated retention of possession and includes an inquiry into his contemplated manner of relinquishing possession, or control, of the property wrongfully taken.

On this approach, it has been held that when a defendant takes the tools of another person with intent to use them temporarily and then to leave them wherever it may be that he finishes with his work, the factfinder is justified in the conclusion that defendant had specific intent to deprive the owner permanently of his property. *State v. Davis*, 38 N.J.L. 176 (1875).

Similarly, it has been decided that a defendant who wrongfully takes the property of another intending to use it for a short time and then to relinquish possession, or control, in a manner leaving to chance whether the owner recovers his property is correctly held specifically to intend that the owner be deprived permanently of his property. *State v. Smith*, 268 N.C. 167, 150 S.E.2d 194 (1966).

The rationale underlying these decisions is that to negate, as a matter of law, the existence of specific intent to deprive permanently the owner of his property, a wrongful taker of the property of another must have in mind not only that his retention of possession, or control, will be "temporary" but also that when he will relinquish the possession, or control, he will do it in some manner (whatever, particularly, it will be) he regards as having affirmative tendency toward getting the property returned to its owner.[2] In the absence of such thinking by the defendant, his state

---

[2] Since we are here dealing with specific intent of the wrongdoer, the legal criterion is in subjective terms: whether or not defendant actually has in his mind the thought of relinquishing possession, or control, of the wrongfully taken property in a manner which will, *as defendant thinks of it*, be an affirmative step toward a recovery of the property by its owner. Whether the manner in which defendant in fact relinquishes his possession, or control, has, or has not, a reasonable tendency in all the circumstances (objectively) to assist in a recovery of the property by the owner may be *evidence* of defendant's actual state of mind. Evidence, however, must be distinguished from the ultimate fact legally required to be proved by evidence.

of mind is fairly characterized as indifference should the owner never recover his property; and such indifference by a wrongdoer who is the moving force separating an owner from his property is appropriately regarded as his "willingness" that the owner never regain his property. In this sense, the wrongdoer may appropriately be held to entertain specific intent that the deprivation to the owner be permanent.

In *Commonwealth v. Salerno*, Mass., 255 N.E.2d 318 (1970) the Massachusetts Court adopted this principle, holding that:

> "One who takes property without the authority of the owner and . . . (with) indifference whether the owner recovers possession may be found to intend to deprive the owner of it permanently." (p. 321)

We agree.

On this basis, the evidence in the present case clearly presented a jury question as to defendant's specific intent. Although defendant may have stated to the owner, Prout, that defendant

> "would take care of * * * [the automobile] and see [that] * * * [Prout] got it back as soon as possible",

Defendant himself testified that

> "[i]n my mind it was just to get out of the area. * * * Just get out of the area and leave the car and get under cover somewhere."

This idea to "leave the car" and "get under cover somewhere" existed in defendant's mind as part of an uncertainty about where it would happen. Because defendant was " * * * sort of desperate during the whole day", he had not "really formulated any plans about destination."

Such testimony of defendant, together with other evidence that defendant had already utterly abandoned another vehicle (the station wagon) in desperation, plainly warranted a jury conclusion that defendant's facilely uttered statements to Prout were empty words, and it was defendant's true state of mind to use Prout's Chevelle and abandon it in whatever manner might happen to meet the circumstantial exigencies of defendant's predicament—without defendant's having any thought that the relinquishment of the possession was to be in a manner having some affirmative tendency to help in the owner's recovery of his property. On this finding the jury was warranted in a conclusion that defendant was indifferent should the owner, Prout, never have back his automobile and, therefore had specific intent that the owner be deprived permanently of his property.

* * *

The entry is:

Appeal denied.

Notes and Questions

1. The *Gordon* court's interpretation of what larceny (and robbery, when it incorporates larceny) requires is questionable and, most likely, wrong. The court probably confused what the jury must find in order to justify conviction and what evidence must exist in the record of the conviction for an appellate court reviewing the conviction to uphold the jury's finding. This distinction was drawn more carefully in *Commonwealth v. Moore*, 36 Mass.App.Ct. 455, 632 N.E.2d 1234 (1994). The court set out the facts:

> The defendant [took] a Chevy pickup truck owned by one Duquette from an alleyway behind a drinking establishment in Brockton. A police officer took up pursuit, and when the defendant stopped at an intersection, the officer attempted to get into the vehicle for the purpose of taking the defendant into custody. As the officer was reaching for a door handle, the defendant (according to the officer's testimony) grabbed hold of the officer's wrist (the assault and battery on a police officer offense) and took off. The officer attempted to mount the running board and to free himself, but he was unsuccessful. The officer was dragged some distance (about one hundred yards) with his left leg on the ground. As the vehicle was swerving and "swaying back and forth," the officer was continually being slapped against it (the assault and battery with a dangerous weapon offense). Eventually, the officer dropped off and became unconscious. He suffered a concussion and other injuries.

At trial on the charge of larceny of the truck, the trial judge instructed the jury that it could find the defendant guilty if it found either an intent permanently to deprive the owner of his property or an indifference to whether the owner recovered his property. Despite *Commonwealth v. Salerno*, relied upon by the *Gordon* court, the *Moore* tribunal found reversible error. It stressed that *Salerno* had said that one who takes property with indifference whether the owner recovers it "may" be found to have the intent necessary for larceny. It then explained:

Although indifference to whether the owner recovers possession of the property *may* indicate that a defendant had the requisite intent to permanently deprive the owner of possession, such indifference is not an alternative to the intent to permanently deprive. It does not automatically suffice to prove the mental element of larceny; it merely may serve as the evidentiary basis from which the jury may infer that an intent to deprive permanently exists.

(emphasis in original). Thus *Moore* makes clear that an intent to deprive is required. It further establishes, however, that if a jury finds the required intent and the record contains testimony strongly suggesting indifference, an appellate court will assume the jury decided to infer intent to permanently deprive from that indifference and affirm the conviction to respect the jury's judgment that such an inference is proper on the facts of the case.

2. What is really a specialized application of mistake of law doctrine (discussed generally in Chapter 13) has been raised as a "defense" of "claim of right" by some defendants charged with property crimes. Traditional application of claim of right doctrine in the larceny context is illustrated by *State v. Varszegi*, 33 Conn.App. 368, 635 A.2d 816 (1993), certif. denied, 228 Conn. 921, 636 A.2d 851 (1994):

> The defendant was the landlord of commercial property at 1372 Summer Street in Stamford. One of the defendant's tenants was Executive Decisions Support, Inc., a computer software company headed by Catherine Topp. Topp, in her capacity as president of the company, personally signed the lease with the defendant. The lease contained a default clause authorizing the defendant to enter the tenant's premises, seize the tenant's personal property and sell it as a way of recovering unpaid rent or other charges. The defendant claimed Topp had failed to pay her rent for March, April and May of 1990.
>
> On Saturday May 5, 1990, the defendant entered Topp's office by picking the lock. He proceeded to remove two of Topp's computers and attached printers. On Monday May 7, 1990, Topp arrived at work and noticed that the lock on her office door had been tampered with. Upon entering and noticing her computers were missing, Topp called the Stamford police. After the completion of an initial investigation at the scene by Officer

Frank Pica, Topp telephoned the defendant, who admitted that he had taken her computers as a consequence of her failure to pay three months rent. Pica then took the phone from Topp and identified himself. The defendant advised Pica that he was Topp's landlord and expressed his belief that his actions were proper and legal. Upon hearing this, Pica expressed doubt as to the lawfulness of the defendant's conduct, at which point the defendant reiterated his belief that his actions were in accordance with his lease.

> At this point, Pica called his supervisor, Sergeant Ralph Geter. Geter arrived shortly thereafter and telephoned the defendant, who again identified himself as Topp's landlord and again admitted having taken the computers in question. Geter informed the defendant that he had no right under the law to confiscate Topp's computer equipment and that he should make arrangements with Topp to return the goods. No such arrangements were made and the defendant sold the computers on May 23, 1990.

Reversing Varszegi's conviction for larceny, the court explained:

> "The 'animus furandi,' or intent to steal, is an essential element of the crime of larceny at common law." 50 Am.Jur.2d, Larceny § 35. Hornbook law articulates the same premise. "Since the taking must be with felonious intent . . . taking under a bona fide claim of right, however unfounded, is not larceny. . . . [A]lthough ignorance of the law is, as a rule, no excuse, it is an excuse if it negatives the existence of a specific intent. Therefore, even if the taker's claim of right is based upon ignorance or mistake of law, it is sufficient to negative a felonious intent. A fortiori, a mistake of fact, if it is the basis of a bona fide claim of right, is sufficient." J. Miller, Handbook of Criminal Law (1934) § 114(a), p. 367.
>
> * * *
>
> Particularly apposite to the present case is the comment in American Jurisprudence that, "[i]t is generally held that because of lack of a felonious intent, one is not guilty of larceny who in the honest belief that he has the right to do so, openly and avowedly takes the property of another without the latter's consent, as security for a debt bona fide claimed to be

due him by the owner, or even to apply or credit it to the payment thereof."

Applying this law, the court continued:

> [T]he defendant claims that he did not possess the specific felonious intent to commit larceny but rather acted in good faith pursuant to a lease that gave him, as the landlord, authority to enter the premises, impound the lessee's property, sell it and apply the proceeds to the unpaid rent or other charges. [This provision was in fact not enforceable. Eds.] * * *
>
> We hold that there was insufficient evidence introduced at trial to prove that the defendant knew that he had no right to take the lessee's computers. During the initial phone conversation with Topp, the defendant made no attempt to conceal either his identity or that he had in fact taken the computers. The defendant emphatically stated during this conversation that the default clause in the lease provided him with the authority to impound her property based on her failure to pay the three months rent due. Moreover, the officers testifying at trial each stated that the defendant never wavered from his contention that his actions were lawful, even when faced with the threat of criminal prosecution. The defendant's unfaltering and consistent statements to all parties involved that he acted in good faith in seizing Topp's computers were not contradicted by the testimony of any witness.
>
> * * *
>
> * * * [T]he defendant's claim that he acted in good faith was not countered by any evidence, direct or circumstantial, that he intended to steal the computers. The state contends, however, that the defendant's weekend entry into Topp's office by picking the lock and his subsequent impounding of the computers without leaving a note was enough evidence from which the jury could have reasonably found the requisite intent. Significantly, none of the foregoing evidence contradicted the defendant's claim that he acted in good faith in taking the computers based on the default clause in the lease. In fact, the defendant testified that he entered the office on the weekend so as to avoid an awkward confrontation. When asked by Topp where the computers were on the following Monday, the defendant concealed nothing. * * *

> Moreover, the state contends that even if the defendant believed in good faith that he had the right to take his tenant's personal property to secure overdue rent payments, once he was told by three members of the police force that he was acting illegally, he could no longer reasonably maintain an honest though mistaken belief that he was acting lawfully. We do not agree. Police officers are not imbued with the authority or prerogative to declare provisions of civil contracts void, thereby converting good faith to a felonious intent.

3. Modern theft statutes often incorporate much the same culpable mental state requirement as existed under traditional larceny. Many follow the approach of the Model Penal Code, reprinted at page 280, under which the general theft provision—section 223.2.—requires that the person act "with purpose to deprive [the other person of the property]." "[D]eprive" is then defined in section 223.0(1). As applied to the facts of *Gordon*, this would probably require that the prosecution prove that Gordon acted with the purpose of disposing of the property so as to make it unlikely that the owner would recover it. Could the prosecution have proved this in *Gordon*?

   A few jurisdictions have taken different approaches. Maine, for example, defines the "intent to deprive" required for theft as including the conscious object "to use or dispose of the property under circumstances that make it unlikely that the owner will recover it or that manifest an indifference as to whether the owner will recover it." Me.St.Ti. 17-A, § 352(3). Georgia requires the intent to deprive the other of the property but defines deprive as meaning, "to withhold property of another permanently or temporarily." Ga.St.Ann. § 16-8-1(1)(B).

4. The culpable mental state requirement of larceny or theft has given rise to such difficulty regarding the takings of vehicles that many jurisdictions have crimes consisting of the use of vehicles without the culpable mental state necessary for larceny or theft. The New York statute is fairly typical:

   > § 165.5 Unauthorized use of a vehicle * * *
   >
   > A person is guilty of unauthorized use of a vehicle * * * when * * * [k]nowing that he does not have the consent of the owner, he takes, operates, exercises control over, rides in or otherwise uses a vehicle. * * *

   The crime provided for by these statutes is often informally called "joyriding."

B. EMBEZZLEMENT

Embezzlement was not a crime at common law. If one came into possession of property with the owner's consent and subsequently absconded with it, no crime was made out because there had not been a trespassory taking. As the *Olivo* court indicated, the problem thus posed had been dealt with in part by the doctrine of constructive possession under which servants normally had only custody of their master's property rather than possession. Owners were also said to retain constructive possession of lost property or property delivered to another for very limited purposes. However, these fictions were not applied in the famous case of The *King v. Bazeley*, 168 Eng.Rep. 117 (1799). Bazeley, a bank clerk, had received money for deposit to the owner's account. Instead of transferring it to the bank's possession by moving it to the cash drawer or vault he pocketed the money. This was held not to be larceny because possession had been willingly surrendered by the owner but never received by the bank. To fill this gap, that very year, Parliament enacted the first embezzlement statute.

Embezzlement is generally defined as the unlawful conversion of the property of another already in the possession of the defendant, with the intent to defraud.

Under many modern statutes, the conduct that traditionally gave rise to the separate offense of embezzlement is now one way of committing the general property crime of theft.

1. The Act of Conversion

In order to complete the crime of larceny, the defendant must convert the property. Relatively little litigation has developed over whether defendants charged with embezzlement have done enough to or with the property to be said to have converted it. In the case reprinted in this subsection, however, the court addresses whether the defendant was proved to have "appropriated" the property within the meaning of a specialized embezzlement statute in California. Despite the terminology difference, the case raises the contents of the act requirement in embezzlement and related crimes.

People v. Redondo

Court of Appeal, California, 1993
19 Cal.App.4th 1428, 24 Cal.Rptr.2d 143.

VARTABEDIAN, Associate Justice.

Defendant, Andres C. Redondo, was a deputy sheriff for the Merced County Sheriff's Department. He was convicted of felony embezzlement and misdemeanor theft. These charges arose when defendant used his assigned sheriff's department vehicle to steal a lawnmower. Defendant appeals, * * * asserting that his felony embezzlement conviction could not properly be based on his "momentary" usage of his patrol vehicle to steal the lawnmower. * * *

[W]e validate the embezzlement conviction, finding[] however, the evidence supported a misdemeanor rather than a felony embezzlement.

Facts

In the early morning hours of July 14, 1991, Merced Police Sergeant Wallace L. Broughton was patrolling an area of commercial buildings when he saw a sheriff's department car backed up to the Small Engine Doctor repair shop. He saw defendant standing behind the vehicle and saw the handle of a lawnmower sticking out the driver's side of the trunk. It looked as if defendant was tying the trunk down. Sergeant Broughton recognized defendant, having known him for 10 years. Since a burglar alarm had gone off earlier in the area, Broughton thought defendant had caught a burglar. Broughton turned his car around to come back and talk to defendant.

Defendant was leaving the area when Broughton came back. Defendant took off speeding and Broughton pursued He lost track of defendant and then saw headlights leaving an orchard. Broughton stopped defendant at 3:24 A.M. and asked him if he stole a lawnmower. Defendant denied all knowledge of the lawnmower and said he was on his way to a call at the hospital. The lawnmower was not in defendant's car when Broughton stopped him. He allowed defendant to leave.

Broughton called the chief of police. He and other officers found the lawnmower in an orchard later that morning. The lawnmower was one being repaired at the engine repair shop. The owner of the shop had left it outside the night before on the washpad.

The tread on the tires of defendant's car matched the tire tracks in the orchard where the lawnmower was found and the tire tracks at the engine repair shop. Dirt and paint chips were removed from the trunk of defendant's car. A comparison of dirt from the engine repair shop and the items removed from defendant's trunk were consistent with the mower having been in the trunk of defendant's car.

The vehicle driven by defendant was assigned to him by the Merced County Sheriff's Department. It was owned by the county and had a salvage value of $1,000.

* * *

Discussion

* * *

II. Temporary Use of Governmental Property

Defendant's conviction under section 504 was based on his fraudulent appropriation of his official vehicle to steal the lawnmower. Section 504 provides:

> "Every officer of this state, or of any county * * * thereof * * * who fraudulently appropriates to any use or purpose not in the due and lawful execution of his trust, any property which he has in his possession or under his control by virtue of his trust, or secretes it with a fraudulent intent to appropriate it to such use or purpose, is guilty of embezzlement."

Defendant argues that his use of the vehicle was purely incidental to the target offense and such momentary use of property cannot constitute embezzlement of the property. Defendant contends that in order for the taking to be a violation of section 504, it must be made with the intent to permanently deprive the owner of the property for at least an extended period of time.

In order to prove a violation of section 504, it must be shown that the defendant "is (1) an officer of a city or other municipal corporation or subdivision thereof or a deputy, clerk, or servant of such an officer (2) who fraudulent appropriated property in his possession and control entrusted to him for a use or purpose not in a lawful execution of that trust. These elements 'may be proved by circumstantial evidence and reasonable inferences drawn from such evidence.'"

People v. Harby (1942) 51 Cal.App.2d 759, 125 P.2d 874 is most closely on point to the facts presented here. In *Harby*, a city councilperson used a city-owned automobile to travel more than 4,000 miles on a pleasure trip. He was charged with willful or corrupt misconduct in office in violation of section 504 and Los Angeles Municipal Code section 63.106. The appellate court found the defendant had embezzled property from the city. "To drive a city-owned automobile on a 4,000 mile pleasure jaunt was so clearly an appropriation of the vehicle to a private use that illustration and authority seem supererogatory. His only right to the Chrysler was to use it in performing the city's business." "Such a journey without authorization required a use of the car that was inconsistent with its owner's rights and inconsistent with the nature of the trust reposed in appellant and therefore it was an embezzlement." The appellate court commented that "the journey subjected the automobile to substantial detriment. It was therefore to the extent of its use an embezzlement of the property of the city."

Although defendant's journey here was substantially briefer than the defendant's journey in *Harby*, his use was without authorization and was clearly inconsistent with the owner's rights and inconsistent with the nature of the trust reposed in defendant. Defendant not only used the automobile to steal the lawnmower, but used it to evade Sergeant Broughton at high speeds. By doing so, he subjected the automobile to detriment.

In *People v. Dolbeer* (1963) 214 Cal.App.2d 619, 29 Cal.Rptr. 573, the defendant enlisted the aid of a phone company employee to provide him with a daily list of new phone company subscribers. After defendant was given the list, he quickly copied and returned them to the employee. The appellate court found the lists were property because they were physical goods and had a value. The appellate court also found that even though the lists were returned promptly, an embezzlement had occurred and the defendant appropriated the lists with the intent to defraud.

Here, defendant's use of the vehicle was for a very brief period of time, but defendant appropriated the property to a purpose not in the due and lawful execution of his trust. Section 504 defines a violation in broad terms as "*any* use or purpose not in the due and lawful execution of his trust." (Emphasis added.) Defendant's utilization of the car, although brief, was an appropriation not in the public interest.

III. Felony or Misdemeanor Embezzlement

Section 514 defines the punishment for one convicted of embezzlement. It provides:

> "Every person guilty of embezzlement is punishable in the manner prescribed for theft of property of the value or kind embezzled * * *."

The following stipulation was entered into by the parties:

> "Mr. Redondo was at the time of this offense, a Detective of the Merced sheriff's department, that he was a deputy of Sheriff Sawyer who's an officer of this county, that the vehicle that he was driving was the assigned—his assigned vehicle, and it was the property of this county, and that the value of that vehicle was approximately a thousand dollars, which is based upon a salvage value from the county persons who keep track of that."

Defendant asserts that the amount of the theft should be limited to the reasonable value of the temporary use of the vehicle between 3 and 6 A.M. Defendant argues that such use was less than $400, the amount necessary to prove grand theft, and therefore his conviction should be reduced to a misdemeanor. Defendant made the same argument at sentencing, and the court rejected it.

* * *

In the previously discussed case of *People v. Harby,* in finding the defendant had embezzled government property by using the city-owned automobile for private purposes, the court held that there was an embezzlement of the property of the city "to the extent of its use." Where government property is used rather than taken in a more permanent sense, value of the use is the appropriate test for determining a monetary equivalent of what was embezzled. To hold otherwise would have some absurd results. For example, if an employee used a FAX machine once for an unauthorized FAX, should that employee be found to have embezzled the entire value of the machine? We think not. If so, an employee who used the FAX machine hundreds of times or took the FAX machine would be guilty of the same offense as the one-time user. This would ignore the differing culpabilities of the defendants recognized by the petty theft/grand theft dichotomy. Defendant did not by his acts expose the county to the loss of the automobile; the county's loss was the loss of the use of that automobile for a certain amount of time. The value of the loss of use suffered by the county must exceed $400 to make the offense a felony.

The only evidence presented at trial established the salvage value of the automobile at $1,000. No evidence was presented as to the value of the limited use of the automobile. It certainly had value, but we have no reason to believe the value is anything near $400. Because the evidence failed to establish embezzlement of public property to the extent of more than $400 in value, we reduce the embezzlement to a misdemeanor.

Disposition

Defendant's embezzlement conviction is hereby reduced to a misdemeanor, and the trial court shall resentence him accordingly. In all other respects, the judgment is affirmed.

2. The Culpable Mental State: The Intent to Defraud

Embezzlement usually does not require the intent to permanently deprive the owner of the property as is required for larceny or modern theft, but rather the "intent to defraud." Generally, courts have assumed that intent to defraud is a less rigorous requirement than the traditional intent to steal required for larceny, but this assumption that it is a minimally demanding requirement has left some question as to what is actually meant by intent to defraud.

State v. Joy

Supreme Court of Vermont, 1988
149 Vt. 607, 549 A.2d 1033.

DOOLEY, Justice.

Following a jury trial in the Washington District Court, defendant Gailon Joy was convicted of one count of embezzlement in violation of 13 V.S.A. § 2531. Defendant appeals his conviction. We affirm.

Defendant Joy was president and sole shareholder of Credit Management Services Corporation (CMS), a debt collection agency. At all relevant times defendant had exclusive control over, and directed the activities of, CMS. CMS contracted with various businesses and credit institutions to collect delinquent accounts for a percentage of the amount collected. Once CMS contracted with a client, CMS was entitled to forty percent of any amount collected on a delinquent account. CMS was entitled to this percentage regardless of whether the debtor paid CMS or settled with the client directly.

As a matter of practice, when CMS received a payment from a debtor, it would deposit the money with a Barre bank and within a month an invoice detailing the transaction would be sent to the client. If monies were due the client, a check would accompany the invoice.

In addition to the bank account with the Barre bank (the Barre account) CMS maintained an account with a Montpelier bank (the Montpelier account). CMS drew on its account with the Montpelier bank to pay its operating expenses, including overhead and payroll expenses.

In late 1980 or early 1981 CMS, suffering financial difficulties, began transferring funds from the Barre account to the Montpelier account to cover its operating expenses. These transfers occurred under defendant's direction. Defendant instructed his bookkeeping personnel to credit client accounts when debts were collected, but not to prepare invoices if there were insufficient funds in the Barre bank account.

In June, 1981, CMS entered into a contract with Stacey Fuel and Lumber Company (Stacy) whereby CMS was to collect several delinquent accounts. On August 14, 1981, CMS received a check from one of Stacey's debtors in the amount of $1,920.25. CMS never forwarded any of this money to Stacey, nor did it inform Stacey that the money had been received. Stacey terminated its relationship with CMS in August, 1982. Subsequently, Stacey received notice that CMS had filed for bankruptcy and that Stacey had been listed as a creditor of CMS.

On February 17, 1984 the State filed an information charging defendant with * * * embezzlement * * * related to the $1,920.25 payment received by CMS for Stacey. Defendant was convicted * * * and filed a timely notice of appeal.

Defendant * * * argues that the trial court erred in its instructions to the jury regarding intent. * * *

* * * [D]efendant suggests that the trial court improperly refused to charge the jury that "[t]he mere fact that C.M.S. Corporation failed or was unable to pay its creditors is not a sufficient showing of intent to justify conviction [of embezzlement]." Defendant also argues that the trial court erred in failing to instruct the jury that, while intent to repay is not a defense, the jury should consider defendant's intent to repay in determining whether defendant possessed the requisite fraudulent intent to make out the crime of embezzlement. Based on these two claims, defendant also assigns error to the fact that the trial judge instructed the jury "without qualification" that intent to repay is not a defense to a charge of embezzlement.

* * *

Defendant's main objection to the charge is that it failed to state that the jury could consider intent to repay as evidence that the defendant had no fraudulent intent. The elements of embezzlement are detailed in 13 V.S.A. § 2531, which states in pertinent part that:

> An officer, agent, bailee for hire, clerk or servant of a banking association or an incorporated company, . . . who embezzles or fraudulently converts to his own use, or takes or secretes with intent to embezzle or fraudulently convert to his own use, money or other property which comes into his possession or is under his care by virtue of such employment, notwithstanding he may have an interest in such property, shall be guilty of embezzlement. . . .

The law is clear that intent to repay is not a defense to embezzlement under a statute like ours. See, e.g., 3 Wharton's Criminal Law § 397, at 405–07 (14th ed. 1980). Further, the proposition that defendant's intent to repay should have been considered by the jury in its determination of whether or not he possessed the necessary *mens rea* is inconsistent with the state of the law. A leading authority on criminal law has observed that "[g]iven a fraudulent appropriation or conversion, an embezzlement is committed even if the defendant intends at some subsequent time to return the property or to make restitution to the owner." 3 Wharton's Criminal Law § 397, at 405–06 (footnote omitted). Likewise, the Supreme Court of Illinois, in a case quite similar to the instant case, held that "[t]he intention to restore or replace does not make an intentional purloining, secretion or appropriation of the money of another any the less an embezzlement." *People v. Riggins*, 13 Ill.2d 134, 140, 148 N.E.2d 450, 453 (1958) (citation omitted); accord *Commonwealth v. Bovaird*, 373 Pa. 47, 60, 95 A.2d 173, 178 (1953).

The rationale for this rule was stated by the Pennsylvania Supreme Court in *Commonwealth v. Bovaird*:

> Where one is charged with embezzlement or fraudulent conversion, the intention to abstract the money and appropriate it to his own use has been fully executed upon its wrongful taking; the ability and intention to indemnify the party from whom it has been withdrawn remains unexecuted, and such intention, even if conscientiously entertained, may become impossible of fulfillment. The crime is consummated when the money is intentionally and wrongfully converted, temporarily or permanently, to the defendant's own use.

Thus, we are not persuaded by defendant's argument that it was error for the trial judge to refuse to instruct the jury that defendant's intent to repay was relevant to the existence or nonexistence of fraudulent intent; there clearly was no error on this point.*

The trial judge properly charged the elements of the offense of embezzlement. Regarding intent, the judge stressed that "there must be a fraudulent intent and the State must prove fraudulent intent beyond a reasonable doubt." And the court properly noted that "the intent to embezzle is a state of mind which can be shown by words or conduct."

Defendant also argues that the trial court erred by not instructing the jury that a mere inability or failure to pay creditors is not sufficient to demonstrate the fraudulent intent necessary for the crime of embezzlement. For the same reasons that intent to repay is not relevant to the existence of fraudulent intent, neither is the ability or inability to repay.

Based on the foregoing analysis, we conclude that no grounds for reversal exist in this case.

AFFIRMED.

---

* Some authorities have observed that intent to return the identical property taken is evidence of lack of fraudulent intent, or that intent to repay may be relevant to sentencing, but neither of these situations is the case before us now.

Notes and Questions

1. What is the intent to defraud? Could Joy have argued that the prosecution failed to prove it? Specifically, is it sufficient that the accused embezzler intended in some way to deceive the victim? Or, perhaps, is it necessary that the accused be aware of some risk that the property or value will be lost to the owner and intentionally subject the owner to that risk of loss? In *Joy*, the jury was given the following instruction regarding the *mens rea* it had to find:

> Along with [a] conversion, there must be a fraudulent intent, and the State must prove fraudulent intent beyond a reasonable doubt. Fraudulent intent means to act with a willful and corrupt motive, that is, to act in bad faith. And the intent to embezzle is a state of mind which can be shown by words or conduct. Ordinarily, there can be no embezzlement by merely keeping money belonging to another without fraudulent intent to deprive the other of his property. Nor can there ordinarily be an embezzlement by merely doing something the unexpected result of which is to deprive the owner of his property. However, if one wrongfully and intentionally misappropriates the property of another, such as money, it is not a defense that he intended at a later date to return the property or pay back the rightful owner. Again, fraudulent intent must be determined from the surrounding facts and circumstances.

Arguing that this was accurate, the prosecution in its appellate brief quoted *United States v. Waronek*, 582 F.2d 1158, 1161 n. 4 (7th Cir. 1978): "[T]he "felonious" intent with which embezzlement is committed consists of the intent to appropriate or convert the property of the owner * * *."

2. In *State v. DeWall*, 343 N.W.2d 790 (S.D.1984) (per curiam), the facts were as follows:

> At 4:00 P.M. one afternoon appellant and her cousin looked over some used cars on Russ DeVine's car lot in Watertown, South Dakota. Appellant and her cousin asked Mr. DeVine if they could test drive a 1980 Citation. DeVine gave appellant permission to take the car to a local motel where appellant's mother worked. Appellant and her cousin drove by the motel and stopped at some other local businesses.

When they returned to DeVine's car lot it was closed. After filling the car up with gas, appellant and her cousin took a three hundred mile drive through South Dakota and Minnesota. When they arrived back in Watertown in the early morning hours, appellant told her cousin to return the car to DeVine's lot and lock the keys in it.

DeWall's conviction for embezzling the car was upheld over a contention that the trial judge erred in failing to instruct the jury that embezzlement under South Dakota law required an intent to deprive the owner of the property. Embezzlement, the court held, requires only an intent to defraud.

3. In *Walsh v. State*, 110 Nev. 1385, 887 P.2d 1239 (1994) (per curiam), the facts were as follows:

Walsh entered into an oral contract with Bill J. King ("King") to repair some body damage to King's truck. King delivered his truck to Walsh and asked that it be repaired by the following day. After beginning work on the truck, Walsh drove it off the premises to go to a nearby gas station. On his return from the gas station, Walsh had an accident. As a result, King's truck was destroyed.

Walsh was convicted of embezzlement. On appeal, the Nevada Supreme Court held that Walsh's conviction could only be upheld, if at all, under an embezzlement statute that required proof that the accused acted "with intent to steal [the property] or to defraud the owner * * * thereof." Because Walsh lacked this "intent to steal," the court concluded, his conviction must be reversed. If Nevada's law had been like that of Vermont applied in *Joy*—and thus required only an intent to defraud—would Walsh have been guilty of the crime? Even if Walsh had the necessary intent to defraud, arguably his misuse of the truck was not sufficient for a conversion of it, even under *Redondo*.

C. FALSE PRETENSES

Editors' Introduction: False Pretenses, the Law's Reluctance to Criminalize Nonpayment of Debts, and Check Problems

The essence of common law larceny was that it involved a trespassory taking, that is, a misappropriation of another's property against his will. The essence of embezzlement was the misappropriation of another's property rightfully in the possession of the offender. What then of the duplicitous criminal who obtains title to the tangible personal property of another through the owner's willing transfer of the property in reliance upon the actor's false statements or actions? An easy example would be where the owner sells the property in exchange for counterfeit money. At common law there was an offense of cheating by false tokens, which covered such conduct. It did not, however, cover the situation where the property was given because of false *statements*. This conduct was criminalized by Parliament's creation in 1757 of the statutory crime of false pretenses, which involved the fraudulent causing of another to part with title to property by means of the false representation of facts known to the offender to be false.

Larceny could be committed, under *King v. Pear*, 168 Eng.Rep. 208 (1779), by taking property by means of deception. Thus, larceny potentially overlapped with false pretenses. The key theoretical distinction between false pretenses and larceny by trick is whether the thief, through his trickery, acquired *title* to the property from the owner (making the crime false pretenses) or merely *possession* (in which case the crime committed is larceny by trick). *Bell v. United States*, 462 U.S. 356, 103 S.Ct. 2398, 76 L.Ed.2d 638 (1983).

False pretenses did not require the intent to steal as demanded by larceny. Instead, like embezzlement, this offense demanded only an intent to defraud.

American criminal statutes often include a version of false pretenses, sometimes as a specific offense. The Model Penal Code (see page 282) provides separately in section 223.3 for "Theft by Deception." Modern statutes sometimes make the behavior constituting this separate offense under the Model Penal Code one manner of committing a broad general crime such as theft.

American courts' interpretation and application of false pretenses-like crimes have been influenced by a widely shared perception that simple failure to pay debts and disputes about contractual obligations should not give rise to criminal liability. In part, this is because such actions do not involve the moral blameworthiness that should be required for criminal liability. In addition, however, the courts have believed that a risk of criminal liability will discourage desirable commercial activity. Further, imprisonment for "debt" also raises serious constitutional considerations, and conviction in these cases may result in prohibited imprisonment for debt.

A major result of American courts' attitude toward this crime was the manner in which they construed the false pretense necessary for criminal liability. The New York Court of Appeals explained:

> The gravamen of [false pretenses] was obtaining property, with the intent permanently to deprive the owner, by fraudulently inducing the owner to part with both possession and title through the use of false statements about some prior or existing facts. As adopted in New York and many other jurisdictions, the crime of larceny by false pretenses did not apply to the act of obtaining money or property by a false promise to do something (such as repaying a loan or delivering goods) in the future. Although a promise accompanied by an intention not to perform could theoretically have been viewed as a false statement of an existing fact, most courts, including this one, took the narrowest possible view and held that such conduct did not constitute the crime of larceny by false pretenses. The judicial reluctance to criminalize such conduct was principally derived in concerns about jailing individuals for mere nonpayment of debt and in the courts' sensitivity to the potential chilling effect that criminalizing such conduct might have on business.

People v. Norman, 85 N.Y.2d 609, 617–18, 650 N.E.2d 1303, 1307–08, 627 N.Y.S.2d 302, 306–07 (1995).

The decision reprinted in this section reflects one court's abandonment of this approach. As the Iowa statute applied in this case illustrates, statutes permitting criminal liability to be based on a promise made with the knowledge that it would not be carried out sometimes attempt to safeguard against misuse of these crimes by specifying that the prosecution's proof of the accused's intent must include more than simply evidence that the accused did not in fact perform as he promised.

As also illustrated by the decision that follows, special problems are created when prosecution is based on claimed misrepresentations arising from or relating to a check, and these are increased if the check was postdated. Special statutory provisions have sometimes been enacted to deal with check-related situations and, as is discussed in the next case, these may overlap with the modern version of false pretenses.

Consideration of these situations requires that several distinctions be drawn. First, a careful distinction must be drawn between crimes consisting of simply making or issuing a "bad" check, on the one hand, and, on the other hand, crimes consisting of obtaining property or services by means of such a bad check. Crimes of the first sort usually carry a rather low penalty and arguably serve in part as a means of assisting those who receive bad checks to encourage the check writer to make good the check. Crimes of the second sort usually carry a more serious penalty and it is these offenses that courts see as posing the risks just discussed. The defendant in the case that follows was not charged with a crime of the first sort.

A second distinction that should be drawn in these situations is between statutory provisions that define the elements of the crime that might be charged, on the one hand, and, on the other hand, statutory provisions that provide the prosecution with procedural help in litigation. In the decision that follows, the Iowa Supreme Court discusses Iowa's "theft by check" statute and its provision for certain situations in which the criminal intent required for theft by check may be "impl[ied]." This is not an element of the charged crime, but rather a procedural device to aid prosecution under this specific crime.

Under such a provision, a jury is often told that it *may*—although it need not—infer that a defendant acted with criminal intent (as, for example, with knowledge that a check would not be paid when presented for payment) if the prosecution proves that the check was in fact dishonored for insufficient funds, the defendant was given certain notice, and the defendant failed to make the check good within a particular period of time. The jury must still find that the prosecution has proved that the defendant acted with the requisite culpable mental state, but it may infer that he did so from proof of his failure to make the check good under the circumstances described. This device is often called a presumption, because the jury is told it *may*—but need not—infer or "presume" the required fact (knowledge that the check would not be paid) from a different one proved by the prosecution (the accused failed to make the check good after being given notice and opportunity to do so).

State v. Hogrefe

Supreme Court of Iowa, 1996
557 N.W.2d 871.

LAVORATO, Justice.

Sherman Paul Hogrefe appeals from conviction and sentence for theft by deception. * * *

I. *Background Facts and Proceedings.*

[Hogrefe is a 1986 graduate of South Dakota State with a major in agribusiness. For several years he worked for American Cyanamid selling chemicals but in January of 1991 he quit and started a small farm.

Later in 1991, Hogrefe borrowed $425,000 from Midwest Soya International, Inc. (Midwest) and Pattison Grain to purchase Pursuit, a herbicide, for resale. He purchased and resold the Pursuit, but "forgot" what he did with the proceeds. Midwest and Pattison Grain were not repaid from those proceeds as they expected. The debt, due December 1, 1991, was secured by a security interest in Hogrefe's crops and a mortgage on his home.

In December of 1991, Hogrefe apparently developed a plan for repayment and approached two employees of North Iowa Cooperative Elevator (NICE), Richard Houge and Jim Dunbar. Hogrefe agreed to purchase 500 gallons of Pursuit for $262,220. At a meeting in mid-December—the "first transaction"— Hogrefe wrote four checks to NICE for a total of $262,000. These checks were postdated December 22. Hogrefe and Dunbar on behalf of NICE understood that they were to be cashed at different times.

On December 24, Houge wrote Hogrefe a NICE check for $230,000. The nature of and reason for this payment were the subject of conflicting testimony. Hogrefe signed the check over to Midwest to repay his debt to it.

On December 26, Hogrefe and Houge met at Houge's request. At this "second transaction" Hogrefe wrote three checks to NICE for a total of $231,500. Two were dated December 28 and one was dated December 29. Houge was to hold these checks until Hogrefe approved their deposit.

NICE ordered the Pursuit from American Cyanamid through distributor United Purchasers Association (UPA) on December 30. The Pursuit arrived at NICE on January 2. Hogrefe picked it up that same day, and gave it to Pattison Grain, apparently in repayment of the initial loan to Hogrefe from Pattison Grain.

In mid-January, Hogrefe promised Hough that he would obtain 1,000 gallons of Pursuit and give it to NICE in exchange for the money and Pursuit he had obtained from NICE. Later in January, Hogrefe misrepresented to law enforcement authorities that 1,000 gallons of Pursuit had been stolen from him and he attempted to collect insurance reimbursement. Investigation revealed that the claim was fraudulent since he never had the Pursuit. In a separate case, Hogrefe was convicted of filing a false report based on this action.

UPA billed NICE for the Pursuit. NICE assigned to UPA the three checks written to NICE by Hogrefe on December 26 in the second transaction. When UPA attempted to cash the checks, they were returned for insufficient funds. The four checks Hogrefe wrote to NICE earlier in December (in the first transaction) were also presented for payment at a time not clear from the testimony, and those checks were also not honored because Hogrefe's funds were insufficient.

Hogrefe later sought bankruptcy. NICE submitted a claim for the debt due it from Hogrefe.]

The State charged Hogrefe with one count of first-degree theft by deception * * *. A jury convicted Hogrefe * * *. The district court sentenced Hogrefe to an indeterminate sentence not to exceed ten years.

II. *Sufficiency of the Evidence to Support Submission of the Marshalling Instruction on Theft by Deception.*

* * *

[The trial judge gave the jury a "marshalling instruction," an instruction which summarizes the evidence and explains how the law applies to that evidence. In this instruction,

the judge told the jury that it could convict Hogrefe on any of three theories: (a) that in the first transaction he received money from NICE (the $230,000) in exchange for the checks written in mid-December; (b) that in both transactions combined he received money (the $230,000) and chemicals (the 500 gallons of Pursuit) from NICE in exchange for the checks written at both times; or (c) that in the second transaction he received chemicals (again the Pursuit) from NICE in exchange for the checks written at that time.]

Hogrefe contends the district court erred in giving this instruction. * * * In support of his contention, Hogrefe relies heavily on one of our recent theft by check cases where we said:

> Our holdings establish that when there is an understanding between the parties that a check is not cashable [no money in the account to cover the check] at the time it is received, but will be made so at some time in the future, the representations made are only promises, there is no deception and, thus, no criminal liability results under section 714.1(6) [theft by check]. If, however, the surrounding circumstances at the time a check is given, including the statements made, are representations that sufficient funds exist at the time to cover the check, then criminal liability may result even though a check is postdated. Our focus remains on the representations made at the time a check is delivered.
>
> Under our approach, a postdate is only *evidence* that a check was intended as a promise of future payment and does not alone relieve a defendant of criminal responsibility. It must also be established that both parties understood that a check was not cashable when delivered before criminal liability is precluded as a matter of law. Where both parties do not understand that a postdated check is not cashable until a future date, the question of guilt should be submitted to the fact finder. It is then up to the fact finder to determine whether the maker deceived the party receiving the check by presenting a check that the maker knew, at the time of delivery, would not be paid when presented to the bank it was drawn upon.

State v. McFadden, 467 N.W.2d 578, 581 (Iowa 1991) (citation omitted). We pointed out in *McFadden* that the gist of the theft by check offense is obtaining something of value through deception. If the victim knows the check is worthless when the victim takes it, the victim has not been deceived. In these circumstances, criminal liability for theft by check is precluded as a matter of law.

Hogrefe points out that at the time all seven checks were written, he told Houge there were not sufficient funds in his account to cover the checks and that Houge was to hold the checks until told to deposit them. Thus, Hogrefe concludes, the district court—based on our decision in *McFadden*—should not have instructed the jury to consider the seven checks on the question of deception.

Hogrefe makes an additional argument as to the three checks he gave Houge several days following the $230,000 advance. Houge asked for these checks, Hogrefe argues, because Houge had second thoughts about advancing him the $230,000. Hogrefe's point is that he had already obtained the $230,000 before he had written the three checks. In short, NICE through Houge never advanced the $230,000 in reliance on the three checks. Or, in the words of paragraph one of the marshalling instruction, Hogrefe never "received cash . . . from NICE in exchange" for the three checks. For this additional reason, Hogrefe insists the district court should not have instructed the jury to consider these three checks because the checks were not evidence of deception.

The State responds that Hogrefe's arguments raise "nothing more than a red herring." The State points out that Hogrefe is relying on our use of the term "deception" in the context of a theft by check offense, whereas here we are dealing with a theft by deception offense. The State relies heavily on our holding in *State v. West*, 252 N.W.2d 457 (Iowa 1977), dealing with "theft by false pretenses," the historical precursor to "theft by deception." As the State implies, Hogrefe simply wants us to define deception in theft by deception cases the same way we define deception in our theft by check cases.

Hogrefe's contentions raise a sufficiency of the evidence objection to the marshalling instruction. Our rule is that parties to a lawsuit are entitled to have their legal theories submitted to the jury if such theories are supported by substantial evidence. Evidence is substantial to support submission of an instruction to the jury when a reasonable mind would accept the evidence as adequate to reach a conclusion. In determining whether there is substantial evidence to support submission of an instruction to the jury, we view the evidence in the light most favorable to the party requesting the instruction.

Because there is a substantial overlap between "theft by deception" and "theft by check," we think a discussion of the two offenses and their treatment of checks would help in our analysis of the issue Hogrefe raises.

A. Historical Background.

We have never interpreted theft by deception. Some historical background, therefore, is helpful. Iowa Code section 714.1(3), theft by deception, replaced sections criminalizing theft by "false pretenses." In enacting section 714.1(3),

theft by deception, the legislature—for the most part—followed the lead of the American Law Institute Model Penal Code (1980) [hereinafter Model Penal Code] in its definition of theft by deception. So the Model Penal Code commentaries on the definition are persuasive authority in our interpretation of our own theft by deception statute.

* * * Iowa Code section 714.1(3) provides that a person commits theft when that person "obtains the labor or services of another, or a transfer of possession, control, or ownership of the property of another, or the beneficial use of property of another by deception." Iowa Code § 714.1(3).

Iowa Code section 702.9(5) defines deception as "[p]romising payment, the delivery of goods, or other performance which the actor does not intend to perform or knows that the actor will not be able to perform." Iowa Code § 702.9(5). This same section goes on to say "[f]ailure to perform, standing alone, is not evidence that the actor did not intend to perform." Iowa Code § 702.9(5).

[Former] Iowa Code section 713.1 (1975) [now replaced by section 7.14(1)(3)] defined "false pretense" as follows: If any person designedly and by false pretense . . . and with intent to defraud, obtain from another any money, goods, or other property . . . he shall be imprisoned . . . .

The change in language from theft by "false pretenses" to theft by "deception" clarified the legislature's intent to criminalize every instance of a person obtaining another person's property by deception. Before, in other jurisdictions, convictions for theft by false pretenses were challenged if the deception involved a promise to pay in the future. For example, in *Chaplin v. United States,* 157 F.2d 697, 698-99 (D.C.Cir.1946), the court held that a liquor dealer who asked for money to buy liquor tax stamps and promised to repay the cash advanced, could not be convicted of theft by false pretenses. The defendant used only a small portion of the advance to purchase stamps and never repaid any amount. The defendant's promises were held to "relate to a future transaction" and, therefore, did not and could not constitute a "false *pretense* [which] must relate to a past event or existing fact." (emphasis added).

Many federal and state courts, however, rejected the *Chaplin* rationale that the promise of future payment made without the intent to fulfill this promise could not be a false pretense. See, e.g., *People v. Ashley*, 42 Cal.2d 246, 262, 267 P.2d 271, 281 (1954) ("[A] promise made without intention to perform is a misrepresentation of a state of mind, and thus a misrepresentation of existing fact, and is a false pretense. . . .").

We clearly rejected the *Chaplin* rationale in *West*—a false pretenses case. We stated the issue this way: "Does a promise to perform an act in the future, made with no intent to perform, constitute a misrepresentation under the false pretenses statute * * *?" We concluded it did. We held that the promisor's intention at the time of promising, as well as the promisor's ability to fulfill the promise, are facts which may constitute a false pretense.

In *West*, we overruled turn of the century precedent which implied that promises of future payment could not be a false pretense. The false promises rationale embraced in *West* was carried over to the definition of deception in section 702.9(5) (Deception consists of knowingly "[p]romising payment, the delivery of goods, or other performances which the actor does not intend to perform or knows that the actor will not be able to perform."). Accord Model Penal Code § 223.3 cmt. 3(b) (false promises are part of definition of "deception" in theft by deception offense).

Theft by check and theft by deception clearly overlap. [That part of the theft statute creating the offense of theft by check provides:

A person commits theft when the person * * * [m]akes, utters, draws, delivers, or gives any check, share draft, draft, or written order on any bank, credit union, person or corporation, and obtains property or service in exchange therefor, if the person knows that such check, share draft, draft or written order will not be paid when presented.

Whenever the drawee of such instrument has refused payment because of insufficient funds, and the maker has not paid the holder of the instrument the amount due thereon within ten days of the maker's receipt of notice from the holder that payment has been refused by the drawee, the court or jury may infer from such facts that the maker knew that the instrument would not be paid on presentation. Notice of refusal of payment shall be by certified mail, or by personal service in the manner prescribed for serving original notices.

Whenever the drawee of such instrument has refused payment because the maker has no account with the drawee, the court or jury may infer from such fact that the maker knew that the instrument would not be paid on presentation.]

A person who obtains another's property by writing a bad check could be charged with theft by check and theft by deception involving a check. * * * Our cases have never explained the reason for this apparent overlap.

When the two statutes are compared, however, the reason for some overlap is apparent. The two charges differ only as to how intent at the time of promising may be proved by the State, that is, what inferences are acceptable. Under the theft by deception statute and the definition of deception, promised payment evidenced by a check may constitute theft if the promisor never intended to pay. But, the "[f]ailure to perform, standing alone, is not evidence that the actor did not intend to perform." Iowa Code § 702.9(5). The mere fact of nonpayment of a check is not sufficient. Something more must be shown to prove criminal intent.

Checks may be returned for a variety of reasons; not all of those reasons necessarily deserve criminal punishment. The court must make an inquiry as to all the surrounding facts to determine the intent with which the check (or promise) was made.

Section 714.1(6) (theft by check), on the other hand, sets out several specific, statutorily-defined circumstances that may, standing alone, imply the criminal intent of the promisor as a check writer. If the check was refused by the drawee because the account was closed, or if the drawee refuses payment because of a lack of funds on deposit and the maker is given the prescribed notice, then the fact finder may infer that the maker knew it would not be paid when the check was written. Iowa Code § 714.1(6).

Theft by check may be proven by the drawee's nonpayment for certain, limited reasons. Theft by deception requires, on the other hand, a more thorough inquiry of all the facts and circumstances surrounding the defendant's promise or other form of deception * * *. When, as here, the deception alleged relates to the defendant's promise, the inquiry centers on (1) whether the defendant intended to perform or (2) whether the defendant knew he or she would not be able to perform. Proof as to either prong depends in most cases on circumstantial evidence.

The theft by check statute establishes a clear scheme for dealing with a common means of theft (bad checks) with potentially difficult questions of proof. Theft by deception is meant as a catch-all crime to encompass the full and ever changing varieties of deception. Factual scenarios may overlap, but the legal schemes in which they are situated are complementary rather than redundant.

Our case law surrounding these two complementary statutes appears contradictory on the question whether a promise to pay in the future can be the basis of a theft charge. * * * The line of cases Hogrefe cites supports his contention. We stated in *McFadden*—a theft by check case—that if it is established that both parties understood a check was not cashable when delivered (the check was postdated for instance), then "criminal liability is precluded as a matter of law." * * *

* * * [T]his line of cases * * * that Hogrefe cites in support of his argument * * * seriously undermines theft by deception as an all-encompassing statute. It rewards crafty criminals for no rational purpose * * *.

* * *

Our solution to this dilemma is clear. Under either charge—theft by deception or theft by check—a postdated check can be evidence of deception even though both parties knew the check was not good at the time the defendant issued it. In these circumstances, criminal liability should attach if at the time the defendant issued the check, the defendant (1) never had the intention to pay the check or (2) knew he or she would not be able to pay it. We now overrule our prior theft by check cases holding otherwise. Our solution is consistent with the interplay of theft by deception laws and theft by check laws found in sections 223.3 and 224.5 of the Model Penal Code.

B. The Merits.

With these principles in mind, we turn to two questions we must answer in resolving Hogrefe's sufficiency of the evidence challenge to the marshalling instruction on theft by deception. First, was there sufficient evidence to establish deception on the part of Hogrefe when he issued the checks? Second, if there was, did Hogrefe obtain the Pursuit and cash from NICE by such deception?

1. *Was there sufficient evidence to establish deception on the part of Hogrefe when he issued the checks?* With this question we focus on Hogrefe's intention and knowledge at the time he gave the seven postdated checks. The postdated checks constituted a promise on Hogrefe's part to pay the checks in the future. Was there, therefore, substantial evidence that at the time Hogrefe issued the checks to NICE he either (1) had no intention to pay them or (2) knew he would not be able to pay them?

Viewing the evidence in the light most favorable to the State, we think the jury could reasonably find from the circumstantial evidence presented that—at the very least—Hogrefe knew he would not be able to pay the checks when he issued them.

Hogrefe was financially in trouble when he approached Houge and Dunbar. He had obligated himself to pay back $425,000 by December 1. He had no means to do so because he had purchased and resold chemicals with the $425,000 but could not remember what had happened to the sales proceeds. He had secured the payment of the $425,000 with a mortgage on his house and a security interest on his crops.

It was at this point, when Hogrefe was in trouble financially, that he approached NICE in hopes of securing enough money to pay back the $425,000. The jury could reasonably ask: If Hogrefe did not have the financial wherewithal to pay back $425,000, how could he honestly believe he could pay back about $500,000 ($262,000 in the first transaction and $231,500 in the second transac-

tion) to NICE? In short, Hogrefe had an antecedent debt he was desperate to pay, and he used the chemicals and money he obtained from NICE to pay off the debt with no apparent way of paying back NICE. Hogrefe's unsuccessful insurance scam and subsequent bankruptcy serve as further circumstantial evidence supporting a finding that Hogrefe knew when he sought the $500,000 from NICE that he could not pay back such a sum of money.

The position of the Model Penal Code on theft by deception supports our analysis. * * * Comment 1 to section 223.3 pertinently states:

Theft by deception under section 223.3 requires proof of purpose. The actor must have the purpose to obtain the property of another, and he must have a purpose to deceive. If the actor believes in the accuracy of the impression he seeks to convey, he will not be guilty of a violation of section 223.3 even if his belief is unreasonable. On the other hand, paragraph (1) makes it clear that the actor's own state of mind may be the subject of the deception. It is not necessary for the prosecution to prove that the defendant affirmatively disbelieved the representations he made. If he creates the impression that he believes something to be true when in fact he has no belief on the subject, he has purposely deceived as to the state of his mind.

The jury could reasonably find from the circumstantial evidence we have sketched out above that Hogrefe was creating an impression that he did or would have the means to repay NICE for the almost $500,000 in chemicals and cash he received when in fact he had no such belief.

That brings us to the second question we must answer.

2. *Did Hogrefe obtain chemicals and cash from NICE by deception?* This question focuses on the language "[o]btains . . . transfer of possession, control, or ownership of the property of another, or the beneficial use of property of another, by deception" in section 714.1(3). The Model Penal Code defines "obtains" to mean in relation to property, "to bring about a transfer or purported transfer of a legal interest in the property, whether to the obtainer or another." Model Penal Code § 223.0(5). As one can see, this definition follows closely the language after the word "obtained" in section 714.1(3).

(a) *The first transaction with NICE.* As recalled, in the first transaction, Hogrefe agreed to buy 500 gallons of Pursuit from NICE and wrote four checks for $262,200 as payment for the 500 gallons. All four checks were dated December 22, 1991. Hogrefe gave the checks to Houge * * * with the understanding that the checks were to be cashed at different times. The chemicals were ordered on

December 30 and arrived at NICE's Plymouth facility on January 2. Hogrefe picked up the Pursuit that day and delivered it to Pattison Grain as final payment on the $425,000 obligation. NICE presented the four checks for payment at some point but the checks were returned for insufficient funds.

The jury could easily find that Hogrefe obtained the chemicals on the strength of the four postdated checks he wrote, checks that Hogrefe knew he could not cover. Thus, with regard to this transaction, we conclude there was substantial evidence from which the jury could find that Hogrefe obtained the 500 gallons of Pursuit by deception.

(b) *The second transaction with NICE.* The second transaction with NICE presents a problem. As recalled, December 24—two days after Hogrefe wrote the four postdated checks to NICE for the 500 gallons of Pursuit— Houge wrote Hogrefe a check from the NICE account for $230,000. On the same date, Hogrefe signed over the check to Midwest as part payment on the $425,000 advance.

Two days later on December 26, * * * [a]t Houge's request, Hogrefe gave Houge three postdated checks made out to NICE for $231,500. Two checks were dated December 28 and one was dated December 29. Houge was to hold all three checks until Hogrefe approved their deposit.

* * *

Clearly, Hogrefe did not obtain the $230,000 on the strength of the three postdated checks he gave Houge. The checks could not, therefore, support a theft by deception charge. Nevertheless, * * * the marshalling instruction * * * instructed the jury that they could consider these checks on the theft by deception charge. * * * The [instruction] gives the jury three options. The jury could find that Hogrefe received (1) cash for checks (the second transaction), (2) both cash and chemicals for checks (both transactions) or (3) chemicals for checks (the first transaction).

What we have then is a marshalling instruction that allows the jury to consider three theories of culpability, only one (chemicals for checks) of which is supported by the evidence. With a general verdict of guilty, we have no way of determining which theory the jury accepted. Because there was insufficient evidence to support an instruction to consider all the checks, the district court erred in giving the marshalling instruction.

III. *Disposition.*

Because the district court erred in giving the marshalling instruction, we reverse and remand for a new trial.

REVERSED AND REMANDED.

Notes and Questions

1. Jurisdictions differ on the necessary and possible consequences of a transaction involving a postdated check. In *State v. Stooksberry*, 872 S.W.2d 906 (Tenn.1994), the court held that a postdated check is simply not a "check," because a check must be payable on demand. Thus a postdated check could not serve as the basis for prosecution under a statute prohibiting the passing of a check to obtain items or services knowing that there are not sufficient funds for payment of it. However, in *State v. Fitanides*, 141 N.H. 534, 141 A.2d 352 (1966), the court held that a postdated check is a check for purposes of a bad check crime consisting of issuing or passing a check knowing or believing that it will not be paid. *Fitanides* indicated, however, that conviction requires proof that the defendant knew the check would not be paid when it was presented for payment *after the date on the check*. Thus proof that the defendant knew at the time he issued or passed the check that there were not, *at that time*, funds adequate for its payment would not be sufficient.

   Whether a check was in fact postdated may be a matter of dispute. If the check itself is introduced into evidence, that document will ordinarily establish the date placed on it by the defendant. Witnesses may differ, however, on when the check was issued or passed, and the prosecution's evidence may prove that a check claimed by the defendant to have been postdated was actually passed on or after the date specified on the check.

2. *Hogrefe* reflects the general rule that under statutes requiring that a bad check be used to obtain items or services, the check must have been passed to the victim before the items or services were provided to the defendant. However, some situations may provide flexibility regarding what can be relied upon by the prosecution. In *State v. Archameau*, 187 Wis.2d 502, 523 N.W.2d 150 (1994), for example, the statute covered issuance of a bad check except "for past consideration." Archameau was convicted on proof that he gave a bad check to Precision Auto Body, which then released a vehicle it had repaired. He argued that the check was given for the repairs already made when the check was issued, and thus it was for only "past consideration." The court, however, noted that under Wisconsin law Precision Auto Body had a statutory possessory lien on the car, which meant it was entitled to retain the car until the repair bill was paid, and that this lien is lost when the lienholder gives up possession. The evidence showed that

Archameau gave Precision Auto Body the check for not only its past work but also for its release of the vehicle and thus for surrender of its lien. The release of the car was *present* rather than *past* consideration and the conviction was therefore proper.

3. The deception required for false pretense-like offenses is often defined, sometimes by statute, as excluding "puffing." Section 223.3 of the Model Penal Code, reprinted at page 282, does so as well. This term was defined for the jury in *Line v. State* 674 P.2d 1345, 1353 n. 5 (Alaska App.1983):

> Deception * * * does not [include] "puffing." ["Puffing"] is defined as the making of extravagant praise, commendation or claim, for exam-

ple, a seller's praise of the virtues of something offered for sale, which is unlikely to deceive reasonable people in the group addressed.

The rationale for applying an objective standard to such puffing has been explained as designed to meet the problem posed by mass advertising, in which the message cannot be tailored to the intellectual or critical capacity of specific persons who may be exposed to it. Without an objective standard, the law would create unfortunate "pressure for communication in terms suitable to the most stupid." *Commonwealth v. Joy,* 253 Pa. Super. 177, 184, 383 A.2d 1288, 1292 (1978), quoting from Model Penal Code § 206.2, Comment 8, p. 71 (Tent. Draft No. 2, 1954).

D. THEFT: CONSOLIDATED ACQUISITION OFFENSES

Dissatisfaction with hairsplitting under traditional property crime law has led to efforts at consolidating the various theft offenses. The following provisions of the Model Penal Code have served as a basis for many modern statutory provisions.

MODEL PENAL CODE[*]

Official Draft, 1985

Section 223.0. Definitions

In this Article, unless a different meaning plainly is required:

(1) "deprive" means: (a) to withhold property of another permanently or for so extended a period as to appropriate a major portion of its economic value, or with intent to restore only upon payment of reward or other compensation; or (b) to dispose of the property so as to make it unlikely that the owner will recover it.

* * *

(4) "movable property" means property the location of which can be changed, including things growing on, affixed to, or found in land, and documents although the rights represented thereby have no physical location; "immovable property" is all other property.

(5) "obtain" means: (a) in relation to property, to bring about a transfer or purported transfer of a legal interest in the property, whether to the obtainer or

another; or (b) in relation to labor or service, to secure performance thereof.

(6) "property" means anything of value, including real estate, tangible and intangible personal property, contract rights, chose-in-action and other interests in or claims to wealth, admission or transportation tickets, captured or domestic animals, food and drink, electric or other power.

(7) "property of another" includes property in which any person other than the actor has an interest which the actor is not privileged to infringe, regardless of the fact that the actor also has an interest in the property and regardless of the fact that the other person might be precluded from civil recovery because the property was used in an unlawful transaction or was subject to forfeiture as contraband. Property in possession of the actor shall not be deemed property of another who has only a security interest therein, even if legal title is in the creditor pursuant to a conditional sales contract or other security agreement.

Section 223.1. Consolidation of Theft Offenses; Grading; Provisions Applicable to Theft Generally

(1) *Consolidation of Theft Offenses.* Conduct denominated theft in this Article constitutes a single offense. [The 1962 Proposed Official Draft included the following language at this point: "embracing the separate offenses heretofore known as larceny, embezzlement, false pretense, extortion, blackmail, fraudulent conversion, receiving stolen property, and the like."]

(2) *Grading of Theft Offenses.*

    (a) Theft constitutes a felony of the third degree if the amount involved exceeds $500, or if the property stolen is a firearm, automobile, airplane, motorcycle, motorboat, or other motor-propelled vehicle, or in the case of theft by receiving stolen property, if the receiver is in the business of buying or selling stolen property.

    (b) Theft not within the preceding paragraph constitutes a misdemeanor, except that if the property was not taken from the person or by threat, or in breach of a fiduciary obligation, and the actor proves by a preponderance of the evidence that the amount involved was less than $50, the offense constitutes a petty misdemeanor.

(3) *Claim of Right.* It is an affirmative defense to prosecution for theft that the actor:

    (a) was unaware that the property or service was that of another; or

    (b) acted under an honest claim of right to the property or service involved or that he had a right to acquire or dispose of it as he did; or

    (c) took property exposed for sale, intending to purchase and pay for it promptly, or reasonably believing that the owner, if present, would have consented.

(4) *Theft From Spouse.* It is no defense that theft was from the actor's spouse, except that misappropriation of household and personal effects, or other

property normally accessible to both spouses, is theft only if it occurs after the parties have ceased living together.

Section 223.2. Theft by Unlawful Taking or Disposition

(1) *Movable Property.* A person is guilty of theft if he unlawfully takes, or exercises unlawful control over, movable property of another with purpose to deprive him thereof.

(2) *Immovable Property.* A person is guilty of theft if he unlawfully transfers immovable property of another or any interest therein with purpose to benefit himself or another not entitled thereto.

Section 223.3. Theft by Deception

A person is guilty of theft if he obtains property of another by deception. A person deceives if he purposely:

(1) creates or reinforces a false impression, including false impressions as to law, value, intention or other state of mind; but deception as to a person's intention to perform a promise shall not be inferred from the fact alone that he did not subsequently perform the promise; or

(2) prevents another from acquiring information which would affect his judgment of a transaction; or

(3) fails to correct a false impression which the deceiver previously created or reinforced, or which the deceiver knows to be influencing another to whom he stands in a fiduciary or confidential relationship; or

(4) fails to disclose a known lien, adverse claim or other legal impediment to the enjoyment of property which he transfers or encumbers in consideration for the property obtained, whether such impediment is or is not valid, or is or is not a matter of official record.

The term "deceive" does not, however, include falsity as to matters having no pecuniary significance, or puffing by statements unlikely to deceive ordinary persons in the group addressed.

Section 223.4. Theft by Extortion

A person is guilty of theft if he obtains property of another by threatening to:

(1) Inflict bodily injury on anyone or commit any other criminal offense; or

(2) accuse anyone of a criminal offense; or

(3) expose any secret tending to subject any person to hatred, contempt or ridicule, or to impair his credit or business repute; or

(4) take or withhold action as an official, or cause an official to take or withhold action; or

(5) bring about or continue a strike, boycott or other collective unofficial action, if the property is not demanded or received for the benefit of the group in whose interest the actor purports to act; or

(6) testify or provide information or withhold testimony or information with respect to another's legal claim or defense; or

(7) inflict any other harm which would not benefit the actor.

It is an affirmative defense to prosecution based on paragraphs (2), (3) or (4) that the property obtained by threat of accusation, exposure, lawsuit or other invocation of official action was honestly claimed as restitution or indemnification for harm done in the circumstances to which such accusation, exposure, lawsuit or other official action relates or as compensation for property or lawful services.

Section 223.7. Theft of Services

(1) A person is guilty of theft if he obtains services which he knows are available only for compensation, by deception or threat, or by false token or other means to avoid payment for the service. "Services" includes labor, professional service, transportation, telephone or other public service, accommodation in hotels, restaurants or elsewhere, admission to exhibitions, use of vehicles or other movable property. Where compensation for service is ordinarily paid immediately upon the rendering of such service, as in the case of hotels and restaurants, refusal to pay or absconding without payment or offer to pay gives rise to a presumption that the service was obtained by deception as to intention to pay.

(2) A person commits theft if, having control over the disposition of services of others, to which he is not entitled, he knowingly diverts such services to his own benefit or to the benefit of another not entitled thereto.

E. COMPUTER-RELATED OFFENSES
Editors' Introduction: Computer-Related Crimes

Since the late 1970s, a new type of criminal offense focusing upon the use of computers has developed. As Hollinger and Lanza-Kaduce, The Process of Criminalization: The Case of Computer Crime Laws, 26 Criminology 101 (1988) have noted, this rapid development of a new type of crime is an exception to the general pattern in American and English law, under which crimes developed much more gradually. Florida and Arizona enacted computer crime statutes in 1978, and the vast majority of jurisdictions have followed.

Although computer crime laws cover a wide range of activities, the most important aspects of this new type of criminal liability result from the development of a new form of intangible property as a result of widespread use of computers. Information may, of course, be stored in computers and this may be done for a variety of reasons, including the use of that information in operating the computer and its related systems, the analysis of that information by means of the computer, and retention of that information and its limited dissemination to others for particular reasons and under limited circumstances. There was a widespread assumption that this information deserved protection and that some interferences with computer-stored information were serious enough to deserve criminal punishment. However, there was also reason to doubt that traditional criminal offenses would provide this sort of protection.

A leading case supporting this concern was *Lund v. Commonwealth*, 217 Va. 688, 232 S.E.2d 745 (1977), in which Lund, a graduate student, had—without authorization—obtained access to a computer and used more than $26,000 worth of computer time. He was charged with larceny by trick under Virginia law, which required that the crime involve "property which may be the subject of larceny." Under Virginia larceny law, the appellate court held, only concrete articles of personal property can be the subject of larceny, in part because only such items are capable of being taken and carried away as is required for larceny. The court concluded that labor and services— and hence the unauthorized use of a computer—cannot be the subject of larceny, and therefore Lund was not guilty of that offense.

Many jurisdictions have created the crime of larceny or theft of services, and *Lund* suggested that under such statutes unauthorized use of a computer might sometimes be covered. Nevertheless, these larceny of service statutes presented other problems. Many, like the New York statute, require that the services be ones that are being offered for payment to the public. Thus, the New York statute did not permit the conviction of an employee who used for his own personal purposes a computer owned by his employer. The computer was used by the employer for internal business purposes and its use was not offered for payment to the public. *People v. Weg*, 113 Misc.2nd 1017, 450 N.Y.S.2d 957 (1982).

In part as a result of concern that traditional criminal provisions did not adequately protect the new property interests that developed as a result of widespread utilization of computers, most jurisdictions created new and quite elaborate computer crime provisions. The California statute, appearing in the state's Penal Code, illustrates the type of legislation that resulted:

§ 502. Unauthorized access to computers, computer systems and computer data

(a) It is the intent of the Legislature in enacting this section to expand the degree of protection afforded to individuals, businesses, and governmental agencies from tampering, interference, damage, and unauthorized access to lawfully created computer data and computer systems. The Legislature finds and declares that the proliferation of computer technology has resulted in a concomitant proliferation of computer crime and other forms of unauthorized access to computers, computer systems, and computer data.

The Legislature further finds and declares that protection of the integrity of all types and forms of lawfully created computers, computer systems, and computer data is vital to the protection of the privacy of individuals as well as to the well-being of financial institutions, business concerns, governmental agencies, and others within this state that lawfully utilize those computers, computer systems, and data.

* * *

(c) * * * [A]ny person who commits any of the following acts is guilty of a public offense:

(1) Knowingly accesses and without permission alters, damages, deletes, destroys, or otherwise uses any data, computer, computer system, or computer network in order to either (A) devise or execute any scheme or artifice to defraud, deceive, or extort, or (B) wrongfully control or obtain money, property, or data.

(2) Knowingly accesses and without permission takes, copies, or makes use of any data from a computer, computer system, or computer network, or takes or copies any supporting documentation, whether existing or residing internal or external to a computer, computer system, or computer network.

(3) Knowingly and without permission uses or causes to be used computer services.

(4) Knowingly accesses and without permission adds, alters, damages, deletes, or destroys any data, computer software, or computer programs which reside or exist internal or external to a computer, computer system, or computer network.

(5) Knowingly and without permission disrupts or causes the disruption of computer services or denies or causes the denial of computer services to an authorized user of a computer, computer system, or computer network.

(6) Knowingly and without permission provides or assists in providing a means of accessing a computer, computer system, or computer network in violation of this section.

(7) Knowingly and without permission accesses or causes to be accessed any computer, computer system, or computer network.

(8) Knowingly introduces any computer contaminant into any computer, computer system, or computer network.

* * *

For purposes of paragraph (8), the statute defines a "computer contaminant" as:

any set of computer instructions that are designed to modify, damage, destroy, record, or transmit information within a computer, computer system, or computer network without the intent or permission of the owner of the information. They include, but are not limited to, a group of computer instructions commonly called viruses or worms, which are self-replicating or self-propagating and are designed to contaminate other computer programs or computer data, consume computer resources, modify, destroy, record, or transmit data, or in some other fashion usurp the normal operation of the computer, computer system, or computer network.

Section 502(b)(10).

The scheme for grading the seriousness of an offense under the California statute is quite complex. A violation of paragraph (1), (2), (4), or (5) is punishable by imprisonment not exceeding 16 months, a fine not exceeding $10,000, or both. A violation of paragraph (3), (6), (7), or (8) is punishable under a range of options from only a fine not exceeding $250 up to the same penalties as constitute the maximum punishment for violating paragraphs (1), (2), (4), or (5). In the case of a violation of paragraph

(3), (6), (7), or (8), the punishment category is determined by whether an offense is a second or subsequent offense, whether there was injury caused and, if so, the amount of the victim expenditure, and the value of the computer services involved. Section 502(d). Under section 502(b):

> (8) "Injury" means any alteration, deletion, damage, or destruction of a computer system, computer network, computer program, or data caused by the access.
> (9) "Victim expenditure" means any expenditure reasonably and necessarily incurred by the owner or lessee to verify that a computer system, computer network, computer program, or data was or was not altered, deleted, damaged, or destroyed by the access.

As the California statute illustrates, "computer crime" can consist of any of a wide range of conduct. It includes not only wrongful accessing of a computer or computer data but also interfering with others' use of computer services, wrongfully obtaining data from a computer, damaging computer equipment or software, introducing a contaminant into a computer system, and wrongfully using computer services. In addition, the offense may under section 502(c)(1) consist of using a computer to commit certain other criminal offenses.

At the federal level, the major computer-specific crimes are those created by the "Hacker Statute," The Computer Fraud and Abuse Act of 1986 and its amendments, codified in 18 U.S.C. 1030. This statute covers certain conduct involving computers implicating federal interests, that is, computers used by the federal government or financial institutions regulated by federal law or in interstate or foreign commerce or communication. As is the case under the California statute, the federal legislation criminalizes a number of types of computer-related behavior. Prohibited conduct includes accessing a protected computer and causing damage, and transmitting (without authorization) a program, code, or command to a protected computer and causing damage. In addition, the statute in 18 U.S.C. § 1030(a)(4) provides that a person commits a crime if that person accesses a protected computer without authorization and with intent to defraud and thereby obtains "anything of value" except less than $5,000 worth of use of the computer itself.

Computer-specific offenses pose in this technically sophisticated context some of the same problems posed by other crimes, including the questions of what conduct is required to commit the offense and what culpable mental state is demanded. Often these crimes make clear that the legislatures intended to include within the crimes conduct by defendants that does not necessarily actually cause the ultimate harm with which the legislature was ultimately concerned but rather conduct that creates a sufficient risk that this harm will result. Thus the question sometimes becomes whether defendants have done enough to create a sufficient risk of that harm being caused.

Accessing as the Act Required

One common type of computer crime consists of using—or, often, "accessing"— a computer for the purpose of committing a criminal offense. Section 502(c)(1) of the California Penal Code is an example of this sort of offense.

A major question concerning the scope of liability under these offenses is what constitutes the prohibited act of "accessing." The principal case reprinted next—*State v. Allen*—raises this as well as other issues.

The meaning of accessing was addressed generally in *State v. Rowell*, 121 N.M. 111, 908 P.2d 1379 (1995), a prosecution under that portion of the New Mexico Computer Crimes Act creating the crime of "accessing" a computer with the intent to commit fraud. The prosecution's evidence showed that Rowell telephoned victims misrepresenting himself to be a lawyer distributing an award from a class action lawsuit and asking the victims to send a cash advance for expenses. It also showed that Rowell's telephone calls were processed by various computerized switches. Consequently, the prosecution contended, by placing the telephone calls Rowell accessed computers and because he did this with intent to commit fraud he committed a computer offense. Under the statute, "computer" does not include "any * * * device which might contain components similar to those in computers but in which the components have the sole function of controlling the device for the single purpose for which the device is intended * * *." N.M. Stat. § 30-45-2(B). Rowell's conviction was reversed. The switches in the telephone equipment, the court reasoned, were used only for a single purpose of processing telephone calls and the computerized components performed the sole function of controlling the switches for that purpose. Moreover, this result is consistent with the legislative purpose in enacting the Computer Crimes Act, which was to punish and deter crimes committed through the abuse of computer sophistication. Rowell's use of the telephone system was not conduct of this sort and was more like "persons who drive cars with computer 'brains' on their way to committing a larceny."

In the course of its discussion, the New Mexico court discussed and distinguished other cases relied upon by the prosecution as supporting its contention that Rowell's use of the telephone system and its computerized switches was a computer crime:

> [A] few other jurisdictions have held that particular uses of a telephone may constitute the accessing of a computer. In *Commonwealth v. Gerulis*, 420 Pa.Super. 266, 616 A.2d 686 (1992), appeal denied, 535 Pa. 645, 633 A.2d 150 (1993), the court held that accessing a "voice mailbox" was accessing a computer because the mailbox was created by a computer, and messages in the mailbox were stored on computer disks. In *People v. Johnson*, 148 Misc.2d 103, 560 N.Y.S.2d 238 (N.Y. City Crim.Ct.1990), the court held that the use of a telephone credit card number was not the mere use of a solitary telephone "but rather a telephone inextricably linked to a sophisticated computerized communication system." Finally, in *State v. Riley*, 121 Wash.2d 22, 846 P.2d 1365 (1993), the Washington Supreme Court held that the switch used to process telephone calls was a computer under the Washington statute.
>
> Although cited by the State, these cases do not support its position. The defendant in *Gerulis* had used a telephone to access computer-generated voice mailboxes. She then entered data into the mailboxes and changed the password for each so that the authorized users could not gain access to them. It was defendant's manipulation of the voice mailbox that violated the Pennsylvania statute, not the mere use of the telephone. Similarly, the defendant in *Johnson* was convicted of

unauthorized use of a computer. Johnson was charged with illegally accessing the long-distance network with stolen calling-card numbers. In this situation the telephone network—the computers that operate the system—was the "victim" of the crime. Finally, the defendant in *Riley* used a computer and modem to enter random six-digit numbers at forty-second intervals into a local telephone company's general access number in an attempt to discover long-distance access codes. The court held that, in accessing the company's long distance switch, Riley had accessed a computer. The court expressly stated, however, that his actions "were not equivalent to placing a telephone call." We conclude that, although these cases are similar to Rowell's and shed some light on the nature of computer crimes, they are not determinative. All three of these cases involved the manipulation of computer technology and abuse of that technology for the defendants' gain. By contrast, the computer network in this case was a passive conduit through which the defendant's criminal activity passed. Thus, instead of supporting the State's position, these cases actually undermine its position.

Accessing Particular Information or Software

Computer crime statutes attempt to define and penalize access to computers under certain circumstances. However, when is access impermissible and thus possibly a crime?

If a person has legitimate access to a particular piece of computer hardware, that is, a computer or computer terminal, can that person commit computer crime by accessing specific information by means of that computer?

The issue was raised in *People v. Lawton*, 48 Cal.App.4th Supp. 11, 56 Cal.Rptr.2d 521 (1996). Defendant Jeffrey Lawton, an unemployed aerospace software engineer, was charged with unauthorized access to a computer or computer system or network under subdivision (c)(7) of California Penal Code section 502. The Ventura County Library Services Agency uses a mainframe computer with more than 200 terminals. Some of these terminals are located in the Camarillo Public Library and are available for use by library patrons for the sole purpose of accessing the computerized catalog of books. The prosecution's evidence showed that Lawton used library terminals to access more than the catalog and achieved access to both the operating system (UNIX) and the "Universe," or database, level. Lawton argued that one who uses a computer terminal with permission cannot violate subdivision (c)(7) by using that terminal to access levels of software beyond the scope of the permission given. The crime can only be committed by achieving unauthorized access of computer *hardware*, he contended. Rejecting this, the court noted that computer systems and computer networks as defined by the statute consist of both hardware and software. Although Lawton had permission to use the hardware he used—the terminal—he did not have permission to access the software in the agency's computer system or network. Explaining further its result, the court continued:

[Lawton's] interpretation would * * * clash * * * with the overall statutory intent to comprehensively protect the integrity of private, commercial and governmental computer systems and data.

[A]dopting [Lawton's] argument would carve a giant loophole in the statute not intended by its drafters. Public access computer terminals are increasingly common in the offices of many governmental bodies and agencies, from courthouses to tax assessors. We believe subdivision (c)(7) was designed to criminalize unauthorized access to the software and data in such systems, even where none of the other illegal activities listed in subdivision (c) have occurred.

To the extent that "mere browsing" in this fashion may cause little or no harm, the statute appropriately sets modest penalties for unaggravated behavior [of this sort].

Other statutes make this result clearer. Under the federal statute, for example, most violations are provided for in terms requiring that the person either access a computer without authorization or exceed authorization to access the computer. Whatever questions arose under the California statute on the facts of *Lawton*, it seems clear that Lawton exceeded his authorization to access the computer at issue in that case.

State v. Allen

Supreme Court of Kansas, 1996
260 Kan. 107, 917 P.2d 848.

LARSON, Justice:

In this first impression case, we are presented with the question of whether a person's telephonic connections that prompt a computer owner to change its security systems constitute felony computer crime * * *.

[Anthony A. Allen was charged under K.S.A. 21-3755, which provides:

(b) Computer crime is:

(1) Intentionally and without authorization gaining or attempting to gain access to and damaging, modifying, altering, destroying, copying, disclosing or taking possession of a computer, computer system, computer network or any other property * * *.

Computer crime which causes a loss of at least $500 is a felony. The complaint alleged that Allen

did then and there intentionally and without authorization gain access and damage a computer, computer system, computer network or other computer property which caused a loss of the value of at least $500.00 but less than $25,000.00 * * * .]

The charges against * * * Allen arose from several telephonic connections he made with Southwestern Bell Telephone Company's computers in early 1995. After preliminary hearing, the trial court dismissed the complaint, finding no probable cause existed to believe Allen had committed any crime.

The State has appealed * * *.

Allen admitted to Detective Kent Willnauer that he had used his computer, equipped with a modem, to call various Southwestern Bell computer modems. The telephone numbers for the modems were obtained by random dialing. If one of Allen's calls were completed, his computer determined if it had been answered by voice or another computer. These were curiosity calls of short duration.

The State presented no evidence which showed that Allen ever had entered any Southwestern Bell computer system. Detective Willnauer was unable to state that Allen had altered any programs, added anything to the system, used it to perform any functions, or interfered with its operation. Willnauer specifically stated he had no evidence that the Southwestern Bell computer system had been damaged.

Ronald W. Knisley, Southwestern Bell's Regional Security Director, testified Allen had called two different types of

Southwestern Bell computer equipment—SLC-96 system environmental controls and SMS-800 database systems.

The telephone numbers for the SLC-96 systems were thought to be known only to Southwestern Bell employees or agents on a need-to-know basis. Access to the SLC-96 systems required knowledge of a password. If one connected to the system it displayed "KEYWORD?" without any identification or warning. No evidence existed that Allen attempted to respond to the prompt.

Testimony confirmed Allen also called and connected 28 times with the SMS-800 systems at several different modem numbers. Each call but two was under 1 minute. Upon connection with this system, a person would see a log on request and a "banner." The banner identifies the system that has answered the incoming call and displays that it is Southwestern Bell property and that access is restricted. Entry into the system itself then requires both a user ID and a password which must agree with each other. No evidence indicated Allen went beyond this banner or even attempted to enter a user ID or password.

Knisley testified that if entry into an SMS-800 system were accomplished and proper commands were given, a PBX system could be located which would allow unlimited and nonchargeable long distance telephone calls. There was no evidence this occurred, nor was it shown that Allen had damaged, modified, destroyed, or copied any data.

James E. Robinson, Function Manager responsible for computer security, testified one call to an SMS-800 system lasted 6 minutes and 35 seconds. Although the system should have retained information about this call, it did not, leading to speculation the record-keeping system had been overridden. Robinson speculated Allen had gained entry into the system but admitted he had no evidence that Allen's computer had done anything more than sit idle for a few minutes after calling a Southwestern Bell modem number.

Robinson testified that Southwestern Bell was unable to document any damage to its computer equipment or software as a result of Allen's activities. However, as a result of its investigation, Southwestern Bell decided that prudence required it to upgrade its password security system to a more secure "token card" process. It was the cost of this investigation and upgrade that the State alleges comprises the damage caused by Allen's actions. Total investigative costs were estimated at $4,140. The cost of developing deterrents was estimated to be $1,656. The cost to distribute secure ID cards to employees totaled $18,000. Thus, the total estimated damage was $23,796.

In closing arguments, the State admitted Allen did not get into the computer system, nor did he modify, alter, destroy, copy, disclose, or take possession of anything. Instead, the State argued Allen's conduct in acquiring the unlisted numbers and calling them constituted an "approach" to the systems, within the meaning of K.S.A. 21-3755(a)(1), which questioned the integrity of the systems and resulted in the altered or added security precautions.

In its oral ruling, the trial court noted K.S.A. 21-3755 was unclear. The court then held the mere fact Allen made telephone calls, a legal activity, which resulted in the connection of two modems, was insufficient to prove he had "gained access" to Southwestern Bell's computer systems as the * * * charge required. In addition, the court held Southwestern Bell's investigative expenses and voluntary security upgrade costs did not constitute damage to the computer systems or other property as defined in the statute.

The legal standard to be applied in a preliminary hearing is clear. If it appears from the evidence presented that a crime has been committed and there is probable cause to believe the defendant committed it, * * * the defendant [is to] be bound over for trial. If there is not sufficient evidence, the defendant must be discharged. From the evidence presented, the trial court must draw the inferences favorable to the prosecution, and the evidence need only establish probable cause. "Probable cause at a preliminary hearing signifies evidence sufficient to cause a person of ordinary prudence and caution to conscientiously entertain a reasonable belief of the accused's guilt."

Felony computer crime as it is charged in this case * * * required the State to prove three distinct elements: (1) intentional and unauthorized access to a computer, computer system, computer network, or any other property (as property is defined in [the statute]); (2) damage to a computer, computer system, computer network, or any other property; and (3) a loss in value as a result of such crime of at least $500 but less than $25,000. The trial court found that the State failed to show probable cause as to each of these elements.

Did the trial court err in ruling there was insufficient evidence to show Allen gained "access" to Southwestern Bell's computers?

After finding the evidence showed Allen had done nothing more than use his computer to call unlisted telephone numbers, the trial court ruled there was insufficient evidence to show Allen had gained access to the computer systems. Although a telephone connection had been established, the evidence showed Allen had done nothing more. The trial court reasoned that unless and until Allen produced a password that permitted him to interact with the data in the computer system, he had not "gained access" as the complaint required.

The State argues the trial court's construction of the statute ignores the fact that "access" is defined in the statute as "to approach, instruct, communicate with, store data in, retrieve data from, or otherwise make use of any resources of a computer, computer system or computer network." By this definition, the State would lead us to believe that any kind of an "approach" is criminal behavior sufficient to satisfy a charge that Allen did in fact "gain access" to a computer system.

The problem with the State's analysis is that [the statute] does not criminalize "accessing" (and, thus, "approaching") but rather "gaining or attempting to gain access." If we were to read "access" in this context as the equivalent of "approach," the statute would criminalize the behavior of "attempting to gain approach" to a computer or computer system. This phrase is lacking in any common meaning such that an ordinary person would have great difficulty discerning what conduct was prohibited, leading to an effective argument that the statute was void for vagueness.

The United States Department of Justice has commented about the use of "approach" in a definition of "access" in this context: "The use of the word 'approach' in the definition of 'access,' if taken literally, could mean that any unauthorized physical proximity to a computer could constitute a crime." National Institute of Justice, Computer Crime: Criminal Justice Resource Manual, p. 84 (2d ed.1989).

We read certain conduct as outside a statute's scope rather than as proscribed by the statute if including it within the statute would render the statute unconstitutionally vague. Consequently, although K.S.A. 21-3755 defines "access," the plain and ordinary meaning should apply rather than a tortured translation of the definition that is provided.

* * *

Webster's defines "access" as "freedom or ability to obtain or make use of." Webster's New Collegiate Dictionary, p. 7 (1977). This is similar to the construction used by the trial court to find that no evidence showed that Allen had gained access to Southwestern Bell's computers. Until Allen proceeded beyond the initial banner and entered appropriate passwords, he could not be said to have had the ability to make use of Southwestern Bell's computers or obtain anything. Therefore, he cannot be said to have gained access to Southwestern Bell's computer systems as gaining access is commonly understood. The trial court did not err in determining the State had failed to present evidence showing probable cause that Allen had gained access to Southwestern Bell's computer system.

Did the trial court err in ruling that no evidence showed Allen had damaged any computer, computer system, computer network, or any other property?

The State acknowledges it cannot meet the damage element of the crime it has charged by any means other than evidence showing Allen's actions resulted in expenditures of money by Southwestern Bell. It is crystal clear there is absolutely no evidence Allen modified, altered, destroyed,

copied, disclosed, or took possession of anything. The State's evidence clearly shows Allen did not physically affect any piece of computer equipment or software by his telephone calls. All the State was able to show was that Southwestern Bell made an independent business judgment to upgrade its security at a cost of $23,796. The State argues this is sufficient.

The State's argument is clearly flawed. The trial court reasoned by a fitting analogy that the State is essentially saying that a person looking at a no trespassing sign on a gate causes damage to the owner of the gate if the owner decides as a result to add a new lock. The trial court has clearly and correctly pointed to the correct analysis of this issue.

The State's circular theory is that if someone incurs costs to investigate whether an activity is criminal, it becomes criminal because investigative costs were incurred. Although computer crime is not, for obvious reasons, a common-law crime, it nevertheless has a common-law predicate which helps us to understand the legislature's intent. K.S.A. 21-3755 was not designed to update criminal trespass or malicious mischief statutes to the computer age but "to address inadequacies in the present theft statute related to prosecution of computer related crimes. Specifically, present theft statutes make prosecution difficult among crimes in which the computer owner was not actually deprived of the computer or its software."

Theft * * * is not concerned with mere occupation, detention, observation, or tampering, but rather requires [a risk of] permanent deprivation. The intent required for theft is an "intent to deprive the owner permanently of the possession, use, or benefit of the owner's property." One may have wrongful intent, such as intent to trespass, without having the intent required for a theft. In addition, at common law, the thing of which the victim was deprived had to be something of value. The second element of computer crime mirrors this common-law requirement of the deprivation of something of value in a larceny action. As in a larceny action, the extent of the deprivation determines the severity level of the crime. This element of computer crime, as with other theft statutes, cannot be satisfied where there is no deprivation as in this case.

* * *

Southwestern Bell's computer system was not "damaged" in the sense the statute requires. Southwestern Bell was not deprived of property in the manner required to support a criminal charge. The fact an independent business judgment that Southwestern Bell's computer systems might be accessible was made after Allen's conduct was discovered does not support the second and third elements of the crime charged. The trial court correctly determined the State failed to meet its probable cause burden on these issues as well.

Affirmed.

Note

Some computer offenses are clearly designed to protect the privacy of the subjects of information to which the computers permit access. Does a person commit a crime if the person uses a computer merely to get information about a subject and thus in some sense violates that subject's privacy?

The issue as it is presented by federal criminal law was raised in *United States v. Czubinski*, 106 F.3d 1069 (1st Cir. 1997). Czubinski, an Internal Revenue Service employee, was given access to the IRS computer system for purposes of responding to taxpayer inquiries concerning their returns. He used his access to browse through the returns of various persons who had made no inquiry of him, but the government's evidence failed to show that he either used the information he thus obtained for any particular purpose or intended to do so. He was convicted of violating the Computer Fraud and Abuse Act of 1986 by exceeding his authorized access to a computer covered by the federal statute, with intent to defraud, and thereby "obtaining anything of value." By the further explicit terms of the statute, the thing of value thus obtained must be something more than just the use of the computer. In the absence of any evidence showing that the information he obtained was rel-

evant to some sort of fraudulent scheme, the court held, the government failed to show that the information was a thing of value within the meaning of the statute. The fact that the information simply satisfied Czubinski's curiosity about the people involved was not sufficient to show that it was "of value" within the meaning of the statute.

If this situation had arisen so as to be subject to the California statute reprinted at page 284, would Czubinski have been guilty? Under section 502(c)(7), a person commits an offense if that person knowingly and without permission accesses any computer or computer system. Czubinski's permission to access the IRS computer was arguably limited to doing so as he perceived necessary to do his work, so the access proved by the government was without permission under the statute.

Congress responded to *Czubinski*, by passing the Taxpayer Browsing Protection Act in 1997. As a result, 26 U.S.C. § 7213A now imposes criminal liability upon any officer or employee of the United States who, except as authorized, willfully "inspect[s]" a federal tax return. The offense is punishable by not more than one year imprisonment, and any convicted federal employee must be dismissed.

F. ROBBERY

Robbery, a common law felony, is traditionally defined as a larceny aggravated by the fact that the taking of the property is from the person or in the presence of the owner by the use or the threatened imminent use of force. Under modern criminal codes, robbery often remains a separate and very serious offense. In fact, the seriousness of the offense has resulted in extensive litigation by defendants seeking to avoid conviction for it.

Robbery consists of some form of a property crime (or an attempt to commit such a crime) and what is generally a criminal assault or battery. Yet a robbery is treated far more seriously than either the underlying property or assaultive crime, or the combination of the two together. Why? Explaining why the Proposed Federal Criminal Code made robbery one of the few crimes carrying very high penalties, a staff member of the drafting Commission stated:

> The * * * great potentiality for violence and human harm is the most outstanding characteristic of the crime. * * * It is the willingness of a robber to use or threaten immediate injury for pecuniary gain and the inability of the ordinary citizen to defend himself against a sudden encounter with such violence which makes robbery one of the most terrifying crimes with which we must deal.

Milton Stein, Comment on Robbery: Section 1721, II Working Paper of the National Commission on Reform of Federal Criminal Laws 903, 906–07 (1970).

A major issue as to the conduct required for robbery is the proximity that must be shown between the use or threatened imminent use of force and the taking. This is considered in the principal case reprinted in Section 1; the court's opinion discusses the varying ways courts have addressed the matter.

Because robbery incorporates larceny, robbery as a general rule requires the intent to deprive as does larceny. Some jurisdictions, however, have adopted the view that robbery, although not larceny or theft, should cover all completed or attempted takings of property, if accompanied by force or threats, whether or not the person had the intent to permanently deprive the owner of that property.

Somewhat different issues are presented depending upon whether a prosecution is for robbery by force or robbery by threats. Consequently, this section treats these two aspects of robbery separately.

MODEL PENAL CODE[*]

Official Draft, 1985

§ 222.1. Robbery

(1) *Robbery Defined.* A person is guilty of robbery if, in the course of committing a theft, he:

    (a) inflicts serious bodily injury upon another; or

    (b) threatens another with or purposely puts him in fear of immediate serious bodily injury; or

    (c) commits or threatens immediately to commit any felony of the first or second degree.

    An act shall be deemed "in the course of committing a theft" if it occurs in an attempt to commit theft or in flight after the attempt or commission.

(2) *Grading.* Robbery is a felony of the second degree, except that it is a felony of the first degree if in the course of committing the theft the actor attempts to kill anyone, or purposely inflicts or attempts to inflict serious bodily injury.

1. Robbery by Force

When a criminal defendant's actions might constitute robbery only because of the defendant's use of force (rather than threats), two major issues might be posed. One is whether his or her actions constituted sufficient "force" to serve as the foundation for robbery. The other is whether there was a sufficient relationship between the use of that force and the actual or attempted taking of the property. The case reprinted next explores primarily the second issue, and the first is addressed in the notes that follow.

State v. Arlt

Intermediate Court of Appeals of Hawaii, 1992
9 Haw.App. 263, 833 P.2d 902.

ATANABE, Judge.

Jeffery Arlt (Defendant) appeals his September 24, 1991
conviction of First Degree Robbery. * * *

Facts

The facts in this case are essentially undisputed. In February
1990, Defendant, who had recently turned eighteen, and his
two friends, Charles and Chance Dunn, came to Hawaii
from California for a two-week vacation. On the evening of
February 28, 1990, after consuming several drinks at a luau,
Defendant and his friends decided to cap off the evening
with beer and tequila. The trio wandered into the Beach
Market superette on Ena Road in Waikiki to purchase the
liquor. When owner Suk Joo Kim (Kim) refused to sell the
boys the liquor without proper identification, Defendant
grabbed the bottle of tequila he had placed on the cash register counter and fled the store. Kim then pressed a silent
alarm button and told the Dunn brothers to wait until the
police arrived. The brothers, however, walked out of the
store shortly thereafter. Kim then changed from slippers to
sneakers, locked the store, and went looking for the boys.
Eventually, he caught up with the two brothers in a parking
lot about 100 meters from the store and asked them to sit
down and wait on the sidewalk area. Charles Dunn
remained seated, but Chance Dunn managed to run away.

Chance then found Defendant, and the two returned to
Kim. Chance took the bottle from Defendant and placed it
on a newspaper stand. When Kim asked for the bottle,
Defendant picked up the bottle and held it out to Kim saying, "here is your bottle." A "very angry" Kim extended his
hand to receive the bottle and said, "give me." At that point,
Defendant thought that Kim was going to hit him.
Defendant claims that he then swung the bottle in an
attempt to deflect Kim's arm. However, Kim ducked and the
bottle struck him on the head. The bottle broke, either
when it struck Kim's head or when it fell to the ground after
the blow.

The boys then fled in a panic and quickly hailed and
jumped into a taxi. Subsequently, Kim caught up with the
cab and jumped in front of it to block the boys' escape. The
police arrived immediately thereafter and arrested
Defendant and Charles.

* * *

On April 24, 1990, Defendant was indicted * * *. After
a jury trial in the First Circuit Court, Defendant was convicted as charged. Defendant was subsequently sentenced
to eight years' incarceration as a youthful offender and
ordered to pay $1,871.21 in restitution.

Defendant timely appealed * * *.

Discussion

* * *

Defendant's main point on appeal is that there was insufficient evidence at the trial to convict him of Robbery in the
First Degree.

Defendant was charged with violating HRS § 708-
840(1)(b)(i) (1985), which provides:

> **Robbery in the first degree.** (1) A person commits the
> offense of robbery in the first degree if, in the course of
> committing theft:
>
> . . . . .
>
> (b) He is armed with a dangerous instrument and:
> (i) He uses force against the person of anyone present
> with intent to overcome that person's physical resistance
> or physical power of resistance; . . .

In order to sustain a conviction * * *, four material elements must be proved beyond a reasonable doubt:

(1) That the defendant was in the course of committing
   theft;
(2) That the defendant was armed with a dangerous
   instrument;
(3) That the defendant used force against the person of
   anyone present;
(4) That the defendant did so with intent to overcome
   that person's physical resistance or physical power of
   resistance.

Defendant contends in substance that since the undisputed evidence shows that he stole the liquor bottle and
found his way to a place of temporary safety without use or
threat of force, and since any force or violence in the case
was used only after he was attempting to return the liquor
bottle to its owner, the crimes for which he should have
been charged were, at most, theft and assault, but not the
singular offense of robbery. In other words, Defendant contends that he was not "in the course of committing theft"
when he used force against Kim, and, therefore, the elements of First Degree Robbery have not been proved.

The State, on the other hand, argues that the theft was still in progress when Defendant struck the store owner, Kim. The State speculates that after Defendant stole the tequila, he returned to "free" his friend, Charles, who would be able to identify Defendant to police. The State contends that Defendant used the tequila bottle, a dangerous instrument, so he could effect a perfect getaway. Hence, the entire occurrence was a continuing transaction and Defendant was guilty of robbery.

The contentions of the parties require us to closely examine the nature of the crime of robbery, under the Hawaii Penal Code.

Under the common law, in order for a defendant to be guilty of robbery, the prosecution had to prove that the defendant took the property by means of force or violence or by putting the victim in fear. The force or intimidation employed was the gist of the offense. * * * The courts did not agree, however, as to whether the use of force or intimidation to retain possession of property taken or to facilitate escape, rather than to physically take the property, supplies the element of force or intimidation necessary to the offense of robbery.

Some courts held that the use of force or intimidation makes the offense a robbery only if it is used prior to or concurrently with the physical act of taking the property. Thus, the use of force closely following the moment when a thief gets his hands on the property may support a conviction of robbery on the ground that the force and taking were contemporaneous or parts of a single transaction. However, the use of force or intimidation to retain the property or attempt to escape with it will not supply the element of force or intimidation necessary to make the offense a robbery.

Other courts, employing a different perspective, generally regarded the occurrence as a continuing transaction. These courts thus held that the use of force or intimidation to retain property, or to effect the retention of property in an escape attempt, or even to escape after property taken has been abandoned, does supply the element of force or intimidation necessary to make the offense a robbery.

This conflict in case law was obviated by the Hawaii legislature when it enacted the Hawaii Penal Code, patterned after the Model Penal Code, in 1972. Specifically, the legislature enacted HRS § 708-842, which defines the phrase "in the course of committing a theft" for purposes of a robbery offense, as follows:

Robbery; "in the course of committing a theft." An act shall be deemed "in the course of committing a theft" if it occurs in an attempt to commit theft, in the commission of theft, *or in the flight after the attempt or commission.* [Emphasis added.]

The commentary to said section * * * states:

The nature and operation of this section is concisely explained by the Model Penal Code:

This provision is unusual only insofar as it makes classification of robbery depend in part on behavior after the theft might be said to have been accomplished. The thief's willingness to use force against those who would restrain him in flight strongly suggests that he would have employed it to effect the theft had there been need for it. No rule-of-thumb is proposed to delimit the time and space of "flight," which should be interpreted in accordance with the rationale. The concept of "fresh pursuit" will be helpful in suggesting realistic bounds between the occasion of the theft and a later occasion when the escaped thief is apprehended.

Previous Hawaii statutory law failed to provide a standard for the determination of the duration of the "theft" aspect of a robbery—a standard which is needed in order to determine when the employment of force or threatened force converts the "theft" into a "robbery." [Footnote omitted.]

The legislature thus clearly intended that in Hawaii, a robbery conviction may be predicated on the use or threatened use of force or violence to retain possession of stolen property during the flight after the theft. On this basis, the State argues that Defendant's flight after the theft commenced when he left the market and did not end until he got caught in the taxi. Defendant was therefore in the course of committing theft when he struck Kim with the stolen bottle.

The undisputed evidence indicates, however, that when Defendant fled the store with the stolen bottle, he used absolutely no force against Kim. Further, when Kim was struck, Defendant was not fleeing with the stolen property, but was actually returning the bottle to Kim. The bottle had previously been taken from Defendant's hands and placed on a newspaper stand. Moreover, Kim admitted that he asked Defendant to give him the bottle and stretched his hand to receive the bottle, before he was struck. Based on the factual circumstances shown on the record before us, we conclude that the theft of the tequila bottle was completed when Defendant snatched the bottle and left the store's premises without the use of force or threatened use of force. The force that Defendant subsequently used upon Kim did not occur "in the course of committing theft," but while Defendant was returning the bottle to Kim and, accordingly, did not convert the theft to robbery.

Other courts, confronted with similar situations, have reached a similar conclusion. In *State v. Jackson,*

40 Or.App. 759, 596 P.2d 600 (1979), for example, the defendant, using a tire iron, had broken open the glove box of victim's car which contained over $500, but had not taken it. While the victim was pulling the defendant from the car, the defendant hit the victim with a tire iron a number of times. The victim then wrestled the tire iron from the defendant, who fled. Oregon, like Hawaii, had adopted the approach of the American Law Institute (ALI) Model Penal Code under which theft becomes robbery if force is used either in the taking or in the retention of the property taken. Oregon had also expanded upon the ALI version by including attempts to commit theft within the scope of the crime of robbery. In concluding that robbery was not proved, the Oregon Court of Appeals said:

> This case does not involve force used in the course of attempting to commit theft. Rather, it involves force used in flight following an abandoned attempt to commit theft. There is no "retention" and hence no extension of the course of the attempt into the flight stage. Because the defendant had abandoned his attempt to commit theft prior to the use of force, his acts do not come within the requirement of the statute that force be used "in the course of committing or attempting to commit theft." In other words, for there to be robbery, there must be a relationship, not a mere concurrence, of force and theft. The revised statute merely extends that idea to the accomplishment of attempted theft and to the retention of the fruits of successful theft; it does not change the requirement that there be a connection between the two elements. Because in this case the force was not used until after the completion and termination of the attempted theft and because there were no fruits of the theft for defendant to use force to retain, the force did not occur "in the course of committing or attempting to commit theft."

Similarly, in *Ex parte Sapp*, 497 So.2d 550 (Ala.1986), the Supreme Court of Alabama held that robbery was not proved where a defendant left a store with a jacket, returned approximately five or ten minutes later wearing the jacket, and engaged in violence in attempting to escape thereafter. Applying a statute similar to HRS § 708-840(1)(b), the court held that:

> [t]he armed force . . . was not used "in the course of committing" the theft or "in immediate flight after the . . . commission," but took place after the theft itself clearly had ceased. In short, the statutes applicable here have not transposed theft into robbery.

Because there is insufficient evidence on the record to indicate that Defendant was "in the course of committing a theft" when he struck Kim, the elements of First Degree Robbery have not, as a matter of law, been proved. Defendant's conviction of First Degree Robbery must therefore be vacated.

* * *

The issue then arises as to what remedy is appropriate to correct Defendant's erroneous robbery conviction.

* * * [W]here there is a reversal of a conviction for insufficiency of evidence, the conviction can be modified to reflect a lesser crime for which there is evidence and which the fact finder necessarily found occurred, if the lesser crime was alleged in the accusatory instrument. * * *

In the case at bar, the indictment charged that Defendant was "in the course of committing theft" when he used force against Kim with intent to overcome Kim's physical resistance or his power of physical assistance, thereby committing Robbery in the First Degree. The jury's verdict that Defendant was guilty as charged makes clear that it found him guilty of Theft, a lesser-included offense of First Degree Robbery. Additionally, the trial court specifically instructed the jury that it could find Defendant guilty of Theft in the Fourth Degree, which was an included offense of Robbery in the Second Degree, which was in turn an included offense of Robbery in the First Degree. Therefore, Defendant had a fair adjudication of guilt on the crime of theft. Finally, Defendant has conceded that he was guilty of theft during his testimony at trial. There is thus sufficient evidence on the record to find Defendant guilty of Theft in the Fourth Degree.

We believe there is also sufficient evidence on the record to find Defendant guilty of Assault in the Third Degree. However, since Defendant was not specifically charged with Assault in the Third Degree, and since * * * Assault in the Third Degree is not a lesser-included offense of Robbery in the First Degree * * *, Defendant was never fairly put on notice that he could be convicted of assault. Therefore, we are unable to direct an entry of a judgment convicting Defendant of Assault in the Third Degree.

Conclusion and Order

We therefore vacate Defendant's conviction as to First Degree Robbery and * * * remand this case to the First Circuit Court with instructions to enter a judgment convicting Defendant of Theft in the Fourth Degree and resentencing him accordingly.

Notes and Questions

1. The policy rationale for expanding robbery in the manner described in *Arlt* was addressed in *State v. Handburgh*, 119 Wash.2d 284, 830 P.2d 641 (1992). In *Handburgh*, the defendant took a bicycle while the victim was elsewhere but used force when the victim

returned and sought to retrieve the bicycle. Nevertheless, the Washington Supreme Court construed its robbery statute as covering the situation. Force used to *retain* property *taken* under circumstances not constituting robbery, it held, was covered by its statute. Turning to the wisdom of such an approach, it continued:

> Commentators note this deviation from the common law and broadening of the definition of robbery is warranted and desirable, because " '[t]he thief's willingness to use force against those who would restrain him in flight suggests that he would have employed force to effect the theft had the need arisen.' " W. LaFave & A. Scott, Criminal Law § 8.11, at 786 (2d ed. 1986) (quoting 2 American Law Institute, Model Penal Code & Commentaries § 222.1, at 104 (Official Draft & Rev. Comments, 1980)).

2. A longstanding but continuing problem in robbery law is defining when a larceny or theft from the person of the victim—"pickpocketing" or "purse snatching"—constitutes robbery because the taking of the property is by force. The problem is illustrated by *Winn v. Commonwealth*, 21 Va.App. 179, 462 S.E.2d 911(1995), in which the facts were as follows:

> The victim was walking through the parking lot of a Ukrop's Grocery Store * * * at approximately 8:30 P.M. on November 13, 1993, after having purchased groceries. As the victim walked toward her car, accompanied by a Ukrop's employee, she heard footsteps behind her. Appellant appeared from behind the victim and "took" her purse from her. The purse strap, which was worn over the victim's shoulder, was "very strongly" removed and the purse taken from under her arm. The victim testified that there was no struggle between her and appellant and that the entire event lasted mere seconds. Although the victim and the Ukrop's employee immediately chased appellant, he escaped with the purse. He was thereafter apprehended.

In holding the evidence insufficient to convict Winn of robbery, the appellate court explained:

> "The touching or violation necessary to prove [robbery] may be indirect, but cannot result merely from the force associated with the taking." Instead, "[v]iolence or force requires a physical touching or violation of the victim's person." * * *

Appellant admits he took the victim's purse with the intent to steal it. The focus of appellant's insufficiency claim is based wholly upon the evidence related to proof of the essential element of robbery—that the actor used violence or intimidation directed against the victim to effect the taking. Appellant argues he used no more force than was necessary to accomplish the removal of the purse from the victim's shoulder and arm. Absent the violence/intimidation element, appellant contends he could only have been convicted of larceny from the person * * *, which carries a less severe punishment.

The Commonwealth asserts that because the victim testified appellant "took" her purse "very strongly" and ran with it, the trial court could have reasonably inferred appellant used violence to effectuate the taking. We disagree with the Commonwealth. Although no Virginia cases have decided whether a "purse snatching" is a robbery or a larceny from the person, we are guided by the decisions of other jurisdictions. Some states have held that the mere snatching of another's purse constitutes robbery, yet most states have determined that such a "sudden taking of property from the person of another does not in itself involve such force, violence, or putting in fear as will constitute robbery," and instead constitutes larceny. These jurisdictions have held that there must be "additional circumstances at the time of the snatching tending to transform the taking from a larceny to a robbery." For example, these circumstances are present when a struggle ensues, where the victim is knocked down, or where the victim is put in fear—in other words, where the defendant employs violence or intimidation against the victim's person. See, *e.g.*, *State v. Sein*, 124 N.J. 209, 590 A.2d 665, 668 (1991)(following "predominant view [that] there is insufficient force to constitute robbery when the thief snatches property from the owner's grasp so suddenly that the owner cannot offer any resistance to the taking"); *State v. Williams*, 202 Conn. 349, 521 A.2d 150, 155 (1987) (affirming robbery conviction where purse snatching left bruises on the victim's shoulder; jury could have inferred that the victim offered resistance to the force exerted to wrench the shoulder strap from her).

Under this general rule, the *Winn* court held, the facts failed to show robbery. No evidence proved that Winn touched the victim's person at any time or that the victim resisted the removal of the purse, it explained. The prosecution urged that the victim's testimony that the purse strap "was 'very strongly' removed" sufficed to show the use of force, but the court responded that "the 'very strong' force employed by appellant was the force necessary to remove the purse from the victim's shoulder, not the force associated with violence against or resistance from the victim."

2. Robbery by Threat

Robbery by threat poses issues analogous to those raised under robbery by force. Thus a major concern is what constitutes a threat sufficient for robbery, and this is explored in the following case.

Bivins v. Commonwealth

Court of Appeals of Virginia, 1995
19 Va.App. 750, 454 S.E.2d 741.

KOONTZ, Judge.

James Manuel Bivins (Bivins) appeals his conviction for robbery of a convenience store clerk. Bivins asserts that the evidence was insufficient to show that he accomplished the taking by intimidation, rendering his crime larceny rather than robbery. Clarifying our holding in *Harris v. Commonwealth*, 3 Va.App. 519, 351 S.E.2d 356 (1986), we agree and reverse Bivins' conviction.

In the early morning hours of August 22, 1992, Bivins entered the Orange Market in Roanoke County. After transacting some business with Donna LaPrade (LaPrade), the clerk, Bivins reached across the counter and took the cash drawer out of the register. As Bivins reached across the counter, LaPrade jumped back. She testified that she had been one foot away from Bivins and was "scared." [The relevant portion of the testimony is:

Q: What did you do when [Bivins] reached across the counter?

A: I jumped backwards.

Q: Why did you jump backwards.

A: Because I didn't know if he was going for me or if he was going for the cash drawer.

Q: How did you feel at that time?

A: Scared.]

On cross-examination, Laprade testified that she had previously described this incident to an investigating police officer as follows: "[Bivins] did it, he did it kind of easy—he just, you know, politely reached over the counter [and took the cash drawer]."

Robbery, a common law offense in Virginia, is defined as "the taking, with intent to steal, of the personal property of another, from his person or in his presence, against his will, by violence or intimidation." The act of violence or intimidation must precede or be concomitant with the taking. The alternative elements of violence or intimidation have been further defined as the use of "force, threat or intimidation."

Violence or force requires a physical touching or violation of the victim's person. The touching or violation necessary to prove the offense may be indirect, but cannot result merely from the force associated with the taking. *Johnson v. Commonwealth*, 65 Va. (24 Gratt.) 555, 557 (1873) (taking of money from hand of victim with no greater force than was required to take bills is larceny from the person). Threat requires an overt expression, by words or conduct, of a present intention to commit an immediate act of violence or force against the victim. The Commonwealth concedes that Bivins' actions did not constitute a use of violence, force or a threat. Accordingly, Bivins can only be guilty of robbery if the evidence shows that he accomplished the taking by intimidation.

Intimidation is defined as "[u]nlawful coercion; extortion; duress; putting in fear."[2] Black's Law Dictionary 831 (6th ed. 1990). "To take or attempt to take, 'by intimida-

---

[2] To avoid confusion, we note that "extortion," as used here, * * * is a separate crime from robbery, the distinction being the immediacy of the harm expressed or implied by the threat or intimidation. See, e.g., *State v. Planes*, 274 N.J.Super. 190, 643 A.2d 658, 660 (Law Div.1994) (threat of future harm is characteristic of theft by extortion, as opposed to robbery).

tion' means willfully to take, or attempt to take, by putting in fear of bodily harm." Id. at 822. Intimidation results when the words or conduct of the accused exercise such domination and control over the victim as to overcome the victim's mind and overbear the victim's will, placing the victim in fear of bodily harm. Intimidation differs from threat in that it occurs without an express threat by the accused to do bodily harm. *Commonwealth v. Brachbill*, 363 Pa.Super. 615, 527 A.2d 113, 116 (1987) ("the legal and common definitions of intimidation invoke a notion of conduct which is directed toward affecting future behavior whether or not a threat is part of that conduct").

The Commonwealth relies upon *Harris* for the proposition that "[t]here is no requirement in Virginia that the 'fear' induced by the defendant's intimidating words or conduct be judged by an objective standard of reasonableness." In *Harris*, the victim was harassed by three men, forced to submit to a search, and surrendered personal belongings at Harris' request. After the taking was completed, Harris threatened to shoot the victim. Harris asserted that none of the acts prior to or concomitant with the taking of the victim's property constituted threats of violence which intimidated the victim.

We held that the atmosphere of intimidation created by Harris and his companions, even if not accompanied by "[t]hreats of violence or bodily harm," was sufficient to prove that the taking was accomplished by intimidation. However, in *Harris* we went on to say that intimidation "must result from the words or conduct of the accused rather than the temperamental timidity of the victim." [S]ee also *People v. Flynn*, 123 Misc.2d 1021, 475 N.Y.S.2d 334, 337 (Sup.Ct.1984) ("[i]t is the actual behavior of any such persons, not their number or mere presence, that is determinative" of whether a robbery by force or intimidation is intended). Thus, where the victim's fear results from the taking itself, the taking is not accomplished through intimidation. The crime committed is larceny, not robbery. See *People v. Thomas*, 119 Ill.App.3d 464, 75 Ill.Dec. 1, 2, 456 N.E.2d 684, 685 (1983) ("the offense of robbery . . . is not related to the force used on the object taken but to the force or intimidation directed at the person of the victim").

Whether the subjective fear induced by the accused's actions facilitated the taking or merely resulted from the taking will depend on the facts of the individual case. The intent of the accused, if it is merely to take, while not determinative, is a factor in this calculus. Thus, in *Harris* we concluded that "the trier of fact was entitled to infer that [the victim] actually surrendered his property to Harris because of fear of bodily harm induced by Harris' intimidating words and conduct."

Here, LaPrade's fear, while believable, was based solely upon Bivins' sudden movement to seize the cash drawer. This action-reaction combination is comparable to an unresisted purse-snatching, rather than a robbery by intimidation.

LaPrade's assertion that she "didn't know if he was going for me or if he was going for the cash drawer" does not, as the Commonwealth asserts, show that Bivins' actions prohibited LaPrade from interfering with his taking the cash drawer.

Even viewing the evidence in the light most favorable to the Commonwealth, we hold that the record is insufficient to prove that Bivins accomplished a robbery by intimidation. Rather, his actions merely produced an understandable, subjective reaction of fear in the victim of a sudden and unexpected larceny. Her fear, while engendered by Bivins' conduct, was incidental to the crime itself. It arose from the victim's temperament rather than by design or conduct of the accused.

For these reasons we reverse Bivins' conviction for the "Orange Market" robbery and remand for further proceedings if the Commonwealth be so advised.

Reversed and remanded.

Notes and Questions

1. Robbery by threats is generally required to involve a threat of *immediate* harm, yet courts have been quite generous in permitting juries to infer such a threat. This is illustrated by *State v. Planes*, 274 N.J.Super. 190, 643 A.2d 658 (1994), in which the facts were as follows:

   > On the evening of September 13, 1992, Defendant, Raul Planes, and two confederates were in the process of burglarizing and stealing an automobile owned by Michael Boyajian. While his two confederates were engaged inside the automobile, Mr. Planes stood watch outside. Michele Zurn, a local resident, was out walking her dog and came upon the crime in progress. Mr. Planes turned to Ms. Zurn and said, "You better keep your mouth shut, or I'll get you. You got to walk that mutt sometime." * * * [When asked] "Did you feel frightened for your life?" Ms. Zurn responded, "Yes, this guy was acting drunk, God only knows if he was on drugs, I took it very serious."
   >
   > After the encounter with Mr. Planes, Ms. Zurn ran away, but managed to see Mr. Planes and his two confederates ride off in the stolen automobile. Ms. Zurn called the police. The automobile and its occupants were stopped soon thereafter, and Ms. Zurn made an on scene identification.

   Was this sufficient to at least create a jury issue as to whether Planes was guilty of robbery? The New Jersey court held that it was:

A person is guilty of robbery if, in the course of committing a theft, he: * * * threatens another with or purposely puts him in fear of *immediate* bodily injury * * *. N.J.S.A. 2C:15-1. (emphasis added)

The robbery provisions in the *New Jersey Code of Criminal Justice* and the *Model Penal Code* are substantially the same. The practice commentary to the *Model Penal Code* talks in terms of an immediate or imminent threat, either express or implied, calculated to communicate menace to the victim if the actor's wishes are not honored. The timing of the harm is crucial. The threatened harm must be more immediate than "future". A threat of "future" harm is characteristic of theft by extortion, as opposed to robbery. The question of when a threat is immediate or future, in the robbery context, has been dealt with in only a few reported decisions. * * *

In the case at bar, Ms. Zurn was frightened by Mr. Planes' threats and fled. It is not however, the fear created in Ms. Zurn that controls, but Mr. Planes' intent when he made those threats. The State must prove that it was Mr. Planes' purpose to convey to Ms. Zurn that immediate harm would result if resistance is encountered.

Mr. Planes issued these threats during the course of a theft, to a woman alone on a dark street, with an apparent purpose to facilitate the commission of a burglary and theft. He attempted to coerce Ms. Zurn into immediate and future silence concerning the criminality that she observed. These threats were calculated to create fear and even terror in Ms. Zurn. * * *

It is not required that Mr. Planes used threatening words of art. To judge a threat to another, in the robbery context, in technical terms of tense, syntax or grammar would allow too much leeway to an artful and articulate robber. The threat, in the totality of the circumstances presented, should be judged by a trier of fact.

Perhaps a jury might conclude that Planes intended only to convey to Ms. Zurn that, if at some future time she cooperated with authorities regarding the crime Planes and his companions were committing, he would harm her. If so, apparently the jury should not convict Planes of robbery. Defense counsel might argue in support of such a position that Planes did not fear that Ms. Zurn (even as assisted by her "mutt") would interfere with the crimes, as for exam-

ple by attracting the attention of others. Thus, defense counsel might contend, Planes had no reason to suggest to Ms. Zurn that he would do her immediate harm.

2. Traditional law requires that when the prosecution charges robbery by threat or intimidation, it must prove that the threat was successful in the sense that the victim was actually put in fear. In *People v. Davison*, 32 Cal.App.4th 206, 212, 38 Cal.Rptr.2d 438, 440 (1995), the court explained further: "Although the victim need not explicitly testify that he or she was afraid in order to show the use of fear to facilitate the taking, there must be evidence from which it can be inferred that the victim was in fact afraid, and that such fear allowed the crime to be accomplished." The result, however, may be different under modern statutes. The issue was presented in *State v. Birch*, 479 N.W.2d 284 (Iowa 1991), in which the facts were as follows:

[O]n July 24, 1990, at approximately 11:00 A.M., defendant entered a pharmacy in Cedar Rapids. He was wearing a mask at the time. He threw a bag on the counter and asked the pharmacist for certain prescription medications. He stated that "he didn't want anybody to get shot."

The pharmacist responded to defendant's request by inquiring how anyone would be shot, given the fact that defendant did not have a gun. At this point, defendant suggested that he had a gun concealed on his person. The pharmacist then requested to see the gun, and when it was not produced, ordered the defendant to leave the store. Defendant did then leave the store while the pharmacist was calling the police.

Birch was convicted of robbery under a statute that provided in part:

A person commits a robbery when, having the intent to commit a theft, the person does any of the following acts to assist or further the commission of the intended theft or the person's escape from the scene thereof with or without the stolen property:

1. Commits an assault upon another.

2. Threatens another with or purposely puts another in fear of immediate serious injury.

Noting that the first method of committing robbery requires an assault, the court observed that under Iowa law fear is "peculiarly attributable to the perpetration of an assault." If fear was required for the second method as well, the second method would be little different from the first. Therefore, a threat need not put the victim in actual fear, the court reasoned. Consequently Davison was found guilty of robbery, although he failed to make much of an impression upon the druggist.

Under such a statute, the focus is upon the thief's intent rather than the thief's success. Thus in *State v. Planes*, discussed in note 1, the court made clear that to establish a threat the prosecution must prove that it was the defendant's purpose to convey to the victim that immediate harm would result. If the defendant acted with such intent, it is of no consequence that the victim did not believe the defendant.

3. To the extent that robbery incorporates larceny (or, under modern statutes, theft), a showing of "claim of right" sufficient to require acquittal of larceny or theft (see the discussion at page 265) would logically seem to require the same result in robbery cases. Courts, however, have struggled to avoid applying claim of right law to robbery, as is illustrated by *Jupiter v. State,* 328 Md. 635, 636, 616 A.2d 412, 413 (1992). In *Jupiter*, the facts were as follows:

> After a day's duck hunting, and after helping three friends drink two and one-half cases of beer, * * * John Mitchell Jupiter (Jupiter), went to Captain John's Crab House and Marina and asked to purchase a six-pack of beer. Warren Yates (Yates), the owner of Captain John's, refused to do so. Yates told Jupiter that he was refused service because he was intoxicated. Jupiter then asked if Yates would sell him a single beer, and Yates again refused. Jupiter went to his vehicle parked outside and then reentered Captain John's carrying a shotgun. It was later determined that there was one shell in the chamber. Jupiter placed the shotgun on the counter, pointed it at Yates, and asked, "Are you going to sell it to me now?" Yates said, "Yes, sir," and produced a six-pack of Budweiser from a cooler behind the counter. Jupiter put a twenty dollar bill on the counter. Yates took the bill and gave Jupiter sixteen dollars change. An employee of Captain John's telephoned the police.

Convicted of robbery, Jupiter appealed. Rejecting his claim that he was entitled to acquittal, the court noted that Jupiter was visibly intoxicated and therefore Yates was prohibited by state statute from selling the beer to him. It then continued:

Jupiter * * * argues that he had a "claim of right" to the beer. * * * [He] * * * contends that those who force merchants of goods to sell their goods do not commit robbery because the merchants have been forced only to do what the merchants held themselves out as willing to do. The argument appears to be that Jupiter did not have the *mens rea* for robbery because he had a good faith claim of right to acquire the goods by paying for them; i.e., he relied upon the "supposed consent" of the seller to yield the goods upon tender of the full price.

* * * [C]laim of right as a defense to robbery has been limited * * *. There are strong public policy reasons why self-help, involving the use of force against a person, should not be condoned. For that reason most courts have tended to apply claim of right strictly under those circumstances. Courts have held that the defense does not apply unless the defendant was attempting to retrieve a specific chattel that was the subject of a prior claim of right; the defendant may not attempt to take money or property of equivalent value. Courts have held that the defense does not apply where the defendant attempted to retake the proceeds of illegal activity. A few courts have suggested that the claim of right defense should be abrogated altogether as a defense to robbery, although there is no consensus on this point.

These limitations on the defense are sometimes logically problematic. Courts rarely explain how removing the defense in robbery cases is consistent with the *mens rea* for the included crime of larceny, or why other criminal proscriptions, such as the ones against assault or extortion are insufficient deterrents. Nonetheless, the public policy underlying these decisions is sound. In a complex and crowded world, legal process is necessarily the preferred alternative.

We need not undertake to describe specific instances in which the claim of right defense should not apply to robbery, and we decline the State's invitation to abrogate the defense altogether. It is sufficient for the purposes of this case to hold that the defense is not applicable to robbery when the transaction that the robbery effects would be illegal even if it were consensual.

3. Carjacking

Editors' Note: "Carjacking" as a New Robbery-Like Offense

"Carjacking" as a separate crime is a fairly new development in criminal law. Generally, carjacking consists of taking a motor vehicle from the possession of another by force or intimidation. A number of states make this a separate offense that, as applied to many situations, obviously overlaps with robbery.

The Anti Car Theft Act of 1992 in a sense "federalized" this new offense. As a result of that legislation, a person commits a federal offense if

(a) he takes a motor vehicle from the person or presence of another (or attempts to do so);

(b) by force and violence or by intimidation;

(c) with the intent to cause death or serious bodily injury; and

(d) the motor vehicle has been transported, shipped, or received in interstate or foreign commerce.

18 U.S.C. § 2119. As a general matter, the federal crime is punishable by not more than 15 years imprisonment. If serious bodily injury results, the imprisonment may be for not more than 25 years and if death ensues the punishment may be imprisonment for up to life or death.

These new crimes are, in part, the result of legislative perception that existing robbery does not cover all of what has become an especially troublesome sort of criminal activity. In addition, however, creation of a new crime served as a means of increasing the penalties applicable to such conduct as was covered by prior law. The 1992 federal legislation was signed by a president who had previously asserted, "I want thugs who take cars at gunpoint to stay in a cell so long that when they get out they're too old to drive."

Mens Rea *Required*

Most versions of carjacking, like the federal statute, do not require that the perpetrator act with the intent to permanently deprive the victim of the property. To the extent that robbery requires such a culpable mental state, then, carjacking extends more serious criminal liability to conduct that previously was not robbery. Some versions of the crime stress this aspect. The California statute, Cal. Penal Code § 215(a), for example, defines the crime in terms of acting "with the intent to either permanently or temporarily deprive [the victim] of the motor vehicle." Maryland even more explicitly provides, "It is not a defense to the offense of carjacking * * * that the defendant did not intend to permanently deprive the owner of the motor vehicle." Md. Code, art. 27, § 348A(e).

The various state formulations of the offense differ from the federal crime in that state versions do not require "the intent to cause death or serious bodily injury" demanded by the federal offense. Many, such as the California statute, require only that the vehicle be taken "by means of force or fear"; these provisions may be construed as requiring that the defendant have intended either the use of force on, or the development of fear in, the victim, but not the more serious *mens rea* demanded by the federal offense. Virginia, however, arguably requires more than most states; it requires that if the taking is undertaken by threat it must be "by assault or otherwise putting a person in fear of serious bodily harm, or by the threat or presentation of firearms, or other deadly weapon." Alternatively, the taking can be accomplished by "by means of partial strangulation, or suffocation, or by striking or beating, or by other violence to the person." Va.Stat. § 18.2–58.1.

Because carjacking crimes borrow concepts and terminology from more traditional offenses, especially larceny and robbery, these new statutory crimes involve some of the same issues as have traditionally been presented by the older offenses. The background of these new crimes, however, may suggest a different resolution of the old issues than would be the case under traditional robbery or larceny law. This is presented, for example, by whether particular defendants have exercised sufficient control over the vehicle to complete the crime.

Seizure or Taking of Vehicle Required

The state versions differ in what they require be accomplished for the crime to be complete. The California version and many others require that the defendant have completed a "taking" of the vehicle. Virginia requires a "seizure or a seizure of control of a motor vehicle," while Maryland provides that the offense occurs when the perpetrator "obtained unauthorized possession or control of" the vehicle. Some but not all statutes are like the federal provision, and cover not only the successful taking but also an *attempt* to so take the vehicle. Obviously those statutes providing for liability for attempted takings are considerably broader than the others.

Carjacking is clearly an offense that is conceptualized in large part in terms of the assaultive aspect of the defendant's actions on the victim. Various versions differ, however, in what relationship of the victim to the vehicle is required. The federal statute requires only that the taking have been from "the person or presence of another." New Jersey and Virginia require that the victim have been "in possession or control of the vehicle." California, in contrast, requires either that the taking have been of a vehicle "in the possession of another, from his or her person or immediate presence" *or* of a vehicle "from the person or immediate presence of a passenger of the motor vehicle * * *." The significance of this explicit reference to passengers is addressed later in this note.

The New Jersey statute requires that the defendant, while in the course of an unlawful taking of a vehicle, use force upon an occupant or person in possession or control of the vehicle. In *State v. Williams*, 289 N.J.Super. 611, 674 A.2d 643, certif. denied, 145 N.J. 375, 678 A.2d 716 (1996), the victim was a passenger in the vehicle and—according to the defendant's version—when he was shoved by the defendant he had gotten out of the vehicle and was standing nearby. Even on the defendant's version of the facts, the court held, the victim was an "occupant" when he was shoved. Interpreting the statute so as to best achieve the legislature's broad aim "to enhance the punishment applicable to persons who use force or intimidation 'to gain possession of [a] motor vehicle,'" the court held that the victim need not be within the actual structure of the vehicle if the victim has temporarily stepped out of the car.

The courts have differed on how rigorously to interpret and apply the requirement of a taking or seizure of the vehicle. They vary particularly regarding the extent to which they interpret carjacking as similar to traditional crimes such as robbery.

In *Keyser v. State*, 22 Va.App. 747,473 S.E.2d 93 (1996), the court took a quite traditional approach. The victim had returned to her car, which she had left with the motor running and transmission in neutral. As she attempted to shut the car door, the defendant grabbed the door, pulled it open, and attacked the victim. She first tried unsuccessfully to get the car moving and then fended off the defendant with a pair of scissors. The statute requires that the defendant have seized the vehicle or seized control of it. Keyser's conviction was reversed because the evidence failed to establish that he completed a seizure of the car. Clearly the evidence showed an attempt to seize the car, but the court noted that the statute did not include an attempt to consummate a seizure.

In *People v. Montero*, 48 Cal.App.4th 1524, 56 Cal.Rptr.2d 303 (1996), vacated and remanded for reconsideration of another issue, —- Cal.4th ——, 66 Cal.Rptr.2d 122, 940 P.2d 709 (1997), in contrast, the court rejected traditional law as a basis for interpreting California's new carjacking statute. The victim was accosted by the defendant when the victim stopped his car at a stop sign. Ordered from his car, the victim as he got out used his knee to hit a "kill" switch hidden under the dashboard; this prevented the car from being started. The defendant got behind the wheel but was unable to start the car and unsuccessfully demanded that the victim tell him how to start it. Convicted of carjacking under the California statute, Montero noted that under California law both robbery and unlawful taking of a vehicle require some movement of the vehicle and argued that under the carjacking statute he could not have seized the car since he did not move it. Rejecting this contention, the court stressed that modern law has generally and wisely abandoned the common law's emphasis upon the need for some asportation to complete larceny or its modern equivalent. Especially in the carjacking situations, it stressed, movement of the car is not necessary to assure that the crime does not punish merely "bad thoughts." Montero's efforts to start the car demonstrated objectively violent conduct within the legislative contemplation, coupled with the necessary intent. The court added:

> Carjacking is a violent, assaultive crime, in which particularly vulnerable victims, trapped in their cars, are confronted, often, as here, with weapons, and forced from their cars. We are confident any carjacking victim, and the Legislature, would consider the carjacking complete where, as here, the victim is dragged from his car at knife point and driven away by pistol-whipping, abandoning his car to his attacker, who then tries to move it but is prevented from doing so by the victim's artifice in activating a kill switch. Whether the victim prevents the car's movement by taking his keys, or the attacker is so inept that he cannot start it before fleeing to avoid being caught makes no difference. Smaller, lighter personal property would always have been taken by that point. Only the car's bulk prevents it from being

taken without starting. Moreover, the terrorized victim who is forced to flee has lost his car just as surely as if he watches the attacker drive it away.

A "taking" under the carjacking statute, the court concluded, is satisfactorily proved by evidence of some movement or "seizure of possession and control by forceful dispossession of the victim's possession and control."

Multiple Convictions Permitted

The courts have tended to construe carjacking statutes so as to permit multiple convictions in some situations, apparently on the rationale that the legislatures intended to maximize the total criminal punishment that can be visited upon those who engage in this particularly reprehensible conduct. In *People v. Hamilton*, 40 Cal.App.4th 1137, 47 Cal.Rptr.2d 343 (1995), review denied (1996), the defendant held a gun on the driver of a Mercedes and his passenger, who had both just gotten out of the vehicle. The defendant was convicted of *two* carjackings, one involving the driver and the other the passenger. The court upheld the two convictions, noting that robbery case law permitted multiple convictions of robbery for the taking of one item from several victims and the apparent legislative intent to be no more lenient with carjackers than with robbers. Moreover, it held, the California carjacking statute specifically provides that a passenger is protected by the statute, and thus a passenger is a victim of carjacking just as is the driver from whom the vehicle is directly taken. Carjacking reflects legislative concern with the high risk of violence created by the situations covered, and if a vehicle has multiple occupants, all of the occupants are subjected to the risk that was the focus of legislative concern. Perhaps, however, other statutes that do not explicitly provide for protection of both those in possession *and* passengers would not be similarly interpreted.

In *Hamilton*, the prosecution argued that the legislative history of carjacking showed a legislative intent to punish carjacking as severely as possible. That this is the case, and that courts are tending to accept this as a basis for interpreting the statutes, is suggested by the interrelationship of new carjacking and old robbery.

Carjacking as Also Robbery

Many—but not all—carjackings are also robbery. If a particular perpetrator's actions constitute both robbery and carjacking, many jurisdictions will permit conviction for both. Some statutes seem to explicitly authorize this, as for example by specifying that a sentence for carjacking may be imposed to run consecutively to a sentence for another conviction arising out of the same conduct, Md. Code § 348A(d), or the same transaction, Mich. Stat. § 750.529a(2). The District of Columbia Court of Appeals, in the absence of such a provision, reached the same result, so a defendant can be convicted of both carjacking and robbery, *Pixley v. United States*, 692 A.2d 438 (D.C.App.1997) or both carjacking and unauthorized use of a vehicle, *Allen v. United States*, 697 A.2d 1 (D.C.App.1997).

Constitutionality of Carjacking Statutes

The effect of the carjacking statutes, of course, is often to dramatically increase the punishment for conduct that was previously punishable but at a lower level. In *Williams*, discussed earlier, the New Jersey court responded to Williams' contention that the mandatory penalties—imprisonment between 10 and 30 years with a 5-year disqualification from parole eligibility—violated the constitutional prohibition against cruel and unusual punishment:

> We are entirely satisfied that the punishment imposed by the statute conforms with contemporary standards of decency and is neither grossly disproportionate to the offense nor substantially unrelated to an appropriate penological objective. In reaching this conclusion, we afford substantial deference to the authority of the Legislature to determine the types and limits of punishments for crimes. We do not view the crime committed here as an isolated event unassociated with a pressing public problem. Carjacking is a calculated crime, and the Legislature could reasonably have concluded that the needs of society dictate that the punishment more nearly fit the offense than the offender. The Legislature clearly gave priority to punishment as a deterrent to others and as an aid to law enforcement. We find no illegality in the sentence imposed.

G. EXTORTION

Robbery and extortion are both aggravated forms of larceny. In the former the taking is from or in the presence of the person by means of violence or intimidation. However, where the intimidation is not a threat of immediate harm to the possessor or someone in her company or is not of physical harm, the surrender of the property in response would not constitute robbery. Extortion and blackmail statutes have been created to cover these situations. These very similar offenses have sometimes been distinguished by a statutory requirement that for extortion the accused be a public official, whereas blackmail involves acts by private citizens. Generally, however, the two terms are used interchangeably.

Extortion is commonly defined so as to be significantly broader than robbery in several ways. First, extortion often imposes no requirement that the threat be of immediate harm as is generally demanded for robbery. Second, the sorts of harm threatened that will suffice for extortion are generally much broader than the physical harm that must be threatened for robbery. Finally, robbery requires that the property be obtained or taken from the person or presence of the victim. Extortion imposes no such requirement.

Under modern statutes such as the Model Penal Code, theft by extortion provision, section 223.4, reprinted at page 282, extortion is made one type of theft and requires that the accused have actually obtained the property at issue. The New York larceny statute, for example, defines one manner of committing larceny by providing: "A person obtains property by extortion when he compels or induces another person to deliver such property to himself or to a third person by means of instilling in him a fear that, if the property is not so delivered, the actor or another will [do or cause certain things]." New York Penal Law section 155.05(e).

Often, however, the offense is structured so as to focus upon the threat rather than upon successful obtaining of the property. Thus the crime at issue in the case reprinted in this section criminalizes threatening another with the intent to achieve certain objectives, that is, to extort money or other advantages to cause the victim "to do an act against his will."

To the extent that an accused has employed threats of violence or of false accusations of crime it is relatively easy to understand why the conduct should be criminalized. However, what if the accused threatens to reveal the truth about the victim unless the victim acts to the benefit of the accused. Should not all persons have the right to make such truthful revelations? Indeed, some persons—journalists or informers for the Internal Revenue Service—are paid for it. Do not all persons have the right to seek recompense for being of service to others? The following case illustrates some of these quandaries.

State v. Harrington

Supreme Court of Vermont, 1969
128 Vt. 242, 260 A.2d 692.

HOLDEN, CHIEF JUSTICE.

The respondent John B. Harrington has been tried and found guilty of the offense of threatening to accuse Armand Morin of Littleton, New Hampshire, of the crime of adultery. The indictment charges that the threat was maliciously made with the intent to extort $175,000 and to compel Morin to do an act against his will in violation of 13 V.S.A. § 1701.[a]

* * * [T]he respondent challenges] the sufficiency of the evidence to sustain the conviction.

At the time of the alleged offense the respondent was engaged in the general practice of law in a firm with offices in Burlington, Vermont. Early in March, 1968, he was consulted by Mrs. Norma Morin, the wife of the alleged victim, Armand E. Morin. Mrs. Morin had separated from her husband because of his recent and severe physical abuse.

Prior to their separation they owned and operated the Continental 93 Motel in Littleton, New Hampshire, where the Morins maintained a residential apartment. The respondent learned the marital estate of the parties had a net value of approximately $500,000. Mrs. Morin reported to the respondent that her husband had also been guilty of numerous marital infidelities with different women at the motel. Mrs. Morin also disclosed that she had been guilty of marital misconduct which apparently had been condoned.

During the first conference the respondent advised Mrs. Morin that, because of her residence in New Hampshire, she could not undertake divorce proceedings in Vermont for at least six months and for her to obtain a divorce in New Hampshire it would be necessary that she obtain counsel from that state. Mrs. Morin indicated she wished to retain Mr. Harrington to represent her.

On one of the subsequent conferences a friend of Mrs. Morin's, who accompanied her to the respondent's office, suggested that an effort should be made to procure corroborative evidence of Mr. Morin's marital misconduct. To this end, the floor plan of the motel was discussed and a diagram prepared. At this time a scheme was designed to procure the services of a girl who would visit the motel in an effort to obtain corroborative evidence of Morin's infidelity.

---

[a] A person who maliciously threatens to accuse another of a crime or offense, or with an injury to his person or property, with intent to extort money or other pecuniary advantage, or with intent to compel the person so threatened to do an act against his will, shall be imprisoned in the state prison not more than two years or fined not more than $500.00.

After some screening, a Mrs. Mazza, who had been suggested by the respondent, was selected to carry out the assignment. The respondent explained to Mrs. Mazza the purpose of her employment and the results she was expected to accomplish and provided her with a "cover story" to explain her registration and presence as a guest at the Continental 93 Motel. Warning Mrs. Mazza against enticement and entrapment, the respondent instructed the employee to be "receptive and available," but not aggressive. The agreement with Mrs. Mazza was that she would be paid one hundred dollars at the time she undertook the assignment and one hundred dollars when her mission was completed.

Mrs. Morin was without funds at the time. A contingent fee agreement was signed by Mrs. Morin and the firm of Harrington and Jackson, by the respondent. The agreement was dated March 5, 1968 and provided that in the event a satisfactory property settlement was obtained, the respondent's firm was to receive twelve and a half percent of the settlement, in addition to reimbursement for expenses advanced by counsel. Electronic listening and recording equipment was ordered and delivered by air.

On the afternoon of March 6 the respondent and two office associates traveled to St. Johnsbury in two vehicles. Mrs. Mazza continued on to Littleton unaccompanied. She registered on arrival at the Continental 93 Motel under the name of Jeanne Raeder. She called the respondent at St. Johnsbury from a public telephone and informed him of her room number and location. Mrs. Mazza later delivered the key to her room to the respondent to enable him to procure a duplicate. The respondent, representing that he was a book salesman, registered at the motel and procured a room directly above that occupied by Mrs. Mazza. He was accompanied by a junior associate and an investigator,— both employed by the respondent's law firm.

During the next day Mrs. Mazza attracted Mr. Morin's attention. The sequence of events which followed led to an invitation by Morin for her to join him at his apartment for a cocktail. Mrs. Mazza accepted. Later she suggested that they go to her room because Mr. Morin's young son was asleep in his quarters. Morin went to Mrs. Mazza's room about midnight. Soon after the appointed hour the respondent and his associates entered the room. With one or more cameras, several photographs were taken of Morin and Mrs. Mazza in bed and unclothed. Morin grabbed for one camera and broke it.

During the time of her stay at the motel Mrs. Mazza carried an electronic transmitter in her handbag. By means of this device, her conversations with Morin were monitored by the respondent and his associates.

The respondent and his companions checked out of the motel at about one in the morning. Before doing so, there was a brief confrontation with Morin. According to Morin's testimony, the respondent demanded $125,000. Morin testified—"at that time I made him an offer of $25,000 to return everything he had, and in a second breath I retracted the offer."

The following day the respondent conferred with Mrs. Morin and reported the events of the trip to New Hampshire. He asked Mrs. Morin to consider reconciliation over the weekend. On March 11, 1968, Mrs. Morin informed the respondent she decided it was too late for reconciliation. With this decision, the respondent dictated, in the presence of Mrs. Morin, a letter which was received in evidence as State's Exhibit 1. * * *

The communication is designated personal and confidential. The following excerpts are taken from the full text:

[The initial paragraphs propose a separation agreement and a Mexican divorce based on incompatibility.]
"Mrs. Morin is willing to give up the following:
"1. All of her marital rights, including her rights to share in your estate.
"2. All of her right, title, and interest, jointly or by reason of marital status, that she has in and to, any or all property of the marriage, including the Continental 93 Motel, the three (3) farms in Vermont, the capital stock that you own, the house in Lindenville, the joint venture in land in East Burke, all personal property except as is specifically hereinafter mentioned and in short, all rights that she may now have or might acquire in the future, as your wife. Furthermore, any such settlement would include the return to you of all tape recordings, all negatives, all photographs and copies of photographs, that might in any way, bring discredit upon yourself. Finally, there would be an absolute undertaking on the part of your wife not to divulge any information of any kind or nature which might be embarrassing to you in your business life, your personal life, your financial life, of your life as it might be affected by the Internal Revenue Service, the United States Customs Service, or any other governmental agency."

The letter goes on to specify the terms of settlement required by Mrs. Morin, concerning custody of the minor child, her retention of an automobile and the disposition of certain designated personal effects. It further provides:

"5. Mrs. Morin would waive all alimony upon receipt of One Hundred Seventy Five Thousand Dollars ($175,000)—."

The sum of $25,000 is specified to be paid at the signing of the separation agreement, with the balance due according to a schedule of payments over the period of eighteen months.

The letter continues:

"— At the present time Mrs. Morin is almost without funds. She did have the $200 that you gave her when she left and she does have the $1500 in Canadian bills from the 'found' money. Because of her shortage of money, and, because she is badly missing David, and finally, because she cannot continue for any substantial period of time to live in the present vacuum, the writer must require prompt communication from you with respect to the proposed settlement contained herein. This letter is being dictated on March 11 and you should have it in your possession by March 13, at the latest. Unless the writer has heard from you on or before March 22, we will have no alternative but to withdraw the offer and bring immediate divorce proceedings in Grafton County. This will, of course, require the participation by the writer's correspondent attorneys in New Hampshire. If we were to proceed under New Hampshire laws, without any stipulation, it would be necessary to allege, in detail, all of the grounds that Mrs. Morin has in seeking the divorce. The writer is, at present, undecided as to advising Mrs. Morin whether or not to file for 'informer fees' with respect to the Internal Revenue Service and the United States Customs Service. In any event, we would file, alleging adultery, including affidavits, alleging extreme cruelty and beatings, and asking for a court order enjoining you from disposing of any property, including your stock interests, during the pendency of the proceedings.

"The thought has been expressed that you might, under certain circumstances, decide to liquidate what you could and abscond to Canada or elsewhere. The writer would advise you that this would in no way impede Mrs. Morin's action. You would be served by publication and under those circumstances, I am very certain that all property in New Hampshire and in Vermont, would be awarded, beyond any question, to Mrs. Morin.

"With absolutely no other purpose than to prove to you that we have all of the proof necessary to prove adultery beyond a reasonable doubt, we are enclosing a photograph taken by one of my investigators on the early morning of March 8. The purpose of enclosing the photograph as previously stated, is simply to show that cameras and equipment were in full operating order.—"

It was stipulated that the letter was received by Morin in Littleton, New Hampshire, "in the due course of the mail."

Such is the evidence upon which the respondent was found guilty. * * *

[T]he respondent maintains his letter (State's Exhibit 1) does not constitute a threat to accuse Morin of the crime of adultery. He argues the implicit threats contained in the communication were "not to accuse of the CRIME of adultery but to bring an embarrassing, reputation ruining divorce proceeding, in Mr. Morin's county of residence unless a stipulation could be negotiated." (Brief of Respondent-Appellant, p. 13.)

In dealing with a parallel contention in *State v. Louanis*, 79 Vt. 463, 467, 65 A. 532, 533, the Court answered the argument in an opinion by Chief Judge Rowell. "The statute is aimed at blackmailing, and a threat of any public accusation is as much within the reason of the statute as a threat of a formal complaint, and is much easier made, and may be quite as likely to accomplish its purpose. There is nothing in the statute that requires such a restricted meaning of the word 'accuse'; and to restrict it thus, would well nigh destroy the efficacy of the act."

The letter, marked "personal and confidential," makes a private accusation of adultery in support of a demand for a cash settlement. An incriminating photograph was enclosed for the avowed purpose of demonstrating "we have all the proof necessary to prove adultery beyond a reasonable doubt." According to the writing itself, cost of refusal will be public exposure of incriminating conduct in the courts of New Hampshire where the event took place.

In further support of motion for acquittal, the respondent urges that the totality of the evidence does not exclude the inference that he acted merely as an attorney, attempting to secure a divorce for his client on the most favorable terms possible. This, of course, was the theory of the defense.

At the time of the writing, the respondent was undecided whether to advise his client to seek "informer fees." One of the advantages tendered to Morin for a "quiet" and "undamaging" divorce is an "absolute undertaking" on the part of the respondent's client not to inform against him in any way. The Internal Revenue Service, the United States Customs Service and other governmental agencies are suggested as being interested in such information. Quite clearly, these veiled threats exceeded the limits of the respondent's representation of his client in the divorce action. Although these matters were not specified in the indictment, they have a competent bearing on the question of intent.

Apart from this, the advancement of his client's claim to the marital property, however well founded, does not afford legal cause for the trial court to direct a verdict of acquittal in the background and context of his letter to Morin. A demand for settlement of a civil action accompanied by a malicious threat to expose the wrongdoer's criminal conduct, if made with intent to extort payment, against his will, constitutes the crime alleged in the indictment.

The evidence at hand establishes beyond dispute the respondent's participation was done with preconceived design. The incriminating evidence which his letter threatens to expose was wilfully contrived and procured by a temptress hired for that purpose. These factors in the proof are sufficient to sustain a finding that the respondent acted maliciously and without just cause, within the meaning of our criminal statutes. The sum of the evidence supports the further inference that the act was done with intent to extort a substantial contingent fee to the respondent's personal advantage.

* * * The evidence of guilt is ample to support the verdict and the trial was free from errors in law.

Judgment affirmed.

Notes and Questions

1. Although defendant Harrington did not put his argument in these terms, he was actually contending that he had (or should have had) a defense of claim of right, as would be available under the last paragraph of section 223.4 of the Model Penal Code, reprinted on page 283. Some state's statutory provisions for extortion or its equivalent make express provision for such a defense. Vermont, of course, had no such statutory defense. Perhaps, however, the court could have read a defense of this sort into the statute, possibly by holding that a defendant who acts pursuant to a claim of right does not threaten "maliciously" as required by the statute.

2. As the court recognized in *State v. Greenspan*, 92 N.C.App. 563, 374 S.E.2d 884 (1989), American jurisdictions that recognize a claim of right defense consisting of proof that the defendant actually—and perhaps reasonably—believed that he was entitled to the money or property he sought to obtain by the threat made are particularly reluctant to apply it to situations in which the defendant fails to show a firm and objective basis for believing that he had a legal right to the specific sum of money or property he sought.

   Greenspan was shown to have contacted a person who had made harassing telephone calls to

Greenspan and to have offered not to press criminal charges if that person would pay him a specified amount of money. Greenspan was convicted of a crime consisting of "threatening * * * with the intention thereby wrongfully to obtain anything of value." He claimed that the requirement of an intent to obtain *wrongfully* the money at issue was not met, because he believed he was entitled to the money as compensation for the wrong done to him by the person threatened. Rejecting Greenspan's contention, the court explained:

   > Among those jurisdictions that have recognized the defense, it has most often been recognized in cases where, assuming that the victim was in fact guilty, the defendant was clearly entitled to some form of compensation. The cases cited by defendant are illustrative. In *State v. Burns*, 161 Wash. 362, 297 P. 212, aff'd per curiam on rehearing, 161 Wash. 362, 1 P.2d 229 (1931), the defendant demanded the return of funds that had been embezzled by the victim. In *Mann v. State*, 47 Ohio St. 556, 26 N.E. 226 (1890), the defendant demanded compensation for property destroyed by the victim. In the present case, however, defendant's entitlement to any money from the victim would depend upon defendant's ability to prevail in a civil action for damages. Even assuming that defendant could prevail in such an action, the amount of damages he would recover is a matter of speculation; yet the evidence shows that defendant asked for the specific sums of $750 and $500.

3. The breadth of extortion crimes has caused several courts to declare at least parts of these crimes unconstitutional as criminalizing speech protected by the First Amendment to the United States Constitution. In *State v. Weinstein*, 182 Ariz. 564, 898 P.2d 513 (Ariz.App.1995), for example, the Arizona court held unconstitutional an extortion statute defining the crime as obtaining or seeking to obtain property or services by means of a threat to "[e]xpose a secret or asserted fact, whether true or false, tending to subject anyone to hatred, contempt or ridicule or to impair his business or credit." Noting that the legislature had considered and failed to enact a provision like that in the Model Penal Code creating a defense of honest claims of restitution or indemnification, the court noted that if enforced as written the crime would create felony liability for:

- a homeowner to notify his contractor that if the contractor does not arrange to have a subcontractor return to fix shoddy work, he will report him to the Registrar of Contractors;

- a new car owner, frustrated with the repeated breakdown of his vehicle, to inform the dealer that if the dealer does not replace the car or refund his money, he will report him to the Better Business Bureau and write a letter informing his friends not to patronize the dealership;

- a store owner to tell a customer to pay a delinquent bill or else he will report the customer to a credit reporting agency;

- an attorney to send a demand letter on behalf of a client stating that the recipient must perform certain duties under a contract or face suit;

- a mother to inform her former husband that if he does not pay back child support, she will report him to the court, where he risks incarceration.

Chapter 11

CRIMES AGAINST THE HABITATION

CHAPTER CONTENTS

At common law there were two felony offenses designed to protect the special sense of security placed in the dwellings. These crimes—burglary and arson—are the subject of this chapter. Other prohibitions such as criminal trespass and malicious mischief may today be employed to protect this same interest but they are not defined in terms of dwellings as the specific object of concern. As is developed later in this chapter, even burglary and arson are now often so broadly defined that they are arguably mischaracterized under present law as offenses against the habitation.

A. BURGLARY

Editors' Introduction: Traditional Burglary Issues

The elements of burglary at common law were: (a) a breaking and (b) entering of (c) the dwelling of (d) another (e) at night (f) with the intent to commit a felony within. Each of these elements was of importance and the subject of significant litigation.

As can be seen from the Model Penal Code provision that follows and the case reprinted in this section, the elements of burglary have been greatly altered by modern statutes. The result of these changes is often to expand very significantly the behavior covered by the crime.

Perhaps this expansion of burglary has made it into a crime without an adequate rationale. The question was discussed in *People v. Salemme*, 2 Cal.App.4th 775, 3 Cal.Rptr.2d 398 (1992) review denied. Salemme was convicted of burglary on proof that he entered the victim's home with intent to therein commit the offense of selling him fraudulent securities. Rejecting Salemme's claim that this stretched burglary beyond acceptable scope, the court responded:

> It is true that * * * one of the purposes of California's burglary laws is to protect against the dangers to personal safety created by the "usual burglary situation." However, * * * the primary purpose is to protect a possessory right in property. Thus if there is an invasion of the occupant's possessory rights, the entry constitutes burglary regardless of whether the actual or potential danger exists.
>
> * * *
>
> In effect, defendant would write into [the burglary statute] the requirement that the perpetrator must intend to commit a felony which poses a physical danger to the victim, rather than "any felony" as specified by the Legislature. This interpretation is not compelled by the purpose of the burglary statutes * * * and would constitute impermissible judicial legislation. Moreover, it creates an unworkable test. Whether a felonious entry poses a physical danger to the victim is fact specific; it depends not on the particular felony, but on the sophistication of the perpetrator, the potential for detection, and the reactions of the victim and perpetrator if the felonious purpose is detected. It is not unreasonable to envision a fraudulent securities transaction where, upon probing questioning about the purchase, the victim discovers the illegality, attempts to call the police, and is attacked by the perpetrator. Other than speculation, how is one to determine whether such a potential threat existed in this case? On the other hand, there are residential burglaries which pose no physical danger to the victim, as where the perpetrator breaks into a house knowing the occupants are away on vacation. Would defendant argue this is not a burglary simply because it poses no physical threat to the victims?

Justice Blease, one member of the court, added for himself:

> Although the burglary statute is aimed at protecting a possessory interest of the occupant in property, neither the statute nor the cases which interpret it limit the offense to the situation in which that interest is invaded. * * *
>
> The consequences are visited upon the defendant in this case. The offense of sale of fraudulent securities ordinarily, as here, poses no threat to the security or other property interest of the occupant of the structure in which the offense fortuitously is committed. Nonetheless the entry of the structure with the intent to do so is burglary. By this measure a burglary would occur in most cases of a completed security fraud since the commission of the fraud is most likely conducted indoors in a structure within the compass of the burglary statute.

* * * [S]uch a result strike[s] me as arbitrary. That could be avoided if the specific property interests of the occupant in personal safety and the protection of the property and its contents were made the purpose of the burglary statute. I differ with my colleagues in their apparent conclusion that the sale of fraudulent securities to an unsuspecting occupant who consented to the entry invades a property interest in the structure entered. * * * [S]weeping offenses such as security fraud into the domain of burglary [also results in] the untoward application of the serious felony sanctions and the limitation on discretion to grant probation which attend burglary of an inhabited dwelling. These heavy penalties are trivialized when they are imposed because of the happenstance that an offense, no more culpable by reason of the locale, occurs in a residence.

Nevertheless, the statute and the case law are to the contrary. * * *

Traditional law limited burglary in a number of ways, although modern criminal law has modified most of these limitations. The two subsections that follow raise several limiting aspects of traditional burglary: the requirement that entry be by "breaking" and the need for "entry" into at least a protected portion of premises protected by the crime. Several additional traditional limitations, however, can be considered somewhat more summarily.

Requirement That the Place Entered Be the Dwelling of Another

The common law offense of burglary was limited to entries of dwellings. Although modern statutes do not limit burglary to entry of such structures, burglary of dwellings or structures used for living purposes is often treated more seriously. Even in this context, the common law concept of a dwelling has generally been rejected.

Perkins v. State, 682 So.2d 1083 (1996), illustrates the problem. Perkins was convicted of second degree burglary, consisting of burglary of a dwelling. The house he entered had been built in 1953 by the present owner and was unoccupied at the time of the entry. The owner lived in the house for many years, but moved out several months before the entry. He had no intent to return to the house as an occupant; he periodically rented the house, however, and hoped to rent or sell it in the future "for someone to live in." Holding that Perkins could be convicted of burglary of a dwelling, the court explained:

Prior to 1982, the courts had to rely on the common law definition of "dwelling" as that word was used in the statutory crime of burglary of a dwelling. For example, in *Smith v. State*, 80 Fla. 315, 85 So. 911 (1920), we held that under the common law a house was not a "dwelling" where the owner, who had occupied the home with his family, had moved out nine months before the burglary. We focused on the requirement that the house be occupied or that the owner intend to return in explaining the common law:

Temporary absence of the occupant does not take away from a dwelling house its character as such, but it must be made to appear that such occupant left the house animo revertendi ["With intention to return." Black's Law Dictionary, 80 (5th ed. 1979)] in order to constitute an unlawful breaking and entry of the house during such absence burglary.

(citations omitted). Thus, we held that the common law definition of "dwelling" contemplated that a structure be occupied and not merely capable of or suitable for occupation. However, [the burglary statute] was amended in 1982 and now provides in pertinent part:

> "Dwelling" means a building or conveyance of any kind, either temporary or permanent, mobile or immobile, which has a roof over it and is designed to be occupied by people lodging therein at night, together with the curtilage thereof.

Under the statutory definition, *Perkins* held, the "design[]" of the building controls and occupancy is not critical. Because the structure entered by Perkins was clearly designed to be occupied by persons overnight, it was held a dwelling even though the owner in a sense abandoned it.

The common law crime also covered other structures related to the main house and within the "curtilage"—the area immediately surrounding and used in connection with the main living house. Because modern statutes almost always expand the crime to cover buildings or structures, this aspect of traditional burglary law has little current significance.

Modern statutes often expand the places covered to other "structures" and even places such as railroad cars and vehicles.

As developed in the second case reprinted here, *State v. Gregory*, the crime traditionally and currently often covered entering not only the covered places as a whole but also separate areas within the protected places.

Requirement That Entry Be in the Nighttime

Traditional common law burglary required that entry be in the nighttime. The traditional approach to determining whether an entry was in the nighttime for burglary purposes was taken in *State v. Lefebvre*, 609 A.2d 957 (R.I.1992):

> The question presented by this case is whether the evidence was sufficient to establish that the breaking and entering took place during the nighttime. The general rule is set forth in 2 Wharton's Criminal Law and Procedure § 431 at 54 (Anderson 1957):
>
>> "In the absence of statute, the determination of night is not the setting and rising of the sun. Instead, it is deemed day although the sun has not yet risen or after it has set, if it is sufficiently light to discern a person's face. That is, visibility by daylight determines the existence of day."

In the case at bar [victim] Martel testified that when she became aware of defendant's presence, it was dark outside but she was able to see in her bedroom from the light cast by a street lamp that was located directly in front of the house and shone into her bedroom. All evidence concerning time was approximate.

The trial justice took judicial notice that the time of sunrise on the day in question was 5:13 A.M. This court [has] in determining whether an offense had been committed in the nighttime, used as an aid G.L.1956 § 31-24-1, which required that vehicle lights shall be displayed from one-half hour after sunset until one-half hour before sunrise. Applying this aid to the determination of the ability to discern a person's face, we are of the opinion that the state's evidence was sufficient to survive a motion for judgment of acquittal.

Probably the two major issues in burglary law concern the means by which entry must be accomplished and the conduct necessary to complete the necessary entry. These are developed in the two subsections that follow. Modern burglary statutes, of course, often affect resolution of these issues. Many such statutes follow the approach of the Model Penal Code provision reprinted next. Where entry on real estate or into a structure is not burglary, it is often a less serious offense frequently called trespass. The Code's trespass provision is therefore also reprinted.

MODEL PENAL CODE*

(Official Draft, 1985)

§ 221.0. Definitions

In this Article, unless a different meaning plainly is required:

(1) "occupied structure" means any structure, vehicle or place adapted for overnight accommodation of persons, or for carrying on business therein, whether or not a person is actually present.

(2) "night" means the period between thirty minutes past sunset and thirty minutes before sunrise.

§ 221.1. Burglary

(1) *Burglary Defined.* A person is guilty of burglary if he enters a building or occupied structure, or separately secured or occupied portion thereof, with purpose to commit a crime therein, unless the premises are at the time open to the public or the actor is licensed or privileged to enter. It is an affirmative defense to prosecution for burglary that the building or structure was abandoned.

(2) *Grading.* Burglary is a felony of the second degree if it is perpetrated in the dwelling of another at night, or if, in the course of committing the offense, the actor:

(a) purposely, knowingly or recklessly inflicts or attempts to inflict bodily injury on anyone; or

(b) is armed with explosives or a deadly weapon.

Otherwise, burglary is a felony of the third degree. An act shall be deemed "in the course of committing" an offense if it occurs in an attempt to commit the offense or in flight after the attempt or commission.

(3) *Multiple Convictions.* A person may not be convicted both for burglary and for the offense which it was his purpose to commit after the burglarious entry or for an attempt to commit that offense, unless the additional offense constitutes a felony of the first or second degree.

§ 221.2. Criminal Trespass

(1) *Buildings and Occupied Structures.* A person commits an offense if, knowing that he is not licensed or privileged to do so, he enters or surreptitiously remains in any building or occupied structure, or separately secured or occupied portion thereof. An offense under this Subsection is a misdemeanor if it is committed in a dwelling at night. Otherwise it is a petty misdemeanor.

(2) *Defiant Trespasser.* A person commits an offense if, knowing that he is not licensed or privileged to do so, he enters or remains in any place as to which notice against trespass is given by:

(a) actual communication to the actor; or

(b) posting in a manner prescribed by law or reasonably likely to come to the attention of intruders; or

(c) fencing or other enclosure manifestly designed to exclude intruders.

An offense under this Subsection constitutes a petty misdemeanor if the offender defies an order to leave personally communicated to him by the owner of the premises or other authorized person. Otherwise it is a violation.

1. The Breaking Requirement

Traditionally, burglary required that the entry be by breaking. Obviously the offense covered only the most egregious violations of the privacy of the dwelling. As the case in the next subsection illustrates, modern statutes often eliminate the requirement of a breaking. Given the definition of breaking, however, this is perhaps a less dramatic change than might first appear. Some jurisdictions, moreover, retain the requirement, at least for some burglary offenses.

As illustrated by the following case, modern burglary generally requires—as it did under the common law offense—that the accused have had the necessary intent to commit an offense at the time of the entry.

Bruce v. Commonwealth

Court of Appeals of Virginia, 1996
22 Va.App. 264, 469 S.E.2d 64.

ELDER, Judge.

Donnie Lee Bruce (appellant) appeals his conviction for breaking and entering his estranged wife's residence armed with a deadly weapon, with the intent to commit assault, in violation of Code § 18.2-91.[1] Appellant contends that the evidence was insufficient to prove the elements of the charge. Disagreeing with appellant, we affirm his conviction.

I. Facts

Appellant and Deborah Bruce (Deborah), although married, lived in separate residences during late 1993. Deborah lived with the couple's son, Donnie Bruce, Jr. (Donnie) and Donnie's girlfriend at Greenfield Trailer Park in Albemarle County, Virginia. Although appellant stayed with Deborah at the residence during a period of time in September or October of 1993, his name was not on the lease, he was not given a key to the residence, and he did not have permission to enter the residence at the time of the alleged offense.

On December 5, 1993, at approximately 2:00 P.M., Deborah, Donnie, and Donnie's girlfriend left their residence. Earlier that morning, Donnie told appellant that Deborah would not be home that afternoon. Upon departing, Donnie and Deborah left the front door and front screen door closed but unlocked. The front door lacked a knob but had a handle which allowed the door to be pulled shut or pushed open.

After Deborah, Donnie, and Donnie's girlfriend left their residence, a witness observed appellant drive his truck into the front yard of the residence and enter through the front door without knocking. Appellant testified, however, that he parked his truck in the lot of a nearby supermarket and never parked in front of the residence. Appellant stated that the front screen door was open and that the front door was open three to four inches when he arrived. Appellant testified that he gently pushed the front door open to gain access and entered the residence to look for Donnie.

While preparing to leave the residence, appellant answered a telephone call from a man with whom Deborah

was having an affair. The conversation angered appellant, and he threw Deborah's telephone to the floor, breaking it. Appellant stated that he then exited through the residence's back door, leaving the door "standing open," and retrieved a .32 automatic gun from his truck, which was parked in the nearby supermarket parking lot. Appellant returned to the residence through the open back door. Appellant, who testified that he intended to shoot himself with the gun, went to Deborah's bedroom, lay on her bed, and drank liquor.

When Deborah, Donnie, and Donnie's girlfriend returned to their residence, appellant's truck was not parked in the front yard. Upon entering the residence, Donnie saw that someone was in the bathroom, with the door closed and the light on. When police arrived soon thereafter, they found appellant passed out on Deborah's bed and arrested him.

On May 24, 1994, a jury in the Circuit Court of Albemarle County convicted appellant of breaking and entering a residence, while armed with a deadly weapon, with the intent to commit assault. Appellant appealed to this Court.

II. Proof of Requisite Elements

In order to convict appellant of the crime charged, the Commonwealth had to prove that appellant broke and entered into his wife's residence with the intent to assault her with a deadly weapon. Under the facts of this case, the Commonwealth satisfied this burden.

> Breaking, as an element of the crime of burglary, may be either actual or constructive. . . . *Actual breaking* involves the application of some force, slight though it may be, whereby the entrance is effected. Merely pushing open a door, turning the key, lifting the latch, or resort to other slight physical force is sufficient to constitute this element of the crime.

Bright v. Commonwealth, 4 Va.App. 248, 252, 356 S.E.2d 443, 445 (1987) (emphasis added). "Where entry is gained by threats, fraud or conspiracy, a *constructive breaking* is deemed to have occurred." *Jones v. Commonwealth*, 3 Va.App. 295, 299, 349 S.E.2d 414, 416–17 (1986) (emphasis added). "[A] breaking, either actual or constructive, to support a conviction of burglary, must have resulted in an *entrance* contrary to the will of the occupier of the house." *Johnson* [*v. Commonwealth*, 221 Va. 872, 876, 275 S.E.2d 592, 595 (1951)] (emphasis added).

Appellant's *initial entry* into Deborah's residence constituted an actual breaking and entering. Sufficient credible

---

[1] Code § 18.2-91 states, "[I]f any person [in the daytime breaks and enters a dwelling house] with intent to commit larceny, assault and battery or any felony other than murder, rape or robbery, he shall be guilty of statutory burglary." [Doing this with intent to commit murder, rape, or robbery is a more serious offense under Virginia law. Eds.]

evidence proved that appellant applied at least slight force to push open the front door and that he did so contrary to his wife's will. However, as the Commonwealth concedes on brief, appellant did *not* possess the intent to assault his wife with a deadly weapon at this time. The Commonwealth bears the burden of "proving beyond a reasonable doubt each and every constituent element of a crime before an accused may stand convicted of that particular offense." The Commonwealth therefore had to prove appellant intended to assault his wife when he re-entered the residence with his gun.

We hold that the Commonwealth presented sufficient credible evidence to prove the crime charged. On the issue of intent, the jury reasonably could have inferred that the phone call from Deborah's boyfriend angered appellant, resulting in his destruction of the telephone and the formation of an intent to commit an assault with a deadly weapon upon Deborah. Viewed in the light most favorable to the Commonwealth, credible evidence proved that appellant exited the back door of the residence, leaving the door open, moved his truck to a nearby parking lot, and re-entered the residence carrying a gun with the intent to assault Deborah.

Well-established principles guide our analysis of whether appellant's exit and re-entry into the residence constituted an actual or constructive breaking. As we state above an "[a]ctual breaking involves the application of some force, slight though it may be, *whereby the entrance is effected.*" "In the criminal law as to housebreaking and burglary, [breaking] means the tearing away or removal of any part of a house or of the locks, latches, or other fastenings intended to secure it, or otherwise exerting force to gain an entrance, with criminal intent. . . ." Black's Law Dictionary 189 (6th ed. 1990). Virginia, like most of our sister states, follows the view that "breaking out of a building after the commission of a crime therein is not burglary in the absence of a statute so declaring."[2] In this case, appellant *exited* the back door of the residence on his way to retrieve the gun from his truck. In doing so, the appellant did not break for the purpose of escaping or leaving. Rather, by opening the closed door, he broke in order to facilitate his re-entry. At

the time he committed the breaking, he did so with the intention of re-entering after retrieving his firearm. Although appellant used no force to effect his re-entry into the residence, he used the force necessary to constitute a breaking by opening the closed door on his way out. Even though no prior case involves facts similar to the instant case, the breaking and the entry need not be concomitant, so long as the intent to commit the substantive crime therein is concomitant with the breaking and entering.[3]

Sound reasoning supports the conclusion that a breaking from within in order to facilitate an entry for the purpose of committing a crime is sufficient to prove the breaking element of burglary. The gravamen of the offense is breaking the close or the sanctity of the residence, which can be accomplished from within or without. A breaking occurs when an accomplice opens a locked door from within to enable his cohorts to enter to commit a theft or by leaving a door or window open from within to facilitate a later entry to commit a crime. Professor LaFave states, "if one gained admittance without a breaking but committed a breaking once inside, there could be no burglary unless there then was an entry through this breaking . . . [and] the entry may be separate in time from the breaking." Wayne R. LaFave, Handbook on Criminal Law § 96, at 711 (1972).

Accordingly, a breaking occurred when appellant opened the back door of the victim's residence, even though the breaking was accomplished from within. Thus, because the evidence was sufficient to prove an intent to commit assault at the time of the breaking and the entering, the Commonwealth proved the elements of the offense. Thus, we affirm appellant's conviction.

Affirmed.

Notes and Questions

1. Traditional law found a constructive breaking when entry was accomplished with the consent of the occupants but that consent was obtained by fraud. Modern statutes dispensing with the need for a breaking nevertheless often require that the entry be

---

[2] "This is true because a common-law burglary required the breaking to be for the purpose of effecting an entrance, and not for the purpose of escape. * * *

As one noted scholar writes:

It was disputed whether one who gained entry without a breaking, but committed a breaking in order to leave, was guilty of burglary. The correct view was that of Hale, who explained that the burglary indictment charged "fregit intravit" (breaking and entering), so that "fregit & excivit" (breaking and leaving) would not suffice. This would also be in

accord with the rationale for requiring a breaking as part of the offense. . . . In this country, courts have continued to follow the original distinction in defining what constitutes a sufficient breaking.

Wayne R. LaFave, Handbook on Criminal Law § 96, at 709 (1972) (citations omitted).

[3] See Torcia, Wharton's Criminal Law § 321, at 247 ("The breaking and entering need not occur on the same night; the defendant may break on one night and enter on another night, so long as he enters through the opening made by his prior break.").

without effective consent. Where burglary statutes are broad enough to cover structures such as stores and businesses, a person who enters such premises during business hours generally does so with consent. Many jurisdictions nevertheless apply a version of the traditional fraud/constructive breaking rule and hold that a person who enters a place open to the public but conceals his or her intention to commit a crime in the premises has obtained no *effective* consent. The consent given, the courts hold, was obtained by fraud and thus was ineffective. See *Clark v. State*, 22 Va.App. 673, 472 S.E.2d 663 (1996), aff'd on rehearing en banc, 24 Va.App. 253, 481 S.E.2d 495 (1997).

2. The dwelling entered must be that of "another." This has been construed, however, to essentially mean *only* of another, because burglary is generally not committed if the person entering is a resident with a right to enter even if he or she enters with the intent to commit a crime against another person living there. Thus, one roommate who entered the living room of a shared apartment with the intent to commit a felony assault against another roommate who was there did not commit burglary. *People v. Gauze*, 15 Cal.3d 709, 125 Cal.Rptr. 773, 542 P.2d 1365 (1975).

The courts often hold that this exemption applies only if the accused had an absolute right to enter the place, and burglary is committed if that right is qualified or limited. If a defendant enters premises in violation of a court order giving the other spouse possession of those premises, his or her actions can constitute burglary. In *Peck v. State*, 539 N.W.2d 170

(Iowa 1995), for example, Peck's wife had begun a dissolution of marriage proceedings and caused him to be served with an order restraining him "from coming upon any premises occupied by the petitioner and minor children." Peck nevertheless returned to and entered the marital home three days after being served with the order and at a time when he knew his wife and children were there moving out. A jury could properly find that because of the court order, the court held, he had no right to enter the premises and thus was guilty of burglary in doing so.

Even in the absence of a formal separation, if a married couple has in fact separated so that the former marital abode is given to the separate possession of one spouse, the other spouse can commit burglary by entering that place. *Folsom v. State*, 668 So.2d 114 (Ala.Crim.App.1995) (jury properly found defendant committed burglary when he entered residence owned by wife and in which he had lived with her, because he had left the premises and returned the keys to her). In *Bruce*, the parties and the court assumed that the premises were the dwelling of Deborah Bruce and not the defendant, so the defendant could commit burglary by entering them.

These cases are arguably best read as dealing less with whether the place entered is that "of another" than with a requirement that the entry be trespassory or without right. Thus Gauze, in *People v. Gauze,* described earlier in this note, escapes conviction for burglary although he entered the dwelling of another because he entered that dwelling pursuant to his right to do so. His right to enter, in turn, was based upon his status as a co-resident of the premises.

2. The Requirement of "Entry" into a Protected Part of the Structure

Although burglary is generally thought of as entry into a structure as a whole, the offense can also be committed by entry into a part of a protected dwelling. This was the case at common law and is often made explicit in modern statutes. The rationale for this was explained by a California court in *People v. McCormick*, 234 Cal.App.3d 253 285 Cal.Rptr. 504 (1991), upholding a trial judge's instructions to the jury that in a prosecution for burglary by entering with intent to steal, "The intent [to steal the personal property of another] need not be in the mind of the person at the time of the initial entry into the structure, if he subsequently forms the intent and enters a room within the structure." Under the California statute defining burglary, the offense is committed by entry into a "room." The court continued:

[A]s our Supreme Court has stated: "'Burglary laws are based primarily upon a recognition of the dangers to personal safety created by the usual burglary situation—the danger that the intruder will harm the occupants in attempting to perpetrate the intended crime or to escape and the danger that the occupants will in anger or panic react violently to the invasion, thereby inviting more violence. The laws are primarily designed, then, not to deter the trespass and the intended crime, which are prohibited by other laws, so much as to forestall the germination of a situation dangerous to personal safety.'" Just as the initial entry into a home carries with it a certain degree of danger, subsequent entries into successive rooms of the home raise the level of risk that the burglar will come into contact with the home's occupants with the resultant threat of violence and harm. Applying the plain language of the statute therefore serves rather than frustrates the policy of the law.

What areas constitute separate parts of a dwelling or structure, sufficient so that entry into those parts of the dwelling or structure constitute burglary, has given rise to some difficulty. The principal case that follows raises such a problem.

The following case also presents the question of what constitutes the "entry" required for burglary. In *Hebron v. State*, 331 Md. 219, 627 A.2d 1029 (1993), the Maryland court noted that it had never been called upon to define entry as used in that state's burglary law. It continued, developing the general meaning of that term:

> The Commentators give the term a uniform meaning. According to Rollin M. Perkins and Ronald N. Boyce, Criminal Law, 253 (3rd ed. 1982), entry occurs when "any part of . . . [the trespasser's] person is within the house. . . ." LaFave and Scott proclaim that "[i]t [is] sufficient if any part of the actor's person intruded, even momentarily, into the structure." Wayne R. LaFave and Austin W. Scott, Jr., Substantive Criminal Law, 710 (1972). Put another way,
>
> > There is an entry when any part of the defendant's person passes the line of the threshold. Thus, there is an entry when the defendant, after opening a closed door, steps across the threshold; when, after breaking the glass of a door or window, he reaches inside to unlock the door or window or to steal property; when, in the course of breaking the glass of a door or window, his finger, hand, or foot happens to pass through the opening; or when, in the course of pushing open a closed door or raising a closed window, his finger or hand happens to pass the line of the threshold.
>
> 3 Charles E. Torcia, Wharton's Criminal Law, § 332, at 202–03 (14th ed. 1980) (footnotes omitted).
>
> Courts in other jurisdictions have similarly defined "entry." See, e.g., *Sears v. State*, 713 P.2d 1218 (Alaska 1986) (The intruder enters by entry of his whole body, part of his body, or by insertion of any instrument that is intended to be used in the commission of a crime). We hold that the term "entering," as used in [our burglary statute,] requires that some part of the body of the intruder or an instrument used by the intruder crosses the threshold, even momentarily, of the house.

The court also noted that in some jurisdictions the term entry is defined by statute, often as including entry by instruments varyingly described as " any part of any instrument" (Delaware) or "[a]ny physical object connected with the body" (Arizona).

State v. Gregory

Court of Appeals of New Mexico, 1993
Certiorari Denied, 1994
117 N.M. 104, 869 P.2d 292.

HARTZ, Judge.

Defendant appeals a judgment and sentence on one count of burglary * * *. We affirm.

The essential facts are undisputed. Defendant removed mail from Harry Parsons' post office box in the United States Post Office in Fort Sumner, New Mexico. The boxes are located in a lobby that is open to the public. The back of each box opens into the post office's mail sorting room, which is not open to the public.

NMSA 1978, Section 30-16-3 (Repl.Pamp.1984) states: "Burglary consists of the unauthorized entry of any . . . structure . . . with the intent to commit any felony or theft therein." Defendant contends that his conduct did not constitute burglary because the post office box is not a "structure" within the meaning of the statute.

We reject Defendant's argument. In *State v. Sanchez*, 105 N.M. 619, 621–22, 735 P.2d 536, 538–39 (Ct.App.), cert. denied, 105 N.M. 618, 735 P.2d 535 (1987), we held that a separately secured area of a building otherwise open to the public is a "structure" within the meaning of the burglary statute. See *State v. Harris*, 101 N.M. 12, 19, 677 P.2d 625, 632 (Ct.App.1984) (affirming separate burglary convictions when defendant broke into two different government agencies that were located in the same building); *State v. Ortega*, 86 N.M. 350, 524 P.2d 522 (Ct.App.1974) (affirming burglary convictions for breaking into locked storage lockers within a building). Here the separately secured area that constitutes a structure is the area consisting of the mail sorting room and the post office boxes.

Defendant's memorandum in opposition raises two factual questions. First, it argues that this Court does not know whether there is a door on the mail-sorting-room side of the mailbox. We find this assertion perplexing in light of the admission in Defendant's docketing statement that "the back of each mail box opens into the mail sorting room." Given that description, we conclude that the mail boxes and the sorting room are part of one structure.

Second, the memorandum contends that it is not known whether "it is physically possible to enter the sorting room through the mail box." Apparently he questions whether a person could get into the sorting room through a box. But the size of the box is irrelevant. A burglary can be accomplished by an entry through an opening that could not accommodate a human being. See *State v. Jacobs*, 102 N.M. 801, 802–05, 701 P.2d 400, 401–04 (Ct.App.1985) (burglary accomplished by lowering bomb through a roof vent).

Defendant also seems to suggest that the mail box and sorting room cannot be part of the same structure because the post office has no possessory interest in the box. We are not sure why that would be legally relevant if it were true, but it is patently false. The post office has a possessory interest in all of its premises.

Finally, we find this case clearly distinguishable from *State v. Bybee*, 109 N.M. 44, 781 P.2d 316 (Ct.App.1989). That decision held that a separately locked soft drink vending machine located outside a grocery store is not a "structure" protected by the burglary statute. The box here, however, unlike the vending machine, is not an isolated object. The back of the vending machine did not open into a room. We are not saying that a box itself is a structure; rather, the structure here is the area encompassing both the boxes and the sorting room.

Defendant's conviction is affirmed.

Notes and Questions

1. There is general agreement that entry can be by an instrument, although there is some difference of view on the circumstances under which this occurs:

   > At common law, the term "enter," when used in reference to the crime of burglary, had an established meaning. Under the common law definition of burglary, no "entry" occurs when an instrument is used solely to facilitate a

subsequent entry and not to achieve a criminal purpose inside the structure. Thus,

"there is no entry when a stick, being used by the defendant merely to break a window, happens to pass through the opening; when, after breaking the glass of a door or window, he pokes a stick inside for the purpose of unlatching the door; when the defendant throws a boulder at a window, and it smashes the window and lands on the inside, it having been thrown merely for the purpose of making an opening; or when the defendant, while standing outside, fires a bullet which smashes the lock of a door and lands inside, the gun having been discharged merely for the purpose of breaking the lock." 3 Wharton's *Criminal Law,* § 333 [(14th ed. 1980 & Supp. 1993)].

However, an "entry" does occur when an instrument intrudes into the structure for the purpose of consummating a criminal intent. Thus,

"there is an entry when the defendant, after breaking a window, pokes a stick inside for the purpose of impaling and stealing a fur coat; when, after breaking a window, the defendant pushes the barrel of a gun through the opening for the purpose of shooting and killing the occupant; *or when the defendant, while standing outside, fires a bullet which pierces a window and lands inside, the gun having been discharged for the purpose of killing the occupant.*" 3 Wharton's Criminal Law, supra, § 333. (Emphasis supplied.)

* * * We conclude that the term "entry," as used in the burglary statutes, is utilized in its common law sense. * * * Therefore, an "entry" can be accomplished by even the slightest intrusion into a building by any part of a person's body, or by an instrument, if the instrument is used to enable the person introducing it to consummate a criminal objective.

State v. Williams, 127 Or.App. 574, 578–79, 873 P.2d 471, 473–74, review denied 319 Or. 274, 877 P.2d 1203 (1994) (emphasis removed). Under the California burglary statute, however, entry can be by an instrument being used only to gain entry. *People v. Moore,* 31 Cal.App.4th 489, 491–92, 37 Cal.Rptr.2d 104, 105–06 (1994), review denied.

Under the general approach, entry occurs when the defendant inserts into the structure a part of the barrel of a gun, which he intends to use to shoot someone inside the structure. *State v. Barlowe,* 337 N.C. 371, 377, 446 S.E.2d 352, 356 (1994). *Williams* held that the defendant entered the home of a person who had testified against him by firing bullets into the home, because he did this with an intent sufficient to render his conduct tampering with a witness. The court observed:

Defendant complains that this holding is unduly broad, because it allows a person to be prosecuted for burglary if that person criminally harasses occupants of a house by shouting threats from the sidewalk, calling on the telephone or accessing a home computer. However, the question of whether an intangible medium such as sound waves or electronic impulses can accomplish an "entry" within the meaning of the burglary statutes is not before us at this time and is an issue on which we express no opinion.

2. Insofar as burglary applies to places other than structures, such as vehicles, the traditional definition of entry has to be somewhat modified. In *Braswell v. State,* 671 So.2d 228 (Fla.App.), review denied, 679 So.2d 773 (Fla.1996), the defendant reached into the open bed of a pickup truck and took an item. Did he commit burglary of the truck under a statute defining the offense as "entering * * * in * * * a conveyance with the intent to commit an offense therein?" After reviewing case law from other jurisdictions, the court held that Braswell did "enter" the truck. It declined to distinguish some other case as arising out of statutes defining the crime as entering a vehicle "or any part thereof." However, in *In re Young K.,* 49 Cal.App.4th 861, 57 Cal.Rptr.2d 12 (1996), the subject of the deliquency proceeding was alleged to be delinquent because he removed the headlights from a parked car. Because he committed "entry into the headlamp housings of an automobile to steal its headlamps," the prosecution claimed, he committed burglary of the vehicle. In response, the court explained:

According to the People, a forced entry into a headlamp housing with the intent to steal headlamps qualifies as an auto burglary * * * because this entry is akin to an entry into the "boundary" of a building in that it "passes the line of the threshold" of the vehicle * * *.

The flaw in the People's analogies is obvious. Under [our statutes], an entry into almost any four-sided structure is a burglary without regard to whether the structure was locked—but an entry into a vehicle is a burglary only if the vehicle was locked. For this reason, we need not engage in the mental gymnastics required to dissect rules regarding boundaries, reasonable expectations, or antiquated curtilage concepts to decide whether an "entry" into a car's headlamp housings constitutes a burglary.

Unlike the car's interior or its trunk, headlamp housings can be "entered" without regard to whether the car is locked, and we view the theft of headlights the same as we would the theft of windshield wipers or hubcaps. These are thefts (or attempted thefts) or auto tampering or acts of vandalism, not burglaries.

Suppose the statute had not required the vehicle to be locked? In *Braswell,* the court noted that under earlier Florida decisions "siphoning gasoline from an automobile did not constitute burglary of a conveyance, because there was no entry[;] stealing hubcaps did not establish burglary of a conveyance, because there was no entry[; but] lifting a radiator from an engine compartment of a vehicle lacking a hood did constitute burglary of a conveyance, because the statute requires entry of only a portion of the defendant's body into the vehicle."

B. ARSON

Arson at common law was the malicious burning of a dwelling of another. Dwelling was defined for purposes of arson, as it was for burglary, to include more than just residences. Outbuildings commonly associated with and in near proximity to the residence were held to be within the meaning of the term.

Perhaps the most troublesome aspect of the traditional crime was determining whether there was an actual "burning" of a part of a structure sufficient to give rise to the crime. The effect of modern statutes on this requirement is explored in *Lockwood v. State,* reprinted later in this subsection. Traditional arson required that the defendant act with the culpable mental state of "malice," which, like burning, was a term of art. This is addressed in the first case that follows.

Modern statutes often eliminate some of these problems by defining the offense not as causing any particular damage to or even an effect on the target property but instead as starting a fire with the intent of causing such harm. The Model Penal Code provision that follows is such a statute. Under these statutes, arson becomes a crime consisting of action that is viewed as posing a sufficient risk that the target harm will occur.

Some modern statutes expand the crime of arson to almost maximum conceivable breadth. California, for example, defines arson as including the "willful and malicious" burning of "any property." Cal.Penal Code § 451. "Property," in turn, is defined in § 450 as including "real property or personal property, other than a structure or forest land." In *People v. Reese*, 182 Cal.App.3d 737, 227 Cal.Rptr. 526 (1986), the defendant was convicted of felony murder in the course of arson; the arson relied upon by the prosecution was the defendant's burning of the clothing of the victim, and this was held within the terms of the statute.

MODEL PENAL CODE*

Official Draft, 1985

§ 220.1. Arson and Related Offenses

(1) *Arson.* A person is guilty of arson, a felony of the second degree, if he starts a fire or causes an explosion with the purpose of —

(a) destroying a building or occupied structure of another; or

(b) destroying or damaging any property, whether his own or another's, to collect insurance for such loss. It shall be an affirmative defense to prosecution under this paragraph that the actor's conduct did not recklessly endanger any building or occupied structure of another or place any other person in danger of death or bodily injury.

(2) *Reckless Burning or Exploding.* A person commits a felony of the third degree if he purposely starts a fire or causes an explosion, whether on his own property or another's, and thereby recklessly:

(a) places another person in danger of death or bodily injury; or

(b) places a building or occupied structure of another in danger of damage or destruction.

* * *

(4) *Definitions.* "Occupied structure" means any structure, vehicle or place adapted for overnight accommodation of persons, or for carrying on business therein, whether or not a person is actually present. Property is that of another, for the purposes of this section, if anyone other than the actor has a possessory or proprietary interest therein. If a building or structure is divided into separately occupied units, any unit not occupied by the actor is an occupied structure of another.

Richmond v. State

Court of Appeals of Maryland, 1992
326 Md. 257, 604 A.2d 483.

KARWACKI, Judge.

* * *

On February 5, 1987, a fire broke out in a two story apartment building located at Dallas Place in Temple Hills. The building contained approximately ten units. The fire originated in the ground floor apartment of Martha Gobert and quickly spread to the apartment located across a common hallway, occupied by Wanda Pfeiffer, and to the apartment located above the Gobert unit, occupied by Evelyn Saunders. All three apartment units were substantially damaged before the fire could be extinguished.

An official investigation of the fire disclosed that Guy L. Richmond, Jr., the appellant, had arranged for three of his confederates to set fire to Gobert's apartment. Richmond and Gobert worked for the same employer, and Richmond recently had been suspended from his job because of a work place grievance filed against him by Gobert.

On October 19, 1987, after a bench trial before the Circuit Court for Prince George's County, Richmond was convicted of three separate counts of [arson] * * * for procuring the burning of the "dwelling houses" of Gobert, Pfeiffer, and Saunders. Thereafter, he was sentenced to 15 years imprisonment on each count with the terms to run consecutively. * * *

[The Maryland arson statute, Maryland Code, Article 27, § 6 provides:

"Any person who wilfully and maliciously sets fire to or burns * * * any dwelling house, or any kitchen, shop, barn, stable or other outhouse * * * whether the property of himself, or of another, shall be guilty of arson, and upon conviction thereof, be sentenced to the penitentiary for not more than thirty years."]

* * *

Richmond contends that the burning of three apartments was the result of one criminal act, that it is but one offense proscribed by Art. 27, § 6 * * *.

It is manifest from the language employed in Art. 27, § 6 that the General Assembly intended the unit of prosecution to be "any dwelling house" burned. The issue before us is not thereby resolved, however, because the term "dwelling house" is not defined in the statute; we must determine whether each individual apartment unit burned constitutes a separate dwelling house.

* * * Maryland has retained the common law definition of arson in Art. 27, § 6. Sir William Blackstone explained the reasons why arson is considered such a serious crime:

"ARSON, ab ardendo, is the malicious and wilful burning of the house or outhouses of another man. This is an offense of very great malignity, and much more pernicious to the public than simple theft: because, first, it is an offense against that right, of habitation, which is acquired by the law of nature as well as by the laws of society; next, because of the terror and confusion that necessarily attends it; and, lastly, because in simple theft the thing stolen only changes it's [sic] master, but still remains in esse for the benefit of the public, whereas by burning the very substance is absolutely destroyed."

4 W. Blackstone, Commentaries *220. Thus, at common law, arson is an offense against the security of habitation or occupancy, rather than against ownership or property. 3 C. Torcia, Wharton's Criminal Law § 345 (14th ed. 1980). Expounding on what constitutes a "dwelling house," Blackstone stated that "if a landlord or reversioner sets fire to his own house, of which another is in possession under a lease from himself or from those whose estate he hath, it shall be accounted arson; for, during the lease, the house is the property of the tenant." 4 W. Blackstone, Commentaries *221–22 (footnote omitted). Thus, since each leased apartment is the property of a separate tenant, and a burning of that property, whether by the landlord or some other individual, constitutes arson, each separate apartment burned constitutes a separate unit of prosecution.

The language of Art. 27, § 6 further confirms the conclusion that each individual apartment burned constitutes a separate dwelling house and a separate offense of arson. Section 6 states that "[a]ny person who wilfully and maliciously sets fire to or burns or causes to be burned or who aids, counsels, or procures the burning of *any* dwelling house" shall be guilty of arson (emphasis added). We have previously construed the use of the word "any" in a criminal statute to mean "every" and to support a legislative intent authorizing multiple convictions. * * *

Richmond next contends that the State was required to prove that he possessed the specific intent to burn, or *mens rea* that the act of burning shall have been "wilful and malicious" as to each apartment unit * * *. The intent requirement as stated by Perkins and Boyce undermines that proposition:

"Lord Coke, writing in the early 1600's said that the 'law doth sometime imply, that the house was burnt maliciously and voluntarily,' giving as an illustration the instance of a fire spreading and causing damage beyond that actually intended. It is not common-law arson for a dweller to burn his own dwelling, and this has given rise to the outstanding example of unintentional arson; for if such a fire obviously creates an unreasonable fire hazard for other nearby dwellings, and any of these is actually burned, common-law arson has been committed even if the wrongdoer did not actually intend the consequence and may have hoped it would not happen. An intentional act creating an obvious fire hazard to the dwelling of another, done without justification, excuse or mitigation, might well be characterized as 'wilful' (a word of many meanings), and would certainly be malicious, but as the law has developed it is a mistake to assume that the phrase 'wilful and malicious,' when found in the definition of common-law arson, adds some distinct requirement not included in the word 'malicious' alone."

R. Perkins and R. Boyce, Criminal Law 274-75 (3d ed. 1982) (footnotes omitted). See M. Wingersky, Clark and Marshall on the Law of Crimes 898–99 (1958) ("[O]n the principle that a man is presumed to have intended the natural and probable consequences of his voluntary acts, if a man does an unlawful act, the natural tendency of which is to set fire to and burn a house, and such a consequence follows, the burning is to be regarded as intentional and malicious."); 3 C. Torcia, Wharton's Criminal Law, § 348 (14th ed. 1980) ("[T]he 'reckless' burning of the dwelling house of another may amount to arson, as where the defendant in burning his own house or other property on a windy day causes the dwelling house of another, which is in close proximity thereto, to be burned.") Consequently, setting a fire with reckless and wanton disregard for the consequences satisfies the wilful and malicious requirement of Art. 27, § 6. Clearly, setting fire to one apartment in a multiple unit apartment building satisfies this requirement. * * *

JUDGMENTS AFFIRMED, WITH COSTS TO BE PAID BY APPELLANT.

People v. Lockwood

Appellate Court of Illinois, 1992
240 Ill.App.3d 137, 608 N.E.2d 132, 181 Ill.Dec. 59.

Justice McMORROW delivered the opinion of the court:

Following a jury trial, defendant was convicted of aggravated arson and sentenced to 12 years imprisonment. On appeal, he contends that the State failed to prove him guilty beyond a reasonable doubt * * * .

The evidence adduced at trial is as follows. Gloria Snow testified that she lived in the first floor apartment of a building on North Harding Avenue in Chicago with her two daughters, Robresta and Aurelius; and that her granddaughter was visiting on the night of January 12, 1990. Shortly after 10 P.M., defendant, who had been dating Robresta, came to the apartment * * *. As defendant was leaving, Robresta arrived. They went into Robresta's room to talk, but within a short time they began fighting. When Gloria went to the room, she saw defendant "hitting [Robresta], shoving her around." After a struggle, Gloria came between him and Robresta and finally pressured defendant to leave. She then locked both the outer door to the building and the apartment door.

When the doorbell rang, Gloria looked out her living room windows from which the street and outer door to the vestibule of the building are visible, and saw defendant at the front door "laying" on the bell. Gloria knocked on the window and told him to stop ringing the bell and to leave. Defendant responded that he was going to stay there all night if necessary. While continuing to ring the bell, he said that if she did not allow Robresta to come out and talk to him, "I'm gonna take all of you out. I will get you out," and then he left. Approximately 30 minutes later, defendant returned and began ringing the bell again. He told Gloria to send Robresta out, but Gloria refused. Defendant then went to his car and took out a brown bag. He came to the front of the house and began shaking liquid on the sidewalk in front of the door and under the front windows. He also shook some liquid into the vestibule through the mail slot. He then gathered some leaves and paper and put them in a pile near the corner of the door, removed a lighter from the glovebox of his car, walked back to the house and set the papers and leaves on fire. Gloria saw flames from the pile of debris and smelled strong gasoline fumes. She hollered to Robresta to call the police. Defendant went to his car and started it, but a police car drove up, preventing him from leaving. One of the officers ran to the house and stomped out the fire.

At the time of these events, Katie Buckhalter, the owner of the building, and her daughter, Kimberly, were in their second-floor apartment. After the police arrived, Gloria and the Buckhalters went down the stairs to the vestibule. The hallway and the rug were flooded with gasoline and the door and floor were "black and burnt" [sic]. Gloria and Katie brought down cleaning supplies and mopped up the gasoline and scrubbed the floor and door. * * *

On cross-examination, Gloria stated that Robresta went down to the vestibule with a pot of water which she splashed on the fire in the hallway as the police officer was stomping on the fire outside. When she opened the door, the fire in the hallway "poofed up." The fire department was never called. After the police had interviewed everyone in the building, they left. Gloria believed at that time that "everything was over" and did not learn until later that they should not have cleaned the hallway. The linoleum in the hallway was not replaced after the incident. * * *

Robresta McSwain testified that [when she] opened the apartment door, the fire in the hallway "went up," and she almost fell into it because the hallway was filled with gasoline. She ran back into the apartment and filled a pan with water to pour on the fire. She also ran upstairs to alert the Buckhalters that there was a fire. After the police left, they cleaned up the gasoline and scrubbed the door. * * *

Officer Kostecki testified that he and his partner arrived at the scene within minutes of receiving a radio call. * * * When he saw that the front door of the building was on fire, he quickly exited his vehicle, went up to the door and stomped and beat out the fire. * * * After defendant was placed under arrest, Kostecki returned to the building. He recovered a rug, which was saturated and smelled of gasoline, from the vestibule. * * * On cross-examination, Kostecki stated he did not see any fire on the inside of the building. There was liquid on the floor but he did not know if it was gasoline or water.

* * *

William Tyrrell, employed as a technician with the police department crime laboratory testified that tests established that a soil sample and the antifreeze container recovered from the scene contained gasoline. He also tested the hallway rug and found the presence of gasoline. On cross-examination, Tyrrell stated that he did not conduct tests to determine the amount of gasoline in or on any of the items. Following Tyrrell's testimony, the State rested.

* * *

Defendant * * * contends that his conviction for aggravated arson was improper because the State failed to prove an essential element of the offense. Specifically, with reliance on *People v. Oliff* (1935), 361 Ill. 237, 197 N.E. 777 * * *, defendant asserts that the State was required to prove that the building was burned. He argues that the evidence established only that a fire was started on the ground outside of the front door and that it was stomped out by a police officer before any burning damage occurred.

In *Oliff* the defendant argued that the charred and scorched condition of the ceiling, walls and floor of a building was not sufficient to constitute a burning necessary to prove arson. The supreme court held that for there to be a burning there must be a wasting of the fibers of the wood, no matter how small in extent. The *Oliff* court further stated that the charring of a wall or floor is sufficient to constitute a burning.

* * *

Although we believe that the evidence, reviewed below, was sufficient to satisfy the definition of a burning under *Oliff,* defendant's argument that the "essential element of burning" was not proved, misapprehends the law. The statutes in effect when *Oliff* [was] decided defined arson as the burning of a structure. However, under the current statute, arson occurs when, by fire or explosive, a person knowingly damages the property of another without the person's consent. Aggravated arson occurs when in the course of committing arson, a person knowingly damages, partially or totally, any building or structure of another without his consent, and he knows or reasonably should know that one or more persons are present in the building. Neither provision uses any form of the word "burn."

At trial, the State presented testimony that the building was damaged by the fire. Gloria Snow testified that defendant gathered papers and leaves in the corner of the front entrance, shook liquid on them and set them afire. She further stated that defendant also poured gasoline into the mail slot and that there was a fire in the vestibule, onto which her daughter, Robresta, threw a pot of water, and that the floor was blackened. Kimberly Buckhalter and her mother, Katie Buckhalter, both testified that the front door was burned, the tile in the vestibule was blackened and a portion of the throw rug was burned. Officer Kostecki testified that when he arrived at the scene he saw "the front door * * * on fire." He extinguished the fire not only by stomping on it with his feet but also by striking at it with a rag he found nearby. Officer Cruz testified that when he drove up, the front door of the building appeared to be on fire.

Defendant also argues that the testimony that there was a fire in the hallway was contradicted by Officer Kostecki who testified that he did not see any fire inside. We note, however, that it was not until after Kostecki extinguished the fire outside that he entered the building. He testified that he was met at the doorway by a young woman carrying a pot. The vestibule smelled strongly of gasoline and the rug was saturated. Although he did not know whether the liquid on the floor was water, gasoline or both, his testimony is supportive of the residents' testimony that Robresta threw a pot of water onto the hallway floor to extinguish a fire there.

Further, the State introduced photographs of the premises taken after cleaning efforts by the residents. It appears from the photographs in the record that the wood on the bottom of the door and on the frame around the door was charred and scorched, rather than merely "smudged and discolored" by smoke as defendant argues. The inside of the door opposite the damaged outside section also appears scorched and blackened, and the vestibule tile at that location was also blackened. Viewing the evidence in the light most favorable to the prosecution, as we are bound to do, we find that the evidence was sufficient to sustain the jury's verdict.

* * *

For the reasons stated, defendant's conviction and sentence are affirmed.

AFFIRMED.

Notes and Questions

1. Another traditional arson "burning" issue was considered under a modern arson statute in *Williams v. State*, 600 N.E.2d 962 (Ind.App.1993). Evidence showed that the defendant, after a fight at a New Years Eve party, set a fire in his host's basement. When the host opened the door to the basement, smoke billowed out and the partygoers had to leave the house. The court added further:

> The house was then evacuated and one of the guests, William Sanders, put out the fire by throwing dirty laundry onto the flames to smother it. The only physical damage caused by the fire, besides the burned clothes, was smoke throughout the house and soot and smoke damage to one of the walls in the basement.

After a jury trial, Williams was convicted of felony arson under a statute defining the crime as knowingly or intentionally, by means of fire or explosive, damaging the dwelling of another person without his or her consent. Rejecting Williams' contention that he had not been proved to have damaged the house within the meaning of the statute, the court explained:

> It is Williams' contention that this offense requires proof of burning or charring as was the case at common law. Traditionally the common law rigidly required an actual burning. The fire must have been actually communicated to the object to such an extent as to have taken effect upon it. In general, any charring of the wood of a building, so that the fiber of the wood was destroyed, was enough to constitute a sufficient burning to complete the crime of arson. However, merely singeing, smoking, scorching, or discoloring by heat were not considered enough to support a conviction.
>
> The State contends that the word "damages" in our present statute is not tied to the common law definition of the word "burning" and should therefore be construed in its plain and ordinary sense. Any damage, even smoke damage, would therefore be enough to satisfy the requirements of the statute. We agree with the State.
>
> First, in construing statutes, words and phrases must be given their plain, ordinary, and usual meaning, unless a contrary purpose is clearly shown by the statute itself. In this case, there is no indication from the statute that any special meaning is to be given to the word "damages." Webster's Third New International Dictionary (1976), defines damage to mean: "loss due to injury: injury or harm to person, property, or reputation: hurt, harm." In this case, there is clearly some harm done to the basement wall by the smoke damage and soot.
>
> Secondly, other states with similar statutes have held that smoke damage is enough to meet a requirement of "damage" in their statutes. * * *

2. Some arson statutes do not even require actual damage to the building or property protected. New Jersey's arson statute, for example, defines the crime as being committed by a person who purposely starts a fire and thereby recklessly places a building of another in danger of damage or destruction. N.J.S.A. 2C:17-1b.

   What constitutes the required starting of a fire that must be done purposely? *State v. M.N.*, 267 N.J. Super. 482, 631 A.2d 1267 (1993), was a juvenile court proceeding in which 12-year-old M.N. was alleged to have committed arson of a garage. Evidence showed that on his way to school (which took him through several residential yards) he found a book of matches and lit the matches one by one and then discarded them. One apparently ignited a fire in some leaves that communicated to the garage and ultimately did $100,000 worth of damage. The trial judge found that M.N. purposely struck the match and thus purposely started the fire. On appeal, the appellate court found that the evidence was insufficient. In part, the court reasoned that—at least under the circumstances—the burning match was not a "fire" sufficient to meet what was required by the arson statute. It also, however, found that the evidence failed to show that M.N. was reckless regarding whether a building of another would be placed in danger of damage or destruction by the fire he started.

Chapter 12

THE INCHOATE CRIMES

Editors' Introduction: The Inchoate or Preparatory Crimes

This chapter deals with an extensive body of law that has evolved to permit the imposition of punishment in the absence of any result whatever. The offenses of attempt, solicitation, and conspiracy are all "inchoate," or anticipatory, in the sense that they consist of uncompleted activity directed toward objectives that are almost invariably criminal in nature. Chapter 12 deals with these three offenses and the defenses specially directed to them.

Conspiracy raises a number of special problems. These are attributable, in large part, to the fact that conspiracy can serve functions other than that of being an inchoate offense. When the prosecution seeks a conviction for conspiracy as well as for the completed offense that was its objective, conspiracy may also serve as a means of aggravating the defendants' actual or potential punishment. Also, as is discussed in Chapter 6, Section B, conspiracy doctrine may be used to attach liability to one individual for the crimes committed by her or his confederates in a more expansive manner than would be possible under the traditional law of complicity.

Does the inchoate nature of these offenses suggest anything concerning the objectives that should be pursued in formulating the substantive law defining these offenses? The drafters of the Model Penal Code offered the following:

> [A]ttempt, solicitation and conspiracy to commit crime [involve] conduct which has in common that it is designed to culminate in the commission of a substantive offense but either has failed to do so in the discrete case or has not yet achieved its culmination because there is something that the actor or another still must do. The offenses are inchoate in this sense.
>
> These, to be sure, are not the only crimes which are so defined that their commission does not rest on proof of the occurrence of the evil that it is the object of

the law to prevent; many specific, substantive offenses also have a large inchoate aspect. This is true not only with respect to crimes of risk-creation, such as reckless driving, or specific crimes of preparation, like those of possession with unlawful purpose. It is also true, at least in part, of crimes like larceny, forgery, kidnapping and even arson, not to speak of burglary, where a purpose to cause greater harm than that which is implicit in the actor's conduct is an element of the offense. It may be thought, indeed, that murder is the only crime which by its definition calls for proof that the full evil that the law endeavors to prevent has come to pass. * * *

Since these offenses always presuppose a purpose to commit another crime, it is doubtful that the threat of punishment for their commission can significantly add to the deterrent efficacy of the sanction which the actor by hypothesis ignores—that is threatened for the crime that is his object. There may be cases where this does occur, as when the actor thinks the chance of apprehension low if he succeeds but high if he should fail in his attempt, or when reflection is promoted at an early stage that otherwise would be postponed until too late, which may be true in some conspiracies. These are, however, special situations. Viewed generally, it seems clear that general deterrence is at most a minor function to be served in fashioning provisions of the penal law addressed to these inchoate crimes; that burden is discharged upon the whole by the law dealing with the substantive offenses.

Other and major functions of the penal law remain, however, to be served. They may be summarized as follows:

First. When a person is seriously dedicated to commission of a crime, there is obviously need for a firm legal basis for the intervention of the agencies of law enforcement to prevent its consummation. In determining that basis, there must be attention to the danger of abuse; equivocal behavior may be misconstrued by an unfriendly eye as preparation to commit a crime. It is no less important, on the other side, that lines should not be drawn so rigidly that the police confront insoluble dilemmas in deciding when to intervene, facing the risk that if they wait the crime may be committed while if they act they may not yet have any valid charge.

Second: Conduct designed to cause or culminate in the commission of a crime obviously yields an indication that the actor is disposed towards such activity, not alone on this occasion but on others. There is a need, therefore, subject again to proper safeguards, for a legal basis upon which the special danger that such individuals present may be assessed and dealt with. They must be made amenable to the corrective process that the law provides.

Third. Finally, and quite apart from these considerations of prevention, when the actor's failure to commit the substantive offense is due to a fortuity, as when the bullet misses in attempted murder or when the expected response to solicitation is withheld, his exculpation on that ground would involve inequality of treatment that would shock the common sense of justice. Such a situation is unthinkable in any mature system, designed to serve the proper goals of penal law.

Model Penal Code, Comments to Article 5, 24–26 (Tent. Draft No. 10. 1960).[*]

A. ATTEMPTS

Until quite recently, according to Sayre, Criminal Attempts, 41 Harv.L.Rev. 821 (1928), the criminal law included no generalized doctrine that attempts to commit crime were, in themselves, criminal. Although some few early convictions for unsuccessful efforts to commit especially heinous crimes are reported, these, according to Professor Sayre, were based on an earlier doctrine that the intention is to be taken for the deed (*voluntas reputabitur pro facto*). The danger of imposing liability upon mere intent was too great to permit resort to this maxim often. Professor Sayre dates the modern doctrine of attempts from *Rex v. Scofield*, Cald. 397 (1784), where it was declared that "[t]he intent may make an act, innocent in itself, criminal; nor is the *completion* of an act, criminal in itself, necessary to constitute criminality." Many issues vital to the law of attempts seem unsettled and resistant to ready resolution.

The drafters of the Model Penal Code addressed the general policy considerations relevant to the issues presented by attempt:

> The literature and decisions dealing with the definition of a criminal attempt reflect ambivalence as to how far the governing criterion should be found in the dangerousness of the actor's conduct, measured by objective standards, and how far in the dangerousness of the actor, as a person manifesting a firm disposition to commit a crime. Both criteria may lead, of course, to the same disposition of a concrete case. When they do not, we think * * * that the proper focus of attention is the actor's disposition * * *. Needless to say, we are in full agreement that the law must be concerned with conduct, not with evil thoughts alone. The question is what conduct, when engaged in with a purpose to commit a crime or to advance towards the attainment of a criminal objective, should suffice to constitute a criminal attempt?
>
> In fashioning an answer we must keep in mind that in attempt, as distinct from solicitation and conspiracy, it is not intrinsic to the actor's conduct that he has disclosed his criminal design to someone else; nor is there any natural line that is suggested by the situation like utterance or agreement. The law must deal with the problem presented by a single individual and must address itself to conduct that may fall anywhere upon a graded scale from early preparation to the final effort to commit the crime.
>
> We think, therefore, that it is useful to begin with any conduct designed to effect or to advance towards the attainment of the criminal objective and to ask when it ought not to be regarded as a crime, either because it does not adequately manifest the dangerousness of the actor or on other overriding grounds of social policy.

Model Penal Code, Comment to § 5.01, 26 (Tent. Draft No. 10, 1960).

1. Elements of the Offense

The crime of attempt consists of two elements, one addressing the accused's conduct and the other his or her state of mind. Basically, the accused must have, with the required state of mind, progressed sufficiently toward the attempted offense. Most issues in attempt cases involve the appropriate formulation of the criterion for determining when conduct is sufficient to constitute an attempt and the application of that criterion to the sorts of facts presented by particular prosecutions. These are the problems addressed in *United States v. Jackson*, reprinted in this subsection.

Consider the function served by imposing a requirement that an accused have progressed a particular distance toward success. By definition, the crime of attempt does not require that the accused have actually caused the serious harm that is the basis for concern, that is, the object crime. To some extent, then, attempt as well as the other inchoate offense pose some risk of punishing persons for evil thoughts that in fact would never progress into fruition. On the other hand, the closer that attempt defendants must be shown to have come to actually committing the object crime, the more difficult it will be for law enforcement to intervene and prevent them from actually causing the harm inherent in their criminal objective. Moreover, a stringent requirement that attempt defendants come close to completing their attempted crimes may reduce the value of attempt law as a deterrent.

The major function of the conduct requirement in attempt law is to balance these considerations. First, it must adequately assure that particular persons' intentions are sufficiently firm and strongly held that society can be reasonably certain that these actors would, in the absence of the state's intervention, ultimately have committed the object crimes that are the subject of their intent. On the other hand, it should also avoid unrealistically limiting the authority to intervene in dangerous situations where serious harm to other citizens can be prevented by apprehending such actors and prosecuting them for attempt.

Traditionally, courts said that attempt requires that the defendant have gone beyond "preparation" (which is *not* sufficient for attempt) into "perpetration" of the crime (which *is* sufficient). These terms, though, are obviously not self-defining. Distinguishing preparation from the beginning of the perpetration that creates criminal liability is the major traditional problem in attempt law.

Modern attempt law, however, clearly places increased emphasis upon the culpable mental state requirement for attempt. Arguably the courts are quite unlikely to find that a defendant did not progress far enough if the defendant's conduct, considered in light of the circumstances, adequately shows the defendant had the intent to complete the attempted offense.

United States v. Jackson

United States Court of Appeals, Second Circuit, 1977
560 F.2d 112, cert. denied, 434 U.S. 941, 98 S.Ct. 434, 54 L.Ed. 301 (1977).

FREDERICK VAN PELT BRYAN, SENIOR DISTRICT JUDGE:

* * * [Robert Jackson, William Scott and Martin Allen were convicted of conspiracy to rob the Manufacturers Hanover Trust branch bank and of attempting to rob this bank on June 14 and June 21, 1976. On appeal, appellants do not contest the sufficiency of the evidence on the conspiracy count but they] assert that, as a matter of law, their conduct never crossed the elusive line which separates "mere preparation" from "attempt." This troublesome question was

recently examined by this court in *United States v. Stallworth*, 543 F.2d 1038 (2d Cir.1976), which set forth the applicable legal principles.

I.

The Government's evidence at trial consisted largely of the testimony of Vanessa Hodges, an unindicted co-conspirator, and of various FBI agents who surveilled the Manufacturers Hanover branch on June 21, 1976. Since the facts are of critical importance in any attempt case, we shall review the Government's proof in considerable detail.

On June 11, 1976, Vanessa Hodges was introduced to appellant Martin Allen by Pia Longhorne, another unindicted co-conspirator. Hodges wanted to meet someone who would help her carry out a plan to rob the Manufacturers Hanover branch located at 210 Flushing Avenue in Brooklyn, and she invited Allen to join her. Hodges proposed that the bank be robbed the next Monday, June 14th, at about 7:30 A.M. She hoped that they could enter with the bank manager at that time, grab the weekend deposits, and leave. Allen agreed to rob the bank with Hodges, and told her he had access to a car, two sawed-off shotguns, and a .38 caliber revolver.

The following Monday, June 14, Allen arrived at Longhorne's house about 7:30 A.M. in a car driven by appellant Robert Jackson. A suitcase in the back seat of the car contained a sawed-off shotgun, shells, materials intended as masks, and handcuffs to bind the bank manager. While Allen picked up Hodges at Longhorne's, Jackson filled the car with gas. The trio then left for the bank.

When they arrived, it was almost 8:00 A.M. It was thus too late to effect the first step of the plan, viz., entering the bank as the manager opened the door. * * * Allen and Hodges left the car and walked over to the bank. The peered in and saw the bulky weekend deposits, but decided it was too risky to rob the bank without an extra man.

Consequently, Jackson, Hodges, and Allen drove to Coney Island in search of another accomplice. In front of a housing project on 33rd Street they found appellant William Scott, who promptly joined the team. Allen added to the arsenal another sawed-off shotgun obtained from one of the buildings in the project, and the group drove back to the bank.

* * * Allen entered the bank to check the location of any surveillance cameras, while Jackson placed a piece of cardboard with a false license number over the authentic license plate of the car. Allen reported back * * * [the location of the sole camera. Scott next entered and returned to report that the weekend deposits were being separated and that a number of patrons were now in the bank. Hodges then suggested that the robbery be rescheduled] for the following Monday, June 21. Accordingly, they * * * returned

to Coney Island where, before splitting up, they purchased a pair of stockings for Hodges to wear over her head as a disguise and pairs of gloves for Hodges, Scott, and Allen to don before entering the bank.

Hodges was arrested on Friday, June 18, 1976 on an unrelated bank robbery charge, and immediately began cooperating with the Government. After relating the events on June 14, she told FBI agents that * * * [the robbery was now set for June 21, and gave descriptions of the robbers, their firearms, and their vehicle, including the use of a cardboard license plate.]

At the request of the agents, Hodges called Allen on Saturday, June 19, and asked if he were still planning to do the job. He said that he was ready. On Sunday she called him again. This time Allen said that he was not going to rob the bank that Monday because he had learned that Hodges had been arrested and he feared that federal agents might be watching. Hodges nevertheless advised the agents that she thought the robbery might still take place as planned with the three men proceeding without her.

At about 7:00 A.M. on Monday, June 21, 1976, some ten FBI agents took various surveilling positions in the area of the bank. At about 7:39 A.M. the agents observed a [car with three black male occupants appear and drive repeatedly past the bank. The appearance of the car and its occupants conformed to Hodges' description. The car stopped several times. Once, an occupant emerged to stand in front of the bank; at another time the front license plate was removed. After parking near the bank for almost thirty minutes the car started past the bank again when the appellants detected the surveillance. The car accelerated but was overtaken and the occupants arrested.] * * *

* * * The agents then observed a black and red plaid suitcase in the rear of the car. The zipper of the suitcase was partially open and exposed two loaded sawed-off shotguns, a toy nickel-plated revolver, a pair of handcuffs, and masks. A New York license plate was seen lying on the front floor of the car. All of these items were seized.

In his memorandum of decision, Chief Judge Mishler characterized the question of whether the defendants had attempted a bank robbery as charged in counts two and three or were merely engaged in preparations as "a close one." After canvassing the authorities on what this court one month later called a "perplexing problem," Chief Judge Mishler applied the following two-tiered inquiry formulated in *United States v. Mandujano*, 499 F.2d 370, 376 (5th Cir. 1974), cert. den. 419 U.S. 1114, 95 S.Ct. 792, 42 L.Ed.2d 812 (1975):

> First, the defendant must have been acting with the kind of culpability otherwise required for the commission of the crime which he is charged with attempting. * * *

Second, the defendant must have engaged in conduct which constitutes a substantial step toward commission of the crime. A substantial step must be conduct strongly corroborative of the firmness of the defendant's criminal intent.

He concluded that on June 14 and again on June 21, the defendants took substantial steps, strongly corroborative of the firmness of their criminal intent, toward commission of the crime of bank robbery and found the defendants guilty on each of the two attempt counts. These appeals followed.

II

* * *

Chief Judge Kaufman, writing for the court [in *United States v. Stallworth*] selected the two-tiered inquiry of *United States v. Mandujano*, supra, "properly derived from the writings of many distinguished jurists," as stating the proper test for determining whether the foregoing conduct constituted an attempt. He observed that this analysis "conforms closely to the sensible definition of an attempt proffered by the American Law Institute's Model Penal Code." * * *

The draftsmen of the Model Penal Code recognized the difficulty of arriving at a general standard for distinguishing acts of preparation from acts constituting an attempt. They found general agreement that when an actor committed the "last proximate act," i.e., when he had done all that he believed necessary to effect a particular result which is an element of the offense, he committed an attempt. They also concluded, however, that while the last proximate act is *sufficient* to constitute an attempt, it is not necessary to such a finding. The problem then was to devise a standard more inclusive than one requiring the last proximate act before attempt liability would attach, but less inclusive than one which would make every act done with the intent to commit a crime criminal. See Model Penal Code § 5.01, Comment at 38–39 (Tent. Draft No. 10, 1960).

The draftsmen considered and rejected the following approaches to distinguishing preparation from attempt, later summarized in *Mandujano*:

(a) The physical proximity doctrine—the overt act required for an attempt must be proximate to the completed crime, or directly tending toward the completion of the crime, or must amount to the commencement of the consummation.

(b) The dangerous proximity doctrine—a test given impetus by Mr. Justice Holmes whereby the greater the gravity and probability of the offense, and the nearer the act to the crime, the stronger is the case for calling the act an attempt.

(c) The indispensable element test—a variation of the proximity tests which emphasizes any indispensable aspect of the criminal endeavor over which the actor has not yet acquired control.

(d) The probable desistance test—the conduct constitutes an attempt if, in the ordinary and natural course of events, without interruption from an outside source, it will result in the crime intended.

(e) The abnormal step approach—an attempt is a step toward crime which goes beyond the point where the normal citizen would think better of his conduct and desist.

(f) The *res ipsa loquitur* or unequivocality test—an attempt is committed when the actor's conduct manifests an intent to commit a crime.

The formulation upon which the draftsmen ultimately agreed required, in addition to criminal purpose, that an act be a substantial step in a course of conduct designed to accomplish a criminal result, and that it be strongly corroborative of criminal purpose in order for it to constitute such a substantial step. The following differences between this test and previous approaches to the preparation-attempt problem were noted:

First, this formulation shifts the emphasis from what remains to be done—the chief concern of the proximity tests—to what the actor *has already* done. The fact that further major steps must be taken before the crime can be completed does not preclude a finding that the steps already undertaken are substantial. It is expected, in the normal case, that this approach will broaden the scope of attempt liability.

Second, although it is intended that the requirement of a substantial step will result in the imposition of attempt liability only in those instances in which some firmness of criminal purpose is shown, no finding is required as to whether the actor would probably have desisted prior to completing the crime. Potentially the probable desistance test could reach very early steps toward crime—depending upon how one assesses the probabilities of desistance—but since in practice this test follows closely the proximity approaches, rejection of probable desistance will not narrow the scope of attempt liability.

Finally, the requirement of proving a substantial step generally will prove less of a hurdle for the prosecution than the *res ipsa loquitur* approach, which requires that the actor's conduct must itself manifest the criminal purpose. The difference will be illustrated in connection with the present section's requirement of corroboration.

Here it should be noted that, in the present formulation, the two purposes to be served by the *res ipsa loquitur* test are, to a large extent, treated separately. Firmness of criminal purpose is intended to be shown by requiring a substantial step, while problems of proof are dealt with by the requirement of corroboration (although, under the reasoning previously expressed, the latter will also tend to establish firmness of purpose).

Model Penal Code § 5.01, Comment at 47 (Tent. Draft No. 10, 1960).

The draftsmen concluded that, in addition to assuring firmness of criminal design, the requirement of a substantial step would preclude attempt liability, with its accompanying harsh penalties, for relatively remote preparatory acts. At the same time, however, by not requiring a "last proximate act" or one of its various analogues it would permit the apprehension of dangerous persons at an earlier stage than the other approaches without immunizing them from attempt liability.

* * *

In the case at bar, Chief Judge Mishler anticipated the precise analysis which this Court adopted in the * * * *Stallworth* case. He then found that on June 14 the appellants, already agreed upon a robbery plan, drove to the bank with loaded weapons. In order to carry the heavy weekend deposit sacks, they recruited another person. Cardboard was placed over the license, and the bank was entered and reconnoitered. Only then was the plan dropped for the moment and rescheduled for the following Monday. On that day, June 21, the defendants performed essentially the same acts. Since the cameras had already been located there was no need to enter the bank again, and since the appellants had arrived at the bank earlier, conditions were more favorable to their initial robbery plan than they had been on June 14. He concluded that on both occasions these men were seriously dedicated to the commission of a crime, had passed beyond the stage of preparation, and would have assaulted the bank had they not been dissuaded by certain external factors, viz., the breaking up of the weekend deposits and crowd of patrons in the bank on June 14 and the detection of the FBI surveillance on June 21.

We cannot say that these conclusions which Chief Judge Mishler reached as the trier of fact as to what the evidence before him established were erroneous. * * * [T]he criminal intent of the appellants was beyond dispute. The question remaining then is the substantiality of the steps taken on the dates in question, and how strongly this corroborates the firmness of their obvious criminal intent. This is a matter of degree.

On two separate occasions, appellants reconnoitered the place contemplated for the commission of the crime and possessed the paraphernalia to be employed in the commission of the crime-loaded sawed-off shotguns, extra shells, a toy revolver, handcuffs, and masks which was specially designed for such unlawful use and which could serve no lawful purpose under the circumstances. Under the Model Penal Code formulation, approved by the *Stallworth* court, either type of conduct, standing alone, was sufficient as a matter of law to constitute a "substantial step" if it strongly corroborated their criminal purpose. Here both types of conduct coincided on both June 14 and June 21, along with numerous other elements strongly corroborative of the firmness of appellants' criminal intent.[8] The steps taken toward a successful bank robbery thus were not "insubstantial" as a matter of law, and Chief Judge Mishler found them "substantial" as a matter of fact. We are unwilling to substitute our assessment of the evidence for his, and thus affirm the convictions for attempted bank robbery.

Notes and Questions

1. There is widespread agreement that attempt is a "specific intent" crime and that it requires "intent in fact." See, for example, *People v. Ratliff*, 41 Cal.3d 675, 224 Cal.Rptr. 705, 715 P.2d 665 (1986) (in attempted murder prosecution, jury must be told that it must find defendant had not merely the intent to shoot but the intent to kill). This seldom seems to pose much of a problem of discerning the standard for whether the required *mens rea* was present, although some fact situations present significant difficulties.

2. Proof of the culpable mental state necessary for attempt was at issue in *Smallwood v. State*, 106 Md.App. 1, 661 A.2d 747 (1995), rev'd, 343 Md. 97, 680 A.2d 512 (1996). While he was imprisoned, Smallwood was diagnosed as infected with HIV, human immunodeficiency virus, and was informed of this diagnosis. After he was released, Smallwood robbed and without using a condom vaginally penetrated three woman without their consent. He was charged with attempted murder and after waiving jury trial was tried before a judge. The trial judge noted that attempted murder requires intent to kill. Smallwood's intent to kill his victims, the judge

---

[8] After securing the extra man they needed on June 14, the gang returned to the bank with their weapons ready and the car's license plate disguised for the getaway. Hodges' testimony was that they were ready to rob the bank at that time, but eventually postponed the robbery because conditions did not seem favorable.

reasoned further, could and would be inferred from Smallwood's knowledge of his HIV positive status and his knowledge as to how the virus is transmitted. Observing that Smallwood "also had sufficient time to consider the consequences of his act," the judge found him guilty. This was upheld by a split intermediate appellate court but reversed by Maryland's highest court. The final court explained:

> Smallwood * * * was properly found guilty of attempted murder * * * only if there was sufficient evidence from which the trier of fact could reasonably have concluded that Smallwood possessed a specific intent to kill at the time he assaulted each of the three women. * * * An intent to kill may be proved by circumstantial evidence. * * * Therefore, the trier of fact may infer the existence of the required intent from surrounding circumstances such as "the accused's acts, conduct and words." As we have repeatedly stated, "under the proper circumstances, an intent to kill may be inferred from the use of a deadly weapon directed at a vital part of the human body."
>
> The State [contends] that the facts of this case are sufficient to infer an intent to kill. The State likens Smallwood's HIV-positive status to a deadly weapon and argues that engaging in unprotected sex when one is knowingly infected with HIV is equivalent to firing a loaded firearm at that person. * * * The State's analysis, however, ignores several factors. * * *
>
> First, we must consider the magnitude of the risk to which the victim is knowingly exposed. The inference [of intent to kill drawn from the shooting of a firearm] rests upon the rule that "[i]t is permissible to infer that 'one intends the natural and probable consequences of his act.'" Before an intent to kill may be inferred based solely upon the defendant's exposure of a victim to a risk of death, it must be shown that the victim's death would have been a natural and probable result of the defendant's conduct. It is for this reason that a trier of fact may infer that a defendant possessed an intent to kill when firing a deadly weapon at a vital part of the human body. When a deadly weapon has been fired at a vital part of a victim's body, the risk of killing the victim is so high that it becomes reasonable to assume that the defendant intended the victim to die as a natural and probable consequence of the defendant's actions.

> Death by AIDS is clearly one natural possible consequence of exposing someone to a risk of HIV infection, even on a single occasion. It is less clear that death by AIDS from that single exposure is a sufficiently probable result to provide the sole support for an inference that the person causing the exposure intended to kill the person who was exposed. While the risk to which Smallwood exposed his victims when he forced them to engage in unprotected sexual activity must not be minimized, the State has presented no evidence from which it can reasonably be concluded that death by AIDS is a probable result of Smallwood's actions to the same extent that death is the probable result of firing a deadly weapon at a vital part of someone's body. Without such evidence, it cannot fairly be concluded that death by AIDS was sufficiently probable to support an inference that Smallwood intended to kill his victims in the absence of other evidence indicative of an intent to kill.

* * *

> In this case, we find no additional evidence from which to infer an intent to kill. Smallwood's actions are wholly explained by an intent to commit rape and armed robbery, the crimes for which he has already pled guilty. For this reason, his actions fail to provide evidence that he also had an intent to kill.
>
> The cases cited by the State demonstrate the sort of additional evidence needed to support an inference that Smallwood intended to kill his victims. The defendants in these cases have either made explicit statements demonstrating an intent to infect their victims or have taken specific actions demonstrating such an intent and tending to exclude other possible intents. * * * The defendant in *Weeks v. State*, 834 S.W.2d 559 (Tex.App. 1992), [for example,] * * * was convicted of attempted murder after he spat on a prison guard. In that case, * * * [t]here was * * * evidence that at the time of the spitting incident, Weeks had stated that he was "going to take someone with him when he went" * * *.

3. The mental state requirement for attempt generally limits those offenses for which an attempt prosecution will lie. If a crime requires proof that the accused caused a particular result, the general rule is that a defendant can be convicted of attempting to

commit that crime only upon proof that he intended to cause that result. Therefore, if the crime requires less than intent, it cannot be the basis of an attempt prosecution.

In *State v. Dunbar*, 117 Wash.2d 587, 590, 817 P.2d 1360, 1361 (1991), for example, the underlying facts were that the prosecution was prepared to prove that in a gang-related drive-by shooting, Dunbar fired several shots from a moving car into a crowd standing in a parking lot. Had the shots killed anyone, Dunbar could have been convicted of first degree murder under a Washington statute, which provides that a person commits this offense if he causes the death of a person "[u]nder circumstances manifesting an extreme indifference to human life

[and by] conduct which creates a grave risk of death to any person * * *." In fact, no one was killed by Dunbar's shots. Could he be convicted of *attempted* first degree murder?

Dunbar, following the general rule, held not. Because first degree murder requires a result (the death of a person) but does not require proof of a specific intent to cause that result, Washington law does not include a crime of attempted first degree murder by creation of a grave risk of death. Similarly, where assault on a police officer consists of *recklessly* causing bodily injury to a police officer, there is no recognizable crime of attempted reckless assault on a police officer. *State v. Hemmer*, 3 Neb.App. 769, 531 N.W.2d 559 (1995).

2. *The Defense of Impossibility*
Editors' Note: Impossibility of Success as Precluding Liability for Attempt

A defendant prosecuted for attempted commission of a crime may have a defense of impossibility, consisting of proof that despite having gone far enough toward the commission of the crime with a sufficient culpable mental state, the defendant could not have in fact committed the crime that was attempted. The defense, in other words, consists of proof that success was impossible.

The underlying policy question of whether any such defense should be available presents the conflict between subjective and objective approaches to liability more sharply than probably any other in the substantive criminal law. A defendant who could not successfully complete the intended crime has arguably not demonstrated by actual action that he or she poses a high risk of successfully committing the crime. This exacerbates the general concern of the criminal law that punishment not be inflicted for an evil state of mind without proof of demonstrated dangerousness.

An example of the bizarre facts often involved in cases presenting impossibility issues is *People v. Dluglash*, 41 N.Y.2d 725, 395 N.Y.S.2d 419, 363 N.E.2d 1155 (1977). Dluglash had been charged with the murder of one Michael Geller. It was clear from the evidence that Dluglash had fired about five shots into the head of Geller as Geller lay on the floor after having been shot several times in the chest by Dluglash's friend, Joe Bush. The defense's theory—that Geller was dead from Bush's shots at the time defendant fired—was rejected by the jury, which convicted Dluglash of intentional murder.

New York's highest court held, first, that the prosecution had failed to prove Geller was alive when shot by Dluglash. Thus, the murder conviction had to be reversed. The court then moved to whether the jury's verdict should be modified to reflect a conviction for the lesser included offense of attempted murder. To answer this question the court examined the doctrine of impossibility to determine whether that doctrine precluded conviction for attempted murder.

Dluglash began by dividing impossibility into the two traditional categories: factual and legal. In the former, the defendant's intention is thwarted because of his or her mistake as to the physical nature of an indispensable instrument or circumstance. Common examples are the shooting of a stump believing it to be one's intended victim, or pulling the trigger of a gun held to the victim's head when, unknown to the defendant, the gun is unloaded, or the picking of an empty pocket. In such cases convictions for attempt have been almost uniformly affirmed.

Legal impossibility is said to be present when the actions performed by, or to be performed by, the defendant, even if fully consummated as he or she desires, would not constitute the crime. Such impossibility is traditionally a defense to attempt. The most common example of this class of cases is where the defendant receives property that had been stolen and that the defendant believes to be stolen but that, unknown to the defendant, has been recovered by the police. Some courts have said that once such property has been recovered by the police it has lost its stolen status and hence by accepting the property a person cannot commit the offense of receipt of stolen goods. Moreover, the defendant's actions cannot be attempted receipt of stolen property because the actions begun or even completed by the defendant—receipt of the formerly stolen property—cannot as a matter of law constitute the crime purportedly attempted: receipt of stolen property. Commission of the crime purportedly attempted by this conduct, in other words, is "legally impossible." See, for example, *United States v. Dove*, 629 F.2d 325 (4th Cir.1980).

In a further refinement of nomenclature, cases such as *Dove* are sometimes described as involving mixed fact and legal impossibility issues, in contrast to "true" legal impossibility.

Such true legal impossibility cases simply do not arise in real life. These are cases in which the defendant's only mistaken perception was about the substantive criminal law. Suppose, for example, a defendant believes that the jurisdiction has a statute making anyone who smokes cigars in any courthouse guilty of a crime. She goes into a courthouse, pulls out a cigar, strikes a match, and is apprehended. There is in fact no crime consisting of smoking a cigar in a courthouse. She was not mistaken about whether she could accomplish the required result; she could in fact have set fire to the cigar. She was not mistaken about any attendant factual circumstances; she did not understand the cigar to be anything other than what it actually was. Is she guilty of criminal attempt? The argument *for* liability is that she has actually demonstrated a willingness to violate what she understands to be the law, and this makes her both morally culpable and demonstrably dangerous.

The *Dluglash* court acknowledged that the distinctions drawn by courts between factual and legal impossibility were very fine and technical and bore little relationship to the dangers posed to society by defendants thus thwarted in the achievement of their evil aims. It noted that in 1967 the New York legislature had decided to jettison the traditional doctrine and to adopt the policy of the Model Penal Code. Under this approach, analysis is focused upon the actor's state of mind rather than upon the external considerations of his or her conduct and situation. One who attempts a crime will be liable for it despite the fact that it was factually or legally impossible of achievement "if such crime could have been committed had the attendant circumstances been as such person believed them to be." (N.Y.Penal Law, § 110.10.) Thus, if Dluglash believed Geller to be alive when he shot him, proof that Geller was in fact dead at the time would give Dluglash no defense to a charge of attempted murder.

The court concluded that the evidence was sufficient to support the jury's finding that the defendant believed his victim was alive when he fired the shots into his head. Obviously the jury had so found, because the defendant's belief as to Geller being alive was necessary to holding him guilty of murder. Dluglash's conviction therefore was modified to one for attempted murder.

As indicated by the discussion of *Dluglash*, under the subjective approach to legal impossibility the courts look to the defendant's intention—for example, to sell heroin—and if it was to commit a crime and the defendant's conduct went beyond preparation, that conduct will constitute an attempt even though the defendant unwittingly possessed a noncontrolled substance for purposes of sale. This is the design of Model Penal Code § 5.01, reprinted at, page 346, which has been widely adopted.

Some jurisdictions have explicitly and completely abolished any defense of impossibility. A Colorado statute, for example, provides:

> Factual or legal impossibility of committing the offense is not a defense if the offense would have [been] committed had the attendant circumstances been as the actor believed them to be * * *.

Col.Rev.Stat. § 18-2-101 (1).

At least some commentators express concern about the total abolition of the impossibility defense. They stress the importance of objective manifestations of criminality so as to minimize the danger of punishment for evil thoughts alone. To return to the hypothetical case of the "attempted" sale of heroin just mentioned, they would stress that the defendant's conduct—possession of, and attempts to sell a noncontrolled substance—provides equivocal signals of criminality. Rather than risk the misidentification of such persons as criminals, or as more serious criminals than they are in fact, the objectivists would stress the importance of the defendant's conduct as demonstrating culpability without regard to his or her intent. Their theoretical case is strongest when the hypothetical defendants have adopted such ill-suited, inadequate means for the achievement of their criminal purposes—such as sticking pins in a voodoo doll to bring about another's death or injury—as to suggest that the actor poses no danger to the public.

Most courts recently considering these matters have tended to reserve decision on whether legal impossibility might in some unusual circumstances be a defense but they have tended to characterize the cases that actually come before the courts as involving only factual impossibility, which is no defense.

In *Grill v. State*, 337 Md. 91, 651 A.2d 856 (1995), for example, Grill had purchased from an undercover officer a bag of an innocuous substance believing it to be heroin. She was charged with attempted possession of heroin, and argued in defense that it was impossible for her to commit possession of heroin by possessing the substance involved in the transaction. Noting that it had never decided whether legal impossibility is a defense, the court found no need to address that issue as the case presented only factual impossibility that clearly was no defense.

In cases like *Grill*, the defendant has done all that the defendant believes necessary to actually complete the offense. Courts have, however, taken the same approach in cases where this was not the situation. In *People v. Reed*, 53 Cal.App.4th 389, 61 Cal.Rptr.2d 658 (1996), review denied, for example, Reed arrived at a motel with sex toys for what he believed would be a meeting with a woman and two young children. He anticipated that the woman would permit him to engage in sexual acts with the children. In fact, the woman meeting him was a police officer and she was accompanied by no children. Convicted of attempted child molestation, he argued that factual impossibility cases did not apply because in his situation there had in fact been no potential child victims who could have been harmed. That his intended victims, unlike those in other cases, were "imaginary," the court held, was "a distinction without a difference." He had no impossibility defense, despite the fact that, unlike *Grill*, he had not done everything he thought necessary to complete the attempted crime of child molestation.

Courts such as those that decided *Grill* and *Reed* would most likely limit any impossibility defense to true legal impossibility situations. They would almost certainly characterize the "formerly stolen goods" cases—in which the defendant accepts goods recovered from thieves by the police—as involving only factual impossibility and thus permitting conviction for attempted receipt of stolen property.

The Model Penal Code, as *Dluglash* suggests, would preclude conviction for attempt only in true legal impossibility situations. It would accomplish this, however, without explicit provision for a defense of impossibility.

Under the Code, a person is guilty of attempt only if that person engages in conduct constituting a substantial step toward conduct that *under the circumstances as the person believes them to be* would be a crime, or engages in conduct that would constitute a crime *if the attendant circumstances were as the person believes them to be*. Grill would be guilty of attempted possession of heroin because she engaged in conduct that would have been possession of heroin if the attendant circumstances were as she believed them to be. Reed would be guilty of attempted child molestation, because he took a substantial step toward conduct—sexual acts with others—that would be a crime if the circumstances—the victims' ages—had been as he believed them to be.

The hypothetical cigar-wielder in the true legal impossibility hypothetical set out earlier would not be guilty of attempt under the Model Penal Code. This, however, would not be because of an impossibility defense. What she planned to do—smoke the cigar in the courthouse—would not in actual fact be a crime if she were able to do it. Her mistaken belief that this would be a crime does not make up for the need for the defendant's objective to be, if the circumstances were as the defendant believes them to be, in fact a crime under the substantive law as it in fact is.

In addition, the Model Penal Code in section 5.05(2) would recognize general discretionary power in a trial court to reduce the grade of an offense or dismiss charges altogether if the judge decides that the facts on which an attempt charge is based are "so unlikely to result or culminate in the commission of a crime" that neither the defendant nor his or her conduct present a "public danger" justifying an offense of the seriousness of criminal attempt. This is designed to provide for possible, but highly unlikely, cases in which a defendant has chosen such inherently impossible methods to attempt a crime that the facts suggest the defendant, whatever his or her moral blameworthiness, lacks the ability to pose an actual and serious threat of completing such offenses in the future.

To the extent that impossibility is a defense, this is a doctrine specific to attempt law. Any such defense as exists does not represent a general principle applicable to other crimes. Thus, the law is clear that there is no defense to burglary consisting of proof that the defendant's commission inside the premises of the crime he or she intends to commit there is "impossible."

3. The Defense of Renunciation
Editors' Note: Renunciation or Abandonment as Precluding Liability for Attempt

Should a person who has proceeded beyond preparation in an effort to commit an offense and has done so with the *mens rea* required for attempt be able to escape criminal liability by abandoning or renouncing the venture? In most other situations, the criminal law denies defendant's exculpation on these grounds. Certainly, if a person is proven to have stolen a car he will not be legally absolved because he subsequently returns it, and one who has committed an assault will not be exculpated by his willingness to compensate his victim. Why should this principle not also apply to the law of attempt?

A defense might be justified for at least two reasons. First, it might encourage people to desist from attempts and thereby reduce the incidence of the ultimate harm with which attempt is concerned—eventual successful completion of other offenses. On the other hand, perhaps people who begin criminal conduct are quite unlikely to be aware of or responsive to the law's offer of exculpation if they abandon an attempt to commit an offense. To the extent that an incentive of this sort might be effective, it can alternatively be provided by denying such defendants a defense but grading attempt as a less serious offense than the completed crime. This would provide an incentive for abandonment without sacrificing the law's ability to act against those who attempt.

A defense might also be justified on the ground that a showing of abandonment tends to negative the dangerousness of the actor. Abandonment might suggest that the actor's criminal resolve was not firm or that it was accompanied by other characteristics that discouraged him or her from finally acting on even a firm resolve. Thus, the defense would tend to filter out those attempters whose conviction and punishment would not serve the underlying purpose of penalizing those who pose a high enough risk of actually completing the crimes attempted.

The creation of such a defense is also arguably consistent with the emergence of greater subjectivity in the definition of attempt. Greater emphasis upon an attempt defendant's culpable mental state is accompanied by a reduction in the need for conduct that objectively establishes the defendant's dangerousness. Perhaps this increasing emphasis on accused's subjective intent to commit an offense is justified only if it is mitigated by a defense that permits some attempt defendants to establish that despite their subjective intentions their actions—considered as a whole, including their abandonment of their intentions—fail to establish that they are sufficiently dangerous to warrant criminal liability.

In other words, the fact that attempt is an inchoate or anticipatory crime might justify providing such a defense here although no such defense is provided to regular crimes that are defined as actually causing a result that has serious social consequences. Perhaps general attempt statutes cast so wide a net of potential liability that devices such as renunciation are desirable techniques to identify those who, although within the net, are not truly blameworthy and dangerous. People who renounce may have criminal propensities, but they may also have values or other inclinations that will ultimately prevent them from fully carrying out those propensities.

The traditional position, nevertheless, is that abandonment of an attempt is not a defense. See, for example, *People v. Staples*, 6 Cal.App.3d 61, 85 Cal.Rptr. 589 (1970); *Stewart v. State*, 85 Nev. 388, 455 P.2d 914 (1969).

Federal criminal law has no controlling statute and the issue has seldom been presented to the federal courts for consideration. In *United States v. Shelton*, 30 F.3d 702 (6th Cir.1994), however, the court considered and rejected an argument that sound policy considerations suggested it should hold that juries should be instructed that a defendant charged with attempt is to be acquitted upon proof of an abandonment manifesting a complete and voluntary renunciation of criminal purpose. The court explained:

> We are not persuaded that the availability of a withdrawal defense would provide an incentive or motive to desist from the commission of an offense, especially since the success of the defense presupposes a criminal trial at which the issue would be submitted to the jury for decision. A remote chance of acquittal would appear to have an even more remote chance of deterring conduct.

The Model Penal Code (see § 5.01(4) reprinted on page 347) would provide for such a defense, and its suggestion has inspired some states to permit a limited defense of this sort. Under the Model Penal Code version the defendant would be required to produce evidence that he abandoned his effort or prevented the commission of the offense "under circumstances manifesting a complete and voluntary renunciation of his criminal purpose." Although the Model Penal Code designates renunciation an affirmative defense, this means only that the burden of production is on the accused. In some jurisdictions providing for the defense, the accused is required to prove renunciation but only by a preponderance of the evidence.

To be successful under the Model Penal Code and similar provisions, the defendant must show that his abandonment was "voluntary" in the sense of an almost religious conversion. This is because only defendants who have so voluntarily abandoned their plans have demonstrated that despite their criminal propensities and their willing to act on those propensities (by going far enough for criminal attempt), they in fact do not pose a serious threat of fully transforming those propensities into final action by completing crimes.

Under this approach, the abandonment cannot have been due to external circumstances such as the threat of imminent apprehension by the authorities or a decision to await a more favorable opportunity. This places a heavy burden on a defendant seeking to establish the defense or even to raise it before the jury.

In *Smith v. State*, 636 N.E.2d 124 (Ind.1994), for example, the evidence showed that Smith approached two truant male high school students, M.B. and J.G., representing himself as a police officer, and directed them to get into his car. Then

> he drove them to a wooded area in Greene County. Smith handcuffed M.B. to a tree. Smith then ordered J.G. to exit the car. Smith held J.G.'s arm behind his back and shoved him into the woods. Smith asked whether J.G. "ever had sex with a boy" and commanded him to disrobe. When J.G. refused, Smith placed his gun to J.G.'s throat and again told him to remove his clothes. J.G. still refused. Smith was startled by the sound of a branch snapping, which was M.B. breaking free from the tree. Smith then took J.G. back to the car and drove him to State Highway 37, where he released him. Meanwhile, M.B. ran to a nearby home and called the police.

He was charged with attempted criminal deviate conduct and convicted. Indiana statutory law contains an abandonment defense to attempt similar to that provided in the Model Penal Code, and on appeal Smith argued that in light of this abandonment defense, the evidence failed to support his conviction. Rejecting this, the Indiana court reasoned:

> Smith contends that his release of J.G. unharmed shows a genuine change of heart and desertion of criminal purpose. J.G. testified, however, that Smith twice commanded him to remove his clothes, held a handgun to his throat to force compliance, and stopped only after he was startled by the sound of M.B. breaking free. This supports the inference that Smith stopped his attack because he feared M.B. had escaped. This evidence was sufficient to overcome defendant's abandonment defense * * *.

4. The Model Penal Code Formulation

The Model Penal Code offers a proposed formulation of the law of attempt that has been widely followed in state statutes. As indicated by *Jackson*, reprinted earlier at page 334, courts have also found the Code's approach attractive in resolving those issues not controlled by statute. Note the position taken by the Code on grading the seriousness of attempts—the Code makes attempts the same grade of offense as the crime attempted.

MODEL PENAL CODE[*]

Official Draft, 1985

Section 5.01. Criminal Attempt

(1) *Definition of Attempt.* A person is guilty of an attempt to commit a crime if, acting with the kind of culpability otherwise required for commission of the crime, he:

  (a) purposely engages in conduct which would constitute the crime if the attendant circumstances were as he believes them to be; or

  (b) when causing a particular result is an element of the crime, does or omits to do anything with the purpose of causing or with the belief that it will cause such result without further conduct on his part; or

  (c) purposely does or omits to do anything that, under the circumstances as he believes them to be, is an act or omission constituting a substantial step in a course of conduct planned to culminate in his commission of the crime.

(2) *Conduct That May Be Held Substantial Step Under Subsection (1)(c).* Conduct shall not be held to constitute a substantial step under Subsection (1)(c) of this Section unless it is strongly corroborative of the actor's criminal purpose. Without negativing the sufficiency of other conduct, the following, if strongly corroborative of the actor's criminal purpose, shall not be held insufficient as a matter of law:

  (a) lying in wait, searching for or following the contemplated victim of the crime;

  (b) enticing or seeking to entice the contemplated victim of the crime to go to the place contemplated for its commission;

  (c) reconnoitering the place contemplated for the commission of the crime;

  (d) unlawful entry of a structure, vehicle or enclosure in which it is contemplated that the crime will be committed;

  (e) possession of materials to be employed in the commission of the crime, which are specially designed for such unlawful use or which can serve no lawful purpose of the actor under the circumstances;

  (f) possession, collection or fabrication of materials to be employed in the commission of the crime, at or near the place contemplated for its commission, where such possession, collection or fabrication serves no lawful purpose of the actor under the circumstances;

(g) soliciting an innocent agent to engage in conduct constituting an element of the crime.

(3) *Conduct Designed to Aid Another in Commission of a Crime.* A person who engages in conduct designed to aid another to commit a crime that would establish his complicity under Section 2.06 if the crime were committed by such other person, is guilty of an attempt to commit the crime, although the crime is not committed or attempted by such other person.

(4) *Renunciation of Criminal Purpose.* When the actor's conduct would otherwise constitute an attempt under Subsection (1)(b) or (1)(c) of this Section, it is an affirmative defense that he abandoned his effort to commit the crime or otherwise prevented its commission, under circumstances manifesting a complete and voluntary renunciation of his criminal purpose. The establishment of such defense does not, however, affect the liability of an accomplice who did not join in such abandonment or prevention.

Within the meaning of this Article, renunciation of criminal purpose is not voluntary if it is motivated, in whole or in part, by circumstances, not present or apparent at the inception of the actor's course of conduct, that increase the probability of detection or apprehension or that make more difficult the accomplishment of the criminal purpose. Renunciation is not complete if it is motivated by a decision to postpone the criminal conduct until a more advantageous time or to transfer the criminal effort to another but similar objective or victim.

Section 5.05 Grading of Criminal Attempt * * *;
Mitigation in Cases of Lesser Danger, * * *

(1) *Grading.* Except as otherwise provided in this Section, attempt * * * [is a crime] of the same grade and degree as the most serious offense that is attempted * * *.

(2) *Mitigation.* If the particular conduct charged to constitute a criminal attempt * * * is so inherently unlikely to result or culminate in the commission of a crime that neither such conduct nor the actor presents a public danger warranting the grading of such offense under this Section, the Court shall exercise its power * * * to enter judgment and impose sentence for a crime of lower grade or degree or, in extreme cases, may dismiss the prosecution.

B. SOLICITATION

Since *Rex v. Higgins*, 102 Eng.Rep 269 (1801), solicitation to commit a felony (and apparently at least some misdemeanors) has been recognized as a common law offense. In most American jurisdictions the balance of countervailing considerations has been struck so as to permit prosecution for solicitation, although many statutes limit the offense to solicitations to commit relatively serious crimes.

The Model Penal Code, section 5.02 (reprinted on page 351), would criminalize soliciting another—that is, commanding, encouraging, or requesting another—to commit any offense. The drafters acknowledged divergent views on the question of whether solicitors posed a great enough danger to justify criminalization. They concluded that in some ways the solicitation was more dangerous than a direct attempt, because it threatens to bring about cooperative criminal ventures, led by a solicitor "more intelligent and masterful * * * than * * * his hirelings." Comment to § 5.02 of the Model Penal Code 365–66 (1985). The Code's offense is somewhat limited, however, by its requirement that the accused have solicited with the purpose of promoting or facilitating the crime and its provision (in section 5.02(3)) of a defense of renunciation.

Criminal liability for solicitation reflects a more expansive exercise of the government's authority than either conspiracy or attempt. A solicitation defendant need not have done anything except communicate to others or, under provisions such as section 5.02(2) of the Model Penal Code, *attempt* to communicate to others. Some are concerned that such offenses might be used to criminalize free speech protected by the First Amendment to the United States Constitution.

In addition, the nature of solicitation causes some to question whether one who has merely solicited another has adequately demonstrated his or her blameworthiness and dangerousness. The fact that such a person has elected not to commit the crime him- or herself but to seek another to commit it is arguably some evidence that the person has only a relatively weak commitment to seeing the crime completed. Further, solicitation situations always involve the possibility that the moral (or practical) judgments of the persons solicited will intervene and prevent the occurrence of the actual offense.

Nevertheless, there is widespread agreement that even an unsuccessful effort to hire or otherwise persuade another person to commit an offense justifies criminal liability. It threatens apprehension on the part of members of the community, and calls for giving law enforcement officers the authority to intervene in the situations. A person's demonstrated willingness to solicit another does provide considerable indication that the person is both morally blameworthy and socially dangerous.

Despite the general consensus as to the wisdom of criminalizing solicitation, concern continues as to potential governmental overreaching and the ease with which such a charge can be made given that mere words may suffice. In response to these concerns a number of techniques have been developed to limit the scope of solicitation statutes. State statutes are frequently limited to solicitations to commit extremely serious felonies. For example, see Texas Penal Code § 15.03(a) (solicitation of capital felonies and felonies of the first degree). Another limitation is to require corroboration either by another person or by the circumstances under which the solicitation was committed. Examples are California Penal Code § 653f and Colorado Revised Statutes § 18-2-301(l). Section 1003(l) of the final draft of the ill-fated Proposed Federal Criminal Code would have imposed still another limitation. It would have required that the solicitant commit an overt act in response to the solicitation. The drafters thought this necessary to avoid resting liability upon speech alone.

Meyer v. State

Court of Special Appeals of Maryland, 1981
47 Md.App. 679, 425 A.2d 664.
cert. denied, 454 U.S. 865, 102 S.Ct. 327, 70 L.Ed.2d 166 (1981).

WILNER, JUDGE.

[The defendant was in a jail awaiting sentence for the first degree murders of a woman and child allegedly performed under contract with Mr. Lon Lewis, the victims' husband and father. During that time he attempted to arrange to have four more persons killed: his wife, Mr. Lewis, and Detectives Hatfield and Morrissette who had extracted a confession from him concerning the Lewis murders. The person solicited was Frank Mazzone, an undercover State policeman. Meyer was charged with and convicted of four counts of solicitation of murder and given four consecutive twenty year sentences to be served consecutively with the life and thirty years he received for the Lewis murders. * * *

* * *

Appellant's initial contact with regard to his plan was with Joseph Walker, a co-inmate at the Detention Center. He asked whether Walker knew "anyone who did contract killings or hits." Walker responded in the affirmative, whereupon, according to Walker, appellant "asked me if I could arrange for a killing." He did not tell Walker who the victim or victims were to be. Walker passed this information on to a Prince George's County policeman, for whom he had served as an informant. With the concurrence of the State's Attorney's Office, it was arranged for Captain Mazzone, of the State Police, to play the role of Vince Rinaldo, an agent for two "hit men" and, wearing a secret transmitter, to meet with appellant at the Detention Center and find out more about what he had in mind.

Two meetings took place, and in both instances the conversation was recorded and transcribed. At the first meeting, on May 8, 1978, appellant very clearly importuned Mazzone to kill, or to arrange for others to kill, appellant's wife. At the second conversation, on May 15, 1978, there was further discussion about the liquidation of the wife and additional importunings of Mazzone to kill, or to arrange for others to kill, the two police officers and Lon Alec Lewis.

The conversations tended to ramble a bit, but what essentially came through was this:

(1) As to the wife, appellant explained that he was upset with her because she failed to testify in his behalf. She was then living in Puerto Rico, and, in order to facilitate the execution, appellant told Mazzone in some detail what her living arrangements were. He described his wife's appearance and also made arrangements for Mazzone to obtain a picture of her from appellant's apartment.

(2) There was a great deal of discussion about the fee for murdering the wife, the parties finally agreeing on $40,000. Appellant promised a deposit of $1,000 "up front," to be taken from an existing bank account in Minnesota, with the balance to be paid from the proceeds of a $100,000 insurance policy on the wife's life. Indeed, as that policy was about to lapse because of nonpayment of premiums, appellant insisted that the killing take place before May 15. He told Mazzone that he didn't care what method was used, but would leave that up to the actual executioner. Appellant did, in fact, later procure a $1,000 money order payable to Vince Rinaldo which he caused to be sent to Mazzone.

(3) The scheme to kill the two officers and Lewis came up in the second conversation, which was initially prompted by the fact that Mazzone had not yet received the $1,000 deposit. After some discussion about that and some further conversation about the execution of the wife, appellant broached the subject of killing the two officers. He told Mazzone that he didn't want them around as witnesses in the event of a second trial.[2] There was no rush about doing away with the officers; as appellant put it, "I suppose anytime, they say a year before the appeal, so anytime within the next year, so its [sic] not really pushing it."

Notwithstanding the permissible delay in implementation, appellant and Mazzone did arrive at a definite agreement as to their ultimate disposition. Appellant gave Mazzone the names of the officers and told him where they worked. They agreed on a fee of $80,000 for the two officers, over and above the $40,000 for the wife.

(4) Lewis was almost an afterthought. Near the end of the second conversation, appellant indicated a desire to be rid of him as well. This part of the conversation is most relevant:

---

[2] Appellant seemed optimistic that his convictions would be overturned on appeal and was looking ahead to the likelihood of a retrial.

"FRANK (MAZZONE): All right, what do you want to do with him?

GENE (APPELLANT): Uh, same thing with Hatfield or Morrissette [the two officers] if that's * * *.

FRANK: Is he on the street right now?

GENE: No, he's up here—second floor.

FRANK: Does he know your [sic, you're] here?

GENE: Disappears or if he dies, people collect _____ people ask too many questions here.

FRANK: You, you do want him dead, or you don't.

GENE: I do."

Ultimately, it was agreed that Mazzone should wait until Lewis was transferred from the Detention Center to the State prison where the killing would be easier to accomplish.[3] Appellant promised an additional fee of $9,000 for Lewis.

* * * Mazzone never * * * made clear to appellant what his supposed relationship was with whomever was to commit the murders. Indeed, there is nothing in the transcript of the conversations to foreclose the possibility that Mazzone himself would be the actual "hitman." Throughout the conversations, when referring to the killings, Mazzone used the plural pronoun "we"—"Then we do the job," "if *we* got to go to Puerto Rico * * *. . . . . . what do you want to show that *we* did the job? We bring you something back?" "*we* got a standard way *we* do things." By way of contrast, when referring to things he individually would do, such as retrieve the picture of appellant's wife from his apartment, Mazzone used the singular pronoun, "I." In short, although he said nothing directly to dispel any notion that he was merely an agent for others, Mazzone, in his own conversations with appellant, clearly portrayed himself as an integral part of a group willing to carry out contract murders, without indicating who would actually "do the job."

* * *

Appellant * * * asserts, in a somewhat confused fashion, that the imposition of four consecutive sentences was inappropriate since, at best (or worst) only one criminal solicitation was involved. The object or thrust of his argument is clear—he seeks to vacate at least three of the sentences—but the argument itself is ambiguous in terms of both the precise nature of the complaint and the legal theory offered in support of it.

The contention is initially framed * * * as an attack only upon the multiple sentences and not upon the underlying multiple convictions. Yet the basis of his complaint is the assertion that only one criminal act occurred[; this] so obviously relates to the multiple convictions * * * that we must, of necessity, consider and resolve the broader question of whether it was proper to charge, convict, and sentence appellant on four separate counts of solicitation upon the evidence in this case. Consecutive sentences are permissible only for distinct violations of law.

* * * Appellant's most elemental position is that the gist of a criminal solicitation is the incitement, and that the evidence here established but one such incitement, notwithstanding that multiple victims were involved. He draws an analogy in this regard to the crime of conspiracy, the gist of which is the unlawful agreement among the conspirators; and * * * argues that a single agreement to commit more than one unlawful act is still but one conspiracy for which but one punishment may be imposed. The same rule, he claims, applies to a criminal solicitation.

This does seem to be the real issue here— * * * whether there were * * * separate crimes established by the evidence. If, assuming arguendo the validity of appellant's analogy to the crime of conspiracy, the evidence showed only one act of incitement, there would arise only one act of criminal solicitation * * *. If, on the other hand, the evidence sufficed to establish separate and distinct acts of incitement, there would arise several acts of solicitation * * *. Each solicitation would stand entirely on its own under the "required evidence" or any other cognizable test.

We are, to some extent, in truly virgin territory. We have been neither directed to nor able to locate any reported decision in the United States or in the common law nations of the British Commonwealth precisely on point—determining whether an entreaty to kill more than one person constitutes distinct incitements and thus permits conviction and punishment for more than one act of criminal solicitation. * * *

We start with the nature of the crime itself. * * * [T]he forbidden act in a criminal solicitation is "the accused person's parol or written efforts to activate another to commit a criminal offense." [*Cherry v. State*,] 18 Md.App. [252,] 258, 306 A.2d 634. We see no reason why, on the one hand, in a single conversation (much less in two separate conversations as occurred here), a person cannot make successive and distinct incitements, each having a separate object; and we therefore reject the notion that merely because there is but one solicitor, one solicitee, and one conversation, only one solicitation can arise. We similarly reject, however, as being equally simplistic, the "per capita" theory that there are necessarily as many solicitations as there are victims.

---

[3] At the time, Lewis was either awaiting trial or he had already been tried and was awaiting sentence.

[T]he question of whether there is but one solicitation or several depends upon the circumstances. What, in other words, is the solicitor asking the solicitee to do?

The number of victims is important only as it may be evidence of the number of incitements. By way of example, an entreaty made by a solicitor to blow up a building in the hope that two or more particular persons may be killed in the blast could be characterized as one solicitation, notwithstanding that implementation of the scheme might violate several different laws or, because of multiple victims, constitute separate violations of the same law. The multiple criminality of the implementation would not, in that instance, pluralize the incitement, which was singular. * * * But that is quite different from the situation in which the solicitee is being importuned directly to commit separate and distinct acts of murder—to kill, individually, several different specified victims—possibly at different times and places and by different means and executioners. In the latter case, there is not a single incitement but multiple ones, each punishable on its own.

That is the framework within which we must judge this case; and, from the record before us, we find the evidence sufficient to show four separate criminal solicitations based upon four distinct incitements. In point of time, at least three of the incitements were clearly distinct. The deal for the wife was made on May 8; that for Lewis and the two officers was made a week later but in different parts of the conversation. The executions were to occur at different times and places, and possibly by different means and executioners; different (and cumulative) fees were to be paid for these acts. Different motives were involved. Even as between the two officers, the evidence permitted a fair inference that most of these distinguishing attributes were present. In short, the evidence sufficed to permit a finding that it was not a "lump sum" singular deal, but separate and independent incitements to commit four separate and distinct acts of murder against specific named individuals; and thus, neither the separate convictions nor the separate and consecutive sentences were inappropriate.

* * *

JUDGMENTS AFFIRMED; APPELLANT TO PAY THE COSTS.

MODEL PENAL CODE[*]

Official Draft, 1985

Section 5.02. Criminal Solicitation

(1) *Definition of Solicitation.* A person is guilty of solicitation to commit a crime if with the purpose of promoting or facilitating its commission he commands, encourages or requests another person to engage in specific conduct that would constitute such crime or an attempt to commit such crime or would establish his complicity in its commission or attempted commission.

(2) *Uncommunicated Solicitation.* It is immaterial under Subsection (1) of this Section that the actor fails to communicate with the person he solicits to commit a crime if his conduct was designed to effect such communication.

(3) *Renunciation of Criminal Purpose.* It is an affirmative defense that the actor, after soliciting another person to commit a crime persuaded him not to do so or otherwise prevented the commission of the crime, under circumstances manifesting a complete and voluntary renunciation of his criminal purpose.

Notes and Questions

1. Solicitation, like attempt and conspiracy, would be graded by the Model Penal Code the same as the most serious offense solicited except that "An attempt, solicitation or conspiracy to commit a [capital crime or a] felony of the first degree is a felony of the second degree." Model Penal Code § 5.05(l) (1985).

2. Must the solicitation actually be communicated to the solicitant? W. LaFave and A. Scott, Criminal Law 492 (1986), citing cases decided between 1873 and 1912, say no, but comment that some courts would require that a non-communicated solicitation be punished as an attempted solicitation. Compare section 5.02(2) of the Model Penal Code, reprinted at page 351.

3. Does impossibility of any sort prevent liability for solicitation? Should it? In *State v. Keen*, 25 N.C.App. 567, 214 S.E.2d 242 (1975), the defendant argued that because the persons he solicited to kill his wife were law enforcement officers and would not have accepted the invitation, his conviction for solicitation was not permissible. Upholding the conviction, the court stated, "The crime of solicitation * * * is complete with the solicitation even though there could never have been an acquiescence in the scheme by the one solicited."

4. May one who solicits another to commit an offense escape liability by voluntarily renouncing the venture before the crime is committed by the person solicited? The appellate case law is inconclusive. See W. LaFave and A. Scott, Criminal Law 492 (2d ed.1986). The Model Penal Code (see page 351) and some modern statutes would make such a defense sometimes available. Under the Model Penal Code, the defense requires that the defendant have actually prevented the person solicited from committing the crime. Other formulations do not require this. Arizona law, for example, requires proof that the defendant notified the person solicited and made reasonable effort to prevent the crime as by notifying law enforcement authorities. Ariz.Rev.Stat. § 13-1005(B).

When is such a defense established? In *People v. Gordon*, 47 Cal. App.3d 465, 120 Cal.Rptr. 840 (1975), defendant—an attorney acting on behalf of an undisclosed client—solicited a police officer to plant narcotics on another individual. The next day, she called the police officer and told him that she had decided not to be a party to the scheme, as she did not want to take a chance on ruining her political career. The officer made several subsequent contacts with defendant, but she refused to set up a meeting between her client and the officer. Affirming her conviction for solicitation, the court held: "Since the crime was fully committed * * *; it is no defense that the defendant later withdrew or failed to consummate the crime which was the object of the solicitation." If the Model Penal Code provision had been applicable, would she have had a defense?

C. CONSPIRACY
Editors' Introduction: Use and Abuse of Conspiracy Law

Conspiracy serves several functions in criminal law. It is, like attempt and solicitation, an inchoate crime for which a defendant may be charged, tried, convicted, and punished even if its criminal purposes are not achieved. However, it is also a substantive offense that justifies conviction and punishment in addition to any liability for any offense committed as the object of the conspiracy. Further, it is sometimes a vehicle for making one person liable for the crimes of other individuals. The so-called *Pinkerton* rule discussed in Section B of Chapter 6, provides that under certain circumstances all conspirators are liable for crimes committed by one member of the conspiracy.

Conspiracy prosecutions often involve complex procedural issues that are beyond the scope of direct concern here. However, in part because of these procedural aspects of conspiracy—and in part because of the nature of the crime of conspiracy itself—some have expressed serious misgivings regarding the continued vitality of conspiracy doctrine as a part of substantive criminal law. The numerous issues that must be faced in considering conspiracy law should be evaluated in light of these concerns. They were perhaps most effectively put by Mr. Justice Jackson in his concurring opinion in *Krulewitch v. United States*, 336 U.S. 440, 445-454, 69 S.Ct. 716, 719-723, 93 L.Ed. 790, 795-800 (1949):

> [A] present drift in the federal law of conspiracy * * * warrants some further comment because it is characteristic of the long evolution of that elastic, sprawling and pervasive offense. Its history exemplifies the "tendency of a principle to expand itself to the limit of its logic." The unavailing protest of courts against the growing habit to indict for conspiracy in lieu of prosecuting for the substantive offense itself, or in addition thereto, suggests that loose practice as to this offense constitutes a serious threat to fairness in our administration of justice.
>
> The modern crime of conspiracy is so vague that it almost defies definition. Despite certain elementary and essential elements, it also, chameleon-like, takes on a special coloration from each of the many independent offenses on which it may be overlaid. It is always "predominantly mental in composition" because it consists primarily of a meeting of minds and an intent.
>
> The crime comes down to us wrapped in vague but unpleasant connotations. It sounds historical undertones of treachery, secret plotting and violence on a scale that menaces social stability and the security of the state itself. "Privy conspiracy" ranks with sedition and rebellion in the Litany's prayer for deliverance. Conspiratorial movements do indeed lie back of the political assassination, the *coup d'etat,* the *putsch,* the revolution, and seizures of power in modern times, as they have in all history.
>
> But the conspiracy concept also is superimposed upon many concerted crimes having no political motivation. It is not intended to question that the basic conspiracy principle has some place in modern criminal law, because to unite, back of a criminal purpose, the strength, opportunities and resources of many is obviously more dangerous and more difficult to police than the efforts of a lone

wrongdoer. It also may be trivialized, as [for example] where the conspiracy consists of the concert of a loathsome panderer and a prostitute to go from New York to Florida to ply their trade and it would appear that a simple Mann Act prosecution would vindicate the majesty of federal law. However, even when appropriately invoked, the looseness and pliability of the doctrine present inherent dangers which should be in the background of judicial thought wherever it is sought to extend the doctrine to meet the exigencies of a particular case.

Conspiracy in federal law aggravates the degree of crime over that of unconcerted offending. The act of confederating to commit a misdemeanor, followed by even an innocent overt act in its execution, is a felony and is such even if the misdemeanor is never consummated. The more radical proposition also is well-established that at common law and under some statutes a combination may be a criminal conspiracy even if it contemplates only acts which are not crimes at all when perpetrated by an individual or by many acting severally.

Thus the conspiracy doctrine will incriminate persons on the fringe of offending who would not be guilty of aiding and abetting or of becoming an accessory, for those charges only lie when an act which is a crime has actually been committed.

* * *

[T]here are procedural advantages from using [conspiracy] which add to the danger of unguarded extension of the concept.

An accused, under the Sixth Amendment, has the right to trial "by an impartial jury of the State and district wherein the crime shall have been committed." The leverage of a conspiracy charge lifts this limitation from the prosecution and reduces its protection to a phantom, for the crime is considered so vagrant as to have been committed in any district where any one of the conspirators did any one of the acts, however innocent, intended to accomplish its object. The Government may, and often does, compel one to defend at a great distance from any place he ever did any act because some accused confederate did some trivial and by itself innocent act in the chosen district. Circumstances may even enable the prosecution to fix the place of trial in Washington, D.C., where a defendant may lawfully be put to trial before a jury partly or even wholly made up of employees of the Government that accuses him.

When the trial starts, the accused feels the full impact of the conspiracy strategy. Strictly, the prosecution should first establish *prima facie* the conspiracy and identify the conspirators, after which evidence of acts and declarations of each in the course of its execution are admissible against all. But the order of proof of so sprawling a charge is difficult for a judge to control. As a practical matter, the accused often is confronted with a hodgepodge of acts and statements by others which he may never have authorized or intended or even known about, but which help to persuade the jury of existence of the conspiracy itself. In other words, a conspiracy often is proved by evidence that is admissible only upon assumption that conspiracy existed. The naive assumption that prejudicial effects can be overcome by instructions to the jury all practicing lawyers know to be unmitigated fiction.

The trial of a conspiracy charge doubtless imposes a heavy burden on the prosecution, but it is an especially difficult situation for the defendant. The hazard from loose application of rules of evidence is aggravated where the Government institutes mass trials. * * *

A co-defendant in a conspiracy trial occupies an uneasy seat. There generally will be evidence of wrongdoing by somebody. It is difficult for the individual to make his own case stand on its own merits in the minds of jurors who are ready to believe that birds of a feather are flocked together. If he is silent, he is taken to admit it and if, as often happens, co-defendants can be prodded into accusing or contradicting each other, they convict each other. * * *

As Justice Jackson made clear, conspiracy shares the doctrinal problems examined in connection with the other inchoate offenses, attempt and solicitation. There is no necessity that a result be shown. This departure from the model concept of the elements of crime raises questions as to the actor's commitment to the criminal goal and his or her dangerousness. Conspiracy prosecutions and convictions can be founded on evidence revealing much less corroboration of criminal intent than would suffice for an attempt. This is also true of solicitation, but the use of that crime tends to be limited to words and conduct intended to bring about only the most serious of felonies. The criticism of conspiracy is, however, based on more than the theoretical difficulties it shares with other inchoate crimes. The history of its use is an important reason for the bad odor in which it is held in some quarters. It has been employed in both England and the United States to suppress combinations of workers and political subversives, as well as those of businesses and others seeking more traditional criminal ends.

Given these criticisms, how is the continued vitality of conspiracy to be explained? In part the answer lies in the same considerations that justify liability for attempt and solicitation: it provides a predicate for state intervention without having to await the commission of the object harm; and it reflects a sense of justice that would be offended if the failure of a criminal scheme served to exculpate one whose *mens rea* and conduct, albeit minimal, identifies his or her as a danger to the rest of us.

In addition there are reasons peculiar to conspiracy itself. The very procedural advantages that disturb civil libertarians serve as powerful weapons that those charged with the duty of crime control are understandably loathe to surrender. Conspiracy also reflects the realities of our more complex society. Modern technology and the enormous increase in our population have resulted in revolutionary changes in the ways in which work, education, leisure, and most other human activities have been organized. Parallel changes have occurred in criminal activity. Although the purse snatcher and burglar may continue to operate as individuals, interstate mail fraud, auto theft rings, and, preeminently, international purveyors of illicit drugs reflect the need for elaborate, far-flung organizations involving many players. The existence of such organizations explains the continuing appeal of conspiracy.

1. *Elements of the Offense*

The two traditional elements of the crime of conspiracy are the agreement between or among the participants and the intent or state of mind required concerning the objective of the agreement. Although the performance of an overt act pursuant to the agreement was not an element of the original common law crime of conspiracy, modern statutes impose such a requirement with sufficient frequency that an overt act needs to be considered a potential additional element in contemporary analysis.

a. Agreement

Editors' Introduction: Agreement and the Overt Act Requirement in Conspiracy Law

The essence of conspiracy is the agreement between or among the parties, although as developed next, an overt act by one of the parties is sometimes required. The problems raised by the requirement of an agreement are to some extent simply problems of proof: What constitutes sufficient evidence of the agreement required by the crime? In addition, however, traditional law has found "defenses" to charges of conspiracy where the facts are regarded as establishing the logical impossibility of two "guilty" minds having actually met in agreement. This is developed in subsection (1)(a)(3).

Before addressing these matters, it is useful to consider the more basic question of what is necessary to establish that an agreement exists and that a specific person is a party to that agreement. Must the person be shown to have made a relatively specific commitment to participate in the scheme that is the subject of the discussion? This was considered in *Cleaver v. United States*, 238 F.2d 766, 771 (10th Cir. 1956), which addressed the question of whether one Webster was a member of a conspiracy to commit burglary that the court acknowledged was proved by the prosecution:

> Webster * * * did not participate in the planning or the commission of the burglary, although he was present during a number of the conversations among the various conspirators. Mere knowledge, approval of or acquiescence in the object or purpose of the conspiracy, without an intention and agreement to cooperate in the crime is insufficient to constitute one a conspirator.

Cleaver is correct that mere presence at the scene of the planning of a crime will not by itself support the finding of an agreement that is crucial to a conspiracy conviction. Even knowledge and approval of others' criminal plans does not make one a co-conspirator.

Does the requirement of an agreement by itself offer sufficient protection from governmental abuse of conspiracy? A major theme of Justice Jackson's attack on conspiracy in *Krulewitch*, see pp. 353–355, is that the definition of the offense is too vague. One response to that claim is that the prosecution is required to establish the existence of an agreement. The agreement, in the view of defenders of conspiracy, is a sufficiently unambiguous act to allay concerns stemming from vagueness. This answer might be more fully reassuring if the agreement requirement could only be satisfied by showing an express meeting of the minds that was formally memorialized. Obviously this is not required for all civil contracts, much less those aimed at the achievement of illicit ends. Instead, of necessity, the law permits triers of fact to infer from circumstantial evidence that the defendant knowingly agreed to join one or more others in a concerted effort to bring about a common end. In practice, the task of proving an agreement may be a small obstacle to the prosecution and, therefore, a minor protection against the dangers that may be posed by the vagueness of conspiracy.

The common law crime of conspiracy required no more than that the act of agreement have been completed. A number of American jurisdictions, though, have required that, in addition to the agreement, the prosecution prove the commission of an overt act by at least one member of the agreement. This is the case under the federal criminal conspiracy statute, 18 U.S.C.A. § 371, which requires proof that "one or more of * * * [the] persons [agreeing did an] act to effect the object of the conspiracy." Some statutes imposed a selective requirement. The Arizona statute, for example, requires proof of an overt act except where the object of the conspiracy is to commit burglary while armed, arson of an occupied structure, or any felony upon the person of another. Ariz.Rev.Stat. § 13-1003.

The Supreme Court summarized the basic law applicable to the overt act requirement under the federal statute as follows:

> It is not necessary that an overt act be the substantive crime charged in the indictment as the object of the conspiracy. Nor, indeed, need such act, taken by itself, even be criminal in character. The function of the overt act in a conspiracy prosecution is simply to manifest "that the conspiracy is at work," and is neither a project still resting solely in the minds of the conspirators nor a fully completed operation no longer in existence.

Yates v. United States, 351 U.S. 298, 334, 77 S.Ct. 1064, 1084–85, 1 L.Ed.2d 1356, 1384 (1957).

There are two major issues posed by this aspect of conspiracy law. The first, of course, is whether sound policy dictates that conspiracy be so defined as to include proof of an overt act as well as an agreement. This second issue is related. What standard should be used to determine whether, under an overt act requirement, specific acts are sufficient? This relates to the rationale for the overt act requirement. What criterion for determining the sufficiency of overt acts best accomplishes the purpose of this requirement?

As to the first issue, it is clear that proponents of an overt act requirement see it as one more way to overcome the danger of misidentification, which they believe is inherent in the vagueness of conspiracy. It is an additional manifestation of the actor's purpose and offers some reassurance that the agreement poses a real danger of consummation. It is also said:

> to allow an opportunity to the conspirators to repent and to terminate the unlawful agreement before any decisive act is done in furtherance of it. The requirement of the allegation and proof of such an overt act "* * * affords a locus poenitentiae, so that before the act is done either one or all of the parties may abandon their design, and thus avoid the penalty prescribed by the statute."

People v. Olson, 232 Cal.App.2d 480, 42 Cal.Rptr. 760, 767 (1965). Any formal requirement of an overt act may simply recognize what prosecutors realize is the practical need for proof of such an act to persuade juries to convict in conspiracy cases. A committee proposing that the Illinois conspiracy statute be amended so as to include a requirement of an overt act observed:

Heretofore, in Illinois, the agreement alone has constituted sufficient conduct to support a charge of conspiracy * * *. In actuality, however, no case has been found in which some activity pursuant to the agreement has not been present. This leads to the conclusion that prosecutors find proof of the agreement without subsequent activity too difficult, or consider the agreement alone too inconsequential, to warrant criminal prosecution.

Illinois Criminal Code of 1961, Committee Comments to Section 8-2.

As to the second issue, it is clear that where an overt act is required it is a burden easily satisfied. Very minor conduct that is undertaken in furtherance of the conspiracy will be sufficient. Certainly the overt act need not itself be criminal.

What constitutes an act in furtherance can, however, pose some difficulties in unusual cases. It has been held that a payment to a co-conspirator to secure his or her agreement to the conspiracy is *not* an overt act required by law. *People v. Teeter*, 86 Misc.2d 532, 382 N.Y.S.2d 938 (1976), aff'd 62 A.D.2d 1158, 404 N.Y.S.2d 210 (1978). On the other hand, if the basic agreement has clearly been achieved, mere conversations among the confederates concerning implementation are likely to be sufficient. See *United States v. Arnione*, 363 F.2d 385 (2d Cir.1966), cert. denied, 385 U.S. 957, 87 S.Ct. 391, 17 L.Ed.2d 303 (1966). Because so little has been required, some have argued that the requirement should be strengthened so as to require proof that each person charged as a conspirator took some significant action in furtherance of the object offense.

Overt acts can have significant procedural consequences. Venue might be found in any district in which any overt act was performed, for example, a matter that can be of considerable advantage to the prosecution. Similarly, an overt act will extend the statute of limitations, which again can be advantageous to the government.

The following subsections present several distinguishable aspects of conspiracy law's agreement requirement. First, the definition of the agreement that must be proved is addressed. Next, the need to distinguish among possibly separate agreements is considered. The final subsection turns to defensive contentions that are based on the need for an agreement.

(1) General Requirement of an Agreement

An agreement is of considerable importance to the definition of criminal conspiracy. No further conduct confirming blameworthiness and dangerousness is required, except for the minimal demands of the overt act element in those jurisdiction imposing it. Proof of the agreement, then, is the major means of allaying concern that the crime of conspiracy punishes only for thoughts or propensities.

Because of the nature of conspiratorial behavior, of course, eyewitness testimony to the achieving of an explicit agreement is often unavailable to the prosecution. Conspiracy law tends to accommodate this. As noted by the Arkansas Supreme Court in *Griffin v. State*, 248 Ark. 1223, 1225, 455 S.W.2d 882, 884 (1970):

[I]t is not necessary that an unlawful combination, conspiracy or concert of action to commit an unlawful act be shown by direct evidence, and * * * it may be proved by circumstances. * * * It may be inferred, even though no actual meeting among the parties is proved, if it be shown that two or more persons pursued by their acts the same unlawful object, each doing a part, so that their acts, though apparently independent, were in fact connected.

Given the obvious difficulties of proving agreements for criminal purposes, it is necessary that the prosecution be permitted considerable leeway in how it may establish this element. This view has been given its clearest expression in the context of federal prosecutions under the Sherman Antitrust Act. A doctrine has been developed that permits agreements to restrain commerce to be inferred from proof that presumptive competitors pursued uniform business conduct. Indeed, it has been said that it is sufficient if the competitors knew of a cooperative plan of action that required concerted action to be successful and, knowing that the plan would result in a restraint of commerce, participated. As Mr. Justice Stone, writing for the Supreme Court, observed:

> It is elementary that an unlawful conspiracy may be and often is formed without simultaneous action or agreement on the part of the conspirators. Acceptance by competitors, without previous agreement of an invitation to participate in a plan, the necessary consequence of which, if carried out, in restraint of interstate commerce, is sufficient to establish an unlawful conspiracy under the Sherman Act.

Interstate Circuit v. United States, 306 U.S. 208, 227, 59 S.Ct. 467, 474, 83 L.Ed. 610, 620 (1939).

United States v. Brown

United States Court of Appeals, Second Circuit, 1985
776 F.2d 397.

FRIENDLY, CIRCUIT JUDGE:

[The defendant and his codefendant, Valentine (a fugitive at the time of trial), were charged with conspiring to distribute heroin and with distribution of heroin. The basis for the prosecution was the purchase by New York City Police Officer William Grimball of a "joint" of "D" (a "joint" is $40 worth of "D" or heroin) while working undercover in Harlem. The jury convicted the defendant of conspiracy but was unable to reach a verdict on the substantive count.]

Officer Grimball was the Government's principal witness. He testified that early in the evening of October 9, 1984, he approached Gregory Valentine on the corner of 115th Street and Eighth Avenue and asked him for a joint of "D". Valentine asked Grimball whom he knew around the street. Grimball asked if Valentine knew Scott. He did not. Brown "came up" and Valentine said, "He wants a joint, but I don't know him." Brown looked at Grimball and said, "He looks okay to me." Valentine then said, "Okay. But I am going to leave it somewhere and you

[meaning Officer Grimball] can pick it up." Brown interjected, "You don't have to do that. Just go and get it for him. He looks all right to me." After looking again at Grimball, Brown said, "He looks all right to me" and "I will wait right here."

Valentine then said, "Okay. Come on with me around to the hotel." Grimball followed him to 300 West 116th Street, where Valentine instructed him, "Sit on the black car and give me a few minutes to go up and get it." Valentine requested and received $40, which had been prerecorded, and then said, "You are going to take care of me for doing this for you, throw some dollars my way?," to which Grimball responded, "Yeah."

Valentine then entered the hotel and shortly returned. The two went back to 115th Street and Eighth Avenue, where Valentine placed a cigarette box on the hood of a blue car. Grimball picked up the cigarette box and found a glassine envelope containing white powder, stipulated to be heroin. Grimball placed $5 of prerecorded buy money in the cigarette box, which he replaced on the hood. Valentine picked up the box and removed the $5. Grimball returned to his car and made a radio transmission to the backup field team that "the buy had went down" and informed them of the locations of the persons involved. Brown and Valentine were arrested. Valentine was found to possess two glassine envelopes of heroin and the $5 of prerecorded money. Brown was in possession of $31 of his own money; no drugs or contraband were found on him. The $40 of marked buy money was not recovered, and no arrests were made at the hotel.

[The prosecution had Grimball qualified as an expert on the basis of several seminars on drug control and his participation in street buys. He then] testified that the typical drug buy in the Harlem area involved two to five people. As a result of frequent police sweeps, Harlem drug dealers were becoming so cautious that they employed

> people who act as steerers and the steerer's responsibility is basically to determine whether or not you are actually an addict or a user of heroin and they are also used to screen you to see if there is any possibility of you being a cop looking for a bulge or some indication that would give them that you are not actually an addict. And a lot of the responsibility relies [sic] on them to determine whether or not the drug buy is going to go down or not.

Officer Grimball [testified further] that based on his experience as an undercover agent he would describe the role that Ronald Brown played in the transaction as that of a steerer. When asked why, he testified * * *, "Because I believe that if it wasn't for his approval, the buy would not have gone down."

[Brown claimed that the trial judge erred in permitting Grimball to testify to an opinion that Brown was a steerer and thus acted pursuant to a prior agreement with Valentine. The court found no need to finally resolve the propriety of this testimony, because other evidence was sufficient to convict Brown.]

In considering the sufficiency of the evidence, we begin with some preliminary observations. One is that, in testing sufficiency, "the relevant question is whether, after viewing the evidence in the light most favorable to the prosecution, *any* rational trier of fact could have found the essential elements of the crime beyond a reasonable doubt." * * *

The second observation is that since the jury convicted on the conspiracy count alone, the evidence must permit a reasonable juror to be convinced beyond a reasonable doubt not simply that Brown had aided and abetted the drug sale but that he had agreed to do so. On the other hand, the jury's failure to agree on the aiding and abetting charge does not operate against the Government; even an acquittal on that count would not have done so.

A review of the evidence against Brown convinces us that it was sufficient, even without Grimball's characterization of Brown as a steerer, although barely so. Although Brown's mere presence at the scene of the crime and his knowledge that a crime was being committed would not have been sufficient to establish Brown's knowing participation in the conspiracy, the proof went considerably beyond that. Brown was not simply standing around while the exchanges between Officer Grimball and Valentine occurred. He came on the scene shortly after these began and Valentine immediately explained the situation to him. Brown then conferred his seal of approval on Grimball, a most unlikely event unless there was an established relationship between Brown and Valentine. Finally, Brown took upon himself the serious responsibility of telling Valentine to desist from his plan to reduce the risks by not handing the heroin directly to Grimball. A rational mind could take this as bespeaking the existence of an agreement whereby Brown was to have the authority to command, or at least to persuade. Brown's remark, "Just go and get it for him," permits inferences that Brown knew where the heroin was to be gotten, that he knew that Valentine knew this, and that Brown and Valentine had engaged in such a transaction before.

The mere fact that these inferences were not ineluctable does not mean that they were insufficient to convince a reasonable juror beyond a reasonable doubt. * * * When we add to the inferences that can be reasonably drawn from the facts to which Grimball testified the portion of his expert testimony about the use of steerers in street sales of narcotics, which was clearly unobjectionable once Grimball's qualifications were established, we conclude that the Government offered sufficient evidence, apart from Grimball's opinion that Brown was a steerer, for a reasonable juror to be satisfied beyond a reasonable doubt not only that Brown had acted as a steerer but that he had agreed to do so.

We do not read *United States v. Tyler*, 758 F.2d 66 (2 Cir.1985), as being to the contrary. The court read the evidence as showing "no more than that Tyler helped a willing buyer find a willing seller." Since there was no basis for inferring a prior contact between Tyler, the introducer, and Bennett, the seller, Tyler could properly be convicted only as an aider or abettor, not as a conspirator. Here a jury could reasonably infer prior arrangements or an established working relationship between Brown and Valentine. * * * . Brown's conversation with Valentine in the presence of Grimball establishes that he knew precisely what the transaction was. * * *

Affirmed.

OAKES, CIRCUIT JUDGE (dissenting):

While it is true that this is another $40 narcotics case, it is also a conspiracy case, and by the majority's own admission one resting on "barely" sufficient evidence. But evidence of what? An agreement—a "continuous and conscious union of wills upon a common undertaking," in the words of Note, *Developments in the Law-Criminal Conspiracy*, 72 Harv.L.Rev. 920, 926 (1959)? Not unless an inference that Brown agreed to act as a "steerer" may be drawn from the fact that he said to Valentine (three times) that Grimball "looks okay [all right] to me," as well as "[j]ust go and get it for him." And the only way that inference may be drawn so as to prove guilt beyond a reasonable doubt is, in my view, with assistance from the "expert" testimony of the ubiquitous Officer Grimball. It could not be drawn from Brown's possession, constructive or otherwise, of narcotics or narcotics paraphernalia, his sharing in the proceeds of the street sale, his conversations with others, or even some hearsay evidence as to his "prior arrangements" with Valentine or "an established working relationship between Brown and Valentine" * * *. There is not a shred of evidence of Brown's "stake in the outcome"; indeed, Brown was apprehended after leaving the area of the crime with only thirty-one of his own dollars in his pocket, and no drugs or other contraband. He did not even stay around for another Valentine sale, though the majority infers, speculatively, that Brown and Valentine had engaged in "such a transaction before."

When * * * numerous other inferences could be drawn from the few words of conversation in which Brown is said to have engaged, I cannot believe that there is proof of *conspiracy,* or Brown's membership in it, beyond a reasonable doubt * * *.

This case may be unique. * * * But * * * it * * * seems to me, * * * to borrow a phrase from Justice Jackson's *Krulewitch* concurrence, to "constitute[ ] a serious threat to fairness in our administration of justice." If today we uphold a conspiracy to sell narcotics on the street, on this kind and amount of evidence, what conspiracies might we approve tomorrow? The majority opinion will come back to haunt us, I fear.

* * * Precisely because this is another $40 narcotics case, I would draw the line. This case effectively permits prosecution of everyone connected with a street sale of narcotics to be prosecuted on two counts—a conspiracy as well as a substantive charge. And evidence showing no more than that a defendant was probably aware that a narcotics deal was about to occur will support a conspiracy conviction * * *.

Accordingly, I dissent.

Notes and Questions

1. If the substantive crime has actually been committed, the law need not impose liability for conspiracy to vindicate the policies that support inchoate crimes. The effect of a rule permitting dual conviction and penalties is, of course, that crimes committed by collective action are punishable by a significantly higher penalty than those committed individually. Is this defensible on policy grounds? In *Callanan v. United States*, 364 U.S. 587, 81 S.Ct. 321, 5 L.Ed.2d 312 (1961), the Supreme Court rejected an argument that Congress had intended that a defendant who committed conspiracy to obstruct commerce by extorting money and the substantive crime of obstructing commerce by extorting money should be punishable for only one of those offenses created by the Hobbs Anti-Racketeering Act. Explaining the apparent legislative reasoning, the Court stated:

   [C]ollective criminal agreement—partnership in crime—presents a greater potential threat to the public than individual delicts. Concerted action both increases the likelihood that the criminal object will be successfully attained and decreases the probability that the individuals involved will depart from their paths of criminality. Group association for criminal purposes often, if not normally, makes possible the attainment of ends more complex than those which one criminal could accomplish. Nor is the danger of a conspiratorial group limited to the particular end towards which it has embarked. Combination in crime makes more likely the commission of crimes unrelated to the original purpose for which the group was formed. In sum, the danger which a conspiracy generates is not confined to the substantive offense which is the immediate aim of the enterprise.

   The Model Penal Code embraces the "minority" view that conviction for both an offense and conspiracy to commit only that offense should not be permitted. See Model Penal Code § 1.07(l)(b) (Official Draft 1985).

2. As the material in Section A(2) of this chapter developed, legal but not factual impossibility may be a defense to a charge of attempt. It seems clear that factual impossibility will not be accepted as a defense to conspiracy. *United States v. Brantley*, 777 F.2d 159, 164 (4th Cir.1985) (defendant, a South Carolina sheriff, could be convicted of conspiracy to commit

extortion in violation of Hobbs Act even though the bribe he accepted to permit the operation of a high stakes gambling club for nonresidents came from an undercover FBI agent and there was never any chance that interstate commerce might thereby be affected).

There is some authority that legal or inherent impossibility precludes conviction for conspiracy. *Ventimiglia v. United States*, 242 F.2d 620 (4th Cir. 1957). However, most courts hold that impossibility—whether legal or factual as those terms are used in attempt law discussions—has no effect on guilt of conspiracy. In *State v. Moretti*, 52 N.J. 182, 244 A.2d 499 (1968), cert. denied, 393 U.S. 952, 89 S.Ct. 376, 21 L.Ed.2d 363 (1968), the court offered the following explanation for the different treatment accorded impossibility in attempt and conspiracy:

> [A] conspiracy charge focuses primarily on the *intent* of the defendants, while in an attempt case the primary inquiry centers on the defendants' *conduct* tending towards the commission of the substantive crime. The crime of conspiracy is complete once the conspirators, having formed the intent to commit a crime, take any step in preparation; mere preparation, however, is an inadequate basis for an attempt conviction regardless of the intent. Thus, the impossibility that the defendants' conduct will result in the consummation of the contemplated crime is not as pertinent in a conspiracy case as it might be in an attempt prosecution.

3. Should withdrawal be a defense to a charge of conspiring to commit a crime? If so, what should be required for an effective withdrawal? Withdrawal has generally not been a defense. This traditional view was explained in *United States v. Read*, 658 F.2d 1225, 1232–33 (7th Cir.1981):

> Withdrawal marks a conspirator's disavowal or abandonment of the conspiratorial agreement. By definition, after a defendant withdraws, he is no longer a member of the conspiracy and the later acts of the conspirators do not bind him. The defendant is still liable, however, for his previous agreement and for the previous acts of his co-conspirators in pursuit of the conspiracy. Withdrawal is not, therefore, a complete defense to the crime of conspiracy. Withdrawal becomes a

complete defense only when coupled with the defense of the statute of limitations. A defendant's withdrawal from the conspiracy starts the running of the statute of limitations as to him. If the indictment is filed more than five years after a defendant withdraws, the statute of limitations bars prosecution for his actual participation in the conspiracy. He cannot be held liable for acts or declarations committed in the five years preceding the indictment by other conspirators because his withdrawal ended his membership in the conspiracy. It is thus only the interaction of the two defenses of withdrawal and the statute of limitations which shields the defendant from liability.

If, however, a jurisdiction requires an overt act by one of the conspirators before the crime of conspiracy is complete, Developments in the Law—Criminal Conspiracy, 72 Harv.L.Rev. 922, 957 (1959) suggests that a withdrawal by one of the actors before the commission of the overt act would seem to preclude liability for crimes committed by the co-conspirators.

4. Insofar as withdrawal has legal significance, what is required for an effective withdrawal? One court has said that the defendant:

> must abandon the illegal enterprise in a manner reasonably calculated to reach coconspirators. Mere cessation of participation in the conspiracy is not enough. However, a defendant need not take action to stop, obstruct or interfere with the conspiracy in order to withdraw from it.

United States v. Lowell, 649 F.2d 950, 957 (3d Cir.1981).

Contrast the positions of *Read* (discussed in note 3) and *Lowell* with that expressed in section 5.03(6) of the Model Penal Code (reprinted at page 378), which provides for a defense of renunciation. The Model Penal Code would make this an affirmative defense, and thus require the defendant to bear the burden of persuasion by a preponderance of the evidence. In contrast, the court in *Read* held that inasmuch as withdrawal negates an essential element of the crime—membership—to place any burden on the defendant other than that of going forward with evidence of withdrawal would violate due process.

The Model Penal Code would require that the defendant have prevented the commission of the object crime; it demands that the defendant have "thwarted the success of the conspiracy." If a conspirator withdraws and, for reasons unrelated to his withdrawal or subsequent activity, the other members of the group fail to commit the object crime, he apparently remains liable for conspiracy.

A further effect of withdrawal is that declarations of one conspirator made during and in furtherance of the conspiracy but after a conspirator's withdrawal cannot be offered against him under a well-established exception to the hearsay rule. Perhaps more significantly, an effective withdrawal prevents a conspirator from being held liable for substantive crimes committed by other members of the scheme. This is discussed in Chapter 6, Section B.

---

(2) Number of Agreements

Editors' Note: The Party and Object Dimensions of Agreements and the Number of Conspiracies in a Situation

Complex multiparty situations giving rise to conspiracy charges may require careful analysis to determine whether they present a single, large conspiracy or instead a number of smaller, perhaps overlapping, conspiracies. This may be important for a number of reasons. If the evidence shows a different number or pattern of agreements than was alleged in the charging instrument, there may be a fatal variance between the instrument and the prosecution's proof at trial; the defendants may consequently be entitled to acquittal.

Whether a defendant was a member of the same conspiracy as another person may be important to resolving a variety of matters. Whether a defendant who conspired is guilty of the crimes committed by another person who conspired depends in part upon whether the two persons were part of the *same* conspiracy. Whether (if an overt act is required) an overt act by another person will constitute the overt act sufficient to make the defendant guilty of conspiracy turns in part upon whether the person acting was a member of the same conspiracy as the defendant.

If the facts present several overlapping conspiracies, one or more persons may be members of more than one and thus subject to several charges of conspiracy rather than only one. Careful analysis may therefore be necessary to determine whether a defendant is guilty of several crimes based on membership in several distinguishable conspiracies.

Disputes over the number of conspiracies shown by the evidence at trial are traditionally among the most commonly raised points on appeal. The normal pattern in practice is that the prosecution alleges a single conspiracy and the defendants claim that, if anything, more than one has been established. Presumably the prosecution favors a single conspiracy because it binds more defendants together in a way that will make the acts and words of each more readily admissible against all others. In those instances in which the prosecution alleges multiple conspiracies, perhaps in an effort to obtain multiple sentences, the defendants may claim that there was only one.

There are two aspects of agreements that might be used to define them and thus also to distinguish among different agreements: the parties and the object or objective to the agreement[s]. Case law does, to some extent, distinguish the effect of differences in these two dimensions of criminal agreements.

Party Dimension

With respect to the party dimension of agreements, it is clear that there is no need to show that the defendant knew all of the parties to a particular conspiracy, much less that he or she explicitly agreed with each. Where the prosecution shows that the defendant joined an illicit scheme of obvious complexity courts will readily infer that the defendant must have realized that others, their identities albeit unknown to him, must be participating. Consequently, the defendant will be held to have been a member of a single, large conspiracy that included these persons, even though they were unknown to him. His participation in only one aspect of a complex criminal operation will not mean that the activities of the unknown others in other aspects in furtherance of the overall scheme constitute a separate conspiracy. *Blumenthal v. United States*, 332 U.S. 539, 556–57, 68 S.Ct. 248, 256, 92 L.Ed. 154 (1947).

The classic example of emphasis upon the party dimension of agreements to analyze a conspiracy situation is *United States v. Bruno*, 105 F.2d 921 (2d Cir.) rev'd, 308 U.S. 287, 60 S.Ct. 198, 84 L.Ed. 257 (1939), where a single conspiracy was found to exist involving New York narcotics smugglers, middlemen who paid the smugglers and distributed to retailers, and two groups of retailers—one in New York and the other in Texas and Louisiana—selling to addicts. This was upheld despite the absence of any evidence of cooperation or even communication between the two retail groups. Thus, a Texas retailer might be guilty of crimes committed by the New York middlemen in furtherance of the conspiracy as well as the conspiracy itself. Yet the Texas retailer, who may not even know of the existence of the person for whose crimes the retailer can be convicted, may well have had no impact whatsoever on the commission of those crimes. Thus the propriety of making the Texas retailer guilty of those crimes is questionable.

The alternative position that there were two conspiracies in *Bruno*—one involving smugglers, wholesalers, and New York retailers, and the other involving smugglers, wholesalers and Louisiana/Texas retailers—is similarly not free from difficulty. Under that view would there be a separate conspiracy for each distinct group of retailers? Why not a separate conspiracy for the smugglers, wholesalers, and each individual retailer in the absence of evidence of a meaningful mutual dependence among the retailers? The potential multiplication of liability—the possibility of multiple prosecutions, convictions, and sentences—poses very serious problems. These difficulties are avoided if the situation is treated as involving only one large conspiracy.

Object Dimension

Clearly the objectives of those who agree must also be considered in defining and distinguishing among criminal agreements. *Braverman v. United States*, 317 U.S. 49, 63 S.Ct. 99, 87 L.Ed. 23 (1942), and a case almost a half-century later illustrate an emphasis upon the object dimension of agreements in analyzing a conspiracy situation.

The *Braverman* defendants were charged with seven conspiracies each having as its objective the violation of a different provision of the Internal Revenue laws. The evidence revealed a long-standing collaboration among the defendants to manufacture, transport and distribute distilled spirits. The defense moved, at the beginning and end of the trial, to require the government to elect one of the seven counts of the indictment upon which to proceed, contending that the proof could not establish more than one agreement. Despite the evidence that there was one overall agreement involving commission of all the crimes, the government and the lower courts took the view that the defendants were guilty of one criminal conspiracy for each crime they contemplated being committed under the scheme. The Supreme Court reversed. Mr. Chief Justice Stone wrote: "the precise nature and extent of the conspiracy must be determined by reference to the agreement which embraces and defines its objects. Whether the object of a single agreement is to commit one or many crimes, it is in either case that agreement which constitutes the conspiracy which the statute punishes. The one agreement cannot be taken to be several agreements and hence several conspiracies because it envisages the violation of several statutes rather than one."

Almost forty years later the defendants in *Albernaz v. United States*, 450 U.S. 333, 101 S.Ct. 1137, 67 L.Ed.2d 275 (1981), relied on *Braverman* in seeking relief. They had entered an agreement to import marihuana and to distribute it. They were charged and convicted, and received consecutive sentences for a conspiracy to import marihuana and a conspiracy to distribute it. The Supreme Court distinguished *Braverman* on the ground that although the agreement there had multiple objectives it violated a single statute—the general federal conspiracy provision. Here, Congress had created two distinct conspiracy provisions that are directed at separate evils posed by drug trafficking. "'Importation' and 'distribution' of marihuana impose diverse societal harms, and * * * Congress has in effect determined that a conspiracy to import drugs and to distribute them is twice as serious to do either object singly." This decision, the Court held, was within the constitutional authority of Congress.

Recent Analyses

Generally, recent judicial treatment of conspiracy situations has made some traditional analyses and the use of "figurative analogies" from older case law less important. *United States v. Morris*, 46 F.3d 410, 415 (5th Cir.), cert. denied, 515 U.S. 1150, 115 S.Ct. 2595, 132 L.Ed.2d 892 (1995).

However, current law still requires determining how many conspiracies arise out of particular conduct, and the courts continue to combine consideration of both parties and objects. These general principles were stressed in *Doolin v. State*, 650 So.2d 44 (Fla.App.1995). Doolin was convicted of two charges of conspiracy, conspiracy to kidnap and conspiracy to commit aggravated battery. The proof showed one agreement to kidnap the victim and then to break her ankles and knees. Rejecting the prosecution's contention that "[a]ppellant cannot seriously suggest that conspirators who discuss and plot the commission of more than one distinct offense have engaged in only one conspiratorial act," the court explained:

> [T]he state has completely misconceived the nature of the offense of criminal conspiracy. The essence of the offense is the agreement to commit a criminal act or

acts, and if a single agreement exists, only one conspiracy exists even if the conspiracy has as its objectives the commission of multiple offenses; and the conspiracy continues to exist until consummated, abandoned, or otherwise terminated by some affirmative act.

Because only one agreement was shown, the court reversed the dual convictions and remanded for entry of judgment on only one count. As the *Doolin* concurrence noted, however, the multiple nature of the criminal objectives can be considered in sentencing. Multiple convictions are, of course, proper in such situations if the evidence in fact shows multiple, distinct agreements.

(3) Defenses Based on the Requirement of an Agreement

The essence of conspiracy is agreement. Some courts consider this requirement of a meeting of guilty minds so important that situations regarded as inconsistent with a union of criminal minds will be used to preclude conviction for conspiracy or even to invalidate a conviction already obtained.

Issues arising under this aspect of conspiracy law generally involve the assertion, as in the case that follows, that the disposition of actual or potential charges against other members of an alleged conspiracy requires acquittal of the remaining member, because the disposition of the charges against the other members is logically inconsistent with the existence of a criminal agreement involving the remaining member.

Regle v. State

Court of Special Appeals of Maryland, 1970
9 Md.App. 346, 264 A.2d 119.

MURPHY, CHIEF JUDGE

On September 28, 1968, Sergeant Frank Mazzone, a Maryland State Police officer working under cover, was advised by other police officers that Michael Isele, a police informer, had informed them that he had been invited by the appellant Regle to participate in a robbery. Mazzone immediately contacted Isele, whom he previously knew, and together they went to see the appellant. Isele introduced Mazzone to the appellant as a prospective participant in the planned robbery. After some discussion, the appellant invited Mazzone to participate in the robbery. While appellant did not then specify the place to be robbed, he indicated to Mazzone that Richard Fields had been involved with him in planning the robbery, and that he would also participate in the crime. Appellant, Mazzone, and Isele then met with Fields and the robbery plan was outlined by appellant and Fields. The need for guns was discussed and appellant and Fields spoke of the necessity of killing two employees at O'Donnell's restaurant, the situs

of the proposed robbery. The four men then drove in Isele's car to appellant's home where appellant phoned Kent Chamblee for the purpose of purchasing a shotgun. Thereafter, the men drove to Chamblee's home, purchased the gun from him, and tested it in his presence. While Chamblee knew that the shotgun was to be used "for a job," he did not accompany the others when they then drove to the restaurant to perpetrate the robbery. Upon arriving there, Mazzone told appellant that he first wanted to "case" the restaurant. This being agreed, Mazzone and Isele went into the restaurant while appellant and Fields went to a nearby bar to await their return. Once inside the restaurant, Mazzone contacted police headquarters and requested assistance. Thereafter, he and Isele left the restaurant and rejoined appellant and Fields. While several police cars promptly responded to the scene, Mazzone found it necessary, in the interim, to reveal his identity as a police officer and to arrest appellant and Fields at gunpoint. At the same time he also arrested Isele in order "to cover him." After the arrest, appellant made an incriminating statement to the effect that he and Fields had planned the robbery and that he had invited Isele to participate in the crime.

Appellant, Fields, and Chamblee were thereafter jointly indicted for conspiracy to rob with a dangerous and deadly weapon and for carrying a deadly weapon openly with intent to injure. Appellant was separately tried by a jury, found guilty on both counts, and sentenced to twenty years on the conspiracy charge, and two years, concurrent, on the weapons offense.

The docket entries indicate that the conspiracy indictment against Chamblee was *nol prossed* prior to appellant's trial. It also appears that at his trial appellant established through the testimony of a police officer that Fields had been examined by State psychiatrists at the Clifton Perkins State Hospital and found "not guilty by reason of being insane at the time of the alleged crime." The State did not rebut the officer's testimony, although the record indicates that two of the State psychiatrists who had examined Fields were then present in court.

Against this background, appellant contends that since the indictment against Chamblee was *nol prossed,* only he and Fields were charged as conspirators; and that because Fields was found insane at the time of the commission of the crime and thus was not a person legally capable of engaging in a criminal conspiracy, his own conviction cannot stand since one person alone cannot be guilty of the crime of conspiracy.

Conspiracy * * * is defined as a combination by two or more persons to accomplish a criminal or unlawful act, or to do a lawful act by criminal or unlawful means. The gist of the offense is the unlawful combination, resulting from the agreement, rather than the mere agreement itself, and no overt act is required to constitute the crime. In other words, as succinctly stated by the Supreme Court of New Jersey in *State v. Carbone*, 10 N.J. 329, 91 A.2d 571, 574, the "gist of the offense of conspiracy lies, not in doing the act, nor effecting the purpose for which the conspiracy is formed, nor in attempting to do them, nor in inciting others to do them, but in the forming of the scheme or agreement between the parties." Concert in criminal purpose, it is said, is the salient factor in criminal conspiracy. Criminal conspiracy is a partnership in crime—"It is the coalition of manpower and human minds enhancing possibilities of achievement aimed at the objective that present a greater threat to society than does a lone offender." Clark and Marshall Crimes (6th Edition) Section 9.00. In short, it is *the existence* of the conspiracy which creates the danger.

As one person cannot conspire or form a combination with himself, it is essential in proving the existence of a criminal conspiracy to show "the consent of two or more minds," viz., it must be shown that at least two persons had a meeting of the minds—a unity of design and purpose—to have an agreement. * * *

In view of these principles, it is the well settled general rule that one defendant in a prosecution for conspiracy cannot be convicted where all of his alleged coconspirators, be they one or more, have been acquitted or discharged under circumstances that amount to an acquittal. * * * The rationale underlying the rule appears clear: that it is illogical to acquit all but one of a purported partnership in crime; that acquittal of all persons with whom a defendant is alleged to have conspired is repugnant to the existence of the requisite corrupt agreement; and that regardless of the criminal animus of the one defendant, there must be someone with whom he confected his corrupt agreement, and where all his alleged coconspirators are not guilty, a like finding as to him must be made. * * *

Generally speaking, it would appear that so long as the disposition of the case against a coconspirator does not remove the basis for the charge of conspiracy, a single defendant may be prosecuted and convicted of the offense, even though for one reason or another his conspirator is either not tried or not convicted. Consistent with this rule, the authorities all agree that the death of one conspirator does not of itself prevent the conviction of the other, where the conspiracy between them is shown by the evidence. In *Hurwitz v. State*, [200 Md. 578, 92 A.2d 575], a case in which all but one of the conspirators were granted immunity from prosecution on a ground not inconsistent with their participation in the conspiracy, the court held that such grant of immunity was not equivalent to acquittal and would not require reversal of the conviction of the one remaining conspirator. The same rule has been applied where one of two conspirators enjoyed diplomatic immunity and therefore could not be prosecuted for the conspiracy. *Farnsworth v. Zerbst*, 98 F.2d 541 (5th Cir.). In *Adams v. State*, 202 Md. 455, 97 A.2d 281, it was held that conviction of one defendant in a conspiracy case was proper despite failure to convict of any of the other conspirators where it was alleged and shown that there were persons unknown to the prosecution with whom the convicted defendant had conspired. And while the cases are generally divided on the question whether the entry of a *nolle prosequi* as to one of two alleged conspirators compels an acquittal of the remaining conspirator, the better reasoned view would appear to support the proposition that it does not, at least where the *nolle prosequi* was not entered without the coconspirator's consent after the trial had begun (which then would have amounted to an acquittal and precluded reindictment). In *Hurwitz*, it was held that the entry of a "stet" to a coconspirator's indictment was not tantamount to an acquittal and did not compel the discharge of the only remaining conspirator.[1]

Some cases suggest that the rule that acquittal of all save one of the alleged conspirators results in the acquittal of all applies only to acquittals on the merits. Other cases—while recognizing that acquittals are not always tantamount to a declaration of innocence—nevertheless conclude that an acquittal is in effect a judicial determination, binding on the State, that the acquitted defendant was not a participant in a criminal conspiracy. The State urges that where the acquittal of one of the alleged conspirators is based solely on the fact that he was insane at the time of the crime, the remaining conspirator should nonetheless be held responsible for the offense. * * * We think the cases relied upon by the [State] stand for the proposition that it is no defense to one who participates either as a principal or aider or abettor in the actual commission of the substantive criminal offense that the principal offender was insane at the time of the crime. The principle would appear similar to the rule that a coconspirator may be convicted of any crime committed by any member of a conspiracy to do an illegal act if the act is done in furtherance of the purpose of the conspiracy. The conspiracy being established, the fact that the member who committed the crime was insane at the time would thus not exonerate the others from complicity in the commission of the substantive offense.

We do not find these cases controlling of the primary question before us, namely, whether *under an indictment for conspiracy,* one conspirator may be convicted of the offense where the only other conspirator was shown to be insane at the time the agreement between them was concluded. Conspiracy to commit a crime is a different offense from the crime that is the object of the conspiracy. One necessarily involves joint action; the other does not. By its nature, conspiracy is a joint or group offense requiring a concert of free wills, and the union of the minds of at least two persons is a prerequisite to the commission of the offense. The essence of conspiracy is, therefore, a mental confederation involving at least two persons; the crime is indivisible in the sense that it requires more than one guilty person; and where the joint intent does not exist, the basis of the charge of conspiracy is necessarily swept away. In short, the guilt of both persons must concur to constitute that of either. It is upon this premise that the authorities all agree that if two persons are charged as conspirators and one is an entrap-

per, or merely feigns acquiescence in the criminal intent, there is no punishable conspiracy because there was no agreement on the part of the one to engage in a criminal conspiracy.[2] For like reasons, we hold that where only two persons are implicated in a conspiracy, and one is shown to have been insane at the time the agreement was concluded, and hence totally incapable of committing any crime, there is no punishable criminal conspiracy, the requisite joint criminal intent being absent.

The evidence in the record before us plainly shows that appellant and Fields planned to commit a robbery at O'Donnell's restaurant. There is some evidence in the record to suggest that Chamblee may also have been a conspirator although the State made little effort at the trial to establish his involvement in the conspiracy. Since an insane person is mentally incapable of forming a criminal intent, it is clear that if Fields was actually insane at the time of the offense, he could not be found guilty of engaging in a criminal conspiracy. It does not appear however, that Fields was ever tried and acquitted of the conspiracy charge. But the only evidence in the record—the testimony of the police officer—is that Fields was found by State psychiatrists upon examination to have been insane at the time of the commission of the offense. While such testimony is hardly the equivalent of the expert medical evidence required to prove insanity, the trial judge, in his charge to the jury, stated as a fact that Fields "was found to be insane." Assuming this to be the true situation, it is unlikely that Fields will ever be brought to trial on the conspiracy charge.

As to Chamblee, the docket entries indicate the entry of a *nolle prosequi* to his conspiracy indictment. We cannot ascertain, therefore, whether, in the circumstances in which it was entered, the *nolle prosequi* operated as an acquittal or not. It appears, however, from colloquy between counsel and with the court that Chamblee was permitted to plead to a lesser offense than conspiracy, possibly with the understanding that he would not thereafter be charged with that offense.

In his * * * instructions to the jury, the trial judge, after fully defining the crime of conspiracy, stated that under Maryland law where only two parties are involved in the alleged conspiracy, and one is found not guilty, "the other could not be tried because one person cannot conspire except with another to commit a crime." He further advised the jury that there has to be "an outright finding of not guilty" but such was not the case with Fields

---

[1] By the Maryland stet procedure, the prosecutor indicates that he does not choose at that time to further prosecute the indictment.

[2] This would not be true, however, if after elimination of the alleged entrapper, there are at least two other parties to the conspiracy.

who was merely found to be insane and for that reason not brought to trial. With reference to Chamblee, the trial judge instructed that he had not been found not guilty of conspiracy; that he did not believe that Chamblee had been prosecuted for that offense.

[The instructions were error.] We thus deem it essential in the interest of justice that appellant's conspiracy conviction be reversed and that the State be afforded the opportunity to retry the case in light of the principles of law which we consider relevant and controlling. If, upon retrial, the State intends to charge only Fields and appellant as conspirators, and the evidence properly shows that Fields was legally insane at the time the agreement to perpetrate the robbery was concluded, then even though Fields has not been acquitted of the offense of conspiracy by a judicial determination that he was insane, nevertheless the requisite joint criminal intent being absent, appellant cannot properly be convicted of engaging with Fields in a criminal conspiracy. If Fields is shown so to be insane, but the facts show that the conspiracy indictment against Chamblee was not *nol prossed* under circumstances amounting to an acquittal, then the State may undertake to adduce evidence showing that Chamblee was a conspirator, with appellant, in the plan to commit the robbery.

Notes and Questions

1. *Regle* applied a rule that requires acquittal of a remaining alleged conspirator upon proof that all other members of the alleged conspiracy have been acquitted or discharged under circumstances that amount to an acquittal. Some courts have held that an alleged conspirator is shown to have been functionally acquitted upon a showing that the conspirator was a police undercover officer who never intended to carry out the criminal objective. Under this approach, if A is charged with conspiring with B to murder C and B is shown to have been an undercover officer, A must be acquitted.

   In *United States v. Escobar de Bright*, 742 F.2d 1196 (9th Cir.1984), the court suggested that a conspiracy charge was inappropriate in such circumstances for both formal and policy reasons. It

stressed, as did the *Regle* court, that there cannot be the required agreement unless at least two persons have a meeting of the minds as to the achievement of the illicit objective. On the policy front it contended that the dangers of group criminality—increased probability of success, future criminal acts of the group, and difficulty of detection—are nonexistent where the alleged other conspirator is a government agent. Finally, the judges in *de Bright* expressed a special concern that another rule would encourage the government to "manufacture" conspiracies in a manner condemned by the defense of entrapment.

2. If Regle had been charged with conspiring with Fields, Chamblee, and others unknown, many courts would hold, as *Regle* itself suggested, that Regle need not be acquitted due to the showings regarding Fields and Chamblee because that evidence is consistent with Regle having conspired with the unknown conspirators. Of course, the prosecution must show that at least one such conspirator actually existed and did agree with the defendant. See *United States v. Lance*, 536 F.2d 1065, 1068 (5th Cir.1976) ("[A] person can be convicted of conspiring with persons whose names are unknown as long as the indictment asserts that such other persons exist and the evidence supports their existence.").

3. A and B are charged with conspiracy to commit grand theft. A pleads guilty. B stands trial and is acquitted. A is then sentenced to imprisonment. Are A's conviction and sentence void? Is the answer dictated by *Regle? Eyman v. Deutsch*, 92 Ariz. 82, 373 P.2d 716 (1962), held yes, but other—and probably most—courts would hold otherwise. These courts reason that acquittal of all other conspirators requires acquittal of the remaining conspirator only because of the offensiveness of jury inconsistency. Thus, the rule is not applied when the acquittal was in a different proceeding before a different jury. In such cases, there are many possible explanations for acquittal of the other conspirators and conviction of the remaining one other than offensive inconsistency. See *Cortis v. Kenney*, 995 F.2d 838 (8th Cir. 1993).

Editors' Note: The Unilateral View of Conspiracy and Acquittal of All Other Conspirators

Section 5.03 of the Model Penal Code, reprinted at page 377, is often regarded as the basis for a very different conceptual approach to conspiracy than is taken under traditional law. Acceptance of this new approach may make a difference in the resolution of issues as were presented in *Regle*.

Traditional law, as *Regle* illustrated, has emphasized the need for at least two persons to actually agree, and thus has taken a "bilateral" approach. This is often distinguished from what is generally called the "unilateral" approach of the Model Penal Code.

The Code's basic approach was described and discussed in the Comment to Section 5.03(l):

> *Unilateral Approach of the Draft.* The definition of the Draft departs from the traditional view of conspiracy as an entirely bilateral or multilateral relationship, the view inherent in the standard formulation cast in terms of "two or more persons" agreeing or combining to commit a crime. Attention is directed instead to each individual's culpability by framing the definition in terms of the conduct which suffices to establish the liability of any given actor, rather than the conduct of a group of which he is charged to be a part—an approach which * * * we have designated "unilateral."
>
> One consequence of this approach is to make it immaterial to the guilt of a conspirator whose culpability has been established that the person or all of the persons with whom he conspired have not been or cannot be convicted. Present law frequently holds otherwise, reasoning from the definition of conspiracy as an agreement between two or more persons that there must be at least two guilty conspirators or none.

Model Penal Code, Comment to § 5.03(l), 102 (Tent. Draft No. 10, 1960).

If this approach had been taken in *Regle*, the court would only have inquired whether the evidence showed that Regle agreed with others that they would commit robbery. Whether those others entered into an agreement under circumstances making them criminally responsible for conspiracy would be of no significance.

In some states that have adopted language drawn from the Model Penal Code with its shift in emphasis to the individual's culpability, the courts have upheld convictions for unilateral conspiracies, that is, conspiracies in which there was only one criminally guilty participant. However, some courts have resisted what appear to have been legislative decisions to adopt the unilateral approach. See *People v. Foster*, 99 Ill.2d 48, 75 111 Dec. 411, 457 N.E.2d 405 (1983) (no change in the law will be found in the absence of explicit legislative statement adopting unilateral view). Courts have a tendency to regard the traditional requirement of at least a bilateral meeting of two guilty minds as inherent in the very notion of a criminal conspiracy.

Judicial resistance to the unilateral approach was explicit in *State v. Pacheco*, 125 Wash.2d 150, 882 P.2d 183 (1994), in which the defendant was charged with conspiring to commit murder and delivery of a controlled substance. He contended that the evidence failed to show a conspiracy because his sole alleged co-conspirator was a police undercover agent who never actually agreed to commit the offenses. Washington has a statute similar to section 5.04 of the Model Penal Code. The crime of conspiracy is, however, defined as requiring that the accused "agree[] with one or more persons to [commit an offense]." Considered as a whole, the *Pacheco* majority concluded, this did not change the prior law regarding the basic requirement of an agreement:

> As a general rule, we presume the Legislature intended undefined words to mean what they did at common law.
>
> [Our statute] expressly requires an agreement, but does not define the term. Black's Law Dictionary defines agreement as, "[a] meeting of two or more minds; a coming together in opinion or determination; the coming together in accord of two minds on a given proposition". Black's Law Dictionary 67 (6th rev. ed. 1990). Similarly, agreement is defined in Webster's as "1a: the act of agreeing or coming to a mutual agreement . . . b: oneness of opinion . . .". *Webster's Third New International Dictionary* 43 (1986). The dictionary definitions thus support the Defendant's argument.
>
> * * *
>
> [T]he Legislature adopted the unilateral approach to [a] limited extent * * *. However, the element of the "requisite corrupt agreement", or the bilateral agreement, is still necessary * * *. Indeed, the essence of a conspiracy is the agreement to commit a crime. We will not presume the Legislature intended to overturn this long-established legal principle unless that intention is made very clear.
>
> Additionally, the unilateral approach fails to carry out the primary purpose of the statute. The primary reason for making conspiracy a separate offense from the substantive crime is the increased danger to society posed by group criminal activity. However, the increased danger is nonexistent when a person "conspires" with a government agent who pretends agreement. In the feigned conspiracy there is no increased chance the criminal enterprise will succeed, no continuing criminal enterprise, no educating in criminal practices, and no greater difficulty of detection.
>
> Indeed, it is questionable whether the unilateral conspiracy punishes criminal activity or merely criminal intentions. The "agreement" in a unilateral conspiracy is a legal fiction, a technical way of transforming nonconspiratorial conduct into a prohibited conspiracy. When one party merely pretends to agree, the other party, whatever he or she may believe about the pretender, is in fact not conspiring with anyone. Although the deluded party has the requisite criminal intent, there has been no criminal act.
>
> * * *
>
> Another concern with the unilateral approach is its potential for abuse. In a unilateral conspiracy, the State not only plays an active role in creating the offense, but also becomes the chief witness in proving the crime at trial. * * * [T]his has the potential to put the State in the improper position of manufacturing crime. At the same time, such reaching is unnecessary because the punishable conduct in a unilateral conspiracy will almost always satisfy the elements of either solicitation or attempt. The State will still be able to thwart the activity and punish the defendant who attempts agreement with an undercover police officer.

b. The State of Mind Required

The United States Supreme Court has noted:

> In a conspiracy, two different types of intent are generally required—the basic intent to agree, which is necessary to establish the existence of the conspiracy, and the more traditional intent to effectuate the object of the conspiracy.

United States v. United States Gypsum Co., 438 U.S. 422, 443 n. 20, 98 S.Ct. 2864, 2876 n. 20, 57 L.Ed.2d. 854, 873 n. 20 (1978). The first of the types of intent distinguished by the Court was treated earlier in Section C(1)(a)(1) of this chapter as part of the requirement of an agreement. This subsection deals with the second type of intent, the state of mind regarding effectuation of the object of the agreement.

Perhaps the issue can best be discussed in terms of a simple hypothetical: A, aware that B and C are illicitly distilling whiskey, agrees to sell B sugar. This can reasonably be construed as an agreement involving A, B, and C; A has agreed to do something that is part of the scheme, and the production of illicit whiskey is the objective of the scheme. A clearly had that type of intent necessary for formulation of the agreement. But what was the required state of mind in regard to the criminal object, that is, the illicit production of whiskey, and did A have that state of mind? Must A have desired that whiskey actually be produced? Is it sufficient if he was aware that production of whiskey would result from the scheme? Or might it be sufficient if A was simply aware of a substantial and unjustifiable risk that a result of the venture would be the production of whiskey? Does this end the inquiry? Or might it also be necessary to prove that A was aware (or was aware of a risk) that the scheme constituted a criminal offense under federal law?

In *Gypsum,* the defendants were charged with conspiracy to fix the price of gypsum board in violation of the Sherman Act. There was no dispute that the defendants, six major manufacturers and some of their officials, had exchanged price information. The question was the intent with which this was done. The Supreme Court first concluded that the Sherman Act, although an economic regulatory scheme, was not intended to be a strict liability offense. A mental element was needed given, in particular, the vagueness of the Act's prohibitions in the context of complex business dealings any of which might have anticompetitive effects despite the good faith business judgments underlying the actions. The Court's majority then concluded that the level of intent required would be "knowledge" rather than "purpose." To require the government to prove that it was the defendants' conscious desire to bring about the anticompetitive effect, the majority reasoned, would be unduly burdensome. Rather, all important objectives would be satisfied if the government were required to show that the defendants had engaged in the conduct charged with knowledge that the proscribed effects would most likely follow.

Gypsum involved an interpretation of only one specific federal crime. It does not control with regard to the culpable mental state regarding the effectuation of the agreement's objective that is required by other criminal conspiracy provisions, especially those created by state statute.

People v. Lauria

California Court of Appeal, 1967
251 Cal.App.2d 471, 59 Cal.Rptr. 628.

FLEMING, ASSOCIATE JUSTICE

In an investigation of call-girl activity the police focused their attention on three prostitutes actively plying their trade on call, each of whom was using Lauria's telephone answering service, presumably for business purposes.

On January 8, 1965, Stella Weeks, a policewoman, signed up for telephone service with Lauria's answering service. Mrs. Weeks, in the course of her conversation with Lauria's office manager, hinted broadly that she was a prostitute concerned with the secrecy of her activities and their concealment from the police. She was assured that the operation of the service was discreet and "about as safe as you can get." It was arranged that Mrs. Weeks need not leave her address with the answering service, but could pick up her calls and pay her bills in person.

On February 11, Mrs. Weeks talked to Lauria on the telephone and told him her business was modeling and she had been referred to the answering service by Terry, one of the three prostitutes under investigation. She complained that because of the operation of the service she had lost two valuable customers, referred to as tricks. Lauria defended his service and said that her friends had probably lied to her about having left calls for her. But he did not respond to Mrs. Weeks' hints that she needed customers in order to make money, other than to invite her to his house for a personal visit in order to get better acquainted. In the course of his talk he said "his business was taking messages."

On February 15, Mrs. Weeks talked on the telephone to Lauria's office manager and again complained of two lost calls, which she described as a $50 and a $100 trick. On investigation the office manager could find nothing wrong, but she said she would alert the switchboard operators about slip-ups on calls.

On April 1 Lauria and the three prostitutes were arrested. Lauria complained to the police that this attention was undeserved, stating that Hollywood Call Board had 60 to 70 prostitutes on its board while his own service had only 9 or 10, that he kept separate records for known or suspected prostitutes for the convenience of himself and the police. When asked if his records were available to police who might come to the office to investigate call girls, Lauria replied that they were whenever the police had a specific name. However, his service didn't "arbitrarily tell the police about prostitutes on our board. As long as they pay their bills we tolerate them." In a subsequent voluntary appearance before the Grand Jury Lauria testified he had always

cooperated with the police. But he admitted he knew some of his customers were prostitutes, and he knew Terry was a prostitute because he had personally used her services, and he knew she was paying for 500 calls a month.

Lauria and the three prostitutes were indicted for conspiracy to commit prostitution * * *. Subsequently the trial court set aside the indictment as having been brought without reasonable or probable cause. The People have appealed, claiming that a sufficient showing of an unlawful agreement to further prostitution was made.

To establish agreement, the People need show no more than a tacit, mutual understanding between coconspirators to accomplish an unlawful act. Here the People attempted to establish a conspiracy by showing that Lauria, well aware that his codefendants were prostitutes who received business calls from customers through his telephone answering service, continued to furnish them with such service. This approach attempts to equate knowledge of another's criminal activity with conspiracy to further such criminal activity, and poses the question of the criminal responsibility of a furnisher of goods or services who knows his product is being used to assist the operation of an illegal business. Under what circumstances does a supplier become a part of a conspiracy to further an illegal enterprise by furnishing goods or services which he knows are to be used by the buyer for criminal purposes?

The two leading cases on this point face in opposite directions. In *United States v. Falcone*, 311 U.S. 205, 61 S.Ct. 204, 85 L.Ed. 128 [(1943)], the sellers of large quantities of sugar, yeast, and cans were absolved from participation in a moonshining conspiracy among distillers who bought from them, while in *Direct Sales Co. v. United States*, 319 U.S. 703, 63 S.Ct. 1265, 87 L.Ed. 1674 [(1949)], a wholesaler of drugs was convicted of conspiracy to violate the federal narcotic laws by selling drugs in quantity to a codefendant physician who was supplying them to addicts. The distinction between these two cases appears primarily based on the proposition that distributors of such dangerous products as drugs are required to exercise greater discrimination in the conduct of their business than are distributors of innocuous substances like sugar and yeast.

In the earlier case, *Falcone*, the sellers' knowledge of the illegal use of the goods was insufficient by itself to make the sellers participants in a conspiracy with the distillers who bought from them. Such knowledge fell short of proof of a conspiracy, and evidence on the volume of sales was too vague to support a jury finding that respondents knew of the conspiracy from the size of the sales alone.

In the later case of *Direct Sales,* the conviction of a drug wholesaler for conspiracy to violate federal narcotic laws was affirmed on a showing that it had actively promoted the sale of morphine sulphate in quantity and had sold codefendant physician, who practiced in a small town in South Carolina, more than 300 times his normal requirements of the drug, even though it had been repeatedly warned of the dangers of unrestricted sales of the drug. The court contrasted the restricted goods involved in *Direct Sales* with the articles of free commerce involved in *Falcone.* "All articles of commerce may be put to illegal ends," said the court. "But all do not have inherently the same susceptibility to harmful and illegal use. * * * This difference is important for two purposes. One is for making certain that the seller knows the buyer's intended illegal use. The other is to show that by the sale he intends to further, promote and cooperate in it. This intent, when given effect by overt act, is the gist of conspiracy. While it is not identical with mere knowledge that another purposes unlawful action, it is not unrelated to such knowledge. * * * The step from knowledge to intent and agreement may be taken. There is more than suspicion, more than knowledge, acquiescence, carelessness, indifference, lack of concern. There is informed and interested cooperation, stimulation, instigation. And there is also a 'stake in the venture' which, even if it may not be essential, is not irrelevant to the question of conspiracy."

While *Falcone* and *Direct Sales* may not be entirely consistent with each other in their full implications, they do provide us with a framework for the criminal liability of a supplier of lawful goods or services put to unlawful use. Both the element of *knowledge* of the illegal use of the goods or services and the element of *intent* to further that use must be present in order to make the supplier a participant in a criminal conspiracy.

Proof of *knowledge* is ordinarily a question of fact and requires no extended discussion in the present case. The knowledge of the supplier was sufficiently established when Lauria admitted he knew some of his customers were prostitutes and admitted he knew that Terry, an active subscriber to his service, was a prostitute. In the face of these admissions he could scarcely claim to have relied on the normal assumption an operator of a business or service is entitled to make, that his customers are behaving themselves in the eyes of the law. Because Lauria knew in fact that some of his customers were prostitutes, it is a legitimate inference he knew they were subscribing to his answering service for illegal business purposes and were using his service to make assignations for prostitution. On this record we think the prosecution is entitled to claim

positive knowledge by Lauria of the use of his service to facilitate the business of prostitution.

The more perplexing issue in the case is the sufficiency of proof of *intent* to further the criminal enterprise. The element of intent may be proved either by direct evidence, or by evidence of circumstances from which an intent to further a criminal enterprise by supplying lawful goods or services may be inferred. Direct evidence of participation, such as advice from the supplier of legal goods or services to the user of those goods or services on their use for illegal purposes * * * provides the simplest case. When the intent to further and promote the criminal enterprise comes from the lips of the supplier himself, ambiguities of inference from circumstance need not trouble us. But in cases where direct proof of complicity is lacking, intent to further the conspiracy must be derived from the sale itself and its surrounding circumstances in order to establish the supplier's express or tacit agreement to join the conspiracy.

In the case at bench the prosecution argues that since Lauria, knew his customers were using his service for illegal purposes but nevertheless continued to furnish it to them, he must have intended to assist them in carrying out their illegal activities. Thus through a union of knowledge and intent he became a participant in a criminal conspiracy. Essentially, the People argue that knowledge alone of the continuing use of his telephone facilities for criminal purposes provided a sufficient basis from which his intent to participate in those criminal activities could be inferred.

In examining precedents in this field we find that sometimes, but not always, the criminal intent of the supplier may be inferred from his knowledge of the unlawful use made of the product he supplies. Some consideration of characteristic patterns may be helpful.

1. Intent may be inferred from knowledge, when the purveyor of legal goods for illegal use has acquired a stake in the venture. (*United States v. Falcone*). For example, in *Regina v. Thomas* (1957), 2 All.E.R. 181, 342, a prosecution for living off the earnings of prostitution, the evidence showed that the accused, knowing the woman to be a convicted prostitute, agreed to let her have the use of his room between the hours of 9 P.M. and 2 A.M. for a charge of £3 a night. The Court of Criminal Appeal refused an appeal from the conviction, holding that when the accused rented a room at a grossly inflated rent to a prostitute for the purpose of carrying on her trade, a jury could find he was living on the earnings of prostitution.

   In the present case, no proof was offered of inflated charges for the telephone answering services furnished the codefendants.

2. Intent may be inferred from knowledge, when no legitimate use for the goods or services exists. The leading California case is *People v. McLaughlin*, 111 Cal.App.2d 781, 245 P.2d 1076, in which the court upheld a conviction of the suppliers of horse-racing information by wire for conspiracy to promote book-making, when it had been established that wire-service information had no other use than to supply information needed by bookmakers to conduct illegal gambling operations.

In *Shaw v. Director of Public Prosecutions*, [1962] A.C. 220, the defendant was convicted of conspiracy to corrupt public morals and of living on the earnings of prostitution when he published a directory consisting almost entirely of advertisements of the names, addresses, and specialized talents of prostitutes. Publication of such a directory, said the court, could have no legitimate use and serve no other purpose than to advertise the professional services of the prostitutes whose advertisements appeared in the directory. The publisher could be deemed a participant in the profits from the business activities of his principal advertisers.

Other services of a comparable nature come to mind: the manufacturer of crooked dice and marked cards who sells his product to gambling casinos; the tipster who furnishes information on the movement of law enforcement officers to known lawbreakers. * * * In such cases the supplier must necessarily have an intent to further the illegal enterprise since there is no known honest use for his goods.

However, there is nothing in the furnishing of telephone answering service which would necessarily imply assistance in the performance of illegal activities. Nor is any inference to be derived from the use of an answering service by women, either in any particular volume of calls, or outside normal working hours. Night-club entertainers, registered nurses, faith healers, public stenographers, photographic models, and free lance substitute employees, provide examples of women in legitimate occupations whose employment might cause them to receive a volume of telephone calls at irregular hours.

3. Intent may be inferred from knowledge, when the volume of business with the buyer is grossly disproportionate to any legitimate demand, or when sales for illegal use amount to a high proportion of the seller's total business. In such cases an intent to participate in the illegal enterprise may be inferred from the quantity of the business done. For example, in *Direct Sales,* supra, the sale of narcotics to a rural physician in quantities 300 times greater than he would have normal use for provided potent evidence of an intent to further the illegal activity. In the same case the court also found significant the fact that the wholesaler had attracted as customers a disproportionately large group of physicians who had been convicted of violating the Harrison Act. In *Shaw v. Director of Public Prosecutions,* almost the entire business of the directory came from prostitutes.

No evidence of any unusual volume of business with prostitutes was presented by the prosecution against Lauria.

Inflated charges, the sale of goods with no legitimate use, sales in inflated amounts, each may provide a fact of sufficient moment from which the intent of the seller to participate in the criminal enterprise may be inferred. In such instances participation by the supplier of legal goods to the illegal enterprise may be inferred because in one way or another the supplier has acquired a special interest in the operation of the illegal enterprise. His intent to participate in the crime of which he has knowledge may be inferred from the existence of his special interest.

Yet there are cases in which it cannot reasonably be said that the supplier has a stake in the venture or has acquired a special interest in the enterprise, but in which he has been held liable as a participant on the basis of knowledge alone. Some suggestion of this appears in *Direct Sales,* supra, where both the knowledge of the illegal use of the drugs and the intent of the supplier to aid that use were inferred. In *Regina v. Bainbridge* (1959), 3 W.L.R. 656 (CCA 6), a supplier of oxygen-cutting equipment to one known to intend to use it to break into a bank was convicted as an accessory to the crime. In *Sykes v. Director of Public Prosecutions* [1962] A.C. 528, one having knowledge of the theft of 100 pistols, 4 submachine guns, and 1960 rounds of ammunition was convicted of misprision of felony for failure to disclose the theft to the public authorities. It seems apparent from these cases that a supplier who furnishes equipment which he *knows* will be used to commit a serious crime may be deemed from that knowledge alone to have intended to produce the result. Such proof may justify an inference that the furnisher intended to aid the execution of the crime and that he thereby became a participant. For instance, we think the operator of a telephone answering service with positive knowledge that his service was being used to facilitate the extortion of ransom, the distribution of heroin, or the passing of counterfeit money who continued to furnish the service with knowledge of its use, might be chargeable on knowledge alone with participation in a scheme to extort money, to distribute narcotics, or to pass counterfeit money. The same result would follow the seller of gasoline who knew the buyer was using his product to make Molotov cocktails for terroristic use.

Logically, the same reasoning could be extended to crimes of every description. Yet we do not believe an inference of intent drawn from knowledge of criminal use properly applies to the less serious crimes classified as misdemeanors. The duty to take positive action to dissociate oneself from activities helpful to violations of the criminal law is far stronger and more compelling for felonies than it is for misdemeanors or petty offenses. In this respect, as in others, the distinction between felonies and misdemeanors, between more serious and less serious crime, retains continuing vitality. In historically the most serious felony, treason, an individual with knowledge of the treason can be prosecuted for concealing and failing to disclose it. In other felonies, both at common law and under the criminal laws of the United States, an individual knowing of the commission of a felony is criminally liable for concealing it and failing to make it known to proper authority. But this crime, known as misprision of felony, has always been limited to knowledge and concealment of felony and has never extended to misdemeanor. * * * We believe the distinction between the obligations arising from knowledge of a felony and those arising from knowledge of a misdemeanor continues to reflect basic human feelings about the duties owed by individuals to society. Heinous crime must be stamped out, and its suppression is the responsibility of all. Venial crime and crime not evil in itself present less of a danger to society, and perhaps the benefits of their suppression through the modern equivalent of the posse, the hue and cry, the informant, and the citizen's arrest, are outweighed by the disruption to everyday life brought about by amateur law enforcement and private officiousness in relatively inconsequential delicts which do not threaten our basic security. * * *

With respect to misdemeanors, we conclude that positive knowledge of the supplier that his products or services are being used for criminal purposes does not, without more, establish an intent of the supplier to participate in the misdemeanors. With respect to felonies, we do not decide the converse, viz. that in all cases of felony knowledge of criminal use alone may justify an inference of the supplier's intent to participate in the crime. The implications of *Falcone* make the matter uncertain with respect to those felonies which are merely prohibited wrongs. But decision on this point is not compelled, and we leave the matter open.

From this analysis of precedent we deduce the following rule: the intent of a supplier who knows of the criminal use to which his supplies are put to participate in the criminal activity connected with the use of his supplies may be established by (1) direct evidence that he intends to participate, or (2) through an inference that he intends to participate based on, (a) his special interest in the activity, or (b) the aggravated nature of the crime itself.

When we review Lauria's activities in the light of this analysis, we find no proof that Lauria took any direct action to further, encourage, or direct the call-girl activities of his codefendants and we find an absence of circumstances from which his special interest in their activities could be inferred. Neither excessive charges for standardized services, or the furnishing of services without a legitimate use, nor any unusual quantity of business with call girls, are present. The offense which he is charged with furthering is a misdemeanor, a category of crime which has never been made a required subject of positive disclosure to public authority. Under these circumstances, although proof of Lauria's knowledge of the criminal activities of his patrons was sufficient to charge him with that fact, there was insufficient evidence that he intended to further their criminal activities, and hence insufficient proof of his participation in a criminal conspiracy with his codefendants to further prostitution. Since the conspiracy centered around the activities of Lauria's telephone answering service, the charges against his codefendants likewise fail for want of proof.

In absolving Lauria of complicity in a criminal conspiracy we do not wish to imply that the public authorities are without remedies to combat modern manifestations of the world's oldest profession. Licensing of telephone answering services under the police power, together with the revocation of licenses for the toleration of prostitution, is a possible civil remedy. The furnishing of telephone answering service in aid of prostitution could be made a crime. Other solutions will doubtless occur to vigilant public authorities if the problem of call-girl activity needs further suppression.

The order is affirmed.

Note

The Model Penal Code, in section 5.03(1) reprinted at page 377, would require that each conspiracy defendant have acted "with the purpose of promoting or facilitating * * * commission [of the crime]." Explaining and supporting that position, the drafters stated:

> *The Requirement of Purpose.* The purpose requirement is crucial to the resolution of the difficult problems presented when a charge of conspiracy is leveled against a person whose relationship to a criminal plan is essentially peripheral. Typical is the case of the person who sells sugar to the producers of illicit whiskey. He may have little interest in the success of the distilling operation and be motivated mainly by the desire to make the normal profit of an other wise lawful sale. To be criminally liable, of course, he must at least have knowledge of the use to which the materials are being put, but the difficult issue presented is whether knowingly facilitat-

ing the commission of a crime ought to be sufficient, absent a true purpose to advance the criminal end. In the case of vendors conflicting interests are also involved: that of the vendors in freedom to engage in gainful and otherwise lawful activities without policing their vendees, and that of the community in preventing behavior that facilitates the commission of crimes. The decisions are in conflict, although many of those requiring purpose properly emphasize that it can be inferred from such circumstances as, for example, quantity sales, the seller's initiative or encouragement, continuity of the relationship, and the contraband nature of the materials sold. * * *

* * *

Thus, it would not be sufficient * * * if the actor only believed that the result [required by a crime] would be produced but did not consciously plan or desire to produce it. For example—* * * if two persons plan to destroy a building by detonating a bomb,

though they know and believe that there are inhabitants in the building who will be killed by the explosion, they are nevertheless guilty only of a conspiracy to destroy the building and not of a conspiracy to kill the inhabitants. While this result may seem unduly restrictive from the viewpoint of the completed crime, it is necessitated by the extremely preparatory behavior that may be involved in conspiracy. Had the crime been completed or had the preparation progressed even to the stage of an attempt, the result would be otherwise. As to the attempt, knowledge or belief that the inhabitants would be killed would suffice. * * *

Model Penal Code, Comment to § 5.03, 107–10 (Tent. Draft No. 10, 1960).*

2. Model Statutory Formulations

The Model Penal Code, in the provisions reprinted here, offers a comprehensive statutory framework for criminal conspiracy law. The general approach of the Code is discussed in detail in the Editors' Note in Section C(3).

MODEL PENAL CODE*

Official Draft, 1985

Section 5.03. Criminal Conspiracy

(1) *Definition of Conspiracy.* A person is guilty of conspiracy with another person or persons to commit a crime if with the purpose of promoting or facilitating its commission he:

   (a) agrees with such other person or persons that they or one or more of them will engage in conduct which constitutes such crime or an attempt or solicitation to commit such crime; or

   (b) agrees to aid such other person or persons in the planning or commission of such crime or of an attempt or solicitation to commit such crime.

(2) *Scope of Conspiratorial Relationship.* If a person guilty of conspiracy, as defined by Subsection (1) of this Section, knows that a person with whom he conspires to commit a crime has conspired with another person or persons to commit the same crime, he is guilty of conspiring with such other person or persons, whether or not he knows their identity, to commit such crime.

(3) *Conspiracy With Multiple Criminal Objectives.* If a person conspires to commit a number of crimes, he is guilty of only one conspiracy so long as such multiple crimes are the object of the same agreement or continuous conspiratorial relationship.

* * *

(5) *Overt Act.* No person may be convicted of conspiracy to commit a crime, other than a felony of the first or second degree, unless an overt act in pursuance of such conspiracy is alleged and proved to have been done by him or by a person with whom he conspired.

(6) *Renunciation of Criminal Purpose.* It is an affirmative defense that the actor, after conspiring to commit a crime, thwarted the success of the conspiracy, under circumstances manifesting a complete and voluntary renunciation of his criminal purpose.

Section 5.04. Incapacity, Irresponsibility or Immunity of Party to Solicitation or Conspiracy

(1) Except as provided in Subsection (2) of this Section, it is immaterial to the liability of a person who solicits or conspires with another to commit a crime that:

(a) he or the person whom he solicits or with whom he conspires does not occupy a particular position or have a particular characteristic which is an element of such crime, if he believes that one of them does; or

(b) the person whom he solicits or with whom he conspires is irresponsible or has an immunity to prosecution or conviction for the commission of the crime.

(2) It is a defense to a charge of solicitation or conspiracy to commit a crime that if the criminal object were achieved, the actor would not be guilty of a crime under the law defining the offense or as an accomplice * * *.

Section 5.05. Grading of Criminal * * * Conspiracy; Mitigation in Cases of Lesser Danger * * *

(1) *Grading.* Except as otherwise provided in this Section, conspiracy [is a crime of] the same grade and degree as the most serious offense that is * * * an object of the conspiracy. * * *

(2) *Mitigation.* If the particular conduct charged to constitute a criminal * * * conspiracy is so inherently unlikely to result or culminate in the commission of a crime that neither such conduct nor the actor presents a public danger warranting the grading of such offense under this Section, the Court shall

exercise its power * * * to enter judgment and impose sentence for a crime of lower grade or degree or, in extreme cases, may dismiss the prosecution.

Notes and Questions

1. How should criminal conspiracy be graded for purposes of punishment? Compare the approach of section 5.05 of the Model Penal Code with that of section 15.02(d) of the Texas Penal Code, which provides that a criminal conspiracy is graded as one category lower than the most serious offense that is the object of the conspiracy.

2. Traditionally, the crime of conspiracy has included not only agreements to commit felonies and misdemeanors but also combinations to commit "unlawful" acts or lawful acts by "unlawful" means, even if these acts or means were not criminal. It has been said, however, that this has been interpreted to encompass only agreements to engage in conduct that is patently fraudulent, prejudicial to the public welfare, or so oppressive of individuals as to be injurious to the public welfare. Developments in the Law—Criminal Conspiracy, 72 Harv.L.Rev. 922, 942–44 (1959). This approach is still reflected in some state statutes, such as section 182(5) of the California Penal Code, which makes criminal any conspiracy "to commit any act injurious to the public health, to public morals, or to pervert or obstruct justice, or the due administration of the Laws." In *Musser v. Utah*, 333 U.S. 95, 68 S.Ct. 397, 92 L.Ed. 562 (1948), the Supreme Court indicated that a Utah statute prohibiting conspiracies "to commit any act injurious to the public health, to public morals, or to trade or commerce, or for the perversion or obstruction of justice or the due administration of the laws" might be unconstitutionally vague. In remanding the case to permit the state court to consider this question, the majority stated:

> [The statute] would seem to be warrant for conviction for agreement to do almost any act which a judge and jury might find at the moment contrary to his or its notion of what was good for health, morals, trade, commerce, justice or order.

The state supreme court found the statute unconstitutional. *State v. Musser*, 118 Utah 537, 223 P.2d 193 (1950). See also *State v. Bowling*, 5 Ariz.App. 436, 427 P.2d 928 (1967), holding invalid a similar statute.

3. RICO: An Alternative to Traditional Conspiracy Law
Editors' Note: Federal and State RICO Crimes

As a result of congressional concern with organized crime's infiltration of legitimate businesses, many jurisdictions have adopted broad statutory programs aimed at what is loosely called organized criminal activity. These programs include new crimes that supplement and perhaps replace conspiracy crimes.

These new crimes share with conspiracy a concern regarding the concerted nature of criminal conduct. Often, they are used by prosecutors in situations where previously conspiracy might have been the preferred, and perhaps the only, possible basis for criminal action against the subjects. Detailed consideration of these new crimes is clearly not a part of *basic* criminal law and thus is beyond the scope of this book. Nevertheless, the current significance of conspiracy law cannot be evaluated without at least taking notice that it has been supplemented, and perhaps to some extent superseded, by this new aspect of criminal liability.

Federal RICO Crimes

This movement was stimulated in 1970, when Congress enacted the Racketeer Influenced and Corrupt Organizations Act of 1970, codified as 18 U.S.C. § 1961 et seq. The Act is popularly known as "RICO." Many states have enacted similar legislation creating state crimes, sometimes called "racketeering," engaging in "organized criminal activity," or simply RICO crimes.

Although the occasion for RICO was congressional concern with the infiltration of legitimate businesses by Mafia-type organizations, the provisions enacted cover far more than those situations. "Congress drafted RICO broadly enough," the United States Supreme Court noted in *H.J. Inc v. Northwestern Bell Telephone Co.*, 492 U.S. 229, 248–49, 109 S.Ct. 2893, 2905, 106 L.Ed.2d 195 (1989), "to encompass a wide range of criminal activity, taking many different forms and likely to attract a broad array of perpetrators, operating in many different ways."

RICO introduced into federal criminal law the concepts of (a) "enterprise," (b) "racketeering activity," and (c) "pattern" of such activity. The federal RICO crime requires proof that a defendant engaged in racketeering activity that constituted a pattern and that was in some way related to an enterprise.

An "enterprise" is an entity or group associated together for a common purpose of engaging in a course of conduct. "Racketeering activity" includes any of a wide variety of federal and state crimes (often called "predicate crimes"), including violent and drug conduct punishable as a state crime by more than one year imprisonment.

A pattern of racketeering activity requires proof that (a) the defendant committed at least two predicate offenses; (b) these offenses are related; and (c) "the predicates themselves amount to, or * * * they otherwise constitute a threat of, *continuing* racketeering activity." The last demand reflects congressional focus on enterprise-related activities that amount to or threaten *long-term* criminal activity.

A criminal RICO violation can be proved in any of four specific, alternative ways.

(1) acquiring or maintaining an interest in an enterprise through a pattern of racketeering activity;

(2) investing proceeds of a pattern of racketeering activity in an enterprise;

(3) conducting or participating in the affairs of an enterprise, by means of a pattern of racketeering activity; or

(4) conspiring to do (1), (2), or (3).

In traditional conspiracy, the agreement is the means by which the defendants seek to commit the crimes, and it is this concerted effort toward criminal activity that the criminal law regards as making conspiracy more dangerous and culpable than individual criminal conduct. To some extent, in RICO crimes the enterprise is substituted for the agreement. Yet RICO is not limited to conspiracy-like situations in which the accuseds use the organization—the enterprise instead of the agreement—as a means of committing the offenses. Even if the enterprise is itself entirely "legitimate"—it has no criminal objectives—a defendant can commit a crime by investing the proceeds of racketeering activity in the enterprise. More commonly, the government relies upon proof that the defendant engaged in racketeering activity and by means of this activity participated in some way in the affairs of the enterprise. Thus the enterprise can be in essence a victim of the basic criminal conduct.

The Supreme Court refused to read the definition of "enterprise" to exclude entities having *only* criminal purposes. Although Congress may have focused on infiltration of legitimate enterprises, the crime it created was not so limited. *United States v. Turkette*, 452 U.S. 576, 101 S.Ct. 2524, 69 L.Ed.2d 246 (1981). Thus, an entirely criminal conspiracy can itself be an enterprise under RICO. Although RICO developed out of congressional concern with organized crime's infiltration of essentially legitimate businesses, it covers what are essentially illegitimate businesses as well. Most federal prosecutions seem to be based on organizations that are almost entirely illegitimate in nature and operation, even though this was not the focus of the congressional investigation that gave rise to RICO.

The Supreme Court also refused to require that the predicate offenses be characteristic of organized crime in the traditional, apparently "Mafia-like," sense or even that they be characteristic of an organization dedicated to the repeated commission of criminal offenses, that is, organized-crime-type situations. See *H.J. Inc.*, previously cited.

Prosecutors often regard a RICO prosecution as giving them advantages they would not have if required to prosecute just for the predicate offenses or for conspiracy to commit those predicate offenses. Some of these advantages are quite procedural and technical. Generally, however, a RICO prosecution may permit prosecutors to claim and prove a broader course of conduct than would be possible in a conspiracy case. A provable "enterprise," in other words, may be larger than a provable "conspiracy." In a RICO case, the prosecution may be able to prove a great deal of criminal behavior by a great number of persons, even if in a conspiracy prosecution it would be unable to show that all of these people engaged in all of this criminal behavior as part of a single criminal conspiracy.

State RICO-Like Crimes

State provisions often follow the general pattern of the federal RICO statute but frequently also differ in some specific ways. The New Jersey RICO or "racketeering" crime, for example, consists essentially of some involvement in the affairs of an enterprise through a pattern of racketeering activity. The involvement can be by conducting or participating in the affairs of the enterprise, either directly or indirectly. A pattern of racketeering activity requires at least two interrelated "incidents of racketeering conduct," which in turn is defined as including any of numerous criminal offenses under New Jersey law. Among these offenses sufficient as predicates are murder, gambling, promotion of prostitution, robbery, theft, burglary, and drug offenses except for possession of small amounts of marijuana.

Differences between federal criminal liability under RICO itself and state RICO-like crimes may be quite subtle. The New Jersey Supreme Court, for example, concluded in *State v. Ball*, 141 N.J. 142, 169, 661 A.2d 251, 264–65 (1995), that the legislative history of that state's RICO statute shows an intention to cover not only the sort of long-term criminal activity that is the target of the federal RICO provisions but also short-term criminal activity. As a result, the pattern of criminal conduct required under the state crime does not include as heavy an emphasis on continuity as is required under the federal RICO statute.

RICO provisions may in a sense, then, provide a sort of "super conspiracy" crime. In addition, however, these statutory programs supplement criminal liability with other weapons for discouraging the targeted conduct. They provide for civil liability, sometimes with enhanced damages to penalize with special rigor those found liable. Often they permit forfeiture to the government of property and money related to violations. Those threatened by racketeering activity may, in addition, obtain injunctive relief, in which a court orders persons not to engage in prohibited conduct and can punish them for contempt of court if they nevertheless do so.

Given the comparative significance of these noncriminal aspects of RICO provisions, some argue that RICO programs are not primarily criminal in nature. Instead, under this view, they emphasize noncriminal means of discouraging the targeted organized criminal behavior, and their criminal aspects are, comparatively evaluated, relatively unimportant.

PART 4

DEFENSES

Chapter 13

MISTAKE AND DEFENSES IN GENERAL

CHAPTER CONTENTS

Editors' Introduction: Elements of Crime, Defensive Matters, Allocation of Burdens, and Constitutional Considerations

This chapter and the three that follow deal with defensive matters that apply to all or at least many crimes. Defenses that are unique to particular crimes, such as impossibility as a defense to attempt, are considered in connection with those crimes to which the defenses apply. The defensive doctrines, and the issues that arise in the cases, are easier to discuss if there is some agreement on terminology and the substantive and procedural issues often arising. Some of the procedural issues were discussed in Chapter 1, but they may usefully be reconsidered now in light of the specific defensive doctrines to be covered in this and the following chapters.

Terminology: Defense, Defensive Theories and Arguments, and Similar Matters

The term "defense" is often used loosely and inconsistently. Best defined, however, a defense is a matter not arising from or directly related in a conceptual sense to the elements of a crime. Thus, it is interjected into a case only if the accused raises it.

Self-defense in an intentional murder prosecution is a defense in this sense. It is unrelated to the elements of the charged crime, because for murder the prosecution must show only that the accused, acting with intent to kill, caused the death of the victim. Nothing in the prosecution's evidence needs to show that the defendant was not motivated by a desire to defend himself against harm. Such a murder defendant's claim of self-defense either admits or assumes that the prosecution has adequately proved the elements of the charged offense and relies upon additional factual information as a basis for seeking acquittal.

A murder defendant's claim of alibi, on the other hand, is not a defense in this sense. A murder defendant who relies on an alibi may admit or at least not contest the prosecution's claim that someone killed the victim and did so with intent to kill. The defense claim of alibi, however, contradicts the prosecution's evidence that it was the defendant who did this. Although the defense may offer additional evidence—testimony by a witness that the defendant was elsewhere than at the scene when the victim was killed—this evidence does not raise any issues not raised by the prosecution's initial evidence of guilt. Rather, the defense is essentially asking that the jury consider the defendant's evidence in deciding whether the prosecution has proved each and every element of the crime beyond a reasonable doubt.

Such a defendant can logically argue to the jurors that they should acquit even if they do not actually and ultimately believe the defense alibi witness is telling the truth. The defendant can argue accurately that if the jurors think there is a high enough likelihood that the alibi witness is telling the truth to raise a reasonable doubt as to whether the prosecution's evidence establishes that the defendant was the killer, they must acquit.

This use of evidence and argument in a defensive manner is sometimes called "negating" (or perhaps "negativing") an element of the charged crime. It involves a defendant relying upon evidence the defendant has produced to counter or contradict evidence the prosecution has produced in its effort to carry its burden of proof on the elements of the crime. A defendant who produces and relies upon such evidence—an alibi witness, for example—does not undertake to prove anything on which the defendant has any technical burden of proof. The defendant seeks to negate the prosecution's proof that he or she was the perpetrator—often, for example, the testimony of eyewitnesses who testify that they saw a person they can now identify as the defendant commit the crime—by laying the basis for a two-pronged defensive strategy. The defendant will argue that given a variety of reasons for suspecting that the prosecution's witnesses are not accurately relating the facts and for believing that the defense alibi witness is accurately relating what that witness observed, the jury should find at a minimum that there is a reasonable doubt that it was the defendant who killed the victim.

There is, of course, no magic in terminology. Confusion is probably minimized, however, if matters such as alibi are called defensive theories or arguments rather than defenses. The term defenses is best reserved for those contentions that rely on matters going beyond the elements of the crime. Defenses and defensive theories or arguments as so defined can be referred to collectively as "defensive matters."

Some doctrines are often referred to as *affirmative* defenses. This label suggests not only that the matter is a defense as previously defined but also one on which a defendant has the burden of proof or persuasion. In fact, this may or may not be true under existing law, but it is an appropriate use of the term despite inconsistencies in the actual uses made of it.

The discussion in Chapter 1 of *United States v. Vuitch* (at page 11) made clear the need to distinguish a final category of elements. If the statute defining a crime specifies that the conduct prohibited is not a crime in certain exceptional situations, the statute will often be construed as creating "exceptions." Many courts regard such exceptions as almost identical to elements of the charged crime, although different in name. Thus the prosecution must often negate these exceptions in the charging instrument and prove at trial beyond a reasonable doubt that the defendant's conduct was not within this exception.

In *Vuitch*, for example, the statute defining the crime of abortion there being applied provided that the described conduct—producing an abortion—was criminal "unless done as necessary for the preservation of the mother's life or health and under the direction of a competent licensed practitioner of medicine." The Supreme Court's opinion in *Vuitch* indicated that this created an exception and therefore the indictment should have included an allegation negating this exception, that is, an allegation of facts making the exception inapplicable. Thus the government should have alleged that Vuitch's actions were not necessary to preserve the life or health of Inez M. Fradin and were not done under the direction of a competent licensed practitioner of medicine. At trial, of course, the government was required to prove this beyond a reasonable doubt, just as if the negative of the exception was an element of the crime.

Justification or Excuse

Traditionally, distinction has been drawn between defensive doctrines that involve "justification" and those that involve "excuse." The former, under this division, involve a conclusion that the act committed by the defendant was justified and thus not wrongful conduct. Doctrines of excuse, on the other hand, do not go to the justification or acceptability of the conduct but rather establish that the defendant has an excuse for engaging in wrongful conduct and thus is not criminally liable. See G. Fletcher, Rethinking Criminal Law 759 (1978). In practice, those doctrines regarded as ones establishing excuses, such as insanity, are ones permitting a defendant to rely on peculiar misperceptions of reality as showing that despite her wrongful conduct the defendant ought not to be held criminally accountable.

Although formerly there were important differences in result between establishment of an excuse and of a justification, these no longer exist. J. Miller, Handbook of Criminal Law 255 (1934). However, the distinction may still be of value in conceptualizing the various doctrines discussed in this and the following chapters.

Constitutional Considerations Generally

As with many other issues arising from substantive criminal law, those relating to defensive matters have at least possible federal constitutional dimensions. This is true regarding the burdens of proof or persuasion, the burdens of proceedings with evidence, the right to a jury instruction, and the necessary contents of any jury instruction that is given.

The Fifth and Fourteenth Amendments' guarantee of due process means that in a criminal case, the prosecution must prove all elements of the charged crime beyond a reasonable doubt. *In re Winship*, 397 U.S. 358, 90 S.Ct. 1068, 25 L.Ed.2d 368 (1970). This right and the Sixth Amendment right of criminal defendants to trial by jury are "interrelated" and together demand that a criminal conviction rest upon a jury determination that the defendant is guilty of every element of the crime charged, beyond a reasonable doubt. *United States v. Gaudin*, 515 U.S. 506, 509. 115 S.Ct. 2310, 2313, 132 L.Ed.2d 444, 449–50 (1995); *Sullivan v. Louisiana*, 508 U.S. 275, 277, 113 S.Ct. 2078, 2081, 124 L.Ed.2d 182 (1993).

A jury instruction that creates too high a risk of obscuring for the jury the prosecution's burden of proof on each element of the crime violates these rights, and this rule clearly applies to those instructions relating to the culpable mental state required by the charged offense. In *Sandstrom v. Montana*, 442 U.S. 510, 99 S.Ct. 2450, 61 L.Ed.2d 39 (1979), for example, an instruction that "[t]he law presumes that a person intends the ordinary consequences of his voluntary acts" was held violative of due process on this ground.

Despite this case law, it is clear that legislatures have very broad authority within constitutional limits to generally define the elements of crimes and defenses to crimes, and more specifically to determine whether a particular matter should be incorporated into the elements of a crime or rather made a possible defense. Making a matter a defensive one, of course, means that the prosecution does not always have the burden of proving it beyond a reasonable doubt.

Burglary provides an example. Traditionally, burglary—as developed in Chapter 11—consists of entry by breaking in the nighttime of the dwelling of another with the intent to commit a felony inside the dwelling. Ordinarily, the prosecution must prove all of these matters beyond a reasonable doubt. Suppose, however, a legislature decided to eliminate the intent to commit a felony inside the dwelling as an element of burglary *and* to create a new defense to burglary consisting of proof that the defendant's intention in entering was something—anything—other than committing a felony inside the dwelling. Suppose further that this legislature placed the burden on a burglary defendant to prove this defense. Unless the federal constitution imposes some limits upon legislatures' power to do this sort of thing, it is arguable that the federal constitutional rule that the prosecution always be required to prove all elements of the crime beyond a reasonable doubt is easily circumvented by simply changing what constitutes the elements of a crime.

Whether a legislature could make this change in burglary law is put into some doubt by *Mullaney v. Wilbur*, 421 U.S. 684, 95 S.Ct. 1881, 44 L.Ed.2d 508 (1975). In *Mullaney*, the Supreme Court held that a Maine murder defendant's right to due process under *Winship* was violated by a jury instruction concerning the difference between murder, which requires malice aforethought, and voluntary manslaughter, defined as a killing upon a heat of passion resulting from sudden provocation. The instruction told the jury that malice aforethought is presumed from the fact of killing. Thus, the jury was told, if it found Mullaney killed the victim it should presume malice and convict him of murder unless the defendant proved that he had killed in the heat of passion upon sudden provocation. The defect in the instruction, the Court suggested, was that it required the defendant to prove "the critical fact in dispute": whether the killing was in the heat of passion upon sudden provocation.

New York has separated its two major homicide offenses, murder and manslaughter, and required proof of intent to kill for murder. A murder defendant who seeks to be convicted only of manslaughter *after the jury has found proof beyond a reasonable doubt of intent to kill* must prove he or she acted under "extreme emotional disturbance." (Extreme emotional disturbance as distinguishing murder from manslaughter is discussed further in Chapter 7.) This placement of the burden of proof on the defendant regarding the defensive matter necessary to reduce to manslaughter what would otherwise be murder was held constitutionally permissible in *Patterson v. New York*, 432 U.S. 197, 97 S.Ct. 2319, 53 L.Ed.2d 281 (1977), decided two years after *Mullaney*.

Mullaney was not overruled in *Patterson*. *Patterson* suggested that *Mullaney* did not indicate that a state could not place the burden of proof on a defendant to prove the "critical fact" distinguishing murder from manslaughter. Rather, *Patterson* offered that *Mullaney* meant only that *if* a state places the burden of proof regarding such a critical fact on the prosecution, it may not also, and indirectly, shift that burden to a defendant by an instruction on a presumption. Thus, *Mullaney* may mean only that legislatures are free to allocate matters like provocation in homicide or the intended objective in burglary between the prosecution and the defense as those legislature see fit. However, if the burden of proof on such a matter is placed on the defendant, this must be done overtly and directly, as New York did regarding extreme emotional disturbance, and not *sub rosa* and indirectly as Maine attempted to do in *Mullaney* by means of a presumption.

Some, however, read *Mullaney* as authority for the proposition that some matters, such as the provocation that traditionally separates voluntary manslaughter from murder, are ones that are so inherently a part of major crimes that due process prevents legislatures from making these matters defensive ones on which criminal defendants have the burden of persuasion. If this interpretation is correct, perhaps the intent to commit an offense in the premises is so critical to burglary (and to distinguishing it from the less serious offense of criminal trespass) that due process prohibits the legislative manipulation described in the hypothetical just set out.

Constitutional Limits on Burdens of Proof for Defenses

The distinction previously drawn between elements of the crime and defensive matters is important only if the federal constitution permits placement of the burden of proof regarding at least some defensive matter on defendants. What federal constitutional limits are there, if any, upon placement of the burdens regarding defenses and other defensive matters?

Although *Winship* established that federal constitutional due process requires that the prosecution have the burden of proof on elements of the crime, it is equally clear that legislatures and courts have considerable flexibility in assigning the burden of proof on defenses as those were previously defined. In *Leland v. Oregon*, 343 U.S. 790, 72 S.Ct. 1002, 96 L.Ed. 1302 (1952), for example, the Supreme Court held that Oregon did not violate due process requirements by making insanity a defense and placing the burden of proof on the defendant—by proof beyond a reasonable doubt— when insanity is an issue in a prosecution. In a homicide prosecution, due process is not violated if the burden of proof on self-defense is placed on the defendant. *Martin v. Ohio*, 480 U.S. 107, 107 S.Ct. 1098, 94 L.Ed.2d 267 (1987).

Jury instructions on a defense, especially one on which the defendant has the burden of proof, must not obscure the prosecution's obligation to prove the elements of the crime. This possibility becomes a particular problem when a defendant relies upon the same or similar facts as both challenging the sufficiency of the prosecution's evidence on one or more elements of the crime charged and as establishing a defense on which the defendant has the burden of proof.

Martin v. Ohio, just briefly discussed, illustrates the problem. Defendant Martin was charged with aggravated murder, defined under Ohio law as purposefully and with prior calculation and design causing the death of another. The evidence showed that the defendant shot and killed her husband after he saw a gun in her hand and came after her. Martin contended that the evidence showed she was motivated by a perception that the fatal shot was necessary to save herself from harm and that this showed both self-defense and that the prosecution failed to prove she acted "with prior calculation and design" as required by the crime charged. Ohio law placed the burden of proof regarding self-defense on the defendant and the Supreme Court held this was constitutionally permissible. Ohio law placed the burden of proof regarding whether one accused of aggravated murder acted "with prior calculation and design" on the prosecution.

Martin argued that the trial court's jury instructions on self-defense obscured the jury's due process obligation to acquit her if the self-defense evidence raised a reasonable doubt as to whether she acted with prior calculation and design. All the Justices appeared to agree that due process would be violated *if* the jury instructions in fact obscured this. They split 5-to-4, however, on whether in fact the jury instructions regarding self-defense were too likely to be construed by the jury as placing on Martin the burden of proving the absence of "prior calculation and design." In finding that the jury instructions were not likely to be so misread by the jurors, the majority explained:

The * * * instructions were sufficiently clear to convey to the jury that the State's burden of proving prior calculation did not shift and that self-defense evidence had to be considered in determining whether the State's burden had been discharged. * * *

It would be quite different if the jury had been instructed that self-defense evidence could not be considered in determining whether there was a reasonable doubt about the State's case, i.e., that self-defense evidence must be put aside for all purposes unless it satisfied the preponderance standard. Such an instruction would relieve the State of its burden and plainly run afoul of *Winship*'s mandate. The instructions in this case could be clearer in this respect, but when read as a whole, we think they are adequate to convey to the jury that all of the evidence, including the evidence going to self-defense, must be considered in deciding whether there was a reasonable doubt about the sufficiency of the State's proof of the elements of the crime.

Constitutional Limits on Burdens of Proceeding Regarding Defensive Matters

Winship, *Martin*, and the other cases previously discussed deal with the burden of proof or persuasion. As the discussion in Chapter 1 made clear, this burden must be distinguished from the burden of going forward (or "proceeding") with the evidence. If a matter on which the prosecution has the burden of proof is also one on which the defendant has the burden of proceeding on the evidence, matters are somewhat more complicated. In such cases, the jury is simply told nothing about the matter *unless* the defendant introduces (or identifies as having been introduced by the prosecution) sufficient evidence to create an issue for the jury. When a trial judge determines that sufficient evidence has been introduced to so "raise" an issue, the judge is then required to instruct the jury on the matter and, in doing so, to instruct the jury that the prosecution must prove the matter beyond a reasonable doubt.

In regard to self-defense, for example, a jurisdiction could take the position (as many do) that the jury in a homicide prosecution should be told nothing about self-defense unless the accused introduces or identifies evidence sufficiently suggesting he or she acted in self-defense to raise an issue on the matter. If the accused does raise the issue, however, the jury would be told to acquit the defendant unless the prosecution proved beyond a reasonable doubt that he or she did *not* act in self-defense.

"Placing upon the defendant the burden of going forward with evidence on an affirmative defense is normally permissible," the Supreme Court made clear in *Simopoulos v. Virginia*, 462 U.S. 506, 510, 103 S.Ct. 2532, 2535, 76 L.Ed.2d 755, 760 (1983).

The Court has not, however, addressed whether defendants' federal constitutional rights to due process and jury trial impose any limits upon placing on a defendant the burden of going forward with evidence on a matter conceptually related to the elements of the charged offense. Almost certainly, however, this is constitutionally permissible as long as the jury instructions do not obscure the prosecution's duty to prove all elements of the crime.

Defendants' Right to Jury Instructions on Defensive Arguments or Theories

Whether the U.S. Constitution ever prohibits placing upon defendants the burden of going forward with evidence on a matter conceptually related to the elements of the charged offense—a defensive theory or argument—turns in part on whether defendants are entitled to any jury instruction at all on a defensive theory regarding the sufficiency of the prosecution's evidence on an element of the crime. If defendants are not entitled to any jury instructions at all, arguably there could be no constitutional barrier to giving them such an instruction only when they have raised the matter. The issue arises most often regarding defensive theories as to why the prosecution's proof of the required culpable mental state is insufficient.

The courts could reason that jury instructions carefully explaining to the jury the culpable mental state required and the prosecution's burden of proof on that matter provides adequate assurance that the jury will take into account the defendant's defensive theory. Even further, the courts could regard jury instructions on particular defensive theories as undesirable because those instructions might mislead the jury or because the judge's specific comments on a particular defensive theory might be misunderstood by the jury as suggesting that the judge regards the defendant's defensive claim as actually or potentially meritorious.

In *Martin*, for example, suppose Martin had requested a jury instruction on the defensive theory that her testimony regarding self-defense, although perhaps insufficient to establish the affirmative defense of self-defense, nevertheless raised a reasonable doubt as to whether she acted "with prior calculation and design." All of the justices were apparently agreed that the jury instructions could not tell the jury not to consider the self-defense evidence for this purpose. They agreed further that the instructions could not create too high a risk that the jurors would misunderstand them as prohibiting consideration of the self-defense evidence on whether the accused acted with prior calculation and design. However, the case simply did not present the question of whether, and if so, when, Martin or other defendants like her are entitled to instructions explicitly explaining such a defensive theory or argument.

In *Martin*, the defendant's state conviction was being challenged in a federal court, so the defendant was limited to federal constitutional arguments. Even if federal constitutional requirements do not demand an instruction on a defensive theory, of course, the Ohio courts could conclude that sound reasons exist for requiring such an instruction as a matter of state law.

These issues are most important regarding the doctrines of mistake presented in the material that follows. The basic question, of course, is what significance the criminal law should give to a defendant's mistake regarding various matters of law and fact. Also consider, though, the procedural implications of the various alternatives. If the law permits defendants to use mistake to negate the prosecution's proof of *mens rea*, for example, should a defendant have the right to have a jury specifically told to consider defense evidence, if it decides that evidence is credible, for this purpose? Or, is it sufficient that the judge makes clear to the jury that the prosecution must prove the elements of the charged offense, including the culpable mental state required?

As discussed in Chapter 1, jurisdictions are divided on the wisdom and necessity of jury instructions on various specific defensive theories. Some courts believe that specific instructions are undesirable because the instructions may confuse and mislead jurors or possibly even unintentionally suggest to jurors that a defendant has the burden of proof on something that in fact he or she does not have to prove.

Similar issues arise again in connection with intoxication, which is addressed in Chapter 15. A number of jurisdictions bar criminal defendants from arguing to juries that evidence suggesting the defendant was voluntarily intoxicated at the time of the conduct proved at least raises a reasonable doubt as to whether the prosecution has proved beyond a reasonable doubt that the defendant acted with the culpable mental state required by the charged offense. Generally in intoxication cases the prosecution seeks a jury instruction telling the jurors that they are *not* to consider defense evidence of intoxication in deciding particular matters.

In *Montana v. Egelhoff*, 518 U.S. 37, 116 S.C.t 2013, 135 L.Ed.2d 514 (1996), discussed in detail in Chapter 15, the justices of the United States Supreme Court failed to agree even on the appropriate standard for determining the federal constitutionality of such jury instructions.

Mistake as a Defensive Matter

This chapter, however, deals with mistake. Many discussions of mistake distinguish between mistake of "fact" and mistake of "law," and therefore this chapter does so as well. This disctinction may be somewhat misleading; the Model Penal Code provision, reprinted after this introduction, does not so subdivide the area.

As a general rule, a defendant's failure to address a matter—ignorance—or an erroneous conclusion regarding a matter addressed—mistake—is relevant to criminal liability only under limited circumstances. In *United States v. Barker*, 514 F.2d 208, 264–65 (D.C.Cir.1975), cert. denied, 421 U.S. 1013, 95 S.Ct. 2420, 44 L.Ed.2d 682 (1975), Judge Wilkey, dissenting, summarized the law:

> It is a commonplace of criminal law that an honest "mistake of fact" negates criminal intent, when the defendant's acts would not constitute a crime if the facts were as he supposed them to be. Conversely, a "mistake of law" is generally held not to excuse the commission of an offense, even though the defendant was unaware his action was prohibited. The frequent difficulty of distinguishing "law" from "fact," as well as the reluctance of modern courts to hold individuals criminally liable when they acted with honest and innocent purpose, however, has led to some erosion of the principle that "everybody is presumed to know the law." When presented with a mistake on the borderline between law and fact, or a case in which the imposition of strict liability would be particularly unjust, the courts have tended either to characterize the defendant's error as factual in nature or to find a way to declare an exception to the "mistake of law" doctrine.
>
> * * *
>
> * * * An error as to the legality of a particular activity, even if based upon the assurance of a government official, has always been treated as a mistake of law in Anglo-Saxon jurisdictions. * * * [T]raditionally a defendant has been allowed a mistake of fact defense only when he was in possession of facts, albeit erroneous,

about his activity which, if true, would have rendered it legal. If he is not in the possession of such facts, but relies instead entirely on the erroneous assertion of a government official or private individual as to the legality of the activity, his mistake is one of law.

To some extent, this is an oversimplification. Some mistakes are held to preclude criminal liability only if, in addition to being honestly held, they are found to have been reasonable ones. And, as Judge Wilkey indicated, there is some, perhaps a growing, tendency to find exceptions that bar criminal conviction because of ignorance or mistake whether or not criminal intent has been negated or disproved.

MODEL PENAL CODE[*]

Official Draft, 1985

Section 2.04. Ignorance or Mistake.

(1) Ignorance or mistake as to a matter of fact or law is a defense if:

(a) the ignorance or mistake negatives the purpose, knowledge, belief, recklessness or negligence required to establish a material element of the offense; or

(b) the law provides that the state of mind established by such ignorance or mistake constitutes a defense.

(2) Although ignorance or mistake would otherwise afford a defense to the offense charged, the defense is not available if the defendant would be guilty of another offense had the situation been as he supposed. In such case, however, the ignorance or mistake of the defendant shall reduce the grade and degree of the offense of which he may be convicted to those of the offense of which he would be guilty had the situation been as he supposed.

(3) A belief that conduct does not legally constitute an offense is a defense to a prosecution for that offense based upon such conduct when:

(a) the statute or other enactment defining the offense is not known to the actor and has not been published or otherwise reasonably made available prior to the conduct alleged; or

(b) he acts in reasonable reliance upon an official statement of the law, afterward determined to be invalid or erroneous, contained in (i) a statute or other enactment; (ii) a judicial decision, opinion or judgment; (iii) an administrative order or grant of permission; or (iv) an official interpretation of the

> public officer or body charged by law with responsibility for the interpretation, administration or enforcement of the law defining the offense.
>
> (4) The defendant must prove a defense arising under Subsection (3) of this Section by a preponderance of evidence.

A. IGNORANCE OR MISTAKE OF FACT

A defendant's contention that he was simply *ignorant* regarding a factual matter—in other words, that he was not aware of certain factual information—is never a "defense" in any sense. Such a contention may, of course, call attention to the fact that the prosecution has failed to prove the culpable mental state required for the charged crime.

Ignorance or passive unawareness in this sense is often distinguished in legal discussion from the defendants' in a sense affirmative *mistake* regarding a matter of fact. A claim of mistake does not rest on mere passive unawareness but rather assumes the defendant addressed the matter and reached an affirmative conclusion that in retrospect was clearly wrong. Legal discussions generally assume that a defendant's evidence of such a mistake regarding a matter of fact may have more exculpatory significance than a claim of mere ignorance.

As Judge Wilkey's summary of mistake law set out in the introduction suggested, a defendant's contention that he was mistaken regarding a matter of "fact" is generally regarded as a challenge to the sufficiency of the prosecution's proof that the defendant acted with the necessary culpable mental state. Simple logic suggests that if a mistaken belief regarding a matter of fact is inconsistent with harboring the culpable mental state required, the jury should acquit the defendant if it gives the defense evidence sufficient credibility to raise a reasonable doubt as to whether the prosecution has proved the required culpable mental state.

Nevertheless, as is reflected in the first case reprinted in this subsection, *Wilson v. Tard*, courts (and statutes) sometimes regard mistake of fact as significant only if it was reasonable in an objective sense. Some authorities apparently regard a requirement of reasonableness as applying only if it is offered to negate the culpable mental state required by a crime demanding only "general intent." If a mistake is offered to negate a "specific intent," on the other hand, it need not be reasonable but only "honestly" held. See R. Perkins, Criminal Law 940–41 (2d ed. 1969).

In some sense, mistake of fact is really a procedural question concerning when if ever a defendant is entitled to have the jury instructed on a particular defensive theory challenging the sufficiency of the prosecution's evidence. In *Wilson*, consider whether the trial judge would have erred if that judge had not addressed mistake of fact at all in the instructions to the jury. If the judge had properly instructed the jury regarding the culpable mental state required by aggravated manslaughter, perhaps there was no need to tell the panel anything about mistake of fact.

On the other hand, if an instruction on mistake is given, obviously it should not confuse or mislead the jury. In *Wilson*, would an instruction complying with Judge Stern's directives but still limited to *reasonable* mistakes mislead the jury? The prosecution might seek such an instruction, hoping that the jury would conclude that any mistake Wilson had was unreasonable and then, following the instruction, simply disregard it. Would this violate Wilson's right to have the jury determine whether the prosecution had proved beyond a reasonable doubt that he acted with recklessness?

Wilson v. Tard

United States District Court, District of New Jersey, 1984
593 F. Supp. 1091.

STERN, DISTRICT JUDGE.

Christopher Wilson petitions for issuance of a writ of habeas corpus pursuant to 28 U.S.C. § 2254, alleging that the jury instructions given in his manslaughter trial prejudiced his constitutional right to be presumed innocent until the state had proven every element of the crime with which he was charged beyond a reasonable doubt.

* * *

Facts

Petitioner was indicted by a Union County Grand Jury on charges of aggravated manslaughter[1]. * * * He pleaded not guilty to both counts and was tried before the Honorable A. Donald McKenzie, J.S.C., and a jury from March 9–12, 1981. Petitioner was charged in connection with the October 15, 1980, shooting death of his friend Rodney Brown while they and two other men were discussing which of them should be the first to use some heroin in their possession. Petitioner did not dispute that he had shot Brown, but at trial he raised as a defense an alleged mistake of fact.[2] Petitioner contended that he had pointed the gun at his friend in a joking attempt to frighten him. He testi-

fied that he had removed the magazine of bullets from the gun before he aimed it, and contended that because of his unfamiliarity with the weapon he believed he had disarmed it. However, one bullet remained in the chamber of the gun; when petitioner aimed the gun at his friend and pulled the trigger, it discharged and fatally injured the victim. Petitioner argued, however, that his belief that the gun was unloaded when he pulled the trigger was a reasonable mistake under the circumstances, and that therefore he did not possess the level of mental culpability, recklessness, necessary to find him guilty of manslaughter.

In his instructions to the jury, the trial court stressed that since the cause of Brown's death was not disputed, determination of petitioner's state of mind was critical to the state's proof of the offense of manslaughter. After first stating that the burden of proving each element of the offense beyond a reasonable doubt lay on the prosecution, the judge instructed the jury that the defense of mistake which the defendant had raised was an exception to the state's burden of proving all elements of the crime. After summarizing New Jersey's statute on mistake, he told the jury that the burden lay on the defendant to "prove by a

---

[1]New Jersey law provides that aggravated manslaughter occurs "when the actor recklessly causes death under circumstances manifesting extreme indifference to human life," § 2C:11-4a, N.J.Stat.Ann. "Simple" manslaughter occurs when homicide is committed "recklessly." § 2C:114b.

Section 2C:2-2, N.J.Stat.Ann., defines "recklessly" in the following way:

A person acts recklessly with respect to a material element of an offense when he consciously disregards a substantial and unjustifiable risk that the material element exists or will result from his conduct. The risk must be of such a nature and degree that, considering the nature and purpose of the actor's conduct and the circumstances known to him, its disregard involves a gross deviation from the standard of

conduct that a reasonable person would observe in the actor's situation.

Aggravated assault is defined by § 2C:12-lb(4), N.J.Stat.Ann., as "knowingly under circumstances manifesting extreme indifference to the value of human life point(ing) a firearm" at another "whether or not the actor believes it to be loaded."

[2]In relevant part, § 2C:2-4a provides that

Ignorance or mistake as to a matter of fact or law is a defense if the defendant reasonably arrived at the conclusion underlying the mistake and: 1) It negatives the culpable mental state required to establish the offense; or 2) The law provides that the state of mind established by such ignorance or mistake constitutes a defense.

preponderance of the evidence" that he was mistaken in his belief that the gun was not loaded, and that "he arrived at the conclusion reasonably." He stated that the mistake would be a defense if the jury could find that "the defendant reasonably arrived at that conclusion underlying the mistake and it negates the culpable mental state required to establish the offense."

The judge further explained that if the jury concluded that defendant's mistake did negate the culpable mental state for manslaughter it should consider, pursuant to § 2C:2-4b, N.J.Stat.Ann., whether the defendant was guilty of aggravated assault.[3]

The jury returned after one hour and forty-five minutes of deliberation and said it was "unclear about the definition of mistake as it pertains to a reduction in charge from simple manslaughter to aggravated assault." The jury was reinstructed, but it returned forty-five minutes later for another explanation of "defensive mistake." After a further hour and fifteen minutes of deliberation, the jury returned a verdict—finding defendant not guilty of aggravated manslaughter but guilty of the lesser-included charge of simple manslaughter, as well as guilty of the possession of a handgun charge.

* * *

Petitioner appealed his conviction to the Superior Court of New Jersey, Appellate Division, on several grounds. Among them was his contention that the burden of proof for the defense of mistake of fact had been misallocated to him in the jury charge. On April 14, 1983, the Appellate Division affirmed petitioner's conviction. As to petitioner's argument that the jury charge was in error, the court stated: "One who deliberately aims and discharges a firearm directly at another human being, thereby causing the latter's death, cannot, as a matter of law, be found to have been reasonable in his mistaken belief that the gun was unloaded or to have acted other than recklessly. The defense in question should not even have been submitted to the jury." *State of New Jersey v. Christopher Wilson*, Nos. A-3703-80T4, A-3704-80T4, April 14, 1983 (Superior Court of New Jersey, Appellate Division, Per Curiam) at 3.

* * *

---

[3] N.J.Stat.Ann. § 2C:2-4b states that

> Although ignorance or mistake would otherwise afford a defense to the offense charged, the defense is not available if the defendant would be guilty of another offense had the situation been as he supposed. In such case, however, the ignorance or mistake of the defendant shall reduce the grade and degree of the offense of which he may be convicted to those of the offense of which he would be guilty had the situation been as he supposed.

I.

We turn first to the decision of the Appellate Division, which amounts to a holding that one who aims a gun at another person and deliberately pulls the trigger has acted recklessly *per se*; in other words, petitioner's mental state is to be presumed from the act itself. By concluding that petitioner's mistake of fact defense should not even have been submitted to the jury, the Appellate Division drew a conclusive presumption from petitioner's acts, which amounts to "an irrebuttable direction by the court" to the factfinder to find that petitioner acted recklessly "once (it is) convinced of the facts triggering the presumption." See *Sandstrom v. Montana*, 442 U.S. 510, 517, 99 S.Ct. 2450, 2456, 61 L.Ed.2d 39 (1979).

Such a presumption, relieving the state from having to prove an element of the crime, conflicts with the principle, set out by the Supreme Court in *In re Winship*, 397 U.S. 358, 364, 90 S.Ct. 1068, 1073, 25 L.Ed.2d 323 (1970) that "the Due Process Clause protects the accused against conviction except upon proof beyond a reasonable doubt of every fact necessary to constitute the crime with which he is charged."

It is clear that the New Jersey statute makes the existence of the mental state of recklessness an essential element of the crime of manslaughter. In fact, it was the only element of the offense at issue in petitioner's trial, since he admitted to causing the death of the victim. Therefore, by directing a finding of recklessness based upon petitioner's acts, the Appellate Division would deny petitioner a necessary constitutional protection. Its reasoning cannot stand.

II.

Since we find that the Appellate Division erred in the grounds it stated in denying petitioner's challenge to the jury instructions, it is necessary for us to consider whether, in those instructions, the trial court erred in assigning the burden of persuasion as to mistake to the defendant and, if so, whether such an error was of constitutional dimension. We now hold that the trial judge's instruction, allocating the burden of proving the mistake of fact defense to petitioner, constitutes a violation of due process.

In *Mullaney v. Wilber*, 421 U.S. 684, 95 S.Ct. 1881, 44 L.Ed.2d 508 (1975), the Supreme Court held that the requirement of *Winship*—that the prosecution prove all elements of the crime beyond a reasonable doubt—necessarily barred the state from shifting to the defendant the burden of disproving any element of the crime charged. * * *

Applying the holding of *Mullaney v. Wilber* to this case, we conclude that, in shifting the burden of proof to petitioner to establish a defense of mistake, the trial court improperly shifted to him the burden of disproving a material element of the offense.

* * *

It is clear that under New Jersey law recklessness and mistake of fact have a mirror relationship * * *; they are "two inconsistent things; thus by proving the latter the defendant would negate the former." A showing that the actor made a reasonable mistake would establish that he did not act recklessly.

In the case before us, in advancing the argument that he had reasonably believed that the gun was unloaded when he pulled its trigger, petitioner had raised a defense whose proof would negate the mental element necessary to constitute manslaughter. Thus, under *Mullaney* he should have borne only the burden of raising the issue, not that of proving it. The state was required to refute this defense beyond a reasonable doubt as an inseparable part of proving beyond a reasonable doubt that petitioner had acted recklessly and thus was guilty of manslaughter. By shifting to petitioner the burden of proving his defense by a preponderance of the evidence, the trial court unconstitutionally relieved the state of its burden of proving all the elements of the crime beyond a reasonable doubt.

This violation of his constitutional rights entitles petitioner to a new trial. The writ of habeas corpus shall issue.

Notes and Questions

1. Suppose the *Wilson* jury had concluded that Wilson in fact mistakenly believed that the gun was unloaded but that a reasonable person in the situation would nevertheless not have been confident that this was the case and therefore would not have pointed the gun at another person and pulled the trigger. The New Jersey statute, like many other formulations of the doctrine of defense or ignorance of fact, limits the rule to those situations in which the accused entertained a reasonable mistake. Logically, if the jury concluded that Wilson entertained such an unreasonable perception, could it also logically conclude that the prosecution had proved beyond a reasonable doubt that he acted recklessly? The trial judge's instructions apparently told the jury to convict Wilson in such a situation. Did this aspect of the instructions violate the *Winship* requirement that the prosecution prove each element of the offense beyond a reasonable doubt?

   As the Editors' Introduction to theis chapter developed, federal constitutional considerations may be operative here. The Wisconsin Court of Appeals has commented:

[T]he objective standard of reasonableness may be unconstitutional. The prosecutor's burden of proof in mistake of fact cases would be more relaxed since an unreasonable act performed without intent could result in criminal liability. The resultant effect would be contrary to *In re Winship*, 397 U.S. 358, 90 S.Ct. 1068, 25 L.Ed.2d 368 (1970), which found that due process required proof beyond a reasonable doubt of every element of an offense.

State v. Bougneit, 97 Wis.2d 687, 692 n. 4, 294 N.W.2d 675, 678 n. 4 (1980). Reconsider this after reading the first case reprinted in the next subsection, *Cheek v. United States*, and again after reading the material on intoxication in Section B of Chapter 15.

2. Howard, The Reasonableness of Mistake in the Criminal Law, 4 U.Queens L.J. 45 (1961), suggests that the disagreement concerning whether a mistake need be reasonable results from a failure to distinguish mistake as a defense to a crime requiring general intent and mistake offered as a defense to a crime for which negligence is sufficient. In the former case, Howard suggests, no reasonableness is necessary; in the latter, only a reasonable mistake logically bars liability. If a jurisdiction has adopted the general position that negligence will constitute sufficient culpability only in exceptional situations, can it also accept a rule—such as that embodied in the New Jersey statute—that mistakes of fact must, as a general matter, be reasonable? Perhaps the existence of such a statute indicates that despite indications elsewhere to the contrary, the jurisdiction has not really adopted a requirement that more than negligence is generally required for criminal liability.

3. If Wilson did mistakenly and reasonably believe the gun was unloaded and therefore cannot be convicted of either aggravated or simple manslaughter under New Jersey law, could he be convicted of aggravated assault, as described in footnote 2 of Judge Stern's opinion?

4. A sexual assault defendant's claim of a mistaken belief that the victim consented is addressed in Chapter 9.

B. IGNORANCE OR MISTAKE OF LAW

As Judge Wilkey's discussion of mistake generally indicated (see the Editors' Introduction), ignorance of or mistake concerning "law" is often said not to affect criminal liability. In other words, mistake as to the law as well as "ignorance of the law" is thus said to be "no excuse." This, of course, is consistent with the notion that ignorance or mistake should affect criminal liability only if it shows the lack of criminal "intent." Generally, the prosecution need not allege or prove that the defendant knew, or even that the defendant should have known, of the existence and meaning of the law under which he or she is being prosecuted. Because mistake as to law does not negate any aspect of the required culpable mental state, it does not affect criminal liability.

The wisdom and acceptability of this view was discussed by Judge Hancock of the New York Court of Appeals:

> Suppose the case of a man who has committed an act which is criminal not because it is inherently wrong or immoral but solely because it violates a criminal statute. He has committed the act in complete good faith under the mistaken but entirely reasonable assumption that the act does not constitute an offense because it is permitted by the wording of the statute. Does the law require that this man be punished? * * *
>
> There can be no question that under the view that the purpose of the criminal justice system is to punish blameworthiness or "choosing freely to do wrong", our supposed man who has acted innocently and without any intent to do wrong should not be punished. Indeed, under some standards of morality he has done no wrong at all. Since he has not knowingly committed a wrong there can be no reason for society to exact retribution. Because the man is law-abiding and would not have acted but for his mistaken assumption as to the law, there is no need for punishment to deter him from further unlawful conduct. Traditionally, however, under the ancient rule of Anglo-American common law that ignorance or mistake of law is no excuse, our supposed man would be punished.
>
> The maxim "ignorantia legis neminem excusat" finds its roots in Medieval law when the "actor's intent was irrelevant since the law punished the act itself" and when, for example, the law recognized no difference between an intentional killing and one that was accidental. Although the common law has gradually evolved from its origins in Anglo-Germanic tribal law (adding the element of intent [*mens rea*] and recognizing defenses based on the actor's mental state—e.g., justification, insanity and intoxication) the dogmatic rule that ignorance or mistake of law is no excuse has remained unaltered. Various justifications have been offered for the rule, but all are frankly pragmatic and utilitarian—preferring the interests of society (e.g., in deterring criminal conduct, fostering orderly judicial administration, and preserving the primacy of the rule of law) to the interest of the individual in being free from punishment except for intentionally engaging in conduct which he knows is criminal.
>
> The societal interests mentioned in the literature include: facilitating judicial administration, encouraging knowledge and obedience to law and preservation of integrity of legal norms. Justice Holmes, for example, stressed society's interests in deterrence, noting that acceptance of ignorance or mistake of law as a defense

would encourage ignorance at the expense of the public good. See, Holmes, The Common Law, at 48 [1881]. John Austin justified "ignorantia legis" on the ground that if the defense were permitted, the courts would be confronted with questions about defendant's mental state which they could not solve. Austin, Lectures on Jurisprudence, at 496-501 [4th ed. 1873] * * *.

Today there is widespread criticism of the common-law rule mandating categorical preclusion of the mistake of law defense. The utilitarian arguments for retaining the rule have been drawn into serious question but the fundamental objection is that it is simply wrong to punish someone who, in good-faith reliance on the wording of a statute, believed that what he was doing was lawful. It is contrary to "the notion that punishment should be conditioned on a showing of subjective moral blameworthiness". This basic objection to the maxim "ignorantia legis neminem excusat" may have had less force in ancient times when most crimes consisted of acts which by their very nature were recognized as evil (*malum in se*). In modern times, however, with the profusion of legislation making otherwise lawful conduct criminal (*malum prohibitum*), the "common law fiction that every man is presumed to know the law has become indefensible in fact or logic".

People v. Marrero, 69 N.Y.2d 382, 392–95, 507 N.E.2d 1068, 1073–75, 515 N.Y.S.2d 212, 217–19 (1987) (Hancock, J., dissenting) (footnote modified into text).

As Judge Wilkey also noted, however, even under the traditional view the distinction between mistakes of fact and those of law is not always clear. Sometimes, it is possible that the existence or meaning of a statute, constitutional rule, or proposition of common law may be a fact within the meaning of the rule that ignorance or mistake of fact may negate *mens rea*. The drafters of the Model Penal Code observed:

> [T]he general principle that ignorance or mistake of law is no excuse is usually greatly overstated; it has no application when the circumstances made material by the definition of the offense include a legal element. The law involved is not the law defining the offense; it is some other legal rule that characterizes the attendant circumstances that are material to the offense.

Model Penal Code, Comment to § 2.02, p. 131 (Tent. Draft No. 4, 1955).

Moreover, there is some tendency on the part of legislatures and courts to provide for limited defenses of ignorance or mistake of law, even when that mistake or ignorance does not logically indicate the absence of the state of mind required by the crime charged.

Constitutional considerations may operate here. *Lambert v. California*, 355 U.S. 225, 78 S.Ct. 240, 2 L.Ed.2d 228 (1967), discussed in the Editors' Introduction to Chapter 4, may be read as demanding that in some situations defendants be afforded at least the opportunity to assert unawareness of certain matters of law defensively. Other Supreme Court case law is discussed in the notes following *Ostrosky v. State,* reprinted in Section B(2) of this chapter.

1. Ignorance or Mistake Regarding Law Incorporated into the Culpable Mental State Required

In a few unusual situations, the culpable mental state required by a crime includes a demand that the actor have been aware of some legal matters, that is, some "law." If this is the case, mistake or even ignorance that raises a reasonable doubt whether the prosecution has proved the required awareness prevents conviction.

Under the approach of the Model Penal Code, reprinted at page 394, this is provided for by section 2.04(1)(a). For those jurisdictions that have separate statutory provisions dealing with mistakes of law and fact, it is arguable that defendants such as John Cheek, the accused in the case reprinted next, are invoking mistake of fact doctrine by treating law as a fact.

Cheek v. United States

Supreme Court of the United States, 1991
498 U.S. 192, 111 S.Ct. 604, 112 L.Ed.2d 617.

Justice WHITE delivered the opinion of the Court.

Title 26, § 7201 of the United States Code provides that any person "who willfully attempts in any manner to evade or defeat any tax imposed by this title or the payment thereof" shall be guilty of a felony. Under 26 U.S.C. § 7203, "[a]ny person required under this title . . . or by regulations made under authority thereof to make a return . . . who willfully fails to . . . make such return" shall be guilty of a misdemeanor. This case turns on the meaning of the word "willfully" as used in §§ 7201 and 7203.

I

Petitioner John L. Cheek has been a pilot for American Airlines since 1973. He filed federal income tax returns through 1979 but thereafter ceased to file returns. He also claimed an increasing number of withholding allowances— eventually claiming 60 allowances by mid-1980—and for the years 1981 to 1984 indicated on his W-4 forms that he was exempt from federal income taxes. In 1983, petitioner unsuccessfully sought a refund of all tax withheld by his employer in 1982. Petitioner's income during this period at all times far exceeded the minimum necessary to trigger the statutory filing requirement.

As a result of his activities, petitioner was indicted for 10 violations of federal law. He was charged with six counts of willfully failing to file a federal income tax return for the years 1980, 1981, and 1983 through 1986, in violation of § 7203. He was further charged with three counts of willfully attempting to evade his income taxes for the years

1980, 1981, and 1983 in violation of 26 U.S.C. § 7201. In those years, American Airlines withheld substantially less than the amount of tax petitioner owed because of the numerous allowances and exempt status he claimed on his W-4 forms. The tax offenses with which petitioner was charged are specific intent crimes that require the defendant to have acted willfully.

At trial, the evidence established that between 1982 and 1986, petitioner was involved in at least four civil cases that challenged various aspects of the federal income tax system. In all four of those cases, the plaintiffs were informed by the courts that many of their arguments, including that they were not taxpayers within the meaning of the tax laws, that wages are not income, that the Sixteenth Amendment does not authorize the imposition of an income tax on individuals, and that the Sixteenth Amendment is unenforceable, were frivolous or had been repeatedly rejected by the courts. During this time period, petitioner also attended at least two criminal trials of persons charged with tax offenses. In addition, there was evidence that in 1980 or 1981 an attorney had advised Cheek that the courts had rejected as frivolous the claim that wages are not income.[4]

---

[4] The attorney also advised that despite the Fifth Amendment, the filing of a tax return was required and that a person could challenge the constitutionality of the system by suing for a refund after the taxes had been withheld, or by putting himself "at risk of criminal prosecution."

Cheek represented himself at trial and testified in his defense. He admitted that he had not filed personal income tax returns during the years in question. He testified that as early as 1978, he had begun attending seminars sponsored by, and following the advice of, a group that believes, among other things, that the federal tax system is unconstitutional. Some of the speakers at these meetings were lawyers who purported to give professional opinions about the invalidity of the federal income tax laws. Cheek produced a letter from an attorney stating that the Sixteenth Amendment did not authorize a tax on wages and salaries but only on gain or profit. Petitioner's defense was that, based on the indoctrination he received from this group and from his own study, he sincerely believed that the tax laws were being unconstitutionally enforced and that his actions during the 1980–1986 period were lawful. He therefore argued that he had acted without the willfulness required for conviction of the various offenses with which he was charged.

In the course of its instructions, the trial court advised the jury that to prove "willfulness" the Government must prove the voluntary and intentional violation of a known legal duty, a burden that could not be proved by showing mistake, ignorance, or negligence. The court further advised the jury that an objectively reasonable good-faith misunderstanding of the law would negate willfulness, but mere disagreement with the law would not. The court described Cheek's beliefs about the income tax system and instructed the jury that if it found that Cheek "honestly and reasonably believed that he was not required to pay income taxes or to file tax returns," a not guilty verdict should be returned.

After several hours of deliberation, the jury sent a note to the judge that stated in part:

> "'We have a basic disagreement between some of us as to if Mr. Cheek honestly & reasonably believed that he was not required to pay income taxes.
>
> . . . . .
>
> "'Page 32 [the relevant jury instruction] discusses good faith misunderstanding & disagreement. Is there any additional clarification you can give us on this point?'"

The District Judge responded with a supplemental instruction containing the following statements: "[A] person's opinion that the tax laws violate his constitutional rights does not constitute a good faith misunderstanding of the law. Furthermore, a person's disagreement with the government's tax collection systems and policies does not constitute a good faith misunderstanding of the law."

At the end of the first day of deliberation, the jury sent out another note saying that it still could not reach a verdict because "'[w]e are divided on the issue as to if Mr. Cheek

honestly & reasonably believed that he was not required to pay income tax.'" When the jury resumed its deliberations, the District Judge gave the jury an additional instruction. This instruction stated in part that "[a]n honest but unreasonable belief is not a defense and does not negate willfulness," and that "[a]dvice or research resulting in the conclusion that wages of a privately employed person are not income or that the tax laws are unconstitutional is not objectively reasonable and cannot serve as the basis for a good faith misunderstanding of the law defense." The court also instructed the jury that "[p]ersistent refusal to acknowledge the law does not constitute a good faith misunderstanding of the law." Approximately two hours later, the jury returned a verdict finding petitioner guilty on all counts.[5] [A sentence of a year and one day imprisonment was imposed. Eds.]

Petitioner appealed his convictions, arguing that the District Court erred by instructing the jury that only an objectively reasonable misunderstanding of the law negates the statutory willfulness requirement. The United States Court of Appeals for the Seventh Circuit rejected that contention and affirmed the convictions. In prior cases, the Seventh Circuit had made clear that good-faith misunderstanding of the law negates willfulness only if the defendant's beliefs are objectively reasonable; in the Seventh Circuit, even actual ignorance is not a defense unless the defendant's ignorance was itself objectively reasonable. In its opinion in this case, the court noted that several specified beliefs, including the beliefs that the tax laws are unconstitutional and that wages are not income, would not be objectively reasonable. Because the Seventh Circuit's interpretation of "willfully" as used in these statutes conflicts with the decisions of several other Courts of Appeals, we granted certiorari.

II

The general rule that ignorance of the law or a mistake of law is no defense to criminal prosecution is deeply rooted in the American legal system. Based on the notion that the law is definite and knowable, the common law presumed that every person knew the law. This common-law rule has

---

[5] A note signed by all 12 jurors also informed the judge that although the jury found petitioner guilty, several jurors wanted to express their personal opinions of the case and that notes from these individual jurors to the court were "a complaint against the narrow & hard expression under the constraints of the law." At least two notes from individual jurors expressed the opinion that petitioner sincerely believed in his cause even though his beliefs might have been unreasonable.

been applied by the Court in numerous cases construing criminal statutes.

The proliferation of statutes and regulations has sometimes made it difficult for the average citizen to know and comprehend the extent of the duties and obligations imposed by the tax laws. Congress has accordingly softened the impact of the common-law presumption by making specific intent to violate the law an element of certain federal criminal tax offenses. Thus, the Court almost 60 years ago interpreted the statutory term "willfully" as used in the federal criminal tax statutes as carving out an exception to the traditional rule. This special treatment of criminal tax offenses is largely due to the complexity of the tax laws. In *United States v. Murdock*, 290 U.S. 389, 54 S.Ct. 223, 78 L.Ed. 381 (1933), the Court recognized that: "Congress did not intend that a person, by reason of a bona fide misunderstanding as to his liability for the tax, as to his duty to make a return, or as to the adequacy of the records he maintained, should become a criminal by his mere failure to measure up to the prescribed standard of conduct." The Court held that the defendant was entitled to an instruction with respect to whether he acted in good faith based on his actual belief. In *Murdock*, the Court interpreted the term "willfully" as used in the criminal tax statutes generally to mean "an act done with a bad purpose," or with "an evil motive."

Subsequent decisions have refined this proposition. In *United States v. Bishop*, 412 U.S. 346, 93 S.Ct. 2008, 36 L.Ed.2d 941 (1973), we described the term "willfully" as connoting "a voluntary, intentional violation of a known legal duty," and did so with specific reference to the "bad faith or evil intent" language employed in *Murdock*. Still later, *United States v. Pomponio*, 429 U.S. 10, 97 S.Ct. 22, 50 L.Ed.2d 12 (1976) (per curiam), addressed a situation in which several defendants had been charged with willfully filing false tax returns. The jury was given an instruction on willfulness similar to the standard set forth in *Bishop*. In addition, it was instructed that "[g]ood motive alone is never a defense where the act done or omitted is a crime." The defendants were convicted but the Court of Appeals reversed, concluding that the latter instruction was improper because the statute required a finding of bad purpose or evil motive.

We reversed the Court of Appeals, stating that "the Court of Appeals incorrectly assumed that the reference to an 'evil motive' in United *States v. Bishop*, supra, and prior cases," "requires proof of any motive other than an intentional violation of a known legal duty." As "the other Courts of Appeals that have considered the question have recognized, willfulness in this context simply means a voluntary, intentional violation of a known legal duty." We concluded that after instructing the jury on willfulness, "[a]n addition-

al instruction on good faith was unnecessary." Taken together, *Bishop* and *Pomponio* conclusively establish that the standard for the statutory willfulness requirement is the "voluntary, intentional violation of a known legal duty."

III

Cheek accepts the *Pomponio* definition of willfulness, but asserts that the District Court's instructions and the Court of Appeals' opinion departed from that definition. In particular, he challenges the ruling that a good-faith misunderstanding of the law or a good-faith belief that one is not violating the law, if it is to negate willfulness, must be objectively reasonable. We agree that the Court of Appeals and the District Court erred in this respect.

A

Willfulness, as construed by our prior decisions in criminal tax cases, requires the Government to prove that the law imposed a duty on the defendant, that the defendant knew of this duty, and that he voluntarily and intentionally violated that duty. We deal first with the case where the issue is whether the defendant knew of the duty purportedly imposed by the provision of the statute or regulation he is accused of violating, a case in which there is no claim that the provision at issue is invalid. In such a case, if the Government proves actual knowledge of the pertinent legal duty, the prosecution, without more, has satisfied the knowledge component of the willfulness requirement. But carrying this burden requires negating a defendant's claim of ignorance of the law or a claim that because of a misunderstanding of the law, he had a good-faith belief that he was not violating any of the provisions of the tax laws. This is so because one cannot be aware that the law imposes a duty upon him and yet be ignorant of it, misunderstand the law, or believe that the duty does not exist. In the end, the issue is whether, based on all the evidence, the Government has proved that the defendant was aware of the duty at issue, which cannot be true if the jury credits a good-faith misunderstanding and belief submission, whether or not the claimed belief or misunderstanding is objectively reasonable.

In this case, if Cheek asserted that he truly believed that the Internal Revenue Code did not purport to treat wages as income, and the jury believed him, the Government would not have carried its burden to prove willfulness, however unreasonable a court might deem such a belief. Of course, in deciding whether to credit Cheek's good-faith belief claim, the jury would be free to consider any admissible evidence from any source showing that Cheek was aware of his duty to file a return and to treat wages as income, including evidence showing his awareness of the relevant provisions of the Code or regulations, of court decisions rejecting his interpretation of the tax law, of authoritative rulings of the Internal Revenue Service, or of any contents of the personal income tax return forms and accompanying instructions that made it plain that wages should be returned as income.[6]

We thus disagree with the Court of Appeals' requirement that a claimed good-faith belief must be objectively reasonable if it is to be considered as possibly negating the Government's evidence purporting to show a defendant's awareness of the legal duty at issue. Knowledge and belief are characteristically questions for the factfinder, in this case the jury. Characterizing a particular belief as not objectively reasonable transforms the inquiry into a legal one and would prevent the jury from considering it. It would of course be proper to exclude evidence having no relevance or probative value with respect to willfulness; but it is not contrary to common sense, let alone impossible, for a defendant to be ignorant of his duty based on an irrational belief that he has no duty, and forbidding the jury to consider evidence that might negate willfulness would raise a serious question under the Sixth Amendment's jury trial provision. It is common ground that this Court, where possible, interprets congressional enactments so as to avoid raising serious constitutional questions.

It was therefore error to instruct the jury to disregard evidence of Cheek's understanding that, within the meaning of the tax laws, he was not a person required to file a return or to pay income taxes and that wages are not taxable income, as incredible as such misunderstandings of and beliefs about the law might be. Of course, the more unreasonable the asserted beliefs or misunderstandings are, the more likely the jury will consider them to be nothing more than simple disagreement with known legal duties imposed by the tax laws and will find that the Government has carried its burden of proving knowledge.

B

Cheek asserted in the trial court that he should be acquitted because he believed in good faith that the income tax law is unconstitutional as applied to him and thus could not legally impose any duty upon him of which he should have

been aware. Such a submission is unsound, not because Cheek's constitutional arguments are not objectively reasonable or frivolous, which they surely are, but because the *Murdock–Pomponio* line of cases does not support such a position. Those cases construed the willfulness requirement in the criminal provisions of the Internal Revenue Code to require proof of knowledge of the law. This was because in "our complex tax system, uncertainty often arises even among taxpayers who earnestly wish to follow the law," and "[i]t is not the purpose of the law to penalize frank difference of opinion or innocent errors made despite the exercise of reasonable care."

Claims that some of the provisions of the tax code are unconstitutional are submissions of a different order. They do not arise from innocent mistakes caused by the complexity of the Internal Revenue Code. Rather, they reveal full knowledge of the provisions at issue and a studied conclusion, however wrong, that those provisions are invalid and unenforceable. Thus in this case, Cheek paid his taxes for years, but after attending various seminars and based on his own study, he concluded that the income tax laws could not constitutionally require him to pay a tax.

We do not believe that Congress contemplated that such a taxpayer, without risking criminal prosecution, could ignore the duties imposed upon him by the Internal Revenue Code and refuse to utilize the mechanisms provided by Congress to present his claims of invalidity to the courts and to abide by their decisions. There is no doubt that Cheek, from year to year, was free to pay the tax that the law purported to require, file for a refund and, if denied, present his claims of invalidity, constitutional or otherwise, to the courts. Also, without paying the tax, he could have challenged claims of tax deficiencies in the Tax Court, with the right to appeal to a higher court if unsuccessful. Cheek took neither course in some years, and when he did was unwilling to accept the outcome. As we see it, he is in no position to claim that his good-faith belief about the validity of the Internal Revenue Code negates willfulness or provides a defense to criminal prosecution under §§ 7201 and 7203. Of course, Cheek was free in this very case to present his claims of invalidity and have them adjudicated, but like defendants in criminal cases in other contexts, who "willfully" refuse to comply with the duties placed upon them by the law, he must take the risk of being wrong.

We thus hold that in a case like this, a defendant's views about the validity of the tax statutes are irrelevant to the issue of willfulness and need not be heard by the jury, and, if they are, an instruction to disregard them would be proper. For this purpose, it makes no difference whether the claims of invalidity are frivolous or have substance. It was therefore not error in this case for the District Judge to instruct the jury not to consider Cheek's claims that the tax

---

[6] Cheek recognizes that a "defendant who knows what the law is and who disagrees with it . . . does not have a bona fide misunderstanding defense," but asserts that "a defendant who has a bona fide misunderstanding of [the law] does not 'know' his legal duty and lacks willfulness." Brief for Petitioner 29, and n. 13. The Reply Brief for Petitioner, at 13, states: "We are in no way suggesting that Cheek or anyone else is immune from criminal prosecution if he knows what the law is, but believes it should be otherwise, and therefore violates it."

laws were unconstitutional. However, it was error for the court to instruct the jury that petitioner's asserted beliefs that wages are not income and that he was not a taxpayer within the meaning of the Internal Revenue Code should not be considered by the jury in determining whether Cheek had acted willfully.[7]

IV

For the reasons set forth in the opinion above, the judgment of the Court of Appeals is vacated, and the case is remanded for further proceedings consistent with this opinion.

It is so ordered.

Justice SOUTER took no part in the consideration or decision of this case.

Justice SCALIA, concurring in the judgment.

I concur in the judgment of the Court because our cases have consistently held that the failure to pay a tax in the good-faith belief that it is not legally owing is not "willful." I do not join the Court's opinion because I do not agree with the test for willfulness that it directs the Court of Appeals to apply on remand.

As the Court acknowledges, our opinions from the 1930's to the 1970's have interpreted the word "willfully" in the criminal tax statutes as requiring the "bad purpose" or "evil motive" of "intentional[ly] violat[ing] a known legal duty." It seems to me that today's opinion squarely reverses that long-established statutory construction when it says that a good-faith erroneous belief in the unconstitutionality of a tax law is no defense. It is quite impossible to say that a statute which one believes unconstitutional represents a "known legal duty."

Although the facts of the present case involve erroneous reliance upon the Constitution in ignoring the otherwise "known legal duty" imposed by the tax statutes, the Court's new interpretation applies also to erroneous reliance upon a tax statute in ignoring the otherwise "known legal duty" of a regulation, and to erroneous reliance upon a regulation in ignoring the otherwise "known legal duty" of a tax assessment. These situations as well meet the opinion's crucial test of "reveal[ing] full knowledge of the provisions at issue and a studied conclusion, however wrong, that those provi-

sions are invalid and unenforceable." There is, moreover, no rational basis for saying that a "willful" violation is established by full knowledge of a statutory requirement, but is not established by full knowledge of a requirement explicitly imposed by regulation or order. Thus, today's opinion works a revolution in past practice, subjecting to criminal penalties taxpayers who do not comply with Treasury Regulations that are in their view contrary to the Internal Revenue Code, Treasury Rulings that are in their view contrary to the regulations, and even IRS auditor pronouncements that are in their view contrary to Treasury Rulings. The law already provides considerable incentive for taxpayers to be careful in ignoring any official assertion of tax liability, since it contains civil penalties that apply even in the event of a good-faith mistake. To impose in addition criminal penalties for misinterpretation of such a complex body of law is a startling innovation indeed.

I find it impossible to understand how one can derive from the lonesome word "willfully" the proposition that belief in the nonexistence of a textual prohibition excuses liability, but belief in the invalidity (i.e., the legal nonexistence) of a textual prohibition does not. One may say, as the law does in many contexts, that "willfully" refers to consciousness of the act but not to consciousness that the act is unlawful. Or alternatively, one may say, as we have said until today with respect to the tax statutes, that "willfully" refers to consciousness of both the act and its illegality. But it seems to me impossible to say that the word refers to consciousness that some legal text exists, without consciousness that that legal text is binding, i.e., with the good-faith belief that it is not a valid law. Perhaps such a test for criminal liability would make sense (though in a field as complicated as federal tax law, I doubt it), but some text other than the mere word "willfully" would have to be employed to describe it—and that text is not ours to write.

Because today's opinion abandons clear and longstanding precedent to impose criminal liability where taxpayers have had no reason to expect it, because the new contours of criminal liability have no basis in the statutory text, and because I strongly suspect that those new contours make no sense even as a policy matter, I concur only in the judgment of the Court.

Justice BLACKMUN, with whom Justice MARSHALL joins, dissenting.

It seems to me that we are concerned in this case not with "the complexity of the tax laws," but with the income tax law in its most elementary and basic aspect: Is a wage earner a taxpayer and are wages income?

The Court acknowledges that the conclusively established standard for willfulness under the applicable statutes

---

[7] Cheek argues that applying to him the Court of Appeals' standard of objective reasonableness violates his rights under the First, Fifth, and Sixth Amendments of the Constitution. Since we have invalidated the challenged standard on statutory grounds, we need not address these submissions.

is the "'voluntary, intentional violation of a known legal duty.'" That being so, it is incomprehensible to me how, in this day, more than 70 years after the institution of our present federal income tax system with the passage of the Income Tax Act of 1913, 38 Stat. 166, any taxpayer of competent mentality can assert as his defense to charges of statutory willfulness the proposition that the wage he receives for his labor is not income, irrespective of a cult that says otherwise and advises the gullible to resist income tax collections. One might note in passing that this particular taxpayer, after all, was a licensed pilot for one of our major commercial airlines; he presumably was a person of at least minimum intellectual competence.

The District Court's instruction that an objectively reasonable and good-faith misunderstanding of the law negates willfulness lends further, rather than less, protection to this defendant, for it adds an additional hurdle for the prosecution to overcome. Petitioner should be grateful for this further protection, rather than be opposed to it.

This Court's opinion today, I fear, will encourage taxpayers to cling to frivolous views of the law in the hope of convincing a jury of their sincerity. If that ensues, I suspect we have gone beyond the limits of common sense.

* * * I therefore dissent.

Note

On remand, Cheek was retried. The trial judge instructed the jury as follows:

> A defendant does not act willfully if he believes in good [faith] that he is acting within the law or that his actions comply with the law. Therefore, if defendant actually believed that what he was doing was in accord with the tax statutes, he cannot be said to have had the criminal intent to willfully evade or defeat taxes or to willfully fail to file tax returns. This is so even if defendant's belief was not objectively reasonable as long as he held the belief in good faith. Nevertheless, you may consider whether the defendant's stated belief about the tax statutes was reasonable as a factor in deciding whether he held that belief in good faith.

He was again convicted, and a sentence of a year and one day imprisonment plus a fine of $62,000 was imposed. On appeal, this was held to adequately reflect the Supreme Court's holding. *United States v. Cheek,* 3 F.3d 1057 (7th Cir.1993), cert. denied, 510 U.S. 1112, 114 S.Ct. 1055, 127 L.Ed.2d 376 (1994).

2. Ignorance or Mistake Regarding the Law Defining the Charged Offense

Most criminal defenses do not require that the actor have known and understood the substantive criminal law and that the actor's conduct constitutes a crime under this law. Despite the criminal law's emphasis on culpable mental state, the culpable mental states required by most crimes demand awareness of only facts, not law. This is reflected in the often-repeated statement that "All persons are presumed to know the law."

Nevertheless, criminal defendants sometimes assert as a defense that they misunderstood the law defining the crime charged and, as a result, believed that their conduct was not criminal in nature. It may still be true that mere passive ignorance of the law making one's conduct a crime is never a defense. Statutes in some jurisdictions, however, provide for a limited defense based on an affirmative but mistaken belief that one's anticipated conduct would not be a crime within the meaning of the criminal law. Case law, including the case reprinted here, suggests that in some limited situations an affirmative mistake of this sort about the law may prevent liability even in the absence of a statutory provision. Constitutional considerations may require such a defense.

In terms of the Model Penal Code's provisions, these cases raise the matter provided for in section 2.04(3), reprinted at page 394.

Some defendants, like the accused in *People v. Marrero*, discussed in the notes after the following case, make no reference to constitutional law and simply argue that they misunderstood the words defining the crime or the definition of those words. Others, like the defendant in the following case, make no claim to have misunderstood what the statutory law meant but argue that they misunderstood either constitutional or procedural law as making the statute unenforceable, as least against them in their situations. As the following case demonstrates, courts have tended to treat these two types of mistake in the same manner.

To the extent that a doctrine requiring acquittal as discussed in this subsection exists, it is a "defense" rather than a "defensive theory" or "argument" as those terms are distinguished in the Editors' Introduction to this chapter. Further, the concerns by courts and legislatures that this defense will be abused in practice has led most authorities to treat it as an *affirmative* defense and thus to place upon an accused the burden of proving it. As demonstrated by the case that follows, courts' concern regarding such abuse may even persuade them to bar the trial jury from considering this matter, if that can be constitutionally done.

Ostrosky v. State

Court of Appeals of Alaska, 1985
704 P.2d 786.

COATS, JUDGE.

This case raises the question of the extent to which a defendant can rely on mistake of law as a defense to a fish and game violation.

Harold Ostrosky and his two daughters were convicted of fishing without a valid limited entry permit in 1979. Ostrosky's daughters moved for post-conviction relief, contending that the Limited Entry Act violated equal protection. Judge Victor D. Carlson found the act unconstitutional and vacated the convictions on August 14, 1981. Ostrosky was allowed to join in the action, and his conviction was set aside on August 25, 1981.[a] The state appealed. This court certified the case to the supreme court, and the supreme court accepted the case for decision.

On July 3, 1983, Ostrosky was fishing with a drift gill net in open waters off Naknek. Trooper Gary Folger, acting as a fish and wildlife protection officer, boarded Ostrosky's boat and checked it for fish. Despite Ostrosky's admission that he had no permit, the trooper did not arrest Ostrosky or try to stop him from fishing.

On July 7, 1983, while the state's appeal in Ostrosky's earlier case was still pending, the state filed an emergency request with the supreme court for a stay of the effect of Judge Carlson's ruling in that case.[b] The request alleged that "irreparable harm" would result if the stay were not granted, because Ostrosky had continued to fish the waters of Bristol Bay without a permit, creating a "serious potential for violence" in the area and "undermining the fishermen's confidence in the limited entry system." * * * Chief Justice Edmond Burke, acting as a single justice, entered an order granting the stay pending the announcement by the supreme court of a decision in Ostrosky's case. The order states, "the intent of this order is to permit the continued

---

[a] When Judge Carlson granted relief to defendant Ostrosky's daughters on August 14, he filed a long "memorandum of decision" explaining his grounds for regarding the statute as unconstitutional; major portions of this memorandum are set out as footnote 3 of *State v. Ostrosky*, 667 P.2d 1184 (Alaska 1983). On August 25, Judge Carlson entered a brief order in response to defendant Ostrosky's petition; this order first permitted Ostrosky to join in the case filed by his daughters and, second, set aside Oskrosky's conviction "for the reasons set forth in the memorandum of decision filed August 14, 1981."

[b] A "stay" is an order that bars enforcement or effectiveness of the action stayed. Thus the order ultimately entered by Chief Justice Burke granting the stay had the effect of rendering Judge Carlson's ruling temporarily ineffective. Since Judge Carlson's stayed order had vacated Ostrosky's conviction, the effect of the stay was to put matters back as they were before that order. Thus the stay "unvacated" Ostrosky's conviction.

enforcement of the Limited Entry Act pending this court's decision on the merits." On July 8, 1983, Trooper Folger cited Ostrosky for fishing without a permit on that date, for fishing without permit on July 3, and for illegal possession of salmon.

On July 19, 1983, the Alaska Supreme Court reversed Judge Carlson's ruling and upheld the Limited Entry Act. After the supreme court's decision, Ostrosky filed a motion to dismiss in the present case alleging that, at the time he was charged with violating the Limited Entry Act, the Act had been declared unconstitutional in a case in which he was a party. Ostrosky argued that he was entitled to rely on Judge Carlson's ruling. Judge Carlson ruled that Ostrosky had no right to rely on his earlier decision and that by fishing, Ostrosky had taken the risk that the earlier decision would be reversed by the supreme court.

Ostrosky then asked the court to instruct the jury that reasonable reliance on a judicial decision was a defense to this prosecution. Judge Carlson denied this request. He also ruled that Ostrosky could not present testimony concerning reasonable reliance on a judicial decision since that testimony would be irrelevant. Ostrosky at this point made an offer of proof that he would testify that at the time he was fishing he believed that he was fishing legally. He represented that he relied on Judge Carlson's decision declaring the Limited Entry Act unconstitutional and that he had read an article in the Fisherman's Journal which reported that a magistrate in Kenai had also ruled that the Limited Entry Act was unconstitutional. He also indicated that after Judge Carlson's ruling declaring the Limited Entry Act to be unconstitutional, Ostrosky had talked to his attorney who had assured him that he would not be arrested for fishing without a permit during the 1983 season.

After Judge Carlson ruled Ostrosky's defense of mistake of law was irrelevant and that he would not give a jury instruction on this defense, Ostrosky agreed to a court trial on the condition that his objection to this ruling would be preserved for appeal. Ostrosky was convicted following a court trial. He now appeals to this court.

[The Limited Entry Act is Chapter 43 of Title 16 of the Alaska Statutes. The statutory provision creating the crime of which Ostrosky was convicted is Alaska Stat. Sec. 16.43.970(a):

(a) A person who violates a provision of this chapter or a regulation adopted under this chapter is, upon conviction, guilty of a class B misdemeanor * * *.

20 AAC 05.100(a), a regulation adopted under the chapter, provides:

(a) It is unlawful for any person to operate gear, within water subject to the jurisdiction of the state, for the commercial taking of any fishery resource without a valid * * * entry permit card issued by the [Alaska Commercial Fisheries Entry Commission] authorizing that person to operate that type of gear in that fishery * * *.

Eds.]

The defense of reasonable reliance on a statute or judicial decision is discussed in W. LaFave and A. Scott, Criminal Law § 47, at 366-67 (1972):

An individual should be able reasonably to rely upon a statute or other enactment under which his conduct would not be criminal, so that he need not fear conviction if subsequent to his conduct the statute is declared invalid. A contrary rule would be inconsistent with the sound policy that the community is to be encouraged to act in compliance with legislation. Thus, just as it is no defense that the defendant mistakenly believed the statute under which he was prosecuted to be unconstitutional, it is a defense that he reasonably relied upon a statute permitting his conduct though it turned out to be an unconstitutional enactment.

For essentially the same reason, the better view is that it is a defense that the defendant acted in reasonable reliance upon a judicial decision, opinion or judgment later determined to be invalid or erroneous. The clearest case is that in which the defendant's reliance was upon a decision of the highest court of the jurisdiction, later overruled, whether the first decision involved the constitutionality of a statute, the interpretation of a statute, or the meaning of the common law. A contrary rule, whereby the subsequent holding would apply retroactively to the defendant's detriment, would be as unfair as ex post facto legislation.

Under the majority view, reasonable reliance upon a decision of a lower court is likewise a defense. Thus, if the lower court has found a repealer statute constitutional, has declared the relevant criminal statute unconstitutional, or has enjoined enforcement of the statute, there may be a basis for reasonable reliance. However, in the case of lower court decisions there is more likely to arise a question of whether the reliance is reasonable. It has been suggested, for example, that reliance should not be a defense when it was known that the decision of the lower court was on appeal.

We note also that the Model Penal Code provides for mistake of law as an affirmative defense. [See Section 2.04(3), reprinted at page 394.]

* * *

We note that the revised [Alaska] criminal code, which appears to attempt to codify defenses to criminal acts, does not provide for a defense of mistake of law. AS 11.81.620(a) provides:

> (a) Knowledge, recklessness, or criminal negligence as to whether conduct constitutes an offense, or knowledge, recklessness, or criminal negligence as to the existence, meaning, or application of the provision of law defining an offense, is not an element of an offense unless the provision of law clearly so provides. Use of the phrase "intent to commit a crime", "intent to promote or facilitate the commission of a crime", or like terminology in a provision of law does not require that the defendant act with a culpable mental state as to the criminality of the conduct that is the object of the defendant's intent.

The commentary to the code indicates that this section is intended to codify "the universal principal that ordinarily ignorance of the law is not a defense." In tracing AS 11.81.620(a) * * * we discover [it] * * * is derived from * * * from New York Penal Law § 15.20(l). New York Penal Law § 15.20 provides for a defense of reasonable mistake of law. Therefore, it appears probable that the drafters of the revised criminal code were aware of the New York provision and did not include it in the revised criminal code. This could mean that the legislature did not intend to allow a mistake of law defense in the revised code. It could also mean that the legislature overlooked the provision or wanted to leave the defense of mistake of law for later court determination. Since the commentary is silent, it is difficult for us to ascertain the legislative intent.

Furthermore, even if we were to conclude that the legislature rejected a defense of reasonable mistake of law in the revised code, that would not mean that the legislature intended that rejection to apply to fish and game offenses. AS 11.81.620(a) only applies to those offenses set forth in Title 11 [, the criminal code].

The state concedes that "most courts and commentators recognize that a person should be able to rely upon a judicial decision, even if that decision is later overruled." However, the state argues that we should hold that the defense of reasonable reliance on a court decision should be limited to decisions by the state appellate courts or the United States Supreme Court.

In the absence of any statutory or case law establishing or rejecting such a defense, we conclude that a concern for due process of law requires us to establish at least a limited defense. Fish and game laws regulate legitimate activity. Violations of those regulations are malum prohibitum, not malum in se. As the court stated in *Kratz v. Kratz*, 477 F.Supp. 463, 481 (E.D.Pa.1979):

> It would be an act of "intolerable injustice" to hold criminally liable a person who had engaged in certain conduct in reasonable reliance upon a judicial opinion instructing that such conduct is legal. Indeed, the reliance defense is required by the constitutional guarantee of due process as illuminated by the Supreme Court in *Marks v. United States*, 430 U.S. 188, 97 S.Ct. 990, 51 L.Ed.2d 260 (1977), *Cox v. Louisiana*, 379 U.S. 559, 85 S.Ct. 476, 13 L.Ed.2d 487 (1965) and *Raley v. Ohio*, 360 U.S. 423, 79 S.Ct. 1257, 3 L.Ed.2d 1344 (1959). [Footnotes omitted.]

However, we believe that the defense of reasonable mistake of law must be a limited defense in light of the fact that the general rule of law is that mistake of law is not a defense. The policy behind this rule is to encourage people to learn and know the law; a contrary rule would reward intentional ignorance of the law. The traditional rule of law that mistake of law is not a defense is based upon the fear "that its absence would encourage and reward public ignorance of the law to the detriment of our organized legal system, and would encourage universal pleas of ignorance of the law that would constantly pose confusing and, to a great extent, insolvable issues of fact to juries and judges, thereby bogging down our adjudicative system." *United States v. Barker*, 546 F.2d 940, 954 (D.C.Cir.1976) (Merhige, District J., concurring).

* * *

An earl[y] version of [Model Penal Code § 2.04(4) provided]:

> The reasonableness of the belief claimed to constitute the defense [permitted by Subsection (3)] shall be determined as a question of law by the Court.

§ 2.04(4) (Tentative Draft No. 4, 1955). We believe that the 1955 Tentative Draft provision sets forth a reasonable procedure for a trial court to follow in deciding whether a defense of mistake of law has been established.

We hold that a defense of mistake of law is an affirmative defense which the defendant must prove to the court by a preponderance of the evidence. We believe that this procedure will allow a defendant in a criminal case to obtain relief in cases where it would be unfair to hold him to knowledge of the law. Making the defense an affirmative defense argued to the court should protect against abuses of the defense and should ultimately make the law in this area more uniform as judges make decisions concerning what is a reasonable mistake of law. The determination of whether the defense applies requires a legal, technical application of due process considerations, a task within the judicial function. This determination will often depend on an understanding of the legal precedential value of decisions of courts at various levels, and of the appeals process. There is great potential for confusion and distraction if the jury were required, for instance, to determine whether it was reasonable to rely on a superior court decision reversing a district court decision (but in accord with the decisions of another district judge) which is being appealed to the supreme court.

The state would have us rule as a matter of law that it was unreasonable for Ostrosky to rely on Judge Carlson's decision that the Limited Entry Act was unconstitutional. The state argues that since the decision was a trial court decision it was not binding on other courts and, since the decision was on appeal, Ostrosky should have been aware that the decision could be reversed. There is support in the cases and commentary on this issue which suggests that normally it might be unreasonable to rely on a decision of a trial court which is on appeal. However, the question of whether a person's reliance on a lower court decision is reasonable or not is in the first instance a question for the trial court. We are not prepared to rule, as a matter of law, that in every case it would be unreasonable to rely on a lower court decision which is on appeal.

We note that in this case Ostrosky does not just represent that he relied on the ruling of the superior court. The

court ruling involved was a case in which Ostrosky was a party. He also claims that his attorney assured him that the decision meant that he could fish.[8] When Ostrosky started fishing, Trooper Folger did not cite him or warn him not to fish. Furthermore, the papers filed with the courts by the Department of Law in July of 1983, taken on their face, indicate that the Department of Law was operating under the assumption that it needed to stay Judge Carlson's decision in order to enforce the Limited Entry Act. If we look at these factors alone, in the light most favorable to Ostrosky, it appears that he has a sufficient claim of reasonable mistake of law to at least allow him to have a hearing on this issue. We therefore remand the case to allow Ostrosky to develop his defense of reasonable mistake of law at a hearing.

---

[8] The drafters of the Model Penal Code did not provide for a mistake of law defense based solely upon the advice of an attorney, and we are not today recognizing such a defense. We hold only that when a defendant is seeking to establish the defense of reasonable reliance on a judicial decision, the fact that he consulted an attorney and was told that the decision meant he could embark on a contemplated course of conduct is probative evidence of the reasonableness of the reliance.

Ostrosky v. State

Court of Appeals of Alaska, 1986
725 P.2d 1087.

COATS, Judge.

In *Ostrosky v. State*, 704 P.2d 786 (Alaska App.1985), * * * we remanded the case to allow Ostrosky an opportunity to further develop his defense. After a hearing on remand, Superior Court Judge Victor D. Carlson concluded that Ostrosky had not established the defense by a preponderance of the evidence and reimposed Ostrosky's original sentence. Ostrosky appeals * * * Judge Carlson's rejection of the defense. * * *

At the hearing on remand, Ostrosky called Frederick Paul, the attorney who represented him in his challenges to the Limited Entry permit system. Paul testified that he first met Ostrosky in 1978, when Ostrosky was charged with twelve counts of fishing without a permit. * * *

Through the course of the * * * proceedings, Paul and Ostrosky frequently discussed their commonly-held belief that the Act was unconstitutional. When the state appealed in Ostrosky's case, Paul filed a brief in response to the state's

appeal, believing Ostrosky would prevail on appeal. Paul and Ostrosky talked regularly about the appeal. When asked if he told Ostrosky he could go fishing during this period, Paul answered

> No, I did not. I should explain that I don't think it's a function of a lawyer to make that kind of a decision for a client. I think that's the client's decision. I told him all the factors involved . . . [T]here's certain areas of law that I don't think . . . a lawyer has any business telling a client to do or not do something. I could tell him the consequences, and that's what I did.

Paul further testified that he knew the state had never applied for a stay of Judge Carlson's decision while the appeal was pending, and this was one of the "factors" he discussed with Ostrosky.

On cross-examination, Paul explained that he told Ostrosky his fishing was not a crime under Judge Carlson's ruling, assuming there was no reversal on appeal. Ostrosky understood that there was a risk of reversal. Paul also told Ostrosky that "while technically, he was—he could be found guilty, . . . there would be some amelioration." Paul also testified that there were no other cases that he knew of challenging the constitutionality of the entire Limited Entry Act.

Ostrosky also testified at the hearing on remand. He stated that he had been fishing commercially for thirty-seven years. When Judge Carlson set aside Ostrosky's 1979 conviction by written order declaring the Limited Entry Act unconstitutional, Ostrosky read the decision and agreed with it.

Ostrosky testified that he also relied on an article in the February 1982 issue of Fisherman's Journal. The article was titled "Kenai Magistrate Bases Decision on Ostrosky Case," and it explained that Magistrate Jess Nicholas had dismissed a fishing prosecution based upon Judge Carlson's decision in the Ostrosky case. Ostrosky stated also that he was aware the state had appealed Judge Carlson's decision, that he read the brief submitted by Paul in the appeal, and that he discussed the brief with Paul. Finally, Ostrosky testified that he knew that on July 8, 1983, the supreme court issued a stay of Judge Carlson's decision, at the state's request and testified that he did not fish after July 8.

On cross-examination, Ostrosky admitted that the article in the Fisherman's Journal also noted that the state planned to appeal Magistrate Nicholas' decision. When Ostrosky told Paul that he was going to fish in the 1983 season, Paul told him he ran the risk of being cited and prosecuted. Paul also told Ostrosky there was a "slight chance" that Judge Carlson's decision would be reversed by the supreme court. According to Ostrosky's testimony, Ostrosky understood that if Judge Carlson's decision were reversed he would stand convicted of the 1979 offense. Paul never told Ostrosky that he would be immune from prosecution. Ostrosky knew that, if the Alaska Supreme Court found the limited entry system constitutional and the United States Supreme Court refused to hear the case, he would "have to bear the consequences." Ostrosky was also aware that, just prior to July 3, 1983, a friend named George Gottschalk, was cited for fishing without a permit. Ostrosky wasn't aware of anyone else being cited. Ostrosky testified that it was his belief that Judge Carlson's decision gave Gottschalk and others without permits the right to fish. In 1983, Ostrosky had not been stopped or cited prior to the July 3 incident. Although he fished in 1982, he was never stopped or cited in that year. When he sold fish to processors, Ostrosky either got cash or, if the processors refused to pay without seeing a valid permit, told the processors to defer payment until after the supreme court decision came down.

At the close of the evidence, Ostrosky argued that he had acted reasonably. The state argued that Ostrosky had failed to meet his burden of establishing by a preponderance of the evidence that his reliance on the 1981 order was reasonable.

Judge Carlson * * * [stated]:

> An objective standard is what is to be applied. I find that on the face of the record, that no reasonable person could reasonably rely upon the trial court's decision in this case. It was on appeal, that fact was generally known, there was no legal advice that the defendant could fish with impunity. I find that there's no reasonable mistake of law, the defendant knew what the law was and he was not advised by his lawyer that he could fish, he was only advised of the consequence of his actions. Specifically, he was not told that he could fish with impunity. I find he's failed to prove by a preponderance of the evidence that he made a reasonable mistake of law. In fact, the defendant was a civil disobedient, and he took the risk and knew he was taking the risk and accepting the responsibility for what he was doing. I find it's unreasonable to rely upon a ruling of the trial court in general, and specifically in this case, the decision was on appeal, and he knew this. He was testing the law, as shown by the record in this case and his related cases. The defendant is aware of legal proceedings, as shown by his letters to the editor, and other public statements which he has made, of which judicial notice can be taken because they're of common knowledge in the community, and his arguments and testimony in this case and the other fishing cases in which he's been involved. Therefore, the—I find that there is no reasonable mistake of law.

We agree with Judge Carlson that Ostrosky failed to establish by a preponderance of the evidence the defense of reasonable mistake of law. In our decision remanding this case, we refused to rule that, as a matter of law, it is unreasonable to rely on a lower court decision that is on appeal. We noted, however, that there is support in the cases and commentary on this issue that suggests that normally such reliance might be unreasonable. The logic behind this position can be seen from Ostrosky's own case: Ostrosky understood there was a risk of reversal and that reversal would render his conduct on July 3, 1983, unlawful. Where there is a known risk that the conduct will ultimately be held unlawful, the policies behind the defense itself begin to dissipate. The defense is designed to recognize good faith reliance, not to encourage gambling, on the outcome of criminal appeals. See, e.g., 2 P. Robinson, *Criminal Law Defenses* § 183, at 387 (1984) ("The excusing condition for the defense requires that the actor not know his conduct is criminal and, indeed, honestly believe *that there is no risk of criminality*") (emphasis added). Our intent was merely to place the decision in the trial judge's hands.

We noted also in our prior decision that "[i]f other courts, particularly the superior courts, had held the Limited Entry Act constitutional, this would tend to undermine Ostrosky's defense of reasonable reliance, particularly if he was aware of those decisions." In fact, the superior court apparently rejected identical constitutional challenges made by Ostrosky in both his 1978 and 1979 cases. It was only in the third decision by a superior court that the challenge proved successful. This circumstance further undermined Ostrosky's defense.

Finally, we noted in our previous decision that "when a defendant is seeking to establish the defense of reasonable reliance on a judicial decision, the fact that he consulted an attorney and was told that the decision meant he could embark on a contemplated course of conduct is probative of evidence of the reasonableness of the reliance." As Judge Carlson correctly noted, rather than assuring Ostrosky that he could embark on the contemplated course of conduct, Paul specifically warned Ostrosky of the risk of reversal of Judge Carlson's 1981 order and the consequences of that reversal. Judge Carlson was not mistaken in concluding that Ostrosky was unreasonable in disregarding this risk.

Ostrosky argues in his reply brief that, because he had a favorable trial court ruling in his case, the defense of reasonable reliance was established as a matter of law. This argument appears to center on the fact that, even though the state had appealed, the state had not requested a stay of Judge Carlson's decision. However, Judge Carlson's 1981 order was simply to vacate Ostrosky's 1979 conviction. The "stay" ultimately requested by the state and issued by the supreme court had no legal effect on the ability of the state to prosecute those who fished in closed waters, despite the affidavit offered in support of the stay indicating that in fact a stay was needed. As Judge Carlson properly concluded at Ostrosky's 1983 trial, it was essentially irrelevant that a stay had not been requested as of July 3, 1983. While a mistaken belief that a stay was needed would be relevant to this defense, Ostrosky does not contend that this belief was communicated to him by anyone other than perhaps Paul. Moreover, it appears from other testimony that both Ostrosky and Paul understood that, regardless of the fact that no stay had been requested, if Judge Carlson's order were reversed, any fishing in 1983 would be chargeable.

* * *

The conviction is AFFIRMED. * * *

Notes and Questions

1. Ostrosky sought federal habeas corpus relief on the ground that his Alaska conviction violated his federal constitutional right to due process. The United States District Court granted relief but this was reversed on appeal. *Ostrosky v. Alaska*, 913 F.2d 590 (9th Cir.1990). The federal appellate court construed his argument as that Alaska law denied him notice that the State would be permitted to enforce against him a statute held unconstitutional in his own prior judicial proceedings. Rejecting this, the court reasoned that under Alaska law a decision by a superior court judge does not bind other superior court judges and that Ostroky had actual knowledge of this. Alaska has authority to define the defense of mistake of law as it wishes, and federal due process entitled Ostrosky to nothing more than he received in the Alaska proceedings.

Ostrosky also claimed in his federal action that he had a right to have his claim of mistake of law decided by a jury. The Court of Appeals did not reach the merits of this contention, but rather held that Ostrosky waived any such right as he might have had by failing to pursue a jury trial in the original prosecution.

2. The majority in *Ostrosky* gave very limited significance to the defendant's claim that his attorney had assured him that his contemplated action would not be criminal. It has been stated that the cases "uniformly hold" that such advice from a private counsel does not constitute a defense. W. LaFave and A. Scott, Criminal Law 419-20 (2d ed. 1986). Would a rule permitting defendants to rely on advice of a lawyer encourage ignorance of the law or would it encourage desirable—and often or sometimes successful—efforts to ascertain it? Would it create a substantial danger of collusion between defendants and attorneys pursuant to which attorneys would falsely testify that they had been consulted and had advised that the contemplated conduct was not criminal?

3. The due process considerations that influenced the *Ostrosky* court were apparently those also raised in *Bsharah v. United States*, 646 A.2d 993 (D.C.Ct.App. 1994). Defendants Bsharah and White were found to have illegally carried pistols on the Washington D.C. Metro. They testified in defense that when they had boarded the train for Washington at Arlingon, Virginia, the station manager advised them—incorrectly—that because they were licensed under federal law as dealers in firearms, it was lawful for them to take those guns into the District of Columbia. Finding no error in the trial judge's holding that this testimony raised no issue as to mistake of law requiring submission to the jury, the court explained:

The defense advanced by White and Bsharah appears to have originated in two Supreme Court cases. In *Raley v. Ohio*, 360 U.S. 423, 79 S.Ct. 1257, 3 L.Ed.2d 1344 (1959), the defendants were convicted of contempt for refusing to answer certain questions put to them by a state investigating commission, even though they had relied on prior assurances by the chairman of the same commission that they were entitled to assert their Fifth Amendment privilege against self-incrimination. Unknown to the chairman, his advice was contrary to state law. Nevertheless, the Supreme Court reversed the convictions because of the chairman's erroneous assurance to the defendants that they could lawfully refuse to answer. The key to the Court's decision was the fact that the chairman "clearly appeared to be the agent of the State in a position to give such assurance." A few years later, in *Cox v. Louisiana*, 379 U.S. 559, 85 S.Ct. 476, 13 L.Ed.2d 487 (1965), the Court reversed the convictions of a group of picketers who had been demonstrating across the street from a courthouse, contrary to state law, because the local chief of police had given them permission to picket at that location. Again the Court based its decision on the fact that the defendants had been misled by "the highest police officers in the city."

The instant case is different because the Metro station manager had no authority, real or apparent, to give these appellants any advice whatever about the District of Columbia firearms laws. He could, perhaps, advise them about transit regulations and subway schedules, but on the subject of firearms he could speak with no more authority than any ordinary citizen. In the words of the Supreme Court, he was not an "agent of the State in a position to give [any] assurance" about the legality of carrying guns in the District of Columbia. *Raley v. Ohio*, supra, 360 U.S. at 437, 79 S.Ct. at 1266. His lack of authority was fatal to appellants' defense * * *.

4. In *People v. Marrero*, 69 N.Y.2d 382, 507 N.E.2d 1068, 515 N.Y.S.2d 212 (1987), the defendant was charged with possession of a handgun. In defense, he proved that he was a federal corrections officer and believed that he came within an exception to the New York statutory prohibition against carrying handguns without permits. He testified that he relied upon his reading of the New York statute as well as interpretations by fellow officers and teachers. New York has enacted a mistake statute, N.Y. Penal Law § 15.20, similar to section 2.04 of the Model Penal Code. The New York legislature did not, however, include the requirement from section 2.04(3)(b) that the official statement of the law relied upon be "afterwards determined to be invalid or erroneous." Consequently, section 15.20 provided that a defendant has a defense if he engages in conduct "under a mistaken belief that it does not * * * constitute an offense, [where] such mistaken belief is founded upon an official interpretation of the law contained in (a) a statute or other enactment * * *." He contended that his belief that carrying a handgun was not a crime was based on an official statement of the law contained in the statute itself and that the jury should therefore be instructed that his reading of the statute could give rise to the defense. Holding that Marrero had not raised a jury question under section 15.20, the New York Court of Appeals read its statute as if the legislature had explicitly included the phrase, "afterward determined to be invalid or erroneous." As so read, the statute permitted a defense only upon a statute that in fact authorized the defendant's conduct but was later "invalidated." Because the handgun law never *in fact* authorized Marrero to carry a handgun, his reliance upon his interpretation of it could not give rise to a defense under section 15.20.

The *Marrero* court's willingness to take considerable liberty with the statutory language was clearly based upon its perception that the mistake of law defense should be quite narrow and that the legislature must have agreed. It explained:

> We recognize that some legal scholars urge that the mistake of law defense should be available more broadly where a defendant misinterprets a potentially ambiguous statute not previously clarified by judicial decision and reasonably believes in good faith that the acts were legal. Professor Perkins, a leading supporter of this view, has said: "[i]f the meaning of a statute is not clear, and has not been judicially determined, one who has acted 'in good faith' should not be held guilty of crime if his conduct would have been proper had the statute meant what he 'reasonably believed' it to mean, even if the court should decide later that the proper construction is otherwise." (Perkins, Ignorance and Mistake in Criminal Law, 88 U.Pa.L.Rev. 35, 45.) * * *

We conclude that the better and correctly

construed view is that the defense should not be recognized, except where * * * the misrelied-upon law has later been properly adjudicated as wrong. Any broader view fosters lawlessness. * * *

Strong public policy reasons underlie the legislative mandate and intent which we perceive in rejecting defendant's construction of New York's mistake of law defense statute. If defendant's argument were accepted, the exception would swallow the rule. Mistakes about the law would be encouraged, rather than respect for and adherence to law. There would be an infinite number of mistake of law defenses which could be devised from a good-faith, perhaps reasonable but mistaken, interpretation of criminal statutes, many of which are concededly complex. Even more troublesome are the opportunities for wrongminded individuals to contrive in bad faith solely to get an exculpatory notion before the jury. These are not in terrorem arguments disrespectful of appropriate adjudicative procedures; rather, they are the realistic and practical consequences were the dissenters' views to prevail. Our holding comports with a statutory scheme which was not designed to allow false and diversionary stratagems to be provided for many more cases than the statutes contemplated. This would not serve the ends of justice but rather would serve game playing and evasion from properly imposed criminal responsibility.

5. What reliance on what sources at least raises a jury issue regarding a defendant's claim that he mistakenly believed his actions were not criminal? In *Commonwealth v. Twitchell*, 416 Mass. 114, 617 N.E.2d 609 (1993), the defendants were charged with manslaughter on the basis of their failure, grounded in religious beliefs, to provide medical treatment for their child. The Massachusetts Attorney General had issued an opinion that the court concluded could be read as stating that state constitutional considerations barred any criminal prosecution on the basis of religiously motivated failure to provide medical care for a child. Although the Twitchells had been unaware of the opinion, they were aware of a Christian Science publication that quoted the opinion, although without attribution. Reversing the convictions, the Massachusetts court concluded that under the United States Supreme Court case law discussed in note 3 and a sound version of mistake of law doctrine, the Twitchells were entitled to a jury determination of whether they reasonably relied on an official misinterpretation of the law.

Chapter 14

DEFENSE OF SELF AND RELATED MATTERS

CHAPTER CONTENTS

Among the most commonly invoked defenses are those based upon claims that what would ordinarily be criminal conduct was engaged in for the purpose of protecting the actor himself, other persons, or property. As a practical matter, these defenses are generally limited to situations in which the defendant is charged with an assaultive crime, such as battery, assault, or one of the homicide offenses.

A. SELF-DEFENSE

Editors' Introduction: The Defense of Self-Defense and the Deadly/Nondeadly Force Distinctions

There is universal agreement that force used by persons to defend themselves is, sometimes at least, insufficient to give rise to criminal liability. As the court in *United States v. Peterson*, 483 F.2d 1222 (D.C. Cir.1973), summarized:

> Self-defense * * * is as viable now as it was in Blackstone's time * * *. But * * * the right of self-defense arises only when necessity begins, and equally ends with the necessity * * *

Most of the issues in self-defense law concern the proper limits upon the defense in order to reasonably assure that it is available only when sufficient necessity existed.

As a general rule, whether an assault or homicide defendant has a meritorious defense of self-defense hinges on what the defendant believed at the time of the conduct constituting the charged crime rather than on reality. Whether the defendant actually had to kill to prevent harm to herself, in other words, does not control. Rather, the law focuses upon whether the defendant *believed* she had to kill to prevent such harm.

In addition, however, the law imposes a requirement that the defendant's belief have been objectively reasonable. A defense is denied, then, to a defendant who actually—and thus "honestly"—but unreasonably believed she had to kill to save her own life. Given the criminal law's general and heavy emphasis upon the accused's actual and subjective mental state, considered in detail in Chapter 4, why is it acceptable with regard to self-defense and related matters to require accuseds to live up to what society expects of a reasonable person? There are several possible answers.

First, defenses are less directly or importantly related to moral blameworthiness than are the elements of crimes. Consequently, reliance upon a purely subjective approach regarding defenses is less important to limiting criminal liability to the truly blameworthy.

Second, a subjective standard may be more effective here than elsewhere in changing people's behavior. There may be something about defensive matters that makes people more receptive to being influenced by the threat of criminal liability. For example, the modern tendency to limit manslaughter to reckless killings is in part based on the assumption that persons who do not subjectively realize that their conduct poses a risk of death to others are not likely enough to respond to the threat of criminal liability for causing death. However, perhaps persons who contemplate attacking another because they subjectively believe they must act in self-defense are more responsive to the law's message: that they had best carefully consider their situation because if their belief is objectively unreasonable, they may well incur criminal liability.

Third, perhaps defenses like self-defense raise matters sufficiently subject to false claims that an objective requirement provides a necessary safeguard against unjustified claims of the defenses. Defendants may be so free to claim self-defense based on their own self-serving testimony at trial, for example, that an unqualified defense could be improperly invoked by any assault or homicide defendant willing to commit perjury at trial. Requiring that a defendant's perception of the need for self-defense have been one a reasonable person would have developed in the situation may provide a safeguard against this special risk of abuse of defenses.

The actual answer may be a combination of these factors. The special risk of abuse and particular reason to believe people may respond to an objective reasonableness requirement may be worth the cost, given that the attenuated relationship between defenses and moral blameworthiness makes that cost relatively low.

Whatever the explanation, the law's insistence upon objective reasonableness in regard to the defenses covered in this chapter is well established and universally accepted.

The two subsections in Section A present somewhat specialized problems in applying self-defense law. Several more general aspects of self-defense law, however, can usefully be considered as a preliminary matter.

Special efforts have been made to limit the defense when the defendant used "deadly force." This situation, of course, arises most often in homicide cases when the force used by the defendant in fact caused the death of the victim. The first two matters to be covered apply to claims that deadly force was used in self-defense, and attention is then turned to defining deadly force for purposes of these rules. Next, the effect of being the aggressor in a conflict is considered. Finally, the "perfect" defense of self-defense is compared with the limited, or "imperfect," defense sometimes available in homicide prosecutions.

Prerequisites for Using Deadly Force in Self-Defense

The criminal law of self-defense is often stated as permitting deadly force in self-defense only by one who reasonably believes that he is being assaulted or threatened with *deadly* force. In *State v. Fullard*, 5 Conn.App. 338, 497 A.2d 1041 (1985), for example, Fullard had stabbed Heggs with a knife, killing him. In evaluating Fullard's claim of self-defense, the court commented, a critical question for the jury was whether Fullard "reasonably believed that Heggs was using or about to use deadly physical force, or was inflicting or about to inflict great bodily harm."

Although there is no hard-and-fast rule, this requirement that the accused have reasonably perceived an attack with deadly force may—as a practical matter—often mean that a defendant can convince a judge or jury that he used deadly force in proper self-defense only if he can show that his assailant was armed with a deadly weapon. In *Howard v. State*, 390 So.2d 1070 (Ala.Crim.App.) writ denied, 390 So.2d 1077 (Ala.1980), for example, the court approved the following jury instruction:

> [A]n assault with the hand or fist never justifies or excuses a homicide under ordinary circumstances, and it is for you to decide whether the facts in this case are within the ordinary reason or not.

Similarly, in *Biniores v. State*, 16 Ark.App. 275, 701 S.W.2d 385 (1985), the trial court rejected Biniores' claim of self-defense to the fatal shooting of Moss. Although there was testimony that Moss kept saying, "These hands can kill!," the court noted no evidence that Moss had a weapon or that Biniores thought he did and held that the trial court could easily have found that Biniores acted too hastily in shooting Moss.

If a victim is attacked with force not amounting to deadly force and nondeadly force would not be effective as a defensive measure, the victim must either submit to the injury or resort to deadly force at the risk of incurring criminal liability. R. Perkins and R. Boyce, Criminal Law 1118 (3d ed. 1982). Submission, of course, does not bar the victim from pursuing after-the-fact remedies against the assailant, including criminal prosecution. The purpose of this is to "maximize social gain by preserving the life of the aggressor," even if the innocent victim is required to bear the personal cost of injury. LaFond, The Case for Liberalizing the Use of Deadly Force in Self-Defense, 6 U.Puget Sound L.Rev. 237, 241 (1983).

LaFond argues that this state of the law greatly impedes the ability of female, aged, and young victims to establish before a judge or jury that they were, in fact, threatened with deadly force by an unarmed adult male assailant and therefore were entitled to use deadly force in self-defense. Moreover,

> Maximizing the preservation of human life by inexorably distributing a significant personal burden of physical harm and psychic scarring to many innocent victims chosen at random by violent aggressors may no longer accord with society's sense of social good. * * * [S]ociety today would not choose to preserve the lives of violent aggressors at the expense of physical and psychic harm to innocent victims.

LaFond proposes that one who honestly and reasonably believes that he is threatened by another with unlawful violence be permitted to use in self-defense any force, including deadly force, which he honestly and reasonably believes "is necessary to protect himself effectively."

Need to Retreat Before Using Deadly Force

What is the effect upon a criminal defendant's claim of self-defense if the prosecution's evidence shows that the defendant could have retreated rather than use force against the person harmed? The Connecticut Supreme Court summarized the law:

> It is generally agreed that one who can safely retreat is not required to do so before using nondeadly force in self-defense. A tension among competing interests exists, however, if deadly force is required, and raises the question of whether the defender has a duty to retreat. One early English authority wrote, regarding the common law on the duty of retreat, that "[t]he minuteness of the law contained in the authorities . . . is a curious relic of a time when police was lax and brawls frequent, and when every gentleman wore arms and was supposed to be familiar with the use of them." Sir James Fitzjames Stephen, Bart., A Digest of the Criminal Law (7th Ed.1926) pp. 202-203 n. 4.

Today, the majority of American jurisdictions holds that a person who is not the initial aggressor need not retreat, even though he can do so safely, before using deadly force upon an assailant whom he reasonably believes will kill him or do him serious bodily harm. This position rests on the rationale that a person who is not the initial aggressor should be permitted to stand his ground in the face of a deadly assault, and that to retreat may be considered to be cowardly and dishonorable. See J. Beale, "Retreat from a Murderous Assault," 16 Harv.L.Rev. 567, 577 (1903).

Anderson v. State, 227 Conn. 518, 529–30, 631 A.2d 1149, 1154–55 (1993).

Most American jurisdictions have rejected a specific requirement of retreat. The position rejecting the duty of retreat is often called the "true man" rule. This was explained in *State v. Rutland*, No. 90-A-1515 (Ohio App.1991) (not reported):

In the notorious case of *Erwin v. State* (1876), 29 Ohio St. 186, 199, the Ohio Supreme Court pondered:

"Does the law hold a man who is violently and feloniously assaulted responsible for having brought such necessity upon himself, on the sole ground that he failed to fly from his assailant when he might have safely done so? * * * [A] true man, who is without fault, is not obliged to fly from an assailant, who, by violence or surprise, maliciously seeks to take his life or do him enormous bodily harm."

The frontier mind of the 1800's believed that an assault was an attack on the "true man's" dignity as well as his physical well-being.

The "true man" rule is sometimes put quite vigorously. In *State v. Renner*, 912 S.W.2d 701 (Tenn.1995), for example, the Tennessee Supreme Court explained, "Under the 'true man' doctrine, one need not retreat from the threatened attack of another even though one may safely do so. Neither must one pause and consider whether a reasonable person might think it possible to safely flee rather than to attack and disable or kill the assailant." However, it is clear that a defendant's awareness of the availability of an opportunity to retreat may still be relevant to whether a right of self-defense existed. It may bear, for example, on whether the threatened harm was imminent enough to justify the force used and whether the defendant used more force than would reasonably be regarded as necessary under the circumstances. Moreover, at least some courts are attracted by the rationale of the "retreat" approach. In *Rutland*, the Ohio court observed that "as society progressed, the duty to retreat, with its attendant emphasis on the preservation of life (even at the expense of personal humiliation) called into question the continued viability of the "true man" doctrine."

Those jurisdictions applying the "retreat rule" require retreat only when retreat is possible in safety. In *Anderson*, for example, the Connecticut Supreme Court noted that its retreat rule requires retreat but only when the person knows that by retreating he can avoid the necessity of using deadly force "with complete safety." By requiring the prosecution to prove awareness of an opportunity to retreat in *complete* safety, the legislature was carefully and significantly limiting the requirement, and thus error occurs if the trial judge instructs the jury only that the prosecution must prove an opportunity to retreat in "safety."

Retreat jurisdictions generally do not require retreat when a person is attacked in that person's dwelling. This "castle doctrine" was explained in *United States v. Peterson*, 483 F.2d 1222, 1236 (D.C.Cir.1973), as based on notions of a special privacy interest in the dwelling and of the likelihood that further retreat would only further endanger the victim. A victim attacked in his dwelling, in other words, is already in the place to which he might otherwise be expected to retreat if attacked.

Assuming that one should have a duty to retreat before using deadly force and that this duty should not apply when one is attacked in one's dwelling, do the rationales for the general rule and the "castle" exception suggest that one attacked in one's dwelling by a "co-dweller" should have to retreat? Explaining its holding that retreat may be required in the face of an attack by a co-dweller, the District of Columbia Court of Appeals stated:

> [A]ll co-occupants, even those unrelated by blood or marriage, have a heightened obligation to treat each other with a degree of tolerance and respect. That obligation does not evaporate when one co-occupant disregards it and attacks another.

Cooper v. United States, 512 A.2d 1002, 1006 (D.C.Ct.App.1986). *State v. Laverty*, 495 A.2d 831, 833 (Me.1985), applied what the court characterized as the majority approach, and held that under the retreat rule one attacked in one's dwelling by a co-dweller need not retreat. This position may rest upon the attacked co-dweller's interest in remaining in the home. As the New York court remarked early in the century, requiring a dweller to retreat may impose upon him or her an especially difficult burden. "Whither shall he flee, and how far, and when may he be permitted to return?" *People v. Tomlins*, 213 N.Y. 240, 244, 107 N.E. 496, 498 (1914).

The "castle" tends to be narrowly defined in retreat jurisdictions. Thus, the dwelling in which one attacked need not retreat does not include the vestibule of the apartment building, *Commonwealth v. Correa*, 437 Pa.Super. 1, 10, 648 A.2d 1199, 1230 (1994), appeal denied, 540 Pa. 617, 657 A.2d 487 (1995), or the hallways of an apartment building, *Commonwealth v. Jefferson*, 36 Mass.App.Ct. 684, 686, 635 N.E.2d 2, 4 (1994), review denied, 418 Mass. 1106, 639 N.E.2d 1081 (1994).

Definition of Deadly Force

What constitutes the use of deadly force so as to trigger the special self-defense requirement applicable to that type of force? Section 3.11(2) of the Model Penal Code, reprinted at page 427, offers a definition. It then further provides that a threat to use deadly force if necessary is not itself the use of deadly force, even if the threat is made "by the production of a weapon."

Stewart v. State, 672 So.2d 865 (Fla.App.1996), raised the issue in the context of defensive display of a firearm. Stewart and the victim, each driving vehicles, passed close to each other in a parking lot. At a nearby stop sign, the two exchanged expressions of disapproval of the other's conduct and, the evidence showed, Stewart finally waved an unloaded, holstered pistol in the air for the victim to see and then drove off. Stewart testified that he exhibited the pistol only because the victim got out of his vehicle and approached Stewart's vehicle "yelling and swearing," causing Stewart to fear that the victim would attack him. During his trial for assault, Stewart first sought an instruction on the use of nondeadly force in self-defense. When that was unsuccessful, he requested an instruction on deadly force in self-defense. His second request was refused as well. Finding that the trial judge erred, the appellate court held that Stewart had raised an issue for the jury as to whether his conduct was proper self-defensive use of *nondeadly* force. Explaining that it was using the Model Penal Code for "guidance" in defining deadly and nondeadly force, the court continued:

> When the evidence does not establish that the force used by a defendant claiming the right to use force in the defense of unlawful force is deadly or nondeadly as a matter of law, the jury should be allowed to decide the question. See *Garramone* [v. *State*], 636 So.2d [869,] 871 [(Fla. 4th DCA 1994)] (jury, not judge, should decide if pushing or throwing a fully clothed individual over the railing of a six-teen foot bridge into the intracoastal waterway at night constituted deadly or non-deadly force * * *). See also *Cooper v. State*, 573 So.2d 74 (Fla. 4th DCA 1990) (question of whether the driving of a vehicle in a manner that it hits someone is deadly force should be submitted to jury). If, however, the type of force used is clearly deadly or nondeadly, only the applicable instruction should be given. See *Miller v. State*, 613 So.2d 530 (Fla. 3d DCA 1993) (the firing of a firearm into the air, even as a so-called warning shot, constitutes the use of deadly force as a mat-ter of law).
>
> [Stewart's] actions did not amount to the use of deadly force and he was enti-tled to an instruction concerning the use of nondeadly force. The appellant's con-duct in waving the firearm * * * amounts to a forcible felony [but] it does not in this case amount to the use of deadly force. Deadly force occurs when the natural, probable, and foreseeable consequences of the defendant's acts are death. If the appellant had fired the weapon, or was stopped as he attempted to, he would have been using deadly force even if the gun was not pointed at the victim. Discharge of a firearm has been held as a matter of law to constitute deadly force because a firearm is by definition a deadly weapon which fires projectiles likely to cause death or great bodily harm. The appellant's evidence indicates that he did not, however, fire the pistol but only waved it. When a weapon is fired it is likely to cause death or great bodily harm but that is not the case when a gun is waved. It is the nature of the force that must be evaluated and the mere display of a gun without more does not constitute deadly force.

The appellate court's determination that the force he used was nondeadly was to Stewart's advantage, because under Florida law a jury instruction regarding deadly force would have told the jury that Stewart was required to retreat before using defen-sive deadly force.

The Model Penal Code defines deadly force in terms of the actor's mental state; it would treat force used as deadly force only if the actor either had the purpose of causing death or serious bodily injury or knew that the force created a substantial risk of such a result. However, the Code also provides that purposefully firing a firearm "in the direction of another person" is deadly force, apparently even if the shooter intended only a warning and unqualifiedly believed his shot would not hit anyone. *Stewart's* recitation that firing a warning shot *into the air* is deadly force as a matter of law confirms that some—probably most—jurisdictions define deadly force more broadly than would the Model Penal Code.

Most jurisdictions would follow something closely akin to the standard applied in *Stewart*: "Deadly force occurs when the natural, probable, and foreseeable consequences of the defendant's acts are death." This is the approach taken in *Fersner v. United States*, reprinted in Section B of this chapter.

Stewart involved only the display—and not the pointing or apparent aiming—of a firearm. In an unreported case, an Ohio defendant argued that pointing a loaded rifle at another, in the absence of evidence that the pointer intended anything other than a threat to use the rifle if necessary, could not be deadly force. Consistent with *Stewart's* suggestion that the nature of such force is often a jury issue, the Ohio court concluded that the jury could have found that on the facts of the case the pointing of the rifle was the use of deadly force. *State v. Bunsie*, 1996 Westlaw 477173 (Ohio App.1996) (unreported), appeal not allowed, 77 Ohio St.3d 1516, 674 N.E.2d 370 (1997).

Effect of Being the Aggressor

Another traditional limitation on the defense of self-defense is the rule that one who provokes an altercation or is the aggressor in it is not entitled to use force in self-defense during the altercation. This rule is based on the proposition that killings in self-defense are permissible only where necessary. "Quite obviously, a defensive killing is unnecessary if the occasion for it could have been averted * * *." *United States v. Peterson*, 483 F.2d 1222, 1231 (D.C.Cir.1973).

What constitutes "aggression" or "provoking the difficulty" has given rise to some dispute. In *Howard v. United States*, 656 A.2d 1106 (D.C.Ct.App.1995), for example, Howard was prosecuted for several assaults on Womack and others that occurred at the home of Boone. In finding no error in the trial court's refusal to instruct the jury on self-defense, the court explained:

> After [a] confrontation at the Farmers' Market, Howard and Willis had returned to Howard's house, armed themselves with a considerable amount of firepower, and driven to Lonnie Boone's house. Thus, even if Kevin Womack had made the first move for a gun once Howard and Willis had arrived, armed, at Boone's house, the degree of initiative appellants had taken in creating the confrontation precluded a claim of self-defense. See *Brown* [v. *United States*], 619 A.2d [1180,] 1182 [D. C.1992)] (quoting *Rowe* [v. *United States*], 125 U.S.App.D.C. [218,] 219, 370 F.2d [240,] 241 [(1966)]) ("[a] defendant cannot successfully claim self-defense when 'he [or she] left an apparently safe haven to arm himself [or herself] and return to the scene.'") Indeed, as we stressed in *Nowlin* [v. *United States*, 382 A.2d 9 (D.C.1978)]:

appellant had no legitimate claim to the defense of self-defense, *since he had voluntarily placed himself in a position which he could reasonably expect would result in violence.* Self-defense "is not available to one who finds trouble by going out of his way to look for it." R. Perkins, Criminal Law 1008 (2d ed. 1969).

Some courts, however, have drawn a further distinction. Being the "aggressor" deprives one of the right to use self-defense. This must be distinguished, according to some courts, from seeking out another person for purposes of accomplishing a peaceful resolution of differences. This may be done even if the seeker fears a possible violent response, and the seeker may—without forfeiting the right to use force in self-defense—"arm himself" in order to protect himself from the violent response.

In *Brown v. State*, 698 P.2d 671 (Alaska App. 1985), for example, Brown and Miller argued; threats may have been made by Miller. Miller left for a bar. Brown sought Miller out in the bar, with the intent, according to Brown's testimony, to talk to Miller and convince Miller that there was no basis for Miller's hostile attitude. Specifically, Brown testified, he wanted to persuade Miller that Brown had not interfered in Miller's marriage. Brown took along a .22 rifle; he testified he knew Miller was armed and was "afraid of going just barehanded." During a confrontation in the bar, Brown shot and killed Miller. At Brown's trial for murder, the judge refused to instruct the jury on self-defense. This was found error on appeal because case law dealing with aggression in starting a fight was held inapplicable.

> Relying on *Bangs v. State*, 608 P.2d 1, 5 (Alaska 1980), the state claims that Brown became an initial aggressor and forfeited his right to claim self-defense when he armed himself and sought to confront Miller.
>
> In *Bangs*, a heated exchange took place between Bangs and his eventual victim, Troyer, during which Troyer grabbed Bangs and attempted to choke him. Bangs escaped, walked rapidly to his nearby trailer, grabbed a loaded revolver and returned to the scene of the struggle. Bangs testified that he pointed his gun at Troyer, cocked it, and challenged Troyer to "come on." When Troyer lunged at him, Bangs shot. The Alaska Supreme Court * * * held that * * * he was not entitled to a self-defense instruction, because he had been the initial aggressor.
>
> We do not believe the holding in *Bangs* to be dispositive in the present case. * * * In * * * *Bangs* undisputed evidence established that [Bangs] anticipating resistance, procured [a gun] for the sole purpose of armed confrontation with [his] intended [victim and] challenged [his victim] to physical combat with the apparent purpose of provoking a response. * * * By contrast, in this case there was evidence that Brown * * * did not confront Miller to seek combat or challenge Miller for the purpose of provoking a physical response.
>
> *Bangs* does not deprive a defendant of the right generally recognized at common law to "seek his adversary for the purpose of a peaceful solution as to their differences."
>
> * * *
>
> Viewing the evidence in the light most favorable to Brown, we believe that there is some evidence that Brown did not provoke a dispute with Miller under circumstances that he knew or should have known would result in

mortal combat. Brown was therefore entitled to have his self-defense claim—weak as it may have been—properly determined by the jury.

Some courts, however, appear to give no significance to this distinction between aggression and seeking out another for peaceful resolution of differences. For example, in *Howard v. United States*, discussed earlier in this introduction, the District of Columbia court of appeals gave no significance to defendant Howard's trial testimony that his objective in going to Boone's house was to "just call everything off and let everything be. I mean let it be, let's not have no problems." He took weapons "[b]ecause I know those guys and Derrick [Ross] had a gun, and I was not going around there without my protection."

An aggressor who withdraws can then use force in self-defense. Withdrawal can be accomplished by actually leaving the conflict or, at least sometimes, by expressing a clear desire to break off the conflict.

What constitutes withdrawal, however, is sometimes a problem. In *State v. Diggs*, 219 Conn. 295, 592 A.2d 494 (1991), for example, the court described the situation:

> The conflict between the defendant and the victim was ignited when the victim, after parking his car on Gregory Street, approached a group of youths, including the defendant, that had gathered around the front porch of 541 Gregory Street. At that time words were exchanged between the victim and the defendant. Thereafter, the defendant jumped from the porch and retrieved the .22 caliber rifle that the defendant knew had been placed under the porch earlier in the evening by a friend. The defendant then confronted the victim with the rifle. The victim's cousin, Rayford Scott, who had come to Gregory Street with the victim, crossed the street and attempted to defuse an argument that had clearly gotten out of hand. The victim and the defendant continued to argue and to threaten, however, and the victim threw a punch at the defendant. There is conflicting evidence as to whether the punch landed on the defendant. Nevertheless, after the punch was thrown, the defendant shot the victim. The single bullet pierced the victim's right side, striking his heart and lungs and causing massive internal bleeding and death.

Defendant Diggs sought to have the jury instructed that he may have regained his right of self-defense in either of two ways. First, he argued that he testified that at one point he walked across the small front lawn of 541 Gregory Street away from the house, and this—despite the fact that no words of withdrawal were said—constituted evidence of an actual withdrawal. Second, he relied upon evidence that he admonished Scott, the victim's cousin, to "tell your cousin to get out of my face" and "come and get your cousin" and warned the victim to "get back before I shoot." This, he contended, constituted an effective communication to the victims of his original aggression that he intended to withdraw from the encounter and this was as effective as an actual withdrawal. Holding that the defense evidence did not even raise an issue on withdrawal under either theory, the court explained:

> All of the defendant's communications of an alleged intent to withdraw from the conflict with the victim took place while the defendant kept the rifle in his hands and trained on the victim. "'As long as a person keeps his gun in his hand pre-

pared to shoot, the person opposing him is not expected or required to accept any act or statement as indicative of an intent to discontinue the assault.'" *State v. Huemphreus*, 270 N.W.2d 457, 462 (Iowa 1978), quoting 40 C.J.S., Homicide § 121; see *State v. Muhammad*, 757 S.W.2d 641, 643 (Mo.App.1988) ("Go on, go on leave me alone" insufficient to support withdrawal instruction). The defendant's communications were more in keeping with a demand that the victim withdraw in order to avoid being shot than an expression of the defendant's intent to break off and withdraw from the encounter himself.

"Imperfect" Defenses in Homicide Prosecutions

As a general rule, self-defense is a complete defense in the sense that if it is successful, the defendant is acquitted completely and has no criminal liability. In homicide cases, however, some jurisdictions recognize what are often called "imperfect" defenses generally related to claims of self-defense or defense of others or property. These defenses are called imperfect because they have the effect not of exculpating the accused of all criminal liability but rather of reducing the seriousness of the offense for which the accused can be convicted.

Under this approach, one who killed in the honest belief that the killing was necessary in self-defense but who exceeded the scope of the legal right of self-defense is generally regarded as guilty only of manslaughter. This applies to one who acted before force was reasonably necessary or who used more force than reasonably could have appeared necessary to prevent the threatened harm. See *Sanchez v. People*, 172 Colo. 168, 470 P.2d 857 (1970). W. LaFave and A. Scott, Criminal Law 665 n. 5 (2d ed. 1986) suggest that such killings are best regarded as voluntary manslaughter because they are intentional but mitigated killings. If manslaughter is appropriate because the defendant acted recklessly or negligently in assessing his right to do what he did, however, involuntary manslaughter would be a more appropriate category.

MODEL PENAL CODE*

Official Draft 1985

Section 3.04. Use of Force in Self-Protection

(1) *Use of Force Justifiable for Protection of the Person.* Subject to the provisions of this Section and of Section 3.09, the use of force upon or toward another person is justifiable when the actor believes that such force is immediately necessary for the purpose of protecting himself against the use of unlawful force by such other person on the present occasion.

---

(2) *Limitations on Justifying Necessity for Use of Force.*

    (a) The use of force is not justifiable under this Section:

        (i) to resist an arrest which the actor knows is being made by a peace officer, although the arrest is unlawful; or

        (ii) to resist force used by the occupier or possessor of property or by another person on his behalf, where the actor knows that the person using the force is doing so under a claim of right to protect the property, except that this limitation shall not apply if:

            (A) the actor is a public officer acting in the performance of his duties or a person lawfully assisting him therein or a person making or assisting in a lawful arrest; or

            (B) the actor has been unlawfully dispossessed of the property and is making a re-entry or recaption justified by Section 3.06; or

            (C) the actor believes that such force is necessary to protect himself against death or serious bodily harm.

    (b) The use of deadly force is not justifiable under this Section unless the actor believes that such force is necessary to protect himself against death, serious bodily harm, kidnapping or sexual intercourse compelled by force or threat; nor is it justifiable if:

        (i) the actor, with the purpose of causing death or serious bodily harm, provoked the use of force against himself in the same encounter; or

        (ii) the actor knows that he can avoid the necessity of using such force with complete safety by retreating or by surrendering possession of a thing to a person asserting a claim of right thereto or by complying with a demand that he abstain from any action which he has no duty to take, except that:

            (A) the actor is not obliged to retreat from his dwelling or place of work, unless he was the initial aggressor or is assailed in his place of work by another person whose place of work the actor knows it to be; and

            (B) a public officer justified in using force in the performance of his duties or a person justified in using force in his assistance or a person justified in using force in making an arrest or preventing an escape is not obliged to desist from efforts to perform such duty, effect such arrest or prevent such escape because of resistance or threatened resistance by or on behalf of the person against whom such action is directed.

    (c) Except as required by paragraphs (a) and (b) of this Subsection, a person employing protective force may estimate the necessity thereof under the circumstances as he believes them to be when the force is used, without retreating, surrendering possession, doing any other act which he has no legal duty to do or abstaining from any lawful action.

* * *

Section 3.09. Mistake of Law as to Unlawfulness of Force or Legality of Arrest; Reckless or Negligent Use of Otherwise Justifiable Force; Reckless or Negligent Injury or Risk of Injury to Innocent Persons

(1) The justification afforded by Sections 3.04 to 3.07, inclusive, is unavailable when

(a) the actor's belief in the unlawfulness of the force or conduct against which he employs protective force or his belief in the lawfulness of an arrest which he endeavors to effect by force is erroneous; and

(b) his error is due to ignorance or mistake as to the provisions of the Code, any other provision of the criminal law or the law governing the legality of an arrest or search.

(2) When the actor believes that the use of force upon or toward the person of another is necessary for any of the purposes for which such belief would establish a justification under Sections 3.03 to 3.08 but the actor is reckless or negligent in having such belief or in acquiring or failing to acquire any knowledge or belief which is material to the justifiability of his use of force, the justification afforded by those Sections is unavailable in a prosecution for an offense for which recklessness or negligence, as the case may be, suffices to establish culpability.

(3) When the actor is justified under Sections 3.03 to 3.08 in using force upon or toward the person of another but he recklessly or negligently injures or creates a risk of injury to innocent persons, the justification afforded by those Sections is unavailable in a prosecution for such recklessness or negligence towards innocent persons.

Section 3.11. Definitions

In this Article, unless a different meaning plainly is required:

(1) "unlawful force" means force, including confinement, which is employed without the consent of the person against whom it is directed and the employment of which constitutes an offense or actionable tort or would constitute such offense or tort except for a defense (such as the absence of intent, negligence, or mental capacity; duress; youth; or diplomatic status) not amounting to a privilege to use the force. Assent constitutes consent, within the meaning of this Section, whether or not it otherwise is legally effective, except assent to the infliction of death or serious bodily harm.

(2) "deadly force" means force which the actor uses with the purpose of causing or which he knows to create a substantial risk of causing death or serious

bodily harm. Purposely firing a firearm in the direction of another person or at a vehicle in which another person is believed to be constitutes deadly force. A threat to cause death or serious bodily harm, by the production of a weapon or otherwise, so long as the actor's purpose is limited to creating an apprehension that he will use deadly force if necessary, does not constitute deadly force.

(3) "dwelling" means any building or structure, though movable or temporary, or a portion thereof, which is for the time being the actor's home or place of lodging.

1. Defending Against an Unlawful Arrest

Self-defense poses special problems when it is based on a claim that force was used to prevent action the defendant knew was part of an effort to arrest the defendant. This is especially the case when the facts indicate the defendant knew that the person seeking to make the arrest was a police officer. As the following case makes clear, courts and legislatures have tended to limit the defense in this context although the issues presented generate conflicting and strong feelings.

State v. Valentine

Supreme Court of Washington, 1997
132 Wash.2d 1, 935 P.2d 1294.

ALEXANDER, Justice.

Ronald Valentine [was convicted] on a charge of third degree assault, a charge that was based on an allegation that Valentine assaulted a law enforcement officer while the officer was engaged in performance of his official duties. Valentine contends on appeal that the trial court erred in instructing the jury that "[t]he use of force to prevent an unlawful arrest which threatens only a loss of freedom . . . is not reasonable." * * *

In the early afternoon of May 16, 1990, in downtown Spokane, Spokane Police Officer Rick Robinson observed what he believed was a "suspicious subject on the corner at First and Jefferson." Upon making this observation, Robinson radioed another Spokane police officer, John Moore, and asked him if he knew the person standing at First and Jefferson "wearing a black coat." Moore proceeded to that location and observed a person wearing a black

jacket enter a car. Although Moore was unable to immediately identify that person, he followed the car as the person drove it away.

According to Moore, the car soon made a turn without signaling. Moore, who was driving an unmarked car, advised Robinson over his radio that he was going to stop the car. He then attempted to do so by placing a rotating blue light on his dashboard, flashing his headlights, and honking his horn. While attempting to stop the automobile, Moore recognized that the driver of the car he was following was Ronald Valentine. [Moore testified at trial that he was acquainted with Valentine because he had cited him on two prior occasions for front license plate violations.] Moore broadcast over his police radio that he was following Valentine and that Valentine was not heeding Moore's efforts to stop him. Shortly thereafter, Valentine stopped his automobile and Moore pulled his car in behind him.

Officer Robinson also pulled in behind Moore as did several other officers who had overheard the radio broadcasts.

All of the police officers who arrived at the scene testified at trial. Their version of the events that transpired after the traffic stop varied dramatically from Valentine's version of events. Moore said that upon confronting Valentine he asked to see his license and registration. This, he indicated, prompted Valentine to ask, "Why?" Moore said that he then told Valentine that he was being cited for failing to signal for a turn. According to Moore, Valentine said that since Moore had given him a ticket a few days earlier, he had all the information that he needed. Moore said that he again asked for the driver's license and registration and Valentine responded by saying that "you . . . cops are just harassing me. I'm Black, and I'm tired of the harassment." After what Moore said was his third request of Valentine to produce his driver's license and registration, Valentine produced it.

Moore testified that he asked Valentine for his current address and that Valentine told Moore to "[l]ook it up." Moore then asked Valentine if he was going to cooperate and sign a citation and, according to Moore, Valentine said that he would not do so. Moore then informed Valentine that he was being placed under "arrest for failure to cooperate . . . . [and] refusing to sign an infraction."

Moore also testified that after Valentine walked to the front of the car to show Moore that the car Valentine had been driving had a front license plate, Valentine returned to his car door, opened it, and started to reach inside the car. Moore said that he told Valentine to stay out of the car and grabbed Valentine's left arm to prevent him from reaching into the car. Robinson also claimed that he grabbed Valentine's right arm in a similar effort to keep Valentine from entering his car. Valentine, according to Moore, responded to their actions by spinning toward Moore and punching him in the side of the head. Robinson also claimed that he was hit in the ensuing skirmish.

Spokane Police Officers Jones, Webb, and Yates all testified that they joined the scuffle when Valentine began to struggle with Moore and Robinson. They said that they eventually subdued Valentine and forced him to the ground. Yates, who indicated that he had decided to assist Moore in effecting the traffic stop when he heard over the radio that it was Valentine who was being pursued,[3] testified that when he became involved in the fracas, he felt Valentine's hand on his gun butt. He said that in order to

subdue Valentine, he had to apply a "carotid hold"[4] to Valentine's neck.

Valentine was eventually placed in handcuffs and was transported to jail. A nurse supervisor at the jail refused to admit Valentine because of his apparent injuries. Valentine was then taken to a hospital where Moore presented him with a citation for failing to signal for a turn. Valentine signed the citation. Valentine was later booked into the Spokane County Jail where he was charged by information with two counts of third degree assault, it being alleged that he assaulted Moore and Robinson while they were performing "official duties."

Valentine testified at trial on his own behalf. He claimed that because his turn signals were not functioning, he used hand signals to indicate his intention to turn. He also said that he stopped his car as soon as it was possible for him to do so. Valentine indicated that before reaching inside his car, he told Moore he was going to lock his car in order to protect some personal items. He denied that he told Moore to look up his address for himself. He also said that he did not throw the first punch, asserting that any blows he delivered were in self-defense and amounted to reasonable force to protect himself from an illegal arrest. Valentine contended that he would have signed a citation on the scene if he had been presented with one. Valentine was found guilty of assaulting Moore and not guilty of assaulting Robinson.

I

Valentine asks us to decide whether the trial court erred in instructing the jury regarding the employment of force to resist an unlawful arrest. Instruction 17 reads as follows:

> A person unlawfully arrested by an officer may resist the arrest; the means used to resist an unlawful arrest must be reasonable and proportioned to the injury attempted upon the party sought to be arrested. *The use of force to prevent an unlawful arrest which threatens only a loss of freedom, if you so find, is not reasonable.*

(emphasis added).

Valentine claims that the instruction is faulty insofar as it informs the jury that a person may not use force to resist an unlawful arrest which threatens only a loss of freedom. He asserts that it is the law in this state that reasonable and proportional force may always be employed to resist an

---

[3] Yates had been involved in a verbal confrontation with Valentine in a tavern the day before the incident leading to this appeal. Yates testified that the tavern incident "probably could have been" discussed with other officers at roll call, about two hours before the incident.

[4] The carotid hold is a hold applied to the neck area. It is designed to inhibit the supply of blood to the brain, and when applied correctly, the victim of the hold will lose consciousness.

unlawful arrest. Valentine bases his argument to a large extent on this court's opinion in *State v. Rousseau*, 40 Wash.2d 92, 241 P.2d 447 (1952). * * * In our review of the law, beginning with *Rousseau*, we have discovered that cases from our court and from the Court of Appeals have created confusion as to whether one who is illegally arrested may resist the arrest when the arresting officer's acts threaten only a loss of liberty. * * *

In *Rousseau*, a 1952 case, we recited the common law rule prevalent in most jurisdictions at the time: "It is the law that a person illegally arrested by an officer may resist that arrest, even to the extent of the taking of life if his own life or any great bodily harm is threatened."

* * *

[Reviewing the law in the jurisdictions whose decisions were cited in *Rousseau*, the court concluded that in many of those jurisdictions the common law rule had been abandoned since *Rousseau*. Eds.] Thus, the theoretical footings on which we based our decision in *Rousseau* have eroded with the passage of time. It is therefore meet and fitting that we reconsider now the bases for our decision in *Rousseau*. * * *

1. *Historical Background of the Common Law Rule.* The English common law right forcibly to resist an illegal arrest was established almost three hundred years ago in *The Queen v. Tooley*, 92 Eng.Rep. 349, 351–52 (1909). * * * [T]he *Tooley* rule has come down to us as a rule permitting an arrestee to use the necessary force (but no more) to resist an unlawful arrest.

   To understand why an unlawful arrest was such a great provocation as to affect "all people out of compassion," it is necessary to look at the historical evidence of the state of English prisons in the eighteenth century.

2. *English Prisons.* Professor Sam Bass Warner of Harvard Law School was instrumental in the 1940's in setting forth the historical background leading to the abandonment of the *Tooley* rule in the majority of states. "The [*Tooley*] rule developed when long imprisonment, often without the opportunity of bail, 'goal [sic] fever,' physical torture, and other great dangers were to be apprehended from arrest, whether legal or illegal." Sam B. Warner, The Uniform Arrest Act, 28 VA.L.REV. 315, 330 (1942).

   * * * Others have also chronicled the deplorable conditions of English jails * * *. As one commentator put it, "Where imprisonment was often the equivalent of a death sentence, or at least, a living death, one can understand why men resisted unlawful arrest." One can also understand why, as the *Tooley* court said, an unlaw-

ful arrest was a great provocation affecting "all people out of compassion." The common law rule set out in *Tooley* plainly resulted from conditions that no longer exist.

3. *Modern Arrest and Incarceration.* In Washington today the law provides those arrested with numerous protections that did not exist when the common law rule arose. Reasonable bail is available. At any critical stage in a criminal prosecution a defendant has a right to appointed counsel under both the federal constitution's Sixth Amendment and our state constitution's article I, section 22 (amend. X). * * * [T]he Fourth Amendment requires a prompt judicial determination of probable cause as a prerequisite to an extended pretrial detention following a warrantless arrest. None of these rights was available in 1709. "[T]he right to resist developed when the procedural safeguards which exist today were unknown." *State v. Hatton*, 116 Ariz. 142, 568 P.2d 1040, 1045 (1977).

   Not only has criminal procedure advanced to protect the rights of the accused, jails themselves are no longer the pestilential death traps they were in eighteenth century England. * * *

   Thus, "[i]n this era of constantly expanding legal protection of the rights of the accused in criminal proceedings, an arrestee may be reasonably required to submit to a possibly unlawful arrest and to take recourse in the legal processes available to restore his liberty." *Commonwealth v. Moreira*, 388 Mass. 596, 447 N.E.2d 1224, 1227 (1983). "The concept of self-help is in decline. It is antisocial in an urbanized society. It is potentially dangerous to all involved. It is no longer necessary because of the legal remedies available." *State v. Koonce*, 89 N.J.Super. 169, 214 A.2d 428, 436 (1965). We agree.

4. *The Trend Away From the Common Law Rule.* In 1966, the right to resist an unlawful arrest was recognized in 45 out of 50 states. * * * By 1983, however, 25 of those 45 states had revoked the common law rule either by statute or decision, and today, only 20 states have it in place, while resisting even an unlawful arrest is prohibited by law in 30 states. "[T]his common law principle has suffered a devastating deluge of criticism." *State v. Thomas*, 262 N.W.2d 607, 610 (Iowa 1978) (rule is "an anachronistic and dangerous concept"). * * *

   Courts addressing the question have set out many cogent and compelling reasons for consigning the common law rule to the dustbin of history. For example:

* * *

While defendant's rights are no doubt violated when he is arrested and detained a matter of days or hours without probable cause, we conclude the state in removing the right to resist does not contribute to or effectuate this deprivation of liberty. In a day when police are armed with lethal and chemical weapons, and possess scientific communication and detection devices readily available for use, it has become highly unlikely that a suspect, using reasonable force, can escape from or effectively deter an arrest, whether lawful or unlawful. His accomplishment is generally limited to temporary evasion, merely rendering the officer's task more difficult or prolonged. Thus self-help as a practical remedy is anachronistic, whatever may have been its original justification or efficacy in an era when the common law doctrine permitting resistance evolved. . . . Indeed, self-help not infrequently causes far graver consequences for both the officer and the suspect than does the unlawful arrest itself. Accordingly, the state, in deleting the right to resist, has not actually altered or diminished the remedies available against the illegality of an arrest without probable cause; it has merely required a person to submit peacefully to the inevitable and to pursue his available remedies through the orderly judicial process.

People v. Curtis, 70 Cal.2d 347, 450 P.2d 33, 36–37, 74 Cal.Rptr. 713 (1969).

* * *

More important [than the existence of civil remedies], however, are the unwarranted dangers to civil order caused by this lingering artifact. Peace officers are today lethally armed and usually well trained to efficiently effect arrests. Resultantly, the resister's chances of success are seriously diminished unless he counters with equal or greater levels of force. The inevitable escalation of violence has serious consequences for both participants and innocent bystanders.

* * *

Thomas, 262 N.W.2d at 611. We agree with all of these sentiments. * * *

In the final analysis, the policy supporting abrogation of the common law rule is sound. That policy was well enunciated * * * in *State v. Westlund*, 13 Wash.App. 460, 467, 536 P.2d 20, 77 A.L.R.3d 270, review denied, 85 Wash.2d 1014 (1975), where the court said:

[T]he arrestee's right to freedom from arrest without excessive force that falls short of causing serious injury or death can be protected and vindicated through legal processes, whereas loss of life or serious physical injury cannot be repaired in the courtroom. However, in the

vast majority of cases * * * resistance and intervention make matters worse, not better. They create violence where none would have otherwise existed or encourage further violence, resulting in a situation of arrest by combat. Police today are sometimes required to use lethal weapons for self-protection. If there is resistance on behalf of the person lawfully arrested and others go to his aid, the situation can degenerate to the point that what should have been a simple lawful arrest leads to serious injury or death to the arrestee, the police or innocent bystanders. Orderly and safe law enforcement demands that an arrestee not resist a lawful arrest and a bystander not intervene on his behalf unless the arrestee is actually about to be seriously injured or killed.

We f[ind] these policy reasons "convincing" * * *.

[W]e hold that, although a person who is being unlawfully arrested has a right, as the trial court indicated in instruction 17, to use reasonable and proportional force to resist an attempt to inflict injury on him or her during the course of an arrest, that person may not use force against the arresting officers if he or she is faced only with a loss of freedom. We explicitly overrule *Rousseau* and other cases that are inconsistent with our holding in this case.

* * *

[I]f the rule were, as the dissent suggests it should be, that a person being unlawfully arrested may always resist such an arrest with force, we would be inviting anarchy. While we do not, as the dissent appears to suggest, condone the unlawful use of state force, we can take note of the fact that in the often heated confrontation between a police officer and an arrestee, the lawfulness of the arrest may be debatable. To endorse resistance by persons who are being arrested by an officer of the law, based simply on the arrested person's belief that the arrest is unlawful, is to encourage violence that could, and most likely would, result in harm to the arresting officer, the defendant, or both. In our opinion, the better place to address the question of the lawfulness of an arrest that does not pose harm to the arrested person is in court and not on the street.

* * *

Affirmed.

DURHAM, C.J., and DOLLIVER, GUY, JOHNSON[, SMITH] and TALMADGE, JJ., concur.

SANDERS, Justice, dissenting.

Ronald Valentine was brutally beaten during the course of an unlawful arrest for a minor traffic infraction. Now this court affirms the criminal conviction of the victim despite the common law rule which clearly provides Valentine a viable legal defense. Mr. Valentine would not give up his liberty without a fight. Neither should we.

This dissent is worth the fight because a great and fundamental principle is at stake. * * *

* * *

Claiming a new-found enlightenment not apparent to legal generations which preceded it, the majority * * * opines that the established common law rule has outlived its usefulness in our brave new world where resistance to unlawful infliction of state coercive power is not only futile, but also invites "anarchy." Apparently the majority believes the unlawful use of state force is not anarchy but order. Yet I suggest such circumstances are not new, nor is the seeming futility of individual resistance to the overwhelming, yet still unlawful, police power of the state. It is an age-old tale. Mr. Valentine does not need courts to tell him who is going to win a physical confrontation with the police. But he does need this court to recognize and protect his legal rights.

* * *

For the reasons which follow I would hold that Valentine's proposed instruction, not the court's, accurately states the law and that as a matter of great principle, as if prudence and legal necessity do not suffice, the rule of law which recognizes a citizen's right to use reasonable force to resist an unlawful arrest should not be lightly cast aside but held tightly to the breast within which beats liberty's very heart.

* * *

Historical Right to Resist Unlawful Arrest

The right to be free from unlawful arrest dates back to the Magna Carta and perhaps before. See Magna Carta, § 39 ("No free man shall be seized or imprisoned . . . except by the law of the land."). Unlawful arrest has always been considered a serious affront. The law has, from the start, deemed an unlawful arrest an assault and battery.

Because this is so, the common law recognized the victim's legal right to forcibly resist. * * * [T]he principle upon which the rule was founded that an individual may resist an unlawful arrest with reasonable force is rooted in political philosophy and is no way dependent upon a trivial factual inquiry into the conditions of one's local jail. * * * I also challenge the factual assumption that our age is any kinder or gentler than preceding ones when it comes to arrest and incarceration. One can scarcely find a better example of this than Valentine himself.

In America the tradition of resisting unlawful authority has been embraced from the early days of resisting imperial British power during the Revolution through the civil rights movement. It is fundamental.

* * *

The age-old rule which recognizes the right to resist unlawful assertions of state power is an important deterrent to tyranny. With the rule limited to cases where the police are exceeding and abusing their authority, the police officers involved in the excess should be deterred, knowing that their abuse may spark resistance.

* * *

It may be true, as the majority posits, [that] those who resist an unlawful arrest, like Valentine, will often be the worse for it physically; however, that is not to say that their resistance is unlawful. The police power of the state is not measured by how hard the officer can wield his baton but rather by the rule of law. Yet by fashioning the rule as it has, the majority legally privileges the aggressor while insulting the victim with a criminal conviction for justifiable resistance.

Unlawful Arrest in Practice

Modern judicial decisions have adopted procedures to deter unlawful search and seizure * * *.

Allowing police to arrest wrongfully and then prosecute the victim for righteous resistance is wrong for the same reason entrapment is wrong. It was only the injustice of the police misconduct that induced the outraged victim to resist.

* * *

At oral argument the city admitted its officers would repeat the same conduct "if this kind of factual circumstance ever arose again." There is no acknowledgment of wrongdoing, let alone remorse. And the majority provides no incentive for contrition.

Nevertheless, the majority suggests victims of illegal arrest should not be allowed to resist by physical force because their rights can be "vindicated through legal processes." But this claim misses the mark: the rights of the victim have already been violated by the illegal arrest. The remaining question is whether the victim who instinctively resists the injustice is to be doubly wronged by suffering the second indignity of a criminal conviction.

* * *

While criminal prosecution of those resisting arrest is common, prosecution of officers abusing their authority is rare. The police department itself does the preliminary investigation of possible abuse and usually the case will not go forward unless the department so recommends. A recent study reveals "of all alleged instances of police misconduct, prosecution occurred in only one quarter of 1% of the cases." Laurie L. Levenson, The Future of State and Federal Civil Rights Prosecutions: The Lessons of the Rodney King Trial, 41 UCLA L.Rev. 509, 535 (1994). Additionally, in the very few cases actually prosecuted, the fact that the police themselves conducted the initial investigation coupled with the "code of silence" often renders effective prosecution impossible.

* * *

Many other jurisdictions prefer the common law rule to mandatory abject submission to unlawful arrest. There is no indication these jurisdictions are plagued by "anarchy."

* * *

Conclusion

The majority's rule makes the unlawful arrest of Valentine irrelevant; however, that is the predicate fact which lawfully justifies reasonable resistance and is Valentine's recognized and legitimate defense to the assault charge. * * * Valentine was absolutely entitled to submit the question of the reasonableness of his response to a false arrest to a jury of his peers.

Apparently the majority thinks it is neither a major injury nor affront to be arrested unlawfully by agents of the government when "only liberty" is at stake. I disagree.

MADSEN, Justice, [concurs in the dissent].

Notes and Questions

The *Valentine* court treated the issue before it as if it was only that of the right to resist an unlawful arrest because of its illegal nature. Many courts, however, distinguish between resisting an unlawful arrest itself because of its unlawful nature and resisting the use of excessive force by an officer making an arrest or taking other action. In *Commonwealth v. French*, 531 Pa. 42, 611 A.2d 175 (1992), the Pennsylvania Supreme Court explained:

> [T]he remedy of a future lawsuit fails to address the exigent nature of a situation in which one's life and limb are in danger. * * * [W]hile an arrestee's liberty interest can be adequately protected through legal channels when there has been an unlawful arrest, one's bodily integrity is not adequately protected by those same means when an arresting officer uses excessive force. This distinction between resisting an arrest and resisting the use of excessive force by an arresting officer is sufficiently compelling for us to conclude that the use of excessive force by an arresting officer may trigger the right to use force in self protection * * * (or * * * in protection of others).

Justice McDermott, concurring, explained further:

> When * * * unnecessary force is used [in making an arrest] one may use such force as appears necessary to protect life or limb and not be guilty of the offense of resisting arrest.

There is a distinction, however, between resisting arrest initially and thereby raising the level of police force necessary to effect arrest, and protecting oneself from initial or subsequent illegal force; and one may raise the level of necessary police force, by continued resistance, to a level which would be illegal force were it used initially. In other words, one cannot find justification, if by their own acts, they exacerbate what they are required to do peacefully into a dangerous condition for themselves and others; hence, one is never authorized to resist a legal arrest or profit by their resistance.

Nevertheless, the policy reasons that persuaded many courts and legislatures to provide that force can never be used to resist an unlawful arrest itself have convinced some courts to limit the right to use force to resist excessive force by police officers. Thus, in *French* the Pennsylvania Supreme Court held that force can be used—that is, that the force is not itself criminal—only if it is used to resist force used by an officer that is both unlawful *and deadly*. In explanation, the court offered that "An arresting officer's use of excessive force capable of causing less than serious bodily injury or death can be vindicated by recourse to subsequent legal remedies."

Justice Zappala disagreed with the *French* majority and adopted the rationale of Judge Wieand, dissenting in the lower court. Judge Wieand argued that normal rules of self-defense should apply to force used to resist excessive force by an officer and these normal rules would permit the use of force to resist even nondeadly but excessive force by an officer. He explained:

> The application of normal principles of self-defense to situations where police use excessive force will not * * * "encourage unnecessary violence" or "invite . . . escalating retaliatory conduct." The statute defining the [self-defense] defense has included limitations which will prevent the use of force and violence by persons who are arrested by the police. Before a citizen is justified in using even slight force against a police officer, the citizen must have a reasonable belief that such force is immediately necessary to protect himself/herself or another against bodily injury inflicted as a result of excessive force used by the police. The degree of force permitted in self-defense, moreover, would be only that force reasonably necessary to protect against bodily injury. I am confident that the law of self-defense as defined by the legislature will be adequate to preserve the public peace and protect police officers against citizen violence in the performance of their duties. It will also serve to protect citizens against the use of excessive force by the police.

If in *Valentine* the courts had distinguished between the right to use force to resist excessive force and that to resist an unlawful arrest, would Valentine have been able to make a credible argument that his conduct was within his right to use force to resist excessive force? The *Valentine* dissenter summarized in more detail than the majority the substance of Valentine's version of the events which led to his actions:

> Valentine testified that as he was closing the window of his car to secure it he heard Moore say to Robinson, "Let's get him now." Officer Robinson testified that he focused on Valentine's arms, twisting them behind his back while wrenching the thumb to the wrist. Moore simultaneously rushed Valentine and cracked him in the face with a police radio, splintering Valentine's glasses and breaking the radio. According to Valentine's testimony, he was not only arrested but was physically battered before he hit Moore. Officer Yates, who had exchanged words with Valentine in the tavern, came from behind and slammed Valentine's head into Valentine's car. Officers Jones and Webb joined in. One requested handcuffs, to which Yates reportedly responded: "Don't worry about the cuffs because we're going to kill him." Webb worked on twisting Valentine's other arm behind his back while Yates was applying an artery chokehold which renders the victim unconscious * * *.

Officers Robinson and Moore testified that they grabbed Valentine to prevent him from entering the car. Perhaps a jury could find that Valentine reasonably believed that the actions of Robinson and Moore were excessive, possibly on the ground that they had not sought to prevent Valentine from entering the car by other methods, such as making clear to him that doing so was unacceptable.

A major argument against recognizing a right to resist excessive force, especially excessive nondeadly force, is that it requires an impossible distinction. Apparently the rule permitting force to resist excessive force permits one like Valentine to resist only to the point of preventing excessive force but not to prevent the arrest. This distinction may be impossible to make. Valentine arguably could not have been expected to resist the officers' use of excessive force but nevertheless submit to the arrest. If Valentine's version of the events is accepted, arguably he could reasonably have concluded that the only way to prevent the officers from using excessive force was to make it impossible for them to reach him by escaping from their custody. If this is so, the right to resist excessive force would seem to become, at least in some situations, a right to resist the arrest or other police action that is being accomplished by the excessive force.

2. Self-Defense Killings by a Battered Spouse

The following case raises issues concerning self-defense in the context of a specialized situation: when one kills one's spouse who has over a sustained period of time inflicted psychological and physical harm upon the "killing" spouse. Consider, in connection with the case, whether generally appropriate limitations upon the right of self-defense adequately assure appropriate results in cases of this sort. To the extent that they do not, what remedial action is most appropriate?

State v. Norman

Supreme Court of North Carolina, 1989
324 N.C. 253, 378 S.E.2d 8.

MITCHELL, Justice.

The defendant was tried * * * upon a proper indictment charging her with the first degree murder of her husband. The jury found the defendant guilty of voluntary man-slaughter. The defendant appealed from the trial court's judgment sentencing her to six years imprisonment.

The Court of Appeals granted a new trial, citing as error the trial court's refusal to submit a possible verdict of acquittal by reason of perfect self-defense. Notwithstanding the uncontroverted evidence that the defendant shot her husband three times in the back of the head as he lay sleeping in his bed, the Court of Appeals held that the defendant's evidence that she exhibited what has come to be called "the battered wife syndrome" entitled her to have the jury consider whether the homicide was an act of perfect self-defense and, thus, not a legal wrong.

* * *

At trial, the State presented the testimony of Deputy Sheriff R.H. Epley of the Rutherford County Sheriff's Department, who was called to the Norman residence on the night of 12 June 1985. Inside the home, Epley found the defendant's husband, John Thomas Norman, lying on a bed in a rear bedroom with his face toward the wall and his back toward the middle of the room. He was dead, but blood was still coming from wounds to the back of his head. A later autopsy revealed three gunshot wounds to the head, two of which caused fatal brain injury. The autopsy also revealed a .12 percent blood alcohol level in the victim's body.

Later that night, the defendant related an account of the events leading to the killing * * *. The defendant told Epley that her husband had been beating her all day and had made her lie down on the floor while he slept on the bed. After her husband fell asleep, the defendant carried her grandchild to the defendant's mother's house. The defendant took a pistol from her mother's purse and walked the short distance back to her home. She pointed the pistol at the back of her sleeping husband's head, but it jammed the first time she tried to shoot him. She fixed the gun and then shot her husband in the back of the head as he lay sleeping. After one shot, she felt her husband's chest and determined that he was still breathing and making sounds. She then shot him twice more in the back of the head. The defendant told Epley that she killed her husband because "she took all she was going to take from him so she shot him."

The defendant presented evidence tending to show a long history of physical and mental abuse by her husband due to his alcoholism. At the time of the killing, the thirty-nine-year-old defendant and her husband had been married almost twenty-five years and had several children. The defendant testified that her husband had started drinking and abusing her about five years after they were married. His physical abuse of her consisted of frequent assaults that included slapping, punching and kicking her, striking her with various objects, and throwing glasses, beer bottles and other objects at her. The defendant described other specific incidents of abuse, such as her husband putting her cigarettes out on her, throwing hot coffee on her, breaking glass against her face and crushing food on her face. Although the defendant did not present evidence of ever having received medical treatment for any physical injuries inflict-

ed by her husband, she displayed several scars about her face which she attributed to her husband's assaults.

The defendant's evidence also tended to show other indignities inflicted upon her by her husband. Her evidence tended to show that her husband did not work and forced her to make money by prostitution, and that he made humor of that fact to family and friends. He would beat her if she resisted going out to prostitute herself or if he was unsatisfied with the amounts of money she made. He routinely called the defendant "dog," "bitch" and "whore," and on a few occasions made her eat pet food out of the pets' bowls and bark like a dog. He often made her sleep on the floor. At times, he deprived her of food and refused to let her get food for the family. During those years of abuse, the defendant's husband threatened numerous times to kill her and to maim her in various ways.

The defendant said her husband's abuse occurred only when he was intoxicated, but that he would not give up drinking. She said she and her husband "got along very well when he was sober," and that he was "a good guy" when he was not drunk. She had accompanied her husband to the local mental health center for sporadic counseling sessions for his problem, but he continued to drink.

In the early morning hours on the day before his death, the defendant's husband, who was intoxicated, went to a rest area off I-85 near Kings Mountain where the defendant was engaging in prostitution and assaulted her. While driving home, he was stopped by a patrolman and jailed on a charge of driving while impaired. After the defendant's mother got him out of jail at the defendant's request later that morning, he resumed his drinking and abuse of the defendant.

The defendant's evidence also tended to show that her husband seemed angrier than ever after he was released from jail and that his abuse of the defendant was more frequent. That evening, sheriff's deputies were called to the Norman residence, and the defendant complained that her husband had been beating her all day and she could not take it anymore. The defendant was advised to file a complaint, but she said she was afraid her husband would kill her if she had him arrested. The deputies told her they needed a warrant before they could arrest her husband, and they left the scene.

The deputies were called back less than an hour later after the defendant had taken a bottle of pills. The defendant's husband cursed her and called her names as she was attended by paramedics, and he told them to let her die. A sheriff's deputy finally chased him back into his house as the defendant was put into an ambulance. The defendant's stomach was pumped at the local hospital, and she was sent home with her mother.

While in the hospital, the defendant was visited by a therapist with whom she discussed filing charges against her husband and having him committed for treatment. Before the therapist left, the defendant agreed to go to the mental health center the next day to discuss those possibilities. The therapist testified at trial that the defendant seemed depressed in the hospital, and that she expressed considerable anger toward her husband. He testified that the defendant threatened a number of times that night to kill her husband and that she said she should kill him "because of the things he had done to her."

The next day, the day she shot her husband, the defendant went to the mental health center to talk about charges and possible commitment, and she confronted her husband with that possibility. She testified that she told her husband later that day: "J.T., straighten up. Quit drinking. I'm going to have you committed to help you." She said her husband then told her he would "see them coming" and would cut her throat before they got to him.

The defendant also went to the social services office that day to seek welfare benefits, but her husband followed her there, interrupted her interview and made her go home with him. He continued his abuse of her, threatening to kill and to maim her, slapping her, kicking her, and throwing objects at her. At one point, he took her cigarette and put it out on her, causing a small burn on her upper torso. He would not let her eat or bring food into the house for their children.

That evening, the defendant and her husband went into their bedroom to lie down, and he called her a "dog" and made her lie on the floor when he lay down on the bed. Their daughter brought in her baby to leave with the defendant, and the defendant's husband agreed to let her babysit. After the defendant's husband fell asleep, the baby started crying and the defendant took it to her mother's house so it would not wake up her husband. She returned shortly with the pistol and killed her husband.

The defendant testified at trial that she was too afraid of her husband to press charges against him or to leave him. She said that she had temporarily left their home on several previous occasions, but he had always found her, brought her home and beaten her. Asked why she killed her husband, the defendant replied: "Because I was scared of him and I knowed when he woke up, it was going to be the same thing, and I was scared when he took me to the truck stop that night it was going to be worse than he had ever been. I just couldn't take it no more. There ain't no way, even if it means going to prison. It's better than living in that. That's worse hell than anything."

The defendant and other witnesses testified that for years her husband had frequently threatened to kill her and to maim her. When asked if she believed those threats, the defendant replied: "Yes. I believed him; he would, he would

kill me if he got a chance. If he thought he wouldn't a had to went to jail, he would a done it."

Two expert witnesses in forensic psychology and psychiatry who examined the defendant after the shooting, Dr. William Tyson and Dr. Robert Rollins, testified that the defendant fit the profile of battered wife syndrome. This condition, they testified, is characterized by such abuse and degradation that the battered wife comes to believe she is unable to help herself and cannot expect help from anyone else. She believes that she cannot escape the complete control of her husband and that he is invulnerable to law enforcement and other sources of help.

Dr. Tyson, a psychologist, was asked his opinion as to whether, on 12 June 1985, "it appeared reasonably necessary for Judy Norman to shoot J.T. Norman?" He replied: "I believe that . . . Mrs. Norman believed herself to be doomed . . . to a life of the worst kind of torture and abuse, degradation that she had experienced over the years in a progressive way; that it would only get worse, and that death was inevitable. . . ." Dr. Tyson later added: "I think Judy Norman felt that she had no choice, both in the protection of herself and her family, but to engage, exhibit deadly force against Mr. Norman, and that in so doing, she was sacrificing herself, both for herself and for her family."

Dr. Rollins, who was the defendant's attending physician at Dorothea Dix Hospital when she was sent there for evaluation, testified that in his opinion the defendant was a typical abused spouse and that "[s]he saw herself as powerless to deal with the situation, that there was no alternative, no way she could escape it." Dr. Rollins was asked his opinion as to whether "on June 12th, 1985, it appeared reasonably necessary that Judy Norman would take the life of J.T. Norman?" Dr. Rollins replied that in his opinion, "that course of action did appear necessary to Mrs. Norman."

Based on the evidence that the defendant exhibited battered wife syndrome, that she believed she could not escape her husband nor expect help from others, that her husband had threatened her, and that her husband's abuse of her had worsened in the two days preceding his death, the Court of Appeals concluded that a jury reasonably could have found that her killing of her husband was justified as an act of perfect self-defense. The Court of Appeals reasoned that the nature of battered wife syndrome is such that a jury could not be precluded from finding the defendant killed her husband lawfully in perfect self-defense, even though he was asleep when she killed him. We disagree.

The right to kill in self-defense is based on the necessity, real or reasonably apparent, of killing an unlawful aggressor to save oneself from *imminent* death or great bodily harm at his hands. Our law has recognized that self-preservation under such circumstances springs from a primal impulse and is an inherent right of natural law.

In North Carolina, a defendant is entitled to have the jury consider acquittal by reason of perfect self-defense when the evidence, viewed in the light most favorable to the defendant, tends to show that at the time of the killing it appeared to the defendant and she believed it to be necessary to kill the decedent to save herself from imminent death or great bodily harm. That belief must be reasonable, however, in that the circumstances as they appeared to the defendant would create such a belief in the mind of a person of ordinary firmness. Further, the defendant must not have been the initial aggressor provoking the fatal confrontation. A killing in the proper exercise of the right of *perfect* self-defense is always completely justified in law and constitutes no legal wrong.

Our law also recognizes an *imperfect* right of self-defense in certain circumstances, including, for example, when the defendant is the initial aggressor, but without intent to kill or to seriously injure the decedent, and the decedent escalates the confrontation to a point where it reasonably appears to the defendant to be necessary to kill the decedent to save herself from imminent death or great bodily harm. Although the culpability of a defendant who kills in the exercise of *imperfect* self-defense is reduced, such a defendant is *not justified* in the killing so as to be entitled to acquittal, but is guilty at least of voluntary manslaughter.

The defendant in the present case was not entitled to a jury instruction on either perfect or imperfect self-defense. The trial court was not required to instruct on *either* form of self-defense unless evidence was introduced tending to show that at the time of the killing the defendant reasonably believed herself to be confronted by circumstances which necessitated her killing her husband to save herself from *imminent* death or great bodily harm. No such evidence was introduced in this case, and it would have been error for the trial court to instruct the jury on either perfect or imperfect self-defense.

The jury found the defendant guilty only of voluntary manslaughter in the present case. As we have indicated, an instruction on imperfect self-defense would have entitled the defendant to nothing more, since one who kills in the exercise of imperfect self-defense is guilty at least of voluntary manslaughter. Therefore, even if it is assumed arguendo that the defendant was entitled to an instruction on imperfect self-defense—a notion we have specifically rejected—the failure to give such an instruction was harmless in this case. Accordingly, although we recognize that the imminence requirement applies to both types of self-defense for almost identical reasons, we limit our consideration in the remainder of this opinion to the issue of

whether the trial court erred in failing to instruct the jury to consider acquittal on the ground that the killing was justified and, thus, lawful as an act of *perfect* self-defense.

The killing of another human being is the most extreme recourse to our inherent right of self-preservation and can be justified in law only by the utmost real or apparent necessity brought about by the decedent. For that reason, our law of self-defense has required that a defendant claiming that a homicide was justified and, as a result, inherently lawful by reason of perfect self-defense must establish that she reasonably believed at the time of the killing she otherwise would have immediately suffered death or great bodily harm. Only if defendants are required to show that they killed due to a reasonable belief that death or great bodily harm was imminent can the justification for homicide remain clearly and firmly rooted in necessity. The imminence requirement ensures that deadly force will be used only where it is necessary as a last resort in the exercise of the inherent right of self-preservation. It also ensures that before a homicide is justified and, as a result, not a legal wrong, it will be reliably determined that the defendant reasonably believed that absent the use of deadly force, not only would an unlawful attack have occurred, but also that the attack would have caused death or great bodily harm. The law does not sanction the use of deadly force to repel simple assaults.

The term "imminent," as used to describe such perceived threats of death or great bodily harm as will justify a homicide by reason of perfect self-defense, has been defined as "immediate danger, such as must be instantly met, such as cannot be guarded against by calling for the assistance of others or the protection of the law." Black's Law Dictionary 676 (5th ed. 1979). Our cases have sometimes used the phrase "about to suffer" interchangeably with "imminent" to describe the immediacy of threat that is required to justify killing in self-defense.

The evidence in this case did not tend to show that the defendant reasonably believed that she was confronted by a threat of imminent death or great bodily harm. The evidence tended to show that no harm was "imminent" or about to happen to the defendant when she shot her husband. The uncontroverted evidence was that her husband had been asleep for some time when she walked to her mother's house, returned with the pistol, fixed the pistol after it jammed and then shot her husband three times in the back of the head. The defendant was not faced with an instantaneous choice between killing her husband or being killed or seriously injured. Instead, *all* of the evidence tended to show that the defendant had ample time and opportunity to resort to other means of preventing further abuse by her husband. There was no action underway by the decedent from which the jury could have found that the defendant had reasonable grounds to believe either that a felonious assault was imminent or that it might result in her death or great bodily injury. Additionally, no such action by the decedent had been underway immediately prior to his falling asleep.

Faced with somewhat similar facts, we have previously held that a defendant who believed himself to be threatened by the decedent was not entitled to a jury instruction on either perfect or imperfect self-defense when it was the defendant who went to the decedent and initiated the final, fatal confrontation. *State v. Mize*, 316 N.C. 48, 340 S.E.2d 439 (1986). In *Mize*, the decedent Joe McDonald was reported to be looking for the defendant George Mize to get revenge for Mize's alleged rape of McDonald's girl friend, which had exacerbated existing animosity between Mize and McDonald. After hiding from McDonald for most of the day, Mize finally went to McDonald's residence, woke him up and then shot and killed him. Mize claimed that he feared McDonald was going to kill him and that his killing of McDonald was in self-defense. Rejecting Mize's argument that his jury should have been instructed on self-defense, we stated:

> Here, although the victim had pursued defendant during the day approximately eight hours before the killing, defendant Mize was in no imminent danger while McDonald was at home asleep. When Mize went to McDonald's trailer with his shotgun, it was a new confrontation. Therefore, even if Mize believed it was necessary to kill McDonald to avoid his own imminent death, that belief was unreasonable.

The same reasoning applies in the present case.

Additionally, the lack of any belief by the defendant—reasonable or otherwise—that she faced a threat of imminent death or great bodily harm from the drunk and sleeping victim in the present case was illustrated by the defendant and her own expert witnesses when testifying about her subjective assessment of her situation at the time of the killing. The psychologist and psychiatrist replied affirmatively when asked their opinions of whether killing her husband "appeared reasonably necessary" to the defendant at the time of the homicide. That testimony spoke of no imminent threat nor of any fear by the defendant of death or great bodily harm, imminent or otherwise. Testimony in the form of a conclusion that a killing "appeared reasonably necessary" to a defendant does not tend to show all that must be shown to establish self-defense. More specifically, for a killing to be in self-defense,

the perceived necessity must arise from a reasonable fear of imminent death or great bodily harm.

Dr. Tyson additionally testified that the defendant "believed herself to be doomed . . . to a life of the worst kind of torture and abuse, degradation that she had experienced over the years in a progressive way; that it would only get worse, and that death was inevitable." Such evidence of the defendant's speculative beliefs concerning her remote and indefinite future, while indicating she had felt generally threatened, did not tend to show that she killed in the belief—reasonable or otherwise—that her husband presented a threat of imminent death or great bodily harm. Under our law of self-defense, a defendant's subjective belief of what might be "inevitable" at some indefinite point in the future does not equate to what she believes to be "imminent." Dr. Tyson's opinion that the defendant believed it was necessary to kill her husband for "the protection of herself and her family" was similarly indefinite and devoid of time frame and did not tend to show a threat or fear of *imminent* harm.

The defendant testified that, "I knowed when he woke up, it was going to be the same thing, and I was scared when he took me to the truck stop that night it was going to be worse than he had ever been." She also testified, when asked if she believed her husband's threats: "Yes . . . . [H]e would kill me if he got a chance. If he thought he wouldn't a had to went to jail, he would a done it." Testimony about such indefinite fears concerning what her sleeping husband might do at some time in the future did not tend to establish a fear—reasonable or otherwise—of *imminent death or great bodily harm* at the time of the killing.

We are not persuaded by the reasoning of our Court of Appeals in this case that when there is evidence of battered wife syndrome, neither an actual attack nor threat of attack by the husband at the moment the wife uses deadly force is required to justify the wife's killing of him in perfect self-defense. The Court of Appeals concluded that to impose such requirements would ignore the "learned helplessness," meekness and other realities of battered wife syndrome and would effectively preclude such women from exercising their right of self-defense. Other jurisdictions which have addressed this question under similar facts are divided in their views, and we can discern no clear majority position on facts closely similar to those of this case. * * *

The reasoning of our Court of Appeals in this case proposes to change the established law of self-defense by giving the term "imminent" a meaning substantially more indefinite and all-encompassing than its present meaning. This would result in a substantial relaxation of the requirement of real or apparent necessity to justify homicide. Such reasoning proposes justifying the taking of human life not upon the reasonable belief it is necessary to prevent death or great bodily harm—which the imminence requirement ensures—but upon purely subjective speculation that the decedent probably would present a threat to life at a future time and that the defendant would not be able to avoid the predicted threat.

* * * The relaxed requirements for perfect self-defense proposed by our Court of Appeals would tend to categorically legalize the opportune killing of abusive husbands by their wives solely on the basis of the wives' testimony concerning their subjective speculation as to the probability of future felonious assaults by their husbands. Homicidal self-help would then become a lawful solution, and perhaps the easiest and most effective solution, to this problem. See generally Rosen, The Excuse of Self-Defense: Correcting A Historical Accident on Behalf of Battered Women Who Kill, 36 Am.U.L.Rev. 11 (1986) (advocating changing the basis of self-defense acquittals to excuse rather than justification, so that excusing battered women's killing of their husbands under circumstances not fitting within the traditional requirements of self-defense would not be seen as justifying and therefore encouraging such self-help killing); Mitchell, Does Wife Abuse Justify Homicide?, 24 Wayne L.Rev. 1705 (1978) (advocating institutional rather than self-help solutions to wife abuse and citing case studies at the trial level where traditional defenses to homicide appeared stretched to accommodate poignant facts, resulting in justifications of some killings which appeared to be motivated by revenge rather than protection from death or great bodily harm). It has even been suggested that the relaxed requirements of self-defense found in what is often called the "battered woman's defense" could be extended in principle to *any type of case* in which a defendant testified that he or she subjectively believed that killing was necessary and proportionate to any perceived threat. Rosen, [supra, at 44].

In conclusion, we decline to expand our law of self-defense beyond the limits of immediacy and necessity which have heretofore provided an appropriately narrow but firm basis upon which homicide may be justified and, thus, lawful by reason of perfect self-defense or upon which a defendant's culpability may be reduced by reason of imperfect self-defense. As we have shown, the evidence in this case did not entitle the defendant to jury instructions on either perfect or imperfect self-defense.

For the foregoing reasons, we conclude that the defendant's conviction for voluntary manslaughter and the trial court's judgment sentencing her to a six-year term of imprisonment were without error. Therefore, we must reverse the decision of the Court of Appeals which awarded the defendant a new trial.

REVERSED.

MARTIN, Justice, dissenting.

* * *

At the heart of the majority's reasoning is its unsubstantiated concern that to find that the evidence presented by defendant would support an instruction on self-defense would "expand our law of self-defense beyond the limits of immediacy and necessity." Defendant does not seek to expand or relax the requirements of self-defense and thereby "legalize the opportune killing of allegedly abusive husbands by their wives," as the majority overstates. Rather, defendant contends that the evidence as gauged by the existing laws of self-defense is sufficient to require the submission of a self-defense instruction to the jury. The proper issue for this Court is to determine whether the evidence, viewed in the light most favorable to the defendant, was sufficient to require the trial court to instruct on the law of self-defense. I conclude that it was.

In every jury trial, it is the duty of the court to charge the jury on all substantial features of the case arising on the evidence * * *.

A defendant is entitled to an instruction on self-defense when there is evidence, viewed in the light most favorable to the defendant, that these four elements existed at the time of the killing:

(1) it appeared to defendant and he believed it to be necessary to kill the deceased in order to save himself from death or great bodily harm; and

(2) defendant's belief was reasonable in that the circumstances as they appeared to him at the time were sufficient to create such a belief in the mind of a person of ordinary firmness; and

(3) defendant was not the aggressor in bringing on the affray, i.e., he did not aggressively and willingly enter into the fight without legal excuse or provocation; and

(4) defendant did not use excessive force, i.e., did not use more force than was necessary or reasonably appeared to him to be necessary under the circumstances to protect himself from death or great bodily harm.

The first element requires that there be evidence that the defendant believed it was necessary to kill in order to protect herself from serious bodily harm or death; the second requires that the circumstances as defendant perceived them were sufficient to create such a belief in the mind of a person of ordinary firmness. Both elements were supported by evidence at defendant's trial.

Evidence presented by defendant described a twenty-year history of beatings and other dehumanizing and degrading treatment by her husband. In his expert testimony a clinical psychologist concluded that defendant fit "and exceed[ed]" the profile of an abused or battered spouse, analogizing this treatment to the dehumanization process suffered by prisoners of war under the Nazis during the Second World War and the brainwashing techniques of the Korean War. The psychologist described the defendant as a woman incarcerated by abuse, by fear, and by her conviction that her husband was invincible and inescapable:

Mrs. Norman didn't leave because she believed, fully believed that escape was totally impossible. There was no place to go. * * * [S]he had left before; he had come and gotten her. She had gone to the Department of Social Services. He had come and gotten her. * * * [S]he believed the law could not protect her; no one could protect her, and I must admit, looking over the records, that there was nothing done that would contradict that belief. She fully believed that he was invulnerable to the law and to all social agencies that were available; that nobody could withstand his power. As a result, there was no such thing as escape.

When asked if he had an opinion whether it appeared reasonably necessary for Judy Norman to shoot her husband, this witness responded:

Yes. . . . I believe that in examining the facts of this case and examining the psychological data, that Mrs. Norman believed herself to be doomed . . . to a life of the worst kind of torture and abuse, degradation that she had experienced over the years in a progressive way; that it would only get worse, and that death was inevitable; death of herself, which was not such, I don't think was such an issue for her, as she had attempted to commit suicide, and in her continuing conviction of J.T. Norman's power over her, and even failed at that form of escape. I believe she also came to the point of beginning to fear for family members and her children, that were she to commit suicide that the abuse and the treatment that was heaped on her would be transferred onto them. This testimony describes defendant's perception of circumstances in which she was held hostage to her husband's abuse for two decades and which ultimately compelled her to kill him.

This testimony alone is evidence amply indicating the first two elements required for entitlement to an instruction on self-defense.

In addition to the testimony of the clinical psychologist, defendant presented the testimony of witnesses who had actually seen defendant's husband abuse her. These witnesses described circumstances that caused not only defendant to believe escape was impossible, but that also convinced *them* of its impossibility. * * *

In *State v. Mize*, 316 N.C. 48, 53, 340 S.E.2d 439, 442 (1986), this Court noted that if the defendant was in "no imminent danger" at the time of the killing, then his belief that it was necessary to kill the man who had pursued him eight hours before was unreasonable. The second element of self-defense was therefore not satisfied. In the context of the doctrine of self-defense, the definition of "imminent" must be informed by the defendant's perceptions. It is not bounded merely by measurable time, but by all of the facts and circumstances. Its meaning depends upon the assessment of the facts by one of "ordinary firmness" with regard to whether the defendant's perception of impending death or injury was so pressing as to render reasonable her belief that it was necessary to kill.

Evidence presented in the case sub judice revealed no letup of tension or fear, no moment in which the defendant felt released from impending serious harm, even while the decedent slept. This, in fact, is a state of mind common to the battered spouse, and one that dramatically distinguishes Judy Norman's belief in the imminence of serious harm from that asserted by the defendant in *Mize*. Psychologists have observed and commentators have described a "constant state of fear" brought on by the cyclical nature of battering as well as the battered spouse's perception that her abuser is both "omnipotent and unstoppable." See Comment, The Admissibility of Expert Testimony on the Battered Woman Syndrome in Support of a Claim of Self-Defense, 15 Conn.L.Rev. 121, 131 (1982). Constant fear means a perpetual anticipation of the next blow, a perpetual expectation that the next blow will kill. "[T]he battered wife is constantly in a heightened state of terror because she is certain that one day her husband will kill her during the course of a beating. . . . Thus from the perspective of the battered wife, the danger is constantly 'immediate.'" Eber, The Battered Wife's Dilemma: To Kill or To Be Killed, 32 Hastings L.J. 895, 928–29 (1981). For the battered wife, if there is no escape, if there is no window of relief or momentary sense of safety, then the next attack, which could be the fatal one, is imminent. In the context of the doctrine of self-defense, "imminent" is a term the meaning of which must be grasped from the defendant's point of view. Properly stated, the second prong of the question is not whether the threat was in fact imminent, but whether defendant's belief in the impending nature of the threat, given the circumstances as she saw them, was reasonable in the mind of a person of ordinary firmness.[1]

* * *

The third element for entitlement to an instruction on self-defense requires that there be evidence that the defendant was not the aggressor in bringing on the affray. * * *

Where the defendant is a battered wife, there is no analogue to the victim-turned-aggressor, who * * * turns the tables on the decedent in a fresh confrontation. Where the defendant is a battered wife, the affray out of which the killing arises can be a continuing assault. There was evidence before the jury that it had not been defendant but her husband who had initiated "the affray," which the jury could have regarded as lasting twenty years, three days, or any number of hours preceding his death. And there was evidence from which the jury could infer that in defendant's mind the affray reached beyond the moment at which her husband fell asleep. Like the ongoing threats of death or great bodily harm, which she might reasonably have perceived as imminent, her husband continued to be the aggressor and she the victim.

Finally, the fourth element of self-defense poses the question of whether there was any evidence tending to show that the force used by defendant to repel her husband was not excessive, that is, more than reasonably appeared to be necessary under the circumstances. This question is answered in part by abundant testimony describing defendant's immobilization by fear caused by abuse by her husband. Three witnesses, including the decedent's best friend, all recounted incidents in which defendant passively accepted beating, kicks, commands, or humiliating affronts without striking back. From such evidence that she was paralyzed by her husband's presence, a jury could infer that it reasonably appeared to defendant to be necessary to kill her husband in order ultimately to protect herself from the death he had threatened and from severe bodily injury, a foretaste of which she had already experienced.

* * *

It is to be remembered that defendant does not have the burden of persuasion as to self-defense; the burden remains with the state to prove beyond a reasonable doubt that defendant intentionally killed decedent without excuse or justification. If the evidence in support of self-defense is sufficient to create a reasonable doubt in the mind of a rational juror whether the state has proved an intentional killing without justification or excuse, self-defense must be submitted to the jury. This is such a case.

Notes and Questions

1. In *Norman* the admissibility of expert testimony concerning the battered woman syndrome was apparently not contested by the parties. Where challenges have been made to the admissibility of such testimony, the courts have divided although most appear to regard such testimony as admissible. Compare *Mullis v. State*, 248 Ga. 338, 282 S.E.2d 334 (1981) (holding such testimony inadmissible because the expert's testimony would address matters that are not difficult for jurors to comprehend by themselves) with *State v. Kelly*, 97 N.J. 178, 478 A.2d 364, 372 (1984) (holding such testimony admissible).

2. Under the minority rule requiring retreat before the use of deadly force, demanding retreat by one domestic partner before using deadly force in defense against the other partner may be especially questionable. The New Jersey Supreme Court held that its statutory retreat rule applied to a woman who was attacked by her battering husband in her separate bedroom. Nevertheless, it urged the legislature to reconsider the matter in light of contemporary knowledge regarding domestic violence. *State v. Gartland*, 149 N.J. 456, 694 A.2d 564 (1997). One court has held that a trial court's failure to tell the jury that a homicide defendant without fault attacked in her own home by her husband had no duty to retreat violated the defendant's constitutional right to due process of law. *State v. Brown*, 117 N.C.App. 239, 450 S.E.2d 538 (1994), cert. denied, 339 N.C. 616, 454 S.E.2d 259 (1995) and 340 N.C. 115, 456 S.E.2d 320 (1995).

3. The Georgia Supreme Court has held that in battered person cases the standard instruction on self-defense should be supplemented by additional instructions to assist the jury in evaluating the battered person's defense of self-defense. *Smith v. State*, 268 Ga. 196, 486 S.E.2d 819 (1997). The court suggested that the instruction read as follows:

> I charge you that the evidence that the defendant suffers from battered person syndrome was admitted for your consideration

---

[1] This interpretation of the meaning of "imminent" is reflected in the Comments to the Model Penal Code: "The actor must believe that his defensive action is immediately necessary and the unlawful force against which he defends must be force that he apprehends will be used on the present occasion, but he need not apprehend that it will be immediately used." Model Penal Code § 3.04 comment (ALI 1985).

in connection with the defendant's claim of self-defense and that such evidence relates to the issue of the reasonableness of the defendant's belief that the use of force was immediately necessary, even though no use of force against the defendant may have been, in fact, imminent. The standard is whether the circumstances were such as would excite the fears of a reasonable person possessing the same or similar psychological and physical characteristics as the defendant, and faced with the same circumstances surrounding the defendant at the time the defendant used force.

B. DEFENSE OF OTHERS

Force is generally not regarded as criminal when it is used in defense of a third person. However, the courts have shown some inclination to impose more limits upon the right to use force in defense of others than have been imposed upon the right of self-defense.

Is there any justification for this? Perhaps it is more reasonable to expect persons to follow legal limits on the use of force when they perceive a risk to others. One who perceives his own safety at risk is, perhaps, unlikely to be influenced by the threat of criminal liability should he act unreasonably. However, one who perceives only the safety of another at risk may be more susceptible to the threat of the criminal sanction.

Moreover, there may be more of a risk that one acting in defense of another will act improperly, that is, will use force to assist another who is not in fact entitled to defend himself. Although a person will generally be acquainted with those facts that determine whether he is entitled to defend himself, a person is less likely to know which party to a fight between two others is at fault and is therefore barred from using protective force.

Fersner v. United States

District of Columbia Court of Appeals, 1984
482 A.2d 387.

FERNN, ASSOCIATE JUDGE:

A jury, rejecting appellant's claim of self-defense, convicted him of second-degree murder while armed and carrying a dangerous weapon. The trial court sentenced him to consecutive prison terms of fifteen years to life on the murder charge and of three to nine years on the weapon charge. On appeal, he argues that the trial court erred in refusing to give an instruction on the use of deadly force in defense of a third person. We affirm.

On the evening of July 31, 1980, appellant and several of his acquaintances gathered in a parking lot behind the Brentwood Village apartments. The decedent, Maurice Winslow, approached them. Earlier, several of the women in the group, including Winslow's girlfriend, had been together at various bars. Winslow had learned that the women were going to one particular bar, but as it turned out they had stayed only a few minutes and thus apparently were not at the bar where Winslow believed he would find them. Winslow asked one of the women, Diane Aull, why she had lied to him (presumably about where the women were planning to go). One witness testified that appellant's girlfriend, Geraldine Barnes, told Aull she did not have to answer Winslow. Barnes testified that she had said nothing to Aull. In any event, Winslow struck Barnes with his hand or fist.

Barnes then went over to appellant, who was seated in a van a short distance away, and told him that Winslow had hit her for no reason. Appellant then walked toward Winslow, who by this time was engaged in an altercation with another woman in the group, Laverne Reed. Accounts of the altercation varied greatly as to whether Winslow or Reed had instigated the fight, whether Reed struck Winslow, and whether Winslow was slapping, punching, kicking, or stomping Reed. The witnesses agreed, however, that Winslow hit Reed at least once before appellant approached him. Reed suffered facial lacerations as a result of the incident.

After appellant and Winslow had exchanged a few words, Winslow turned around and went to his car to get something, which he then put into his pocket. Appellant returned to his own car and put on his tool belt which contained several tools, including a hatchet. Winslow went back toward Reed and Aull. Appellant then approached Winslow and, soon thereafter, struck him either once or twice on the head with the hatchet. Winslow fell to the ground.

The witnesses disagreed about what Winslow was doing immediately before appellant struck the initial blow. Rosie Johnson testified that Winslow was standing in a threatening posture in front of Diane Aull and having a heated discussion with her. Aull corroborated this account, saying that Winslow had just knocked Reed down but had turned back to Aull before appellant hit him. In contrast, Reed herself testified that Winslow, at the time he was struck, had already knocked her to the ground and was beating her. Similarly, Harry Jenkins testified that Winslow, at the moment of the first blow from appellant's hatchet, was kicking and stomping on Reed, saying he would break her neck. Appellant and William Kenney presented still another story. They testified that Winslow, with knife in hand, was facing appellant at the time Winslow received the first blow. Isaac Batts similarly testified that Winslow, while facing appellant, was beginning to remove an object from his own pocket. Finally, Barnes testified that Winslow had turned away from beating Reed to face appellant, in response to a remark by appellant.

The witnesses agreed that after Winslow fell to the ground, appellant struck him again three to eight times as he lay there. According to the testimony of Johnson, Aull, and appellant, Miles Jenkins told appellant to stop, and he did. Winslow then attempted to get up from the ground. At this point, according to government witnesses, Reed began to hit Winslow with the bicycle frame, then appellant pushed her aside and attacked Winslow again with the hatchet. Appellant also testified that after Winslow attempted to get up, appellant hit him again with the hatchet.

Medical testimony indicated that Winslow had suffered at least 13 hatchet blows to the back of his head. Winslow died of his injuries the next day.

II.

In addition to asking for a jury instruction on self-defense, which the trial court granted (based on Kenney's, Batts', Barnes' and appellant's testimony), appellant requested an instruction on the use of force in defense of a third person, Laverne Reed (based on Reed's and Jenkins' testimony). The court denied this request.[2]

The trial court correctly observed that the right to use force in defense of a third person is predicated upon that other person's right of self-defense. The court went on to say, however, that appellant's right to use force in the defense of Ms. Reed, as well as his right to determine the amount of force necessary, turned exclusively on Reed's own perception—not on appellant's perception—of the situation:

> It seems to me the key to the situation with Ms. Reed is her own testimony because it is quite clear that, under the law, that any intervenor on her behalf only has the same right of self-defense that she does. I cannot find that as a matter of law from Ms. Reed's testimony that she had the right to use deadly or dangerous weapon force. I do not find anything from which anyone could conclude that she was, from her own testimony, in imminent danger of serious bodily harm or death of the type that is needed to justify that defense. I will not give that instruction.

In other words, the court concluded first that Reed—based on her own testimony that Winslow struck her approximately nine times causing facial bleeding—would not have been entitled to use deadly force in self-defense. For that reason, the court next concluded, as a matter of law, that appellant was not entitled to use deadly force in defense of Reed, irrespective of his own reasonable perceptions of what was happening to her.[4]

[T]his court has not resolved, whether one who properly comes to the defense of another can be protected by his or her own perceptions, including a reasonable mistake of fact, about the degree of force necessary. Disagreeing with

---

[2] Appellant's own testimony supported only a self-defense instruction, since he said he responded with his hatchet when Winslow confronted him with a knife. That testimony does not preclude appellant's request for an instruction on defense of a third person; "a defendant is entitled to an instruction on any issue fairly raised by the evidence, whether or not consistent with the defendant's testimony or the defense trial theory."

[4] Apparently because deadly force was used against Winslow, the trial court did not address the question whether Reed—or appellant on Reed's behalf—could have used nondeadly force against Winslow.

the trial court, we conclude that when the use of force in defense of a third person is justified, the intervenor is entitled to use the degree of force reasonably necessary to protect the other person on the basis of the facts as the intervenor, not the victim, reasonably perceives them.

We arrive at this conclusion by first examining the factors to be considered in determining whether an act of self-defense is legally permissible and then by applying this analysis to defense of a third person. The right of self-defense, and especially the degree of force the victim is permitted to use to prevent bodily harm, is premised substantially on the victim's own reasonable perceptions of what is happening. Criminal Jury Instructions for the District of Columbia, No. 5.14 (3d ed. 1978) (self-defense-amount of force permissible). The victim's perceptions may include, for example, an enhanced sense of peril based on personal knowledge that the attacker has committed prior acts of violence. Indeed, the victim's personal perceptions are so significant that they may justify the use of reasonable, including deadly, force in self-defense "even though it may afterwards have turned out that the appearances were false." Criminal Jury Instructions, *supra*, No. 5.15. In sum, the victim's subjective perceptions are the prime determinant of the right to use force—and the degree of force required—in self-defense, subject only to the constraint that those perceptions be reasonable under the circumstances.

Given the subjective aspect of the right of self-defense, we find no rational basis for permitting an intervenor to come to the defense of a third person, with all the attendant risks, but conditioning that right on the victim's rather than the intervenor's reasonable perceptions. Obviously, in attempting to determine what the intervenor's perceptions actually and reasonably were, the trier of fact will find relevant the victim's own perceptions. But when it comes to determining whether—and to what degree—force is reasonably necessary to defend a third person under attack, the focus ultimately must be on the intervenor's, not on the victim's, reasonable perceptions of the situation.

It follows that an intervenor may be entitled to use more, or less, force than the victim reasonably could use, depending on their respective perceptions and available resources. For example, an intervenor may reasonably be entitled to use greater force than the victim herself would perceive necessary if the intervenor knows, while the victim does not, that the attacker has killed before. On the other hand, when an intervenor on behalf of a victim of an unarmed assault has strength considerably superior to that of the attacker, the intervenor may reasonably be limited to less force than would a slightly-built victim who has access to a knife. In the present case, therefore, even if Reed herself could not reasonably have perceived that deadly force was necessary in her own self-defense, this does not pre-clude a finding that appellant reasonably perceived that his use of deadly force was necessary to protect her.

III.

We turn to the facts. An accused is entitled to a requested instruction on the defense theory of the case "if there is 'any evidence fairly tending to bear upon the issue * * *', however weak." The question, therefore, is whether there is any evidence of record fairly tending to show that appellant reasonably believed there was a need to use deadly force—specifically, enough force to kill Winslow—to prevent death or serious bodily harm to Laverne Reed.

As properly adapted from standard jury instruction 5.14 on the amount of force permissible in self-defense, the requested instruction as to defense of a third person * * * would include two additional explanations. First, the court would have to instruct on the use of deadly force:

> A person may use a reasonable amount of force in defense of another person, including, in some circumstances, deadly force. "Deadly force" is force which is likely to cause death or serious bodily harm. A person may use deadly force in defense of another person if [he] [she] actually believes at the time of the incident that that person is in imminent danger of death or serious bodily harm from which [he] [she] can save that person only by using deadly force against the assailant, and if [his] [her] belief is reasonable.

Second, the court would have to put the use of deadly force in perspective by also cautioning the jury about the use of excessive force:

> Even if the defendant was justified in using force in defense of another person, [he] [she] would not be entitled to use any greater force than [he] [she] had reasonable grounds to believe and actually did believe to be necessary under the circumstances to save the other person's life or avert serious bodily harm.
>
> In determining whether the defendant used excessive force in defending another person, you may consider all the circumstances under which [he] [she] acted. The claim of defense of a third person is not necessarily defeated if greater force than would have seemed necessary to a calm mind was used by the defendant in the heat of passion generated by an assault upon the third person. A belief which may be unreasonable to a calm mind may be actually and reasonably entertained in the heat of passion.

There was some evidence, particularly Reed's testimony that Winslow was "beating" her and Jenkins' testimony that Winslow was "kicking" and "stomping" on Reed and threatening to break her neck, fairly tending to show that Reed in fact was threatened with serious bodily harm at the time appellant intervened. Appellant and other witnesses testified, moreover, that on previous occasions Winslow had threatened others with injury and death and that he had beaten up several persons, including his girlfriend. Finally, there was testimony indicating that Reed, who was intoxicated and lying on the ground, was unable to defend herself effectively. This evidence would be sufficient to support a jury finding that appellant reasonably believed Reed was in imminent danger of serious bodily harm, and thus that appellant was entitled to use deadly force.

The inquiry does not end here, however. In order to provide a basis for the instruction on defense of a third person, appellant also had to point to evidence fairly tending to show that he reasonably believed the particular deadly force he used to avert serious bodily harm to Reed—a hatchet blow to Winslow's head—was necessary, not excessive, under the circumstances.

While we must accept as true, for purposes of evaluating appellant's right to the requested instruction, that Winslow was "kicking," "stomping," or "beating" on Reed[9]—and threatening to break her neck—at the time appellant felled Winslow with one or two hatchet blows,[10] we can easily say on this record, as a matter of law, that appellant did not have "reasonable grounds to believe"— even if acting "in the heat of passion"—that hatchet blows to Winslow's head were necessary to defend Reed. Even if appellant was entitled to use deadly force—i.e., force "likely to cause death or serious bodily harm"—there are, as this definition implies, degrees of deadly force. On some occasions, it may be reasonable only to cause serious bodily harm not threatening life itself. This is such a case. Under the circumstances here, appellant obviously could have saved Reed by striking Winslow with the blunt side of the hatchet elsewhere on the body, with less damaging (here fatal) results. As a matter of law, therefore, appellant used excessive force; it was not necessary for appellant to use an amount of deadly force that was likely to kill Winslow.

Affirmed.

Notes and Questions

1. Probably the leading case for the proposition that one acting in defense of another should have a defense only where the person aided was in fact entitled to act in self-defense is *People v. Young*, 11 N.Y.2d 274, 229 N.Y.S.2d 1, 183 N.E.2d 319 (1962) (per curiam). Young had come upon two middle-aged men struggling with an 18-year-old youth in the street. He intervened on behalf of the youth, injuring one of the older men. It ultimately turned out that the men were police officers making a valid arrest and the youth was improperly resisting them, but even the officers acknowledged that Young had no way of knowing that the men were officers or that they were making an arrest. Young was convicted of assault, and the New York Court of Appeals, relying upon "[t]he weight of authority," affirmed the conviction. Permitting persons such as Young to intervene on behalf of others without requiring them to act at their own peril, it reasoned, "would not be conducive to an orderly society."

2. Perhaps an argument can be made that the right to use force to defend others should be limited to force used to defend family members or others with whom the defendant has a close personal relationship. Nevertheless, as the Virginia court of appeals said in *Foster v. Commonwealth*, 13 Va.App. 380, 385, 412 S.E.2d 198, 201 (1991), "[g]enerally, * * * the privilege [to use force to defend another] is not limited to family members and extends to anyone, even a stranger * * *."

---

[9] Although there was testimony that Winslow earlier had struck Reed with a bicycle frame, no witness testified that he was using any weapon at the time of appellant's intervention. The witnesses who testified that Winslow pulled a knife on appellant did not claim to have seen this knife before or during the altercation with Reed. At most, the evidence could be taken to show that at the time he first struck Winslow with the hatchet, appellant reasonably believed Winslow had concealed some sort of weapon about his person after going to his car.

[10] Clearly, after the first two hatchet blows, all other blows occurred after Reed had been rescued. Any justification of those later blows would have to be a matter of appellant's own self-defense, for which he received an instruction that did not spare him from conviction.

MODEL PENAL CODE*

Official Draft, 1985

Section 3.05. Use of Force for the Protection of Other Persons

(1) Subject to the provisions of this Section and of Section 3.09 [reprinted at page 427], the use of force upon or toward the person of another is justifiable to protect a third person when:

(a) the actor would be justified under Section 3.04 in using such force to protect himself against the injury he believes to be threatened to the person whom he seeks to protect; and

(b) under the circumstances as the actor believes them to be, the person whom he seeks to protect would be justified in using such protective force; and

(c) the actor believes that his intervention is necessary for the protection of such other person.

(2) Notwithstanding Subsection (1) of this Section:

(a) when the actor would be obliged under Section 3.04 to retreat, to surrender the possession of a thing or to comply with a demand before using force in self-protection, he is not obliged to do so before using force for the protection of another person, unless he knows that he can thereby secure the complete safety of such other person; and

(b) when the person whom the actor seeks to protect would be obliged under Section 3.04 to retreat, to surrender the possession of a thing or to comply with a demand if he knew that he could obtain complete safety by so doing, the actor is obliged to try to cause him to do so before using force in his protection if the actor knows that he can obtain complete safety in that way; and

(c) neither the actor nor the person whom he seeks to protect is obliged to retreat when in the other's dwelling or place of work to any greater extent than in his own.

---

*Copyright 1985 by the American Law Institute. Reprinted with the permission of the American Law Institute.

C. DEFENSE OF PROPERTY

Greater limitations tend to be imposed upon the right to use force in defense of property than are imposed upon either the right of self-defense or defense of others. In large part, of course, this is because the actor's interest—the continued security in his property—is regarded as less important than the interests at issue in the other situations. Are there other considerations? Perhaps it is more reasonable to expect the law to be successful in preventing violence when that violence is—or may be—used to protect only property interests.

State v. Nelson

Supreme Court of Iowa, 1983
329 N.W.2d 643.

SCHULTZ, JUSTICE.

This is an appeal by defendant, Gregory Irvin Nelson, from his conviction of false imprisonment in violation of Iowa Code section 710.7 (1981). On appeal, defendant claims that * * * his request for an instruction on the justification defense of "defense of property" should have been given * * *. We hold * * * that the trial court correctly refused to instruct on the defense of property. We therefore affirm.

The facts in this case are rather unusual. Nelson and codefendant, Georgia Stigler, are brother and sister. Reuben Stigler, one of the victims of the alleged false imprisonment, is the husband of Georgia. He, Georgia, and Georgia's twelve-year-old child from an earlier marriage lived together in a house that Georgia owned. Georgia rented a room of this house to Nelson. Nelson, who is single and partially disabled, is a devotee of military training, guns, and shooting, and had an extensive gun collection.

On the night of February 26, 1981, Nelson returned to his room and discovered that four of his guns, $1000, and other miscellaneous items had been stolen. Nelson told Georgia of the theft as soon as she came into the house. Shortly thereafter, Georgia found Reuben and she accused him of being involved in the theft. She told Reuben that the theft would be reported to the police if the items were not returned by morning.

Reuben testified that he and his friend, Russell Hill, went to a tavern where they recovered three of the stolen guns. They then brought the guns to the Stigler house. This partial recovery apparently did little to soothe the indignation of the codefendants.

The State's evidence indicates that when Reuben and Hill entered the house they were held at gunpoint by the codefendants and others. This situation continued for some

hours, during which time various phone calls were made in an effort to recover the stolen items. Finally, Reuben and Hill made a dramatic escape from the home; according to Reuben, they upset a table and he dove through a closed window while Hill fled through the rear door. At this time the house was surrounded by police and the codefendants were soon arrested.

The State presented evidence from the victims and from the victims' relatives who had received phone calls that the defendants threatened to kill Reuben and Hill if the remainder of Nelson's property and money was not returned. Nelson testified that although he made threats of bodily injury, he held but did not point his gun at the victims. In regard to the threat to kill, he testified: "I never threatened to kill them. There's a semantic difference there. I said I should."

Defendant unsuccessfully requested that the trial court instruct the jury on the justification defense of defense of property. On appeal he claims the court's refusal to give such instruction was error. We hold that such instruction was not justified under the facts of this case.

The defense of justification of use of force in defense of property is codified in Iowa Code section 704.4, which in pertinent part states: "[a] person is justified in the use of reasonable force to prevent or terminate criminal interference with his or her possession or other right in property." We must determine, under this statutory definition, whether the defense of justification exists under the facts of this case. If we determine that there are substantial facts which if proved would satisfy this section, then it becomes the province of the jury to determine the validity of these facts.

The issue presented* * * is whether a justification defense exists under section 704.4 for a defendant who has at an earlier time been deprived of possession of his property by a wrongful taking committed out of his presence, and who then attempts by the use of force to recover the property, although the property is elsewhere. We hold that under this fact situation the defense is unavailable.

In interpreting a statute we look to its language, and if its meaning is clear, we are not permitted to search beyond its express terms. The express terms of section 704.4 provide a defense in situations where the defendant attempts "to prevent or terminate criminal interference." If the criminal interference has occurred out of the presence of the defendant at an earlier time, and the property, the reason for the interference, is no longer present, force can no longer be used to prevent or stop the crime. No language in section 704.4 approves of after-the-fact vigilante action.

Another tool of statutory construction is the examination of the statute's purpose. The obvious purpose of this statute is to prevent the imposition of a penalty upon a person who out of necessity is acting to retain his property or to prevent its injury. Thus, the purpose of the statute is not to recover property but to prevent wrongful interference with it. When the injured party is not present at the time of wrongful taking, or the property is elsewhere, there is no necessity or urgency that would call for the use of force to prevent the wrongful activity.

Other authority supports this interpretation of the statute. In a defense based on necessity, a justification defense, it was held in *State v. Marley*, 54 Haw. 450, 472, 509 P.2d 1095, 1108–09 (1973), that elements of a justification defense are (1) that a direct causal relationship must be reasonably anticipated to exist between the defender's action and the avoidance of harm, (2) that the harm to be prevented must be imminent, (3) that there is no alternative available which does not involve violation of the law, and (4) that the criminal act that defendant seeks to prevent or terminate must be committed in defendant's presence. In *Marley* the court, commenting on the element of presence, stated:

> Prevention or termination of the commission of a crime is only one of several "justification" defenses. Some of the others are self-defense, defense of another, and defense of property. Each of these justification defenses obviously and inevitably requires that the criminal act to be counteracted occur in the presence of the actor. * * * To rule that a full justification defense to the prosecution for commission of crime is established even absent a presence requirement would be to create a very dangerous precedent, for it would make each citizen a judge of the criminality of all the acts of every other citizen, with power to mete out sentence.

See also W. Lafave & A. Scott *Criminal Law* § 402 (recapture of a chattel by force after an interval has elapsed is not

justified); id. § 406 (a requirement of justification defense is that the criminal act that defendant seeks to prevent or terminate be committed in defendant's presence).

Applying this construction to the statute, we find no evidence that defendant's acts were for a purpose other than to regain possession of property that had been taken in his absence and had not been returned. After defendant discovered the theft, all that he knew was that the property was gone. He was not present during the taking and he only suspected the identity of the culprit. Nor did the return of part of the property, after threats were made, restart the timetable of the crime so that defendant could "prevent or terminate" its occurrence. Thus, defendant was not entitled to the instruction he requested.

* * *

Affirmed.

Notes and Questions

1. Force is generally regarded as permissible if it is used immediately after the dispossession or in "hot pursuit" of the dispossessor:

   > If force is allowed to defend possession, it is only a small extension to allow similar force to be used to regain possession immediately after its loss. * * * Moreover, it is an ancient principle of the common law, commended by common sense, that when property is taken on fresh pursuit it is deemed to be taken at the beginning of the pursuit. The retaking is not any the less immediate because the fresh pursuit turns out to be a protracted chase.

   Model Penal Code § 3.06, Comment, at 44 (Tent. Draft No. 8, 1958).

2. If Nelson had confronted Reuben and Hill immediately after the taking of the guns and other items, would he have been permitted to hold Reuben and Hill at gunpoint? Would he have been permitted to threaten to shoot them? Could he have displayed or exhibited a firearm as part of such a threat if he did not point it at them? It is often said that there is no right to use deadly force or to "endanger life or inflict serious bodily harm" in order to defend property. *State v. Deans*, 71 N.C.App. 227, 233, 321 S.E.2d 579, 583 (1984), review denied, 313 N.C. 332, 329 S.E.2d 386 (1985). The definition of deadly force was addressed earlier in the chapter at page 420.

   Even if the use of a firearm is not the use of deadly force inherently improper to defend property, it may be excessive nondeadly force on the facts of the particular case. In *State v. Murphy*, 7 Wn.App. 505, 500 P.2d 1276 (1972), for example, the defendant armed himself with a pistol and confronted trespassers on his property with the gun in his hand dropped at his side. In finding no right to engage in such behavior to eject trespassers, the court explained:

> Mr. Murphy's action in arming himself with a revolver was well calculated to excite apprehension of great bodily harm in the minds of

the two persons who, he believed, were harassing his business interests. * * * There is a recklessness—a wanton disregard of humanity and social duty—in the threatened use of deadly force to repel what at most could be considered a petty inconvenience, which is essentially wicked and which the law abhors. The law forbids such a menacing of human life for so trivial a cause.

Editors' Note: Self-Defense, Defense of the Dwelling, and the Colorado "Make My Day" Legislation

If the property that a person defends with force is that person's dwelling, the person may be able to use force in more circumstances than would otherwise be the case without incurring criminal liability. This is because such a person may have not only the right to defend the person's own property but also the different right to defend the habitation or dwelling. The actual and appropriate content of this right is a matter of considerable dispute.

The traditional right to defend the dwelling gave a person the right to use all force reasonably believed necessary, including deadly force, to repel a person reasonably believed to be attempting to force entry into the dwelling. The old rule may have applied only if the entry was sought "by force." This has traditionally meant that the entry must be such as would amount to a breach of the peace; entering premises after being warned not to do so but without force would not make the entry such a breach of the peace. *Carroll v. State*, 23 Ala. 28 (1853). However, under some more modern versions of the rule, it applies regardless of the manner of entry and even where the facts do not indicate an effort to make a "manifestly violent" entry. *Brockwell v. State*, 545 S.W.2d 60, 65 (Ark.1976).

What must the occupants fear from the intruder to trigger the right to defend the dwelling with deadly force? In *State v. W.J.B.*, 166 W.Va. 602, 276 S.E.2d 550 (1981), the West Virginia court noted the split among jurisdictions and rejected the rule that would require the occupants to reasonably fear at least *serious* bodily injury from the intruder. The court explained:

> A number of courts with the approval of commentators have taken the position that the occupant of a dwelling is not limited in using deadly force against an unlawful intruder to the situation where the occupant is threatened with serious bodily injury or death, but he may use deadly force if the unlawful intruder threatens imminent physical violence or the commission of a felony and the occupant reasonably believes deadly force is necessary. * * *

We believe that there are sound policy reasons for permitting the homeowner to repel with deadly force a violent intrusion into his home where he has reasonable grounds to believe the intruder will commit a felony or personal injury on the occupant and that deadly force is the only means available to prevent it. First, there is still basic vitality to the ancient English rule that a man's home is his castle, and he has the right to expect some privacy and security within its confines. This rule arises from a societal recognition that the home shelters and is a physical refuge for the basic unit of society the family. * * *

Second, we believe that from the standpoint of the intruder the violent and unlawful entry into a dwelling with intent to injure the occupants or commit a felony carries a common sense conclusion that he may be met with deadly force, and that his culpability matches the risk of danger. We also recognize that there is often a certain vulnerability to the occupant of a dwelling who is forced to confront the unlawful intruder in the privacy of his home, without any expectation of a public response or help.

* * *

In attempting to clarify our rule in regard to self-defense in the home, we do not mean to suggest that a homeowner is now free to shoot any stranger who approaches his door or that he may answer the pounding on the door with gunfire. Even an unlawful intrusion will not be sufficient when coupled only with a vague suspicion that the intruder may intend to commit a felony or physically assault the occupant. There must be a reasonable basis for the occupant's belief.

The relationship between the right to defend the dwelling and the right of self-defense is often confused and unclear. This confusion is in part due to the rules in some jurisdictions that otherwise require retreat before using deadly force in self-defense is not required if the attack occurs in the dwelling. Distinguishing between the two defenses, some courts conclude that the right to use force in defense of the dwelling applies only to prevent entry and does not apply if a resident discovers an intruder already in the house. *State v. Brookshire*, 353 S.W.2d 681 (Mo.1962), explained:

> It is apparent that the rules pertaining to the defense of habitation authorize certain protective acts to be taken * * * at the time when and place where the intruder is seeking to cross the protective barrier of the house. But once the intruder has crossed that barrier without resistance from the occupant of the house there is no occasion to kill him in order to keep him out because he is already in, and the occupant is not authorized by law to punish for the wrongful entry. Therefore, * * * a homicide then occurring is justifiable only under the usual rules of self-defense or to prevent therein the commission of a felony * * *.

There is, however, authority to the contrary as well. See *People v. Stombaugh*, 52 Ill.2d 130, 284 N.E.2d 640 (1972).

The differences between the two defenses and the additional immunity from criminal liability conferred by the right to defend the dwelling were illustrated by *State v. McCuiston*, 514 N.W.2d 802 (Minn.App.1994), review denied, in which the facts were as follows:

> McCuiston lived with his five-year-old son in the upstairs part of a triplex across the alley from the victim[, Fontaine]. There was a crack house on McCuiston's

block, and McCuiston had purchased the shotgun to protect his son from crime in the neighborhood.

McCuiston * * * was out walking with his son when the victim verbally accosted them, yelling racial epithets and threatening to chase McCuiston out of the neighborhood. McCuiston is a five foot, six inch tall, 126-pound African American; the victim was a six foot, one inch tall, 178-pound Caucasian. McCuiston gave his son the house keys and told him to run home. McCuiston continued to walk home with the victim yelling at him.

At his house, McCuiston climbed the stairs to the porch, entered, and locked the porch screen door. He was unable to lock the storm door because his son had the keys. McCuiston went upstairs to make certain his son was safe. When he heard someone pulling and kicking on the downstairs screen door, he grabbed his shotgun, walked downstairs, and called to his neighbor to telephone the police. McCuiston did not have a telephone at his residence.

On the porch, the shouting continued. The victim was yelling that he was not afraid of McCuiston; McCuiston was yelling for someone to call the police. McCuiston said he shot the victim as the victim made a gesture to enter McCuiston's house. * * * McCuiston testified as follows concerning his perceptions at the time he fired the fatal shot:

A. Then Mr. Fontaine [the victim]—I said—I told him—I tried to bluff him, I said, "The police on their way, man. You better go home." He said, "F--- the police and f--- you black m----- f-----s and get the f--- out of my way." And, when he said that, he came at me with both hands.

Q. Did you feel threatened at this point?

A. Yes, sir.

Q. Okay. Exactly how did you feel when you saw Mr. Fontaine coming at you?

A. I had a decision to make. I wasn't about to be no statistic or my child's life wasn't going to be put in danger. I had a decision to make. Either let him in my house for coffee and doughnuts or keep him from coming in.

At McCuiston's murder trial, the trial judge instructed the jury on the law of self-defense but refused to instruct it on McCuiston's possible right to use force to defend his dwelling. The jury convicted McCuiston and on appeal the trial judge was held to have erred. Under Minnesota law, the use of deadly force is permitted when necessary to "preventing the commission of a felony in the actor's place of abode." The appellate court observed that it shared the prosecution's concern that the statutory defense of dwelling "may exceed what most people would think permissible under the law," but concluded that it must enforce the statutory law as enacted. "The gravamen of McCuiston's defense was that the victim was about to force his way into McCuiston's house, not that the victim was necessarily about to inflict death or great bodily harm on McCuiston." He had a right to have the jury instructed to acquit him if it found he acted within the defense of dwelling rule, and a jury convinced that McCuiston had no right to kill in self-defense might find he was justified in acting under the right to defend the dwelling.

Despite the misgivings of the *McCuiston* court, some legislatures have been convinced that persons' interest in the security of their habitation is sufficiently important to justify an even broader right to use defensive force than is recognized under most current law. Colorado, for example, has enacted a statute which provides:

> any occupant of a dwelling is justified in using any degree of physical force, including deadly physical force, against another person when that other person has made an unlawful entry into the dwelling, and when the occupant has a reasonable belief that such other person has committed a crime in the dwelling in addition to the uninvited entry, or is committing or intends to commit a crime against a person or property in addition to the uninvited entry, and when the occupant reasonably believes that such other person might use any physical force, no matter how slight, against any occupant.

Colo. St. § 18-1-704.5(2). This is widely described as the "make-my-day" law, with reference to a motion picture situation in which an aggressive police detective, played by actor Clint Eastwood, invited a suspect to resist arrest by suggesting, "Go ahead. Make my day!"

MODEL PENAL CODE*

Official Draft 1985

Section 3.06. Use of Force for the Protection of Property

(1) *Use of Force Justifiable for Protection of Property.* Subject to the provisions of this Section and of Section 3.09 [reprinted at page 427], the use of force upon or toward the person of another is justifiable when the actor believes that such force is immediately necessary:

   (a) to prevent or terminate an unlawful entry or other trespass upon land or a trespass against or the unlawful carrying away of tangible, movable property, provided that such land or movable property is, or is believed by the actor to be, in his possession or in the possession of another person for whose protection he acts; or

   (b) to effect an entry or re-entry upon land or to retake tangible movable property, provided that the actor believes that he or the person by whose authority he acts or a person from whom he or such other person derives title was unlawfully dispossessed of such land or movable property and is entitled to possession, and provided, further, that:

      (i) force is used immediately or on fresh pursuit after such dispossession; or

---

(ii) the actor believes that the person against whom he uses force has no claim of right to the possession of the property and, in the case of land, the circumstances, as the actor believes them to be, are of such urgency that it would be an exceptional hardship to postpone the entry or re-entry until a court order is obtained.

(2) *Meaning of Possession.* For the purposes of Subsection (1) of this Section:

(a) a person who has parted with the custody of property to another who refuses to restore it to him is no longer in possession, unless the property is movable and was and still is located on land in his possession;

(b) a person who has been dispossessed of land does not regain possession thereof merely by setting foot thereon;

(c) a person who has a license to use or occupy real property is deemed to be in possession thereof except against the licensor acting under claim of right.

(3) *Limitations on Justifiable Use of Force.*

(a) *Request to Desist.* The use of force is justifiable under this Section only if the actor first requests the person against whom such force is used to desist from his interference with the property, unless the actor believes that:

(i)   such request would be useless; or

(ii) it would be dangerous to himself or another person to make the request; or

(iii) substantial harm will be done to the physical condition of the property which is sought to be protected before the request can effectively be made.

(b) *Exclusion of Trespasser.* The use of force to prevent or terminate a trespass is not justifiable under this Section if the actor knows that the exclusion of the trespasser will expose him to substantial danger of serious bodily injury.

(c) *Resistance of Lawful Re-entry or Recaption.* The use of force to prevent an entry or re-entry upon land or the reception of movable property is not justifiable under this Section, although the actor believes that such re-entry or reception is unlawful, if:

(i)   the re-entry or reception is made by or on behalf of a person who was actually dispossessed of the property; and

(ii) it is otherwise justifiable under paragraph (1)(b) of this Section.

(d) *Use of Deadly Force.* The use of deadly force is not justifiable under this Section unless the actor believes that:

(i) the person against whom the force is used is attempting to dispossess him of his dwelling otherwise than under a claim of right to its possession; or

(ii) the person against whom the force is used is attempting to commit or consummate arson, burglary, robbery or other felonious theft or property destruction and either:

(1) has employed or threatened deadly force against or in the presence of the actor; or

(2) the use of force other than deadly force to prevent the commission or the consummation of the crime would expose the actor or another in his presence to substantial danger of serious bodily injury.

* * *

Chapter 15

DEFENSES RELATING TO CAPACITY

CHAPTER CONTENTS

Editors' Introduction: Challenges to Criminal "Capacity" and the Requirements of Criminal Liability

Some defensive matters permit defendants to challenge their *capacity* to engage in morally blameworthy activity and thus to incur criminal responsibility. These matters are covered in this chapter. The conceptual relationship between some of these defensive matters and the requirements of criminal liability, especially *mens rea*, is rather complex and deserves some initial consideration.

Mistake of fact, covered in Chapter 13, permits a defendant to use specific evidence to challenge whether, on the specific facts of the case, the prosecution has proved that the defendant acted with the culpable mental state required by the crime charged. Some of the doctrines covered in this chapter, in contrast, permit a defendant to escape conviction because he or she lacked the capacity to form the culpable mental state required for criminal liability. The major formulation of the insanity defense, for example, in some sense permits a defendant to challenge his or her ability to develop an awareness that the conduct constituting the crime was prohibited by the criminal law. This does not, however, permit the defendant to challenge whether the prosecution has proved the required *mens rea*.

Generally speaking, as developed in Chapter 4, criminal law does not require proof that a defendant knew the governing criminal law and understood that his or her conduct violated that law. Further, as developed in Chapter 13's discussion of mistake of law, criminal law does not even permit a defendant to escape liability by affirmatively showing that he or she mistakenly believed the criminal law was such as to permit this conduct. The criminal law "presumes" or "assumes" that all persons can and do know the criminal law and can and do apply it so as to determine before the fact whether their contemplated actions will be criminal. This is not really a presumption in the ordinary technical legal sense, because a defendant is not permitted to rebut it by showing that he or she did not know the law prohibiting the conduct charged or did not determine that the criminal law prohibited that conduct.

As developed in this chapter, however, criminal law has generally permitted a criminal defendant to establish that because of mental impairment he or she *lacked the underlying ability—the capacity*—to determine that the conduct was prohibited by the criminal law. Of course, this is not actually showing that the person lacked the capacity to form the *mens rea* required for criminal liability, because the defense permits the defendant to challenge his or her capacity to form a culpable mental state (knowledge that the conduct was wrong), which is so fundamental it is assumed and need not be proved (and is not subject to challenge) in ordinary criminal prosecutions.

This use of evidence—to challenge a lack of *capacity*—must be distinguished from the use of similar evidence to challenge whether the prosecution has in the particular case satisfactorily proved that the defendant in actual fact had the *mens rea* required by the crime charged. Those jurisdictions embracing what is often called the "diminished capacity" rule, considered in Section C(2) of this chapter, permit defendants to use evidence of mental impairment in this way as an alternative to relying upon it to raise the defense of insanity. Obviously, the two doctrines—insanity and diminished capacity—might easily be confused. The risk of confusion is increased by the fact that defendants raising diminished capacity may argue that their evidence of mental impairment shows they in fact lacked the *mens rea* required by the crime charged *because* it shows they lacked the capacity to form that culpable mental state.

Thus, some of the defensive matters covered in this chapter require a distinction among various ways of using evidence, as, for example, testimony that the defendant was mentally ill. Such evidence might be usable to show that (a) the defendant lacked the capacity to form the *mens rea* required by the crime charged (as, for example, the intent to kill in a murder case); (b) the defendant did not in fact form the intent required by the crime charged (although presumably remaining capable of doing so); and (c) the defendant lacked the capacity to understand the charged conduct was legally wrong (as, for example, that he or she could not understand that killing the victim was prohibited by the law).

Some matters covered may not require consideration of all possibilities. No jurisdiction, for example, permits criminal defendants to use evidence of voluntary intoxication to establish that they lacked the capacity to understand their conduct was wrong or to control their actions. The major issue in voluntary intoxication law is whether defendants should always or perhaps only sometimes be permitted to rely on evidence of voluntary intoxication to challenge whether they have been proved to have acted with the *mens rea* required by the crime charged.

A. INFANCY

Editors' Introduction: The Common Law
Presumptions of Incapacity, Juvenile Court
Jurisdiction, and the Defense of Infancy

A criminal defendant's conviction may be precluded because of the defendant's age. Infancy defense law, however, is complicated by modern efforts to channel many young persons who commit antisocial acts into programs separate from the adult criminal justice system.

The background of the traditional infancy defense was developed by Judge Charles Moylan of the Maryland Court of Special Appeals:

> The case law and the academic literature alike conceptualize the infancy defense as but an instance of the broader phenomenon of a defense based upon lack of moral responsibility or capacity. The criminal law generally will only impose its retributive or deterrent sanctions upon those who are morally blameworthy—those who know they are doing wrong but nonetheless persist in their wrongdoing.
>
> After several centuries of pondering the criminal capacity of children and experimenting with various cut-off ages, the Common Law settled upon its current resolution of the problem by late Tudor and early Stuart times. As explained by LaFave & Scott, Criminal Law, (2d ed. 1986), at 398, the resolution was fairly simple:
>
>> "At common law, children under the age of seven are conclusively presumed to be without criminal capacity, those who have reached the age of fourteen are treated as fully responsible, while as to those between the ages of seven and fourteen there is a rebuttable presumption of criminal incapacity."
>
> The authors make clear that infancy was an instance of criminal capacity generally:
>
>> "The early common law infancy defense was based upon an unwillingness to punish those thought to be incapable of forming criminal intent and not of an age where the threat of punishment could serve as a deterrent" (footnote omitted).
>
> Id. at 399.

In re Devon T., 85 Md.App. 674, 584 A.2d 1287 (1991).

In the early years of the century, American jurisdictions created specialized juvenile courts with original jurisdiction over young persons accused of criminal conduct. To the extent that young persons are not criminally prosecuted but rather are made the subjects of proceedings to determine whether they are "delinquent," the existence of a substantive law defense applicable in ordinary criminal prosecutions became moot. Consequently, attention turned to whether in juvenile delinquency proceedings there should be an infancy defense or its equivalent. Judge Moylan continued in *Devon T.*:

> Under the initially prevailing philosophy that the State was acting in delinquency cases as parens patriae (sovereign parent of the country), the State was perceived to be not the retributive punisher of the child for its misdeeds but the paternalistic guardian of the child for its own best interests. Under such a regime, the moral responsibility or blameworthiness of the child was of no consequence. Morally

responsible or not, the child was in apparent need of the State's rehabilitative intervention and the delinquency adjudication was but the avenue for such intervention.

This was the philosophy that persuaded this Court * * * to forbear from extending the defense of infancy to juvenile court proceedings as an inapposite criterion. * * *

Over the course of the century, however, buffeted by unanticipated urban deterioration and staggering case loads, the reforming vision of * * * the * * * founders of the [juvenile court] movement faded. Although continuing to stress rehabilitation over retribution more heavily than did the adult criminal courts, delinquency adjudications nonetheless took on, in practice if not in theory, many of the attributes of junior varsity criminal trials. The Supreme Court * * * acknowledged this slow but inexorable transformation of the juvenile court apparatus into one with increasingly penal overtones. It ultimately guaranteed, therefore, a juvenile charged with delinquency most of the due process protections afforded an adult charged with crime. * * *

In terms of the applicability of the infancy defense to delinquency proceedings, the implications [of this development] * * * are clear. A finding of delinquency, unlike other proceedings in a juvenile court, unmistakably connotes some degree of blameworthiness and unmistakably exposes the delinquent to, whatever the gloss, the possibility of unpleasant sanctions. Clearly, the juvenile would have as an available defense to the delinquency charge 1) the fact that he was too criminally insane to have known that what he did was wrong, 2) that he was too mentally retarded to have known that what he did was wrong, or 3) that he was too involuntarily intoxicated through no fault of his own to have known that what he did was wrong. It would be inconceivable that he could be found blameworthy and suffer sanctions, notwithstanding precisely the same lack of understanding and absence of moral accountability, simply because the cognitive defect was caused by infancy rather than by one of the other incapacitating mechanisms.

As illustrated by the reprinted decision that follows, the infancy defense is generally recognized in juvenile proceedings and it is in those cases that most infancy defense issues arise.

Many jurisdictions have provisions permitting juvenile courts to "waive" their exclusive jurisdiction over certain young persons. Generally, of course, this is authorized for those alleged delinquents at the upper end of the age range for juvenile court jurisdiction and is to be used when the young person is not appropriate for juvenile programs or where those programs would not adequately protect society from the unusual dangers posed by the youth. A juvenile over whom the juvenile court waives its jurisdiction is generally "transferred" to the regular criminal system and can be prosecuted as an adult. Does such a transferred young person, criminally prosecuted as an adult, have access to a defense of infancy?

The Model Penal Code would provide for no infancy defense to supplement its provisions for juvenile court jurisdiction, but it also would provide that juvenile court jurisdiction could be waived (and the youth prosecuted as an adult) only if at the time of the conduct the youth was 16 or 17 years old. Model Penal Code § 4.10 (Official Draft 1985). Legislative concern with juvenile crime has resulted in authorization in many jurisdictions for prosecution as adults of youths younger than this.

Some jurisdictions vary the age of responsibility with the crime. In New York, for example, section 30.00 of the Penal Law provides that generally only persons less than 16 years old are not responsible for crimes by reason of infancy. Persons 14 or 15, however, are responsible for certain crimes, including certain burglaries, arsons, kidnappings, and sexual offenses. Persons 13, 14, or 15 years old are responsible for certain second degree murders.

Generally, legislative provision for transfer of young persons from juvenile to adult court means that the legislature did not intend an infancy defense to be available in the adult criminal prosecution. A North Carolina court concluded, for example, that legislative authorization for the transfer to adult court for adult prosecution of a youth 13 years old at the time of the crime implicitly rejected the common law infancy defense. Thus, in his adult trial such a defendant could not invoke even a rebuttable presumption of incapacity. *State v. Green*, 124 N.C. App. 269, 477 S.E.2d 182 (1996), review denied, 345 N.C. 644, 483 S.E.2d 714 (1997).

As a general rule, however, a criminal defendant is not to be convicted if he or she is of an age that makes the acts constituting the charged crime the basis of a potential juvenile delinquency proceeding. This is the modern version of the traditional infancy defense applied in ordinary criminal prosecutions.

Although infancy is often termed a "defense," the relationship between age require-ments and the jurisdiction or authority of the various courts has meant that it is often treated somewhat differently than traditional defenses. Most defenses, such as self-defense and insanity, must be raised in the trial court by a plea of not guilty or the accused loses any right to rely on them. A defendant cannot argue for the first time on appeal or in a post-conviction habeas corpus attack (discussed in Chapter 1) that he could have but did not assert a defense to the charges. A defensive theory relying on the age of the defendant, however, is treated differently.

New York courts, for example, hold that a guilty plea is a "nullity" if entered by a criminal defendant who was in fact of such a young age that he was within the juris-diction of the juvenile court. *People v. McFadden*, 194 A.D.2d 566, 598 N.Y.S.2d 567 (1993). At least one court has held that a criminal defendant who misrepresents to the criminal trial court that he is of an age beyond juvenile court jurisdiction nevertheless can later attack his conviction by habeas corpus on the ground that because of his age the trial court lacked "jurisdiction" to convict him. *Ex parte McCullough*, 598 S.W.2d 272 (Tex.Crim.App.1980).

Other courts, however, may be unwilling to give infancy this dramatic effect. In *Twyman v. State*, 459 N.E.2d 705 (Ind.1984), for example, the Indiana Supreme Court held that if a defendant misrepresents that he is above the age of juvenile court juris-diction, pleads guilty, and fails to appeal, he has "waived" his rights as a juvenile and cannot eight years later attack his conviction on the ground that he was below the age of criminal court jurisdiction.

If in an ordinary criminal prosecution a defendant contends that he is of an age that gives the juvenile courts rather than the regular criminal courts jurisdiction over him, the prosecution must prove that the defendant is of an age rendering him subject to adult criminal prosecution and conviction for the crime charged against him. In *People*

v. *Parra*, 191 A.D.2d 465, 594 N.Y.S.2d 286 (1993), for example, the prosecution failed to carry its burden by introducing only a faxed copy of the birth certificate on file with the defendant's high school, which indicated that he had been born in 1974. The defendant himself had submitted to the trial court what appeared to be an original Colombian birth certificate indicating that he was born in 1976, which would have made him too young for conviction in adult court of the crime charged.

Whatever infancy defense is generally available may not apply if the crime charged suggests the legislature intended by the specific crime charged to cover young people otherwise generally exempted from criminal responsibility. A New York court, for example, held the state's infancy defense unavailable in a prosecution for an offense consisting of operation of a boat by a person under 18 years of age. *People v. Ullman*, 159 Misc.2d 548, 609 N.Y.S.2d 750 (1993).

State v. Linares

Court of Appeals of Washington, 1994
75 Wash.App. 404, 880 P.2d 550.

AGID, Judge.

Carlos Linares and Isaac Pam appeal their juvenile [court] convictions on the grounds that the court erred in * * * concluding that they were capable of committing the crimes with which they were charged.

* * *

RCW 9A.04.050 establishes a statutory presumption of incapacity where a child is between 8 and 12 years old. The statutory presumption of incapacity applies in juvenile proceedings. The State has the burden of rebutting the presumption of incapacity by clear and convincing evidence. The standard of review on appeal is whether there was evidence from which a rational trier of fact could find capacity by clear and convincing evidence

* * *

A. Linares

Linares was arrested after breaking into an elementary school with two other boys. He was 11 years old at the time. Officer David Sweeney, one of the arresting officers, read Linares his *Miranda* rights. Linares signed a form indicating that he understood and waived these rights and proceeded to give a statement to Sweeney admitting his involvement in the crime and acknowledging that the conduct was wrong. Linares was charged with, and ultimately found guilty of, burglary * * * and theft * * *.

At Linares' capacity hearing, Officer Sweeney testified that Linares admitted entering the school and taking a radio. He also testified that Linares made the following

statement: "I know what I did is wrong. Those things didn't belong to me. I wasn't supposed to be inside the school." Besides Sweeney's testimony, the court heard testimony from Linares, Yolanda Gonzales, Linares' teacher for 2 years, Jaynie Pleasants, a school psychologist, and James Matthews, one of Linares' former teachers. Gonzales testified that after the incident Linares told her

that he and a friend—a cousin and his brother had gone into a school. And I asked him why. And he said because they wanted to play inside; because it was raining outside, and they wanted to go in and play ball.

She also testified that Linares told her he knew what he had done was wrong and that he took responsibility for it. She explained that Linares understands rules, but not the consequences of breaking those rules. She also testified that Linares has learning disabilities and was receiving special education at the time.

Pleasants testified that she has observed and tested Linares in conjunction with his special education requirements. He was tested in February 1991; the results of those tests showed that his verbal IQ was in the low-average range and his performance IQ was slightly above the mean for his age.[9] She concluded that Linares "has a lot of

---

[9] Pleasants explained that verbal IQ relates to information learned through auditory processing and performance IQ relates to visual/spatial information.

difficulty processing and getting into long-term memory things". She also testified that, on a comprehension subtest designed to measure a child's understanding of cultural and social information, Linares scored below a 7-year-old level. Pleasants concluded that Linares may understand that "criminals . . . do wrong things," but he would not understand that they actually broke the law or what the consequences of doing so were. In her opinion, Linares did not have the capacity to understand the crimes with which he was charged.

Matthews was Linares' teacher when he was in the second grade and had seen him almost every day since at school. He described Linares as an "agreeable" person who "doesn't want to go against what the other kids are doing." He testified that the fact Linares is bilingual has made it harder for him to learn.

Linares testified at the capacity hearing. He was asked a series of questions by his attorney about his understanding of his rights and the criminal justice system. To each question asked he simply replied "no." The State asked only a few questions on cross examination. The trial court found that the State had met its burden of rebutting the statutory presumption of incapacity * * * because the * * * evidence was clear, cogent, and convincing that Linares had the capacity to understand it was wrong both to enter a locked school and to take things.

B. Pam

On May 26, 1991, the Renton police received a report that three boys were throwing rocks at an office building and breaking windows. One of the boys was Isaac Pam, who was 11 years old at the time. Officer Scott Phipps located the boys and read each boy his *Miranda* rights. Pam gave a statement to Phipps in which he admitted throwing rocks at the building. Pam was charged with, and ultimately found guilty of, malicious mischief * * *.

At Pam's capacity hearing, Officer Phipps testified that he asked Pam if he knew why he was being stopped. Pam replied that "he believed that it was in regards to . . . throwing rocks at a building." Phipps further testified that they

> first discussed who was throwing the rocks and how many rocks were thrown, and he had indicated that he had also thrown rocks at the same building the day before, on, I believe it was, the 25th, and had broken out some windows, both—both this day and the day before.
>
> When we finished discussing that, I asked him if he realized his actions were wrong; he stated that he did realize that. We talked about did he think he was going to get in trouble from his parents; he stated yeah, he was going to be in trouble, and he knew when he was

doing it that it was something that he could get in trouble for. I also—we discussed the fact that there are laws in our state, and did he realize that it was against the law to break windows, and he said that he did understand that.

Pam did not testify at the capacity hearing and the State did not present any witnesses besides Phipps.

Discussion

Linares argues that the State did not rebut the statutory presumption of incapacity because it did not establish that he appreciated the quality of his acts at the time he committed them or that he understood the consequences of his acts. He contends that the concept of wrongfulness as used in the context of a juvenile's capacity to commit a crime must include the requirement that the juvenile understand the basic legal prohibition against such action. He also argues that, although the evidence may have shown that he knew his actions were morally wrong, there was no evidence to show that he knew his actions were legally prohibited.

In addressing this issue, we find it instructive to refer to cases interpreting the insanity defense. Although not perfectly analogous, the insanity and infancy defenses have similar origins and functions in the criminal law. Both belong to a class of defenses that focus on the actor's lack of capacity to form the *mens rea* of a crime. If the actor lacks that capacity, he or she is legally incapable of committing the crime and for that reason is relieved of all criminal responsibility for the act.

The wording of the insanity statute is similar to that of the infancy statute and the case law interpreting the former assists us in our analysis of the latter. * * * Apart from the requirement under the insanity defense that an actor suffer from a mental disease or defect, the differences between the statutes are procedural rather than substantive. * * * We interpret the requirement * * * that a child "know [the act or neglect] was wrong" to have essentially the same meaning as the requirement [in the insanity standard] that a defendant be "unable to tell right from wrong with reference to the particular act charged."

* *˙ *

Capacity determinations, by their nature, are fact-specific inquiries and must be determined on a case by case basis. In addition to the nature of the crime, the following factors are relevant in determining whether a child knew the act he or she was committing was wrong: (1) whether the child evinced a desire for secrecy, (2) the child's age, (3) prior conduct similar to that charged, (4) any consequences that attached to that conduct, and (5) acknowledgment that the behavior is wrong and could lead to detention.

We conclude that there was sufficient evidence presented

in Linares' case to enable a rational trier of fact to find capacity by clear and convincing evidence. In addition to Linares' statement to Officer Sweeney, the court considered his statement to Gonzales and the testimony of Linares' teachers and a school psychologist regarding his level of maturity and intellectual development. Although some of these witnesses felt Linares did not understand the legal prohibitions against his acts, none testified that he did not understand that his conduct was wrong. The court was also able to observe Linares' demeanor when he took the stand at the hearing. Linares' conduct during and after the break-in is also highly probative in establishing that he appreciated the wrongfulness of his conduct.[14] The finding of capacity is further supported by the fact that Linares was 11 years old at the time of the incident, the upper end of the age range in which a child is presumed incapable of committing a crime.

The State did not meet its burden in Pam's case. Apart from the fact that Pam was 11 years old at the time of the incident, there was no other evidence presented at the hearing besides his custodial statement on which the court could have based its capacity finding. Pam did not testify at the hearing, and the court did not have an opportunity to observe his demeanor. The court did not hear testimony from any other witness besides Officer Phipps. Although in his statement to Phipps following the incident Pam acknowledged that his actions were wrong, that is insufficient evidence from which a rational trier of fact could have concluded that Pam appreciated the wrongfulness of his act at the time it was committed.

* * * [O]nce the children were separated and given *Miranda* warnings it must have been obvious to Pam that he had done something wrong. Furthermore, when the police showed up, the children did not try to hide what they had done, lie, or otherwise evidence a desire for secrecy. Nor had they suffered any consequences from the similar behavior the day before, acts which Pam readily admitted. We hold that a child's after-the-fact acknowledgment that he or she understood that the conduct was wrong is insufficient, standing alone, to overcome the presumption of incapacity by clear and convincing evidence.

The disposition in *Linares* is affirmed and the disposition in *Pam* is reversed.

Note

Traditionally, criminal defendants charged with rape could invoke a specific defensive matter based on their age. The

Massachusetts Supreme Judicial Court explained in *Commonwealth v. Walter R.*, 414 Mass. 714, 610 N.E.2d 323 (1993):

> Under English common law, a child under fourteen years of age was conclusively presumed incapable of committing rape. Although the exact origin of the presumption is not clearly established, various courts have identified two rationales. The most commonly cited rationale is that young males in pre-industrial England usually did not reach puberty until the age of fourteen and therefore were not sexually able to engage in natural intercourse prior to that chronological age. The other rationale * * * is that the presumption was created to protect young males from the penalty mandated for rape at common law: death.
>
> Most American jurisdictions have rejected the conclusive presumption and adopted instead a rebuttable presumption. Evidence that the juvenile has reached puberty may rebut the presumption in these jurisdictions.

In *Walter R.*, the Massachusetts court for the first time addressed whether to adopt the common law approach and declined to do so even for delinquency proceedings in juvenile court:

> We conclude that there is no sound legal or medical basis for a presumption that an individual under fourteen is incapable of rape, as defined at common law. Whatever basis the original justifications for the presumption once had, they are inapplicable today.
>
> The rationale * * * that the presumption was created to protect youthful offenders from the harshness of the death penalty, no longer carries any weight in Massachusetts. First, the crime of rape is not punishable by death. Second, the Commonwealth employs a system for dealing with youthful offenders which affords them greater protections than the adults have under the traditional system.
>
> To the extent the common law presumption rested on an assumption that males under the age of fourteen were not sexually mature, current medical information suggests otherwise. Over the past century, the onset of puberty has gradually occurred at a younger age, and currently begins between the ages of ten and twelve. See S.R. Ambron & N.J. Salkind, Child Development 468 (4th ed. 1984).

Because, as addressed in Chapter 9, under modern law rape or its equivalent can generally be committed by means other than penile penetration, a rule based on the presumed capacity to accomplish penile penetration is particularly inappropriate. Of course, in a criminal prosecution

---

[14] Upon seeing police, Linares dropped a radio he was carrying. At the police station he lied to Sweeney, claiming that stolen items found on his person were his belongings.

for rape alleged to have occurred by penile penetration the prosecution must show that the accused in fact so penetrated the victim and this necessarily involves a showing that the defendant was physically capable of performing that

act. Evidence that the defendant did so penetrate the victim permits a conclusion that he was capable of doing so, and the evidence need not in any direct way address separately the question of capacity.

B. INTOXICATION

Editors' Introduction: Intoxication, Criminal Liability, and the Constitutionality of Barring Criminal Defendants from Defensive Reliance upon Exculpatory Evidence

Criminal law's treatment of intoxication reflects considerable ambivalence regarding the significance of intoxication in evaluating the blameworthiness of an offender's conduct and, to the extent that intoxication might be exculpatory, the best manner of giving this effect.

Most of the controversy regarding intoxication revolves around what is characterized as "voluntary" intoxication. This must be distinguished from involuntary intoxication and the effect of a "settled condition" brought about by the use of intoxicants; these are discussed in the Editors' Note following the decision reprinted in this section. The definition of involuntary intoxication discussed there makes clear that voluntary intoxication is any intoxication resulting from a person's voluntary consumption of a substance that the person knows is intoxicating, in the absence of actual duress. It is not limited to intoxication resulting from a person's conscious decision to become intoxicated. Thus, a person who voluntarily consumes a known intoxicant and becomes intoxicated is treated as voluntarily intoxicated even if that person intended to limit consumption to a sufficiently limited amount of the substance to avoid intoxication.

In *Montana v. Egelhoff*, 518 U.S. 37, 116 S.Ct 2013, 135 L.Ed.2d 361 (1996), Justice Scalia's plurality opinion (analyzed in more detail later in this introduction) traced the development of American voluntary intoxication law:

> By the laws of England, wrote Hale, the intoxicated defendant "shall have no privilege by this voluntarily contracted madness, but shall have the same judgment as if he were in his right senses." 1 M. Hale, Pleas of the Crown *32–33. According to Blackstone and Coke, the law's condemnation of those suffering from *dementia affectata* was harsher still: Blackstone, citing Coke, explained that the law viewed intoxication "as an aggravation of an offense, rather than an excuse for any criminal misbehaviour." 4 W. Blackstone, Commentaries *25–26. This stern rejection of inebriation as a defense became a fixture of American law as well. * * *
>
> * * * Over the course of the 19th century, courts carved out an exception to the common-law's traditional across-the-board condemnation of the drunken offender, allowing a jury to consider a defendant's intoxication when assessing whether he possessed the mental state needed to commit the crime charged, where the crime was one requiring "specific intent." * * * This exception was "slow to take root, * * * even in England. * * * Eventually, however, the new

view won out, and by the end of the 19th century, in most American jurisdictions, intoxication could be considered in determining whether a defendant was capable of forming the specific intent necessary to commit the crime charged.

As Justice Scalia indicated, at early common law voluntary intoxication was never a defense in the sense that it permitted or required the acquittal of a criminal defendant whose guilt was established. Under at least "new" common law, however, evidence of voluntary intoxication was admissible and could be relied upon by a defendant charged with a crime requiring "specific intent," to show that he or she was incapable of forming that culpable mental state or, perhaps, simply did not have that mental state. If the crime charged required only "general intent," on the other hand, the accused's voluntary intoxication was of no defensive significance whatsoever.

American jurisdictions have often followed the new common law rule, although determining what culpable mental states are "specific intents" has proven to be a difficult task. The difficulty presented by the term specific intent was discussed in detail in the Editors' Introduction to Section A of Chapter 14. When statutory frameworks were revised following the Model Penal Code approach, jurisdictions sometimes followed that model's recommendation formulated in section 2.08 of the Code, reprinted in this section.

The Model Penal Code's basic approach to defining culpable mental state requirements renders meaningless the traditional distinction between general and specific intents, and section 2.08 thus makes no effort to limit defendants' use of intoxication to such specific intent crimes. Rather, it proposes to limit defendants' use of intoxication according to the level of the culpable mental state required, as the "level" dimension of states of mind is defined in the Editors' Introduction to Part A of Chapter 4. A defendant can rely upon evidence of voluntary intoxication in an effort to persuade the jury that the prosecution has failed to prove he or she acted with the culpable mental state required by the crime if, but only if, the culpable mental state at issue requires either purpose or knowledge. If the culpable mental state requires only recklessness (or negligence), on the other hand, a defendant cannot rely on evidence of voluntary intoxication for this purpose even if that evidence seems logically to show that he or she did not act with the required recklessness.

Legislatures as well as courts, however, have been increasingly reluctant to authorize exculpatory significance to be given to voluntary intoxication. Some post-Model Penal Code statutes consequently limited the permissible use of evidence of voluntary intoxication even more than section 2.08. The Alaska legislature, for example, has provided:

> Sec. 11.81.630. Intoxication as a defense.
>
> Voluntary intoxication is not a defense to a prosecution for an offense, but evidence that the defendant was intoxicated may be offered whenever it is relevant to negate an element of the offense that requires that the defendant intentionally cause a result.

Other jurisdictions have barred criminal defendants from relying on voluntary intoxication either as a "defense" or to negate *any* culpable mental state. In 1881, for example, the Texas legislature provided that "[n]either intoxication, nor temporary insanity of mind produced by the voluntary recent use of ardent spirits, shall constitute any excuse in this State for the commission of crime, nor shall intoxication mitigate either the degree or penalty of crime * * *." In *Evers v. State*, 20 S.W. 744, 746 (Tex.Crim.App.1892), the Texas court indicated that the statute was a response to a case in which Porter, "a traveling actor," was shot down without provocation and his killer acquitted on grounds of temporary insanity caused by drunkenness.

The rationales for these restrictive approaches to intoxication have been discussed at some length by the courts. In *Bieber v. State*, 856 P.2d 811 (Col.1993), cert. denied, 510 U.S. 1054, 114 S.Ct. 716, 126 L.Ed.2d 680 (1994), for example, the Colorado Supreme Court explained:

> [U]nderlying the intoxication statute [limiting the defense of intoxication to the negation of *mens rea* in specific intent crimes], we have found strong policy concerns * * *. In *People v. DelGuidice*, 199 Colo. 41, 46, 606 P.2d 840, 844 (1980) [holding that a second degree murder defendant charged with "knowingly" killing the victim could not rely on voluntary intoxication to challenge that he acted "knowingly"], we stated that:
>
> > The Colorado common law and statutory rule which makes evidence of voluntary intoxication incompetent to disprove general intent when that mental state is an element of a criminal charge is supported by weighty policy choices about the extent to which drunkenness can excuse criminal responsibility.
>
> We addressed those policy choices more specifically in *Hendershott v. People*, 653 P.2d 385, 396 (Colo.1982), as follows:
>
> > The concept of self-induced intoxication, by definition, requires that the defendant be aware at the outset that the substance he is about to ingest may affect his mental faculties. It is a matter of common knowledge that the excessive use of liquor or drugs impairs the perceptual, judgmental and volitional faculties of the user. Also, because the intoxication must be "self-induced," the defendant necessarily must have had the conscious ability to prevent this temporary incapacity from coming into being at all. Self-induced intoxication, therefore, by its very nature involves a degree of moral culpability. The moral blameworthiness lies in the voluntary impairment of one's mental faculties with knowledge that the resulting condition is a source of potential danger to others . . . . It is this blameworthiness that serves as the basis for *DelGuidice*'s rule of exclusion. Thus, when a defendant chooses to knowingly introduce intoxicants into his body to the point of becoming temporarily impaired in his powers of perception, judgment and control, the policy enunciated in *DelGuidice* prohibits him from utilizing his intoxication as a defense to crimes requiring the *mens rea* of "knowingly," "willfully," "recklessly" or "with criminal negligence." * * * (Citation and footnotes omitted).

Limitations upon defendants' ability to rely on evidence of intoxication raise constitutional considerations. An Indiana statute purported to limit the exculpatory effect of voluntary intoxication by providing that such intoxication "is a defense only to the extent that it negates an element of the offense referred to by the phrase 'with intent to' or 'with an intention to.'" Ind. Code § 35-41-3-5(b). In *Terry v. State*, 465 N.E.2d 1085 (Ind.1984), the Indiana Supreme Court held the statute ineffective, apparently on constitutional grounds:

> Any factor which serves as a denial of the existence of *mens rea* must be considered by a trier of fact before a guilty finding is entered. Historically, facts such as age, mental condition, mistake or intoxication have been offered to negate the capacity to formulate intent. The attempt by the legislature to remove the factor of voluntary intoxication, except in limited situations, goes against this firmly ingrained principle. We thus hold Ind.Code § 35-41-3-5(b) is void and without effect.

Most courts, in contrast, have been quite receptive to legislative efforts to limit the exculpatory significance of voluntary intoxication. In *DelGuidice*, the Colorado Supreme Court upheld application of that state's statute to a second degree murder defendant over an attack based on due process. More recently, the Hawaii Supreme Court upheld application of the Hawaii statute in a prosecution for attempted murder. *State v. Souza*, 72 Haw. 246, 813 P.2d 1384 (1991).

The United States Supreme Court finally addressed the federal constitutional question in *Montana v. Egelhoff*, 518 U.S. 37, 116 S.Ct 2013, 135 L.Ed.2d 351 (1996). Egelhoff had been prosecuted for what Montana law called deliberate homicide, a crime requiring that the accused have purposefully or knowingly caused the death of another human being. Evidence at trial indicated that he was found in a car with the bodies of the two victims and that an hour after his discovery his blood-alcohol content was .36 percent. Pursuant to the Montana statute, the jury was instructed that it could not consider his intoxicated condition in determining whether he acted purposefully or knowingly as required by the crime charged. He argued that evidence of intoxication was logically relevant to whether the prosecution had proved the culpable mental state required and that due process was violated by his inability to rely on this relevant evidence. The Montana Supreme Court had held that the Montana statute deprived Egelhoff of due process.

The United States Supreme Court reversed but no single explanation received a majority vote of the nine justices. Five opinions were filed in the case, but none received the five votes necessary to make an opinion that of the Supreme Court. Further, the justices split on several complicated and interrelated issues regarding the content of due process, the effect of the Montana statute on Montana criminal law, and the United States Supreme Court's authority to ignore the Montana courts' characterization of Montana law. The detailed differences among the justices in *Egelhoff* go far beyond what is necessary to understand the substantive criminal law governing the defensive significance of voluntary intoxication. However, those differences do help to make clear the complexity of the basic policy judgments involved and the difficulty of developing from *Egelhoff* or other authority an appropriate federal constitutional standard for determining when a state's limits on criminal defendants exceed what should be regarded as within the state's prerogative.

The plurality *Egelhoff* opinion written by Justice Scalia and joined by three other members of the Court[a] did not attempt a comprehensive consideration of the extent to which due process entitles a criminal defendant to rely on evidence logically relevant to whether the prosecution has proven his or her guilt of the crime charged. A defendant seeking to establish a federal constitutional right to rely on such evidence, Justice Scalia stressed, has the "unusually heavy burden" of establishing that the right to have the jury consider the evidence at issue is a "fundamental principle of justice" so as to be part of the federal guarantee of due process. In determining whether the principle asserted by Egelhoff—that the defendant is entitled to have a jury consider logically relevant evidence of intoxication in determining whether he or she had the required mental state—is such a fundamental principle of justice, historical practice is the "primary guide." By the end of the 19th century, the majority of American jurisdictions permitted intoxication to be considered in determining whether a criminal defendant was capable of forming the specific intent required by a charged criminal offense. However, Justice Scalia noted, the original common law position was to the contrary and "fully one-fifth of the States either never adopted the 'new common-law' rule * * * or have recently abandoned it." He concluded:

> Although the rule allowing a jury to consider evidence of a defendant's voluntary intoxication where relevant to *mens rea* has gained considerable acceptance, it is of too recent vintage, and has not received sufficiently uniform and permanent allegiance to qualify as fundamental, especially since it displaces a lengthy common-law tradition which remains supported by valid justifications today.

Because the rule is not fundamental, it is not a part of due process. Montana's application to Egelhoff of its restrictive approach, therefore, did not violate Egelhoff's federal constitutional due process right.

Justice O'Connor, writing for herself and three other dissenters, argued that federal constitutional due process "demands that a criminal defendant be afforded a fair opportunity to defend against the State's accusations." This means, she reasoned, that a defendant like Egelhoff cannot be prevented from presenting—and presumably having the jury consider—"relevant, probative evidence." Montana law treats evidence of voluntary intoxication as relevant to criminal defendant's subjective mental states but bars juries from considering it "for the express purpose of improving the State's likelihood of winning a conviction against a certain type of defendant." This, she concluded, violates due process.

Justice O'Connor conceded that a state such as Montana has authority to define crimes—and the culpable mental states required by specific crimes, in particular—so that voluntary intoxication is not logically relevant to whether they are committed. She read the *Egelhoff* opinion of the Montana Supreme Court as reaching two distinct conclusions. First, it construed the statute as leaving the culpable mental states of deliberate homicide and other Montana crimes such that evidence of intoxication is

---

[a] The significance of a plurality opinion is addressed in an editors' footnote to the discussion of *Powell v. Texas* in Chapter 3.

logically relevant to whether the mental states existed. Second, the Montana court's opinion held that the statutes barred defendants from relying on this concededly relevant evidence. Because the interpretation of state law is a matter within the exclusive authority of the state courts, Justice O'Connor noted, the United States Supreme Court is without authority to conclude that the Montana Supreme Court misinterpreted Montana substantive criminal law. Therefore, she reasoned, the Montana statute as construed by the Montana courts bars defendants from relying on evidence logically relevant to their guilt or innocence as defined by state law and thus violates what she construed as the requirements of due process.

The fifth—and "swing"—vote to reverse the Montana court's holding that the Montana statute as applied to Egelhoff violated his due process rights was that of Justice Ginsburg. She appeared to agree with the dissenters that the case turned largely on whether the Montana statute redefined the culpable mental states required for Montana crimes or rather barred defendants from relying on evidence relevant to those mental states. The Montana statute *could* be construed as redefining the culpable mental state required by deliberate homicide and other offenses, she reasoned. Because that interpretation would save its constitutionality, she adopted it. She did not address the dissenters' position that the Montana courts had construed the statute differently and the United States Supreme Court was required to simply accept this characterization of state law by a state court.

The significance of the various opinions is further complicated by Justice Scalia's footnote comment that the plurality did not find Justice Ginsburg's approach necessary. Montana could implement its policy judgment to hold intoxicated persons fully responsible, he suggested, in either of two ways. First, it could define the substantive requirements of particular crimes so as to make intoxication irrelevant to whether they were committed. Second, it could accomplish the same result by leaving the culpable mental states defined as unqualifiedly requiring particular subjective awareness— as, for example, a purpose to cause death or knowledge that death would result—but barring defendants from relying upon logically relevant evidence of intoxication to counter the prosecution's evidence that the defendants acted with those culpable mental states. Either approach was permissible, the plurality concluded, so there was no need to determine which approach Montana had taken.

Justice Ginsburg's refusal to join Justice Scalia's plurality opinion is probably significant only if Justice Ginsburg might find other statutory provisions relating to intoxication too clearly barring defendants from relying on evidence that the state's definitions of crimes makes relevant to those crimes' culpable mental states. If she were to find a state statute to be one of this sort, her *Egelhoff* opinion suggests that she might join the *Egelhoff* dissenters and thus create a majority of five justices to hold that such an approach violated due process. Her refusal to read the Montana statute as doing this, however, indicates that she is quite unlikely to find any other statutory provision to be one of this sort.

A state substantive law rule might bar a defendant from relying on evidence logically suggesting he lacked a required culpable mental state but in a manner not condoned by a "lengthy common-law tradition." Such a rule might nevertheless be within due process limits because sound policy considerations supported the legislative decision to bar such evidence from criminal trials. *Egelhoff*, does not, of course, resolve this. Justice Scalia's plurality opinion strongly suggested that the four justices joining that opinion would have been willing, had the historical argument not been so clearly determinative, to uphold the Montana approach as based on sufficiently strong policy grounds as to justify it:

> It is not surprising that many States have held fast to or resurrected the common-law rule prohibiting consideration of voluntary intoxication in the determination of *mens rea*, because that rule has considerable justification—which alone casts doubt upon the proposition that the opposite rule is a "fundamental principle." A large number of crimes, especially violent crimes, are committed by intoxicated offenders; modern studies put the numbers as high as half of all homicides, for example. Disallowing consideration of voluntary intoxication has the effect of increasing the punishment for all unlawful acts committed in that state, and thereby deters drunkenness or irresponsible behavior while drunk. The rule also serves as a specific deterrent, ensuring that those who prove incapable of controlling violent impulses while voluntarily intoxicated go to prison. And finally, the rule comports with and implements society's moral perception that one who has voluntarily impaired his own faculties should be responsible for the consequences.
>
> There is, in modern times, even more justification for [such] laws * * * than there used to be. Some recent studies suggest that the connection between drunkenness and crime is as much cultural as pharmacological—that is, that drunks are violent not simply because alcohol makes them that way, but because they are behaving in accord with their learned belief that drunks are violent. See, e.g., Collins, Suggested Explanatory Frameworks to Clarify the Alcohol Use/Violence Relationship, 15 Contemp. Drug Prob. 107, 115 (1988); Critchlow, The Powers of John Barleycorn, 41 Am. Psychologist 751, 754–755 (July 1986). This not only adds additional support to the traditional view that an intoxicated criminal is not deserving of exoneration, but it suggests that juries—who possess the same learned belief as the intoxicated offender—will be too quick to accept the claim that the defendant was biologically incapable of forming the requisite *mens rea*. Treating the matter as one of excluding misleading evidence therefore makes some sense.

The *Egelhoff* plurality, then, seemed to acknowledge that the Montana rule may mean that a few defendants might be unjustly convicted because they were found guilty, although in fact and because of voluntary intoxication they did not act with the required culpable mental state. The plurality regarded this cost as acceptable, however, because the rule excluding consideration of intoxication accomplishes other and important objectives. It facilitates imprisoning and thus incapacitating dangerous (although not culpable) persons. It also may prevent juries from being confused and misled by inaccurate but superficially credible claims by defendants that because of their intoxication they acted without the required culpable mental state.

Egelhoff underlines the difficulty of formulating appropriate constitutional standards for determining legislatures' authority to create criminal liability without a culpable mental state and to limit defendants' ability to rely on particular kinds of evidence to challenge the prosecution's proof of whatever culpable mental states are required. This was explored to some extent in Chapter 10; some of the issues raised in that chapter may be affected by *Egelhoff*.

If Montana could bar Egelhoff from relying upon voluntary intoxication to challenge the prosecution's contention that he killed his victims purposefully or knowingly, arguably New Jersey may bar the defendant in *Wilson v. Tard*, reprinted at page 396, from relying on an unreasonable mistake of fact to challenge the prosecution's contention that he killed his victim with recklessness. Justice Ginsburg, for example, might argue that the New Jersey mistake of fact statute requiring a mistake of fact to be reasonable amounts to an implicit and indirect reformulation of the culpable mental states such as recklessness.

Despite *Egelhoff*, a majority of American jurisdictions do permit defendants to rely on evidence of voluntary intoxication in challenging the prosecution's proof that they acted with the culpable mental state required by at least some crimes. At least some states, however, might well respond to the result in *Egelhoff* by restricting defendants' ability to use voluntary intoxication in a defensive manner.

How do judges and juries actually respond to defendants' efforts to offer intoxication evidence as negating a required culpable mental state? Despite concerns that juries might be misled by false claims that intoxication prevented defendants from forming required mental states, conventional wisdom among lawyers is that criminal defendants usually face a difficult task in persuading juries that voluntary intoxication evidence raises a reasonable doubt as to whether those defendants acted with required culpable mental states. Jurors may often be persuaded that defendants' contentions are simply not believable. Or they may be persuaded to ignore the formal law and convict defendants even if the defense evidence raises such a doubt as to whether the defendants acted with the theoretically necessary *mens rea*. Juries, at least in some cases, may be receptive to the reasoning that the fault involved in becoming intoxicated is an adequate and appropriate substitute for the *mens rea* the law demands to assure blameworthiness.

The principal case that follows was litigated under the broad Indiana rule resulting from *Terry*, holding—as discussed earlier in this introduction—that the legislature lacked power to limit those mental states defendants could negate with evidence of voluntary intoxication. Thus, it reflects application of an approach permitting evidence of voluntary intoxication to be used to negate *any* mental element required by the crime charged. In *Terry* itself the Indiana Supreme Court commented that its holding—expanding defendants' ability to defensively use evidence of intoxication—might not be as prodefendant as might appear:

> The potential of this defense should not be confused with the reality of the situation. It is difficult to envision a finding of not guilty by reason of intoxication when the acts committed require a significant degree of physical or intellectual skills. As a general proposition, a defendant should not be relieved of responsibility when he was able to devise a plan, operate equipment, instruct the behavior of others or carry out acts requiring physical skill.

The decision reprinted in this subsection reflects unusually vigorous scrutiny by an appellate court of a jury's decision to reject such a contention. If the jury in the reprinted case was willing to reject the intoxication defense found so credible by the appellate majority, perhaps a rule permitting defendants to rely on voluntary intoxication is unrealistic because it will simply not be accepted by juries.

The reprinted case also provides an opportunity to consider how cases should be handled under the restrictive approach taken by Montana and left enforceable by the vote of the United States Supreme Court in *Egelhoff*. Suppose the reprinted case was tried under the Montana attempted murder statute and the jury was instructed, as it was in *Egelhoff*, that the defendant's intoxication was not to be considered in determining whether he acted with the required culpable mental state. Suppose further the jurors returned after some deliberation and informed the judge that they were convinced on the basis of the intoxication evidence that Wilson had not acted with intent to kill. They added, however, that they were confused as to how to proceed because they had also been told that they should convict only if they found the prosecution had proved intent to kill. Could a reasonable and helpful instruction be developed to help the jurors with their conceptual problem?

In *Egelhoff*, Justice Ginsburg, quoting from briefs in the case, offered the following interpretive summary of Montana law:

> [I]n a prosecution for deliberate homicide, the State need not prove that the defendant "purposefully or knowingly cause[d] the death of another" in a purely subjective sense. To obtain a conviction, the prosecution must prove only that (1) the defendant caused the death of another with actual knowledge or purpose, *or* (2) that the defendant killed "under circumstances that would otherwise establish knowledge or purpose 'but for' [the defendant's] voluntary intoxication."

If (2) in fact reflects what the law asks the jurors to consider, perhaps regardless of whatever is or is not constitutionally required, fairness to the jurors requires the law to tell them this explicitly and as clearly as possible.

Weaver v. State

Court of Appeals of Indiana, 1994
627 N.E.2d 1311.

SHIELDS, Judge.

Jordan Weaver appeals his convictions of attempted murder, a class A felony; confinement, a class B felony; battery, a class C felony; two counts of battery, a class A misdemeanor; resisting law enforcement, a class A misdemeanor; and criminal mischief, a class A misdemeanor. We affirm in part and reverse in part.

ISSUES

Weaver raises * * for our review * * * [whether] * * * the evidence [is] sufficient to support Weaver's conviction of attempted murder?

* * *

FACTS

On the afternoon of April 2, 1991, Jordan Weaver took two "hits" of LSD. Weaver was feeling the effects of the drug very heavily when his girlfriend, Wendy Waldman, picked him up at a friend's house later that day. During the evening, Wendy and Weaver met some acquaintances of theirs, Kurt Steigerwald, Kris Hettle, Jessica Godley, and Tracie Glanzman. Wendy told the group she was worried about Weaver because he was "tripping" on LSD and was acting very oddly. The group decided to take Weaver to a secluded place, the Alverna Retreat, to keep him out of trouble.

Once at the Retreat, Weaver's behavior was very erratic. He began arguing with Wendy when she tried to get him to sit down. He wrestled with Kurt, kissed or licked his neck, and bit Wendy's finger when she tried to separate the two of them. Weaver kissed Jessica and then tried to strangle her, calling her Wendy. Kurt hit Weaver with a tire jack, and then Kris put him in a choke hold to get him away from Jessica. The group unsuccessfully tried to restrain Weaver and lock him in the trunk of the car to take him to the hospital, and even considered hitting him with the car in order to stop him. Weaver then attacked Wendy, repeatedly slamming her head into the pavement and kicking her; the rest of the group drove away to get help.

As he tried to drive away from the Retreat, Weaver crashed Wendy's car, turning it over on its side. He then made his way to a nearby neighborhood and jumped through the closed bay window of the house owned by Barbara and Michael Blickman. Mr. Blickman hit Weaver over the head with a chair and then with a chair leg; a scuffle then ensued between Weaver and the Blickmans which progressed out into the Blickmans' driveway. The police arrived and, after a struggle, placed Weaver under arrest.

* * *

Weaver argues the evidence is insufficient to sustain his conviction of the attempted murder of Wendy Waldman. Specifically, Weaver argues that the State failed to disprove his defense of voluntary intoxication. We agree.

Ind.Code 35-41-3-5 (1988) provides that voluntary intoxication is a defense only to the extent that it negates the intent element of an offense, in this case the intent to murder Wendy. The defendant has the burden of establishing a factual predicate for the defense of voluntary intoxication. Specifically, Weaver had the burden of presenting evidence of intoxication "that, if believed, is such that, [sic] it could create a reasonable doubt in the mind of a rational trier of fact that the accused entertained the requisite specific intent." Here, Weaver clearly met this burden, as there is ample evidence that, at the time he assaulted Wendy, Weaver was extremely intoxicated from the two hits of LSD

he had taken earlier that day and that he had exhibited erratic behavior over the course of the evening. Thus, the State had the burden of establishing beyond a reasonable doubt that the defendant was not so intoxicated as to negate his ability to form the required intent. Whether the State has met that burden is a question of fact for the jury, and, as with any sufficiency question, we will uphold the jury's determination if there is evidence of probative value from which a reasonable trier of fact could infer beyond a reasonable doubt that Weaver was not too intoxicated to form the intent to murder Wendy.

In order to determine whether the jury could reasonably have found that Weaver had the intent to commit murder when he attacked Wendy, we must look at the evidence of Weaver's behavior just before, during, and just after the attack. We will examine this evidence in light of the general proposition that "a defendant should not be relieved of responsibility when he was able to devise a plan, operate equipment, instruct the behavior of others or carry out acts requiring physical skill." *Terry v. State* (1984), Ind., 465 N.E.2d 1085, 1089.

The record contains uncontroverted evidence that Weaver took two "hits" of "thick" LSD[1] in the afternoon of April 2, 1991, and was experiencing an "extreme trip" by the time Wendy picked him up that evening. In fact, the effect of the LSD was so strong that he told Wendy he did not think he was able to go out with her that evening. Weaver nevertheless went to a restaurant with Wendy. Once there, Weaver was incapable of reading the menu and ordering; instead, he gave the waitress money before either he or Wendy had ordered, then said he was not hungry, prompting Wendy to "make up an excuse to get out" of the restaurant. A short time later, Wendy and Weaver met up with Kurt Steigerwald, Kris Hettle, Jessica Godley, and Tracie Glanzman. Kurt described Weaver's appearance at that time as follows: "he looked pretty dazed out, he didn't act normal . . . it didn't seem to me that he had any idea what was really going on." The group decided to take Weaver to the Alverna Retreat because he "was not in the right state of mind and we really didn't want him to get in trouble. . . . We basically wanted somewhere away from people, kind of quiet, for his own protection."

Once at the Retreat, Weaver refused to sit down with the others and began arguing with Kurt and Wendy. He then "came over and basically laid on top of" Kurt, and

---

[1] The record indicates that LSD is sold in doses, called "hits," which consist of small squares of paper dipped in LSD. The LSD Weaver took on the day in question was "tripple dipped" and "thicker" than usual, meaning that each "hit" contained more LSD than a normal "hit" would.

began kissing or licking Kurt's neck. When Wendy tried to help Kurt, Weaver bit her fingers; Kris, Kurt, and Weaver then struggled on the ground, with Weaver finally hitting Kurt in the eye. Weaver then got into Kurt's car next to Jessica, whom he kissed. He then began choking Jessica, calling her Wendy and threatening to kill her. Kris and Kurt hit him twice on the head with a tire jack in order to stop him, but this had no effect on Weaver. Kris and Kurt finally got Weaver off of Jessica by putting him in a choke hold and throwing a blanket over him.

At this point, the group decided to take Weaver to the hospital because they thought he was "overdosing." They tried to restrain him by locking him in the trunk of the car; however, they were unsuccessful. In fact, Weaver was in such a frenzy that they considered hitting him with the car to stop him. However, before they could restrain him, he attacked Wendy. After the attack, he apparently tried to drive away from the Retreat in Wendy's car, which had been left running by the others. However, he went only a short distance before hitting a bush and overturning the car; it appears that he then got out of the wrecked car by kicking through the windshield. Weaver somehow made his way on foot to a nearby neighborhood, where he jumped through a closed window into the home of Michael and Barbara Blickman. Once inside, Weaver walked toward Mr. Blickman, who hit him over the head with a chair and then tackled him to the floor. As the two men struggled on the floor, Mrs. Blickman hit Weaver in the back with a chair leg; Weaver shouted obscenities at Mrs. Blickman. The struggle finally ended outside on the Blickmans' driveway, where Weaver was arrested by police officers who had been called to the scene.

Dr. Michael Evans, a toxicologist who interviewed Weaver regarding his experiences on the night in question, testified that, based on his conversation with Weaver, Weaver was experiencing "a bad trip, [an] acute psychotic reaction." Dr. Evans testified that during a "bad trip"

> the person begins to lose contact with reality and in a sense of not only seeing these things [hallucinations], but they can't distinguish reality from what they're seeing and envisioning. It no longer becomes a trip. They no longer are observing it, they are part of it. . . . [Y]ou lose sense of reality. It alters your perception so much that you lose reality.

"The basic presupposition upon which the [voluntary intoxication] defense rests is that intoxication can be so severe as to render a person incapable of forming or entertaining the criminal intent required to commit a crime, yet not so severe as to render such person incapable of the conduct required to commit the crime." *Street v. State* (1991), Ind., 567 N.E.2d 102, 104. Thus, the fact that Weaver was

physically able to attack Wendy, somehow get from the Alverna Retreat to the Blickmans' neighborhood, and struggle with the Blickmans is simply not sufficient evidence to disprove his intoxication defense, which involves the question of mental incapacitation because of intoxication. We see nothing in the evidence of record from which a jury could reasonably find that Weaver was capable of forming the intent to kill when he attacked Wendy. For example, there is no evidence that Weaver committed any acts of "physical dexterity and mental calculation" similar to those which have been found sufficient to disprove the defense of voluntary intoxication in other cases. See, e.g., *Gregory v. State* (1989), Ind., 540 N.E.2d 585, 594 (defendant got ladder from garage, climbed up to his mother's bedroom window, unlatched window, climbed in and stabbed his mother); *Gibson v. State* (1987), Ind., 516 N.E.2d 31, 33 (defendant denied taking part in robbery, left stolen goods behind in an abandoned house, and tried to escape); *Boze v. State* (1987), Ind., 514 N.E.2d 275, 279 (defendant pulled out a knife, threatened police officer, ran through woods and hurdled a fallen tree in attempt to escape). In each of these cases, there was evidence from which the jury reasonably found that the defendant formed a plan of action and carried it out; there is no such evidence here.

There is no doubt that Weaver was acting under the influence of LSD, and none of his actions indicate that he was able to devise a plan, operate equipment, instruct the behavior of others or carry out acts requiring physical skill. Further, we are obligated to honor the legislature's judgment that voluntary intoxication ought to relieve a defendant from criminal liability under certain circumstances, that is, when the defendant's intoxication prohibits him from forming the requisite *mens rea*. Our review of the facts of this case has convinced us that if the defense of voluntary intoxication does not apply as a matter of law here, it is an illusory defense.

The State failed to carry its burden of disproving Weaver's voluntary intoxication defense, and his conviction of attempted murder must be reversed.

* * *

Judgment of conviction of attempted murder reversed; in all other things, the judgment is affirmed.

SULLIVAN, J., concurs.

SHARPNACK, Chief Judge, * * * dissenting.
* * * I respectfully dissent as to the resolution of the issue of the defense of voluntary intoxication, upon which the majority reverses. Two aspects of the majority's treatment of this issue trouble me. First, I believe the majority depreciates the jury's determinative role in evaluating the facts on this issue. Second, I question the majority's use of the standard

formulated in *Terry v. State* for determining when a defendant may not be relieved of responsibility for his acts.

At the outset, I recognize that this is a very difficult case to consider and that there is an abundance of evidence to support the conclusion that Weaver was under the influence of LSD during the time that the material events occurred. I also agree with the majority analysis of the applicability of the defense of voluntary intoxication * * *. However, where the majority finds "nothing in the evidence of record from which a jury could reasonably find that Weaver was capable of forming the intent to kill when he attacked Wendy," I must disagree. I believe that the majority has inadvertently reweighed the evidence and, in the process, has discounted the evidence and inferences that reasonably could be drawn therefrom and from which the jury could have (and did) conclude that Weaver not only had the capacity to form the intent to kill Wendy but acted with that intent in his attack on her.

Without rehashing the evidence at length, it is clear that the evidence demonstrated that Weaver was able to walk without difficulty; was able to respond (albeit poorly) to threats, cajoling, and physical attacks; was able to get into the back seat of a car and attempt to throttle a girl in spite of being under attack at the time; was able to lift Wendy and hurl her to the ground, to kick her, and to bang her head on the ground; was able to get into Wendy's car and operate it in leaving the scene of his attack on her; was able, after the car overturned, to free himself from the car by kicking out the windshield; was able to make his way to and into the Blickman house, struggle with the Blickmans, and respond with verbal abuse to Mrs. Blickman's exhortations; and was able to continue the struggle with the police when they arrived.

There was also evidence that Weaver's recollection of the events was more complete at the hospital than when he testified at trial. The jury heard his testimony at length about the effects of an LSD "trip" and what he remembered of the night in question, which was in fair detail except as to the critical events. The jury also witnessed his apparent disorientation and inability to respond to questions after having testified at length and responsively. The jury was free to conclude that Weaver's apparent disability on the stand was not genuine.

There is no precise set of hoops that a defendant must jump through in order to have the capacity to form a criminal intent. It is the totality of the facts that is determinative. The issue is not whether LSD influenced Weaver's behavior. We know from our experience that alcohol and other drugs are influencing factors in many physical assaults. The issue is whether the influence of LSD was enough to deprive Weaver of the ability to act with intent.

The jury reasonably could have concluded, for exam-

ple, that Weaver was capable of intending to escape from the scene of his attack on Wendy, which could be seen as demonstrating his comprehension of the nature of what he had done, and was capable of getting into the car and starting off on his flight. If he had the capacity to intend and initiate that, he had the capacity to intend, for whatever distorted motive, to kill Wendy.

The jury was thoroughly and correctly instructed as to the law applicable to the case, including the defense of voluntary intoxication. The jury specifically requested more information about that defense and was reinstructed. A jury having heard and seen all the evidence in this case, having been properly instructed, and having conscientiously reached its verdict, ought not have an appellate court tell it that it got it all wrong.

The majority quotes *Terry v. State* (1984), Ind., 465 N.E.2d 1085, for the proposition that "a defendant should not be relieved of responsibility when he was able to devise a plan, operate equipment, instruct the behavior of others or carry out acts requiring physical skill." Since *Terry*, however, the Indiana Supreme Court has held that "where the evidence shows a defendant had the ability to engage offensively in physical combat, to disengage and leave the scene, and to find his way to a friend's home seeking aid, his intoxication was not so great as to relieve him from responsibility for his acts." *Ferguson v. State* (1992), Ind., 594 N.E.2d 790, 792. This standard, which does not require that the defendant devise a plan or instruct the behavior of others, appears to focus the intoxication defense analysis on behavioral manifestations of intent rather than mental processes. I believe that the evidence supports the jury's verdict under either analysis, but especially so under *Ferguson* * * *.

In this difficult and tragic case, I would affirm.

Notes and Questions

1. On review by the Supreme Court of Indiana, an unanimous court adopted the analysis of Chief Judge Sharpnack, vacated the Court of Appeals' opinion, and affirmed the judgment of the trial court. 643 N.E.2d 342 (Ind.1994).

2. *Weaver* was litigated and decided under *Terry*, holding that the statutory effort to limit voluntary intoxication to disproving certain mental states was ineffective. Many jurisdictions, however, would limit the efforts of defendants such as Weaver to challenges to specific intents. If Indiana followed this approach, which of the crimes with which Weaver was charged would be specific intent crimes? Would any sound policy be served by limiting the significance of Weaver's intoxication to those charged crimes requiring a specific intent? "Specific intent" is

discussed in Section A of Chapter 4.

The matter was considered at length by the Maryland Court of Special Appeals in *Wieland v. State*, 101 Md.App. 1, 643 A.2d 446 (1994), in which the defendant was charged with multiple crimes, including carrying a handgun with intent to injure another person, assault by intent to frighten upon one Ullah, and assault by attempting to commit a battery upon his brother, Bryan Wieland. The jury was instructed to consider his intoxication in determining his guilt of the first offense but no such instruction was given regarding the others. Maryland applies the general rule that intoxication can be relied upon only if the crime is a specific intent crime. Application of that rule to the facts in *Wieland*, the court commented, involves "a very subtle nuance of *mens rea* analysis which is on the very cutting edge of legal thought." It continued:

> *Shell v. State* [307 Md. 46, 62–63, 512 A.2d 358 (1986)] approved the definition of and description of specific intent that this Court made in *Smith v. State*, 41 Md.App. 277, 305–306, 398 A.2d 426, cert. denied, 284 Md. 748 (1979):
>
> > A specific intent is not simply the intent to do the immediate act but embraces the requirement that the mind be conscious of a more remote purpose or design which shall eventuate from the doing of the immediate act. Though assault implies only the general intent to strike the blow, assault with intent to murder, rob, rape or maim requires a fully formed and conscious purpose that those further consequences shall flow from the doing of the immediate act. To break and enter requires a mere general intent but to commit burglary requires the additional specific intent of committing a felony after the entry has been made. A trespassory taking requires a mere general intent but larceny (or robbery) requires the specific animus furandi or deliberate purpose of depriving the owner permanently of the stolen goods. This is why even voluntary intoxication may negate a specific

intent though it will not negate a mere general intent.

> > …
>
> > The larger class "specific intent" includes such other members as 1) assault with intent to murder, 2) assault with intent to rape, 3) assault with intent to rob, 4) assault with intent to maim, 5) burglary, 6) larceny, 7) robbery and 8) the specific-intent-to-inflict-grievous-bodily harm variety of murder. Each of these requires not simply the general intent to do the immediate act with no particular, clear or undifferentiated end in mind, but the additional deliberate and conscious purpose or design of accomplishing a very specific and more remote result.

Applying this approach to the issues before it, the court first held that assault of the intended frightening variety is a specific intent crime. It requires a threatening gesture and the general intent to make that gesture. It also, however, requires an intent to engender apprehension of imminent bodily harm in the mind of the apparent victim, and this second mental element "is quintessentially a specific intent." The court then held that assault of the attempted battery variety is not a specific intent offense, because this kind of assault requires no more than an intent to commit a battery, that is, to hit the victim. Because the intent concerns a result that is "immediate" rather than "more remote," it is only a general intent.

Wieland purported to apply a rule that a specific intent is an intent to cause something other than the *actus reus* of the crime. Its analysis of the attempted battery type of assault, however, ignored that hitting the victim is not part of the *actus reus* of assault, although it is a part of the *actus reus* of battery.

3. In some jurisdictions permitting voluntary intoxication to be considered on whether the defendant had the *mens rea* required, such intoxication is regarded as an affirmative defense. Arguably, however, placing the burden of proof on the defendant regarding this matter is inconsistent with the constitutional need for the prosecution to have the burden of proof on all elements of the crime, including any required culpable mental state.

Editors' Note: Involuntary Intoxication and Settled Conditions Arising from Use of Intoxicants

Intoxication defense law is complicated by the need to distinguish the rules regarding voluntary intoxication from other rules that essentially permit insanity to be raised by two intoxication-related conditions. One is involuntary intoxication and the other is a settled condition resulting from the use of intoxicants.

Involuntary Intoxication

If intoxication is "involuntary," it is generally treated quite differently. Even jurisdictions in which explicit statutory provision is made for voluntary intoxication and no statute addressing involuntary intoxication has been enacted, courts are often willing to recognize that involuntary intoxication—unlike its voluntary counterpart—can give rise to a defense to criminal liability. This is because the rationale for the law's disfavor with claims to exculpation based on voluntary intoxication does not apply when the underlying intoxication is involuntary in nature. See *Torres v. State*, 583 S.W.2d 746, 749 (Tex.Crim.App.1979), recognizing a defense of involuntary intoxication despite the legislature's provision that voluntary intoxication is not to be considered in determining criminal liability.

Whether involuntary intoxication exculpates a criminal defendant is generally determined by using whatever test the jurisdiction applies for insanity. *People v. Caulley*, 197 Mich.App. 177, 186–88, 494 N.W.2d 853, 858–59 (1992), appeal denied 442 Mich. 885, 502 N.W.2d 39 (1993); *Torres*, 583 S.W.2d at 749. The Utah legislature abolished the insanity defense and provided that mental illness would exculpate a defendant only if it demonstrates that the defendant lacked the mental state required by the offense at issue; see the discussion in Section C of this chapter. A defendant seeking to raise involuntary intoxication argued that his defense should not be judged by this standard but rather on the basis of the pre-legislation insanity defense, under which he would be entitled to acquittal if as a result of his intoxication he lacked the capacity to conform his conduct to the requirements of law. The Utah Supreme Court rejected this, and followed the general rule that the effect of involuntary intoxication is tied to the effect that the jurisdiction gives to mental illness. See *State v. Gardner*, 870 P.2d 900, 902 (Utah 1993). The legislative rationale for limiting the exculpatory significance of mental illness, *Gardner* suggests, most likely also applies to involuntary intoxication.

When is intoxication involuntary so as to invoke what is sometimes the more flexible involuntary intoxication rule? The courts generally limit involuntary intoxication to situations in which the defendant was unaware that the substance he was ingesting was intoxicating or in which he was compelled by quite direct action of others to ingest a substance he knew was intoxicating. Intoxication is *not* rendered involuntary simply because the defendant did not intend to become intoxicated or to become severely intoxicated. Cf., *People v. Larry*, 144 Ill.App.3d 669, 494 N.E.2d 1212, 1218 (1986), appeal denied. Evidence that another person secretly put a drug in Alka Seltzer the defendant consumed, then, would render the resulting intoxication involuntary. *Torres*, 585 S.W.2d at 749–50. Intoxication would be involuntary if it resulted from a prescription medication that the defendant took without knowledge that it was intoxicating. *Caulley*, 197 Mich.App. at 188, 494 N.W.2d at 859. However, *Larry* suggests that intoxication resulting from smoking marijuana laced with PCP would not be involuntary where the evidence indicated the defendant knew the marijuana had been adulterated but "didn't bother" to inquire further. One court has suggested that intoxication resulting from the combination of a prescription drug and alcohol would not be involuntary where the defendant ignored a warning that he should not mix the medication with alcohol. *Spriggs v. State*, 878 S.W.2d 646, 650 (Tex.App.1994).

Defendants claiming that intoxication was involuntary because it was the result of underlying alcoholism have generally been unsuccessful. See *People v. Starowicz*, 207 A.D.2d 994, 994–95, 617 N.Y.S.2d 100, 101, appeal denied 84 N.Y.2d 1016, 647 N.E.2d 133 (1994).

Settled Conditions

Defendants seeking exculpation on the basis of intoxicant-related considerations may also invoke what has been called the "settled insanity" doctrine. The Colorado Supreme Court explained:

> The doctrine of "settled insanity" * * * may be traced back to English law of the early 19th century. Hale, Pleas of the Crown, Ch. IV. It was first recognized in federal court in the United States in *United States v. McGlue*, 26 Fed.Cas. 1093 (C.C.Mass.1851). It was accepted in state courts even earlier. See, e.g., *Haile v. State*, 30 Tenn. 154 (1850). * * *
>
> The doctrine of "settled insanity" draws a distinction between voluntary intoxication, universally recognized as not constituting a defense, and "insanity" arising from the long-term use of intoxicants but separate from immediate intoxication. The reasoning behind this distinction has been set forth in many jurisdictions. For example, in *People v. Lim Dum Dong*, 26 Cal.App.2d 135, 78 P.2d 1026, 1028 (1938), the court stated as follows:
>
> There is, in truth, no injustice in holding a person responsible for his acts committed in a state of voluntary intoxication. It is a duty which every one owes to his fellow men, and to society, to say nothing of more solemn obligations, to preserve so far as lies in his power, the inestimable gift of reason. If it is perverted or destroyed by fixed disease, though brought on by his own vices, the law holds him not accountable, but if, by a voluntary act, he temporarily casts off the restraints of reason and conscience, no wrong is done him if he is considered answerable for any injury which, in that state, he may do to others or to society . . . It must be "settled insanity", and not merely a temporary mental condition . . . which will relieve one of the responsibility of his criminal act.
>
> We recognize that the substantial weight of precedent from other jurisdictions that have considered the "settled insanity" defense lies in acceptance of that doctrine. * * *

Bieber v. People, 856 P.2d 811, 815 (Col.1993).

In *Bieber*, Bieber was charged with murder, robbery, and theft on the basis of an episode during which he brandished a gun, and claimed that he was a prisoner of war and that he was being followed by Communists. He approached Ellis, a stranger sitting in his truck, shot Ellis, and drove the truck away. At trial, Bieber produced expert testimony that his actions were caused by "amphetamine delusional disorder." His expert testified:

> A delusional disorder is a mental disorder which is characterized by delusional beliefs. A delusional belief is a belief held by an individual that is out of character for their sociocultural economic background and is held in a very rigid way and the person doesn't change their belief in the face of reasoning.
>
> And it's a false belief. That is what a delusion is. There's a number of causes of delusional thinking. One cause of delusional thinking is what used to be called amphetamine psychosis. It's now called amphetamine delusional disorder.
>
> And what that is from, some people when they use amphetamines on a chronic basis, begin to get very paranoid and delusional. And if that happens, it's associated with the use of amphetamines. It's called an amphetamine delusional disorder.

Bieber sought and was denied a jury instruction as follows:

> Insanity produced by long-continued use of amphetamines affects responsibility in the same way as insanity produced by any other cause if the mental disease or defect causing the insanity is "settled".
>
> "Settled" does not mean permanent or incurable, but means that the mental disease or defect resulting in insanity exists independently of the contemporaneous use of the drug. One who is actually insane does not lose the defense of insanity simply because, at the time he committed the act in question, he may also have been intoxicated. It is immaterial that the use of amphetamines may have caused the insanity, as long as the insanity was of a settled nature and qualifies as insanity as defined in [these instructions].

A majority of the Colorado Supreme Court found no error in rejection of these instructions, reasoning that the "settled insanity" defense is not a part of Colorado law. Colorado has a comprehensive statute limiting the exculpatory effect of voluntary intoxication. This statute specifically states that intoxication is not itself a mental disease or defect for purposes of the insanity defense. The Model Penal Code's section 2.08(3) (reprinted at page 480) contains a similar provision. So-called settled insanity such as Bieber's claimed amphetamine delusional disorder is intoxication within the meaning of the statute, the court reasoned, which defines intoxication as "a disturbance of mental or physical capacities resulting from the introduction of any substance into the body." Hence, it cannot give rise to insanity. This, the majority continued, makes good sense:

> We do not see any qualitative difference between a person who drinks or takes drugs knowing that he or she will be momentarily "mentally defective" as an immediate result, and one who drinks or takes drugs knowing that he or she may be "mentally defective" as an eventual, long-term result. In both cases, the person is aware of the possible consequences of his or her actions. We do not believe that

in the latter case, such knowledge should be excused simply because the resulting affliction is more severe. * * * As a matter of public policy * * * we cannot excuse a defendant's actions, which endanger others in his or her community, based upon a mental disturbance or illness that he or she actively and voluntarily contracted. There is no principled basis to distinguish between the short-term and long-term effects of voluntary intoxication by punishing the first and excusing the second. If anything, the moral blameworthiness would seem to be even greater with respect to the long-term effects of many, repeated instances of voluntary intoxication occurring over an extended period of time.

Justice Lohr, joined by two other members of the court, dissented on the ground that the statute should be read as permitting the court to authorize settled insanity as a defense. Moreover, the dissenters argued that this would be appropriate:

> In contrast to the majority's position, I believe that when a person suffers from an actual disease or defect of the mind, regardless of whether it is attributable to prior alcohol or drug use, so that he meets the legal definition of insanity, and when that condition exists independent of any intoxicated state, any limitations on the ability to assert intoxication as a defense are inapplicable.
>
> The validity and significance of the distinction between settled insanity and the immediate and transient effects resulting from ingestion of alcohol or other drugs are underscored by the wealth of authority from other jurisdictions that recognize the doctrine of settled insanity as a defense.

MODEL PENAL CODE[*]

Official Draft, 1985

Section 2.08. Intoxication

(1) Except as provided in Subsection (4) of this Section, intoxication of the actor is not a defense unless it negatives an element of the offense.

(2) When recklessness establishes an element of the offense, if the actor, due to self-induced intoxication, is unaware of a risk of which he would have been aware had he been sober, such unawareness is immaterial.

(3) Intoxication does not, in itself, constitute mental disease within the meaning of Section 4.01 [providing for the defense of insanity].

(4) Intoxication which (a) is not self-induced or (b) is pathological is an affirmative defense if by reason of such intoxication the actor at the time of his conduct lacks substantial capacity either to appreciate its criminality

[wrongfulness] or to conform his conduct to the requirements of law.

(5) *Definitions.* In this Section unless a different meaning plainly is required:

   (a) "intoxication" means a disturbance of mental or physical capacities resulting from the introduction of substances into the body;

   (b) "self-induced intoxication" means intoxication caused by substances which the actor knowingly introduces into his body, the tendency of which to cause intoxication he knows or ought to know, unless he introduces them pursuant to medical advice or under such circumstances as would afford a defense to a charge of crime;

   (c) "pathological intoxication" means intoxication grossly excessive in degree, given the amount of the intoxicant, to which the actor does not know he is susceptible.

Notes

1. Probably the most difficult issue posed by the Model Penal Code as well as by other statutory formulations relates to the question of whether intoxication should be permitted to "disprove" recklessness when that is sufficient for culpability. The drafters of the Model Penal Code assert that their position—that intoxication should not be permitted to show lack of recklessness—is in accord with prevailing law. Noting that the usual statement of the rule is that intoxication can be used to disprove a "specific" intent but not to disprove "general intent," they explain that the "obscure, unanalyzed distinction between specific and general intent" creates difficulty in applying this distinction. Model Penal Code, Comments to § 2.08, pp. 4–5 (Tent. Draft No. 9, 1959). The actual result of judicial decisions, they conclude, is that recklessness is generally sufficient for *mens rea* and intoxication is generally inadmissible to disprove it. However, when purpose or knowledge, as defined in § 2.02, is required, such evidence is generally held usable. W. LaFave and A. Scott, Criminal Law 389, 392–93 (2nd ed.1986) find this to be the present majority approach.

   As the discussion of specific intent in Chapter 4 indicates, this is inconsistent with some definitions of the terms specific and general intent. LaFave and Scott urge that these concepts be avoided in consideration of the effect of intoxication upon a defendant's liability.

2. As to the basic decision of whether defendants should be able to use intoxication to show the absence of recklessness, the commentary to the Model Penal Code defends the Code's position as follows:

   > Those who oppose a special rule [making intoxication unavailable to "disprove" recklessness] draw strength initially from the presumptive disfavor of any special rules of liability. * * * [They] draw further strength from the proposition that it is precisely the awareness of the risk in recklessness that is the essence of its moral culpability—a culpability dependent on the magnitude of the specific risk advertently created. When that risk is

greater in degree than that which the actor perceives at the time of getting drunk, as is frequently the case, the result of a special rule is bound to be a liability disproportionate to culpability. * * *

The case thus made is worthy of respect, but there are strong considerations on the other side. We mention first the weight of the prevailing law * * *. Beyond this, there is the fundamental point that awareness of the potential consequences of excessive drinking on the capacity of human beings to gauge the risks incident to their conduct is by now so dispersed in our culture that we believe it fair to postulate a general equivalence between the risks created by the conduct of the drunken actor and the risks created by his conduct in becoming drunk. Becoming so drunk as to destroy temporarily the actor's power of perception and of judgment is conduct which plainly has no affirmative social value to counterbalance the potential danger. The actor's moral culpability lies in engaging in such conduct. Added to this are the impressive difficulties posed in litigating the foresight of any particular actor at the time when he imbibes and the relative rarity of cases where intoxication really does engender unawareness as distinguished from imprudence. These considerations lead us to propose, on balance, that the Code declare that unawareness of a risk of which the actor would have been aware had he been sober be declared immaterial.

Model Penal Code § 2.08, comment (Tent.Draft No. 9, 1959).

C. DEFENSES AND OTHER DOCTRINES RELATED TO MENTAL IMPAIRMENT
Editors' Introduction: Psychological Impairment and Criminal Liability

Perhaps the most perplexing problem of substantive criminal law has been the task of accommodating some offenders' psychological abnormality in the decision as to whether, or to what extent, to hold persons criminally responsible for their conduct. This section explores two possible vehicles for this task. The first is the traditional defense of insanity. The second is the doctrine of diminished capacity, under which a defendant's psychological abnormality is considered in determining whether the defendant had the state of mind required by the crime charged.

Competency to Stand Trial Distinguished

Both of these doctrines need to be distinguished from another issue often presented in criminal litigation that also involves an inquiry into defendants' mental condition. It is a violation of due process as well as the procedural requirements of virtually all states to place on trial a defendant who is incompetent to stand trial. *Pate v. Robinson,*

383 U.S. 375, 86 S.Ct. 836, 15 L.Ed.2d 815 (1966). There is widespread agreement that a defendant is incompetent within the meaning of this rule if, because of psychological abnormality, he lacks present ability to consult with his lawyer with a reasonable degree of understanding or if he lacks a reasonable as well as factual understanding of the proceedings. *Dusky v. United States*, 362 U.S. 402, 80 S.Ct. 788, 4 L.Ed.2d 824 (1960). The competency inquiry, then, focuses upon defendants' mental condition *at the time of trial*; the questions concerning responsibility considered in this section are concerned with defendants' mental condition *at the time of the commission of the acts constituting the alleged offense*.

There is a far more fundamental difference, however. Incompetency to stand trial is not a defense or even a defensive theory in the sense that doctrines of these types address the merits of the charges pending against the accused. Rather, it is simply a bar to trial of the defendant and therefore to disposition of the charges. If, after a determination of incompetency, a defendant is restored to a condition in which he or she no longer suffers from disabilities rendering him incompetent, the defendant may at that point be tried upon the still pending charges.

Both insanity and diminished capacity, on the other hand, are defensive matters. If either is successfully asserted by a defendant, the charges are permanently resolved and there is no danger of a subsequent retrial and conviction.

Basic Policy Concerns

In discussing the matters covered in this section, it is important to begin with a consideration of what objectives the law is or ought to be pursuing by means of the doctrines at issue. Among those policy objectives that might be considered proper ones are the following:

1. *Exculpation of the Nonblameworthy.* Insofar as criminal liability involves a judgment of ethical reprehensibility, it is desirable to have doctrines that prevent the conviction of those who are not in fact blameworthy despite their past conduct and their dangerousness. Not only does exculpation avoid what some argue is the stigmatization resulting from criminal conviction, but it also may prevent the infliction of punishment containing at least an element of senseless revenge.

2. *Channeling Offenders into Appropriate Systems.* To some extent, the insanity defense serves not only to prevent criminal liability but also to channel a defendant who asserts it into the mental health system. This may be seen as desirable for several reasons. It is arguable that it implements society's interest in preventing further offenses by the defendant. Admission to the mental health system may result in an offender being provided with "treatment" that is more appropriate to that person's needs than any therapy available in the correctional system. Moreover, such action may provide society with the means of retaining the defendant as long as he or she presents a danger. A defendant sentenced under criminal provisions must usually be released at the expiration of the sentence no matter how dangerous he or she is believed to be at that time; one committed to psychiatric facilities following exculpation under the doctrines discussed here may sometimes be retained until—and if—it is determined that he or she no longer poses a danger to society. Further, it is

argued that society's interests in protection are accomplished at less cost to offenders, because treatment in the mental health system is less stigmatizing and less
disabling in other ways. For example, it may have less effect upon offenders' subsequent employment opportunities.

3. *Reinforcement of General Notions of Responsibility.* Some argue that the concept of
   criminal irresponsibility and its litigation in occasional cases tends to reinforce the
   sense of responsibility held by most members of the community. By the process
   of attempting to identify exceptional cases in which defendants will be regarded as
   irresponsible, the community reaffirms its commitment to the general rule of
   responsibility and this process of reaffirmance itself tends to cause members of the
   community to act in a responsible way.

4. *Avoidance of Misuse of Exculpatory Doctrines.* In addition to the general objectives
   just outlined, it seems clear that society has a strong and legitimate interest in
   avoiding the misuse of any exculpatory doctrines that the law might adopt. For
   example, an exculpatory rule might in theory be justifiable on the ground that it
   excuses persons who are not in fact blameworthy. It might also, however, be subject to the objection that in practice so many blameworthy defendants are able to
   falsely claim the benefits of the rule that the costs of the rule exceed its benefits.
   Closely related to this is the danger that a rule might pose questions that, in the
   context of individual cases, are either impossible of resolution or are so expensive
   and time-consuming to resolve that society cannot afford to have the judicial system spend time on efforts to address the questions. Some formulations of the
   insanity defense or the diminished responsibility rule might be subject to such
   objections.

Overall Significance of Insanity Defenses

It is important to keep insanity and related matters in reasonable perspective. The
National Advisory Commission on the Insanity Defense reported several "myths" relating to the insanity defense, including widespread beliefs that "many criminal defendants plead insanity and most are acquitted" and that "the insanity defense causes
major problems for the criminal justice system." Myths and Realities: A Report of the
National Commission on the Insanity Defense 14–15 (1983). A public opinion survey
conducted after the 1982 acquittal on insanity grounds of John Hinckley, the attempted assassin of President Reagan, found that over 87 percent of those questioned agreed
that the insanity defense is a loophole that allows too many guilty people to go free.
Hans and Slater, John Hinckley, Jr. and the Insanity Defense: The Public's Verdict, 47
Public Opinion Q. 202, 207 (1983).

   In reality, it is clear that defenses based upon mental abnormality are seldom raised.
When they are raised, they most often fail. The National Advisory Commission developed information indicating, for example, that in New York the insanity defense is
raised about once in every 600 to 700 cases and is successful in about 25 percent of
the cases in which it is raised. The commission concluded:

   [D]espite the exaggerated attention insanity acquittals receive in the media, in legislatures, and in the legal and psychiatric literature, the consensus of the experts

in the field is that the insanity defense is an extremely rare event and a successful insanity defense is even more rare.

It is difficult to imagine how a defense which is invoked so infrequently can be largely responsible for the problems which exist in our criminal justice system. While it is painfully obvious to many Americans that our criminal justice system suffers from various major problems, it should also be apparent that the existence and use of the insanity defense is not one of them. * * * Given the small numbers, the insanity defense event may not even be part of the problem.

Criminal responsibility matters, such as the insanity defense, do, however, pose interesting and difficult questions concerning basic assumptions regarding criminal behavior and the law's potential effect on that behavior. Because of this, the manner in which criminal responsibility issues are resolved often has great symbolic value for those holding strong views regarding these matters. Further, the fact that many members of the public perceive criminal responsibility issues to be a major practical problem for the criminal justice system is itself important, even if that perception is incorrect. Public disenchantment with the system cannot help but have an adverse effect upon the system in many ways.

1. The Defense of Insanity
Editors' Introduction: Development of the Insanity Defense

Traditionally, discussions of the insanity defense have focused upon the appropriate standard to be used for determining which defendants to exculpate on the ground of insanity. Although in the ideal world the legal standard *should* be the primary determinant of how specific cases come out, this may not be the result in the imperfect environment of the criminal justice system. How particular trial judges exercise their inevitable discretion to admit or exclude offered expert testimony, for example, may have more effect upon the outcome of cases than does the content of jury instructions. Jurors may, moreover, fail to accurately apply the standard given to them in the judge's instructions because they do not understand it or perhaps because they find it so contrary to their intuitive sense of what justice requires. As the American Psychiatric Association observed, "the exact wording of the insanity defense has never, through scientific studies or the case approach, been shown to be the major determinant of whether a defendant is acquitted by reason of insanity." American Psychiatric Association Statement on the Insanity Defense, 140 Am.J. Psychiatry 681, 684 (1983).

Nevertheless, consideration of insanity matters must at least begin with the legal criterion and how it should be applied to particular cases. Especially in light of relatively recent changes in insanity standards, it is useful to consider separately whether, and how, the standards should provide for evaluating defendants whose illnesses resulted in cognitive impairment and other defendants whose illnesses arguably gave rise to volitional or control disabilities. This consideration is made in the two subsections that follow. First, however, it is necessary to consider the manner in which the current standards developed, some alternatives to the presently used approach, and some procedural aspects of inquiry into a criminal defendant's sanity.

The Benchmark: The M'Naghten Rule

Any discussion of insanity must begin with Daniel M'Naghten's Case, 10 Cl. & F. 200, 8 Eng.Rep. 718 (1843), which is the basis for the traditional standard. M'Naghten, in an apparent effort to kill Sir Robert Peel, shot and killed Edward Drummond, Peel's private secretary. At the trial, defense testimony tended to show that the defendant experienced delusions that others were pursuing and seeking to kill him and that he fired the fatal shot believing that this would bring him peace from his persecution. The jury acquitted. Public outcry was so great that the matter was taken up in the House of Lords and the judges gave an opinion on the question of the nature and extent of unsoundness of mind excusing the commission of a crime of the sort involved.

Lord Chief Justice Tindal delivered the opinion, in which all but one of the judges concurred. He first addressed the proper questions to be submitted to a jury when a criminal defendant sets up insanity as a defense:

> [T]he jurors ought to be told in all cases that every man is to be presumed to be sane, and to possess a sufficient degree of reason to be responsible for his crimes, until the contrary be proved to their satisfaction; and that to establish a defense on the ground of insanity, it must be clearly proved that, at the time of the committing of the act, the party accused was labouring under such a defect of reason, from disease of the mind, as not to know the nature and quality of the act he was doing; or, if he did know it, that he did not know he was doing what was wrong.

Turning to a more specific question, the opinion addressed whether a person who commits an offense in consequence of "an insane delusion as to existing facts." It answered:

> [T]he answer must of course depend on the nature of the delusion: but [assuming] that he labours under [a] partial delusion only, and is not in other respects insane, we think he must be considered in the same situation as to responsibility as if the facts with respect to which the delusion exists were real. For example, if under the influence of his delusion he supposes another man to be in the act of attempting to take away his life, and he kills that man, as he supposes, in self-defense, he would be exempt from punishment. If his delusion was that the deceased had inflicted a serious injury to his character and fortune, and he killed him in revenge for such supposed injury, he would be liable to punishment.

Under this approach, the M'Naghten rule, a defendant is entitled to acquittal on insanity grounds only if that defendant proves: (a) he was suffering from "disease of the mind;" (b) this caused "a defect of reason;" and (c) as a result either (i) the defendant did not know the nature and quality of the act constituting the crime, or (ii) the defendant did not know that the act constituting the crime was "wrong."

Liberalization of Insanity: Loss of Control

The M'Naghten rule has been subjected to severe criticism, primarily on the ground that it fails to adequately identify all those impaired persons who cannot justly be held responsible for their conduct. As the California Supreme Court explained:

> Principal among [the deficiencies of *M'Naghten*] is the test's exclusive focus upon the cognitive capacity of the defendant * * *. As explained by Judge Ely of the Ninth Circuit: " * * * This formulation * * * fails to attack the problem presented in a case wherein an accused may have understood his actions but was incapable of controlling his behavior."
>
> *M'Naghten's* exclusive emphasis on cognition would be of little consequence if all serious mental illness impaired the capacity of the affected person to know the nature and wrongfulness of his action. * * * Current psychiatric opinion, however, holds that mental illness often leaves the individual's intellectual understanding relatively unimpaired, but so affects his emotions or reason that he is unable to prevent himself from committing the act. * * * To ask whether such a person knows or understands that his act is "wrong" is to ask a question irrelevant to the nature of his mental illness or to the degree of his criminal responsibility.

People v. Drew, 22 Cal.3d 333, 341–42, 149 Cal.Rptr. 275, 278 79, 583 P.2d 1318, 1322–23 (1978).

In response to such criticisms of the *M'Naghten* rule, a number of American jurisdictions modified it or rejected it as the sole determinant of a defendant's right to acquittal on insanity grounds. Often this was accomplished by adding an additional alternative means by which the defense of insanity could be established. In some jurisdictions, this supplementation was by means of an "irresistible impulse" test. In *Parsons v. State*, 81 Ala. 577, 2 So. 854 (1887), for example, the Alabama court held that juries were to be told that defendants were to be found not guilty by reason of insanity if they were "moved to action by an insane impulse controlling their will or their judgment."

The Supreme Court, however, in 1952 rejected the argument that legislative adoption of "the 'right and wrong' test of legal insanity in preference to the 'irresistible impulse' test" violates due process of law:

> Knowledge of right and wrong is the exclusive test of criminal responsibility in a majority of American jurisdictions. The science of psychiatry has made tremendous strides since that test was laid down in M'Naghten's Case, but the progress of science has not yet reached a point where its learning would compel us to require the states to eliminate the right and wrong test from their criminal law. Moreover, the choice of a test of legal insanity involves not only scientific knowledge but questions of basic policy as to the extent to which that knowledge should determine criminal responsibility. The whole problem has evoked wide disagreement among those who have studied it. In these circumstances it is clear that adoption of the irresistible impulse test is not "implicit in the concept of ordered liberty."

Leland v. Oregon, 343 U.S. 790, 800–01, 72 S.Ct. 1002, 1008–09, 96 L.Ed. 1302, 1310 (1952).

In 1968, the Supreme Court in *Powell v. Texas*, discussed in Section A of Chapter 3 in the notes following *Robinson v. California*, refused to construe *Robinson* as holding that the Eighth Amendment's prohibition against cruel and unusual punishment means that a chronic alcoholic cannot be criminally convicted for behavior that is an involuntary result of his or her disease or condition. The plurality's unwillingness to find a federal constitutional right to be free from conviction for this sort of involuntary conduct was almost certainly motivated in part by its perception that any such holding would also require a holding that the Eighth Amendment requires acquittal of a mentally impaired defendant who shows that the charged crime was the involuntary result of this impairment. Thus, *Leland* would have to be overruled. *Powell* is widely construed as reaffirming *Leland*'s holding that the federal constitution does not require an insanity defense that can be based on lack of control.

In 1962, the Proposed Official Draft of the American Law Institute's Model Penal Code proposed a formulation that restated the *M'Naghten* rule but also added an alternative that permitted acquittal on the basis of volitional impairment:

Section 4.01. Mental Disease or Defect Excluding Responsibility
   (1) A person is not responsible for criminal conduct if at the time of such conduct as a result of mental disease or defect he lacks substantial capacity either to appreciate the criminality [wrongfulness] of his conduct or to conform his conduct to the requirements of law.
   (2) As used in this Article, the terms "mental disease or defect" do not include an abnormality manifested only by repeated or otherwise antisocial conduct.

The major change that this would make (beyond restating the *M'Naghten* rule in modern terminology) would be to also permit a defendant to base an insanity defense upon an impairment that did not affect reasoning or cognitive abilities but did impair control or volitional capacity.

A defendant who could not, as a result of mental impairment, control his conduct could be found to have "lack[ed] the substantial capacity * * * to conform his conduct to the requirements of law" within the meaning of section 4.01(1). The drafters explained this potentially significant expansion of the defense:

[The formulation] accepts the view that any effort to exclude the nondeterrables from strictly penal sanctions must take account of the impairment of volitional capacity no less than of impairment of cognition * * *. It also accepts the criticism of the "irresistible impulse" formulation as inept in so far as it may be impliedly restricted to sudden, spontaneous acts as distinguished from insane propulsions that are accompanied by brooding or reflection. * * * [It deems] the proper question on this branch of the inquiry to be whether the defendant was without capacity to conform his conduct to the requirements of law. * * * The application of the principle will call, of course, for a distinction between incapacity, upon the one hand, and mere indisposition on the other. Such a distinction is inevitable in the application of a standard addressed to impairment of volition. We believe that the distinction can be made.

Model Penal Code, Comment to § 4.01, at 157–58 (Tent. Draft No. 4, 1955).

This apparently invigorated the movement for reform of insanity law, because the Model Penal Code's formulation was widely adopted by both courts and legislatures. By 1982, all the federal circuits and at least 29 states defined the defense of insanity so as to provide for acquittal on the basis of volitional impairment of some sort. American Bar Association Standing Committee on Association Standards for Criminal Justice and Commission on the Mentally Disabled, Report with Recommendations to the House of Delegates 10, reprinted in Reports With Recommendations to the House of Delegates, 1983 Midyear Meeting (1983).

The Movement Away from Volitional Impairment

On June 21, 1982, a Washington, D.C. jury found John W. Hinckley, Jr., not guilty by reason of insanity on all charges arising out of his efforts the prior year to assassinate President Reagan. The verdict was widely regarded as improper by a public that saw Hinckley as sane. See Hans and Slater, John W. Hinckley, Jr. and the Insanity Defense: The Public's Verdict, 47 Public Opinion Q. 202 (1983).

The Hinckley acquittal stimulated reconsideration of a number of matters related to criminal responsibility litigation. Among these was proper placement of the burden of persuasion on insanity. The Hinckley jury was instructed that because the insanity issue had been raised, the government had the obligation of proving sanity beyond a reasonable doubt. Some saw the Hinckley acquittal as confirming that the ready availability of prodefendant expert testimony and the confusing nature of that testimony permits almost any defendant with imagination and financial backing to raise a reasonable doubt as to his or her sanity in a jury's mind. Hinckley's acquittal, in this view, suggested the need for more widespread adoption of the position taken by some jurisdictions, under which the defendant has the burden of proving, usually by a preponderance of the evidence, that he or she was insane within the meaning of the defense. This is discussed further later.

Most importantly, however, the Hinckley verdict provided the impetus for widespread abandonment of volitional impairment as a basis for an insanity defense. Many saw the jury's verdict of acquittal as the result of confusion engendered by large amounts of psychiatric testimony rendered admissible—these observers believed—because of Hinckley's ability to challenge his volitional capacity. This perceived risk of jury confusion (and therefore improper acquittals) provided the occasion for a reconsideration of whether expert testimony bearing upon an offender's past ability to control his conduct was as reliable as had been assumed during the rise of the defense of volitional impairment. Dix, Criminal Responsibility and Mental Impairment in American Criminal Law: Response to the Hinckley Acquittal in Historical Perspective, 1 Law and Mental Health, International Perspectives 1 (1984).

Perhaps most amazing was the uniformity with which professional organizations attacked the volitional aspect of many existing insanity standards. The American Bar Association House of Delegates approved "in principle a defense of nonresponsibility for crime which focuses solely on whether the defendant, as a result of mental disease or defect, was unable to appreciate the wrongfulness of his or her conduct at the time of the offense charged." Summary of Action Taken by the House of Delegates, 1983 Midyear Meeting 3 (1983). The American Medical Association urged the abolition of any "special defense" and its replacement by provision for acquittal when, as a result of mental disease or defect, the defendant lacked the state of mind or *mens rea* required by the offense charged. Insanity Defense in Criminal Trials and Limitations of Psychiatric Testimony, Report of the Board of Trustees, 251 J.Am.Medical Assoc. 2967 (1984).

The American Psychiatric Association indicated a preference for an insanity standard along the lines of that favored by the American Bar Association. In explanation, it noted:

> Many psychiatrists * * * believe that psychiatric information relevant to determining whether a defendant understood the nature of his act, and whether he appreciated its wrongfulness, is more reliable, and has a stronger scientific basis than, for example, does psychiatric information relevant to whether a defendant was able to control his behavior. The line between an irresistible impulse and an impulse not resisted is probably no sharper than that between twilight and dusk. Psychiatry is a deterministic discipline that views all human behavior as, to a large extent, "caused." The concept of volition is the subject of some disagreement among psychiatrists. Many psychiatrists, therefore believe that psychiatric testimony * * * about volition is more likely to produce confusion for jurors than is psychiatric testimony relevant to a defendant's appreciation or understanding.

American Psychiatric Association Statement on the Insanity Defense, 140 Am.J. Psychiatry 681, 685 (1983). The Association also challenged the apparent assumption that a purely cognitive standard would deprive many volitionally-impaired persons of an opportunity for exculpation:

> In practice there is considerable overlap between a psychotic person's defective understanding or appreciation and his ability to control his behavior. Most psychotic persons who fail a volitional test for insanity will also fail a cognitive-type test when such a test is applied to their behavior, thus rendering the volitional test superfluous in judging them.

Legislative action has been widespread and generally has involved redefinition of the criterion for insanity along the lines of a modernized version of the *M'Naghten* rule offered by Professor Richard J. Bonnie. See Bonnie, The Moral Basis of the Insanity Defense, 69 J.Am.B.Assoc. 194 (1983). This corresponds to the formulations urged by the American Bar Association and the American Psychiatric Association.

Perhaps the most significant legislative action was the federal Insanity Reform Act of 1984. Until this enactment, the substance of the insanity defense as it applied in prosecutions for federal crimes had been left to judicial development. The United States Supreme Court had not addressed the matter, but all of the intermediate courts of appeals had embraced a version of the Model Penal Code's formulation. As a result of the 1984 legislation, Title 18 of the United States Code now contains the following provision:

§ 20. Insanity defense

(a) Affirmative defense.—It is an affirmative defense to a prosecution under any federal statute that, at the time of the commission of the acts constituting the offense, the defendant, as a result of a severe mental disease or defect, was unable to appreciate the nature and quality or the wrongfulness of his acts. Mental disease or defect does not otherwise constitute a defense.

(b) Burden of proof.—The defendant has the burden of proving the defense of insanity by clear and convincing evidence.

The House Report on the measure explained:

Conceptually, there is some appeal to a defense predicated on lack of power to avoid criminal conduct. If one conceives the major purpose of the insanity defense to be the exclusion of the nondeterrables from criminal responsibility, a control test seems designed to meet that objective. Furthermore, notions of retributive punishment seem particularly inappropriate with respect to one powerless to do otherwise than he did.

Richard J. Bonnie, Professor of Law and Director of the Institute of Law, Psychiatry and Public Policy at the University of Virginia, while accepting the moral predicate for a control test, explained the fundamental difficulty involved:

Unfortunately, however, there is no scientific test for measuring a person's capacity for self-control or for calibrating the impairment of such capacity. There is, in short, no objective basis for distinguishing between offenders who were undeterrable and those who were merely undeterred, between the impulse that was irresistible and the impulse not resisted, or between substantial impairment of capacity and some lesser impairment. Whatever the precise terms of the volitional test, the question is unanswerable or can be answered only by "moral guesses." To ask it at all, in my opinion, invites fabricated claims, undermines equal administration of the penal law, and compromise its deterrent effect.

H.R.Rep. No. 98-1030, 98th Cong., 2nd Sess. 226–27 (1984), reprinted in [1984] U.S.Code Cong. & Adm.News 3182.

Until 1979, the California Supreme Court had adhered to the *M'Naghten* rule. In *People v. Drew*, supra, however, the court adopted the Model Penal Code formulation. However, in June 1982, the California electorate adopted "Proposition 8," which, among other things, established a statutory definition of insanity that embodied a purely cognitive test. See Cal. Penal Code § 25(b).

The National Commission on the Insanity Defense, established by the National Mental Health Association, arrived at a conclusion clearly contrary to the trend. The Commission acknowledged that psychiatric testimony on volition might confuse a jury, but, it concluded, if the burden of proof on insanity is placed on the defendant, "the adjudicative difficulties perceived by others in the volitional test ought to be minimized or eliminated." It recommended, therefore, that the insanity test include both cognitive and volitional elements or prongs. Myths & Realities: A Report of the National Commission on the Insanity Defense 36 (1983).

Other Approaches: Product
or Durham Rule

Some believe that jury instructions should be less directive than those previously considered. Since *State v. Pike*, 49 N.H. 399 (1870), for example, New Hampshire has submitted insanity cases to juries with only directions to determine whether the defendants were mentally ill and, if so, whether the crimes were the products of those mental illnesses. See *State v. Abbott*, 127 N.H. 444, 503 A.2d. 791 (1985).

In a landmark decision, *Durham v. United States*, 214 F.2d 862 (D.C.Cir.1954), the United States Court of Appeals for the District of Columbia adopted this approach for criminal litigation in the District. Judge David Bazelon's opinion relied heavily upon what the court perceived as the need for a broad rule that, in implementation, would impose no impediment to expert witnesses' efforts to convey to juries all of their information concerning defendants' behavior and its causes.

Administration of the *Durham* rule, however, proved difficult. In *McDonald v. United States*, 312 F.2d 847 (D.C.Cir.1962), the court responded by promulgating a definition of the mental disease or defect required. This was defined as "any abnormal condition of the mind which substantially affects mental or emotional processes *and substantially impairs behavior controls*." With this definition, the *Durham* rule required volitional impairment, but as a part of the definition of the underlying impairment rather than as part of the necessary impact of that impairment on the defendant. Thus it arguably differed little in substance from overtly volitional tests, but was less direct and therefore potentially more confusing to jurors.

In *United States v. Brawner*, 471 F.2d 969 (D.C.Cir.1972), the court abandoned the *Durham* rule in favor of the Model Penal Code (or ALI) formulation. The major difficulty, reasoned the court, was that the *Durham* rule required expert testimony to address the issue of "productivity," that is, whether the crime charged was the product of the defendant's abnormality. It also required juries to address that question. Unfortunately, neither experts nor jurors had any definition of "productivity." As a result, experts tended to rely upon their own definitions of the term, which inevitably incorporated their own ethical and personal views and values. These experts tended, however, to testify as if their conclusions were simply the result of objective application of their professional expertise. Juries would then tend to rely upon this testimony, without realizing that the testimony represented personal value judgments not within the witnesses' area of professional expertise. What the court perceived as the need to reduce, in insanity litigation, "undue dominance by the experts giving testimony," was a major consideration in the court's *Brawner* action. The court explained:

> The ALI's formulation retains the core requirement of a meaningful relationship between the mental illness and the incident charged. The language used in the ALI rule is sufficiently in the common ken that its use in the courtroom, or in preparation for trial, permits a reasonable three-way communication—between (a) the law-trained judges and lawyers; (b) the experts and (c) the jurymen— without insisting on a vocabulary that is either stilted or stultified, or conducive to a testimonial mystique permitting expert dominance and encroachment on the jury's function.

Other Approaches: General "Justice" Standard

Virtually all modern formulations of the insanity defense attempt to focus juries' attention on specific possible effects of a defendant's impairment. This may pose jurors with an impossible task because even with the help of experts, such matters as a defendant's prior ability to control his or her actions simply cannot be resolved. If this is so, perhaps it would be better to make clear to juries that they cannot hope to make specific decisions on "objective" or "scientific" grounds and that they must address the issues as ethical ones. Chief Judge Bazelon, author of the District of Columbia's landmark *Durham* opinion previously discussed, so suggested in a concurring *Brawner* opinion:

> [The ALI test] asks the jury to wrestle with such unfamiliar, if not incomprehensible, concepts as the capacity to appreciate the wrongfulness of one's actions, and the capacity to conform to the requirements of law. The best hope for our new test is that jurors will regularly conclude that no one—including the experts—can provide a meaningful answer to the questions posed by the ALI test. And in their search for some semblance of an intelligible standard, they may be forced to consider whether it would be just to hold the defendant responsible for his actions. By that indirect approach, our new test may lead jurors to * * * make the "intertwining moral, legal, and medical judgments" on which the resolution of the responsibility question properly depends * * *.
>
> Our instruction to the jury should provide that a defendant is not responsible *if at the time of his unlawful conduct his mental* or *emotional processes or behavior controls were impaired to such an extent that he cannot justly be held responsible for his act.* This test would ask the psychiatrist a single question: what is the nature of the impairment of the defendant's mental and emotional processes and behavior controls? It would leave for the jury the question whether that impairment is sufficient to relieve the defendant of responsibility for the particular act charged.
>
> The purpose of this proposed instruction is to focus the jury's attention on the legal and moral aspects of criminal responsibility, and to make clear why the determination of responsibility is entrusted to the jury and not the expert witnesses.

Other Approaches: The Mens Rea *Approach*

As previously discussed, the American Medical Association urged after the Hinckley acquittal that any special defense of insanity be abolished and replaced by provision for acquittal when a defendant, as a result of mental disease or defect, lacked the state of mind or *mens rea* required as an element of the crime charged. This has been done in several states: Idaho, Montana, and Utah.

Montana, for example, has abolished the insanity defense and provided for the jury to return a verdict of acquittal on the ground that "due to a mental disease or defect [the defendant] could not have had a particular state of mind that is an essential element of the offense charged." Mont.Code Ann. § 46-14-201(2).

In addition, the Montana Code authorizes a trial court to take evidence of impairment into account at sentencing. At the time of sentencing, the trial court is to consider evidence of mental impairment and may make a finding that at the time of the crime the defendant suffered from a mental disease or defect that rendered him unable to appreciate the criminality of his conduct or to conform his conduct to the requirements of law. If the trial court makes such a finding, the convicted defendant is to be committed for placement in an "appropriate institution" for a definite time not to exceed the maximum term of imprisonment that could be imposed. During that period of institutionalization, the defendant may return to the sentencing court and upon a showing that he has been cured of the mental disease or defect the court may modify the commitment.

Although Montana's replacement of the defense with the *mens rea* approach came in 1979, before the Hinckley verdict and the recommendations of the American Medical Association, the association's justifications for its position are helpful to an understanding of this approach. In defense of the *mens rea* approach, the association explained that an insanity defense could not be an effective device for assuring acquittal of those who cannot be expected to conform to the law and thereby assuring the moral integrity of the law. Assuming that any insanity defense must rest primarily upon psychiatric models, the Association's report continued:

> A defense premised on psychiatric models represents a singularly unsatisfactory, and inherently contradictory, approach to the issue of accountability. By necessity, psychiatrists tend to view all human behavior as a product of deterministic influences. This deterministic orientation cannot be reconciled with the concept of free will * * *.
>
> The essential goal of an exculpatory test for insanity is to identify the point at which a defendant's mental condition has become so impaired that society may confidently conclude that he has lost his free will. Psychiatric concepts of mental illness are ill-suited to this task * * *. Because free will is an article of faith, rather than a concept that can be explained in medical terms, it is impossible for psychiatrists to determine whether a mental impairment has affected the defendant's capacity for voluntary choice, or caused him to commit the particular act in question. Accordingly, since models of mental illness are indeterminant in this respect, they can provide no reliable measure of moral responsibility.
>
> * * *
>
> Even under a truncated test of insanity limited to cognitive impairments, the inscrutable cause-and-effect relationship between mental illness and free will remains the central question. * * * Meaningful reform can be achieved only if the focus of the inquiry is shifted away from the elusive notion of free will, and its relationship to mental disease, and back to the relatively objective standards of *mens rea* where it fell traditionally.

Insanity Defense in Criminal Trials and Limitations of Psychiatric Testimony, Report of the Board of Trustees, 251 J.Am.Medical Ass. 2967, 2978 (1984).

Courts in all three of the *mens rea* jurisdictions have upheld their limited defenses against constitutional challenges. A split Utah Supreme Court, for example, upheld that state's statute in *State v. Herrera*, 895 P.2d 359 (Utah 1995). Relying heavily upon *Leland v. Oregon* (discussed at page 487) and *Powell v. Texas* (discussed at page 40), the court found that federal constitutional considerations do not demand an insanity defense. It explicitly rejected the contention that an affirmative defense of insanity "is so grounded in our legal system that its abolition offends our fundamental principles of law and justice and therefore offends due process." Whatever minimal standards are demanded by due process are satisfied by permitting defendants to challenge whether they acted with the *mens rea* required. On this basis the Utah court distinguished several earlier decisions holding unconstitutional the abolition of the insanity defense without giving defendants the right to rely on mental impairment as negating the necessary culpable mental state.

Other Approaches: "Guilty but Mentally Ill" Alternative

Responding to criticisms that the insanity defense forces juries and judges to make a rigid "all or nothing" judgment, some jurisdictions have retained a defense of insanity but, in addition, provided juries with the alternative of finding a defendant "guilty but mentally ill." The following Michigan statute is the prototype of these approaches:

> 768.36. Guilty but mentally ill
> Sec. 36. (1) If the defendant asserts a defense of insanity the defendant may be found "guilty but mentally ill" if, after trial, the trier of fact finds all of the following beyond a reasonable doubt:
> (a) That the defendant is guilty of an offense.
> (b) That the defendant was mentally ill at the time of the commission of that offense.
> (c) That the defendant was not legally insane at the time of the commission of that offense.

A defendant who is found "guilty but mentally ill" may be sentenced to any punishment that could be imposed upon a defendant who is convicted of the same offense. If the defendant is sentenced to imprisonment, he is to be specially evaluated and any treatment necessary is to be provided, including transfer to a hospital run by the Department of Mental Health. In the event that the parole board considers the defendant for parole, the Board is directed by the statute to obtain information from the facility administering treatment to the defendant. In the event that probation is imposed as a penalty—and if treatment is recommended after an evaluation of the defendant—such treatment is to be made a condition of probation.

The American Psychiatric Association was "extremely skeptical" of this approach:

> "Guilty but mentally ill" offers a compromise for the jury. Persons who might otherwise have qualified for an insanity verdict may instead be siphoned into a category of "guilty but mentally ill." * * *
> The "guilty but mentally ill" approach may become the easy way out. Juries may avoid grappling with the difficult moral issues inherent in adjudicating guilt or innocence, jurors instead settling conveniently on "guilty but mentally ill." * * *

There are other problems * * *. In times of financial stress, the likelihood that meaningful treatment for persons "guilty but mentally ill" will be mandated and paid for by state legislatures is slight. * * *

Alternatively, whatever limited funds are available for the treatment of mentally ill inmates may be devoted to "guilty but mentally ill defendant," ignoring the treatment needs of other mentally ill but conventionally sentenced prisoners who require mental health treatment in prison.

American Psychiatric Association Statement on the Insanity Defense, 140 Am.J.Psychiatry 681, 684 (1983).

In *People v. Robles*, 682 N.E.2d 194, 224 Ill.Dec. 633 (App.1997), the Illinois intermediate appellate court held the Illinois "not guilty by reason of insanity" procedure unconstitutional. It relied heavily upon the 1989 conclusions of the Illinois Governor's Commission to Revise the Mental Health Code of Illinois, which had recommended abolition of the program. *Robles* explained:

> In calling for the abolition of the GBMI verdict, the Commission reasoned that it had failed to achieve its intended goals and that it had caused a number of negative consequences. The Commission initially determined that there was little evidence that the enactment of the GBMI statute had reduced the number of acquittals by reason of insanity. As to the mental health treatment GBMIs receive in prison, the Commission concluded: "[T]he actual treatment provided for GBMI's is identical to other prisoners. No special units or programs have been established for the small group; they are not housed in any special facility; and no GBMI is currently confined in a [Department of Mental Health and Developmental Disabilities] facility."
>
> The Commission also focused on two negative consequences of a GBMI verdict. First, it found that GBMIs were stigmatized in the general prison population and, as a result, maltreated. Second, the Commission noted potential jury confusion caused by the verdict and described anecdotal evidence of a jury's confusion when deliberating a case involving GBMI instructions.

Holding the statute unconstitutional, the court continued:

> [A] statute that encourages compromise verdicts based upon jurors' misperceptions and misunderstandings is a violation of due process.
>
> The wording of the GBMI statute would seem to indicate that there is some sort of significance to the phrase "but mentally ill." * * *
>
> Yet * * * a GBMI verdict does not reflect diminished culpability or criminal responsibility. Moreover, a GBMI verdict is identical to a "guilty" verdict in terms of potential punishment and/or psychiatric treatment. Further, as of 1989, the psychiatric treatment afforded those found GBMI was identical to that of other prisoners. There were no separate facilities for them at any penal institutions, and none were receiving treatment in a psychiatric facility. We are aware of no evidence that any of this has changed significantly in the intervening years. From this, we conclude that the GBMI statute has no practical effect.
>
> * * *
>
> We have little doubt that conscientious jurors who are confronted with this continuum of verdicts assume that the GBMI verdict represents a distinct and sep-

arate position on this continuum. In all probability, they further assume that the GBMI verdict indicates that some sort of ameliorative disposition will be afforded the defendant. We find that these misconceptions and misunderstandings encourage a compromise verdict of GBMI, which is devoid of any substance.

The Illinois Supreme Court has agreed to review the case. *People v. Robles*, 174 Ill.2d 586, 686 N.E.2d 1170, 227 Ill.Dec. 14 (1997).

Other Reforms in Criminal Responsibility Litigation

Although much attention has been focused upon the criterion for determining insanity, other—perhaps less dramatic—changes may eliminate or at least reduce the problems found by many with the current administration of the defense.

Burden of Proof. If the burden of proof of sanity rests upon the prosecution, expert testimony—even if objectively incredible—may convince many juries that a reasonable doubt exists. The federal statute (reprinted at page 491), as well as many others, respond to this concern by placing the burden on the defendant; the federal legislation requires proof by the unusually high burden of clear and convincing evidence.

Conclusory Expert Testimony. Juries may be inappropriately dominated by defense experts for any of several reasons. Such experts may testify solely in conclusory terms that a defendant was insane, for example. Juries, left without any basis on which to evaluate that conclusion, may uncritically assume that insanity has been established.

In order to address this perceived problem, the federal legislation added the following provision to Rule 704 of the Federal Rules of Evidence:

(b) No expert witness testifying with respect to the mental state or condition of a defendant in a criminal case may state an opinion or inference as to whether the defendant did or did not have the mental state or condition constituting an element of the crime charged or a defense thereto. Such ultimate issues are matters for the trier of fact alone.

Under this provision, defense experts may testify to their observations of the accused and many of the professional opinions they reached based on their examination. They may not, however, be asked whether, in their opinion, the defendant was insane at the time he or she committed the act constituting the crime. The purpose is to force experts to testify to the underlying bases for their ultimate conclusions by prohibiting them from testifying to the conclusions themselves, and thus to encourage juries to objectively consider whether the experts' observations and reasoning support ultimate conclusions regarding sanity or insanity.

There are some who go further and argue that mental health professionals have little, if any, appropriate role in the decision-making process regarding responsibility for criminal conduct. Morse, Failed Explanations and Criminal Responsibility: Experts and the Unconscious, 68 Va.L.Rev. 971 (1982), challenges the scientific validity of psychodynamic explanations of human behavior and argues that its employment leads to misguided decisions and compromises the integrity of the criminal justice system. Some of these critics of the status quo would bar all expert testimony on insanity. Most commentators, though, including Bonnie & Slobogin, The Role of Mental Health Professionals in the Criminal Process: The Caw for Informed Speculation, 66 Va.L.Rev. 427 (1980), believe that despite the considerable difficulties, experts should continue to be used.

Bifurcation of Trial Proceedings When Responsibility Is Challenged. Some jurisdictions direct that when a defendant claims to be not guilty because of insanity, trial proceedings are to be "bifurcated." Under Minnesota's Rules of Criminal Procedure, for example, if a defendant gives notice of intent to rely on defense of not guilty by reason of mental illness or deficiency, the trial court is to separate the trial into two stages. At the first, the jury will hear evidence on and be asked to decide whether—without regard to sanity—the defendant is guilty of the crime charged. If the jury finds the defendant guilty, the trial proceeds to the second stage at which the same jury hears evidence on and is asked to decide whether the defendant was insane at the time of the crime. If at the first stage the jury finds the defendant not guilty, of course, the trial ends and the defendant is free. Such procedures separate or bifurcate consideration of the defendant's factual guilt from consideration of whether despite that guilt the defendant is to be exonerated on insanity grounds.

This bifurcated procedure arguably has several advantages. First, it protects defendants against being uncritically convicted by juries that may be unconvinced that the prosecution has proven guilt but are persuaded by insanity evidence that the defendant is extremely dangerous and should be locked up. Second, a bifurcated procedure separates the responsibility question from other issues arising in such cases and thus arguably permits desirable focusing of attention on that issue. Finally, information elicited from accuseds by compelled mental examinations can be used by the prosecution only on the issue of responsibility, with the result that such compelled examinations intrude less upon the interests protected by the privilege against compelled self-incrimination.

Bifurcated trial proceedings give rise to difficulty when a defendant relies upon a psychological abnormality as a basis for challenging the persuasiveness of the prosecution's evidence that he or she acted with the culpable mental state required for liability. If the defendant also (and alternatively) relies upon an insanity defense, the matter may become quite complicated. In such cases, the issues of guilt–innocence and responsibility are not as clearly differentiated as the bifurcated trial procedures assume will be the case. *State v. Provost*, reprinted in the second subsection that follows, involved a defendant who sought to introduce such evidence in the first stage of Minnesota's bifurcated trial.

Jury Consideration of Acquittal Consequences. Should a trial jury be told of the consequences of acquitting the defendant on insanity grounds? The United States Supreme Court considered the matter in regard to trials in federal court in *Shannon v. United*

States, 512 U.S. 573, 114 S.Ct. 2419, 129 L.Ed.2d 459 (1994). Shannon sought an instruction telling the jury about the consequences under the Insanity Defense Reform Act of 1984 (the IDRA), discussed in detail later in this introduction, of an insanity acquittal. He argued that jurors may mistakenly believe that an acquitted defendant will simply be released into society. If those jurors believe the defendant is dangerous, they may seek to prevent such a release by convicting even though they believe the evidence indicates that the defendant should be found not guilty by reason of insanity.

Rejecting Shannon's argument, the Supreme Court noted that as a general rule juries are not to be told the consequences of their verdicts. This is because juries' role in criminal trials is only to find the facts and decide defendants' guilt, and thus jurors have no reason to consider or even know about the procedural consequences of the jury's verdict. Juries can be instructed to ignore the consequences of their verdicts and there is no reason to believe they are less inclined or able to do this in insanity cases than in others. If juries are to be told of the consequences of an insanity acquittal, it continued, there is no principled way to limit this approach to the insanity situation. Thus, juries would have to be told of such matters as mandatory minimum or maximum sentences and parole, and "the rule against informing jurors of the consequences of their verdicts would soon be swallowed by the exceptions." Moreover, the Court noted, an instruction might backfire, because the jury would have to be told that the only assured hospitalization would be for a short period. It thus might vote to convict to eliminate the possibility that a dangerous defendant would be released after this short period.

A few jurisdictions do require that juries be told the consequences of insanity acquittals. This is required by statute in Connecticut, for example. The Connecticut Supreme Court has held, however, that a trial judge may also instruct the jury to base its decision on the evidence and not on its knowledge of the possible consequences of its verdict. *State v. Wood*, 208 Conn. 125, 144, 545 A.2d 1026, 1035–36 (1988).

Terminology. Some and perhaps much of the adverse public reaction to the Hinckley verdict may be attributed to public misunderstanding of the term, "not *guilty* by reason of insanity." To the extent that the verdict suggests a lack of proof that the defendant engaged in the conduct at issue, it of course ran counter to the facts and common sense. As a result, it has been suggested that the term, "not responsible by reason of insanity" be substituted for the term, "not guilty by reason of insanity." Myths & Realities: A Report of the National Commission on the Insanity Defense 34–35 (1983). To the extent that a need of this sort exists, substituting the phrase, "guilty but insane" might better serve the need.

Postacquittal Confinement and Treatment

Generally, the verdict in a criminal case is either guilty or not guilty. In a case involving an insanity defense, however, the jury is often told that if it finds the defendant entitled to acquittal on insanity grounds, this should be reflected by the return of a special verdict of not guilty by reason of insanity. The return of such a verdict usually triggers a procedure for confinement of the acquitted defendant, often in a high-security mental hospital.

These procedures vary from jurisdiction to jurisdiction. The procedure enacted by Congress in 1984, as part of the Insanity Reform Act of 1984, for hospitalization of defendants acquitted on insanity grounds in federal court is reasonably typical.

Under the federal statute, 18 U.S.C.A. § 4243, all defendants acquitted in federal court trials by reason of insanity are to be automatically committed to a "suitable facility." Within 40 days, a hearing is to be held on whether further hospitalization is appropriate. At this hearing, the defendant has the burden of proving that his or her release "would not create a substantial risk of bodily injury to another person or serious damage of property of another due to a present mental disease or defect." If the crime of which the defendant was acquitted involved bodily injury to another, serious damage to the property of another, or a substantial risk of such injury or damage, the defendant's burden is by clear and convincing evidence.

In other cases, the burden is by a preponderance of the evidence. If the court finds that the defendant failed to meet his or her burden, the defendant is to be committed for further confinement. Subsequently, the court may hold hearings on whether a committed defendant should be discharged. At these hearings, discharge is to be ordered only if the defendant establishes, by the same burdens previously discussed, that the release would no longer create a substantial risk of bodily injury to another person or serious damage to property of another. If the court finds that the defendant can be safely released only if he or she continues treatment, the court can order release conditioned upon the defendant complying with such treatment.

In *Jones v. United States*, 463 U.S. 354, 103 S.Ct. 3043, 77 L.Ed.2d 694 (1983), the Supreme Court considered and rejected several constitutional challenges to such postacquittal commitment schemes. Jones had been committed following his insanity acquittal on a charge of attempted petit larceny, which consisted of attempting to steal a jacket from a department store. Under the applicable law, a defendant was required to prove insanity by a preponderance of the evidence. Had Jones been convicted, his penal sentence could not have exceeded one year. After over one year of hospitalization, Jones sought his release.

The Supreme Court found no constitutional deficiency in Jones' commitment and retention, and rejected Jones' contention that the maximum term of incarceration available as punishment upon conviction limited the maximum term of hospitalization that may be required upon an insanity acquittal:

> His confinement rests on his continuing illness and dangerousness. * * * There simply is no necessary correlation between severity of the offense and length of time necessary for recovery. The length of the acquittee's hypothetical criminal sentence therefore is irrelevant to the purpose of his commitment.

Justice Brennan, joined by Justices Marshall and Blackmun, dissented. They argued that an insanity acquittee may, under the Constitution, be confined longer than the maximum penal sentence available for the crime only if the government affirmatively shows that continued confinement is justified under the standards and procedures used for involuntary civil commitment of mentally ill persons not charged with a crime. Justice Stevens agreed. Under those normal civil commitment procedures, the burden—as a matter of federal constitutional law under *Addington v. Texas*, 441 U.S. 418, 99 S.Ct. 1804, 60 L.Ed.2d 323 (1979)—is upon those seeking commitment to show by "clear and convincing evidence" that involuntary treatment is justified.

An insanity acquittee's continued confinement is constitutionally required, however, to rest on the impairment that led to his acquittal. In *Foucha v. Louisiana*, 504 U.S. 71, 112 S.Ct. 1780, 118 L.Ed.2d 437 (1992), Foucha had been charged in the Louisiana courts with burglary and discharge of a firearm. He was acquitted on grounds of insanity and hospitalized. Four years later, a hearing was held on whether to release him. The testimony at that hearing was that Foucha had suffered from a drug-induced psychosis but had recovered from that condition. He also had an antisocial personality, an untreatable "condition" that the testimony indicated was not a mental disease. Given this last fact, and indications that Foucha had been involved in several altercations while in the hospital, the physicians did not "feel comfortable in certifying" that he would not be a danger to himself or others. He was denied release. The Supreme Court held that his continued retention violated both due process and equal protection, because the basis for institutionalizing him as an insanity acquittee—the mental illness that generated his criminal conduct—had disappeared.

Editors' Note: The Need for a Sufficient Impairment

Most difficulties in applying insanity criteria arise in determining whether an accused's mental impairment had a sufficient impact on the conduct constituting the charged crime to justify acquittal. A defendant's claim to insanity acquittal may, however, be barred without inquiry into the effect of his impairment if the underlying impairment is not sufficient to give rise to the defense. *M'Naghten* itself required that a defendant show that at the time of the conduct he had a "disease of the mind." The Model Penal Code formulation of the defense requires a "mental disease or defect." Revisions of the insanity standard since Hinckley have tended to increase the importance of the long-standing requirement of a sufficient underlying impairment as a means of limiting inappropriate claims of insanity without complicated and difficult inquiries into the effects of particular impairments. The federal statute (reprinted at page 491) and similar state statutes now require a "*severe* mental disease or defect."

Whether an impairment had a sufficient impact upon a defendant's cognitive (or volitional) capacity is important only if the impairment is one that can give rise to the defense. There is general agreement that "disease of the mind" under *M'Naghten* or "mental illness or defect," whether severity is required or not, includes both what is commonly called mental retardation as well as mental illness. What limits, if any, the law places upon the impairments that can be sufficient, however, has troubled the courts.

Generally, the question is assumed to be whether the defendant's condition must come within any particular diagnostic categories used by mental health professionals.

In *State v. Coombs*, 18 Ohio St.3d 123, 124, 480 N.E.2d 414, 416 (1985), for example, the appellate court commented that the trial court would have erred had it used a standard requiring that a defendant prove a disorder amounting to a psychosis or a neurosis.

Nevertheless, mental health professionals and some courts assume that a defendant relying upon a mental illness must establish that the impairment would justify a diagnosis of psychosis. This assumption may be accurate under statutes after Hinckley. In its statement on the insanity defense, the American Psychiatric Association made the following recommendation:

> Definitions of mental disease or defect sometimes, but not always, accompany insanity defense standards. * * * Allowing insanity acquittals in cases involving persons who manifest primarily "personality disorders" such as antisocial personality disorder (sociopathy) does not accord with modern psychiatric knowledge or psychiatric beliefs concerning the extent to which such persons do have control over their behavior. Persons with antisocial personality disorders should, at least for heuristic reasons, be held accountable for their behavior. The American Psychiatric Association, therefore, suggests that any revision of the insanity defense standards should indicate that mental disorders potentially leading to exculpation must be *serious*. Such disorders should usually be of the severity (if not always of the quality) of conditions that psychiatrists diagnose as psychoses.

American Psychiatric Association Statement on the Insanity Defense, 140 Am.J. Psychiatry 681, 685 (1983).

The Sociopath, "Antisocial Personality," and Others with "Personality Disorders." There is widespread agreement that a condition justifying "only" the diagnosis of sociopath, psychopath, or antisocial personality cannot serve as a basis for an insanity defense.

Section 4.01(2) of the Model Penal Code standard (reprinted at page 488) was arguably designed to embody this position. Perhaps, however, it does not accomplish this task. In adopting the Model Penal Code provision, the California Supreme Court observed:

> [A]lthough [subdivision 2] was designed to deny an insanity defense to psychopaths and sociopaths, it does not have that precise effect. What it does is prevent consideration of a mental illness if that illness is manifested only by a series of criminal or antisocial acts. If that illness manifests itself in some other way as well, then it can be considered as a "mental disease" under the ALI test, and instances of criminal or antisocial conduct can be ascribed to that disease or cited as evidence of its severity. * * * Whether this requirement denies the insanity defense to a person with an "antisocial personality" will depend upon the individual case, and on the ability of the psychiatrist to base a diagnosis upon facts additional to a list of defendant's criminal or antisocial acts.

People v. Fields, 35 Cal.3d 329, 369–70, 197 Cal.Rptr. 803, 829–30, 673 P.2d 680, 706 (1983). Turning to the wisdom of the subdivision's objective, the court continued:

If a pattern of antisocial behavior is sufficient basis for an insanity defense, then a substantial proportion of serious criminal offenders would be able to assert this defense. It may be that few would succeed in persuading a jury. But the assertion of the insanity defense by recidivists with no apparent sign of mental illness except their penchant for criminal behavior would burden the legal system, bring the insanity defense into disrepute, and imperil the ability of persons with definite mental illness to assert that defense. * * * To classify persons with "antisocial personality" as insane would put in the mental institutions persons for whom there is currently no suitable treatment, and who would be a constant danger to the staff and other inmates. Mental hospitals are not designed for this kind of person; prisons are.

The federal statute, reprinted at page 491, may limit the insanity defense more than does subdivision 2 of the Model Penal Code formulation. That was most likely the intent of the requirement that a defendant's proof include evidence of "a *severe* mental disease or defect." The House Committee report explained:

The provision that the mental disease or defect must be "severe" was added * * * as a Committee amendment. * * * The concept of severity was added to empha-size that nonpsychotic behavior disorders or neuroses such as an "inadequate per-sonality," "immature personality," or a pattern of "antisocial tendencies" do not constitute the defense.

H.R.Rep. No. 98-1030, 98th Cong., 2d Sess. 229 (1984), reprinted in [1984] U.S.Code Cong. & Adm.News 3182. Perhaps courts will restrict defendants on grounds of this sort. See *Commonwealth v. Christy*, 540 Pa. 192, 204, 656 A.2d 877, 882, cert. denied, 481 U.S. 1059, 116 S.Ct. 194, 95 L.Ed.2d 857 (1995) (defendant's evidence that he suffers from a "personality disorder" and has an "antisocial personality" would not have been admissible on whether he was insane under the *M'Naghten* test).

Substance Addiction. Can substance addiction form the basis for a defense? Probably not.

In *Commonwealth v. Tate*, 893 S.W.2d 368 (Ky.1995), the defendant, charged with robbery, offered expert testimony that he was addicted to drugs and his need to obtain money for drugs overcame his ability to conform to the law prohibiting robbery. This was properly excluded as resting on an insufficient impairment, the Kentucky Supreme Court held after surveying the case law. The general rule, the court observed, is that drug addiction alone, "without other physiological or psychological involve-ment," does not constitute a mental illness. Given that the condition of addiction results from the voluntary use of drugs, the court reasoned, the legislature could not have intended to permit this condition to support a defense.

The *Tate* court left open the possibility that a jury question would be raised if such a defendant introduced evidence that at the time of the robbery he needed a "fix" and because of this need he was unable to comply with legal requirements. A jury could find, the court apparently concluded, that the condition of needing a fix as a result of drug addiction is a mental illness sufficient to support a claim of insanity.

Gambling Disorders. Defendants relying on claimed pathological gambling as a basis for an insanity defense have generally been unsuccessful. This is not, however, because courts have held that the impairment is inherently insufficient to support a defense.

In *United States v. Runnells*, 1993 WL 124493 (4th Cir.), cert. denied, 508 U.S. 931, 956, 113 S.Ct. 2458, 3061, 125 L.Ed.2d 672, 743 (1993) (per curiam) (unreported), the Fourth Circuit summarized its case law as holding that a defendant seeking to rely on pathological gambling as a basis for a defense of insanity must first demonstrate substantial acceptance in the field of psychiatry or psychology of a causal link between pathological gambling and the criminal conduct charged in his case. Runnells himself had been charged with 24 felony counts that included conspiracy, filing false tax returns, bankruptcy fraud, criminal contempt, and obstruction of justice. His own expert conceded that a pathological gambler's inability to control his impulses had not been successfully used an a defense against legal charges. Because Runnells had failed to establish the necessary causal link, the trial court did not err in excluding his offered testimony.

Multiple Personality Disorders. Defendants claiming to be suffering from multiple personality disorder (MPD) have presented the courts with particular problems. There seems to be general agreement that this condition is sufficiently serious that it might serve as the basis of an insanity defense. The Washington Supreme Court, however, has noted that some mental health professionals are "intensely skeptical" about many reported cases of MPD and believe that in most instances MPD is consciously simulated to avoid criminal responsibility. *State v. Wheaton*, 121 Wash.2d 347, 351–52, 850 P.2d 507, 509 (1993).

Controversy has focused upon the proper approach to assessing responsibility if a defendant suffering from MPD proves that at the time of the offense his "host," "core," or dominant personality was neither conscious nor in "executive control" of the defendant's body but rather control was being exercised by one or more of his or her "alter personalities." In *Commonwealth v. Roman*, 414 Mass. 235, 606 N.E.2d 1333 (1993), the defendant introduced evidence that when she possessed heroin as charged, her behavior was under the control of "Vicky," a noncore personality. She argued that the jury should have been told to focus upon whether her core personality, Norma, lacked substantial capacity to control Vicky and to cause Vicky to conform to the law. Rejecting this approach, the Massachusetts court held that a criminal defendant must be viewed as a single personality and her responsibility assessed on that basis.

A different approach was directed by *United States v. Denny-Shaffer*, 2 F.3d 999 (10th Cir.1993). Defendant Denny-Shaffer was charged with transporting in interstate commerce a child who had been kidnapped. A defense expert testified that she suffered from MPD and that when the child was abducted two of her alter personalities (Rina and Bridget) but not her host personality were present; the expert was unable, however, to offer an opinion as to whether those alter personalities were insane under the federal standard. The trial judge took the view that such a defendant must raise the insanity of the personality in control at the time of the act and because Denny-Shaffer had not done this, there was no issue of insanity for submission to the jury. Reversing, the Tenth Circuit Court of Appeals rejected *Roman's* analysis as well as that used by the trial judge. The critical question, held the court, is whether the defendant has shown that the host or dominant personality lacked the ability to appreciate the nature and quality of the acts or the wrongfulness of those acts.

Urban Psychosis. How much flexibility the concept of mental illness has was tested in *State v. Morgan*, 195 Wis.2d 388, 536 N.W.2d 425 (App.1995). Felicia Morgan was prosecuted for several robberies and an intentional murder committed when she was 17 years old. The State's theory was that Morgan and a 15-year-old companion had gone on a 15-minute crime spree ending in the killing of another young woman to secure a leather trenchcoat the victim was wearing. Defense counsel offered at both the guilt and responsibility phases of the bifurcated trial extensive testimony that Morgan had experienced numerous instances of violence in her home and neighborhood and as a result suffered from posttraumatic stress disorder. The evidence was excluded at the guilt stage, despite her contention that it tended to show she lacked the *mens rea* required by the charged offenses, and was admitted at the second stage of the trial; the jury nevertheless rejected her claim of insanity. In the course of finding no reversible error, the appellate court noted:

> While she does not use the phrase in her appellate brief, Morgan's counsel has elsewhere used the phrase "urban psychosis" to describe her criminal defense theory for Morgan's actions * * *. We reach no conclusions on the psychiatric accuracy or clinical reliability of such a term, but note that we are unable to locate any academic or judicial support for, or recognition of, such an "urban psychosis" defense. Accordingly, this court will not be the first to give such recognition to an unfounded legal concept.

a. The Cognitively Impaired Offender
Editors' Introduction: Insanity Under Cognitive Tests

Most American jurisdictions limit the insanity defense to those defendants able to demonstrate that their underlying impairments affected their cognitive capacities. This subsection focuses upon determining whether a defendant's cognitive impairment of this sort justifies an insanity acquittal. Impairments that affect control or volition are considered in the next subsection.

The cognitive capacities that are relevant to a defendant's sanity under cognitive approaches include the abilities to perceive and ascertain reality and to reason about that reality. Generally, cognitive insanity standards provide for acquittal only of those defendants who prove that at the time of the crimes they did not know or appreciate that their conduct was in some sense wrongful. There are two major problems in applying these standards

Defining "Wrong"

As the principal case reprinted in this subsection demonstrates, a major issue under the cognitive insanity standards has been the meaning of the word "wrong." Must a defendant show that his mental impairment prevented him from understanding that his action was *legally* wrong, or is it sufficient that he establishes that his mental impairment prevented him from understanding that his action was *morally* wrong in some sense of that term?

This issue is presented most dramatically in the cases where defendants' evidence suggests that as a result of mental illness they believed that God not only authorized them to commit the crimes but also directed them to do so. These cases are sometimes, as in the principal case, called "deific command" cases. If a jury believes the defense evidence in such a case, it may conclude that the defendant retained the ability to understand that his act would be legally wrong, in the sense that it would lead to apprehension by police, prosecution in the courts, and perhaps conviction. However, the jury may also conclude that the defendant, believing that God directed him to commit the crime, had lost the ability to understand that his act was morally wrong.

The leading such case is *People v. Schmidt*, 216 N.Y. 324, 110 N.E. 945 (1915), in which Schmidt was prosecuted for the murder of Anna Aumuller. Defense experts testified that Schmidt reported that he had heard the voice of God telling him that to atone for his past sinful life, he was required to kill Aumuller. The experts reported that Schmidt believed that when he killed the victim he was in the "visible presence" of God, who directed him to kill her. Prosecution experts, on the other hand, testified that Schmidt was feigning mental illness and had no such beliefs at all. The trial judge instructed the jury to acquit Schmidt if it concluded he was mentally ill and as a result did not know that his act was wrong. It refused, however, to define "wrong," and the jury convicted.

The New York appellate court held, first, that the trial judge erred in not defining "wrong." If a defendant as a result of a mental impairment believes his actions directed by God, it reasoned, he does not know these actions are morally wrong and should be acquitted, and this should be explained to the jury. Thus at least in these "deific decree" cases, wrong means morally wrong under New York law.

Ironically, however, this was held next not to require reversal of Schmidt's conviction. In an effort to persuade the trial judge to grant a new trial, Schmidt had filed an affidavit stating that he caused Aumuller's death while performing an unlawful abortion on her. In order to avoid implicating others involved in the abortion (and thus in the death as manslaughter), he added, he falsely claimed to have killed Aumuller intentionally believing that he could feign insanity and thus avoid conviction for murder. Because he admitted fabricating the entire basis for any insanity defense at all, the appellate court reasoned, he had no right to a new trial because of the trial judge's error in instructing the jury on insanity.

The New York court acknowledged that some guilty defendants would undoubtedly raise fabricated claims that their crimes were motivated by delusional beliefs that God directed those crimes. "We can," the court responded, "safely leave such fabrications to the common sense of juries." The jury in *Schmidt* itself may have rejected the insanity defense because it insightfully recognized that Schmidt had been merely faking symptoms of mental impairment.

"Know" Versus "Appreciate"

Some modern formulations of a cognitive insanity defense, including the Connecticut one applied in the principal case, somewhat expand the defense beyond what is provided in the original *M'Naghten* formulation by replacing "know" with "appreciate." How does this enlarge the defense?

"Appreciating" that something is wrong requires more than simply "knowing" that it is wrong. A defendant whose mental illness permits him to intellectually "know" that his planned actions are wrong may nevertheless be unable to "appreciate" its wrongfulness because he has such a distorted perception of the situation. The Alabama Court of Criminal Appeals has approved a jury instruction regarding "appreciate" that states:

> A person's capacity to appreciate the criminality of his conduct is not the same as his ability to know right from wrong. A person may indeed know that doing the act that constitutes an offense is wrong and still not appreciate its wrongfulness because he does not fully comprehend or is not fully sensible to what he is doing or how wrong it is.

Brown v. State, 686 So.2d 385, 402 (Ala.Cr.App.1995).

Some defendants believe this expansion of the defense is extremely significant. In *Ivery v. State*, 686 So.2d 495 (Ala.Crim.App.1996), for example, Ivery was shown to have killed the clerk in a convenience store during a robbery. His expert testimony at trial indicated that he suffered from paranoid schizophrenia. As a result of the delusions caused by this mental illness, Ivery believed himself to be the "ninja of God" and to have been instructed by God to kill people at will and to take their money as the spoils of victory. His defense lawyer argued to the jury that the key to the case was the wording of the Alabama insanity defense, which provided that the defendant should be acquitted if he did not appreciate the criminality of his acts. One expert had acknowledged that despite his mental illness, Ivery "in a[n] abstract sense, * * * does know it is wrong to kill people." But, he continued, because of his delusional ideas Ivery "thinks he is an exception." The expert explained his own perception of the difference between "know" and "appreciate" by using an automobile analogy. He offered that both a child and an adult know what an automobile does, but their knowledge is in different degrees; the adult better appreciates the functions of an automobile than does the child. Ivery's lawyer argued to the jury, "[B]efore you can conclude that [Ivery is sane], you've got to focus in on the word 'appreciation.'" "[T]hat's the key word, appreciate," he maintained.

In *Ivery*, the jury rejected Ivery's defense of insanity and found him guilty. This may have been because the jury believed the prosecution expert witnesses who testified that Ivery was faking his mental illness entirely. It also may have been because the jurors believed the defense witnesses but nevertheless decided that Ivery's delusions did not cause him to fail to appreciate the criminality of his act of killing.

While reading the following case, consider whether the distinctions between "legally wrong" and "morally wrong" and between "know" and "appreciate" may be too difficult for jurors to understand in a way that permits them to use the critical terms to resolve particular cases. Or, perhaps the concepts reflected in some of the terms are so subtle that jurors will often lack sufficient information to make the judgments that are required by insanity standards that use these terms.

State v. Wilson

Supreme Court of Connecticut, 1997
700 A.2d 633, 242 Conn. 605.
Before BORDEN, BERDON, NORCOTT, KATZ, PALMER, MCDONALD and PETERS, JJ.

PALMER, J.

This appeal requires us to define the term "wrongfulness" for purposes of the affirmative defense of insanity * * *. A jury convicted the defendant, Andrew Wilson, of murder * * *.

The following facts are undisputed. The defendant and the victim, Jack Peters, were acquainted through the victim's son, Dirk Peters, with whom the defendant had attended high school. In early 1993, the defendant began to exhibit symptoms of a mental disorder manifested by a delusional belief that Dirk, assisted by the victim, systematically was destroying the defendant's life. Specifically, the defendant believed that, in 1981, Dirk had poisoned him with methamphetamine and had hypnotized him in order to obtain control of his thoughts. The defendant believed that Dirk had been acting with the approval of the victim, who, the defendant also believed, was the mastermind of a large organization bent on controlling the minds of others. The defendant further believed that Dirk and the victim were responsible for the defendant's loss of employment, sexual inadequacy, physical weakness and other incapacities, as well as the deaths of the defendant's mother and several family dogs. In addition, the defendant blamed the victim and Dirk for the breakup of the defendant's relationship with a former girlfriend.

Beginning in approximately February, 1993, the defendant began contacting law enforcement authorities to inform them of the conspiracy by the victim and Dirk to destroy his life and the lives of others. He informed the police that Dirk was continuing to drug and brainwash people, and that Dirk should be stopped. He blamed the victim and Dirk for his own drug involvement and claimed that they were ruining other people's lives as well. In May and June, 1993, the defendant repeatedly called the police, requesting their assistance in combating the mind control conspiracy by the victim and Dirk. The police informed him that it was impossible to investigate his allegations.

On August 5, 1993, the defendant went to see the victim at his home in the city of Greenwich. He quarreled with the victim and then shot him numerous times with a semiautomatic revolver that he had purchased two days earlier from a gun dealer in the city of New Haven.

Later that day, the defendant entered the Greenwich police headquarters and stated that he had shot the victim because he "had to do it." The defendant thereafter gave a sworn statement to the police in which he indicated, among other things, that: (1) his life had been ruined by Dirk, who had drugged, hypnotized and brainwashed him; (2) the victim had assisted Dirk in these activities; (3) Dirk and the victim were responsible for the defendant's schizophrenia; (4) the conduct of Dirk and the victim required "drastic action" and "drastic retribution"; and (5) the defendant had shot the victim repeatedly at the victim's home earlier that day.

At trial, the defendant raised his mental illness as an affirmative defense under § 53a-13. The jury, however, rejected the defendant's claim of insanity and convicted him of murder. The trial court rendered judgment sentencing the defendant to sixty years imprisonment. This appeal followed.

The primary issue raised by this appeal is whether the trial court improperly failed to give an instruction defining the term "wrongfulness" under § 53a-13(a). Section 53a-13(a) provides that "[i]n any prosecution for an offense, it shall be an affirmative defense that the defendant, at the time he committed the proscribed act or acts, lacked substantial capacity, as a result of mental disease or defect, either to *appreciate the wrongfulness of his conduct* or to control his conduct within the requirements of the law." (Emphasis added.) In this case, the defendant requested that the trial court instruct the jury that wrongfulness is comprised of a moral element, so that "an accused is not criminally responsible for his offending act if, because of mental disease or defect, he believes that he is morally justified in his conduct—even though he may appreciate that his act is criminal." The trial court, however, refused to [so] instruct the jury * * *. The defendant argues that the court's failure to charge the jury on this moral component of the insanity defense requires reversal. * * *

I

* * *

* * * In 1967 * * * the General Assembly adopted the American Law Institute's Model Penal Code test for insanity * * *. The Model Penal Code test provides, in language nearly identical to that now contained in § 53a-13(a), that "[a] person is not responsible for criminal conduct if at the time of such conduct as a result of mental disease or defect he lacks substantial capacity either to appreciate the criminality [wrongfulness] of his conduct or to conform his conduct to the requirements of law." (Brackets in original.)

For purposes of this appeal, three features of the Model Penal Code test are noteworthy. First, * * * this test encompasses * * * both a cognitive and a volitional prong. Under the cognitive prong, a person is considered legally insane if, as a result of mental disease or defect, "he lacks substantial capacity . . . to appreciate the criminality [wrongfulness] of his conduct." Under the volitional prong, a person also would be considered legally insane if "he lacks substantial capacity . . . to conform his conduct to the requirements of law." Because the defendant does not claim that the trial court misinstructed the jury on the volitional prong of the insanity test, we need not consider the application of the volitional prong in our analysis.

Second, the Model Penal Code test focuses on the defendant's actual appreciation of, rather than merely his knowledge of, the wrongfulness of his conduct. The drafters of the Model Penal Code purposefully adopted the term "appreciate" in order to account for the defendant whose "detached or abstract awareness" of the wrongfulness of his conduct "does not penetrate to the affective level." As Herbert Wechsler, chief reporter for the Model Penal Code, stated * * *: "To appreciate the wrongfulness of conduct is, in short, to realize that it is wrong; to understand the idea as a matter of importance and reality; to grasp it in a way that makes it meaningful in the life of the individual, not as a bare abstraction put in words."

The third important feature of the Model Penal Code test, and the most relevant for purposes of this appeal, is its

alternative phrasing of the cognitive prong. By bracketing the term "wrongfulness" and juxtaposing that term with "criminality," the drafters purposefully left it to the individual state legislatures to decide which of these two standards to adopt to describe the nature of the conduct that a defendant must be unable to appreciate in order to qualify as legally insane. The history of the Model Penal Code indicates that "wrongfulness" was offered as a choice so that any legislature, if it wishes, could introduce a "moral issue" into the test for insanity.

* * *

There is little dispute in this case that, by choosing the term "wrongfulness" instead of "criminality," the legislature intended to import this moral element into Connecticut's insanity statute. * * *

The more difficult question * * * is how properly to define the moral element inherent in the term "wrongfulness" under § 53a-13(a). The defendant contends that morality must be defined in purely personal terms, such that a defendant is not responsible for his criminal acts as long as his mental disease or defect causes him personally to believe that those acts are morally justified, even though he may appreciate that his conduct is wrong in the sense that it is both illegal and contrary to societal standards of morality. * * *

[T]he defendant's efforts to define morality in purely personal terms are inconsistent with the Model Penal Code, judicial precedent, and the assumptions underlying our criminal law.

The text accompanying § 4.01 of the Model Penal Code, upon which § 53a-13 is modeled, suggests that its drafters intended that the moral element of "wrongfulness" be measured by a defendant's capacity to understand society's moral standards. In his model jury charge, for example, Professor Wechsler suggests the following language: "[A] person may have knowledge of the facts about his conduct and of the immediate surrounding circumstances and still be rendered quite incapable of grasping the idea that it is wrong, *in the sense that it is condemned by the law and commonly accepted moral standards.*" (Emphasis added.) * * * [W]e conclude that the drafters of § 4.01 did not intend that a defendant who appreciates both the illegality and the societal immorality of his actions be relieved of criminal responsibility due to his purely personal, albeit delusional, moral code.

Moreover, the large majority of other jurisdictions that have considered the cognitive prong of the insanity defense has chosen a societal, rather than a personal, standard. * * *

Finally, with respect to the fundamental policies that undergird our criminal law, defining the moral element of wrongfulness according to a purely personal standard tends to undermine the "moral culture on which our societal norms of behavior are based." There may well be cases in which a defendant's delusional ideation causes him to harbor personal beliefs that so cloud his cognition as to render him incapable of recognizing the broader moral implications of his actions. In such cases, the defendant would be entitled to be acquitted under the cognitive prong of the defense.

Those cases involving the so-called "deific command," in our view, fall into this category. * * * [W]e are hard pressed to envision an individual who, because of mental disease or defect, truly believes that a divine power has authorized his actions, but, at the same time, also truly believes that such actions are immoral. An individual laboring under a delusion that causes him to believe in the divine approbation of his conduct is an individual who, in all practicality, is unlikely to be able fully to appreciate the wrongfulness of that conduct.

A defendant should not be relieved of criminal liability, however, if his mental illness does not deprive him of substantial capacity to appreciate the boundaries of societal morality and if he elects to transgress those boundaries in pursuit of a delusional personal belief system that he appreciates society would not itself accept. To permit otherwise "would seriously undermine the criminal law [by allowing] one who violated the law to be excused from criminal responsibility solely because, in his own conscience, his act was not morally wrong."

Accordingly, we reject the personal test as an improper method of measuring a defendant's capacity to appreciate the moral element inherent in the term "wrongfulness." Consistent with the considerations discussed above, this test is flawed because it fails to account for principles of societal morality that the Model Penal Code test incorporated, other jurisdictions have embraced, and our criminal law assumes.

[W]e disagree * * * that, in rejecting a purely personal test, we have given "short shrift" to the intentions of the Model Penal Code drafters by denigrating the importance of the term "appreciate." The assumption upon which this assertion rests is that a deluded individual who acts in accordance with a personal code of morality may "know" that society morally would condemn his actions, but can never "appreciate" that moral condemnation. We reject this unsupported proposition. We acknowledge that an individual's delusion may distort his sense of personal morality to the point that he no longer has the capacity to appreciate that society morally condemns his conduct. That a particular individual may establish that he suffers from such a delusion does not mean, however, that every delusional individual who harbors a personal moral code also lacks

the capacity to appreciate the social immorality of his actions. Rather, the question of whether a defendant's delusional moral code prevents him from appreciating the social immorality of his actions is an issue of fact to be decided on a case-by-case basis. Thus, in our view, an individual who both appreciates the social immorality of his conduct and is able, as a matter of volition, to conform his actions to the requirements of law should not be absolved from criminal responsibility, as a matter of law, upon proof that he instead acted in accordance with a divergent personal belief system.

[T]he test endorsed by the state is superior to the personal test. According to the state, a defendant can succeed under the cognitive prong of the insanity defense if he can demonstrate that, at the time of the prohibited conduct, he lacked substantial capacity to appreciate that his actions were contrary to societal morality. Although we agree with the state that the defendant's appreciation of morality must be defined in terms of his appreciation of society's moral standards[,] the state's test is insufficient in one important respect. Consider, for example, a defendant who, because of a mental delusion, misperceives reality and, on the basis of that misperception, engages in criminal conduct that he believes is necessary to advance a greater social good, but who, at the same time, also appreciates that society is unaware of the need to bring about this social good and, because of this ignorance, would not condone his actions. For example, a defendant might, because of a mental delusion, believe that his infant child suffers from a rare condition that will cause her to die unless she ingests certain medication that he can obtain only through theft. This hypothetical defendant might appreciate that society, objectively speaking, would disapprove of him stealing the medication but, nevertheless, may believe that, if society knew of his child's condition, it would no longer view his theft of the medication as immoral. Under the state's test, such an individual would probably not be considered legally insane because he retains substantial capacity to appreciate that, objectively speaking, society does not approve of his actions.

In our view, such an approach represents an overly restrictive interpretation of what the legislature intended by choosing the term "wrongfulness" instead of the term "criminality." * * * "[W]rongfulness" was chosen in order to connote a moral element with a meaning independent of illegality. Under the state's test, however, moral wrongfulness would be measured strictly in terms of society's objective disapproval; to the extent that this objective disapproval is embodied in the criminal code, the state's test renders morality and criminality virtually synonymous. We are unwilling to negate the legislature's choice of the term "wrongfulness" by treating these otherwise distinct terms as virtually identical.

We conclude, rather, that a defendant does not truly "appreciate the wrongfulness of his conduct" as stated in § 53a-13(a) if a mental disease or defect causes him both to harbor a distorted perception of reality and to believe that, under the circumstances as he honestly perceives them, his actions do not offend societal morality, even though he may also be aware that society, on the basis of the criminal code, does not condone his actions. Thus, a defendant would be entitled to prevail under § 53a-13(a) if, as a result of his mental disease or defect, he sincerely believes that society would approve of his conduct if it shared his understanding of the circumstances underlying his actions. This formulation appropriately balances the concepts of societal morality that underlie our criminal law with the concepts of moral justification that motivated the legislature's adoption of the term "wrongfulness" in our insanity statute.

A jury instruction on the cognitive prong of § 53a-13(a) should set forth this formulation as clearly as possible. The trial court should inform the jury that a person may establish that he was legally insane if he proves that, at the time he committed the prohibited conduct, due to mental disease or defect he suffered from a misperception of reality and, in acting on the basis of that misperception, he did not have the substantial capacity to appreciate that his actions were contrary to societal morality, even though he may have been aware that the conduct in question was criminal. The trial court should instruct the jury further that, in deciding whether the defendant had substantial capacity to appreciate that his conduct was contrary to societal morality, it must not limit its inquiry merely to the defendant's appreciation that society, objectively speaking, condemned his actions. Rather, the jury should be instructed that it must also determine whether the defendant maintained a sincere belief that society would condone his actions under the circumstances as the defendant honestly perceived them. Finally, the trial court also should instruct the jury that, if it finds that the defendant had the substantial capacity to appreciate that his conduct both violated the criminal law and was contrary to society's moral standards, even under the circumstances as he honestly perceives them, then he should not be adjudged legally insane simply because, as a result of mental disease or defect, he elected to follow his own personal moral code.

II

* * *

The state contends that the defendant was not entitled to an instruction defining the term "wrongfulness" under § 53a-13(a) because he failed to adduce sufficient evidence to support such an instruction. According to the state, the evidence submitted on the defendant's behalf did not establish,

in accordance with the wrongfulness test discussed above, that his "delusion deprived him of a substantial capacity to appreciate that the [killing] of the victim was wrong under society's moral standards." Although the state does not seriously dispute that the defendant suffered from a mental disease that caused him to misperceive reality, the state claims that the evidence merely tended to show, in accordance with the purely personal standard we have rejected, that the defendant had followed his own subjective moral calculus in seeking revenge for the perceived actions of the victim and Dirk. * * *

At trial, the defense called several expert witnesses to testify regarding their examinations of the defendant and the conclusions drawn therefrom. Jay Berkowitz, a psychiatrist employed by the department of correction and working at the Bridgeport correctional center (center), testified that he had conducted a ninety minute interview and psychiatric evaluation of the defendant after the defendant's arrival at the center. Berkowitz testified that the defendant had expressed remorse for killing the victim but felt that it was something that he had to do in order to save other people. Sue Anne O'Brien, a psychiatric nurse who also worked at the center, testified that she had spoken with the defendant for approximately ninety minutes. O'Brien testified that the defendant believed that he had "saved all of us from this evil thing [that] was occurring," and she quoted the defendant as stating, "'I saved you. I saved everyone here. I've saved the world.'"

Another expert witness, Leslie Kurt, a forensic psychiatrist, testified extensively with respect to her examination and diagnosis of the defendant, with whom she had met in a series of six interviews for a total of nearly twelve hours. Kurt stated that the defendant believed that the victim had used methamphetamine and hypnosis to gain control over people and had done nothing to prevent the intensely evil crimes of Dirk. According to Kurt, the defendant likened the victim to Sirhan Sirhan, Jim Jones and Charles Manson, and expressed a belief that he had a higher moral duty to stop the victim and Dirk. Kurt described the defendant's belief in a higher moral duty as something akin to a person believing, during World War II, that he or she had a moral obligation to assassinate Adolf Hitler even though that person understood that this killing would be illegal.

On the basis of this testimony, we conclude that the defendant presented sufficient evidence from which a jury reasonably could have found, by a preponderance of the evidence, that, due to a mental disease or defect, the defendant misperceived reality and, in acting on the basis of that misperception, did not substantially appreciate that his actions were contrary to societal morality. It is true, as the state maintains, that the defendant tried repeatedly, albeit unsuccessfully, to convince the police that the activities conducted by the victim and Dirk were dangerous and unlawful. Thus, it reasonably could be said that the defendant understood that society, unpersuaded of the danger posed by the victim, did not condone his actions. The test that we have adopted, however, requires a fact finder to look beyond the defendant's appreciation of society's objective disapproval of his actions and to inquire whether the defendant, as a result of mental disease or defect, truly believed that society, if it were aware of the circumstances as he honestly perceived them, would have condoned his actions.

It is also true, as the state argues, that other evidence tended to show that the defendant might not have acted in furtherance of society's moral standards at all, but was instead motivated by a desire to seek retribution for wrongs he mistakenly believed the victim and Dirk had perpetrated against him. This countervailing evidence, however, goes to the weight of the defendant's proof, and not to whether the defendant was entitled to a jury instruction correctly defining the term "wrongfulness." * * *

The judgment is reversed and the case is remanded for a new trial.

BORDEN, NORCOTT and PETERS, JJ., concur.

KATZ, J., concurring.
* * *
* * * I disagree with the majority * * * that the defense should not apply to an individual who is mentally ill and because of that illness believes that society's rules do not apply to his or her actions. It is my belief that such a person is not capable of appreciating the legal and social import of his or her acts, and, therefore, should not be held criminally responsible.

Societal morals are reflected by the criminal code. * * * Because murder is an offense against good morals, it has been made a crime. The test adopted by the court today attempts to create a distinction between issues of legality and morality, but by focusing on a societal standard it has, I believe, conflated the two in much the same way as does the state in its test, which this court has properly rejected.

* * * I am concerned with the defendant who: (1) suffers from a mental disease or defect; and (2) knows that society would condemn his action under any set of facts; but (3) is unable, because of his mental illness, to appreciate that societal condemnation. I agree with the majority that an individual who is mentally ill and who, although ill, is yet able to fully appreciate societal morality, should be held criminally responsible for his or her illegal acts, absent a claim of lack of volition. Where we differ, however, is that I consider that, as a matter of law, an individual who, as a

result of his or her mental illness, believes that his or her personal moral code allows him or her to act against societal mores cannot appreciate that societal condemnation and, therefore, cannot be held criminally responsible.

Indeed, I wonder whether this particular defendant could meet the requirements of the majority's test and could convince a jury that society, knowing what he believed, would have approved of his actions. In this case, the defendant did everything in his control to notify law enforcement authorities, as well as other members of society, of the facts about the victim as he believed them, and society, knowing what the defendant believed, nevertheless declined to act. How, then, could the defendant argue that society would approve of his conduct? Even if the defendant were to claim that society failed to act only because it did not believe him, the defendant nevertheless has acted in the face of society's disapproval. Rather than interpreting society's reaction as a signal that he may be wrong in his assumptions about the victim and his justification for his actions, he has assumed that society is wrong for not believing him. As I interpret the majority's test, under these circumstances, this defendant, deluded as he may be, cannot claim insanity as a defense. Contrary to the majority's position that these circumstances raise a jury issue[,] I believe that these circumstances, under the majority's test, preclude the jury's consideration of the insanity defense.
* * *
[Justice Berdon also concurred only in the result, agreeing generally with Justice Katz's conclusions although for slightly different reasons than she relied upon.]

MCDONALD, J., dissenting.
* * *
The majority now approves a jury instruction that provides a definition of wrong as something against societal morality, but not objectively speaking. * * * Under this formula, a person who knows murder is wrong in the eyes of society and knows society does not share his perception that his victim needs to be killed may be excused if he believes, because of mental illness, that society would condone the killing if it, too, saw that need. This should not be written into our law. If the defendant recognizes his conduct is both criminal and wrong in the eyes of society, as murder clearly is[,] public safety demands that he be held responsible for his actions. I do not agree that it should be a defense that the defendant believes society did not approve of his conduct only because society failed to appreciate a needed "greater social good" which would come from those same actions.

It is hoped that we can still rely on the common sense of jurors, coping with these enigmatic instructions, to safeguard us.

Accordingly, I respectfully dissent.

<u>Work</u>

<u>Criminal Law</u>:
- ~~Do 1 page paper on To Kill a Mockingbird~~
- ~~Prepare for Oral Presentation~~
- ~~Read more Cases~~

<u>Judicial Process</u>
- ~~Do 2 Essays for Monday~~
- ~~Read Material + Articles~~

<u>Constitutional Law</u>
- ~~Read Cases~~

<u>Sports in History</u>
- Start Paper on Black Sox ~~Scandal and Gambling in Baseball~~
- ~~Watch Hoop Dreams and do Paper.~~

<u>Baseball</u>
- ~~Do Marlins Lists~~
- ~~Redo Spikes List + Make Call~~
- ~~Look Over Apparel List~~
- ~~Call Fusco - for Uniform + Ad~~
- ~~Contact Kelly's~~

Note

A quite traditional approach to applying a narrow cognitive insanity standard to a defendant's delusional belief that a spouse was having an affair is illustrated by *Chancellor v. State*, 165 Ga.App. 365, 301 S.E.2d 294 (1983). Chancellor was tried for the murder of a woman she believed, because of her mental illness, was having an affair with her husband. The trial court refused to instruct the jury on insanity by "delusional compulsion." Finding no error, the appellate court first concluded that under Georgia law it is no defense to murder that the deceased was an illicit lover of the defendant's spouse. Turning to the insanity issue, it reasoned:

> Before such a defense is available it must appear that the defendant was acting under a delusion which, if true, would justify her act. Since the delusion allegedly suffered by appellant (the adulterous affair between her husband and the victim) does not justify homicide a charge on delusional compulsion was not authorized.

b. The Volitionally Impaired Offender

Many American jurisdictions have limited their insanity defense criteria so as to preclude the defense from being based upon impairments that cause only so-called volitional impairments. A major rationale for this approach is that claims of volitional impairment are seldom if ever meritorious. Moreover, they are difficult to address and resolve and create a considerable risk of so confusing and confounding trial courts that those tribunals will sometimes erroneously acquit because of the confusion.

Consider the arguments for and against permitting the defense to be based on volitional impairment in light of the following case. The opinion is that of the trial judge to whom the case was submitted after the defendant waived his right to trial by jury. Is the defendant's claim of being so nonblameworthy as to require acquittal so frivolous that defendants should be barred from making such claims (as they now are in most jurisdictions)? Would the evidence in the case have so confused a jury that it gave rise to a significant risk that a jury would have mistakenly acquitted?

United States v. Pollard

United States District Court, Eastern District of Michigan, 1959
171 F.Supp. 474, set aside, 282 F.2d 450 (6th Cir.1960),
mandate clarified, 285 F.2d 81 (6th Cir.1960).

LEVIN, DISTRICT JUDGE.

The defendant, Marmion Pollard, having waived indictment, the Government instituted this prosecution on a three-count information charging him * * * with the attempted robbery of the Chene-Medbury Branch of the Bank of the Commonwealth and the 24th-Michigan Branch of the Detroit Bank & Trust Company on May 21, 1958, and the attempted robbery on June 3, 1958, of the Woodrow Wilson-Davison Branch of the Bank of the Commonwealth. These banks * * * are located in Detroit, Michigan.

On arraignment * * * a plea of not guilty was entered. The case was then assigned to me for trial.

Prior to trial, I was advised that a psychiatric report of a psychiatrist retained by the defendant indicated that the defendant was, at the time of the offenses, suffering from a diseased mind which produced an irresistible impulse to commit the criminal acts. Subsequently, a report was submitted to the Government by each of two psychiatrists who had examined the defendant at its request. These reports, which were made available to me, agreed with the conclusion of the defendant's psychiatrist. It then appeared to me that it would be in the interest of justice to secure a psychiatric evaluation of defendant's state of mind based upon more extensive study. I was particularly desirous of having such a study made inasmuch as the psychiatric reports submitted to me were based on interviews that did not exceed a maximum of two hours with each of the three psychiatrists. I, thereupon * * * entered an order that the defendant be sent to the United States Medical Center at Springfield, Missouri. After a study of thirty days, the Medical Center submitted a report which was introduced in evidence. The gist of the report may be set out as follows:

> During the period under inquiry, "a dissociative state may have existed and that his [defendant's] actions may not have been consciously motivated.
>
> "It is, therefore, our opinion that during the period in question, Pollard, while intellectually capable of knowing right from wrong, may have been governed by unconscious drives which made it impossible for him to adhere to the right.
>
> "* * * We readily acknowledge our inability either to marshal sufficient objective facts or formulate a completely satisfactory theory on which to base a solid opinion as to subject's responsibility during the period in question." [2]

The defendant elected to be tried by the Court without a jury. During the trial, the following facts appeared:

The defendant is an intelligent, twenty-nine year old man. In 1949, he married and, during the next four years, three sons and a daughter were born of this marriage. He was apparently a well-adjusted, happy, family man. In 1952, he became a member of the Police Department of the City of Detroit and continued to work as a policeman until he was apprehended for the acts for which he is now being prosecuted. In April, 1956, his wife and infant daughter were brutally killed in an unprovoked attack by a drunken neighbor.

On May 21, 1958, one day before he remarried, at about 11:00 A.M., defendant entered the 24th-Michigan

Branch of the Detroit Bank & Trust Company. He paused for a few moments to look over the bank and then proceeded to an enclosure in which a bank official was at work. He told the official, whom he believed to be the manager, that he wanted to open a savings account. He then walked through a swinging gate into the enclosure, sat down at the desk, pulled out a gun and pointed it at the official. He ordered the official to call a teller. When the teller arrived, the defendant handed a brown paper grocery bag to him and told him to fill it with money. While it was being filled, defendant kept the bank official covered. The teller filled the bag with money as ordered and turned it over to the defendant. Thereupon, defendant ordered the bank official to accompany him to the exit. As both the defendant and bank official approached the exit, the official suddenly wrapped his arms around the defendant, who then dropped the bag and fled from the bank and escaped.

About 4:00 P.M., on the same day, he entered the Chene-Medbury Branch of the Bank of the Commonwealth and walked to a railing behind which a bank employee was sitting. He pointed his gun at the man and told him to sit quietly. The employee, however, did not obey this order but instead raised an alarm, whereupon the defendant ran from the bank and again escaped.

After the defendant was apprehended by the Detroit Police under circumstances which I shall later relate, he admitted to agents of the Federal Bureau of Investigation that after his abortive attempts to rob the two banks, he decided to rob a third bank and actually proceeded on the same day to an unnamed bank he had selected but decided not to make the attempt when he discovered that the bank was "too wide open"—had too much window area so that the possibility of apprehension was enhanced.

On June 3, at about 3:00 P.M., the defendant entered the Woodrow Wilson-Davison Branch of the Bank of the Commonwealth and went directly to an enclosure behind which a male and female employee were sitting at desks facing each other. Defendant held his gun under a jacket which he carried over his right arm. He ordered the woman employee to come out from behind the railing. In doing so, she grasped the edge of her desk. Defendant, in the belief that she may have pushed an alarm button, decided to leave but ordered the woman to accompany him out of the bank. When they reached the street, he told her to walk ahead of him, but not to attract attention. Defendant noticed a police car approaching the bank and waited until it passed him, then ran across an empty lot to his car and again escaped.

On June 11, 1958, he attempted to hold up a grocery market. He was thwarted in the attempt when the proprietor screamed and, becoming frightened, the defendant

---

[2] Not only is this report, in the light most favorable to the defendant, inconclusive but in part is based upon facts which were not substantiated during the trial. The personal and social history section of the report states that after his wife's death "it was noted by his supervisors that he [defendant] became less efficient, less interested, more withdrawn and a noticeably less effective policeman". However, the police department records introduced in evidence reveal that the defendant's police work covering the period of inquiry, if anything, was more effective than his service prior to the death of his wife

fled. In so doing, he abandoned his automobile in back of the market where he had parked it during the holdup attempt. Routinely, this car was placed under surveillance and later when the defendant, dressed in his Detroit Police Officer's uniform, attempted to get in it, he was arrested by detectives of the Detroit Police Force.

After his apprehension, the defendant confessed to eleven other robberies, or attempted robberies.

The three psychiatrists who submitted the written reports, all qualified and respected members of their profession, testified that in their opinion the defendant, at the time he committed the criminal acts, knew the difference between right and wrong and knew that the acts he committed were wrong but was suffering from a "traumatic neurosis" or "dissociative reaction", characterized by moods of depression and severe feelings of guilt, induced by the traumatic effect of the death of his wife and child and his belief that he was responsible for their deaths because by his absence from home he left them exposed to the actions of the crazed, drunken neighbor. They further stated that he had an unconscious desire to be punished by society to expiate these guilt feelings and that the governing power of his mind was so destroyed or impaired that he was unable to resist the commission of the criminal acts. In their opinion, however, the defendant was not then, nor is he now, psychotic or committable to a mental institution.

Three of defendant's fellow police officers, called as defense witnesses, testified that during the period in which the defendant committed the criminal acts he had a tendency to be late for work; that at times he was despondent; and that he occasionally seemed to be lost in thought and did not promptly respond to questions directed to him. One of the officers testified that on one occasion, he repeatedly beat the steering wheel of the police car in which they were riding, while at the same time reiterating the name of his murdered wife. However, none of them found his conduct or moods to be of such consequence that they believed it necessary to report the defendant to a superior officer.

Defendant's present wife, who impressed me as an intelligent person, testified that on two occasions defendant suddenly, and for no reason apparent to her, lapsed into crying spells and that he talked to her once or twice about committing suicide. She also testified that during one such period of depression he pointed a gun at himself; that she became frightened and called the police; that the police came, relieved him of his gun, and took him to the precinct police station; and that after his release he appeared jovial and acted as if nothing had happened. Defendant's brother-in-law stated that the defendant had always been a very happy person but that he became noticeably despondent after the death of his wife and child and expressed a desire

to commit suicide because he now no longer had a reason for living.

A police lieutenant of the Detroit Police Department testified that the defendant's police work, during the period with which we are now concerned, as evidenced by his efficiency rating and his written duty reports, was, if anything, more effective than his service prior to the death of his wife.

Counsel for defendant contends that since all the medical testimony was to the effect that the defendant was suffering from an irresistible impulse at the time of the commission of the offenses, this Court must accept this uncontroverted expert testimony and find him not guilty by reason of insanity.

I have great respect for the profession of psychiatry. Vast areas of information have been made available through its efforts. I have found much comfort in having the assistance of psychiatrists in the disposition of many cases on sentence. Yet, there are compelling reasons for not blindly following the opinions of experts on controlling issues of fact. Expert testimony performs a valuable function in explaining complex and specialized data to the untutored lay mind. When the experts have made available their knowledge to aid the jury or the Court in reaching a conclusion, their function is completed. The opinions and judgments or inferences of experts, even when unanimous and uncontroverted, are not necessarily conclusive on the trier of the facts and may be disregarded when, in the light of the facts adduced, such judgments, opinions or inferences do not appear valid. The jury, in determining the probative effect to be given to expert testimony, is not to disregard its own experience and knowledge and its collective conscience. It follows that this is also true of the judge sitting without a jury.

The psychiatrists, as I hereinbefore related, testified that the defendant suffered from severe feelings of depression and guilt; and that in their opinion he had an irresistible impulse to commit criminal acts, an unconscious desire to be apprehended and punished; and that he geared his behavior to the accomplishment of this end. However, his entire pattern of conduct during the period of his criminal activities militates against this conclusion. His conscious desire not to be apprehended and punished was demonstrably greater than his unconscious desire to the contrary. After his apprehension, despite searching interrogation for over five hours by Detroit Police Officers and by agents of the Federal Bureau of Investigation, he denied any participation in criminal conduct of any kind. It was only after he was positively identified by bank personnel that he finally admitted that he did attempt to perpetrate the bank robberies. I asked one of the psychiatrists to explain this apparent inconsistency. In answer to my question, he stated that although the defendant had an unconscious desire to be apprehended and punished, when the possibility of apprehension became direct and immediate, the more dominating desire for self-preservation asserted itself. This explanation may have merit if applied to individual acts. However, the validity of a theory that attempts to explain the behavior of a person must be determined in light of that person's entire behavioral pattern and not with reference to isolated acts which are extracted from that pattern. The defendant's pattern of behavior of May 21, 1958, discloses that the desire for self-preservation was not fleeting and momentary but continuing, consistent and dominant. What, then, becomes of the theory of irresistible impulse? Looking to the events of that day, I am asked to believe, first, that the defendant, acting pursuant to an irresistible impulse, selected a bank site to rob, entered the bank to accomplish that end, purposely failed in the attempt and when the end he sought, apprehension, was in view, escaped because of the dominance, at the moment of ultimate accomplishment, of the stronger drive for self-preservation. I must then believe that when the defendant knew he was apparently free from detection, his compulsive state reasserted itself and that he again went through the steps of planning, abortive attempt and escape. And if I acquiesce in this theory, what other psychiatric theory explains his subsequent conduct—his plan to rob a third unnamed bank and the rejection of that plan because of his subjective belief that the possibility of apprehension would be too great? If the theory remains the same, then it appears that in the latter case, the fear of apprehension and punishment tipped "the scales enough to make resistible an impulse otherwise irresistible." It is a logical inference that, in reality, the other robbery attempts were made as the result of impulses that the defendant did not choose voluntarily to resist because, to him, the possibility of success outweighed the likelihood of detection which is in essence a motivation for all criminal conduct. The impulse being resistible, the defendant is accountable for his criminal conduct.

Psychiatrists admit that the line between irresistible impulse and acts which are the result of impulses not resisted is not easy to trace. To the extent that the line may be traced, the distinguishing motivation of the action, whether the act is performed to satisfy an intrinsic need or is the result of extrinsic provocation, is a determining factor. Admittedly, motivations may be mixed. However, all the facts have clearly established that defendant's criminal activity was planned to satisfy an extrinsic need by a reasoned but anti-social method. The defendant had financial problems of varying degrees of intensity throughout his life. He had financial difficulties during his first marriage. He was now embarking upon a second marriage. He was about to

undertake the responsibility of supporting not only a wife and himself, but also four children, three of them the product of his first marriage. In statements given to agents of the Federal Bureau of Investigation admitting his criminal activity, he stated: "Inasmuch as I was about to marry my second wife, I decided that I would not lead the same type of financially insecure life that I led with my first wife. I needed about $5,000 in order to buy a house. My only purpose in deciding to rob a bank was to obtain $5,000 and if I obtained the money, I did not intend to continue robbing." Defendant's entire pattern of conduct was consistent with this expressed motivation.

Life does not always proceed on an even keel. Periods of depression, feelings of guilt and inadequacy are experienced by many of us. Defendant was a devoted husband and loving father. His feelings of despondency and depression induced by the brutal killing of his wife and infant daughter were not unnatural. How else the defendant should have reacted to his tragic loss I am not told. His conduct throughout this crucial period did not cause any concern among his colleagues. All stated unequivocally that in their opinion he was sane. Significant also is the fact that his present wife married him on May 22, 1958, after a year of courtship. It is a permissible inference that defendant's conduct relative to his mental condition, as related by her, did not suggest to her that the defendant was insane.

I am satisfied beyond a reasonable doubt that the defendant committed the acts for which he is now charged and that when he committed them he was legally sane.

I, therefore, adjudge the defendant guilty of the three counts of the information.

Notes

1. On appeal, the trial judge's decision was reversed. In view of the "unanimous testimony of the government's medical experts * * * and appellant's expert witnesses" and the testimony of the lay witnesses, the appellate court explained, the presumption of sanity was overcome and the government failed to sustain its burden of proving sanity under the federal rule. *Pollard v. United States*, 282 F.2d 450, mandate clarified, 285 F.2d 81 (6th Cir. 1960).

2. Perhaps there is no realistic possibility of obtaining "scientific" testimony concerning the extent to which particular offenders were or were not prevented by their impairments from exercising volitional control with regard to antisocial actions in which they were inclined to engage. Recall that the American Medical Association's report on the insanity defense asserted

that "by necessity," psychiatrists must view human behavior as determined by causes other than free will or volitional choice; see page 494. The matter was reviewed by Howard and Conway, Can There Be an Empirical Science of Volitional Action?, 41 Am.Psychologist 1241 (1986). The authors concluded that the consensus in psychological research "has been that concepts such as self-determination or volitional behavior are either illusory or unscientific." They suggested, however, that research can be designed to probe the extent to which choice affects behavior and that despite difficulties such research should be undertaken. Why "should [psychologists] * * * take the difficult and risky steps of conducting research on human volition?" Among the reasons identified by Howard and Conway was the need to respond to the disenchantment toward psychology harbored by those in other disciplines, including law as well as philosophy and theology, that often entertain volitional models of human behavior.

2. Diminished Capacity

The doctrine frequently referred to as "diminished capacity" can be stated with deceptive simplicity; it simply provides that in deciding whether a defendant acted with the state of mind required by the offense under consideration, the trier of fact may consider, among other things, any psychological impairment of the defendant and the extent to which that impairment affected his "capacity" to entertain the state of mind at issue.

As the discussion earlier in this chapter indicated, such a doctrine is sometimes proposed, and in some jurisdiction has been accepted, as a complete alternative to the insanity defense. More commonly, however, it is considered for adoption in addition to a defense of insanity. Arguably, the desirability of the doctrine differs, or at least presents different considerations, depending upon whether it is offered as an alternative to, or as a companion of, the "complete" defense of insanity.

Prior to the United States Supreme Court 1996 decision in *Montana v. Egelhoff*, discussed in the Editors' Introduction to Section B of this chapter at page 467, at least some courts were receptive to the argument that federal due process considerations barred exclusion of expert testimony that a defendant—because of mental impairment—did not have the *mens rea* required by the charged offense. *United States v. Skodnek*, 896 F.Supp. 60 (D.Mass.1995) (all expert testimony to this effect cannot be excluded without violating due process). However, as was developed in that Editors' Introduction, *Egelhoff* may settle the federal constitutional question.

The case law in this area, including the opinions in the principal case that follows, can easily generate confusion regarding the terminology used by various judges: diminished capacity, diminished responsibility, and—as used in the principal case—"strict *mens rea* use of psychiatric testimony." Terminology is addressed further in the notes after the principal case. As a preliminary matter, however, it is useful to keep in mind that American courts often use the term "diminished capacity" to refer to a "rule" or position that permits a criminal defendant to introduce evidence of mental impairment in support of a contention that this evidence establishes that the prosecution has failed to show the defendant acted with the culpable mental state required by the crime charged. Despite suggestions to the contrary in the material, this is in substance no different from what is sometimes called the "strict *mens rea* use of psychiatric testimony."

State v. Provost

Supreme Court of Minnesota, 1992
490 N.W.2d 93.

SIMONETT, Justice.

Defendant-appellant Provost was convicted of first degree murder following a bifurcated trial where he pleaded not guilty and not guilty by reason of insanity. [The bifurcated trial procedure is discussed in the Editors' Introduction to Section C(1) of this chapter, at page 498.]. On appeal, defendant claims * * * error in prohibiting him from presenting expert psychiatric testimony during the first (or guilt) phase of the trial. * * *

Defendant Robert Provost, Jr., and Barbara Larson were married in August 1987, soon after they graduated from high school. During the fall of 1989, their relationship, never a happy one, worsened; defendant became increasingly violent, assaulting Barbara, destroying her possessions, and threatening to kill her. In December 1989 he threatened to burn her, as in the movie "The Burning Bed."

At about 12:30 P.M. on December 29, 1989, defendant walked into the Blaine City Police Station. After waiting patiently for the receptionist to wait on someone else, he asked to be locked up because he had burned his wife. Defendant told the police officers who talked to him that he had burned his wife, that he wanted to get help for her fast, and that they should call an ambulance. As he spoke, defendant became very upset and agitated, pacing back and forth in the lobby and sometimes refusing to answer questions. At one point he said, "Help her!" As they talked, the officers detected the smell of gasoline and noticed that the hair on defendant's face and neck was singed.

The officers tried to get defendant to tell them where his wife was; and he eventually told the officers that she was in the Carlos Avery Wildlife Refuge. Defendant also mentioned having made a 911 telephone call. Upon checking, the police found that there had been a telephone call earlier in the day reporting a woman needing help in the Carlos Avery area, and that an officer had then driven through that area but was unable to find anyone needing help.

Because the defendant appeared unable to give coherent directions to his wife's location, and because the officers believed she might be injured and in need of help, they asked defendant if he could show them where his wife was. He indicated that he could. Defendant was then handcuffed and placed in the police car. As they drove along, the officers asked defendant for directions, and at one point asked for the wife's name. Defendant shouted at the officers to hurry and to go faster, saying that his wife was hurt.

Following defendant's directions, the officers found Barbara Provost's badly burned body and a dented gas can in the middle of a dirt road in the Carlos Avery Wildlife Refuge. Defendant was then transferred to Chisago County authorities * * *.

Prior to trial, defense counsel notified the State of his intention to call Dr. Turnquist, a psychiatrist, during the first or "guilt" phase of the trial, to testify that Provost did not intend to kill his wife. In response, the prosecution moved for an order in limine to prevent defendant from calling Dr. Turnquist. The trial court issued an order restricting the psychiatrist's testimony "to factual observations relevant to intent and premeditation, and a discussion of normal psychological processes involved in intent formation and premeditation." Faced with these limitations, defense counsel elected not to call his expert in the first trial stage. To preserve his claim of error for a later appeal, defense counsel made an offer of proof as to what his expert's testimony would have been.

During the first phase of the trial, the coroner testified that Barbara Provost had died of smoke inhalation, that her body was extensively burned with a 3- or 4-inch hole in the chest, and that the severity of the burns indicated use of an accelerant. Also during the first phase of the trial, defendant testified to taking a gas can from his parents' garage and putting it in his car, and then forcing his wife into the car. He related taking his wife to the Carlos Avery Wildlife Refuge, pouring gasoline on her, lighting her on fire, dousing her with gasoline again, and then leaving her in the snow. At the close of his direct testimony, after denying he intended to kill his wife, defendant added, "I still believe that she is alive."

In the second trial stage, the defense called Dr. Kevin Turnquist and Dr. Jeffrey Boyd. Dr. Turnquist, a psychiatrist, diagnosed defendant as suffering from chronic and subchronic undifferentiated schizophrenia, and gave an opinion that defendant did not know the nature of his acts on December 29, 1989. Dr. Boyd's psychological testing confirmed the diagnosis of chronic undifferentiated schizophrenia. He testified that schizophrenia can impair a person's volition and the capacity to control one's behavior. The State called three expert witnesses: Dr. Michael Farnsworth, a psychiatrist; Dr. Douglas Fox, a psychologist; and Dr. Carl Schwartz, a forensic psychiatrist. Each of the State's expert witnesses testified that defendant understood that he was burning his wife and that he knew it was wrong.

* * *

III.

* * *

The trial court's order in limine limited the expert to testifying [at the first stage of the trial] on factual observations relevant to intent and premeditation, and a discussion of the normal psychological processes involved in forming intent and premeditation. Confronted with these restrictions, defense counsel elected not to call his expert during the first phase of the trial. Instead, to preserve his claim of error on appeal, counsel made an offer of proof as to what his expert would have said.[3]

On appeal, defendant * * * asserts that denying a defendant the right to present relevant psychiatric opinion evidence on the element of intent is a violation of his federal right to due process and a fair trial, arguing * * * that a *per se* exclusion of this type of evidence, irrespective of its competency, relevance and helpfulness, interferes impermissibly with his right to present a defense.

* * *

[D]efendant contends that [we] should not preclude expert psychiatric testimony on whether a mentally ill defendant subjectively premeditated and intended the death of the victim. Presumably the expert testimony is not being offered to show diminished capacity or diminished responsibility, but only to show whether the defendant, in fact, formed the guilty mind which is an element of the crime charged. This approach is sometimes called the "strict *mens rea* model." Two law review articles which propose this model are Arenella, The Diminished Capacity and Diminished Responsibility Defenses: Two Children of a Doomed Marriage, 77 Colum.L.Rev. 827 (1977); and Morse, Undiminished Confusion in Diminished Capacity, 75 J.Crim.L. & Criminology 1 (1984) (hereinafter referred to respectively as Arenella or Morse). Relying in part on these two articles, the dissent in this case makes a good argument for a strict *mens rea* use of psychiatric testimony, but even so we are not persuaded this approach is appropriate.

The role of psychiatry in determining criminal culpability has generated no end of judicial writing, and there is no wish here to repeat what has been said many times elsewhere.[4] To respond to the arguments raised by the dissent and by the defendant, it is necessary, however, to explain in some detail our position and how we arrive at it.

A.

It might be well to begin with how criminal intent is typically proven:

> It is not always easy to prove at a later date the state of a man's mind at that particular earlier moment when he was engaged in conduct causing or threatening harm to the interests of others. He does not often contemporaneously speak or write out his thoughts for others to hear or read. He will not generally admit later to having the intention which the court requires. So of course his thoughts must be gathered from his words (if any) and actions in the light of all the surrounding circumstances. Naturally, what he does and what foreseeably results from his deeds have a bearing on what he may have had in mind.

LaFave & Scott, Substantive Criminal Law § 3.5, pp. 317–18 (2d ed. 1986).

Even when mental illness impairs a defendant's capacity for forming criminal intent, such intent is still determined from what a defendant says and does. Take this case. Notwithstanding defendant's obvious mental illness and bizarre behavior, and although no psychiatric testimony was admitted into evidence during the first stage of the trial, the evidence of both premeditation and intent to kill was overwhelming.

Nevertheless, the dissent argues that psychiatric opinion testimony is somehow helpful in determining what defendant really intended and should have been admitted. Perhaps if relevancy were simply a matter of logic, we might agree, but it is not. * * * Minn.R.Evid. 403 * * * provides that relevant evidence may be excluded if its probative value is substantially outweighed by other considerations, including prejudice and confusion of the issues. * * * Consequently, to conclude that psychiatric testimony may have some relevance to a guilty mind is only the beginning, not the end, of any inquiry into admissibility of that testimony.

---

[3] Defense counsel's offer of proof was as follows: "Dr. Turnquist would say: the defendant is schizophrenic, and that typically a schizophrenic person has a thought disorder, that it can loosen associations, that their determination of cause and effect and consequences thus can be impaired, and that should be considered by the jury as to whether or not he intended the death of Barbara Provost."

[4] Our research has indicated some 42 states which have discussed the admissibility of psychiatric opinion evidence as it bears on *mens rea*. Twenty-four of these states, in one fashion or another, have allowed such testimony, while 18 states have taken a contrary view. * * * The use of psychiatric testimony on the issue of *mens rea* is also recognized by the Model Penal Code, § 4.0 (1962) and by the American Bar Association Criminal Justice Mental Health Standards, Standard 7-6.2 (1989). * * *

Even jurisdictions that allow psychiatric testimony on *mens rea* appear to acknowledge that logic has its limits; most of these jurisdictions "illogically" restrict admissibility to crimes involving "specific intent" as distinguished from something called "general intent," and a few limit this testimony to homicide. Indeed, if one were to be perfectly logical about it, psychiatric opinion testimony on how the mind subjectively forms intent should be admissible even in the case of a perfectly sane defendant who is suffering from no mental abnormality.

It is sometimes suggested that expert testimony is needed to dispel the old notion that mental illness is really not an illness at all but simply a moral failing. There is, however, hardly a family in these modern times that has not had some experience with mental illness. The fact is jurors understand and accept that mental illness is a real illness. They also understand that people with mental illness can, and do, function in our society without committing crimes. The question in these cases is not whether the defendant is mentally ill, but rather what the defendant, mentally ill or not, subjectively "had in mind."

Psychiatric opinion testimony, in any event, should not be allowed to show diminished capacity or diminished responsibility. The role of the court and jury is to determine whether the facts of a particular case fit the crime as defined by the legislature. In assessing this "fit," it is generally assumed that all those who commit the same acts with the same *mens rea* are guilty of the same offense, regardless of differences in upbringing, mental condition, or environmental background, so long as they understand the nature of their act and that it was wrong. In other words, all defendants who are not insane are held to a certain minimal standard of conduct. The criminal law seeks to match legal responsibility with moral culpability in a consistent and fair manner, while at the same time providing adequate societal controls so that members of the public may live in relative peace and security.

The doctrines of diminished capacity and diminished responsibility run counter to these basic societal assumptions. The diminished capacity approach "opens the courtroom doors to virtually unlimited psychiatric testimony," and does not lend itself to a consistent and principled administration of criminal justice. The diminished responsibility approach seeks to make the punishment fit the crime by, in effect, changing the crime (or at least by transferring the sentencing function from the judge to the jury). Diminished responsibility, as Arenella points out, separates sane offenders into two subgroups, namely: a group of "normal" fully culpable criminal offenders and a group of mentally abnormal but sane offenders with reduced culpability. Not only has our legislature not recognized such sub-

groups, but it is questionable whether psychiatry is able to tell into which subgroup a particular offender belongs.

The dissenting opinion would avoid the twin pitfalls of diminished capacity and diminished responsibility by limiting psychiatric opinion testimony to strict *mens rea*, i.e., only to whether in fact the defendant formed a guilty mind. But if psychiatric opinion testimony is admitted on the issue of whether the defendant *did or didn't* have the requisite guilty mind, the jury will inevitably take the testimony as an invitation to consider whether the defendant *could or couldn't* have a guilty mind. Indeed, why else (so jurors would quite properly wonder) would the psychiatrist be testifying? Cautioning the jury not to consider diminished capacity or responsibility would only cause confusion. The law cannot giveth psychiatric testimony on the one hand and taketh it away with the other.

In addition to the diminished capacity spill-over effect, another factor severely limits the probative value of psychiatric opinion testimony. If expert testimony is admissible to negate *mens rea*, it is also admissible to affirm *mens rea*. This leads to unprofitable disagreements between the experts hired by both sides. See, e.g., Morse, supra, at 37 ("Trial and appellate courts are literally bombarded by irrelevant, confusing, and prejudicial testimony from mental health professionals who either do not understand what the law requires of them or who have not-so-hidden agendas.").

* * *

B.

[Our case law] disallows * * * "expert psychiatric opinion testimony."

First of all, psychiatric opinion testimony is not admissible on whether, in fact, the defendant had the capacity to form the requisite subjective state of mind. This testimony impermissibly introduces diminished capacity into the jury's deliberations. The testimony is also inconsistent with the premise of the guilt stage of the bifurcated trial, namely, that the defendant is capable of forming the *mens rea* but simply has not done so. * * *

Nor is psychiatric opinion testimony admissible on the ultimate question of whether in fact the defendant had the requisite *mens rea* when he committed the crime. Because *mens rea* is a legal construct, a medical opinion is being improperly elicited on a mixed question of law and fact. * * * Equally important, any probative value of such opinion testimony is substantially outweighed by the confusion and prejudice engendered by the "semantic jousting" of the experts. * * *

In our view, psychiatric opinion testimony is not helpful on whether a person capable of forming a specific intent did in fact formulate that intent. Though a subjective state of mind may at times be difficult to determine, there is no mystery to *mens rea*, the latinism notwithstanding. Jurors in their everyday lives constantly make judgments on whether the conduct of others was intentional or accidental, premeditated or not. Thus, to do something intentionally is to do it with the purpose of accomplishing that something. To set a person on fire with the purpose of ending that person's life is to torch with intent to kill. The psychiatrist may look at what the defendant said and did to give an opinion whether the torching was done with intent to kill or to hurt, but the factfinder can do this too; indeed, it is the factfinder's job to do it, not the expert's as a thirteenth juror.

Arguably, psychiatric opinion testimony might still be useful in explaining generally about the characteristics and origins of mental illness and disorders; but these opinions, in the initial stage of a bifurcated trial, are of minimal usefulness to a jury already aware that the defendant's conduct is mentally abnormal. To add conflicting descriptions of the defendant's condition by disagreeing experts adds very little to help the jury determine the defendant's subjective state of mind. See Morse, supra, at 52 ("knowing that the defendant suffers from paranoid schizophrenia would add no additional, legally relevant information.") Whether defendant suffers from "undifferentiated schizophrenia" or from a "personality disorder" (as the disagreeing experts testified in this case during the second stage), the fact remains that the defendant still has the capacity to form intent, and the question is what was the intent that was formed. In legal terms, this psychiatric opinion testimony has, at best, minimal relevance, the probative value of which is substantially outweighed by counterconsiderations.

* * *

To sum up, we hold the following rules shall govern the admissibility of psychiatric opinion testimony in the first stage of the bifurcated trial:

1) Psychiatric opinion testimony on the ultimate question of whether in fact the defendant had the requisite subjective *mens rea* is inadmissible.

2) Psychiatric opinion testimony on whether the defendant, in fact, had the capacity to form the requisite subjective *mens rea* is inadmissible.

3) Other psychiatric opinion testimony is generally inadmissible except in a few cases, such as to explain a particular mental disorder characterized by a specific intent different from the requisite *mens rea*, or where aspects of a defendant's past mental illness history are relevant. The trial judge should require an offer of proof outside the hearing of the jury on the admissibility of the proffered expert testimony or parts thereof, carefully weighing the relevancy and

probative value of the proffered evidence, if any, against the likelihood of prejudice or confusion.

C.

This case affords a good illustration of how the foregoing evidentiary rules are applied. According to the defendant's offer of proof, the defense psychiatrist would have testified "the defendant is schizophrenic, and that typically a schizophrenic person has a thought disorder, that it can loosen association, that then determination of cause and effect and consequences thus can be impaired." This offer of proof was properly rejected.

The offered testimony lacked sufficient probative value. It consisted of a diagnosis of a mental condition and an opinion on how schizophrenics typically function, which really added nothing to what the defendant "had in mind," which is the issue under consideration in the first phase. Indeed, the defendant's testimony in this case was that he had the capacity to form a specific intent and that he in fact formed a specific intent; he claims only that his intent was an intent to hurt, not an intent to kill. Expert testimony that defendant had a "thought disorder" has no probative value on which intent the defendant actually had in mind when he torched his wife. In the offer of proof the expert did not give an opinion on the ultimate issue of *mens rea*; if he had, such an opinion would have been inadmissible. * * *

We need only add that exclusion of psychiatric opinion testimony on *mens rea* from the guilt phase of a bifurcated trial is not a denial of constitutional due process. * * *

Affirmed.

GARDEBRING, Justice (dissenting in part).

* * *

* * * [M]y reading of * * * [our case law] * * * is that it left open the possibility that * * * expert psychiatric testimony on the elements of intent and premeditation might be relevant and thus admissible. * * *

In order to determine whether the trial court's action in curtailing the scope of the proffered testimony was correct, I would have us look at whether the testimony would have been relevant to the existence of intent. To convict appellant of murder in the first degree, the state must prove that appellant caused the death of his wife, and that he did it with premeditation and intent to effect her death. * * *

Minn.R.Evid. 401 defines relevant evidence as that "having *any* tendency to make the existence of any fact * * * more probable or less probable than it would be without the evidence." (Emphasis added.) As noted in the committee comment, the test is one of logic and assessment of probative value, and represents a liberal approach to relevancy, and thus admissibility.

I am convinced that, although not by any means dispositive on questions of intent and premeditation, expert psychiatric testimony can have a bearing, can have a tendency to make their existence "more probable or less probable." This evidence is appropriately weighed and considered by the jury, along with the physical facts of the incident, in determining whether the state has proved the necessary elements of the crime.

* * *

As with all other expert testimony, the admissibility of a particular expert's testimony and opinion on the *mens rea* elements in the first phase of a bifurcated trial will be governed by the requirements of the Minnesota Rules of Evidence. Expert testimony concerning the defendant's mental disease or defect and its bearing on the existence of a specific *mens rea* should be admissible only if it meets the tests of evidence normally applied to offers of expert testimony.

* * *

* * * I would conclude that evidence, including expert opinion testimony, concerning the defendant's mental disease or defect at the time of the alleged offense, is admissible to negate the existence of a necessary specific *mens rea*. As the majority concedes * * *, this position is consistent with the conclusion reached by the majority of jurisdictions which have considered this issue, and is in conformity with the Model Penal Code and American Bar Association Criminal Justice Mental Health Standards.

This determination is consistent with our traditional approach to admissibility of evidence based on our faith in the jury's ability to meaningfully assess the weight assigned to particular pieces of testimony. * * *

While I would conclude that some expert testimony may be relevant to the issues of intent and premeditation in the first part of a bifurcated trial, the content of that testimony must be narrowly tailored to address only the issues of defendant's actual *mens rea*, the particular intent and premeditation the defendant possessed at the time of the offense. It may not address any general *capacity* to intend or premeditate. By limiting the evidence in this way, I would adopt what has been called the "strict *mens rea*" model of the admissibility of evidence to negate the elements of a charged crime.

Further, I want to stress what I am *not* advocating today. I do not advocate the adoption of a new affirmative defense. The admissible evidence under this rule would simply go to negating an element of the required prima facie case.

I would not adopt the "diminished capacity" doctrine. No evidence which merely shows a defendant may be merely less *capable* of entertaining the required *mens rea* is admissible.

I would not adopt the "diminished responsibility" doctrine. No evidence which is offered to show that a defendant is somehow less responsible for his or her actions because of a mental disease is admissible. Each defendant must take full responsibility for the crime he or she committed.

However, if a defendant charged with murder in the first degree *did not* possess the required *mens rea* elements of intent and premeditation, and that lack is proved by relevant evidence, including psychiatric evidence, then he or she is not guilty of that crime, although possibly still guilty of a lesser crime not requiring the proof of those specific *mens rea* elements. * * *

For these reasons, I would allow the admission of psychiatric evidence on the issue of intent for the limited purpose of negating its presence.

Notes and Questions

1. Best defined, "diminished responsibility" would relate to criminal responsibility as that is defined in the law governing insanity, but provide for some legal effect to be given to proof that a defendant's responsibility is diminished but not lacking. American courts, however, sometimes use the phrase "diminished responsibility" to refer to the doctrine at issue in *Provost*.

   Would a doctrine of diminished responsibility be desirable? The English Homicide Act, 5 & 6 Eliz. II, ch. 11, § 2 established such a doctrine for purposes of homicide cases. Under this statute, a defendant shown guilty of murder is to be convicted only of manslaughter if the defense shows that at the time of the killing the defendant "was suffering from such abnormality of mind * * * as substantially impaired his mental responsibility for acts and omissions in * * * the killing."

   If such an approach is desirable, might it be better provided for by a statute along the following lines:

   > § _. Diminished responsibility
   >
   >   1. An offender shall be regarded as being of diminished responsibility if the trier of fact finds that at the time of the offense he was suffering from a mental disease or defect and that this substantially reduced his ability to appreciate the nature and quality or wrongfulness of his acts [or his ability to conform to the requirements of law], although not to the extent necessary to establish the defense of insanity.
   >
   >   2. Upon a finding of diminished responsibility, [the offense shall be treated for sentencing purposes as one degree lower than would otherwise be the case] [any sentence of

imprisonment imposed may not exceed, in minimum and maximum terms, two-thirds of the minimum and maximum that are generally authorized for the offense].

2. In those jurisdictions in which it has been adopted, the doctrine of diminished capacity is often limited in application. Pennsylvania, for example, appears to restrict it to first degree murder. *Commonwealth v. Garcia*, 505 Pa. 304, 311, 479 A.2d 473, 477 (1984). More commonly, it is limited to "specific intent" crimes, but the difficulty of adequately defining "specific intent" sometimes makes the substance of this limitation somewhat unclear.

Limitations imposed upon the defense in some jurisdictions seem designed to limit its application to those situations in which there is a lesser included offense of the crime charged that lacks the specific intent required by the crime charged. This would mean that the doctrine could only be invoked in those situations where its application would result in conviction of the defendant of a lesser offense. Such a limitation, the court suggested in *State v. Thompson*, 695 S.W.2d 154, 159 (Mo.App.1985), is necessary to prevent the doctrine from becoming a "complete" defense and thus a substitute for insanity. A defendant who escapes conviction for a crime to which the doctrine applies will often, it is assumed, be guilty of a different (and less serious) offense to which it does not apply. Thus the doctrine permits *reduction* of the seriousness of the offense of which the impaired offender is found guilty.

3. The Model Penal Code proposed a quite broad and apparently unqualified acceptance of the diminished capacity approach:

> Section 4.02. Evidence of Mental Disease or Defect Admissible When Relevant to Element of the Offense * * *
>
> (1) Evidence that the defendant suffered from a mental disease or defect is admissible whenever it is relevant to prove that the defendant did not have a state of mind that is an element of the crime.

The comments acknowledged that as of the time of the drafting of this provision—1955—"there is a sharp division of authority throughout the country." But they continued:

> Some jurisdictions decline for reasons of policy to accord evidence of mental disease or defect an admissibility extensive with its relevancy to prove or disprove a material state of mind. We see no justification for such a limitation of this kind. If states of mind such as deliberation or premeditation are accorded legal significance, psychiatric evidence should be admissible when relevant to prove or disprove their existence to the same extent as any other evidence.

Model Penal Code, Comments to § 4.02 193 (Tent. Draft No. 4, 1955).

Editors' Note: California's Experimentation with Diminished Capacity

The California version of diminished capacity has had an interesting history, composed in large part of efforts by the California Supreme Court to integrate a diminished capacity approach with creative development of the statutory definitions of several homicide offenses (reprinted at page 153). The court's objective appears to have been to create a system of diminished responsibility for homicide, as *diminished responsibility* was distinguished from *diminished capacity* in note 1 after *Provost*.

The California doctrine is sometimes referred to as the *Wells-Gorshen* Rule because of the two early cases in which it was recognized, *People v. Wells*, 33 Cal.2d 330, 202 P.2d 53, cert. denied 338 U.S. 836, 70 S.Ct. 43, 94 L.Ed. 510 (1949), and *People v. Gorshen*, 51 Cal.2d 716, 336 P.2d 492 (1959).

In *Wells*, the court held that the trial court erred in excluding psychiatric testimony offered to prove the absence of the malice aforethought required by the crime charged, serious assault by a prison inmate with malice aforethought. In *Gorshen*, the defendant had been charged with murder. The trial court permitted psychiatric testimony to the effect that despite Gorshen's acknowledged intent to shoot the victim, he lacked malice aforethought as required for murder because of sexual hallucinations and other symptoms of abnormality. This was approved on appeal.

The California court's subsequent decisions between 1964 and 1974, building on *Wells* and *Gorshen*, can be read as an effort to redefine the states of mind required by the homicide offenses so as to make diminished capacity an appropriate and effective vehicle for accommodating the seriousness of the offenses for which homicide defendants are convicted and the culpability of their conduct given evidence of substantial psychological impairment.

In *People v. Wolff*, 61 Cal.2d 795, 40 Cal.Rptr. 271, 394 P.2d 959 (1964), the court addressed the standard for determining whether a defendant engaged in the premeditation required for first degree murder. Such premeditation, it held, requires that the defendant "maturely and meaningfully reflect upon the gravity of his contemplated act." Psychiatric testimony and the defendant's age in the case (the defendant had been 15 years old at the time he killed his mother) established the absence of premeditation under this standard:

> He knew the difference between right and wrong; he knew that the intended act
> was wrong and nevertheless carried it out. But the extent of his understanding,
> reflection upon it and its consequences, with realization of the enormity of the
> evil, appears to have been materially—as relevant to appraising the quantum of
> his moral turpitude and depravity—vague and detached.

Thus, the conviction for first degree premeditated murder was not supported by the evidence and was reduced by the court to second degree murder.

In several cases, the court considered the meaning of malice aforethought as it related to the nature and quantity of evidence of mental aberration necessary to establish that a killing is manslaughter rather than murder. In *People v. Conley*, 64 Cal.2d 310, 49 Cal.Rptr. 815, 411 P.2d 911 (1966), the court added a new requirement to the state of mind required for murder: "[a]n awareness of the obligation to act within the general body of laws regulating society * * *." It then explained *Gorshen* as involving evidence tending to establish that although the defendant premeditated within the meaning of first degree murder, he acted without malice because his abnormality had caused him to forget "about God's laws and human laws and everything else."

In *Conley*, a defense psychologist testified at trial that at the time of the killing Conley was in a "dissociative state" and because of "personality fragmentation" did not function with his normal personality. Other evidence indicated he was intoxicated at the time of the killings. On the basis of this testimony, the court concluded a jury could find that although Conley deliberated and premeditated the killing, his abnormality (and his intoxication) showed he may have acted without malice aforethought. The failure to instruct the jury concerning this possibility was therefore error.

Although *Conley* added a new cognitive dimension to the *mens rea* required for murder, it did not address the extent to which evidence of volitional impairment might be relevant to the absence of malice aforethought. This issue was addressed in *People v. Poddar*, 10 Cal. 3d 750, 111 Cal.Rptr. 910, 518 P.2d 342 (1974). At Poddar's trial for the killing of a woman associate, substantial evidence of his abnormality was introduced. The jury was instructed on second degree murder and manslaughter and was told that diminished capacity could negate the malice aforethought necessary for murder, but the trial judge refused to instruct the jury more specifically on the relationship between impaired mental processes and malice aforethought. Poddar's proposed instructions explaining the need for an understanding of the duty that the law imposed and an ability to conform one's conduct to the comprehended duty were refused. The resulting conviction for second degree murder was reversed on appeal. Addressing the question of the relevance of diminished capacity to murder when the prosecution relies upon malice implied from acts committed with a "wanton disregard for human life," the court explained:

> The effect * * * which a diminished capacity bears on malice in a second degree murder-implied malice case is relevant to two questions: First, was the accused because of a diminished capacity unaware of a duty to act within the law? A person is, of course, presumed to know the law which prohibits injuring another. Second, even assuming that the accused was aware of this duty to act within the law, was he, because of a diminished capacity, unable to act in accordance with that duty?

Because the instructions did not apply the evidence to the underlying issues with sufficient specificity, the court erred in refusing more specific instructions.

Poddar, then, seemed to leave no doubt that impairment of *volition* could establish the absence of the malice aforethought required for murder, at least in some circumstances. A defendant "unable to act in accordance with [what he knew was the] duty [to act within the law]" was entitled to be acquitted of murder (because proof of malice aforethought would be missing) but could be convicted of manslaughter.

California continued throughout this period to follow the *M'Naghten* standard for the defense of insanity. As compared to many other jurisdictions, then, the state had a comparatively narrow complete defense of insanity. The *Wolff–Conley–Poddar* case law appeared to reflect a perception by the California Supreme Court that the law should give defendants only a limited opportunity for complete acquittal on grounds of psychological abnormality but it should also make a creative effort to reduce the seriousness of the homicide offense for which some impaired killers were responsible. That reduction should reflect essentially reduced, but still present, responsibility for the criminal conduct.

Thus, an impaired person who killed but was sane under *M'Naghten* might under *Wolff* avoid liability for first degree murder if his mental impairment showed he failed to maturely and meaningfully reflect upon the gravity of the act of killing his victim. His liability might be reduced even further—from second degree murder to manslaughter—under *Poddar* in either of two ways. First, if the evidence showed the defendant suffered from a cognitive impairment that caused him to lack intellectual awareness of his obligation act within the law, he would be guilty of manslaughter rather than murder. Second, if the evidence showed a volitional impairment, which was totally irrelevant to sanity/insanity, that rendered him unable to act within the duty to follow the law (which he intellectually understood), he would be guilty of murder rather than manslaughter.

Obviously the California court sought to distribute proved and sane but impaired killers among first degree murder, second degree murder, and manslaughter, depending upon the degree of their responsibility.

The public, however, rebelled. In 1981, legislation responded to these case law developments. Some modification was also made by 1982 and 1984 legislation. The California Penal Code's definition of malice, necessary for murder, contained in § 188 (reprinted at page 153), was supplemented by the addition of the following paragraph:

> When it is shown that the killing resulted from the intentional doing of an act with express or implied malice as defined above, no other mental state need be shown to establish the mental state of malice aforethought. An awareness of the obligation to act within the general body of laws regulating society is not included within the definition of malice.

The definition of first degree murder, contained in § 189 (reprinted at page 153), was supplemented by the addition of the following:

> To prove the killing was "deliberate and premeditated," it shall not be necessary to prove the defendant maturely and meaningfully reflected upon the gravity of his or her act.

In addition, the following sections were added to the California Penal Code:

§ 21. Manifestation of intent; evidence of lack of capacity or ability to control conduct

(a) The intent or intention is manifested by the circumstances connected with the offense.

(b) In the guilt phase of a criminal action * * * evidence that the accused lacked the capacity or ability to control his conduct for any reason shall not be admissible on the issue of whether the accused actually had any mental state with respect to the commission of any crime. * * *

§ 28. Evidence of mental disease, mental defect or mental disorder

(a) Evidence of mental disease, mental defect, or mental disorder shall not be admitted to show or negate the capacity to form any mental state, including, but not limited to, purpose, intent, knowledge, premeditation, deliberation, or malice aforethought, with which the accused committed the act. Evidence of mental disease, mental defect, or mental disorder is admissible solely on the issue of whether or not the accused actually formed a required specific intent, premeditated, deliberated, or harbored malice aforethought, when a specific intent crime is charged.

(b) As a matter of public policy there shall be no defense of diminished capacity, diminished responsibility, or irresistible impulse in a criminal action

* * *

(d) Nothing in this section shall limit a court's discretion, pursuant to the Evidence Code, to exclude psychiatric or psychological evidence on whether the accused had a mental disease, mental defect, or mental disorder at the time of the alleged offense.

§ 29. Mental state; restriction on expert testimony; determination by trier of fact

In the guilt phase of a criminal action, any expert testifying about a defendant's mental illness, mental disorder, or mental defect shall not testify as to whether the defendant had or did not have the required mental states, which include, but are not limited to, purpose, intent, knowledge, or malice aforethought, for the crimes charged. The question as to whether the defendant had or did not have the required mental states shall be decided by the trier of fact.

The California Supreme Court addressed the effect of the revisions in *People v. Saille,* 54 Cal.3d 1103, 820 P.2d 588, 2 Cal.Rptr.2d 364 (1991). The court noted that there was "initially some confusion" as to the relationship between section 25, subdivision (a) (providing that evidence of impairment is not admissible to show or negate capacity to form a mental state) and section 28 (providing that evidence of mental illness is admissible on whether an accused actually formed a specific intent). Courts and commentators have concluded, it added, that "the two sections are complementary and that both are operative."

The last sentence of section 188, *Saille* continued, directly repudiates the expanded definition of malice aforethought developed in *Conley* and *Poddar.* Therefore malice under California law no longer includes an awareness of the obligation to act within the general body of laws regulating society and the capability of acting in accordance with such awareness. It added, however:

Sections 22 and 28 state that voluntary intoxication or mental condition may be considered in deciding whether the defendant actually had the required mental state, including malice. These sections relate to *any* crime, and make no attempt to define what mental state is required.

In a murder prosecution based on the theory that the defendant acted with intent to kill, that is, express malice, the defendant can still use evidence of mental impairment to raise a reasonable doubt as to whether he acted with that intent. If the defendant raises such a reasonable doubt, he cannot be convicted of a crime more serious than involuntary manslaughter.

Under the statutory reforms responding to the *Wells–Gorshen* case law, a California defendant charged with murder can still introduce expert testimony that he or she was psychologically impaired at the time of the crime although not insane within the meaning of the insanity defense. The nature of the testimony such a defendant can submit to the jury, and the arguments the defendant can make on the basis of it, are far more limited than before 1981.

Testimony that the defendant was volitionally impaired and thus was unable to follow what he or she understood were legal obligations is simply inadmissible under the terms of section 21(b). Thus *Poddar's* holding that volitional impairment could reduce but not eliminate responsibility—by rendering the accused guilty of manslaughter rather than murder—was negated.

An expert testifying about a homicide defendant's cognitive impairment, moreover, cannot testify in terms of the defendant's *capacity* to form the malice aforethought required for murder, but can testify in support of the argument that the defendant did not *actually* form that malice aforethought required. Expert testimony suggesting that the defendant's mental impairment caused him to actually be unaware of his duty to act within the law is not admissible, because, under section 189 as amended, awareness of that duty is no longer a part of the *mens rea* required for murder. *Conley's* interpretation of malice aforethought as requiring awareness of this duty was thus negated. Because no awareness of this duty is required, the statutory revisions also rejected *Poddar's* opportunity for a defendant to reduce his liability to manslaughter by showing a cognitive impairment that prevented him from being aware of that duty.

Finally, under section 29, the expert cannot expressly testify that in the expert's opinion the defendant did not actually act with malice aforethought. The expert can testify to what he believes the defendant knew, understood, and intended. Defense counsel can argue to the jury that the jury should reason from the expert's testimony that the defendant did not actually act with malice aforethought. An expert cannot, however, testify explicitly to an opinion as to whether the defendant did or did not have the mental state required by murder.

A California defendant charged with premeditated first degree murder can similarly offer expert testimony about his or her mental impairment and its effects to support the contention that he or she did not actually premeditate. Because premeditation now under section 189 no longer requires that the person "maturely and meaningfully" reflect upon the gravity of the killing, testimony suggesting that the defendant did not actually so reflect on the killing is no longer admissible. Under section 29, a defense expert witness cannot explicitly testify that in the expert's opinion the defendant did not premeditate before killing the victim. The expert must testify in other terms about the defendant's mental processes and defense counsel must argue to the jury that it should infer from the expert's factual conclusions that the defendant did not actually premeditate.

As the California legislature expressly stated in section 28(b), these changes were intended to abolish the "defense" of diminished capacity or diminished responsibility that had developed under *Wells, Gorshen,* and their progeny. Defendants' limited remaining right to rely on mental impairment and expert testimony in support of contentions that they never "actually formed"—in the language of section 28(a)—the *mens rea* required by the charged offense is sometimes, perhaps facetiously, called "diminished actuality."

Saille also rejected the argument that the legislative modification of the *Wells–Gorshen* diminished responsibility approach raised a due process problem:

The Legislature can limit the mental elements included in the statutory definition of a crime and thereby curtail use of *mens rea* defenses. If, however, a crime requires a particular mental state the Legislature may not deny a defendant the opportunity to prove he did not possess that state. The abolition of the diminished capacity defense and limitation of admissible evidence to actual formation of various mental states [does] not violate the due process right to present a defense. If there is no due process impediment to the deletion of malice as an element of the crime of felony murder, there is likewise no problem here.

Chapter 16

Other Defenses

CHAPTER CONTENTS

This chapter considers three defensive matters that arise from quite different concerns and reflect very different exculpatory considerations.

As with other areas of criminal law, it is necessary to address the extent to which federal and state constitutional considerations limit the flexibility available to courts and legislatures in regard to these defensive doctrines. In each of these areas, it is useful to consider whether constitutional doctrines require that a defense be made available to defendants and what if any limitations constitutional doctrines impose upon any such defense as is made available. To some extent, federal constitutional considerations may define the outer perimeter within which policy choices may be made on the state legislative or judicial level.

A. NECESSITY, DURESS, AND JUSTIFICATION GENERALLY
Editors' Introduction: The Defenses of Necessity and Duress and the General Principle of Justification

Necessity is generally used to describe situations in which the accused was motivated to commit a crime by a perception that doing so was necessary to prevent some evil or harm greater than would result from the crime.

In a sense, necessity is a general principle that is reflected in other more specific defensive doctrines that cover more particular situations. Self-defense, as considered in Chapter 13, for example, consists of a showing that the defendant believed that committing the crime was necessary to avoid harm to the defendant himself, a greater evil than the crime and its injury to the victim. Necessity as a separate defense, then, is something of a residual doctrine, to be considered after other, more specific doctrines—such as self-defense—have been found inapplicable. If a defendant's motivation does not fit within any other defense, it may come within the relatively broad and flexible defense of necessity.

This breadth of the doctrine of necessity is reflected in its embodiment in section 3.02 of the Model Penal Code, reprinted later in this section. Section 3.02 does not label the defense as that of "necessity," but rather calls it "Justification Generally," and only secondarily uses the term, "Choice of Evils." This reflects the basic nature of the defense.

In the case that follows, *United States v. Bailey*, the United States Supreme Court indicated that modern cases have blurred the traditional distinction between necessity and duress. Although the lower federal court in this case may have merged the two, it is at least arguable that in most jurisdictions the distinction between the two matters remains much clearer than the Supreme Court suggested.

Duress

Duress, as the *Bailey* Court noted, arises from coercion to commit the crime applied by another person. In a sense, then, duress—like self-defense—is simply a specific application of the general principle reflected in necessity. The defendant is exculpated from criminal liability because he chose to commit the crime to avoid a greater evil than would flow from his commission of the crime; the avoided evil in the duress scenario is the harm that the person applying the duress would do if the defendant did not commit the offense.

Duress must be distinguished from the basic requirement of voluntary conduct, considered in Chapter 3. If an accused's physical conduct is shown to have been actually and literally generated by another, the accused has not performed any voluntary act upon which any criminal liability whatsoever can be based. In *Bailey*, for example, if the defendants could have shown that the jail guards had dragged them, screaming "No, I want to stay!," out of the jail, the court would have had no need to consider possible defenses to specific crimes such as escape, because the defendants' acts of leaving custody would not have been voluntary. As a practical matter, duress is thus limited to situations in which the defendant is motivated in committing the crime by a threat by another person to do harm if the defendant does not commit the crime. The other person may have already done some harm to emphasize the threats, but it is the threat of future harm that provides the potentially exculpating motivation.

In *Bailey*, there seems to have been little basis for regarding the defendants as having any claim of a defense of duress, so defined. The evidence they relied upon appears not to have included any suggestion that jail guards (or any others) threatened to burn them, deny them medical care, or to otherwise harm them in any way *if they did not at least attempt to escape.* Perhaps the defendants believed the appeal of their defensive contention would be increased if they could appear to make it come within duress as well as necessity.

Necessity

The doctrine of necessity has been most widely discussed in regard to situations in which a human life was taken in order to prevent the death of others. Several early cases offer conflicting approaches to determining whether necessity can ever justify a person taking the life of another to save her own life and, if this is conceivably permissible, when this can be done.

One of the two leading early cases, *United States v. Holmes,* 26 Fed.Cas. 360 (No. 15,383) (C.C.E.D.Pa.1842), involved an American vessel that struck an iceberg in April, 1842. Nine crew members and thirty-two passengers got into the ship's longboat commanded by the first mate. Twenty-four hours after the ship had sunk, the weather worsened and the longboat appeared about to sink. The mate commanded that some of the passengers be thrown overboard, although he directed his crew not to part man and wife and not to throw over any women. Fourteen men and two women went overboard and perished; the women may have jumped into the sea after their brother was ejected from the boat. After daylight the next morning, two men who had hidden themselves were discovered and thrown into the sea. At no point had the passengers been consulted concerning these actions. All passengers and crew members aboard the longboat were saved the next day when the boat was sighted by another ship. One of the crew members was indicted and tried for manslaughter. The trial judge instructed the jury as follows:

> Where * * * a case does arise, embraced by [the] "law of necessity," the penal
> laws pass over such case in silence * * *. For example, suppose that two persons
> who owe no duty to one another that is not mutual, should by accident, not

attributable to either, be placed in a situation where both cannot survive. Neither * * * would * * * commit a crime in saving his own life in a struggle for the only means of safety * * *.

But * * * the slayer must be under no obligation to make his own safety secondary to the safety of others * * *. [On shipboard, officers and sailors have a duty to protect passengers.] Should [an] emergency become so extreme as to call for the sacrifice of life, there can be no reason why the law does not remain the same. The passenger, not being bound either to labour or to incur the risk of life, cannot be bound to sacrifice his existence to preserve the sailor's. The captain, indeed, and a sufficient number of seamen to navigate the boat, must be preserved; for, except these abide in this ship, all will perish. But if there be more seamen than are necessary to manage the boat, the supernumerary sailors have no right, for their safety, to sacrifice the passengers * * *.

But, in addition, if the source of the danger has been obvious, and destruction ascertained to be certainly about to arrive, although at a future time, there should be consultation, and some mode of selection fixed, by which those in equal relations may have equal chance for their life * * *. [T]he selection is [to be] by lot.

The defendant was convicted and sentenced to six months at hard labor and a fine of $20. After the president refused a pardon, the penalty was remitted.

Holmes suggested that in at least some limited situations, necessity would apply to one who takes the life of another to save his own life. The other leading decision, however, indicates otherwise. In July of 1884, three English seamen—Dudley, Stephens, and Brooks—and a 17-year-old youth were forced to abandon an English yacht in an open boat. After twenty days, eight without any food at all, Stephens and Dudley killed the youth over the objections of Brooks. All three fed upon the youth's body and were rescued four days later. Dudley and Stephens were charged with murder. The jury found the basic facts of the case as stated but disclaimed an ability to determine whether the acts constituted murder. On referral to the court, the facts were held to constitute murder. *Regina v. Dudley and Stephens*, 14 Q.B.D. 273 (1884). The court explained:

[T]he temptation to the act which existed here was not what the law has ever called necessity. Nor is this to be regretted. Though law and morality are not the same, and many things may be immoral which are not necessarily illegal, yet the absolute divorce of law from morality would be of fatal consequence; and such divorce would follow if the temptation to murder in this case were to be held by law an absolute defense of it. It is not so. To preserve one's life is generally speaking a duty, but it may be the plainest and highest duty to sacrifice it * * *. It is not needful to point out the awful dangers of admitting the principle which has been contended for. Who is to be the judge of this sort of necessity? By what measure is the comparative value of lives to be measured? Is it to be strength, or intellect, or what? * * * We are often compelled to set up standards we cannot reach ourselves, and to lay down rules which we could not ourselves satisfy. But a man has no right to declare temptation to be an excuse, though he might himself have yielded to it, nor allow compassion for the criminal to change or weaken in any manner the legal definition of the crime.

The defendants were sentenced to death but this was later commuted by the Crown to six months' imprisonment.

Both *Holmes* and *Dudley and Stephens* reflect the courts' reluctance to recognize a broad necessity defense or at least to give juries broad discretion in addressing whether defendants should be acquitted on general necessity grounds. This same attitude is obvious in *Bailey*, which holds that the defendants in that case were not entitled to have juries even consider whether to acquit them because they were motivated by fear of conditions in the jail. What is the basis for this judicial attitude?

Perhaps it flows from a distrust of juries. Arguably *Bailey* reflects in part a concern that if the courts recognize jury issues in escape cases of the sort before the Court, skillful defense lawyers will be able to persuade juries to ignore the formal legal requirements and acquit defendants on more general equitable grounds. In addition, however, *Bailey* and similar cases probably reflect the courts' reluctance to make specific criminal trials a forum for addressing what are really broader political issues. If defendants like Bailey are entitled to have the jury consider their proposed defenses, arguably criminal trials will permit or even require extensive testimony on and inquiry into such matters as jail conditions generally, what conditions are "reasonable" in light of competing demands for public funds, and similar matters. At least some courts are undoubtedly convinced that although these are important questions of public policy, the places to develop and debate them do not include criminal trials of defendants who have escaped from jails.

United States v. Bailey

Supreme Court of the United States, 1980
444 U.S. 394, 100 S.Ct. 624, 62 L.Ed.2d 575.

MR. JUSTICE REHNQUIST delivered the opinion of the Court.

In the early morning hours of August 26, 1976, respondents Clifford Bailey, James T. Cogdell, Ronald C. Cooley, and Ralph Walker, federal prisoners at the District of Columbia jail, crawled through a window from which a bar had been removed, slid down a knotted bedsheet, and escaped from custody. Federal authorities recaptured them after they had remained at large for a period of time ranging from one month to three and one-half months. Upon their apprehension, they were charged with violating 18 U.S.C. § 751(a), which governs escape from federal custody. At their trials, each of the respondents adduced or offered to adduce evidence as to various conditions and events at the District of Columbia jail, but each was convicted by the jury. The Court of Appeals for the District of Columbia Circuit reversed the convictions by a divided vote * * *. We granted certiorari, and now reverse the judgments of the Court of Appeals.

* * *

I

All respondents requested jury trials and were initially scheduled to be tried jointly. At the last minute, however, respondent Cogdell secured a severance. * * *

The prosecution's case in chief against Bailey, Cooley, and Walker was brief. The Government introduced evidence that each of the respondents was in federal custody on August 26, 1976, that they had disappeared, apparently through a cell window, at approximately 5:35 A.M. on that date, and that they had been apprehended individually between September 27 and December 13, 1976.

Respondents' defense of duress or necessity centered on the conditions in the jail during the months of June, July, and August 1976, and on various threats and beatings directed at them during that period. In describing the conditions at the jail, they introduced evidence of frequent fires in "Northeast One," the maximum-security cellblock occupied by respondents prior to their escape. Construed in the light most favorable to them, this evidence demonstrated that the inmates of Northeast One, and on occasion the guards in that unit, set fire to trash, bedding, and other objects thrown from the cells. According to the inmates, the guards simply allowed the fires to burn until they went out. Although the fires apparently were confined to small areas and posed no substantial threat of spreading through the complex, poor ventilation caused smoke to collect and linger in the cellblock.

Respondents Cooley and Bailey also introduced testimony that the guards at the jail had subjected them to beatings and to threats of death. Walker attempted to prove that he was an epileptic and had received inadequate medical attention for his seizures.

Consistently during the trial, the District Court stressed that, to sustain their defenses, respondents would have to introduce some evidence that they attempted to surrender or engaged in equivalent conduct once they had freed themselves from the conditions they described. But the court waited for such evidence in vain. Respondent Cooley, who had eluded the authorities for one month, testified that his "people" had tried to contact the authorities, but "never got in touch with anybody." He also suggested that someone had told his sister that the Federal Bureau of Investigation would kill him when he was apprehended.

Respondent Bailey, who was apprehended on November 19, 1976, told a similar story. He stated that he "had the jail officials called several times," but did not turn himself in because "I would still be under the threats of death." Like Cooley, Bailey testified that "the FBI was telling my people that they was going to shoot me."

Only respondent Walker suggested that he had attempted to negotiate a surrender. Like Cooley and Bailey, Walker testified that the FBI had told his "people" that they would kill him when they recaptured him. Nevertheless, according to Walker, he called the FBI three times and spoke with an agent whose name he could not remember. That agent allegedly assured him that the FBI would not harm him, but was unable to promise that Walker would not be returned to the D.C. jail.[2] Walker testified that he last called

the FBI in mid-October. He was finally apprehended on December 13, 1976.

At the close of all the evidence, the District Court rejected respondents' proffered instruction on duress as a defense to prison escape.[3] The court ruled that respondents had failed as a matter of law to present evidence sufficient to support such a defense because they had not turned themselves in after they had escaped the allegedly coercive conditions. After receiving instructions to disregard the evidence of the conditions in the jail, the jury convicted Bailey, Cooley, and Walker of violating § 751(a).

Two months later, respondent Cogdell came to trial before the same District Judge who had presided over the trial of his co-respondents. When Cogdell attempted to offer testimony concerning the allegedly inhumane conditions at the D.C. jail, the District Judge inquired into Cogdell's conduct between his escape on August 26 and his apprehension on September 28. In response to Cogdell's assertion, that he "may have written letters," the District Court specified that Cogdell could testify only as to "what he did * * * [n]ot what he may have done." Absent such testimony, however, the District Court ruled that Cogdell could not present evidence of conditions at the jail. Cogdell subsequently chose not to testify on his own behalf, and was convicted by the jury of violating § 751(a).

By a divided vote, the Court of Appeals reversed each respondent's conviction and remanded for new trials.

II

Respondents contend that they are entitled to a new trial because they presented (or, in Cogdell's case, could have presented) sufficient evidence of duress or necessity to submit such a defense to the jury. The majority below did not confront this claim squarely, holding instead that, to the extent that such a defense normally would be barred by a prisoner's failure to return to custody, neither the indictment nor the jury instructions adequately described such a requirement.

Common law historically distinguished between the defenses of duress and necessity. Duress was said to excuse criminal conduct where the actor was under an unlawful

---

[2] On rebuttal, the prosecution called Joel Dean, the FBI agent who had been assigned to investigate Walker's escape in August 1976. He testified that, under standard Bureau practice, he would have been notified of any contact made by Walker with the FBI. According to Dean, he never was informed of any such contact.

[3] Respondents asked the District Court to give the following instruction:

"Coercion which would excuse the commission of a criminal act must result from:

"1) Threatening [sic] conduct sufficient to create in the mind of a reasonable person the fear of death or serious bodily harm;

"2) The conduct in fact caused such fear of death or serious bodily harm in the mind of the defendant;

"3) The fear or duress was operating upon the mind of the defendant at the time of the alleged act; and

"4) The defendant committed the act to avoid the threatened [sic] harm."

threat of imminent death or serious bodily injury, which threat caused the actor to engage in conduct violating the literal terms of the criminal law. While the defense of duress covered the situation where the coercion had its source in the actions of other human beings, the defense of necessity, or choice of evils, traditionally covered the situation where physical forces beyond the actor's control rendered illegal conduct the lesser of two evils. Thus, where A destroyed a dike because B threatened to kill him if he did not, A would argue that he acted under duress, whereas if A destroyed the dike in order to protect more valuable property from flooding, A could claim a defense of necessity.

Modern cases have tended to blur the distinction between duress and necessity. In the court below, the majority discarded the labels "duress" and "necessity," choosing instead to examine the policies underlying the traditional defenses. In particular, the majority felt that the defenses were designed to spare a person from punishment if he acted "under threats or conditions that a person of ordinary firmness would have been unable to resist," or if he reasonably believed that criminal action "was necessary to avoid a harm more serious than that sought to be prevented by the statute defining the offense." The Model Penal Code redefines the defenses along similar lines. See Model Penal Code § 2.09 (duress) and § 3.02 (choice of evils).

We need not speculate now, however, on the precise contours of whatever defenses of duress or necessity are available against charges brought under § 751(a). Under any definition of these defenses one principle remains constant: if there was a reasonable, legal alternative to violating the law, "a chance both to refuse to do the criminal act and also to avoid the threatened harm," the defenses will fail. Clearly, in the context of prison escape, the escapee is not entitled to claim a defense of duress or necessity unless and until he demonstrates that, given the imminence of the threat, violation of § 751(a) was his only reasonable alternative.

In the present case, the Government contends that respondents' showing was insufficient on two grounds. First, the Government asserts that the threats and conditions cited by respondents as justifying their escape were not sufficiently immediate or serious to justify their departure from lawful custody. Second, the Government contends that, once the respondents had escaped, the coercive conditions in the jail were no longer a threat and respondents were under a duty to terminate their status as fugitives by turning themselves over to the authorities.

Respondents, on the other hand, argue that the evidence of coercion and conditions in the jail was at least sufficient to go to the jury as an affirmative defense to the crime charged. As for their failure to return to custody after gaining their freedom, respondents assert that this failure should be but one factor in the overall determination whether their initial departure was justified. According to respondents, their failure to surrender "may reflect adversely on the bona fides of [their] motivation" in leaving the jail, but should not withdraw the question of their motivation from the jury's consideration.

We need not decide whether such evidence as that submitted by respondents was sufficient to raise a jury question as to their initial departures. This is because we decline to hold that respondents' failure to return is "just one factor" for the jury to weigh in deciding whether the initial escape could be affirmatively justified. On the contrary, several considerations lead us to conclude that, in order to be entitled to an instruction on duress or necessity as a defense to the crime charged, an escapee must first offer evidence justifying his continued absence from custody as well as his initial departure and that an indispensable element of such an offer is testimony of a bona fide effort to surrender or return to custody as soon as the claimed duress or necessity had lost its coercive force.

First, we think it clear beyond peradventure that escape from federal custody as defined in § 751(a) is a continuing offense and that an escapee can be held liable for failure to return to custody as well as for his initial departure. Given the continuing threat to society posed by an escaped prisoner, "the nature of the crime involved is such that Congress must assuredly have intended that it be treated as a continuing one." *Toussie v. United States,* 397 U.S. 112, 115, 90 S.Ct. 858, 860, 25 L.Ed.2d 156 (1970). * * *

The Anglo-Saxon tradition of criminal justice, embodied in the United States Constitution and in federal statutes, makes jurors the judges of the credibility of testimony offered by witnesses. It is for, them, generally, and not for appellate courts, to say that a particular witness spoke the truth or fabricated a cock-and-bull story. An escapee who flees from a jail that is in the process of burning to the ground may well be entitled to an instruction on duress or necessity, "'for he is not to be hanged because he would not stay to be burnt.'" *United States v. Kirby,* 7 Wall. 482, 487, 19 L.Ed. 278 (1869). And in the federal system it is the jury that is the judge of whether the prisoner's account of his reason for flight is true or false. But precisely because a defendant is entitled to have the credibility of his testimony, or that of witnesses called on his behalf, judged by the jury, it is essential that the testimony given or proffered meet a minimum standard as to each element of the defense so that, if a jury finds it to be true, it would support an affirmative defense—here that of duress or necessity.

We therefore hold that, where a criminal defendant is charged with escape and claims that he is entitled to an instruction on the theory of duress or necessity, he must proffer evidence of a bona fide effort to surrender or return to custody as soon as the claimed duress or necessity had lost its coercive force. We have reviewed the evidence examined elaborately in the majority and dissenting opinions below, and find the case not even close, even under respondents' versions of the facts, as to whether they either surrendered or offered to surrender at their earliest possible opportunity. Since we have determined that this is an indispensable element of the defense of duress or necessity, respondents were not entitled to any instruction on such a theory. Vague and necessarily self-serving statements of defendants or witnesses as to future good intentions or ambiguous conduct simply do not support a finding of this element of the defense.[11]

III

[W]e believe that we are * * * faithful * * * to [the] policy of "allowing the jury to perform its accustomed role" as the arbiter of factual disputes. The requirement of a threshold showing on the part of those who assert an affirmative defense to a crime is by no means a derogation of the importance of the jury as a judge of credibility. Nor is it based on any distrust of the jury's ability to separate fact from fiction. On the contrary, it is a testament to the importance of trial by jury and the need to husband the resources necessary for that process by limiting evidence in a trial to that directed at the elements of the crime or at affirmative defenses. If, as we here hold, an affirmative defense consists of several elements and testimony supporting one element is insufficient to sustain it even if believed, the trial court and jury need not be burdened with testimony supporting other elements of the defense.

Because the respondents failed to introduce evidence sufficient to submit their defenses of duress and necessity to the juries, we reverse the judgments of the Court of Appeals.

Reversed.

MR. JUSTICE MARSHALL took no part in the consideration or decision of these cases.

MR. JUSTICE STEVENS, concurring.

The essential difference between the majority and the dissent is over the question whether the record contains enough evidence of a bona fide effort to surrender or return to custody to present a question of fact for the jury to resolve. On this issue, I agree with the Court that the evidence introduced by defendants Cooley, Bailey, and Cogdell was plainly insufficient. Vague references to anonymous intermediaries are so inherently incredible that a trial judge is entitled to ignore them. With respect to Walker, however, the question is much closer because he testified that he personally telephoned an FBI agent three times in an effort to negotiate a surrender. But since he remained at large for about two months after his last effort to speak with the FBI, I am persuaded that even under his version of the facts he did not make an adequate attempt to satisfy the return requirement.

The fact that I have joined the Court's opinion does not indicate that I—or indeed that any other Member of the majority—is unconcerned about prison conditions * * *. Because we are construing the federal escape statute, however, I think it only fair to note that such conditions are more apt to prevail in state or county facilities than in federal facilities. Moreover, reasonable men may well differ about the most effective methods of redressing the situation. In my view, progress toward acceptable solutions involves formulating enforceable objective standards for civilized prison conditions, keeping the channels of communication between prisoners and the outside world open, and guaranteeing access to the courts, rather than relying on ad hoc judgments about the good faith of prison administrators, giving undue deference to their "expertise" or encouraging self-help by convicted felons.[8] In short, neither my agreement with

---

[11] Contrary to the implication of Mr. Justice Blackmun's dissent describing the rationale of the necessity defense as "a balancing of harms," we are construing an Act of Congress, not drafting it. The statute itself, as we have noted, requires no heightened *mens rea* that might be negated by any defense of duress or coercion. We nonetheless recognize that Congress in enacting criminal statutes legislates against a background of Anglo-Saxon common law and that therefore a defense of duress or coercion may well have been contemplated by Congress when it enacted § 751(a). But since the express purpose of Congress in enacting that section was to punish escape from penal custody, we think that some duty to return, a duty described more elaborately in the text, must be an essential element of the defense unless the congressional judgment that escape from prison is a crime be rendered wholly nugatory. Our principal difference with the dissent,

therefore, is not as to the existence of such a defense but as to the importance of surrender as an element of it. And we remain satisfied that, even if credited by the jury, the testimony * * * could not support a finding that respondents had no alternatives but to remain at large until recaptured anywhere from one to three and onehalf months after their escape. To hold otherwise would indeed quickly reduce the overcrowding in prisons that has been universally condemned by penologists. But that result would be accomplished in a manner quite at odds with the purpose of Congress when it made escape from prison a federal criminal offense.

[8] It would be unwise, and perhaps counterproductive to immunize escapes that would otherwise be unlawful in the hope that they would motivate significant reforms. * * *

much of what Mr. Justice Blackmun has written, nor my dis-agreement with the Court about related issues, prevents me from joining its construction of the federal escape statute.

MR. JUSTICE BLACKMUN, with whom MR. JUSTICE BRENNAN joins, dissenting.

* * *

I * * * agree with the Court * * * that the jury generally should be instructed that, in order to prevail on a necessity or duress defense, the defendant must justify his continued absence from custody, as well as his initial departure. I agree with the Court that the very nature of escape makes it a continuing crime. But I cannot agree that the only way continued absence can be justified is by evidence "of a bona fide effort to surrender or return to custody." The Court apparently entertains the view, naive in my estimation, that once the prisoner has escaped from a life- or health-threat-ening situation, he can turn himself in, secure in the faith that his escape somehow will result in improvement in those intolerable prison conditions. While it may be true in some rare circumstance that an escapee will obtain the aid of a court or of the prison administration once the escape is accomplished, the escapee, realistically, faces a high proba-bility of being returned to the same prison and to exactly the same, or even greater, threats to life and safety.

The rationale of the necessity defense is a balancing of harms. If the harm caused by an escape is less than the harm caused by remaining in a threatening situation, the prisoner's initial departure is justified. The same rationale should apply to hesitancy and failure to return. A situation may well arise where the social balance weighs in favor of the prisoner even though he fails to return to custody. The escapee at least should be permitted to present to the jury the possibility that the harm that would result from a return to custody out-weighs the harm to society from continued absence.

Even under the Court's own standard, the defendant in an escape prosecution should be permitted to submit evi-dence to the jury to demonstrate that surrender would result in his being placed again in a life- or health-threaten-ing situation. The Court requires return to custody once the "claimed duress or necessity had lost its coercive force." Realistically, however, the escapee who reasonably believes that surrender will result in return to what concededly is an intolerable prison situation remains subject to the same "coercive force" that prompted his escape in the first instance. It is ironic to say that that force is automatically "lost" once the prison wall is passed.

The Court's own phrasing of its test demonstrates that it is deciding factual questions that should be presented to the jury. It states that a "bona fide" effort to surrender must be proved. Whether an effort is "bona fide" is a jury ques-tion. * * *

Finally, I of course must agree with the Court that use of the jury is to be reserved for the case in which there is sufficient evidence to support a verdict. I have no difficulty, however, in concluding that respondents here did indeed submit sufficient evidence to support a verdict of not guilty, if the jury were so inclined, based on the necessity defense. Respondent Bailey testified that he was in fear for his life, that he was afraid he would still face the same threats if he turned himself in, and that "[t]he FBI was telling my people that they was going to shoot me." Respondent Cooley testi-fied that he did not know anyone to call, and that he feared that the police would shoot him when they came to get him. Respondent Walker testified that he had been in "con-stant rapport," with an FBI agent, who assured him that the FBI would not harm him, but who would not promise that he would not be returned to the D.C. jail. Walker also stat-ed that he had heard through his sister that the FBI "said that if they ran down on me they was going to kill me."

Perhaps it is highly unlikely that the jury would have believed respondents' stories that the FBI planned to shoot them on sight, or that respondent Walker had been in con-stant communication with an FBI agent. Nevertheless, such testimony, even though "self-serving," and possibly extreme and unwarranted in part, was sufficient to permit the jury to decide whether the failure to surrender immediately was justified or excused. * * *

Notes

1. Defendants charged with crimes arising out of protests against facilities and persons performing abortions have generally been unsuccessful in getting the courts to permit them to argue necessity defenses to juries. Often the courts reason that the occurrence of abortions pursuant to the women's federal consti-tutional right to abortions is not an "evil" or a legally recognizable harm that can serve as the basis for a necessity defense. *Judge v. State*, 659 N.E.2d 608 (Ind.App.1995).

2. An important limitation on the defense of necessity is the requirement that the harm to be avoided have appeared imminent. This was illustrated by *Commonwealth v. Leno*, 415 Mass. 835, 616 N.E.2d 453 (1993), in which the defendants were charged with criminal possession of hypodermic needles and syringes without a prescription. Massachusetts is one of a minority of states that prohibits distribution and possession of these items without medical authoriza-tion. The defendants were AIDS activists whose activities occurred in connection with needle exchange programs for drug users. They offered extensive expert testimony regarding the effective-ness of needle exchange programs in preventing

AIDS and sought to have the jury instructed on the necessity defense, contending that they reasonably believed their commissions of the charged crimes were necessary to avoid drug users' deaths by AIDS. Holding that the trial court properly refused to permit the defendants to develop this defense, the appellate court explained:

> The defense of * * * necessity is not applicable unless a person is "faced with a clear and imminent danger, not one which is debatable or speculative." * * *
>
> The prevention of possible future harm does not excuse a current systematic violation of the law in anticipation of the eventual overall benefit to the public. * * * The defendants did not show that the danger they sought to avoid was clear and imminent, rather than debatable or speculative. * * * The defendants' argument raises the issue of jury nullification, not the defense of necessity. We decline to require an instruction on jury nullification.

3. There is general agreement that a defendant cannot invoke necessity on grounds that were considered by the legislature that adopted the charged crime and rejected as a basis for exonerating those who commit the crimes. Thus, defendants charged with marijuana offenses have been precluded from invoking necessity on the ground that their use of the substance was necessary to alleviate medical symptoms where state legislatures have enacted legislation providing for limited experimental dispensation of marijuana by physicians to certain patients. By providing for some medical uses of the substance, the courts reason, the legislatures implicitly barred use of the necessity defense to avoid criminal liability for other medical uses. *Kauffman v. State*, 620 So.2d 90 (Ala.Crim.App.1992).

    At least one court has held that a legislature's consideration of and *failure* to adopt such legislation similarly reflected an intention to make the necessity defense unavailable for any medical use of marijuana. *Commonwealth v. Hutchins*, 410 Mass. 726, 575 N.E.2d 741 (1991).

4. What *does* raise at least a jury issue under necessity? In *Toops v. State*, 643 N.E.2d 367 (Ind.App.1994), the evidence at Toops' trial for driving while intoxicated showed these facts:

> In the late evening hours of October 30, 1992, Terry Toops, Warren Cripe and Ed Raisor were present at Toops's home in Logansport, Indiana drinking beer. Around 3:00 A.M. the following morning the trio

decided to drive to a store in town. Because he was intoxicated, Toops agreed to allow Cripe to drive Toops's car. Toops sat in the front passenger seat and Raisor sat in the rear. Toops began to feel ill during the drive and stuck his head out the window for fresh air. In the meantime, Sheriff's Deputy Michael Day and Town Marshall Gary Layer were on routine patrol when they observed a person later identified as Toops hanging out the car window. The officers decided to investigate and made a u-turn to follow the car. Cripe saw the patrol car turn around and panicked because he was a minor and had been drinking. He let go of the steering wheel and jumped into the back seat of the car. The car began to career out of control, leaving its lane, veering into the northbound lane of traffic then veering back into the southbound lane. Toops finally slid into the driver's seat and brought the car under control.

> The officers overtook the car and noted that Toops, whom they had originally seen hanging out of the car window, was now seated behind the steering wheel. The officers also noted that Cripe and Raisor were seated in the back seat of the car. At the officers' request, Toops submitted to a breath test which revealed a [blood alcohol concentration] of .21%. As a result Toops was arrested and charged with various alcohol related traffic offenses.

The trial judge declined to instruct the jury concerning the defense of necessity, and the appellate court held this error:

> There is no question that the evidence presented in this case raised a jury question as to whether Toops's control of the car while intoxicated, an illegal act, was necessary to prevent a greater harm, namely: an automobile collision potentially resulting in personal injury or property damage.

5. Duress is generally not available to a prosecution for an intentional killing, on the ground that a reasonable person would always refuse to intentionally kill another, whatever the cost to himself. As the court recognized in *State v. Lassen*, 679 S.W.2d 363 (Mo.App.1984), the courts are disagreed on whether the defense applies in a felony murder prosecution where it would be available as a defense to the underlying felony that makes the unintended killing murder.

Statutes sometimes limit the duress defense even further. Under the Iowa statute, for example, the defense—called "compulsion"—is unavailable for "any act by which one intentionally or recklessly causes physical injury to another." Iowa Code Ann. § 704.10. Under an Indiana statutory provision, the defense is not available to charges of "offenses against the person." Ind.Code § 35-41-3-8. Thus, it is no defense to robbery or attempted robbery. *Armand v. State*, 474 N.E.2d 1002 (Ind.1985).

6. The Model Penal Code would make duress unavailable if the defendant recklessly placed himself in a situation in which it was probable that he would be subjected to duress. This limitation, or a similar one, will probably be applied even in the absence of a specific statutory provision of this sort. When is duress thus rendered unavailable? In *Williams v. State*, 101 Md.App. 408, 646 A.2d 1101 (1994), cert. denied, 651 A.2d 855 (Md. 1995), the defendant was shown to have participated with two others in the attempted robbery of the Reverend Chris Hale. In his defense, Williams testified that to repay a debt he had been induced to make a drug run for a local drug dealer. The other participants in the robbery, he explained, had abducted him and threatened to kill him if he did not reveal the location of the dealer's stash house. He led them to the Reverend Hale's apartment and participated in the attempted robbery representing that this was the stash house, all in an effort to stall and thus avoid being killed himself. The trial court nevertheless refused to permit the jury to consider a duress defense to attempted robbery. On appeal this was held not to be error, because Williams' testimony did not raise the defense of duress. Adopting the approach of the Model Penal Code, the court held that by voluntarily associating himself with the drug dealer and thus making himself readily identifiable as knowledgeable about the dealer's operation, Williams "contributed mightily" to the situation giving rise to the threats against him and thereby rendered any duress defense unavailable.

Necessity is similarly unavailable if the defendant wrongfully created the need to choose between commission of a crime and a greater evil. *Jones v. City of Tulsa*, 857 P.2d 814 (Okla.Crim.App.1993).

MODEL PENAL CODE[*]

Official Draft 1985

Section 2.09. Duress

(1) It is an affirmative defense that the actor engaged in the conduct charged to constitute an offense because he was coerced to do so by the use of, or a threat to use, unlawful force against his person or the person of another, that a person of reasonable firmness in his situation would have been unable to resist.

(2) The defense provided by this Section is unavailable if the actor recklessly placed himself in a situation in which it was probable that he would be subjected to duress. The defense is also unavailable if he was negligent in placing himself in such a situation, whenever negligence suffices to establish culpability for the offense charged.

(3) It is not a defense that a woman acted on the command of her husband, unless she acted under such coercion as would establish a defense under this

[*]Copyright 1985 by the American Law Institute. Reprinted with the permission of the American Law Institute.

Section. [The presumption that a woman, acting in the presence of her husband, is coerced is abolished.]

(4) When the conduct of the actor would otherwise be justifiable under Section 3.02, this Section does not preclude such defense.

Section 3.02. Justification Generally: Choice of Evils

(1) Conduct which the actor believes to be necessary to avoid a harm or evil to himself or to another is justifiable, provided that:

    (a) the harm or evil sought to be avoided by such conduct is greater than that sought to be prevented by the law defining the offense charged; and

    (b) neither the Code nor other law defining the offense provides exceptions or defenses dealing with the specific situation involved; and

    (c) a legislative purpose to exclude the justification claimed does not otherwise plainly appear.

(2) When the actor was reckless or negligent in bringing about the situation requiring a choice of harms or evils or in appraising the necessity for his conduct, the justification afforded by this Section is unavailable in a prosecution for any offense for which recklessness or negligence, as the case may be, suffices to establish culpability.

B. ENTRAPMENT
Editors' Introduction: Federal Entrapment Law and the Subjective/Objective Approaches to Entrapment

The defense of entrapment has given rise to a great deal of discussion concerning not only the appropriate or acceptable role of undercover police work in law enforcement but also the role that defenses to criminal liability ought to play in regulating law enforcement conduct. There are two very different approaches to conceptualizing the rationale and purposes of the defense and, consequently, to defining the standard for determining whether entrapment occurred. As with other areas of criminal law, the possibility that constitutional requirements affect the entrapment defense is often a topic of discussion.

The leading line of cases consists of several decisions of the United States Supreme Court, beginning with *Sorrells v. United States*, 287 U.S. 435, 53 S.Ct. 210, 77 L.Ed. 413 (1932), which developed and applied the defense of entrapment to federal criminal offenses. Congress has enacted no statute addressing entrapment in federal criminal prosecutions, so the federal courts have responsibility for recognizing and defining the defense as it applies in such cases.

In *Sorrells*, the Supreme Court adopted the traditional "subjective" formulation of the entrapment defense. Sorrells had been approached during Prohibition by an undercover police agent who had been a member of Sorrell's military unit during World War I. At several points during their discussion of war experiences, the agent asked if Sorrells could get him some liquor. Sorrells demurred to the first two requests but after the third left and returned with some liquor. He was arrested and tried for possession and sale of the liquor. The trial court refused to instruct the jury on a defense of entrapment or to direct a verdict of acquittal on that basis. Reversing, Chief Justice Hughes formulated the issue for the Court:

> It is well settled that the fact that officers or employees of the government merely afford opportunities or facilities for the commission of the offense does not defeat the prosecution. Artifice and stratagem may be employed to catch those engaged in criminal enterprises. * * * A different question is presented when the criminal design originates with the officials of the government, and they implant in the mind of an innocent person the disposition to commit the alleged offense and induce its commission in order that they may prosecute.

In the latter situations, Chief Justice Hughes continued, Congress must have intended a defense to exist:

> "[G]eneral terms descriptive of a class of persons made subject to a criminal statute may and should be limited, where the literal application of the statute would lead to extreme or absurd results, and where the legislative purpose gathered from the whole act would be satisfied by a more limited interpretation."
>
> We think that this established principle of construction is applicable here. We are unable to conclude that it was the intention of the Congress in enacting this statute that its process of detention and enforcement should be abused by the instigation by government officials of an act on the part of persons otherwise innocent in order to lure them to its commission and to punish them. We are not forced by the letter to do violence to the spirit of the statute.

The trial court erred, the majority concluded, in failing to submit the issue of entrapment to the jury.

Sorrells was reaffirmed in *Sherman v. United States*, 356 U.S. 369, 78 S.Ct. 819, 2 L.Ed.2d 848 (1958). Justice Frankfurter concurred in *Sherman*, and developed a position previously articulated by Justice Roberts concurring in *Sorrells*. He rejected the *Sorrells'* basis for the defense—that Congress could not have intended federal crimes to cover persons who were entrapped into committing them—and suggested a much different rationale. Entrapment, Justice Frankfurter urged, should not be regarded as resting upon some presumed legislative intention but rather upon a power of courts to exercise supervisory jurisdiction over the administration of criminal justice. Consistent with this, he continued, whether entrapment exists should be regarded as an issue for the judge rather than a guilt–innocence issue to be decided by the trial jury.

Justice Frankfurter also reasoned that his rationale suggested a different criterion for determining whether entrapment had occurred. Under the majority's approach, he emphasized, no entrapment occurs if the evidence shows "a general intention or predisposition to commit, whenever the opportunity should arise, crimes of the kind solicited * * *." This, he urged, was inappropriate:

> [A] test that looks to the character and predisposition of the defendant rather than the conduct of the police loses sight of the underlying reason for the defense of entrapment. No matter what the defendant's past record and present inclinations to criminality, certain police conduct to ensnare him into further crime is not to be tolerated by an advanced society.

The proper test, he concluded, would ask whether the officers, in holding out inducements, acted in such a manner as is likely to induce to the commission of crime "those engaged in criminal conduct and ready and willing to commit further crimes should the occasion arise." No entrapment occurs if this is the case. However, if the officers act in such a manner as is likely to induce to the commission of crime "those persons * * * who would normally avoid crime and through self-struggle resist ordinary temptations," then entrapment occurs. He added:

> This test shifts attention from the record and predisposition of the particular defendant to the conduct of the police and the likelihood, objectively considered, that it would entrap only those ready and willing to commit crime. It is as objective a test as the subject matter permits * * *. It draws directly on the fundamental intuition that led in the first instance to the outlawing of "entrapment" as a prosecutorial instrument.

The Supreme Court revisited the issue in *United States v. Russell*, 411 U.S. 423, 93 S.Ct. 137, 36 L.Ed.2d 366 (1973). Shapiro, a federal officer, had offered to supply the defendants—experienced methamphetamine producers—with phenyl-2-propanone to be used in the manufacture of methamphetamine, in return for one half of the methamphetamine produced. Shapiro conditioned his offer upon being shown the laboratory the defendants were using and a sample of methamphetamine they had already produced there. In a sense, then, his offer was one that only predisposed suspects could accept. Shapiro actually provided some of the substance and was present during the manufacturing process, and obtained most but not all of the methamphetamine produced by the phenyl-2-propanone he provided. The jury was instructed on entrapment but nevertheless convicted.

Justice Stewart argued in a *Russell* dissent that the Court should adopt the approach previously urged by Justices Roberts and Frankfurter. The *Russell* majority, however, refused to reject the *Sorrells* and *Sherman* approach. It reaffirmed that the defense, under federal law, is based on the notion that Congress could not have intended its crimes to include unpredisposed persons who engage in the prohibited conduct only because they were induced by the government itself to do so. No legitimate basis for the Court to develop a broader defense exists, *Russell* reasoned. Moreover, Justice Rehnquist explained for the majority, it does not seem "particularly appropriate" to grant immunity to a person who has planned and committed a crime simply because government undercover agents have subjected him to inducements that might have seduced other—and unpredisposed—persons into committing the crime but that had no significant effect on this particular defendant.

Russell's "principal contention," the majority indicated, was that the entrapment defense should be regarded as resting on federal constitutional grounds. Due process, Russell argued, should bar a defendant's prosecution upon proof that the pretrial investigation involved unacceptable involvement by the police in criminal activity. Specifically, he contended that by supplying the phenyl-2-propanone, Shapiro had "supplied an indispensable means to the commission of the crime that could not have been obtained otherwise, through legal or illegal channels." Supplying such material, Russell's argument went, should be unacceptable police conduct that constitutionally bars prosecution. Rejecting this, the majority noted that the record before it established that phenyl-2-propanone was in fact available to the defendants from other sources; Russell therefore had not brought himself within the rule for which he argued. The Court nevertheless continued:

> While we may some day be presented with a situation in which the conduct of law enforcement agents is so outrageous that due process principles would absolutely bar the government from invoking judicial processes to obtain a conviction, the instant case is distinctly not of that breed. Shapiro's contribution of propanone to the criminal enterprise already in process was scarcely objectionable. The chemical is by itself a harmless substance and its possession is legal. While the government may have been seeking to make it more difficult for drug rings * * *, to obtain the chemical, the evidence * * * shows that it nonetheless was obtainable. The law enforcement conduct here stops far short of violating that "fundamental fairness, shocking to the universal sense of justice," mandated by the Due Process Clause of the Fifth Amendment.

Russell's dictum that under due process police involvement in the offense being investigated might bar prosecution for that offense has given rise to numerous efforts by defendants to establish that police involvement in their investigations was constitutionally unacceptable. Such efforts were not encouraged, however, by *Hampton v. United States*, 425 U.S. 484, 96 S.Ct. 1646, 48 L.Ed.2d 113 (1976). Hampton testified that a federal informant had provided the heroin that Hampton was charged with selling and had initially suggested selling it. The trial court refused to instruct the jury that Hampton should be acquitted if the jury found that the heroin had been supplied to Hampton by a government informer. Hampton was convicted and he appealed. The Supreme Court affirmed.

In a plurality opinion, Justice Rehnquist explained that Hampton's predisposition rendered entrapment unavailable to him. Further, even if his testimony regarding the informant's involvement by providing the drug was credited, none of Hampton's federal constitutional rights had been violated. Under the *Russell* dictum, he offered, due process comes into play only if the government's involvement violates a protected right of the defendant. This cannot happen, he suggested, if the government undercover agent and the defendant act "in concert." Justice Powell, joined by Justice

Blackmun, concurred in the result but indicated an unwillingness to join some of Justice Rehnquist's language rejecting the likelihood that outrageous police behavior in such situations might offend due process.

Justice Brennan, joined by Justices Stewart and Marshall, dissented in *Hampton* on the ground that either due process or federal entrapment doctrine should bar conviction where the subject of the charge is the sale of contraband provided to the defendant by a government agent.

Sorrells and its progeny set the courts of the county off on what the New Mexico Supreme Court in *Baca v. State*, 106 N.M. 338, 742 P.2d 1043 (1987), called the often confusing search for the perfect definition of entrapment. Two models have dominated discussion.

One, based on *Sorrells*, is the subjective approach. It is subjective because the defendant's actual predisposition to commit crimes of the sort involved in the case is a determinative factor. Whether entrapment occurred is determined by two related matters. First, the defendant must not have been predisposed to commit the crime and, second, the defendant must have been induced or persuaded by law enforcement officers or their agents to commit that crime. A showing of predisposition means no entrapment occurred, no matter what the law enforcement officers did. The case reprinted in this section was tried under the federal subjective approach, and the Court sets out the trial judge's very typical instructions to the jury regarding entrapment.

The Supreme Court's adoption of the subjective approach for purposes of federal criminal law is not, of course, in any manner binding on the states. However, the Court's repeated reaffirmance of that approach lends support to the proposition that state courts should follow the high tribunal's lead on the ground that the Court's position is based on sound policy and reason.

The other model is based on Justice Roberts' position in *Sorrells,* which was embraced by the Model Penal Code provision, reprinted at page 554. This objective approach would involve no subjective inquiry into whether or not the defendant was predisposed. Whether entrapment occurred, rather, is determined by inquiring whether the police conduct is sufficiently likely to cause unpredisposed persons in general to commit the offense.

Justice Brickley of the Michigan Supreme Court has commented on the relative merits of the two approaches:

> In our view, each test has its flaws. The objective test has two. First, it encourages the courts to play a supervisory role over another branch of government, not to determine whether there has been illegal or unconstitutional practices engaged in by law enforcement, but * * * whether the law enforcement technique was "reprehensible." This often requires the courts to second-guess investigative techniques and law enforcement alternatives for which they obviously do not have expertise. Secondly, it sacrifices the conviction of an offender who is very much disposed toward the crime committed, but was fortunate enough to be snared by judicially disfavored law enforcement measures.

By the same token, the subjective test, in focusing on the predisposition of the defendant, suffers, theoretically at least, in going beyond the statutory requirement of guilt to find mitigating circumstances * * * that logically speaking should not interfere with a finding of guilt. The subjective test also has the flaw of all subjective tests: attempting to determine the workings of the human mind in an individual situation.

People v. Jamieson, 436 Mich. 61, 78–79, 461 N.W.2d 884, 890–91 (1990) (plurality opinion). The Michigan Supreme Court has embraced the objective approach, although it conceded that a majority of jurisdictions follow *Sorrells* and the subjective test. See *People v. Juillet*, 439 Mich. 34, 53, 475 N.W.2d 786, 793 (1991) (plurality opinion).

Jurisdictions differ on whether entrapment is an issue for the court or the jury. Under the subjective approach, entrapment establishes that the accused is not guilty of the crime charged and as a matter relating to guilt or innocence, it is therefore often— and perhaps constitutionally must be—submitted to the jury if the evidence raises an issue regarding the matter. Jurisdictions following the objective approach, on the other hand, frequently treat the issue as one for the court rather than the jury. The Michigan Supreme Court explained its rationales for treating entrapment as an issue for the judge rather than the jury in *People v. D'Angelo*, 401 Mich. 167, 173–76, 257 N.W.2d 655, 658–60 (1977). Juries should decide guilt or innocence, the court reasoned. Entrapment, however, is properly based not on the innocence of the defendant but rather on the need to condemn and discourage improper law enforcement conduct, and this is properly a concern of the judge. Moreover, specific rulings by trial judges will be more effective than general jury verdicts in developing standards for law enforcement conduct and making clear when and how officers fall short of those standards. Finally, leaving entrapment issues to the judge will avoid confusing and contaminating the jury's resolution of the basic issue posed for it: the defendant's guilt or innocence.

Under the subjective approach of *Sorrells*, in contrast, entrapment means that the defendant's conduct is not within the crime, that is, that the defendant is innocent. Thus, it poses a guilt-or-innocence issue that should—and perhaps under the Sixth Amendment right to jury trial must—be resolved by the jury.

It is common ground under both approaches to entrapment that, as Chief Justice Hughes indicated in *Sorrells*, officers' action in merely providing a suspect with an opportunity to commit an offense is not entrapment. Beyond this, however, little can be said with confidence as to what is and is not entrapment. As the principal case that follows illustrates, the Supreme Court, despite its repeated reaffirmation of the subjective approach, is divided on what requires a finding of entrapment under that approach.

Jacobson v. United States

Supreme Court of the United States, 1992
503 U.S. 540, 112 S.Ct. 1535, 118 L.Ed.2d 174.

Justice WHITE delivered the opinion of the Court.

On September 24, 1987, petitioner Keith Jacobson was indicted for violating a provision of the Child Protection Act of 1984, which criminalizes the knowing receipt through the mails of a "visual depiction [that] involves the use of a minor engaging in sexually explicit conduct. . . ." Petitioner defended on the ground that the Government entrapped him into committing the crime through a series of communications from undercover agents that spanned the 26 months preceding his arrest. Petitioner was found guilty after a jury trial. The Court of Appeals affirmed his conviction, holding that the Government had carried its burden of proving beyond reasonable doubt that petitioner was predisposed to break the law and hence was not entrapped.

Because the Government overstepped the line between setting a trap for the "unwary innocent" and the "unwary criminal," *Sherman v. United States*, 356 U.S. 369, 372, 78 S.Ct. 819, 821, 2 L.Ed.2d 848 (1958), and as a matter of law failed to establish that petitioner was independently predisposed to commit the crime for which he was arrested, we reverse the Court of Appeals' judgment affirming his conviction.

I

In February 1984, petitioner, a 56-year-old veteran-turned-farmer who supported his elderly father in Nebraska, ordered two magazines and a brochure from a California adult bookstore. The magazines, entitled Bare Boys I and Bare Boys II, contained photographs of nude preteen and teenage boys. The contents of the magazines startled petitioner, who testified that he had expected to receive photographs of "young men 18 years or older." On cross-examination, he explained his response to the magazines:

"[PROSECUTOR]: [Y]ou were shocked and surprised that there were pictures of very young boys without clothes on, is that correct?

"[JACOBSON]: Yes, I was.

"[PROSECUTOR]: Were you offended?

. . . . .

"[JACOBSON]: I was not offended because I thought these were a nudist type publication. Many of the pictures were

out in a rural or outdoor setting. There was—I didn't draw any sexual connotation or connection with that."

The young men depicted in the magazines were not engaged in sexual activity, and petitioner's receipt of the magazines was legal under both federal and Nebraska law. Within three months, the law with respect to child pornography changed; Congress passed the Act illegalizing the receipt through the mails of sexually explicit depictions of children. In the very month that the new provision became law, postal inspectors found petitioner's name on the mailing list of the California bookstore that had mailed him Bare Boys I and II. There followed over the next 2 1/2 years, repeated efforts by two Government agencies, through five fictitious organizations and a bogus pen pal, to explore petitioner's willingness to break the new law by ordering sexually explicit photographs of children through the mail.

The Government began its efforts in January 1985 when a postal inspector sent petitioner a letter supposedly from the American Hedonist Society, which in fact was a fictitious organization. The letter included a membership application and stated the Society's doctrine: that members had the "right to read what we desire, the right to discuss similar interests with those who share our philosophy, and finally that we have the right to seek pleasure without restrictions being placed on us by outdated puritan morality." Petitioner enrolled in the organization and returned a sexual attitude questionnaire that asked him to rank on a scale of one to four his enjoyment of various sexual materials, with one being "really enjoy," two being "enjoy," three being "somewhat enjoy," and four being "do not enjoy." Petitioner ranked the entry "[p]re-teen sex" as a two, but indicated that he was opposed to pedophilia.

For a time, the Government left petitioner alone. But then a new "prohibited mail specialist" in the Postal Service found petitioner's name in a file, and in May 1986, petitioner received a solicitation from a second fictitious consumer research company, "Midlands Data Research," seeking a response from those who "believe in the joys of sex and the complete awareness of those lusty and youthful lads and lasses of the neophite [sic] age." The letter never explained whether "neophite" referred to minors or young adults. Petitioner responded: "Please feel free to send me more information, I am interested in teenage sexuality. Please keep my name confidential."

Petitioner then heard from yet another Government creation, "Heartland Institute for a New Tomorrow" (HINT), which proclaimed that it was "an organization founded to protect and promote sexual freedom and freedom of choice. We believe that arbitrarily imposed legislative sanctions restricting your sexual freedom should be rescinded through the legislative process." The letter also enclosed a second survey. Petitioner indicated that his interest in "[p]reteen sex-homosexual" material was above average, but not high. In response to another question, petitioner wrote: "Not only sexual expression but freedom of the press is under attack. We must be ever vigilant to counter attack right wing fundamentalists who are determined to curtail our freedoms."

"HINT" replied, portraying itself as a lobbying organization seeking to repeal "all statutes which regulate sexual activities, except those laws which deal with violent behavior, such as rape. HINT is also lobbying to eliminate any legal definition of 'the age of consent.'" These lobbying efforts were to be funded by sales from a catalog to be published in the future "offering the sale of various items which we believe you will find to be both interesting and stimulating." HINT also provided computer matching of group members with similar survey responses; and, although petitioner was supplied with a list of potential "pen pals," he did not initiate any correspondence.

Nevertheless, the Government's "prohibited mail specialist" began writing to petitioner, using the pseudonym "Carl Long." The letters employed a tactic known as "mirroring," which the inspector described as "reflect[ing] whatever the interests are of the person we are writing to." Petitioner responded at first, indicating that his interest was primarily in "male-male items." Inspector "Long" wrote back:

"My interests too are primarily male-male items. Are you satisfied with the type of VCR tapes available? Personally, I like the amateur stuff better if its [sic] well produced as it can get more kinky and also seems more real. I think the actors enjoy it more."

Petitioner responded:

"As far as my likes are concerned, I like good looking young guys (in their late teens and early 20's) doing their thing together."

Petitioner's letters to "Long" made no reference to child pornography. After writing two letters, petitioner discontinued the correspondence.

By March 1987, 34 months had passed since the Government obtained petitioner's name from the mailing list of the California bookstore, and 26 months had passed since the Postal Service had commenced its mailings to petitioner. Although petitioner had responded to surveys and letters, the Government had no evidence that petitioner had ever intentionally possessed or been exposed to child pornography. The Postal Service had not checked petitioner's mail to determine whether he was receiving questionable mailings from persons—other than the Government—involved in the child pornography industry.

At this point, a second Government agency, the Customs Service, included petitioner in its own child pornography sting, "Operation Borderline," after receiving his name on lists submitted by the Postal Service. Using the name of a fictitious Canadian company called "Produit Outaouais," the Customs Service mailed petitioner a brochure advertising photographs of young boys engaging in sex. Petitioner placed an order that was never filled.

The Postal Service also continued its efforts in the Jacobson case, writing to petitioner as the "Far Eastern Trading Company Ltd." The letter began:

"As many of you know, much hysterical nonsense has appeared in the American media concerning 'pornography' and what must be done to stop it from coming across your borders. This brief letter does not allow us to give much comments; however, why is your government spending millions of dollars to exercise international censorship while tons of drugs, which makes yours the world's most crime ridden country are passed through easily."

The letter went on to say:

"[W]e have devised a method of getting these to you without prying eyes of U.S. Customs seizing your mail. . . . After consultations with American solicitors, we have been advised that once we have posted our material through your system, it cannot be opened for any inspection without authorization of a judge."

The letter invited petitioner to send for more information. It also asked petitioner to sign an affirmation that he was "not a law enforcement officer or agent of the U.S. Government acting in an undercover capacity for the purpose of entrapping Far Eastern Trading Company, its agents or customers." Petitioner responded. A catalogue was sent, and petitioner ordered Boys Who Love Boys, a pornographic magazine depicting young boys engaged in various sexual activities. Petitioner was arrested after a controlled delivery of a photocopy of the magazine.

When petitioner was asked at trial why he placed such an order, he explained that the Government had succeeded in piquing his curiosity:

"Well, the statement was made of all the trouble and the hysteria over pornography and I wanted to see what the material was. It didn't describe the—I didn't know for sure what kind of sexual action they were referring to in the Canadian letter. . . ."

In petitioner's home, the Government found the Bare Boys magazines and materials that the Government had sent to him in the course of its protracted investigation, but no other materials that would indicate that petitioner collected or was actively interested in child pornography.

Petitioner was indicted * * *. The trial court instructed the jury on the petitioner's entrapment defense,[1] petitioner was convicted, and a divided Court of Appeals for the Eighth Circuit, sitting en banc, affirmed, concluding that "Jacobson was not entrapped as a matter of law." We granted certiorari.

II

There can be no dispute about the evils of child pornography or the difficulties that laws and law enforcement have encountered in eliminating it. Likewise, there can be no dispute that the Government may use undercover agents to enforce the law "It is well settled that the fact that officers or employees of the Government merely afford opportunities or facilities for the commission of the offense does not defeat the prosecution. Artifice and stratagem may be employed to catch those engaged in criminal enterprises." *Sorrells v. United States*, 287 U.S. 435, 441, 53 S.Ct. 210, 212, 77 L.Ed. 413 (1932).

In their zeal to enforce the law, however, Government agents may not originate a criminal design, implant in an innocent person's mind the disposition to commit a criminal act, and then induce commission of the crime so that the Government may prosecute. Where the Government has induced an individual to break the law and the defense of entrapment is at issue, as it was in this case, the prosecution must prove beyond reasonable doubt that the defendant was disposed to commit the criminal act prior to first being approached by Government agents.[2]

Thus, an agent deployed to stop the traffic in illegal drugs may offer the opportunity to buy or sell drugs, and, if the offer is accepted, make an arrest on the spot or later. In such a typical case, or in a more elaborate "sting" operation involving government-sponsored fencing where the defendant is simply provided with the opportunity to commit a crime, the entrapment defense is of little use because the ready commission of the criminal act amply demonstrates the defendant's predisposition. Had the agents in this case simply offered petitioner the opportunity to order child pornography through the mails, and petitioner—who must be presumed to know the law—had promptly availed himself of this criminal opportunity, it is unlikely that his entrapment defense would have warranted a jury instruction.

But that is not what happened here. By the time petitioner finally placed his order, he had already been the target of 26 months of repeated mailings and communications from Government agents and fictitious organizations. Therefore, although he had become predisposed to break

---

[1] The jury was instructed:

"As mentioned, one of the issues in this case is whether the defendant was entrapped. If the defendant was entrapped he must be found not guilty. The government has the burden of proving beyond a reasonable doubt that the defendant was not entrapped.

"If the defendant before contact with law-enforcement officers or their agents did not have any intent or disposition to commit the crime charged and was induced or persuaded by law-enforcement officers o[r] their agents to commit that crime, then he was entrapped. On the other hand, if the defendant before contact with law-enforcement officers or their agents did have an intent or disposition to commit the crime charged, then he was not entrapped even though law-enforcement officers or their agents provided a favorable opportunity to commit the crime or made committing the crime easier or even participated in acts essential to the crime."

---

[2] Inducement is not at issue in this case. The Government does not dispute that it induced petitioner to commit the crime. The sole issue is whether the Government carried its burden of proving that petitioner was predisposed to violate the law before the Government intervened. The dissent is mistaken in claiming that this is an innovation in entrapment law and in suggesting that the Government's conduct prior to the moment of solicitation is irrelevant. The Court rejected these arguments five decades ago in *Sorrells*, when the Court wrote that the Government may not punish an individual "for an alleged offense which is the product of the creative activity of its own officials" and that in such a case the Government "is in no position to object to evidence of the activities of its representatives in relation to the accused. . . ." Indeed, the proposition that the accused must be predisposed prior to contact with law enforcement officers is so firmly established that the Government conceded the point at oral argument, submitting that the evidence it developed during the course of its investigation was probative because it indicated petitioner's state of mind prior to the commencement of the Government's investigation.

This long-established standard in no way encroaches upon Government investigatory activities. * * *

the law by May 1987, it is our view that the Government did not prove that this predisposition was independent and not the product of the attention that the Government had directed at petitioner since January 1985.

The prosecution's evidence of predisposition falls into two categories: evidence developed prior to the Postal Service's mail campaign, and that developed during the course of the investigation. The sole piece of preinvestigation evidence is petitioner's 1984 order and receipt of the Bare Boys magazines. But this is scant if any proof of petitioner's predisposition to commit an illegal act, the criminal character of which a defendant is presumed to know. It may indicate a predisposition to view sexually-oriented photographs that are responsive to his sexual tastes; but evidence that merely indicates a generic inclination to act within a broad range, not all of which is criminal, is of little probative value in establishing predisposition.

Furthermore, petitioner was acting within the law at the time he received these magazines. Receipt through the mails of sexually explicit depictions of children for non-commercial use did not become illegal under federal law until May 1984, and Nebraska had no law that forbade petitioner's possession of such material until 1988. Evidence of predisposition to do what once was lawful is not, by itself, sufficient to show predisposition to do what is now illegal, for there is a common understanding that most people obey the law even when they disapprove of it. This obedience may reflect a generalized respect for legality or the fear of prosecution, but for whatever reason, the law's prohibitions are matters of consequence. Hence, the fact that petitioner legally ordered and received the Bare Boys magazines does little to further the Government's burden of proving that petitioner was predisposed to commit a criminal act. This is particularly true given petitioner's unchallenged testimony that he did not know until they arrived that the magazines would depict minors.

The prosecution's evidence gathered during the investigation also fails to carry the Government's burden. Petitioner's responses to the many communications prior to the ultimate criminal act were at most indicative of certain personal inclinations, including a predisposition to view photographs of preteen sex and a willingness to promote a given agenda by supporting lobbying organizations. Even so, petitioner's responses hardly support an inference that he would commit the crime of receiving child pornography through the mails. * * *

On the other hand, the strong arguable inference is that, by waving the banner of individual rights and disparaging the legitimacy and constitutionality of efforts to restrict the availability of sexually explicit materials, the Government not only excited petitioner's interest in sexually explicit materials banned by law but also exerted substantial pres-

sure on petitioner to obtain and read such material as part of a fight against censorship and the infringement of individual rights. For instance, HINT described itself as "an organization founded to protect and promote sexual freedom and freedom of choice" and stated that "the most appropriate means to accomplish [its] objectives is to promote honest dialogue among concerned individuals and to continue its lobbying efforts with State Legislators." These lobbying efforts were to be financed through catalogue sales. Mailings from the equally fictitious American Hedonist Society, and the correspondence from the non-existent Carl Long, endorsed these themes.

Similarly, the two solicitations in the spring of 1987 raised the specter of censorship while suggesting that petitioner ought to be allowed to do what he had been solicited to do. The mailing from the Customs Service referred to "the worldwide ban and intense enforcement on this type of material," observed that "what was legal and commonplace is now an 'underground' and secretive service," and emphasized that "[t]his environment forces us to take extreme measures" to insure delivery. The Postal Service solicitation described the concern about child pornography as "hysterical nonsense," decried "international censorship," and assured petitioner, based on consultation with "American solicitors," that an order that had been posted could not be opened for inspection without authorization of a judge. It further asked petitioner to affirm that he was not a government agent attempting to entrap the mail order company or its customers. In these particulars, both government solicitations suggested that receiving this material was something that petitioner ought to be allowed to do.

Petitioner's ready response to these solicitations cannot be enough to establish beyond reasonable doubt that he was predisposed, prior to the Government acts intended to create predisposition, to commit the crime of receiving child pornography through the mails. The evidence that petitioner was ready and willing to commit the offense came only after the Government had devoted 2 1/2 years to convincing him that he had or should have the right to engage in the very behavior proscribed by law. Rational jurors could not say beyond a reasonable doubt that petitioner possessed the requisite predisposition prior to the Government's investigation and that it existed independent of the Government's many and varied approaches to petitioner. * * *

Law enforcement officials go too far when they "implant in the mind of an innocent person the *disposition* to commit the alleged offense and induce its commission in order that they may prosecute." *Sorrells v. U.S.*, 287 U.S. 435, at 442, 53 S.Ct. 210, at 212-213, 77 L.Ed. 413 (emphasis added). Like the *Sorrells* court, we are "unable to conclude that it was the intention of the Congress in enacting this statute that its processes of detection and enforcement should be abused by the instigation by government officials of an act on the part of persons otherwise innocent in order to lure them to its commission and to punish them." When the Government's quest for convictions leads to the apprehension of an otherwise law-abiding citizen who, if left to his own devices, likely would have never run afoul of the law, the courts should intervene.

Because we conclude that this is such a case and that the prosecution failed, as a matter of law, to adduce evidence to support the jury verdict that petitioner was predisposed, independent of the Government's acts and beyond a reasonable doubt, to violate the law by receiving child pornography through the mails, we reverse the Court of Appeals' judgment affirming the conviction of Keith Jacobson.

It is so ordered.

Justice O'CONNOR, with whom THE CHIEF JUSTICE and Justice[s] KENNEDY [and SCALIA] join, * * *, dissenting.

Keith Jacobson was offered only two opportunities to buy child pornography through the mail. Both times, he ordered. Both times, he asked for opportunities to buy more. He needed no Government agent to coax, threaten, or persuade him; no one played on his sympathies, friendship, or suggested that his committing the crime would further a greater good. In fact, no Government agent even contacted him face-to-face. The Government contends that from the enthusiasm with which Mr. Jacobson responded to the chance to commit a crime, a reasonable jury could permissibly infer beyond a reasonable doubt that he was predisposed to commit the crime. I agree. * * *

The Court, however, concludes that a reasonable jury could not have found Mr. Jacobson to be predisposed beyond a reasonable doubt on the basis of his responses to the Government's catalogs, even though it admits that, by that time, he was predisposed to commit the crime. The Government, the Court holds, failed to provide evidence that Mr. Jacobson's obvious predisposition at the time of the crime "was independent and not the product of the attention that the Government had directed at petitioner." In so holding, I believe the Court fails to acknowledge the reasonableness of the jury's inference from the evidence, redefines "predisposition," and introduces a new requirement that Government sting operations have a reasonable suspicion of illegal activity before contacting a suspect.

* * *

This Court has held previously that a defendant's predisposition is to be assessed as of the time the Government agent first suggested the crime, not when the Government agent first became involved. *Sherman v. United States*, 356 U.S. 369, 372–376, 78 S.Ct. 819, 820–823, 2 L.Ed.2d 848 (1958). Until the Government actually makes a suggestion of criminal conduct, it could not be said to have "implant[ed] in the mind of an innocent person the disposition to commit the alleged offense and induce its commission. . . ." *Sorrells v. United States*, 287 U.S. 435, 442, 53 S.Ct. 210, 212–213, 77 L.Ed. 413 (1932). Even in *Sherman v. United States*, supra, in which the Court held that the defendant had been entrapped as a matter of law, the Government agent had repeatedly and unsuccessfully coaxed the defendant to buy drugs, ultimately succeeding only by playing on the defendant's sympathy. The Court found lack of predisposition based on the Government's numerous unsuccessful attempts to induce the crime, not on the basis of preliminary contacts with the defendant.

Today, the Court holds that Government conduct may be considered to create a predisposition to commit a crime, even before any Government action to induce the commission of the crime. In my view, this holding changes entrapment doctrine. Generally, the inquiry is whether a suspect is predisposed before the Government induces the commission of the crime, not before the Government makes initial contact with him. There is no dispute here that the Government's questionnaires and letters were not sufficient to establish inducement; they did not even suggest that Mr. Jacobson should engage in any illegal activity. If all the Government had done was to send these materials, Mr. Jacobson's entrapment defense would fail. Yet the Court holds that the Government must prove not only that a suspect was predisposed to commit the crime before the opportunity to commit it arose, but also before the Government came on the scene.

The rule that preliminary Government contact can create a predisposition has the potential to be misread by lower courts as well as criminal investigators as requiring that the Government must have sufficient evidence of a defendant's predisposition before it ever seeks to contact him. Surely the Court cannot intend to impose such a requirement, for it would mean that the Government must have a reasonable suspicion of criminal activity before it begins an investigation, a condition that we have never before imposed. The Court denies that its new rule will affect run-of-the-mill sting operations, and one hopes that it means what it says. Nonetheless, after this case, every defendant will claim that something the Government agent did before soliciting the crime "created" a predisposition that was not there before. For example, a bribe taker will claim that the description of the amount of money available was so enticing that it implanted a disposition to accept the bribe later offered. A drug buyer will claim that the description of the drug's purity and effects was so tempting that it created the urge to try it for the first time. In short, the Court's opinion could be read to prohibit the Government from advertising the seductions of criminal activity as part of its sting operation, for fear of creating a predisposition in its suspects. That limitation would be especially likely to hamper sting operations such as this one, which mimic the advertising done by genuine purveyors of pornography. * * *

The crux of the Court's concern in this case is that the Government went too far and "abused" the "processes of detection and enforcement" by luring an innocent person to violate the law. Consequently, the Court holds that the Government failed to prove beyond a reasonable doubt that Mr. Jacobson was predisposed to commit the crime. It was, however, the jury's task, as the conscience of the community, to decide whether or not Mr. Jacobson was a willing participant in the criminal activity here or an innocent dupe. * * * There is no dispute that the jury in this case was fully and accurately instructed on the law of entrapment, and nonetheless found Mr. Jacobson guilty. Because I believe there was sufficient evidence to uphold the jury's verdict, I respectfully dissent.

Notes and Questions

1. Several courts have read *Jacobson* as developing federal entrapment law by creating a requirement of "positional predisposition." Under *United States v. Hollingsworth*, 27 F.3d 1196 (7th Cir.1994) (en banc), *Jacobson* requires that once entrapment is raised by proof that the defendant was induced to commit the crime, the government must show that the defendant was "so situated by reason of previous training or experience or occupation or acquaintances that it is likely that if the Government had not induced him to commit the crime some criminal would have done so." Under this approach, it is not enough for the government to show only that the defendant was "'willing,' in the sense of being psychologically prepared, to commit the crime" without regard to whether he would have had the occasion to do so had not the Government intervened.

    In *United States v. Knox* (and *Brace*), 112 F.3d 802 (5th Cir.1997) (rehearing en banc granted), for example, the defendant Brace was the minister of a church in financial difficulties. His efforts to solicit investors were responded to by federal undercover officers who offered money they represented came from cocaine producers. Brace's acceptance of the money constituted money laundering under federal law. The government's response to his claim of entrapment emphasized his enthusiastic response to the offer despite being told the source of the money. (Brace told the officers that he had prayed for guidance and God had responded that He had helped to put the deal together.) The defense, in contrast, emphasized evidence indicating that Brace was an isolated cleric, naive, ignorant, and inefficient. It argued that given his "position," he would never—but for the government—have encountered an opportunity to launder money, in part because no drug dealers would have approached anyone like him to launder their money.

    The court agreed and reversed Brace's conviction, holding that the government's effort to meet its burden to disprove entrapment focused upon Brace's mental disposition and ignored the situational aspect developed in *Hollingsworth*. The government produced no evidence that real drug dealers could or would use a church to launder money and that even if they would, that they would approach someone as naive and ignorant as Brace. The court acknowledged that drug dealers *might* seek out churches to launder money and might find a willing although naive and inexperienced pastor an invaluable asset in their plans. However, it stressed that the government had introduced no evidence at trial that this was in fact the case. Thus, the government failed to prove that when approached, Brace "was in a position to launder money." Essentially, the prosecution "failed to establish that Brace would have laundered money absent government involvement * * *," and therefore failed to show positional predisposition as required by *Hollingsworth*.

2. Even under the position taken by Justices Roberts, Frankfurter, and Stewart, the only basis on which law enforcement conduct can be found to have given rise to entrapment is its tendency, as a general matter, to induce nonpredisposed persons to form the intent to commit crime. Law enforcement conduct that is offensive for other reasons cannot justify a finding that the defendant was entrapped. Some commentators and a few courts have argued that entrapment should be formulated so as to permit acquittal of a defendant on the ground that the law enforcement conduct leading to their commission of the crime was offensive for other reasons.

    In *State v. Sainz*, 84 N.M. 259,261,501 P.2d l247, 1249 (App.1972), for example, the New Mexico Court of Appeals adopted the following formulation of the entrapment defense:

When the state's participation in the criminal enterprise reaches the point where it can be said that except for the conduct of the state a crime would probably not have been committed or because the conduct is such that it is likely to induce those to commit a crime who would normally avoid crime, *or, if the conduct is such that if allowed to continue would shake the public's confidence in the fair and honorable administration of justice,* this then becomes entrapment as a matter of law.

Sainz was overruled by the New Mexico Supreme Court in *State v. Fiechter,* 89 N.M. 74, 547 P.2d 557 (1976), but in *Baca v. State,* 106 N.M. 338, 742 P.2d 1043 (1987), that court concluded that "something more than an objective standard is needed to define entrapment." As a result, it held that "a criminal defendant may successfully assert the defense of entrapment, either by showing lack of predisposition to commit the crime for which he is charged, or, that the police exceeded the standards of proper investigation * * *."

3. Generally, a defendant is permitted to argue inconsistent positions to a jury in a criminal case. Many courts have treated entrapment differently and held that a defendant may not deny commission of the crime charged and also assert entrapment. This rule may even be applied to require that a defendant take the stand and admit commission of the acts constituting the crime before entrapment will be regarded as having been raised. See *State v. Montano,* 117 Ariz. 145, 571 P.2d 291 (1977).

   In *Mathews v. United States,* 485 U.S. 58, 108 S.Ct. 883, 99 L.Ed.2d 54 (1988), the Supreme Court held that for purposes of federal prosecutions defendants would not be barred from relying on entrapment by inconsistency between denials that they committed the crimes and entrapment. The government argued that permitting defendants to argue inconsistent positions—that they did not commit the charged crime but if they did they were entrapped—would encourage defendants to commit perjury. Entrapment does not always have to assume full criminal guilt, the Court responded, and emphasized the facts of *Mathews* in which the defendant sought to argue

that he lacked the *mens rea* required by the crime charged but if that was proven, he was entitled to acquittal on entrapment grounds. Further, practical considerations such as the likelihood of offending a jury by testifying in a manner inconsistent with the evidence will discourage defendants from committing perjury. On balance, the Court concluded, the danger of encouraging perjury is not great enough to justify a special prohibition against inconsistent positions regarding only the defense of entrapment.

Mathews was not a constitutional decision and determined only the rule for federal criminal prosecutions. Some state courts, however, have found the Supreme Court's reasoning persuasive and have adopted the *Mathews* approach as a matter of state entrapment law. Other courts have rejected the *Mathews* reasoning. The Arizona Supreme Court, for example, adhered to its longstanding rule that defendants must admit guilt of the crime to argue entrapment. It did so for what it explained were two reasons:

> First, the *Mathews* rule fosters perjury and more litigation. Under *Mathews,* a defendant may take the stand and testify that he did not do the act. The jury is instructed not only on the elements of entrapment but the elements of the crime itself. To allow a defendant to testify as to two defenses that cannot both be true is equivalent to sanctioning a defendant's perjury.
>
> Second, allowing inconsistent defenses may confuse the jury. What must the jury think when the defendant testifies that he had nothing to do with the sale of narcotics and then the defendant's attorney tells the jury that, yes, the defendant did commit the crime but was entrapped? * * * Entrapment is a proper defense under these circumstances only if the accused is lying. We do not believe that the defendant has a right to lie at trial or a right to solicit his attorney's aid in executing such a defense strategy. * * *

State v. Soule, 168 Ariz. 134, 135–37, 811 P.2d 1071, 1072–74 (1991), cert. denied, 502 U.S. 1038, 112 S.Ct. 888, 116 L.Ed.2d 791 (1992).

MODEL PENAL CODE*

Official Draft 1985

Section 2.13. Entrapment

(1) A public law enforcement official or a person acting in cooperation with such an official perpetrated an entrapment if for the purpose of obtaining evidence of the commission of an offense, he induces or encourages another person to engage in conduct constituting such offense by either:

    (a) making knowingly false representations designed to induce the belief that such conduct is not prohibited; or

    (b) employing methods of persuasion or inducement which create a substantial risk that such an offense will be committed by persons other than those who are ready to commit it.

(2) Except as provided in Subsection (3) of this Section, a person prosecuted for an offense shall be acquitted if he proves by a preponderance of evidence that his conduct occurred in response to an entrapment. The issue of entrapment shall be tried by the Court in the absence of the jury.

(3) The defense afforded by this Section is unavailable when causing or threatening bodily injury is an element of the offense charged and the prosecution is based on conduct causing or threatening such injury to a person other than the person perpetrating the entrapment.

C. LAW ENFORCEMENT
Editors' Introduction: Criminal Liability for Action Taken to Enforce the Law

When criminal responsibility exists for conduct committed for the purpose of enforcing the law is a seldom addressed matter. This is undoubtedly in part because whatever the formal law is or might be, criminal charges are seldom pursued by prosecutors against police officers or others who engage in activity with this objective in mind.

As the principal case in this section demonstrates, however, more litigation has occurred concerning the *civil liability* for damages of police officers and their employers for actions of the officers. As a result, it is necessary to carefully distinguish among the bodies of law that relate to this sort of conduct. The principal case, as well as many other appellate decisions, address the circumstances in which a police officer's conduct gives rise to civil liability. However, it does not necessarily follow that because the officer (or the officer's employer) is liable in a civil action for damages that the officer may be successfully prosecuted for a crime. Perhaps criminal prosecution is also possible, but this is not necessarily the case. The two matters—civil liability and criminal liability—are governed by different bodies of law.

Primary concern here, of course, is with the potential *criminal* liability of a police officer for conduct engaged in for purposes of law enforcement. Generally speaking, this may arise in several types of situations.

Use of Possibly Excessive Force

One consists of those situations such as the on that gave rise to the principal case. In these situations, the officer uses force for purposes of making an arrest, a detention of some other sort, or a search. Such force constitutes a crime—assault, battery, or if death results murder or manslaughter—unless the officer has a defense. Criminal statutes often address at least some of these situations. Many jurisdictions, for example, have extensive statutory provisions dealing with the use of force to make an arrest or to perform other law enforcement functions. These provisions give officers a defense to a criminal charge based on conduct permitted by their terms. State statutes are often modeled after section 3.07 of the Model Penal Code, reprinted after this introduction. In cases of this sort, the task is to determine whether the officer acted within the provision.

Exceeding Specific Authorizations

The second and third types of situations usually involve scenarios in which officers as part of an investigation or pursuit engage in what would generally be criminal activity. Sometimes this activity is part of the conduct being investigated; officers engaged in undercover drug investigations, for example, may possess, deliver, or even manufacture drugs in the course of their investigation. At other times, the officers' conduct is not what is being investigated. An undercover officer engaged in a drug investigation may participate in a burglary to gain the confidence of her targets. An officer pursuing a suspect may violate the criminal prohibition against speeding.

Sometimes the conduct in these two types of situations is not addressed by any specific statute or legal rule. These are situations of the third type, considered next. In other cases, the officer's conduct is addressed by, but may exceed, statutory provisions authorizing conduct of the type involved. These are situations of the second type. Drug laws sometimes include an exemption for law enforcement conduct, for example, often based on the Uniform Controlled Substance Act. This is illustrated by Washington's statutory provisions governing controlled substances, which include section 69.50.506(c):

> (c) No liability is imposed by this chapter upon any authorized state, county or municipal officer, engaged in the lawful performance of his duties.

A similar statute was held in *State v. Francisco*, 790 S.W.2d 543 (Tenn.Cr.App.1989), to apply where a sheriff's narcotics detective was found in possession of cocaine. The defendant testified that in the course of his work he had made a large purchase of cocaine. He was delivering it to his superiors in small increments over a period a time to avoid further criticism by his supervisor that he was spending too much money for drug purchases and making too few arrests. Although he admitted falsifying dates and quantities in the reports he had filed, he added that he believed the entire deceptive procedure was necessary in order to successfully apprehend a major drug dealer. The jury was instructed that Francisco should be acquitted if the jury found that he possessed the cocaine while "engaged in the lawful performance of his duties." It convicted him. On appeal, the court held that the evidence supported the jury's determination that despite the statute his possession of the cocaine was criminal, given the evidence that his possession of the cocaine was not incident to the lawful performance of his duties. Further, the trial judge did not err in refusing to tell the jury that Francisco was entitled to acquittal simply because he was a peace officer engaged in his lawful duties when he possessed the cocaine. "For the possession to be lawful," the court explained, "it must be incident to, not merely contemporaneous with, the performance of his duties."

Francisco apparently rested on the jury's right to reject Francisco's testimony in its entirety. Thus, the jury could have concluded that he had no intention of turning the cocaine over to his superiors at all and possessed it with no exculpatory state of mind. The appellate court's action therefore left unclear whether the detective's possession of the cocaine would be criminal if his testimony was believed. Neither the statute nor the court's opinion make clear whether the detective's possession of the cocaine would have become unlawful, unauthorized, or both—and thus a crime—if he was retaining it for eventual but piecemeal delivery to his superiors pursuant to reports that falsified some details regarding how he obtained it.

Under these statutes, then, generally criminal conduct—such as possession of cocaine—committed by an officer who believes this conduct is reasonably necessary to achieve a legitimate law enforcement task within her duties is noncriminal only if it is both "authorized" and "lawful." Often, however, it is unclear what defines the lawfulness of such conduct and what authorization is required to meet the first demand. If Detective Francisco's testimony is believed, for example, perhaps the difference between what regulations and practice in his department required and his possession of the cocaine was not great enough to render his possession not "authorized" under the statute. The appellate decision just described, however, leaves this uncertain.

Conduct Within Defense of Public Duty or General "Justification"

The final type of situation involves cases in which a police officer, for law enforcement purposes, engages in what would generally be criminal activity where that is not covered by a statutory provision such as those permitting the use of force for law enforcement or more specific activity such as possession and sale of drugs.

The little case law available indicates that in situations of the second sort, courts will be receptive to the argument that some sort of defense of law enforcement must be recognized. The leading case is *Lilly v. West Virginia*, 29 F.2d 61 (4th Cir.1928). Mack B. Lilly was a federal prohibition agent who was chasing a car his investigation had

convinced him was illegally transporting liquor. Lilly was driving in excess of the
speed limit imposed by city ordinance and struck a pedestrian who was attempting to
cross the road at a marked crosswalk in Huntington, West Virginia. An ordinance of
the city in which this occurred required that pedestrians be given the right-of-way in
such crosswalks. The pedestrian died and Lilly was indicted in the West Virginia
courts for involuntary manslaughter, apparently on the rationale that he had caused
the death of a person in the commission of misdemeanor violations of the city ordi-
nances. Under a federal statute, his prosecution was removed to and tried in a federal
district court.

Lilly requested that the jury be instructed that he should be acquitted if the jury
determined that at the time of the accident he was acting as a federal law enforcement
agent in reasonable pursuit of the vehicle and was using reasonable care and diligence
for the safety of the public under the circumstances. Not only was this instruction
refused, but the trial judge instructed the jury that:

> Lilly had a right, based on information he had, to catch that car if he could * * *;
> but * * * that did not give him any right to break any law of the state of West
> Virginia or the city of Huntington to do it.

Lilly was convicted and appealed. The appellate court found that the trial judge had
erred. Crimes such as those created by the Huntington speed and right-of-way ordi-
nances, it concluded, should be construed as inapplicable to "public officials engaged
in the performance of a public duty where speed and right of way are a necessity." As a
result, it continued:

> The officer in this case was warranted in attempting to make the arrest under the
> circumstances, and he is by reason thereof exempted from the limitations of the
> speed prescribed by the city ordinance at issue; provided the jury believed that he
> acted in good faith in what he did, and with the prudence, care, and caution that
> a reasonable person would have exercised under the circumstances in which he
> was placed; the degree of care required being commensurate with the dangers'
> existing, and to be increased in proportion to such dangers should there be an
> increase thereof.

Under modern codes, general provisions for a defense of justification are often construed as applicable to claims that action taken for law enforcement purposes is not
criminal. Many of these general provisions are based upon Section 3.03(1) of the Model
Penal Code, titled Execution of Public Duty, which provides:

> [C]onduct is justifiable [and the actor has an affirmative defense to a criminal
> charge based on that conduct] when it is required or authorized by * * * the law
> defining the duties or functions of a public officer or the assistance to be rendered
> to such an officer in the performance of his duties * * *.

The comment to this section states that it is intended to provide a defense to persons
such as a police officer who exceeds posted speed limits in apprehending a fugitive,
that is, in situations like *Lilly*. Because the precise duties of various public officers are

so numerous and vary so much, the comment indicates, a catalog of specific situations would be "unwieldy." Model Penal Code and Commentaries, Comment to § 3.03 (Official Draft 1985).

Under this approach, the question becomes whether the law defining an officer's duties or functions authorizes the conduct at issue. Such a matter was raised in *Aucoin v. State*, 548 So.2d 1053 (Ala.Cr.App.1989), cert. denied. Aucoin was convicted of theft from an insurance company based on evidence that he and codefendant Harris staged a fake automobile accident and represented to an insurance company that damages to a vehicle actually caused earlier had been caused in that accident. Aucoin, at the time, was a constable. At trial, he testified that although he participated in the scheme he did so while engaged in undercover police work as a means of gaining the confidence of another officer he was investigating for drug-related offenses. He unsuccessfully asked that the trial judge instruct the jury under a statute somewhat like section 3.03 of the Model Penal Code. The Alabama statute exempted from criminal penalties conduct "performed by a public servant in the reasonable exercise of his official powers, duties or functions."

Finding no error, the appellate court held that Aucoin's testimony did not raise a jury issue on whether his conduct was a reasonable exercise of his official functions. It explained:

> Even if the appellants were working undercover on an investigation of another officer, defrauding an insurance company was not a reasonable means to investigate the officer for drug-related offenses. The insurance company was not informed of the investigation, or what its role in the investigation would be, until the appellants were themselves being investigated. Furthermore, there was no testimony at trial from a higher authority that the appellant's method of investigating the other officer had been decided upon or approved.

Thus, the court apparently held that even if Aucoin's testimony was credible, and Aucoin did in fact engage in the scheme as a part of his undercover investigation, his decision to commit the crime of theft was so clearly and obviously an unreasonable means of pursuing the law enforcement objectives involved that no jury could properly find it a *reasonable* exercise of his official functions within the meaning of the statutory defense.

A leading authority comments that "[p]resumably" certain kinds of conduct are so serious that they do not come within a defense of the sort under discussion here. W. LaFave and A. Scott, Criminal Law 477 (2d ed. 1986). It is not at all clear, however, where the line will be drawn, again because the infrequency of prosecutions in such situations means that very little relevant case law exists.

Undercover activity such as the defendant in *Aucoin* claimed was involved in that case presents special problems. This is considered further in an Editors' Note following the principal case in this section.

MODEL PENAL CODE[*]

Official Draft 1985

Section 3.07. Use of Force in Law Enforcement.

(1) Use of Force Justifiable to Effect an Arrest. Subject to the provisions of this Section and of Section 3.09, the use of force upon or toward the person of another is justifiable when the actor is making or assisting in making an arrest and the actor believes that such force is immediately necessary to effect a lawful arrest.

(2) *Limitations on the Use of Force.*

    (a) The use of force is not justifiable under this Section unless:

        (i) the actor makes known the purpose of the arrest or believes that it is otherwise known by or cannot reasonably be made known to the person to be arrested; and

        (ii) when the arrest is made under a warrant, the warrant is valid or believed by the actor to be valid.

    (b) The use of deadly force is not justifiable under this Section unless:

        (i) the arrest is for a felony; and

        (ii) the person effecting the arrest is authorized to act as a peace officer or is assisting a person whom he believes to be authorized to act as a peace officer; and

        (iii) the actor believes that the force employed creates no substantial risk of injury to innocent persons; and

        (iv) the actor believes that:

            (A) the crime for which the arrest is made involved conduct including the use or threatened use of deadly force; or

            (B) there is a substantial risk that the person to be arrested will cause death or serious bodily injury if his apprehension is delayed.

* * *

(5) *Use of Force to Prevent Suicide or the Commission of a Crime.*

    (a) The use of force upon or toward the person of another is justifiable when the actor believes that such force is immediately necessary to prevent such other person from committing suicide, inflicting serious bodily injury upon himself, committing or consummating the commission of a crime involving or threatening bodily injury, damage to or loss of property or a breach of the peace, except that:

(i) any limitations imposed by the other provisions of this Article on the justifiable use of force in self-protection, for the protection of others, the protection of property, the effectuation of an arrest or the prevention of an escape from custody shall apply notwithstanding the criminality of the conduct against which such force is used; and

(ii) the use of deadly force is not in any event justifiable under this Subsection unless:

(A) the actor believes that there is a substantial risk that the person whom he seeks to prevent from committing a crime will cause death or serious bodily injury to another unless the commission or the consummation of the crime is prevented and that the use of such force presents no substantial risk of injury to innocent persons; or

(B) the actor believes that the use of such force is necessary to suppress a riot or mutiny after the rioters or mutineers have been ordered to disperse and warned, in any particular manner that the law may require, that such force will be used if they do not obey.

(b) The justification afforded by this Subsection extends to the use of confinement as preventive force only if the actor takes all reasonable measures to terminate the confinement as soon as he knows that he safely can, unless the person confined has been arrested on a charge of crime.

Editors' Note: Related Defense of "Crime Prevention"

A defendant charged with an assaultive crime may have what is often called the defense of "crime prevention." Section 3.07(5) of the Model Penal Code, previously reprinted, includes within the right to use force in "law enforcement" situations in which force is used to prevent the commission of an offense. Some discussions regard this as a separate doctrine that in effect creates a defense consisting of a showing that the defendant was motivated in the assault or homicide charged by a desire to prevent what the defendant perceived was the victim's commission of a criminal offense.

This defense, where it exists, is closely related not only to law enforcement but also to self-defense and related matters discussed in Chapter 14. Sometimes, a defendant unable to invoke the defenses of self-defense, defense of others, or defense of property may nevertheless be able to establish that he or she believed the victim about to do harm to the defendant, another, or property that would be a crime. This may permit the defendant to come within a somewhat broader defensive doctrine permitting the use of force to prevent such criminal offenses.

Common law permitted the use of force to prevent the commission of a crime that would be a felony or a breach of the peace, the Alaska Supreme Court noted in *State v. Sundberg*, 611 P.2d 44 (Alaska 1980). Under modern statutory law, *Sundberg* continued, this is not always still the case. Oklahoma, for example, provides by statute that any person may make "[l]awful resistance" to the commission of any "public offense." 11 Okla.Stat. § 31.

In some situations, this defense may be available where others are not. In *State v. Korzep*, 165 Ariz. 490, 799 P.2d 831 (1990), for example, the Arizona Supreme Court held that the jury at Roberta Korzep's manslaughter trial should have been instructed not only on self-defense law but also on her right under an Arizona statute to use force to prevent the commission of various crimes, including aggravated assault. Korzep was shown to have fatally stabbed her husband as he struck her with his fists. The court noted that Korzep might have had several advantages under the law defining her right to prevent assault by her husband that she would not have had under Arizona self-defense law: Self-defense law required an immediate threat to the actor's safety and retreat before the use of deadly force; neither was required under the right to use force to prevent the listed crimes, which demanded only that the accused's use of force have been "reasonable." Moreover, the statute creating the right to use force to prevent crimes created a presumption that a person motivated by a desire to prevent a crime acts reasonably, whereas self-defense law contained no such advantage for an accused.

Similarly, in *Brown v. State*, 486 S.E.2d 178 (Ga. 1997), defendant Brown, about to go to trial for murder, was held entitled to present evidence that the victim had attempted to molest Brown's 5-year-old daughter. This might establish, the court reasoned, that Brown had a statutory right to use deadly force to prevent that molestation. Georgia law permits the use of deadly force in defense of another only if the person using the force reasonably believes that the deadly force is necessary to prevent death or "great bodily harm" to the third person "*or* to prevent the commission of a forcible felony." Child molestation, the Georgia court held, is a "forcible felony" that Brown might have used deadly force to prevent. Presumably, then, Brown would be entitled to acquittal on felony prevention grounds (but not on self-defense grounds) if he reasonably believed the victim would otherwise commit child molestation on his daughter but without doing great bodily harm to her.

Although the question appears not to have been litigated, a defendant apparently may invoke the defense without having been aware that the victim's conduct, which she sought to avoid, would have been a crime. In the case previously discussed, Roberta Korzep would most likely not have had to establish that when she stabbed her husband, she knew his assault on her would be a crime (or, specifically, the felony of aggravated assault). It is apparently enough that she was motivated by a desire to prevent his conduct, that her perception was objectively reasonable, and that *in fact* his conduct would have been aggravated assault.

Carjacking as a new robbery-like crime of particular offensiveness was discussed in Chapter 10 at page 302. At least one jurisdiction has adopted a specific and broad right to use deadly force to prevent this offense.

In 1997, the Louisiana legislature amended that state's justifiable homicide statute. Previously, the statute had characterized as justifiable those killings (among others) committed by persons inside dwellings or places of business who reasonably believed the killings were necessary to prevent unlawful entry into the premises or to compel unlawful intruders to leave the premises. This was widely known as the "shoot the burglar" law. The 1997 amendment, popularly known as the "shoot the carjacker" law, expanded the provision so that it read in part as follows:

> § 20. Justifiable homicide
> A homicide is justifiable:
>
> * * *
>
> (3) When * * * committed against a person whom one reasonably believes is attempting to use any unlawful force against a person present in a motor vehicle while committing or attempting to commit a burglary or robbery of such * * * motor vehicle. The homicide shall be justifiable even though the person does not retreat from the encounter.
>
> (4) When committed by a person lawfully inside a * * * a motor vehicle * * * against a person who is attempting to make an unlawful entry into the * * * motor vehicle, or who has made an unlawful entry into the * * * motor vehicle, and the person committing the homicide reasonably believes that the use of deadly force is necessary to prevent the entry or to compel the intruder to leave the * * * motor vehicle. The homicide shall be justifiable even though the person committing the homicide does not retreat from the encounter.

This is apparently the first statutory provision to focus specifically and directly upon the right to use force to prevent what have come to be known as "carjackings." According to a victims' advocacy spokesperson, the Louisiana statute was preceded by three cases in which victims of violent incidents were charged with crimes for defending themselves. Victims of carjackings, she added, should not—if they live through the incidents—"be hassled by the legal system." A critic of the new provision responded, "Essentially, its just a law that allows you to kill car thieves." Louisiana Law Allows Force on Carjackers, New York Times, Aug. 17, 1997, p. A19.

Tennessee v. Garner

Supreme Court of the United States, 1985
471 U.S. 1, 105 S.Ct. 1694, 85 L.Ed.2d 1.

JUSTICE WHITE delivered the opinion of the Court.

* * *

I

At about 10:45 P.M. on October 3, 1974, Memphis Police Officers Elton Hymon and Leslie Wright were dispatched to answer a "prowler inside call." Upon arriving at the scene they saw a woman standing on her porch and gesturing toward the adjacent house. She told them she had heard glass breaking and that "they" or "someone" was breaking in next door. While Wright radioed the dispatcher to say that they were on the scene, Hymon went behind the house. He heard a door slam and saw someone run across the back yard. The fleeing suspect, who was appellee-respondent's decedent, Edward Garner, stopped at a 6-feet-high chain link fence at the edge of the yard. With the aid of a flashlight, Hymon was able to see Garner's face and hands. He saw no sign of a weapon, and, though not certain, was "reasonably sure" and "figured" that Garner was unarmed. He thought Garner was 17 or 18 years old and about 5' 5" or 5' 7" tall. While Garner was crouched at the base of the fence, Hymon called out "police, halt" and took a few steps toward him. Garner then began to climb over the fence. Convinced that if Garner made it over the fence he would elude capture, Hymon shot him. The bullet hit Garner in the back of the head. Garner was taken by ambulance to a hospital, where he died on the operating table. Ten dollars and a purse taken from the house were found on his body.

In using deadly force to prevent the escape, Hymon was acting under the authority of a Tennessee statute and pursuant to Police Department policy. The statute provides that "[i]f, after notice of the intention to arrest the defendant, he either flee or forcibly resist, the officer may use all the necessary means to effect the arrest." Tenn.Code Ann. § 40-7-108 (1982). The Department policy was slightly more restrictive than the statute, but still allowed the use of deadly force in cases of burglary. The incident was reviewed by the Memphis Police Firearm's Review Board and presented to a grand jury. Neither took any action.

Garner's father then brought this action in the Federal District Court for the Western District of Tennessee, seeking damages * * * for asserted violations of Garner's constitutional rights. * * * After a 3-day bench trial, the District Court entered judgment for all defendants. * * * It * * * concluded that Hymon's actions were authorized by the Tennessee statute, which in turn was constitutional. * * *

The Court of Appeals reversed and remanded. [It concluded that section 3.07 of the Model Penal Code, reprinted on page 559, stated the standard for determining whether the force used to make an arrest renders the arrest "unreasonable" and therefore in violation of the Fourth Amendment requirement that seizures of the person be "reasonable." On the facts of this case, it continued, the officers could not use deadly force unless they had probable cause to believe that the suspect had committed a felony and posed a threat to the safety of the officers or a danger to the community if left at large. As applied to this case, the Tennessee statute was unconstitutional because it permitted the use of force that was prohibited by the federal constitutional standard. Since the District Court had applied an incorrect standard in deciding for the defendants, the appellate court reversed and remanded for further proceedings in the District Court.]* * * The State of Tennessee, which had intervened to defend the statute, appealed to this Court.

II

Whenever an officer restrains the freedom of a person to walk away, he has seized that person.

A

A police officer may arrest a person if he has probable cause to believe that person committed a crime. Petitioners and appellant argue that if this requirement is satisfied the Fourth Amendment has nothing to say about how that seizure is made. This submission ignores the many cases in which this Court, by balancing the extent of the intrusion against the need for it, has examined the reasonableness of the manner in which a search or seizure is conducted. To determine the constitutionality of a seizure "[w]e must balance the nature and quality of the intrusion on the individual's Fourth Amendment interests against the importance of the governmental interests alleged to justify the intrusion." * * *

B

The * * * balancing process * * * demonstrates that, notwithstanding probable cause to seize a suspect, an officer may not always do so by killing him. The intrusiveness of a seizure by means of deadly force is unmatched. The suspect's fundamental interest in his own life need not be elaborated upon. The use of deadly force also frustrates the interest of the individual, and of society, in judicial determination of guilt and punishment. Against these interests are ranged governmental interests in effective law enforcement. It is argued that overall violence will be reduced by encouraging the peaceful submission of suspects who know that they may be shot if they flee. Effectiveness in making arrests requires the resort to deadly force, or at least the meaningful threat thereof. "Being able to arrest such individuals is a condition precedent to the state's entire system of law enforcement." Brief for Petitioners 14.

Without in any way disparaging the importance of these goals, we are not convinced that the use of deadly force is a sufficiently productive means of accomplishing them to justify the killing of nonviolent suspects. The use of deadly force is a self-defeating way of apprehending a suspect and so setting the criminal justice mechanism in motion. If successful, it guarantees that that mechanism will not be set in motion. And while the meaningful threat of deadly force might be thought to lead to the arrest of more live suspects by discouraging escape attempts, the presently available evidence does not support this thesis. The fact is that a majority of police departments in this country have forbidden the use of deadly force against nonviolent suspects. If those charged with the enforcement of the criminal law have abjured the use of deadly force in arresting nondangerous felons, there is a substantial basis for doubting that the use of such force is an essential attribute of the arrest power in all felony cases. Petitioners and appellant have not persuaded us that shooting nondangerous fleeing suspects is so vital as to outweigh the suspect's interest in his own life.

The use of deadly force to prevent the escape of all felony suspects, whatever the circumstances, is constitutionally unreasonable. It is not better that all felony suspects die than that they escape. Where the suspect poses no immediate threat to the officer and no threat to others, the harm resulting from failing to apprehend him does not justify the use of deadly force to do so. It is no doubt unfortunate when a suspect who is in sight escapes, but the fact that the police arrive a little late or are a little slower afoot does not always justify killing the suspect. A police officer may not seize an unarmed, nondangerous suspect by shooting him dead. The Tennessee statute is unconstitutional insofar as it authorizes the use of deadly force against such fleeing suspects.

It is not, however, unconstitutional on its face. Where the officer has probable cause to believe that the suspect poses a threat of serious physical harm, either to the officer or to others, it is not constitutionally unreasonable to prevent escape by using deadly force. Thus, if the suspect threatens the officer with a weapon or there is probable cause to believe that he has committed a crime involving the infliction or threatened infliction of serious physical harm, deadly force may be used if necessary to prevent escape, and if, where feasible, some warning has been given. As applied in such circumstances, the Tennessee statute would pass constitutional muster.

III

A

It is insisted that the Fourth Amendment must be construed in light of the common-law rule, which allowed the use of whatever force was necessary to effect the arrest of a fleeing felon, though not a misdemeanant. * * * Most American jurisdictions also imposed a flat prohibition against the use of deadly force to stop a fleeing misdemeanant, coupled with a general privilege to use such force to stop a fleeing felon.

The State and city argue that because this was the prevailing rule at the time of the adoption of the Fourth Amendment and for some time thereafter, and is still in force in some States, use of deadly force against a fleeing felon must be "reasonable." It is true that this Court has often looked to the common law in evaluating the reasonableness, for Fourth Amendment purposes, of police activity. On the other hand, it "has not simply frozen into constitutional law those law enforcement practices that existed at the time of the Fourth Amendment's passage." Because of sweeping change in the legal and technological context, reliance on the common-law rule in this case would be a mistaken literalism that ignores the purposes of a historical inquiry.

B

It has been pointed out many times that the common-law rule is best understood in light of the fact that it arose at a time when virtually all felonies were punishable by death. "Though effected without the protections and formalities of an orderly trial and conviction, the killing of a resisting or fleeing felon resulted in no greater consequences than those authorized for punishment of the felony of which the individual was charged or suspected." American Law Institute, Model Penal Code § 3.07, Comment 3, p. 56 (Tentative Draft No. 8, 1958) (hereinafter Model Penal Code Comment). Courts have also justified the common-law rule by emphasizing the relative dangerousness of felons.

Neither of these justifications makes sense today. Almost all crimes formerly punishable by death no longer are or can be. And while in earlier times "the gulf between the felonies and the minor offenses was broad and deep," today the distinction is minor and often arbitrary. Many crimes classified as misdemeanors, or nonexistent, at common law are now felonies. These changes have undermined the concept, which was questionable to begin with, that use of deadly force against a fleeing felon is merely a speedier execution of someone who has already forfeited his life. They have also made the assumption that a "felon" is more dangerous than a misdemeanant untenable. Indeed, numerous misdemeanors involve conduct more dangerous than many felonies.

There is an additional reason why the common-law rule cannot be directly translated to the present day. The common-law rule developed at a time when weapons were rudimentary. Deadly force could be inflicted almost solely in a hand-to-hand struggle during which, necessarily, the safety of the arresting officer was at risk. Handguns were not carried by police officers until the latter half of the last century. Only then did it become possible to use deadly force from a distance as a means of apprehension. As a practical matter, the use of deadly force under the standard articulation of the common-law rule has an altogether different meaning—and harsher consequences—now than in past centuries. * * *[13]

---

[13] It has been argued that sophisticated techniques of apprehension and increased communication between the police in different jurisdictions have made it more likely that an escapee will be caught than was once the case, and that this change has also reduced the "reasonableness" of the use of deadly force to prevent escape. We are unaware of any data that would permit sensible evaluation of this claim. Current arrest rates are sufficiently low, however, that we have some doubt whether in past centuries the failure to arrest at the scene meant that the police had missed their only chance in a way that is not presently the case. In 1983, 21% of the offenses in the FBI crime index were cleared by arrest. The clearance rate for burglary was 15%.

C

In evaluating the reasonableness of police procedures under the Fourth Amendment, we have also looked to prevailing rules in individual jurisdictions. The rules in the States are varied. Some 19 States have codified the common-law rule, though in two of these the courts have significantly limited the statute. Four States, though without a relevant statute, apparently retain the common-law rule. Two States have adopted the Model Penal Code's provision verbatim. Eighteen others allow, in slightly varying language, the use of deadly force only if the suspect has committed a felony involving the use or threat of physical or deadly force, or is escaping with a deadly weapon, or is likely to endanger life or inflict serious physical injury if not arrested. Louisiana and Vermont, though without statutes or case law on point, do forbid the use of deadly force to prevent any but violent felonies. The remaining States either have no relevant statute or case-law, or have positions that are unclear.

It cannot be said that there is a constant or overwhelming trend away from the common-law rule. In recent years, some States have reviewed their laws and expressly rejected abandonment of the common-law rule. Nonetheless, the long-term movement has been away from the rule that deadly force may be used against any fleeing felon, and that remains the rule in less than half the States.

This trend is more evident and impressive when viewed in light of the policies adopted by the police departments themselves. Overwhelmingly, these are more restrictive than the common-law rule. The Federal Bureau of Investigation and the New York City Police Department, for example, both forbid the use of firearms except when necessary to prevent death or grievous bodily harm. For accreditation by the Commission on Accreditation for Law Enforcement Agencies, a department must restrict the use of deadly force to situations where "the officer reasonably believes that the action is in defense of human life * * * or in defense of any person in immediate danger of serious physical injury." A 1974 study reported that the police department regulations in a majority of the large cities of the United States allowed the firing of a weapon only when a felony presented a threat of death or serious bodily harm. Boston Police Department, Planning & Research Division, The Use of Deadly Force by Boston Police Personnel (1974). Overall, only 7.5% of departmental and municipal policies explicitly permit the use of deadly force against any felon; 86.8% explicitly do not. K. Matulia, A Balance of Forces: A Report of the International Association of Chiefs of Police 161 (1982) (table). In light of the rules adopted by those who must actually administer them, the older and fading common-law view is a dubious indicium of the constitutionality of the Tennessee statute now before us.

D

Actual departmental policies are important for an additional reason. We would hesitate to declare a police practice of long standing "unreasonable" if doing so would severely hamper effective law enforcement. But the indications are to the contrary. There has been no suggestion that crime has worsened in any way in jurisdictions that have adopted, by legislation or departmental policy, rules similar to that announced today. Amici noted that "[a]fter extensive research and consideration, [they] have concluded that laws permitting police officers to use deadly force to apprehend unarmed, non-violent fleeing felony suspects actually do not protect citizens or law enforcement officers, do not deter crime or alleviate problems caused by crime, and do not improve the crime-fighting ability of law enforcement agencies." Brief for Police Foundation et al. as *Amici Curiae* 11. The submission is that the obvious state interests in apprehension are not sufficiently served to warrant the use of lethal weapons against all fleeing felons.

Nor do we agree with petitioners and appellant that the rule we have adopted requires the police to make impossible, split-second evaluations of unknowable facts. We do not deny the practical difficulties of attempting to assess the suspect's dangerousness. However, similarly difficult judgments must be made by the police in equally uncertain circumstances. Nor is there any indication that in States that allow the use of deadly force only against dangerous suspects, the standard has been difficult to apply or has led to a rash of litigation involving inappropriate second-guessing of police officers' split-second decisions. Moreover, the highly technical felony/misdemeanor distinction is equally, if not more, difficult to apply in the field. An officer is in no position to know, for example, the precise value of property stolen, or whether the crime was a first or second offense. Finally, as noted above, this claim must be viewed with suspicion in light of the similar self-imposed limitations of so many police departments.

IV

* * *

Officer Hymon could not reasonably have believed that Garner—young, slight, and unarmed—posed any threat. * * * [T]he fact that Garner was a suspected burglar could not, without regard to the other circumstances, automatically justify the use of deadly force. Hymon did not have probable cause to believe that Garner, whom he correctly believed to be unarmed, posed any physical danger to himself or others.

The dissent argues that the shooting was justified by the fact that Officer Hymon had probable cause to believe that Garner had committed a nighttime burglary. While we agree that burglary is a serious crime, we cannot agree that it is so dangerous as automatically to justify the use of deadly force. The FBI classifies burglary as a "property" rather than a "violent" crime. Although the armed burglar would present a different situation, the fact that an unarmed suspect has broken into a dwelling at night does not automatically mean he is physically dangerous. This case demonstrates as much. In fact, the available statistics demonstrate that burglaries only rarely involve physical violence. During the 10-year period from 1973–1982, only 3.8% of all burglaries involved violent crime.[23]

The judgment of the Court of Appeals is affirmed, and the case is remanded for further proceedings consistent with this opinion.

So ordered.

JUSTICE O'CONNOR, with whom THE CHIEF JUSTICE and JUSTICE REHNQUIST join, dissenting.

* * *

For purposes of Fourth Amendment analysis, I agree with the Court that Officer Hymon "seized" Garner by shooting him. Whether that seizure was reasonable and therefore permitted by the Fourth Amendment requires a careful balancing of the important public interest in crime prevention and detection and the nature and quality of the intrusion upon legitimate interests of the individual. * * *

The public interest involved in the use of deadly force as a last resort to apprehend a fleeing burglary suspect relates primarily to the serious nature of the crime. Household burglaries represent not only the illegal entry into a person's home, but also "pos[e] real risk of serious harm to others." According to recent Department of Justice statistics, "[t]hree-fifths of all rapes in the home, three-fifths of all home robberies, and about a third of home aggravated and simple assaults are committed by burglars." Bureau of Justice Statistics Bulletin, Household Burglary 1 (January 1985). During the period 1973–1982, 2.8 million such violent crimes were committed in the course of burglaries. * * *

Because burglary is a serious and dangerous felony, the public interest in the prevention and detection of the crime is of compelling importance. * * * Although some law

enforcement agencies may choose to assume the risk that a criminal will remain at large, the Tennessee statute reflects a legislative determination that the use of deadly force in prescribed circumstances will serve generally to protect the public. Such statutes assist the police in apprehending suspected perpetrators of serious crimes and provide notice that a lawful police order to stop and submit to arrest may not be ignored with impunity. * * *

Against the strong public interests justifying the conduct at issue here must be weighed the individual interests implicated in the use of deadly force by police officers. The majority declares that "[t]he suspect's fundamental interest in his own life need not be elaborated upon." This blithe assertion hardly provides an adequate substitute for the majority's failure to acknowledge the distinctive manner in which the suspect's interest in his life is even exposed to risk. For purposes of this case, we must recall that the police officer, in the course of investigating a nighttime burglary, had reasonable cause to arrest the suspect and ordered him to halt. The officer's use of force resulted because the suspected burglar refused to heed this command and the officer reasonably believed that there was no means short of firing his weapon to apprehend the suspect. Without questioning the importance of a person's interest in his life, I do not think this interest encompasses a right to flee unimpeded from the scene of a burglary. * * * The legitimate interests of the suspect in these circumstances are adequately accommodated by the Tennessee statute: to avoid the use of deadly force and the consequent risk to his life, the suspect need merely obey the valid order to halt.

A proper balancing of the interests involved suggests that use of deadly force as a last resort to apprehend a criminal suspect fleeing from the scene of a nighttime burglary is not unreasonable within the meaning of the Fourth Amendment. Admittedly, the events giving rise to this case are in retrospect deeply regrettable. No one can view the death of an unarmed and apparently nonviolent 15-year old without sorrow, much less disapproval. Nonetheless, the reasonableness of Officer Hymon's conduct for purposes of the Fourth Amendment cannot be evaluated by what later appears to have been a preferable course of police action. The officer pursued a suspect in the darkened backyard of a house that from all indi-

---

[23] The dissent points out that three-fifths of all rapes in the home, three-fifths of all home robberies, and about a third of home assaults are committed by burglars. These figures mean only that if one knows that a suspect committed a rape in the home, there is a good chance that the suspect is also a burglar. That has nothing to do with the question here, which is whether the fact that someone has committed a burglary indicates that he has committed, or might commit, a violent crime.

The dissent also points out that this 3.8% adds up to 2.8 million violent crimes over a 10-year period, as if to imply that today's holding will let loose 2.8 million violent burglars. The relevant universe is, of course, far smaller. At issue is only that tiny fraction of cases where violence has taken place and an officer who has no other means of apprehending the suspect is unaware of its occurrence.

cations had just been burglarized. The police officer was not certain whether the suspect was alone or unarmed; nor did he know what had transpired inside the house. He ordered the suspect to halt, and when the suspect refused to obey and attempted to flee into the night, the officer fired his weapon to prevent escape. The reasonableness of this action for purposes of the Fourth Amendment is not determined by the unfortunate nature of this particular case; instead, the question is whether it is constitutionally impermissible for police officers, as a last resort, to shoot a burglary suspect fleeing the scene of the crime.

* * *

Whatever the constitutional limits on police use of deadly force in order to apprehend a fleeing felon, I do not believe they are exceeded in a case in which a police officer has probable cause to arrest a suspect at the scene of a residential burglary, orders the suspect to halt, and then fires his weapon as a last resort to prevent the suspect's escape into the night. I respectfully dissent.

Notes and Questions

1. The principal case does not address whether Officer Hymon is guilty of a criminal offense under Tennessee law based upon his actions in shooting and killing Garner. The only issue presented by the litigation is whether his actions constituted an unreasonable arrest under the Fourth Amendment and therefore created civil liability for damages under the federal Civil Rights statute. It was not necessary, as a result of the case, that Tennessee change its law concerning when a police officer has a defense to a criminal prosecution based upon the officer's efforts to apprehend a suspect for purposes of arrest.

   As a matter of state criminal law policy, the state of Tennessee (that is, its legislature or courts) could conclude that the considerations relied upon by the majority of the Supreme Court in *Garner* are either unconvincing or inapplicable to the question of whether officers should be guilty of criminal conduct in such situations. Or, Tennessee might conclude that there are other considerations bearing upon whether officers should be guilty of crime that were not implicated in the issue addressed in *Garner*. In any case, Tennessee remained free, despite the United States Supreme Court decision in *Garner*, to provide that as a matter of Tennessee substantive criminal law, officers who use deadly force to arrest a suspect do not commit a crime if they have probable cause to believe the suspect committed a felony and

they reasonably believe that the deadly force was necessary to make the arrest.

In actual fact, however, Tennessee in 1985 amended the statute on which Officer Hymon relied to read as follows:

40-7-108. Resistance to Officer

(a) If, after notice of the intention to arrest the defendant, he either flees or forcibly resists, the officer may use all the necessary means to effect the arrest.

(b) Notwithstanding subsection (a), deadly force is authorized to effect an arrest only if all other reasonable means of apprehension have been exhausted, and, where feasible, warning has been given the defendant, by identifying himself or herself as such officer, or an oral order to halt, or an oral warning that deadly force might be used, and;

    (1) The officer has probable cause to believe the defendant has committed a felony involving the infliction or threatened infliction of serious physical harm to the officer or to any person in the presence of the officer; or

    (2) The officer has probable cause to believe that the defendant poses a threat of serious physical harm, either to the officer or to others unless he is immediately apprehended.

Some changes have been made to the statute by subsequent legislation, but it remains substantively quite similar.

Several other jurisdictions whose statutory law was cited in *Garner* as codifying the common law rule have modified those statutes so as to accommodate *Garner*. 1986 Idaho Sess.Laws ch. 303, codified as Idaho Code §§ 18-4011, 19-610; 1986 Wash.Laws ch. 209, codified as Wash.Rev.Code § 9A.16.040. In other jurisdictions, however, statutes clearly part of the substantive criminal law continue to provide that a police officer has a defense to criminal charges when those charges are based upon force used to make an arrest under circumstances permitted by the common law rule. See, for example, Ala.Code § 13A-3-27; Conn.Gen.Stat. § 53a-22. Nothing in or resulting from *Garner* requires Alabama or Connecticut to provide by statute that an officer who uses necessary deadly force to apprehend a violent felony suspect is guilty of a crime.

Editors' Note: Criminal Liability for Actions Taken in Undercover Investigations

The potential criminal liability of officers or others engaged in undercover law enforcement work has proven to be an especially difficult problem. Iowa has enacted a relatively comprehensive statutory provision that appears to have been aimed at primarily this sort of activity:

> Section 704.11 Police Activity
>
> A peace officer or person acting as an agent of or directed by any police agency who participates in the commission of a crime by another person solely for the purpose of gathering evidence leading to the prosecution of such other person shall not be guilty of that crime or of the crime of solicitation provided that all of the following are true:
>
> 1. He or she is not an instigator of the criminal activity.
> 2. He or she does not intentionally injure a nonparticipant in the crime.
> 3. He or she acts with the consent of superiors, or the necessity of immediate action precludes obtaining such consent.
> 4. His or her actions are reasonable under the circumstances.
>
> This section is not intended to preclude the use of undercover or surveillance persons by law enforcement agencies in appropriate circumstances or manner. It is intended to discourage such activity to tempt, urge, or persuade the commission of offenses by persons not already disposed to commit offenses of that kind.

This statute is the exception rather than the rule, however. In most jurisdictions, no specific statutory provisions address as an overall matter what conduct that would otherwise be criminal does not create criminal liability because it is related to law enforcement undercover work.

Some courts have assumed without much question that an undercover officer or an informer may, without committing an offense, engage in drug transactions that would otherwise be criminal. See, for example, *State v. Georgalis*, 421 So.2d 676 (Fla.App.1982) (uncontested evidence that defendant was acting as confidential informant to Federal Drug Enforcement Administration and because of his cooperation was entitled to engage in conduct at issue required dismissal of charges of trafficking in marijuana and methaqualone); *Kirkpatrick v. State*, 412 So.2d 903, 906–07 (Fla.App.1982). Yet whether this is actually the case is not entirely clear.

Activity involving drugs may be affected by the statutory provisions in some controlled substance statutes discussed in the Editors' Introduction to this section. These provisions state that criminal liability is not imposed under the drug laws "upon any authorized state, county or municipal officer, engaged in the lawful performance of his duties." What is necessary for activity by an officer to be authorized, and what activities constitute the lawful performance of an officer's duties, has presented special problems when an officer's actions involve undercover investigations or informants.

Some cases are clear. In *State v. Glazer*, 223 Kan. 351, 574 P.2d 942 (1978), for example, the prosecution showed that a state attorney general's investigator conspired to have drugs brought into the state to frame innocent persons for drug offenses and to sell to finance the scheme, all in order to further the gubernatorial ambitions of the investigator's employer and the investigator's own career opportunities. This conduct far exceeded the officer's authority and the statute provided no defense.

In other situations, the courts have been less definite. This is undoubtedly in large part because of uncertainty as to what determines whether particular undercover activity is "lawful" and whether it is "authorized" within the meaning of these statutory defenses.

The North Dakota Supreme Court, for example, has suggested that this language would not immunize an officer's actions in taking drugs confiscated in an investigation and giving them to informants for sale to suspects, at least in the absence of evidence that this was authorized by a superior officer. *State v. Kummer*, 481 N.W.2d 437, 443 (N.D. 1992). In contrast, a Texas court has held that this language did authorize undercover officers' possession and delivery of marihuana (from an undetermined source) to suspects in the course of a drug investigation. *Leos v. State*, 847 S.W.2d 665, 667 (Tex.App.—Texarkana 1993), rev'd on other grounds, 883 S.W.2d 209 (Tex.Crim. App.1994). A Michigan court has indicated that such a provision would not immunize an officer's actions in taking drugs confiscated in an investigation and offering them to informants in return for cooperation and information, at least in the absence of evidence that this was officially authorized in some way. *People v. Iaconneli*, 112 Mich.App. 725, 757, 317 N.W.2d 540, 553, vacated in part on other grounds, 116 Mich.App. 176, 321 N.W.2d 684 (1982).

Further, these statutes state only that actual officers' actions do not give rise to criminal liability. Thus, they make no provision regarding immunity for informants or others working with officers. In *State v. McReynolds*, 80 Wash.App. 894, 912 P.2d 514 (1996), the defendant—charged with delivery of cocaine—had been recruited as an informant by officers. He testified that to the extent he was involved in the transactions, he regarded it as part of his work for the officers. Further, he unsuccessfully asked that he be regarded as potentially within the immunity conferred by the Washington statute set out at page 555, and that the jury be told

> Delivery of a controlled substance is lawful * * * if when the delivery occurs, the Defendant believes that he is acting as an agent of [an] * * * authorized * * * officer, engaged in the lawful performance of his duties.

The appellate court expressed some doubt that given the language of the statute, a nonofficer informant could ever be immunized. However, it noted further that the evidence showed that McReynolds had signed an acknowledgment that he had been advised that he was not to violate any laws and was not to possess, sell or deliver drugs except as specifically directed by a detective. The detectives who dealt with him testified that they warned him not to use or sell drugs and not to become involved in any drug deals. "[H]e ignored these warnings," the court stressed, "at his own risk." The court thus assumed that any defense as might be available would require the informant to reasonably believe that he was acting pursuant to directions of an authorized officer, and McReynold's testimony provided no basis for a jury to conclude that any belief of this sort he may have had was reasonable.

Most of the few courts to address the liability of confidential informants for criminal activity have taken essentially the same approach as the *McReynolds* court. Without so deciding and with considerable reservation, they have assumed that such informants *might* have a defense based on an objectively reasonable belief that their actions were authorized by the police officers for or under whom they worked. These courts, though, have been extremely reluctant to conclude that particular defendants even raised issues as to whether their beliefs that their conduct was authorized were reasonable.

State v. Farnsworth, 447 A.2d 1216 (Me.1982), illustrates this approach. Farnsworth was prosecuted for driving under the influence of intoxicating liquor. He testified that he frequently worked as a police informant on drug and theft matters and at the time of the offense he was going to a drug purchase in his capacity as an informer. He further testified that officers had told him he would be "covered" with respect to drug transactions. The officers knew he had a serious drinking problem, he continued, and therefore his "cover" included exemption from liability for the offense charged. The trial judge, however, refused to instruct the jury that any possible defense was raised by this testimony. Affirming, the appellate court found no need to consider whether any legal doctrine might provide a defense in such situations because, it reasoned, any such defense would require an objectively reasonable belief that the crime committed was authorized by police. Farnsworth could not reasonably have construed the officers' representation to include authority to drive while intoxicated. Because there was no evidence that the officers had "given him permission" to commit the offense charged, no instruction to the jury was necessary.

Some courts have treated claims of this sort as raising only a possible issue of mistake regarding the law defining the charged offense, covered in Chapter 13. Because the defendants have never relied upon the sort of basis as could possibly give rise to such a defense, the claims are rejected. See, for example, *United States v. Duggan*, 743 F.2d 59, 83–84 (2d Cir.1984) (testimony by defendants, representatives of Provisional Irish Republican Army, that they reasonably and in good faith believed that person representing himself to be CIA agent had authority to authorize gun running scheme presented only mistake of law that was not defense to charge of federal weapons laws violation). Some courts give these claims even less significance. In *Stoner v. State*, 442 N.E.2d 983 (Ind.1982), for example, the felony murder defendant claimed that he went along with the fatal burglary to gain the confidence of his cofelon-roommate, as part of his actions pursuant to his agreement that he would function as a "clandestine agent" for the police who had previously arrested him on drug charges. The appellate court analyzed the case as involving only a possible mistake of fact (addressed in Chapter 13). It held that because Stoner's mistaken belief did not in any way tend to negate the *mens rea* required for the crime charged, it raised no possible defense.

Perhaps federal constitutional considerations discussed in detail elsewhere might apply to some of these situations. Several decisions of the United States Supreme Court, discussed in Section B of Chapter 13 at page 412 have been widely regarded as establishing that a criminal prosecution is barred if a person in a position of authority represented to the accused that the conduct at issue was not criminal. In *Cox v. Louisiana*, 379 U.S. 559, 85 S.Ct. 476, 13 L.Ed.2d 487 (1965), a bar to prosecution was created by evidence that the local chief of police had told protesters that certain activity was not prohibited by the law under which prosecution was eventually brought. If a police officer represents to an informer that the officer has authority to "authorize" the informer to commit crimes to facilitate obtaining information, arguably prosecution for such crimes should be barred by the due process rationale applied in *Cox*. On the other hand, perhaps any reliance placed by an informant on such representation by an officer no higher in authority than a detective is not objectively reasonable, as is arguably required by *Cox*.

General justification provisions immunizing conduct taken pursuant to a public duty, discussed in the Editors' Introduction to this section, might apply to some such situations. In *Baird v. Commonwealth*, 709 S.W.2d 458 (Ky.App.1986), the defendant was convicted of possession of a handgun by a convicted felon. He testified that he had purchased the handgun at the request of a police detective, who had asked him to attempt to acquire the recently stolen weapon. When he found the officer was away on a fishing trip, Baird testified, he retained the gun pending the officer's return. It was found in his possession when he was stopped by officers for other, unrelated reasons and searched. The officer testified only that Baird had engaged in undercover work for him and that he had "generally" requested that Baird make inquiries into the possibility of obtaining the gun. Baird was held entitled to have the jury instructed concerning the defense of justification under a statute based on and similar to section 3.03 of the Model Penal Code, set out in the Editors' Introduction. Thus, he apparently would be entitled to acquittal if, but only if, he established that his possession of the firearm was at least authorized by the law defining the assistance to be rendered to a public officer in the officer's performance of his duties.

A rare judicial opportunity to consider limitations upon the defense created for undercover law enforcement work by statutory provisions based on section 3.03 of the Model Penal Code arose in *People v. Mattison*, 75 A.D.2d 959, 428 N.Y.S.2d 355 (1980). At Mattison's trial for armed robbery, the prosecution's evidence showed that he acted as a lookout while one Dennis Mageese committed a robbery. Mattison, however, took the witness stand and testified that he was a paid informant for Investigator Freeman of the New York State Police. Freeman, he testified, had asked him to procure evidence that would lead to Mageese's conviction. Mattison reported to Freeman that Mageese had suggested the commission of a burglary and robbery and had procured a gun. Freeman responded—according to Mattison—that Mattison should "stick with it" and "when you have something solid give me a ring." Mattison testified, however, that he did not find out Mageese's specific plans until shortly before the robbery and he agreed to participate only to secure evidence. All of this was contradicted by testimony presented by the prosecution. Nevertheless, Mattison requested the trial judge to instruct the jury under the New York statute that provided that conduct was "justified" and thus not criminal if it was "performed by a public servant in the reasonable exercise of his official powers, duties or functions." New York Penal Law § 35.05. The trial judge refused and Mattison was convicted.

Finding no error, the *Mattison* appellate court concluded that the statute was intended primarily to apply to crimes that did not require *mens rea*. It then continued:

> Regardless of its precise scope, * * * the defense would never apply to an accusation requiring a particular criminal intent, such as larceny, because if an intent to steal were established, a public servant could hardly assert that the theft was undertaken as a "reasonable exercise" of official functions. By way of contrast, a public servant accused of speeding * * * might validly contend that his duties and the circumstances of the situation justified his action.

In the alternative, the appellate court found another reason why the instruction need not have been given:

> [T]here was no reasonable view of the evidence which would permit the jury to find [Mattison] acted as a public servant or within his official function. Although paid for information on an occasional basis, there was no proof that defendant was hired as an employee, nor was it shown that Freeman delegated any specific police functions to him. Significantly, defendant [during his testimony] did not elaborate on his alleged "functions" pertaining to this matter, and activity beyond reporting information to Freeman could not be regarded as reasonable incidents of his supposed "duties."

Thus, the court apparently regarded any defense as available only to persons in some formal sense employed by law enforcement agencies. The discussion did not make clear how formally authorized such employment would have to be to bring a person such as Mattison within any defense.

The result in *Mattison* may perhaps be best explained in terms of the seriousness of the offense—armed robbery—which the defendant claimed was committed for law enforcement purposes. If (see Editors' Introduction, page 558) there are certain offenses that are so serious they cannot come within those defenses applicable to law enforcement conduct, it seems quite likely that armed robbery is among them. The court did not explicitly rely on the seriousness of the crime charged in reaching its result. Perhaps, however, its suggestion that the defense could possibly be available only to charges of crimes not "requiring a particular criminal intent" was designed to limit the defense to charges of relatively non-serious offenses.

It is widely assumed that the availability of a defense to involvement in a crime is tied to entrapment doctrine, that is, that an officer (or informer) has a defense for undercover involvement unless the officer or informer engages in what under the circumstances is entrapment. However, there seems little express authority for the proposition that an officer loses any otherwise available defense immediately when and if the officer's conduct crosses the line and becomes entrapment. Perhaps, if the conduct of officers or informants constitutes entrapment, it is not "lawful" or "authorized by * * * the law" within the meaning of such provisions as section 3.03 of the Model Penal Code or the Washington statute setting out situations in which the controlled substance statute does not impose liability.

Index